THE JESUITS

The Jesuits

A HISTORY

MARKUS FRIEDRICH

TRANSLATED BY
JOHN NOËL DILLON

PRINCETON UNIVERSITY PRESS

PRINCETON & OXFORD

This is a translation of *Die Jesuiten: Aufstieg, Niedergang, Neubeginn* by Markus Friedrich, copyright © 2016 by Piper Verlag GmbH, München/Berlin

Published by Princeton University Press
41 William Street, Princeton, New Jersey 08540
6 Oxford Street, Woodstock, Oxfordshire OX20 1TR

press.princeton.edu

Library of Congress Cataloging-in-Publication Data

Names: Friedrich, Markus, author. | Dillon, John Noël, translator.
Title: The Jesuits : a history / Markus Friedrich ; translated by John Noël Dillon.
Other titles: Jesuiten. English
Description: Princeton : Princeton University Press, [2022] | Includes bibliographical references and index.
Identifiers: LCCN 2021012468 (print) | LCCN 2021012469 (ebook) | ISBN 9780691180120 (hardback) | ISBN 9780691226194 (ebook)
Subjects: LCSH: Jesuits—History.
Classification: LCC BX3702.3 .F7513 2022 (print) | LCC BX3702.3 (ebook) | DDC 271/.53—dc23
LC record available at https://lccn.loc.gov/2021012468
LC ebook record available at https://lccn.loc.gov/2021012469

British Library Cataloging-in-Publication Data is available

Editorial: Ben Tate, Josh Drake
Jacket Design: Karl Spurzem
Production: Danielle Amatucci
Publicity: Maria Whelan, Carmen Jimenez

Jacket art: St. Ignatius of Loyola before Pope Paul III. Anonymous, 16th century. Scala / Art Resource, NY

This book has been composed in Arno.

Printed on acid-free paper. ∞

Printed in the United States of America

10 9 8 7 6 5 4 3 2 1

For Frieda

CONTENTS

List of Illustrations ix

List of Abbreviations xi

Prologue: Ignatius of Loyola Founds an Order 1

1 The Inner Life and Structure of the Society 20

2 The Society, the Churches, and the Faithful 131

3 *Saeculum* and the Kingdom of God:
The Jesuits "in the World" 260

4 The Global Society 427

5 A World without the Society of Jesus:
Hostility, Suppression, Revival 575

Epilogue: The Modern Society 621

Acknowledgments 673

Afterword to the English Edition 675

Translator's Note 677

Notes 679

Works Cited 751

Names Index 829

Subject Index 845

LIST OF ILLUSTRATIONS

1. Ignatius of Loyola, painted by Jacopino del Conte, 1556.   4

2. Portraits of Ignatius and the first companions, 1590.   7

3. Fresco from the Collegio Romano (presumably eighteenth century).   59

4. Etching by Peter Paul Rubens from *Exercitia Spiritualia S. P. Ignatii Loyolae.*   76

5. Fresco of the IHS monogram from the rooms of Ignatius of Loyola in Rome.   118

6. Casuists at work: the deliberations of experts in moral theology.   175

7. Penitential sermon and procession.   230

8. A Jesuit missionary preaches to a penitent crowd.   231

9. View of the city of Rome and the Society of Jesus headquarters.   269

10. The castle in Kissing.   278

11. Standardized accounting form of the Society of Jesus.   284

12. Public award ceremony for outstanding students.   318

13. Giovanni Battista Riccioli, *Almagestum Novum* (Bologna 1651).   369

14. Two examples of Jesuit fortress architecture.   371

15. Paul Hoste, *L'art des armées navales* (1697).   372

16. Francesco Lana Terzi's design for an airship (1670).   373

17. Jesuit map of Paraguay.   375

18. Drawing by Georg Josef Kamel (1703).   377

19. Jean Dubreuil's stage design (1679).   392

20. Model of the city of Munich by Jakob Sandtner (1570).   415

21. The Jesuit college of Roanne under construction.   419

22. Andrea Pozzo, ascension of St. Ignatius of Loyola.   421

23. Hieronymus Wierix, *Auferstandener Christus*.   424

24. Sculptural adaptation of *Auferstandener Christus*.   425

25. Emblems from *Imago primi saeculi Societatis Iesu*.   428

26. Mission village inhabitants leave the vice of
    alcohol at a cross.   501

27. The birth of Jesus Christ in Jerónimo Nadal's
    Adnotationes et meditationes (1595).   536

28. Ai Rulüe/Giulio Aleni's birth of Jesus (1640).   537

29. Nicolas Trigault in Chinese dress.   541

30. Gabriel Malagrida depicted in the caricature
    "Les Moins Devoilés."   593

31. Drawing of the mission station of St. Mary, 1841,
    by Nicholas Point.   634

ABBREVIATIONS

ACDF Archivio della Congregazione per la dottrina della Fede

AD Archives départementales

AFSJ Archives françaises de la Société de Jésus

AN Archives nationales, Paris

ARSI Archivum Romanum Societatis Iesu

BayHStA Bayerisches Hauptstaatsarchiv, Munich

BN Biblioteca Nazionale, Rome

BnF Bibliotèque nationale de France, Paris

Braunsberger Braunsberger, Otto, ed. *Beati Petri Canisii Societatis Jesu, Epistolae & Acta*. 8 vols. Freiburg 1896–1923

CG Padberg, John W., Martin D. O'Keefe, and John McCarthy. *For Matters of Greater Moment: The First Thirty Jesuit General Congregations*. St. Louis, MO, 1994 (cited by General Congregation, decree, and page number)

Clm *Codex latinus monaciensis*. Bayerische Staatsbibliothek, Munich

Const *The Constitutions of the Society of Jesus and Their Complementary Norms: A Complete English Translation of Official Latin Texts*, translated by George E. Ganss, S.J. St. Louis, MO, 1996

DBI *Dizionario Biografico degli Italiani*. 84 vols. thus far. Rome 1960–present

DHCJ   O'Neill, Charles E., ed. *Diccionario histórico de la Compañía de Jesús. Biográfico-Temático.* 4 vols. Rome 2001

Duhr   Duhr, Bernhard. *Geschichte der Jesuiten in den Ländern Deutscher Zunge.* 4 vols. in 6. Freiburg 1913–28

EpIgn   *S. Ignatii de Loyola Epistolae.* 12 vols. Rome 1964–68

EpMixt   *Epistolae mixtae ex variis Europae locis.* 5 vols. Rome 1898–1901

EpNad   *Epistolae et Monumenta P. Hieronymi Nadal.* 6 vols. Rome 1898–1964

EpSalm   *Epistolae P. Alphonsi Salmeronis.* 2 vols. Madrid 1906–7

Ex   Ignatius of Loyola, *The Spiritual Exercises*, in *Saint Ignatius of Loyola. Personal Writings. Reminiscences, Spiritual Diary, Select Letters including the text of the Spiritual Exercises*, trans. Joseph A. Munitz and Philip Endean, 281–361. London 1996

FontNarr   *Fontes narrativi de S. Ignatio de Loyola et de Societatis Iesu initiis.* 4 vols. Rome 1943–65

FontRicc   D'Elia, Pasquale, ed. *Fonti Ricciane.* 3 vols. Rome 1942–49

GE   *The Constitutions of the Society of Jesus and Their Complementary Norms: A Complete English Translation of Official Latin Texts*, translated by George E. Ganss, S.J. St. Louis, MO, 1996

Imago   *Imago primi saeculi.* Rome 1640

Inst   *Institutum Societatis Iesu.* 3 vols. Florence, 1892–93

JR   Thwaites, Reuben Gold, ed. *The Jesuit Relations and Allied Documents: Travels and Explorations of the Jesuit Missionaries in New France, 1610–1791.* 73 vols. Cleveland 1896–1901

Leibniz Leibniz, Gottfried Wilhelm. *Werke*. Akademie Edition in nine series. Berlin 1923–present

LittQuadr *Litterae quadrimestres ex universis praeter Indiam et Brasiliam locis* [. . .] *Romam missae*. 7 vols. Rome 1895–1932

MonBor *Monumenta Borgia*. 7 vols. Madrid 1898–2009

MonBras *Monumenta Brasiliae*. 5 vols. Rome 1956–68

MonFab *Fabri Monumenta*. Madrid 1914

MonInd *Documenta Indica*. 18 vols. Rome 1948–88

MonMex *Monumenta Mexicana*. 8 vols. Rome 1956–91

MonPaed *Monumenta Paedagogica*. 7 vols. Rome 1965–92

MonPeru *Monumenta Peruana*. 8 vols. Rome 1954–86

MonRib *Monumenta Ribadeneira*. 2 vols. Madrid 1920–23

Pastor von Pastor, Ludwig. *Geschichte der Päpste*. 16 vols. Freiburg 1886–1933

PolChron Polanco, Juan Alfonso de. *Vita Ignatii Loiolae et rerum Societatis Jesu historica*. 6 vols. Madrid 1894–98

RAA Rijksarchief te Antwerpen, Beveren

Ratio *Ratio Studiorum*, in MonPaed 5:353–454

Reminisc. Ignatius of Loyola, *Reminiscences (Autobiography)*, in *Saint Ignatius of Loyola. Personal Writings. Reminiscences, Spiritual Diary, Select Letters Including the Text of the Spiritual Exercises*, trans. Joseph A. Munitz and Philip Endean, 3–67. London 1996

Schatz Schatz, Klaus. *Geschichte der deutschen Jesuiten (1814–1983)*. 5 vols. Munster 2013

SJ Society of Jesus

Sommervogel Sommervogel, Carlos, ed. *Bibliothèque de la Compagnie de Jésus. Bibliographie, histoire*. 9 vols. Leuven 1960 (repr.)

THE JESUITS

Ignatius of Loyola Founds
an Order

ON MAY 20, 1521, troops of the French king Francis I under the leadership of André des Fois reached Pamplona in the northern Spanish kingdom of Navarra. The soldiers met little resistance as they stormed the city. Much of the garrison had abandoned their posts and fled before the superior numbers of the French. Only the citadel of Pamplona created difficulties. A few daring defenders believed they could withstand the enemy. After a fierce battle and heavy artillery fire, though, resistance in the citadel collapsed. Pamplona became French, albeit not for long. The fortune of war soon turned against Francis I, and the events of the early summer of 1521 ultimately proved to be no more than an insignificant episode in the long political and military struggle between the two superpowers France and Spain, which shaped European politics for two hundred years after 1494.[1]

The French bombardment of the citadel of Pamplona nonetheless had epoch-making consequences. That, at least, is how the Jesuits saw it, whose story is told in this book. The origin of this Catholic order, the Societas Iesu, or Society of Jesus, is intimately connected to the events of 1521. One of the bold, or rather reckless, holdouts in the citadel was a Basque nobleman about thirty years old, Iñigo López de Oñaz y Loyola. He was allegedly the one who had instigated the desperate defense: he had gone to the captain of the citadel and protested against the cowardice of the retreating Spanish soldiers. The—admittedly, understandable—flight of the vastly outnumbered Spaniards offended his strong sense of honor, bravery, and virtue. He was willing to risk life and limb in the struggle against the French. His daring infected some of the remaining soldiers. Iñigo personally led the resistance, but then a cannonball severely wounded both his legs. After he was knocked out, his men's morale dissipated. Pamplona fell with Iñigo.

But Iñigo survived his grievous injuries. His French adversaries recognized his valor and tended to his wounds. Days after the battle, he was carried home on a litter to his family's castle in Loyola. Several gruesome operations on his shattered leg followed. Some were necessary for medical reasons; others were ordered by Iñigo himself for cosmetic reasons. The healing process had left a piece of bone protruding below his knee; its removal was excruciatingly painful. Iñigo limped the rest of his life because of these operations. Thus, the fall of Pamplona had already changed the Basque nobleman outwardly, but the events were also the cause, or at least the spark, of a profound inner change. Iñigo's long confinement to his sickbed and recovery triggered a critical assessment of his life up to that point.

From his birth (presumably in 1491) to the year 1521, Iñigo had led a life that was in many respects typical of the Spanish nobility of the late Middle Ages. He was born in Guizpoca, a Basque region in the former Kingdom of Navarre directly south of the Pyrenees. The Loyolas were a respected and well-connected family in the region and can be traced back for centuries to the year 1180. Over their long history, the Loyolas acquired not only a noble title but also extensive landholdings. No fewer than six abbeys and ten chapels were committed to their care.[2] Such seigneurial rights over villages and churches were the traditional basis of noble wealth and power. This regional power base then translated into superregional connections. Iñigo's family enjoyed good relations with the high Spanish nobility and important royal officials, from which Iñigo himself benefited at a very early age. As a young man he—like many an ambitious young nobleman—put himself in the orbit and under the protection of a higher-ranking family. Beginning in 1505, Iñigo lived in Arévalo under the patronage of the treasurer of Castile, Don Juan Velázquez de Cuéllar. There, he was able to acquaint himself with courtly life and culture as a boy and young man. He also learned how to cultivate contacts with the rich and powerful. These were skills that Iñigo would demonstrate again and again throughout his life.

Iñigo's family was shaped by religion and military service. Numerous Loyolas fell in battle on campaign for the kings of Spain, while other uncles, brothers, and nephews became churchmen. Iñigo himself had presumably received minor holy orders to open the door to a position in the church. His world was shaped by the chivalric Christian values of late medieval noble culture. Iñigo's piety was as deeply rooted as it was perfunctory, as morally rigorous in principle as it was malleable in practice, at once institutional and individual. At Cuéllar's court, the young man lived in an environment that reflected the many facets of this chivalric Christian culture. On the one hand, it was a center of mystic and introverted Franciscan devotion, which we shall meet again later. On the other, it was a strikingly unscrupulous world. Iñigo was a tempestuous young man himself and quick to draw his sword. He and his peers jealously guarded what they called "honor"—their own, their families', their wives', and that of the church and its saints. A hearty helping of machismo was de rigueur, and nobles like Iñigo interpreted official moral precepts very liberally, as needed. Illegitimate children were no rarity in Iñigo's family.

All that changed after Pamplona, in the latter half of 1521, as Iñigo recovered in Loyola. The trauma of his injuries made him question his existence up to that point. He changed his ways entirely and set forth on a spiritual and physical journey of self-discovery, at the end of which, nearly twenty years later, he founded a religious community: the Society of Jesus, the Jesuit order. Iñigo himself told the tale of his transformation after 1521 at the end of his life in 1556, in his so-called *Autobiography*, in which he describes himself in the third person as "the pilgrim." This text is a transcript, reworked by a scribe, of an oral account that was interrupted several times. It strives to be more edifying than biographical, painting an impressive picture of a man seeking and finding a religious vocation.[3] In the process, the Basque nobleman Iñigo López de Oñaz y Loyola became the churchman and future saint Ignatius of Loyola (fig. 1).

FIGURE 1. The founder of the Society of Jesus, Ignatius of
Loyola, in a contemporary painting. © akg-images.

This spiritual rediscovery, according to a famous anecdote, was triggered by chance. In the *Autobiography*, we learn that Ignatius had always
enjoyed reading late medieval romances to pass the time. When he
asked for such books on his sickbed, he was brought some religious
works instead—the only reading material to be found in Loyola. For
lack of an alternative, and perhaps somewhat disappointed and reluctant, Ignatius picked up two books that were very popular at the time:
the *Vita Christi* by Ludolph of Saxony and the *Legenda Aurea* by Jacobus
da Varagine. Much to his surprise, this literature he had previously neglected had profound consequences for him. These works, which merely
reinforced the conventional worldview of countless other readers and
listeners, called Ignatius's entire life into question. Among the saints
whose acquaintance he now made on the pages of these books, he was
most impressed by the medieval monastic founders Sts. Francis and

Dominic. He felt challenged by their religious efforts; he wanted to emulate their spiritual chivalry. It soon became apparent to everyone present that Ignatius had changed. Against his family's wishes, he left Loyola and took to the road as a wandering ascetic. He stopped at various pilgrimage sites in Spain. He prayed for a whole night before the famous statue of the Virgin of Montserrat west of Barcelona. He lived in nearby Manresa for nearly nine months, a time that was—in his own words—full of "illumination." From Barcelona, Ignatius traveled in extreme poverty to Rome; from there, he reached Venice and finally made the crossing to the Holy Land. Ignatius wanted to stay at the biblical sites, potentially as a minister for other pilgrims. But the Franciscan Custodian of the Holy Land sent the penniless Ignatius back to Europe.

In the first phase of his "new" life after 1521, Ignatius was very hard on himself. He was full of doubt and reservations that manifested themselves in a kind of compulsion to confess. He believed he constantly had to perform feats of spirituality. The first stages of his search for the right spiritual orientation thus were characterized by radical asceticism. At times, he stopped cutting his hair and nails, wore only the coarsest clothing, went barefoot or wore shoes in which he had deliberately cut holes, fasted to the point of starvation, confessed daily. It was not until after his pilgrimage to Jerusalem—and his eventful return to Spain amid the chaos of war—that he embarked on a new stage of this quest. He decided to broaden his worldview with a significant acquisition: an academic education. Since the early thirteenth century, new centers of knowledge and learning had sprung up across Europe: universities. Spain was involved in this trend from the start. The first Iberian university was founded in Salamanca in 1218. Admittedly, the European nobility long felt ambivalent about these new centers of learning and their new forms and standards of truth and education. Life at court, as Ignatius himself had experienced in Arévalo, may have presumed a high level of education and knowledge, but not necessarily the Latin erudition of intellectuals, professors, and theologians. Ignatius had not thus far encountered higher education in an academic sense.

Yet it was precisely a university education that he now set out to acquire. Well over thirty years old, Ignatius first had to learn the basics of

Latin in Barcelona before he could actually study at an institution of higher learning. He took up the challenge of academic study with gusto. Yet despite several years in residence at the universities of Alcalá de Henares (1526), Salamanca (1527), and especially Paris (from 1528 on), Ignatius never truly felt at home in the early modern academy. Even though his followers sometimes described him admiringly as "our father, the theologian," Ignatius himself preferred to rely on expert assistants to devise theoretical platforms and dogmatic positions—and his new order soon put a large number of them at his disposal.[4] Ignatius cannot really be assigned to either of the two dominant intellectual cultures in Europe circa 1540, humanism and scholasticism, although he was intimately familiar with both.

Be that as it may, his student years were an extraordinarily fruitful time for him, and they have left many traces in the prehistory and early history of the Society of Jesus. The didactic method Ignatius learned in Paris became the model for the Society's educational projects. And even if Ignatius himself remained relatively untouched by university training and academic theology, he still came into constant contact with people more thoroughly steeped in academic culture and thought than himself. A series of qualified theologians were among Ignatius's closest companions. They founded the Society together with him in 1540 and gave it a reputation for outstanding scholarly ability from the very start. Diego Laínez and Alfonso Salmerón, for example, two Jesuits from day one, were among the few people who participated in all three sessions of the Council of Trent from 1545 to 1563.[5]

For Ignatius and his order, the years he spent traveling and studying in Spain and France were also key in another way. Ignatius gained important experience in engaging people on a spiritual level. During this period, he not only met the nine companions who ultimately constituted the first generation of Jesuits together with himself—Pierre Favre (also known as Peter Faber), Francis Xavier, Claude Jay, Paschase Broët, Simão Rodrigues, Alfonso Salmerón, Diego Laínez, Nicolás Bobadilla, and Jean Codure (fig. 2). If we are to believe his autobiography, the future founder of the order engaged in spiritual conversations with people of all walks of life after he was wounded in Pamplona. He talked

FIGURE 2. The first generation of Jesuits "at a glance." © akg-images/Album/Oronoz.

constantly with men and women, rich and poor, lay and clergy—some people even soon sought Ignatius out themselves, while he spoke to others as chance dictated. As his autobiography suggests, Ignatius's own tortured spiritual life made him particularly adroit at understanding the inner life of those he conversed with. People thus eagerly approached him for advice and guidance. This role as "spiritual father" remained very important to Ignatius for the rest of his life. A growing store of psychological experience, gradually acquired through these countless encounters, helped him sharpen his conversational skills even more. In a complicated process that lasted decades until 1540, Ignatius turned these experiences from everyday life into a method for meditation and spiritual self-examination. He ultimately compiled his notes and other scraps of text he was constantly writing into a little book, the famous *Spiritual Exercises*. In them, Ignatius sets forth how one could gain clarity about the spiritually correct way to lead one's life by completing a program of approximately four weeks of prayer, meditation, and self-discovery. The *Exercises*, which were finished by the time the Jesuit order was founded, became the new community's most important spiritual foundation. They exerted a profound influence on Christendom for a very long time.

Ignatius also came to know the dangers, limitations, and difficulties of dealing with people during his student days. He clashed with the Inquisition and other church authorities—often in connection with his conversational efforts to win over others to his ideas of religious life. Ignatius and his followers were criticized for presuming to undertake such pastoral work without formal ecclesiastical or academic qualifications. They also were repeatedly suspected of harboring unorthodox ideas. Spanish Catholics feared that new devotional practices might break with established norms. Religious introspection often led to intense mysticism—there was a radical side to fervent devotion. Some aspects of this new religious culture seemed beneficial and good to church superiors; others were frowned upon. One diffuse group, known as the *alumbrados*, the "illuminated," was even persecuted. More than once, it seemed to the authorities that Ignatius might sympathize with these dangerous views. Even though such accusations were regularly dismissed as unfounded, the experience made it clear to Ignatius that he had to obtain the church's official blessing for his concept of devotion and pastoral ministry.

Ignatius stayed in Paris until 1535. Then, for the last time in his life, he returned home for a few months. Although he no longer presented himself as a member of the prestigious house of Loyola, his countrymen immediately recognized him and tried in vain to treat him according to his traditional social status. But Ignatius had long since distanced himself from his origins. He came home as a spiritual reformer. He preached and ministered to the common people as a man of God, he reformed a monastery, then he set out for Venice, where he had arranged to meet his friends from Paris. The fact that this small group held together though separated by great distances and time shows how strong was the bond they had forged in Paris. In contrast to Ignatius's earlier circle of friends in Spain, separation did not spell the end of their relationship; the group had developed a genuine sense of solidarity from their years together in Paris. That solidarity culminated in a particularly significant event. On Montmartre in Paris in 1534, Ignatius and six other future Jesuits took three vows: of poverty, chastity, and obedience—they constituted the nucleus of the future order, even if at the time they did not yet attach any institutional consequences to their vows.

Ignatius and his friends thus met in Venice. They planned to embark for the Holy Land together as pilgrims and aspired to perform ministries that were "beneficial to souls." This formula would become typical for the ministry and purpose of the Jesuit order. It succinctly describes the central feature of the future order, "apostolicity," that is, emulation of the pastoral ministry of the apostles, who once traveled from city to city proclaiming the Christian faith.[6] At least in Ignatius's retrospective account, the companions' plans for Jerusalem in the 1530s already closely corresponded to the program of the future order. But Ignatius had learned from his first trip to Palestine fifteen years earlier. He knew how difficult it was to work in the Holy Land. He and his friends accordingly devised a backup plan: in the event that it proved impossible to stay in or near Jerusalem, they would travel back to Italy and offer their services directly to the pope. They resolved to do likewise if it proved impossible to cross the Mediterranean. There were good reasons why Ignatius viewed traveling to Jerusalem and serving the pope as interchangeable. He regarded the Holy Land, where Jesus of Nazareth had lived and worked, as the birthplace of the apostolic mission itself. There, one could best perceive the will of Jesus Christ, and it was from there that Christ sent his apostles out into the world, "recommend[ing] them to be ready to help everyone." After Jesus, however, the pope, as his representative and head of the church, was the most competent person to authorize such apostolic enterprises. What Jerusalem embodied so prominently for Ignatius could be realized, at least in outline, from Rome.[7]

It was wise of Ignatius and his group to make an alternative plan. A political and military storm was brewing in the waters of the Levant, and their fears came true: Ignatius's second visit to the Holy Land never took place. The Venetians and Ottomans went to war again in 1537, and crossing the Mediterranean was out of the question for the foreseeable future. After some hesitation, the group finally went with their second option and traveled to Rome in the fall of 1537. Shortly before reaching the city gates, Ignatius had a famous vision in the small chapel of La Storta: he saw God the Father and Jesus, and the former promised to support Ignatius and his traveling companions in Rome.

On arriving in the Eternal City, Ignatius was only two more steps away from founding the Jesuit order. First, he and his companions had to decide to institutionalize their still informal community, which was held together by their personal ties and shared experiences. In a series of discussions over the summer of 1538, they deliberated whether to take this step. They answered in the affirmative. The second step accordingly was to obtain the blessing of the pope—only he could legally authorize religious groups and new ecclesiastical corporations. Pope Paul III was reigning in Rome at the time, and he was well-disposed toward the newcomers. Although the College of Cardinals was generally wary of new religious orders, its assessment of the future Society of Jesus was overwhelmingly positive. It seemed in keeping with the progressive religious sentiment that prevailed in Rome at the time.

In the decades after the devastating sack of Rome by the troops of Emperor Charles V in 1527, the leading role of the pope and Rome in the Christian world underwent a metamorphosis. New religious ideas and groups were being discussed. The growing threat of the Reformation in Germany and England also made waves in the Catholic world. In the fall of 1539, therefore, Paul III provided the Society of Jesus with a formal legal basis, albeit initially only in oral form. After significant resistance in the College of Cardinals was overcome yet again, the pope's oral confirmation was reiterated in writing on September 28, 1540. Paul III issued the bull *Regimini militantis ecclesiae*, the papal document that transformed the loose band of ten men into a corporation under canon law, an institution with its own legal personality, in short: an order—the *Societas Iesu*. Ignatius became its first superior general.

The last clearly defined stage of Loyola's life thus began in 1540. His migratory wandering was at an end. Ignatius spent the remaining sixteen years of his life almost exclusively in Rome or its immediate surroundings as the head of his new order. At least in geographic terms, he had reached his destination. He now, however, faced entirely new tasks and challenges. Yet again he had to adjust to a new role. He had gained some administrative experience during his youth in the service of the treasurer of Castile, but directing a rapidly growing and soon globally active institution was something new. He soon recognized that institutional responsibility and organizational tasks had their own difficulties and challenges and could not easily be reconciled with his previous spiritual lifestyle. He still tried to achieve inner clarity in meditation and prayer when deliberating important decisions. A series of records from the year 1544 gives a vivid glimpse of the spiritual struggle and strain that bore down on Ignatius at such times, affecting those around him. The entire house held its breath for days as Ignatius pondered the structure of the Society in meditation and prayer.[8] But, in general, Ignatius's thoughts now revolved less around himself and his own spirituality and more around the question of how he should exercise his new executive powers and shape his order.

The most important step in this direction was the composition of the *Constitutions*, the founding charter of the Jesuit order. Ignatius worked on it with several collaborators for a decade and a half until shortly before his death. One of these collaborators, the Spaniard Juan Alfonso de

Polanco (1517–76), was appointed secretary in 1547, thus becoming Ignatius's most important adviser in all organizational matters.[9] The *Constitutions* make up a thick book of more than eight hundred paragraphs in which the spirituality and basic ecclesiastical policy of the young order were translated into administrative procedures and institutions. Although supplemented and changed in numerous particulars, this work still shapes the structure of the Society today. Largely finished by 1552, the *Constitutions* were promulgated and elucidated within the lifetime of the order's founder by another important collaborator, Jerónimo Nadal, while he spent years crisscrossing Europe. It was through this process of slow and gradual promulgation and explication that new members of the order in Spain, Portugal, France, and Germany came to realize more clearly what Ignatius actually intended. There were definitely surprises for some new Jesuits. The Society had grown so rapidly that in some places its true nature remained obscure. Not everyone who enthusiastically joined the Society stayed when they learned in detail what it was all about.[10]

By the time Ignatius died, in 1556, his fellow brothers had established missions in Asia, Africa, and South America. From the ten Jesuits in 1540, there now were approximately a thousand members. And growth continued at a breakneck pace. In light of this tumultuous expansion, it is no surprise that open questions and points of ambiguity remained. The organizational and even the spiritual framework of the Society had to be modified several times in the decades and centuries after Ignatius, and it had to be defended and upheld especially against alternative visions. The history of the Jesuit order is therefore also one of inner diversity, differences, and even outright conflict. Serious altercations arose even among the first ten companions, especially between Ignatius and Simão Rodrigues, who was finally deposed as provincial of Portugal after a bitter dispute in 1553. Nicolás Bobadilla also often took positions contrary to Ignatius's own.

The first signs of hostility from outside began to appear in the final years of Ignatius's life. Paul IV, elected pope in 1555, was no friend of the founder of the Society of Jesus, and Ignatius anticipated the difficulties that loomed ahead. In a climate of suspicion, the order became involved at least marginally in two Inquisition trials in Rome. Giovanni Morone,

cardinal of the Roman church and the Jesuits' patron, and Bartolomé de
Carranza, the future archbishop of Toledo, were arrested in 1557 and 1558,
respectively, in Rome and Valladolid for allegedly heterodox beliefs.
Whereas Morone was released and rehabilitated after the death of Paul IV
in 1559, Carranza languished in prison nearly two decades before he too
was acquitted. The early Jesuits had a positive, close relationship with both
of these men, which put them in a dangerous position under Paul IV.

In these circumstances, it was difficult to arrange the succession after
Ignatius's death on July 31, 1556. It took two years until the First General
Congregation of the Society of Jesus met in Rome in 1558 to elect a new superior general. The delay was caused not least by the fact that Pope Paul IV
was currently waging war and the Papal States were occupied by Spanish
troops. It moreover was disputed how the Society should elect a new superior general after Ignatius's death. The *Constitutions* contained highly
detailed guidelines on the subject, but were they already in force if they
had not yet been officially adopted? Bobadilla in particular agitated
against the *Constitutions*, initially finding an ally in Paul IV. The pope also
wanted to overturn Ignatius's measures in several other particulars concerning the everyday spiritual life of the Society and its administration.
He considered the new order too unusual and demanded that it adhere
more strictly to established traditions. For example, he faulted the Jesuits
for failing to sing the liturgical hours in choir.

Since Paul IV enjoyed considerable support within the Society, the
situation escalated into a crisis. The First General Congregation in 1558
proved to be an important moment of consolidation during this difficult
phase. Despite adverse conditions inside and outside the Society, the
General Congregation succeeded in officially adopting the *Constitutions*, thereby making them binding. Paul IV died shortly thereafter in
1559, so the changes he had imposed never took effect. The order had
been permanently established, its legal and spiritual framework had
been defended, and its constitutional institutions had survived their
first serious test.

Despite the unmistakable changes that accompanied each of the
three major phases of the life of Ignatius of Loyola, they should not be
distinguished too rigidly from one another. The year 1521 was definitely

a turning point in Ignatius's life. But the *Autobiography* exaggerates when it makes his real life begin in Pamplona. The influence of Ignatius's aristocratic childhood and youth lasted far longer than one might infer from the single sentence with which Ignatius dismissed his former life in retrospect. Research on Ignatius of Loyola thus took a major step forward when scholars in the middle of the twentieth century began to inquire about the influence of Loyola's noble and chivalric heritage on his later life. Historians at the time discovered a "chivalric" and "secular saint" in Ignatius.[11] His rebirth after Pamplona did not simply erase his former habits, skills, and customs. Ignatius's ability to win the ear and sympathy of the rich and powerful as superior general, a skill he put to prominent use throughout his life, was surely a product of his aristocratic socialization—Ignatius remained a nobleman even as a Jesuit. And his constant spiritual quest, the pious competition that decisively shaped the spirituality of the Jesuit order, may have been a religious reinterpretation of the medieval ideal of the Christian knight (*miles christianus*) Ignatius had grown up with. And despite his spiritual conversion, all his life Ignatius clung to a central value of chivalric society: even his admirers noted his "great appetite for honor and glory."[12] The inner and outer changes that Ignatius experienced in 1521 were dramatic, and his new role as the superior general of a rapidly growing organization enriched his life and thought in important ways, but that does not mean that we should presume his personality completely changed in the process. Ignatius imparted to his order an exciting combination of old and new, secular and spiritual values. That had highly ambivalent, long-term consequences: both the many strengths and many flaws of the Society had their roots here.

Ignatius founded his order in an age of profound change for Europe. The people of the early modern period—from roughly 1500 to 1800—witnessed far-reaching revolutions in both political and religious life. Ignatius himself observed many of these changes directly and modified his order accordingly, but others had only just begun, and other, later developments could hardly have been foreseen. The future would have to reveal how well Ignatius's successors adapted to new circumstances.

By 1550, it was clear that Europe was moving toward ever greater state power, concentrated in the hands of monarchs. The creeping bureaucratization of power since the late Middle Ages was unmistakable. Step by step, modern states took shape. This process also influenced the church: the old question of the relationship between politics and religion, between secular and ecclesiastical power, was soon asked again with new urgency in light of the growing boldness of kings and princes.

The Society of Jesus was also a child of the Age of Reformation. Ignatius was not even aware of it initially; Protestantism was not especially important to him prior to 1540. But the Reformation permanently changed the Catholic Church. The pillars of the Catholic response to the Reformation were erected at the famous Council of Trent, which met in three sessions from 1545 to 1563.[13] Trent and a series of parallel reforms similar in spirit were decisive in ensuring that the Catholic Church emerged from the insecurity and setbacks of the Reformation modernized, effective, and confident. A new, more militant, more urgent identity had developed. The popes seized ever more power and created new and more efficient administrative institutions. At best, Ignatius himself could foresee these developments only in their infancy, but the Jesuit order ultimately became one of the most important proponents of this renewed Catholicism, which began to make itself felt in the latter half of the sixteenth century. In the long term, the revitalized Catholicism of the post-Reformation period proved to be especially significant to the *Societas Iesu*.

———

This book tells the story of the Jesuit order over the centuries since its foundation. It proceeds in three major chronological steps. The "rise" of the Society of Jesus stands at the center of chapters 2 to 5. These chapters cover the period from the foundation of the order to the middle of the eighteenth century. By then, it was undeniable that it would only get harder for the Society to present itself as a useful and beneficial part of contemporary culture and society. The Jesuits continued to apply themselves to their mission with energy and devotion, but the significance of their accomplishments was often no longer obvious to contemporaries.

Radical, outright hostility toward Ignatius's successors reared its head in many places. The roots of this animosity reached as far back as the sixteenth century, but this anti-Jesuit movement escalated during the quarter century after 1750. It ultimately led to the suppression of the Society by Pope Clement XIV in 1773. The "decline" of the order had reached its nadir. Chapter 5 examines this phase.

But the end proved to be temporary. In 1814, the Society was restored, after the political, religious, and social life of Europe had been radically changed by the French Revolution and the ensuing Napoleonic Wars. "Rebirth" became possible, and the Jesuits' first thought was to revive the old institutions. But the world had become a different place. Nationalism, atheism, scientific discoveries, liberalism, Marxism—the list of new challenges was long, and so it took some time before the Society found a new place of its own. In searching for its identity, the Society of Jesus of the nineteenth century moved primarily in a conservative direction, although the Society's unease with reactionary extremes is often obvious. The order remained an uncommonly complex institution even during this phase. The book's epilogue gives a brief overview of the slow recovery of the Society from 1814 to today.

At the provisional end of this revival stands the Society of Jesus in its present form. Today, the Society of Jesus is often perceived as a progressive, innovative, and unconventional branch of the Roman Catholic Church. This manifestation of the Society first appeared after the Second World War. If we look back at the latter half of the twentieth century, the Jesuits played a leading part in many groundbreaking changes to the Catholic world—for instance, greater emphasis on the poor and on inculturation, a more accessible appearance, and alternatives to the strict focus of the church on the pope. Some Jesuits supported these innovations in a very conspicuous and sometimes even radical manner. They are often the most famous men of the Society today. But the Society of Jesus has arguably exerted an even greater, longer-lasting influence by virtue of its moderate, liberal middle. Many of these Jesuits give the church a contemporary, engaged face without veering toward radical extremes. Pope Francis, the Jesuit on the throne of St. Peter, is a modern exponent of this changed Society of Jesus.

Perhaps the greatest challenge of writing a history of the Jesuits is that it essentially has to be a world history in a nutshell. There is scarcely any sphere of human life, any region of the world, left untouched by the Jesuits over the centuries. No book about them can therefore be complete. Yet a series of topics have always stood at the center of the history of the Society over the centuries and despite all its caesuras and changes: the Jesuit mission, education, knowledge, and spirituality as embodied in the *Spiritual Exercises*. In light of this enormous variety, I have striven to the best of my ability to give a representative survey of these core areas of the history of the Society. But readers will also regularly find at least brief mention of more unusual and episodic activities. This is in fact one of the major goals of this book: to present the Jesuit order as an incredibly diverse institution, so as to contradict still current clichés about it. There neither was nor is *the* stereotypical Jesuit, and there neither was nor is *the* Society of Jesus, except in a legal and institutional sense. To quote an old Jesuit joke: "three Jesuits, four opinions." The cultural and religious pursuits, accomplishments, and projects of this order are incredibly diverse, but they may also be contradictory and sometimes even irreconcilable. This great variety naturally also raises the question of what holds the Society of Jesus together, how one can conceive of it as a whole at all. Both these problems will constantly recur: on the one hand, variety and openness; on the other, a search for unity and an integrated, common identity.

The book's chapters proceed thematically in a broad chronological arc—from 1540 to 1773 and from 1814 to Pope Francis. Aside from well-known caesuras, there is no standard chronology of the history of the Jesuit order. Developments in different cultural spheres and in corners of the world influenced by the Jesuits always had their own peculiar dynamic. Triumphs and disasters often occurred simultaneously in different places. In many areas, the sixteenth century was a dynamic period of new beginnings and major initiatives; in others, change did not come until the eighteenth century—it is virtually impossible to establish a universal chronology of the Jesuit order. Only for specific areas of

Jesuit history can we make out a relatively clear developmental trajectory at all.

The second objective of the following chapters is to show how the Jesuits frequently built on earlier theological, pastoral, and devotional traditions, which they distilled in a very promising and concise way, adapting them to contemporary needs. The Jesuits did not appear ex nihilo, and many of their projects and procedures can scarcely be understood without reference to earlier and parallel developments. This conclusion is in no way intended to diminish or question the achievements and unique profile of this very special order. But connecting the Society of Jesus to earlier efforts and parallel trends considerably helps us understand its own approaches and strategies.

———

This is a historian's book. I am interested in the Society of Jesus insofar as it was an institution that was (and is) very important to the historical development of Europe and the world. My goal is to assess and also account for the Society's historical role; to trace how the Society of Jesus achieved such powerful influence and became a key player in so many social, religious, cultural, and political areas. I have done so with a sober and detached view. In this history—as in every history—there is neither anything to defend nor anything to attack. This book concerns itself with historical processes, not religious truths. My comments are also not predicated on the premise that there is something "hidden" in the Society of Jesus, waiting to be discovered. The Jesuits neither were nor are some shadow power at the Vatican, an organization with a secret, hidden structure. There is nothing about them to unmask. Hence this book distances itself from various religious, political, and other conspiracy theories. From a historical perspective, the only legitimate question is how and when such conspiracy theories arose and why certain people in certain circumstances believe them, even today. That is the question I will take up later.

This book has just as little to defend or glorify as it has to expose or attack. In many cases, Jesuits skirted the border of immorality, and some

members of the order occasionally crossed it. Such episodes are important and are duly told in this book. They not only illustrate the internal
contradictions of the Society of Jesus but also show how the order always remained a product of its times. For all their strengths and weaknesses, the Jesuits were always beholden to the assumptions and limitations of their age. The order not only shaped history but also was and is
a reflection of the times. The elevation of individual personages from
the Society to Catholic "saints"—besides Ignatius himself, one thinks
especially of the missionary Francis Xavier, although there are many
more—seems to have conferred a timeless and exemplary quality on
their lives. But such a devotional or hagiographic perspective has no
place in this book. Uncritical enthusiasm for and veneration of the great
figures of the Society are not the point.

The following chapters stand on the shoulders of an immense body
of literature. The body of scholarship on the Society of Jesus is completely unmanageable, particularly since it frequently is dedicated to
local or regional contexts. Many earlier scholarly works remain unsurpassed for their abundance of material, but they often suffer from bias.
What the Jesuits themselves have written about their order is usually
amply documented, but is pervaded by a more or less obvious basic
sympathy. What opponents of the Society have written is not infre-
quently astute and stimulating, but it normally fails to do justice to the
self-conception of the men concerned. Only in recent decades has interest in the Jesuit order grown significantly outside the narrow confines
of ecclesiastical and historical circles. This has helped make the analysis
considerably more objective. Most scholarly works on the Society of
Jesus today are written by historians approaching the Society with new
questions. It goes without saying that the Society of Jesus is now regarded as a serious subject of historical study, which has helped us better
understand many aspects of early modern and modern history. I have
attempted to the best of my ability to acquaint myself with this recent
research and to combine it with the usable findings of earlier, more or
less polemical scholarship.

1

The Inner Life and Structure
of the Society

THE JESUITS were proud of their order—proud of its members, its special qualities, and its unconventional features. They were also proud of how quickly their order spread and how prominent it soon became in the world. The Society of Jesus indeed grew rapidly after 1540, and not a few Jesuits seemed so confident of victory that this self-certainty became part of the Jesuit mentality.[1] That is the impression one gets, for example, when opening the *Imago primi saeculi* of 1640, an opulent, folio-sized luxury volume set in crisp type and illustrated with numerous fine etchings. The *Imago* was a celebratory text commissioned by the Jesuits of Antwerp on the occasion of the hundredth anniversary of the founding of the Society, and it unmistakably reflects its authors' confident pride. The *Imago* is second to none as a document of the Jesuits' confidence in success—and it was also criticized outside and even inside the order for its lavishness. Be that as it may, it accurately reflects the mentality of many Jesuits after long years of virtually unabated success.[2]

Ignatius of Loyola himself laid the groundwork for the growth of his order very carefully in his sixteen years as superior general. He had set out to establish detailed, binding rules to govern the Society of Jesus in both spiritual and organizational terms. In the process, and in collaboration with his two most important associates, Juan de Polanco and Jerónimo Nadal, he ensured that his unique personal charisma translated into a viable structure. The *Spiritual Exercises* and the *Constitutions* served as authoritative foundational texts that described both the spiritual and organizational sides of the Society in detail. Ignatius did everything conceivable to guarantee the continuity of the order. Some turbulence occurred after his death, from 1556 until the conclusion of the First General Congregation in 1558, but these two years did not cause any lasting breaks. In contrast to many other religious orders, for the Society of Jesus the loss of the charismatic founder ultimately proved to be only a moderate crisis. The rapid success of the new order continued virtually unbroken after 1556 and even accelerated.

The first section of this chapter gives a succinct overview of the most important stages and regions in which the Society of Jesus spread across Europe. On the one hand, it is intended to illustrate the enormous geographic extent of the Jesuits' presence. On the other, it should become clear that the nature and special identity of the Society were by no means universally embraced. Many contemporaries harbored reservations and harshly criticized the methods of the new order.

The second section introduces the men who joined the Society: Who were they, and what were their motives? And, fundamentally: How did one become a Jesuit? The third section then gives an overview of Jesuit religious life and the pillars of Jesuit spirituality. Here we will see the spiritual compass that a Jesuit lived by, and what religious values shaped his conception of self and the world. We also will encounter the Jesuits' claim that there actually was something like "our way of proceeding"— the *Imago primi saeculi* itself sang the praises of this "typically Jesuit" way over several hundred pages.

After spirituality, our view will shift to the structure and constitution of the Society—precisely the aspects that are traditionally regarded as the keys to the enormous success of the Society of Jesus. No other order in the history of Western Christendom gave so much thought and dedicated so much energy to regulating its internal administration. The Jesuit order became a bureaucratic machine—at least that is how its enemies saw it, and that is what many leading Jesuits seem to have intended. It is not for nothing that Superior General Claudio Acquaviva himself once declared that the Society should function like "clockwork."[3]

In practice, everyday operations usually fell far short of this ideal, but there was no shortage of efforts to optimize the internal procedures of the Jesuit order.

Historians normally set their sights only on the successful and loyal members of the Jesuit order. But, as the final section of this chapter shows, controversy constantly simmered beneath the surface of the Society of Jesus. In no way did every young man who joined the Society thrive there. And by no means did every Jesuit who was admitted meet his superiors' expectations. Hence, the history of the Society is also a history of disappointment, dismissal, and disillusionment. A study of the inner life of this religious order would be incomplete without discussing the dissatisfaction and dejection, the turpitude and abject indecency of some of its members and their associates. With several thousand members and hundreds of communities, it is no wonder that disputes constantly broke out in the Society of Jesus.

Growth in Europe

When the Jesuit order was founded in 1540, it had ten members. By Ignatius's death in 1556, that number had grown to a thousand.[4] But it was the founder's successors who witnessed and guided the massive expansion of the Society. The first of these was Diego Laínez (r. 1558–65), an adept theologian and one of Ignatius's closest confidants. Laínez was the only one of Ignatius's first companions to become superior general. After Laínez's death in 1565, Francisco de Borja (r. 1565–72) was elected at the Second General Congregation. Borja came from the highest echelon of the Spanish nobility, and he had already lent the Jesuits his energetic support as Duke of Gandía. He was arguably the Jesuit superior general who was inclined the most toward mysticism and devotional introspection; accordingly, he always paid particularly close attention to the spiritual side of the Society's development. Under Laínez and Borja, the number of Jesuits quadrupled.

The order thus grew rapidly from the very start. But this growth was neither consciously planned nor completely even. The lifetime of the founder was by no means the period that witnessed the greatest numbers of new members; while Ignatius led the Society, it grew by approximately 62 Jesuits per year. The order's most significant growth occurred, instead, under Claudio Acquaviva (r. 1581–1615), when it gained up to 309 men annually. By 1600, there consequently were already 8,519 Jesuits. It was Acquaviva who obviously maximized the attractiveness of the order. And it was by this point in time, at the latest, that the rapid developments of the past sixty years had led to an erosion of clear guidelines. A generation after Ignatius's death, the incredible vitality that could be observed everywhere had to be brought under stricter control.

Acquaviva governed the Society of Jesus for thirty-four years and consolidated the order over this long period. The final form of many Jesuit projects can be traced back to his term in office. He helped the Society find its pedagogical identity with the universal educational program set forth in the *Ratio studiorum* of 1599; he approved an obligatory guide to the *Spiritual Exercises* in the form of an official handbook (also published in 1599). Acquaviva's name is further associated with numerous administrative rules and literary projects. Not least, during his long term as superior general, he ensured that his vision of a rigorously organized, worldly, proselytizing, focused, and centralized Society of Jesus became reality, despite internal resistance.

Not all Jesuits were on board with Acquaviva's vision. He was harshly criticized in some quarters. Spanish adversaries in particular railed against his allegedly "tyrannical" leadership. At the Fifth General Congregation in 1593, they tried to pass constitutional amendments that would have dramatically changed the Society, but the superior general from the family of the Dukes of Atri in southern Italy successfully asserted his policy. In his peculiar way, he made sure that the many initiatives of the stormy early years remained coherent despite their ferocious individual dynamics. The Society of Jesus that Acquaviva erected on the foundation laid by Ignatius and his immediate successors went on to shape Europe for the next 150 years.

Under Acquaviva's cautious successor, Muzio Vitelleschi (r. 1615–45), less turbulent times followed, despite the Thirty Years' War. After the Society survived a succession of three superiors general in just six years between 1646 and 1652, Goswin Nickel (r. 1652–64), Gianpaolo Oliva (r. 1664–81), and Charles de Noyelle (r. 1682–86) presided over a period of slower growth. Now the annual number of new recruits was only 40 to 50 Jesuits, so that by 1679 the Society had a total of 17,655 members. The late seventeenth century is often considered a period of growing problems for the order, which even experienced crises in certain areas. Andalusia, for example, registered a precipitous drop in numbers.[5] Within the Society, the generalate of Tirso González (r. 1687–1705) was marred by fierce infighting over his unusual theological positions and his authoritarian leadership style. The overall situation did not improve until after 1700. Michaelangelo Tamburini (r. 1706–30) and Franz Retz (r. 1730–50) led the Society in its final phase of expansion. The first half of the century that gave birth to the Enlightenment was a phase in which the attractiveness of the Society increased yet again—the order grew on average by 95 Jesuits per year. In 1750, the Society reached its absolute peak membership with 22,589 Jesuits. Thereafter, membership collapsed: by 1758, only 17,879 members remained. Growing hostility toward the order in Portugal, France, Spain, and soon all across Europe made itself felt. The appeal of the Society of Jesus was rapidly dwindling at the end of the early modern period.

All these Jesuits had to live and work somewhere, and so the proliferation of Jesuit houses was no less rapid. In 1540, the Society still lacked permanent quarters; at the time of Ignatius's death, it had 79 houses. That number soon exploded to several hundred—at the Society's greatest geographic extent in 1710, there were no fewer than 612 colleges worldwide and approximately 500 other communities, excluding temporary missions. A network of significantly over 1,100 more or less permanent, more or less elaborate Jesuit outposts and communities spanned the globe. At Ignatius's death, the order had divided the world into 12 provinces; in 1616, there were 32; and prior to 1773, that number had risen to a grand total of 37.

Behind these numbers—people, provinces, houses—lie the fates of countless individuals and unique local developments. The lives of the Jesuits in Europe varied greatly throughout the early modern period.[6] Until approximately 1750, for example, Portugal was very fertile ground for the Jesuits.[7] King João III became the first major patron of the young order. As early as 1539, even before the Society had been formally founded, João had instructed his ambassador in Rome to ask Loyola to send Jesuits. It was in Portugal in 1552 that a Jesuit—Diego Miró—first became court confessor. And it was in the service of the king of Portugal that the first Jesuit missionaries set out for Asia (Francis Xavier) and Brazil (Manuel da Nóbrega).

In Portugal, it was Simão Rodrigues—like Francis Xavier, one of Ignatius's earliest companions—who was initially of paramount importance. But he and Ignatius soon clashed, ultimately resulting in Rodrigues's demotion and almost in his expulsion from the Society. It was not until decades later, under the fourth superior general, Everard Mercurian (r. 1573–80), that a kind of reconciliation with the headquarters in Rome was reached. In early 1542, Rodrigues received the old monastery of Santo Antão in Lisbon in exchange for other properties that the king had transferred to him. Ten years later, this site became the Jesuit college in the capital. Almost simultaneously, in 1541, the Jesuits established a house in the university city of Coimbra, and in 1555 the Society took over the royal university there (the Real Collegio). The Jesuits also founded a new university under the aegis of Cardinal Henrique, the king's brother, in Évora in 1551. The influx of new members in Portugal was initially immense. By 1579, the small country with its 550 Jesuits had twice as many members as the German provinces combined.

Over the long term, however, developments in Portugal took an ambivalent turn for the Jesuits. When King Sebastião, João's grandson, fell in battle against the Muslims at Alcácer Quibir, Morocco, in 1578, the Jesuits were blamed for the youthful ambition of the idealistic ruler they had largely educated. Sixty years of Spanish rule in Portugal followed until 1640, a period in which the Jesuits enjoyed much less influence. Only two new establishments—a professed house in Vila Viçosa (1601) and the college of Santarém—were founded during this phase. The number of new members declined, and two of the three novitiates closed (Évora and Coimbra; only Lisbon survived).

The Jesuits were sympathetic observers of the upheaval of 1640, when the Portuguese dynasty of the Braganças ended Spanish rule, but they did not participate directly. Over the following decades, members of the Society again came into close proximity to the king of Portugal. The Jesuits supported the new dynasty as best they could. Besides sermons, celebrations, and other activities, it is the propagandistic pamphlet *Restauração de Portugal prodigiosa* (1643) penned by the Jesuit João de Vasconcelos that best reflects the Society's loyalist position. Under João IV, Jesuits were entrusted with delicate diplomatic missions. But their influence remained variable and precarious, and they competed ever more fiercely with the Inquisition. Later kings, especially Afonso VI (1643–83; r. 1656–83), were much warier of the Society. Serious conflict with the Inquisition broke out. Although it took a variety of forms, the dispute revolved primarily around the relationship between the Catholic Church and Christians with Jewish ancestry. In this regard, the Jesuits were relatively open, whereas the Inquisition strictly opposed all cooperation. Pedro II (1648–1706; regent since 1668, king from 1683) had greater faith in the Jesuits, but like all his predecessors since 1640, he was not a major supporter of the Society.

In Portugal as in the rest of Europe in the later seventeenth and eighteenth centuries, relatively few new houses were established—the Society had reached a certain level of saturation. Powerful financial backers, moreover, now kept their distance. The order's ties to the high nobility of Portugal were largely severed after 1700. In 1712, King João V (1689–1750; r. since 1706) explicitly emancipated himself from the staff of Jesuits that had surrounded him in his youth. The new monarch brought his royal power to bear on the Jesuits—and other churchmen—more frequently than before. Still, at least one Jesuit, Giovanni Battista Carbone (1695–1750), was able to win João's political confidence, serving him as an adviser and emissary (particularly in ecclesiastical matters). Despite the growing distance between the Jesuits and the court, however, it was still a major break when in 1759 the campaign to suppress the Society began precisely in Portugal.[8]

Italy had become the new order's home in tandem with Portugal. The authors of the *Imago primi saeculi* considered Italy the center of the Society of Jesus. Loyola may have been Spanish, and the Society long retained a Spanish character, but the Italianization of the Society of Jesus was well underway by the generalship of Acquaviva. The superiors general of the seventeenth and eighteenth centuries came predominantly from Italy. A German (Goswin Nickel), a Belgian (Charles de Noyelle), a Spaniard (Tirso González), and a Bohemian (Franz Retz) were the exceptions, not the rule. Rome had served as the center of the Jesuit order since 1540. It was here that the superior general resided; here, where the most important churches and institutions, like Il Gesù or the Collegio Romano, were to be found; here, where the Jesuits were directly connected to the church hierarchy. The order quickly spread to other Italian cities, and soon the peninsula was dotted with Jesuit houses. In 1640, there were 116 colleges and more than three thousand members in Italy.

The Jesuits arrived early in the parts of southern Italy under Spanish rule. Messina on the island of Sicily was a particularly important foothold with respect to the development of the Jesuit school system. In the north, in Spanish Milan, relations with Carlo Borromeo, the grand archbishop and church reformer, proved quite tempestuous. Nevertheless, the Jesuit houses in Milan soon proved to be important centers for all northern Italy.

The main exception to the broadly successful expansion of the Society of Jesus in Italy was its long ambivalent and, frankly, dysfunctional relationship with Venice. The order had arrived in the City of Bridges in 1550 but was banned in 1606. Conflict had broken out between the city and the pope over the question of whether clergymen who had committed a crime could be tried before a secular, municipal court. When Paul V excommunicated the city, the Jesuit *patres* were expelled in turn because they had intransigently taken the position of the Roman Curia. The Jesuits were not permitted to return to Venice until 1657.

Italy remained a bastion of strength for the Society in the seventeenth and eighteenth centuries. The Collegio Romano, with its international staff, was still considered the intellectual center of all Christendom. The Jesuits were also well-connected with numerous leading intellectual, social, and artistic figures—Gian Lorenzo Bernini, for example, the great sculptor and architect of baroque Rome, was a close friend of the Jesuit Cardinal Sforza Pallavicino and Superior General Gianpaolo Oliva. It was not until the mid-eighteenth century that the picture began to change, at least in some regions. Depending on the political alignment of various Italian principalities, the principles of the Enlightenment began to be asserted more forcefully. In the now Austrian territories of central and northern Italy, ministers such as Karl Joseph von Firmian implemented Enlightened absolutist regimes as embodied in Austria by Maria Theresa and especially by her son Joseph II. Many of the Jesuits' traditional preferences in culture, religion, and public order came in for criticism.

The rulers of Spain reacted to the arrival of the new order much more warily than the king of Portugal and sundry Italian princes.[9] Emperor Charles V—Charles I as king of Spain—kept his distance. The most important Spanish archbishop, Cardinal Juan Martínez Silíceo of Toledo (r. 1546–57), was even a bitter adversary. Conflict with the Inquisition ensued, leading in 1559 to a genuine crisis in connection with the imprisonment of Bartolomé de Carranza, when church authorities in Valladolid and Seville took action against several members of the Society.

It thus was no surprise that the first two Jesuits to come to Spain— Antonio de Araoz, a nephew of Ignatius's sister-in-law, and Pierre Favre, one of the founder's first companions—did so at the request of the king of Portugal, not the king of Spain. João III sought spiritual support for his daughter Maria, who had married the Spanish crown prince Philip (II). Araoz was initially a key figure in establishing the Society in Spain, but his fame was soon overshadowed by the spectacular rise of the Duke of Gandía, Francisco de Borja. Borja joined the Society as a widower in 1548, subsequently became superior general in 1565, and was ultimately sainted in 1671.

Serious conflict soon broke out between Borja and Araoz. Araoz was a strong, willful personality, who chafed at competition with the former duke. There were also significant differences in their spiritual orientations, since Borja's mystical inclinations jarred with Araoz's pious style. It was Borja, however, not Araoz, who became the dominant Jesuit figure in Spain, using his noble connections to gain access to the court— not to Charles V himself but to his daughters Maria and especially

Joanna (Juana) of Austria, who ruled the country from 1554 to 1559 as her father's representative and her brother's (Philip II) regent. She was captivated by Borja and other early Jesuits in Spain and became an important patroness. Uniquely, the daughter of the emperor and sister of the king was even officially admitted to the Society under a pseudonym—the only female Jesuit in history.

Thus, despite numerous difficulties and deep mistrust, the Society of Jesus also spread rapidly in Spain. Already by 1543, Francisco de Villanueva had received a house in Alcalá de Henares, which became a college in 1545. Araoz came to Valencia in 1544 with six young Jesuits. Gandía, Borja's ancestral home, was another important stronghold. A Jesuit presence in Madrid followed in 1560, established with the aid of Leonor de Mascareñhas, a Portuguese woman from a very influential family friendly to the Jesuits. With the support of both daughters of Charles V, this eventually became the great Colegio Imperial. In 1553, when the first college in Andalusia was founded in Córdoba, the Jesuit presence in the southern Iberian Peninsula expanded rapidly. Important houses were opened in Seville and Granada in 1554, then again in Córdoba in 1558, Cádiz in 1564, Málaga in 1571, and many more in between and thereafter. The wave of new houses continued until around 1630.[10]

After the era of expansion, the latter half of the seventeenth century was a period in which the Society of Jesus in Spain both enjoyed great power and experienced grave crises. Even more houses were established, albeit not as many as in decades past. High-placed personages protected and sponsored the Jesuits, such as the Duke of Lerma, Francisco Gómez de Sandoval (1553–1625). Philip III's leading minister, Sandoval, was the grandson of Francisco de Borja and tried to exploit this family connection to win symbolic capital for himself. In 1629, the next king, Philip IV, founded a university in Madrid both for and with the Jesuits, summoning Jesuit professors from across Europe to staff it. The construction of a college (beginning in 1682) in Loyola, Ignatius's home, was an especially powerful symbol of this era. Some Jesuits acquired formidable political power as the confessors of ministers and queens, especially Eberhard Nithard (1607–81), an Austrian who had accompanied Mariana of Austria, the wife of Philip IV, to Spain as her confessor.

But the Jesuits tellingly never became the confessors of the kings in Spain of the sixteenth and seventeenth centuries.

The late seventeenth century was a phase of stagnation and decline. The number of Spanish Jesuits plummeted, and their intellectual cachet within the Society declined. Civil war–like unrest in Catalonia and the independence of Portugal created tension, conflict, and the unpleasant necessity of choosing political sides. As a severe economic crisis swept across the Iberian Peninsula, these decades were a time of grinding poverty for many small colleges.

When the French Bourbons came to power in 1701, during the War of the Spanish Succession, conditions changed dramatically yet again for the Jesuits. Broadly speaking, the Society quickly befriended the new ruling dynasty. The following decades of the eighteenth century were initially a period of prosperity, in terms of both new members and new houses. Now the kings of Spain themselves were counseled by Jesuit confessors like Guillaume Daubenton (1648–1723) and Gabriel Bermúdez (1667–1749).

The situation in France was even more complicated. Even the authors of the *Imago primi saeculi* had to admit that "access [was] more difficult" there than elsewhere.[11] When Henry II granted the Jesuits official permission to establish themselves in his kingdom in 1551, grave religious disputes already loomed on the horizon. Protestantism was on the rise in France, and its adherents fought a bloody, decades-long civil war with several Catholic parties, sometimes fighting on three fronts. The new order was thus thrust into a highly fraught situation from the very start. All in all, the Jesuits were not exceptionally active in these religious civil wars.[12] But individual members of the Society quickly adopted more or less extreme anti-Protestant positions. In 1561, Superior General Laínez was present at the Colloquy of Poissy in France, clashing with the Calvinist leaders around Theodore Beza. A few years later, Edmond Auger (1530–91), the Jesuit provincial of Aquitaine, was a welcome face among the leaders of the Catholic camp.[13] At any rate, the Protestants blamed his sermons for the outbreak of Catholic violence in Bordeaux in 1572.

Auger was one of those erratic Jesuits who made the early years of the Society so colorful in various parts of Europe. On the one hand, he won immense influence at court for the Jesuit community, enabling the Society of Jesus to establish fourteen colleges in France by 1580, despite the tense situation. On the other, Auger's stature made it hard for his superiors to control him. Then, in the mid-1580s, he became a problem for the Catholic extremists (the so-called Catholic League) because he still supported Henry III, whom they now no longer considered sufficiently Catholic. Jesuits like Claude Matthieu, Jacques Commolet, and Henri Samier, however, were actively collaborating with these extremists. This partisanship on behalf of the radical Catholic party became a serious problem for the Society in 1589, just when the situation seemed to be settling down.

It was then that a new king, Henry IV, ascended the French throne. Henry was actually a Protestant who owed his kingdom to a tragic accident: his predecessor, Henry III, had been murdered without male issue. Henry IV had converted to Catholicism to become king. The Jesuits initially remained skeptical, since the new ruler pursued a policy that promoted religious tolerance. Henry IV also touted the religious autonomy of France. With their strong attachment to Rome, however, the Jesuits embodied the complete opposite of this "Gallicanism." Thus, in 1594, the Society was tried before the Parlement of Paris. It was whispered that the Jesuits wanted to have the formerly Protestant king assassinated—whispers that grew louder when an unsuccessful assassination attempt was made on Henry in 1594. The Jesuits had nothing to do with it, but the Society was still outlawed in large parts of France.[14]

Central and northern France remained off limits to the Jesuits for nine years; they were not allowed to return until 1603. It was Henry IV himself who called them back, demonstrating his domestic strength with this royal act of clemency while simultaneously making the Society utterly dependent on his favor. Proximity to the monarch became a special feature of the French branches of the order. The king demonstrated this new solidarity between himself and the Society by founding the great Jesuit college of La Flèche. But in 1610 another attempt was made on Henry's life, this time successfully. The king had been assassinated and history seemed to repeat itself. Again the Jesuits stood in the crossfire of criticism, but this time they were not expelled, despite new trials. The Jesuit superiors in France escaped this drastic measure by issuing a declaration that they would henceforth follow the ecclesiastical-political "doctrine of Paris"—this meant that they largely recognized the autonomy of France.[15] This laid the basis for reliable royal patronage in the succeeding decades. Yet the Society remained permanently under special scrutiny. Cardinal Richelieu always kept a vigilant, critical eye on the Jesuits.

Many French Jesuits gradually came around to the fact that they had to accept a compromise between Rome and Paris in this difficult situation. Gallicanism, willy-nilly, became part of the everyday reality of the Society's French provinces. Many French Jesuits soon internalized the lesson that survival in France under the king's protection meant occasionally distancing oneself from Rome. Under Louis XIV, French Jesuits repeatedly had to take sides, since the king was involved in grave disputes both with Innocent XI and with the Jesuit Curia in Rome. The French Jesuits tried to maneuver as long as they could, but ultimately most of them were inclined to accommodate the position of the king in cases of doubt, despite their personal scruples and reservations.[16] And so the alliance between the French Society of Jesus and the kings of France survived these times of conflict. It would not finally collapse until the middle of the eighteenth century, when the Society became ever more conspicuously a pawn in the escalating political power struggle between the king and the *parlements*. The *parlements* called for the suppression and ultimately the abolition of the Society of Jesus. Hoping that such a concession might bring about domestic peace, after long hesitation Louis XV finally granted their wish in 1762/3. The history of the Jesuits in France was thereby (for the time being) over.

Like France, the Holy Roman Empire of the German Nation, which comprised the entirety of Central Europe, was divided into rival confessions when the Jesuits arrived. The first Jesuit to set foot in Germany after the founding of the Society was Pierre Favre, who attended the Colloquy of Worms and Regensburg between the Catholics and Lutherans in 1540/1. In 1542, Claude Jay and Nicolás Bobadilla were also on hand. Bobadilla was the first Jesuit to come to Vienna in 1542 and to Prague in 1544—presumably accompanying the German king Ferdinand I. In 1543 and 1544, Jay established contacts in Dillingen, Ingolstadt, and Augsburg, where he soon was made a theological adviser at the Council of Trent by Bishop Truchsess of Waldburg. In 1544, Favre established the first, albeit temporary, home for the Society on German soil in Cologne. The order's first regular residence in the Holy Roman Empire was established in Vienna in 1551. In the spring of 1543, Favre met the Dutchman Peter (Petrus) Canisius in Mainz, winning him over to the Jesuit order. Canisius was extremely important for the subsequent expansion of the Society of Jesus in the empire. The *Imago* concluded, not without reason, that "the Society and, if you believe the heretics, Religion [i.e., Catholicism] owed no one in Germany more than it did to him."[17]

Shortly before his death in 1556, Ignatius founded two German provinces in the wake of these early successes, the provinces of Upper Germany and the Rhine. New houses were quickly established within this framework. Cologne was expanded and Prague reopened in the same year; Munich followed in 1559; Trier was added in 1560, Mainz and the first house in the Kingdom of Hungary (Trnava) in 1561, and the college in Speyer in 1571. In 1562, Austria was split off as a separate province. The first college in Poland was established at Braniewo in 1564, and many more soon followed, so that a separate province of Poland could be founded ten years later. Piotr Skarga (1536–1612) was the most important Polish Jesuit of this early phase; he found a patron in King Sigismund III. Bohemia followed almost contemporaneously with houses at Olomouc in 1566 and Brno in 1573. A separate province was created there too in 1623. The province of Austria, however, remained the largest in Europe, since it included Hungary as well. Around the same time, the Jesuits made inroads into an especially complex border region and religious melting pot: Transylvania, where the Society was active for several years after 1579.[18] Here the Society of Jesus encountered not only Muslims but also various groups of Protestant, Orthodox, and Romanian Christians. The Jesuits' expulsion from 1588 to 1595 put a temporary stop to their plans, but a lasting presence was successfully established under the auspices of Alfonso Carillo (1556–1628).

The Thirty Years' War was a devastating interlude for many branches of the Society in the Holy Roman Empire. The Jesuits had to flee Prague in 1620, for example, only to be restored in 1622. Then in 1648, shortly before the end of the war, they had to fear the depredations of the Swedes yet again.[19] Many houses in the empire were at least temporarily abandoned on account of the chaos of war; others were severely damaged. Membership plummeted. The Jesuits were also the victims of numerous wars in the Holy Roman Empire during the latter half of the seventeenth century. The Upper Rhine in particular suffered serious damage as a result of the eastern expansionism of Louis XIV—the houses in Baden and Speyer, for example, were affected by the war.

The decades after 1620 thus were a phase of constant reconstruction. During this century of warfare, the Jesuits were focused more on restoring previous conditions than on attempting anything new. New houses were rare, as at Mannheim in 1720 or Bruchsal in 1753 and a few colleges in Hungary. Nonetheless, it was not merely a time of stagnation. The gaps in membership caused by the great war had been filled in the Lower Rhine area by about 1700. Ever more missions fanned out from Münster, Paderborn, and Hildesheim to Protestant northern Germany and northern Europe. Over time, footholds were established in Hamburg, Bremen, Glückstadt, and Lübeck, as well as in Berlin and Dresden.

The Holy Roman Empire remained a battleground for most European wars of the eighteenth century, and the Jesuits experienced their fair share of these conflicts. The Jesuits of Bavaria, for example, suffered greatly during the War of the Austrian Succession (1740–48). Maria Theresa in Vienna had demanded—without success but not without reason—that the Jesuit houses in Austrian-controlled Tyrolia be split off from the province of Upper Germany, which was dominated by the hostile Bavarians, and incorporated in the province of Austria. The Jesuits of the Holy Roman Empire also felt the wave of anti-Jesuit sentiment that swept across Europe, even though the ever more numerous enemies of the Society in Germany were far less able to take political action against the Society of Jesus than in France or Portugal. Yet even here the traditional alliances with the ruling dynasties of the Wittelsbachs (in Bavaria, Neuburg, and various bishoprics like Cologne or Liège) and the Habsburgs (Vienna, Innsbruck, Graz, Klagenfurt) had undeniably begun to fray. Maria Theresa never openly opposed the Society, but she still sought to emancipate herself from the Jesuits with respect to school policy.[20] Yet the first half of the Age of Enlightenment was indisputably a high point for the Society of Jesus in Austria and elsewhere. The number of Jesuits rose until shortly before the suppression of the Society in 1773; in 1767, there were 1,906 Jesuits in Austria alone.

When the Society was founded, the territory of modern Belgium and the Netherlands still belonged to the Holy Roman Empire and the possessions of the (Spanish) Habsburgs. The Netherlands, however, became increasingly Protestant after the 1560s and won their political independence from Spain in 1648. Although a very large Catholic minority remained, the country was regarded as Reformed, and so the Jesuits were only ever active there as missionaries, lacking a full-fledged infrastructure. Things were different in early modern Belgium. The Society took root there in 1542, after some young Jesuits who had studied in Paris were driven out by the French on account of their Spanish origins. They fled northward, to Leuven. Among them was Francisco de Estrada, a gifted preacher, whose sermons caused a sensation. The Society quickly attracted prospective members. In 1547, this group of young Jesuits and sympathizers came together under the leadership of the novice Cornelis Wischaven as Belgium's first Jesuit community. This early group, whose members were officially admitted by Ignatius in Rome in 1548, helped the Society spread rapidly. Pastoral excursions soon reached Mechelen, Brussels, and other cities. In 1553, a second house was founded in Tournai. After long negotiations with the Spanish governors in Brussels, the order was officially established in the country in 1556, although it was initially subject to some restrictions. New houses followed in Dinant and Cambrai, and a small establishment was founded in Antwerp in 1563. At the same time, the college in Leuven was virtually expanded into a university, and a first-rate intellectual center soon blossomed there. Robert Bellarmine began teaching in Leuven in 1569. When a separate Belgian province was founded in 1564, further communities followed. The college of Douai, founded in 1575, evolved into the province's leading institution. When Ernest of Bavaria of the House of Wittelsbach became bishop of Liège, the Society of Jesus profited from its close collaboration with the dynasty there, too.

This first wave of foundations was impressive, and yet circumstances in Belgium were anything but simple. The Dutch struggle for religious and political independence had begun. Protestants and Catholics, Dutch and Spanish intermittently fought one another with extreme brutality. Where Protestant and anti-Spanish forces gained the upper hand, the Jesuits were (temporarily) expelled. There were even difficulties with the local Spanish representatives. The Duke of Alba, governor from 1567 to 1573, was ill-disposed to the Society. Not until one of his successors took office, Alessandro Farnese in 1579, was more sympathy forthcoming from the Spanish. Farnese secured full authorization for the Society in 1584. This period of consolidation was followed by a wave of new establishments around 1600, including such important colleges as that of Brussels, founded in 1604. The time was ripe for the province to be partitioned. In 1612, the French part, the Povincia Gallo-Belgica, was split off from the Flemish, the Provincia Flandro-Belgica. The ensuing decades were a phase of breakneck growth. As early as 1621, each province had more members by itself than had existed in the formerly undivided Belgium. The Habsburg regents who governed Belgium were very friendly toward the Jesuits. Many new houses were opened until the 1630s. It was during this phase of triumphant expansion that the Antwerp Jesuits celebrated the jubilee of the Society in 1640 with the *Imago primi saeculi*.

This period of impressive growth gradually petered out in Belgium after the middle of the century. Under Louis XIV, Belgium was the scene of constant military conflict, as France and the Netherlands found themselves increasingly at odds. The University of Leuven became a prominent center of anti-Jesuit theology. The Jansenists, bitter opponents of the Jesuits, moreover established a strong presence in Belgium, which sapped public goodwill toward the Society of Jesus. Thus, the Society's activity and membership appreciably declined after the middle of the century. Despite the good financial start that many colleges enjoyed on account of the Habsburg governors, the order's economic base had largely crumbled by 1700. The Jesuits' many lavish buildings also devoured their resources.

The *Imago* thus was not wrong: wherever there were Catholics, there also seemed to be a Jesuit house nearby one hundred years after the founding of the Society. But how did things look in Protestant Europe? Even the countries that had joined the Reformation were by no means impenetrable to the Jesuits. In these places, the Jesuits often worked as the direct representatives of the papal Curia. Antonio Possevino, for example, a Jesuit with many exceptional gifts, acted as a papal diplomat on religious-political missions in Protestant northern, northeastern, and eastern Europe several times in the late sixteenth century. In the 1560s, he was engaged in the struggle against the Calvinists in Piedmont and Valtellina; in 1580, he traveled to Scandinavia on a papal mission and shortly thereafter was involved in negotiations between Poland and Russia concerning the status of Catholicism in both kingdoms.[21] The particulars of Possevino's achievements were sundry and varied, yet hardly any other personality better symbolizes the Society's effort to (re)assert Catholicism in Protestant Europe in alliance with the popes of the day.

Working conditions in the predominantly Protestant regions of Europe varied dramatically in the early modern period. In many northern German cities, a small handful of Jesuits had operated more or less unmolested—albeit often bitterly antagonized—since the early seventeenth century, either unofficially in the retinue of an imperial or French ambassador or even in the context of an established "mission." In 1594, the Jesuits also began to operate in the northern provinces of the United Netherlands, which had progressively embraced Calvinism since 1568.[22] Although many harsh laws against Catholics were on the books there, they were seldom enforced. The Jesuits' influence in the Netherlands persisted until the early eighteenth century, when the Society was expelled.

In Scandinavia, in contrast, and especially in England, the Jesuits could only exist undercover.[23] Whereas the Society of Jesus maintained only an intermittent and sporadic presence in early modern Sweden, the Protestant British Isles eventually became a separate province despite these impediments. The Society made its first contacts there on the margins: a very brief preliminary visit by two Jesuits took place in fall 1541. Soon afterward, Paschase Broët and Alonso Salmerón were sent as papal legates to Ireland to support the Catholic cause there. This mission, however, did not leave behind a lasting tradition. In 1562 and 1566, the Jesuits Nikolaas Floris de Gouda and Edmund Hay traveled to Scotland to speak with Mary Stuart, the Catholic Scottish queen and cousin of the Protestant English queen Elizabeth I. Each time, the Jesuits sought (in vain) to launch an offensive pro-Catholic policy in Protestant-leaning Scotland. Around the same time, David Wolfe, Edmund Daniel, and William Good were active in Ireland again. Wolfe stayed eleven years, five of which he spent in a Dublin jail. He had previously ministered to Catholics as a traveling priest and performed episcopal duties. Daniel, in contrast, did not survive his deployment: he was executed by the English, becoming the first Jesuit to die for his faith in Europe.

The Society of Jesuit was not active in England itself for the first forty years of its existence. After England had permanently converted to Protestantism under Queen Elizabeth in 1558, life became hard for the roughly 10 percent of remaining Catholics who refused to convert or flee. Catholics were increasingly suspected of high treason; it was prohibited to recognize the authority of the pope in 1559. Further laws against the "Papists" followed. A mission thus seemed too risky to the Jesuits, as their Irish and Scottish experiences also seemed to indicate. Exiled English Catholics in Belgium and Rome were unable to convince the cautious Superior General Everard Mercurian (r. 1573–80) to send Jesuits to England until the last months of his generalship.

Three Jesuits thus set out for England in 1580: Robert Persons, Edmund Campion, and Ralph Emerson. The first martyrdom on this mission occurred not long afterward, when Campion was publicly executed in London on December 1, 1581. He would not be the only one: by 1679, twenty-seven further members of the Society had followed him to their deaths. The Act against Jesuits and Seminarists was passed in 1585, declaring membership in the order tantamount to high treason for an Englishman. Given these perilous circumstances, there were never more than about a dozen Jesuits active in England at a time during this early phase of the mission. These trying circumstances led some English Jesuits to believe that the very survival of Catholicism could be guaranteed only by political or even military action. After fleeing Ireland, David Wolfe began organizing a Catholic rebellion on the island, for which he hoped to gain the support of the Spanish court in Madrid. Persons had similar plans. Broadly speaking, the Jesuits had high hopes for the Spanish Armada, with which Philip II of Spain tried and failed to conquer England in 1588.

The threat level remained high in the early seventeenth century. The Gunpowder Plot of 1605 and various other supposedly Catholic conspiracies against the English monarchs led to temporary spikes in anti-Catholic efforts, but in other phases, the more time passed, the more (relative) tolerance came to prevail. In 1619 and 1623, Superior General Muzio Vitelleschi was able to elevate the English mission to a vice-province and then to a full province. There may have been a good hundred Jesuits in England by 1620, who were now able to found houses and schools. "Greater calm [prevailed] under king Charles I," the authors of the *Imago* duly remarked about the 1620s and 1630s.[24] Of course, violence against individual communities remained a possibility—for instance, in 1628, the Society's quarters in London were attacked. The period of domestic unrest after 1640 during the English Civil War and then under Oliver Cromwell spelled a serious setback for the Society. When the monarchy was restored under Charles II in 1660, the king promised tolerance, but it was a promise that could not be kept unconditionally. Since yet another supposedly Catholic assassination attempt was "uncovered" in the Popish Plot of 1678–1681, the allegedly guilty Jesuits had to pay the price: although it could not be proved that they were involved, eight members of the Society died on the scaffold as did a similar number in prison.

On the one hand, the Jesuits maintained a solid presence in eighteenth-century England, with well over one hundred members; on the other, they played virtually no part in public life whatsoever, since their Catholic flock had by and large retreated from view. English Catholics had shrunken to an insignificant minority and were moreover plagued by fierce infighting. The Jesuits and the secular clergy regarded one another with deep antipathy. Thus, for all the tranquility after the Glorious Revolution of 1688, it was an era of growing insignificance. Conditions in Ireland under Protestant British rule largely corresponded to those in England, if on a smaller scale.

Another form of ministering to the spiritual needs of England and Ireland was far less dangerous in this period. Since a large number of Catholics had fled the Protestant Reformation and had settled on the Continent since the middle of the sixteenth century, there was an influential English Catholic diaspora there. In order to support them and to train clergymen from among their numbers—who might then return to their homeland as missionaries—colleges were established specifically for English Catholics everywhere on the Continent, most of them under Jesuit management. In 1579, after some back-and-forth, the Society took over the English seminary—known as English College (Collegium Anglorum)—in Rome; and in Belgian Saint-Omer, the Society concentrated its efforts on the British Isles to a considerable extent. A seminary there trained future English priests. Similar institutions existed in Spain and Portugal in cities like Valladolid, Seville, and Lisbon. Specialized colleges for Scandinavia were also established under Jesuit direction, notably a "Nordic Seminary" in Linz, Austria.[25] The Germanicum (1552) and the Hungaricum (1578) were founded in Rome for the same purpose at the direct instigation of Ignatius himself.[26]

The authors of the *Imago primi saeculi* thus were not wrong when they proudly and confidently noted in 1640 that Europe "had received the Society in very many places."[27] The network of Jesuit houses became even more close-knit in the following century, and the number of members likewise grew. It was an eventful process that made the Society of Jesus ubiquitous across Catholic and Protestant Europe. This upward trend of course had peaks and valleys, winners and losers, steps forward and backward, phases of crisis and phases of dynamic growth. It is important to note that the expansion of the Society was not at all planned in advance, let alone steered centrally from Rome. New houses, of course, had to be approved by the superior general in Rome, but in many cases local and regional circumstances dictated where and in what form Jesuits came together to live. The expansion of the Society thus played out as a series of compromises, complicated negotiations, and costly experiments. In the end, though, an impressive network of several hundred communities small and large emerged. Houses, provinces, institutions—these admittedly constituted only one side of the

Society. The actual protagonists of the history of the order are the Jesuits themselves, the persons and personalities who worked in these establishments.

Life in the Service of the Society

The first generation of Jesuits consisted of Ignatius himself and his famous nine companions. They had a decisive influence on the early history of the Society of Jesus. Ignatius had met these nine men and won them over in widely different circumstances over time. He had lodged with Francis Xavier and Pierre Favre as a student in Paris since 1529. Rodrigues had heard of Ignatius there and deliberately sought him out in 1530; Jay, Broët, and Codure, who already knew each other, were the last to join the group. They were brought over by Favre in 1535.

Ignatius's first companions were a highly heterogeneous group. There were men from Spain, the Basque Country, France, Navarre, and Savoy. There were glaring political differences, as well: the families of Francis Xavier and Ignatius, for example, had stood on opposite sides of the war in 1521. Like Ignatius himself, Xavier came from the old nobility and had been accustomed to an aristocratic lifestyle.[28] Salmerón and Favre, in contrast, came from humble backgrounds. Favre was the first priest among the companions. He read the mass in 1534 at which they confirmed their commitment to live together as a community. Laínez and Salmerón were the best scholars in the group and vastly superior to Ignatius in academic theology. Favre was a gentle, deeply pious, introspective, and simple character who indefatigably went about his work—he traveled constantly—with humility and modesty. Rodrigues and Bobadilla, in contrast, soon articulated bold alternative visions of the future of the Society.

The nine "first companions," some of whom are now venerated by the Catholic Church as saints, were important role models for the Society after its founding in 1540, although they were all soon overshadowed by Ignatius himself—somewhat unfairly from a historical perspective.[29] It is far less well-known, however, that Ignatius was acquainted with many more people both before and after he made contact with these men. But his attempts to win over these people to his vision of spirituality were unsuccessful. As early as 1524/5, a small circle of friends had gathered around him in Barcelona, accompanying him to Alcalá. Ignatius placed high hopes in some of the earlier people he attracted, only to be bitterly disappointed more than once. One of his initially enthusiastic followers, Jean Bochet, briefly joined the new order in 1541 but soon afterward was executed in Spain as a bandit and highwayman. Diego de Cáceres was at the deliberations in Rome in 1539 and also joined the Society, but he is not considered part of the first generation—in 1542, he "left" the young Society of Jesus to work as a spy for France. Diego Hoces, a loyal follower, died before the decisive date of 1540.[30]

These difficult experiences probably led Ignatius to select new members of the Society with the utmost care. All Catholic orders have certain admission requirements, and all of them stipulate a phase of examination and preparation before an aspirant is formally admitted to the community. But the recruitment and selection of future Jesuits were especially close to Ignatius's heart. Hardly any other order examines potential entrants as long or as intensely as the Society of Jesus. Detailed passages in the *Constitutions* describe the prerequisites that a future Jesuit must meet, and the long way from initial, provisional admittance as a novice to final entry into the Society as a full member. Not everyone could—or should—become a Jesuit.

Jesuits and Their Families: Origins, Recruitment, and Ties

Whoever wanted to join the Society of Jesus first had to meet certain legal, social, physical, and intellectual requirements.[31] The *Constitutions* stipulate that no murderers or persons with physical handicaps or deficient intellectual gifts could be admitted. In reality, Ignatius himself used wide discretion in enforcing these measures, for instance, admitting men with missing fingers or eyes. Illegitimate children could also find a home in the Society. Other aspirants, such as Louis Le Valois, were initially admitted but subsequently expelled on account of sickness—only to be readmitted after the health problems in question subsided.[32] The admission of interested parties who had previously belonged to another order was a more difficult question, but exceptions could be made here, too. All candidates, of course, had to be unmarried when they were admitted to the Society, but that by no means meant that husbands and fathers could not join after their spouses' death. Francisco de Borja, Duke of Gandía, joined as a widower. The lay brother Alonso Rodríguez (1532–1617), one of the most famous intellectuals of the order and later also canonized, joined the Society of Jesus in 1571, just shy of his fortieth birthday, after the death of his wife, as the father of three children (who had died young).

It was fiercely debated within the Society whether people born outside Europe could be admitted—that is, indigenous peoples, mestizos (children born to one European and one indigenous parent), and Creoles (children born to two European parents overseas).[33] The Jesuits were not entirely at liberty to answer this question for themselves. The popes and Iberian kings had passed numerous—partly contradictory and inconsistent—laws concerning the admission of people born to non-European forefathers to ecclesiastical office.[34] The Councils of Lima in 1550 and 1567 had forbidden Indios and mestizos to hold ecclesiastical office. Gregory XIII then allowed them to be ordained in 1577, which Philip II subsequently prohibited again, only to allow it after all in 1588.

The Jesuits themselves were hardly less inconsistent. The provincial congregation of Peru unapologetically declared against mestizos in 1582. But there also was dissent, and at least individual children of indigenous parents were admitted at a relatively early date. The great administrator and author José de Acosta (1539–1600) is a good example of this ambivalent attitude that mingled skepticism and hostility with occasional concessions. In his standard work on the mission to the Americas, he declared that it was "not appropriate to elevate Indians to higher ecclesiastical ranks," yet he acknowledged "that we cannot deny that some are our equals in the blamelessness of their lives and our superiors in their command of the Indian language." The knowledge of languages was indeed a key argument in favor of consecrating mestizos. But mestizos and natives who were admissible, in Acosta's view, were "rare."[35] As provincial of Peru, he personally admitted some of these select few to the Society in 1582/3. One member of this group was the mestizo Blas Valera, whose life is a famous and inscrutable case. It is clear that he fell out with his superiors. He was imprisoned, accused of immoral conduct, and finally sent to Europe to answer to the superior general in Rome.[36] The background to the case was apparently Valera's all too heartfelt sympathy for indigenous culture and religion, which he considered compatible with Christianity; this view roused the resentment of many of his confreres.

Even over the long term, the Jesuits had little enthusiasm for creating an indigenous clergy and a fortiori admitting natives to the Society of Jesus. In Japan, a handful of natives had been admitted as priests around 1610. Similar concessions were deliberated in China around the same date, but the sons of the Middle Kingdom were ultimately excluded from the priesthood and entrance into the Society—some Chinese were admitted only as lay helpers.[37] This policy was maintained until younger missionaries took a different view in the last quarter of the seventeenth century. They were much more open to indigenous priests as members of the order. In 1688, three Chinese priests were admitted to the Society, but a tradition of indigenous members failed to materialize. Just a single Indian joined the order as a priest prior to 1773.[38] On this point, the Jesuits were fundamentally at odds with the official policy of the papal missionary authority, the congregation De Propaganda Fide, which proved to be much more liberal.

The Society of Jesus was also initially very cool toward Creoles.[39] General Mercurian had already assented to a restrictive policy regarding Creoles when he wrote that "indigenous people should be admitted into the Society only seldom and only after they have been tested extensively and for a long time."[40] His successor Acquaviva confirmed this policy in 1588. Even at the end of the late seventeenth century, the Jesuit missionary António Vieira wrote a hateful document in which he used extraordinarily harsh terms to contrast the inferiority of Brazilian Creoles with the superiority of Jesuits born in Portugal.[41] It was easy to exclude Creoles in the beginning, since there were so few of them, but the interest of the growing numbers of them could not be denied forever.[42] Around the turn of the seventeenth century, ethnically Spanish settlers in the New World began to develop a Creole identity of their own. Entrance and admission to ecclesiastical office was an important point to them. The Jesuit leadership in Rome also relaxed its position and now wished for the peaceful coexistence of metropolitan and Creole Jesuits. Former superior general Vincenzo Carafa lamented in 1647: "Nothing causes me greater concern in those provinces than the lack of unity and charity [of Jesuits] toward one another, especially between those who were born there and those who come from Europe."[43] A degree of distrust on the part of both groups thus persisted, although the number and importance of Creole Jesuits constantly increased with the explicit endorsement of the leadership of the Society. By 1654, if not earlier, more Creole than Spanish novices were being trained in Peru. A Creole Jesuit, Leonardo de Peñafiel, became provincial of the Andes for the first time in 1656.

Becoming a Jesuit was also made very difficult early on for men from Jewish backgrounds. It was decided in 1593 that no conversos—that is, men from formerly Jewish families, regardless of when they converted to Christianity—could become Jesuits.[44] At least in theory, prospective members had to conduct detailed genealogical research back four or five generations to prove their eligibility.[45] This was how General Acquaviva, who himself had little personal sympathy for conversos, responded to Spanish pressure. Entrenched suspicion of Christianized Jewish and Muslim minorities (who had been forced to convert) was a major factor in Spain. Throughout the early modern period, extremely harsh restrictions on these groups remained in effect. The Spanish nobility, for example, was explicitly ordered to shun conversos so as not to taint their own *limpieza de sangre* (purity of blood). Many Jesuits in Portugal, Spain, and Italy shared these discriminatory views and said as much publicly—men like Antonio de Araoz, the first provincial of Spain, and Benedetto Palmio, a provincial and highly respected authority in Italy. This group's view carried the day in 1593. Thereafter, conversos were excluded from the Society. Although there was initial resistance to this prohibition in the seventeenth century, and knowledgeable Jesuits like those of Seville testified that it would be virtually impossible to recruit new members on account of the ubiquity of formerly Jewish families, this discrimination against conversos remained official policy until 1946.[46]

The exclusion of conversos was a question of great practical importance for the Society of Jesus. Prior to 1593, there was in fact a notably high number of men from formerly Jewish families in the Jesuits' ranks. Despite opinions to the contrary in Spain and Italy, which made themselves felt virtually from the start, Ignatius himself took a very favorable view of conversos. The first decades of the history of the Society witnessed many leading Jesuits who came from an ex-Jewish milieu or held liberal views. Diego Laínez, Antonio Possevino, and Juan de Polanco are just a few members who belonged to the large group of prominent converso-Jesuits. In addition to Ignatius, Jerónimo Nadal and Francisco de Borja were also champions of the pro-converso line. They did not shy away from bringing down on themselves the ire of the king of Spain, the Spanish Inquisition, and the most important Spanish archbishop, Juan Martínez Silíceo of Toledo. Many of the spiritual pillars of the Society that inspired Ignatius and Borja—for instance, the theology of the highly controversial mystic Juan de Valdés—derived from a converso context. The Society, however, bade farewell to this tradition of openness step by step after Borja's death in 1572. Polanco's otherwise self-evident election to superior general was then prevented because his family had once been Jewish. Acquaviva's concessions to the Spanish line in 1593 sealed the fate of the early pro-converso phase of the Society.

The requirements for admission to the Society of Jesus were far less discriminatory in social terms. Men from the high nobility of Europe, like Borja, rubbed elbows in the Society with brothers from humble backgrounds and even from the underclass. Pierre Chaumonot, for example, a celebrated Jesuit missionary in Canada, lived for years as a young tramp and vagabond on the streets of France and Italy before he became a Jesuit in Rome. For people like him, the institutions of the Catholic Church were one of very few "channels of mobility" in the early modern period that enabled at least limited social climbing.[47] Chaumonot himself was well aware of this; he wrote the following about his first weeks in the order:

O what joy! O what happiness for me to find myself among fifty novices, all young men of distinguished birth, excellent spirit and character, and handsome bodies. I would not have been more than their
valet or kitchen boy had they and I stayed in the (secular) world! . . .
Great God! Who would have ever imagined that a poor bumpkin like
me would be admitted to such a holy, such an illustrious Society as
the Society of Jesus, your son![48]

Similar stories are easy to find both within the Society and within the
Catholic Church as a whole. Tirso González, an important Jesuit missionary in Spain and later superior general, grew up in extreme poverty
and had worked as a shepherd in his boyhood.

The vast majority of Jesuits, of course, came from neither the top nor
the bottom of the society of estates, but rather from the middle. Research on the social history of the Society largely remains a desidera-
tum, but it is at least clear that clergymen in both the Catholic and the
Protestant churches came predominantly from the urban and middle
social strata in the early modern period. Middle and high officials, no-
taries and teachers, and even the sons of merchants and well-to-do artisans were just as much a part of the typical pool of new Jesuit recruits
as the sons of the petty nobility.[49] This was the case not least because
this clientele was the most important source of customers for the many
Jesuit schools, which were a vital source of new recruits. Recruitment,
of course, was not the explicit goal of the schools, let alone the only
purpose they served; the Jesuits even temporarily prohibited the admission of students to the Society. But it is undeniable that the Jesuits frequently recruited novices from the classes they taught, as Polanco himself once admitted in 1551.[50]

Outside Jesuit classrooms, recruitment also relied on family
traditions—up to 10 percent of all Jesuits are thought to have had relatives
in the Society.[51] We sometimes can describe such relationships virtually
as family networks. For example, three brothers from the Gagliardi
family—Achille, Ludovico, and Leonetto—became Jesuits, and likewise three brothers from the Khabes family of Vienna joined the order
in the early eighteenth century. The Acosta family from Spain arguably

epitomized such collective decisions to join the Society: in 1551, not only did the aforementioned José join, but also four of his brothers and his widowed father.[52] Many Jesuits were also connected to other religious orders by family ties. The Jesuit Miguel Godínez (born Michael Wadding), for example, had a famous brother among the Franciscans: Lucas Wadding, one of the most important historians of his day. And Pierre Bernard's family mirrored the diverse world of Catholic orders: in addition to Pierre, another brother joined the Jesuits, while two others became Capuchins and yet another went to the Carmelites.[53] Some families seem to have taken to the religious life more or less en masse. Younger male relatives in such cases were doubtless inspired by the example of their elders.

But families were not always overjoyed when their younger male members decided in favor of a religious life in the Jesuit order. Ignatius himself was repeatedly confronted with family conflicts between parents and children thinking of becoming novices.[54] Pierre Ayrault, a French legal scholar, even filed a lawsuit against the Jesuits when his son René joined the Society in Paris. He detailed his case at length in a book that soon found a broad audience.[55] There were similar incidents elsewhere: a German nobleman from Trier complained in 1609 or 1610 that his son had joined the Society of Jesus.[56] In some cases, relatives even resorted to violence to pry their children or nephews away from the Society. For example, in the Italian city of Nola in 1575, relatives and guardians of the young Carlo Carafa abducted him from his novitiate with "lively force" to prevent him from joining the Society.[57] A strikingly similar case, again featuring the use of force and tumultuous scenes, took place in Paderborn in 1618.[58] By no means all fathers and mothers in the early modern period were excited when their sons resolved to become Jesuits.

There were many reasons for parents' unease and their resultant opposition to their sons' plans.[59] Ayrault, for example, although a Catholic himself, was principally averse to the Society of Jesus as a Gallican official in France under Henry IV. Other contemporaries criticized joining the Society as a religious fad and a sign of misguided devotion. Such claims were leveled especially against new orders like the Jesuits and

Capuchins. Ayrault and the aforementioned German nobleman from Trier viewed their sons' secret entrance into the order moreover as an act of contempt for their paternal authority. As stated in the case from Trier, the son's actions were especially wrong because he had acted "without consulting his parents." At the same time, the boy's father openly admitted that he had other plans for his son, namely, military service, the traditional calling of the nobility. The father of the future Jesuit Pierre Coton, who rose to the highest honors in the early seventeenth century as the confessor of two French kings, also at first saw his hopes for his son bitterly dashed when the young man joined the Society. And other parents felt the need for their sons' everyday presence in one way or another, like the mother of Peter Canisius after her husband's death in 1544.[60]

Parents and other relatives opposed young men's entrance into the Society especially for economic reasons. Since Jesuits were forbidden to have any possessions yet were still entitled to receive inheritances, it naturally was asked what they intended to do with their share of the family property. Grave suspicion of the Society might quickly arise in such circumstances. In the eyes of many family members, their family property was in jeopardy. Again and again, the Jesuits were accused of attempting to persuade wealthy new members to donate their property to the order. Not a few Jesuits really bequeathed their assets to the Society of Jesus, but it was forbidden to pursue such bequests proactively, as the superiors of the order insisted time and again.[61] Quite independent of the question to whom a new member wanted to leave his present and future possessions, the necessary arrangements upon his admission to the Society had to be clarified with legal experts in the province and Rome. This process might drag on for a long time, particularly in the case of wealthy young men. Over the years and decades, the Society of Jesus became entangled in many complicated legal disputes over its members' property.

Parental resistance was especially fierce when sons were intent on joining the Society at a very young age. Young men normally joined the order between the ages of sixteen and twenty, but there were exceptions both young and old.[62] The Jesuits often hesitated to admit older men, since it seemed unlikely that older aspirants could be won over completely to the ways of the Society of Jesus.[63] In such cases, it was essential that the candidates had special social or intellectual qualifications. With youths, in contrast, the legal situation had to be taken into careful consideration, since regulations on the minimum age of new members varied according to secular and ecclesiastical law. In France, a minimum age of twenty was established in 1560 and subsequently lowered. Canon law, however, ruled that the consent of an adult novice was no longer necessary after the age of eighteen or twenty.[64] But ideally, as Ignatius himself wrote, when young men aspired to join the Society, one should always take care that "their parents are satisfied."[65] Diego Laínez also ordered that one should avoid conflict with candidates' parents at all costs.[66]

In the event, though, that the cooperation of a candidate's parents was not readily forthcoming, the Jesuits had various means and arguments at the ready. Pierre Favre responded to the protestations of Canisius's mother by arguing that she should esteem his spiritual progress in the Society higher than her own merely "fleshly" delight in the presence of her son. Louis Bourdaloue, one of the Society's famous preachers, delivered a speech on the subject in 1700, taking a somewhat different tack to win over reluctant parents.[67] Bourdaloue argued that parents should not overestimate their own authority in such matters. A true vocation, after all, was a mystery that parents could not easily recognize. Even Mary and Joseph did not immediately realize what a special future was intended for their son Jesus. This example was intended as a lesson to induce mothers and fathers in early modern France to show restraint. In brief, he concluded, "A Christian father cannot make himself the arbiter of his children's vocation without committing obvious injustices."

While Bourdaloue admonished parents to show restraint and respect for the religious fervor of their sons, Nicolaus Lancicius, a Polish Jesuit, exhorted young men to take resolute, courageous action.[68] He explicitly advised aspirants to forgo discussing their choices with their families because parents and relatives would only respond with worldly arguments. If parents then forbade their sons to join the Society, they could openly be ignored. Lancicius then suggested a series of arguments that potential candidates might use to refute their relatives' objections. He constantly pitted service to God against the allures of the world: whoever was called to the blessed life in the order could not dedicate himself to the superficial aspirations of earthly existence. If necessary, Lancicius provided aspirants with even more drastic arguments. Opponents of entering the Society could be countered with the argument that Luther had also rejected religious orders—hence chastising critical parents, albeit implicitly, for disbelief.

It remains unclear how successful such strategies were in defending an aspiring Jesuit's vocation against skeptical parents and relatives. It appears, however, that many parents nonetheless yielded to a real spiritual need that their children felt. Carlo Carafa, who had been abducted from the novitiate in Nola, ultimately overcame his relatives with "deep sighs and frequent tears," because he showed genuine signs of a true vocation during his confinement. The father from Trier's change of heart is described in very similar terms, but far more soberly and hence more credibly. Although he conveyed his disappointment so vehemently, as mentioned earlier, he took a more conciliatory tone in the end. His resistance was broken down not least by the realization that his son's decision was first and foremost in response to a "divine impulse." In this case too, it seems, a family ultimately yielded after detecting plausible signs of a true spiritual vocation.

Even when a novice joined the Society of Jesus with his family's blessing, his relationship with his parents and family fundamentally changed. The *Constitutions* approvingly cite verse 19:29 of the Gospel of Matthew, which promises one hundredfold in reward for leaving one's mother and father (among others) to follow Christ.[69] Love for one's parents and relatives, of course, did not necessarily have to cease entirely, but it had to be transformed. At most, "moderate" affection for one's family was allowed, but it should be exclusively "spiritual" in terms of Christian charity. Hence Jesuits were supposed to behave toward their parents as if their mothers and fathers had already died.[70] They were supposed to focus not on their parents, siblings, and other relatives but rather on their fellow brothers and superiors in the Society. Contact with their families thus had to be monitored and was subject to several restrictions. Jesuits had to request permission when they wanted to contact their families by letter or meet them in person.[71] By no means all such meetings were allowed. Ignatius himself could take a hard line, if he believed that visits might jeopardize the "spiritual progress" of a young Jesuit. In 1553, for example, Ignatius wrote to Nicholas Peter Cesari in Naples that he would not permit his son Octavius to travel to see his mother because he did not consider the young man emotionally stable enough. Although Ignatius explicitly acknowledged the mother's longing to see her son, he nonetheless refused to soften his position.[72] Other leading figures of the Society saw things similarly. Lorenzo Maggio, for instance, viewed young Jesuits' abiding affection for their parents as a threat that might undermine their concentration on their spiritual duties.[73]

Several documents suggest that many dedicated and successful Jesuits had internalized this limited but broad separation from their families to a surprising degree. Theodore Moretus, a Belgian Jesuit in Bohemia, wrote home in 1635, immediately after he had taken his final vows, "I want those who were once my relatives to consider me dead and even buried," only to ask them to send cordial greetings to his mother. Rejection and affection were tangled in a complex relationship.[74] The case of Eusebius Truchsess was the same. He reported in 1663 that his sister had asked him to stay with her longer in Cologne when he visited her. He initially refused, but then gave in after careful consideration, not least on account of a raging outbreak of the plague.[75] Truchsess accepted the tension between his secular responsibilities and feelings for his family and his spiritual responsibilities and feelings for the Society. He essentially weighed the two against one another. A certain distance from his familial roots, prescribed by the Society and soon internalized by Truchsess himself, is unmistakable.

That did not, however, result in a categorical separation. Family ties were reassessed, not cut. Not all affection toward one's family was forbidden, only "immoderate" feelings.[76] At the novitiate of Paris, the superiors were accordingly warned against excessive "cruelty" on this point. Young aspirants there were permitted to communicate with their parents, albeit seldom.[77] Ignatius himself stressed that there was no need to go out of one's way to alienate one's parents. Specifically, he considered it absurd that Francesco Adorno no longer spoke of his "father" since joining the Society, but rather of "the one they say was my father."[78]

Many leading Jesuits thus saw no need to cut family ties completely. When the Society in France was searching for missionaries to send to the Far East in 1653, two Jesuits who had been selected were nonetheless left home when their parents intervened—precisely because the Society refused to take a poor and widowed noblewoman's son away from her in this way.[79] In individual cases, at least, the Society's leadership also broke the rule that Jesuits traveling to see their parents had to be accompanied, if allowed to go at all, and granted exceptional leave.[80] For the most part, Jesuits seem to have remained more or less closely connected to their families even after joining the Society; family affairs certainly are a strikingly consistent subject of their letters and other statements.[81] Not only prior to but also during and after a Jesuit's admission to the Society of Jesus, his family background exerted an often decisive influence. The Society could help one overcome social barriers and required a new Jesuit to change his relationship with his former social and familial milieu, but life in this spiritual community was by no means completely detached from society outside.

Life as a Jesuit: Stations, Stages, Careers

It is hard to say how and for what reasons young men were inspired to break with their families and dedicate themselves to a strange, new world. What lurked behind the "divine impulse" to live as a Jesuit? What did this impulse look like, and how did it manifest itself? How did the idea of living as a Jesuit become plausible to young men? Contemporary theorists stressed that God and man arrived at the decision jointly—the novice definitely had to take an active part in the decision to join.[82] That sometimes meant it might take quite a long time, amid inner conflict and even vehement rejection, before a future Jesuit finally decided in favor of the Society. Jerónimo Nadal, who later became so influential, is a famous example of a Jesuit who wrestled with his decision for a long time before committing to the order. It took years before Ignatius and Francis Xavier could convince him that he genuinely had a vocation to join the new order. Nadal had long turned a deaf ear to their efforts. But at length—and here Nadal's autobiographical account is paradigmatic—he was "moved in the spirit." He thereby—and this too is a typical expression—"acknowledged the grace of God," that is, his vocation, which had long been present.[83]

Other famous Jesuits described the decision to join much more prosaically in hindsight. Some candidates, like Martin Delrio, who joined late as a twenty-eight-year-old, had already informed themselves about the Society and even read the *Constitutions*.[84] Others, such as Robert Bellarmine, depict their path to the Society as a systematic process of self-discovery. Bellarmine mentions neither a divine vocation nor any other kind of inner agitation. In his case, the decision to join the Society was allegedly the result of cool contemplation and introspection.[85] The method that Bellarmine supposedly applied in scrutinizing his inner self clearly recalls the *Spiritual Exercises* of the founder of the order. Other Jesuits also retrospectively stylized their entrance into the Society of Jesus in strikingly Ignatian language. Pierre Ayrault defended this existential step to his father by citing the "consolation" of the soul that it gave him—this, too, a key concept of the *Exercises*.[86] Evidently, as the decades passed, adopting Jesuit spirituality not only colored the self-perception of many members of the Society but also shaped their idea of a genuine vocation to spiritual life.

At any rate, it was not hard for people to come into contact with the Society of Jesus even as children. Bellarmine explicitly states in his autobiography that his mother had known Paschase Broët, Ignatius's early companion, and was so sympathetic to the new order thereafter that she would have gladly seen all five of her children become Jesuits.[87] Other children first came into contact with the Society by attending one of the schools it ran. Julien Maunoir (1606–83), for example, attended the local college in Rennes, the capital of Brittany, and soon felt drawn to life in the order. When Pierre Coton, the provincial at the time, came to visit in 1626, the then nineteen-year-old Maunoir approached him and asked to be admitted. Coton, who presumably knew of the young man's religious fervor, assented. Maunoir joined the Society and was soon sent to Paris for training.[88]

Maunoir appears to have been accepted as a novice directly by the provincial. His biographer, at any rate, makes no mention of a three-week probation that he would have served shortly before his novitiate, as would have been customary at the time. Soon "houses of probation" were established for the purpose of such nonbinding trials with the Society. The criteria for admission from probation to the novitiate were the subject of heated discussion.[89] Maunoir seems to have skipped this probational phase, perhaps because he was already well known to the *patres* in Rennes. But despite this head start, his career as a Jesuit ran into trouble before it had even begun: his name was not on the list of those admitted at the novitiate on the rue de Mézières, on the Rive Gauche of Paris, where all aspiring Jesuits resided. The Jesuit officials told Maunoir that, without an official note in their files, they could not admit him—Coton had apparently neglected to inform the officials in Paris. Maunoir was nonetheless admitted provisionally until the confusion could be cleared up (which he attributed to the influence of God), but the episode illustrates what was already an important feature of the Jesuit order: the administration of its membership obeyed complex and carefully observed bureaucratic rules.

In the early years after 1540, novices did not yet live in specialized, independent establishments but rather together with other members of the Society. In many places, this remained the case for a long time—as, for instance, in Villagarcía in Spain or Strasbourg in France.[90] But as a rule, novices were trained at separate institutions, so-called novitiates. The first one was founded in Messina in 1550; another in Simancas followed in 1554. In 1565, the Second General Congregation decided to require that novitiates be established for the entire order. The famous novitiate on the Quirinal Hill of Rome was founded in 1566.[91] Pioneering rules were issued by General Mercurian in 1580, and the training of young aspirants at novitiates was formalized and regulated under Acquaviva, culminating in an important decree of 1608. The novitiate where Maunoir joined the Society in Paris was founded in 1610 in response to these measures.

Novitiates served to introduce boys to the Society, to familiarize them with Jesuit life, and to integrate them into the order's culture.[92] Not least, novitiates enabled the Jesuits themselves to get to know the candidates and assess their suitability for the Society of Jesus. The rhythm of life in the Society was marked by regular evaluations of the personal development of novices and full members to determine where they might best be placed. Hence it is no surprise that the duration of the novitiate was dramatically extended to give the superiors more time to assess young candidates: whereas the novitiate often lasted a year for the medieval religious orders, it lasted two years for the Jesuits.[93] Some of the other new orders of the sixteenth century, such as the Theatines, also extended the novitiate to two years.[94] These orders had obviously become much more discriminating in selecting the next generation. The Jesuits were especially careful in this regard. By no means all novices successfully completed these two years of assessment. One well-known case, for example, was Guillaume Postel, a famous French scholar who became a Jesuit novice in 1544 at the age of thirty-five, only to be dismissed soon afterward.[95]

The daily life of Maunoir and other aspiring novices in Paris was governed by "little rules, of which there was a very great number."[96] The smallest everyday minutiae were regulated. For example, complicated procedures were followed to determine who was allowed to speak with whom in their free time.[97] Such rules were intended "to break one's own will." For the same reason, the entire day was planned out in exact, minute detail, from rising at 4:00 a.m. to bedtime at 9:00 p.m. Novices sometimes moved from one task to the next every fifteen minutes at the ringing of a bell. This incessant activity, as restless as it was devout, served to instill "uniform" behavior and basic religious virtues in Jesuit novices.[98] In Paris, their days were filled with various forms of religious reflection: prayer, meditation, introspection, religious lectures, and reading. Practically every action, every posture, every moment was charged with religious significance and connected to God. That applied especially to the time set aside for "recreation," which was supposed to be spent predominantly in conversation about edifying subjects.

Specialized superiors played a major part in this formation of young men in the Jesuit spirit. "Masters of novices," or *patres magistri*, tended to the everyday activities and spiritual formation of the candidates.[99] Their interpersonal qualities and ability to work with and influence novices were extremely important. For example, Pierre Chaumonot, mentioned earlier, found the master of novices in Rome "too serious and too severe" in 1632. But when he was transferred to Florence, he met Fr. Lidanus Colanelli (1587–1674), to whom he could "open his heart much more" because he was a man of "charming gentleness."[100] Such close personal ties were crucial during the two years of one's novitiate. Masters of novices had an enormous influence on the worldview of the next generation of Jesuits and thus a significant effect on the subsequent evolution of the Society.

Novices were made to live in relative isolation from the world so that their personality could be molded more effectively. Leaving the grounds of the novitiate was considered exceptional, although there were always various occasions for doing so—regular visits to a nearby estate for recreation, walks to the local college, shopping at the market. The novitiate was "a place where we should be very comfortable to forget the world and be forgotten by it"—that was viewed as conducive to training the next generation of Jesuits.[101] The regular rhythm of life during the novices' first year, however, was sometimes interrupted. The *Constitutions* mention a series of special "testing experiences" during the novitiate that helped the superiors determine the real suitability of aspirants: for example, the young men might have to work in a hospital for a month or take a monthlong pilgrimage without any money whatsoever.[102] Although Ignatius himself had intended these tests to be used selectively, they in fact became much more common.[103]

Like other aspiring Jesuits, Julien Maunoir completed his novitiate in two years. At its conclusion, he and all the other candidates who had been admitted took their "simple vows," which conferred on them a kind of provisional membership in the Society. The next stage of their career in the Society now began: a long period of study. First, the young Jesuits studied the cultural foundations of the day—classical languages and literature and philosophy—at one of the many colleges of the Society. Beginning in 1627, Maunoir attended the famous institution at La Flèche, where he studied philosophy for three years.[104] In 1630, he then was sent to Quimper in Brittany and later to Tours, where as a "regent" he spent several years teaching young students Latin and other elementary subjects.[105] After working as a teacher for several years, Maunoir himself resumed learning and studying: he commenced four years of mandatory theological study, which he completed in Bourges.[106] Maunoir was now a *scholasticus*. Again, he and other rising Jesuits lived side by side with a far greater number of students who were not pursuing a religious career. As a scholastic, both his age and his knowledge now made him part of a very distinct and important group in the life of colleges.[107] Scholastics like Maunoir were responsible, among other things, for supporting the teachers instructing the younger students.

Jesuits normally were ordained in their final year of studying theology.[108] That was also true for Maunoir—he became "Father Maunoir" in 1638.[109] There were various disputes over the precise point at which ordination should occur. Pope Pius V, for example, criticized the fact that ordination took place before the men in question were full members of the Society. Indeed, even after completing their study of theology and receiving ordination, rising Jesuits were still not done with their formation. Maunoir took the final step in the summer of 1639, when he entered his "second novitiate," also known as the "tertianship" (*tertiatus*)—a third year of intense examination.[110] This phase of the novitiate, which future Jesuits were required to complete after several years of study and other training, was a real innovation of the Society of Jesus.[111] Ignatius and Polanco themselves had broached the idea, and Generals Borja and Mercurian took the first steps toward formalizing and institutionalizing the practice. In 1567, presumably the first separate house specifically intended for Jesuits in their tertianship was founded in Andalusia. General Acquaviva took special interest in the tertianship and gave it its final form. He made it a general practice and integrated it permanently into Jesuit life.

The men who by this point had spent more than ten years training for the Society, performing various tasks of teaching, administration, and ministry, were now supposed to resume contemplating the spiritual dimension of Jesuit life, just as they had done at the beginning of their careers—but now in far greater depth.[112] After long years of training,

FIGURE 3. Novitiate and tertiate as school of humility: Luigi Gonzaga washes dishes. © P. Pegoraro/PUG.

it was thought, the men's spiritual fervor, humility, and piety might have cooled. Tending to the sick and poor, begging, working with simple people, and serving in the kitchen or garden were intended to help these Jesuits rekindle their spirituality (fig. 3). In overseas missions, Jesuit superiors also feared spiritual exhaustion in light of the often overwhelming difficulty of life there. Here especially it was crucial to reignite the pursuit of "spiritual perfection" in one's third year of training.[113] The goal of the tertianship was to progress "from theory to practice, from maxims to actions."[114] After a candidate had committed outwardly to the Society of Jesus, he should now, at last, commit inwardly.[115] Ignatius and Polanco themselves described the tertianship as the decisive "school of affects" (*schola affectuum*).

The Jesuits who instructed the tertians and who directed and shaped this final year of the novices' spiritual formation were of paramount importance for the spiritual culture of the Society of Jesus. Louis Lallemant (1578–1635), for example, molded a whole generation of influential Jesuits at the tertian house of Rouen from 1626 to 1635, among them Vincent Huby, Jean Rigoleuc, Paul Le Jeune, and Jean-Joseph Surin.[116] Although conditions in Rouen were perhaps atypical, even elsewhere the tertianship was a phase of intense, advanced spiritual concentration for experienced, seasoned adults. In order to meet these Jesuits' special needs, the tertianship was also ideally located at a remove from where the candidates had spent the two years of their novitiate.[117] The tertianship represented the final phase of training and examination for a future Jesuit.

The entire time up to the end of their tertianship, these young men usually viewed themselves as Jesuits and performed a variety of pastoral and instructional duties. Yet their status in the Society was precarious. This seemed strange to many contemporaries and to the men themselves. The simple vows the Jesuits had taken after their novitiate, on which alone their membership in the Society was based up to this point, created a very one-sided affiliation. The obligations of each party differed dramatically: the aspiring candidate could no longer unilaterally leave the Society, whereas the order, in contrast, could abruptly dismiss him at any time.[118] The Jesuits wanted to maintain high standards among their members by thoroughly testing and carefully selecting them, and so they considered it a valuable precedent that "Our Holy Parent Ignatius readily dismissed disobedient members from the Society."[119] The precarious legal position of Jesuits prior to their profession was intended to maintain the quality of the Society's personnel.

The idea of simple vows first emerged in the sixteenth century and was hotly debated.[120] The status they conferred easily roused the suspicion of the Jesuits who took them, since an element of unpredictability and precariousness clung to their careers for years.[121] The young men's status also clashed with the existing legal and social categories of ecclesiastical life. This is especially clear with respect to property rights. Since aspiring Jesuits could be dismissed from the Society at any time, they retained certain property and inheritance rights that enabled them to return to secular life.[122] That, however, produced the strange scenario in which members of a religious order might still have possessions. Were *scholastici* then really members of the Society in the true sense of the word, with all associated legal rights and duties? Pope Gregory XIII, a great friend of the Society, attempted to resolve this quandary in two important documents of 1583 and 1584. He decided that scholastics should be regarded as full members of the Society without distinction.[123] But even after the question was settled, conflicts still constantly broke out.[124]

At the end of the tertianship, it was time for the Society to decide what would become of the men. In essence, there were three (or four) categories of Jesuits: "professed fathers," who took three or four solemn vows; "spiritual coadjutors" (*coadjutores spirituales*), who took the three simple vows; and lay brothers or "temporal coadjutors" (*coadjutores temporales*)—a Jesuit was not simply a Jesuit.[125] Taking solemn vows, the "profession," was actually the norm in Catholic orders; for centuries, entrants to an order confirmed their membership by taking the three solemn vows of poverty, chastity, and obedience. In the Society of Jesus, candidates could take these three solemn vows or supplement them with the famous fourth vow, that of obedience to the pope. The first option, profession with the three vows, hardly played a part in the subsequent history of the Jesuit order; it remained the exception. A typical "full Jesuit" almost always took all four solemn vows. Julien Maunoir belonged to this group. The third category of Jesuits, spiritual coadjutors, in contrast, were not permitted to take the solemn vows after their tertianship and ordination. Instead, they publicly took their simple vows a second time. Spiritual coadjutors constituted a large group that held a lower status in the Society.[126]

This complicated and idiosyncratic internal hierarchy was a relic of the Society's chaotic early years. Many adult priests with poor theological training were among the first people attracted to the newly founded order after 1540. Ignatius wanted to admit these priests in light of the order's acute need for personnel, but the difference between them and the highly educated core members around the founder was simply all too apparent. The primary difference between this group and the Jesuits proper thus was their level of education. As the Jesuits themselves soon took charge of educating their eventual successors, the proportion of members trained outside the Society—and often poorly educated for that reason—declined. The next logical step would have been to regard the rank of spiritual coadjutor simply as a transitional phenomenon that would be abolished in time. But that did not happen: on the contrary, by circa 1615, spiritual coadjutors had come to make up more than 40 percent of the total membership: although education had improved, full membership in the Society was still denied to a growing number of Jesuits. During the first half of the early modern period, it was argued that Jesuits with "outstanding" theological expertise deserved special distinction. Acquaviva himself set the highest standards and made the highest demands on the intellectual attainment of new recruits. It is open to doubt, however, whether this corresponded to Ignatius's original intentions. As a matter of fact, Ignatius had merely sought to respond to a temporary social reality. Conditions did not change until the seventeenth and especially the eighteenth century. When the Society was suppressed, there were hardly any spiritual coadjutors left.

Thus, in the eyes of many contemporaries, there was a dizzying number of forms of membership in the Society of Jesus: novices, scholastics, professed fathers, spiritual coadjutors. What all these men had in common was the fact that they were destined for the priesthood and were indeed ultimately ordained. But there were also many Jesuits who were not priests. The decision over who would join the order as a lay brother was usually made after the novitiate.[127] There were lay brothers in most Catholic orders; among the Jesuits, these men were called temporal coadjutors, "worldly helpers" (*coadjutores temporales*). Their job was not pastoral but rather consisted of supporting Jesuit priests in a material and physical capacity. It was often "competence in the affairs of everyday life" that was prized in this group. Coadjutors were bakers, shoemakers, cooks, brewers, gardeners, and porters.[128] Ignatius originally had not provided for any such helpers for everyday needs. The first ten Jesuits performed all these incidental tasks themselves, everything from letter writing to cleaning.[129] But already by 1541, we hear of attendants assisting the Jesuits. Diego Miró reported to Ignatius in 1543 that he "had taken on two or three (newcomers) and others very well suited to serving, and those who are for serving, we took only on the explicit condition that they would always have to serve."[130] The establishment of this special group was sanctioned by the papal brief *Exponi nobis* in 1546. From individual cases, an entire membership category in the Society had been created.

Temporal coadjutors were very important to the Society of Jesus: in some provinces, 40 to 50 percent of all Jesuits in the seventeenth century were lay brothers. They made up about a third of the Society at the time, and still a quarter in the eighteenth century.[131] But their influence extended far beyond mere numbers: in addition to everyday housekeeping and the provisioning of the colleges, many of the Jesuits' cultural and scholarly accomplishments can be traced back to them. Most of the great artists of the Society were temporal coadjutors: that is true of the painter and architect Andrea Pozzo (1642–1709) and many of his colleagues, such as Corrado Guden (1658–1743) from Flanders, a gifted joiner.[132] Many temporal coadjutors joined the Society later in life, in middle age, often after they had plied their trades for years.[133] Some of the Society's most important spiritual authors came from this group as well, such as the mystic Alonso Rodríguez, who actually worked as a porter at the entrance of the college of Majorca.

Despite the everyday importance and cultural and scholarly significance of temporal coadjutors, their standing in the Society was by no means straightforward. Understandably, it was very important to them that they were perceived as the peers of the other Jesuits, despite the fact that they had not studied or been ordained. This started with external matters, such as clothing. In the sixteenth century, for instance, temporal coadjutors were permitted to wear a biretta, the distinctive square cap with three raised corners that indicated one's status as a clergy-man.[134] But bitter disputes over this symbol of equality raged in the Society. Although it had originally been decided that temporal coadju-tors should be identifiable by their clothing in light of their special status as members of a religious order, some Jesuits now proposed that they should be forbidden to wear the symbolic cap of clergymen. We can clearly observe a growing need for differentiation within the order.[135] In consequence, internal distinctions of status came to be marked more conspicuously. At the Seventh General Congregation, in 1615, lay brothers were explicitly forbidden to wear a biretta. Temporal coadju-tors and other members of the Society who opposed this emphasis on distinctions of rank protested vociferously but ultimately in vain.[136] The "clear differentiation" between the different groups of Jesuits was to be unmistakable. At roughly the same time, educational opportunities for lay brothers were also limited.[137] In 1681, temporal coadjutors feared that they might even be formally ousted from the Society; at least, they complained that they would be viewed simply as servants.[138]

Jesuits enjoyed various employment opportunities according to their rank and the current stage of their education. Where Jesuits were sent and how they were employed, and how they subsequently led their lives and made their careers, depended on a variety of factors that can hardly be generalized. In theory, it was the superiors' prerogative to decide where and in what capacity a Jesuit would be placed. Jesuits were sup-posed to be "indifferent" with respect to their duties. In practice, how-ever, efforts were made to accommodate special talents and interests that emerged over the course of a Jesuit's long training. Maunoir, for example, was employed in various pastoral capacities during his years of study, but it quickly became clear that he was especially inclined toward life as a wandering missionary, and his intimate familiarity with western central France and Brittany was likewise noted. With other Je-suits, it was obvious early on that they were especially well-suited to serve as scholars or professors. And still others showed administrative talent and subsequently served for years or even decades as superiors in various positions. Over the course of the early modern period, we can see that overall, besides the generalists in the Society, several specialized fields emerged that often occupied the Jesuits engaged in them for life. I will explore several such specializations later.

As for where a Jesuit was stationed, conspicuous patterns likewise emerged. First and foremost, the Jesuit order viewed itself very much as an international institution in which regional identities should not be a factor, and many Jesuits realized this ideal in practice. This was necessarily the case for the first generation, when it was up to Spanish, French, and Dutch Jesuits to establish the Society in Germany. But this principle was also observed later and, in essence, remains true today. An international cast not only filled (and fills) positions of leadership and roles in the central administration of the Society in Rome. Many Jesuits at large showed equally great mobility. And yet even shortly after 1540 it was undeniable that an opposite trend had also emerged, becoming more pronounced over time. Jesuits were proud of their regional and cultural backgrounds and even flaunted them, going so far as to articulate a sense of superiority over their fellow brothers. The recruitment and placement of Jesuits soon became heavily regionalized. In Austria, for example, almost three-quarters of the Jesuits there in the seventeenth century had local origins; Bohemia was no different. The situation in Westphalia was similar: most Jesuits active there came from the region, were educated there, and died locally.[139] Maunoir's career after completing his tertianship likewise fits this picture of close regional ties.

Spirituality and Religious Practice

What was imparted to the Jesuits during their long training went far beyond academic material. During their novitiate and tertianship, they learned above all, and by no means exclusively, what it meant to understand and live the Catholic faith as a Jesuit. The years of study before they took their final vows served to instill in the men of the Society a very specific understanding of Christianity. The most important model was Ignatius of Loyola himself, who had set forth the main parameters of his conception of God and the world in the *Spiritual Exercises*, as well as in many of his letters. His successors elaborated on his ideas, quarreled over various emphases, and yet all shared a handful of basic convictions. Even though there was undeniable variation in the details of the religious life, there still existed a kind of core spiritual identity that virtually all Jesuits naturally and enthusiastically embraced out of true conviction and years of daily practice.

Core Elements of Jesuit Spirituality

Jesuit piety was characterized by several basic convictions that were distilled into pithy formulas. These phrases condensed the fundamental spiritual principles of the Society of Jesus: a Jesuit had to be "indifferent" to his career because "the whole world was his home" and he should "seek God in all things." He also had to strive unstintingly for "more" (*más/magis*) spiritual attainment while staying true to "our way of proceeding," which meant he had to stay "active in contemplation." All this would help a Jesuit "help the souls" of his neighbors, which was ultimately the Society's special contribution "to the greater glory of God." Every Jesuit would have immediately recognized these formulas and acknowledged them as expressions of the fundamental spiritual identity of the Society of Jesus. So easily recognizable, these phrases became virtual trademarks and defining features of the Society, while their axiomatic brevity distilled the elaborate and profound spiritual thoughts behind them.

"Helping souls" epitomized the actual purpose of the Society. The founding bull issued by Paul III in 1540 at the instigation of the first Jesuits had regarded helping souls by "propagating the faith" more specifically as the primary goal of the Society.[140] The *Constitutions* took up the thought and declared up front that "the end [i.e., purpose] of this Society is to devote itself with God's grace to the salvation and perfection of the members' own souls, but also with that same grace to labor strenuously in giving aid toward the salvation and perfection of the souls of their neighbors."[141] Jerónimo Nadal, whom Ignatius dispatched to explain the nature and spirituality of the new order authoritatively across Europe, made this point crystal clear at many Jesuit houses: "We are called on by God to help souls, and undoubtedly more so those that are bereft of human aid."[142] Three generations later (1651), Scipione

Paolucci unequivocally declared: "This goal of helping the souls of others is not secondary and incidental, but rather the foremost substantial and essential one."[143]

This concept of helping souls went hand in hand with the belief that, first, Ignatius himself and, second, the Society he founded were "instruments" of God that would improve the world by leading it to him.[144] Hence it was self-evident that the Society of Jesus was an apostolic community, a religious order that explicitly followed in the footsteps of the apostles and felt duty bound to spread and strengthen the Christian faith among men. The early church was a major source of inspiration, and the apostle Paul in particular an important model. He had virtually elevated incessant, indefatigable effort to proclaim the gospel to a way of life.[145] Apostolic ministry, the proactive effort to promote Christianity among men, had long been a prominent feature of classical Western monasticism, but among the Jesuits—even more so than in the mendicant Dominican and Franciscan orders—it became the overriding purpose of life.

Of course, the *Constitutions* also stressed that the Jesuits had to attend to the spiritual health of their own souls. Again, it was Nadal in 1557 who devised a formula to describe how a Jesuit should ideally reconcile both goals. A Jesuit should "feel and contemplate the presence of God and an affection for spirituality in all things, all actions, and all conversations, being at the same time *contemplative in action* (which [Ignatius] used to explain by saying one should find God in all things)."[146] The original context was rather incidental: Nadal was merely describing Ignatius's special experience of prayer. But the expression stuck, was taken up, and was soon generalized.[147] Both Nadal and, as the formula became established, later Jesuits insisted that contemplation should by no means be neglected but rather should always be constructive in reference to Christian action.

Christian thinkers had long understood contemplation and action as antithetical—even mutually exclusive. The antithesis was familiar to many Jesuits, and they often vividly described the difficulty of balancing spiritual introspection and action for one's neighbor. The following anecdote is related about Pierre Champion, for example, a famous author from the Society in the late seventeenth century: "The inner life has such great appeal to him that he wondered whether he should give up missionary work and dedicate himself more seriously to the repose of contemplation." But Champion finally realized "that he should employ himself in apostolic endeavors, as his vocations [as a Jesuit] prescribed, and that God did not want him to lead a more withdrawn life."[148] All Jesuits faced this dilemma. They developed their own preferences and personal devotional styles of dealing with it. Louis Lallemant at the tertiate of Rouen, for example, took pains to ensure that no one neglected the aspect of contemplation in Nadal's formula. Concentrating exclusively on pious deeds—thus neglecting the inner life and the guidance of the Holy Spirit—was disastrous in his view.[149] Yet he too emphasized that the one aspect could not exist without the other among the Jesuits. It was generally believed that the success of the Jesuits' apostolic mission derived from their intense inner focus on God, which could be perfected only through effective effort on their neighbor's behalf.

Nadal had explained the relationship between spiritual contemplation and pious action on behalf of one's neighbor in another very influential expression, "finding God in all things," that became a cornerstone of the Jesuit interpretation of the world. Ignatius used the expression in the *Constitutions* to describe what members of the Society were actually supposed to do.[150] He explained that one should not love things of the world for their own sake; instead, one should venerate the Creator through his creation. Juan de Polanco elaborated on this point in a letter of 1551: one should "practice looking for God in everything, in talking with someone, walking, seeing, tasting, hearing, understanding, and in everything we should do, because it is true that His divine majesty is in everything through his presence, power, and essence." Polanco further argued that this "meditation" on God was relatively easy because it was based on concrete objects and did not necessarily attempt to penetrate to "abstract divine truths."[151] The idea that God could be recognized everywhere in his creation was hardly spectacular—it was a traditional Christian concept that had been introduced to the Jesuits by the influential theology of St. Thomas Aquinas.[152] Martin Luther had written in a similar vein. What mattered most to Ignatius, however, was the belief that a Jesuit could find total fulfillment by living and working not beyond the material world but rather in it and alongside its inhabitants.

Among the Jesuits, the exhortation to find and venerate God in "all" things and in all Christian endeavors was combined with the admonition that no member should harbor special preferences of his own.[153] That is why the incredibly important requirement of "indifference" was imposed on every Jesuit. One should not prefer health to sickness, regard poverty as superior to wealth, or vice versa. Put in these terms, the precept might sound like old news—the traditional monastic orders were also characterized by aloofness to earthly things, and new concepts of inner balance and dispassion (*apatheia*) had been developed throughout the history of philosophy.[154] But among the Jesuits, this indifference was not to be confused with escapism. On the contrary, it was not the things of the world that were indifferent; instead, the Jesuits' relationship to these things should be indifferent.[155] The Jesuits did not strive to become a motor and source of individual determinations, but rather to let their own will be determined by God. As a French Jesuit once noted, "It is for God to find me, and for me to suffer everything. I believe this is the surest path to attain perfection: to ask for nothing and to refuse nothing, but rather to agree and love all the states and circumstances that divine will chooses."[156]

The requirement of indifference entailed several difficulties. The Jesuits discovered this at the end of the seventeenth century, when the so-called Quietists (intended as a disparaging nickname) thought that the faithful should be so indifferent to themselves that they should not even desire salvation.[157] This was wrong in the Jesuits' opinion: for all their indifference, they still clung to every person's obligation to strive for the good. Indifference did not mean that members of the Society should refrain from thinking about their careers and their activities, nor did it mean that a Jesuit should not have an opinion about the respective advantages and disadvantages of various options. Indifference meant that a Jesuit should remain so detached from his own standpoint that he did not insist on it. Indifference was a call not to unreflecting, egoless obedience but to emancipation from one's own impulses and desires. One should be as if "at the center of a pair of scales."[158] That also entailed that a Jesuit should not remain in a state of indifference forever. Once a decision had been made (but not as a result of the Jesuit's own feelings), then a Jesuit had to proceed resolutely on the path chosen for him and thus make the choice completely his own.[159]

The question remained as to who helped an indifferent Jesuit decide. The answer was obvious: God. In everyday life, of course, it was usually one's superior (who in Ignatius's view essentially served as a proxy for God) who determined in very practical terms how and where each member of the order would be employed.[160] A superior certainly could also take one's predilections and skills into consideration. On an organizational level, the Society could not afford to disregard its members' special gifts and desires, despite the fact that such concerns were supposed to be nonfactors on an individual, spiritual level.

The personal indifference that was required of every Jesuit pertained to all things, tasks, and places. The apostolic mission that was demanded of every member targeted the entire world. Permanent availability and permanent readiness to change locations and cultures thus were also cornerstones of Jesuit spirituality.[161] Again it was Nadal who devised the most incisive formula when he stressed that traveling (*peregrinatio*) was a fundamental part of Jesuit existence. "Through this, the entire world becomes our abode," he wrote, succinctly summarizing the universalism of constant availability. "For the Society, the whole world must be home." This quintessential formula recurs again and again in Nadal's subsequent writings. What he means, Nadal explains, is that "wherever they can be sent on ministry to bring help to souls, that is these theologians' most outstanding and most sought-after abode." In this instance, too, the point was not whether every Jesuit actually spent his life wandering—as we have seen, many did not. Rather, for Nadal, who himself traveled tirelessly, the spiritual principle was more important. Jesuits were required to adopt a pious attitude of constant availability, openness to sudden reassignment, and alertness to spiritual distress, which also required shifting personnel and resources. Jesuits should be spiritually at peace within themselves, yet always restless. That presumes a spiritual attitude that was categorically distinct from the old monastic principle of *stabilitas loci*.

From this spiritual principle, we may bridge the gap to another one that takes the following form in an exhortation by Father Jerónimo

Lopez to the young Tirso González in the year 1652/3: "If you could enter Heaven with ten thousand [saved] souls, do not be content with only four thousand, just as merchants are not content with one million [in profit] if they can make two."[162] The mercantile simile that underpins this exhortation may not have been the rule for Jesuit piety, but it illustrates a fundamental point of Ignatian spirituality: Jesuits always went for "more" (*más/magis*). They refused to content themselves with what was merely good but strove instead for something *greater*. This Jesuit commitment to incessant improvement and their pride in undertaking not merely efficient but *especially* efficient actions are ubiquitous in the writings of Ignatius and his followers.[163] The principle is reflected nowhere better than in the universally applied motto of the Society: everything happens not merely to the *great* but rather "to the *greater* glory of God," *ad maiorem Dei gloriam*, routinely abbreviated AMDG.

This individual commitment to a constant, spiritual "more" was implemented throughout the Society. Ignatius and Polanco constructed a system of government for the Society of Jesus that was conceived so as to extract the maximum benefit from available resources in a universal perspective. It is from this spiritual preference for *magis*, for the greater benefit, that the pronounced centralism of the Society of Jesus derived. That insistence on "more" also drove the Jesuits' notable tendency to quantify their spiritual successes. The Jesuits were asked to count systematically and regularly everything they had accomplished: confessions, communions, last rites, conversions—everything. Large tables were occasionally prepared that enabled one to see at a glance everything that had been accomplished. In at least this bureaucratic realization of the spiritual principle, the Society was not far removed from the mercantile aftertaste that the *magis* had acquired for López and González.[164]

All these elements of the Jesuit self-conception, which manifested themselves in formulaic spiritual maxims, could ultimately be subordinated to and integrated in the overarching category of "our way of proceeding." The Jesuits made very frequent use of the Spanish formula *nuestro modo de proceder* and its countless variants. The expression served equally as a code, as shorthand for everything that made up the Jesuits' common spiritual orientation and what distinguished them from other orders. It originated with Ignatius, who often spoke of "my" or "our way of proceeding."[165] The phrase accordingly occurs nine times in the *Constitutions*.[166] In defining this "way," the *Constitutions* evoke many of the cornerstones of Jesuit spirituality again and again—action, pastoral ministry, flexibility.

But more interesting than attempting to distill a precise definition of the Jesuit way of proceeding from the sources is the fact that *nuestro modo* was a formula that could be used to practice spiritual identity politics. One could justify rejecting something by arguing that it was incompatible with "our way of proceeding."[167] That was also true of people. "If you do not accept the spirit and way of proceeding of the Society, then it would be much better if you were outside it," Ignatius wrote to a difficult brother.[168] Even administrative questions were soon assessed with the help of this formula.[169] Whoever cited "our," and not some other, way of proceeding thereby intimated a priori that he was in possession of or at least was standing in the tradition of authentic Jesuit spirituality. But this contention stood on shaky ground because it was often fiercely disputed what "our" way (still) was and was not (anymore).[170] Moreover, a certain degree of flexibility was both inevitable and explicitly desired in light of the enormous cultural differences across Europe and especially in the missions.[171] Hence talk of "our" way of proceeding realized its potential as a framework not because it necessarily referred to precise elements of Jesuit spirituality but because it posited such a thing as a typical Jesuit identity that could serve as an authoritative standard of "Jesuit compatibility." In this way, "our way" was less an immutable and ahistorical quantity. Instead, through constant exchange and reference to "our way of proceeding," the Jesuits reinforced their members' conviction that the multifaceted and global Society of Jesus truly had a core identity.

The Spiritual Exercises

If anything really stood at the heart of the Society of Jesus, it was the *Spiritual Exercises* of Ignatius. At first glance, the *Exercises* were an unassuming little book on which the founder of the order had worked since his conversion in 1521. But this little book had a big impact. For the Jesuits, it became the most important reference for their own faith. Antonio

Possevino used a metaphor to express the value of the *Exercises*: "The *Constitutions* and *Rules* in the Society give, as it were, the material, but the *Exercises* are like the form and the soul that give these life and being."[172] Vincenzo Carafa, the seventh superior general, described the *Exercises* in 1646 as the "principles" and "cornerstones" of the rise and preservation of the Society.[173] Through a variety of uses—whether for introspection at the beginning of one's career, whether as a source of spiritual refreshment or as a quarry of material for everyday meditation—the *Spiritual Exercises* became *the* key religious practice that shaped the identity of the Society of Jesus over the sixteenth century.

The text and the religious experiences that underlay it were largely finished before the founding of the Society itself.[174] The *Exercises* were primarily the product of Ignatius's inner experiences since his serious injury at Pamplona. After he received important impulses in Montserrat, he composed many of the central passages of the *Exercises* over the following months in Manresa. The period between Manresa and Salamanca passed without significant work on the text, which was expanded and rearranged in Paris between 1527 and 1535. A clumsy, preliminary Latin version was also composed in Paris. When Loyola set out for Spain again in 1535, large parts of the *Exercises* had already existed in written form for years. Ignatius had hoped to present the booklet to his friends as an epitome and distillation of his spirituality, and he did so. The finishing touches were added or fully fleshed out in Italy after 1536, and the Latin translation was significantly refined. When the Society officially came to life in 1540, its spiritual foundation had already been laid in a tried and tested, and permanent, literary form.

Although a large part of the substance of the *Exercises* undoubtedly can be traced to Ignatius and his spiritual experiences, several of Ignatius's companions—Pierre Favre, Alfonso Salmerón, Polanco, perhaps Jean Codure—also left their mark in the latter phases of redaction. In 1547, André des Freux composed an official translation in elegant, humanistic Latin; it was printed and remained the authorized version of the *Exercises*.[175] Pope Paul III officially recognized and sanctioned the *Exercises* in 1548. The Society did not publish the original Spanish version until 1615.

The *Spiritual Exercises* consist essentially of instructions for a four-week program of meditation, prayer, and spiritual introspection. The *Exercises* do not propound a doctrine as much as they delineate a procedure, a method. One does not read them; one practices them. The Jesuits also did not do so alone: normally, the *Exercises* took the form of cooperation between the meditating Jesuit and a spiritual director. This person was very important because he guided the spiritual progress of the practitioner. The goal of the process was to give the person who made the *Exercises* spiritual clarity about his life. To accomplish that, it was necessary to get to know one's own inner life and to find out what impulses and predilections one could trust. Vice versa, one had to "rid [the soul] of all disordered attachments."[176] The notion that there were wrong and misleading impulses was very important to Ignatius; the *Exercises* were supposed to help one identify and rid oneself of them. The human soul would then be equipped to find and undertake the right way of life. The point was to find out what God wanted for the practitioner and how he should lead his life.[177] It must be stressed that, for all a Jesuit's individual efforts, Ignatius still viewed this inner process as totally dependent on God. In ideal conditions, Ignatius set a period of four weeks for completing this process. But the instructions are very flexible, with respect to both the details of the process and its duration—Ignatius recognized that not everyone would embark on the *Exercises* with the same needs and circumstances.

To fulfill their purpose, the *Exercises* proposed a well-organized series of inner (and outer) activities: prayer, imagination, self-discovery, and all in specific, precisely described postures in the practitioner's own room, day and night. The bulk of the text consists of very specific recommendations, suggested meditation topics, and instructions on meditating. One might, for example, meditate on the categories of mortal and venal sin. The sin of Lucifer and the transgression of Adam and Eve could be considered further. It might also be helpful to visualize Christ's conversation with one of the thieves on the cross. The text even suggests imagining hell in detail as a guide to self-discovery. The text also contains symbolic scenes that the practitioner was supposed to play out in his head as precisely and realistically as possible so that this inner experience might enable him more clearly to discern his standing with God.

The "Meditation on the Two Standards" is famous: the practitioner should imagine a battlefield in the greatest possible detail, where the troops of God and the troops of Satan meet. An apocalyptic battle, painted down to the last detail—where would one stand?

On the path to self-discovery, "examining one's conscience, . . . meditating, contemplating, praying vocally and mentally" all were essential.[178] This plan was at once very traditional and highly innovative. The last three practices mentioned—meditation (*meditatio*), contemplation (*contemplatio*), and prayer (*oratio*)—were classic components of Western mysticism, although contemplation and prayer usually appeared in the opposite order. The fact that Ignatius explicitly mentions spoken and silent prayer together implies a valorization of the latter. Since the Middle Ages, silent prayer had risen in importance as an alternative to traditional, communal, vocal prayer. Silent prayer enabled one to fulfill one's religious obligations in a secular, and particularly an urban, environment.[179] In this way, laymen in emerging urban centers could be integrated more effectively into prayer-focused, fervently religious lifestyles. Ignatius seized on this trend. Many contemporaries, however, viewed this innovation as dangerous, since Ignatius seemed to be tearing down the well-established boundary between laity and clergy.[180]

Ignatius's heavy emphasis on self-discovery was unusual. In the first week of the *Exercises*, the aspiring practitioner was instructed to follow elaborate procedures to take stock of his life up to that point. The practitioner should make himself a subject of his own introspection; he should "[demand] of oneself an account of the particular point proposed for correction and reform, running over each hour or each period of time, beginning from the hour of rising, up to the hour and moment of the present exam."[181] Ignatius repeatedly stresses that the practitioner must constantly observe himself during the *Exercises*.[182] To achieve an overview of one's spiritual progress, he even devised a record-keeping system that called for practitioners to draw a longer or shorter line for every sin according to the severity of each transgression. In this way, they could judge at a glance whether and to what extent they had improved (fig. 4). At the end of the first week, they were to make a general confession to ask forgiveness for the sins they had recognized.

FIGURE 4. Peter Paul Rubens' depiction of the graphic writing system
of moral-theological self-assessment (following the *Spiritual Exercises*
of Ignatius). From *Exercitia Spiritualia S. P. Ignatii Loyolae,
Fundatoris Ordinis Societatis Jesu* [. . .] (Antwerp 1689), 67.
© Staats- und Stadtbibliothek Augsburg, Th Pr 1275.

Whereas the purpose of the first week was to take stock of one's past way of life, the remaining three weeks were dedicated to searching for a new orientation. "Electing" the best option for one's life became the most important subject, and numerous passages of the text revolve around it. Whether by distinguishing between "three times in any of which a sound and good election can be made" or by meditating on the "Two Standards" of the devil and Christ, between which one had to decide, spiritual self-discovery ultimately led to the right decision in accordance with the will of God. Constant visualization of Jesus Christ served as a positive source of inspiration. Episodes from his life make up a majority of the meditation themes of the final weeks of the *Exercises*. At the end of the four weeks, the practitioner ideally has completed a "journey," transporting him via the life of Jesus Christ from a sinner giving an account of his life to a new orientation focused on God.

Reflecting and meditating on Jesus and specifically on the Passion took on a powerful dynamic of its own in the early modern period among the Jesuits both in the context of the *Exercises* and independently. Virgilio Cepari argued in 1600 that "this meditation on the Passion was more productive than others, because this seems to me to be an experience in which the remedies for every evil may be found."[183] Andreas Brunner, a somewhat younger contemporary from southern Germany, was convinced that detailed reflection on the Passion would instill true piety: reflecting on Christ's "fear and bloody sweat on the Mount of Olives" would lead to "hatred and disgust for sin," Brunner remarked. Through and during meditation, one should identify with Jesus as he suffered, thereby feeling the force of sin virtually physically. Meditating Jesuits were further encouraged to apply the implements of Christ's martyrdom to their own soul:

> The nails of his hands and feet
> Stick in your heart! Now they are sweet
> Because they have tasted his blood.
> Lay the thorns also on your heart;
> Whereby the passion will be longer,
> The fiery heart will smolder more.[184]

The vividness of these imagined visions was crucial. While meditating, the Jesuit should envision the tiniest details of Jesus's suffering. In 1670, the Jesuit preacher Philipp Kisel of Worms calculated that Christ had shed exactly 97,035 drops of blood on the cross, every one of which was grounds for a sinner to repent.[185]

With this specificity, even allowing for the exuberance of the times, these authors still were essentially in line with the *Exercises*. Visualizing the meditation scenes as vividly and realistically as possible was especially important to Ignatius. Again and again in his little book, he urges the practitioner to imagine the episodes he was meditating on—whether they were biblical or not—as realistically as possible. The meditator should hear, see, and taste what happened in his mind. Ignatius described this visualization as the "composition of place" (*compositio loci*).[186] It was an essential part of the preparations for every meditation over the four weeks. Behind this practice lay the firm conviction that the senses—even when engaged inwardly through the imagination—could open up the way to faith for a practitioner. This conviction shaped the Society of Jesus for a long time. The Jesuits' fascination with sensual forms of apostolic ministry, which will be discussed in detail later, is rooted in this conviction of Ignatius's.[187]

Various examples document how the *Exercises* functioned in specific contexts. The notes made by Juan Alfonso de Vitoria, who made the *Exercises* in 1549, are still extant today.[188] He divided the question of whether he should join a religious order and, if so, which one, into several steps. For every subquestion, Vitoria then collected reasons for and against. After completing this evidently very methodical procedure, in which he sought to give an honest account of his personal habits, preferences, and character, the young man reached the conclusion that he should and would become a Jesuit. When the *Exercises* were taken seriously, their investigative method helped clarify the practitioner's uncertainty about his path in life. That was also the case for Peter Canisius, who made the *Exercises* in Cologne with Pierre Favre. In hindsight, he believed the *Exercises* helped him find the right path. He wanted "to ascertain the good, pleasing, and perfect will of God for me."[189] Julien Maunoir also noted that the "Meditation on the Two Standards" had confirmed his desire to become a Jesuit. He had heard God "call" him and "decided to give everything up to follow him."[190] Paolo Segneri reports analogously that the *Exercises* stirred his soul "to move suddenly from thoughts of fear to love." Segneri described the effect of the *Exercises* as a dramatic transformation of his inner disposition, amounting to a refocusing of his feelings and efforts on true spiritual goals pleasing to God. He had heard "a voice within"—probably divine in nature—and he had been witness to a "clear light" during the *Exercises*, which ultimately inspired him to undertake a "serious and absolute reform of my way of life."[191] These passages and their language also show how, for many Jesuits, the *Exercises* were more than merely a decision-making and personality-shaping technology. They were also an occasion for immediate, intense, and sometimes ecstatic encounters with God.[192]

The *Exercises* were assigned particularly for novices and, later, for the tertianship to facilitate such clarification about one's individual path in life and to test the vocation of young men.[193] The goal was to test and thereby validate the candidate's desire to join the Society. The *Exercises* and the insights they afforded served as "proof" of the firmness of the practitioner's decision. In the earliest period, when the Society was still under construction, the Jesuits experimented with the nature and duration of the *Exercises*. In Spain, the full, four-week program often already appears to have been the rule, while Leonhard Kessel, the superior in Cologne, typically administered only a brief, abridged version of the *Exercises*. Hence the period prescribed for the *Exercises* might vary widely in length, from one week to (exceptionally) sixty-four days, which was how long Andrés Carvalho needed for the meditations. It was under the generalships of Everard Mercurian and Claudio Acquaviva that this spiritual practice took an increasingly fixed form. In the late 1570s, at first handwritten copies and then an official printed version of rules for the superintendents of novices circulated.[194] These gave more precise guidelines for administering the *Exercises*. It was Acquaviva who finally prescribed the full, monthlong period of reflection for all aspirants. The unabridged, four-week *Exercises* were regarded as the "preeminent" spiritual practice on the path toward ultimate confirmation in one's tertianship. A body of instructional literature dedicated specifically to the *Exercises* grew in this context.[195] At the same time, after various preliminary steps, an official and authoritative handbook on administering and making the *Exercises* was published.[196]

The Jesuits themselves might even take a somewhat ambivalent view of the *Exercises*. In light of the intensity of the introspection they called for, some Jesuits would have preferred to skip the *Exercises* altogether, for example, citing physical infirmities. For others, concentrating on the *Exercises* caused various other complaints after a few days. Léon Enrique wrote that "many people fell sick during the *Exercises*."[197] Many other Jesuits, in contrast, happily integrated the *Exercises* into their lives and completed them repeatedly either in full or at least sections at a time. The *Exercises* were increasingly viewed as a way for Jesuits engaged in ministry to enjoy a spell of spiritual reinforcement and rest once a year. Under the title "Mortifications," the *Exercises* and other devotional practices were recommended during the summer to help Jesuits refocus outside their daily work routines. Claudio Acquaviva suggested retreating for a week of the *Exercises* to draw strength prior to the taxing phase of Lenten preaching. On a different occasion, Acquaviva emphasized that the *Exercises* would give one strength in moments of hostility and should therefore be regularly repeated.[198] Jesuit missionaries, often pushed to the brink overseas, welcomed the idea of regular periods of rest: "Because they have so many distractions, so many obstacles to spiritual retreat in the houses and residences, the superiors should see to it that the brothers scattered in the residences meet annually for one or two months in the novitiate or college to overcome all the difficulties that arise."[199] The idea was quickly taken up in Europe. The Sixth General Congregation in 1608 made the *Exercises* of at least eight or ten days obligatory annually for all Jesuits. Subsequent general congregations inculcated the practice and regulated additional details.[200] Guides were published that explained how one might squeeze the four-week *Exercises* as sensibly as possible into briefer periods with as little loss of substance as possible.[201]

Other authors went even further and tried to transform the *Exercises* into a kind of lifelong form of daily meditation. The *Exercises* were cut up into separate parts to be meditated in isolation.[202] They became a constant, everyday practice. Achille Gagliardi wrote in 1600, "It absolutely must be stressed that the *Exercises* should last one's entire life uninterrupted, doing them during the daily hour of prayer, during examinations, and during all the actions of the day; for in this way all the evils will be rooted out, and all the virtues will grow as one's vocation [to the Society] ripens."[203] Whereas the *Exercises* had originally introduced a temporary "monastic" element of seclusion for about four weeks, they became the exact opposite in Gagliardi's view: a constant part of everyday life. Other authors took up this idea. Giovanni Ceccotti, an experienced Jesuit who was intimately familiar with the *Exercises*, created 365 days of meditations from the *Exercises* by adding further material. That went hand in hand with a complete reorganization of the meditations that Ignatius had proposed—not a trace of the four-week structure was left.[204] This changed the character of the *Exercises* dramatically. A concentrated decision-making period was transformed into an everyday practice of reflection and moral-religious self-centering.

We are relatively well-informed about the sources and diverse traditions that influenced the *Exercises* of Ignatius in one way or another. Parallels to other texts are constantly being identified.[205] First, we must not overlook the fact that Ignatius's experiences from his time at the court of Isabella of Castile influenced how he constructed certain scenes. The image of the king fighting the forces of the infidel may have been inspired by the crusading rhetoric of Ferdinand II of Aragon.

With respect to literary influences, first and foremost is the *Vita Christi* by Ludolph of Saxony, a fourteenth-century Carthusian monk. Ignatius read the *Vita* in a very liberal, loose Spanish translation that Ambrosio Montesino O.F.M. had made in 1502/3.[206] Ludolph's book was a well-known classic of late medieval devotional literature. No fewer than two hundred editions in various European languages were made in the two centuries since it appeared. Hence, it is unsurprising that this book was also available in Ignatius's home—not exactly a hotbed of avant-garde literature. Along with the *Vita Christi*, the future founder of the Society read on his sickbed the no less popular collection of saints' lives compiled in the thirteenth century by Jacobus da Varagine under the title *Flos Sanctorum*.

When Ignatius says in his autobiography that he read these religious texts only because his beloved romances were unavailable, this antithesis he draws between the two genres should not obscure the profound parallels they share. The Jesus of the *Vita Christi* is a dashing hero. Ignatius thus threw himself into a contest in chivalric, courtly terms, into a kind of spiritual tournament against the saints whose life stories he could read in the *Flos Sanctorum*. On several occasions, Ignatius mentions that he had aspired to "surpass" the pious deeds of Dominic or Francis.[207] The spiritual ideal that motivated Ignatius for so long combined values from his chivalric background with the pious message of these influential books: the holy ministry of Christ was the essence of religious life, but one should also constantly strive for "more" (*magis*), thus integrating competition and self-improvement into one's personal spiritual practice.

Ludolph also stressed that one must meditate daily on the life of Jesus Christ, albeit in manageable portions. Immersion in the exemplary deeds of Jesus would motivate the contemplator to self-improvement. Ludolph further emphasized that while reflecting on the life of Christ, people should picture the context of his actions. These meditations thus abounded in imagery. Landscapes, buildings, situations—Ludolph's readers were supposed to imagine the setting of the holy deeds of Jesus Christ in exhaustive detail. Some meditations in the *Spiritual Exercises*, such as the famous motif of the "Two Standards," thus may derive from Loyola's personal experiences while reading Ludolph.[208]

At the next station after Ignatius's sickbed, the Benedictine abbey of Montserrat, he received further spiritual influences that left traces behind in the *Spiritual Exercises*. At Montserrat, he encountered an intense Benedictine piety that Abbot García de Cisneros had molded a few years earlier.[209] Two texts from this milieu, the important *Exercitatorio* by García de Cisneros himself and a loose and creative epitome of it under the title *Compendio breve* exhibit striking parallels to the *Exercises*. The *Compendio* in particular contains phrases and rules of meditation that colored the content, language, and presentation of the *Spiritual Exercises*. The very title itself—*Exercitia*—might be borrowed from Cisneros. In 1641, in the context of the centennial anniversary of the Society of Jesus, a controversy that would flare up again and again between the Jesuits and Benedictines broke out over the question of whether Cisneros should be viewed as the real author of the *Exercises*.[210]

Whether he was conscious of it or not, the different texts that Ignatius came into contact with during those first years after Pamplona imparted to him a broad tradition of Christian literature. The *Vita Christi*, for example, drew heavily on Bernard of Clairvaux, as well as on various Eastern texts. The exhortation to keep a written account of sins and virtues might ultimately derive from John Climacus, a seventh-century monk on Mount Sinai.[211] Cisneros's *Exercitatorio* further transmitted fundamental concepts of *Devotio moderna*, a religious reform movement that rapidly spread across Germany and the Low Countries in the fifteenth century.[212] Gerard of Zutphen in particular is frequently cited as a reference point for Ignatian piety.

Finally, we must discuss a third work of medieval devotional literature: Thomas à Kempis's *Imitatio Christi* from the fifteenth century.[213] Ignatius probably first encountered the popular text of the *Imitatio* in Manresa. Various evidence shows that he held this book in high regard all his life. As in the *Vita Christi*, the *Imitatio* also treats Jesus's life as a model one should emulate. Its fundamental understanding of Christian life as spiritual military service, as serving and fighting for God, linked the *Imitatio* to other works of late medieval piety and influenced the *Exercises*. The *Imitatio* may have made the greatest impression, however, with its general insistence on the contemplative elements of Christian piety. Other aspects of Ignatian piety, such as the prominence of grief, joy, and temptation, also had parallels in the *Imitatio*, if they did not originate there.

Ignatius's student days in Alcalá and Paris also influenced the form of the *Exercises*. When Ignatius was studying in Alcalá in 1525, a new edition of the writings of Erasmus of Rotterdam was produced there by none other than Ignatius's personal friend Miguel de Eguía.[214] There are in fact striking parallels between the *Spiritual Exercises* and various works of Erasmus that may potentially derive from Ignatius's direct reading of works by the humanist in Alcalá (there is, however, still no consensus about the significance of these parallels). The conditions that

Ignatius experienced in Paris also played a part in the composition of the *Exercises*. Some passages of the *Exercises* draw on documents from a synod that met in Sens in 1528. It is moreover obvious that Ignatius's theological expertise, which had grown apace since his formal education, also influenced the *Exercises*.[215]

The traditional material that flowed into the *Exercises* thus encompassed the entire spectrum of contemporary spirituality—from slivers of academic theology to ecclesiastical legal texts to popular devotional literature and the charismatic founder's own intense experiences. But not all of these influences continued to affect subsequent generations. The spirituality of the sixteenth and seventeenth centuries was treacherous terrain in which mistrust ran rampant. The Jesuits had to position themselves in this broad field with exacting precision.

Between Asceticism and Mysticism

Giovanni Ceccotti had firm ideas about the purpose of the *Exercises*: "[Their] 'fruit' is understood to be some specific virtue gathered from what occurs in the present week's meditations."[216] For him, the *Exercises* were techniques for working on oneself, for laborious moral and spiritual improvement. For Peter Canisius, in contrast, the *Exercises* had been completely different, far more ecstatic. The meditations had produced a state of physical rapture in Canisius: he trembled as he meditated on the Ascension of Christ. Canisius was confident that by attaining this state of ecstasy he truly could see the scene of the Ascension, hear the song of the angels, and even smell something—the imagination produced a real sensual experience.[217]

Allowing for some simplification, these two different experiences with the *Exercises* may be taken as representative of two extremes of early modern Catholic piety: a workmanlike piety of small steps, based on the fulfillment of religious duty and the virtuous practice of spiritual habits (ascesis); and a piety that aspired to obtain direct, immediate access to God, for example, in a vision or an ecstatic state of grace (mysticism). The pious heavy lifting of ascesis was regarded as a tedious test of one's patience; mysticism, in contrast, was "easier" because it was an abrupt path to God. Mystical closeness to God depended on the gift of special grace, which might be granted to anyone but was always the exception.[218] Typical bywords of the mystics included spiritual concepts like "love of God," "self-annihilation," "the innermost depths of the soul," "contemplation and unification with God," and "devotion." Subjects such as overcoming the stirrings of one's soul and enrapturing the human spirit with the utterly transformative presence of God were very important. The inner world of man, where encounters with God supposedly took place, was crucial. But there was always at least the latent threat that mystics might devalue and thus set themselves above external authorities—the church, the sacraments, even the Bible.[219] It was also asked whether God let himself be reached through or only contrary to essential human capabilities (will, reason, feelings). Was withdrawal from the world indispensable to mysticism or not?[220]

The early modern Catholic Church was torn between asceticism and mysticism. In principle, the church wanted to recognize mysticism, but it also was extremely wary because mysticism was so difficult to control. This ambivalent attitude of the church carried over to the Society of Jesus. On the one hand, the Society was marked by a strong ascetic tendency that today, in hindsight, often seems characteristic of the Jesuits. Works on this form of devotion by Jesuit writers like Eusebius Nieremberg or Alonso Rodríguez became international classics. Rodríguez, for example, dedicated several hundred pages of his treatise *Practice of Perfection and Christian Virtues* (*Ejercicio de perfección y virtudes cristianas*, first published in 1609) to describing how Jesus Christ perfected his own virtues, dominated his vices, and thereby led a more pious life through hard work on himself. Rodríguez sought to give readers a practical guide to improving their everyday lives and faith: How can one be chaste? How should one conduct oneself with relatives? How can one live one's daily life in a way pleasing to God? These were the key questions for Rodríguez when he wrote about "Christian perfection." This straightforward, practice-oriented, active devotion resonated widely both inside the Society of Jesus and beyond. Rodríguez's book was published, translated, and adapted more than three hundred times. Many other authors from the Society wrote similar works (as did many non-Jesuits). They thus continued to influence the image of the Jesuits in their own eyes and those of others down to the modern era. The strict, rigid piety that characterized the Society of Jesus in the nineteenth century under General Jan Roothaan (r. 1829–53) drew inspiration directly from Rodríguez. There was no place here for ecstatic experiences and meditation.[221]

But besides this ascetic tendency, there was another way in which the Society was profoundly influenced by the legacy of mysticism. It began with Ignatius himself, whose spirituality was heavily influenced by contemporary trends that were on the margins of or even went beyond accepted forms of Catholic devotion.[222] His various interrogations and trials before the most diverse ecclesiastical tribunals may not have resulted in conviction, but he was hardly untouched by the new forms of intensive devotional mysticism. Even at the end of his life, he used mystic ideas and terms to describe the religious experiences of his wandering years in his autobiography. The text is full of references not only to "visions" but also to still more intense "illumination" (*iluminación*); that is, the experience of a clarity transmitted directly from God (*entendimiento*). Ignatius was so unshakably certain of these moments of illumination that he placed them even over the Bible: "If there weren't Scripture to teach us these matters of faith, he would be resolved to die for them solely on the basis of what he has seen."[223]

The product of this certainty was a kind of independence from the established liturgical and sacramental forms of devotion—the *Exercises*, for example, largely do without the sacraments.[224] Ignatius also showed confident detachment from traditional penitential and devotional practices (confession, flagellation, etc.). Instead of adhering strictly to established rules, he considered it legitimate to "search about and make many kinds of experiments" to attain spiritual perfection. "Most holy gifts" and "divine impressions and illumination" often stood at the heart of his faith.[225] Hence he believed from the start that he was entitled and able to override the established rules of Catholic devotion and to speak and preach about matters of the faith without theological training.[226] In the eyes of many contemporaries, these aspects of his faith brought him dangerously close to the controversial *alumbrados*, a group of devout laymen and clergy who had been declared heterodox and persecuted by the church for the direct relationship with God they claimed.[227] This relative openness to contemplative devotional practices remained intact after 1540. Ignatius continued to maintain a friendly correspondence with Juan de Ávila, who was also accused of holding views similar to those of the *alumbrados*.[228] In Spain, the "*alumbrados*' manner of speaking" remained widespread among the Jesuits.[229] The very first book produced by a Jesuit (namely, by Peter Canisius) was an edition of sermons by the controversial Rhenish mystic Johannes Tauler in 1543.

The Carmelite nun Teresa de Ávila was an especially powerful catalyst for the transmission of mystic and meditative practices to the Society of Jesus.[230] Teresa is regarded as one of the most influential religious voices of the early modern period. She had very close ties to Ignatius's order. She met Francisco de Borja personally twice, and these encounters made a deep impression on both of them. Teresa was also under the spiritual tutelage of various Jesuits for many years. The saint from Ávila profited from the Jesuits' spirituality and found that many aspects of the *Exercises* helped her channel her own spiritual experiences. The Jesuits took her inner state seriously and attempted to help her with pastoral guidance. We can identify no fewer than twenty-three Jesuits who served as counselors for the Spanish saint. Teresa herself influenced many Jesuits in turn with her ideas and religious language, both during her lifetime and far more profoundly afterward. Balthasar Álvarez, one of her confessors and a controversial Jesuit author, may have adopted important aspects of his own spirituality from Teresa. Elements of Carmelite spirituality cropped up repeatedly in the Jesuit order. When the Jesuit Raymundo Prat was on his deathbed in Manila in 1605, he had his fellow brothers sing a poem composed by Teresa and set to music to comfort him.[231]

Contemplative and more pronouncedly eremitic forms of spirituality received strong support under Francisco de Borja, the third superior general of the Society of Jesus.[232] The former duke himself was a fixture of religious circles that focused on the inward, contemplative aspects of piety (*recogimiento*). For example, he was in close contact with the Franciscan Juan de Tejeda, whose teachings were regarded as extreme and viewed very critically by contemporaries. At the college of Gandía, the chief city of Borja's duchy, some Jesuit fathers embraced teachings that went beyond the pale of what was tolerated. The fifteenth-century Italian mysticism of Girolamo Savonarola was also known within Borja's circle. Even the fiercely contested messianic thinking of Joachim of Fiore from the twelfth century could be found in Gandía. Borja was declared the "Angel Pope," a key figure in Joachim's thought. The Jesuits otherwise wanted nothing to do with Joachimite messianism. Ignatius felt that these ideas were so inappropriate that he wrote a long, very frank letter against them in 1549. As much as he had been influenced by the alternative spirituality of Spain, Ignatius was unwilling to entertain these prophetic variants.[233]

Many of these mystic and highly contemplative Spanish strains of spirituality spread through the Society of Jesus to Italy and all of Europe. For example, the Jesuit order became a refuge for students and scholars of Juan de Ávila. One of them was Gaspar de Loarte, who was ultimately transferred to Genoa in northern Italy.[234] Through Loarte, these Spanish ideas came into contact with their Italian counterparts.[235] Francesco Adorno, sometime provincial of the province of Lombardy, was very open to mystical ideas and acknowledged that he had "read many of these texts."[236]

Other Jesuits around the year 1600 also praised mystical experiences. Virgilio Cepari, for example, wrote much-read books about two revered Jesuit mystics, Aloysius Gonzaga (1568–91) and John Berchmans (1599–1621), in which he expatiated at length on their contemplative, detached, and ecstatic spirituality.[237] Cepari described communicating with God directly through contemplation. An immediate divine presence was possible. In this state of rapture, "pure love" of God reigned in man, a love of God without any ulterior motive—a typically mystic conceit. Outright "ecstasies" could result from this state. Cepari believed it was both possible and, as the royal road of spirituality, desirable that "each person is elevated by the light and grace that God shares with them to function outside their natural state of being." It was supposedly not unusual for people with such experiences "to step completely outside themselves." The senses and mind were thus shut off for a moment. In conclusion, Cepari longs—in latent contradiction to the principles of his order—for a reclusive life of contemplation: "O, what torment this active life is for him who knows it well. How often have I envied you, because you have the good fortune to live [in a monastery] far from this worldly chaos and you can and should attend to perfecting your-selves."[238] Cepari's ideas were widespread in the Jesuit order. Robert Bellarmine, one of the Jesuits' most important theologians, also bene-fited from them. On his deathbed, Bellarmine supposedly found great consolation in reading his confrere Cepari's book.

But whoever flirted with mystic, contemplative, and alternative forms of spirituality was playing with fire, as Achille Gagliardi discovered in Milan when he caused a major scandal in the late sixteenth century. In 1584, he had begun mentoring a noblewoman of great devotion, Isabella Berinzaga.[239] Gagliardi's famous work *Breve compendio di perfezione cris-tiana* (Brief compendium of Christian perfection) was the fruit of this collaboration, which drew attention to itself for its clear call to mystic "self-annihilation" (*annihilatione*).[240] The goal of Gagliardi's piety was the "deification" (*deificazione*) of man—a dangerous concept. This dei-fication he described in typically mystic terms as an "ecstasy of the will and not of the intellect." He wanted not only to pay homage to God with the mind but also to change the entire person. He writes, "Penetrating theological concepts and similar such divine matters . . . is only for few people and is not necessary." Here we glimpse the anti-intellectual po-tential of this spiritual tradition. Gagliardi sought to submit his will to God utterly. He may not have regarded visions and mystic states of rap-ture to be strictly necessary, but his religious practices and his collabora-tion with Berinzaga were viewed critically, and the *Breve compendio* was censored. In 1601, Gagliardi's works were prohibited on account of their "novel manner of speaking."[241]

His ideas nonetheless were very popular and spread quickly both inside and outside the Society. Even Protestants like Pierre Poiret (1646–1719) cited Gagliardi with approval. The mystic Maria Maddalena de' Pazzi (1566–1607) also owned a copy of the *Breve compendio*.[242] The French Jesuit Pierre Coton, who was educated in Milan and maintained a correspondence with de' Pazzi, brought the text back home with him across the Alps in 1600. Étienne Binet, likewise a Jesuit, translated the *Breve compendio* into French. But Gagliardi's text had reached France by other means in 1597, thanks to none other than Pierre de Bérulle (1575–1629), who published his own French translation.

Bérulle, who was not a Jesuit, became one of the most important religious authorities of the seventeenth century and left a lasting impression on Catholic spirituality. He not only knew and appreciated Gagliardi's book but also was deeply inspired by contemplative spirituality. In 1602, he made the *Exercises* in Verdun under the direction of Lorenzo Maggio, who himself was one of Gagliardi's prominent sympathizers.[243] Bérulle in turn had a cousin, Madame Acarie, who was one of the driving forces behind the founding of the Discalced Carmelites in France. She had received the stigmata and was influenced by the Capuchin mystic Benoît.[244] In 1600, Acarie's residence in Paris became the center of a circle of believers who advocated an intense form of Catholic spirituality and had been heavily influenced by Teresa de Ávila. Not only was Bérulle a regular in Madame Acarie's circle, but the Jesuit Pierre Coton, mentioned previously, was also routinely present. Coton remained a confidant of Bérulle, even though the latter's relationship with the Society remained ambivalent with respect to church organization, in contrast to spirituality.[245] Jesuits so inclined thus had no trouble becoming part of a religious milieu that brought together laity and clergy, men and women, members of religious orders and secular priests, Carmelite nuns and followers of Ignatius notwithstanding all their other differences.

Coton was simultaneously the provincial of Francia and the confessor of Louis XIII, high offices that gave him great influence on the development of the Society in France. Hence it is unsurprising that this introspective Catholic spirituality became naturalized in many French Jesuit houses.[246] A large number of young Jesuits embraced contemplative spiritual trends. Some, like Barthélémy Jacquinot and Jean-Jerôme Baiole, cultivated mystic ideas.[247] This tradition reached its peak under the influence of the aforementioned Louis Lallemant at the tertiate of Rouen, who molded an outright "school" of profoundly pious young Jesuits who all advocated intense, occasionally even ecstatic, spirituality.[248]

One of the Jesuits profoundly influenced by Lallemant was Jean-Joseph Surin, a tragic figure. Surin was born in Bordeaux in 1600. At the age of sixteen, he joined the Society of Jesus and received the usual education. Surin was sickly and had a sensitive personality. He spent two decades of his life, from 1637 to 1657, suffering from mental illness. In 1645, he even attempted suicide. Only at the end of his life, before his death in 1665, did he at last find mental and spiritual clarity. Yet despite his dramatic biography, Surin left behind an extensive and very influential oeuvre of spiritual texts.[249] He prized contemplation and regarded it as his duty to mentor others with similar mental states. He drew a sharp distinction between the accomplishments of theologians, on the one hand, and mystics, on the other—the anti-intellectual undertones can hardly be missed.[250] In Surin's view, sanctity could not be achieved solely through human endeavor but rather was a gift of grace to be obtained from God. These were two "very different things." Virtue as the result of human effort was important, but it was only half the battle. Surin thus explicitly rejected the widespread practice of asceticism, as represented by Alonso Rodríguez, mentioned earlier.[251] Merely performing pious penitential exercises was pointless. The "extraordinary gifts" of God were still necessary. These alone created an "intimate familiarity with God," the "fervor of charity," and the "permanent attention of the heart to God." Without true "love" for God, all was in vain.[252] Surin accordingly did not want to privilege a form of prayer that relied on various methods of human reason, but rather prayer "in which God himself can do the most." One should not consider God only with the intellect, but should savor him sensually.[253] Contemplative prayer, in Surin's view, should also play a significant part in the Jesuit order. Surin cited the founder of the Society himself as an example.[254]

Questions concerning prayer were a frequent source of strife in the Jesuit order. Different methods of praying were in competition with one another in the early modern Catholic world, just as they were within the Society of Jesus. Whereas with traditional "vocal prayer" (*oratio vocalis*) the faithful addressed requests and statements to God aloud or quietly, the highly controversial "mental prayer" (*oratio mentalis*) utilized images and feelings to experience divine love as a mental state. Mystically inspired Jesuits like Balthasar Álvarez and Antonio Cordeses were especially fascinated by this form of prayer in the 1560s and 1570s. By praying in this way, Cordeses writes, "the heart leaped like a fish in water."[255] Language, reason, and intellect ultimately fell short in the realm of religion; Cordeses sought "secret stirrings of the most fervent love"—again the latent anti-intellectual danger of this contemplative spirituality rears its head. At almost the same time, Diego Álvarez de Paz and Francisco Suárez (1548–1617), the latter one of the greatest theologians and philosophers of the Society, were also impressed by the mystic experiences of mental prayer.[256] The Irish-born Jesuit Miguel Godínez (1591–1644) held similar views later in the same century.[257] He too regarded the goal of piety not so much as the recognition of truth as the emotional and existential assumption of truth and the focus of man on this truth. One should "answer Christ's love for us with love."[258]

But the views held by Jesuits like Cordeses or Álvarez rubbed their superiors the wrong way. The label *mysticus* was rarely intended as a compliment.[259] Everard Mercurian and Muzio Vitelleschi are regarded as superiors general who resorted to more or less drastic measures to suppress mystic ambitions within the Society. Mercurian composed a pointed circular in 1573 against "unusual" forms of spirituality in Spain. Two years later, at a stroke, he prohibited practically all classics of Christian mysticism, from Johannes Tauler to Mechthild of Magdeburg to Hendrik Herp.[260] Half a century later, his successor, Vitelleschi, sternly warned the Jesuits of Lallemant's school against pursuing such interests. Some of them left the Society in frustration. Jean de Labadie (1610–74), for example, turned his back on the order in 1639 and supported the Huguenots in southern France and Calvinist pietists in the Netherlands before ending up as a Reformed separatist and millenarian in Altona.[261]

Vitelleschi railed against mystic Jesuits like Labadie, who supposedly led a life "of pure spirit and had attained a state of beatific vision and other stories totally foreign to the spirit of the Society."[262] The unusual spirituality of Labadie and brothers with similar views seemed to the superior general to be incompatible with the goals and principles of the Society of Jesus. It was alleged against other mystics that their spirituality "does not extend itself very well to those exercises of the active life, it is not appropriate to the Company, whose end is this [the active life]."[263] Conservative Jesuits feared the tendency of mysticism toward "inactivity" and to the passive "enjoyment" of closeness to God. The mystics were reputed to reject key aspects of Jesuit spirituality— "meditation" and "formal prayer and other such pious practices."[264] Mysticism furthermore undermined confidence in reason and human will, in science and rational theology, and posed a threat to engagement on behalf of the faithful—these were pillars of the Jesuit self-conception. These reservations and skepticism of mysticism thus also reflected an effort to protect the identity of the Society: *activus in contemplatione* was one of its guiding principles, after all.

It remains an open question as to whether Mercurian and Vitelleschi really wanted to banish mysticism from the Society entirely or merely limit it. Despite all their prohibitions, the medieval classics and major contemporary authors continued to be widely read in the Society of Jesus.[265] And yet the skeptical superiors' intervention resulted in a kind of general compromise: nearly all mystic authors from the Jesuit order henceforth took great pains to ensure that adopting mystic practices did not lead to escapism and pure contemplation. Miguel Godínez, for instance, explicitly stressed that contemplation was compatible with an active life—he was not advocating a detached existence as a hermit. Godínez also maintained an open interest in combining contemplative mysticism with the Society's typical scholasticism and scientific theology.[266] Maximilian Sandaeus (van der Sandt), in his treatise *Theologia mystica* (1627), even tried to adapt "the formulae of the mystics' manner of speaking precisely to that of the scholastics," as he explained in a lexicon of mysticism he subsequently prepared (*Pro theologia mystica clavis* [Key to mystical theology], published in 1640).[267] He thus translated the often poetic, metaphoric, and unusual language of mysticism into the intellectual world of Jesuit scholasticism. Jean de Brébeuf, Paul Le Jeune, Antoine Daniel, and Isaac Jogues from Lallemant's school also struck a successful balance between mysticism and worldly engagement, albeit in a different way. They were all profoundly influenced by their teacher's mysticism, but they all led very active lives—in contrast to Surin, for example—in the ministries of the Society, namely, as missionaries in Canada.[268] All this was ultimately a kind of compromise made by many other contemporary mystics, but it was especially important to the Jesuits. It meant no less than integrating the experience and idiom of mystic contemplative spirituality into the realm of accepted Orthodox Catholicism.[269]

Obedience and Self-Initiative

Lorenzo Tristano, a master builder and Jesuit, once had a remarkable personal encounter with Ignatius at the Roman headquarters of the Society of Jesus:

> Master Lorenzo used to say that our Blessed Father [Ignatius] taught him how to obey, and he did it in this way. With his walking stick, Our Blessed Father drew a window that he was to make in a large, old wall: "And make it neither too large nor too small." In the meantime the Father Procurator of the Casa passed by and said to him, "Master Lorenzo, this window is too small; make it a little larger." He simply enlarged it. When he was done, Our Blessed Father returned and saw that the window was larger than the window he designed. He said, "Brother, what have you done? It's larger than the one I designed for you." He responded, "Father, the Father Procurator told me to make it larger." He made him redo it and make it small. When he was done, Our Blessed Father returned and said, "Brother, undo it again and make it as you had before." And he redid it in this way, without saying a word. And from then on he obeyed blindly.[270]

Stories like these are told again and again among the Jesuits. They illustrate a key virtue highly prized within the Society of Jesus: obedience. Obedience, of course, had always been one of the most important traits of Christian monks. Together with Poverty (Matthew 19:21) and Chastity (Matthew 19:12), Obedience was the third "evangelical counsel": it was not strictly necessary for one's salvation to practice them—the laity did not submit to them—but according to Catholic thought they represented a special ministry to God, as was befitting of monks (Matthew 19:16). Every order had adopted chastity, poverty, and obedience in their own way, and the Jesuits were no different. But while the meaning and significance of chastity seemed self-evident, or at least was relatively seldom discussed in detail, Ignatius and his successors devoted much more attention to poverty and especially to obedience. The Society of Jesus made *oboedientia* a central pillar of its self-conception. Episodes like the one experienced by Tristano illustrated the importance and nature of obedience to young Jesuits.

Generations of Jesuits drew on a series of memorable expressions to describe the nature and significance of obedience in their order. Some of these phrases had circulated for a long time but now acquired special prominence. The foundation was laid by Ignatius, who commented on obedience in several of his letters. According to him, not only obedience in deed was important, but also obedience of the will and mind.[271] As related with praise by Tristano, obedience should be "blind," that is, unconditional, without hesitation, opposition, or inner resistance. According to a saying that is equal parts famous and infamous, derived from Franciscan models, Ignatius wrote that the obedience Jesuit should be like a "corpse" (*perinde ac cadaver*), like a piece of inanimate material, bound to carry out his superior's orders with no power to resist.[272]

These famous phrases were not primarily concerned with social practice. Obedience was understood first and foremost as a mental virtue, a pious challenge, a spiritual opportunity. Seen in this light, obedience pertained first of all to the religious relationship that every single Jesuit had with himself, with his ego, his own person. According to this view, being obedient meant not blindly trusting and following one's own inner feelings and impulses. Obedience was the counterpart to indifference. In a spiritual sense, it was an act of active self-relativization and the humiliation of human nature, especially the will as its supreme expression. Obedience meant stepping out of oneself, an act of self-sacrifice and thus an act of devotion to God. Like the Rule of St. Benedict and Bernard of Clairvaux, Ignatius regarded actions taken on one's own initiative as indicative of pride (*vana gloria*), that original sin with which Loyola himself, on his own admission, struggled all his life.[273] Obedience was both an expression of and a means to achieving humility as the opposite of pride. Obedience freed a Jesuit of this sin. Obedience of one's own free will was freedom for God to Ignatius's mind:

> Try then, dear brothers, to set aside completely your own wishes. With great liberality, offer the liberty that He gave you to your Creator and Lord present in his ministers. Consider that it is no small privilege of your freedom of will to be able to return it completely in obedience to the One who gave it to you. You do not destroy it in this way; rather you bring it to perfection as you put your own wishes in line with the most sure rule of all rightness, the will of God. For you the interpreter of that will is the superior who rules you in the place of God.

With obedience, a person performed "nothing less than a holocaust." With obedience, "one puts aside all that one is, one dispossesses oneself of all that one has, in order to be possessed and governed by divine Providence by means of a superior."[274]

Despite all the spiritual underpinnings of obedience, Ignatius and his successors never lost sight of its social aspect. Obedience was and is a form of relations between two (or more) agents. Obedience was always obedience to someone. Within the order, the superiors commanded obedience, for they were the representatives of God. Ignatius himself had stressed that point, exhorting his brothers, "When the voice of your superior is heard giving an order, recognize it not as the voice of the person you know, but as the voice of Christ."[275] His successors took up this thought. An eighteenth-century text states, "It is piety that perfects obedience, by ensuring that one sees nothing but God in one's superiors and that one has the feelings of a son toward them," as toward God the Father.[276]

Hence, as Ignatius stressed, there was a multilevel hierarchy of claims on one's obedience: obedience to one's immediate superior, to one's indirect superior, and ultimately to the superior general, and, at least for the professed, explicitly toward the pope as stipulated in the famous fourth vow. The chain of superiority and subordination went even farther: it was an all-encompassing principle. Everything in nature was part of a hierarchy that culminated with God. Ignatius formulated this view as follows: "For example, among the angels there is a subordination of one hierarchy to another, and similarly in the heavens and in the movements of all bodies there is a pull from the higher to the lower, and among the higher, each in its due order, up to the supreme mover."[277] The unity of the Jesuit order was the most important social consequence of this hierarchy and the Jesuits' complete submission to it. *Unio*— solidarity and unity—was the ideal result when every member of the order surrendered his will and obediently took his assigned place.

Ignatius was realistic enough to foresee that future Jesuits would always struggle to see the true will of God in the commands of a given superior. He responded with several suggestions. On the one hand, he tried to give practical advice to help Jesuits obey more readily even in difficult situations. He encouraged them not to be skeptical of their superiors but rather to place inexhaustible trust in them. A Jesuit should never attempt to find reasons to disobey an order but should always look for additional reasons for carrying it out.[278] On the other hand— and this is often overlooked—Ignatius also established several counterpoints to obedience. For one, there was the fundamental purpose of the *Spiritual Exercises*.[279] This consisted of scrutinizing one's inner convictions and ideas and choosing and reinforcing "true" impulses, that is, those pleasing to God. This search for and trust in "true, inner movements" in the faithful's soul sent by the Holy Spirit was very much at odds with strict obedience or at least supplemented it with a radical alternative. Ignatius never organized his thoughts into a complete system on this point, and so contradictions and unclarity remain. But already in the letter on obedience that he sent to the Jesuits in Portugal in 1548, which subsequently became a fundamental text for the Society, he formulated clear, if also limited and narrowly defined, grounds for disputing a superior's order.

On the other side of the equation, Loyola and his successors also required autonomous decision-making and judicious independence from those who took orders from the Society of Jesus. It was obvious in everyday administration that the superiors could never know every last detail on the ground. That was also true of the superior general himself: for example, the German head of the Society, Goswin Nickel, confessed in 1662 that other Jesuits had "more experience in southern Italian affairs, because I have never seen these places," counting on local experts instead.[280] In light of the openly acknowledged limitations on superiors' competence, the ability to determine the best course of action oneself in cases of doubt was one of the leadership qualities sought in a Jesuit. Jesuits were supposed to obey blindly, but they were also expected to show shrewd self-reliance and confident autonomy. Anxiously awaiting orders was frowned upon, especially when it resulted in wasted opportunities.

We thus may conclude the following: episodes like Tristano's as he built a window were (as the text also explicitly said) intended as "instruction," meant to convey the spiritual side of obedience. No one in the Society of Jesus seriously planned to lead and manage the administration of the Society with such behavior. The essence and scope of "obedience" in the Jesuit order were far more flexible and complex than the image of zombie-like obedience would suggest on an all too simplistic reading.

How Jesuit obedience might manifest concretely was thus the subject of complex negotiations from case to case.[281] And how the imperative of obedience was put into practice within the Society of Jesus was also highly variable and disputed. Some Jesuits demanded a kind of right to have a say in life-altering decisions. "It seems to me with good reason that [the superior] should first ascertain my wish in a case like this and not immediately resort to commands," Paolo Segneri (1624–94) complained in February 1692, for example, when he was made the court preacher of Pope Innocent XII against his will.[282] Segneri wanted his voice to be heard about whether he would hold certain offices in the church, and he got his way: the sources show that he confidently negotiated with the pope and superior general himself.

A rather less well-known Jesuit, Jacob de Vos, took similar action in the Netherlands in 1681/2. He likewise wanted a say in decisions that would affect his life. "I do not think it is disobedient for a religious to give his reasons, to indicate his feeling of horror, to pour forth his prayers humbly."[283] For relatively insignificant members of the Society, the superiors could always play the ultimate trump card: it was possible to give specific instructions explicitly "by virtue of holy obedience."[284] This seldom-uttered phrase, to be used only with caution, was the harshest form of command available to Jesuit superiors. Disobeying such commands was tantamount to flagrant insubordination and was regarded as a violation of the fundamental values of the Society.

Some Jesuits like Segneri, however, enjoyed so much autonomy by virtue of their offices or prestige that such an effort to exact obedience would have been simply impossible and fatuous. This also applied to Jesuits in the circle of powerful princes and kings. Eberhard Nithard (1607–81), the confessor of Mariana of Austria, the widow of Philip IV and regent of Spain after his death in 1665, was just such a case. He had so much political influence over the church and politics on the Iberian Peninsula that even Superior General Gianpaolo Oliva was forced to acknowledge that he was "exempt from obedience to the Society."[285] Nithard could take the liberty of deciding for himself what action he wished to take. In doing so, he considered his situation in Madrid at least as much as the wishes and requests of the superior general. Oliva, in turn, realistically recognized his own weak position and avoided a power struggle with Nithard purely for pragmatic reasons: the Society simply profited too much from Nithard's influence at court.

Hence the everyday execution of superiors' commands, in obedience or disobedience, was always subject to complex compromises. Where and when disobedience began, where the border between tolerable self-assertion and intolerable obstinacy ran, was never clearly defined in the Jesuit order. Instead, whether an action was labeled and regarded as (dis)obedience always depended on a variety of local factors, the availability of viable alternatives, and the identity of the persons concerned. Whether Nithard and de Vos were particularly recalcitrant characters is the wrong question. Instead, we should highlight the fact that even such personalities embraced and accepted certain aspects of the Jesuit culture of obedience—and then interpreted them in their own way. Thus, with respect to conditions in Madrid, it must be emphasized that Nithard had long acted entirely in accordance with the will of the Society and his superiors when he agreed to mentor the queen dowager. In cases like his and in many more, it was not simply a matter of obedience versus disobedience. Nithard's transgressions resulted precisely from his fulfillment of his superiors' instructions.

Law, Constitution, and Organization

After only a few years, the ever-denser web of laws by which the new order was governed seemed like a "labyrinth" to Nicolás Bobadilla, Ignatius's friend and early companion.[286] Some regulations came down from the popes, but most were the work of the Jesuits themselves, who were and remained productive legislators. The Jesuits attempted to organize the inner workings of their community with an abundance of rules and norms of varying scope and binding force. Calls for rules and regulations were heard frequently in the Society. Many Jesuits viewed legislation as an appropriate way to respond to new situations and uncertain circumstances. In contrast to Bobadilla, many members of the Society of Jesus were confident in the power of new, ever more detailed regulations to bring order and harmony.

The right of the Society to issue rules for its own members was one of the pillars of its autonomy. Pope Paul III had granted the order this right in the founding bull *Regimini militantis ecclesiae* of 1540.[287] Like every order of the Catholic Church, the Society of Jesus was a distinct legal sphere in which specific laws, regulations, and conventions prevailed. The Jesuit legal sphere consisted of several components: canon law provided a major external juristic framework that included rulings by the papal court and documents issued by the popes (bulls, briefs, constitutions). Many rules of canon law were older, general norms that did not apply to the Jesuits exclusively or even primarily. Other sources of canon law, in contrast, especially papal bulls and briefs, were specific in nature and explicitly concerned only the Jesuits. These sources frequently established special rules or granted exceptions from general measures. The Jesuits began to collect the legal texts that they and the popes had issued for the Society at an early date. Juan Alfonso de Polanco himself, Ignatius's secretary and his most important Roman collaborator, preserved the foundational documents in the order's archive.[288] In 1635, the Society subsequently began to publish several authoritative compilations of its legal foundations, the so-called *Institutum Societatis Iesu*. In its final form in 1892, it filled three large, thick volumes set in tiny type. Practically every Jesuit house also maintained its own manuscript collection of important rules, letters from the generals, excerpts of regulations, and epitomes of individual norms. These handbooks were usually composed with local conditions in mind. The superiors had such collections made so that they would always have the most important documents at hand in a usable form.[289]

The oldest component of the *Institutum* is a relatively brief document, the *Formula Instituti*, in which Ignatius set down his thoughts on the function and form of the future society for the first time in 1539. He presented this sketch to Paul III, who incorporated it more or less verbatim in the bull *Regimini militantis ecclesiae*, which confirmed it. The *Formula* succinctly presents the quintessence of the Society of Jesus. For the next few years, it was the only basis on which the Society developed. But Ignatius soon got to work defining far more precisely how his order should be built and function. What the *Formula* had indicated in broad strokes had to be elaborated and explained in detail. Once the Society had been founded, regulations were needed in new areas that had not been covered by the *Formula*, and Ignatius felt a more detailed basic text was needed. He began working on such a text very soon, but the work stagnated. He needed an assistant to put the project in motion. At last, Ignatius found an energetic collaborator in legal and organizational matters in Polanco, who was named secretary in 1547.[290]

With Polanco's help, the work proceeded more quickly. By the mid-1550s, Ignatius and Polanco were able to present a preliminary draft of their regulatory work; the text was officially approved in 1558, two years after the founder's death—the *Constitutions* of the Society of Jesus now had binding force. By the modern numeration, this fundamental work contains no fewer than 827 paragraphs, some of them quite extensive, which are in turn divided into ten parts along with various prefatory remarks. Even today, interpretation of the *Constitutions* oscillates between a spiritual and an organizational and legal understanding.[291] Viewed as a classic of Western religious literature, the *Constitutions* represent an attempt to motivate and guide the reader to exhibit specific pious behavior. As a spiritual text, the *Constitutions* exhort and call on the reader to adopt a specific mental attitude. Last but not least, they served to convey to members of the Society of Jesus a sense of the order's nature and identity. For this purpose, the *Constitutions* were first supplemented by epitomized lists of rules as early as the late sixteenth century and soon receded from view. The *Constitutions* were reduced to a set of fixed practices and reference points. This normative formalization peaked in the nineteenth and early twentieth centuries.

In addition to spiritual guidelines, the *Constitutions* detail the Society's complex organizational structure. They regulate countless everyday procedures, such as the admission of new members and their subsequent training and education. The *Constitutions* give the Society of Jesus its outward appearance. At first glance, it is as clear as it is simple. The order is divided into three or four levels. The first, lowest level consists of the individual Jesuit establishments in cities and villages—as we have seen, their number exploded in no time at all. There were several types of highly distinct institutions in the Society. We can distinguish a first group of a relatively small number of Jesuit houses dedicated to special functions in the context of Jesuit education—houses of probation for candidates, novitiates for the instruction of provisional members, and tertiates for Jesuits shortly before full admission.

Viewed over the long term, the type originally intended as the standard model, the "professed house," was also not particularly numerous.[292] Full-fledged members of the Society were supposed to live at these institutions in a spiritual community and use them as a base for their pastoral ministry. Ignatius's wish, as reflected in the *Constitutions*, was that the inhabitants of these professed houses would live in absolute poverty. That meant that not only every Jesuit but also the Society as a whole should not have any kind of regular income whatsoever. The Jesuits who lived at a professed house were supposed to provide for their own sustenance with nonrecurring, spontaneous donations. If necessary, they would go begging. This model of house was inspired by the mendicant orders, but it was impossible to overlook the fact that the permanent financial insecurity of professed houses significantly impeded their extensive spiritual commitments. In Rome, the local professed house, the Curia, was chronically underfunded and faced major financial problems—in 1700, it became necessary to launch outright fundraising campaigns for it.[293] Despite such problems, though, local Jesuits sometimes called for new professed houses to be opened to counteract the popular impression that the Society had abandoned its commitment to poverty. The Second and Third General Congregations indeed authorized the founding of several new professed houses. The local college in Valladolid, for example, was converted into a professed house in 1567.[294] But by 1600, leading Jesuits of the next generation, like Pedro de Ribadeneira, realized that the Society could not function broadly and productively on the basis of professed houses alone. The Jesuits were now working in too many areas with too many expenses to forgo regular income. It moreover was clear that only major cities with large populations could guarantee adequate provisioning solely on the basis of spontaneous donations: "Just as there are few large and wealthy towns, there can be only few professed houses." Contrary to Ignatius's original intentions, thus, this unique type of Jesuit institution remained the exception—by 1773 there were just twenty-nine professed houses worldwide. In most provinces there was precisely one such establishment.[295]

It is typical of the precarious situation of professed houses that the house in Valladolid was transformed yet again in 1627. Now it was turned back into a "college." It thus once again became one of the typical institutions outfitted with a school that has since come to epitomize the Jesuits' presence. Enormous sums were sometimes necessary to maintain Jesuit colleges because instruction was free, and a considerable number of members had to be supported as teachers. To make ends meet, the rule of poverty had to be broken—colleges, it was soon decided, needed extensive possessions so they could reliably meet their long-term expenses. These institutions, where in some cases well over a thousand young men studied, might even take on the character of a university. They typically housed large numbers of Jesuits, who performed many other services in addition to their teaching duties. Jesuit colleges were first-rate cultural and religious centers and had a considerable impact on their respective host cities.

Whereas the institutions mentioned thus far had physical locations—buildings or grounds—there soon were more virtual forms that were chronologically and/or spatially more fleeting, often existing only temporarily. A group of Jesuits, for example, might come together for specific "missions" depending on their specific duties. That is why the bases for converting non-Christians in America, Africa, and Asia, where a small group of Jesuits lived in the midst of the indigenous population, often far from all other Europeans, were called "missions." But there were other "missions" in this organizational sense at other places and for other purposes, as for instance when Jesuits served as chaplains with an army in the field or aboard ship. This was called a *missio castrensis*, a military mission.

All Jesuit communities, no matter what type they were, were led by an executive staff. At the top stood a superior appointed usually for three years—the "rector" in the case of a college, the "superior" for other Jesuit communities. He surrounded himself with a number of senior managers. The head of every house had counselors (*consultores*) at hand, who took part in important decisions, attending regular meetings. At colleges, the procurator played an important part: he was responsible for financial and legal affairs and also might employ various assistants in certain circumstances. At other institutions, there were still other specialized Jesuits, such as those who attended to the education of novices ("masters of novices"). Over time, detailed rules were issued for all these officeholders and their assistants, describing their duties, rights, and obligations, as well as rules of conduct. A labyrinth of regulations was the result, as Bobadilla had remarked.

Every Jesuit was assigned to a house and was under the supervision and command of his superior. Jesuit life was essentially communal. No Jesuit lived for himself alone. No one was supposed to travel alone—the Society also adopted that monastic tradition. Hence in 1603, the Jesuits of Lille seriously considered reducing the number of pastoral visits to the countryside rather than permit unaccompanied Jesuits from the local college to make them as before.[296] At first glance, at least, there was no getting around the strict rule of communal life. Yet there were always individual Jesuits whose subordination to the local hierarchies might explicitly be lifted. Pedro de Ribadeneira, for example, who lived in Toledo and Madrid from 1573 until his death in 1611, was explicitly exempted from the authority of a house superior in recognition of his special role as Ignatius's close confidant.[297]

The Jesuits grouped their many individual establishments into larger regional territories called "provinces." This regional structure was also based on older models, although its introduction was a significant departure from the Western monasticism of the High Middle Ages. The loosely organized Benedictines and the other orders derived from them knew nothing of the sort. It was the more rigorously organized mendicant orders of the late Middle Ages that introduced a geographic logic to their structure: the Dominicans were the first to divide their order into provinces. Three hundred years later, the Society of Jesus adopted the practice as natural.

Bit by bit, the Jesuits likewise carved the world into provinces. In 1546, one Spanish and one Portuguese province were founded. A Sicilian province followed in 1551. Spain was partitioned by 1552, and the first German province was established in 1556. Such territories were also quickly established oversees, first in India in 1549, then in Brazil in 1552 and Peru in 1568. At the end of its early modern existence, in 1773, the Society of Jesus comprised a total of thirty-two provinces and vice-provinces, although there often was no obvious difference between the two forms. Far more went into the geographic subdivision of the world, of course, than everyday administrative practicality. For local Jesuits, the administrative consolidation of the houses in a given region into an autonomous (vice-)province was also often a kind of symbolic recognition of their linguistic, cultural, or political distinctiveness. Jesuits thus often fought passionately to have "their" region elevated to a (vice-)province.

The provinces evolved into an important midlevel administrative unit that served a vital coordinating function. They were headed by a superior, the "provincial," who was supported by a relatively small staff of associates. He was accompanied by a secretary (*socius*, his "ally"), who presumably exerted great influence on everyday affairs. There also was a dedicated specialist for administrative and financial affairs at the province level: the provincial procurator. He was responsible for managing the properties and incomes that belonged to the entire province. He also took care of legal and financial questions that arose when new members joined the Society. The provincial also had, just like every local superior, a small group of counselors (*consultores*) recruited primarily from the heads of individual Jesuit communities.

On the one hand, the provincial had considerable influence on local affairs and could intervene in the business of individual communities to impose order or issue commands. He moreover was an immensely important contact for the Roman leadership of the Society for information about conditions on the ground. Hardly any important decisions were made in Rome without consulting the provincials. On the other hand, though, the respective competences of the provincials and rectors had been clearly delimited only for a small number of technical questions. The rectors of powerful, major establishments who were deeply embedded in local and regional networks may have carried considerable weight of their own. And the provincial administration was not, after all, intended to dominate the various communities and individual Jesuits within the province. The provincial and his staff more frequently coordinated, prioritized, and distilled the opinions and views of the individual communities than made decisions over their heads.

Provincials and their *socii* led a taxing life. It was their job to visit every institution in their administrative district once a year. Even in relatively small territories like the Belgian provinces, this meant that the provincial was almost constantly on the move. In larger territories, such as the province of Austria, which included large parts of Bohemia and Hungary, visiting every site was possible only with the greatest exertion. The practice was completely utopian for the massive territories outside Europe with their poorly developed infrastructure. During visitations, the provincial spoke with all the Jesuits at the community in question, inspected the buildings, and discussed current problems with the rector, whether they pertained to the everyday life of the members or were of an administrative or political nature. At the end of the visit, he left behind a booklet with official resolutions and apprised the leadership in Rome of the current situation on the basis of his own impressions.

Besides the annual circuit of the provincials, who stopped sometimes several times en route at conveniently located communities, where they often stayed for weeks at a time during their visitations, there were few integrating institutions on the provincial level. By far the most important one was the provincial congregation, when all the superiors of a province's houses met together with further important Jesuits every three years.[298] The provincial congregation was a conference lasting several days, with ample scope for conviviality. When the *patres* of the Lower Rhine held their meeting in Cologne in 1702, lasting from Sunday to Friday, venison, veal, sauerkraut, and "ox with horseradish" were on the menu.[299] The meetings were opportunities for the Jesuits of a province to discuss, coordinate, and reach decisions. The end result was a "memorial," a document that outlined future measures like a declaration of intent. Furthermore—and this was their official raison d'être—the congregation appointed two members who would be sent to the leadership in Rome at its conclusion. These delegates were also called "procurators," but they should not be confused with the provincial administrators who bore that title.

The chosen procurators then met in Rome with their colleagues from other provinces, as well as with the Jesuit leadership, at the so-called congregation of procurators. This was the only regularly convened forum where members of the entire order could voice their opinion to the leaders. The congregation of procurators was not created until 1568 and lacked a direct basis in the *Constitutions*. These belatedly introduced assemblies in Rome had hardly any powers, although their potential as a platform for the exchange of information and lobbying should not be underestimated. They actually had just one decision to make, although it had potentially far-reaching consequences: every three years, they voted whether a general congregation should be convened. Occasionally, the procurators declared in favor of calling a general congregation— for example, in 1606, which is why the Sixth General Congregation met two years later to discuss whether the Society was in a spiritual and organizational crisis and what might potentially be done about it.

A general congregation was a representative assembly of the Society, for which selected Jesuits traveled to Rome from every province. The general congregation enjoyed supreme legislative power; its decrees were the most important sources of the law for the Society after papal decrees and the *Constitutions*. At a general congregation—one should actually say *only* at a general congregation—Jesuits had the power to exercise direct legislative influence on the form and development of their order.

Why was the rather insignificant institution of the congregation of procurators not invented until 1568? It was a constitutional compromise, a concession to disgruntled members of the Society.[300] They were disgruntled because Ignatius and Polanco had originally ruled that general congregations should be convened only on the death of the superior general. Otherwise, the Society would not have any representative institution. This was very unusual, however, in the history of Western monastic orders. Most other orders convened general congregations or general chapters regularly and often. The Dominicans and Cistercians generally held annual meetings, for example, to discuss current affairs. It was there that everyday politics were practiced. But Ignatius and Polanco had no patience for that. They were skeptical of the very notion that delegates from the entire order should regularly take part in everyday administration and decision-making. They did not consider it desirable to create an institution that might represent the Society of Jesus from below and influence its actual development. Hence in the roughly 480 years of the history of the Society, only thirty-six general congregations have met, the most recent in 2016; merely nineteen had met by 1773. Congregations of procurators, which were not legislative bodies but could convene a general congregation, were a small nod to the older traditions.

There was constant wrangling over the rarity of general congregations. Hardly any other organizational ruling in the *Constitutions* was as controversial as this point. Criticism came from both inside and outside the Society. In the sixteenth century, for example, Juan de Mariana, a Spanish Jesuit historian, theologian, and philosopher—as controversial as he was influential—called for more regular meetings. In the seventeenth century, the advocates of reform made a temporary breakthrough when, in 1646, Pope Innocent X issued the bull *Prospero felicique*, forcing the Society of Jesus to hold a general congregation every nine years—still relatively seldom, but at least now with predictable regularity.[301] This rule was observed for a while but was rescinded in 1746.

Instead of regular general assemblies as had previously been typical of the monastic orders, the Jesuits preferred a strong executive in Rome, which would govern the Society largely free from the influence of representative institutions. The *Constitutions* established a leadership structured like a monarchy, which had few parallels in the history of the Catholic Church. The Society was (and is) led by a superior with universal, general executive competence: the *superior generalis*, superior general, or the Jesuit "general" for short. The term thus originally had nothing to do with the military, even if the Jesuits themselves soon regularly associated the two metaphorically. The general was elected by the general congregation—the death of the head of the Society was accordingly the only occasion on which convening such an assembly was explicitly required. In contrast to most of the older orders, the superior general, once elected, served not for a specific, limited term but for life. It was precisely for this reason that the *Constitutions* considered it unnecessary to hold regular representative assemblies.

In comparison to the older monastic communities of the Middle Ages, this arrangement undoubtedly strengthened the continuity and stability of the Jesuit executive. Some generals directed the Society of Jesus for only a brief time—Luigi Gottifredi, for example, served for only fifty days at the beginning of 1652 before he suddenly died. What was crucial for the Jesuits, however, was the fact that many other superior generals reigned for an extraordinarily long time. Claudio Acquaviva, for example, was in office for 34 years (1581–1615), Muzio Vitelleschi for 31 years (1615–46), Michelangelo Tamburini for 24 years (1706–30), and Lorenzo Ricci, the last early modern general, for 15 years (1758–73) before he died in 1775 on account of the harsh conditions of his imprisonment after the suppression of the Society. In the nineteenth century, Peter Jan Beckx was likewise in office for 34 years (1853–87). Such elected authorities might not have been able to rival secular monarchs, in which the succession was usually based on descent—in France, for example, only eight kings ruled from 1547 to 1774 versus eighteen generals of the Society of Jesus. But compared with other European elective monarchies, the continuity of the Jesuit leadership is very impressive. That is especially true with respect to the most important benchmark, the papacy: from 1534 to 1774, no fewer than thirty different popes reigned.[302]

Comparing superior generals to ecclesiastical and secular kings is instructive and warranted in another aspect, as well. The Jesuits themselves regularly described their order unabashedly, albeit not unreservedly, as a monarchy. The *Constitutions* granted the superior general powers that went far beyond those of the heads of other orders. The text remarks more than once that competences in the Society of Jesus flowed from the top down. Provincials and rectors exercised power not by virtue of their own authority but only to the extent that it was delegated to them by the general. A number of important decisions moreover remained exclusively in the general's hands, at least in theory. He was the one who approved the final admission of new members; he alone could found new communities; he alone appointed local and regional superiors. The general thus was the supreme authority on whose command, or at least on whose assent, almost every decision depended.

Jesuit constitutional thinkers, however, also believed that the monarchic principle behind the structure of the Society was subject to several limitations. They emphasized that the *Constitutions* mitigated the Society's undeniably monarchic structure by incorporating several "aristocratic" aspects. They meant not only the congregations of procurators but also a group of Jesuit officials gathered around the general in Rome: the "assistants," who were at most six in number. These advisers had two functions. First and foremost, they served as the representatives of the major geographic regions in Rome. They were supposed to convey information and interests from the areas in which the Society was active to the leadership in Rome. Initially, there was one assistant each for Spain, Portugal, Germany, and Italy; one for France was added in 1608, and another for Poland in 1755. Provinces outside Europe were assigned to an assistant according to their political affiliation: Brazil, for example, belonged to Portugal, and the Philippines belonged to Spain. The American provinces made several attempts to establish an assistantship of their own, but they never succeeded. In Rome, the assistants were assigned to the general as the representatives and spokesmen of these major geographic areas. They did not have direct executive power and did not compete with the provincials. Their responsibilities were rather of an advisory, informative, and coordinating nature. But their advisory function was always connected to the assistants' second function mentioned in the *Constitutions*. In the event of physical incapacity or flagrant moral turpitude on the part of the general, the assistants could launch a kind of impeachment process. The regulations on this point, in accordance with Ignatius and Polanco's belief in the effectiveness of a strong monarchic central authority, were extremely vague and allusive. At no time in the history of the Society did the assistants come close to carrying out such an impeachment, even when they threatened to do so in certain cases. But at least two superior generals—Claudio Acquaviva in the 1590s and Tirso González in the 1690s—faced very strong opposition on the part of their assistants.

The central leadership of the Society in Rome was rounded out by the secretary and general procurator. For the role of secretary, the person and tenure of Juan de Polanco, beginning in 1547, was of the utmost importance.[303] Although the secretary per se was merely the personal associate of the general, Polanco shaped the position in such a way that the secretary became the linchpin of the entire administration of the order. A growing number of scribes, sometimes an archivist, and occasionally also a historian of the Society worked alongside the secretary. The influence of the secretary and his staff was usually unofficial, derived primarily from the everyday importance of his work, and less so from specific, clearly codified rights. Since he regularly collaborated with the general on everyday business, he was arguably the most well-informed man in the Society. It may be assumed that he also exerted considerable influence on the decisions and opinions of the general. The undeniable importance of the secretaries of the Society of Jesus reflected the general rise to prominence of this profession across Europe.

The general procurator of the Society of Jesus was first and foremost a specialist for legal and procedural questions that came up especially in the order's dealings with the various officials of the papal Curia. He

was also responsible for ensuring that the order correctly followed procedures with legal implications, for example, reviewing contracts. Last
but not least, it was his job to regulate the often-difficult abdication of
property that was incumbent on every Jesuit who joined the Society.
Especially with respect to new members from wealthy families, water-
tight provisions had to be devised for potential inheritances. While his
provincial and local counterparts were preoccupied with the administration of sometimes very extensive economic undertakings, this was
not the general procurator's highest priority. He may have managed a
number of financial investments and some land, but these tasks probably remained in the background. At no point did anyone in Rome conceive of the idea, let alone attempt to realize it, of central financial planning for the entire order. Rome's engagement with the everyday
economy of the Society of Jesus never extended beyond the legal safeguarding of individual financial contracts on the local or provincial
level. The centralism and monarchic principle of the Society were always limited on this point.

The efficiency and success of the Society depended on the smooth
coordination of its three levels of organization—local houses, the provinces, and the central administration in Rome. Individual groups of
Jesuits could not worry excessively about local concerns, nor could
Rome trample local peculiarities with its universal perspective. In order
to avoid both extremes and to ensure harmony, the successors of Ignatius and Polanco relied on bureaucracy. They devised a system of elaborate administrative routines to ensure that the three levels constantly
communicated and coordinated their wishes and desires, while ensuring that neither local conditions nor the global perspective was
neglected.

Personal counseling and visitations were not uncommon in the Jesuit
order. I have already mentioned the regular journey of provincial representatives to the congregation of procurators—and on rare occasions
to a general congregation. Visitators also traveled through the provinces
at the general's behest, stopping at every house and addressing everyday
details big and small in the interest of Rome.[304] When carried out carefully and well, visitations were an extremely effective means of

reforming and coordinating local activities. But drawing inspiration from the *Constitutions*, the Jesuits believed even more adamantly in the efficacy of administrative routines based on written documents. It could be said without exaggeration that the Society of Jesus entrusted its spiritual plans and goals wholly and by and large unreservedly to bureaucratic procedures.

The fact that the Jesuits bureaucratized life in the Society and subordinated it to written documents was, in a sense, in keeping with the times. Corporations big and small in the sixteenth century—states, trading companies, and even the papacy—increasingly relied on written texts to organize their internal processes. While the Society of Jesus, however, may have been following a contemporary trend, we still must acknowledge that the Jesuits made significant progress in bureaucratization at an unusually early date. Ignatius himself had made a habit of relying on written communication after he was wounded, unless we assume that he had already come into contact with record keeping and receipts at the court of the treasurer of Isabella of Castile. Immediately after founding the Society of Jesus in 1540, he introduced the convention of routine letter writing among the first Jesuits.[305] As early as 1542, he deemed it necessary to give his closest confidants, men such as Pierre Favre or Nicolás Bobadilla, detailed instructions on how they had to correspond with him. One by one, the Jesuits in Rome were asked to process, archive, and answer a rapidly growing body of correspondence—now Francis Xavier, now Ribadeneira, now Salmerón.[306] Ignatius quickly realized that his predilection for epistolary correspondence threatened to turn into a herculean task. In late 1542, Ignatius let Pierre Favre know in exasperation how consuming the constant letter writing was—Favre thus should not complain about the few letters of his own he had to write.[307] Named secretary in 1547, Polanco systematically refined these incipient practices.

Letters served a variety of functions for Ignatius. The content of some letters was purely spiritual. In these, the founder sought to raise the spirits of his downtrodden friends, uplift doubting brothers, and bring recalcitrant companions to their senses.[308] Although the more than six thousand letters of Ignatius's correspondence may still be regarded as genuine spiritual literature in light of these texts at least in part, this quality largely vanished from the letters of later superiors general. They knew only a small number of their brothers personally, and their work-days were taken up even more so with the details of their official respon-sibilities. Pastoral correspondence with individual members of the So-ciety they did not know personally was by far the exception.[309] Direct spiritual guidance was unthinkable now. That does not mean, of course, that later superiors general no longer had any interest in reaching their brothers spiritually. Ignatius's successors often resorted to open circular letters to address current spiritual problems. In these circulars, they sometimes elaborated surprisingly extensive and deep thoughts on the most diverse religious topics. Acquaviva wrote about "renewal of the spirit" (*De renovatione spiritus*) in 1583; Carafa, about "means of keeping the original spirit of the Society" (*De mediis conservandi primaevum So-cietatis spiritum*) in 1646. And as late as 1756, Luigi Centurione sent a letter "on the spirit of our vocation" (*De spiritu nostrae vocationis*). Igna-tius, too, had composed several spiritual letters in a style clearly in-tended to make statements of a general import independent of a specific context, even if we can still identify the specific reasons for the letters. This is true above all of his famous letter on obedience from 1553. Origi-nally intended for the houses in Portugal, the letter contains a compre-hensive treatment of Ignatius's thoughts on the difficult subject of Jesuit obedience. Like the circular letters of later generals, this letter quickly became a universally accepted reference. Printed and manuscript trans-lations of it were widespread.[310]

It was above all streams of administrative correspondence that flowed back and forth between the various levels of the Society's hierarchy. This correspondence moved primarily in a vertical direction. There were precise regulations stipulating which officials had to write to which su-perior or subordinate, how often, and on what topics. Some rules, the so-called *formula scribendi* and its supplements, covered the frequency, style, and content of Jesuit bureaucratic correspondence. One funda-mental rule was to differentiate individual questions from one another clearly. Hence, tens of thousands of the Society's surviving administra-tive letters are often no more than a concatenation of more or less disjointed paragraphs dedicated to individual topics. On a number of subjects, individual paragraphs prepared by the scribes no longer sufficed for the superiors: whole letters now were required.

This correspondence communicated decisions, expressed wishes, and described local conditions. Praise and blame were given, and, most important, questions were asked and answered. Correspondence served to ensure the flow of information between the different levels of the hierarchy. The leadership in Rome, after all, had to be in a position in which it could maintain a universal perspective on the Society as it operated globally. That was possible only if it received regular, high-quality information about conditions in individual houses and colleges. Hence the greatest concern of Jesuit bureaucrats was arguably to ensure the quality of their information. Circumstances and persons had to be described fairly, objectively, and reliably. It was for this reason that Polanco took great pains to standardize the retrieval of information. He drew up questionnaires, advocated the use of tables, and circulated lists with useful information. By the early eighteenth century, the Jesuits had adopted cutting-edge administrative technology to guarantee both the type and the quality of the information the Society collected: printed forms.

The Jesuits invested the lion's share of their bureaucratic efforts in personnel planning. We have already encountered the Society's obsession with the quality, education, and development of its members several times—this passion was translated into bureaucratic procedures to an astounding degree. Every Jesuit's mental, spiritual, intellectual, and physical capacity was routinely evaluated. The Society devised elaborate procedures for conducting such examinations. Even the wording of these assessments was prescribed. A kind of grading system with standard content was devised that was then used to answer about a dozen questions about each member. Every three years, local and provincial superiors were required to prepare overviews of the staff under their authority, whom they were required to assess in table form. These catalogues have justly been celebrated as an outstanding example of the bureaucratization of the early modern period.

The details and evolution of these administrative routines are too complicated to recapitulate here in detail. But the spirit and intentions behind these measures are no less obvious; since Polanco's tireless work, the Jesuits firmly believed that the spiritual goals of the Society could be supported by bureaucratic procedures, and that these procedures could significantly help coordinate the levels of the Jesuit administrative hierarchy. The effort was immense, but the potential benefits seemed far greater. In this way, a truly universal and constantly, meticulously updated overview of the state of the Society and its members would be maintained in Rome. The general would be like a man "on a high tower" who could see the entire Jesuit world. He thereby would be capable of making effective, far-reaching decisions. The Jesuits also believed that bureaucratic correspondence would help them avoid an either-or choice between Roman centralism and local autonomy. Rome would indeed determine many things, but on the basis of local input. The systematic transfer of information helped the Society keep up this balancing act between local embeddedness and a global outlook.

That was the plan, at any rate—but resistance, dissatisfaction, obstacles, and other difficulties in implementing it were so great that we should not exaggerate the efficiency of Jesuit bureaucracy. Rome very quickly became a victim of its own success. The more such routines were devised and had to be followed, the more work was needed to carry them out. The generals constantly grumbled not about too little but about too much correspondence. The system was potentially self-destructive. Also, by no means every member of the Society was thrilled with the progress of bureaucratization. Bobadilla's remark about the "labyrinth" of regulations was just one particularly early expression of resistance. Harsh criticism erupted again and again, and most conspicuously under General Claudio Acquaviva, whom his opponents regarded as the incarnation of the centralistic, bureaucratic style of government they detested.

But even in purely practical terms, the Jesuits' faith in bureaucratic administration came up against a bevy of imponderables. Individual Jesuits either could not or would not give objective reports, misjudged situations, or were badly informed. Letters were lost or stolen. And often it just took too long for the mail to arrive anyway. The slow infrastructure of the premodern period often made epistolary correspondence a waiting game. Many a letter was completely outdated when it finally arrived in Rome. That was already the case in Europe, and it was absolutely true for overseas contacts, where one could often expect it to take weeks, months, and sometimes even years for a letter to be delivered. Finally, many Jesuits obviously had no compunction about slyly using these channels of communication to advance their own agenda and interests. Hence the greatly feared and greatly admired bureaucratic administration of the Society constantly fell victim to the very phenomenon that it was intended to overcome: even in the Jesuit order, particular interests frequently dictated the conduct of individual members.

Discontent, Defiance, and Working toward a Common Identity

Ignatius himself and then truly his successors found themselves confronted by a fundamental problem that characterizes every major social organization, but one that was perceived as especially dire by the Jesuits: How was it to deal with dissatisfied or rebellious members and instill a feeling of solidarity among thousands of men pursuing the most diverse tasks scattered across the globe?

Outward symbols are an important means of creating collective identities. Identity and identifiability are closely intertwined. The Jesuits knew this, too. The Society rapidly developed a kind of logo consisting of the three letters IHS surrounded by a circle with a cross superimposed over the central letter (fig. 5).[311] For centuries, the three letters had stood as an abbreviation for the name Jesus (from Greek, Ἰησοῦς or ΙΗΣΟΥΣ). They therefore were a symbol that conveyed a special relationship with Jesus Christ—which, for the Society of Jesus, was undoubtedly true. The monogram was soon put on the Society's official seal, buildings, paintings, and book covers. Anyone could identify something bearing this decoration unambiguously as Jesuit. But what was true of buildings and objects was not true of people. Traditionally, the members of a given religious order were identified by their habit

FIGURE 5. The monogram of the Society of Jesus, with the three letters *IHS* inside a ring of flames. The cross is superimposed at the center, with the three nails sticking out of the Sacred Heart below. © SJ-Bild.

(from Latin, *habitus*), the distinctive clothing of their order. But Ignatius wanted nothing to do with that. The Jesuit order would not have a standard habit.[312] He merely stipulated that his brothers' clothing be moderate and accord with local customs. The result, however, was the loss of an important identifying feature in a religious context—the color and shape of the habit of a religious order were always symbolically charged. Clothing highlighted central aspects of the identity of Benedictines, Dominicans, and Augustinians, among others.

The Jesuits therefore searched for other means to strengthen their identification with the Society. The *Constitutions* contain a detailed chapter dedicated to effecting a "union of hearts." It was obvious that group solidarity and social consciousness constantly had to be cultivated and created anew or at least maintained. A common identity was not a state that would last forever once attained. Integrating the Jesuit order, on the contrary, took relentless work.

Three identity-building strategies were considered especially effective. First of all, many Jesuits in leading positions in Rome firmly believed that standardization and regulation would produce a "union of hearts." This belief was predicated on the notion that it was virtually impossible for thousands of people to maintain a shared identity, if they all were permitted to live their own vision of Jesuit life uninhibited. It was crucial that "the priests of this order, who are separated from one another in the most diverse regions of the world, follow *one and the same* approach in carrying out this ministry," as Polanco remarked as early as 1554.[313] It was for this reason that none other than General Claudio Acquaviva repeatedly tried to impose a degree of uniformity on many areas of Jesuit life around the year 1600. He laid down rules for the educational stages of young members (the tertiate), established a number of administrative procedures, introduced a standard and, in theory, universally valid school system (*Ratio studiorum*), and standardized the *Exercises* by issuing a mandatory guide to using them in 1599.

Acquaviva also believed that the unity (*unitas*) of the Society had to be fostered and supported by uniformity of doctrine (*uniformitas doctrinae*).[314] His generalship witnessed the culmination of deliberations regarding how one might reinforce intellectual homogeneity in the Society. It was decided that the Society would make a selection of mandatory views (*delectus opinionum*) that all Jesuits would be obligated to maintain, thus guaranteeing a certain degree of intellectual uniformity. That did not necessarily mean that Jesuits had to regard all excluded views as wrong, bad, or even heretical but only that their identity should have a kind of fixed intellectual core. This core was composed of the theology of St. Thomas Aquinas and the philosophy of Aristotle. The *Constitutions* themselves obliged the Jesuits to follow these two authorities. The *Ratio studiorum* of 1599 reiterated this endorsement, and, in 1611 and 1613, General Acquaviva again advocated Thomist-Aristotelian "unity of doctrine."[315] For a long time, most Jesuits honored this consensus or at least paid it lip service. Standardization and uniformity were considered important means of reinforcing members' solidarity with one another and their identification with the Society, and of directing their individual worldviews toward a common perspective.

A second means of generating, reinforcing, and maintaining shared perspectives and convictions was the purposeful use of history. Social groups that successfully unite their members around a certain vision of their shared history take a major step forward by fostering identification with the organization.[316] The Jesuit order in particular made every effort to give itself a convincing, generally accessible autobiography.

Ignatius of Loyola himself played a towering part in it. He was stylized so radically as the "ideal Jesuit" that the equally important accomplishments of his nine companions largely disappeared from view.[317] "Every founder of a religious order is like a model for his order which all his children should try to emulate with all their might," wrote Pedro de Ribadeneira, the most important early biographer of the founder of the Society, just a few years after Ignatius's death—and that maxim naturally also applied to Ignatius and the Society of Jesus.[318] It was the second and fourth of Ignatius's successors as leader of the Society of Jesus—the Spaniard Francisco de Borja and the Italian Claudio Acquaviva—who fostered a strong cult of Ignatius. His status as a role model culminated in his canonization by Pope Gregory XIII in 1622. At this time it became a declared goal to transform new Jesuits into the most faithful likenesses of Ignatius possible: Jesuits should become *Ignatiani*. This was also taken quite literally: Ignatius's face, of which there were several more or less contemporary depictions, became a clearly recognizable "Jesuit" type. Portraits of other Jesuits often exhibit facial features that bear a remarkable resemblance to those of Ignatius.[319]

In order to commit the Society to follow Ignatius's example, countless historiographical works, edifying hagiographies, heroic epics, depictions in the most diverse media, and even musical and dramatic productions were made about him. Collections of Ignatius's sayings appeared, and many of his letters circulated.[320] Jesuit authors even turned the searching pilgrim into a pious hero. Liberties were sometimes taken with authenticity. Much was remembered, but hardly everything: Ignatius's rooms at the Jesuit Curia in Rome were painstakingly preserved and lavishly painted with scenes from his life by Andrea Pozzo. Loyola's letters were diligently collected, but the text of the *Autobiography*, which quickly ceased to conform to the public image of the saint on account of its all too open statements, was hidden from the public in 1567.[321] Hence this carefully controlled and obviously curated version of the life of Ignatius, which was considered an appropriate model, was supposed to serve as Jesuits' point of reference, capture their imagination, and bind them together in shared admiration. Drafts of other, alternative biographies, of which there were not a few, were marginalized, if not suppressed. The situation was similar for many other saints and well-known members of the Society. Francis Xavier, Stanislaus Kostka, and Aloysius Gonzaga, for example, were also frequently depicted in a variety of media, including texts, plays, and operas, as paragons of Jesuit culture.

Alongside this hagiographical tradition, the Society of Jesus set in motion an enormous machinery of professional historians to present the evolution of the Society in a way befitting the self-image it sought to project. In 1615, the first volume of an official history of the Jesuit order appeared, its composition undertaken at Rome's behest.[322] The work proceeded slowly, but it was thorough, so that merely the first six parts had been finished by the time the Society was dissolved in 1773, covering its history down to the generalship of Muzio Vitelleschi (r. 1615–45). Analogously, albeit often more succinctly, many provinces produced accounts of their own history.[323] It must be acknowledged that the fruit of these labors was an official account of the history of the Society that deliberately adhered to certain views. "Everything that might offend the provinces or secular persons must be stricken," the instructions frequently read.[324] Yet, despite this tendency toward self-aggrandizement, we should not dismiss the historiography of the Society as mere propaganda. Jesuit authors often drew on extensive archival and library research.[325] They tried to the best of their ability to attain a complete overview of all available information.[326] It moreover very likely was understood that such histories had to be more than mere agglomerations of pious details.[327] Credibility and reliability were also important. The self-history that the Society produced with enormous scholarly effort and at the highest standards of content and style thus showed the Jesuits, through a shrewdly calibrated mixture of accuracy and manipulation, what their community was, how it came about, and how it had evolved. At the same time, it set down what it meant to be a part of the Jesuit order and its tradition.

There was still a third means that was used to promote unity and shared values and ideas: Ignatius himself believed that the Jesuits would grow together spiritually even across great distances and differences if they were constantly informed about the fate and accomplishments of their brothers elsewhere. The dissemination of current, exemplary details from the lives of other members of the Society would "glue together" (*conglutinare*) the men on a global level.[328] Hence the Society devised an edifying news service, reporting in a pious tone, by Jesuits for Jesuits. Every Jesuit house was encouraged to record the most important, most inspirational events at regular intervals, initially three times a year, then twice, and at last—in the final format established in 1565— only annually. These reports were accordingly called the *litterae annuae*. The annual reports of individual houses were collected at the provincial level, edited, and compiled into a whole. Then either several copies were made and sent directly to the other provinces or, as was increasingly the case after 1554, they were sent to Rome, where extensive annual reports covering all the provinces and houses of the entire Society of Jesus were compiled and sometimes also printed.

The evolution of the system was a long process of trial and error.[329] The purpose and result of the project, however, can be clearly discerned through all the details: by carefully disseminating information, the annual reports raised awareness of conditions elsewhere and, by presenting Jesuit achievements and challenges at large, fostered identification with one's fellow brothers near and far. Hence when new *litterae annuae* arrived, the superiors were required to read them aloud at meals as soon as possible so that all members of the house heard the news. At regular intervals, the Jesuits were encouraged to cultivate empathy for the fate of their confreres in a ritualized yet modern way.

These efforts to cultivate group identity and to commit the Jesuits to shared values and models were very progressive. They are still impressive even today for the candor with which the Jesuits discussed problems and potential solutions. The Jesuits were under no illusions about the challenges that they, like every other large, global organization, had to overcome. They equally had no illusions about the fact that reality often fell far short of the ideal to which they aspired. Nothing could be further from the truth than to think of the Society of Jesus as a homogeneous, uniform bloc of like-minded men. On the contrary, the Society was plagued by internal conflict and differences of opinion that regularly erupted into real crises. Both individuals and large groups of Jesuits were dissatisfied with their situation, their fellow brothers, or the order's leadership and articulated that dissatisfaction. There were always outsiders, dissenters, and renegades in the Society. By no means every man who joined the Society of Jesus was happy with this choice in the long run.

Individual reasons were often at fault. Men were unhappy because they disagreed with the rules, obligations, and requirements of life in the Society; because they quarreled with their superiors or confreres; or because their worldview broke with that of the Society. Some Jesuits found it difficult to abide by the cultural guidelines of the Society. Arnoldo Concho in 1557, for example, simply could not understand why he was forbidden to read the works of Erasmus of Rotterdam. He openly threatened to procure this prohibited literature elsewhere.[330] Generally speaking, there were frequent conflicts over obeying the superiors and rules of the Society. Many Jesuits protested when they were ordered to do certain things by their rectors or provincials. Conflict usually derived from specific incidents—individual instructions were disregarded. But not a few Jesuits were capable of finding far more fundamental arguments for insubordination that threatened to elevate individual objections to the status of a general debate. Others were deemed unfit because they had an "all too glowing enthusiasm for spiritual questions," culminating in spiritual overload and mental breakdown.[331]

In addition to obedience, chastity was also a problem. Adam Musch, for example, a *coadjutor temporalis* and tailor in the college of Heiligenstadt, fled the house in 1582 "on account of passionate love for a girl."[332] To avoid such episodes, the superiors were extremely careful when they noticed even a flicker of the threat of "excessive familiarity" between the sexes.[333] Hence behavior like that of Fr. de Vos, the missionary in the Netherlands mentioned earlier, who passed the time with female wards until late in the evening and seemed to enjoy their company, could not be tolerated.[334] How far such "familiarity" went and whether it led to sexual encounters can hardly be extracted from the Society's sources, which give the reader no more than allusions and vague periphrases. Anti-Jesuit and anti-church polemic of the seventeenth and eighteenth centuries alleged that the Jesuits and other priests regularly sexually exploited women, but their lascivious claims were undoubtedly exaggerated. Still, we can detect individual cases in which the Society itself became suspicious. For example, Philippus Mambrianus, rector in Modena, and Hieronymus Bondinarus, a Jesuit also based in Modena and known for exorcisms, were summoned to Rome in 1617, incarcerated, and investigated both inside and outside the order on charges of sexual misconduct.[335] Likewise, several dozen indigenous women reported during an inquisition in 1774 that Fr. Franz Reittemberger (1736–67), a Jesuit missionary to the Mariana Islands in the Pacific, had frequently become intimate with them under the pretense of religious exercises.[336]

Incidents of homosexuality were even more delicate. In addition to the violation of chastity, these cases also introduced moral objections to homosexuality. Homosexuality was quite widespread in the early modern period and was even practiced semi-openly in various contexts, but in the official view of the church and the Society it was nonetheless regarded as contrary to nature. Jakob Marell, S.J. (1649–1727), for example, was actively involved in several homosexual affairs in 1698, and, to his disgrace, predominantly with students at his college.[337] "He sinned with [his own spiritual sons] very often this year and last year, as I have learned from the report of two parties involved," one of his confreres reported to the provincial before describing down to the last detail what had transpired during the abuse. Apparently, Marell had systematically recruited a troop of dependent or willing young men who were compelled or consented to cater to his needs.

Further cases might be mentioned. In the sixteenth century, Giovanni Battista, the brother of Antonio Possevino, was caught several times "touch[ing] the hands, the head, and the face of his students, and some . . . he touched more intimately and often."[338] A young man reported in 1719 that an old Jesuit had come to him in his cell and wanted "such a revolting deed that I do not want to report it out of embarrassment."[339] Pierre François Guyot Desfontaines (1685–1745) was a well-known homosexual shortly after 1700. After attending school with the Jesuits, Desfontaines joined the Society in 1700 and stayed until 1717, when he quit to live as a man of letters in Paris. It was there that he made the acquaintance of Voltaire and immediately picked a literary quarrel with him. His predilection for men got Desfontaines into trouble with the Parisian authorities several times and probably was also one of the reasons why he left the Society.[340]

In other cases, it was not sexuality and chastity that caused internal conflict but rather unstable personalities and unhealthy group dynamics. For example, a case from Granada concerns the lay brother Hernando Gómez Dávila, who in 1616 allegedly attempted to murder another Jesuit, Hernando de Salazar.[341] Gómez Dávila was apparently plagued by mental illness; at any rate, he was repeatedly put in chains in his cell so his outbursts could be contained. It seems as if he had persecutory delusions directed toward Salazar. Salazar was, as Gómez Dávila himself reported, the complete opposite of the poor devil: Salazar was handsome, intelligent, perfect—an "angel." His confreres apparently saw things the same way, and Gómez Dávila was constantly teased and ridiculed for his condition. The young man felt let down by his superiors: they had supposedly treated him with unnecessary harshness. Without downplaying his own guilt for attacking Salazar, the unhappy Jesuit still described an unhealthy, tense, and claustrophobic social atmosphere.

Some missionaries suffered the complete opposite of claustrophobia, living in remote locations without regular contact with their own kind. Mental breakdowns were not unusual in such isolation. Francisco Ortíz, who was active on the west coast of Mexico, is one such example.[342] People who met him thought his erratic behavior, which seemed to vacillate unpredictably between charm and irascibility, was "half crazy." The fact that Ortíz tried to drown his problems in alcohol only made matters worse. Other Jesuits chose even more drastic ways of escaping the unbearable burden of their responsibilities. Cases of suicide were rare in the Society, but they still happened. One missionary in northern India, for example, felt his position was so difficult that "the blood went to his head and he became delirious," at which time he then supposedly attacked himself.[343] Nicolas Trigault, the great missionary to China, hung himself in 1628. Already known to be an instable character, he apparently took internal disputes about how to go about converting China so much to heart that he saw no other way out.[344]

Jesuits in such extraordinary crises could not simply leave the Society after they had taken their simple vows. They could, however, ask their superiors to allow them to be released—unless they simply decided to make a run for it, which also repeatedly happened. Requests for dismissal were common, and in certain phases more than a third of all the men in the Society left in this way. This applied above all to *scholastici* before their final vows, but even ordained priests sometimes left in considerable numbers. It is striking that such separations often occurred years after the end of the novitiate, which was supposed to confirm aspiring Jesuits' vocation. It obviously took much longer than the prescribed two years for interested candidates to make up their minds about themselves and the Society.[345] But by no means all requests for dismissal were granted—at least not until "very detailed and quite specific information about the problems" had been gathered.[346] If only "trivial reasons" were given, the superiors often remained firm.[347] "The fact that the Society's methods of proceeding no longer appeal to you is not sufficient grounds for dismissal," one disillusioned German Jesuit was informed.[348] No one in the Society was interested in bowing to the slightest wavering and indecision of the members.

Some resourceful men appear to have planned their exit from the Society right from the get-go, leaving their superiors feeling not unreasonably as if they had been scammed, as some cases from the 1570s attest. The rectors complained that several Jesuits "only enter the Society in order to become educated, and then they turn their heels to us without ever being the least bit grateful to the Society."[349] Other requests to leave, however, stemmed from genuine doubts in one's vocation. Hence the desire to leave was by no means always an indictment of the Society. Carlo Carafa, for example, whom we met earlier, left the order because he simply could not decide whether he really wanted to live his life there. He nonetheless continued to feel "great respect" for the Society of Jesus, which he rejoined later.[350] Many other cases are known in which members of the Society repeatedly joined and left.

But hardly every Jesuit whose way of life, psyche, and worldview proved incompatible with the Society was willing to put an end to this frustration by voluntarily leaving. For some men, particularly those with personal problems, the order seemed to be more like a kind of last refuge. Potential dismissal then became their constant worry, looming over their lives like the sword of Damocles.[351] That was perhaps exaggerated, but not completely unwarranted: prior to one's profession, the superiors theoretically could dismiss any disagreeable, problematic, or deviant Jesuit at any time, even against his will. And dismissal really was one of the tried-and-true methods used by rectors and provincials to maintain the solidarity of their respective groups. Jesuits consequently were dismissed frequently and sometimes without hesitation.

Yet the decision also was not taken lightly. General Borja, for example, urged Juan de Montoya, the all too uncompromising visitor of Sicily, not to jump the gun but rather always to treat difficult members of the Society with a mixture of "fear and love." It was his spiritual duty to give recalcitrant Jesuits a chance at a "new life" in the Society.[352] Oliver Manaraeus argued in 1604 that one could not revoke admission shortly after it had been granted. The superiors thus often proceeded cautiously and tried to find solutions that were also acceptable to the member's family in cases of inevitable dismissal.[353] Although some Jesuits—for example, Pedro de Ribadeneira—took a harsh, disparaging, or thoroughly disappointed view of those who left willingly or unwillingly, the Society normally did its utmost to find at least halfway amicable solutions that avoided conflict as much as possible.[354]

The Jesuits also precisely calculated the risk that dismissal from the Society could create unrest both inside and outside the community. They often carefully weighed what would be worse for the "reputation" (*fama*) and identity of the Society: the dismissal or retention of renitent men.[355] In certain circumstances, the superiors deemed it better to keep even gross deviants like Jakob Marell in the ranks, particularly when the men were—their respective flaws notwithstanding—still regarded as good Jesuits. Hence, again and again, the superiors resorted to the tactic of retaining even notorious members and perhaps taking them out of the line of fire by transferring them if that could both cover up the crime and guarantee their control of the member in question.[356]

All these deviations from the identity and solidarity that the Society desired to cultivate and project were indeed frequent—whether for sexual indiscretions, disobedience, or mental problems—but they ultimately all were individual cases that could be handled on an individual basis. The solidarity of the Society, however, its "union of hearts," was also threatened by conflict between large groups. The Society of Jesus has been described as a "divided order."[357] There were always two flash points that caused different groups of Jesuits to close ranks in opposition to one another rather than join in solidarity: dissatisfaction with the structure of the Society and the leadership of particular generals, and ethnic and political rivalries.

Many Jesuits accepted the special, unusual structure of their order and were even perhaps a little proud of its peculiarity, making the view of politics and society on which it was predicated their own, at least by force of habit. But over the centuries, there was a very vocal minority that chafed at various organizational details of the Society and at its overall "command structure," especially when superiors supposedly abused their power or wielded it with bias. For that reason every last detail of the constitution of the Society was criticized internally as the decades passed: its system of (rare) congregations, centralism, the nature of the vows, the educational system, its reliance on written communication, lifelong generalships—everything was attacked by numerous members of the order in letters, treatises, and petitions, from the sixteenth to the eighteenth century, and later authors were likewise well versed in the arguments of earlier critics.[358]

When such complaints reached critical mass, and discontent within the Society coincided with political conflict between the pope and particular monarchs, the order's cohesion might dramatically be put to the test. Both in 1590 under Claudio Acquaviva and a hundred years later under General Tirso González, when the kings of Spain and France collaborated, respectively, with the Jesuit opposition, calls were made for the ouster of the superior general and the secession of particular provinces. Both Acquaviva and González were attacked from within their own ranks with the argument that they would make tyrannical use of the general's already too extensive power.

It would go too far to view the profound uneasiness of Spanish and French Jesuits as a coherent reform movement. They had no clear counterplan, no detailed alternative vision. And yet it is impossible to overlook the fact that the Jesuits entertained a certain fascination for the less centralized, less bureaucratic, and less complex command structure and administration of the older religious orders. A need for greater local autonomy was also felt. These alternative ideas could be constantly updated and turned against the Society, when spiritual, ecclesiastical, cultural, political, or personal differences made individual Jesuits or groups of them dissatisfied with the official line.

One of the specific causes for complaints against the Society's Roman leadership and its modus operandi was the much-deplored "vice of nationality" (*vitium nationalitatis*).[359] General Muzio Vitelleschi, for example, gave the following disappointed and concerned diagnosis in 1619: "In the beginning, the Society was not divided into colleges or provinces or even into nations, kingdoms, or regions. Now, however, there is no denying that a certain attachment and zeal betrays itself for what they think will benefit their own provinces."[360] With the passage of time, the fact that, contrary to all guidelines, particular branches of the Society were plagued by rivalry and spectacularly failed to "avoid that sentiment with which nations typically think or speak ill of other nations" and cultures presented ever greater challenges.[361] In this regard, the Society of Jesus was moving in lockstep with the times, as national identities began to coalesce across early modern Europe. The Society, moreover, was often sucked into political and military conflicts—when Spain was at war with France, for instance, the respective Jesuits were expected to be loyal to "their" nation and "their" king.

And so it came about that a tense atmosphere often prevailed between Jesuits of different nationalities. Austrian Jesuits turned their noses up at their Hungarian brothers and prevented them from obtaining their own (vice-)province for centuries. French Jesuit missionaries in China and India refused to serve under Spanish or Portuguese superiors after 1695. In Poland, "turmoil" broke out in 1618 when an Italian was appointed provincial.[362] For decades, the king of Spain prevented non-Spanish Jesuit missionaries from traveling to his colonies, and

Portuguese authorities were dismayed to learn in the late 1750s that there were as many non-Portuguese as Portuguese Jesuit missionaries active in Brazil.[363] Vitelleschi's lament from 1619 had some substance to it. The global "union of hearts" that was supposed to be essential to the identity of the Society was overwhelmed by a strong countercurrent of regional interests and ethnic, political, and cultural animosities.

The superiors had relatively few means of effectively fighting such tendencies. The fact that the Society had inextricably grafted itself onto the political and social fabric of Europe—the Jesuits' success, after all, was based on shrewd assimilation to local conditions—could be neither changed nor overlooked. Spiritual appeals to members of the Society not to let themselves become infected by such particularistic ideas, contrary to the zeitgeist, were frequently made but had limited effect. The leadership also systematically relied on the international exchange of personnel. Roman novices, for example, were sent to Venice, Sicily, or Milan "for their edification and for greater union between the provinces and nations [nazioni] of the Society."[364] How effective such procedures were, however, remains doubtful. Rather than completely defeating "nationalism," the Society probably sought broadly to mitigate existing animosities and balance competing interests and preferences as best it could.

To conclude, an anecdote about the great Jesuit artist Andrea Pozzo, who had become an international celebrity by the end of the seventeenth century, illustrates how carefully the Society proceeded, and indeed had to proceed, to ensure that all its provinces were treated equally. Every Jesuit province where building projects had been planned was practically falling over itself to secure the services of the famous painter and architect. To keep this rivalry and competition under control, General Gianpaolo Oliva was forced to plan well in advance to which house and province he would dispatch Pozzo one by one. Oliva sent Pozzo to the Savoy house in Mondoví, for example, after he had first worked primarily in Milan: such exchange across boundaries, the general remarked, would "maintain ... more intimate communication between those nations that otherwise would have so many outside reasons for some animosity."[365] Personnel policy served to promote Jesuit identity and unity and could not overlook the obstacles, peculiarities, and particular interests of individual regions.

2

The Society, the Churches, and the Faithful

ONE OF THE MOST famous sections of the *Spiritual Exercises* of Ignatius of Loyola consists of eighteen "rules to follow in view of the true attitude of mind that we ought to maintain [as members] within the church militant."[1] In these rules, Ignatius reveals himself as a loyal and dedicated adherent of the Catholic Church, including and in particular its institutional and hierarchical manifestation. He recommends obedience to church superiors, urges that one keep the sacraments, and broadly advocates orienting oneself toward official church doctrine, norms, and precepts. The famous Rule 13 moreover calls on Jesuits "always [to] maintain that the white I see, I shall believe to be black, if the hierarchical church so stipulates." To Ignatius, this seemed both possible and necessary in recognition of the fact that "between Christ our Lord, the bridegroom, and the church, His bride, there is the same Spirit who governs and directs us for the good of our souls." There can be no doubt about the profound attachment of the Society of Jesus to the church, its structures, traditions, institutions, and policies.

But the Roman Catholic Church was anything but monolithic. On the contrary, it was rife with conflict and rivalry and housed a variety of institutions and groups with their own traditions, rules, and interests. There were cardinals, archbishops, bishops, abbots, heads of orders, and superiors all with their own institutions in the background. There were old and young orders, contemplative and less contemplative orders, congregations of men and congregations of women. There were central and regional institutions, and the papal Curia in Rome itself consisted of multiple (frequently rival) branches that often viewed the world church from a completely different perspective from that of diocesan bishops or parish priests. Every new pope, moreover, set different priorities that could often lead to major policy shifts in the Roman church. Sometimes the Jesuits were simply glad when a disagreeable pope died "at the right time" before he influenced the fate of the Society all too dramatically—that was the case, for example, when Sixtus V met his maker in 1590 just before his order that the Society of Jesus change its allegedly pompous name could take effect.[2]

In light of this elaborate institutional complexity, legal competence (under canon law) was always at issue. The inner workings of the early modern Catholic Church were characterized by a tangle of different jurisdictions. Every level of the hierarchy, every group, every organizational unit jealously kept watch to ensure that their rights were upheld and that no rival institutions received too many of their own. A new order like the Society of Jesus, which had received new privileges and powers on an astonishingly comprehensive scale, put existing institutional arrangements under significant pressure. A good example of this is confession: who could hear confession from whom and where, and who was permitted to remit what sins for whom were often fiercely disputed questions. Bishops in particular clashed repeatedly with the Jesuits over competence with respect to confession.

The drive to obtain as advantageous a position for one's own interests as possible in the web of Roman Catholic institutions also determined the thought and actions of the Society of Jesus. At the same time, however, the popes, cardinals, bishops, Roman congregations, orders, and especially the Jesuits themselves were all well aware, every day, that the Roman Catholic Church was embedded in a far greater panorama of Christian diversity. The fact that several Protestant churches had been established since 1517 and were now locked in an existential struggle with the Catholic Church profoundly influenced the Jesuits' (and most Catholics') thoughts and deeds, even if only indirectly. Members of the

Society often encountered representatives of other confessions not only in Germany, England, Hungary, or Holland but also in India, the Caribbean, and the Mediterranean. Many well-educated Jesuits moreover had learned during their training to view their confession as superior to Protestantism—even if they personally rejected the Reformation, it nonetheless became part of many Jesuits' education and spirituality *ex negativo*.

In addition to the Protestant churches, the Catholic Church and the Jesuits became cognizant of another Christian alternative in the sixteenth century: the Eastern churches. This meant, first and foremost, the Orthodox churches of Russia, Lithuania, and Poland. The Jesuits began to forge closer ties to them when Antonio Possevino undertook long missionary journeys as far as Moscow on behalf of the church.[3] When in 1596 the Orthodox bishops of Poland adopted a union with the Roman Catholic Church in Brest (modern Belarus), hope in an even broader, general church union was kindled. The Jesuits in Eastern Europe always bore this goal in mind as they traversed the borderlands between Latin and Greek culture, from Poland to Hungary to Transylvania, over the following decades.[4] Second, early modern Catholics—just like the Protestants, incidentally—reopened dialogue with the ancient Christian churches of the Near East, such as the Copts and Syrian Christians. Some members of these groups were soon living in Europe. The Jesuits played their part in reacquainting the Roman Catholic Church with these long-forgotten, ancient, autonomous Christian traditions.[5]

The Jesuits had to position themselves vis-à-vis all these different Christian actors—Catholic, Protestant, Eastern. They sometimes did so explicitly and rigidly, sometimes cautiously and flexibly. Over time, they struck alliances and conducted hostilities, made friends and foes; some were permanent and dogmatic, others temporary and tactical. While the Jesuits were finding and cultivating their own religious and ecclesiastical identity, they also looked for their place among the many forms of Christianity in early modern Europe and the world. Just as the identity of the Society had never been set in stone, its place in the wide world of Christian churches was likewise an open question.

The Jesuits in the Roman Church

Relations with the Church Hierarchy

In 1537, Ignatius's plans to sail with his first companions to Jerusalem to dedicate himself to guiding pilgrims were dashed. Instead, the group decided to go to Rome to ask the reigning pope, Paul III, for an assignment. Loyalty to the pope has played a very special part in the (self-) perception of the Society ever since. This special relationship with the supreme shepherd in Rome is reflected above all in the Jesuits' famous fourth vow, which even contemporaries often misunderstood. What could it mean? What was lurking behind the relationship between the Society of Jesus and the pope?

The fourth vow reads: "I further promise a special obedience to the sovereign pontiff in regard to the missions, according to the same apostolic letters and the Constitutions."[6] It thus focused above all on the Jesuits' apostolic ministry, especially the deployment of the young order to convert people in Europe and overseas. What fascinated Ignatius and the Jesuits so much about the pope was the universality and globality of Christianity that he embodied. Through their fourth vow, the Jesuits sought to take part in this universal and global perspective. Special obedience to the pope was praised "for having the members dispersed throughout the various parts of the world."[7] It decidedly did not pertain to doctrinal questions or ecclesiastical politics. The goal of the fourth vow, accordingly, was not to transform the Society into an extended arm of papal power with no vision of its own. The vow had nothing to do with the meaning and policies of Catholicism but rather was intended to reflect and guarantee the universal scope that the new order claimed for itself. The vow promised no less, but also no more, than that the Jesuits would "go to whatever provinces [the popes] wished to send them."[8] We thus should not overestimate the direct influence of obedience to the pope on the everyday workings of the Society. It created a basis and an institutional framework for a key aspect of the Jesuit ministry, the worldwide mission, but it did not directly govern conventional, everyday business. The vow played a subordinate part in the internal rules and regulations of the Society.[9] The popes likewise seldom referred to it.

The vow of obedience also did not guarantee a harmonious relationship between the Jesuits and the popes. On the contrary, the Society's relations with the head of the Catholic Church fluctuated dramatically and often enough were cool or even hostile. These sometimes wide shifts were not least a result of the fact that the papacy was an elective monarchy characterized by relatively brief terms of office—constantly changing political loyalties, religious views, and theological emphases were hardwired into the system. Gian Pietro Carafa, who reigned as Paul IV from 1555 to 1559, was famous for his hostility to the Jesuits. Relations between General Acquaviva and Clement VIII in the 1590s were also strained. With other popes, in contrast, the Jesuits found active protection and direct support. Gregory XIII (r. 1572–85), for example, was especially friendly; he confirmed the constitutional structure and spirituality of the Society in a series of important bulls. The Jesuits also rejoiced at the election of Clement XIII (r. 1758–69). They could "scarcely imagine a pope friendlier and more interested in promoting their interests," one Jesuit historian later wrote.[10] The pope indeed did his utmost to defend the Society of Jesus against rising anti-Jesuit sentiment worldwide.

Relations between the Society and the popes were often facilitated, although also sometimes further complicated, when individual Jesuits had close personal ties to high officials in the Curia. Everything depended on whether they could capitalize on their influence in immediate proximity to the pope for the benefit of the Society. Francisco de Toledo (1532–96), for example, was a rather unreliable contact in this respect. First a professor at the Collegio Romano, then active politically in the service of Sixtus V, in 1593 Toledo became the first Jesuit cardinal and an important personage at the papal court toward the end of the sixteenth century.[11] Since Toledo opposed the superior general at the time, Acquaviva, on various matters, his interventions frequently raised rather than lowered tensions between the Society and the Curia.[12] Sforza Pallavicino, half a century later, also enjoyed the "complete confidence of the pope." Alexander VII, then known as Fabio Chigi, had been one of Pallavicino's childhood friends, "so that not a day passes on which they fail to talk two or three times about this or that for three or four hours."[13] Some Jesuits also had family ties to the papal court. Robert Bellarmine, for example, was a nephew of Pope Marcellus II. His elevation to cardinal undoubtedly was indebted to this circumstance.[14] Still other members of the Society of Jesus worked in close quarters with the pope. In the late seventeenth century, Paolo Segneri Sr., a famous missionary and orator, was summoned to the court of Innocent XII—indeed, against his will as we have seen. And General Lorenzo Ricci, elected in 1758, was the confessor and intimate confidant of Cardinal–Secretary of State Torrigiani. His position at court was a key factor behind the initially pro-Jesuit climate under Clement XIII.[15] Jesuits and popes sometimes worked together closely and harmoniously.

By the reign of Gregory XIII, the Society of Jesus had become even more deeply involved in the organizational and administrative work of governing the worldwide church. At the Third General Congregation in 1573, there was still explicit opposition to Jesuits serving in papal institutions,[16] but de facto the Jesuits had already been engaged in the papal administration for years. As early as 1564, for example, several members of the order assisted the papal vicar during his visitation of the diocese of Rome.[17] The Jesuits had also long been involved in the Apostolic Penitentiary. They provided this institution with fifteen to twenty men who served as confessors for visitors to St. Peter's from all over the world.[18] These *poenitentiari minori* necessarily thus included Germans, Frenchmen, Italians, Spaniards, Hungarians, Greeks, Illyrians, Poles, and Englishmen. In 1569, these confessors were brought together in their own house at least partly under the authority of the penitentiary—an unusual arrangement that was the source of frequent tensions. These Jesuits were very close to the papal court: when a pope died, they were responsible for watching over the corpse until it was buried. From 1569 to today, the Jesuits hold the office of "theologian" of the penitentiary and serve the presiding cardinal in an advisory capacity.

The Jesuits' relations with the Inquisition (Sanctum Officium, the Holy Office) were far more complicated. The high offices of the

Inquisition in Rome were controlled almost exclusively by the Dominicans, although individual Jesuits played an influential part in the work
of this important congregation.[19] The great Jesuit theologian Robert
Bellarmine, for example, collaborated as a *consultor* after 1597 and was
an influential member of the Sanctum Officium after his elevation to
cardinal in 1599.[20] Ignatio Tellino (1623–99), an Irishman who became
a Jesuit in Ingolstadt and had taught at the university there, was regarded
in Rome as "initiated in the secrets of the Holy Inquisition."[21] Jesuit
cardinals (Juan de Lugo, Sforza Pallavicino, Giovanni Battista Tolomei)
later sometimes worked in the Sanctum Officium. But overall, in quantitative terms, there were far fewer Jesuits in the Roman Inquisition than
Dominicans or Franciscans.[22] The order was relatively more involved,
in contrast, in the Spanish Inquisition. After the Jesuits began serving
as the confessors of the king in Madrid under the new Bourbon dynasty
in 1701, they also exercised greater influence on the appointment of
Inquisition officials. Beginning in 1701, a Jesuit sat on the council of the
local Inquisition.[23]

The Inquisition and the Society of Jesus had very different responsibilities and priorities as far as deviant behavior was concerned, which
often prevented them from collaborating effectively.[24] The Inquisition,
generally, took a legalistic approach to sin, heresy, and moral lapses,
whereas the Jesuits took a pastoral approach. For the Inquisition, the
search for wrongdoing took center stage, which is why, for instance,
denunciation played such an important part in its methods. Public ab-
juration of heresy, with all its social consequences, was likewise standard procedure. The Jesuits, in contrast, advocated a pastoral concept
of spiritual guidance that focused primarily on inner conversion and the
improvement of the sinner or heretic. It was for this reason that more
than one Jesuit thought the Inquisition's procedure was "savage," not
with respect to its moral aims but rather with respect to its outward
forms and their consequences. Giovanni Battista Faure, S.J., lamented
in 1750 that the Dominicans in the Inquisition showed "imprudent severity" and had practiced "imprudent and inhuman methods."[25] Their
actions needlessly caused the dispute with Luther to escalate out of
control in the sixteenth century. In typical Jesuit fashion, Faure pleaded

instead for a "practice of leniency" and "charity" in dealing with heretics. In this case, Faure most certainly was not speaking as his order's official voice. His book on the subject was banned.[26] Yet his blunt reckoning with the Dominicans in the Inquisition is nonetheless clear, albeit extreme, evidence of the fact that the Jesuits had their own strategies for dealing with sin and sinners who broke with official dogma.

What is true of the Inquisition is also true of many other papal institutions. The Jesuits collaborated with them and sometimes put outstanding personnel at their disposal, but these institutions seldom became mainstays of the papal government. In some cases, tensions escalated so far as to erupt into open rivalry or even obstruction. This can be observed above all in the case of the papal institution for missionary undertakings founded in 1622, the congregation De Propaganda Fide. This relationship proved to be precisely the opposite of what one would have expected, since it was Jesuits like Francisco de Borja who had called for the founding of a papal missionary institution since 1568.[27] Their willingness to cooperate, however, had dissipated by the time Gregory XV founded the congregation in 1622. By then, the Jesuits had set up their own missions according to their own ideas.[28] They worked closely with European monarchs, so that their missionary efforts were relatively decentralized, coordinated separately in Madrid, Lisbon, and Paris. It was precisely this decentralization that the Propaganda Fide sought to counteract. The new papal missionary authority embodied the Vatican's desire to impose stricter control and centralization on the worldwide mission. In 1640, the congregation accordingly decreed that the missionary affairs of all orders would henceforth fall under its jurisdiction. This pertained in particular to the so-called *facultates*, that is, extraordinary ecclesiastical rights such as the power to hear confession or grant dispensations, which members of the Society of Jesus usually received so that they could be flexible and effective in the unusual circumstances of their mission.

Some religious orders, such as the Capuchins, were amenable to these plans and built close ties to the Propaganda Fide. The Jesuits, however, kept their distance. One contemporary witness reported, "The Most Eminent cardinals of the congregation wanted the missionaries of the Society of Jesus that were sent to China and elsewhere to be completely dependent on their will, which the *patres* of the Society vehemently opposed." The Jesuit generals Vitelleschi and Carafa, for example, stubbornly refused to implement the Propaganda Fide's decree of 1640.[29] Conflicts of competence, authority, and jurisdiction broke out anyway between the Jesuits and the Propaganda Fide. The Jesuits definitely made enemies in the process, including Cardinal Giovanni Battista Pamphili, who became Pope Innocent X in 1644. He gave abundant evidence of his pent-up displeasure with the Society in a number of measures.[30] But the Jesuits accepted such risks to ensure that the bases of their missionary operations overseas remained as independent as possible.

This feud with the Propaganda Fide soon led to dramatic upheaval in the Jesuits' mission territories. In the seventeenth century, the cardinals began to rely on "apostolic vicars" to monitor and supervise Catholic life and Christianization in the missions—with the important distinction that they were directly subject to the authority of Rome and often in open competition with Portuguese and Spanish bishops and religious orders with ties to the colonial powers. Holding the rank of bishop, some of these apostolic vicars were on good terms with the Jesuit missionaries who had long been present in their territories, and vice versa. François Laval, for example, active in Canada since 1658, was a friend of the Society of Jesus.[31] When the Propaganda Fide subsequently began to dispatch missionaries of its own, the Jesuits were even capable of heaping praise on them.[32] But conflict with the vicars and their partisans was more frequent.[33] In time, the vicars complained more than once about "act(s) of disobedience on the part of the Jesuits in the form of evasive maneuvers and hair-splitting, although they are subordinate to the vicars"—but precisely that latter point was contested.[34] The secretary of the Propaganda Fide similarly said in 1659 that "one must mistrust the Jesuits, especially the Portuguese."[35] Thus, however close the Jesuits and the Propaganda Fide were in many regards, they still represented different organizational forms and different traditions of the Catholic mission. Cooperation was not utterly impossible, but their relationship was often strained or even hostile.

In addition to the apostolic vicars, papal nuncios were also important representatives of Roman interests in Europe. The nuncios were regular or extraordinary legates of the pope. In terms of function and importance, they were roughly equivalent to the ambassadors of secular princes. The nuncios were very important for articulating the will of the church leadership in Rome locally and vice versa for keeping Rome up to date with local happenings.[36] Nunciatures were established in Luzern, Graz, Vienna, Cologne, Paris, Madrid, and elsewhere. The papal legates there regularly encountered members of the Society of Jesus.

The new order initially benefited from the nuncios.[37] The first Jesuits to come to Germany, Claude Jay, Nicolas Bobadilla, and Pierre Favre, had arrived in the retinue of papal legates there to attend the imperial diets. These early Jesuits, exactly like Peter Canisius later, pleaded for the expansion and reinforcement of the papal diplomatic corps, which they viewed as a powerful means of bringing the unruly state of Christendom north of the Alps more firmly under Roman control. Vice versa, individual Jesuits were also soon viewed as "excellent instruments" and potential partners of the nuncios.[38] Clement VIII, for example, urged several of his legates in 1600 to cooperate closely with the Society of Jesus, especially in Germany. In particular, the perceptive pontifex wrote, they should rely on the Jesuits as informants. "A good and secret correspondence with the Jesuit fathers" was regarded as a necessity for successfully carrying out their mission. The nuncios indeed turned to members of the Society of Jesus more than once as collaborators and even used the Society's houses as temporary living quarters.[39] Obviously, the legates of Clement and other popes were also regularly instructed to intercede with local princes and bishops in support of special requests or projects of the Society.

That does not mean that the relationship between the Jesuits and the nuncios was always friendly and cooperative. Members like Peter Canisius and Martin Leubenstain, the rector in Luzern, criticized the deportment and decisions of individual nuncios. For all the Jesuits' high hopes in the presence of representatives from Rome, they also warned against heedless action when the nuncios sought to impose the Curia's will without knowledge of local conditions.[40] In turn, some papal legates took a critical view of the Jesuits' positions. Gaspare Mattei, the nuncio in Vienna, for example, noted his general reservations against the Society of Jesus in his assessment of the emperor's confessor, Johannes Gans: "In sum, he is a Jesuit, to be frank, but in these tasks we have to rely on them, because they know plenty, can do a lot, and also do good for the Catholic religion. But where the prince's interests and their own are concerned, you have to open your eyes, don't be quick to believe them, because you'll end up being deceived."[41] But as much as such dissonance always occurred and disappointment or indignation might prevail in regard to specific persons or actions, relations between the Jesuits and the nuncios—in contrast to the apostolic vicars—were fundamentally free of rivalry.

Like all religious orders, the Jesuits also stood outside the local diocesan and parish structure under the direction of bishops. That had originally made them attractive: the Jesuits brought a "breath of fresh air" from outside, rattling the established actors and presenting an alternative to well-worn methods. But after the initial shine had worn off and the Jesuits showed their autonomy, this independence could also be taken as competition or insubordination. The global clergy grew more confident over the course of the early modern period, as it recovered from the crisis of the Reformation and was renewed in qualitative terms. The bishops of the eighteenth century in particular vehemently stressed the exclusive right of the priests under their authority to tend to the spiritual well-being of the faithful. The archbishop of Cologne, Josef Clemens, indignantly remarked in 1717 that "the *pastores* are the first shepherds"—decidedly not the priests in the Society of Jesus.[42]

For his own part, Ignatius insisted from the start on maintaining clear institutional distance from the bishops. Hence the *Constitutions* state that no Jesuit was permitted to seek or accept "any dignity or prelacy outside the Society." The Jesuits were not supposed to take over parishes or become bishops, because that was "one of the greatest or the greatest of all" ways of "bringing down and destroying this Society," Ignatius wrote in 1546.[43] General Mercurian sent a memorandum to Gregory XIII during his tenure, citing twelve "reasons why an episcopacy should not be given to anyone from the Society."[44] Specialized literature was dedicated to these problems and how to circumvent them.[45] The Society's success in declining such clerical offices was mixed: by 1773, there were thirteen Jesuit cardinals, and there were just as many bishops from the order. After the revival of the Society of Jesus in 1814, there were roughly as many cardinals as before, but significantly more bishops—at least, more than originally intended. Even after allowing the election of the first Jesuit pope, Francis, Ignatius's order definitely does not view holding high office in the church as its mission. The primary reason for this reluctance was the fact that a secular clerical office would have tied a Jesuit to the place where he held it. That would have undermined the Society's principle of mobility and had major practical and even spiritual consequences.

In spite or perhaps even because of the Jesuits' distance from bishops, the extent of their collaboration with them varied dramatically from case to case. For one thing, it was initially often bishops who were the driving force behind the spread of the Jesuits. In the Holy Roman Empire, the ordinaries hoped that the well-educated, energetic, and engaged members of the Society would stabilize the Catholic faith. In Olomouc, for example, Bishop Vilém Prusinovský z Víckova was a key patron, as was Christoph Andreas von Spaur, bishop of Gurk, who had supported the Jesuits since the 1580s.[46] Likewise in Augsburg, Bishop Otto Truchsess von Waldburg was a major supporter. Admittedly—and this is also typical—his efforts to establish a permanent Jesuit college were initially thwarted by the resistance of Augsburg's cathedral chapter. The need for the new order was hotly disputed within the Catholic clergy. It was not until 1580 that the Society reached an agreement with the city to found the College of St. Salvator and instruction could begin.[47] The bishop of Ermland (Warmia) in Prussia, Stanislaus Hosius, was another major promoter of the Society with pronounced Counter-Reformation goals. In 1565, he arranged the transfer of eleven *patres* to Braunsberg (modern Braniewo), which the Jesuits then used as a base for their efforts to protect, revive, and propagate the Catholic faith in Protestant Prussia.[48]

There were also, however, many episodes in which members of the Society and bishops did not work well together or even quarreled. The local ordinary clergy by no means gave the Jesuits a warm welcome everywhere. Conflicts might arise from theological differences, for instance. François de Caulet, the Jansenist bishop of Parmiers, excommunicated a Jesuit in 1668 on account of his supposedly false doctrine, while the latter defended himself by composing satirical poems and exploiting legal loopholes.[49] Disputes also raged over questions of jurisdiction as rivals vied for power and influence, often in consequence of structural factors. In Prague, a protracted dispute between the Society and the powerful bishop, Ernest Adalbert von Harrach, broke out in 1622.[50] It originally was over the city's university, which was under the Jesuits' direction and was about to be merged with their house. Harrach protested this plan, which he viewed as a threat to his own influence on the university. Although Harrach himself was a product of Jesuit education, the dispute escalated into a grave conflict in the ensuing years. The Jesuits and the bishop personified different religious policies in predominantly Protestant Bohemia. Later, they also clashed over whether the local seminary should be maintained and directed by the bishop or the Society.

The epic battle that the Jesuits in Mexico fought starting in 1657 against the bishop of Puebla and the former viceroy (June–November 1642) Juan de Palafox y Mendoza was similarly complex.[51] This dispute likewise revolved around the question of whether and to what extent the Jesuits should be integrated into the ordinary church structure and thus whether they had to recognize the supremacy of the bishop. The conflict erupted specifically over whether the Jesuits were required to present their papal authorizations to the bishop for inspection. Palafox gruffly demanded it; the Jesuits refused. For both sides, it was a battle of gestures and principles: the bishop knew all along that the Jesuits had valid documents and that they easily could have presented them. But concrete economic interests were also at stake: Did the Jesuits have to pay the tithe to Palafox or not? This economic dispute had smoldered for some time, and the popes had avoided giving an unambiguous ruling. Palafox was broadly interested in strengthening the financial resources of his diocese, and he collected dues with greater rigor. In the case of the Jesuits, he had faced fierce resistance since 1639.

They refused to pay, citing their exceptional legal status. Reciprocal ex-communications and a vigorous political and ecclesiastical tug-of-war ensued. The Jesuits and Palafox finally struck an accord in 1655, but in the same year the Jesuits secured his recall and transfer to the insignificant see of Osma in Spain.

The superior generals normally frowned on such jockeying between Jesuits and ordinaries. From the perspective of the Jesuit leadership, for example, in 1648, they could "not understand why you [i.e., the Jesuits in Mexico] have not shown the bishop [sc. Palafox] the licenses of our colleges in Puebla to hear confession and preach and thus grant him his wish." They should not forget "the great respect and reverence owed to the prelates, just as the examples of Ignatius, Francis Xavier and other saints and great superiors of our Society have taught."[52] The default position most likely embraced cooperation with the bishops, but local and global perspectives might arrive at different assessments within the Society. Due caution was advisable, because such arguments were often only skirmishes in broader conflicts. The Jesuits' success against Harrach depended not least on the support of the emperor in Vienna, who wanted to rein in the power of the prince-bishop of Prague with the Jesuits' help. The Jesuits were maneuvering on a bigger political stage in their battle with Palafox, as well. The bishop of Puebla attempted to subjugate the Society in particular because the Jesuits had allied themselves with the new viceroy Salvatierra, who was locked in a bitter struggle with Palafox for the political future of Mexico. Conflicts over ecclesiastical jurisdiction and political power struggles were intertwined from Prague to Puebla. The authorities in Rome knew that this was a powder keg.

On the ground, in the communities and villages, Jesuits and members of other religious orders had to coordinate their activities with the local parish clergy. The parish priests and chaplains, after all, were personally responsible for the spiritual well-being of their parishioners. Of course, one of the key insights that the Catholic Church had taken away from the Reformation was that the quality of local clergy was often shockingly poor across Europe. The parish was very weak as a social, ecclesiastical-political, and religious entity in the sixteenth century—if it could be recognized as a functioning institution at all.[53] Hence it was initially appealing and acceptable for all parties involved to employ the much better-educated and motivated men from the various orders, especially the Jesuits. It may have constantly led to conflicts, but in many cases at least a kind of "cease-fire" prevailed.[54] By the mid-sixteenth century, the Counter-Reformation church sought to establish a new ideal of the good Catholic priest.[55] The church recognized that the priestly profession needed a new guiding concept and that it had perhaps underestimated the challenges of pastoral care. The complexity of the task of turning simple people into good Christians had become impossible to ignore. Effective spiritual care was now viewed as an "art" that was "neither easy nor soon mastered." Aspiring priests had to be thoroughly prepared for this challenging job.[56] An extensive body of literature about the ideal and self-conception of the "good priest" was produced to help.[57]

The Jesuits also felt obliged to suggest rules of conduct for secular parish priests. According to the oft-reprinted *Manuale parochorum* by Charles Musart, S.J. (first published in 1652), the ideal parish priest should lead an exemplary life and be humble, chaste, generous, moderate and sober, clever, attentive, vigilant, and energetic in the service of God. Musart presents the typical responsibilities of the office and discusses practical suggestions for various everyday contingencies. Again and again, he cites the Jesuit order as a model from which a parish priest could draw inspiration. Other Jesuit writers soon added their own voices, such as Antonio Foresti in 1709 and Franciscus Herzig in 1716. They gave specific advice for dealing with the vow of chastity in moments of crisis and emphasized the importance of a good education for aspiring priests.[58]

In order to raise the quality of the parish clergy, the Council of Trent had issued a famous decree calling for the creation of special educational institutions for secular priests. But the implementation of the decree throughout the early modern period remained patchy and sluggish or was lacking entirely.[59] Even where good seminaries were established, their capacities often proved inadequate. Initially, the Jesuits had no need to engage with such educational institutions. The Second General Congregation explicitly forbade Jesuits to take over seminaries in

1565, although it then permitted them to do so in certain economically advantageous situations.[60] In actuality, however, the Jesuits soon were frequently taking on management or at least teaching responsibilities at numerous seminaries. In Olomouc, they were already in charge of the education of numerous priests at several establishments as early as 1566, for which the pope, the local bishop, the cathedral chapter, and private donors had provided around 120 scholarships by 1618.[61] The Society also deliberately educated priests in Dillingen.[62] The pope financed around two dozen scholarship there, just as in Fulda and Vienna, specifically for candidates for the priesthood. The bishop of Augsburg paid for thirteen more scholarships. In the same year in Milan, the Jesuits also took over the seminary at the request of Cardinal Borromeo. But controversies soon broke out between parts of the clergy and Borromeo, on the one hand, and the Jesuits, on the other. Each side had its own views about the goals and methods of education, and after slightly less than fifteen years, in 1579, the Jesuits gave up the management of this paradigmatic institution by mutual agreement. In Milan, it moreover emerged how fierce competition between different forms of Catholic spirituality might become: Borromeo was dissatisfied with the Jesuit leadership of his seminary because many of the best candidates joined the Society of Jesus rather than the priesthood. Jesuit education had thus certainly prospered, but not in the way originally intended.[63]

Since there were relatively few functioning seminaries in the early modern period, other forms of education were more important. Aspiring priests usually had to study at other educational institutions. Young candidates for the priesthood frequently opted for their local Jesuit colleges, which thus became de facto key institutions for educating the next generation of Catholic clergy. There—exactly as at seminaries under Jesuit influence—aspiring clergymen received largely the same education as all other students. Practical skills necessary for priests occasionally rounded out the curriculum, such as liturgical song, practice delivering sermons, and advice for establishing catechetical instruction in the parish. What Jesuit colleges did not provide was an introduction to the challenges of parish pastoral guidance. Aspiring priests at these educational institutions were not specifically taught how to manage their congregation and its spiritual needs. The Jesuit schools and the seminaries originally planned after the Council of Trent provided an intellectual and moral foundation, not pastoral training.

This began to change when a new kind of seminary emerged in mid-seventeenth-century France. These seminaries focused much more closely on shaping and cultivating the vocation of priests. The most important pioneers of this new movement were not necessarily members of the Society of Jesus. Vincent de Paul or Jean-Jacques Olier, who founded an influential seminary at Saint-Sulpice in Paris, did not belong to the Jesuit order. The *Spiritual Exercises* of Ignatius, however, proved to be an important resource of spiritual inculcation and influenced these new educational establishments in a variety of ways. In 1682, the Twelfth General Congregation of the Society of Jesus subsequently permitted Jesuits in much more open language to become involved in the education of priests, with these new institutions in mind.[64] Numerous seminaries came under Jesuit control or were refounded along Jesuit lines. The Society of Jesus exercised a major and institutionally entrenched, albeit not exclusive, influence on the organized education of priests in the eighteenth century.[65]

Relations with Other Religious Orders

If the Jesuits' relations with the secular clergy were complicated, that is especially true of their relations with the many other Catholic religious orders. It started with the fact that Ignatius's new order resisted categorization according to the existing typology of orders. The extraordinarily complex evolution of Catholic orders down to the seventeenth century can, for simplicity's sake, be divided into roughly three types and stages of development.[66] First, there is monasticism in the true sense of the word, which means above all the Benedictines and a series of contemplative orders that evolved from them. In brief, they practice a form of communal religious life that is characterized by retreat from the world—the Benedictines traditionally lived in separate, largely self-sufficient monasteries and were more or less completely absorbed in their own religious development. The Cluniacs and Cistercians of the

High Middle Ages were the heirs of this tradition. The Carthusians like-wise adhered to this ideal of eremitic life.

In the twelfth and thirteenth centuries, a new kind of monastic community emerged, the mendicant or begging friars. The Franciscans and Dominicans, as well as the Carmelites and the Augustinians, placed pastoral ministry for one's fellow man at the center of their identity. They deliberately settled in the growing cities at the time and soon could be found occupied at universities, in church politics, and in the fight against heresy. They viewed themselves as engaged, proactive communities to a far greater extent than the classical monastic orders. The hallmark of the Dominicans and especially the Franciscans was the principle of poverty, which is why begging became one of their most prominent characteristics. The Franciscans in particular split into a variety of branches over time, often depending on whether one wished to follow the original ideas more or less strictly.

The Jesuits themselves, finally, are the most famous exponent of a third kind of order, that of "clerics regular." This form of religious cohabitation is typical of the sixteenth and seventeenth centuries. Besides the Society of Jesus, this group includes the Theatines, who were founded shortly beforehand, the Piarists, and the Barnabites. These religious communities were grouped together under a common designation to reflect the fact that they no longer lived in actual monasteries but rather strove to be engaged "in the world" and had emancipated themselves from established monastic traditions to a greater extent—the rejection of choral prayer and lack of a standard habit in the case of the Jesuits are just two particularly prominent examples.

The fact that the Jesuits were clerics regular did not mean, of course, that they had no connection to the earlier monastic tradition. On the contrary, Ignatius was familiar with forms of monasticism, and he drew creative inspiration from them. On his own admission, he viewed St. Francis of Assisi and St. Dominic as models and inspirations in the years after his conversion in 1521.[67] Bernard of Clairvaux, one of the most influential figures of the Cistercian order with very pronounced and profound piety, including mystic tendencies, was also an important reference point for Ignatius in matters of monastic life.[68] Polanco and

Ignatius studied the rules of the earlier orders long and hard, compiling extensive excerpts before composing their own *Constitutions*; the legal texts of the Dominicans in particular made a significant impression.[69] Many early Jesuits also had a friendly relationship with the Carthusians. The Carthusian prior of Cologne, Gerhard Kalckbrenner, was an important supporter of the new order in Germany in the 1540s.[70] Pierre Favre held the Carthusians of Cologne in high regard, and Peter Canisius, who had lived in close proximity to the Carthusians as a young man, was another important link. A strikingly high number of men transferred from the Society of Jesus to the Carthusians in the first decades of that order's existence.[71] The positive relationship between the two orders was soon also put on an institutional basis. The Carthusians officially proposed a close association between the two orders in 1544, and at the Fifth General Congregation in 1593, the Society of Jesus entered a special "fraternal compact" with the Carthusians.[72]

Such explicit declarations of solidarity, however, did not rule out the possibility that the orders might occasionally clash and compete. With respect to pastoral capacities and efficiency, all Catholic orders cultivated a confident rivalry. The Jesuits regularly stressed that "our" priests were more effective at satisfying the spiritual needs of the laity than the "monks of other orders." They were proud to keep up with the endeavors of the Franciscans and the Recollects (a new branch of Franciscans) and complimented themselves when one of their own events attracted a bigger crowd than the competition's.[73]

Conflicts over economic and social resources were more serious. Bishops and other authorities often attempted to finance new Jesuit houses and colleges by reassigning monasteries and lands that belonged to older orders deemed less capable of reform. In Laibach, the local Jesuit college was supposed to be funded after 1594 by taking over the property of a Carthusian monastery in decline—but the charterhouse successfully defended itself, and a compromise was eventually found.[74] Other orders were also affected: a house of Franciscans in Münster was threatened with closure in 1574; in 1615 and 1618, the Franciscans lost their monasteries in Andernach and Neuss to the Jesuits.[75] Such takeovers often created bad blood, and from time to time the Jesuits declined to move into old monasteries to avoid conflict—in Vienna, for example, Claude Jay refused to move into a Dominican monastery so as to keep the peace. When several years later Ferdinand I abruptly transferred the local Carmelite monastery to the Jesuits, Ignatius fervently hoped that the transfer could be completed "without the resistance of the brothers," but rather "with their assent."[76] What all these examples show is this: the orders made no concessions to one another. The Catholic orders were institutions embedded in society and fought for their own interests.

Such local squabbles were serious, but they should not be overblown. Conflicts that did not stem from individual problems but instead pitted entire orders against one another were far more problematic. Even in the Middle Ages, some orders viewed each other as hostile rivals—the bitter feud between the Cluniacs and Cistercians is the most famous example. The Jesuits were also entangled in such hostilities. The Dominicans were wary of them from the start: some of the Jesuits' earliest and harshest critics came from the Order of Preachers. First and foremost was Melchor Cano (1509–60), a great theologian from Salamanca, who bitterly mocked the *Spiritual Exercises*.[77] When Cano visited the general chapter of the Dominican order in Rome in 1542, he got to know the Jesuits at first hand and judged them, not without reason, as embodying a model of Catholicism antithetical to the dominant form in Habsburg Spain.[78] The Spanish church relied on the Inquisition as a means of exercising social and religious control, sought to temper the universal ambitions of Rome, and cultivated a strictly controlled, formalized, and ascetic religiosity. The Jesuits, with their focus on Rome and global outlook, and their "way of proceeding" based on subjective decisions of faith, were a poor fit for the model that Cano championed. The Jesuits' relationship with the Dominicans also remained confrontational. The Jesuits and Dominicans took opposing sides in the great controversy over the Catholic doctrine of faith in the early 1600s (*de auxiliis*, concerning divine grace), in the disputes over the Jesuits' doctrine of morality half a century later, and in the rites controversy over the mission to China around 1700. The way in which the Dominicans dominated the Inquisition was yet another explosive issue.[79]

But amicable tones could also be heard. Many Dominicans of the sixteenth century cultivated very cordial contacts with the Jesuit order. The great author Luis de Granada was one of them, as was the theologian Juan de la Peña, who wrote the first defense of the Jesuits, indeed in response to his own confrere Cano.[80] Ignatius himself, as we have seen, mentioned St. Dominic as a model and had often lived in close proximity to Dominicans in both Spain and Paris prior to 1540. As a duke, prior to joining the Society, Francisco de Borja had even founded a Dominican monastery and had a Dominican confessor. In 1578, the Jesuit newcomers to Como received warm cooperation from the Dominicans established there, who voluntarily ceded a church to them.[81] Both sides issued mutual declarations of sympathy and calls for peace in 1646 and 1661.[82] In 1679, the General Chapter of the Preachers decreed that all novices had to make the *Exercises* of Ignatius of Loyola before joining the Dominican order.[83] In the same year, the Jesuit general Oliva instructed the Jesuits of Antwerp to conduct themselves with tact and restraint toward the Friars Preachers.[84] The position taken by the Jesuit cardinal Giovanni Battista Tolomei reflects the broad spectrum of attitudes: "The malevolence and disdain that a few of [the Dominicans] have shown the Society should not extinguish in us all feeling of gratitude toward the very many who are friendly to it."[85] It thus appears that despite all their competitiveness and differences, there were nonetheless many moments and elements of mutual appreciation and cooperation between these two large, ambitious orders.

The Jesuits completely blew it with another order, however: the Carmelites. The Society's relations with the recently reformed, "discalced" branch of the Carmelites were initially very good. Teresa de Ávila, the founder of the reformed community, had close ties to the Jesuits.[86] But friendship between them had cooled by the end of the sixteenth century. On the surface, the strife seemed to be the result of economic rivalry and competition, but there were deeper spiritual differences, slow to emerge, that lurked behind the two orders' growing estrangement. General Mercurian therefore instructed in 1578, "As for dealing with the Carmelites, look . . . for the remedy that seems appropriate to you to avoid any excess." Then a scandal erupted between the orders in the seventeenth century for completely different reasons. The Carmelites had been founded in the twelfth century, but they traced their origins back to the Old Testament prophet Elijah. Mythical origin stories still enjoyed widespread currency in the Middle Ages and even in the sixteenth century. Such venerable tales served to raise the prestige of one's institution. The Carmelites' descent from Elijah had already been contested here and there in the early modern period, but it was the scholarly Jesuits of Antwerp around the great philologist Daniel Papebroch who launched an all-out scholarly assault on the old legend in 1669.[87] The Carmelites were incensed, and so a decades-long war of pamphlets broke out between the two orders, soon escalating to fierce legal wrangling before church officials. In 1695, the Spanish Inquisition prohibited the Jesuits' writings, although this ban was not confirmed in Rome.

From the point of view of the Jesuit leadership, it was an unfortunate conflict. The scholarly arguments raised by the Jesuits of Antwerp against the Elijah legend were unobjectionable, but the leaders still wanted to avoid trouble and controversy at all costs. More than once, the generals involved wrote to Belgium urging discretion. "While we may not confirm the glory of the antiquity that is attributed to this order, we at least should not attack it," Gianpaolo Oliva instructed. The Jesuits should avoid doing anything to insult the Carmelites, and they could surely also leave other various offensive facts unsaid.[88] Still, all hope of containing the controversy was dashed: the Jesuits had made an enemy.[89]

Relations with the Theatines, who had been founded by Gaetano da Thiene and Gian Pietro Carafa in 1524, were strained from the start. As it turned out, contemporaries saw such great similarity between the two orders that the Jesuits were often erroneously labeled "Theatines," especially in Italy.[90] It was even rumored that Ignatius had wanted to become a Theatine in 1535/6, but da Thiene had declined because he predicted that Loyola would found the Society of Jesus instead.[91] In reality, the differences between the Theatines and Ignatius were much greater than this story suggests. Under the influence of Carafa, who quickly eclipsed the mystically inclined da Thiene, the Theatines became an order that sought to carry out the necessary reform of the church by strictly controlling and regulating persons, ideas, and groups. Carafa was skeptical of the widespread search for spiritual renewal at the time—and in his eyes that included Ignatius and his widening search for a new spirituality of his own.[92] Carafa (not da Thiene) actually met Ignatius in Venice in 1536, but in light of their different goals, their conversation was less than encouraging.[93] Ignatius was not very impressed by the Theatines.[94] When Carafa became pope nineteen years later, this tense relationship continued.

The order of the Barnabites had much in common with the early Theatines. Antonio Maria Zaccari, who founded the order, had the same spiritual teacher as Gaetano da Thiene: the mystically inclined Dominican Battista da Crema. But whereas, in the case of da Thiene and the Theatines, da Crema's dramatic and sometimes even prophetic forms of meditation were quickly banished from the order under Carafa's influence, these aspects remained prominent with the Barnabites. Intense charitable engagement was combined with introspective spirituality that aspired to the perfection of the individual. The Barnabites and Jesuits therefore overlapped somewhat with respect to their active ministry, despite the fact that the Barnabites were more open to exalted forms of spirituality. Precisely because the two orders were often found in close proximity on various projects, these differences in their respective backgrounds loomed large.[95] The Barnabites and Jesuits, moreover, constantly battled for the same social contacts, responsibilities, and positions because the Barnabites also soon concentrated on education. In some particulars, they even modeled their own pedagogy on that of the Society of Jesus.[96]

Relations between the Jesuits and Piarists (also known as the Scolopi) were characterized by similar competition. The Piarists were a teaching order officially established by papal bull in 1621. Initially, they were involved in elementary education for the neediest segments of the population of Italy—hence, from that perspective, the order founded by St. Joseph Calasanz was an ideal complement to the Jesuits with their own schools. But the Piarists soon went beyond these initial "competences," and so local Piarist and Jesuit schools were often in direct competition with one another. In Chieti, Cagliari, Messina, and Florence, as well as in Valencia in Spain, the two orders constantly clashed, leading to the involvement of their Roman headquarters as well.[97] When for various reasons the Piarists were dissolved (ultimately only temporarily) in the 1640s by Innocent X, it was a Jesuit, Silvestro da Pietrasanta, who played a key part in the affair as the pope's Apostolic Visitator. The Piarists were furious over da Pietrasanta's attitude and actions and expressed grave mistrust toward him and the Society of Jesus.[98]

In contrast to these rivalries, the Jesuits had a very positive relationship with a number of women's orders.[99] That was the case, for example, with the various branches of Ursuline nuns. The Ursulines were founded in Florence in 1535 by Angela Merici. In 1606, Anne de Xainctonge in Dôle founded another group of Ursulines.[100] These communities were characterized by the nuns' active engagement in pastoral ministry and the propagation of the faith. That was unusual insofar as women's orders were supposed to be cloistered, that is, they were supposed to live apart inside a convent. The church affirmed this rule yet again in 1566. The original Ursulines had circumvented it by living with their families, but they too bowed to the cloister in the seventeenth century, although they could still carry out their most important task, educating girls, at large. Anne de Xainctonge, in contrast, refused to allow her community to be cloistered, and astonishingly her nuns remained exempt.

The Ursulines worked with the Jesuits very closely. In the mission territories of Canada and Louisiana, for example, the nuns assumed responsibility for tending to the female indigenous population.[101] The Ursulines usually focused especially on teaching the catechism and imparted at least a rudimentary education to young girls. The Society of Jesus was the Ursulines' most important pastoral, spiritual, and organizational model. The *Exercises* were prominent in many Ursuline convents, and Jesuits were the Ursulines' preferred confessors and spiritual advisers. Anne de Xainctonge aspired to "succeed Ignatius." Since this was impossible within the Society of Jesus, she adopted as many transferable aspects as possible. The "English Ladies" (Englische Fräulein) or "Jesuitesses" were similar. This teaching order, founded in Flanders in 1609 by Mary Ward, was dedicated primarily to the education of girls; it borrowed heavily from the Jesuits' rules and forms of spirituality.[102] At almost the same time, in 1606, Jeanne de Lestonnac founded another women's community with a pedagogical mission in Bordeaux, the Compagnie de Marie-Notre-Dame. Here, too, Jesuit texts and several members of the Society played a decisive part.[103]

In this way, a series of women's communities grew up to fill the vacuum left by the lack of a female branch of the Society of Jesus. Ignatius himself had strictly rejected the idea of female Jesuits because he believed that hypothetical Jesuitesses would undermine the Society's imperative of mobility, since their male counterparts would be obliged to minister to them. It was feared that the Jesuits would lose their intrinsic flexibility. The superiors thus long hesitated before taking on long-term pastoral duties at convents. Even in their dealings with the Ursulines or the English Ladies, whose approach and spirituality closely resembled their own, a certain diffidence was always palpable on the part of the Jesuits.[104] In this case, as in all others, Ignatius's men kept constant watch over their spiritual, social, and institutional interests and their place in the overall structure of the Catholic Church.

The Society of Jesus and Catholic Spirituality

Just as Catholic Christianity was institutionally diverse, it also hosted a broad palette of distinct theological positions, spiritual nuances, devotional styles, and religious emphases. The Jesuits also searched for—and found—their own special place in Catholic theology and devotion. They favored certain theological theories and rejected others; they praised some theologians and condemned others. They developed a marked predilection for certain forms of devotion, certain saints, and certain religious rituals. Very little of what contemporaries associated with the Jesuits with respect to theology or spirituality had been invented by them *ex novo*. As in so many other areas, the Jesuits frequently took up older and newer developments and then shaped them into particularly loaded and impressive manifestations of the renewed Catholic faith of the Counter-Reformation.

If there is anything that is typical of the Jesuits in a spiritual and theological respect, then it is—notwithstanding all the exceptions in the details—their shared preference for a spirituality that engaged *with* people *in* their everyday life, while conveying confidence and certitude in a generally optimistic tone. Of course, the members of the Society of Jesus also never forgot that the message of Christianity should constantly shake up and unsettle people, jolting them out of the well-worn habits of their everyday lives. The Jesuits were virtuosos at playing up this imperative when they diagnosed a lack of enthusiasm on the part of the faithful. But their spirituality primarily aimed—with some exceptions—to instill a religious consciousness that was not founded on constant fear. Uncertainty and contrition should be only a necessary stage, not the fundamental nature, of Jesuit spirituality.

Despite their predilections, the Jesuits were also always willing to draw on a broad range of different forms of spirituality. Hence, we cannot pin down the Society of Jesus on a single spiritual program. The Jesuits' religious conceptions spanned and effortlessly adapted elements from the entire spectrum of contemporary ideas. On the one end, we find refined forms of a new, exalted, and emotionalized devotion; on the other, many Jesuits practiced with true conviction humble features of popular piety that bordered on superstition. Jesuit spirituality undeniably also had a place in the lives of simple believers.

Profiles of Jesuit Spirituality in the Baroque Period

People of the early modern period experienced the presence and even the omnipotence of God at all times, every day. Women, for example, regularly hoped and prayed for God's help during childbirth: bringing a child into the world in the early modern period was often a matter of life and death. The Jesuits were constantly confronted with this immutable reality:

> A woman, whom the doctors and midwives had given up for lost, bound herself by oath at our instigation that if she gave birth to a boy, she would dedicate him to Saint Ignatius. And lo and behold, no sooner had she sworn the oath, she gave birth to a boy, and she had nothing more urgent to do than name him Ignatius. Another woman struggled greatly in childbirth. When at the suggestion of a respected

woman she made an oath to Saint Ignatius, she gave birth successfully without danger.[105]

Stories like these two from Neuss in 1634 were constantly on the Jesuits'
lips, bearing witness to how immediately relevant the Christian faith
might be in the early modern period. God influenced the events of the
day down to the last details, and the saints of the church like Ignatius of
Loyola and other Jesuits like Francis Xavier or Stanislaus Kostka had
the power to induce God to intervene to help his faithful. It was possible
to influence this supernatural realm by offering something to its inhabitants—an oath, the dedication of a child, a pilgrimage, a physical sacrifice, prayers.

God himself kept close watch to see whether such promises or oaths
were kept according to this transactional concept of religion. He and his
helpers could punish negligence with disaster at any time. That is what
allegedly happened to a noble girl, Katharina von Keudel, in Heiligenstadt in 1603. She had a swelling on her neck and swore an oath to Christ,
whereupon the disease vanished. But the material value of the vow was
apparently too low for God, because a calf that belonged to the young
girl soon died—God had "punished her greed." When Katharina also
failed for two years to undertake the pilgrimage she had promised, "God
in his paternal love let the scar gradually break open again."[106] The story
continues back and forth a while, but even these few details illustrate
the worldview and faith of the Jesuits in Germany, on the front lines
against Lutheranism: it was a world where God reacted like an angry
father to his children's least indiscretions, and one could influence him
almost mechanically with certain behaviors. It is no wonder that the
Jesuit superiors were uncomfortable with such somewhat homespun,
superstitious, and nearly magical ideas.

The pious belief that certain objects might help to catch God's power
and channel it for specific purposes or in crises was also ambivalent. The
belief in such divine aids and their efficacy was as deep-rooted among
the Jesuits as it was in the population:

A sick woman called on Francis Xavier to intercede and found help
and relief. Many feverous persons also recovered their health by

means of his relics. The relics of our Holy Father Ignatius also helped several pregnant women give birth successfully. Another woman found that water that had been blessed in the name of this saint had a healing effect on her. She made a vow and was freed of a dangerous fever by the holy water.[107]

In addition to relics (physical remains of the saints) and holy water, so-called sacramentals (*sacramentalia*) performed the same function: these included blessed coins, rosaries, and other religious objects. The omnipotence of God manifested itself in them and through them in a way that was immediately relevant to everyday life, provided that the faithful and priests combined these aids with true belief in God. Wherever possible, the Jesuits endorsed and encouraged the use of such objects.[108]

In the process, they labored to draw a boundary between these legitimate religious practices and illicit magic. While *sacramentalia* were welcomed, amulets were rejected as implements of superstitious beliefs. The Jesuits also disapproved when the faithful not only revered saints as intercessors before God but also imagined that they could perform miracles themselves. And by no means was every surprising turn for the better in a serious illness actually the result of a supernatural miracle in the Jesuits' view.[109] The Jesuits thus were very critical of certain elements of popular piety that they disqualified as "superstition," and yet they shared the laity's basic belief that God actively guided the universe, that he knew of and influenced the happenings of human life, and that events big and small in people's lives reflected the will and dispensation of God. The providence of God was a firmly acknowledged fact for both the Jesuits and the broad mass of the Catholic faithful. It stabilized the people's mentality and served at the same time as a reason for hope and confidence.

Security and confidence in God were necessary not just on account of the often uncontrollable circumstances of life. A healthy dose of optimism was also helpful in a world that still seemed, at least in the first half of the early modern period, to be teeming with demons, witches, and malevolent spirits. The Jesuits essentially shared this view and participated energetically in scholarly research on demonic powers.[110] First and foremost was the Spanish-Flemish Jesuit Martin Delrio, who published a standard work on demonology in 1599 (reprinted several times thereafter), the *Disquisitionum magicarum libri sex* (Six books of magical inquiries). Delrio was well aware of the fact that it was notoriously difficult to prove incidents of diabolical intervention, witchcraft, and magic. At times, even the learned Jesuits found it difficult to distinguish between demonic possession and merely mortal perversity.[111] But that incited Delrio and his colleagues all the more to find criteria and explanations for how demons and the supernatural functioned and could be identified.

In 1569, for example, the entire province of Upper Germany was in an uproar because two young girls in Augsburg had been treated with multiple exorcisms.[112] The order's Roman leadership was very skeptical. Had it really been determined that evil demons were behind the episode in Augsburg? Had the right steps been taken? Rome was already of the opinion that exorcisms were outside the scope of the Society's typical responsibilities. It therefore sternly admonished Peter Canisius, who had carried out the exorcisms in Augsburg, that he should proceed with extreme caution and act only after thorough consultation with his superiors and theological experts. And in the latter half of the seventeenth century, the Jesuit generals remained skeptical of accepting the "troublesome and dangerous office of exorcist."[113]

In practice, however, these reservations were often pushed aside—the Jesuits and the Catholic faithful's conviction in the existence of demons was too great. The devil seemed ubiquitous. Beginning in the 1580s at the latest, the sources are full of episodes of Jesuits treating possessed people. In some instances, the presence of a priest seemed beneficial. Priests interrogated the demons, who often revealed their names. They used the holy objects mentioned earlier—rosaries, holy water, relics—to put the diabolical spirits under pressure. Prayers and adjurations were indispensable. If necessary—and only then—exorcisms followed, first in simple rooms but, if repetition was necessary, even in a church. After the demons had been defeated, communion, confession, and joint prayer concluded the procedure.[114] This was arguably how the most famous case of demonic possession involving

Jesuits unfolded. It happened in Loudon, western France, in 1634.[115] Several nuns at the Ursuline convent had allegedly been bewitched by the local priest Urbain Grandier, who paid the price by being burned at the stake. Several clerics from various orders—including the Jesuit mystic Jean-Joseph Surin—attempted exorcisms. But the episode ended in disaster for Surin: his confrontation with the possessed nuns ultimately caused him to fall into a state of mental illness that lasted for years.

Surin and his allies tried everything to free the nuns from their bewitchment. They never doubted the phenomenon of witchcraft itself— belief in demons remained part of their basic religious mentality. Some Jesuits, however, doubted the social and legal practice of witch hunts and trials.[116] The Jesuit Friedrich Spee was one of the fiercest opponents of early modern witch hunts. His famous book, *Cautio criminalis*, published in 1631, condemned contemporary excesses with incisive, shrewd argumentation and words that could not be clearer. But he was not the only opponent of witch hunts. One of his most important predecessors (whom he frequently quoted) was Adam Tanner, a theologian and confrere from Innsbruck, who likewise turned against the excesses of witch hunts. In addition to Spee, Tanner influenced his younger confrere Paul Laymann, who also urged caution at the very least. And Bernhard Frey, S.J., also in Bavaria, was an early advocate of the theory that the behavior of "witches" should be viewed in medical terms, that is, as mental illness, rather than in theological terms as diabolical power. Spee's magnum opus increasingly began to bear fruit among his Jesuit brothers by the 1670s.

Spee and Tanner wrote in particular against the legal excesses of the witch hunts: torture and denunciations. Spee openly railed against the perversion of justice, without which it would have been impossible to condemn anyone as a witch. We cannot conclusively say whether or to what extent Spee also disputed the existence of witches; he never explicitly challenged the belief in witches, although he admitted doubts. In contrast to his demonological adversary in the Society, Delrio, he had no interest in the academic discussion of the phenomenon.

Many other Jesuits, however, took the opposite view and participated in witch hunts more or less out of conviction. Peter Canisius praised the

authorities for imprisoning witches and obtaining forced confessions;
Jakob Gretser in Munich, a rival of Tanner's, was also among the supporters of witch trials, as was his confrere Adam Contzen, the court
confessor of Duke Maximilian I. Gregor de Valencia was also on the side
of the persecuting authorities in Bavaria. Delrio likewise advocated torture and the death penalty. And when a fierce witch hunt commenced
in Trier in 1590, the local Jesuits did not stand idly by but rather took
part in the trials. General Acquaviva, of course, was opposed to this
involvement. The Jesuits were expressly forbidden to become involved
in trials held in secular courts. But even as late as 1749, a Jesuit priest in
Würzburg, Georg Gaar, was still defending the recent execution of an
alleged witch. This late example of rigid intransigence was met with
incomprehension in both Austria and Italy, inside and outside the Society. In conclusion, the Jesuits never adopted a consistent policy on
witchcraft, although the Roman leadership urged restraint on the
whole—albeit probably for fear of becoming needlessly entangled in
political and social controversy. That did not, however, stop local representatives of the Society. They were convinced of the constant presence
of demons in their everyday ministry and did everything they could to
make people believe that they as clergymen could master these malevolent powers.

Another "safeguard" of Catholic piety closely connected to the belief
in demons was also heavily promoted by the Jesuits: the veneration of
"guardian angels."[117] Every single person who fought the demons that
were at work everywhere in the world was assisted by his own guardian
angel. This belief had existed for some time. At its root was the conviction that God had assigned an angel to watch over every person, even
pagans and heretics. Prayers were offered to guardian angels already in
the High Middle Ages, but their veneration did not really take off until
the seventeenth century. In several steps taken in 1570, 1608, and 1670, a
church feast was introduced for guardian angels. Now an extensive body
of literature and works of art popularized the image of guardian angels
and seemed to induce people to worship them. The Society of Jesus was
heavily involved in this boom. Pierre Favre was a fervent worshipper of
guardian angels, as was the youthful saint Luigi Gonzaga. The Jesuits

soon founded confraternities of their own for the worship of guardian angels—such as that established in Naples in 1611 by Francesco Albertino.

Albertino published the first Jesuit work about guardian angels in 1612.[118] In it, he not only highlighted their ubiquity—even Mary and the devil had angels by their side—but also stressed the fact that angels were especially "effective" on behalf of those who led a pious life: virgins, clergy, philanthropists, sufferers for Christ. But these angels remained with people even when they sinned. Even after death, they accompanied the person to whom they had been assigned to purgatory and to the Last Judgment itself. "To my guardian angel, the most loyal, most steadfast, and most loving friend," as the Jesuit Paul de Barry dedicated his book *La dévotion aux anges*.[119] For Albertino, what mattered most was the effect that guardian angels had on the human soul: they conveyed prayers to God, helped ward off demons, gave consolation, and taught God's will. Vice versa, the faithful were encouraged to love their guardian angel, communicate with it, and make a point of interacting with it confidentially. They should thank it and turn to it with their prayers. Other Jesuits believed that one should even give one's guardian angel precedence upon entering a doorway.[120]

Angels had always been responsible for protecting one's life and limb, as well as for protecting one's soul from malevolent influences. The Jesuits elaborated this aspect significantly. Guardian angels now were venerated for keeping the faithful on the right path and guiding them to a good—that is a pious, Christian—death. The worship of guardian angels among the Jesuits thus overlapped precisely with their marked obsession with a "good death." Jacques Coret, S.J. (1631–1721), one of the great literary proponents of the cult of angels, wrote two books in 1662 and 1663 about "guardian angels as the companions of the dying."[121] An entire literary genre was dedicated to the "art of dying," with the Jesuits among its foremost exponents; it took the form of books intended to guide the faithful in detail through their final hours and to prepare them for a pious death.[122] The purpose of these guides was to ensure that the dying believer did not doubt God and eternal life out of fear of death in his final hours. Guardian angels were on hand to help.

Guardian angels were explicitly viewed as pillars of strength for the human race, which had been drastically weakened by the Fall of man.[123] They were a divine aid for the devout. Guardian angels, as the Jesuits understood and propagated them, gave the faithful a feeling of security and reliability just as *sacramentalia* and vows did. Guardian angels supported and personified the belief that God was closely tied to the world, and they reinforced the idea that God really looked after mankind and was interested in its prosperity.

In fact, as de Barry wrote, there was hardly anyone that believers should revere more than their own guardian angels. Only Jesus, Mary, and Joseph stood above them in the hierarchy.[124] These three Christian icons were fervently revered in the early modern period with new forms of devotion, and the Jesuits were often involved in developing and disseminating them. Reverence for Joseph was still in its infancy in the early modern period—Jesus's earthly father had not received much attention until the fifteenth century, before his status was subsequently elevated by Teresa de Ávila.[125] Many Jesuits, especially those with a strong proclivity toward the intense spirituality of the Spanish mystic, took up her enthusiasm for Joseph.[126] Joseph was now viewed as an exponent and model of private, inner prayer, from whom one could seek protection and guidance, a view that was connected with Joseph's important function as a helper at the hour of death. The significance of his cult rose insofar as "dying well" became a central focus of the Jesuits and of early modern Catholicism collectively. There also was Joseph's obedience toward God and his widely assumed virginity, both of which made him a moral role model. Thus a rich new spirituality came into being, although it faced hostility in the Society of Jesus from General Vitelleschi, who was highly critical of mysticism. In the long term, however, the cult of Joseph ultimately triumphed even in the Society. It thus was unsurprising that members of the order established ever more chapels to Joseph and even made Mary's betrothed the patron of select cities.[127]

The booming worship of Jesus Christ took an entirely different turn. The rise in the worship of the Sacred Heart of Jesus was especially spectacular.[128] The heart of Jesus had long stood as a symbol of his love and physical suffering on the way to the cross. The mystics of the Middle Ages had taken an interest in it, and the Carthusians had also worshipped Jesus's heart. The Franciscans and Dominicans had also written about it. In seventeenth-century France, this tradition was revived by Cardinal Bérulle, François de Sales, and especially Jean Eudes. The Jesuits thus were neither the first nor the only ones to be interested in the Sacred Heart of Jesus, and yet this devotion in particular became closely associated with them. Peter Canisius had a predilection for the Sacred Heart of Jesus perhaps deriving from the Carthusians of Cologne. After him, the Jesuits Diego Álvarez de Paz and Jean-Baptiste Saint-Jure took serious interest in it. The first sermon on the Sacred Heart of Jesus by the Jesuit Philipp Kisel of Worms was printed in 1666.

The watershed moment, when worship of the Sacred Heart of Jesus transformed into one of the most prominent forms of devotion of the modern age, did not occur until 1670, in the aftermath of the visions of the Sacred Heart experienced by Marguerite-Marie Alacoque (1647–90), a Salesian nun. She was closely connected to the Jesuits: her most important confessor was Claude La Colombiere, S.J. The nun's visions were publicized across Europe and laid the cornerstone for the transformation of worship of the Sacred Heart of Jesus into a mass phenomenon. La Colombiere himself published on the subject repeatedly. Jean Croiset, La Colombiere's successor as Alacoque's confessor, was potentially even more important, publishing his oft-reprinted work *La dévotion au Sacré Cœur de Notre Seigneur Jésus-Christ* (Devotion to the Sacred Heart of Jesus) in 1680. Fifteen years later, in 1695, the Jesuits Thaddäus Schwaller of Einsiedeln and Bernhard Sonnenberg of Munich published the first two books on the subject in the territory of the Holy Roman Empire and Switzerland.[129] Following the example of various French foundations, the Jesuits of Vienna established the first confraternity of the Sacred Heart in the Holy Roman Empire in 1699. Some authors viewed the rapidly proliferating worship of the Sacred Heart of Jesus as the fulfillment of prophecy: "It was foretold that this divine kingdom would be reestablished in these last days."[130] Some credited the Sacred Heart of Jesus with miraculous powers. In 1721, for example, the Sacred Heart relieved Marseille from the plague, a feat that the city commemorated a year later with a thanksgiving feast that resonated widely.[131] Everywhere, the Jesuits were in the vanguard of the spread of the cult of the Sacred Heart of Jesus.

The devotion of the Sacred Heart presented Jesus Christ in a kind of double role: on the one hand, as a wronged king whose commands had been disobeyed by sinful mankind; on the other, as a kind, tender, loving, and amiable savior, who had sacrificed his heart for mankind. Thus, worship of the Sacred Heart of Jesus was broadly a devotion of kindness. In the cult of the Sacred Heart, the Jesuits prayed to God for sympathy with faulty humans because God should "see in them only the blood by which they were redeemed."[132] The Sacred Heart symbolized his love of man and encouraged pious Christians to return that love as comprehensively as possible. The Sacred Heart also, however, emphasized the Passion of Christ, thus serving as a constant incentive to repent. The fundamental elements of the worship of the Sacred Heart of Jesus were mankind's obligation to make atonement, the lovingness of God, and divine mercy. Broadly speaking, this form of devotion was earnest and intimidating, but also pervaded by affection and love, mercy and kindness.

It was not focused on the heart purely in a metaphoric sense: Alacoque and the Jesuits who followed her believed that Jesus wanted to be worshipped "in the form of this corporeal heart."[133] Worship of Jesus in particular and the forms of devotion practiced by the Jesuits in this period placed great emphasis on the body. The idea was to worship the most important protagonists of the Christian faith as human beings in their full human physicality. Hence it was unsurprising that the Jesuits depicted not only symbolic hearts in many illustrations but also anatomically correct body parts for the faithful to contemplate.[134] This realism was intended to help one to establish an intense, personal, emotional relationship with Jesus Christ.

This powerful relationship to Jesus's heart could—and indeed was supposed to—go so far that some authors dreamed of becoming one with it: Alacoque wrote that the devotion of the Sacred Heart would help her lose her own will in the will of Jesus.[135] Like La Colombiere, the Jesuits enthusiastically embraced the idea: "You must give us a heart that is like Your heart; You must give us Your own heart."[136] Such passages make clear how extensively the devotion of the Sacred Heart of Jesus borrowed ideas and formulations from European mysticism that the cult subsequently popularized.[137] Praying to the heart of Jesus in this form is a good example of how Jesuit piety went beyond the transactional religiosity of *sacramentalia* and holy water and widely promoted contemplative and emotional forms of devotion with a certain openness to ecstatic moments of introspection.[138]

It was but a small step from the devout worship of the heart and body of Jesus Christ to the intense cult of the Eucharist, which also changed and spread in the early modern period. Countless confraternities and pious associations came together around the "most blessed sacrament" as early as the sixteenth century.[139] The Feast of Corpus Christi also became an increasingly prominent part of religious life. The feast with its traditional procession, at which the Blessed Sacrament was carried through the streets of cities and villages in a monstrance, had been celebrated officially since 1264. But in response to criticism of the Catholic doctrine of the Eucharist, first by the Protestants and later by the early Enlightenment philosophes, it gained popularity as an ostentatiously Catholic devotion. The Jesuits celebrated it regularly as an explicit defense and illustration of the tenets of the Catholic faith. In 1586, they revived the old custom in Paderborn to great fanfare.[140] In 1597, it again was members of the Society of Jesus who processed through Altötting after a long hiatus. The Jesuits also began to hold such processions in Erfurt in 1607, where the events soon took on massive dimensions. No fewer than 349 costumed lay actors roamed through the city in 1729, depicting biblical and religious scenes.[141] The Jesuits knowingly accepted the risk that such Corpus Christi processions might provoke the Protestants—if that was not their real intent.[142]

The Jesuits and other Catholics of the sixteenth and seventeenth centuries generally promoted the conspicuous exhibition of the Eucharist, even in the face of fierce opposition.[143] In the process, new and even formerly marginal devotions were created and popularized alongside the familiar forms. The most important innovation was the Forty Hours' Devotion, the Quarant'ore.[144] In this devotion, the Blessed Sacrament was publicly exhibited like an icon in a church and prayed to continuously. Something like that was possible only in Catholicism, and so the Quarant'ore was an explicit demonstration of the Catholic doctrine of the Eucharist against the Protestants. The number forty also had symbolic significance. The path from the Last Supper to the Crucifixion had lasted forty hours; Jesus Christ had lain in the grave for forty hours. The devotion of the Eucharist and worship of Jesus were intimately linked.

Early forms of the Quarant'ore had appeared in Zadar around the year 1214, but the mature form first emerged in Milan in 1530. The practice then became widespread in Italy around 1550 and soon reached territories north of the Alps and ultimately overseas. The leading agents of its propagation were the Oratorians, the Capuchins, the Barnabites, and indeed the Jesuits. Forty hours of prayer were often held during emergencies. In 1556, the Jesuits began to favor devotion during Carnival as a counterpoint to the usual merrymaking. Hence, on the one hand, the Quarant'ore was a devotion of fervent prayer and penitent contrition; on the other, it was deliberately used and advertised in advance to win divine support for specific requests.[145] These prayers might be held for spiritual goals (e.g., the reform of Christendom, suppression of heresy), but secular wishes could also be the subject of the Quarant'ore (e.g., harmony among Christian princes, repelling Turkish assaults). Although it at first was occasionally decried as a strange innovation, these prayers to the Blessed Sacrament soon became very popular.[146] This popularity was undoubtedly connected to the fact that the Quarant'ore had ceased to be austere and unforgiving and had been transformed by the Jesuits and Capuchins into a highly elaborate theatrical affair.[147] The Blessed Sacrament was exhibited as if onstage. Lighting effects and a range of structures soon became part of the spectacle. The host was set in biblical and allegorical scenes and images. Music was added to this multimedia exhibition of the Blessed Sacrament for prayer. One admirer of the exhibition in Il Gesù in 1608 remarked, "All of it taken together seemed like an object of Paradise and a reflection of heaven; the soul is satisfied with the greatest delight by the real presence of Christ our Lord, the eye by the elaborate and most devout scenery, and the ears by the sweetest and most harmonious concert of every instrument."[148] In light of this strategy to overload the senses, it was only logical that the greatest artists of the day were hired to design the monumental sets. Bernini, Andrea Pozzo, and many others devised the ever-changing scenery. No expense or effort was spared.[149] Among the Jesuits, the eucharistic devotion of the Quarant'ore seamlessly merged with their inclination to convey important tenets of faith through visual and other sensory media. It was hoped that the faithful would come in great throngs and from all walks of life. The people were amazed, frozen in "sacred shuddering" (*sacro orrore*).[150] That initially gave some authorities cause for concern, since the pious productions seemed a little unpredictable.[151] But the Quarant'ore soon became an established fixture of the religious life of almost all Catholic communities.

Along with Joseph and Jesus Christ (or the Eucharist), Mary was the third axis of the religiosity that the Jesuits propagated and lived by example. Ignatius himself had prayed before the statue of Mary in Montserrat for a long time and dedicated himself to Mary after he set out from Loyola in 1521. Dedicating oneself to the Mother of God was also part of the religious curriculum of many Jesuit pupils.[152] This later escalated into talk of "enslaving oneself in the ministry of Mary"—although it was prohibited by the church. Several opponents feared that this constantly expanding devotion to Mary could lead to her being worshipped by "reckless devotees" (*dévots indiscrets*) with unorthodox exaltation. The Jesuits took the contrary view: they viewed the cult of Mary as one of the most important religious practices of all—on the whole, practitioners were on the right path, they argued, even if there were also incorrect extremes.[153] Worship of Mary as the Immaculata, the woman untouched by original sin on account of her role as the Mother of God, was particularly controversial.[154] The question of whether the Immaculate Conception had actually occurred had not yet been decided doctrinally in unambiguous terms. It was not until 1854 that Pius IX elevated the Immaculate Conception to dogma. In many places, however, Mary had long been revered as the Immaculata by the common people. In the early modern period, the Jesuits became especially resolute partisans.

The early modern dispute over the Immaculata broke out in Seville in 1613. It would preoccupy all Europe for the next three decades. A

Dominican had rejected the Immaculate Conception in a sermon, while the Franciscans and Jesuits were divided. Philip II of Spain established a government commission to review the subject in 1616, the Real Junta de la Inmaculada Concepción. The Spanish government was usually on the side of those in favor, whereas Rome was interested in suppressing the popular excesses of the worship of Mary—and so the matter became a political tug-of-war between Rome and Madrid.

In the midst of this dogmatic uncertainty, the adherents of the Immaculata resorted to drastic means to underline their determination to defend her. The "blood oath" became a widespread practice, whereby the supporters of the cult solemnly swore in an annual ceremony to defend the Immaculate Conception of Mary and the rituals associated with it until their own martyrdom, if need be.[155] The Jesuits were considered major supporters of the practice, although the Society never made the oath obligatory or took it collectively. As the Immaculata became a fiercely debated subject in the Catholic world, the Society of Jesus supported the spread of the oath across Europe. By the mid-1650s, they promoted its popularity in the Holy Roman Empire with the backing of the emperor.[156] In popular religion, the oath was also often connected to very emotional events. In Palermo, for example, the practice began in 1624, when an especially revered Immaculata had saved the city from an outbreak of the plague.[157] The Immaculata, who herself was free of the "plague" of original sin in body and soul, was considered a powerful protectress from the threat of epidemics.[158]

The blood oath came under increasingly fierce criticism around 1700. The great Italian scholar Ludovico Antonio Muratori (1672–1750) was an especially vocal critic who considered this religious practice to be nothing more than "pious obstinacy."[159] But there was more to the attacks on the blood oath than met the eye. Muratori ultimately advocated an entirely different religious culture from that of the Jesuits. He wanted a form of religiosity that was sober, rational, skeptic, lean, and reduced to essentials—a "regulated devotion" (*devozione regolata*) as he himself called it. Muratori articulated his skepticism of extravagant religious practices in a book that bore the telling title *De superstitione vitanda* (On avoiding superstition).

Enlightened rulers like Maria Theresa of Austria, who also kept her distance from the cult of the Sacred Heart of Jesus, shifted over to Muratori's critical line.[160] Catholic groups gradually split over the worship of the Sacred Heart. This devotion was increasingly viewed as "Jesuit"— and, as time went on, that increasingly also meant "outmoded." In the wake of the French Revolution, the Sacred Heart had at last come to symbolize ecclesiastical, antirevolutionary, and usually also monarchist-reactionary views. The Sacred Heart of Jesus had prevailed, yet at the same time it had become a highly controversial, even defiant, emblem of one of the parties. In the nineteenth century, it stood for a conservative and frequently antimodernist brand of Catholicism.[161]

In all the various manifestations and forms of their religiosity, most Jesuits favored and defended a positive outlook that they sought to impart to others. "Gentle and temperate governance" should prevail.[162] Many Jesuits therefore evinced, on the whole, a comparatively open and friendly, relaxed, and easygoing manner. "God does not want to be served in sorrow," Pierre Le Moyne asserted. "Joy is the core of the soul," and therefore also the goal of religion.[163] Le Moyne took this conviction especially far when he called for "effortless devotion" (*dévotion aisée*) in a hotly disputed book. He was outright opposed to becoming an "emaciated phantom who celebrates Lent all year, who has Good Friday every day." Virtue and devotion required moderation and method and could not be allowed to become "forced labor" (*corvée*).[164]

Le Moyne went very far, but even his contemporaries saw that he stood in the tradition of his order. For Nicolas Caussin, for example, that meant that people who lived in luxury at court were by no means obliged to give up all earthly delights. Pious devotion for the Jesuits was not synonymous with radical and extreme asceticism. A passionately pious courtier had to adopt a different faith and way of life from those of a hermit. Sanctity, piety, and faith accordingly manifested themselves in many ways. And the Society of Jesus was constantly attacked for precisely that reason. Opponents of the Jesuits like Jean Neercassel, the apostolic vicar of the Netherlands, railed against the Jesuit principle of "easiness" in matters of faith and devotion.[165] Already contemporaries labeled this form of religiosity, of which Neercassel was merely a prominent advocate, "rigorism." What separated the rigorists and the Jesuits more profoundly was the Jesuits' far greater dose of optimistic and positive confidence in the world and in people. The religiosity that many Jesuits represented and embodied was based on the firm conviction that a link could be forged between the faith and everyday life. That is not to say that the Jesuits were satisfied with the religious status quo. On the contrary, they wanted to improve and invigorate the Christian life of mankind and indeed everywhere and at all times. The Jesuits also knew that a life pleasing to God entailed "hard work and frequent good deeds."[166] But they were not interested in stressing the difficulty, let alone the unattainability, of perfect faith; instead, they sought to win people over by suggesting improvements in their everyday lives.

Morality and Mercy: Jesuits versus Rigorists, Dominicans, and Jansenists

Theological considerations with far-reaching ramifications lay behind the devotion and faith that the Jesuits propagated. And just as the religious and devotional practices of the Society of Jesus were controversial, so too was its theology. Hence the Jesuits were embroiled in several inter-Catholic theological conflicts in the seventeenth and eighteenth centuries. Theologians quarreled over penance, mercy, and the way to achieve salvation. Many of these doctrinal disputes ultimately revolved around the question of how the Catholic image of man and God should look, how one should imagine the basic mechanisms of gaining salvation, and especially what consequences that had on the practice of religion and pastoral ministry in everyday life.

Different views of penance and remorse, for example, lurked behind the conflict between the rigorists and the Jesuits. The two adversaries agreed that divine forgiveness always had to be based on the sinner's penitent remorse for his wrongdoing. But there were two contrary concepts as to what constituted remorse: *attritio* and *contritio*.[167] *Attritio* meant that one regretted one's sins out of *fear* of divine punishment. *Contritio*, in contrast, was a higher form of remorse that stemmed from *love* of God, whom one had injured through sin. The question was whether *attritio* sufficed for the remission of sins in confession or whether the higher form of *contritio* was required. In other words: How high should the spiritual standards for absolution be? Even in the Middle Ages opinions were divided. The Council of Trent had accepted "imperfect *contritio*" in a rather imprecise formula, thus inclining more to *attritio*, albeit in a moderate and watered-down form—the reason being that Luther had radically called for *contritio*. In the seventeenth century, the number of *attritionistae* predominated by far; in the eighteenth century, however, the *contritionistae* gained the upper hand in many places, after the French clergy officially took their side in the conflict in 1700. Whoever advocated *attritio* had to emphasize that absolution took effect by performance of the sacrament (*ex opere operato*), independent of the inner disposition of the person giving confession.

A majority of Jesuits were *attritionistae*. From the pulpit and in numerous printed books, they defended their position in sometimes quite heated disputes.[168] Antoine Sirmond, for example, argued in his much-discussed book of 1641, *Défense de la Vertu* (Defense of virtue), that pure love of God (*contritio*) was not necessary. In response he was fiercely attacked by many *contritionistae*. Prominent *devote* theologians like the Abbé de Saint-Cyran wrote against Sirmond, whose publication they viewed as an affront. Bishop Jean-Baptiste Camus in particular conducted a long literary feud with Sirmond. The Jesuit, for his part, stood his ground and considered demands for *contritio* unrealistic: the "true love" of God that Camus required, and which acted only out of devotion to God and without any self-interested motives, could not be obtained in this life.[169] For rigorist theologians, though, the Jesuits' attitude was far too easygoing and "lax" (*relâché*). With their liberality, the Jesuits did not take the drama of sin seriously enough. By accommodating sinners' needs in their moral teachings, the Jesuits thus supposedly stooped to their level.

Some moral-theological assessments penned by Jesuits, viewed in isolation, in fact could give a ridiculously lax impression. The moral theologian Juan Sánchez, for example, argued in 1643, with respect to sexual offenses, that one had to absolve even a repeat offender "every time that he does penance, and not only when one can actually observe an improvement [in his behavior]."[170] Serious, long-term improvement (*emendatio*) or a real, permanent change of heart on the part of the confessing sinner was not necessary for absolution. Authors like Sánchez almost seemed to be proclaiming something like a right to the remission of sin. The concept of *attritio* and confidence in the automatic effect of the sacrament of confession, without any need for additional spiritual ingredients, peaked in such statements—pure laxity, opponents normally cried in such cases. The Jesuits—according to their rigorist adversaries—all too often took sides with sinners, not with God.

But a much closer look is necessary. Sánchez supported his assessment with reference to Matthew 18:22, the passage in which Jesus teaches his disciples to forgive a sin not just seven times, but even seventy-seven times. In this way, the Spaniard argued, Jesus understood how to deal with "our frailty"—one should not expect too much of people. Sánchez also undertook a careful analysis of the circumstances of sinful deeds in his discussion: he asked whether there were any humanly possible alternatives, whether any exculpatory influences should be assumed, what in particular drove or encouraged the sinner to act, and so on. Before handing down moral judgment, in the opinion of Sánchez and many other Jesuits, one first had to evaluate the specific situation and people concerned, with all their weaknesses and influences, which might prove to be mitigating or explanatory circumstances.

There was a system and method to the Jesuits' moral theology, which largely consisted of the assessment of individual cases (*casus*).[171] Jesuit ethics was case-driven ethics and thus comprised an expansive body of literature and scholarship on specific moral dilemmas, the equally famous and infamous Jesuit science of casuistry. In 1599, casuistry was embedded in the *Ratio studiorum*, the official curriculum of all Jesuit colleges; the subject had already been taught for some time.[172] Soon weekly classes were held everywhere to practice the "solution," discussion, and moral assessment of individual case studies. Designated teachers prepared these classes and instructed the students in the precise analysis of all relevant details.[173] By 1800, nearly thirteen hundred new books had been published on the subject, most of them authored by Jesuits.[174] Over thousands of pages, these thick folios discussed a variety of more or less everyday cases. They covered questions of marital and sexual ethics, aspects of economic life, interconfessional relations, military incidents, and much more. The cases were usually anonymized, generalized, and stripped of recognizable particulars. They thus became universal and thereby transferable and applicable to other contexts. In the form of casuistry, a full-fledged method of moral theology was established that now came into its own as an autonomous subject of study, a distinct theological discipline with its own scholarly literature, its own specialists, and its own discursive profile.[175]

With such courses and a growing body of literature, the Jesuits hoped to train aspiring priests how to interact with confessing sinners, because there seemed to be a shortage of competent confessors who could see the sins confessed to them in the right light. Casuistry was thus also part of the reform of the clergy. Casuistry and the boom in confession went hand in hand in the reformed Catholicism of the Jesuits. This pragmatic emphasis, however, often came at the expense of deeper scrutiny of theological questions. In Asturias, it was decided that "one should disregard theological matters that do not bear on the ethical cases; theological questions should be handled only briefly when the solution of a case depends on them."[176] Spiritual questions after pastoral care had been administered were also usually lacking. It is often difficult to find a link between casuistry and the faith, religious practices, and captivating forms of devotion that we encountered in the previous section.[177]

We may presume that the services of the casuists were in high demand both inside and outside the confessional. Jesuits trained in casuistry and their colleagues obviously served an important purpose as moral-theological consultants in the troubled and contradictory times of the early modern period. Their services were called on again and again. The casuists created moral certainty and relieved one's conscience (fig. 6). The *casus* of the Benedictines of Sts. Ulrich and Afra from Augsburg, for example, is transmitted from southern Germany. The monks had sworn loyalty to the (Lutheran) king of Sweden, Gustavus Adolphus, during the chaos of the Thirty Years' War. Now a panel of experts made up of Jesuits was asked to assess their conduct at the time in ethical and canonistic terms.[178] As a scholarly subject, this instruction in ethics was obviously deeply rooted in the social conditions of an age

FIGURE 6. Casuists at work: an idealized view of the deliberations of experts in
moral theology. Contemporary etching from A. Delamet and G. Fromageau,
Dictionaire des cas de conscience (1773). © Bibliothèque de Port-Royal.

characterized by constant conflicts of loyalty and coercion—Protestants,
incidentally, felt the same need, and an extensive tradition of casuistry
also took root among them.

In deciding *casus,* casuists both inside and outside the Society of
Jesus relied heavily on the opinions of colleagues who were viewed as
experts. Hence, when a casuistic decision had to be made, a large part
of it amounted de facto to weighing the positions that established casuists had taken in similar cases. For that reason alone, casuistry needed
its own specialists, because no one could possibly know all the existing
texts and rulings without extensive study. But what should one do when
different authors reached a different verdict about the circumstances of
a case? Which opinion should one follow in assessing a specific *casus*?
How could one choose from the abundance of opinions? This was the
methodological question at the heart of the whole endeavor, and it was
hotly debated for decades. There were three different strategies for
choosing from existing opinions: probabilism, probabiliorism, and
tutiorism.

A glance at the Latin terms cuts to the heart of the matter—whether
one took the "probable" (*probabilis*), the "more probable" (*probabilior*),

or the "safer" (*tutior*) opinion. Each of these approaches revolved around opinions, not absolute, perfect, securely demonstrable "mathematical" truths. Casuistic ethics was an ethics for troubled times and uncertain circumstances, an ethics with a high level of ambivalence. The critical question was just how much ambivalence one could tolerate when it was necessary to choose a course of action. One group thought that one presumably acted correctly in choosing the course of action or opinion that seemed "probable." The Jesuits, allowing some exceptions, were and are considered firm adherents of this probabilist position, even though probabilism itself was actually invented by a sixteenth-century Dominican, Bartolomé de Medina. The Jesuits Heinrich Busembaum, Tommaso Tamburini, and Honoré Fabri composed highly successful works in the probabilist tradition that were regarded as representative of this approach.

Opposite the probabilists could be found the probabiliorists—especially in the Dominicans' camp, although elsewhere too. They held that one acted correctly when one chose not merely a probable option from two or more, but rather the "more probable" option. There was a vast difference, they believed, as to whether one should take a probable or the more probable view. In 1722, a Dominican publicly preached in Reggio del Calabrio that "all probabilists are heretics, whose leader will roast them all in Hell!"—citing Jesuits like Tommaso Tamburini and others by name.[179]

Finally, the tutiorists suggested that one should not focus on probabilities but rather take the course of action that was the "safest," that is, the option that had the least potential for sin, even if it seemed less "probable" than the others.

Countless questions of detail concerning casuistic method ensued:[180] did the status of an opinion as "probable" have to be certain, or did it suffice if it was "probable"—that is to say: Could one also choose a "probable probability"?[181] And what exactly made an opinion "probable"? How many authors had to hold it, and did the mere number of authorities count or rather the weight of their arguments? In the eyes of radical probabilists, it sufficed when a single opinion was "probable" for someone to take that course of action. In other words, if one could find just a single recognized authority who considered one's preference to be "probable," then one could follow one's own inclination with a clear conscience, even if the rest of the world of moral theology was opposed. Such extreme opinions were not the rule in the Society of Jesus, but they occurred. That was grist for the mill of the Jesuits' enemies, who feared such positions might lead to the collapse of all morality: "There is practically nothing left that would be forbidden to Christians according to the Jesuits, after they have made everything probable," Antoine Arnauld, one of their harshest critics, wrote in 1641.[182] Many contemporaries agreed with him. What the Jesuits advocated under the cover of "ethics" was no ethics at all anymore, so weak and lax were the results.

Arnauld therefore condemned the Jesuits root and branch, but that was far too simplistic: there were countercurrents within the Society of Jesus itself. There were probabiliorist, contritionist, and rigorist Jesuits whose opposition constantly roiled the Society. Nicolas Caussin, for example, an adherent of *contritio*, lost his post as the confessor of Louis XIII not least because he insisted on his position against the attritionist Cardinal Richelieu. There was a long series of probabiliorists who toiled in the shadow of the dominant doctrine. Miguel de Elizalde (1616–78) and Cardinal Sforza Pallavicino (1607–67) were two such men. At least in private letters to Elizalde, Pallavicino ridiculed "this murky chaos of probable opinions."[183] The Jesuit probabiliorists then stepped out of the shadows at the end of the seventeenth century, when Tirso González was elected superior general of the Society.[184] In this eminent position, González immediately attempted to introduce the stricter ethical system to his own order. González's willful actions, which contemporaries often criticized as autocratic, nearly plunged the Society of Jesus into a schism. González's efforts were ultimately in vain; probabiliorism remained a minority opinion. Paul-Gabriel Antoine (1678/9–1743) was, like González, also one of the strictest moral theologians of the Society. Even his colleagues in the eighteenth century regarded him as one of the most rigorist moral theologians of all.[185] Pierre La Quintinye (1627–1712) also advocated rigorist positions against his confreres in Aquitaine in 1666 and 1667.[186] He went to General Oliva and later to the pope because most Jesuits allegedly claimed that whatever a person may have done in good faith could not be so bad and sinful. By that logic, he argued, ignorant heathens and heretics should be forgiven, at least provided that they did not come into contact with Catholics and the "true doctrine."

La Quintinye was alluding to the fundamental question of whether the heathen overseas could commit sins at all before they encountered Christian missionaries. Jesuit missionaries in this case were often regarded as indulgent. António Vieira, for example, the famous missionary to Brazil, admitted that the heathen had lived in "unsurpassable ignorance" (*ignorantia invincibilis*) and that their actions should not therefore be considered sins.[187] This was later called "philosophical sin"—sinful behavior that was not genuine, theological sin by reason of ignorance. Rigorist theologians inside and outside the Society objected to this view—one sin cannot be excused by another, namely, ignorance, they argued. Pope Alexander VIII condemned the concept of "philosophical sin" in 1690: a violation of divine norms even out of sheer ignorance was very probably still a genuine sin and an offense to God.

Precisely the debate about the heathen reveals that, behind their casuistry and antirigorist ethical doctrine, the Jesuits had a theological concept of man and God that they advocated in the most diverse contexts. By and large, the followers of Ignatius took a comparatively optimistic view of mankind. They trusted in human nature, in the reason and will of man. Mankind had, of course, been weakened by the Fall and needed divine aid to gain salvation. But that did not mean that salvation was obtained only *in spite of* man's natural abilities. On the contrary, the Jesuits had no doubt that they could and should build on the given conditions of "normal" human existence. Hence the debate over Jesuit casuistry ultimately revolved around fundamental questions of theological anthropology. It stemmed from different attitudes toward man and his potential: Could human nature serve as the starting point for the process of salvation and even possibly contribute something to it, or was that impossible a priori?

The experts usually formulated this age-old problem of Christianity in terms of the relationship between "human will" and "divine grace."

The question was ancient: the church father Augustine had already laid the groundwork in the fifth century. The subject became urgent again in the sixteenth century in the wake of the Reformation. In making sometimes radical demands, Martin Luther had claimed that mankind was justified "by grace alone" (*sola gratia*). He disputed the power of human will to accomplish anything good pertaining to salvation—it was rather the devil who used human will as his steed. Moreover, according to the Calvinist doctrine of predestination, human involvement in salvation was even more limited. The sixth session of the Council of Trent in 1547 explicitly rebutted these "new" Protestant theologies by resolving that human will could and indeed had to be involved in justification. It was up to human will to accept or to reject the offer of divine grace.

The council's emphatic but very vague anti-Protestant position left (too) many questions open. Even some Catholic theologians believed that this very broad wording attached too much importance to human will and felt that much more emphasis should be placed on the role of divine grace. They usually cited Augustine, who took a very chary view of human will and represented justification as a work of divine grace. Michel Baius, professor of theology in Leuven, was one of the first theologians after Trent who, like Augustine, pleaded for a Catholic theology centered on grace. Controversy broke out in the 1560s over his Augustinian position, which militated against the active role of human will in questions of salvation. His views were finally banned in 1567, although he was not mentioned by name. The Jesuits were bitter adversaries of Baius and his Augustinian doctrine from the start. Robert Bellarmine himself was tasked with the job of critiquing the theologian from Leuven.

The year 1588 was a decisive moment for the positive formulation of a Jesuit position on the role of free will in the process of justification. It was then that the Spanish Jesuit Luis de Molina published a book with the appealing title *Concordia liberi arbitrii cum gratiae donis* (The harmony of free will with the gifts of grace). Put concisely, Molina's position and that of many of his Jesuit followers were interpreted as attributing human free will an active role in salvation of its own accord, insofar as human will could spontaneously agree with divine grace. According to Molina's view of things, God had showered mankind with general grace that was "sufficient" (*gratia sufficiens*) to enable the will—itself involved by grace—to participate in salvation as described earlier. God did this, Molina explained, because in his omniscience he had foreseen how people would act and determined that this general grace would suffice for justification (*post praevisa merita*). Molina thus got himself into a first-rate philosophical quandary: If God foresaw everything, was man still free? Molina proposed to solve this complex problem in a new way by developing a theory of divine *scientia media*: God did not determine human decisions in the future (then mankind would no longer be free), but he could foresee how a free person would behave in certain circumstances by virtue of his or her own free will; he accordingly created the circumstances of their choice. God thus could clearly foresee which person would choose the correct religious attitude and way of life without casting the free will of man in this situation into doubt.

Molina's adversaries—predominantly, but by no means exclusively, from the Dominican order—rejected this intellectual edifice. His theory, in their view, was a grotesque overestimation of human will. The anti-Molinists argued that no pious human act, including agreement with divine plans, could originate in free will. On the contrary, such pious acts were predicated on effective grace (*gratia efficiens*) in a specific situation—thus, no pious action was undertaken without the active support of God, which, however, was conferred only on select people. Advocates of this position viewed every human action in a comparatively strong causal relationship as "predetermined" by God.

Here a deep rift opened up in Catholic theology because the different models adopted dramatically different interpretations of the relationship between God and man. It was no wonder that the Catholic world split along these positions. After disputes over these questions interrupted instruction in Valladolid in 1594, Pope Clement VIII intervened at the insistence of high-ranking Jesuits like Cardinal Francisco de Toledo.[188] He founded a congregation of cardinals *De auxiliis* to solve the problem. The cardinals met for years. At some points, the Dominicans thought victory was within their grasp; at others, the Jesuits did. At last, on September 28, 1607, the case was officially declared closed: Pope Paul V explicitly declined to decide the matter and instead ordered all the parties involved not to publish any further pamphlets. This represented a victory more so for the Jesuits than the Dominicans, since they themselves had always striven to achieve something similar, even if the compromise failed to recognize their own position as correct.

As anyone could have foreseen, the papal decision of 1607 did nothing to put the controversy to rest. In 1610, the influential Jesuit (and casuist) Leonhard Lessius published his *De gratia efficaci* (On effective grace) in Antwerp, a work steeped in the thought of Molina. Paul V and Urban VIII renewed the prohibition on such publications in 1611 and 1625, but again with mixed success. In 1640, again in Leuven, the posthumous book *Augustinus* by the bishop of Ypern, Cornelius Jansen (1585–1638), appeared. In this work, making as broad a use of the works of the church fathers as possible, Jansen created a synthesis of Augustinian theology as he understood it—the very approach itself, namely, enriching the doctrinal discussion with systematic interpretation of patristic sources, was an unprecedented innovation.[189] In terms of content, the text amounted to a critique of the Jesuits and their Molinist views. Jansen, like other anti-Molinist theologians, emphasized the absolute necessity of grace and the inadequacy of human will.

The debate over grace expanded to even greater dimensions with the publication of Jansen's comprehensive work. The nuncio resident in Cologne, Fabio Chigi, attempted to put a stop to the controversies that broke out after *Augustinus* appeared, but he proved unsuccessful.[190] The Jesuits immediately went after the book. Censures were issued in Rome in 1641, 1643, 1653, 1656, and 1665, initially for circumventing the publishing ban on questions of grace and then also for errors of substance. An abridged version of the book made by the theologians of the Sorbonne in 1641 played a decisive part in its condemnation.[191] It was hotly contested between both sides whether the five theses of this abridgment actually appeared in Jansen's *Augustinus* or whether the book should be vindicated from the suspicion of false doctrine. Then, in 1664, the so-called *formulaire* was introduced in France: the entire clergy now had to distance itself in writing from the five "Jansenist" theses by signing a form drawn up with the help of the Jesuit and royal confessor François Annat (1590–1670), which was presented to every priest.

Jansen's *Augustinus* survived this storm of hostility. The determined defense of the work by pious French authors made it impossible to suppress the controversies of 1641 or 1643.[192] Among the spokesmen of the "Jansenist" sympathizers were the *contritionista* Jean Du Vergier de Haranne, the Abbé de Saint-Cyran, an old acquaintance of Jansen's; Pierre Nicole (1625–95); and Antoine Arnauld (1612–94).[193] In 1641, Jansen's book was reprinted in Paris to great success. Arnauld in particular ensured that the dispute merged with older conflicts over the dogma of grace. Key terms of the earlier debate like *gratia efficax* were taken up again but integrated in new contexts and sometimes radicalized.[194] Even prayer required special, "efficient" grace in the view of some Jansenists, which the Jesuits firmly rejected. Because Arnauld wrote his popular anti-Jesuit texts in French, he ensured that the dispute burst out of the confines of specialist doctrinal debate and came to the attention of the broad reading public.

The Jansenists received important backing and close support from the convent of Port-Royal near Paris, with which they had close personal contacts. Angélique Arnauld (1591–1661), Antoine Arnauld's sister, was the abbess there, and Saint-Cyran was an influential spiritual confidant. Angélique had carried out profound spiritual reforms at Port-Royal the substance and style of which anticipated the convictions of the Jansenists. Hence it was unsurprising that Port-Royal became a stronghold of the Jansenist opposition when the public disputes broke out. A dozen "hermits" lived in the dilapidated stables of the convent and indulged their pious inclinations. Antoine Arnauld found refuge and support there when he was censored by the Sorbonne in 1656. Another thinker and author with Jansenist inclinations also took shelter in Port-Royal: Blaise Pascal, who took a stand against the Jesuits, their Molinism, and their lax moral theology in general in 1656/7. It was at Port-Royal that he wrote his famous, bitterly anti-Jesuit, and highly polemical eighteen *Lettres provinciales*, in which he shaped the negative image of the Jesuits for future generations.

In the ensuing decades, the dispute with the Jansenists raged on, although there were also phases of relative quiet—a so-called Peace of the Church beginning in 1669 reigned in France for about ten years.[195] But the conflict escalated again in 1700, exacerbated especially by the prominently anti-Jansenist archbishop of Mechelen in the Spanish Netherlands, Humbert-Guillaume de Précipiano. At the turn of the new century, Précipiano was responsible for the arrest of Pasquier Quesnel, who had become the new Jansenist leader after Arnauld's death. The "Quesnel case" revived the conflicts anew. In 1705, the pope renewed the previous prohibitions on Jansenism; in 1709, the last inhabitants of Port-Royal were deported, and the convent was razed between 1711 and 1713. Even the graves were opened and the corpses exhumed. The whole affair came to a head in the apostolic constitution *Unigenitus* of 1713, in which 101 of Quesnel's Jansenist propositions were condemned. For decades thereafter, controversy raged over this papal document in France—a controversy that intensified anti-Jesuit sentiment in the 1750s shortly before the abolition of the Society in France. The crown's anti-Jansenist efforts became more and more the subject of dispute. Whoever was for Jansenism almost inevitably slipped into an oppositional, antimonarchical role.[196]

Jesuits were actively involved in all these stages of anti-Jansenist agitation: Jacques-Philippe Lallemant, for example, published a book in 1704 titled *Père Quesnel séditieux* (Seditious Father Quesnel). His confrere Guillaume Daubenton—sometime confessor of Philip V of Spain—was one of the masterminds behind *Unigenitus* and was indirectly involved in the persecution and unmasking of Jansenists.[197] In the course of the debates, it became increasingly evident that the fight had long since ceased to be about nuances of Catholic dogma. Different styles, backgrounds, and lifestyles of Catholic Christians collided. The Jesuit Louis Patouillet accordingly accused his adversaries in 1752 of "affecting to lament the extreme decline of these latest times, of depicting our church as covered in darkness"; Ignatius's men, in contrast, strove to be optimistic and argued that one had to look at humankind and the times with a certain sense of confidence.[198]

Despite some short-term victories, over the long term the Jesuits' implacable opposition to the Jansenists probably weakened the Society of Jesus. The Jesuits expended too much energy and talent waging these inter-Catholic wars, and a certain narrowing of their intellectual horizon may have been the result.[199] Since the Jansenists made use of progressive historical and philological arguments, the Jesuits pointedly refused to do so. The unending battles over Jansen's *Augustinus* increasingly absorbed other moral-theological and dogmatic conflicts of the baroque period: the debate over rigorism, the doctrine of grace, and the "superstitious" (in the Jansenists' view) devotions of the Sacred Heart of Jesus and the Immaculata.[200] The all-encompassing controversy between the Jansenists and the Jesuits robbed other questions of their autonomy. The interpretive matrix of the Jansenist conflict threatened to overlay and sublimate all other developments.

Despite a stubborn defense, the Jesuits ultimately could not prevent their opponents from gaining ground.[201] The Jesuits and their sympathizers may have succeeded in establishing a probabilist, antirigorist, and anti-Jansenist devotional culture in Europe by approximately 1700, but their position lost in the long term. After 1700, Catholics in many places began to call for more sobriety and rigor, which suited Muratori's "regulated devotion" very well. Whether it was with respect to the devotion of the Sacred Heart of Jesus, their worship of the Immaculata, their lax and probabilist ethics, or their Molinist doctrine of grace, the Jesuits remained a powerful but increasingly isolated group that faced mounting pressure on all sides. People became skeptical that the Jesuits' devotion and theology really served to "help souls" as they incessantly claimed. For all the criticism, however, that really was what the successors of Loyola were pursuing with their casuistry, baroque spirituality, and devotions.

"Helping Souls": Pastoral Ministry and the Fostering of Christian Life

The Jesuits had been founded as an apostolic community. They wanted to "help souls." In everyday terms, this meant that a majority of the Society's members were engaged in some form of pastoral ministry. Over time, several fields of operation emerged that the Jesuits viewed as characteristic of themselves: these were the "customary ministries" (*consueta ministeria*). Many of these typical ministries concentrated on large groups of people, whereas others pertained to individuals. For some ministries, the Jesuits founded supporting institutions and establishments; others retained a rather informal character. The pastoral care organized and administered by the Society of Jesus was characterized by the insight that one had to take careful cognizance of people's social circumstances and potentially change them. In many places, Jesuit ministry merged with social welfare.

Like many other areas, Jesuit pastoral care also tended to become specialized. We should not exaggerate this development; many members of the Society remained generalists—they heard confession, preached, tended to the sick and poor, and addressed all kinds of spiritual needs for all kinds of people. And yet, as time passed, there were ever more experts for particular *consueta ministeria*, and these experts set the tone in their fields.

The very term "customary" shows that these ministries in fact comprised only a selection of possible areas of pastoral care—there obviously also were "less customary" options. Indeed, the Jesuits helped people's souls in a variety of ways, but there were also groups and activities in which they were involved either not at all or relatively seldom. Caring for orphans is one such case. The Jesuits made initial inquiries and occasionally launched initiatives, but there was no large-scale, broad engagement. Ignatius himself had once spoken with Pope Paul III about founding an orphanage in Rome, but nothing came of it.[202] The Colegio de Niños del Amor de Dios, however, a Jesuit pastoral institute founded in 1595 specifically for children, existed in Valladolid for centuries.[203] In Seville, the Jesuit Francisco de Soto gave a highly esteemed sermon in 1627, in which he emphatically pleaded for better care for exposed infants—by no means a marginal topic in light of the 257 foundlings on average per year there.[204] And when Ignaz Parhamer was made director of an existing orphanage by Empress Maria Theresa and the archbishop of Vienna, Cardinal Christoph Migazzi, the Society assumed responsibility for parentless children there, too.[205] Parhamer's administration in fact proved so successful that the orphanage of Vienna became a model for subsequent Austrian establishments.[206] But these are all more or less singular cases. There was no broad, let alone systematic, Jesuit engagement for orphans. But things were different for many other marginalized social groups.

Prostitutes, Paupers, Soldiers, and Criminals: The Jesuits and the Marginalized

When it came down to "helping souls," Ignatius was not afraid to get his hands dirty. On the contrary, marginalized social groups stood at the center of his work. He was especially happy to work personally for the poor, for outcasts, and for the needy and to mobilize the resources of his new order on their behalf. According to one famous story, Ignatius ran around the streets of Rome ahead of a prostitute in the 1540s so he could drive away prospective clients and, in this way, forestall lewd remarks and lucrative offers.[207] But Ignatius and his successors quickly realized that they wanted to do far more than make such spontaneous and individualized efforts. Friendly persuasion by individual members of the Jesuit order would have had, at best, a limited effect in converting marginal social groups. The Jesuits therefore turned to institutionalized forms of pastoral care. They could pool their resources in large-scale establishments. The Jesuits thus preferred to found pastoral institutions in which needy and vulnerable people were also supposed to live, which made it possible to tend to them more efficiently and measure success more accurately. From the start, Ignatius relied on the cooperation of wealthy, pious laymen to found and maintain such institutions.

Hence, from the very beginning, the pastoral projects of the Society of Jesus made an important contribution to the colorful history of Western Christian social welfare.[208] Giving alms was one of the fundamental virtues of Christian charity by biblical tradition. In the Middle Ages, this individual pious duty on the part of those with wealth was institutionalized across Europe. A patchwork of private and public institutions cared for the sick and poor and provided meals for the hungry: hospitals, poorhouses, hostels for pilgrims, and more. This tradition was continued in the sixteenth century by Christians of all confessions and in most parts of Europe, while it also received new impulses. Even today, however, it remains disputed whether real economic and social changes—whether a consequence of population growth or the result of a rise in the importation of precious metals from the New World—objectively drove up the number of needy persons or whether the intensification of such efforts instead reflected greater attention to poverty and misery. At any rate, it was material hardship that the Jesuits viewed as the root of spiritual lapses. "Poverty was the lesser evil of the poor; far worse was that they virtually did not know or did not recall that they are Christians," one leading Jesuit theorist concluded around 1700.[209] For these people, material support provided both the precondition and the opportunity for inner reform. A "new philanthropy" focused on salvation was taking root. It was with this in mind that Ignatius and his followers devised projects for people in difficult social circumstances.

The best-known example is the Jesuits' social work and ministry to the many prostitutes of Rome.[210] Ignatius founded an institution in 1543, the Casa Santa Marta, where prostitutes open to reform would be provided for from six to twelve months so that they could think about their future. The Jesuits did not run the house themselves. Instead, following the model sketched here, it was put under the direction of an influential confraternity that had been founded specifically for the purpose. The house's ties to the Society of Jesus, at least during the early years, remained very close. The goal of the institution was to change the lives of the women permanently; converted prostitutes were given the option to join a special convent. This had been the traditional escape route for prostitutes who wanted a new life (known as *convertite*) since the Middle Ages. There were special convents dedicated to such women in various cities of Italy and elsewhere in Europe. The two other options available at the Jesuit Casa were more innovative: the confraternity collected donations to provide the former prostitutes with a dowry so they could marry honorably. This was a door opener for reentry into respectable society.[211] As a final option, the Casa arranged for employment in the household of a wealthy noblewoman, who took on the appearance of a benefactor in this way. There were sporadic precedents for this flexible approach that opened up paths out of prostitution other than a convent.[212] The Casa Santa Marta, however, uniquely attached great importance to its residents' free choice about their future life.

The Casa Santa Marta in Rome had an eventful history. It initially enjoyed considerable success. Already by 1547, part of the house had been reserved as a convent of *convertite*. The original idea of serving as a kind of intermediate stop for ex-prostitutes remained intact for a while, but the transformation of the Casa into a convent proceeded apace. The institution ultimately turned into a relatively elitist Augustinian convent where, instead of former prostitutes, the sheltered daughters of well-to-do parents lodged. The focus of the Casa had made a complete 180-degree turn. Nevertheless, we should not underestimate the importance of this institution as a model that was imitated elsewhere. It is probable that Andrea Lippomano supported the arrival of the Society of Jesus in Venice in 1550 precisely in anticipation of this form of social work.[213] The model also resonated outside of Italy. The Jesuits of Seville, for example, reported a similar institution around 1600, the Casa Pia, which, however, proved to be short-lived.[214] In Spain, as in many other places, creating escape routes for prostitutes was often combined with aggressive agitation against prostitution itself. The Jesuits of Granada and Seville refused outright to condone the practice, which had been officially tolerated and even subsidized for centuries. They took bold physical action against clients and the practice of the profession itself, and launched shrewd legal and publicity campaigns locally and in Madrid. In Spain, the Jesuits were at least ostensibly victorious: in 1623, public brothels were prohibited by royal decree.

Ignatius also set in motion the founding of the Casa Santa Catarina, which, in contrast to the Casa Santa Marta, was intended to provide preventative help rather than assist existing prostitutes: it was dedicated to the daughters of prostitutes and, more broadly, to all girls in precarious social circumstances. At the Casa Santa Catarina, these girls were given sustenance and at least a rudimentary education intended to instill Christian values and save them from a life of sin on the streets. The confraternity established to maintain the Casa also provided an acceptable dowry so that the girls could eventually marry. In 1560, Benedetto Palmio, an influential early Jesuit, brought these Roman ideas to Venice, where they meshed well with similar ideas that some wealthy local women had maintained for some time on their own initiative.[215] The fruit of this collaboration between the Jesuits and influential local laymen in Venice was the Casa de Citelle, founded in 1561; its function was similar to that of the Roman Casa Santa Catarina. On June 10 of that year, Palmio led forty girls in a solemn and highly visible procession through the entire City of Bridges to their new abode on the outlying island of Guidecca, directly opposite San Marco. This model radiated outward from Venice. Palmio's specifications were followed in other cities, such as Udine and Milan, where wealthy women financed equivalent institutions in the 1590s.[216] All these institutions were shaped and organized with Jesuit involvement, but their everyday administration was in the hands of laymen and local priests.

The Jesuits proceeded similarly with care for the poor in the seventeenth century. In this area, too, they were part of a broader movement that tried to adapt older charitable institutions for beggars and the needy to the new political, religious, and social climate. Caring for the poor was and remained a predominantly local and decentralized project, even when bishops or royal officials occasionally planned more closely coordinated initiatives. In France, reform-minded clerics like Vincent de Paul therefore attempted to put poor relief on a new local basis by founding confraternities in villages and small communities.[217] The Compagnie de Saint Sacrement had also worked closely with poorhouses since the mid-seventeenth century. The Compagnie was an association of devout laymen (dévots) who were deeply engaged in the social sector. Its members established a large poorhouse in Paris and then soon agitated to found parallel institutions in the rest of the kingdom to relieve it.[218] The French king issued laws in support of these initiatives. In the 1670s, when these efforts threatened to fail, Jesuits like Honoré Chaurand (1617–97) took up these plans and enriched them with their own ideas.[219] It was only at this point that members of the Society of Jesus began to be broadly and systematically involved in poor relief.

Jesuits like Chaurand, André Guévarre, and Pierre-Joseph Dunod developed their own "method" (manière) of founding these institutions.[220]

They moved from village to village, city to city according to a careful plan and held publicity events lasting about two weeks. Sermons, admonitions, and countless conversations—which might at first be complicated and riddled with misunderstandings—served to explain the project on the ground. Finally, the institution was founded in the Jesuits' presence and embedded in local society with statutes and appointed officials. Then the beggars and poor of a city would be rounded up, counted, publicly feted in a symbolic act, and occasionally given new clothes, before they then moved into the newly opened house and the gates of the institution closed behind them. During these campaigns, the Jesuits constantly availed themselves of the assistance of royal officials, bishops, and especially the local clergy. All of this activity was supported by an expertly coordinated publishing initiative in Paris overseen by Gabriel Calloët-Querbrat (b. 1616–20, d. after 1688), a Breton nobleman close to the leading minister Jean-Baptiste Colbert.[221] These vigorous initiatives met with some success. The main protagonists themselves declared in 1688 that 106 such institutions had been founded. Recent research presumes that Chaurand alone founded some 38 poorhouses in Brittany.[222]

The Jesuits were interested in institutions that operated *à la Capucine*, not *à la Benedictine*.[223] This meant that these welfare establishments in small towns or villages did not depend on donations of land or buildings or on an endowment—in many places, efforts to found such houses had failed on account of limited communal and individual resources. Instead, these facilities for the poor would be financed by systematically organized, but sporadic, fundraising campaigns: everyone could give a little bit now and again. "As for furniture, one can find it everywhere [for these institutions] within 24 hours," the Jesuits thought, because "every family has some small thing they do not need that they can set outside the door of the house . . . which the Directors can take away in carts."[224] In Grenoble, where André Guévarre applied this method, no fewer than twenty carts full of furnishings came together in 1712; other sources frequently report such columns of heavily loaded wagons that became a public spectacle as they lumbered toward the local poorhouse.[225] For the Jesuits, it was entirely possible that this precarious financial basis could become permanent if suitably extensive donations could be collected.[226] Sometimes individual benefactors really sponsored an entire *hôpital général*.[227] The decisive factor, however, was the voluntary but directed and skillfully coordinated ad hoc self-organization of the community. Chaurand, for example, was convinced that "one should never use compulsory taxes to support the poor. That angers the people."[228]

The French model caused quite a stir. In 1691 and from 1692 to 1694, Guévarre presented it in Rome to the newly elected Innocent XII and the superior general, Tirso González. The French also attracted a great deal of attention in the Grand Duchy of Tuscany.[229] In Turin, the Duke of Savoy, Victor Amadeus II, who had also just been crowned king of Sicily in 1713, showed interest. The example of Savoy was especially influential, because Guévarre stylized it as a model in his programmatic treatise *La mendicità sbandita* (Banning begging), which he dedicated to Victor Amadeus in 1717. But even in Turin the truth was that older local models were more important and more successful than the Jesuit was willing to admit, as he strove to cast himself, his order, and the king in a flattering light.[230] It was a peculiarity of Jesuit poorhouses, though, that they were not just a "religious house" and "seminary" but also a "manufacture"—which is to say, "all the paupers are taught a trade so that they can sustain themselves throughout their lives without relapsing into the poverty from which they were extracted." With this additional emphasis, Jesuit institutions went beyond the plans of the *dévots* from the Compagnie du Saint-Sacrement and were more in line with the ideas of Minister Jean-Baptiste Colbert. Not all Jesuits shared these views, but in many places they were open to arguments based on economic advantage.[231]

All these institutions dedicated to the welfare of the poor, of prostitutes, and of vulnerable girls aspired to transform their charges' lives completely.[232] This institutionalized care was intended to educate the residents in every aspect of life. It was the steadfast conviction of Jesuits like Guévarre that the best way to bring about material and spiritual improvement in people's lives was to proceed in an orderly, methodical fashion (*con ordine, e con metodo*)—two pillars of Jesuit pedagogy.[233] To that end, Parhamer went so far as to establish a military command structure in the Viennese orphanage and had the boys living there march and conduct field exercises.[234] And in Udine it was held that careful "government" was indispensable for the social and religious well-being of the girls.[235] In keeping with this trend, the Jesuits conceived of their charitable institutions as a sealed-off parallel world that resembled a barracks or prison.[236] This general predilection for institutionalized control, surveillance, and regulation met with little resistance in the Society.[237]

We should not, however, view this Jesuit mindset unfairly as compliant support of fantasies of state power and surveillance, as has been done time and time again. The Jesuits were not simply agents of royal centralization policies; control and surveillance were merely means to an end for them, not ends unto themselves. Men like Chaurand and Calloët-Querbrat may have acted with the permission and official support of Louis XIV, but the king played no part in the execution and success of the campaign, nor in the actual form that individual institutions took.[238] The Jesuits were happy to enjoy the protection of the king and his ministers, but they ultimately acted for their own spiritual motives. That, of course, did not rule out social side effects, such as the enhancement of state power, but that was not the Jesuits' primary goal.

In addition to prostitutes and the poor, the Jesuits and other Catholics paid ever greater attention to soldiers and officers over the course of the early modern period.[239] Warfare changed dramatically during this time, which has previously been described rather misleadingly as a "military revolution." Armies and navies grew to an astonishing degree. Bands of mercenaries were now increasingly joined by standing armies. Beginning in France, the logistical support and administration of the military were significantly expanded. Efforts were made to regulate troops and their conduct more strictly outside of combat. And, not least, the salvation of the soldiers itself became the subject of pastoral endeavors of unprecedented intensity. In 1532, it was decreed that priests were to be present in the armies of Spain, although the execution of the order was far from comprehensive. In consequence, clergymen became embedded in the armies and navies of Europe.

The Jesuits quickly made it their business to tend to the souls of the rank and file.[240] Diego Laínez preached as the "first Jesuit military chaplain" in 1550 at the Spanish victory over the Muslims at Mahdia, southeast of Tunis. Jerónimo Nadal accompanied a Spanish army from Sicily to North Africa in 1551. One of Nadal's companions from the Society drowned in a shipwreck during the crossing. Nadal himself spent long weeks in North Africa hearing confession, preaching, and teaching catechesis to the soldiers. The Jesuit increasingly came to question his decision to minister to the army temporarily. Nadal appears to have decided to travel with the troops without a clear idea of the challenges and potential duties a military chaplain might have to perform. The conclusion of his journey to Africa accordingly rather resembled a bold secret escape from the army.

The Jesuits, however, soon returned to the theater of war in the southern Mediterranean. Already by 1560, a good half dozen of them under the leadership of Anton Vinck were again on board a Spanish-Sicilian expedition on course for Tripoli. The Jesuits had been brought along to tend to the sick, but on at least one occasion they saw open battle. The Jesuits made themselves useful in repelling an attack on their ship, for instance, by hauling gunpowder.[241] In addition to the wars against the Muslims in the Mediterranean, the French Wars of Religion that commenced in the 1560s became proving grounds for the Jesuit ministry to soldiers. Beginning in 1568, Edmond Auger agitated in France in word and deed for military action against the Protestants as an expression of living, genuine Catholicism.[242] At least occasionally, he personally served as a chaplain in the army of the Catholic League at the express wish of the king of France.[243] When Pope Pius V sent a contingent of troops across the Alps to fight the Protestants, Jesuits were with them yet again. Antonio Possevino composed the first Catholic catechism for soldiers in 1569, his famous *Soldato christiano*. Soon German and Swiss Jesuits also accompanied various armies to France as chaplains.[244] In 1587, the Jesuit Thomas Sailly (1553–1623) held the first military chaplaincy officially institutionalized as such in the Spanish army of Alessandro Farnese in the Netherlands.[245] General Claudio Acquaviva published an instruction in 1591 that outlined the conduct and duties of

Jesuit chaplains more precisely.[246] Cardinal Richelieu finally issued an order whereby six Jesuits were to be assigned as chaplains to every large army.[247]

The Jesuits were well aware of the fact that working with fighting men would be an unusually difficult job. Soldiers did not enjoy a good reputation. Possevino considered it necessary in his *Soldato* to warn against various forms of moral indiscretion typically committed by soldiers: homosexuality, irreverence toward holy sites and buildings, and unnecessary violence toward the vanquished.[248] All too often Catholic armies conducted themselves like a swarm of locusts, as Jesuit authors soberly assessed the facts.[249] Sailly also knew that extortion and harassment were typical vices.[250] Another Jesuit concluded with concern, "To be honest, forced recruitment [*l'empressement*] and the agitation of a call to arms are not especially favorable circumstances for our plans."[251]

The Jesuits wanted to change these conditions, which jeopardized both the salvation of individual soldiers and the success of whole campaigns. A "good" or "holy war" as Auger, for example, had mentioned, needed a Christian army through and through. That started with the officers. The good general was a key figure in this project of Christianizing armies: "Just as you ensure that your troops serve the king well, you also should ensure by all means possible that they serve God."[252] The Jesuits were therefore especially pleased when they could see proof of officers' piety. The Jesuits of Paderborn, for instance, were duly proud when a high officer, Othmar von Erwitte, came to the local college on March 17, 1631: "Having bid farewell to Mars [i.e., the war] for a while, he (came) seeking the retreat of the spiritual exercises of Our Holy Father Ignatius and the health of his soul and the tranquility of his conscience, having set all other affairs aside; so that then, once he attained it, he would go forth against the enemy all the more eagerly."[253] Intense devotion and military prowess went hand in hand for the Jesuits. The Jesuit theory of war and Jesuits' ministry to soldiers were predicated on this basic assumption.

Besides the officers, it was the troops in whom the Jesuits were interested the most. The "spiritual education of soldiers" was their foremost goal.[254] The Jesuits relied on a variety of strategies to achieve it. If they could, they typically made use of sounds and images to convey their devotion to the soldiers as effectively and memorably as possible. Thomas Sailly is reported to have obtained permission from his general (and penitent) Alessandro Farnese to have the soldiers pray an Ave Maria every morning after three trumpet blasts and to carry an image of Mary before them on the march for all to see.[255] He also took up an idea of Pope Sixtus V, who had called for the creation of special confraternities of soldiers in the army.[256] Prayers and litanies were also held several times a day. In the Jesuits' opinion, it was essential that the soldiers should examine their conscience daily.[257] In addition to other, similar advice, Sailly also gave the soldiers specific instructions on how to attend field mass.[258]

Soon the Jesuits began to pay greater attention to those existential wartime situations where pastoral care may have been needed most: injury, mortal fear, and death. At the end of later editions of his *Soldato*, Possevino added a "Guide on How to Pray for Soldiers to Prepare Themselves to Die Confidently Before They Embark on Any Undertaking."[259] Ministering to soldiers in these extreme moments regularly came to occupy a central position. In 1595, Nicolò Fabrini reported from Gran, where he and a good dozen more Jesuits were tending to the imperial armies fighting the Turks. He wrote, "We have our hands full with the large number of wounded near us more than ever. The number rose today to 1,500. Eighteen to twenty die daily. It is up to us almost entirely to hear their confession, administer communion to them, stay with them in the throes of death, and often even bury them."[260] Joachim Pleiner, who served as a chaplain in the armies of the emperor and elector of Saxony during the War of the Austrian Succession, reflected on precisely these difficult situations from his own experience in a devotional work composed in 1748. His book was intended to prepare "the soldier in the midst of mortal danger for a Christian death with consolatory advice and gracious prayers." Pleiner was prescient enough in this devotional book to consider the fact that many soldiers in battle would experience such situations probably isolated and alone, and "in the absence of priestly support."[261] Even dying Protestants received care in such situations.[262] In light of that fact, the Jesuits in the armies were also important conveyors of information for family members waiting anxiously at home, even if only to obtain certainty about the sad end of fallen relatives, for instance, in the form of a *dodtenzedl* (death notice).[263]

Spiritual guidance and physical care of the wounded often went hand in hand. Possevino had urged the Jesuits constantly to obtain "tents, beds, any doctor, surgeon, specialist, and necessary medicines and food appropriate for the sick."[264] Although Acquaviva was rather restrained in his instruction of 1591, this remained an essential task. The soldiers' physical and spiritual needs before and after battle were inseparable. Sailly stressed that physical care for wounded soldiers was one's Christian duty, because all combatants in such circumstances numbered among the "weak and sick," who were the preferred objects of Christian charity (*charité*).[265] The Jesuits who accompanied the Bavarian armies on campaign in Bohemia in 1620 regularly cared for the sick.[266] In the seventeenth and eighteenth centuries, it was the responsibility of the Jesuits in the French army to care for the wounded on the front lines of battle in so-called mobile hospitals.[267]

Finally, the Jesuits helped soldiers interpret and assess their grisly actions. Many Jesuit books for military chaplains and soldiers contain extensive passages justifying and explaining war. Possevino, for example, attempted at the very beginning of his *Soldato* to convince the reader of the fundamental righteousness and godliness of war against heretics.[268] Sailly wrote in a similar vein, as also did his confrere Jeremias Drexel in Bohemia in 1620. On the one hand, they knew the horror of war, which was "sweet [only] to those who have not experienced it." As they traveled through the devastated landscape, they wrote down their realization that "war is the face of all possible horrors: this man plunders, that man is plunder, this man is dying, that man lies dead." On the other hand, the same Jesuits adhered to the conventional interpretation that war was useful and necessary, for example, in the struggle against heretics, whose misery one might indeed regard as willed by God. In this way, men like Sailly and Drexel both acknowledged soldiers' experiences and gave them a higher, albeit very one-sided, purpose. To give them "confidence" in their actions—that was the goal of this interpretation of war.[269]

Jesuits were not present only for military operations on land. Since the sixteenth century, they also provided chaplains for the navies of Europe. Before the Spanish fleet set out for Lepanto in 1571, the Jesuits heard the confession of the galley slaves and rowers.[270] Several Jesuits were present at the battle itself.[271] Nearly two dozen members of the Society of Jesus were also aboard the Spanish Armada in 1588.[272] Pierre Champion (1632–1701), who was later renowned as a religious man of letters and devotional author, accompanied the French fleet of the Comte d'Estrées to Cayenne and Tobago as a ship's chaplain.[273] In 1685, schools specifically for naval chaplains were established under Jesuit management in the two most important naval strongholds of the French fleet, Toulon and Brest.[274] Although these institutions were actually financed by the crown, the seminar in Brest suffered from chronic underfunding, leading to an unending series of legal battles with local authorities. Even so, in 1703, a total of 730 chaplains were trained there by the Jesuits.

Working with soldiers was demanding and thus was not exactly one of the most popular or attractive ministries in the Society.[275] Again and again, Jesuits lost their lives as a direct consequence of war. Fifteen of the twenty-three Jesuits who served aboard the Spanish Armada of 1588 perished. Johann Buslidius, who accompanied Duke Maximilian of Bavaria in Bohemia in 1620, stood with him on the general's hill on October 27 so they could observe the enemy—a dangerous business, even if "no one was injured" despite numerous skirmishes. But three days later a young man standing next to the duke was killed by an enemy bullet.[276] It was not for nothing that Thomas Sailly, and presumably many a Jesuit, wore armor for protection.[277]

Even disregarding bullets and swords, the work was demanding and potentially exhausting purely in physical terms. Sickness followed every early modern army and did not spare the Jesuits. In 1595, several members of the Society succumbed to disease on the campaign outside Gran mentioned earlier, including their leader Nicolò Fabrini. The constant mobility exacerbated the hardship. The Jesuits froze and hungered on the Bavarian campaign in Bohemia just like all the other participants on account of the autumn weather and lack of food. They spent more than one sleepless night on the front fully armed. Even the Jesuits were infected by the nervousness and anxiety of the soldiers on the eve of the Battle of White Mountain in November 1620.[278] Such living conditions could easily become physical challenges. When one "had spent so many years at war and moreover had seen so many killed next to and around oneself in the bombardment and siege of so many cities," then it was not easy and by no means straightforward to keep one's faith, good cheer, and optimism.[279]

Prisoners constituted a final major group of particularly needy people on the fringes of early modern society to whom the Jesuits gave particular spiritual and material care. The ministry to incarcerated criminals had obvious biblical roots; Jesus mentions the subject explicitly (Matthew 26:31–46) in a passage leading Jesuits repeatedly cited.[280] Ignatius himself had enjoined his confreres to apply themselves to this kind of spiritual ministry. The founder of the Society potentially had his own experiences in mind. He had been imprisoned twice for several weeks in 1527, in Alcalá de Henares and in Salamanca. Prisoners therefore were never omitted from the list of ways one might typically "help souls." Canisius visited the prison of Vienna together with several lay brothers in 1552.[281] A generation later, Pedro de León (1545–1632) of Seville was one of the most famous Jesuits who took particular interest in prisons and their inmates.[282] He worked for decades in the royal prison of Seville, where up to a thousand men—and women, who lived in a separate area—were incarcerated.[283]

Early modern prisons were godless places, the Jesuits concluded again and again with disgust. Francisco de Estrada, who arrived in Porto in Portugal on a pastoral pilgrimage in 1546, wrote: "We visited the prison, which was in such a spiritual and temporal state that it was necessary to take particular caution, because although Lent had occurred several days before, no one there had confessed, and some died without giving confession, and they had not heard mass for an entire year or even a word to remind them of God and Christ."[284] The inmates themselves were also often considered especially crude and sinful people. Hence, the Jesuits focused above all on making prisons into places where Christianity was practiced more regularly. They were happy if criminals started to listen to them at all. Canisius thus considered it a triumph when he succeeded in raising the frequency of confession in Vienna. The Jesuits ultimately relied on an apparent paradox—the prison should become a place of freedom. One early text summarized the concept behind the Jesuits' prison ministry as follows: "The goal of those [of us] who go to the prisons to help the inmates should be to ensure with both collective and individual exhortations that they receive an opportunity from the physical prison to leave the spiritual prison of sin and make a firm resolution to change their life."[285]

Here, too, religious and material care went hand in hand. Prisoners in early modern prisons frequently had to pay for their own accommodations. Poor inmates, however, had virtually no chance of doing so without working and so fell into a bottomless pit of debt. The Jesuits and all others who wanted to get involved in charitable work in prisons saw great need for action here. In Vienna, the Jesuits therefore not only heard confession and gave the prisoners religious appeals but also gave them shirts, shoes, and coats courtesy of the generous donations of some noblemen. The Viennese Jesuits also tried to improve prison conditions and often held fundraising campaigns to collect money to free debtors from prison, since debtors made up the largest group of prisoners. They frequently called on confraternities created specifically for this purpose, thus involving the laity in this form of charitable aid. In 1579, the French Jesuit Jean Tellier (1545–79) founded the Pietà dei Carcerati in Rome, one of the most renowned confraternities of the Eternal City.[286] The Pietà was one of the first organizations in Rome dedicated exclusively to caring for prisoners. Further confraternities under Jesuit management covered other needs of the prisoners. In Seville, around thirty men from the confraternity of Nuestra Señora de la Visitación under the Jesuits' leadership helped defend the rights of "forgotten prisoners" who otherwise had to survive without recourse to legal assistance. The Jesuits were prepared to level harsh charges against the Spanish judiciary, which exploited and unjustly treated defenseless inmates.[287]

Ministering to prisoners on their way to execution was especially urgent. Pedro de León, for example, accompanied no fewer than 309 condemned men to the gallows.[288] This was the last chance for criminals to reconcile with God before the end. Since executions were usually public in the early modern period and were often witnessed by large crowds, the public repentance of serious criminals was staged as visibly as possible.[289] The criminal had to transform into a penitent sinner, who served as both a model (of remorse and conversion) and a deterrent (by virtue of his crimes and horrific punishment). The offender should accept his death "cheerfully" and "joyfully" because—thanks not least to the ministry of the *patres*—he had now found the right religious attitude.[290] The purpose was to "reconcile [the condemned] with the pyre"; only then could a public execution be an instructive example for the spectators.[291]

The Jesuits' goal was the "good death" of the criminal.[292] A dramatic example from Paderborn illustrates how that might look. In 1643, the Jesuits were counseling a man sitting in prison for murdering twenty-seven victims. Even he finally transformed in exemplary fashion for the final steps of his life:

> And even though he was always visited by our priest, he still stubbornly and brusquely rejected his counsel until at last he realized that all hope of life had been taken from him; then he finally softened after prayers and warnings from Heaven, cast off his ferocity, recanted [Calvinist] heresy, received the sacraments according to the Catholic rite, and bravely and piously suffered the wheel, the breaking of his limbs, and the quartering of his body, thereby amending his deplorable life at least with a good death.[293]

In order to effect the "Christianization" of criminals, an especially intense phase of pastoral care took place between the pronouncement of the sentence and the execution. Time was short, and there were often—as in the example from Paderborn—significant obstacles to overcome. Hence no effort was spared. In Seville, Pedro de León and other pastors spent the final days of the prisoner's life in special quarters with their own altar. The prisoners confessed, took communion, did penance, meditated. Litanies were sung, and mass was read for them before they made their way to the gallows. Very few prisoners will have had such intimate contact with the church in their former lives. If this strategy of overwhelming religious engagement succeeded, an execution transformed into a brilliantly staged act with manifold religious overtones. Clad in white, the offender was conducted in a procession through the whole city to the place of execution accompanied by several clergymen. The Jesuit who had served as his companion in prison was always present. At the foot of the gallows, he heard the prisoner's last confession. Earthly justice and divine forgiveness manifested themselves equally in the criminal's good death.

It appears that ministering to prisoners was institutionalized and routinized to a lesser extent than many other pastoral ministries in the Society. We seldom find individual Jesuits who specialized in this form of "helping souls." Pedro de León himself described it as a "valuable, but unknown ministry."[294] Some sources even suggest that the Jesuits sometimes did not take the call to go to the prisons seriously. At any rate, they were constantly enjoined to set foot in the prisons and even the deepest of dungeons, because "Christ is there."[295] Perhaps it was also "fear of entering and working in the stinking dungeons and dark cells, of working with criminal people, on the one hand, and with people who were badly instructed [in the faith] and of depraved conscience" that posed such a serious obstacle to this ministry.[296] Many Jesuits nonetheless went "into the prisons," as it is always put in these reports. There can be no doubt about that: the ministry to prisoners was one of the "customary ministries" of the Society of Jesus, just like the ministry to prostitutes, paupers, and soldiers. The social, material, and religious support of outsiders, the poor and defenseless, was at the heart of Jesuit identity. It was the Jesuits' duty to attend to such people in need and to acquaint them with the Word of God—not only them but the entire community of the faithful. The traditional means of doing so was the sermon.

The Jesuits as Preachers

In just the forty days of Lent in 1769, no fewer than 1,835 sermons were delivered in Madrid.[297] The intensification of Catholic sermonizing reflected in this enormous number had commenced in the late Middle Ages, but it jumped yet again in the sixteenth century, not least in response to the Reformation, in which sermons played a major part. The Council of Trent took up the topic several times, elevating the sermon to a key element of pastoral ministry. There also was the influence of humanism, from which at least two important ideas derived: one was the call that sermons should focus more closely on the Bible reading of the day; the other was the view that sermons had to influence the audience's life. The primary purpose of a sermon was defined as seizing and moving (*movere*) people.[298] For the Jesuits, a sermon might "defeat kings, check the lusts of powerful men, conquer cities" for the faith, and "impose discipline on profligate lasciviousness"—in brief: influence the audience toward a Christian end.[299] According to General Acquaviva, a sermon above all had to "persuade and stir the emotions"—classic formulas of humanist rhetoric.[300] Sermons should be like cannons that blast through the walls of evil and open the way for people to the good, in the words of Francisco de Borja.[301]

Whence should this persuasiveness come, and how should this shaping of wills, feelings, and ideas occur?[302] First, we should point to a clear charismatic element in the Jesuit understanding of sermons. Many of the great, innovative preachers at the time, like Luis de Granada or Juan de Ávila, were convinced that the Holy Spirit had to contribute to a successful sermon. Within the Society of Jesus, Francisco de Borja, who had studied under Juan de Ávila after all, advocated this conviction in his *Tratado breve del modo de predicar el Santo Evangelio* (Brief treatise on how to preach the Holy Gospel).[303] Rhetorical effectiveness was regarded primarily as a gift of the Holy Spirit, less so as a product of human labor. Of course, for Borja and other Jesuits, that did not mean that one should disregard the human element of preaching. One seventeenth-century author characteristically stressed that "it is necessary to work hard and study much to know how to preach, because a preacher cannot expect God to instill all knowledge directly in him."[304] Human virtuosity and earthly preaching aids were thus in high demand as additional means of reaching audiences effectively.

To that end, Jesuit preachers of the seventeenth century were especially fond of integrating images and props into their sermons. The orator himself was the first "image" that the audience saw—he embodied the same pious way of life that was the point of the sermons. The Jesuits reported that Borja once stood at the pulpit even though sickness had left him barely able to speak—and still his mere presence deeply moved the audience.[305] Already the early Jesuits relied on props to lend emphasis to their words. Crosses, skulls, and nooses underscored their message. In the seventeenth century, this blossomed into a broad tradition of full-fledged dramatic productions on the pulpit. Wolfgang Rauscher from Dillingen composed an entire sermon as an "anatomy or dismemberment of a skull from limb to limb."[306] Hence it was a common expression at the time that one "preached for the eyes," which meant both the eyes of the body and the eyes of the mind, both spiritual and physical seeing at the same time. It thus was nothing unusual when Father Anton Khabes had three pictorial representations of scenes from the Old Testament mounted above the high altar in the church of the Professed House of Vienna in 1745, and then proceeded to preach about them.[307] Sermons became synesthetic spectacles.[308]

The Jesuits also were firm believers in the power of ancient rhetoric to ensure that their message affected the lives of their listeners.[309] Cicero and Quintilian were considered the most important stylistic models for preaching, but it was not clear how far one really had to follow them: Jesuit scholars like the famous Denis Pétau in France or the equally well-read Andreas Schott in Belgium argued that one should follow the ancient systems of rhetoric strictly. Jesuits like Étienne Binet or the aforementioned Nicolas Caussin, however, for all their humanistic education, still viewed their principal business less in terms of scholarly exchange than in terms of successfully "moving the emotions" of their audience; they judged the admissibility of certain rhetorical effects less by the criterion of absolute stylistic fidelity to Cicero than by actual success. They viewed sermons less as a literary productions or printed works of art and more as speeches to be delivered. And "popular preachers" of the seventeenth century, such as Francesco de Geronimo or Gregorio Rocco in southern Italy, who frequently spoke to passersby on the streets, often used an even more simplified style.[310] The Spaniard Miguel Angel Pascual argued in 1698 that the structural principles of a missionary sermon might be completely at odds with a solemn, scholarly sermon or a conventional sermon given by the parish clergy.[311]

Very many preachers of the seventeenth century made use of such rhetorical techniques and tricks that one might describe as "opulent" and "bombastic" in hindsight. The style they cultivated aimed for grand rhetorical gestures, overpowering oratory, and elaborate effects. One of the most extreme forms of these attempts to move an audience with virtuoso oratory was the so-called *concepto*. These were puzzles and ostensibly nonsensical wordplay or even indecipherable pictures ("hieroglyphs") that the speaker worked into his sermon; he then explained their religious significance to the amazement of his audience. Beyond stirring hearts, the audience's wits should also be surprised and impressed.[312] A sermon delivered by the great Jesuit preacher António Vieira in Lisbon on the feast day of Ignatius of Loyola, July 31, 1669, can serve as an example; it was already famous (or infamous) among contemporaries. It went without saying that the founder of the Society would be celebrated and glorified especially lavishly on this day, and Vieira did not disappoint. In exemplary fashion, he made use of a *concepto*, one of those complicated, intricate, ostensibly nonsensical and paradoxical plays on words. Vieira introduced Ignatius as "similarity without similarity" (*semejante sin semejante*). This, at first glance, baffling expression alluded loosely to the biblical passage Luke 12:36 ("Be like those who are waiting for their master to return"), but Vieira's train of thought then carried him far from that starting point. The quintessence of his playful approach to the verse was that Ignatius united in himself the virtues of all other saints. Hence, he was similar to every one of them, but vice versa no other saint was similar to Ignatius with his panoply of virtues. This sermon, which fills twenty-two printed pages, repeatedly circles back to this motif of Loyola's incomparable similarity.[313] With such complexities, baroque preachers tried (especially in educated circles) to thrill, seize, and put their audience under the spell of their message.

These extravagant strategies soon came under the suspicion that they served to further preachers' narcissistic vainglory rather than influence the Christian community. Rhetorical effects were good and well, but they could not be used indiscriminately, overshadowing the actual message of the sermon. A rhetorical middle way was the goal, as exemplified, for instance, by the moderate and pious Ciceronianism of Carlo Reggio's *Orator Christianus* of 1612.[314] General Claudio Acquaviva pointed in the same direction in a circular a year later. The most serious obstacle to a successful sermon was the apparently widespread practice of "preaching oneself and seeking praise rather than looking after the good of one's audience for God."[315] Acquaviva explicitly mentioned the excessive use of "profane authors, stories, hieroglyphs," the vanity of which stood in the way of true piety. He condemned excessive grandiloquence as well as the widespread temptation to indulge in poetic neologisms and exotic phrasing. Nicolas Caussin, who undoubtedly knew Acquaviva's text, took the same line a few years later in 1619, criticizing his contemporaries for "trying to turn churches themselves into backdrops and sermons into theater shows."[316]

The flourishing baroque sermon thus was criticized constantly both inside and outside the Society, especially in the last quarter of the seventeenth century. A more moderate style should prevail, the skeptics argued, instead of the "grand sermon," which was often viewed as ambivalent, exaggerated, and potentially dangerous. Sforza Pallavicino, a Jesuit cardinal and a famous stylistic theorist, railed against preachers who "abandoned the cause [of Christ] on the pulpit to celebrate their own ingenuity and to reap praise." Wolfgang Rauscher, a Jesuit from Dillingen, likewise stressed that he was "averse" to the trendy "crimped" and "marvelous strange" manner of speaking and the "perverse words" of French and Italian sermons. From the Jesuits' own ranks, Louis Bourdaloue (1632–1704) was the preeminent representative of this new, pared-down, "classical" style of sermonizing. Vincent Houdry, a French preacher from the Society with extensive personal experience, was very glad to report in 1714 that sermons had become far more "methodical" than previously. In contrast to the once ubiquitous borrowing of passages from secular, even pagan authors, contemporary preachers "have made the pulpit Christian again . . . albeit less learned."[317]

These trends accelerated still more in the eighteenth century. A multifaced reform movement in preaching commenced—in the eyes of many disgruntled authors, the sermons of the baroque period were an aberration. In 1728, Pope Benedict XIII sent a letter to Spain warning of the rampant narcissism of many sermons. He also harshly criticized *conceptos* in very broad terms. Even the Jesuits who themselves had created the baroque tradition and perpetuated it until well into the Age of Enlightenment soon joined the chorus of reformers. The Spanish Jesuit Antonio Codorniu explicitly subscribed to the reformist demands in his work *El Predicador evangélico*, published in 1740. His compatriot and confrere José Francisco de Isla went so far as to write a whole book, *Crisis de los predicadores y de los sermones* (Crisis of preachers and sermons), that de Isla and many others diagnosed at the time. Codorniu is still more famous for his trenchant and satirical novel of 1758 about a fictional preacher named "Fray Gerundio de Companazas," who continued to cultivate the baroque style.[318]

The second major change inspired by humanism was to tie sermons much more closely to the text of the Bible than had been customary in the Middle Ages. Instead of the "thematic sermons" of the Middle Ages, "homilies" or "postils" were now preferred. Homiletics experts used these terms to indicate a sermon in which the content and structure were based directly on the liturgical readings from the Bible for a given day rather than focused on a given subject.[319] The Bible should no longer merely serve as an excuse for discussing a stand-alone religious subject that the sermonizer then covered with rigorous logic and multiple minor points. Instead, humanist speakers argued that sermons should above all interpret and explain the text of the Bible. Even the structure of a sermon should follow the structure of the underlying passage more closely than had been done previously. The *Constitutions* of the Society of Jesus reflected this position.[320]

Preachers in the Society of Jesus, however, often still remained faithful to the thematic model of sermons. Ludovico Carbone included in his rhetorical treatise of 1595 a detailed chapter about the "questions" or topics that a preacher might address in a sermon.[321] In 1655, António Vieira criticized the idea that the text of the Bible alone could give a sermon a sensible structure:

Today the preaching method called "giving a postil on the Gospel" [*postillar el Evangelio*] is used, whereby they take up many topics and raise many points. And whoever raises many pursuits but follows none only comes back empty handed. . . . A sermon must have one, not many subjects. If a farmer first sows wheat, and on top of the wheat sows rye, and on top of the rye sows barley, what inevitably grows? A fierce thicket, a green mess. . . . If a ship steers one course to the north, another to the east, another to the south, another to the west, how will it make its voyage?[322]

Simply following the Bible—and here Vieira returned to the key Jesuit thought—was no more than "teaching" and "interpreting," whereas a sermon should "convince" and "move." Sermons based exclusively on the Bible missed the point of the spiritual appeal that the Jesuits had foremost in mind.

Houdry was also skeptical of such "homilies"—they simply failed to pack the desired punch. He therefore was relieved to conclude that this form of sermon had been abandoned, because it was difficult to reconcile the needs of a preacher with the text as found in the Bible. Hence, the best method was completely different: every sermon should explore one—and only one—truth or theme, and the sermon should engage directly with the Bible only to the extent that it made sense to do so. With this insistence on "thematic sermons," Jesuits like Houdry also conspicuously distanced themselves from Jansenism, which had called for an outright preaching reform in which the biblical focus of sermons from the pulpit played a major part.[323]

At any rate, early modern contemporaries expected a lot of speakers. The office of preacher might accordingly be challenging. One problem was the sheer number of sermons that a successful preacher regularly had to produce. The Viennese Jesuit Ignaz Wurz wrote in 1770, "A preacher in our lands is truly far too overburdened. Composing 60, 70, even 80 sermons throughout the year is work that, if performed correctly, exceeds almost all human power."[324] Hence it was only understandable that the Jesuits produced and used aids for composing such texts. There were numerous manuals and textbooks a preacher could turn to in preparing his next sermon. There also were numerous printed collections of model sermons from which a preacher might either draw inspiration or deliver unchanged.[325] It was even whispered that a shop in Paris had stockpiled two to three thousand manuscripts of finished sermons that a clergyman could buy.[326] For those who wished to compose their own sermons, the primary focus lay on close reading and intense work with the Bible, because that was the source from which the content of a sermon was supposed to derive, even if it did not come off as a homily or postil.[327] In addition to that, one also had to constantly adduce further arguments and authorities.[328] Jesuit preachers undoubtedly read widely and in depth for this purpose—they read to preach and used the knowledge that they had just gleaned from their readings in their sermons.

Many a preacher will have gratefully used what *La bibliothèque des prédicateurs* by Father Houdry, an eight-volume reference work, put at their disposal: material on hundreds of potential sermon topics could be found there. If a preacher had planned to talk about trust in God as a guideline for Christian life in his next sermon, he could find no fewer than twenty-two pages on the topic in the *Bibliothèque* under the rubric "Confiance en Dieu": quotations from the Bible and other books, illustrative examples, suggested arrangements, and help with arguments.[329] Hence many sermons were composed de facto of excerpts from one's readings and secondhand and thirdhand quotations. That made no difference, however, and was completely normal in the eyes of contemporaries. For all the extravagance of their presentation and form, it was still the purpose of a sermon to reinforce yet again an old, ideally well-known, message.

But despite the abundance of such aids, preparing the next sermon may often have been a race against time for the preacher. Many Jesuits will have fared like José de Errada, who in 1672 worked "until 11 o'clock at night" to finish a sermon for the next day.[330] And when preparation was lacking and a Jesuit preacher first thought about his sermon when he was "putting on the vestments [for mass]" shortly beforehand, criticism and ridicule were not far behind.[331] The sermons of missionaries were a different matter. They often had neither the time nor the opportunity for long-term planning as they moved from place to place. In these circumstances, Jesuit missionaries' ability to speak extemporaneously and improvise was much more sought after, since in content and style their sermons had to adapt to their situation.[332]

What all sermons had in common, however, was the fact that, regardless of how they were prepared, everything depended on the delivery from the pulpit. A sermon was a performative act. The key factor in a sermon was its execution, the act of preaching, as many rhetorical textbooks explicitly stressed.[333] Simply reading words from a prepared text was out of the question. Preachers rather had to be capable of learning their sermons more or less by heart. A good memory was crucial for a good preacher, notwithstanding cleverly prepared notes with large writing and clearly indicated key words.[334] Nothing was more embarrassing than when a preacher lost his place on the pulpit—he was guaranteed to receive humiliating ridicule. Of course, such lapses were completely understandable: sermons in the early modern period could be very long. A speaking time of about sixty minutes was usually recommended, but even longer sermons were not uncommon. In Jülich, for example, the Jesuit missionaries spoke for an hour and a half in 1714.[335] Such extravagant speaking times often led priests to schedule their sermons from the pulpit at a time outside mass itself, so that the sermon became a distinct event in its own right.[336] In light of the length of such sermons, it was no wonder that preaching was considered a strenuous activity.[337] The "profession" of preacher exacted a heavy physical toll. It was said of Houdry that he ended his career at the age of seventy on account of worsening "weakness of voice."[338]

Common Sacraments: Confession and Communion

Sermons were not normally used in isolation in the Society of Jesus. They were rather part of a multipronged pastoral approach for large audiences, as Fr. Jakob Ernfelder reported in a letter from Alsatian Molsheim in 1581:

We preach frequently; people listen attentively and gladly follow our advice. So far, we dedicated almost everything to convincing people that piety could not be implanted again in human hearts without fairly frequent confession and communion. On Easter, the two of us heard 510 confessions. On Pentecost, we counted—which was not at all the customary anymore—84 at the table of the Lord at the first holy communion after Eastertime.[339]

Sermons, confession, and communion constituted a triad and ultimately stood on the firm ground of the Council of Trent, which had explicitly taken up all three topics. As Ernfelder admitted, though, confession and communion had ceased to play a major part in popular religious life in the early modern period. That changed with the arrival of the Jesuits.

A conventional confession in the sixteenth century was rather formal in nature.[340] Time and place were central to the practice: confession was a seasonal affair that usually occurred only once a year, at Easter, the prescribed minimum set by the Fourth Lateran Council in 1215. Confession took place seldom and certainly not in the context of an intense personal relationship between penitent and confessor. In the late Middle Ages, Catholics could largely determine for themselves to whom they wanted to confess, which presumably meant that they tended to avoid awkward personal encounters. Confession was primarily about the dutiful performance of an indispensable ritual. For the faithful, the goal of confessing was first and foremost to receive absolution from the priest at the end. One did what was necessary; there was neither reason nor occasion to think of confession as a process of self-revelation. Confession was also closely linked to the interests of the Inquisition: it was asked whether it might be a useful resource to facilitate the search for and detection of erroneous thoughts and acts. The Inquisition thus broached an understanding of confession focused primarily on its potential to detect, control, and thus repress deviance. Hence traditional, ritualistic confession was viewed with a measure of skepticism and treated like a duty that one had to perform.

The Jesuits, however, took a broader view of the purpose of confession. For them, confession was not (merely) a ritual to obtain grace and not (merely) a strategy to uncover deviants; the Jesuits viewed confession as an opportunity to disclose one's inner spiritual life to a trusted, well-known confessor, who in turn was supposed to use this occasion to give personally tailored counsel and advice as to how one should live.[341] In their eyes, confession no longer served only to mark the end of one's sinful past but also to explore the causes of that sin with an eye to improvement in the future. Going to confession had a therapeutic and pedagogical function that went beyond its sacramental and inquisitorial relevance. In their view, a confessor should always practice *caritas* (charity) and look out for the salvation of a penitent's soul.[342] In a word: the faithful should receive encouragement, solace, and fortification from confession, and not fear an accusation. "Proceeding like an inquisitor" was therefore wrong in the eyes of many Jesuits.[343]

Concretely, this pastoral conception of confession translated into a call for people to go to confession as often as possible. Frequent confession would help one realize the effects of the sacrament—one would come to know one's sins better, which in turn helped one banish mistakes. It also kept one's conscience sharp and attentive.[344] "By confessing repeatedly, one might more easily come to know oneself," as Francis Coster concluded.[345]

By the same token, this Jesuit view led to calls for a comparatively "gentle" confession procedure. The Jesuits did everything in their power to prevent confession from being a fear-inducing event. They tried to ensure to the best of their ability that people did not have reservations about coming to confession because they were afraid of the consequences of their statements. Hence, oral confession conducted as a conversation in a confessional—a form that appeared toward the end of the sixteenth century—was especially attractive to them. It created the necessary privacy for speaking openly about difficult subjects in a protected space.[346] The Jesuits refused to demand public, written recantations— as the Inquisition sometimes did—when they encountered a heretic in the confessional. They also refused to summon the Inquisition, even when they encountered details in the confessional that genuinely concerned the Sanctum Officium. Sins stayed between the penitent, his confessor, and God. Publicity was counterproductive, because it generated "shame" and dampened willingness of the faithful to carry out an honest self-investigation out of fear for their "reputation," as Paolo Segneri Jr. once noted.[347]

In this way, the confessional became the starting point and an integral part of an individual, personal, and devout process of renewal for the Jesuits, which they otherwise associated with the *Spiritual Exercises*. Accordingly, the figure of the confessor transformed from a mere dispenser of guaranteed grace to a far more intimate counselor and spiritual guide. It thus must have pleased the followers of Ignatius when, in 1591, Jacob Müller—one of their former students and an important patron of the Society of Jesus in Regensburg—proposed, expanding on some ideas of Carlo Borromeo, to hang little depictions of Christ's suffering in confessionals that might help a penitent search his conscience. In such contexts, confession and meditation merged.[348]

There moreover were connections between the *Exercises* and the Jesuit conception of confession in the special form of "general" or "whole-life" confession. This type of confession was presumably not invented by Ignatius, but its practice had become part of the *Exercises*.[349] In a sense, this form of confession amounted to a (preliminary) account of one's life.[350] The cumulative realization of all one's sins (to the present) was regarded as a cathartic experience because it increased the pain one felt on account of one's own misconduct—a positive development. Whole-life confession helped one recognize the (poor) state of one's religiosity in dramatic fashion. It therefore was good to make such general confessions more regularly, perhaps once a year. That made it possible to see progress over time, which in turn might help penitents focus their efforts on improving the particularly sinful areas of their lives. The Jesuits also viewed general confession as an important symbolic act that accompanied life-changing situations. Prostitutes had to give general confession to demonstrate their earnestness in entering one of the Society's charitable institutions, as did fellows joining Marian congregations. *Confessio generalis* came to symbolize the awakening of true piety and a pivot toward the spirituality of the Society.

Whole-life confession in particular presupposed thorough self-knowledge. But in general, confessions from which sins were omitted were regarded as defective. Preachers from the Society accordingly always warned in very traditional fashion that forgotten sins invalidated a confession.[351] Because this problem continued to bother the Jesuits, Ignatius gave instructions for how one could visually represent the sins one had uncovered by drawing lines of varying lengths on a paper.[352] The Jesuits are reported to have used such lists to keep track of their own sins.[353] Every day when people examined their consciences, Vincenzo Bruno noted, they might also take notes about the sins they had uncovered.[354] In the process, the Jesuits adapted to penitents' local conditions and capabilities: in Peru, newly baptized indigenous people were expressly advised to use their traditional form of writing, knotted quipus, to record their sins.[355]

With such guidelines in their mental baggage, thousands of Jesuits in the early modern period got to work, hearing confession from countless people in Europe and the New World. They were advised to be in the confessional early in the morning, especially on Sundays and holidays, "because it is disgraceful and unbecoming to keep the penitents waiting long."[356] And that was absolutely necessary advice because on innumerable occasions Jesuits reported from their everyday pastoral life that they heard confession from morning to evening without interruption for days and weeks on end and still were not done. The faithful normally went to confession after the Jesuits had preached or taught catechism— these different forms of pastoral care were seamlessly connected.[357] The Jesuits were especially pleased when individuals who had not confessed in years at last did so under their direction. The Jesuits constantly emphasized that they raised not only the frequency but also the quality of confession—it was thanks to their work that people had ceased to give confession "sacrilegiously."[358] Prior to the Jesuits' arrival, some had (allegedly) "never confessed correctly." By confessing "correctly" to the Jesuits, "they put their lives back in order," as one individual noted.[359] Confession gave people "long desired, but previously unattained peace of mind," which led to the "consolation of souls" or to a "joyous spirit" and "the greatest peace."[360] The Jesuits, moreover, were often psychologically astute enough to recognize that people in such moments of existential renewal might overshoot the goal in their enthusiasm. They therefore refused to permit people to make long-term vows and promises in confession itself or in the glow of absolution.[361] In this way, the Jesuits balanced pastoral pragmatism and realism with their great confidence in the consolatory, admonitory, and cathartic purpose of the sacraments. Confession was a start, but it by no means guaranteed a new life.

None of that, obviously, precluded the Jesuits from resorting to coercion in certain situations—even they neither could nor would break completely with the repressive and disciplinary function of confession in the early modern period. "Force" was certainly combined with confession among the Jesuits—even on a massive scale—at least when people fundamentally refused to go to confession at all.[362] Ignatius's men advocated the use of so-called *schedulae confessionis*, written documents that confirmed one had gone to confession within the obligatory time period, thus supporting the authorities' efforts to enforce mandatory confession.[363] It would be remiss to downplay these aspects of the Jesuits' confessional practice. But despite their support for these control measures, we still find that the Jesuits were interested primarily in other aspects of confession; their focus lay clearly on the new uplifting and consoling pastoral use of confession.

The consoling and encouraging conception of confession that the Jesuits advocated continually gained ground.[364] Yet the seventeenth and eighteenth centuries still witnessed heavy criticism of the Jesuits' "gentle" and pedagogical confessional practice. The rigorist Jansenists wanted to take much stricter action than the "lax" Jesuits. They first targeted the frequency of absolution: penitents had to possess "all-surpassing," "extraordinary" love of God before they could be absolved—but that was hard to attain and even harder to confirm. Restraint therefore was the prime directive.[365] Contritionists like Jean Neercassel, for example, the apostolic vicar in the Netherlands and a declared enemy of the Jesuits, demanded in their sermons: "Catholics should go to confession only two or three times a year and should be more concerned that they show an act of true contrition."[366]

The Jesuits vehemently opposed such rigorist severity. But they also found themselves asking how they might ensure that the effect of conversion—which in their view confession brought about rather than presupposed—would last. The textbook writers therefore set penitents on their way with a series of suggestions for how they might avoid sin in the future.[367] By far the most effective means of extending the grace imparted by confession was, in the eyes of many Jesuit confessors, the practice of receiving communion regularly. In general, confession and communion were closely linked, since it was theoretically possible to receive the Eucharist only after one had confessed.

The practice of receiving communion was handled in a wide variety of ways over the history of the church.[368] In the ancient church, communion was often taken frequently, even daily. This went completely out of style, however, in the High and late Middle Ages even though prominent theologians—Peter Lombard, Thomas Aquinas, Vincent Ferrer, Girolamo Savonarola—recommended that one often approach the altar. The Fourth Lateran Council of 1215 found it necessary to require every Catholic to take communion at least once a year on threat of excommunication. In light of this, calls to receive communion more regularly became a hallmark of church and devotional reformers.[369] The *Imitatio Christi*, which Ignatius himself had read so closely, was decidedly in favor of frequent communion.[370] In the sixteenth century, Francisco de Osuna, Juan de Ávila, and Luis de Granada also declared in favor of frequent communion. Spanish Jesuits were heavily influenced by these thoughts and soon brought them to Italy, where they found a local tradition of frequent communion already in place. The new orders of the Barnabites and Oratorians were also open to it.

Almost from the get-go, the Jesuits set out more or less in solidarity to defend and promote this practice broadly. Many of the congregations they founded practiced frequent communion.[371] Wherever the Jesuits went, "frequent confession and communion were introduced."[372] Nicolás Bobadilla and Cristóbal de Madrid were the first to articulate the significance of frequent communion in theological terms.[373] Many other Jesuit theologians subsequently wrote about the subject, including Francisco de Toledo. The Jesuits insisted on regularly receiving communion because they viewed it as "food for the soul," a defense against human frailty that gave one strength and courage. It was "medicine that purged sin and fortified virtue." Communion, the Jesuits were convinced, was effective per se because Christ was immediately present and "imparted . . . the life of grace on those eating it." Communion brought the believer into the life-giving body of Christ himself—Christ had said, after all, that he was the "bread of life" (John 6:58). In a certain sense, the Jesuits therefore saw no reason to deprive the faithful of communion—excepting the extreme case in which a person had committed a mortal sin for which he (still) had not received absolution. Cristóbal de Madrid accordingly concluded: "Receiving the most holy eucharist from the love of Christ is more useful and profitable than abstaining for fear of irreverence."

Of course, the Jesuits' adversaries and opponents of frequent communion saw things completely differently. In their view, it was *precisely* the unworthiness of most people at most times that should prevent them from going to communion in good conscience. Fear of placing the host in unworthy hands and mouths ruled out frequent communion in their eyes. Abstaining from receiving the sacrament at the altar was a sensible act of penance. The dignity of the Eucharist—and ultimately the dignity of Christ—was more important than any conceivable positive consequences for the faithful. Communion (and confession) presumed the genuine inner conversion. Whenever and as long as that remained in doubt, opponents of frequent communion argued, the Eucharist should be withheld.

Again, it was above all the Jansenists and rigorists who used such arguments against the Jesuits to plead against frequent communion in the seventeenth and eighteenth centuries. The Abbé de Saint-Cyran had previously emphasized that one should not only delay absolution until true *contritio* but also forgo communion—whether as an act of penance or to prepare for and ensure true remorse.[374] But it was Antoine Arnauld's work *De la fréquente communion*, which appeared in 1643 at just under a thousand pages, that became Port-Royal's decisive declaration *against* frequent communion. Without the necessary strictness and restraint, "this holy flesh" would become "poison," Arnauld argued.[375]

This widely read book unleashed a storm of literary polemic that lasted for years. While the Jesuits stressed that the communicant need not be perfect, because the Eucharist helped him to a better state of piety and would "soften his heart," their opponents thought that only someone who was already far along the path to salvation should receive communion. For Arnauld, the Eucharist was predicated on grace; for the Jesuits, it was a reinforcement.[376] Arnauld had as little understanding for the encouraging, fortifying, and healing power of the Eucharist as Saint-Cyran. On the contrary, they both utilized deprivation of communion for pastoral purposes, to encourage the faithful to convert. In everyday pastoral terms, that amounted to limiting access to the Eucharist.

What exactly "frequent" communion meant, meanwhile, was interpreted in a variety of ways within the Society of Jesus. Bobadilla supported daily communion. De Madrid was more reserved and opted for weekly communion as a rule, and this line became the dominant policy. Polanco also supported receiving the sacraments with only "moderate frequency" in 1550. Nadal was of a similar opinion, and in the seventeenth century Jesuit pastors and moral theologians also favored weekly communion.[377] This was a cautious compromise because daily communion—let alone communion several times a day—was often viewed as a symptom of heterodoxy.[378] Daily communion nonetheless remained a possibility in the Society. De Toledo, for example, supported daily communion for advanced believers whose piety was characterized by special "love" for God and the sacrament.[379] His position was taken up in 1632 by the Spanish Jesuit Juan Perlín, who had long served as a missionary in Peru.[380] Again and again, those engaged in active ministry stressed that they omitted no occasion of offering communion to the faithful.[381]

In the early modern period, taking communion was *not* synonymous with attending mass. Communion was often completely independent of mass.[382] Men and women usually went to communion separately.[383] According to Catholic practice, the Eucharist was almost always distributed in one form, namely, bread; in contrast to Protestant practice, the cup of wine was not normally offered. Although Jesuits in confessional border regions and conflict zones sporadically permitted both forms of communion—which would have facilitated rapprochement with the Protestants—Rome remained opposed.[384] The Jesuits adopted this position as their own and tried in their various places of deployment to win even the Lutherans over to the Catholic practice.[385] To encourage the laity to go to communion, the Jesuits resolutely tried to overcome the pangs of conscience and "anxieties" that a Jansenist pastor would have only reinforced.[386] Often elaborate and laborious publicity was necessary. In the Eichsfeld region, the practice of taking communion had become so uncommon that the Jesuits had to go "door to door" to convince people to go in the late sixteenth century.[387] Even in later times, "house visits" were often essential for impressing on the laity the importance of communion.[388] Whether the faithful ever realized the spiritual value of communion that the Jesuits so prominently attached to it remains doubtful at the very least—it sometimes seems as if communicants in many places had to be motivated to take the sacrament with the prospect of the indulgences associated with it.[389] And generally it appears that people were especially interested in going to communion when other incentives beyond receiving the Eucharist were present. Religious festivals, which attracted large numbers of spectators, were such occasions that the Jesuits capitalized on for communion.[390] Processions inspired by the plague may also have helped motivate people to attend the celebration of the liturgy and the Eucharist.[391]

The Jesuits were proud of the crowds they could inspire to take communion. They viewed the number of communicants as direct evidence of the success of their overall pastoral efforts—if catechism was taught well and sermons delivered effectively, the frequency of both confession and communion would rise.[392] Since the number of hosts distributed could easily be counted, thus indicating annual trends, communion numbers became a very important barometer for the Jesuits' ministry. The Jesuits thus noted fairly precisely in the uplifting reports they sent to Rome how many thousands or tens of thousands of hosts had been distributed. Even if we do not entirely trust the numbers, the Jesuits undoubtedly enjoyed some success. In 1615, the people of Munich— viewed statistically—received communion on average five times a year; in 1690, it was seven times a year. In Ingolstadt, the number of times one received the Eucharist allegedly quintupled over the same period.[393] Frequent confession and frequent communion became a mass phenomenon that made it easy to identify active Christians. At least some believers were so inspired by the support and encouragement they received from their confessors that they wanted to keep such a "spiritual director" with them at all times.

Jesuits as "Spiritual Directors":
Long-Term Pastoral Connections

Theologians of the sixteenth and seventeenth centuries—and first and foremost, albeit not exclusively, the Jesuits—viewed the spiritual formation of an individual believer as an extraordinarily complex process that required hard work on oneself and extensive, difficult self-criticism; they accordingly came to view the sanctification of life as a long-term project. By the mid-sixteenth century, it was considered desirable to have a personal companion on this long journey. Thus, a new religious figure gradually came into being. He was very similar to the confessor but differed by virtue of his considerably closer and longer-lasting connection to his clientele: the spiritual director. Spiritual directors met with their protégés frequently, conducted deep conversations with them, or—and we encounter this especially often in the early modern period—corresponded with them by letter. A director suggested ways in which his protégés might experience spiritual growth; he gave solace and encouragement and set an example with his own pious way of life. Spiritual directors had to be familiar enough with the inner life of their protégés so that they could address their specific desires, character traits, and specific personal circumstances; directeurs and their protégés led "related lives."[394] Such mentors also gave their advisees an outsider's perspective and had the advantage of the cumulative experience of a professional observer, enabling them to catch loopholes and dead ends before they were taken, nip negative developments in the bud, and admonish protégés whose religious progress had stagnated. A spiritual director shared in his protégés' suffering and yet gazed critically on their lives from the outside. In light of this close and long-lasting connection, these relationships often transformed into "spiritual friendships," which, however, were by no means exempt from hierarchical considerations, as is apparent from the titles that were conferred on such mentors. Contemporaries regularly described them as "angels" and often also as a "new Moses," a "doctor," or one "blessed with sight in the land of the blind." The directeur spirituel played the part of the teacher guiding obedient, inquisitive students.[395]

The Jesuits neither invented nor developed the practice alone.[396] The concept of spiritual counsel (*consilium*) had already emerged in the High Middle Ages, which is why early modern Europe produced so many important and famous people, men and women alike, from outside the Society of Jesus who had performed this function: people like Teresa of Ávila, François de Sales, and Vincent de Paul or, in Protestant territory, Johann Arndt, Johann Gerhard, and Jakob Philipp Spener. Drawing inspiration from these great figures of Christian devotional history and in collaboration with them, the Jesuits invested even greater resources in this demanding form of pastoral care. They made this "work on their interior" their own.[397] Starting with Ignatius and his personal account of his spiritual growth, the Jesuits had a particular interest in the rigor and methodology of such long-lasting spiritual aid.

How that might play out is illustrated by the guidebook and manual composed by the Jesuit François Guilloré in 1671, in which he sought to give some helpful tips for successful spiritual direction. Guilloré was pursuing a very ambitious goal. His book and spiritual advising itself were "not for people who are already content with living well." Rather, his book and the process of spiritual direction were addressed to "people who are stirred by a desire for sanctity."[398] These were people who wanted to grow in their "inner lives." Spiritual direction was not a pastoral practice that aimed to affect people en masse—in contrast to missions, sermons, and regular communion.

Guilloré often called the recipients of such spiritual counsel "penitents." That already indicates that he conceived of *direction* first and foremost as the correction, improvement, and molding of a pious mindset and attitude. The penitents should learn to overcome themselves and their own will (*abnégation*); they should exercise prescribed acts of devotion (prayer, communion, ascetic exercises); and they should especially "withdraw from the world," which Guilloré wanted them to achieve with days of retreat (*retraites*). Such retreats forged a direct link to the pastoral practice of lay exercises. In light of this molding function, Guilloré defined spiritual direction as a "rule" to which one's protégés should submit. It was a kind of spiritual "slavery and captivity."[399] *Direction* was synonymous with voluntarily giving up one's own will and freedom. The

Jesuits characteristically observed that this religious molding of personality was ultimately an individual affair for which one had to accommodate the penitents' precise needs. Ignatius of Loyola himself had stressed that the *Spiritual Exercises* should be adapted to practitioners' circumstances and needs in every single case.[400] Standing in this tradition, Guilloré viewed spiritual direction as a process that should be geared toward each advisee's "temperament, talent, and inner constitution."[401]

Not everyone could or had to make the highest degree of perfection their goal.[402] Guilloré, like his contemporaries, distinguished between normal and "eminent" souls. Some people were endowed with special, God-given "gifts." When a *directeur* encountered someone with such eminent gifts, then heights of religious attainment far beyond the pious norm became possible. As we have seen, the word "mysticism" must be used with care in connection with the Jesuit order—Guilloré, for example, wanted to prohibit "eminent souls" in particular from perusing mystic literature.[403] But serving as spiritual advisers for such "eminent souls" was one context in which the Society of Jesus came into increasingly close contact with mystic forms of belief. Such contact was both a great opportunity and a considerable risk for all parties involved. The pastoral practice of *direction spirituelle* presumed that mystic grace was fundamentally possible, and probably every *directeur* hoped at least a little to discover gifted people under his care. The director's task was then to mold and channel the abilities of such protégés as their "guardian" (*gardien*).[404]

There are numerous examples of relationships between Jesuits and such "eminent souls." In 1579, the Jesuit Andrea Rossi cultivated a spiritual friendship with Camilla Travaglia in Florence. Rossi and several other Jesuits there also served as spiritual guides for a future saint, the young Maria Maddalena de' Pazzi.[405] The Jesuits involved both were impressed by and benefited from their protégés' spiritual attainment. Travaglia experienced "ecstasy" and "revelations" in Florence, contemporaries report. Rossi was captivated by Travaglia's peculiar mystical abilities. Often such relationships resulted in a reciprocal give-and-take. This is illustrated in the case of another, far more famous spiritual duo that we have already met once before: Achille Gagliardi and Isabella Berinzaga.[406] As with Rossi, here too we see how heavily the Jesuit director was impressed and influenced by his charge's spiritual experiences. Gagliardi made note of Berinzaga's religious growth, which he was able to observe up close as her spiritual director. He did so initially for himself but later transformed his records into a series of epoch-making devotional treatises—a case of spiritual-literary teamwork.[407] The spiritually productive relationship between Marguerite-Marie Alacoque and her Jesuit confessors also fits this type.

Taking such scenarios of spiritual direction to mystical extremes was thus not a rare phenomenon, but it also was hardly the norm. The substance of most of these long-term religious mentoring relationships was far less spectacular. For an example, we may turn to the letters that the Jesuit Louis Le Valois wrote his spiritual protégé Bernardin Gigault, Marquis de Bellefonds (1630–94).[408] Bellefonds was marshal of the French army, a hardened soldier who fought for Louis XIV. On the whole, he was interested in how he might "piously preserve our health for serving God" with his spiritual director's advice. Hence Le Valois constantly exhorted his protégé not to let his very worldly life make him lose sight of his true goal and the important hierarchies between earthly and heavenly existence. In order for Bellefonds to reach his goal, Le Valois gave a kind of running religious commentary on the marquis's life. When Bellefonds was sick, Le Valois wrote of the necessity of always preparing for death and the beyond. When Bellefonds received a new rank or a new title, the Jesuit pointedly refused to show joy or to extend congratulations, but instead urged Bellefonds to cultivate the one true joy, actions pleasing to God. When Bellefonds traveled to court in Versailles, the Jesuit reminded him in his corresponding letter that the court and Christian life were incompatible, and suggested daily meditations on relevant topics. At the turn of the new year, Le Valois proposed a mutual commitment to prayer: Bellefonds should pray that the Jesuit might love his poverty (more), and in return Le Valois would pray that the wealthy nobleman might scorn the treasures of the world. Le Valois regularly addressed his correspondent very frankly, giving advice, for example, about the frequency of communion or warning Bellefonds about specific dangers in his current situation. Sometimes he appealed to Bellefonds as a general and exhorted him to convert his soldiers. However important Bellefonds's service to king and country might be, he should nonetheless always recognize service to God and his own salvation as his most important reference points and conduct himself accordingly. In terms of ascetic discipline, the Jesuit preferred moderation. In tone, Le Valois's letters admonished in broad strokes: he did not normally criticize Bellefonds's actions in detail. Only in the event of an emergency did the spiritual director threaten the general with open criticism. There are no spiritual, mystic heights to be found in their letters. In closing, the Jesuit conceived of his spiritual correspondence with Bellefonds as an ongoing conversation about an ongoing project of Christian living that never completely came to an end.

In all of this, Le Valois did not overestimate his own influence. Sometimes he was forced to admit, "I am not informed of the disposition of your heart and the state of your health."[409] Despite their personal nature, the letters between Le Valois and the marquis maintain a certain distance. In other relationships of spiritual direction, in contrast, social boundaries and distinctions of status threatened to collapse altogether. When the Jesuit confessor of Lucrezia Barberini, Duchess of Modena, died in 1679, she wrote:

> Even if I could put my entire heart, which is full of tears, in this letter, it would not be enough to express my extreme dismay at this very heavy blow that God has dealt me in depriving my soul of my confessor. [My soul] has become an orphan and is in the greatest need. Turning to God, I say to Him: Divine Providence, You who in a particular way gave me a father who fit my soul so perfectly, why do You deprive me of him now? . . . Extend his life and give me death, so that I may have his holy support as I die.[410]

Lucrezia lost one of the mainstays of her life with the death of her confessor.

Such close relationships, verging on dependency, could also have less edifying side effects. Sometimes, a close spiritual directorship might drive a Jesuit confessor right out of the company of his confreres. Juan de Prádanos, the spiritual director of the Duchess Magdalena de Ulloa in Valladolid, was one such case. One of his confreres complained, "He no longer eats at the prescribed hour with the rest of us, and he also does not eat what we all eat. He has to eat at least 20 ounces of meat every day along with half a roasted hen that Lady Magdalena provides him. Appetizers and dessert and everything else must be the best one can find."[411] Superiors in the Society constantly feared not only that spiritual direction might overshoot the mark in material terms, as here, but also that it might lead to inappropriate intimacy. Even if sexual encounters between spiritual directors and their female protégés were probably uncommon, scrupulous care was taken to ensure that the close spiritual relationships that Jesuit confessors often entered into stayed within accepted social boundaries. Whenever Jesuits conducted their relationships with female penitents in such a way that gave rise to rumors, whether intentionally or not, the superiors intervened energetically. Jakob de Vos, for example, a Jesuit and missionary in the Netherlands, was repeatedly warned in 1682 that he should be more cautious in attending to his circle of female devotees: "His relationship with some pious women became ever more intense. He dined luxuriously with them. Three or four times, or indeed still more often, he kept company with them in the evening or at night. After dinner was over, after laughter and jokes, they even played cards."[412] In De Vos's case, as with Prádanos a century earlier, a pastoral relationship had become a social affair. Spiritual intimacy was not only supplemented but sometimes even overridden by the pleasures of companionship. There was a fine line between permissible and objectionable intimacy.

In light of these sundry aspects, spiritual direction was a demanding responsibility. Not all members of the Society and not all priests were equally suited for it. Rather, individual Jesuits became sought-after authorities of considerable renown in this area—spiritual directors gradually emerged as specialists, for which specialized practical literature soon appeared, complete with instructions and ready-made exercises for tutees. Handbooks like the one composed by François Guilloré were used and copied in the process of spiritual direction, gaining immediate spiritual and pastoral relevance in everyday life.[413] The special challenges of spiritual direction, however, also meant that it could not simply be extended to the masses as such. Parish priests, for example, who had extensive pastoral duties, could not advise all their flock in such an intensive way. People began to complain that there were too few spiritual directors and too many laymen without one.[414] Other forms of spiritual direction more suited to the masses had to be found.

Pastoral Care as Mission: Conversion Campaigns in Europe

It was pouring rain when the Jesuit Paolo Segneri Jr. spoke before a large crowd in a meadow one evening in northern Italy in early June 1712. He praised the patience and steadfastness of his audience, given the weather.[415] But he also had come with a special proposal: he wanted to make a pact, an agreement (*accordo*) with them. The purpose of this proposed alliance was as ambitious as it was fundamental: Segneri and his audience, he said, wanted and indeed should attain paradise. But, Segneri stressed, the inhabitants of Modena and neighboring regions could never be certain that they would make it. He could see many shortcomings. One of the main purposes of his visit in 1712 was to "show the ugliness of sin." His listeners should stop "joking" with God and instead take warnings to change their lives seriously. Many times, Segneri spelled out to people "the necessity of converting, of converting now, without postponing indefinitely." He worked at "stirring the emotions [of people] toward our savior in various ways."

On his own testimony, Segneri came to the people of Modena and environs as an "ambassador of God." His presence in northern Italy was a "holy mission"; he viewed himself as a "missionary." This choice of words shows how the Jesuits considered the conversion of non-Christians overseas and efforts to reinforce the faith among nominally Christian peoples of Europe to be different facets of one and the same mission. The Jesuits were reviving earlier efforts in this instance, as well: since the preaching campaigns of the late medieval mendicant orders, pious clergymen had come around to the view that Europe itself was still missionary territory. Therefore, in the fourteenth and fifteenth centuries, men like Vincent Ferrer and Bernardino of Siena crisscrossed often seriously neglected regions of Europe, where they provided for a better understanding of and grounding in Christianity with sermons and catechesis.[416] The Reformation and ensuing Catholic revival only intensified this negative perception of the spiritual backwaters of Europe.[417] Churchmen looked with dismay at the religious condition of the population. Diego Ximenes, secretary of the Society, duly remarked in 1596 in a confidential letter to Pope Clement VIII: "Of the more than 100,000 people living above the gates of Rome in the hills from Tivoli through all Abruzzo, you will scarcely find fifteen or twenty thousand who have explicit faith [fede esplicita], which they must have in order to be saved."[418] Hardly any difference from the Americas or Asia could be seen—Sicily, Brittany, and the mountains of Spain were even regarded as a "European India." Wave after wave of missionaries therefore washed over rural and urban Europe, seeking to fight a "military battle against sin."[419] From the start, large numbers of Jesuits took part in this project with great enthusiasm.

In essence, Ignatius himself was the prototypical Jesuit missionary in Europe. He left Paris for home for the last time in 1535 and dedicated himself to bringing spiritual reform and a new spiritual focus to Azpeitia and environs.[420] The months he spent wandering with his early companions after they put off their trip to Palestine in 1537, first in northern Italy and then from Venice to Rome, were also characterized by more or less lengthy stops in villages and towns where Ignatius and the others pursued their pastoral agenda.[421] Some of the first companions clung to this ideal their entire lives—Nicolás Bobadilla in particular spent decades as a preacher and wandering minister in central and southern Italy.[422] The early missionary work of the Jesuit Silvestro Landini (1503?–54) on Corsica and Capraia was even more influential and controversial than Bobadilla's.[423] Wandering Jesuits like Bobadilla and Landini did not initially view their work as distinct—they did nothing different from what their confreres did in the cities; the difference was merely that they were much more mobile, sought out the most remote settlements, and so had to cultivate a more transient lifestyle. Missions initially were often nothing more than a case-by-case, spontaneous, and improvised expansion of the usual ministries.[424]

The first half of the seventeenth century bore witness to significant refinement of the Jesuit way of proceeding in terms of specialization, systematization, and methodology. Systematic reflections on the European mission began to crop up.[425] In 1590, General Acquaviva issued the first of several groundbreaking instructions intended to ensure that salvation was also brought to people living in the countryside.[426] He prescribed a specific procedure. The mission began with official notification of the local worthies. The missionary's arrival was thus announced and anticipated long in advance.[427] Acquaviva instructed the missionaries to hold a series of sermons and give catechetical instruction in various localities. They could also give further theological or spiritual training to local parish clergy, insofar as it was needed and feasible.[428] The mission thus morphed into a carefully choreographed and staged act of communication.[429] The missionary had to be particularly well-suited to these tasks and trained in the necessary skills.

Processions became an increasingly important element of these European missions. The Jesuits expressly involved the laity in their preparation and execution. The jointly arranged event thus served to tighten the bond between the missionaries and their message and the laity.[430] After circa 1610, processions became closely associated with corporal penitential practices, especially self-flagellation, even outside of Italy. The practice of publicly whipping oneself had once been popular in the Middle Ages but had lapsed into desuetude in many places. Jesuits like Edmond Auger in Paris, Jakob Gretser and Konrad Vetter in Augsburg, and Sertorio Caputo in southern Italian L'Aquila then began— cautiously, but deliberately—promoting corporal penitential practices around 1580. Jesuit missionaries then openly advocated self-flagellation as the next century dawned, for example, by having local cobblers prepare a large supply of whips.[431]

Missions were a spectacle in other ways, too. Dialogues between missionaries and skulls or crosses on the pulpit were popular, as was the clever use of light and darkness. For example, the missionaries might drape the pulpit, church, or cathedra in black. Missionaries also often appeared with a noose around their neck. A complex psychology of faith underpinned such elaborate staging and such theatrical events.[432] The goal was "to strike the people with these spectacles and make the love of Our Lord enter them through the senses right down to the heart."[433] Every human sense had the potential to receive the truths of faith: "We are so crude and corporeal that we are not satisfied when the revelations of the lessons of the Gospel enter through the gateway of the ears but not through that of the eyes. And the sense of sight is so privileged that it not only brings visible sensations more promptly to the soul but also engraves and impresses them more fixedly on it," wrote one experienced missionary from Spain.[434] The Jesuits therefore did everything in their power to make people's eyes serve their purposes. In general terms, the missionaries relied on the pedagogical utility of dramatic surprise. The shock effect of fear was regarded as a pedagogical means that "brought the heart to contrition more easily."[435] Missionaries used direct, provocative appeals to their audiences—"Could you unexpectedly die tonight?" (in a state of sin)—to transform the objective drama of the message into a personal feeling of urgency.[436] This appeal to the emotions of the laity was heightened by the use of binary messages: this life/afterlife, present/eternity, guilt/mercy, sin/forgiveness, light/dark, compassion and love/ignorance and contempt for Christ were favorite antitheses that the missionaries used to explain Christianity and inspire action.[437]

By the seventeenth century, all these elements had converged in a well-conceived and, increasingly, well-articulated method. Popular missions consisted of set pieces that the audience actively expected. Over the long term, this turned the "missionary" into a specialist in the Society, an expert in a field in which colleagues could not simply be thrust without further ado.[438] For all this methodological refinement, however, we still cannot overlook the fact that missionaries had to possess one important skill in particular: the gift of improvisation. Texts and procedures constantly had to be adapted to local conditions. Missionaries also constantly had to anticipate unanticipated, ad hoc problems of a physical nature, such as scarcity of lumber for building altars or stages, or bad weather.[439] In light of these factors, we should highlight the Jesuit missionaries' impressive ability to adapt to local conditions and improvise. And yet despite the rise of specialization, some Jesuits were still driven to serve as missionaries without all this "professional" support. He had spontaneously followed a "sudden inner impulse," Philipp Jeningen said of his unsystematic efforts in the little village of Dalkingen in 1687.[440] Much at the missions not only looked improvised, but also was.

Around 1700, propelled by these developments, the Society reached the pinnacle of its European missionary efforts. A new generation of notable missionaries became celebrities. The French Jesuit Julien Maunoir, who carried the Catholic faith to the remotest corners of Brittany for forty-three years and in 393 individual missions, received international recognition for his success.[441] His contemporary and the most important innovator for the mission in 1700 was Paolo Segneri the Elder (1624–94), who traveled for years in northern Italy with several companions. Segneri perfected the famous penitential processions that featured collective self-flagellation. These penitential practices revolved around Jesus Christ and the story of the Passion—practitioners aspired to reenact Jesus's deeds collectively and at the same time appreciate his sacrifice fully by feeling it themselves. The believers' willingness to engage in self-mortification and their spontaneous weeping—even if it was deliberately triggered by the missionaries—were regarded as "practical confirmation" of the earnestness of their new religious feelings.[442] In good biblical tradition, the blood they shed was thought to seal the faithful's new relationship with God.[443]

Segneri was also the first missionary who began to whip himself while preaching, beginning around 1670.[444] The self-flagellating Jesuit became an anticipated element of every mission in Italy. When Segneri reached certain passages in many of his sermons, he let his vestment drop and began to whip his own back, ideally with a cross in his hand to underscore the connection to Christ. In this way, he placed himself as a sinner on a par with the parishioners and posed as an example of profound contrition and remorse in the hope of inspiring collective emulation.

As this example makes especially clear, Jesuit missions were interactive affairs between the individual missionary and the mass of believers. The collective participation of the laity was supposed to bring individuals to accept truths of the faith in their own everyday lives. The missionaries' exhortations, which shifted from the "I" of the missionary to the "we" of the audience and finally to the "I" of every individual, frequently and exemplarily reflect this structure (figs. 7 and 8).[445]

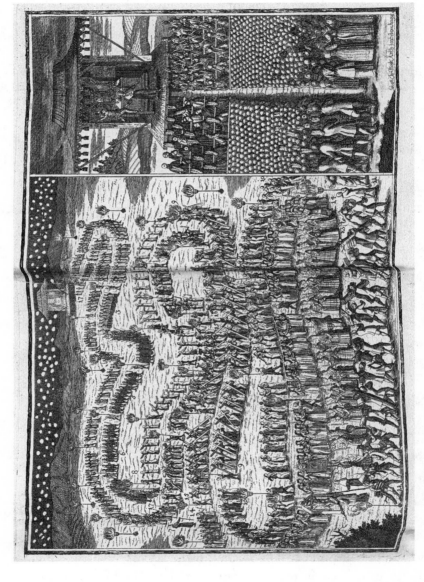

FIGURE 7. Penitential sermons and processions, with self-flagellation, were important elements of Jesuit missions in Europe. Copperplate engraving by Johann Christoph Kolb, ca. 1720. © Bayerische Staatsbibliothek München, Cgm 2624#Beibd.76 a.

FIGURE 8. A missionary with props preaches to a captivated
urban crowd of penitent faithful atop an improvised stage.
Contemporary etching, illustration taken from Louis Châtellier,
La religion des pauvres (Paris 1993).

Segneri also developed the idea of a "central mission." The missionaries did not make every place the focus of a mission in the same way.
They established themselves in a village or city that then served as a
missionary hub for the surrounding area for approximately a week.
With the help of local priests and chaplains, the inhabitants of the surrounding settlements would be led in processions to this central location, where they would come into contact with the mission (i.e., not in
their home settlements).[446] General Acquaviva had proposed a similar
structure to open up territory for missions in 1599,[447] but it was Segneri

who first perfected the combination of temporary centrality and mobile missionary operations. This method became standard for the Jesuits—Alphonsus Ligouri and the Redemptorists he subsequently founded were the first to turn against it and actually try to send missionaries everywhere.[448]

Even the fact that people harbored deep distrust of flagellation outside Italy changed nothing about Segneri's preeminence.[449] His method enjoyed widespread popularity. Jerónimo López introduced the practice to Spain, where the future superior general Tirso González and later, in the eighteenth century, the great Pedro de Calatayud used it.[450] There were successors north of the Alps, too: Duchess Maria Anna of Jülich, a Habsburg by birth, began financing Jesuit missions in Düsseldorf in 1690, and the Italian method was introduced to the Lower Rhine some two decades later under the next duchess, Anna Maria Luisa, a Medici by birth. There, the Jesuits Konrad Herdegen and Georg Loferer adopted a method that borrowed heavily from Segneri for the first time in 1715. Roughly contemporaneously, beginning in 1705, Segneri's loyal helper Flavio Fontana imported the Italian method to Austria, Bavaria, Switzerland, and the Upper Palatinate. He did so at first, remarkably, despite not knowing German, so that his sermons had to be translated sentence for sentence.[451]

As the practice peaked around 1700, criticism also set in. The Benedictine Mauro Alessandro Lazzarelli, for example, complained in 1713 that, with their "pomp" and grandiose appearance, as if at a "ball," the missionaries put whole cities in a "state of agitation" (*stato violento*).[452] "Totally calm," more contemplative alternatives stood at the ready in the form of the Lazarists and other newly founded missionary orders.[453] Self-flagellation in particular came in for heavy criticism in many places, as authorities viewed it as a public nuisance rather than a reasonable religious practice. The elector of Bavaria repeatedly prohibited this missionary practice in the eighteenth century. The fact that the Jesuits constantly flouted such bans undoubtedly roused the authorities' displeasure.[454] Jansenist and enlightened circles strictly rejected flagellation as a form of religious experience.[455] Many authorities also frowned on the Jesuits' practice of holding important parts of their missions in the evening or in the dark at night—partly to heighten the drama, but also quite pragmatically out of respect for working hours—on account of their general mistrust of nighttime activities.[456] Some members of the Society itself also recognized the need for radical change.[457] Ignaz Parhamer's famous mission in Salzburg (1754–58) was an important model of a more reserved, less theatrical approach.[458] In 1766, the Jesuits in the Eifel region also abandoned many of the traditional effects.[459] But such reform efforts remained piecemeal. The Jesuits often found it extremely difficult to adapt their once so successful strategy of transmitting the faith to changed circumstances. That put the Society considerably at odds with the spirit of the times.[460] In 1767, the enlightened ministers Kaunitz and Firmian suppressed the missions in Milan entirely as public nuisances.[461] The exuberant devotion of the Jesuit missions was now considered "Pharisaic" and should make way for a "regulated" and "enlightened devotion" in the style of Muratori.[462]

"And what about the people?" one might ask in conclusion. How did they feel about these temporary, unconventional, fiery missions, which played out as a kind of shock therapy? The Jesuits' own reports regularly sing a paean of praise for the successful missionaries. But we can often tell—and by no means only by reading between the lines—that the intensification of Christian religious fervor hardly received undivided attention everywhere. Again and again, Julien Maunoir discovered that villagers had not even realized that missionaries were there.[463] Missions were sometimes received with open scorn, as for instance when bystanders made themselves crowns of thorns with ridiculous objects to parody penitential processions.[464] Some missionaries could produce comprehensive lists of excuses that people used to explain why they kept away from the missions—lack of time or too great a distance were favorite pretenses.[465] Even obvious failures also constantly manifest themselves. Philipp Jeningen in Swabia, like Julien Maunoir in Brittany, was pelted with stones several times, driven away, and nearly beaten to death because of "mistrust."[466] In the mountains near Salzburg in 1731, the missionaries even got into a brawl with farmers, in which the Jesuits themselves "threatened to strike one person in the face with an actually outstretched open hand."[467] By no means all members of a church community were raring to perform penitential practices or even watch them.[468] Parents in Brittany forbade their children to attend catechism class.[469]

At first glance, one might explain away such failures by arguing that the missions were imposed from outside and carried out by strangers. It was often public authorities or bishops who invited the Jesuits and then supported the mission materially by providing supplies and infrastructure—the streets and alleys of Jülich were improved in 1715, in anticipation of the event.[470] Neither the local clergy nor especially the local laity had as much of a say in initiating missions or choosing their format or theme. Popular missions thus were often regarded as events that were planned and directed by officials for the purpose of controlling the lay population.[471] That would seemingly be a good explanation for popular resistance to them. But just as we cannot completely dismiss this interpretation, we likewise cannot unequivocally accept it. A close reading of the reports and documents shows that Jesuit missionaries sometimes very shrewdly and liberally catered to the thought patterns, religious practices, and basic convictions of the laity. Even as they stressed and lamented the spiritual wastelands of Europe, they also often subtly took sides with the homespun piety of "simple people." The free use of *sacramentalia* mentioned previously is just one well-known example.[472]

In light of this tendency, it is easier to understand why non-Jesuit sources also frequently report that Jesuit missionaries received much attention. Missions became eagerly anticipated events.[473] In 1715 in Düsseldorf, the elector's horse track had to be opened as an additional gathering place to accommodate all the interested spectators. Interest was so great that people in the church even climbed on top of the confessionals to find a seat.[474] Of course, simple curiosity and the appeal of an unusual spectacle would also have played a part. Given the distances involved and the immensity of the task, missionaries visited individual villages at best only once every few years despite their best efforts. Their stay thus was a novelty with scarcity value.[475] But we should also not underestimate at least the short-term efficacy of calls to repent: Julien Maunoir, the famous missionary to Brittany, visited the isolated Île d'Ouessant twice, in 1641 and 1642, and was excited about the lasting changes in people's lives there.[476] In 1645, while participating in a procession, Olive Moëlo, a thirty-six-year-old woman from Caudan in Brittany, even experienced visions.[477] There in fact were constant reports of the hallucinatory effects of missions, proving that the Jesuits definitely achieved their goal of breaking people (productively) out of their everyday routines.[478] In general, the boisterous involvement of the laity is frequently reported. The active support of villagers was indeed even a necessity for Jesuit missionaries.[479] In many places, individual laymen accompanied the missionaries out of pure enthusiasm for days and weeks on end.[480] French historians have long regarded the missionary endeavors of the early modern period, and since the early eighteenth century in particular, as a success story. It was then, they argue, that Europe truly became Christian.[481] But in the Jesuits' view it was in no way only these missions that helped transmit to and inculcate the foundations of fervent devotion in the population at large.

A Counterpoint to Everyday Life: The Exercises for Laymen

One of the Jesuits' most important tools for setting contemporary people on the right path was the Spiritual Exercises of Ignatius of Loyola. We have already learned about the importance of the Exercises for the spiritual training, formation, and identity of members of the Society. The founder himself, however, had intended them for everyone. In accordance with Loyola's wishes, the traditional division between laity and clergy should be set aside with respect to devotional practice—a point that regularly drew the ire of more traditionally minded churchmen and mendicants like Melchor Cano, O.P., or Gian Pietro Carafa (later Pope Paul IV).[482] But Ignatius and the Jesuits viewed the Exercises as a technique, a method, a procedure that people from varied stages and walks of life could successfully apply. A glance at the internal manuals that were composed in the sixteenth century confirms this conviction: there we find mention of Exercises for boys, monks, doctors, lawyers, spouses, women, busy people with little time, highly placed personages, and the uneducated.[483] No group was considered fundamentally unsuitable for making the Exercises, even if the enthusiasm for uneducated practitioners was rather restrained. The official handbook for the *Exercises*, published in 1599, stressed the diversity of these target groups. The then reigning superior general Claudio Acquaviva explicitly urged the regional superiors in a letter to make an inviting and "generous" offer to laymen to make the *Exercises* under the Jesuits' direction. Acquaviva's letter gives the impression that he wanted to do everything in his power to popularize the practice of making the *Exercises*. That, of course, required the superiors' skill as ministers. Some rules in the handbook of 1599 gave tips on how one might cleverly make people interested in the *Exercises*. For instance, one might spark their interest during confession or with carefully chosen remarks in spiritual conversations.[484]

The social expansion of the *Exercises* was initially limited to individual cases. In imitation of Ignatius, the *Exercises* were applied where individuals needed help to make life-changing decisions. A good example from southern Italy is Carlo Carafa. As a young man (as we have seen), he became a Jesuit novice but soon left the Society and led a profligate, albeit very successful, life as a soldier for several years. Shortly before 1600, though, he underwent a new transformation—he wanted to return to his spiritual vocation. The *Spiritual Exercises* were an important factor in this conversion: Carafa begged the Jesuits to let him make them. In his dire existential situation, by practicing the "Christian philosophy" of Ignatius, "he renewed his spirit, put his good intentions on a firm basis, grew in his knowledge of God, ignited with His love, and above all determined the way of life he should lead in the future."[485] Carafa became a priest soon after the thirty days and had a long, renowned pastoral career ahead of him in Naples. The *Exercises* were intended predominantly for such unusual people in extraordinary personal circumstances in the sixteenth and even the seventeenth century.

This well-established application of the *Exercises* remained in use over the long term, but in the seventeenth century it began to be supplemented by a totally different, new form of administering and making the *Exercises*: the *Exercises* were converted into a pastoral resource for the masses. It became conventional to give the *Exercises* in a form suitable for larger groups of people. The roots of this development extended beyond the Society of Jesus. In the 1620s, several exponents of the *dévots* (a strict, devout Catholic milieu in France), men like André Du Val, Pierre Bérulle, and especially Vincent de Paul, began to offer French priests annual courses of religious training, mental preparation, and spiritual renewal.[486] In this way, the idea of collective retreats entered French religious culture. The Jesuits' *Spiritual Exercises* played a part in this development: around 1630, priests from this background began to ask the Jesuits whether they might take part in the *Exercises*.[487] Pope Alexander VII lent the practice additional luster in 1657, when he combined such collective *Exercises* with general absolution—indeed, for both clergy and laity. By this point, the latter had already been integrated in the movement.[488] Around the date of Alexander's general absolution, the Society of Jesus also became involved in the culture of retreats for priests and laymen. From rather tentative local origins, a broad initiative soon emerged. The rather spontaneous beginning was made in Vannes in Brittany.[489] It was there that Jean Rigoleuc, S.J., intended to found a place where priests could study with the help of a local financier named Louis Eudo de Kerlivio. The plan may have failed, but the partnership was only diverted. Instead of a retreat house for clergymen, the first retreat house for laymen was founded, with Vincent Huby, S.J., chosen as its first director in 1663. Under his supervision, the number of visitors who came for a few days of spiritual retreat, completing an abridged version of the *Spiritual Exercises*, increased dramatically. In the first sixteen years of the house's existence, no fewer than eighteen thousand people, some of them coming from far away, supposedly made the *Exercises* with Huby. To accommodate the masses, Huby moved from individual to collective *Exercises*. Soon, around twenty sessions, each lasting eight days, were held annually to cope with the onrush. Huby deliberately stoked this enthusiasm for his spiritual courses, for example, by printing posters to announce the beginning of the *Exercises*.[490] The *Exercises* became a fixed component of (Jesuit) pastoral care that could be applied to masses of people.

This practice rested on two pillars: temporary withdrawal from the world and Ignatian meditation techniques. The first of these aspects appears in the very language the Jesuits used. The *Exercises* at these institutions soon came to be called *retraites*, "retreats" or withdrawal.

Elsewhere, the sessions were called "solitudes."[491] The latter term was intended to convey the experience of religious withdrawal from the world, at least temporarily, to a broad audience.[492] Huby's *retraites* were very pragmatic and sought compromise with the normal beholdenness of many laymen to the world: "There are few people who would feel uncomfortable doing [the *Exercises*]; the only difficulty is finding the time."[493] People had to be pried away from this conventional obligation to everyday business for a little while without demanding permanent withdrawal from the world as the only solution.[494] To a certain extent, these group retreats amounted to the intermittent intrusion of monastic-like life in the everyday world. They were "days of salvation" on which a process of spiritual purification was supposed to begin.[495] The goal was to compensate for the negative consequences of everyday overstimulation in a socially feasible way: "It is necessary to withdraw from the crowd, to withdraw in solitude at least now and then if you want to breath purer air."[496] Great effort was accordingly invested in ensuring that the exercitants were largely isolated; for example, at the retreat house of Paris.[497]

In this environment, one was supposed to become aware of and to "reflect" on vital truths of faith.[498] This was accomplished through meditations in conjunction with Loyola's *Spiritual Exercises* and countless sermons and exhortations. The exercitants meditated jointly on prescribed subjects, speaking out loud. It seems as if the participants gave voice to their thoughts and impressions—ideally conveyed to them by the Holy Spirit.[499] The sermons, which made reference to the topics of the meditations, were tailored to the social background and capacity of the exercitants. Huby strove to express himself in language that made the greatest secrets of faith accessible to even the coarsest people. Questions to the audience lightened up the talks and simultaneously helped determine whether the audience was learning. He liked to use simple rhetorical patterns and dramatic contrasts to get his message across.[500] Finally, the Jesuits in Brittany often made use of pictures during these *Exercises*. At the retreat house in Quimper, a large hall and the chapel were painted with images to which the exercitants' attention was constantly directed as inspiration for their meditations. Huby went even further, resorting to "moralistic paintings or images" and tables of key Christian teachings.[501] The deliberate use of such illustrations answered Ignatius's own call for vivid imagination in the *Exercises*.

Huby thus recast the *Spiritual Exercises* of the founder of the Society in an innovative new form, while still largely adhering to their substance. Never before had there been independent institutions with specialized personnel dedicated exclusively to temporary spiritual retreat. The use of the *Exercises* as a tool for mass pastoral care was also new.[502] But there also was sporadic criticism of these trends. Luis de la Palma, a much-read Jesuit author, explicitly insisted on the traditional four-week *Exercises* in his *Camino espiritual*, first published in 1626 and reprinted several times thereafter. His insistence on the complexity of the *Exercises* was far removed from the optimism of Huby and his imitators, who assumed that the practice could be adapted relatively problem-free.[503]

The model of retreat houses that emerged somewhat haphazardly in Vannes quickly spread far and wide. Julien Maunoir, the missionary to Brittany, regularly offered the *Exercises* in somewhat improvised form for hundreds of people in the parish churches of the region around Quimper.[504] One of his confreres, Jean Jégou, the rector of the Jesuit college in Quimper, began in 1665 to lay the groundwork for a retreat house there in the style of the house in Vannes. The retreat house of Quimper opened in 1670. Houses in Saint-Malo, Nantes, Rennes, Toulouse, Aurillac, Avignon, Paris, and elsewhere soon followed. In many other places, the Jesuits at least made available designated, separate areas for exercitants in their colleges.[505] In this way, a network of more than seventy houses was created, financed by various local arrangements.[506] Allowing for local diversity, we should view all these institutions as part of a shared devotional practice that was available in novel, large-scale form.

The retreat movement in Vannes was proselytory in nature. This is clearly shown by the wide-ranging personal contacts that Rigoleuc and Huby maintained with the Breton missionaries around Julien Maunoir. Group meditation was accordingly regarded as an "abridged mission."[507] This connection between institutionalized *Exercises* for the laity and the popular mission in Europe is unmistakable even for other reasons. The French institutions founded in the wake of Vannes were part of an effort to preserve the results of intermittent, short-term missionary visits.[508] Vice versa, we can observe how missionaries constantly made use of brief, focused *Exercises* in the villages and cities of sparsely populated areas. In the Eifel mountains, for example, the Jesuits annually offered *Exercises* lasting four to eight days at various monasteries and noble residences as they traveled from mission to mission.[509] They occasionally even tried to guide the large crowds that converged to hear their sermons through *Exercises*. It thus was not entirely unreasonable when some observers argued that such "publicity" (*pubblicità*) would strip the *Exercises* of one of their essential qualities—the effort to retreat from the world and from everyday affairs at least temporarily had thus largely been abandoned.[510]

France was decisive for the development of this application of the *Exercises*, but there were independent parallels in Naples. There, Pierantonio Spinelli (1555–1615) integrated the *Exercises* within his large-scale pastoral ministry.[511] As in France, groups of priests there were familiarized more intimately with the *Exercises* around the middle of the century. Carlo Carafa, who profited from the *Exercises* in his own conversion, as we have seen, prescribed regular *Exercises* to a community of clergymen he founded.

Then, in 1677, one of the earliest retreat houses in Italy was founded in Alessandria in the northern part of the country. It was not until 1705, though, that another house was opened in Turin.[512] In 1720, with the founding of the first retreat house in Córdoba, Argentina, the practice reached the Americas.[513] Retreat houses first came to Germany in the 1750s, when one was founded in Vienna.[514]

Confraternities and Marian Congregations

One of the Jesuits' chief concerns was to ensure that the religious change they had set in motion with the *Exercises*, missions, confession, sermons, and spiritual direction remained permanent. The Jesuits were not naive about the fact that genuine, lasting conversions were difficult to attain and even more difficult to preserve. In order to help the faithful maintain the religious progress they had made and potentially even surpass it, the Jesuits made skillful use of social resources in addition to the spiritual techniques already mentioned. One strategy for instilling a more intense devotion in the lives of believers centered around confraternities, also known as sodalities (from *sodales*, "fellows," i.e. members) or congregations. They were associations of laymen for pious purposes. Confraternities were local institutions; they had statutes and a leadership structure and sometimes possessed significant capital. Some confraternities were very elitist; others were open to a broad social spectrum. Some were founded as pious benefit societies for specific causes; others worked generally to create a Christian society. In every case, the goal was to support the spiritual progress of individuals by giving them a grounding in a devout lifestyle.

Confraternities were also hardly a Jesuit invention. This widespread organizational form of lay Christian life had existed since the late Middle Ages.[515] Every city, every village, no matter how small, had confraternities—some major European cities had one or two dozen confraternities that were influenced or led by the Jesuits. They brought people together. The goal was always religious, but confraternities undeniably also served important social functions for their members. The members celebrated, organized, reminisced, ate, and drank together. As they pursued their goals, confraternities often took on a complex symbolic and artistic life of their own—they had their own rituals, ceremonies, meeting rooms, holidays, and sometimes even their own special clothing. For many people in the late Middle Ages and the early modern period, everyday life in a confraternity probably represented their most significant encounter with Christianity. Building on this tradition, the late sixteenth century and especially the seventeenth century experienced a veritable boom in new confraternities.[516]

The Jesuits collaborated closely with older confraternities in many places, particularly in the early years of their ministry. Initially, it sometimes was long-standing congregations that supported and financed newcomers from the Society of Jesus in their endeavors. In Naples, the first Jesuits around Alfonso Salmerón joined several older confraternities, from which the college in Naples received significant infusions of capital.[517] Ignatius's followers soon founded countless congregations of their own—Pierre Favre was the first to do so in 1540, in Parma.[518] These newly founded institutions often perpetuated the earlier tradition, but their activities and devotional profiles aligned more closely with Jesuit values. In general, the Jesuits strove to create a closer relationship between congregations and the clergy than had previously been the case.

The Jesuits cleverly used this organizational form to win social support for particular pious undertakings. Some of congregations they founded, inspired, or merely advised financed and maintained poorhouses and houses for former prostitutes; others were confraternities dedicated to ministering to prisoners and supporting slaves.[519] This method of safeguarding expensive institutions was critically important to Ignatius's men because in principle they refused to accept any financial compensation for their pastoral work—schools not only were free but also offered sermons and other services without pay. Confraternities helped the Jesuits stay true to this unusual principle.[520]

The most important and famous new form of confraternity that the Jesuits introduced was the Marian congregation. This model dates back to the year 1563, when Jean Leunis (1532–84), a Belgian at the Collegio Romano in the Eternal City, founded the first such institution.[521] He conspicuously drew on the rich tradition of confraternities; it was only in the aftermath that something new emerged from this congregation. The Marian congregation founded by Leunis was a sodality for students of the Jesuits' flagship school. In addition to instruction, the members were supposed to study together and do pious works to train in the faith. The Marian congregation thus initially sought to create a close connection between educational and pious purposes. This sodality soon became too full, and analogous confraternities had to be founded. Different groups were set up for different ages—homogeneous membership was an important principle of these new Jesuit institutions. In 1584, the project was officially recognized by Gregory XIII; in 1589, Sixtus V permitted Marian congregations to be founded without the involvement of colleges or students.

The Roman model soon traveled worldwide. In the following years and decades, similar institutions were founded at almost every Jesuit house—in Paris (1565), Douai (1572), Cologne and Dillingen (1574), and Naples (1577).[522] Soon there were Marian confraternities not only for students but also for men (and rarely and, for a long time, informally for women) from the most diverse walks of life outside the scholarly and academic world of schools. Yet again, the Jesuit principle of nuanced and specialized pastoral care prevailed: in Cologne, for example, there ultimately were nine Marian congregations at the Jesuit college (together with two other Jesuit confraternities of a different kind), including congregations for laborers, unmarried men, and Frenchmen.[523] Such confraternities were often known as "civil sodalities," which were intended for a wide range of people usually from the middle class. There also were Marian congregations for the upper classes. Noblemen, high officials, and even princes joined.[524] When the order was abolished in 1773, there were reportedly twenty-five hundred Marian congregations worldwide, some of them with several hundred members.

The most remarkable aspect of this type of confraternity was the fact that all these local institutions could bind themselves to the original mother institution in Rome, as many of them did. A global network of Christian lay organizations was created for which General Claudio Acquaviva issued standard statutes and rules in 1587.[525] This focus on Rome was reinforced by special confederations that individual sodalities established with regional counterparts: the congregation of Erfurt, for example, partnered with similar groups in Augsburg, Bamberg, Mainz, Munich, and many other German cities.[526] This ensured that— even allowing for local variation—a vision of a highly centralized, Rome-oriented, and closely supervised form of Catholicism played a prominent part in the everyday lives of many people. Compared with older confraternities, Marian congregations were strictly organized. Compliance with the rules was enforced with unusual severity. In contrast to older confraternities, the admission of new members to Marian confraternities was essentially in the hands of clergymen—the earnest, religious conviction of the *sodales* had to be checked and confirmed. The membership of Marian congregations therefore often developed into a kind of model clientele for the Jesuits. Candidates for the Jesuit order, other orders, and the global clergy were recruited from their ranks.[527]

As in the case of retreat houses, Marian congregations were intended to provide interested people a space in which they could retreat from the world and from worldly affairs without having to abandon the world entirely.[528] The sodalities aspired to create a spiritual enclave. Members practiced a spirituality that was heavily influenced by Ignatius and the Ignatian tradition. The *Exercises* played an important part, and the members' fraternal devotions duly included meditation. Jesuit confraternities also frequently received communion and confessed.[529] In general terms, Marian congregations were supposed to convey the Jesuit ideal of daily, continuous, and intense work of spiritual self-improvement to a broad segment of the population. The members of these lay associations with close ties to the Society were supposed to stand head and shoulders above their worldly fellows with respect to their piety. That, in the Jesuits' view, required constant spiritual guidance and supervision—it was precisely for that reason that these new congregations cultivated much closer ties to the Jesuit order than had previously been customary.

The confraternities propagated the devotion of Mary that the Jesuits generally prized so highly. Worldwide, it became almost exclusively customary to link new Jesuit confraternities of this kind with aspects of the worship of Mary. The names of the various sodalities highlighted different aspects of the contemporary devotion of the Mother of God—they called themselves, for example, "Immaculata," "the Assumption of Mary," or "Mary, Queen of the Angels." In Düsseldorf, for instance, the Marian *sodales* pledged to follow an extensive spiritual program for each day, week, and year—daily mass, participation in processions and the Quarant'ore, pious undertakings—with a pronounced Marian bent: "All *sodales* [should] not only revere the blessed virgin, Mary the Mother of God with special devotion and appeal for her intercession before the Lord God, but also endeavor to emulate the example of her sublime virtue with a chaste and wholesome way of life and inspire one another to all godliness."[530] Devotion to Mary was combined with the hope for moral improvement, which was explicitly to be realized through the collective nature of the confraternity. Mary, moreover, helped the members in their final hour—the theme of a "good death" in Jesuit ministry crops up here yet again.[531] In this way, too, the congregations helped realize a primary objective of Jesuit piety: "They strive for and attain such great peace of mind."[532]

Even new Jesuit confraternities, however, were never totally subsumed by this religious function. Despite every effort to bring about a more centralized, stricter form of devotion, the sodalities of the Society of Jesus remained essentially local groups focused to a considerable extent on social activities.[533] Communal feasts and banquets remained an important part of fraternal life until well into the eighteenth century. And it was sometimes hard to keep the members participating seriously and engaged. The Jesuits therefore constantly warned pious laymen not to neglect their congregations' regular meetings and sessions— apparently this aspect of the confraternities was particularly liable to fall by the wayside.[534]

The longer these groups existed, the more imperative it was to prevent their inner workings from becoming a source of conflict and squabbles over prestige. The Christian character of the confraternities, the Jesuit Louis Le Valois warned in 1726, should be apparent not only in their activities at large but also in the members' relations with one another. The fact that he insisted on this point so vehemently leads one to suspect that problems had arisen. The ideal and reality sometimes diverged even in Marian congregations. Still, there can be no doubt that confraternities in general and Marian congregations in particular made a profound mark on Catholic life of the early modern period and even down to the twentieth century. Drawing on a long and varied tradition, the Jesuits devised and largely established their own form of confraternity. Pious societies were an especially important institution that served to help people's souls in a lasting and socially relevant way.

Jesuits and Protestants, Protestants and Jesuits

"Fools and heretics are people too. There is a place for mercy."[535] With these words, written in 1620 at the beginning of the Thirty Years' War, the Jesuit Gottfried Lemius of Fulda makes several fundamental facts clear. First, it was obvious to him and to the entire order that the Reformation was wrong. The great reformers like Martin Luther or John

Calvin believed in false doctrines—Protestantism was heresy and had been brought about by diabolical seduction, obstinacy, or evil intentions. One could and must reject their positions uncompromisingly. Yet Lemius and many other Jesuits also recognized that it was important to distinguish between the Protestant clergy and the mass of Protestant faithful. People born in the second generation of the Reformation had often not learned anything else. They could not help it that they held false beliefs. It was pity, not enmity, that the Jesuits felt toward simple Lutherans or Calvinists. Hence, they had two basic ways of interacting with Protestants: open, aggressive, hostile measures to rebuff, refute, and fight them, on the one hand, and, on the other, efforts to lead every last Protestant they could reach back into the bosom of the Catholic Church with spiritual guidance and pastoral care.[536] The Jesuits' Protestant strategies wavered between these two extremes for a long time, and not always without contradiction.

The Protestants only gradually came into the Jesuits' field of view. The Society of Jesus—contrary to a widespread but inaccurate belief— was *not* founded as a counterpoint to the Reformation. *Prior* to 1540, the Reformation had practically made no difference to Ignatius. That changed only after some of the first companions came to Germany in 1540 and wrote in shock about religious conditions there. It was then that the fight against Protestantism became an important subject to the Jesuits. In 1550, Pope Julius III declared "defending the faith" an additional area of responsibility for the Society of Jesus.[537] The Jesuits had not been founded as an anti-Protestant brigade, but by 1550 they already had incorporated a clear Counter-Reformation orientation in their identity. Polanco, for example, was soon certain that the Society had been "received by divine providence among the effective means to remedy so great an evil."[538] Pierre Favre, who was among the first Jesuits to report back from Germany, emphasized that the Catholics largely had only themselves to blame for the spread of heresy. The Catholic Church had often failed Germany. For the Jesuits, the fight against the Lutherans began with frank self-criticism. In many places, there was no priest at all; in others, a single one; women had to jump in as sextons, Favre reported, concluding that he "would not wonder anything more than how it's possible there are not even more Lutherans."[539] Ignatius also thought that the Lutherans' success was "a consequence of those who should have been prepared and of the bad examples and ignorance of Catholics, especially the clergy, that wrought such carnage and destruction in the vineyard of the Lord."[540] There was a lack of a positive Catholic way of life, of convincing role models, of an easily comprehensible and enthusiastically presented theology.[541]

The Jesuits thus viewed Germany's religious problems first and foremost as the result of a dramatic, self-inflicted pastoral crisis—they wanted to bring relief by filling the old church with new life. From now on they wanted to impart "basic theology" to children and simple people in an easily understandable way and without controversy. Catechism and catechesis epitomized this strategy and became the most important means of implementing it.[542]

In focusing on the catechism, the Jesuits shrewdly responded to the Protestants' strategic advantages. Even if catechesis had enjoyed a fresh boom long before the Reformation, Martin Luther's *Small Catechism* and *Large Catechism* of 1529 were undeniably pedagogical milestones in the propagation of Christianity.[543] With the publication of these two texts, the project of propagating the faith through catechism made unprecedented use of the new medium of the printing press. Luther's works were a massive publishing hit: six or seven hundred thousand copies were produced in the sixteenth century alone. The Catholics had nothing comparable at hand to counter them. It was Peter Canisius, a member of the Society of Jesus, who composed the Catholic response to Luther's works in 1555. His *Summa doctrinae Christianae*, however, was repeatedly revised over the ensuing years and supplemented by abridgments of varying length as early as 1556 and 1559. The goal was to make available a published format that was appropriate to every level of comprehension—from children to uneducated adults to advanced readers. In its various versions, Canisius's catechism was used for centuries in hundreds of editions.[544] These books avoided direct confrontation with the Protestants and instead presented the tenets of Catholicism in question-and-answer form. Canisius's catechisms thus were both very much oriented toward the Reformation and yet also focused on propagating the faith in positive terms. It was not least for that reason that his works enjoyed wide popularity outside confessional battle zones. They were joined by countless other catechisms by Jesuit authors over the following decades.[545] With these texts, the Jesuits tried at every opportunity to teach people, and especially children, the basics of the Catholic faith in a form that was easy to understand.

In Ignatius's view, measures to "inculcate firm instruction in Catholic truth" could and should be accompanied by more or less militant reprisals toward the Protestants, especially those in positions of responsibility.[546] Ideally, Ignatius wrote, the authorities would remove all Protestants from public office, confiscate and burn Lutheran writings, and especially dismiss all suspect clergymen and teachers. Jesuits often supported, demanded, and accompanied such explicit Counter-Reformation measures, including the use of force, but they could be imposed only in the special case when a determined ruler personally supported such an uncompromising spiritual program.[547]

Such cases regularly occurred. Starting in 1621, the dukes of Bavaria spared no effort to bring the deeply Protestant Upper Palatinate back to the Catholic faith, and Louis XIV launched an equally heavy-handed campaign to re-Catholicize the diocese of Strasbourg in 1681.[548] The Jesuits usually played an important part in such efforts and often were the driving force behind aggressive Counter-Reformation campaigns. Many Jesuits at the time were inclined to take provocative anti-Protestant positions. They were also not afraid of open, personal confrontation. Since they and their Protestant adversaries were usually equally matched, scurrilous maneuvering for tactical advantages might be the result. Several episodes, for example, are known from the area of Neustadt an der Weinstrasse, which was fiercely contested by the two confessions around the year 1700. The local Calvinist clergy and the Jesuits made life difficult for one another and their respective followers on both sides. The rivals blocked each other's events and pressured some followers not to visit opponents. Enormous effort and energy were poured into such everyday pettiness.[549] There were constant confrontations, threats of violence, and scuffles between members of different confessions. The Jesuits' vocal and markedly anti-Protestant positioning certainly did nothing to help de-escalate the situation—no more than the analogous attitude of their Protestant opponents.

Leading ecclesiastical personalities, however, had to take care that their own flock did not become tired of all this negative propaganda. Where a social and political deadlock prevailed between confessional groups—as, for example, in the imperial city of Osnabruck—and it could not be easily tilted in either party's favor, the people often reached a pragmatic and veritably friendly modus vivendi with their neighbors of the other confession.[550] Jesuit agitation was not received well even by Catholics in such circumstances. Fr. Bernard Löpen, who was involved in Jesuit efforts in Osnabruck, was forced to admit, "There are some among the Catholics who perversely slander my zeal; some, who adhere to my opponents in opposition to myself and ecclesiastical freedom; some, who dare to utter publicly and in the sight of the people of Melle, 'The Father is making a lot of trouble for us.'" Other Catholic (!) contemporaries likewise mentioned Löpen's "unchristian zeal." In such circumstances, whether they liked it or not, the Jesuits thus had to accept and come to terms with the fact that they always had to proceed cautiously so as not to irritate the Catholic population in light of the irreversible biconfessionality of such regions.

One front in this open warfare against the Protestant confession was detailed critique of the opposing side's theology and publications. It took a while, though, before the Jesuits accepted that it was impossible to defeat the Protestants exclusively with Catholic reform and mechanisms of social repression, and that they had to confront the Protestants' ideas, as well. In the early years, Pierre Favre and other pioneering Jesuits had overlooked or underestimated the theological and spiritual potential of Luther's teachings. Closer theological study of Luther's teachings and writings proceeded at best only in fits and starts.[551] Even Nadal's anti-Protestant texts made only very superficial reference to Protestant theology. Salmerón, in contrast, soon absorbed an astonishingly broad body of Protestant literature. And by the latter half of the 1550s, the Jesuits finally became convinced that they had to deal with their adversaries' theologies on an intellectual level in much greater detail, even if they were already convinced of their falsity. In 1554, Ignatius stated that they had to respond to Lutheran publications in kind.[552] The result was the creation of a theological subdiscipline specialized in refuting opposing viewpoints: "controversialist" theology. The key Catholic work of this kind was the brilliant *Disputationes de controversiis* by Robert Bellarmine, a critical masterpiece that coolly analyzed and systematically dissected Protestant theology. Bellarmine penetrated so deeply into the teachings of the German Reformers that his findings alerted the Protestants themselves to holes in their thinking, so that, in a certain sense, he gave positive impetus to Lutheran theology in Germany.[553] The *Disputationes* were reprinted and cited by Catholics, and attacked and refuted by Protestants, many times.[554] In order to ensure that this challenging material also reached the broad mass of priests, the Jesuits soon composed easily accessible handbooks of controversialist theology, which priests could refer to when they needed anti-Protestant arguments in their everyday pastoral work. These works moreover discussed *how* to engage in competent theological dispute and unmasked the Protestants' methods.[555]

The boundary between academic controversialist theology and exclusionary, demonizing, incendiary diatribe was fluid. Attempts to damage one's adversaries in print knew no bounds. In Germany, for example, the Jesuits manipulated Lutheran texts to mislead potential Protestant readers.[556] They also utilized quite refined Latin poetry against the Lutherans—André des Freux, S.J., for instance, wrote numerous *Epigrammata in Haereticos* (Epigrams against heretics).[557] Therein, he compared the Lutherans—with rather less refinement—to excrement so foul that it immediately made the sewer itself want to retch.[558] This tone, however, was nothing out of the ordinary. Both sides produced large quantities of aggressive (usually vernacular) polemic that, notwithstanding all its theological content, was thoroughly coarse and crude.[559]

Jesuits branded their Lutheran adversaries with insults like "fool" or "pig," which the Protestants repaid in kind. On the Lutheran side, the clever reformulation of the German term for a member of the Society from "Jesuiter" (pronounced "yeh-soo-ee-ter") to "Jesu-ider" (pronounced "yeh-soo-ee-der" but meaning "against Jesus," "contra-Jesus") was especially popular; the Jesuits, meanwhile, constantly turned

"Luther" into "Luder" (hussy, slut).[560] The Protestants also often equated the Jesuits with insects, denigrating them as vermin; it was especially popular to identify them with the dreaded plagues of locusts in the Bible.[561] Such all-out attacks not only on the teachings but also on the persons, and indeed almost on the very humanity of the opposing side, were widespread in the religious controversies of the early modern period. It was imperative in this system of verbal violence toward one's confessional adversaries that no attack went unrequited. In practice, the Jesuits attempted to refute at least the most important Protestant works, especially those that could be found "in the hands of every scholar, every political adviser, and every nobleman," from which "the entire Catholic cause suffers great harm."[562]

The Jesuit order supported this culture of confessional warfare almost unreservedly—albeit with important nuances and growing uncertainty. Rome expressed explicit reservations quite early about the extremism of Central European Jesuits' attacks on the Protestants. The generals claimed that some polemicists wrote "not with gentleness and moderation, as would be proper, but rather attacked their targets more bitterly and bitingly in their texts," hence "diminishing the particular benefit of writing" against the heretics.[563] Of course, Jesuits in Germany often took a different view: what seemed unnecessary or even dangerous from the global perspective of the superior general seemed indispensable from the local perspective of Jesuits active in areas with mixed confessional populations. In 1613, for example, a dispute broke out between General Acquaviva and the Jesuit Adam Contzen in Mainz over details of Contzen's controversialist strategy. Contzen dealt with "heretical" texts too recklessly for Acquaviva's taste, writing in a way that would have bewildered readers in Spain or Italy.[564] Contzen did not deny that his books might seem unusual in southern Europe, but he insisted that his strategy was particularly "effective" in Central Europe. Beneath the surface, Rome and Mainz had different priorities in the public fight against Protestant theology.[565]

Jesuit anti-Protestant theologians, moreover, had to convince not only Rome but also, to an increasing degree, their own intended audience. "Polemical sermons again! What good are these jeremiads?

Nobody converts!" said one exhausted contemporary in 1757.[566] There soon would be whole libraries overflowing with religious polemics that no one read anymore, he argued. The Jesuits' aggressive, hostile manner, moreover, seemed out of touch in the tolerant Age of Enlightenment. Controversialist theology fell into an existential crisis—even the Jesuits had to admit it. Yet many of them, like Franz Neumayr of Augsburg, resolutely clung to it and even believed it would continue to thrive: Neumayr, at any rate, was so immodest as to credit the palpable stabilization of Catholicism in the latter half of the seventeenth century to incessant and implacable theological polemics.[567] The value of this literature should not (only) be derived from the number of actual conversions, he argued. More importantly, it served to show respect to God's truth, which for the Jesuits was identical with the truth of Catholicism. The Word of God demanded that it be articulated clearly, and that also entailed the criticism and condemnation of error. "The church of Christ [must] always be in arms."[568] "Keeping silent," it was well known, led to "great evil."[569] In Neumayr's view, it was not controversialist theology that was the problem, but rather unreceptive and bored readers and listers. Refuting Protestant doctrine helped "strengthen the orthodox, convince those in error, convert those in doubt."[570] Despite all its uncertainties, many Jesuits still embraced controversialist theology, even if it may have become a little old-fashioned.

Controversialist theology was not only literary but also oral. The sixteenth century and the first half of the seventeenth century produced a long series of so-called colloquies at which theologians of various confessions appeared, discussed different views, and ideally reached a common position.[571] These were expert debates: theological discussions between laymen of different confessions were frowned upon.[572] In point of fact, these often elaborately staged events usually resulted at best in only formal compromises because neither party was willing or able to acknowledge the superiority of the other's arguments. The Jesuits took part in many of these events as representatives of the Catholic side. They made their first appearances in Germany in 1541 at the Colloquies of Worms and Regensburg. General Laínez himself then took part in the Colloquy of Poissy in France, where he met the great Reformed theologian Theodore Beza, among others. The Jesuits took part in yet another colloquy, held in Regensburg in 1601, just as they did in the exhibition match at Hämelschenburg Castle in 1614, which featured the Jesuit Augustin Turriani of Hildesheim and the professor of theology Georg Calixt of Helmstedt.

These events really were often no more than exhibition matches. It is doubtful—just as with diatribes and controversialist theology—whether the participants believed they might convince their opponents at all or, if so, to what extent. The point was rather to make the other side look bad in front of the audience. At Hämelschenburg Castle, for example, as at many of these staged confessional debates, the opposing sides strove to exert a positive influence on a wavering young nobleman by disavowing and refuting each other. The colloquy was just one step in a long series of events that culminated in the lord of the castle's conversion to Catholicism in late 1621.[573] Other colloquies had abandoned the attempt to win over some third party altogether. Instead, they served to reinforce followers' existing commitment to their chosen beliefs performatively through the ritual of reciprocal refutation. When four disputations took place between several Anglicans and the Jesuit Edmund Campion in London in the summer of 1580, the authorities did everything in their power to give Campion as little a chance as possible: he was not allowed to prepare and did not receive any books, and the Anglicans picked the topics. The point was to demonstrate Campion's inadequacy and that of Catholicism altogether, not to engage in a genuine exchange of ideas.[574]

In light of such experiences, the Jesuits soon ceased to be completely convinced of the utility of such public summits between heavily armed controversialists. When General Mercurian first sent Jesuits as missionaries to England in 1580, he instructed them to avoid public debates, because "it is the characteristic of heretics, even when they are clearly beaten in argument, to be unwilling to give in to anybody."[575] In 1595, a Jesuit in Mühlhausen, Thuringia, declined a debate because he had come neither intending to do so nor had made the necessary preparations.[576] And the Jesuits of Hamburg—a small, embattled minority in a solidly Lutheran city—themselves admitted, "Indeed, at the request of our friends and according to our own judgment, we avoid controversial aspects of faith." A different strategy toward Protestants seemed more effective: covering overarching, general topics of interest to Christians broadly or, as the Jesuits of Hamburg put it, "Relying especially on sacred scripture and moral improvement, having learned from experience that that is more how both the people are gathered and the fruit harvested."[577]

A certain general aversion to aggressive polemic spread in the middle of the seventeenth century—in this case the Jesuits were part of a broader movement.[578] As important as it was to expose the falsity and error of every Protestant conviction, it was even more essential to win the hearts, faith, and will of one's confessional adversaries if one was to propagate Catholicism successfully. Confrontation at all costs could not be the goal.[579] Hence the Jesuits' everyday efforts on behalf of Protestants' souls often were not characterized by polemical and hostile methods but rather by urgent persuasion, for which the "conversion handbooks" that Jesuits in England were sometimes given, for example, recommended a pastoral register.[580] In this regard, guiding the Protestants back into the bosom of the Catholic Church was fundamentally no different from the mission to convert the "heathen" and to reinforce the faith among the only nominally Catholic rural population of Europe.

From the statements quoted here, it also emerges that the actual conversion of Protestants was usually de facto the fruit of one-on-one pastoral care. The Jesuits took advantage of the crises of wavering people—preferably cases of sickness or the moments before death in which they broached general Christian topics in Catholic terms.[581] A psychologically shrewd and well-trained Jesuit should "make use of certain methods and of times that are propitious—as for instance, if he should see him in a fit of melancholy or desolation of soul, he will then be able, under the pretext of consoling him, to speak about human misery and how full this life is of it." One should also pay close attention to the influence of the time of day on a person's mood.[582] Obviously, a clever Jesuit always had to keep an eye out for everyday situations that facilitated religiously relevant conversations. They were not afraid to take very circuitous detours: since England was regarded as the land of science, future missionaries to England were educated in the natural sciences—this was an effortless way to strike up a conversation.[583] And in order to get close to Sir Everard Digby, the English Jesuit John Gerard spent much time playing cards with him—Ignatius's men adapted to the habits of their Protestant targets to a considerable and, even for contemporaries, borderline unethical extent.[584]

When they could do so and considered it promising, the Jesuits sometimes offered social advantages—for example, they secured an eight-year-old boy from Bautzen in Vienna his start as a page in a princely house and then in the empress's bakery. Small pious gifts, such as religious images, could also help open doors.[585] As opportunity arose, the Jesuits also became involved in mixed marriages between Catholics and Protestants, where a certain amount of religious disquiet almost inevitably existed anyway.[586] Some Protestants seem to have been at least inclined to speak well of the Catholic confession, which the Jesuits of course were happy to seize on and use for their own purposes.[587] In other cases, initial reservations had to be overcome before a young man "was easily overcome and convinced by a friendly and salvific conversation and fled to the bosom of the Catholic Church."[588] Sometimes that led to protracted "negotiations" between the Jesuit pastor and the (future) convert, which might not only take an oral form but also be committed to writing.[589]

Even though the Jesuits' reports of such conversions are very summary in nature and presumably exaggerated, giving the events an "inspirational" ring, at least this much is undeniable: the everyday work of persuasion that preceded every Lutheran's or Calvinist's return to the Catholic Church was tailored to individuals and their personal situations. The Jesuits brought people to change confessions not—at least not primarily—by dogmatically condemning Protestant doctrine and pompously expounding their own truth but rather by engaging with the desires, concerns, and events of individual biographies and gently shepherding them in a Catholic direction. The Jesuits normally had no use for the acerbity of controversialist theology in their everyday efforts to convert individuals.[590] This was Lemius's specifically pastoral approach to conversion mentioned at the beginning of this section—the Jesuits were fundamentally confident that their ministry would be incomparably more effective than that of their Protestant opponents because religious truth was ultimately on their side.

A restrained demeanor and empathetic approach to Protestants were not simply promising methods with respect to conversion; in many places they were absolutely necessary for political reasons. The Jesuits had to cope with major impediments in the Protestant states of Europe where they were active. They lived there as a suspect minority and had to rein in their zeal. Indiscreet actions might lead to embarrassing backpedaling at the very least. In 1640, for example, the Swedish troops encamped at Alsatian Oberehnheim forced the Jesuits to retract an openly anti-Lutheran sermon in print.[591] Things took a far graver turn when the Jesuits were physically attacked by the Protestant majority.[592] Openly presenting oneself, let alone doing so combatively, in the Protestant countries of northern Europe—Scandinavia and England—could be fatal. On account of drastic state persecution, the Jesuits there faced acute danger to life and limb.[593]

The Jesuits thus were forced to take to life underground in these areas. It was obvious they could not go about openly as Catholic priests and definitely not as Jesuits. Disguise was the order of the day. Heinrich Schacht, S.J., for example, who spent long years in northern Europe and was even condemned to death in Sweden in 1617 but then pardoned, liked to pose as a mousetrap dealer to hide his identity.[594] Fake names were routinely used to escape lethal detection by the Protestants. Visible "Catholic" acts of faith could endanger one's life. Fr. Robert Valens, who was active in Edinburgh in 1629, vividly described this threat:

> The searchers of the town visit the house monthly, or oftener, and on two occasions have come while I was saying office. I was in considerable danger, and still greater alarm, for they came close to my room where I had some of the sacred furniture exposed to view. The hand of God stayed them from coming farther. I am safe nowhere in the town, for they have divided it in districts among four-and-twenty zealous Puritans, to multiply the chances of catching us, so I now say my hours in the fields, or lurk all day on the hills dressed like a peasant.[595]

In the northern Netherlands, where conditions were not quite as bad, the cautious Jesuits resorted to leaving their secret hiding places only by night. Pastoral care was usually administered after dark.[596] It was impossible to prioritize converting Protestants under these circumstances. The few Jesuits on hand strove instead to minister to the spiritual needs of the "hidden Catholics" and thus prevent them from apostatizing from the Roman Catholic Church under the pressure of this complicated situation.[597]

To escape certain condemnation and probable execution, the Jesuits in England deliberated at length about whether and to what extent one had to tell the truth under interrogation in the event of arrest. Outright lying was prohibited, but the Jesuits, in their plight, explicitly supported ambiguous speech—they were very much allowed to trick the opposing side and hide their identity. "Mental reservation" was the name given to the cryptic tactic of continuing one's spoken sentences in one's head, the added thought making a spoken lie true. Even German Jesuits considered it legitimate to pose as Lutherans in an emergency and go to Protestant communion.[598] Superior General Nickel was not amused and rejected the practice. He knew that this ambivalent behavior would redound on the Jesuits' heads in highly negative fashion. This willingness to dissemble, conceal, and maintain multiple identities helped inspire the distorted, hostile image of the devious Jesuit who hid and disguised his true intentions in order to achieve his real goals all the more effectively in secret.

Despite all the reciprocal and passionately advertised hostility between the Jesuits and Protestants, we also must not overlook the fact that in many places there also were close friendships and everyday interaction, natural cooperation, and mutual esteem. The Protestants were especially fascinated by the cultural achievements of the Society of Jesus. The doors of Jesuit schools were normally also open to Protestants, at least as long as they were not "obstinate" and did not cause a disturbance.[599] Renowned Protestant pedagogues and educational philosophers like Johannes Sturm of Strasbourg in the sixteenth century and Francis Bacon in the seventeenth century praised the Society's colleges. Visiting select Jesuit schools thus was also a popular part of

Protestants' grand tours. When the Protestant Englishman John Bargrave came to Bourges in 1645, he spent several days enthusiastically in the company of several local English Jesuits. He attended various events at the college, and both sides enjoyed the learned conversation among countrymen that chance had made possible there. Solidarity with one's countrymen trumped confessional loyalty. Religious differences were not, however, swept under the carpet. On the contrary, it is striking that Bargrave and the Jesuits talked about theological questions often— indeed sometimes quite contentiously—throughout his visit, but with sportsmanlike competitiveness and in amicable, bonding fashion. Discussing their confessional differences brought the men closer together on a personal level, without either side changing its position.[600]

Cooperative theological relations across confessional boundaries were definitely possible. For Protestants with mystical inclinations, such as the radical Pietist Gottfried Arnold, the mystical works of the Jesuit Maximilian Sandaeus were an important source of information.[601] Jesuit scholars often also had long-standing contact with colleagues from the "enemy" camp. Gottfried Wilhelm Leibniz's wide-ranging interconfessional contacts are well known, but even the English Royal Society esteemed correspondents from the Jesuit order. Philipp Jakob Spener, the most important early leader of German Pietism, revered the Jesuit François de Ménestrier for his heraldic knowledge and even visited him once at the college in Lyon.[602] Vice versa, Theodore Moretus, the Dutch Jesuit and mathematician, had good relations with the Lutheran associates of Otto von Guericke and with physicians in Hamburg.[603]

Jesuit theater and celebrations were also a major attraction. Protestants regularly adopted plays written for the Society's colleges and performed them on Lutheran stages.[604] The Protestant nobility and universities of the Holy Roman Empire enjoyed attending the usually elaborately staged opening ceremonies of the Jesuit colleges at the beginning of the semester—and politely apologized when something unanticipated prevented them from doing so.[605] Even the liturgical ceremonies of Catholic Jesuits attracted the curiosity of bystanders of other confessions. In 1671, more than three hundred Protestants and two margraves of Ansbach traveled from Strasbourg to nearby Molsheim to see the famous Jesuit procession on Good Friday. In 1721, numerous "persons of different faith" took part, "at least as spectators," in the Jesuits' festivities on the Hülfensberge in Thuringia—and indeed "cordially thanked one of our priests."[606]

There thus was much more than fighting, hatred, and contempt when Jesuits and Protestants came in touch with one another, whether in person or as mediated by texts. Friendship, collegiality, and respect were also the order of the day. Ultimately, circumstances dictated how they interacted with one another. Political and social power relations were a major factor when Jesuits and Protestants met. Contact with visitors passing through was vastly different from pastoral ministry in the heart of a Protestant population. Life as an underground priest in England, living in mortal danger, cast the Protestants in a different light from the perspective of a professor in Rome. Whoever spoke openly about Lutherans had different goals in mind from those of a Jesuit who stood at the bedside of a dying Protestant. The situation appeared differently to someone who thought or wrote about "Protestantism" than to someone who met an individual human being. An anti-Protestant element may have very quickly become intrinsic to the worldview of almost all Jesuits, but a variety of factors determined how often and how prominently it manifested itself in daily life. By no means all members of the Society of Jesus felt the need to interpret the world primarily according to anti-Protestant categories as they went about their everyday lives. For many of them, other problems, other topics, and other adversaries were more important and pressing.

3

Saeculum and the Kingdom of God

THE JESUITS "IN THE WORLD"

"HE WHO IS NO GOOD for the world is as little good for the Society; and he who has talent for being useful and living in the world is good for the Society," Ignatius once said.[1] The order that he founded made this principle its own. In this chapter, we will learn what the result of this determination was. We will see how the Jesuits moved in contemporary society and dealt with politics, how they were involved in economic life, and how they became architects and authors, scholars, and teachers.

Ignatius's description of Jesuits "in the world" reflected the conviction that the Jesuits should and could proactively engage with walks of life that at first glance seemed completely or largely incompatible with a religious disposition. Many of the older orders had been founded, after all, so that the monks could *flee* the world. Erudition, school, and urban life were viewed as obstacles on the path toward God. Some Christians of the sixteenth, seventeenth, and eighteenth centuries wanted to escape from the world; with few exceptions, however, the Jesuits never indulged this tendency toward escapism. Despite all the fascination of a more rigorously contemplative, meditative devotion, the Society of Jesus retained the attitude echoed in the sentence of Ignatius's just quoted: the Jesuits did not view the world, at least from a global perspective, as antithetical to a righteous life: the world was their home.

The Jesuits therefore both were supposed to and indeed had to learn and master the rules of the world, and they soon did that so well that many of their opponents began to ask in bewilderment where the search for salvation had gone.

The "world," however, and the everyday lives of people that played out there had a very ambivalent status, even for the Jesuits. The early modern period was an age in which individual sectors of society became ever more conspicuously differentiated. More and more aspects of human life—politics, economics, and science are regarded as excellent examples—came to be viewed as semi- or quasi-autonomous spheres that obeyed a logic of their own. The influence and interpretive dominance of religion, in particular, were no longer self-evident in these areas. And the Jesuits were perfectly capable of accepting a certain autonomy in the everyday business of human life.

But only a certain autonomy: the true emancipation of politics or economics from the overriding perspective of the salvation of mankind was obviously out of the question. A religious framework remained in place and encompassed all human endeavor, just as before. Hence, the Jesuits regarded it as feasible and reasonable to intervene in all these areas as men of God. It is important to emphasize that fact: however much the Jesuits became involved in the "world," they always did so from this spiritual perspective and continued to see themselves foremost as clergymen. They wanted to be involved in commerce, but not as merchants; to live at court, but not as courtiers. Since this distinction was very difficult to maintain, both in theory and in practice, the Jesuits often walked a tightrope in their mission in the "world." At every instance, they ran the risk of conforming too closely to the rules of the world.

In virtually every area of social, cultural, and political life, there were at least some Jesuits who believed, at least for a time, that they could work "to help souls." The Jesuits ultimately tried to penetrate as many areas of early modern society as possible and set about their work. The range of activities that resulted from this effort was often astonishing and today is sometimes difficult to comprehend. It is important to remember, however, that not everything that individual Jesuits regarded as necessary actions in the world—going as far as using scientific skills for military purposes—became the official policy of the entire order. The individual preferences of individual Jesuits and institutional guidelines were in fact often at odds with respect to taking action "in the world." With respect to political or economic involvement, for example, as well as science, the superiors constantly drew clear boundaries or set priorities that differed from those of the men in the field. The Jesuits' place in the world was therefore also always subject to a variety of compromises and negotiations: with Jesuit superiors, with church leadership, and especially with society at large. The history of how the Jesuits played a part in the world and where this engagement took them over time is incredibly variegated. It ultimately says as much about the order as it does about the rest of society. In this chapter, we will see how the Jesuits were engaged in society, the economy, education, scholarship, and contemporary arts.

Nobles and Cities: The Society Finds Its Place

When the limping, haggard, and shabbily dressed Ignatius arrived in Rome with his friends in 1537, he did not know many people there. He and several of his companions found it difficult to make themselves understood at all because—in the famous words of Jesuit historian Georg Schurhammer—they spoke only a broken "mishmash of Italian and Spanish."[2] Hence, it was all the more astonishing how rapidly the first Jesuits established themselves in the most influential social circles of Rome. The newcomers had a handful of contacts in Rome after all, and these helped them make their way. Their relationship with Gasparo Contarini, a cardinal at the papal Curia and a member of the high nobility of Venice, was especially important. The Jesuits had a connection to him through his nephew Pietro, with whom Ignatius and his friends had made contact during their time in Venice.[3] Ignatius and his companions had established amicable ties to further members of the papal Curia even before 1540. One of them, Pietro Codacio, even joined the Society and provided it with its first real estate in the center of the city. Codacio was also important because he was "extremely dear" to the pope.[4]

By adeptly exploiting and cleverly expanding their few existing connections over the following years, the Jesuits laid an enduring social foundation for their subsequent activities. They created an astonishingly dense network of highly placed sympathizers. Their excellent relations with Leonora Osorio, wife of the Spanish ambassador and future viceroy of Sicily, were particularly important. Pierre Favre had already had spiritual discussions with her sister in Spain. Margaret (Madama) of Parma, an illegitimate daughter of Emperor Charles V, and her husband, Ottavio Farnese, were no less important. Powerful groups of religiously engaged laymen with sympathy for the Jesuits coalesced around them, just as they did around Osorio. After a few trying years, these supporters helped foster the young order's social support and influence in the Eternal City.

In Spain, the fate of the young Society of Jesus also initially depended on the goodwill of individual nobles. Charles V was very skeptical of the new order. His two daughters, Maria and Joanna, were the ones who aroused sympathy for the Society in Spain and across Europe. Maria, as the wife of Charles's nephew Maximilian II, became empress herself and was instrumental in establishing the Society in Vienna. This groundbreaking connection to the emperor's daughters was forged by their governess, Leonor de Mascareñas, who wholeheartedly embraced the new order after meeting Pierre Favre in 1541. Leonor, in turn, was related to Pedro de Mascareñas, the Portuguese ambassador in Rome. At the instigation of his relative Leonor, he sought out Ignatius there—and gave a positive account of their meeting to his king, João III. The king of Portugal then became arguably the early Jesuits' most important patron of all and soon made it possible for them to commence their missionary endeavors in Asia.

Building on these initial successes, the Jesuits managed to break into leading social circles almost everywhere in Europe and abroad within a few years, rapidly establishing ties to the rich and powerful. That social savvy is a key aspect of the Jesuit success story. Women remained especially important for helping the Jesuits integrate in society in the early decades of their existence.[5] In Marchena, the residence of the dukes of Arcos, approximately two days' journey east of Seville, the duchess "burned with the holy desire" to found a college in 1553.[6] She and her husband pondered how they might collect the necessary resources for such an institution. At this point, the pious narrative duly records that the noblewoman sold off "a large part of her jewelry, which was very exquisite and of high value," for this purpose.[7] Shortly thereafter, Francisco de Borja, who was incidentally in the area, founded the institution she had longed for.

Noble patronage was nothing unusual for the Jesuits in particular or for the church in general in the late Middle Ages and the early modern period. The institution of *patrocinatus*, the supervision and care of religious institutions, was a central part of the mentality of the Second Estate.[8] Taking on religious obligations and responsibilities was an indispensable item in a nobleman's portfolio; they augmented one's fame and prestige. The need for self-representation and piety were thus two sides of the same coin and inseparably linked. The Jesuits exploited this connection by making a special offer to would-be noble donors: the Society dangled the prospect of a kind of title it could confer on benefactors. Eminent patrons were honored as *fundatores* for founding a new institution or as *benefactores* for providing important support as construction progressed.[9] Women could compete for the title of "Mother of the church," which was conferred on the one who gave the most—a semi-official document made the title conspicuous everywhere. *Fundatores* and *benefactores* at least were long remembered and regularly celebrated by the local Jesuit community. Every house had its own lists and books in which donations were commemorated.[10] The Jesuits were very receptive to the specific wishes and desires of *benefactores*, especially those who made substantial contributions. Conspicuous "gratitude" was in order, as the experienced Jesuit Carlo Scribani wrote.[11] The foundation stories and annual reports of individual houses, which aimed to serve as sources of pious inspiration, therefore had to give prominent accounts of such support.[12] In exceptional cases, the pious sponsors and their families were even mentioned in inscriptions on the facades of the buildings, as, for instance, in Naples in 1586, where above the entrance to the college large letters celebrated the "generosity, patriotism, and piety" of the *fundator* Roberto Carafa.[13] In brief, the Jesuits created a widely recognizable special status for benefactors. The interests of the powerful and the Jesuits often converged on this path, albeit not always without some friction. The Society established its place in society. The superior generals in Rome soon could no longer take refuge from the stream of inquiries about new houses that came pouring in; sometimes they had to make difficult decisions about where they could approve new institutions and where not. More than 150 requests had to be rejected by 1593.[14]

When the Council of Trent urged individual bishops in Italy, France, Germany, and Spain to look for new methods of pastoral care and religious organization, the bishops also began to support the young and dynamic Society of Jesus more enthusiastically. Cardinal Stanislaus Hosius, bishop of Warmia in Prussia, may serve as an example of these episcopal sympathizers.[15] The Jesuits also benefited from the confidence of the church leadership in Paris. Guillaume Duprat, for example, the bishop of Clermont, let some Jesuits live in his official quarters in Paris for a while and later gave them various property holdings in a private capacity.[16] With these resources, supplemented by gifts from other donors, it became possible to maintain an ever-expanding college, albeit only with great effort. The people and soon the Jesuits themselves called this institution the Collège de Clermont, thus immortalizing the founder Duprat until the college was renamed in 1682.

After 1682, the college was known as Louis-le-Grand. This new name was intended to tout the college's prominent new patron far and wide: Louis XIV, the Sun King, had adopted the venerable college, sponsoring new buildings and donating significant sums of money. This was not the first time that a French king took direct responsibility for a Jesuit college. Henry IV, Louis's grandfather, had done the same when he founded a large model Jesuit school in La Flèche, 250 kilometers southwest of Paris, giving it the prestigious name Collège Henri IV.[17] The hearts of the king and his wife were to be buried there after their death. Placing the college in the Society's hands put the Jesuits under a special obligation to remember and pray for the souls of the deceased monarchs. The fact that Henry in particular, the ex-Protestant on the throne of France, took such an interest in the Jesuits is merely a particularly powerful reflection of a broader trend. By 1600 at the latest, the Jesuits had attained such great social recognition and had become so thoroughly embedded in society that they had opened the door to princely courts across Europe.[18]

Ignatius explicitly encouraged his men to foster such close collaboration with the ruling class. While it would be utterly wrong to accuse the Jesuits of lopsidedly elitist preferences—as we have seen, the Society took great pains to tend to marginalized social groups—social elites still were very important for the success of the new order. Ignatius viewed them as potent catalysts for the religious goals, practices, and ideas of the Society of Jesus. Loyola elaborated on this idea in his letters and other texts: in his eyes, the Jesuits' typical pursuit of *magis* (more), their obligation to maximize their spiritual efficiency, necessitated that they attach special value to the rich and powerful.[19] There also were economic reasons: with the beginning of the college system, the Jesuits incurred immense expenses as they founded ever more schools. Colleges that required a large teaching staff but gave instruction for free were very expensive. Ample financial endowments were necessary to found and maintain them, and only social elites controlled the necessary capital.

On the whole, the entanglement with the potentates of the day that the Jesuits sought out and initiated had highly ambivalent consequences. On the one hand, it conferred a preeminent social position on the Society of Jesus in society and rooted it at the center of aristocratic culture. On the other, however, the order became dependent on its patrons, whose support was contingent on personal interests all their own.[20] The newly founded order was by no means always the master of its destiny. As General Muzio Vitelleschi admitted, those who won social prestige by allying themselves with influential and wealthy patrons like the Balbi of Genoa also always had "to keep an eye on the concordat with the Signori Balbi."[21] At least to some extent, the new order was the plaything of the rich and powerful, who were enthusiastic about the Jesuits' ideals but also combined their involvement with their own agenda.

In light of this dependency on the goodwill of local noblemen and wealthy patrons, the Jesuits could not always predict when and where they might settle. The growth of the Society and the precise site of new houses retained an element of unpredictability. And yet it is impossible to overlook the fact that the Jesuits had an ever-clearer idea of where they wanted to found new houses—and where not. In other words: even if the location of new houses did not follow an explicit master plan, we can still clearly identify some basic principles. The Jesuits tried to cover territory as strategically as possible. In particular, they wanted to be present at places that could serve as catalysts for their dissemination. They therefore focused on cities and transit routes. In the *Constitutions*, Ignatius mentioned "large nations, cities, and universities" as particularly suitable places for Jesuit houses because, from there, they would be able to reach the greatest number of people.[22] The Jesuits followed this advice in many places. In Andalusia, for example, by approximately 1600, the Society had "occupied" virtually every city with more than fifteen thousand inhabitants, and by 1650, with twenty-two houses, the Jesuits had a presence in almost every settlement with more than ten thousand inhabitants.[23] In southern Italy around the year 1600, the Jesuits also skillfully proceeded to close geographic gaps in their coverage.[24] Fabio Fabi, the provincial of Naples, even drafted a kind of general map for future settlements—a rare example of a carefully formulated geographic strategy. The Jesuits' special focus on major urban centers set them apart from other orders founded at the same time. The otherwise comparable Capuchins or the Recollects, for instance, concentrated to a much greater extent on smaller cities and nonurban settlements.[25]

The Society of Jesus thus attempted to cover and provide for the population by adapting to the network of European cities. It tried to avoid oversaturation, however, in certain regions; in southern Spain, for example, the Jesuits left certain larger settlements "unoccupied" if there were already several houses in the immediate vicinity. The superiors feared, not without reason, that rivalries might erupt between institutions located too close together, as happened on Sardinia, for example, where the colleges in Sassari and Cagliari feuded over the location of a new university on the island after 1555.[26] It thus was very realistic of General Vitelleschi, when he glanced at the very dense geography of Jesuit settlements in northern Germany in 1631, to urge restraint in subsequent plans.[27]

Among the Jesuits, however, these concerns never transformed into a rigid principle as was the case with the mendicant orders. The Dominicans and Franciscans determined the exact distance that had to be maintained between individual institutions; the Society of Jesus dispensed with such explicit rules. In other regards, however, the new order's urban strategy followed the tradition of the medieval mendicant orders. Whereas the earlier Benedictines, Cluniacs, and Cistercians had established themselves predominantly in remote locations away from urban hubbub, the Dominicans and Franciscans focused on population centers. The mendicants usually built their monasteries, however, on the edge of town; the Jesuits, in contrast, pushed into the heart of metropoles. Ignatius himself wanted houses to be located "not too far away from engagement with the city."[28] In a famous view of the city of Rome in the "official" biography of Ignatius by the Jesuit Pedro de Ribadeneira (fig. 9), the headquarters of the Society is presented as the center of the Eternal City. That was the ideal, and often enough it was realized.

In Rome itself, the Jesuits—along with other new orders—established a new, third spiritual center between the papal poles of St. Peter's and the Lateran Basilica with their long traditions in the heart of the ancient city. The Jesuits likewise pushed their way into the most prominent places in Florence, Antwerp, and Madrid. Here they established massive houses that encompassed whole city blocks and contained a church, living and working quarters, and often the college and schools themselves.[29] Insofar as they had a serious option to do so, the Jesuits deliberated very carefully about where they would settle between the various neighborhoods of a city. In addition to infrastructural and economic factors, the need to organize pastoral care for the urban population optimally was also always a central concern.[30]

Many major cities, both in Europe and overseas, even had several Jesuit institutions. This was true not just in Rome, where there was a veritable network of Jesuit establishments consisting of the various colleges, the professed house, the novitiate, and sundry papal institutions under Jesuit supervision; there were also several Jesuit institutions in Paris and Madrid. Occasionally, there were even several institutions

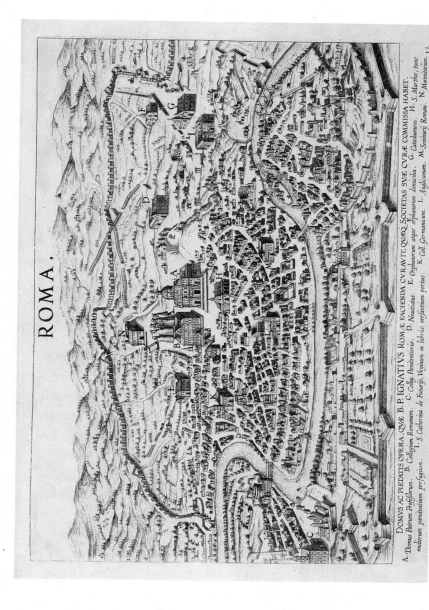

ROMA.

DOMVS AC PIETATIS OPERA, QVÆ B. P. IGNATIVS ROMÆ FACIENDA CVRAVIT; QVÆQ. SOCIETAS SVÆ CVRÆ COMMISSA HABET.

A. *Domus Patrum Professorum.*   B. *Collegium Romanum.*   C. *Colleg. Pænitentiariæ.*   D. *Neophitæ.*   E. *Orphanorum atque orphanarum domicilia.*   G. *Catechumeni.*   H. *S. Martha, tunc mulierum pænitentium perfugium.*   I. *S. Catherina de Funarÿs, Virginum in lubrica versantium portus.*   K. *Coll. Germanicum.*   L. *Anglicanum.*   M. *Seminarÿ Romani.*   N. *Mœnitarium.* 12.

FIGURE 9. "Ignatian Rome": the Eternal City and its Jesuit institutions. Pedro de Ribadeneira, *Vita beati patris Ignatii Loyolae religionis Societatis Iesu fundatoris ad vivum expressa* [. . .] (Antwerp 1610), table 12. © Boston College.

of the same type. There were two colleges, for example, in Lyon and Valladolid, and three in Naples. The Jesuits' dense urban presence could sometimes lead to internal tension. In Valladolid, the colleges of San Ignacio and San Ambrosio became embroiled in a bitter dispute in 1667/8, when San Ambrosio terminated its pastoral collaboration with San Ignacio at Christmastime, alleging it was overextended.[31]

Notable Jesuit authors like the Neapolitan Scipione Paolucci explicitly stressed the urban character of the Society of Jesus. Only cities were suitable places, he argued, "where our men can found a House or College with appropriate dignity and establish themselves permanently."[32] But that by no means meant, Paolucci continued, that the regions between cities dropped from view. Instead, as we have seen, they were integrated in the regional mission. No place was too small or too remote for the missionaries to visit. The ambitious spiritual leaders of the early modern period had long since lost faith in rural priests, but the Jesuits neither could nor would take up permanent residence in little villages or hamlets. It was the new orders of the eighteenth century that took a different tack in this regard. The Jesuits, in contrast, made their urban bases the point of departure for frequent visits to rural territories.

Only novitiates and tertiates were located deliberately in the relative isolation of smaller rural sites. Here, Jesuits in training were supposed to concentrate entirely and completely on themselves. The novitiate for Upper Germany in Landsberg, for example, was located in such a settlement. A quiet place far away from the city had the advantage that "it does not have the noise of business, the annoyance of deals, the restlessness of study."[33] That would be good for the spiritual development of young members, the Jesuits assumed. Jesuits like the unorthodox and rebellious mystic Jean-Joseph Surin could see things the same way for other reasons. Surin viewed long stays in the countryside as a welcome alternative to city life and declared the country the opposite of court, which he regarded as the center of unchristian evil.[34] But such skepticism of cities and courts was ultimately a minority opinion. The Jesuits viewed cities as major pastoral hubs: it was here that they saw especially favorable opportunities to cultivate social contacts.

The Ideal of Poverty and Economic Pursuits

Cooperation with social elites was not exclusively about money, but it was very often about money. Even Jesuits had to eat and drink, live and sleep. They needed rest and help for their own spiritual well-being. Without churches and buildings, even Jesuits could not live and work. But where was all that supposed to come from, and how could the Society pay for it?

The question of how a Catholic order could support its members and finance their pursuits was repeatedly discussed—and fiercely debated— over the course of history. According to the traditional view, life in a religious order should be governed by the three "evangelical counsels" of chastity, obedience, and poverty. But what exactly poverty meant in the context of life in an order was anything but clear. The Jesuits advocated goals and ideals that were definitely not of this world, but they lived and achieved these goals in and with this world. This dichotomy had been inescapable ever since the mendicant orders of the thirteenth century radicalized the call for poverty. Francis of Assisi resolved to combine dedicated engagement in the world with drastic rejection of its economic standards. Countless Franciscans over the centuries demanded strict adherence to this radical life without possessions, while other brothers were more amenable to compromise.

A good three hundred years after Francis, the Jesuits also faced the challenge of reconciling active and deliberate engagement in the world with distance from prevailing economic practices as stipulated by the imperative of poverty. A remarkable document from the first half of 1544 takes up this very issue. The text is a fragment of Ignatius's *Spiritual Diary* that he apparently regularly kept during his prayers and meditations.[35] Precisely the section in which Ignatius wrestled with the question of how one should cultivate poverty over the long term survives. His impressive notes, which often feel very immediate, vividly document the relentlessness, spiritual tension, and mental exertion with which Ignatius tackled this question in prayer and meditation. He ultimately decided in favor of forgoing possessions entirely. The saintly founders of the mendicant orders, above all Francis, exerted a strong appeal on Ignatius since his conversion.

Over the long term, however, the Jesuits neither could nor would abide by this strict position. It was the large-scale takeover of schools that changed the Jesuits' economic behavior. Since the colleges provided for and housed not only the Jesuits who lived there but often also several hundred students for free, and since food and equipment were also necessary, these institutions devoured enormous sums. Schools could not be built on a foundation of absolute poverty. Hence it became necessary to introduce a new type of house, the *collegium* (college). In contrast to the original form of Jesuit houses, the *casa professa* (professed house), colleges were permitted to own land and other regular sources of income like capital gains. Various systems of poverty were established in the Society thereafter.[36]

Step by step, through the usual channels of donations, legacies, purchases, and trade, the Jesuit colleges soon acquired extensive resources.[37] At most houses, this resulted in a dense and often impenetrable web of highly heterogeneous properties and sources of income. In the seventeenth century, the Jesuits in Blois, France, for example, annually received several payments from other monasteries in the city, as well as from the cathedral chapter, in addition to various rents, a pension from the royal treasury, a payment from the royal salt tax, and, after 1710, the proceeds of a small priory nearby, which were collected in turn from a complicated variety of sources. To keep track of it all, they maintained a special account book in which the various assets were clearly described, along with instructions for what had to be done and when each year so that the income was actually collected.[38] Conditions were similarly complicated almost everywhere else.[39]

This rather uncoordinated proliferation of sources of income highlights the fact that the Society of Jesus never pursued something like a coordinated transregional financial strategy. Finance was one of those aspects of life in which the leadership in Rome dispensed with universal planning and initiatives. Rome was content to set general guidelines and review individual decisions and, if necessary, reverse them. In other words, economic activity in the order was always left to single units, normally individual houses or provinces. It was on this level that decisions were made and people were held accountable for potential losses.

The poverty and wealth of the Society were essentially the poverty and wealth of its constituent parts. It was up to regional and local superiors to ensure that their houses had a livelihood.

Opening up the Society to economic pursuits unleashed a constant internal debate over the limits of what was permissible. Complicated questions might arise in this respect. According to the *Constitutions*, for example, professed houses were not supposed to rely on any permanent income, yet they were permitted to own rural houses as places of recreation or infirmaries. But what happened if vines, apples, or olives, for instance, grew in the gardens of such rural houses? The *Constitutions* forbade the Jesuits to draw "revenue" from these rural houses, but the casuists of the seventeenth century saw room for a little leeway here. Juan de Lugo discussed at length what this rule meant. The Jesuits were permitted to eat the fruit, but they were not allowed to produce wine or oil. They could plant grains and vegetables in the gardens of these houses, but they were forbidden to process them into bread. They could keep hens and bees and enjoy the eggs and honey that were produced, but they could not sell these items under any circumstances. They were not allowed to install a fish pond, but if the house was near a stream or lake, they were permitted to fish. Many further details followed. Apparently, even in the seemingly simple case of a professed house, it was impossible to define where "poverty" stopped and "property" started, where "livelihood" stopped and "revenue" began.[40]

Real estate could bring a whole other set of problems with it. In 1589, the Duke of Bavaria gave the Jesuits of Ingolstadt the buildings and rights to the Benedictine monastery of Biburg, which had been dissolved in 1555. But an unusual challenge came attached: Biburg was one of the local ecclesiastical estates (*Landstände*)—in other words, Biburg and now also the Jesuit college of Ingolstadt had a vote in Bavarian politics at the regional diet. Even if the real weight of Biburg's vote was very slight, it still raised a fundamental problem because such political involvement was explicitly prohibited. The Jesuits of Upper Germany discussed with Rome at length what they should do.[41] Many Jesuits of Dillingen wanted to give the property back rather than accept political entanglement. In the end, they kept the property and thus also the associated status of a *Landstand*, but they permanently refrained from exercising their political rights.[42]

The moral quandaries raised by speculation, lending, interest, and the suspicion of usury were especially vexing. Usury remained a vice in the eyes of the early modern church. Monetary transactions were permissible only if they were clearly distinct from usurious practices. In Germany and Austrian, a heated controversy raged in the 1570s and 1580s over whether one was permitted to collect 5 percent interest on rents. The Fuggers supported collecting interest, but Duke William V of Bavaria—"the Pious"—long held the contrary position. The Jesuits were likewise torn. The Curia of the Society and the pope in Rome had to intervene several times. Committees of high-ranking experts repeatedly met to reach a ruling. The result was very conservative: only in certain circumstances was 5 percent interest allowed. Many Jesuits involved in these debates were still fundamentally opposed to collecting interest.[43]

In the long term, however, Catholic theologians and philosophers came to a reassessment of the interest problem in the sixteenth century, starting with the Spanish Dominicans and Jesuits at the University of Salamanca. This had important historical consequences. The view that moderate interest was permissible came to be the Catholic majority opinion. Many Jesuits adopted this compromise as their own.[44] Collecting and paying interest seem to have become largely normalized for them. In 1554, for example, Juan de Polanco repeatedly gave detailed and very forthcoming advice about how an acquaintance of the Paduan Jesuit Giovanni Battista Tavono in Rome might invest his money. With no moral qualms and with obvious expertise, Polanco explained the anticipated profits and the advantages and risks of various investment options.[45] It was clear to many Catholic moral theologians of the sixteenth and seventeenth centuries that money was a legitimate commodity, the price of which was determined by supply and demand. Hence, around the year 1600, Jesuits like Leonard Lessius and Luis de Molina presumed that collecting interest was permissible.[46] When a more pronouncedly rigorist tendency toward strict moral theology emerged around the year 1660, some Jesuits backpedaled. Now, the willingness to collect interest was interpreted as evidence of the Society's laxity, and the Jesuits adapted by making more careful and more conservative decisions about money transactions. The central leadership also intervened when Jesuit publications defended collecting interest all too openly.[47]

In the context of these efforts to establish a nuanced position—and sometimes outside of it—the Jesuits were indeed quite active in the capital markets of early modern Europe. Everywhere, money was lent, invested, given, traded, or donated, or existing funds were transferred for use. In 1650, for example, Johannes Egen donated a sum of 5,000 guldens to the Jesuits of Innsbruck, but this sum had already been lent to the Upper Swabian town of Saulgau, some two hundred kilometers to the northwest, at an interest rate of 5 percent.[48] By accepting the donation, the order nolens volens also accepted all its concomitant circumstances and initially ran into difficulties. Saulgau either could not or would not fulfill its obligations, and negotiations and mediation were necessary before the *patres* in Innsbruck received even a portion of their revenue.

If the Jesuits' own capital was insufficient, they took out credit. In Rome, the extravagant expansion of Il Gesù for the Quarant'ore was financed by a Jesuit confraternity (Congregazione de' Nobili), which in turn derived much of its income from rents, leases, and interest.[49] Curiously, a significant proportion of this interest came from loans that other Jesuit houses had taken out from the Roman confraternity. Such internal loans were a matter of course in the early modern Society of Jesus. Separate institutions regularly lent each other money, and bitter disputes might arise over details of repayment. In 1755, the province of England lent French missionaries in the Caribbean the enormous sum of 327,000 livres—and was dragged into the ensuing debt scandal that enveloped the French provinces in 1760, ultimately becoming a decisive factor in the collapse of the Society in France.[50] The situation was even more complex when the Jesuits took out loans on the free market, which also frequently happened. It often was impossible to maintain the colleges or to carry out building projects without outside money. The Colegio Máximo in Mexico City in the latter half of the seventeenth century had to manage no fewer than "176 loans, mortgages, and accompanying legal fees."[51]

Some houses were completely debt-free, such as Konstanz or Freiburg in 1606. Other colleges, in contrast, like Munich or Augsburg, piled on massive liabilities so that at times almost half of their income had to be spent on debt management.[52] According to their own testimony, the Spanish provinces were no less than 227,000 ducats in debt in the year 1590, at a time when it was possible to purchase several houses in Valladolid for 3,000 ducats.[53] Sometimes such debts were the result of maladministration. In 1650, for example, a royal commission investigated the partial insolvency of the college of San Hermenegildo in Seville, finding that it was primarily the result of the shady dealings by Brother Andrés de Villar Goitia.[54] Structural factors, however, were more often probably to blame for tight fiscal conditions. The original financial arrangements of institutions here and there were too thin. Over the course of the seventeenth century, underfinanced houses across Europe were closed after the initial euphoria behind them evaporated. Other colleges fell victim to their own success, when they outgrew the size originally intended for them. The Jesuits therefore were constantly on the lookout for additional gifts and donations: it was the only way they could finance growth.

Shrewd capital management was a relatively new form of business in the sixteenth century. Agroeconomics, in contrast, was a far more traditional means of achieving sustainability. Until well into the nineteenth century, Europe was profoundly shaped by agriculture. A majority of people's income came directly or indirectly from working the land. "Property" and "income" also initially meant agricultural revenue for the Society of Jesus. The Jesuits acquired land and had it farmed to support their colleges. This had a variety of consequences. In Ettlingen in Baden, the college building itself initially served as its economic hub, but so much noise was generated every day that the "peace and calm that one needs for religious exercises" was now simply out of the question.[55] In light of the agricultural basis of their livelihood, the Jesuits—like society at large—were also subject to uncontrollable external circumstances: bad weather, low prices, the chaos of war, and social unrest could ruin harvests and diminish income.[56] Finally, the agrarian nature of the Jesuit economy had farther-reaching social and political consequences because in early modern society landownership also always entailed authority over the people who lived on the land and farmed it.[57] The Jesuits were thus dragged into the daily happenings of villages and farmsteads: they might become judges of the first instance, authorities over infrastructure, mediators in local conflicts, or the benevolent lords of subjects in distress. None of this was a direct result of their religious endeavors, but rather of the legal and social realities of early modern feudal society.

Conditions in Augsburg illustrate how Jesuit colleges were integrated into rural society and the agrarian economy.[58] The Jesuits in the city on the Lech had initially relied on subventions from the Fuggers, but by the year 1602 they had raised enough capital to buy an entire village for 42,500 guldens: Kissing, some ten kilometers south of the city on the east bank of the Lech. What the Jesuits acquired was a considerable property at the time: Kissing consisted of twelve major farmsteads and more than a hundred smaller farms and a mill. In the same year, the friendly Duke of Bavaria, Maximilian I, conferred the so-called *Hofmark* on the Jesuits, that is, the right to exercise lower judicial authority with all its associated rights, duties, and fees. In subsequent years and decades, they bought or acquired by trade further nearby estates. In 1603, they even acquired the little local castle of Kissing (fig. 10). The village peasants were obliged to pay the *patres* regular and precisely fixed duties in cash and kind—and that was exactly the economic advantage of such a property. In this way, it served its purpose of providing a stable income to support the college of Augsburg. There were further, smaller sources of income in Kissing, such as the fish pond or game, the rights to which the Jesuits held since 1611.

The manorial administration of such a village, particularly in the eyes of the Jesuits, included attention to infrastructure. In Kissing, for example, they took it upon themselves to organize elementary education. Thus a "schoolmaster" is attested there since 1609. By 1688, they had built a schoolhouse. As landlords, the Jesuits were also responsible for organizing—but not for carrying out—local pastoral care. They were involved in the logistics of collecting the tithe, which supported the local priest. In 1698, they reached an arrangement with the priest as to how the renovation of the rectory should be financed.

FIGURE 10. The castle in Kissing (top left), a gem of Jesuit real estate. Michael Wening, *Historico-Topographica Descriptio* (Munich 1701). © Bayerische Staatsbibliothek München, Hbks/F 18-1.

It was wartime that highlighted how closely connected the Jesuits were to their village and how much responsibility they bore for the fate of the people who lived there. When Swedish troops invaded in 1632, the *patres* ransomed their peasants from Swedish captivity by selling the last remaining objects of value in the college: embroidered tapestries. At the end of the war, when not only most farms in the village but also the church had been destroyed or damaged by the ravages of war, the Jesuits were expected, as the landlords, to take part in reconstruction. They invested seventy guldens, for example, to restore the church walls. When French troops occupied the area in 1703 during the War of the Spanish Succession, the Jesuits negotiated with the occupiers to ward off the worst for their peasants.

But their relationship with their subjects was not always harmonious. The feudal rural society of the early modern period was a society of conflict. Landlords and peasants squabbled constantly over their mutual rights and duties. Conflicts over corvée (socage) were especially common.[59] In Kissing, in 1606, the Jesuits ordered their subjects to help them plant a hedge, but the peasants refused, and it took a ruling of the ducal court in Munich to resolve the dispute in the Jesuits' favor. Other quarrels concerned not so much the Jesuits' relations with their subjects as those with neighboring authorities. The exact boundary of the Jesuits' property and jurisdiction, for instance, was unclear. The Jesuits of Augsburg had to fight a century-long legal battle, from 1605 to 1719, until a ducal commission decided the matter. At times, fish were stolen from the Jesuits' pond, or the Jesuits were dragged into the domestic inheritance disputes of their peasants, whose conflicts might affect the Society's property.[60] Such entanglement in village society regularly thrust the Jesuits into costly and complex legal disputes over property, rights, and fees.

In the missionary territories outside of Europe, the agrarian economy also was of paramount importance to the Jesuit colleges, but on a completely different order of magnitude. The kings of Europe had pledged to provide support for the missionaries in their colonies; this was part of the so-called *padronado* (Spanish; cf. Portuguese: *padroado*): secular and ecclesiastical authority over the newly discovered territories should be united under the same princely auspices. In practice, however, the Jesuits quickly found out—like many other missionary orders—that this ambition was never completely achieved. Francis Xavier, for example, did not hesitate to inform the king of Portugal, João III, of the partial failure of this noble idea.[61] In economic terms, this meant that the Jesuits themselves (and their colleagues from other orders) had to acquire economic resources of their own just to meet expenses, whether they wanted to or not. There soon also were donations overseas, but by no means on the same scale as in Europe and only where there was a sufficiently large European population—that was not the case in India, China, or the Amazon. These missions collected donations at home in Europe—not without success—but the amounts that the house of the Duke of Bavaria or members of the Fuggers regularly gave for the mission in China were no more than a drop in the bucket.[62] There also were no old and long-standing sources of ecclesiastical income from monasteries in the colonies that might have been redirected to the Society.[63] Reservations about investing in mining grew in the late seventeenth century, even though—in Mexico, for instance—the Jesuits regularly invested in mines to a limited extent.[64]

Thus, to an even greater extent than in Europe, the Jesuits resorted to agriculture. Everywhere, they quickly came to the conclusion that they had to be more or less self-sufficient and outfit and maintain their missionary efforts on their own. Their experiences in Brazil since the early 1540s may have been decisive here, influencing the missionaries in India, on the Zambezi, and in Mexico and Peru as much as those in the Caribbean and Japan.[65] They first received their lands predominantly from donations, but, by the end of the sixteenth century, increasingly from planned, proactive purchases.[66] In some parts of the New World, the Society of Jesus became one of the greatest landowners of all in this way.[67]

Some estates were let out to tenants; the colleges that owned them lived off the rent, which they often still accepted in kind. Far more remarkably, however, the Jesuits often worked their latifundia personally, and in the most diverse branches of agricultural production. In Argentina, Portugal, and elsewhere, they were among the most important cattle breeders. The college of Rio de Janeiro reportedly owned no fewer than 17,050 heads of cattle in 1701.[68] The Jesuits also bred and sold mules in grand style in Argentina.[69] After some initial hesitation, they got into the production of sugar in Brazil and the Caribbean and built their own plantations— including slaves, as we shall see. In the eighteenth century, Fr. Antoine Lavalette tried to introduce sugar production to the Caribbean island of Dominica so the Society could at last get a handle on its debts on Martinique. This bold plan, however, had disastrous consequences: the endeavor ended in fiscal ruin. The bankruptcy of Lavalette's plantation was one of the catalysts for the suppression of the Society of Jesus in France.[70]

The productivity of these agricultural efforts varied in the extreme. In Baja California, for example, the Jesuits were long unable to feed themselves with their own produce. The natural conditions in this extremely arid region were too poor. For a long time, the missionaries were more or less entirely dependent on agricultural support from the

Mexican mainland, where Jesuit haciendas on the Sea of Cortés usually produced more than what was needed locally. The gardens of Baja California, by contrast, produced just one product in moderate surfeit: wine, which was allegedly of high quality. The Jesuits sent this back to the mainland, usually as payment for services rendered, although they also sold it for cash.

Other agricultural undertakings of the Society, in contrast, brought in tremendous yields that far surpassed their own needs. Jesuit houses initially preferred to sell their surpluses to other Jesuit institutions. In this way, a kind of food supply chain was created within the order, although products were still constantly bought and sold, not normally given.[71] But many products, such as animal skins or sugar, were never intended for direct consumption, but rather were produced with an eye to local, regional, and even international markets. The Jesuits in the missionary territories were irresistibly drawn into commerce with the goods they produced.

The Jesuits were not, however, without scruples. The problem, in terms of canon law, was "profit"—or, rather, the intention of making one. The exchange of goods could be legitimated only if it was conducted in the service of *caritas*. But precisely these categories became more and more controversial with the passage of time.[72] The friendly Pope Gregory XIII declared that the Jesuits' commercial undertakings were "charity" because they served to maintain the order's religious institutions. Other, later popes retracted this interpretation. The Jesuit generals also remained highly skeptical and vigilant over the long term. Still, the kings of Portugal allowed the Jesuits from the beginning to ship at least small quantities of exotic goods—cloth or spices—and sell them at market value, that is, at a profit (and often duty-free). Other initiatives, however, such as the export of brazilwood, were prohibited in Portugal by the now Spanish kings around the year 1600. Later, a large proportion of Jesuit sugar and cocoa production in Brazil was put on the market. It represented, however, only a vanishingly small part of the total exports of these raw materials from the wealthy colony.

The most remarkable involvement of the Society of Jesus in international trade, however, played out on the other side of the world.

Beginning in 1557, China ceased selling its silk products overseas on account of the threat posed by regional pirates, affecting the trade with Japan most of all. The Portuguese soon assumed the role of middlemen in the Far East, which they began to play from their base in Macao. Probably around the last quarter of the sixteenth century, the Jesuits also began to get involved. In the province of Japan, the Society pushed for a share in the silk trade to cover the rising cost of the mission on the island kingdom—a typical case of commerce in the name of *caritas*, they argued. In the long run, however, this business brought them far more trouble and mistrust than profits. Many of their shipments never arrived, and the profits were much smaller than widely anticipated. Using Macao as their base, the Jesuits also shipped other goods across Asia, including sandalwood and various spices. But even though these entanglements in regional and transregional commerce frequently resulted in scandal, we still can observe that the Jesuits' operations were neither massive in scale nor conducted unscrupulously, let alone according to a profit-oriented economic rationale.

Finally, special legal and economic prerogatives helped reinforce the financial basis of the Society. Tax and duty exemptions could be granted. Limitless variations were possible: some benefits affected the Jesuits and all other clergy or religious orders, whereas other privileges were conferred on them exclusively. Jesuit privileges that were conspicuous in everyday business were particularly prone to inspire envy.[73] Exemption from the tithe, for example, which the Jesuits often enjoyed, could lead to major conflicts—their escalating dispute with Bishop Palafox in Mexican Puebla was just one particularly virulent example.

Privileges also carried risks: they ultimately were tokens of a ruler's favor, which he could retract. When kings or princes canceled their generosity on account of their own material needs, the economic basis for the Society's institutions might quickly be jeopardized. The college in Innsbruck, for example, once had to sell some of its land to make payments that were demanded without warning to finance a war.[74] Desperate rulers occasionally also tried to confiscate the property of churches and religious orders by launching large-scale reviews of their legal titles. Philip IV of Spain, as king of Portugal, conducted such reviews there in

1624 and 1634—even the Jesuits had to exert themselves to document the legitimacy of their proprietary claims.[75] Failing that, they had to purchase valid charters from the king and his officials—producing a refreshing shower of one-off income for the royal treasury.[76]

For these and many other delicate economic matters, the Jesuits needed specialists. The great ranches and haciendas of the colonies had their own supervisors and stewards on site, some of whom came from the Society, some of whom were laymen.[77] These men shouldered great responsibility with considerable autonomy. The people actually responsible for organizing, monitoring, and administering Jesuit property with all its income, however, were the procurators. They constituted a network unto themselves within the order. Every house and every province had a procurator. Procurators were also often dispatched to important economic and political hubs. The missions had procurators in the nearest provincial capital and also often one in Europe. These were the men who invested available cash, sold surpluses, took out loans, and dealt with real estate.

Some procurators were very skilled at such transactions and played to their talents with aplomb. Others had to do battle against unfavorable circumstances that hindered the Society's economic development. And still other procurators were incompetent and caused their confreres losses and debt. A certain mistrust of them can be glimpsed repeatedly in the sources. Around 1600, at any rate, General Acquaviva and his advisers in Rome felt that action had to be taken.[78] In 1602, they issued a sternly worded circular *De rebus temporalibus bene administrandis* (The good administration of worldly affairs). The General Congregations of 1646, 1649/50, and 1696/7 took the topic up again and issued instructions accordingly. "Since the abuses in the administration of worldly affairs are almost innumerable, there seems to be virtually no effective remedy that could be applied," they lamented in 1700.[79] To address these problems, the Society invested in developing and reinforcing ever more precise accounting methods. Every unit in the Society—every farm, every house, every province—had to keep records, and the information was routinely summarized and compiled into ever more expansive, up-to-date general audits. To improve this detailed bookkeeping, the leadership of the Society commissioned the Sicilian Jesuit (and

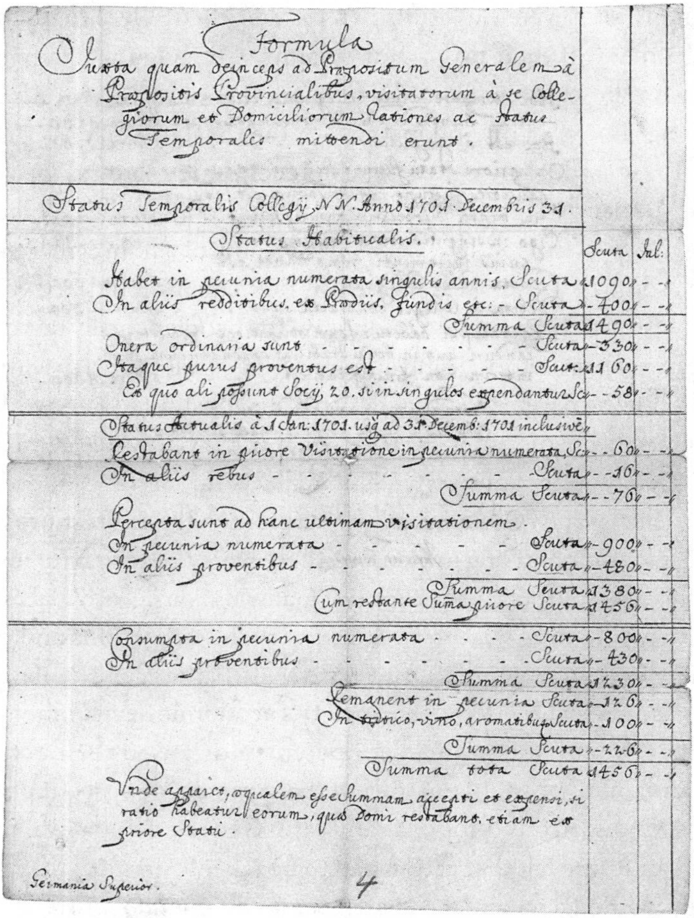

Formula
Iuxta quam deinceps ad Praepositum Generalem à Praepositis Provincialibus, visitatorum à se Collegiorum et Domiciliorum Rationes ac Status Temporales mittendi erunt.

Status Temporalis Collegii, N.N. Anno 1701. Decembris 31.

Status Habitualis.

	Scuta	Jul.
Habet in pecunia numerata singulis annis, Scuta	1090	
In aliis redditibus ex Praediis, fundis etc: Scuta	700	
Summa Scuta	1490	
Onera ordinaria sunt Scuta	330	
Itaque purus proventus est Scuta	1160	
Ex quo ali possunt Socii, 20. si in singulos expendantur Sc.	58	
Status Actualis à 1 Ian: 1701. usq ad 31 Decemb: 1701 inclusive.		
Restabant in priore Visitatione in pecunia numerata, Sc.	60	
In aliis rebus Scuta	16	
Summa Scuta	76	
Percepta sunt ad hanc ultimam visitationem.		
In pecunia numerata Scuta	900	
In aliis proventibus Scuta	480	
Summa Scuta	1380	
Cum restante Summa priore Scuta	1456	
Consumpta in pecunia numerata Scuta	800	
In aliis proventibus Scuta	430	
Summa Scuta	1230	
Remanent in pecunia Scuta	126	
In tritico, vino, aromatibus Scuta	100	
Summa Scuta	226	
Summa tota Scuta	1456	

Unde apparet, aequalem esse Summam accepti et expensi, si ratio habeatur eorum, quae domi restabant, etiam ex priore Statu.

Germania Superior. 4

FIGURE 11. Standardized accounting form of the Society of Jesus. © Bayerisches Hauptstaatsarchiv, BayHStA Jesuitica 887, fol. 4r–v.

procurator) Lodovico Flori (1579/80–1647) to compose a systematic treatise on the subject.[80] The Jesuits, moreover, continued to standardize their method of recording money transfers in their account books. In the seventeenth century, bookkeeping records could take a wide variety of forms. Some property records were even kept in running text—not as columns of numbers. But around 1700, a mandatory accounting form was introduced that procurators were required to fill out annually (fig. 11).

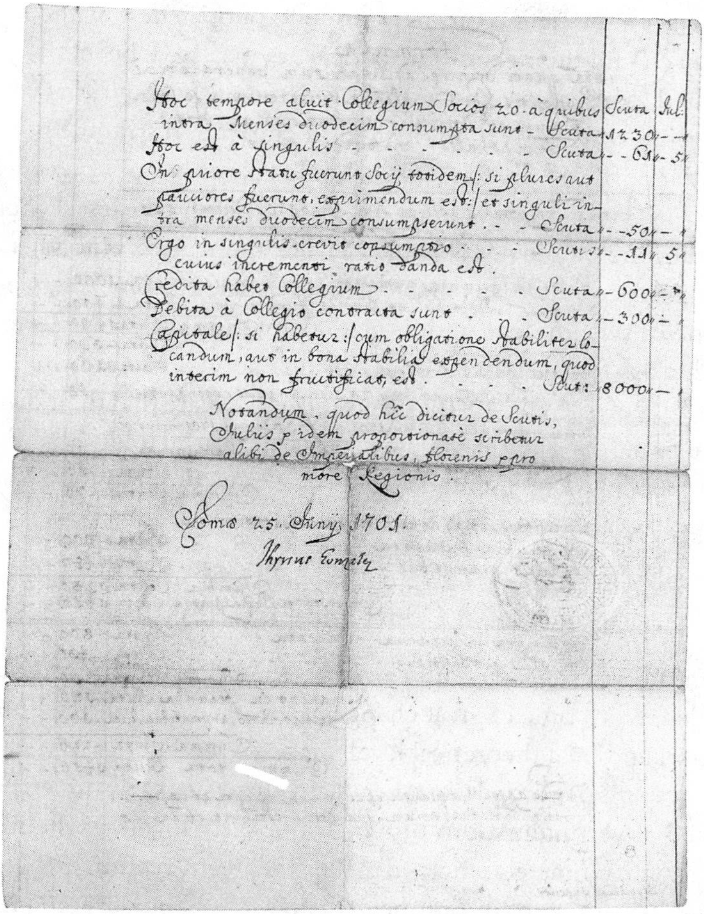

FIGURE 11. (Continued)

Bureaucratic control to raise economic efficiency and an unmistakably Christian approach to business: the Society's agricultural and fiscal
endeavors fell between these two contrary aims. The Jesuits agreed with
the entire Catholic Church in condemning profit-seeking for its own
sake as selfishness. Whoever followed his own "interest" committed
several sins, Paolo Segneri Sr. once preached.[81] Economic engagement
served first and foremost to ensure that critical needs were met, even if
it generated surpluses and profits. The Jesuits accordingly did not

proactively attempt to create new products or open new markets. However successful their economic endeavors may have been, the Jesuits remained "conservative" investors by virtue of their spiritual values.[82] They were constantly admonished to cultivate restraint. In Bavaria around 1600, they were told, "One should take only 4 or 5 percent interest on a loan, not more, because one should rather take less. When selling grain, one should not demand the maximum price, but rather sell at a median price or perhaps slightly higher. It helps inspire [people] if we sell one or two guldens under the maximum price."[83] The Jesuits declined to ask for the highest price for their goods especially in times of famine or emergencies.[84] They thus took great care that their own economic practices did not violate their ethical principles. That did not make them naive humanitarians, but turning a profit in the Society of Jesus always remained only a means to an end.

Jesuits at Court and High Politics

The middle of the sixteenth century, when the Society of Jesus was founded, was a time of great change in the realm of politics, both on a practical and on a theoretical level. Since the end of the Middle Ages, the kingdoms of Europe had taken many small steps toward territorially defined governments, out of which the early forms of the modern nation-state ultimately emerged in the seventeenth century. This fundamental development in European history could be observed in most principalities of central, southern, and western Europe. The growing complexity of the domestic apparatus of power usually was accompanied by the entrenchment of foreign enmities and alliances. One long-term international struggle in particular shaped the sixteenth, seventeenth, and eighteenth centuries and constantly affected the Jesuits: the power struggle between France on one side and the Habsburgs in Austria, Belgium, Italy, and Spain on the other.

These new realities insisted ever more urgently on being expressed in a language of their own, the language of politics, which gradually could be heard ever more clearly in the early modern period. Concepts like "politics," "the state," and "national interest" made their first appearance or became part of the general vocabulary. The rise of such new concepts was indicative of a profound transformation. These new terms showed that "politicians"—also a term invented in the early modern period—were beginning to view their field of work as something distinct. Regulating human coexistence in a community was emancipated, at least somewhat, from an exclusively religious frame of mind.

The emergence of an independent "political" view of human coexistence and the interaction of commonwealths, and the gradual formation and consolidation of the state had dramatic consequences for church and religion. As soon as the state and politics became autonomous fields, the obvious question was what their relationship would be to the church and religion. There had always been a kind of "two-pronged leadership" in Europe in the persons of the (Holy Roman) emperor and the pope, and the relationship between the two institutions had always been tense. But in the early modern period the relationship between religion and politics, as it was then being articulated for the first time, became a fundamental problem. The question became a decisive issue both in political theory and in the everyday practice of government apparatuses. In this respect, the Society of Jesus was founded during a phase of upheaval.

It would undoubtedly be incorrect, however, to claim that politics—the states—had simply bidden farewell to religion and the church in the early modern period. The opposite is correct: until well into the eighteenth century, religion remained a major presence in the political world. It is not for nothing that absolutist France under Louis XIV is today called an "ecclesiastical monarchy."[85] Cardinal-ministers were a constant presence. A series of them stretches from Jiménez in Spain in the late fifteenth century to Melchior Khlesl in Vienna, Cardinals Richelieu and Mazarin in seventeenth-century France, to their successor Fleury, Cardinal Alberoni in Spain, and many more clergymen shortly before the French Revolution. Until the fall of the ancien régime, there normally was a large number of clergymen at the courts of Europe, including many Jesuits.

Jesuits at Court

When Emperor Ferdinand III began to sound out the Protestant and therefore enemy landgrave of Hesse regarding a possible peace agreement in 1639/40 during the Thirty Years' War, one Jesuit was a close observer of the events: Johannes Gans.[86] Born in Würzburg in 1591, Gans was deployed in the Jesuit province of Austria, first as a preacher in Graz and soon afterward in Vienna. At the end of 1636, Ferdinand III appointed him his personal priest. As *Hofbeichtvater*, "court confessor," Gans, like a long line of Jesuits before and after him, heard the emperor's confession and was his direct adviser in all questions of faith, conscience, and spiritual life. He was the emperor's spiritual director, admonishing, encouraging, and consoling him as necessary. In a word: even as court confessor, every Jesuit was exactly what his title claimed: a pastor who had to take care of the soul of a person through confession and spiritual conversation. His duties were first and foremost the same as those of many other pastors in the cities and countryside.[87] Ferdinand II, for example, constantly asked his confessor for guidance on how he might live a truly pious everyday life—how often should he pray? he wanted to know one day.[88]

While, in one sense, there thus was nothing special about a confessor's role at court, in another sense it was anything but ordinary. As court confessors, Jesuits like Gans were not dealing with ordinary people, but rather with the princes and rulers of Europe. And confessors like Gans met "their" princes very frequently. They traveled with them and regularly passed in and out of their chambers. The kings of the early modern period were confronted with this adviser not once every two months like Louis XII of France (1462–1515, r. since 1498) but almost every day.[89] Hence, it is unsurprising that court confessors were confronted with burning questions of contemporary politics and formed their own opinions about them—Johannes Gans's involvement in peace negotiations with Hesse in 1640 is just one of many examples, although a particularly instructive one on account of his interconfessional openness.

What court confessors made of this close contact with "their" princes varied from case to case. Whether a court confessor might influence political decisions was primarily a question of personalities and circumstances. A confessor's character and conception of his office played as much a part as did the ruler's own self-conception. The social milieu of the court was also decisive. This was a particularly delicate aspect because the courts of the early modern period were regarded as treacherous ground for good reason. Everyday life was shaped by intrigues, coalitions, and rivalries between courtiers. More than once, the Jesuits were caught in the crossfire.

In such cases, they could not expect any help from other clergymen at court. Cardinals, bishops, canons, and chaplains were all in competition with one another when it came to bringing their religious wishes before the monarch. Cardinals and major abbots naturally insisted on their eminent positions and were in no way prepared to concede influence to confessors. It is well known, for example, to what ends Cardinal Richelieu went to control and limit the role of other court clergymen—especially that of Jesuit confessors. When Jean Suffren was to become Louis XIII's new confessor, the cardinal gave him specific guidelines in a detailed letter about how he should exercise his office. In essence, he told the Jesuit to content himself with secondary tasks—Richelieu did not tolerate competition.[90] The many clergymen at court thus exerted varied influence. The Jesuits were prominently represented, but they were far from the only mouthpiece for ecclesiastical affairs. Whereas anti-Jesuit polemic falsely and simplistically alleged that Jesuit court confessors regularly controlled their princely penitents, turning them into puppets or at least trying to do so, the reality was far more complex and manifold. The power of Jesuit confessors to influence rulers varied dramatically.

Sometimes, that power was very great. Bernhard von Galen, for example, the prince-bishop of Münster and a military enthusiast, was eager to wage war against the neighboring Netherlands together with Louis XIV in 1672. He consulted his confessor, the Jesuit Theodor Körler, to learn whether he could do so "in good conscience." When a ruler (re)formulated political questions as pastoral questions in this way, the Jesuits responsible did not shrink from answering them—Körler may have raised some nuanced considerations, but he ultimately gave his prince a very clear answer in the affirmative.[91] The Jesuit himself did not single-handedly devise von Galen's aggressive foreign policy, but he certainly influenced the course of events. Other confessors exerted a powerful influence at courts big and small across Europe. The following is related about Johannes Wolf, a largely unknown Jesuit who served as a regimental chaplain around 1700 under the converted prince and imperial field marshal Maximilian Wilhelm of Hanover: "The house is directed by Father Wolf and everything follows his commands."[92] And Jean Arnoux, S.J., persuaded his penitent King Louis XIII of France to take military action against the southern French city of Montauban in 1621.[93] In Munich and Vienna, the two uncompromising Jesuits Adam Contzen and Wilhelm Lamormaini, respectively, were strong and powerful voices in support of the fiercely anti-Protestant Edict of Restitution of 1629. They urged Maximilian, Duke of Bavaria, and Emperor Ferdinand II to issue it over the opposition of other advisers.[94]

Lamormaini in particular served Ferdinand as an interpretive and advisory authority of last resort. "Tomorrow morning," the emperor once explained, "the Hungarian affair will be deliberated, but I will not reach a conclusion because I want to know the opinion of Your Reverence and of our pious Fr. Dominic in this matter after lunchtime." Ferdinand therefore kept the Jesuit informed about current political and military events that had nothing directly or indirectly to do with his actual pastoral role. Conversation between the prince and his Jesuit confessor switched seamlessly from spiritual to secular subjects and back again. Questions such as when he should go to communion the next week harmonized perfectly in Ferdinand's view with information about the last meeting of the court council (*Hofrat*).[95]

The emperor regularly used Lamormaini and other Jesuits as messengers, for instance, to put recalcitrant persons under additional pressure or to deliver delicate, strictly confidential messages for which they occasionally even cited the seal of confession as grounds for keeping them secret.[96] The extensive travels of the Jesuits Francesco Borja and Antonio Possevino to Spain and northern Europe in the sixteenth and seventeenth centuries represent a special case with respect to these diplomatic missions because they took place at the pope's behest. Other

Jesuits traveled for secular rulers. In 1645, for example, Johannes Verveaux, the new confessor in Munich, went to Paris at Duke Maximilian's behest to sound out the feasibility of peace there in conversation with his French counterpart.[97] In the same year, Nithard Biber, the confessor of the elector of Mainz, traveled to the General Congregation in Rome and conducted numerous conversations on behalf of the archbishop at the courts he visited en route, all of which concerned the peace negotiations in Osnabrück and Münster.[98] Jesuits also served the dukes of Modena in the seventeenth century as political middlemen.[99] And Friedrich von Lüdinghausen zu Wolff, confessor of Emperor Leopold I in 1700, was involved in numerous political and religious affairs on the international stage on behalf of Vienna, not least in the negotiations over the elevation of the elector of Brandenburg, Frederick III, to king of Prussia.[100]

In France, where Jesuits had served as the confessors of the kings since about 1600, and often also as the confessors of the influential regents, the reign of Louis XIV in the late seventeenth century was the undisputed high point of a new alliance between the clergy and the monarchy. Among other things, the confessors also exerted major influence on the conferral of ecclesiastical offices. They had a voice in the appointment of approximately 110 bishops and 800 abbots because, once a week, usually on Friday morning, they advised the king precisely on this question in special sessions.[101] In Spain, the Jesuits' influence at court increased especially in the eighteenth century. The Society had been present at the Spanish court since the sixteenth century, providing confessors for leading ministers like the Count-Duke of Olivares and several wives, brothers, sons, and daughters of the monarchs. Hernando de Salazar, the Jesuit confessor of Olivares, wielded especially great political influence. Salazar embraced the role of politician and openly gave his views on political questions, advising his master, for instance, in financial affairs.[102] Salazar also sat on various government committees, just as Eberhard Nithart did several years later. Nithart was the confessor of Mariana, the wife of Philip IV of Spain, and also wielded powerful influence. General Gianpaolo Oliva made an exception for him in 1666, allowing him to bear the title "His Excellence."[103]

But despite these influential positions, the Jesuits in Spain did not gain direct access to the king himself until the Bourbon dynasty succeeded the Habsburgs in 1701. For the next fifty-five years, various members of the Society of Jesus served in Madrid as the confessors and confidants of kings. Under the melancholic but pious and detached Philip V, who reigned with one brief interruption until 1746, the confessors had major influence. Political observers in the capital were agreed that "the Catholic king dares not do or decide anything without involving his confessor," Father Bermúdez. The Jesuits at court, diplomats reported, were "the only and best channel of access" to the unstable ruler.[104] One of the confessors under the next king, Ferdinand VI, the Spanish Jesuit Francisco de Rávago, served as a kind of "minister for ecclesiastical affairs," negotiating an important concordat between Spain and the pope in 1753, among other things. Rávago also took the lead in the conferral of ecclesiastical offices and the organization of the Spanish church. "I have ordered what you propose," Ferdinand frequently noted in regard to his confessor's suggestions in such matters.[105]

But by no means every court confessor wielded such political influence. Self-confident princesses like Liselotte, Madame Palatine, simply ignored their confessors' theological warnings or saw to it that they were publicly ridiculed for their "simplistic" religious positions.[106] Some confessors were, even in the words of their own confreres, simply hopeless: "Nothing can be expected of the ineffectiveness of Fr. Clarke," remarked one about the confessor of Philip V.[107] In Bourbon France, the king's foreign policy was generally taboo for his confessors.[108] And whereas Ferdinand II, as we saw, always tended to view political decisions as questions of conscience, that was not the case under his son and successor, Ferdinand III. Contemporaries observed that he did not want the Jesuits "to dare to interfere in court affairs," but rather "attend to their own business." The new ruler was not averse to the Society of Jesus, but he gave himself greater room to maneuver with symbolic actions, for example, by (moderately) reducing donations for the Jesuits or by celebrating fewer holidays with them.[109] Johannes Gans, mentioned at the beginning of this section, had a much smaller role at court in comparison to his predecessor, Lamormaini.

Just as it is impossible to make out a typical role for Jesuit confessors at court, because ultimately every situation at court was new, it is likewise impossible to identify a coherent Jesuit political profile. Sometimes the Jesuits supported the government, sometimes the opposition, depending on which one they considered legitimate.[110] There were hard-liners and compromisers, hawks and doves among the Jesuits at court; there were flexible tacticians and narrow-minded zealots. In not a single one of the great political crises of the early modern period did the Jesuits really take the same line across Europe. At no point in time did the politically active members of the order pursue a coherently articulated goal, let alone one dictated centrally by the pope. Every situation that necessitated a political decision forced the Jesuits to consider and coordinate three major factors: the well-being of Catholicism as a whole (whatever one understood that to be), concern for one's own local projects, and the interests of one's ruler. Since opinions might be divided on any one of these points both inside and outside the Society of Jesus, a uniform political strategy that court confessors might then shrewdly implement across Europe was simply inconceivable. On the contrary, the order was implicated in numerous political contradictions that sometimes veered into the grotesque. When Louis XIV came into open conflict with the pope and, for different reasons, also with the Jesuit general Tirso González in the late seventeenth century, his confessor Pierre de La Chaise remained faithful to the king—in opposition to the pope and his own superior general. The well-being of the Catholic Church, of the Society, and of France looked very different from the perspective of a Jesuit at the French court than in the eyes of a confrere in Rome or a papal diplomat.[111] In light of the Jesuits' shifting political preferences, dominated as they were by local circumstances, the order as a whole simply cannot be said to have systematically supported the policy of any court or king. It was rather the case that every monarch demanded unconditional loyalty from "his" Jesuits, with the result that Jesuits at different courts had to take different, often antithetical, positions. The events of 1640, when France and Spain were at war, Portugal declared its independence from Spain, and an uprising against Madrid took place in Catalonia with French support, are a perfect example of the bind the Society regularly found itself in when political conflicts broke out.[112] The Society of Jesus had interests on every side. Catalan, Portuguese, Spanish, and French Jesuits all stood at odds. At the Battle of Fuentarrabía in Basque Country, 1638, the victorious Spanish bastion was fortified by the Jesuit Francesco Isasi, while his confrere Georges Fournier supported the defeated general on the French side. During the military conflicts between Portugal and Spain in 1640, Jan Ciermans designed fortifications for the Portuguese, while his confrere Jean-Charles della Faille supported the Spanish siege army as an engineer.[113]

Residence at court thus was often a two-edged sword for the Jesuits. It was very easy to make mistakes and reap harsh criticism—while it was very hard to do the right thing in such circumstances. The history of Jesuit court confessors is also a history of failure, dramatic falls from favor, and banishment in disgrace. Criticism was constant from every quarter, even from the Society itself. It might attach itself to any aspect of one's official conduct, target the substance of confessors' particular proposals, undermine their personal integrity in light of their behavior at court, or concern the spiritual side of events. Jean Arnoux was dismissed by Louis XIII after his counsel to undertake a siege of Montauban had proved unwise, with grave consequences. Pierre Coton, his predecessor, and Nicolas Caussin, one of his successors, were also banished from the court for their political views on French involvement in the Thirty Years' War. Caussin was forced to spend long years in exile in the Jesuit house in Quimper in Brittany. Some one hundred years later, Gabriel Bermúdez was removed from the court in Madrid in dramatic circumstances. Such cases show that a royal confessor's position depended first and foremost on the ruler's favor and was also very often a flash point for wrangling over influence. The Jesuits at court thus were often highly polarizing figures. When Arnoux was dismissed, chief minister Luynes informed him: "I believed . . . that you had some plot to my disadvantage with the king. . . . For which reason I asked His Majesty to see fit that I, no longer having confidence in you, should choose a new confessor."[114] The queen of Spain and second wife of Philip V, Elisabeth Farnese, was also partly responsible for Bermúdez's fall. She considered the Jesuit "a traitor, a Judas" and "loathed" him outright.[115]

The Society of Jesus was well aware of the complexity of its involvement at court. Service as a royal confessor brought with it the opportunity to influence policy and also spoke to the order's determination to miss no opportunity to "help souls." At the same time, however, means had to be devised to reduce the perils of courtly life for the Jesuits immediately involved and for the Society as a whole. The Jesuit leadership therefore repeatedly issued rules of conduct intended to ensure the spiritual health of confessors and preserve the good reputation of the Society. Claudio Acquaviva issued the important *Instruction for the Confessors of Princes* (*Instructio pro confessariis principum*) in 1602. The guidelines contained therein were intended to help Jesuits stay on the straight and narrow. Instructions about conduct (avoid emulating courtly behavior too closely, eat and drink as if one were still in a Jesuit house) were combined with guidance on cultivating relations with the prince—do so respectfully, but pay heed to religious truths. The *Instruction* of 1602 was an important point of reference for the Jesuits' relationship with courtly life because it officially sanctioned the mixture of caution, distance, and the ready assumption of responsibility so typical of the order. It characterized the Jesuits' life at court as a difficult enterprise, the success of which required Jesuits to exhibit tact, spiritual integrity, and strength of character.

The constant call to exercise restraint was an important aspect of these rules. Very early, in the *Spiritual Exercises*, Ignatius himself had stated that it was necessary that a "religious speaks about wars or trade" with restraint.[116] Acquaviva's *Instruction* of 1602 similarly required a Jesuit at court to be aware of the limits of his competence and to steer clear of "outside and political business."[117] And General Vitelleschi wrote time and again that one should absolutely abstain from politics. It was for that reason that he wanted to punish the all too brash pro-French collaborators in the ranks of the Jesuits of Catalonia by transferring them elsewhere—although this plan was probably not carried out.[118]

For cases in which the Jesuits nonetheless intervened, restraint and confidentiality were advised. General Francesco Piccolomini wrote a telling letter to the court confessor in Munich, Johannes Vervaux, in 1650. The subject of the letter was a princely marriage project in which

Vervaux was involved. "I request the aid of Your Reverence in this secret affair," the general told his confidant in Bavaria, "but I do not want you to undertake anything yourself, but rather first ascertain if it has been undertaken and is being pursued by others." A few lines later, the same thought resurfaces: "If you find that it has been undertaken by others, then you may promote the treaty at your discretion [*prudentia*] to the extent that the tenor of our Institute permits. . . . But first do not neglect to inform me about the entire business."[119] Such instructions do not reflect guile or dissimulation, but rather an effort to master the great ambivalence that resulted from the Jesuits' entanglement in contemporary politics. These Jesuits' responsibility to fulfill their pastoral duties and the political and social influence they enjoyed came with grave threats to the standing of the Society and the spiritual health of the Jesuits involved. Involvement at court was equally appealing and terrifying to them. This tension ultimately proved impossible to defuse, and so the Jesuit generals constantly urged restraint in politics, while also approaching various court confessors just as often with very specific plans and requests.[120] Confidentiality, as Piccolomini ordered, combined with circumspection (*prudentia*) and restraint, was the best means of surviving at least somewhat unscathed in this complex arena.

Theoretical Ideas

The authors of the Society of Jesus normally acknowledged two theories that easily came into conflict. On the one hand, they believed that there was a realm of human action in everyday life that did not need to be governed constantly and directly by religious considerations. Many Jesuit political theorists liked to cite the French king Henry IV, who supposedly said, "Priests do not rule princes, but rather are ruled by them."[121] On the other hand, they determined that this political autonomy had to be narrowly circumscribed within a religious framework. All political power ultimately derived from God and had to be justified before him. The Spanish Jesuit Eusebius Nieremberg epitomized this theological embeddedness of politics in 1641 when he gave the book he published at the time the telling title *Theopoliticus*.[122]

With this narrow theological framing of the political, the Jesuits wholly and unanimously took a stand against Niccolò Machiavelli and *Il Principe*, which appeared in 1532. They accused Machiavelli of separating the exercise of power from ethics and religion entirely.[123] The Jesuits of the sixteenth and seventeenth centuries countered Machiavelli by introducing the figure of the "pious" or "Christian" prince.[124]

What these ambivalent reflections on principles meant in detail is illustrated by the Jesuits' view of the role of the pope with respect to secular monarchs. The Jesuits held a complicated intermediate position that compromised between two extremes.[125] Radical pro-papal theorists like the Dominican Francisco Peña in Rome held that the pope not only had sovereignty over all spiritual questions in all Christendom, but also had authority in secular affairs. The king of England, James I, advocated the opposite extreme: in his widely read treatise *Basilikon doron*, published in 1600, James argued that both spiritual and secular authority should and could be placed in the hands of one person—not the pope, but rather the king. James was seconded by Scottish jurist William Barclay, who argued that the two powers were so clearly separated that their respective competences could never overlap.

It was above all Cardinal Robert Bellarmine who situated the Society of Jesus in this tumultuous arena of political-theoretical jockeying with a view of its own. Most Jesuit authors around 1600—such as Luis de Molina, Francisco Suárez, and Robert Persons—held similar views.[126] Bellarmine (like Barclay) presumed that ecclesiastical and secular, papal and royal power were different and separate. The pope, therefore, did not wield secular power directly (contra Peña). He merely ruled over people's consciences. If, however, a secular act by the king affected the consciences and thus the spiritual well-being of his subjects, then the spiritual power of the pope also came into play in secular affairs by this circuitous route. In this *indirect* way, the pope could influence secular affairs after all. Bellarmine's view became famous as encapsulated in the phrase "indirect power" (*potestas indirecta*). The political power of popes and kings rested on completely different foundations, but they might potentially overlap, and if "consciences" were injured in one of the overlapping areas, the spiritual power of the pope was superior.[127]

In Bellarmine's theory, the Jesuits advocated a Christian monarchy that respected the precedence of papal authority without, however, abandoning the direct responsibility of kings for politics. By and large, however, the Jesuits were not interested in letting an "emergency" papal intervention in secular affairs actually occur. Luis de Molina, S.J., for example, argued that the pope should avail himself of his indirect secular power only in the event of imminent danger and should otherwise rely on his spiritual powers of intervention.[128] They nonetheless essentially left the door open for a secular papal policy.

With this view, the Jesuits were able to make yet another point that was important to them: they were opposed, at least in theory, to giving kings excessive power over the church in their kingdoms. This view clashed with efforts to found a "national church" in Spain and France, which had elevated the king to the most important representative of ecclesiastical interests.[129] Enrique Henríquez, for example, an eccentric Spanish Jesuit and theologian, published a controversial work in which he argued in support of the Spanish king's competence in ecclesiastical affairs, especially when church dignitaries showed themselves to be "tyrannical" and power hungry.[130] But such endeavors to place royal powers above the church went against the cultural and political interests of the Roman leadership of the Society (and of the papacy). The Society's official policy was to uphold the primacy of Rome and the popes.[131] Acquaviva therefore saw to it that Henríquez's theories were censored inside and outside the order. But despite such *succès d'estime* by Rome, it remains doubtful whether the quasi-official doctrine of *potestas indirecta* even defeated arguments in favor of national churches within the Society. In France, many Jesuits were by no means inclined to take a unanimous position against the claims of the king. Here, even Bellarmine's view was regarded as "too papist"—authors from the Jesuit order had to walk a fine line here.

Acquaviva also had to deal with another political theory espoused by Jesuits that he vehemently disputed: the right to kill a tyrant. This difficult question became an issue because a majority of Jesuit political theorists presumed that, although political power ultimately derived from God, it did so indirectly, as mediated by "the people."[132] Therefore, most political theorists in the Society of Jesus were certain that the power of princes was limited by fundamental laws, representative bodies, ethical norms, and abstract principles like the "common good." On this basis, the English Jesuit Robert Persons wrote, for example, "The power and authority which the prince has from the commonwealth is in very truth not absolute, but *potestas vicaria* or *deligata* [*sic*] as we Civilians [i.e., Roman jurists] call it rather only vicarious and delegated, that is to say, a power delegate, or power by commission from the commonwealth, which is given with such restrictions, cautels, and conditions."[133]

The Jesuits then discussed extreme inferences. Could one, if necessary, violently resist or even kill a monarch who had blatantly overstepped the limits of the power conferred on him and circumscribed by the "people"? Many Jesuits explored these questions, and some came very close to a positive answer, most notably Juan de Mariana.[134] He legitimated such an act of homicide if it served to execute the public condemnation and deposition of a king in the last resort, to free the people of a tyrant. Suárez also claimed that even a private citizen was at liberty to commit regicide in the last resort so as to carry out the king's deposition by the representatives of the "people," provided no other course of action was viable. An enormous international debate raged around these theories after 1600. Overall, Jesuit authors were actually quite restrained and allowed the assassination of a tyrant almost exclusively as a theoretical option in improbably dramatic circumstances. But in light of the numerous assassinations that took place around 1600—in France, for example—the Society was roundly condemned by its enemies as "regicidal," a stigma that the Society of Jesus never shook off. It made no difference that the doctrine of legitimate tyrannicide was officially condemned again and again. General Acquaviva issued three sharply worded bans against such theses in 1610 and 1614.[135]

The questions of indirect papal power, tyrannicide, and the legitimation of Christian monarchs defined Jesuit political theory until approximately 1630. After the Peace of Westphalia in 1648, it becomes far more difficult to determine how members of the Society of Jesus contributed to the wide-ranging political theory of the day. There is a dearth of famous authors from their midst, as well as topics, theories, and problems with which they might have left their mark on the debate. The old authors from the turn of the seventeenth century, above all Suárez, remained the Jesuits' measure of all things in the eighteenth century. There are hardly any major modern authors from the Society. Innovative theories and burning topics were generated predominantly by a new generation of generally Protestant theorists. Hugo Grotius, Thomas Hobbes, John Locke, Samuel Pufendorf, Christian Thomasius, and others developed a new, secular natural law that became the starting point for the discussion of political theory. This new model tended to separate legal and constitutional questions from theology and religion, albeit to significantly varying degrees. The Jesuits, however, neither could nor would do that, at least not without reservations.[136] Ingaz Schwarz (1690–1763), a Jesuit from Ingolstadt, is a typical example.[137] He was well acquainted with contemporary authorities on natural law, but he broadly opposed their views. He was particularly critical of the great German theorists Christian Thomasius and especially Samuel Pufendorf. Schwarz objected above all to the fact that Pufendorf had effectively emancipated legal theory from theology. Pufendorf's secular natural law, which was no longer based on divine law, but rather on "nature" broadly conceived, had untethered politics from the divine order on which the Jesuits had erected their political theory. Schwarz feared (not without good reason) that "they would adapt religion to the political state rather than adapt the state to religion" on account of this new theory of natural law.[138] Schwarz therefore objected, contrary to Pufendorf, that natural law could not be regarded as autonomous and independent of religious considerations. Whereas Pufendorf distinguished between external actions (natural law) and the judgment of internal attitudes (moral theology), Schwarz viewed Pufendorf's arguments as a "profanation of church power" that he had allegedly produced only "to prop up wretched Protestantism."[139] On this point, Schwarz quite clearly was suffering from the narrow-mindedness of controversialist theology, because Pufendorf was not at all primarily concerned about confessional matters. This ultimately all too trivial insinuation by Schwarz perfectly illustrates how Jesuit authors either could not engage with the new natural law as intellectual equals or failed to see why it necessary to do so. One way or another, in terms of political theory, the followers of Ignatius were clearly out of touch with the current debate after the Thirty Years' War and especially after the appearance of enlightened natural law around the year 1700. Political theory in this case, however, merely reflected the overall trajectory of Jesuit scholarship.

Scholars, Researchers, Pedagogues: The Jesuits and the Early Modern Culture of Knowledge

The Jesuits are frequently regarded as a teaching order. That is correct and yet also misleading. The founders of the Society did not envision becoming involved in education in 1540. The description would also be too narrow in the sense that the order was exclusively preoccupied with teaching and education. It is, of course, correct and applicable insofar as the Society of Jesus became the most important agent of lay and priestly education in the Catholic world within a few years of its founding—at first tentatively and then soon in grand style. Schools, teaching, and care for the (academic) youth all became very prominent within the order, and education began to consume a majority of the Society's resources. Even if the Jesuits were not a teaching order from the start, they *became* an order in which schools were of paramount importance in an astonishingly short time.[140] By embracing pedagogy, Ignatius of Loyola changed not only the character and appearance of the entire Catholic Church but also the focus and nature of the Society he had just founded.

From their engagement in instruction and education, the Jesuits soon experienced the allure of scholarship and the ability to contribute to it. The great schools of the Society, the colleges, became research institutions in addition to their function as places of education. The scholars and scientists who worked there may have remained relatively small in number over the long term, but they were extremely important for the order's self-conception and the perception of the Society by others. There soon was no field of scholarly curiosity in which Jesuits were not engaged in the quest for new knowledge—their interests ranged from history and philology to botany, astronomy, the study of electricity, and various branches of engineering. The Jesuits were virtually predestined to observe the natural world in light of their relatively strong presence overseas. For a long time, Europe relied primarily on the missionaries of the Catholic orders and the usually preeminently well-educated Jesuits for much of its knowledge about the non-European world.

The men of the Society of Jesus, however, found it increasingly difficult to reconcile their cultural profile with current scholarly trends. While the Jesuits were frequently still among the scholarly avant-garde of Europe in the sixteenth and seventeenth centuries, they gradually lost this influential position in the latter half of the early modern period. That of course did not prevent individual scholars from producing outstanding work, but on the whole the cultural profile of Europe changed so radically that it became harder and harder for scholars from the Society to keep pace. In the following sections, we shall see how the Society of Jesus evolved into a teaching order and how it got its start in scholarly research and developed its own scholarly culture, before we consider how the changes introduced by the Enlightenment and modern science exposed the limits of the Jesuit educational and scholarly model.

Getting into Education: A Fundamental Decision and Its Consequences

The Jesuits' commitment to education and scholarship was the outcome of an internal decision. When the Society of Jesus was founded, Ignatius and his first nine fellow Jesuits were already fully educated, learned adult men. The same was true of some of the first members to join after 1540. But it was clear that sooner or later their successors would consist of young men who had not yet received such an education. The Society would have to see to their education directly. Ignatius initially preferred the model of having the young men study at leading European universities during their novitiate, while the Society provided shared living quarters (*collegia*) specifically for members in university cities. The establishments would be financed by sponsors. Seven such institutions were founded—in Paris, Leuven, Cologne, Padua, Alcalá, Valencia, and Coímbra. But all except the last-named failed on account of a lack of local support. At the same time, some members of the order became involved in teaching right from the start: Laínez and Favre in Rome 1537, Favre in Mainz in 1542/3, and Jay in Ingolstadt in 1543/4. As early as 1545, Ignatius gave permission to the Jesuit house in Padua to provide instruction by Jesuits for Jesuits in addition to the courses offered by the local university. In 1546, the Jesuits took over a new college founded specifically for them in Gandía, Spain, where they themselves worked as teachers. The Duke of Gandía, Francisco de Borja, a friend of the order and later himself a Jesuit and superior general, was behind the project. He explicitly requested a school that would also be open to non-Jesuits. Ignatius granted his wish, and so the small institution became the first Jesuit school for the general public.

In hindsight, the year 1548 marked a crucial breakthrough. Building on all these developments, a Jesuit school was founded for members and laymen alike in Messina that would become the model for countless successors. Thanks to the collaboration of the Jesuit Jerónimo Doménech and Leonora Osorio, the wife of the Spanish viceroy and one of the most important advocates of the young order, the plan to establish a public school like that of Gandía was hatched in Sicily. Ignatius had already apparently warmed to this new responsibility, because he appointed a series of preeminent Jesuits to the new school: Peter Canisius was involved, as was the humanist André des Freux, and Jerónimo Nadal took primary responsibility for the idea. Shortly after the schools at Gandía and Messina were founded, the pope conferred the status of *studium generale* on both, elevating them to universities entitled to confer degrees.

From the very start, the Jesuits were determined to offer instruction essentially free of charge to all interested parties without exception. Ignatius himself had approved of the Jesuits' involvement in running schools for outsiders only because he could reconcile it with the pastoral and missionary goals of his order—it was his conviction that the Jesuits would also "help people's souls" with schooling.[141]

The example set by the initiative in Messina spread far and wide in the following months. Already by the subsequent year, 1549, a Jesuit school was founded not only in Palermo but also in Cologne. Further schools were founded in Italy at short intervals. The first peak of this wave of school foundings was the establishment of a college in Rome in the year 1551, for which Francisco de Borja again provided indispensable financial aid. When Ignatius died in 1556, there were already three dozen Jesuit educational establishments in operation. By 1710, there would be 612 Jesuit colleges worldwide. The network of schools maintained by the Society of Jesus may have been one of the biggest of its kind in history.

The Jesuits dedicated comprehensive normative and theoretical reflections to these practical initiatives right from the start.[142] For the two universities of Gandía and Messina, it was necessary to issue statutes that governed the curriculum and established the structure of the institution. Supported by several fellow Jesuits, Nadal and Andrea Oviedo got to work, respectively, in Sicily and Spain. In 1550, work on the *Constitutions* was redoubled, and now education played an important part in the fourth section of the laws of the Society. The college in Rome ultimately became a kind of general model for Jesuit educational institutions. Consequently, a universal curriculum (*ratio studiorum*) was devised there that would apply to all Jesuit schools. In 1558, the curriculum for Rome was finished. Although the idea of making it generally obligatory was entertained, its status as a model ultimately remained unofficial. It would be another forty years—after a vigorous exchange of information and ideas between Rome and the provinces, as well as various drafts in 1569, 1586, and 1591—before the famous *Ratio atque institutio studiorum Societatis Iesu* was issued in 1599. This teaching curriculum was intended to regulate instruction at Jesuit colleges worldwide. The *Ratio* remained unchanged until 1832 and, even then, was only revised. A certain amount of supplementation and adaptation took place, however, in the form of a vigorous body of pedagogical literature to which many authors lent their voices from the seventeenth century on. Francesco Sacchini, Juan Bonifacio, Joseph de Jouvency, and Francis Xavier Kropf were among the Jesuits who composed pedagogical guides for the Society, many of which remained purely internal documents in manuscript form.

The Jesuits' enormous success and the apparent ease with which the Society transformed into an educational institution should not blind us to the fact that this was a sweeping change. The shift toward education, which is evident by 1547/8, represents a major turning point in the history of the Society of Jesus. It has been called, perhaps with some exaggeration, the "second founding" of the order.[143] It is easy to overlook how momentous this change was, since the long history of the Society *with* schools was preceded by a very brief period *without* them. But responsibility for, at first, dozens and soon hundreds of schools—some of them very large—introduced a range of totally new tasks, opportunities, challenges, and necessities that shaped the Jesuits as they perceived and adapted to them. In order to operate schools, the ideas of poverty and property were reconsidered, as we have already seen. Moreover, the colleges embedded the Society, its ideals, and its pursuits more profoundly in local society than was conceivable with the originally intended institution, the professed house. The benefit that the colleges brought the general public was immediately obvious to the people of a city. Jesuits and civic authorities established close ties to one another. In Messina, public officials regarded it as their civic duty to attract the Jesuits.[144] And in Frascati near Rome, the Jesuits were connected directly to the city by contract in 1563: they agreed to provide two teachers for sixty scudi annually. The Jesuits had become publicly remunerated schoolmasters.[145] Their colleges thus also came under the close scrutiny of the magistrates and citizens of the cities in question—after all, no less than the education of the next generation was at stake.

The social embeddedness of the colleges also introduced something else: competition. In light of their other activities, and if professed houses had remained their only establishments, the Jesuits might have attracted only sporadic envy and displeasure and little more. But the schools and colleges entangled the Jesuits in multifaced conflicts of interest. Some critics alleged, for example, that the Jesuits would concentrate on recruiting new priests at their colleges. The fear was by no means unwarranted. In Munich, for instance, about half of all graduates took up ecclesiastical office.[146] This was a thorn in the side of many civic authorities because they had not sponsored the colleges as educational institutions for clergymen. Protestant parents in particular, whose children also frequently attended Jesuit schools, were regularly worried about this prospect. The Jesuits sometimes also had to vie for material resources and institutional influence. In many places, they elbowed their way into an existing educational landscape. Conflicts between Jesuits and established teachers are known from some Italian cities.[147] When the Collegio Romano was founded in Rome, fierce disputes broke out with the traditional schoolmasters, the *maestri dei rioni*. Although the instruction offered by the latter was generally decried as insufficient, they were unwilling to give way to the new competition.[148] To some extent, these older forms of instruction continued to exist alongside the new Jesuit college in Rome. In France, however, the founding of many Jesuit schools meant nothing less than the complete takeover of existing institutions of higher education that had previously been under municipal control. In this case, the Jesuits, with their new pedagogical dynamism, supplanted the older civic tradition that had fallen into crisis in many places during the French Wars of Religion.[149]

The Jesuits and their colleges also ran into fierce competition with universities, especially where they operated large, sophisticated schools with university-like offerings. In Paris, for example, the Jesuit college and the university were and remained bitter enemies for the entire early modern period. The right to confer academic grades in philosophy and theology was reserved to the Sorbonne for the time being. The Jesuits countered with an outstanding selection of classes in the *humaniora*, which lured many students to their classrooms. This rivalry (frequently also underpinned by theological differences) between the major educational institutions of Paris remained a fixture of French history. Allowing for local variation, roughly the same was true of many other old university cities, such as Salamanca, Vienna, or Prague.

Similarly fraught situations arose when the Jesuits took over the management of parts of long-standing universities. Germany offers several examples.[150] Pierre Favre was holding well-attended lectures in Mainz as early as 1542. A year later, he also taught at Cologne for several months.

Claude Jay was teaching at the university of Ingolstadt in Bavaria at the same time. The initially fairly spontaneous and always temporary addition to the curriculum that these Jesuits provided soon turned into a steady job. In late 1549, several chairs on Ingolstadt's faculty of theology were officially and permanently transferred to the Society—Canisius, Salmerón, and Jay thus became the first university professors from the Society of Jesus. The Jesuits may have retreated from this role several times over the following decades, but in 1576 they took over the entire faculty of theology and, in 1585, philosophy as well. The faculty of philosophy, the lowest-ranking at the university, ceased operations, and the philosophy education offered at the Jesuit college of Ingolstadt was declared part of the university. In Cologne, the Jesuits likewise became members of the lowest-ranking faculty, that of philosophy, in 1556 and of theology in 1560, but the Jesuits' presence in theology at Cologne remained rather unobtrusive over the long term. In Trier, Mainz, Freiburg, Erfurt, and Würzburg, the Jesuits achieved a more or less prominent presence or even a complete takeover in the teaching of theology and philosophy over the course of the sixteenth century.

The Jesuits' swift infiltration of German universities was by no means the norm from a European perspective. In Italy, for example, the prestige and popularity of universities derived much more from medicine and law, whereas theology and philosophy were the leading disciplines in the confessional battleground countries of Germany and France. Since the Jesuits, however, had little to do with instruction in medicine and jurisprudence, their course offerings were far less attractive to Italian universities.[151] Attempts at a partial takeover following the example set in Ingolstadt failed both in Turin and in Catania on Sicily. At Padua, perhaps the most famous Italian university of the sixteenth century, the Jesuits made no attempt to take over the established faculty.[152] They founded a college in the city, however, that many viewed as competing with the university. When the university therefore took action against the college, it was the Jesuits who lost: General Acquaviva gave up the location and withdrew his men in 1592.

The resistance to the Jesuits in these cases often stemmed from the fact that these long-established universities had a distinct self-image, exceptionally strong traditions, and a pronounced sense of independence. In many places, the infiltration of the Jesuits, who were subservient to the superior general of the Society in Rome, seemed incompatible with the conception of a university itself. This obviously was not a problem for institutions that had been recently founded specifically for the Jesuits by a prince or commune. In Italy, the universities of Parma (1601) and Mantua (1624) may serve as examples, although Mantua closed soon after it was plundered during the Thirty Years' War. Both universities were established by princes for Jesuit and non-Jesuit professors, just as the Duke of Mantua, Ferdinando Gonzaga, had witnessed during his own studies in Ingolstadt in 1601. Beginning with the complicated and protracted but, by 1563, successful takeover of Dillingen, a series of universities in the Holy Roman Empire were placed completely under the Society's control by their founders. Besides Dillingen, that included Paderborn, Molsheim, Münster, Osnabrück, Graz, and Bamberg. The founding of such universities was often more or less a direct outgrowth of local Jesuit colleges, as for example at Sassari on Sardinia (authorized by Acquaviva in 1612 and confirmed by the king of Spain in 1617).[153] Elevation to a university both implied the recognition of the high quality of the existing structures and represented an opportunity to expand these institutions even further.

But even at universities that were founded with or for the Jesuits, problems could quickly arise. In Alsatian Pont-a-Mousson, for instance, the Duke of Lorrain opened a university for the Jesuits in 1574, which was then supplemented by non-Jesuit faculties of medicine and law. But bitter conflicts soon erupted between the non-Jesuit faculties and the Society, despite the fact that the Jesuits theoretically had authority over the entire university.[154] The jurists and physicians insisted that, as "secular" disciplines, they should not be subordinate to ecclesiastical leadership. The dean of the law faculty, the famous jurist and political theorist Pierre Gregoire de Toulouse, battled the Jesuit university rectors on multiple fronts. Then, in 1699, conflict also broke out with the faculty of medicine, who disputed the influence of the Jesuits (and other orders) on local care for the sick. Secular pharmacists also protested because those from the Society were enjoying too much success.[155] It was not for nothing that the Jesuits had opted *against* adding faculties of law and medicine, but the duke had wanted them, because only then could the new institution function as a beacon of culture. The Jesuits at the University of Sassari and the Jesuit universities of Germany were free of such problems, since they managed without law and medicine over the long term. Jesuit universities in Germany had only two faculties: philosophy and theology. Sporadic lectures on law in Dillingen in the 1630s were no more than a temporary exception.

Getting into higher education at the university and pre-university level not only changed the Society's place in society but also influenced the Jesuits' social and intellectual profile. Since the members of the order served as the teaching staff at its schools, there was a great need for professors. Complaints about a lack of teachers were widespread at an early date.[156] To solve this problem, the Society not only officially recognized schools as one of its primary *ministeria* in 1560, under General Laínez, but also determined that young Jesuits—usually right after completing their studies in the *humanitates*—would then teach introductory classes for a few years, educating the next generation.[157] The result was that practically every Jesuit worked as a teacher for at least a few years of his life in the Society—at least rudimentary pedagogical experience henceforth became part of almost every member's background. The institutionalization of teaching and learning in the Society also inspired many Jesuits to develop and pursue scientific and scholarly interests of their own. The Society needed experts in the fields it taught; it needed textbook authors; it needed men who could link Jesuit instruction professionally to the wider scholarly world. The Jesuits began to take a more active part in the scholarly and cultural discussions of the day.

The colleges soon devoured significant numbers of the Jesuits' personnel. Since the teachers performed pastoral duties, such as giving sermons, hearing confession, or tending to the poor, in addition to instruction, the colleges also became important religious and social centers. Insofar as the colleges were bases for Marian (and occasionally also other) congregations, these institutions also propagated the Jesuits' religious goals and practices beyond the classroom. For all these reasons, the schools in particular came to shape the public profile and general perception of the Society. Vice versa, the Jesuits made use of the public visibility and presence that their colleges gave them to develop their public image. Even though the Jesuits never forgot that the original Jesuit establishment, the professed house, had looked completely different, de facto it was the colleges that defined the image of the Society of Jesus to both outsiders and insiders. One need only think of the elite, architecturally massive institutions in Munich, Paris, Vienna, or Madrid in all their unmistakable urban prominence to see how the order used its colleges to project an image of a confident religious organization embedded in secular society.

Jesuit Schools: Curriculum, Pedagogy, Everyday Routine

The Jesuits' pedagogical endeavors focused primarily on higher education. They normally did not preoccupy themselves with elementary education and vernacular schools—other orders such as the Piarists, for example, were active here. Initially, as in Messina, they also taught the fundamentals of reading and writing. They sometimes continued to do so for a long time, but on the whole the Society of Jesus concentrated on a Latin curriculum and higher studies. Greek was also an important subject among the Jesuits.

The Jesuit curriculum was essentially divided into three parts, as the final form of the *Ratio studiorum* determined in 1599. There were five "lower classes," which constituted the core, then "philosophy," and finally "theology." In many smaller colleges, it is doubtful whether philosophy and theology were regularly offered at all. The vast majority of students undoubtedly left school before specialized instruction in these subjects commenced. Hence the appeal and enormous social influence of the Society's colleges were based above all on the subjects taught in the lower classes. Around the year 1550, the Jesuits adopted the humanist educational program that had been established for a generation or two among both Protestants and Catholics. The subjects were the Latin language (with Greek as a supplement) and, mediated through it, ancient Greco-Roman culture. The humanists generally regarded language as the defining characteristic of mankind, and the Jesuits viewed the texts of antiquity as the unsurpassed pinnacle of the human intellect. Reading and adapting the ancient texts and engaging with the Latin language thus were thought to contribute decisively to the perfection of the individual. For that reason, the students' active ability to express themselves in Latin was a declared goal of Jesuit schools. Latin therefore was to be spoken in the colleges as much as possible, even outside of class. Jakob Pontanus, in his *Progymnasmata*, gave numerous examples of how such Latin conversations might play out during breaks between classes. Only in exceptional cases were the vernacular languages the subject of instruction. In Bordeaux, for example, French was taught as early as 1584 during semester breaks and on holidays for young local Jesuits who spoke only Aquitanian, Basque, or Occitan.[158] But the vernacular did not come into its own as a medium of instruction and a scholarly subject on a larger scale until the eighteenth century—if at all. In Naples, for example, the first efforts to establish independent instruction in Italian were probably made around the year 1750. In southern Germany, even in 1770, German poetry was taught for just half an hour daily, and that took place before instruction officially started.[159]

Students' education thus began with three classes on Latin and Greek grammar. In the first grammar class, morphology and brief fragments of Cicero, four lines long at most, were learned by heart and explained. Then there were translation exercises to teach students how to construct simple sentences. Similar methods were used to teach Greek already in this very first year. The middle grammar class continued this training on an advanced level. The goal of the highest grammar class was the complete mastery of Latin and an advanced knowledge of Greek. Now more extensive and complete texts of Cicero were discussed. Even titillating poets like Ovid and Catullus might be read—in expurgated form—and explained by the teacher, since meter now was also taught. The *Ratio* mentions many more texts as potential reading material.

The three classes in grammar were followed by the *humanitates*, the "humanities." The term is almost untranslatable otherwise: it stood for the subjects that the humanists had declared to be the core of their educational program. In the Jesuit version, this part of one's education focused on perfecting one's knowledge of Latin, acquiring an education in classical literature, and laying the foundation for the fifth class that followed: rhetoric. Caesar, Sallust, Livy, Curtius Rufus, Vergil, Horace, and other ancient authors populated the reading list. Stylistic aspects of Latin were taught and practiced, and students received their first insights into rhetoric by working through the standard Jesuit textbook by Cyprian Soarez. Finally, the students reached the last of the five lower classes, rhetoric. The goal of Jesuit instruction here was "perfect eloquence, which comprises two extremely important skills, oratory and poetry. . . . [Eloquence] not only serves a pragmatic purpose, but also indulges in ornamentation."[160] This gave the impetus for the superior literary and poetic production of numerous students of the Jesuit order. To be precise, students had to master three subjects by the conclusion of the rhetoric course: the rules of speaking, style, and "invention"— that is, the identification and arrangement of rhetorical arguments—all on the basis of classical texts. Again, the *Ratio* held up the orator Cicero as the ideal and recommended that one pay particularly close attention to his works. The *Poetics* of Aristotle might also occasionally be included. Effective composition was taught and critically discussed in detailed lectures. Techniques of argumentation and the structure of speeches were explained. These subjects laid an important foundation for the Jesuits' future engagement as preachers.

In the class on philosophy that followed, the entire spectrum of scholastic philosophy, focusing on Aristotle, was taught. In the first year, the courses covered logic in all its Aristotelian breadth; in the second year, physics, likewise following the model set by the Greek thinker. In the third year of philosophy, students continued with natural philosophy before turning to metaphysics, although the philosophical doctrine of God was excluded on account of its potential contradiction of the Revelation. Now and then, a professor of moral philosophy might independently present and explain Aristotle's *Ethics*, but he had to take great care "that he not turn aside under any circumstances to theological questions."[161] Finally, lectures on Euclidian mathematics might be given, which were intended to help students in the second philosophy class engage with physics. There was room for comments on geography or astronomy, as well. On the basis of these concise measures, Jesuit schools rapidly blossomed into unusually active centers of early modern mathematics.[162]

Finally, theology included a course in casuistry as its most basic subject. The full curriculum, in contrast, consisted of four years of scholastic theology according to Thomas Aquinas (three professors) and several years of exegesis. Students were supposed to study the exegesis of sacred scripture on the basis of authoritative editions that "protect the interpretations of popes and councils" and "reverently follow in the footsteps of the Holy Fathers."[163] There moreover was supposed to be no overlap between scholastic and exegetical or positive theology. Exegesis also had to be given without polemical (for instance, anti-Protestant) motives. Professors of Hebrew first had to impart the necessary linguistic competences.

Further subjects outside the official curriculum were also taught at many Jesuit colleges, often—but not always—integrated in one of the established courses. For example, the *Ratio* did not provide for a separate course in history, remarking merely that the ancient historians were to be read "quite quickly."[164] Instruction in history might nonetheless be quite extensive. Francesco Benci, one of the most famous humanists and orators of the Society of Jesus, indicated at the end of the sixteenth century that in covering ancient authors he would speak at length about the historical contexts necessary to understanding the texts in question.[165] Many ancient historians were covered in the colleges of Upper Germany in 1604; a survey of the subject lists an impressive number of contemporary commentaries.[166] In 1598, the Jesuit Orazio Torsellini (1545–99) even published a history textbook, which became a standard work at many of the Society's colleges in subsequent decades. His *Epitome historiarum* appeared in dozens of editions, translations, and compendiums. After the author's death, other Jesuits (and other scholars) updated the book, bringing it down to the present day.[167] This book imparted to students knowledge of the past that may not have been very detailed or especially advanced, but it nonetheless went significantly beyond what the *Ratio* had stipulated. Other historical works by Jesuit authors were also occasionally used in college classes. From Poland, for example, we know of the use of the complex works of the Roman

Alessandro Donati and the Frenchman Denis Pétau.[168] Joseph de Jouvency stressed the indispensability of historical training in his pedagogical treatise *De ratione docendi et discendi* (Method of teaching and learning) of 1691.[169] Yet history still did not become a separate academic subject at Jesuit schools until the eighteenth century—long after it had become established at Protestant schools. In 1717, the province of Upper Germany published a *Methodus tradendi in schola historiam* (Method for teaching history in school). While this work recognized history as a subject in its own right, it focused entirely on the role of history as a teacher of ethics and religiosity.[170] The *Rudimenta historica* by the Jesuit Maximilian Dufrène, which began to appear in 1727, became the textbook for this course in history. In 1728, history was introduced as a separate subject in Bohemia; Austria followed in 1730, and Poland in 1739. Further subjects, such as geography and heraldry, were integrated in the structure of the *Ratio studiorum* in similar fashion.[171]

This brief survey of the basic contents of the *Ratio studiorum* makes one thing clear: the pedagogical project of the Society of Jesus was not aimed at educating the masses, even if several hundred thousand Europeans attended Jesuit schools over the centuries. The Jesuits' insistence on a Latin curriculum meant, rather, that they would concentrate on the social groups that were prepared and able to endure the rigors of long years of education and were already considering university study.[172] The Jesuits, of course, let no talent that they discovered go unused, and so students from every level of society found their way to the schools. There definitely also were children from impoverished backgrounds among the Jesuits' students—all in all, between 10 and 30 percent of the boys. The fact that the Jesuits offered courses for free was extremely helpful to them. Often, it was priests or monks in small country villages who discovered gifted poor children and brought them to the Jesuits to be educated, but the sons of citizens, officials, and tradesmen made up a majority of the students.

The number of students from the nobility was much smaller, perhaps only 5 percent, although the Jesuits were especially proud of them. "Other things being equal, preference is given to those who are thought to be more valuable to the commonwealth in the future on account of their nobility or other reasons," the college of Paris decreed in 1585.[173] The Jesuits' predilection for high social station was palpable in the colleges; hence the Jesuits were willing to accommodate the pedagogical and social wishes of the nobility, at least somewhat. In Prague and presumably in other colleges as well, the *patres* permitted noble scions to bear swords as a mark of their estate.[174] When the children of influential Polish noblemen moved into their chosen college, the Jesuits held a welcome ceremony to satisfy their families' need to be seen.[175] Jesuits sometimes also served as private tutors, insofar as at least part of young noblemen's education took place outside the college.[176] Subjects peculiar to the nobility, such as heraldry and genealogy, acquired considerable importance in the Jesuit order.

Hence it was no surprise that the order declared itself ready to take over some institutions dedicated specifically to the education of young noblemen, when an engaged prince or churchman from outside proposed such a project. In 1604, the Jesuits took over their first school for young noblemen in Parma. Another such institute was founded in Cagliari in 1614, and by 1620 further institutions stood under the Jesuits' direction in Ferrara, Modena, Mantua, and Florence. There were Jesuit knight academies also north of the Alps, in Graz, Vienna, and Warsaw, as well as in Madrid and Olomouc in Bohemia.[177] In addition to Christian values and the usual academic education, the Jesuits also taught genuine aristocratic skills at these schools. In Parma, for example, the young nobles could go hunting at the expense of the Duke of Parma and were trained in riding, dancing, warfare and fortifications, and music.[178] The Jesuits were not the only ones to jump on this bandwagon: noble and knight academies were becoming popular across Catholic and Protestant Europe.[179]

To a considerable extent, the Jesuits' pedagogical effectiveness and hence the enormous appeal of their schools can be traced back to the fact that they imparted socially established and expected content with notable rigor and efficiency. The conviction that children and young people needed special treatment—a concept adapted from humanist educators but elaborated by the Jesuits—was decisive. We can identify many Jesuit educators who appreciated children as exceptionally important objects of social care, a view that was not widespread at the time. Ignatius himself, as the Spaniard Juan Bonifacio emphasized, had "ordered his old men to become boys again and his orators to stutter" to educate the youth.[180] He regarded youth as an especially "flexible age" and saw in children first and foremost the potential to be influenced in a positive way. Bonifacio explicitly spoke out against the widespread moral prejudice that children were inclined to vice and the "extremely destructive to the Christian commonwealth."[181] Francesco Sacchini, who also composed several pedagogical guides, was likewise full of laudatory amazement at the capacity of children to learn and grow. The Italian Jesuit was also convinced that only outstanding teachers could activate and harness the enormous potential of young people; otherwise, their faculties threatened to lapse into their undesirable opposites.[182] The ideal teacher would calibrate his lessons to the children's capabilities: "Their tender age warrants that they not be burdened too greatly; their innocence warrants that they be shown mercy. And it moreover is completely inappropriate for freeborn children to be kept in servile conditions."[183] Jesuit teachers were convinced that one should not senselessly overburden children—no shoes that were too big for the little ones, as it was said once in Brussels in 1642.[184] In brief: the educational practitioners and theorists from the Jesuit order considered it self-evident that a well-conceived pedagogical program tailored to the abilities of children had unique potential, special significance, enormous importance, and great need.

These fundamental convictions led the Jesuits to adopt a series of pedagogical strategies in their schools. One technique that was not widespread at the time was to divide the students and subject matter into distinct classes. A Jesuit "class," however, was not a cohort of students of a given age but rather was defined by the students' progress through the curriculum. Students advanced from one class to the next not after a year but after successfully mastering the prescribed material. Since students were placed according to their individual ability and the subject matter was structured accordingly, Jesuit education became standardized to an unanticipated degree. At the same time, the material was modularized into a series of successive units that built on one another, which enabled the Jesuits to transfer students and teachers at any time. Teachers were required to follow the prescribed system in terms of both content and pedagogical method—new teachers were not allowed to try out new approaches of their own. There was to be only "one method of instruction."[185]

The clear structure of Jesuit education was complemented by a large number of pedagogical exercises that served to repeat, reinforce, and test course material. The *Ratio studiorum* is full of requirements that the students demonstrate their newly acquired knowledge in written essays and public examinations. It explicitly calls for "competitions" between students. It was remarkable "with how much eagerness and care" the students prepared for this test of their mettle, Polanco reported from Rome in 1567.[186] Public disputations and scholarly exhibition contests were regarded as particularly important aspects of instruction and were therefore part of the weekly routine. The best students were identified, and once a year, outstanding work was put on public display (in the form of *affixiones*). The *Ratio*, moreover, called on teachers to appoint "decurions" (*decuriones*) from among the best students in class. A decurion was a kind of teacher's aide whose job was to supervise ten other classmates.[187] The literary productions of the best students were also posted every other month as placards for all to see.[188] Prizes were also given and were conferred publicly on especially successful graduates (fig. 12). Such acts of recognition served both to commend outstanding young men and to admonish and encourage the rest of the student body, while showing them examples of ideal pious Christians.[189] Last but not least, they also presented the achievements of Jesuit education to a wide audience.

The shrewd use of media also was part of Jesuit education. It was relatively conventional to present historical information in table form, where appropriate, such as pinning chronologies on large sheets of paper to the wall as visual aids.[190] The Jesuits were especially fond of emblems. This art form came into vogue in the sixteenth century and absolutely captivated early modern people. Emblems were a combination of symbolic or allegorical pictures and brief explanatory texts, often in verse. This multimedia format used allegorical pictures as mnemonic

Præmium multorum laborum
est DOCTRINAM obtinuisse.

votorum summa. *Juvenal*.

FIGURE 12. Public award ceremony for outstanding students, a hallmark of Jesuit
pedagogy. © Bibliothèque Royale de Belgique, ms 20327, fol. 106v (1683).

aids, thus fixing the assigned material more firmly in one's memory.
The *Ratio* mentions designing such emblems as an occasional student
exercise—in particular, they were to adorn the outstanding texts by
individual students selected for public display (*affixiones*).

This practice was cultivated intensively in Brussels, for instance. Hundreds of such student emblems survive today. The effort that emblems

entailed seemed unfeasible to some superiors,[191] but the examples from Brussels illustrate how shrewdly this artform was utilized in pedagogy. In 1663, for example, the local Jesuit students designed several emblems to symbolize the basic messages of Cicero's *De Oratore*. In the process, the students not only learned the content that they were representing visually but also practiced one of the essential virtues of rhetoric: they learned how to devise images to illustrate complex circumstances, which an orator was expected to do in every speech. They were urged to search for clever comparisons and surprising similes that reinforced the memory. Individual pedagogical emblems, which sometimes stood out for their friendly satire, supposedly brought visitors to laugh, which was indeed the intent. The image became a bridge linking content and memory.

Humor and playful learning had their place in the everyday life of Jesuit schools. Where appropriate and helpful, the Jesuits integrated productive forms of play into education.[192] For example, pedagogical card games were sometimes used to help students recognize coats of arms in the context of history lessons. The chronological skeleton of history was also sometimes presented in the form of playing cards.[193] Jesuits like Jakob Pontanus also tried to lighten up the pedagogical rigor of Latin class by composing brief, entertaining scenes from everyday life so that their students would practice using the language almost as an afterthought as they worked through them or performed them.

The irony or cheekiness of such teaching aids is sometimes astonishing. Pontanus wrote an educational scene, for instance, in which Cicero appears as the judge of a legal dispute between his daughter "Latinity" and her slanderer, the "barbarized Latin language." The students were supposed to improve their own Latin with the text while at the same time finding themselves accused of *mixobarbaritas* on account of their own imperfect command of the language.[194]

Thus many playful efforts were made to impart material that, taken together, amounted to a "pedagogy of persuasion."[195] Key material was conveyed by way of illustration, covering examples, overwhelming the senses, and teaching collective forms of behavior and mentalities. Education functioned best, to quote Sacchini again, "when it was very pleasant." It was for that reason that one and the same word was used for "school" and "game," he noted: both were called *ludus*.[196] By the same token, pedagogy functioned best when the students were involved in the process. The lecture (*praelectio*) may have remained a key form of instruction that shaped every stage of study, but the Jesuits also placed great emphasis on enthusiasm, on their students' active engagement (*alacritas*). Educators viewed this as an indispensable basis of successful instruction. The aforementioned Francesco Sacchini dedicated an entire section of one of his pedagogical manuals to how one might induce students to take an active part in their own education.[197]

When such more or less subtle pedagogical strategies that relied on control, competition, and imitation failed, the Jesuits occasionally resorted to punishment. Beatings were an especially difficult subject for Ignatius and his successors.[198] The founder flatly refused to permit his confreres to administer beatings. Soon a compromise was reached whereby corporal punishment would be administered by someone appointed from outside the Society, the *corrector*, when it seemed imperative.

And such punishment could not be ruled out, because discipline at early modern schools and universities was often an enormous problem. Students, especially those of university age, were regarded not without reason as an especially uninhibited, volatile, and violence-prone segment of the population. There were regular complaints about them all across Europe, and the insubordinate behavior of young men in most university towns led to serious problems. No one could expect the Jesuits and their educational establishments to be spared. Indeed, like all other places of learning, the Society's colleges were plagued by rebelliousness and misconduct on the part of the students. In Parma, the sacraments could not be left unattended in the chapel for fear of "acts of irreverence" (*irreverenze*).[199] And, in Paris, the Jesuits' rebellious students allegedly pranked their teachers in 1682 with an act worthy of the theater. First, they had images of Ignatius and Francis Xavier painted on their buttocks, did something to warrant corporal punishment, exposed their backsides, and wickedly chuckled to themselves as the naive *patres* marveled at the "miraculous" images on their hides.[200] Such episodes warn us against imagining everyday life in the Jesuit colleges as entirely harmonious and "Christian."

The teaching method employed by the Jesuits was no more an invention than the material that underpinned the curriculum. We can identify at least two important inspirations: humanism and the Brethren of the Common Life. The humanists had built entire educational programs on the belief that emulating ancient culture built character and enabled one to realize his full potential. Guarino Guarini (1374–1460) was one of the first authorities of humanist pedagogy. Pier Paolo Vergerio (1370–1444) and many others soon followed.[201] The Jesuits shared with these predecessors an appreciation of pedagogy and the related conviction that children and young people as individuals both could and indeed must be educated. The order also adopted specific pedagogical practices from the humanists. Pontanus, for example, borrowed the idea of writing vivid scenes from everyday life to help students learn Latin from Erasmus.

In addition to the humanists, the Brethren of the Common Life also influenced Jesuit pedagogy.[202] The Brethren were a religious society that did not take vows but, beginning in the fifteenth century, strove to propagate and exemplify the practice of a simple, devotional form of piety. They were heavily involved in reviving the stagnant system of religious education and founded numerous schools. Many famous personages of the fifteenth century traced their roots back to this milieu, and many humanists were influenced by the Brethren, directly or indirectly. The Protestant school reform of the sixteenth century was also heavily inspired by the Brethren. The practice of dividing students into clearly defined cohorts ("classes") who worked on mastering the same material and possessed roughly the same knowledge can be traced back to the Brethren. Likewise, they also had tested the idea of having outstanding students look after smaller groups of their classmates. School theater also was prominent among the Brethren. One of the university colleges of Paris (a residence that offered courses for the students), the Collège de Montaigu, was heavily influenced by the practices of the Brethren of the Common Life, and it was precisely this college where Ignatius and his companions resided.

A new educational culture evolved at many other Parisian university colleges of the sixteenth century.[203] Teachers experimented by dividing students into classes, by organizing course material in stricter and more modular forms, and by holding public discussions on specific topics (*disputationes*). This efficient "Parisian style" (*style parisien*; Latin, *modus parisiensis*) became the new standard.[204] The Jesuits were also decisively influenced by the Parisian style and mention their Parisian models again and again.[205] They clearly distanced themselves, however, from the subversive undercurrent that was often unmistakable in these movements.[206] Ignatius and his men were interested above all in combining the cultural mission of humanism with the religious and moral mission of an increasingly confessionalized Christianity. They strove to fuse the "basics of grammar and education" with "Christian instruction."[207] They wanted to shape personalities in which education and piety were indissolubly intertwined.

The Jesuits did not stop at imparting religious content and humanist knowledge. Their ambition to shape personalities comprehensively extended beyond the inner life of boys and young men. Their pupils should become smart representatives of a new Christian culture; in this way, their humanist-religious education was enhanced by a complete set of social behaviors.[208] On the one hand, the Jesuits wanted to teach their students to be educated, pious, and proactive individuals; on the other, though, they wanted to socialize them in Christian society in broader terms, as well. To that end, the colleges always had both the individual and the collective in mind—Jesuit education was quite explicitly an education for people "in the world."[209] The Jesuits wanted to train Christian members of a Christian society—in the Jesuit sense— and that included the entire spectrum of social behavior. Here, the Jesuits took up a broad tradition of books of manners and courtesy that had blossomed in Europe in the wake of Baldassare Castiglione's *The Courtier* in 1528. The Jesuits, however, gave this tradition a specifically Catholic Christian face. Léonard Périn, a Jesuit from Pont-à-Mousson, composed a handbook of correct behavior in which he gave direct instructions for numerous specific situations. He even discussed eating at a banquet at the end. Graduates of Jesuit schools were to learn how to behave with moderation and restraint and always to bear in mind what was "appropriate," whether in conversation at table or in serious political or administrative decisions.

The Jesuits also strove to impart a "refined urbanity [*urbanitas*] of manners which is commonly called civility [*civilitas*]," to quote Périn again.[210] "A boorish scholar is like food without salt," wrote Jakob Masen, who was not only an orator but also an educator—the two vocations were closely connected among the Jesuits.[211] Masen wanted "keen" conversation that conveyed appropriate content with incisive wit (*argutia*). This form of communication was so effective because it was stimulating and memorable. The virtue of "urbanity" (*urbanitas*) included stimulating social behavior, characterized by elegant ease and graceful aplomb in dealing with people and situations. In Masen's view, there was something innately "playful" about witty conversation, to return to this central Jesuit concept.

That playfulness, however, remained tied to the constant call for conscious control over one's own actions. The values of order, cleanliness, and purity were emphasized—in many places, part of the students' education included cleaning their rooms.[212] Control and pervasive supervision were the hallmarks of Jesuit schools.[213] The colleges may have felt like crowded and oppressive social spaces with a high degree of peer pressure. In Naples, starting in 1680, all outside auditors at the Jesuit college had to enter their name, surname, and place of domicile in a list as a control measure before they were allowed to attend lectures.[214] Control was the order of the day internally, too. One of the fundamental principles of pedagogy was that the rector and his assistants always should have precise knowledge of the qualities and conduct of the students. Giulio Gori accordingly described the Society's colleges in 1700 as places "where the youths are surrounded by people with the title of confessor who instill the most delicate piety into a student's mind, people who relieve the burden of study, people with the title of teacher who lead them to Parnassus, people who take care of their health. It is a community with many eyes, more than any Argus . . . monitoring the others' progress."[215] The Jesuits' educational ideal thus was characterized by the comprehensive engagement of the total person.[216] Education, devotion, control, and urbanity were supposed to meld into one, and it was precisely this combination that many Jesuit colleges cited to woo students, even in printed treatises designed to attract them.[217] The young men were supposed to grow into ambitious social and personal models of culture and religiosity. And on the whole, the Society's colleges enjoyed great success: in countless cases, including many prominent ones, studying with the Jesuits made possible or at least facilitated successful careers as men of letters, scholars, churchmen, and politicians. Just as the Catholic Reform spread to ever wider segments of the population, so too did the Jesuits' graduates disperse into the society around them, which they decisively shaped often enough by virtue of their leading social positions.

With their fairly static model of education, the Jesuits were not seriously interested in the open-ended development of their students' personalities, as later critics stressed time and again.[218] Therefore, almost the entire cast of Enlightenment philosophes—from Locke to Voltaire to Rousseau—viewed education in the Society of Jesus primarily as a system of surveillance that disregarded natural abilities. The Jesuits supposedly failed to comprehend the pedagogical idiosyncrasy of childhood. The critics also objected that the specific material taught at the Society's schools was "useless" and outmoded. The philosophes wanted to take education beyond the mere transmission of knowledge and instead raise children to be good citizens. In their view, schools should not shield children from the world, but rather guide them to live in it. The methods and interests of the Jesuits, public opinion increasingly held in the eighteenth century, were incompatible with these new goals. To use a contemporary word: the Jesuits would not give one a "modern" education. The fight against the Jesuits in the eighteenth century, in France in particular, was therefore a battle for the pedagogical future of the nation.

Indeed, the Jesuits do not seem to have made an explicit shift in pedagogy to Enlightenment views and sensibilities in their schools. Their teaching practices may often have had more in common with the ideas of the Enlightenment than was alleged, but neither in content nor in form could the Jesuits wholeheartedly embrace the shift in pedagogical culture to a more child-oriented, more natural, and more useful education as proclaimed by the philosophes.[219] Jacob Baegert, a Jesuit and former missionary to Mexico, wrote against the new pedagogy in typical fashion, probably drawing on his own pedagogical experience, which most philosophes lacked: "May God . . . preserve Europe, and especially Germany, from rearing children in the Indian manner, which in part corresponds to the plan of that base-minded zealot J. J. Rousseau in his *Émile*, and also to the moral teachings of some modern philosophers belonging to the same fraternity of dogs."[220] Only a handful of educators in the Society of Jesus engaged constructively with the educational treatises of the philosophes. Jean-Baptiste Blanchard (1731–97) is one such case. His *Préceptes pour l'éducation des deux sexes* (Precepts for the education of the two sexes, 1803), written after the abolition of the Society and published posthumously, is an attempt to reinterpret Rousseau's *Émile* in a Christian sense.[221] Blanchard conceded that teaching subjects like "Latin and geometry" failed to address current needs, and he approvingly brought up many of Rousseau's other observations in long quotations. But outside such isolated efforts of adaptation, the Jesuits' usual position toward the new pedagogy of the Enlightenment, in the wake of Locke, Voltaire, and Rousseau, ranged from indifference to open hostility.

From Teaching to Research: Jesuit Science between Advocacy, Control, and Mistrust

A very short and direct path proceeded in the Society of Jesus from the *transmission* of knowledge in schools to the *creation* of knowledge through innovative research. There was hardly any field of early modern scholarship in which members of the order had not taken a position. The Jesuit researcher, scholar, and author as a type became integral to the Society's self-conception. Even if ultimately only a small proportion of members dedicated most or all of their time to scholarship, their engagement was in many respects nonetheless a direct extension of the founder's earliest thoughts and wishes. All of Loyola's first nine companions had a formal education, and that was how he intended it to be in the future. In the *Constitutions*, Ignatius required members of the Society of Jesus to have a high level of education.[222] In stark contrast to the views of many other religious orders, Ignatius saw no contradiction between piety and education—as long as the former served as the standard for the latter. His followers were to be highly educated members of the European intellectual elite. This seemed necessary to Ignatius so that the Jesuits could carry out their challenging pastoral duties in the widest variety of settings in a well-conceived, theoretically sound fashion.

The establishment of colleges significantly reinforced this view. To maintain the standards of instruction at the flagship schools and, obviously, universities, the Society needed members who could participate in current scholarly debates at the highest level. "To preserve the knowledge of the *litterae humaniores* and cultivate a kind of seminary for future teachers," the *Ratio studiorum* advised provincials to have "at least two or three outstanding scholars of letters and eloquence" in their territories.[223] The same was true mutatis mutandis for philosophers and theologians. The Jesuits, moreover, were generally of the opinion that Christianization could succeed only as a comprehensive cultural project. Hence it was desirable to place members of the Society in as many cultural arenas as possible, and science and scholarship were at the forefront. Intellectual brilliance brought fame and prestige and thus generated social capital, which the Society had no intention of letting slip away: "[The sciences] very often present our members the opportunity of entering into friendship with learned men, and once they [the learned men] have given ear to various mysteries of nature, they listen to them speaking not unwillingly nor uselessly about the Faith and matters pertaining to the salvation of the soul." That at any rate was the justification given in Liège for extensive scientific instruction.[224]

As we have seen in the case of specialist missionaries and preachers, the scholarly "author" also gradually became, at least de facto, a recognized specialist in the Society of Jesus.[225] Well over thirty thousand books by Jesuit authors appeared in print by 1773, and a good two-thirds of them had nothing immediately to do with theology.[226] The designation *scriptor* was sometimes used within the order for Jesuits who wrote and researched. This title first appeared in Rome in 1570 and was common in Germany already by 1573.[227] The Society's leadership repeatedly commissioned Jesuits with literary or scholarly talent to carry out special publishing assignments. Johannes Nádasi, for example, was asked by the Jesuit Curia in Rome to produce the *Litterae annuae* for the order in the 1650s.[228] The scholarly and publishing engagement of Jesuit authors was thus firmly rooted in the norms and culture of the Society. There was an authorized, institutionalized, and thereby religiously sanctioned place within the Society of Jesus for members with such ambitions and gifts.

This open space for individual intellectual endeavor, however, was strictly monitored by the corporate structures of the Society. Jesuit writers had to submit to internal censorship, for which a distinct official hierarchy was soon established.[229] Initially, the order relied on a decentralized procedure, but around 1600 General Acquaviva established a committee of censors with universal competence at the Collegio Romano.[230] The results of the regional monitoring that had previously been utilized, Acquaviva noted, were far too disparate and contradictory. Five Jesuits, the so-called general revisors (*revisores generales*)—one from each assistancy—were henceforth authorized to scrutinize forthcoming publications as their primary job with no further duties. Initially, the revisors really tried to inspect every manuscript that a Jesuit had prepared before it was printed. When this total centralization of the intellectual production of the Society swiftly proved to be unrealistic in light of the gigantic workload it generated, the Jesuits—typically, according to their distinctive organizational logic—turned to a complicated cooperative procedure. Manuscripts henceforth would be read and assessed locally by regional censors in the provinces. The reports detailing the findings of these written assessments would be forwarded to the general in Rome, who then asked the *revisores generales* for their opinion. Only rarely did Rome require original manuscripts. The generals tried very hard to guarantee the quality of the preliminary regional censors by issuing guidelines and instructions.[231] Even though by no means every book written by a Jesuit actually completed the entire journey to the explicit imprimatur of the general, the influence of the

Society's Curia on the publication of finished manuscripts was of paramount importance.[232] Jesuit authors therefore sometimes had to make
complicated maneuvers to ensure that their manuscripts were favorably
received. In 1667/8, for example, the Bolognese Jesuit Giovanni Battista
Riccioli—known today as an astronomer rather than a theologian—
tried to publish a treatise on the Immaculate Conception. On account
of the heated debates over the subject at the time, the project dragged
on for months. Numerous meetings with various cardinals, the superior
general, and even the pope were spent discussing Riccioli's manuscript.[233] A plethora of different interests, sympathies, and institutional
loyalties steered the printing process, and not only in Riccioli's particularly complicated case.

Why the Society viewed such a sophisticated censorship system as
necessary was spelled out very clearly.[234] Only books whose contents
conformed to the officially sanctioned theology and philosophy should
be published. The fact that books by Jesuits still kept landing on the
papal Index of Forbidden Books was extremely embarrassing to the order's superiors, as General Nickel once noted in a sharp letter sent to
Germany in 1654.[235] The interests of princes also had to be taken into
account. Subjects such as the doctrine of grace, on which the pope had
imposed a moratorium, had to be dropped entirely. The censors also
had to ensure that Jesuit publications attained a certain level of quality.
In cases of doubt, preference was shown to experienced authors over
young authors, and the need for texts that merely rehashed known material was critically scrutinized. A minimum stylistic standard was indispensable; that also affected the Society's reputation. Efforts were also
made to suppress excessively combative works, "so nothing happens
that might justly give offense." Dedicatory prefaces also had to be carefully examined. The superiors were supposed to diligently ascertain
whether Jesuit authors had violated the imperative of humility. It was
not the purpose of the Society's publishing efforts to flaunt their social
connections to the world.

Numerous examples of various stages of the censorship process have
been transmitted. Even the most prominent Jesuit scholars had to submit to the process. That was true even for someone like the great

German polymath Athanasius Kircher.[236] The surviving verdicts of the Roman *revisores* about many of his books give us good insight into the everyday process. For one, it is hardly surprising that the censors were sometimes, but by no means always, in agreement. The works of an author also were not judged en masse. Even in the case of a "best-selling" author like Kircher, every new work had to be assessed and approved. And if the censors felt it was necessary, they readily criticized and amended points in Kircher's manuscripts. Their reports also show that their specific suggestions for improvement were often limited to formal and stylistic matters rather than concern regarding the content. In these cases, the *revisores* worked more as proofreaders than censors, and their influence on the form and quality of the works in question may have been rather more positive and constructive.

Censorial review, however, could very easily become a serious problem, as for instance when certain manuscripts were rejected outright. Kircher's book *Scrutinium pestis* (Inquiry into the plague), on the plague of 1657, for example, was initially prohibited because Jesuits theoretically were not supposed to preoccupy themselves with medicine. Only after a second round of readers' reports could the work finally be printed. The censors' verdicts on their famous confrere's works were sometimes very harsh. Kircher's publications on pagan religions were not orthodox enough for them, and they regarded his *Ars magna sciendi* of 1660 quite frankly as bad, albeit intellectually harmless. The fact, however, that the *Ars magna* still appeared in print (after extensive revision) several years later also shows that the censors' reports—at least for prominent members of the order like Kircher—were not necessarily the last word. There were always other means of getting one's way. For example, an author might appeal directly to the superior general himself, who outranked the censors.

Another option was simply to disregard the censors' opinion or to avoid the review process altogether. Kircher appears to have done both. At any rate, the *revisores* sometimes complained that he had not followed their instructions or had smuggled whole sections of his books past their oversight. The "favor and friendship" of the censors also sometimes helped authors illicitly circumvent the Society's stringent publishing criteria.[237] When the Roman superiors or provincial reviewers already had a certain degree of faith in an author, they might have considerable influence on the outcome of the censorship process.[238]

At any rate, it is obvious that Jesuits like Kircher tried to push the boundaries of their intellectual lifestyle as far as they could. For many a scholar and researcher in the Society of Jesus, scholarship and publishing took center stage and supplanted interest in other, pastoral activities.[239] Kircher, for instance, is not known to have done any significant pastoral work in addition to his literary endeavors; he does not seem to have missed it either. Kircher already had a reputation for "excessive" pride in his accomplishments.[240] Men like him were first and foremost scholars, and their scholarly life was often astonishingly similar to that of their peers outside the Society. We should not, however, dismiss this attitude as disingenuous: even if the intellectual pursuits of someone like Athanasius Kircher seemed largely removed from active religious life, his scholarly career nonetheless stemmed from religious motives and was situated within a similar overall framework.

Other Jesuits, in contrast, appear to have had persistent doubts about the value and utility of publishing and scholarship. As early as 1562, Pablo Hernández, the rector of the college of Murcia, Spain, grumbled that "a teacher who has no other [pastoral] position does not meet the requirements of religion."[241] Here lurked genuine potential for conflict. Julien Maunoir captured this ambivalence brilliantly when he wrote,

> It is difficult enough to unite sanctity and science, but this alliance is necessary for a Jesuit. I thus will strive to become a scholar in such a way that does not prevent me from being holy. I also will strive to be holy in such a way that does not prevent me from being a scholar.[242]

Most Jesuits reacted to this ambivalence with a "twofold" strategy, as for instance Louis Le Valois:

> He wrote a book against a point of the new philosophy [of René Descartes] that seemed to him to be dangerous and difficult to reconcile with the principles of the Faith. But whatever talent he may have had for writing, he never made it his profession; and without

neglecting the sundry other duties with which he was tasked, he dedicated himself with indefatigable enthusiasm to the sanctification of souls.[243]

Le Valois thus bowed to the Society's typical demand that he take an active part in contemporary intellectual, cultural, and scholarly debates, as his abilities and gifts suggested. At the same time, however, he insisted that this was not at the heart of his view of pious life in the service of the faith.

The Jesuits repeatedly stressed in a variety of contexts that Jesuit scholars and authors should never seek temporal fame and social recognition with their pursuits.[244] Humility and submission were of paramount importance for intellectually accomplished Jesuits in particular. The pompous, vain scholar was a common, oft-ridiculed caricature of the early modern period. Precisely because this danger seemed so grave, pious Jesuits like Le Valois were plagued by scruples. In conclusion, as much as the institutions and members of the Society of Jesus became preeminent hubs and leaders of the republic of letters and the scientific community of Europe, the Society's intellectual and scholarly engagement was equally embedded in a Christian framework on both an institutional and an individual level. "Since our way of life and the will of our founder lead us forth into the sunshine and dust rather than permit us to retreat into the shade of letters to write books," in the words of the college of Liège, "it would not be surprising if only a few literary monuments produced by the industriousness of our men had come forth into the light."[245] The Jesuits did far more than that.

The Great Institutions of the Society: A Web of Research Centers

The Society of Jesus not only permitted and encouraged scholarly activity but also soon erected a remarkable network of first-rate research institutions. Even in the early modern period, a variety of infrastructure and expensive institutions were needed to conduct efficient scholarly work and research. Hence Jesuit colleges transformed over the decades into veritable research centers. They became centers of European knowledge and scholarship in the early modern period.[246]

The colleges performed many different tasks for Jesuit scholars. It all started because the colleges were best suited to guarantee long-term sustenance for the Society's own "society of scholars."[247] Only they could provide Jesuit scholars with a regular income. The colleges were moreover the most obvious sites for building the infrastructure of research. That included libraries, for example, which the *Constitutions* already had declared a standard feature of the colleges.[248] Rules specifically for the college librarian were devised for the first time in 1546, in Coimbra. Under Acquaviva, general guidelines for the construction, administration, and organization of college libraries were issued.[249]

These guidelines not only reveal practical details—for instance, that the librarian was supposed to dust the books regularly and carefully close the rooms—but also give important evidence of the Society's passion for books. On the one hand, the church's regulations about "forbidden" books were an important factor—libraries may still have held such works, but they were not supposed to be generally accessible. On the other, the category of "utility" was decisive: the librarian should remain bibliographically vigilant and acquire useful or necessary books. Titles deemed useless were to be thrown out—in Paris, for example, "worthless" books were actually sold every year at the beginning of the summer holidays.[250] The colleges' book collections thus were tools that had been prepared with the members' and professors' spiritual and scholarly needs in mind. The potential needs of the students, in contrast, were probably of secondary importance.[251]

The college budget was the first resource for the acquisition of books; a fixed sum was reserved for purchasing books when each institution was founded.[252] Gifts of money or even estates for acquiring books are also frequently attested.[253] Occasionally, as in Madrid, the sales of popular books by Jesuit authors were used to finance new purchases for the library.[254] Jesuit libraries—like many other early modern libraries—also grew on account of books donated by friends and patrons. The college of Paris received several private libraries as gifts, including those of famous contemporary bibliophiles like Guillaume Budé, Cardinal de

Joyeuse, and Achille IV de Harley. Pierre-Daniel Huet, bishop of Avranches and an active ecclesiastical critic of the early Enlightenment, gave his books—some eight thousand of them—to the professed house of Paris. In 1553, King Ferdinand I gave the college of Vienna an important manuscript of the Byzantine church historian Nicephorus.[255] After the Battle of White Mountain in 1621, at the emperor's command, the Jesuits of Bohemia systematically confiscated manuscripts in Protestant hands.[256] In this way and others, the major houses of the Society came into the possession of extensive collections, which might comprise more than ten thousand and occasionally even twenty thousand volumes. In some places, such as Naples, the Jesuit library was regarded as "the biggest and very beautiful in appearance," as Johann Caspar Goethe, the father of the poet, concluded in 1740.[257] Even specialized labor was needed: in Naples, for example, there was a barber right at the college who also worked as a bookbinder.[258] The Jesuits also built or designed typically baroque showrooms for some, though by no means all, of these book collections. In Naples, shelves were built in 1695 that "are perhaps the most elegant in Europe—made of walnut, olivewood, and other woods and of unique craftsmanship."[259]

In many ways, the holdings of Jesuit libraries reflected their specific needs for carrying out their intellectual pursuits.[260] In addition to a solid number of theological works, Jesuit collections were dominated by publications on the sciences, humanities, and especially history, reference works, and contemporary journals. Juristic publications were also well represented. What was largely lacking or at least had not been systematically collected—tellingly in the eighteenth century—were the works of the Enlightenment philosophes, neither their philosophical texts nor their many novels. In contrast to the institutions of other religious orders, it is striking that religious books may have made up a smaller proportion of Jesuit library holdings. Of course, local conditions were often crucial. In Alsatian Ensisheim, for example, located in the immediate vicinity of fierce confessional conflicts, the Jesuits possessed a conspicuously large collection of controversialist anti-Protestant literature—probably to prepare them for confrontations with Lutherans. Forbidden books were also definitely a presence in Jesuit libraries. In

Naples, for example, the library catalogue contained a separate section dedicated to them, listing an impressive number of works that were supposed to be strictly banned.[261] The theological experts of the Society needed their adversaries' books in order to be able to debate and write against them on equal footing. Hence they were permitted to possess and read such works, albeit only with their superiors' special permission: the relevant section of the library was kept *sub clave*, under lock and key.

The major colleges soon also rolled out further research aids. Several Jesuit institutions had scholarly collections of coins or exotica. The college of Anchin in northern France, for example, had six thousand ancient medallions, as well as clothing from China, stuffed birds, and snake skins in the late seventeenth century.[262] In Innsbruck, Burghausen, Landshut, Düsseldorf, and finally Ingolstadt, the Jesuit Ferdinand Orban (1655–1732) assembled an extensive collection for which a museum (today the Orbansaal) was built on the grounds of the college of Ingolstadt.[263] In keeping with the fashion of baroque cabinets of curiosities, the most diverse objects were gathered in Father Orban's collection: there were artisanal rarities and mechanical instruments, textiles and shoes, weapons, coins, cameos, sculptures, vases, paintings, books, minerals, insects, shells, and much more. Even trophies looted from the Turks by Duke Charles of Lorraine at the Battle of Vienna in 1683 found their way into the museum as a gift. It is also remarkable that Orban not only received objects in semicoincidental fashion as gifts and used the channels of the Society and its overseas missionaries to acquire exotic objects, but also exploited contacts even farther afield. In 1704, he turned to none other than (the Protestant) Gottfried Wilhelm Leibniz in Hannover as an intermediary to obtain mathematical instruments from Paris.[264]

Orban's collection initially caused him constant problems with the Society. The value of his pieces was thought to be incompatible with the vow of poverty. Orban also seems to have exhibited his collection inappropriately, for instance, permitting unaccompanied women to view it. The Jesuit superiors' power over the restless Orban was limited, however, because he enjoyed patronage of the highest degree, above all that of Johann Wilhelm, Elector Palatine, who repeatedly interceded on his behalf with the superior general in Rome. Yet again, the superiors found it difficult to prevail over the secular connections of a prominent Jesuit.

Even contemporaries were already comparing Orban, a Jesuit and collector in Germany, to his more famous colleague in Rome, Athanasius Kircher. Over the course of the seventeenth century, Kircher assembled the most famous of all Jesuit college museums, the Museum Kircherianum named after him, which was exhibited in the corridors of the Collegio Romano.[265] There he had collected countless objects from the most diverse contexts: obelisks and objects from nature, preserved animals (a crocodile was especially famous), and machines that he himself had created. Fossils, portrait busts, antiques, and much more could be seen here. The museum was intended as a reflection of nature, yet it also highlighted the creative genius of man and, in particular, of Kircher himself as the designer of the collection's mechanical devices.

In Rome and elsewhere, Jesuit colleges were also prominent for their astronomical observatories.[266] One of the first was built in Avignon in 1631, where Athanasius Kircher was professor for a few years as he made his way from Germany to Rome. A local patron had paid for the necessary tower to be built. Kircher, however, was not content with only an *observatorium* and so conceived of using mirrors inside this tower to project the paths of the planets and stars. In this way, Kircher himself argued, "it reduced the immense volumes of the stars as if into an abridgement [*epitome*] so that it exhibited the marvels of the heavens, which thus far the keenness of the eyes had been unable to penetrate, to be observed and studied in person clearly and without difficulty."[267] Many visitors came to behold these unprecedented wonders. Though not quite as spectacular, the astronomical facilities at other Jesuit colleges were no less remarkable. Ingolstadt, for example, was outfitted with a small "mathematical tower" at almost the same time as Avignon. In Lyon, work began in 1701 on a seven-story tower on top of the college church, to be used for observing the stars. The observatory at the Jesuit college in Vienna was especially important. Founded in 1734, it received an energetic director in Maximilian Hell in 1756. The Jesuits regularly fed the findings they made at their observatories into the contemporary scholarly discussion, for instance, by sharing their observations with state academies.[268] The early modern scientific community was happy to rely on the work of Jesuit astronomers.

To publicize their findings, Jesuit authors and scholars, like all their contemporaries, turned to the printing press. They initially thought of running their own presses. Ignatius himself advocated doing so at the end of his life in 1555,[269] and the Collegio Romano was the first to start. Obtaining usable printing type proved to be more complicated than anticipated, but the press was finally ready to run in October 1556. A German printer known simply as Michele oversaw the work at first. Twenty-four printed works were produced in the first eight years. The press soon added Hebrew letters, and in 1564 the Collegio Romano became the first press in Rome that could print Arabic. Production was initially limited to texts for internal use, such as the *Constitutions* and related rules or papal documents. A printing press was then installed in the Jesuit college of Vienna in 1559. In Spain, with the exception of the royal college in Madrid (1627), the Jesuits established printing presses in their colleges primarily in the eighteenth century.[270] Some of these undertakings were of considerable importance, at least regionally. In Villagarcía de Campos, for example, books were produced by the thousand and then systematically distributed through the regional network of Jesuit houses.

Viewed on the whole, however, the Jesuits' success as printers was rather limited. As early as 1559, Polanco wrote from Rome with resignation, "The Roman members [of the Society] learned from experience that printing is not at all suited to our organization, seeing as it requires great effort and manpower."[271] The press in Vienna was closed after a few years and little impact, and Madrid put out only a handful of printed works. Even the press at the Collegio Romano ceased operations for unknown reasons in 1616. In the same year, the Seventh General Congregation prohibited the Jesuits from participating in the commercial book trade, whether they or external printers had produced the books.[272]

Instead of founding their own presses, the Jesuit leadership recommended in 1559 that authors rely on printers and publishers outside the Society. Over the long term, this was the far more successful route.

Individual Jesuits and individual colleges developed lasting working relationships with several major publishers. In Paris, for example, the prestigious publishing house of Sébastian Cramoisy in the rue Saint-Jacques acted as the Jesuits' house publisher in the 1630s; he had already collaborated very closely with the order in Pont-à-Mousson from 1621 to 1628.[273] Cramoisy produced the many mission reports (*relations*) of the Jesuits in Canada, for example. And decades later, Claude Ménestrier, a famous heraldist and emblematist from the Jesuit order, preferred to work with the publishers Benoît Coral in Lyon and Robert J. B. de la Caille and Étienne Michallat in Paris.[274] Members of the Moretus family also corresponded directly with Belgian Jesuit missionaries, such as those dispatched to China, and may have played a major part in the information policy of the Society.[275] At least one member of the family, Theodore Moretus (1602–67), became a Jesuit himself.[276] Other publishing families sent brothers, cousins, or sons to the Society.[277]

That does not mean, of course, that manuscripts submitted by Jesuits with such connections were automatically printed without the usual business considerations on the part of the publishers. Theodore Moretus, for example, had to take great pains to persuade his cousins in Antwerp to publish his mathematical works.[278] The relationship between printers and book dealers and the Society's authors was also not always entirely amicable. The personal preferences of individual Jesuit authors might clash with the ideas of their superiors, as for instance when Ménestrier wanted to publish with Guillaume Barbier in Lyon, whom the Society regarded as an "enemy of the Jesuits." Compromises thus were sometimes necessary to reconcile the desire for market presence and printing quality with overarching cultural considerations and religious policy. Of course, if it helped the Jesuits propagate their ideals—especially in "enemy territory"—then they had no compunction about hiring printers of rival confessions. The Mennonite Blaeu in Amsterdam, for example, printed several dozen works by the Jesuits Jeremias Drexel and Robert Bellarmine, albeit under a different name.[279]

All these examples show what the great Jesuit colleges might represent in ideal circumstances: places where innovative research was conducted and where unusual and rare things could be seen. As places of knowledge, the colleges became centers in the republic of letters and permanent fixtures of urban life. They were hubs of scholarly exchange, scientific discussion, and academic reflection, and they exerted a virtually magnetic attraction on visitors with scholarly interests: in 1564, two members of the famed Manutius family of Venetian humanists and printers—Paulus (1512–74) and Aldus Jr. (1547–97)—who "had become good friends" of the Jesuits, visited the Collegio Romano. During their visit, "both received the customary welcoming for learned men, with verses in Latin and Greek, which they praised very highly."[280] When Galileo Galilei came to Rome in 1611 to present his telescope to the public, his one burning desire was to be welcomed by the Jesuit astronomers at the Collegio Romano and to gain access to their circle of researchers.[281] More than a century later, in 1723, yet another visitor described the typical, informal meetings of intellectuals that he regularly attended among the Jesuits in Lyon at their great college: "I spent a very pleasant afternoon in the room of Fr. de Colonia, with him and Fr. Lombard. We reasoned and moralized; we discussed freely and with open heart for three and a half hours until evening."[282] The order's colleges in the cultural centers of Europe allowed active Jesuit scholars and authors to dive into the broader intellectual communities of the day.

It would not do justice to the Society's colleges and the Jesuits who worked there to view them merely as local institutions and actors. What made the Society of Jesus special was rather that each of these sites of knowledge was part of an expansive transregional and even global network.[283] It was easy to transfer information and theories, objects and scholarly finds, and especially people and experts within the Society of Jesus, and the order made ample use of that ability. The constant mobility of many teachers, professors, authors, and researchers is striking. In the Society's turbulent early years, educators were often transferred on an annual rhythm, in part so that some well-known professors could be assigned to newly founded colleges. Many Jesuits were only stationed on call.

This constant turnover of teaching staff may have undermined pedagogical continuity and was criticized for that reason by local school directors,[284] but at the same time it fostered the dissemination of knowledge. The transmission of mathematical knowledge within the Society by way of the peregrinations of leading protagonists serves as a good example. The Belgian Jesuit Grégoire de Saint-Vincent studied mathematics in Rome and then promoted teaching the subject back home in Antwerp. After various detours, he eventually became a teacher in Prague. His student Jean-Charles della Faille transplanted this tradition of mathematics to Madrid. The wanderings of another Jesuit mathematician from Antwerp, Theodore Moretus, the scion of the Moretus publishing family mentioned earlier, took him from home to Münster and later to Saint-Vincent in Prague before he then was transferred to Olomouc—on account of the Thirty Years' War—then back to Prague, and finally to Wrocław. Such travels spread Belgian Jesuit mathematics at least as far and wide as printed publications did.[285]

Exotic objects and observations could also circulate fairly easily through the Society's own channels, and the network of Jesuit houses could always be instrumentalized for concerted transregional research projects. For example, when the Jesuits in Paris at the College Louis-le-Grand launched a systematic review of new publications in their journal (*Mémoires de Trévoux*) in the early eighteenth century, all the provinces of Europe were asked to assess new titles locally and send a list of the worthwhile works to Paris.[286] In the case of the *Mémoires*, however, this typical Jesuit approach was only mildly successful. There was significant internal resistance to the idea, and so the Parisian Jesuits' excellent survey of contemporary philosophical and scientific literature probably derived primarily from their personal contacts.[287] It presumably was a combination of numerous very well-outfitted sites of knowledge and far-flung institutional lines of communication that made Jesuit scholars so effective.

Some serious qualification, however, is in order: by no means did every Jesuit college enjoy the same status in the Society's scholarly network. The spectacular examples of Rome, Madrid, Paris, Lyon, Antwerp, and Ingolstadt were not the norm. For each of these major colleges with outstanding libraries of several thousand volumes, there were small Jesuit colleges elsewhere that had no more than a few hundred books in their possession. Only a small minority of Jesuit colleges became prominent centers of research and writing, perhaps three dozen major colleges out of the several hundred that the Society directed.[288] And even these major colleges experienced certain highs and lows. Ingolstadt, for instance, may have had Orban's museum and an observatory in 1752, but both had seen their best days long ago according to the report of the traveling Jesuit Franciscus Cardell.[289] Many other, smaller institutions will have belonged to the intellectual backwaters of Europe, often as permanently as the schools of small, provincial cities. Thus, for example, the missionary to China, Antoine Gaubil, S.J., looked back in 1722 at conditions in his home of Toulouse: "Most of the colleges in the province were poor and did not have good books. There were few Jesuits who corresponded with scholars, and most were content to know something of literature, their philosophy and theology, but without making an effort to know to some extent the mathematics necessary for physics, natural history, scholarly languages, ecclesiastical history, criticism, and other areas that fall within the scope of theology."[290] This sober assessment from the heart of the order may have been realistic.

Cultural Profiles: Late Humanism

The Society of Jesus was founded in a distinguished intellectual milieu in 1540. The Society was the child and proponent of a specific culture of knowledge. Europe in the sixteenth century was dominated by a model of knowledge and science that admitted of a variety of manifestations and gave ample scope for conflict and differences of opinion, yet also served as something of a widely accepted basis that extended beyond confessional boundaries. This hegemonic model rested on two key pillars: late Christian humanism and recently revived late scholasticism. What contemporary scholars—and that applies particularly to the Jesuits—viewed as knowledge; how they generated, ordered, and systematized knowledge; and how they discussed, formulated, transmitted, and reflected on knowledge: all of it was based primarily on humanist and scholastic strategies of thought, research, and argumentation combined in a confessional Christian spirit. The fundamental texts of the *Constitutions* and the *Ratio studiorum* canonized this culture of knowledge.

Since roughly 1300, humanist pioneers like Francesco Petrarca, Coluccio Salutati, Lorenzo Valla, Juan Luis Vives, and Erasmus of Rotterdam had declared the literature and thought of Greco-Roman antiquity the preeminent culture of Europe. They viewed ancient authors like Cicero and Caesar not only as historical personages but also as interlocutors with present-day relevance. The humanists regarded the language, mindset, and culture of antiquity as a model to emulate in their own lives. They therefore created a new culture and mentality in late medieval Europe that was based on the creative adaptation of the ancients. This movement spread to almost every corner of Europe in the centuries prior to the founding of the Society of Jesus. Hence it was unsurprising that the Jesuits encountered Renaissance humanism relatively early. Loyola himself may have come into contact with Renaissance culture as a courtier in his youth.[291] After his conversion in 1521, Ignatius attended schools in Barcelona and Alcalá in which humanist ideas were very popular. Even at the university of Paris, which cannot be regarded as a bastion of humanism, humanist works and ideas could be found at nearby independent colleges.

Thus, it is beyond question that the Society of Jesus came into contact with humanism in a variety of ways right from the start.[292] A string of parallels between the humanist views and those of the Jesuits can be cited: both groups viewed the ultimate purpose of theology not as speculation but rather as a practical way of life and as a tool to guide one's neighbors. With their emphasis on propagating the faith by preaching, the Jesuits saw numerous points of contact in the humanist appreciation of rhetoric; the humanists' confidence that man could be taught to lead a virtuous, religious life influenced the Jesuits' decision to embrace education; the humanists' inclination toward rhetoric suited Ignatius's view that evangelizing always had to be adapted to the specific circumstances and abilities of the audience. Finally, the two groups shared a tendency to assess and judge human behavior from case to case.[293] Humanist ideas also made a profound mark on the fundamental texts of the new order. More than one passage of the *Constitutions* was borrowed from ancient authors, reflecting contemporary enthusiasm for antiquity.[294]

Despite these diverse encounters with humanism, Ignatius himself was not a humanist, that is, someone who had made idealized antiquity the guiding principle of his own life. Nor were Loyola's early companions humanists, strictly speaking. Diego Laínez, for example, once had to be informed in a long letter from Polanco of the benefits of reading ancient literature, which were apparently not obvious to him.[295] Rather than "pure humanism," it was a combination of devotion and humanist learning that was supposed to shape a Jesuit and be transmitted at the Society's schools. Ignatius was accordingly critical of many ancient and humanist texts. Many works by the ancient pagans were acceptable only after they had been "expurgated," that is, after offensive passages had been altered, cut, or abridged—as for example in the case of Horace or Martial.[296] Even this practice, however, sometimes seemed not enough: Ignatius did not want to allow Terence even after "expurgation."[297] Several years later, General Mercurian issued a list of ancient authors that could be assigned only to advanced students to read. A long list of "obscene books—Catullus, Tibullus, Propertius, most of Ovid, Plautus, Terence, Horace, Martial," and others—was forbidden to beginning students.[298]

Loyola's relationship to the great contemporary humanists Juan Luis Vives and Erasmus of Rotterdam was similarly ambivalent. Ignatius may have personally met Vives in Bruges once around the year 1530, but now and again he explicitly prohibited the works of both these authors.[299] Jesuits who engaged with the works of Erasmus or went so far as to defend him were reported within the Society.[300] At other moments, however, the Roman leadership was more open. For one, they wanted to limit the strict ban on Erasmus only to Rome itself, where outright hostility toward the great humanist was palpable around 1550. Outside the Eternal City, the writings of Erasmus were a fixture of Jesuit education. His works could be found in the library of more than one Jesuit college.[301] The Jesuits also disguised their own use of various works by the Dutch scholar by simply citing them without mentioning his name.[302] They shrewdly calculated whether they could use Erasmus or not in certain cases. "Our men should stay away from the books [of Erasmus and Vives], unless their use seems necessary for the greater glory of God"—this formula coined by General Mercurian epitomizes the Jesuits' multifaceted and pragmatic relationship with humanism.[303]

Jesuits like André des Freux, one of Ignatius's close confidants and collaborators, devised a forward-thinking way out of such dilemmas. Des Freux may justifiably be considered a humanist scholar. It was he who carried out the "expurgation" of ancient texts for Ignatius.[304] Des Freux also published a book titled *De utraque copia, verborum et rerum, praecepta* (Instructions on the abundance of both words and subjects) in 1568 in which he explained the expert use of words and stylistic techniques.[305] The book was intended to replace the identically titled work by Erasmus, which was a much-read but little liked resource for learning Latin style in the Jesuit order. Step by step, other Jesuits also published their own textbooks on humanist culture, which soon supplemented or supplanted classical humanist educational material. The Spanish Jesuit Cyprian Soarez published a new—and wildly successful—textbook of rhetoric in 1568.[306] The Jesuit Jakob Pontanus was similarly active in Augsburg. His *Progymnasmata latinitatis* of 1588 replaced Erasmus's *Colloquia*, which was intended to teach students Latin through scenes taken from everyday life.

The textbooks by des Freux, Soarez, Pontanus, and many other Jesuits belonged to a new stage of European humanism. The emergence of humanist textbooks illustrates the integration of the movement in school programs, in which the Jesuits played a very important part. Humanism had become an accepted cultural code in early modern society, which was precisely why it now was to be taught at schools—albeit according to a post-Reformation, strictly Catholic interpretation. That guaranteed it a broad impact, but it also could lead to a certain degree of superficiality because humanistic educational ideals now had to be turned into a subject that could be taught to and learned by a wide audience.[307] Graduates were now expected to know and be able to quote from more or less the entire canon of Greek and Latin literature, whether to write a text of their own or to produce a convincing argument in a public speech. They had to imbibe and digest ancient literature so thoroughly that they could call on the wisdoms it contained at any time.

Doing so required special knowledge technologies. Students were constantly reading great quantities of text. In the process, they worked to transform what they had read into usable excerpts. Humanism in the schools—at any rate, as taught at Jesuit colleges—frequently took the form of "carving up" texts. The Jesuits elevated the process of excerpting, copying, paraphrasing, and compiling to an art form, developing a systematic approach to note-taking.[308] Francesco Sacchini set it in motion in 1614 with his work *De ratione libros cum profectu legendi* (On the method of reading books with profit). The "profitable reading" referred to in the title consisted of reworking ancient literature into the building blocks of arguments that could be used at any time. Several years later, at least two more Jesuits produced similar handbooks of their own. Claude Clement did so in the context of his comprehensive work on library science in 1635, and the German Jesuit Jeremias Drexel in a book on excerpting.[309] Sacchini's guide in particular was widely read and republished in numerous editions and translations until at least 1832. Sacchini recommended that readers first simply take down in order everything that struck them as notable. The next step was then to arrange these notes thematically under key words (*loci communes*, i.e., "commonplaces") in a book. In this way, writers could later look them up whenever they needed to discuss a topic and find suitable aphorisms and text fragments. This organized bounty culled from one's reading over a long and productive scholarly life was a special treasure for humanists from the Society—just as it was for their peers and comrades in arms outside. Prominent personalities like the great scholar and writer Jakob Pontanus even published their private collections of excerpts to spare other, less diligent readers some of the work.[310]

In addition to the transformation of cultural heritage into educational material, the late humanism of the sixteenth and seventeenth centuries was also characterized by an increased reliance on technical and specialist scholarship. The fields of philology and textual criticism and a passion for facts and objects of antiquity—antiquarianism—were among the most important legacies of humanism. These emphases emerged as early as the fourteenth and fifteenth centuries and became the dominant form of humanism in the age in which the Society of Jesus was founded. Humanism thus transformed from a certain mindset into a scholarly field of (ancient) languages, objects, and events. Multiple scholarly branches spread forth from humanist literature.[311] The Jesuits played a considerable part in this process, as many members of the order eagerly took part in the ever more detailed scholarly study of the legacy of antiquity, late antiquity, and early Christianity.

Undoubtedly the scholarly endeavors of the Bollandists in Antwerp are the most famous and most significant Jesuit example of this brand of late humanism. The Bollandists' work was dedicated less to the ancient pagan tradition than to the spiritual foundations of the Roman Catholic faith. To be more specific: they were primarily interested in saints' legends.[312] In 1607, the Flemish Jesuit Heribert Rosweyde devised a plan to systematically collect manuscript reports of the miraculous deeds and lives of the saints and to subject them to critical scholarly scrutiny. He wanted to distinguish authentic, reliable accounts from false, forged, or subsequently invented traditions. In this way, it would be possible to separate real from invented saints and to eliminate the latter. Such a scholarly survey would produce a reliable canon of Catholic saints.[313] Rosweyde's project was a direct response to the humanists' and Reformers' fundamental attack on the Catholic saints, which was often based on the ahistorical nature of many legends.[314] On this methodological basis, he published a critical edition of *Lives of the Saints* (*Vitae patrum*), the most important collection of early Christian martyr legends.[315]

His actual project, in contrast—the complete compilation, sifting, and examination of all hagiographic sources in Belgium—remained unfinished at his death in 1629. Rosweyde left behind, however, a mountain of notes and preliminary work—excerpts, notebooks, copies, all prepared according to the method described earlier. On the basis of this material, the project was continued by his confrere Jean Bolland (1596–1665), under whose leadership the "Bollandists" became a scholarly institution with far-reaching influence. In 1635, the group expanded with the addition of the incredibly diligent and meticulous Gottfried Henschen, S.J. (1600–1682). The most important figure of the next generation was the Jesuit scholar Daniel Papebroch (1628–1714). Whereas

Rosweyde had proposed "only" a complete survey of Belgian sources, under Bolland the plan was expanded to encompass the ambitious goal of a worldwide collection.

The growth of the *Acta Sanctorum* is a perfect illustration of how such projects relied on extensive teamwork. Aides and collaborators, sympathizers and patrons, friends and colleagues were indispensable. From 1660 to 1662, Henschen and Papebroch undertook a long journey through Germany and Italy in search of new manuscripts.[316] What they did not find and inspect personally as they traveled, friends inside and outside the Society of Jesus often made available to them. Papebroch was linked to a wide network of correspondents that included both Protestant experts like Gottfried Wilhelm Leibniz and the Frankfurt Orientalist Hiob Ludolf, and the Catholic scholar Charles du Fresne, Sieur du Cange.[317] Projects like the *Acta Sanctorum* could succeed only if the European community of researchers collaborated across borders, and that also meant across confessional boundaries. Jesuit scholars moved effortlessly in this scholarly world. The European république des lettres accepted the Catholic men of the Society as respected members in turn, often without any hesitation whatsoever.

The seventeenth century was an important phase in the rise of source criticism, and the Bollandists perfectly illustrate the Jesuits' great contributions to this field. This recasting of humanism as the philological science of textual criticism, however, also had dangerous sides. On the one hand, it seemed plausible that one could use these techniques to analyze not only saints' lives and historical sources but also the Bible itself. To a limited extent, the philological analysis of the sacred scripture eventually became acceptable for pious churchmen like the Jesuits and even deemed necessary. On the other hand, the threat of more or less comprehensive skepticism might lurk behind textual criticism. Philology harbored a fundamental mistrust of texts and their reliability, and this skepticism could escalate almost limitlessly. In the last decades of the seventeenth century, such pessimistic views of the sources for the past became ever more common—was text-based knowledge of the historical past even possible? Or were a new science and alternative approach perhaps needed, methods that were not based on texts? One

atypical but fascinating Jesuit cast such fundamental doubt on old manuscripts and contested their value as historical sources so radically that
he annoyed even contemporaries with his skepticism: Jean Hardouin
(1646–1729), an incredibly hardworking scholar of vast erudition.[318]
Over long years, he compiled what was at the time a very modern,
twelve-volume collection of the acts of all church councils, in which he
critically explored the contradictions and inconcinnities of the transmission. It was not long, however, before he took this critical approach to
the gaps and conflicts in the sources to the extreme. Starting on the basis
of individual observations on the works of Augustine, between 1690 and
1692 Hardouin developed the radical thesis that "a certain band of fellows
existed, some centuries ago, who had undertaken the task of concocting
ancient history, as we now have it, there being at that time none in existence." With the exception of Cicero, Pliny the Elder (whom Hardouin
himself had edited), Horace, and parts of Vergil, these "men" had forged
all other ancient text in the Middle Ages. Hardouin granted only Roman
coinage the status of a reliable witness and source. His general suspicion
of textual sources, incidentally, also pertained to such central Christian
authors as Augustine, the entire series of church fathers, and even
Thomas Aquinas: "A very unusual doubt came over me lately, namely
whether there really was a St. Thomas Aquinas."[319] Over the course of
his long life, Hardouin wrote numerous scholarly treatises that attempted
to support his theory of the "invention" of antiquity and the Middle Ages
with references to inconsistencies and contradictions in (allegedly) ancient documents. In the end, Hardouin's theory is striking not only for
its vast scale and his unflagging defense of it, but also for the fact that it
ultimately was nothing more than a radical manifestation of contemporary scholarly practices. Hardouin's views obviously met with
heavy criticism inside the order. Outside it, a storm of indignation broke,
fanned by scholars from the most diverse backgrounds.

The late humanist Christian scholarly world was characterized by the
conviction that there was a uniform and consistent divine truth, which
manifested itself in each and every thing. Thus everything in existence
was connected—cultures and civilizations, metaphysics and empirical
reality, scholarly observation and divine revelation were fundamentally

incapable of contradicting one another, but rather were positively linked. The world of late humanist Jesuits was therefore a world in which China and Egypt, Europe and America, texts and objects, nature and culture, creation and Creator, were all interrelated. How exactly all these distinct pieces of information fit together to constitute a whole, however, was not immediately obvious. There were problems and contradictions because parts seemed impossible to harmonize—but then it was precisely the scholar's task to decipher these connections despite such conflict and paint a coherent, universal image of the world. No one embodied this fascinating but—even for contemporaries—sometimes incomprehensible worldview better than the aforementioned Jesuit polymath Athanasius Kircher, whom contemporaries already regarded as the pinnacle of this culture as it veered off into the absurd.[320]

Kircher was a German who joined the Society of Jesus in Paderborn. He then made an adventurous escape to France during the Thirty Years' War, worked on Malta a while, and finally spent most of his life in Rome. There he produced a rich body of literature and spun such a far-reaching web of correspondence that even his contemporaries marveled at it. Kircher was a universal scholar, who wrote as much about magnetism, volcanos, and the center of the earth as he did about ancient Egypt, modern China, music, and history. Direct observation of nature and scholarly knowledge acquired through reading complemented one another—Kircher climbed Mount Vesuvius to make his own observations and learned Coptic to gain a better understanding of biblical antiquities and history. In his mind, everything pointed ultimately to one another and to God, the Creator.

Kircher's book about Noah's ark (*Arca Noë*), published in 1675, may serve as an example of this method of interpreting the world. In it, Kircher discussed at length the question of how, by whom, and with what resources the ark had been built. The biblical narrative was always the starting point. Kircher began by discussing the very brief and incomplete passages about it in the Old Testament not only in Latin but also in Greek, Arabic, Chaldean, and Syriac versions.[321] Then he explored on a philological basis whether an "ark" was a "ship" (probably not). There followed discussions of the wood used and carpentry. Again, he exploited his wide knowledge of ancient and contemporary works, which supplied him with numerous details on potential types of wood and methods of working it. Comments on the precise location in which the ark was built and the necessary materials followed. Kircher then described how and where various types of animals came on board and were housed—animals that were difficult to control, especially snakes and birds, posed a particular problem. Finally, Kircher seized on the biblical account as grounds to indulge in an extensive scientific discussion. Geological questions, meteorological problems, and above all a plethora of zoological topics had to be addressed.[322] He was captivated by questions about the procreation of animals; for example, of maggots and flies. This type of late humanist, baroque learning was based largely on books, but it by no means shut itself off from the natural world, even if it usually interpreted and perceived that world primarily through texts.

Kircher was thus ultimately an unusually comprehensive exponent of the baroque culture of knowledge, which in many ways was typical of the scholars of the Society of Jesus as a whole. This approach combined the study of texts and nature, secular and religious knowledge, and local and global interests, fitting all of them into a universal framework comprised by the one divine truth. The Jesuits did not invent this cultural-historical configuration, but they profoundly shaped it, exemplarily advocated it, and ardently defended it.

Cultural Profiles: Late Scholasticism

Within the Society of Jesus, the late humanist culture of knowledge merged with a revival of scholasticism. Like humanism, scholasticism is also an old phenomenon. First coming into view in the late eleventh century, it was a method of teaching and discovering "the truth" that was applied predominantly at the newly founded universities. Scholasticism was a style of thinking, a method of proceeding, an intellectual process, as well as a literary form. Scholastic argumentation and writing were characterized by the systematic subdivision of large topics. The certainty of knowledge was predicated on the use of terminology that was as precise and rational as possible. By devising ever more finely nuanced concepts, one could differentiate facts, distinguish different aspects of objects, and tease out different ways of viewing a question. The concept of a "cause," to cite just one example, was usually divided into four aspects: material, formal, final, and efficient (*causa materialis, formalis, finalis, efficiens*). Causes could also be "near" and "far," intermediate causes were possible in between, and so on. This level of nuance was reflected in the style of presentation adopted in scholastic literature. Treatises were divided into individual "questions" (*quaestiones*) with "articles." An author first introduced all previous opinions on a topic, then laid out his own position, and finally refuted all views to the contrary. Special care was always taken to formulate questions and arguments precisely and correctly, as well as to anticipate potential objections, all of which had to be completely dispelled. Whereas the humanists relied on rhetoric, trusting in the power and legitimacy of persuasive strategies and privileging literary thought and writing, the scholastics relied on an austere, often very technical Latin and the power of cool logic to break questions down into the subtlest distinctions. This extreme emphasis on conceptual clarity was a late development of Aristotelian logic. As an intellectual method and style of debate, scholasticism essentially affected every discipline, but, besides jurisprudence and philosophy, it was theology that it influenced especially profoundly.

The Jesuits trusted in scholasticism because they believed in the utility of systematic theology that relied on rational argumentation. In contrast to their medieval predecessors, the Jesuits practiced a thoroughly modernized and enhanced scholasticism. In the sixteenth century, Dominican scholars at the University of Salamanca—especially Francisco de Vitoria (1492–1546), Melchor Cano (1509–60), and Domingo de Soto (1494–1560)—brought Spanish late scholasticism to the forefront of the European intellectual world.[323] Then the Jesuits exercised a formative influence on European late scholasticism as part of a second generation of philosophers and theologians. Francisco de Toledo, a student of de Soto, became an important professor of theology at the Collegio Romano prior to 1600, while another of de Soto's students, Juan de Maldonado, brought the scholasticism of Salamanca to Paris.[324] Yet another generation later, Francisco Suárez (1548–1617) became the dominant personality of the Society in Rome, Alcalá, and Coimbra in the fields of philosophy and theology; he too had been educated and intellectually molded in Salamanca. His works exerted an irresistible influence, dominating the book market for Catholic late scholasticism from approximately 1600 to the end of the nineteenth century and beyond, even exerting a varied influence at Protestant universities.

The revival of theology, philosophy, and jurisprudence that radiated from Salamanca was shaped, on the one hand, by an attempt to preserve the legacy of medieval scholasticism and, on the other, by an effort to integrate new sources that the humanist movement had brought to light.[325] The scholastic ideal of systematic analysis aided by rigorous conceptual logic remained intact but was supplemented by the humanist view that ancient and early Christian sources had to be taken more extensively into consideration and treated more critically. In the field of theology, the result was a sharp upturn in "positive theology." This term designated a methodology that relied much more emphatically on biblical passages and the facts (*posita*) contained therein rather than the systematic arrangement of subjects.[326]

At the same time, the new generation of late scholastic theologians was working intensively on the philological analysis of the text of the Bible. Francisco de Toledo, for example, was highly esteemed for his exegetical works.[327] He moreover played a leading role in the revision of the Latin translation of the Bible (the Vulgate), which was launched under Pope Clement VIII and therefore known as the Clementina. Juan de Maldonado, mentioned previously, was also a famous exegete.[328] Although he by no means rejected scholastic theology as such entirely, we nonetheless can observe a certain distance from dogmatic speculation in many of his remarks. Theology, he felt, should stay grounded in the positive statements of the Bible. With respect to questions of substance, one should refer "not to Plato or Aristotle ... but rather to the prophets and apostles, to the evangelists, to Christ, to the church, to tradition."[329] A good theologian, Maldonado concluded, may need an acute and uncompromising intellect, but, and here we see the difference in his fundamental orientation, "He must have studied Latin and not be ignorant of Greek and Hebrew, so that he does not speak vulgarly or ridiculously. . . . He must be versed in all areas of philosophy . . . But even more important, he must be trained in every area of theology, first and foremost in Sacred Scripture, which is the source of all theology."[330] Here we find the legacy of humanism, whereby an interest in new, "original" sources and philological skills became standard.

Besides the Bible, the church fathers also attained new prominence. As reference points for the new, humanistic field of positive theology, they played a much bigger part than previously in the Middle Ages. Most early Christian church fathers had only recently really been discovered. Many Jesuits fused an outstanding knowledge of patristics onto a scholastic skeleton in their arguments. A systematic approach, dedication to completeness, and logical argumentation all remained intact, and yet the scholastic method took on a new appearance in the process. According to Maldonado, the philosophers' only purpose was to put the finishing touches on the statements of the Bible, church documents, and the church fathers "to the extent that that is necessary."[331] Even if later generations of Jesuit theologians no longer radiated the same passion for the humanist *ad fontes* as Maldonado, the legacy of this enhanced source consciousness survived and remained influential for a long time.

Not only did the scholasticism of the early modern period have to redefine its relationship to the early Christian sources that had been discovered, but scholastic philosophers and theologians of the sixteenth and seventeenth centuries also had to address how they related to their medieval predecessors. Outright schools of thought had already gathered around the most important authors as early as the fourteenth and fifteenth centuries.[332] The Scotists thus followed Duns Scotus in philosophy and theology; the nominalists, William of Ockham; the Thomists, Thomas Aquinas. This varied collection of scholastic philosophical schools continued in the early modern period, but the influence of Thomism grew ever stronger. In the sixteenth century, St. Thomas Aquinas became the universal theological icon of Catholicism par excellence.[333]

But then the problems began. First of all, it was quite obvious to the Jesuits of the sixteenth and seventeenth centuries that Thomas, the great model, had been mistaken about certain questions, and other topics, such as Protestantism, had simply been unknown in his day. Many Jesuits therefore rejected Thomas's doctrine at least on individual points and supplemented them by drawing on other scholastic authorities. In both philosophy and theology, the Jesuits harbored a veiled but still powerful attraction to late medieval Scotism.[334] Second, scholars had wildly different opinions not only about what Thomas had actually said about particular problems but even about what his core ideas were. It was one thing to demand allegiance to Thomas, quite another to determine what that actually meant. Thomas required interpretation, too. And so he was interpreted, indeed in manifold ways and with varying results. In a nutshell, one might say that Thomism "exploded" and splintered into multiple Thomisms. It was virtually the same in philosophy with respect to Aristotle's doctrine and the sundry different Aristotelianisms elaborated since antiquity. Long, glorious battles could be fought over who held the purest, most authentic, and therefore most orthodox interpretation of Thomas and Aristotle. The Jesuits and Dominicans in particular continually clashed in this debate.

Benito Pereira, an extraordinarily influential Portuguese professor of philosophy at the Collegio Roman, may serve as an example of this diversity and the innovative potential of Jesuit philosophy. In his fundamental work, *De communibus omnium rerum naturalium* (On the commonalities of all natural things), published in 1576, Pereira explicitly claimed that he had not written a commentary but rather devised a system in which he had integrated Aristotle's statements. The legacy of late humanism comes to light here too: Pereira was proud that he had cited not only original texts but also a large number of late antique and medieval commentators that the achievements of the late humanists had first made available.[335] He favored a radical version of Aristotelianism that was potentially incompatible with Christianity, being heavily influenced by the Muslim philosopher Averroës, who had risen to prominence with a series of "unchristian" theses in the twelfth century. Pereira was therefore viewed very suspiciously in the order. Achille Gagliardi in Rome went to the pope to denounce him (unsuccessfully), and the lectures taught by Pereira's students in Dillingen were carefully monitored.[336]

In the field of theology, Gregory of Valencia, a Spanish Jesuit educated in Salamanca who taught in late sixteenth-century Ingolstadt, represents the flexible and innovative position of the Society of Jesus.[337] In the preface to his *Commentarii theologici*, he explains at length that he had by and large remained faithful to the classical model set by Thomas Aquinas. Gregory also built his lectures on the works of his great model. But in the same breath he mentions that he also has rearranged, expanded, and abridged numerous points. His text is riddled with references to the church fathers, and a collage of relevant quotations from the Bible frequently stands at the beginning of sections of his argument—which is more than a superficial reflection of humanism. The Jesuits' Thomism was thus far from the conservative adherence to received ways of thinking; it was a modernized approach that was capable of evolution. It is clear to see that, for all its formal conservatism, late scholasticism as expanded by humanism was still capable of developing further in creative fashion.

It was sometimes uncertain, however, as to how much humanism should influence particulars. Jakob Pontanus, for example, argued in 1590 that the *humaniora* should be appreciated for their intrinsic value and continue to be upheld.[338] He feared, however, that the humanities would be increasingly marginalized in the colleges as philosophy and theology dominated ever more. He viewed it ultimately as a generational phenomenon: while he and many older Jesuits considered the humanities to be very important, younger Jesuits had their sights set on a model of knowledge that emphasized the systematic subjects of philosophy and theology.

Despite such nuances, however, the Society of Jesus long stood for an understanding of knowledge and science that synthesized late humanism and late scholasticism. The *Ratio studiorum* was the lasting expression of this combination. One point in particular remained the unquestioned cornerstone of this position: that all knowledge and all sciences stood in a hierarchy that culminated in theology. It was the Jesuits' unshakable conviction that the nontheological disciplines could never be more than the "handmaidens of theology." There could be no real contradiction between the findings of the various subjects because there was only one truth—that of theology. If mathematics or physics arrived at results that differed from those of theology, there were only two conceivable alternatives: either one openly proclaimed a contradiction with theology, which would result in sanctions, or one claimed that the results were not "genuine" truths but rather, for example, only "hypotheses" with a limited claim to truth. It must be stressed that this second option really left Jesuit scholars ample leeway to expand their nontheological interests and pursue them nearly unimpeded. But they ultimately remained tied to a model of knowledge and science that presumed a strict hierarchy of disciplines.

This baroque model was also still alive in the Society of Jesus in the eighteenth century.[339] Jesuit scholastics like the Spaniard Luis de Lossada or the Germans Anton Mayr and Berthold Hauser maintained the tradition in highly impressive fashion. They were more or less well-acquainted with newer ideas, integrated this one or that in their work, but adhered emphatically to the established method. The product of this attitude was often extremely well-thought-out late scholastic surveys. Yet as competent as eighteenth-century Jesuit scholasticism may have been, measured by its own standards, one thing was clear: as the dominant intellectual approach, this worldview and scholarly method faced growing criticism.

Cultural Profiles: The (Catholic) Enlightenment

"Let us be Christians before we are philosophers," the French Jesuit René Rapin proclaimed in his treatise *Réflexions sur la philosophie ancienne et moderne* (Reflections on ancient and modern philosophy) in 1676.[340] He criticized the growing independence and experimentalism of philosophers whose ideas transgressed established intellectual boundaries. His criticism was directed against representatives of the so-called (early) Enlightenment—he names Pierre Gassendi and René Descartes several times.

Today, the umbrella term "Enlightenment" covers several intellectual and cultural developments that began to influence Europe in the mid-seventeenth century and with greater intensity after about 1680. In contradiction to widespread Christian convictions, René Descartes proposed a radical duality of spirit and matter, thus undermining the traditional concept of man and God and the Catholic doctrine of the Eucharist.[341] The Jewish philosopher Baruch Spinoza, in contrast, represented the danger of conflating God with nature for Rapin and his contemporaries: materialism. George Berkeley, for his part, heavily emphasized the spiritual realm and considered the existence of the world unprovable. Nicolas Malebranche, finally, claimed that body and soul, matter and spirit, could work together only because God directly triggered every single act of material bodies when the spirit had a corresponding thought. In one way or another, all these theories contradicted traditional Christian concepts of the world, man, and God. These concepts may have placed body and soul, material and spirit, in a clear hierarchy and relationship of dependence but nonetheless always understood them as interrelated.

Hence it is unsurprising that Rapin and most of his Jesuit confreres had major problems with the early Enlightenment. The Society produced a long series of more or less strictly conservative and purely negative ripostes. Giambattista de Benedictis, for example, waged a fierce literary battle against Jansenist and Cartesian innovations in Lecce and Naples around 1700 and finally became a victim of his own fervor, when he was driven from the city by his enemies.[342] His colleague Louis Le Valois, whom we have already come to know as an author, equaled him in his anti-Cartesian aversion.[343] In the eyes of many, only suppression seemed to help. Descartes's philosophy was explicitly banned from the Society in 1651 and 1706.[344]

But this picture of Jesuit hostility to the Enlightenment is too simple. There also were members of the Society who learned to engage with the new cultural framework of the age in a highly creative and productive way.[345] For a long time, there was no broad, let alone total opposition between the Jesuits and the Enlightenment philosophes. Despite all the bans against his work, Descartes still had sympathizers in the order, including such influential members as Father Charlet, the French assistant to the superior general in Rome, or Father Dinet, the confessor of Louis XIII. Denis Mesland of La Flèche was another important acolyte of the philosopher—until the Jesuit leadership sent him on mission to the Caribbean, potentially on account of his Cartesian convictions.[346] In Spain, Jesuits like Andrés Marcos Burriel in the mid-eighteenth century were deeply involved in a dynamic cultural upheaval that took place in the name of reform inspired by the Enlightenment after the Bourbons came to power in 1701. Burriel was focused above all on the methodological renewal of historiography and the modern historical-critical ideal of scholarship associated with it. The influential confessor of King Ferdinand VI, Father Francisco de Rávago (1685–1783), was likewise convinced that the Society of Jesus should play a major part in the cultural renewal of Spain.[347] The new zeitgeist was undeniably more present in the Society than is often claimed.

There was even a group of Jesuit scholars at the Collegio Romano in the early eighteenth century who were open to the new ideas of the day.[348] One of them was the gifted professor of physics and philosophy Giulio Gori (1686–1764). In his view, the received theological and philosophical positions were soon to be shipwrecked:

> The sails [of the old philosophy] are already torn in more than one place, and the ship, although not yet broken up, is still already yawning somewhat at the bows and is no longer capable of sailing unknown waters to discover new lands. It is forced to survive on what it already has. . . . The hatred that the old-timers have for the new teachings they loathe and their unwillingness to change their position are not, as some think, obstinacy of spirit . . . but rather the impotence of a mind that can no longer learn anything new.[349]

In light of such diagnoses, many Jesuit philosophes resolved to seize on and repurpose transferable aspects of the new philosophy for a Catholic Enlightenment.[350] What was "new" did not necessarily have to be contrasted with the transmitted "old" as praiseworthy "innovation"—instead, it was simply adapted so that the Jesuits became de facto participants in the philosophes' debate without proclaiming their rejection of the old traditions.[351] In this way, many French Jesuits came into contact with at least sections of the philosophy of John Locke.[352] In similarly selective fashion, Bertold Hauser in Dillingen cited the Lutheran natural law thinker and German philosophe Christian Wolff positively and without reservations around 1750.[353] His confrere Benedict Stattler utilized Enlightenment philosophy to develop a new form of Catholic theology that was intended to be acceptable to Protestants.[354] And Sigismund von Storchenau, a Jesuit like Stattler who continued working as a philosophical author and teacher even after 1773, was also a friend and an influential propagator of Wolff's philosophy.[355] Storchenau essentially tried to adapt arguments of the more radical Enlightenment that potentially undermined religion and integrate them into a traditional ecclesiastical model.

The Jesuits, moreover, were very much alive to the fact that the "Enlightenment" was more than a body of ideas and convictions.[356] To be "enlightened" also meant reading journals, discussing in salons, being "gallant" and cultured, and being able to talk about major subjects in pleasantly entertaining fashion. The European Enlightenment was a culture, a milieu, a self-conception, a habitus, a style, a way of life.[357] The absolute supremacy of antiquity as a model, which had held firm in the sixteenth and seventeenth centuries, began to crumble—the "modern" style, as it was called, increasingly prevailed over "the ancients" in ethics, culture, and language. The cultural openness of many Jesuits ensured that they easily come to terms with the new social ideas of the Enlightenment.

Personal relations between men of the Society and important thinkers of the new movement were accordingly common. Gottfried Wilhelm Leibniz, for example, had good contacts with members of the order.[358] Yves-Marie André (1675–1764) was a friend and companion of Malebranche, with whom he corresponded intensely from 1705 to 1715.[359] Guillaume-François Berthier (1704–28) later cultivated Jean-Jacques Rousseau as a contact; although by no means uncritical of Rousseau, Berthier showed genuine affection and appreciation.[360] In Spain in 1744, the Jesuit Andrés Marcos Burriel became one of the most important correspondents and personal friends of Gregorio Mayans, the leading proponent of the Spanish Enlightenment.[361] Even Voltaire, who had attended the Jesuit college of La Flèche, confided as a young man in his "paternal" teacher René-Joseph Tournemine (1661–1739) in difficult situations after his school days. He turned to the Jesuit for advice and support in late 1713, for example, when he was desperately in love with Catherine Olympe du Noyer and had been disinherited by his father for that very reason.[362] The tone of the Jesuits' reception of Voltaire usually remained friendly and laudatory until the 1740s, when the Society clashed with its former pupil on account of his theological radicalization. Roughly contemporaneously, Charles Secondat de Montesquieu also maintained friendships with Jesuits, with Louis-Bertrand Castel among his closest confidants. Montesquieu discussed writings and ideas with the Jesuit, although they also had differences of opinion and sometimes biting ridicule for one another. Still, Montesquieu valued Castel so highly that he—together with another Jesuit—were present at the philosopher's deathbed as his confessor.[363]

Montesquieu, however, is also a good example of the limitations of the philosophes' sympathies. He esteemed and liked individual Jesuits, but he took a skeptical view of the Society as a whole.[364] Montesquieu thus had rather harsh words for other members of the order. His condemnation of Tournemine, the paternal friend of Voltaire just mentioned, is a famous example. Montesquieu came away from a meeting with him only with an impression of "despotism and chicanery"—and other sources also report that Tournemine had a forceful personality and deliberately flouted the conventions of gallant society.[365]

Montesquieu and Tournemine had clashed at an event typical of the Enlightenment: a meeting for learned and philosophical conversation, namely, the société littéraire of Abbé Oliva, the librarian of the Duke of Rohan at the Hôtel de Soubise. Such private discussion groups, which met informally, yet by invitation only, to discuss current intellectual topics, were a mainstay of Enlightenment sociability. Women frequently hosted such salons. Jesuits were regularly present, too. Claude Buffier (1661–1737), for example, was a master of the gallant conventions of the Enlightenment and also was on good terms with Voltaire. He could regularly be found among the best minds of the day and was a welcome guest at the prominent salon of the Marquise de Lambert in Paris.[366] Several years later, not only did the most famous (and some of the more radical) philosophes frequent Madame de Tencin's salon, but many

Jesuits did so as well: Madame de Tencin had close ties to the Society, as did her brother, who had been elevated to cardinal.[367]

Members of the Society of Jesus were not present only at these "little academies": the real, often state-sponsored or at least state-sanctioned "major" academies for the arts and sciences also gladly admitted Jesuits. The famous Royal Society in London, for example, counted the Jesuits Roger Boscovich and the aforementioned Castel among its members and often published Jesuit scientific findings in its journal.[368] Castel was furthermore a member of the French provincial academies of Rouen and Bordeaux, which admitted Jesuits, in contrast to the royal establishments of the capital. Even as late as 1758, a Jesuit, Joseph-Antoine Cerutti (1738–92)—who later joined the Revolution and served as Mirabeau's secretary—won the Academie française's prize for eloquence.[369] All these examples demonstrate how numerous Jesuits were viewed quite naturally as part of the intellectual community of the Enlightenment.

The Jesuits of the Age of Enlightenment also experimented with one of the new media formats of the day, the periodical press. Journals were extremely important supporting media of the Enlightenment, and two major Jesuit projects in Paris aspired to adapt this key medium to their own needs. From 1702 to 1776, the *Lettres édifiantes et curieuses* published thirty-four volumes of letters and reports from Jesuit missionaries overseas. The *Mémoires de Trévoux*, also based in Paris, appeared far more regularly, once a month.[370] The *Mémoires* were the Parisian Jesuits' answer to the most important contemporary journals, the Enlightenment-oriented *Nouvelles de la République de Lettres* published by Pierre Bayle, the Gallican-oriented *Journal des Savants*, and the Jansenist *Nouvelles ecclésiastiques*. Like all these journals, which were generally hostile to the Jesuits, the *Mémoires* consisted of reviews of contemporary works, literary notices, and book excerpts with commentary. The idea for such a scholarly journal of the Catholic Enlightenment was hatched in the context of the French court. Michel Le Tellier, a Jesuit and later the confessor of Louis XIV, played an important part. The Duke of Maine, Louis Auguste, a pious illegitimate son of the Sun King, sponsored the undertaking.

The *Mémoires de Trévoux* was by far the most successful scholarly journal of any Catholic religious order.[371] There were highs and lows, of course, and internal conflicts among the collaborators, but the journal survived and gave voice to the Society's views.[372] Under the leadership of Tournemine, mentioned several times previously, and his immediate successors, the *Mémoires* embodied the Jesuits' moderate inclination toward many Enlightenment arguments, as sketched earlier. This tone of moderate, open assessment of new ideas remained intact under the editor Guillaume François after 1745, but the growing confidence of the philosophes and the radicalization of their ideas eventually led Berthier to adopt a more critical attitude.[373]

Although the *Mémoires* were eagerly read by Jesuits in Spain and even in China, they did not inspire any imitators elsewhere.[374] The *Lettres édifiantes*, however, inspired a long-lived parallel project in German titled *Der Neue Welt-Bott*—this journal likewise made mission reports available to a broad readership in edited form and, if necessary, in translation.[375] In Poland in the mid-1730s, the Jesuits took over the weekly *Kuryer Polski*, the most important newspaper in the country, which had originally been edited by the fathers of the Piarist order. In a print run of a thousand copies, this paper shaped the market for news and information in the kingdom for the following decades. The Jesuits were also involved in the publication of the *Monitor*, a journal that followed the model of the English *Spectator* and adapted the format of Enlightenment weeklies. Further publishing projects were at least discussed by Polish and Lithuanian Jesuits in the mid-eighteenth century.[376]

If one were to attempt to summarize the Jesuits' intellectual engagement with the ideas of the Enlightenment in the middle of the eighteenth century, a statement by Guillaume-François Berthier from the year 1747 could serve as a bellwether:

The new philosophers have earned just praise for relieving philosophy of certain [scholastic] entities, formalities, and other terms signifying nothing, with which, when one knows them and cites them in school in an authoritative tone, one persuades oneself of one's own great erudition. The new philosophers have often successfully destroyed, but they have not always built with the same success. Their new edifices—that is, these new systems vaunted so highly— lack the solidity of the ancient buildings of Roman [i.e., Catholic] architecture.[377]

The Jesuits could, at least to some extent, understand the philosophes' need for a new intellectual beginning; they even could adapt some of their new ideas. But they also wanted "a mixture of old and new," as Tommaso Ceva stated in 1722.[378] The Jesuits therefore never made the Enlightenment completely their own. Hence, the Enlightenment also never became part of the general self-conception and collective identity of the Society, as had been the case with the synthesis of late humanism and late scholasticism. The fundamental texts of the order—the *Ratio studiorum*, the *Constitutions*—were never adapted to the new culture. The official line still ranged from reserved to dismissive. Individual Jesuits nonetheless engaged in highly creative and productive ways with the innovations of the Enlightenment and adapted significant parts of the new ideas in a moderate, theological, Catholic Enlightenment of their own.

This precarious truce gradually gave way to open hostility after the mid-eighteenth century. The Jesuits lost their confident place in the Enlightenment, as the philosophes advertised the radical implications of the new culture ever more openly. The Jesuits and the Enlightenment thinkers increasingly stood opposed as hostile blocs.[379] This was nowhere more evident than in the Society's public battle with Denis Diderot and his *Encyclopédie* in 1751/2.[380] Diderot's great lexicon, which today is regarded as the epitome of the Enlightenment, attracted ample suspicion. It was considered a vehicle for atheist and heretical thought. Even leading proponents of the Enlightenment like Voltaire and Montesquieu were initially skeptical. The editor of the *Mémoires de Trévoux* at the time, Berthier, shared this critical attitude. In 1751 and 1752, he gave predominantly negative reviews of Diderot's "Prospectus," "Discours préliminaire," and the first volume of the *Encyclopédie*. Berthier and other conservative authors criticized the fact that Diderot's texts frequently contained radical ideas hidden in seemingly neutral and objective articles. Overall, this criticism was right on the mark. But the Jesuits around

Berthier never lost sight of the fact that the new lexicon had powerful political supporters; they therefore steered a middle course that combined broad rejection with the recognition of particular points.[381]

These controversies escalated into a symbolic struggle between old and new forces for cultural and intellectual dominance. Opponents and supporters of the Enlightenment coalesced around the two parties. The criticism that the Jesuits and other members of the church leveled at the *Encyclopédie* forged the philosophes together in an alliance despite their respective differences and simultaneously radicalized them. As the leaders of this ecclesiastical-religious countercurrent, the Jesuits became implicated in these highly prominent and polarizing public conflicts as the enemies of the Enlightenment.

The Jesuits could not shake this position in public life for the final two and a half decades of their existence prior to 1773. By midcentury at the latest, they were firmly in the *parti antiphilosophique*—allowing for sporadic, individual exceptions mentioned previously—both in their own estimation and in that of most contemporaries. The Enlightenment, meanwhile, evolved into a broad, culturally dominant movement—and its proponents knew how to market themselves shrewdly to the public at large.[382] Conflicts over forms of devotion, such as the veneration of the Sacred Heart, and over school reform catalyzed the process of the Jesuits' cultural marginalization. Growing enmity and ever more distorted negative stereotypes about the Jesuits split the intellectual elite of Europe. Supporters and opponents of the Enlightenment squared off as ideological adversaries in increasingly implacable opposition for the final third of the eighteenth century.

Cultural Profiles: The Jesuits, Science, and Technology

Another profound change, in addition to the cultural rhythm of humanism, late humanism, late scholasticism, and the Enlightenment, washed over the European culture of knowledge in the early modern period: the way people looked at nature changed, as did the methods with which they sought to explain natural phenomena. Like the Enlightenment, the transformation of the scientific worldview was difficult to reconcile to the late humanist, scholastic Catholicism of the Jesuits. Undaunted, however, the Jesuits made an honest effort to integrate many new findings in astronomy, botany, mechanics, and electricity into their intellectual world. Their enthusiasm for the latest discoveries in the heavens and on earth was not limitless, but still often very great.

This was also true in the case of the Florentine mathematician Galileo Galilei, who became famous all over Europe in 1610 after he published his book *Nuntius sidereus*. Therein he presented the findings of his observations of different celestial bodies with the help of his telescope. Galileo was probably the first European to see and describe irregularities on the surface of the moon, a variety of new stars, and four moons of the planet Jupiter. All these points contradicted the standard cosmological and astronomical model of the late Middle Ages and the sixteenth century, which was based on a synthesis of the ancient authors Aristotle and Ptolemy. According to this earlier model, the earth was the center of the universe, and the celestial bodies rotated around it firmly mounted in spheres and with perfectly regular shapes. The Prussian canon Nicolaus Copernicus had already contradicted this geocentric conception of the universe in 1543; he had wanted to put the sun at the center of the cosmos instead. For a long time, Copernicus's heliocentric theory had not caused any major problems for the Catholic Church, since it was treated only as a thought experiment to optimize mathematical calculations. Some prominent theologians, like the Augustinian monk Diego de Zúñiga or the Carmelite Paolo Foscarini, had even argued that the new doctrine was compatible with the Bible or supported by it.[383] Galileo also took Copernicus's side in his *Nuntius sidereus*—only he no longer wanted to treat this model merely as a mathematical hypothesis but rather presented it as the actual structure of the cosmos in light of his empirical observations.

The Society was initially very sympathetic to Galileo. The Jesuits' faith in the geocentric model almost never wavered around 1600, but they still took great interest in Galileo's new research methods and many of his observations.[384] Galileo himself had learned things from the Jesuits, especially with respect to epistemology and methodology.[385] Christoph Clavius, one of the most influential mathematicians and astronomers of the period, and his students had done important pre-liminary work.[386] Clavius and the other mathematicians at the Collegio Romano were decidedly in favor of using mathematical methods to describe natural phenomena—precisely what appealed to Galileo.[387] These Jesuits were open to fusing mathematics and the observation of nature. Under the rubric of "mixed mathematics" (*mathematica mixta*, i.e., applied mathematics), they pursued interests in music, geodesy, cartography, hydrology, and especially astronomy.

The innovative potential of this Jesuit approach was especially visible to contemporaries in the calendar reform of 1582.[388] This reform was necessary because the ancient Julian calendar was not in perfect har-mony with the astronomical cycles of the sun and moon. Criticism of the calendar's imprecision had grown since the Middle Ages, intensify-ing in the sixteenth century. After taking office in 1572, Pope Gregory XIII finally convened a commission to devise a new calendar, which is still called the Gregorian calendar today. A decades-long controversy erupted between Catholics and Protestants over the validity of the new calendar, which corrected the calculation of the date simply by skipping ten days and introducing the system of leap years. But there was no doubt that it was a scientific improvement, and that was not least thanks to the contribution of the Jesuit Clavius, who was the leading personal-ity on the commission and later defended the calendar again in an important publication of 1603.

Despite such successes, the mathematical observation of nature had fierce competition inside the Society. The Jesuit natural philosophers in particular put up a stubborn resistance. They wanted to treat natural phenomena not quantitatively but rather qualitatively—philosophically. The mathematicians' most important adversary at the Collegio Roman was Benito Pereira, who believed it was pointless to apply mathematics to natural phenomena.[389] Clavius and Pereira thus took diametrically opposed opinions as to whether astronomy—which obtained its find-ings by mathematically based inferences—was a true science with the power to explain the natural world: Clavius said yes; Pereira, no.

Galileo thus had some reason to hope that the Jesuits around Clavius could give his new views a positive reception. Clavius himself may have kept reticent until his death in 1612, but many of his students and allies like Christoph Grienberger (1561–1636), Giuseppe Biancani (1566–1624), and Orazio Grassi (1583–1654) openly accepted at least major parts of Galileo's accomplishments.[390] Grienberger, who himself was a lens grinder, was the first Jesuit to see the moons of Jupiter through a telescope, in late 1610. In 1612, he praised explicitly in print the observations Galileo had made with the telescope. Grienberger remained a sympathizer of Galileo and defended him several times against other Jesuits, as for instance in the controversy between Galileo and the Mantuan Jesuit Mario Bettini over the height of the mountains on the moon or in Galileo's famous conflict with the Jesuit astronomer from Ingolstadt, Christoph Scheiner, over who was the first to observe sunspots. In a letter to Grienberger in 1611, Biancani also exemplarily declared, "I love and admire Galileo not only for his rare erudition and ingenuity, but also for the long-standing friendship that I have cultivated with him since our time in Padua. I still feel obliged by his politeness and courtesy. I think no one has propagated, confirmed, and defended his discoveries, publicly and privately, more fervently than I."[391] Jean Lorin, a Jesuit theologian at the Collegio Romano, also praised many of the brand-new discoveries of the Florentine astronomer—in a commentary on the Bible![392]

It was not until after 1614, when Galileo began to wage a heavy-handed and not always shrewdly managed campaign to popularize Copernicanism that the Jesuits gradually became alienated and broke with him. His views were first critically examined by the Sanctum Officium in Rome in 1616. Jesuits were also involved in this inquiry, particularly Robert Bellarmine as a leading adviser of the papal Inquisition. Bellarmine, however, together with Grienberger and other Jesuits, extended a protective hand over Galileo as far as he could. In a famous, last-second conversation with Galileo on February 26, 1616, Bellarmine attempted to persuade the defendant to recast his theses in a less offensive form.[393] In the end, the Inquisition initially condemned "only" the view that the Copernican model was reality—this was now deemed to contradict the Bible. Copernicanism could, however, still be upheld as a mathematical "hypothesis" that significantly facilitated calculating the orbits of the planets. Galileo himself was not accused of false doctrine in 1616, again thanks to Bellarmine. The Jesuits were certainly not the driving force behind the events of 1616, and it is not unreasonable to ask whether Galileo himself was partly to blame for what happened.[394] Galileo, however, felt betrayed by the Jesuits, and so several conflicts subsequently broke out between him and leading members of the order.

The condemnation of the Copernican model in 1616 increased the pressure not only on Galileo but also on Jesuit scientists. Previously, the respective accuracy of a geocentric or heliocentric model was a relatively obscure mathematical question. Now the Copernican worldview had become the dividing line between old and new, orthodox and heretical, and that had consequences for the Jesuits, too. Although they were actually interested in new scientific ideas, questions, and methods, they now had to demonstrate their distance from Galileo and especially from the Copernican model. And so numerous theologians and exegetes from the Society of Jesus joined the incipient wave of anti-Copernican polemic.[395] The censors within the Society now took more vigorous action when they suspected sympathy with Galileo's ideas.[396] General Acquaviva insisted yet again on Thomism and Aristotelianism in 1611 and 1613. The fight over astronomy also became amalgamated with the conflict over the Immaculate Conception that was breaking out at the same time in Seville. Since the sixteenth century, advocates of the Immaculate Conception had associated Mary metaphorically with the perfect, round, pellucid, pure moon—but that was no longer possible with Galileo's view of the heavens. The consequence was even greater skepticism of his new findings.[397]

The years after 1610 thus significantly curtailed the Jesuits' intellectual freedom. This curtailment, however, was not tantamount to total constraint, and Jesuit researchers did not allow the new parameters to prevent them from participating in the current scholarly debate. Even without the Copernican model, they could still take part in the advancement of the sciences. This became considerably easier for several decades because an alternative to Copernicus and Galileo emerged around 1620: the model of the Danish astronomer Tycho Brahe, which combined geocentric and heliocentric aspects in such a way that all the planets orbited the sun—with the exception of the earth, which instead was orbited by the sun along with the planets orbiting it. The Jesuits made this model their own after Biancani had been the first in the Society to advocate it. Brahe's model could explain many new discoveries virtually as well as the model of Copernicus and Galileo.

On this basis, an impressive series of Jesuit astronomers and mathematicians grew up, first in Parma and then, in the next generation, in Bologna. Foremost was Giovanni Battista Riccioli (1598–1671); then came Riccioli's assistant Francesco Maria Grimaldi (1618–63) and Mario Bettini (1582–1657).[398] Riccioli had studied in Parma since 1620, where the aforementioned Giuseppe Biancani was professor. The Jesuits at the college in Parma at the time were interested in experiments to investigate nature, and Biancani embodied this spirit particularly prominently. Many famous Jesuit astronomers and physicists were his students, including Niccolò Cabeo, Niccolò Zucchi, and Riccioli himself.

All his life at various places—Parma, Mantua, and finally Bologna, where the school of experimentally inclined Jesuits had been moved in 1636—Riccioli investigated geographical, chronographical, hydrographical, mineralogical, and historical questions. His chief interests, however, were astronomy and physics. His works on mechanics revolved around experiments with a pendulum. His astronomical research culminated in one of the most important textbooks on astronomy of the entire early modern period: the *Almagestum novum* of 1651. One part of this epoch-making and oft-cited book consisted of Riccioli's precise observations of the surface of the moon, which he summarized in a detailed map (fig. 13). Broadly speaking, he was an enthusiastic observer, experimentalist, and user of scientific instruments—in a word, an exemplary proponent of the empirical culture of knowledge that blossomed in the sixteenth century.[399]

But the Jesuits had their limits—although it is striking how creatively and liberally Jesuit scientists negotiated them. Like Biancani and Grienberger before him, Riccioli also could not unreservedly support Galileo's views. The Jesuits could recognize heliocentrism only as a very useful mathematical "hypothesis." But within the scope of this acknowledgment as hypothesis, Riccioli could nonetheless fully endorse both Copernicus and Kepler and praise their achievement, even if he disputed the astronomical truth of their theses to the bitter end. And as time went on, many

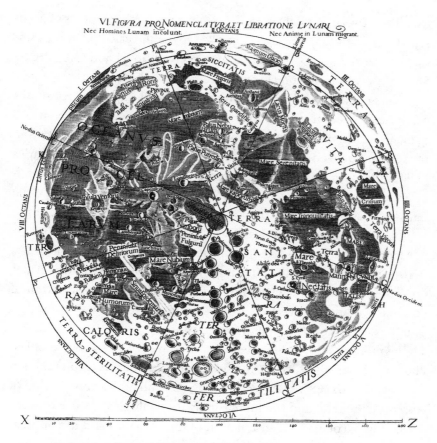

FIGURE 13. Giovanni Battista Riccioli's precise map of the moon, 1651.
© akg/Science Photo Library.

Jesuits simply ceased to refute Copernicus explicitly. Mathematicians like the intractable Honoré Fabri (1608–88) in Rome and Adam Kochański (1631–1700) in Poland supported Copernican heliocentrism even more unabashedly. They taught the heliocentric view quite candidly and sometimes "forgot" to mention its hypothetical status.[400] In the fields of mathematics and mechanics, even a cardinal and Jesuit like Sforza Pallavicino in 1665 could consider himself a "Galileista, at least a bit."[401]

Around the same time as the first Galileo affair in Rome, another Jesuit network of "friends of mathematics" (*philomathematici*) established itself in Antwerp and Leuven, helping illustrate further aspects of Jesuit scientific and technological research.[402] Optics and calculus were prominent here: the Jesuits François Aguilon (1567–1617) and Grégoire de Saint-Vincent (1584–1667) were preeminent scholars in these fields. Aguilon's *Opticorum libri sex* was one of the most important textbooks on optics and color theory and potentially influenced Isaac Newton. Saint-Vincent's treatises on geometry were read by Leibniz in Paris in 1672 and influenced his work on the theory of calculus.[403] Jean-Charles della Faille (1597–1652), a student of Saint-Vincent, conducted research in geometry and maintained interests in cartography. In 1629, della Faille was summoned by the king of Spain (as an inhabitant of the southern Netherlands, the Jesuit was his subject) to the Jesuit college of Madrid and appointed *cosmógrafo mayor* of the Council of the Indies in 1638, in other words, the official geographic expert on this important government body.[404] He had already been involved in the creation of sea charts. He moreover was interested in the mathematical underpinnings of the construction of fortifications.

The military utility of mathematical knowledge was a source of fascination for other Jesuits, too, such as André Tacquet (1612–60) and Jan Ciermans (1602–48).[405] As a result of the overall professionalization of warfare in general and the increasingly technological nature of siege warfare in particular, the installation of fortifications and the optimal positioning of troops and artillery became a mathematical art more and more. The Jesuit Juan Baptista Poza, a man engaged in such matters, thus declared in 1627:

> The reasons for adopting a particular formation or using a particular type of fortification in order to obtain victory or to defend a place, are to be found in the mathematical principles of geometry and perspective, which the art of war makes full use of. And just as it has been approved to be licit for Jesuits to learn and to teach mathematics, it is equally licit [for them] to apply those same principles to military matters.

Out of this same conviction, many Jesuits taught military science across Europe. At Jesuit strongholds in Italy, France, Belgium, and Spain,

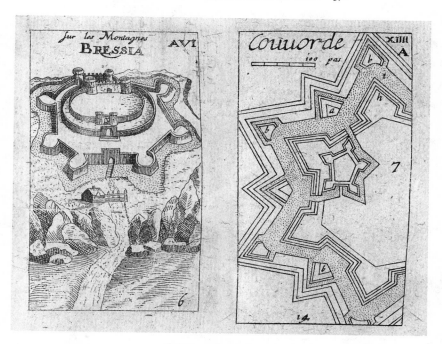

FIGURE 14. Two examples of Jesuit fortress architecture. Georges Fournier,
Traité des Fortifications ou architecture militaire (Mainz 1668).
© Bayerische Staatsbibliothek München, Res/App.mil. 48, plates 6 and 14.

courses were offered in the mathematics of building fortifications, bal-
listics, and pyrotechnics—often at colleges for noblemen, whose graduates had a class-related affinity for warfare (fig. 14).

Jesuit engineers were also prominent in the navies of many European
states. In Lisbon, Jesuit classes gave graduates a thorough education in
navigation until well into the seventeenth century.[406] One of the earliest
and most important theorists of naval tactics was Paul Hoste, S.J. (1652–
1700), who was actively training naval officers in Toulon by 1686. Hoste
was primarily a mathematician, but he combined a scientific approach to
navigation with a passion for putting it into practice. At his own request,
Hoste often sailed with the fleet of Admiral Anne-Hilarion de Costentin,
Comte de Tourville, "to perfect himself in his trade."[407] Shortly before his
death, he published the fruits of his long years of study in three works
dedicated to the tactics of fleets in battle and various other mathematical

FIGURE 15. Paul Hoste improved naval warfare by means of Jesuit *mathematica mixta*. From *L'art des armées navales, ou traité des évolutions navales* (Paris 1697), 202, plate 64. © Deutsches Museum, Libri Rari, 1947C1.

problems of a military nature.[408] In his *Art des Armées navales ou traité des évolutions navales* (Art of naval armies or treatise on evolutions, 1697), he presented numerous schematic illustrations and specific examples of historic naval battles, some of which he had personally experienced, to illustrate the geometric principles of such maneuvers as a chase at sea or sailing in line under various wind conditions (fig. 15).

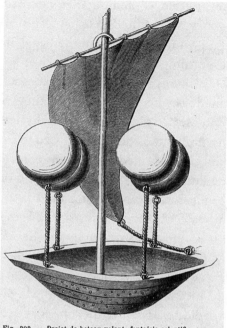

Fig. 292. — Projet de bateau volant, fantaisie scientifique
du jésuite Lana (page 514).

FIGURE 16. Lana Terzi's design for an airship. It
was never built and, in fact, could not have
functioned. *Prodromo overo saggio di calcune
inventioni nuovi premesso all'arte maestra* (Brescia
1670), 252, fig. 2. © akg-images/Florilegius.

Jesuits also thought deeply about shipbuilding and its scientific principles. François de la Maugeraye, S.J., clashed with naval officer Jean-
Antoine de Barras de la Penne over ancient galleys and their methods of
construction, a topic that was still relevant in light of the large fleets of
oared ships in the Mediterranean. Hoste was also involved in pragmatic
debates about shipbuilding. His confrere Francesco Lana Terzi (1631–87)
wanted to build a different means of transportation: he is famous for his
idea of building an airship, which he published in the year 1670 (fig. 16).[409]
The plan was to lift the hull of a ship in the air by means of light copper
spheres out of which the air would be pumped, creating a vacuum. Although the concept was proved unfeasible by Leibniz, and no attempts

to implement it are attested, contemporaries vigorously debated Lana Terzi's idea. He also was permitted to teach technical subjects at the university of Ferrara, which belonged to the Papal States. The Jesuits there were also responsible for regulating the river Po at the behest of various popes.[410] Hydrology was a job that engineers from the Society repeatedly performed elsewhere, too. In 1607/8, they were also involved in planning canals in Mexico City to divert floodwaters.[411]

From hydrology, it often was only a short step to surveying and cartography, and Jesuit scholars made important contributions in these fields, too. Outside Europe, Jesuit missionaries were often the first and for a long time the only Europeans who measured distances with reliable methods and drew maps from them using scientific methods of projection.[412] Nearly a hundred maps drawn by Jesuits survive for central South America. The Jesuits constantly created high-caliber products, such as a map of Paraquaria drawn shortly before 1650 and dedicated to Superior General Vincenzo Carafa (fig. 17). The high-quality original etching featured a dedicatory poem to the superior general that was often tacitly dropped in Protestant reproductions. The *Nouvelle Atlas de la Chine* that Jean-Baptiste Bourguignon d'Anville (1697–1782) put on the market in 1737, which was regarded as a cartographic benchmark for Asia, was based on the preliminary work of French Jesuits.[413] Jesuit information, even if its Jesuit origin was sometimes rendered unrecognizable, found its way into the general store of European knowledge.

Mapping terra incognita outside Europe entailed extensive journeys of exploration. The Jesuits were often among those who knew the land and its peoples best, and so it is no surprise that they were often recruited even for purely scientific expeditions. Gabriel Patino (1662–1729), for example, was the first person to travel the almost two-thousand-kilometer-long Pilcomayo River in South America upstream to its source in 1721. In 1745/6, several members of the order, including the cartographer and navigator José Quiroga, sailed on board a Spanish frigate from Buenos Aires along the continent south just shy of the Strait of Magellan to inspect and map the coastline. This voyage of discovery represented a seamless fusion of religious and political, ecclesiastical, and state interests: whereas the Jesuits wanted to survey the region for

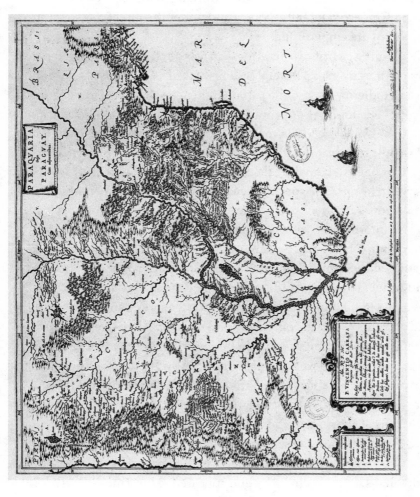

FIGURE 17. The Jesuits fused the roles of missionaries and scholars. In order to keep their bearings in faraway places, they also became outstanding cartographers. Here, a map of Paraguay. Gerard Coeck, *Paraquaria vulgo Paraguay cum adjacentibus.* © Bibliothèque National de France, CPL GE DD-2987 (9440).

new missionary activity, the Spanish military—then in the midst of the War of the Austrian Succession (1740–48)—primarily wanted to counteract the English presence in the South Atlantic. Over several campaigns in China, too, from 1708 to 1716, the Jesuits explored and surveyed almost the entire empire, while working in intimate cooperation with the Chinese state bureaucracy and under the direct, personal supervision of the emperor himself.[414]

The Jesuits' scientific work in biology was often closely connected to their activities overseas. Several Jesuits worked as zoologists. Giovanni Battista Hodierna (1597–1660) studied the eyes of insects under a microscope. His findings appeared in a little book titled *L'Occhio della mosca* (The eye of the fly) in 1644, one of the first books ever to contain microscopic observations.[415] It was botany, however, far more than zoology, that became a favorite field of Jesuit scientists, especially in missionary territories. The special occupational designation *botanicus* was introduced within the order for some of them. Through autopsy and extensive information from indigenous peoples, Jesuits like Pedro Montenegro (1663–1728) and Sigismund Aperger (1678–1772) catalogued and studied the flora of the Gran Chaco in South America.[416] Georg Josef Kamel (1661–1706), after whom the camellia is named and who last worked in the Philippines, was highly esteemed as an expert on the world of plants.[417] Like Montenegro and Aperger, Kamel was still working before the creation of modern botanical taxonomy by the Swede Carl Linnaeus, which went largely unnoticed by Jesuit botanists. Kamel sent many of his botanical observations and dried specimens to Europe, where they circulated in the scholarly community around 1700. The English scientist John Ray, whose *Historia plantarum* of 1704 was celebrated by contemporaries as an important publication, received much of his information about tropical plants of the Pacific from Kamel. Several botanical notices penned by him appeared in the *Transactions of the Royal Society of London*. Drawings and descriptions of local animals—insects, primates, imaginary creatures—supplemented the scientific work of this Jesuit with such wide-ranging interests (fig. 18).

The botanical research by Kamel and many other Jesuits was often closely related to pharmaceutical endeavors. Before Kamel was officially

FIGURE 18. The Jesuit Georg Josef Kamel drew numerous
exotic Asian plants. © akg-images/Science Photo Library/
Natural History Museum, London.

designated a "botanist" in the Society, he was considered an "apothe-
cary." Jesuits' close contact with indigenous peoples overseas, their scientific training, and their social engagement in tending to the sick meant
that they were confronted with medicinal challenges to an especially
high degree and were also often in a position to offer new remedies.[418]
It was no coincidence, for example, that quinine—an antipyretic and
for a long time the most important medication for malaria (which was
still widespread in Europe)—was known as *pulvis Jesuiticus*: "Jesuit
powder." The information and substances that were gleaned from tropical
plants in the gardens of numerous Jesuit colleges were used extensively

in the everyday medical practice of Europe. Jan Bisschop, S.J., a lay brother, scholar, poet, and pharmacist in Ghent, for example, composed a pharmaceutical treatise in 1653 that was reprinted several times, exerting a powerful influence in Belgium.[419]

In the mid-sixteenth century, many Jesuit houses even began to maintain their own pharmacies, which served not only their fellow Jesuits but also soon the population at large. The pharmacy at the Collegio Romano set the bar high: it was frequented by famous personages, princes, and popes.[420] Things frequently looked just as good in the provinces. When a pharmacy was established at the local college in Pont-à-Mousson, it was intended to provide for the city and surrounding area, as well.[421] Several thousand doses of healing medicines were given to hundreds of patients in this Lothringian city over the fifty years prior to the dissolution of the Society. The Jesuit pharmacy in Pont-à-Mousson not only tended to the sick directly on site but also dispatched doctors and specialists regionally. Noblemen and simple folk alike also bought other chemicals from the pharmacists at the college, such as moth poison or "a powder against flies." The Jesuit pharmacists in Pont-à-Mousson always had state-of-the-art scientific apparatuses and literature at their disposal for preparing medicines. That was also true mutatis mutandis for the overseas territories. In the Spanish cities and missionary settlements of South America, for example, there usually was a rudimentary pharmacy and in some cases, like Córdoba or Santiago de Chile, even very large ones, although the Jesuits still often complained about the overall rather scanty medical care.[422]

The pharmaceutical production of medicines in the early modern period often skirted dangerously close to alchemy. On the whole, the Jesuits had an ambivalent relationship with this art, reflecting the opinion of many early modern scholars.[423] Some influential authors, like the demonologist Martin Delrio, had a certain sympathy for alchemy. Delrio at least did not think it was impossible to produce gold, although he also warned that many people had lost everything trying to do so. The natural philosopher Benito Pereira was of a similar opinion. Athanasius Kircher rejected the production of gold as an impossibility and ruthlessly lampooned alchemist artists of transmutation, although he considered the alchemical art of separating and purifying metals and medicinal substances as a noble science—in his case, this judgment was closely connected to his very specific interests in current developments in mining and metallurgy.[424] Kircher himself experimented in this field at the Collegio Romano, which possessed a large laboratory. He even sent some of his recipes to Pope Alexander VII, who was also open to experimenting in alchemy.

Other members of the Jesuit order were perhaps even more optimistic than Kircher. There were persistent rumors around 1600 that François Aguilon had even conducted experiments on the transmutation of metals at the college of Antwerp. Francesco Lana Terzi, the Jesuit inventor of the airship, likewise believed in transmutation, which he claimed he had observed with his own eyes in many experiments.[425] Lana Terzi was fascinated above all by the "greatest art" of alchemy, which consisted in distilling the pure fifth element that could then be transmuted into all other substances.

Niccolò Cabeo (1586–1650), in contrast, was interested more in the philosophical aspects of alchemy, and he was not afraid to invoke the name of the controversial alchemist Paracelsus (1493–1541).[426] Other Jesuits were more enthusiastic about medicinal alchemy. In Belgium, Ignatius Derkennis conducted such extensive experiments that his confreres joked that he had transformed "from a theologian into an alchemist."[427] The little-known Jesuit Johannes Misch was also attracted to alchemical medicine in Hungarian Trnava around 1660.[428] He held convictions similar to those of Jan Baptist van Helmont, a follower of Paracelsus, and also drew inspiration from Oswald Croll, another highly controversial Paracelsist and alchemist. The Jesuits had access to individual works by Paracelsus and other Paracelsists elsewhere, too.[429]

But this optimism aroused mistrust and criticism both inside and outside the Society. Jan Bisschop, just mentioned, dismissed alchemy altogether and recounted an anecdote about a Viennese alchemist who refused to take his own medicines when he once fell sick.[430] Some Jesuits, such as Juan de Pineda in Seville, wanted to ban alchemy outright. Others were less strict, albeit critical. Giovanni Stefano Menochio warned politicians in 1625 not to believe the promises of alchemists, stating that no one should hope to fill the state treasury by manufacturing gold. Although it might have worked sporadically, he argued, the number of those who failed was so much greater that a wise prince should not take such a risk.[431] A generation later, Cardinal Sforza Pallavicino also scoffed at astrologers and alchemists rather than impute to them any power to predict the future.[432] Writing about Kircher's alchemical inclinations, his confrere Adam Kochański noted in 1670 that they excited "much opposition."[433] All in all, alchemy never attained more than a marginal status in the Jesuit order.

In the sixteenth and early seventeenth centuries, enthusiasm for electrical phenomena was not far removed from interest in alchemy.[434] The debate over the origin and transfer of electric currents slowly evolved from earlier discussions of forces of attraction in general and of magnetism in particular. In 1600, *On the Magnet* appeared, an epoch-making work by the English researcher William Gilbert. A few years earlier, however, Father Leonardo Garzoni (1543–92) had published theoretical reflections and practical observations that clearly anticipated Gilbert's work.[435] Within the Society, Niccolò Cabeo took up the mantle and published on both electricity and magnetic attraction. In Cabeo's case, we can observe, on the one hand, the typical effort not to break explicitly with Aristotle and Aristotelian natural philosophy and, on the other, a willingness to tacitly abandon received explanations in preference for new approaches.[436] In the eighteenth century, Jesuits like Giovanni Battista Faure continued the discussion, now also citing Newton's new views on gravitation.[437] Like many European scholars, Faure was frustrated by the Englishman's cryptic allusions to the final details of his doctrine. Like many other Jesuits, he remained cool toward Newton.[438]

Until at least 1700, Jesuit scientists thus still were undoubtedly among the scholarly elite of Europe and maintained collegial relations with many leading scientists, despite the institutionally mandated balancing act they performed between their research interests and official guidelines. It is undeniable, however, that the Jesuits' influence in this area waned with the passage of time. There had always been a certain tension between officially sanctioned teaching material, on the one hand, and particular scientific positions, on the other. This gap grew ever wider and more glaring. It became increasingly difficult to juggle both the old doctrines and the plethora of new theories. In the end, there were too many fronts on which the Jesuits were unable to embrace current developments openly: the Jesuits denied the vacuum and therefore were cut off from countless experimental possibilities that had been tested across Europe since Evangelista Torricelli's experiment with a tube of mercury in 1644.[439] Although atomism became a major topic of scholarly discussion in the mid-seventeenth century, constituting the basis of both Descartes's and later Newton's mechanics, the Jesuits were unable to accept the theory until the mid-eighteenth century on account of its incompatibility with Aristotelian physics; they thus were far behind the times.[440] The Jesuits were also late to adopt the new mathematical tool of differential and integral calculus, which had been developed by Newton and Leibniz in the 1660s and 1680s—perhaps because they showed little interest in algebra generally.[441] Among the Society's other obsolete positions, it was stipulated until about 1700 that natural science in the Jesuit order still fell under the purview of "mathematics."[442] "Physics," in contrast, remained a purely philosophical discipline that attempted primarily to produce philosophical descriptions of things, not to investigate their structures according to natural laws.

Only with delay, and to a certain extent in a belated push for modernization, did the Jesuits also begin to stage spectacular experiments for exhibition, a very popular practice since the seventeenth century (a classic example, for instance, is Otto von Guericke's public demonstration of the force of air pressure with the Magdeburg hemispheres). It was some time before the Jesuits hit upon the idea of staging such "pleasant science" that, "through a thousand lovely experiments," would "disclose the most secret mysteries of nature."[443] They first began to put on scientific demonstrations for the general public and the students at their colleges in the mid-eighteenth century. Experiments with fermentation are known from the Society's schools in Alsace in the eighteenth century. And there are reports of experiments with burning, exploding, and loudly popping powders that were carried out by Father François de la Maugeraye at Louis-le-Grand in Paris. In the eighteenth century, physics then also became an experimental science for the Jesuit order. A course in *physica experimentalis* is first mentioned in the curriculum of Ingolstadt in 1748. Appropriate devices and instruments were systematically acquired.[444] At many Jesuit colleges, research and teaching now went beyond the scholastic tradition.

In this way, at least individual Jesuits could consider themselves leaders of the scientific community even in the mid-eighteenth century. Vincenzo Recatti (1707–75), for example, began to engage with new developments in mathematics in 1752 and published widely recognized works in that field. Recatti openly declared his allegiance to Galileo.[445] His confrere Josef Stepling (1716–78) from Bohemia likewise had modern mathematical interests and maintained an extensive correspondence with Christian Wolff and Leonhard Euler. In 1744, Stepling explicitly took sides with Newton with respect to calculating the orbits of comets.[446] Stepling also corresponded with two of the most important Jesuit scholars of the last decades before the dissolution of the Society of Jesus: the astronomer Maximilian Hell (1720–92) in Vienna and the mathematician Roger Boscovich (1711–87). Boscovich, who had always welcomed Newton's ideas and adhered to heliocentrism, had been on good terms with the progressive-minded Pope Benedict XIV and especially with his Cardinal Secretary Silvio Valenti Gonzaga since 1740. The fact that the pope finally lifted the ban on heliocentrism in 1757 (but did not remove Galileo's works from the Index) may ultimately be attributed to Boscovich's influence.[447] Members of the Society of Jesus thus did not completely disappear from the scientific discussion. Their presence in the scientific community, however, was much smaller than it had been a century earlier. Their influence on the course of scientific research did not completely dissipate, but it declined significantly and was no longer as profound as it had once been.

Through the Senses toward God:
The Jesuits and the Arts

Science and education were not the only subjects dear to the Jesuits' hearts: the fine arts (not called thus until later) were, too. This is true, albeit with varying emphases, for all art forms: from architecture to sculpture, painting, and interior decorating to theater, music, and the most diverse literary genres, the Jesuits accepted that religious content had to be presented in a way that was palpable to the human senses. They viewed this fact not as something bad but rather as a reflection of the fundamental nature of man that should be taken seriously. They thus took a very clear position on the wide spectrum of early modern Catholic Christianity, and it did not escape criticism.

Roughly speaking, there were two positions in Christianity with respect to the appreciation of the arts and sensory perception, on which they were based, after all. On the one hand, one could view the human body as sinful, as the source of all evil, and that absolutely included the senses. The idea of the vice of a lustful glance, for example, was widespread and took many nuanced forms. That usually left little love for the arts. Again and again, images and statues were thus condemned or even destroyed in Christian culture. The theater was also usually heavily criticized by this tradition. The second-century church father Tertullian in particular was the trailblazing pioneer of this attitude. Then again, one could also acknowledge that the physicality of man, including the senses, constitutes an indispensable and productive basis for the transmission of religious and salvific content. In that case, it was regularly emphasized that the senses and sensuality were a double-edged sword that could very much be utilized for pious purposes. In this tradition, the arts—provided they were strictly monitored and controlled—could be used to convey messages to people relevant to their salvation.

It was this latter tradition of closely monitored and regulated, but also positive and often even enthusiastic, use of the arts that early modern Catholicism broadly embraced. The famous decree on sacred images issued by the Council of Trent determined that the use of such images was fundamentally admissible provided that any and all lasciviousness was avoided.[448] Gabriele Paleotti, bishop of Bologna, was a leading proponent of the new ideal and the most important art theorist of Counter-Reformation Catholicism. He presumed without hesitation that "for Christian images there is one end: to persuade to piety and bring people to God."[449] The Jesuits saw things the same way and defended the use of images in religious contexts against real or imagined Protestant hostility. They wanted to convert people not away from but rather with images, thereby "helping souls."

In a certain sense, it was inevitable that the Society would have to address concerns about the arts: whoever wanted to build churches and other buildings also had to think about their architectural and painterly decoration; whoever wrote texts and aspired to convince people with words had to inform himself about their rhetorical delivery. Whoever wanted to reform and improve society had to engage with *every* manifestation of culture, had to adopt a position on *every* way in which the human spirit expressed itself. Hence, beyond the utility of the arts and media for ministry, the Jesuits were always eager to show contemporary poets, painters, architects, and dramatists their own positive examples of the right, appropriately Christian application of the arts.

For the Jesuits, as for many protagonists of early modern Catholicism, this optimistic confidence in artistic sensuality went hand in hand with the firm conviction that there had to be clear limits on artistic freedom. The senses had to help the faith and not distract from it—let alone lure people's souls down the path to perdition. Idolatry, the worship of images, was a constant threat; the Jesuits knew this, too. The arts and sensual pleasure could not become an end unto themselves but had to stay true to their religious mission. All art therefore had to be "decorous"; it had to obey the category of *decorum*.[450] Of course, what might be appropriate was a distinct problem for every art form and moreover changed with contemporary taste and from author to author. The Jesuits were therefore implicated in questions of style almost from the very start and of religious necessity had to engage in debates over the appropriateness of particular works, techniques, styles, and genres. It was easy to fight over style, especially for religious reasons. By the same token, however, we also cannot help but see the Jesuits' enthusiasm for the genuinely aesthetic dimensions of their products. Artistic media and their production followed and follow a logic of their own. Their development is not only determined by external conditions and forces but also, at least to a certain extent, has its own dynamic. For the Jesuits, this dynamic neither could nor should ever be separated from its moral and religious framework—the notion of the autonomy of art was totally alien to them. But within this religious framework, the Jesuits were thoroughly delighted to discuss the aesthetic and artistic perfection of individual pieces. That was true for poetry, drama, music, dance, architecture, painting, and sculpture and equally for all the many other arts and crafts.

Writing, Playing, and Composing

Soon after the Society was founded in 1540, the people in the cities and villages where they worked gave them telling nicknames. In Bologna, for example, Ignatius's men were somewhat derisively called the *preti delle comedie*, the "theater fathers."[451] The moniker alluded to the dramatic performances that the college frequently put on even then.[452] In point of fact, the Jesuits performed and even composed thousands of plays not only in Bologna but at Jesuit schools everywhere prior to 1773.

The passion of the Society of Jesus for the performing arts is regularly attributed to a congenial convergence of the theater and the spirituality of the Society's founder. Drama played a major part in Ignatius's *Exercises*, albeit primarily in the form of virtual drama in the exercitant's imagination. The latter was supposed to envision whole scenes that would play out vividly before his inner eye as if onstage, while he prepared for and carried out the meditations. It then was a small step from mental to real theater: the persuasive power of the theater, which the spectators could behold with their own eyes, was especially great. As Pedro Pablo de Acevedo, one of the first and most important Jesuit dramatists from Spain, wrote in the prologue of one of his plays, "What one sees with the eyes moves us / much more than that to which we give ear."[453] Some 150 years later, in 1730, a French theorist from the order, Charles Porée, made the same point in similar terms: if one merely reads a story, the heroes "are presented to the eyes naked, without color, without decoration, clothed only in words." But on the stage, they appear "wearing their clothing, distinguished by their particular colors, decorated with their insignia." The theater brought the dead figures of written texts to life. Precisely therein lay its special power.[454] There was also, of course, a minority opinion in the Society—just as there was in the church as a whole—that criticized this contemporary enthusiasm for the theater. But this position never won out over the long term.[455]

It was not the *Exercises* that inspired the Society to discover the stage but rather the schools: Jesuit theater was school theater. The first theatrical performance in a Jesuit school is usually placed in Messina, in 1551. In Rome, the great Latinist André des Freux may have inaugurated the tradition of student performances in February 1554, initially in the form of instructional Latin dialogues between students.[456] Ignatius explicitly recommended such dialogues to school rectors.[457]

There were very pragmatic motives for the Jesuits' enthusiasm for pedagogical drama. Rehearsals and performances reinforced the students' identification with the course material and simultaneously strengthened the relationship between the schools and the children's parents. Besides a handful of adults who usually played the leads, the authors tried to involve as many students of all ages as possible, at least in nonspeaking parts. The cast of many plays thus numbered over a hundred people.[458] Dramatic performances were a tried and tested way to profile and embed the Society and its students in the local and regional community.[459] In Paris, newspapers and journals reported such productions.[460] The audience often included princes and noblemen. Jesuit drama was thus, in marked contrast to the Passion and Christmas plays of the late Middle Ages, no longer simply part of the divine service but rather a much more autonomous affair. The performances were not primarily conceived as dramatic reproductions of the events of Easter or Christmas.

Given their fixed place in the schools, Jesuit plays were composed in Latin, a majority of them in prose. The exception to the rule was Spain, where plays were often performed in the vernacular from the 1560s and exclusively so after about 1650.[461] For the often-numerous spectators who understood none or very little Latin, brief summaries were printed in the vernacular, so-called *periochae*.[462] Stunningly, the general unintelligibility of the spoken text did not drive the audience away: on the contrary, the Jesuits knew how to convey important messages and emotions with numerous performative techniques that did not require those in the audience to understand the text.

They were especially eager to convey messages and emotions: the point of Jesuit drama was not only to give their students additional practice in Latin but also to contribute to the students' and the audience's moral and religious edification. Through exemplary actions onstage, Jesuit drama conveyed crucial pastoral teachings to the spectators, and did so in a way that captivated the audience emotionally. The plays were intended to increase the spectators' devotion, convey the certainty of the faith to them, and at the same time present them with the challenges of leading a good, righteous life. To achieve these goals, one could proceed either in a positive, encouraging way or in a negative, deterrent way. Accordingly, some plays were optimistic and presented positive role models, whereas others focused on polemical condemnation. One performance in Munich in 1596 "had the objective of inspiring the students to surrender suspect books. This was successful, because after the end of the play more than 60 books were burned."[463]

The Jesuits liked to show people in conflict situations for the moral edification of their audience. Onstage, ideas had to be painted very deliberately in black and white so that the moral lessons were obvious, argued Charles Porée in 1730.[464] Only a righteous life led to salvation. But the protagonists onstage often had to battle dramatically for hours to achieve that righteous life, as their souls—just like the souls of the audience—were presented as a battleground between God and Satan, salvation and damnation, good and evil. More than once the audience witnessed the Last Judgment onstage, where a guardian angel and an infernal demon vied for the soul of the protagonist before the archangel Michael.[465] The Everyman play fit this formula especially well and was heavily used for that reason in the first few decades of Jesuit drama. Onstage, an anonymous, typified person—an Everyman—was presented wavering between good and evil before he ultimately either was saved or was ensnared by the devil. The Everyman play *Euripus*, by the Minorite Lewin Brecht of Leuven (1502 or 1503–60), was especially important to the Society of Jesus. Beginning in 1555, it was performed frequently across Europe.

Beyond the Everyman, the Jesuits used the most diverse subjects to broadcast their moral and religious messages onstage. Biblical topics were the obvious first choice, but it was often difficult to dramatize biblical episodes. Many interesting passages of the New Testament were also very brief. Dialogue was limited to a few sentences or was lacking entirely. Jesuit playwrights therefore sometimes combined several Bible passages to create a new, original piece with biblical echoes.[466] To make Bible stories like "The Waking of Lazarus" (John 11:1–44) or "The Healing of the Blind Man" (John 9:1–7) suitable for the theater, Jakob Gretser invented several additional acts in the two plays he staged in Freiburg. New characters were introduced to flesh out the brief biblical originals. Additional dialogue revealed what the protagonists experienced, thought, and felt. It was here that Gretser could play to his poetic talent. He powerfully elaborated on the sensations with which the blind man described his first experience of sight—all without a biblical model:

> I see! But what? I don't know.
> I do not know what the sky is, I do not know what the air is.
> I do not know what water is unless I touch it—what color,
>   what a house is.
> I do not know what fire is unless I reach for it.
> If I should meet my parents by chance,
> Unless they should speak, I would not recognize either of them.
> In a word, I do not know what a person is unless he speaks.
> I would not recognize even myself, unless I spoke.[467]

The dramatic change in the formerly blind man brought about by Jesus's miracle is vividly portrayed in this rhetorical presentation. In his *Lazarus*, Gretser depicts the suffering and death of the title character and his relatives' grief in exquisite detail to put the audience under his spell. It was precisely these dramatic techniques that the Jesuits firmly believed helped to convey religious messages and moral attitudes powerfully.

In addition to biblical figures, the Catholic saints also often appeared in school dramas. The martyrs illustrated the exemplary life on which the audience should model their own. Early Christian saints in particular were frequently seen on Jesuit stages.[468] In this way, the Jesuits shrewdly played to a widespread contemporary trend: the original church and its protagonists were in vogue around 1600, not least because ever more ancient and early Christian monuments had been excavated. Many important Jesuit dramatists chose to write about this era that had only recently become known. Bernardino Stefonio's early Christian *Flavia*, for example, was performed at the Collegio Romano in 1600.[469] Such glances at the history of the church could be cast in a highly allegorical form yet also be of local historical significance. In 1688, for instance, the play *The Fortune of Westphalia, or: Westphalia Converted from Paganism to the Christian Faith* was performed in Münster, dramatizing the future bishop Ludger's conversion of Westphalia in the eighth century.[470] Some subjects from remote ecclesiastical history were exotic and may have been unfamiliar to most contemporaries. When Kaspar Rhey, for example, put the history of the Eastern Roman emperor Theodosius II and his wife, St. Eudocia, onstage, he showed himself to be up to date with the state of research in the incipient field of Byzantine studies.[471] The *periochae* proudly report which historical sources the playwrights had drawn on in their research.

The Jesuits were especially fond, however, of putting on plays about contemporary saints and martyrs. In general, the Jesuits regarded current examples as especially effective.[472] They particularly liked to put their own saints onstage. In 1622, the year of his canonization, *Ignatius Conversus* (Ignatius converted) could be seen in Augsburg. The dramatic events from the missions furnished especially rich material for new plays. The bloody and ruthless persecution of the Jesuits and indigenous Christians in Japan around 1600 hit stages in Europe in the most diverse forms.[473] The story of Takayama Ukon, for example, who was not killed but driven into exile in 1587 by the Japanese ruler Hideyoshi, was very popular. At least two different versions and four performances were staged in the Jesuit province of Flanders alone in the late seventeenth century.[474] This play also drew direct connections to the present for those in the audience, to whom the actors cried out, "You are true Japanese, / when you hold your own passions in place of God."

By putting martyrs and other Christian heroes onstage, the Jesuits simultaneously changed the conception of the theater. According to Aristotle, whose views had long served as a model, a hero should be a "middle" person with good and bad qualities. The Christian "hero" of the Jesuits, in contrast, was an unambiguous figure with clearly positive qualities. The suffering of flawless saints at the hands of scoundrels was considered edifying because the sinfulness of man—the central theme of Jesuit drama—could be recognized all the more easily against the backdrop of the martyrs' innocence.[475] With their plays, the Jesuits thus were at the forefront of a general Catholic movement toward Christian heroism. The strikingly graphic depiction of violence, such as that inflicted on the martyrs, was an integral part of this religiously motivated celebration of heroism.[476]

As the seventeenth century wore on, however, contemporaries began to feel that biblical and hagiographic themes had become a bit trite. Jakob Masen (1606–81), the famous Jesuit stylist and an influential drama theorist, advised against biblical subjects.[477] Instead, topics from ancient history became more popular. Denis Pétau wrote a play titled *The Carthaginians* in 1614.[478] In La Flèche in 1621, Pierre Mousson published four dramas with plots taken from ancient history, such as *Croesus* or one about the Persian king Darius. In the college of Paris in 1708, Charles Porrée's *Brutus*, a play about early Roman history, was performed with great pomp.[479] Given the Jesuits' deep humanist roots, this exploitation of "pagan" material is unsurprising. The pagans' behavior, their actions and values, thoughts and feelings could very much correspond to a good Christian's way of life. The distance between the pagans and Christ may have never been bridged, but the Jesuits still saw great parallels to Christian life in the human problems and experiences that shaped the pagans' decisions. Even pagan heroes could represent Christian values; they just did not know they were "Christian."

Many dramas used allegorical figures to broadcast their pedagogical messages. The Church, Heresy, Wisdom, and Stupidity appear as characters in a play from Munich, tellingly titled *On the Use and Misuse of Education* (1585). The play expounds on the Jesuit version of Christian humanism quite directly with speaking figures. Allegorical asides were even regularly inserted in "historical" plays, summarizing the exemplary action for the audience. Dogmatic content, in contrast, was presented rather rarely onstage; when it was presented, it sometimes met with criticism, as happened in Medina del Campo in Spain, where God the Father and God the Son spoke with one another onstage—in the vernacular. In response, Juan Ramírez angrily told General Borja it was "a story that, in some way, disrespects so profound a mystery."[480]

For the theater to overwhelm and deeply move the audience, everything depended on the persuasive power of the production. The Jesuits invested great effort in staging their plays—and precisely there lay the rub: since more than a hundred students were often involved in performances, it frequently proved impossible to have regular instruction during rehearsals. In Parma, where a play was usually chosen on January 1 to be performed during Carnival, hardly a day passed without rehearsal over the intervening weeks.[481] More than one Jesuit criticized the often excessive prominence of the theater in the daily life of the colleges, arguing that too much energy was being invested in the wrong project. In the last quarter of the sixteenth century, the Roman leadership launched a veritable campaign to reduce the cost and lavishness of plays.[482] In his influential discussion in 1650, Jakob Masen criticized "spectacular plays with various machines, where Phaeton steers the chariot of heaven, comets appear, dragons and genies fly through the air, sea battles are produced on the stage."[483]

Masen was not necessarily exaggerating.[484] Jesuits like Jean Dubreuil produced theoretical discussions of stage design and elaborate illusionistic decorations and gave practical advice for a variety of differently equipped production sites (fig. 19).[485] This was necessary because, especially in the early days, many Jesuit dramas were performed on improvised stages without extensive resources. In some places, plays were long performed on open fields—if it rained, the show had to be interrupted.[486] But many colleges marshaled greater resources: they built large stages and put on elaborate productions. In 1732, the scenery for a tragedy at the college Louis-le-Grand in Paris included "a large outdoor courtyard of a magnificent palace," in the middle of which stood "a structure in the foreground supported by columns. . . . Between the columns, groups of figures in white marble were placed. . . . In the center of the decorations is a large and magnificent arcade surmounted by the crest of France," and there were "galleries in an elevated and simple

FIGURE 19. Jesuits as theorists and practitioners of the stage. A drawing from Jean Dubreuil's standard work on stage design. *La perspective pratique, ou se voyent les beautez et raretez de cette science* (Paris 1679).
© Bayerische Staatsbibliothek München, 7329952 4 Math.a.221-3.

architecture, ingeniously interrupted."[487] In Munich, the Colossus of
Rhodes was once constructed onstage, only to come crashing down
soon afterward in a dramatized storm.[488] Burning props were as much
a part of the repertoire of Jesuit drama as scenes of war and nature.[489]
In light of such sensational multimedia spectacles, it was no wonder that
Jesuit plays were often extremely well attended. Some outstanding productions were watched by several thousand spectators. Food and drink
were provided. Tumultuous scenes occasionally played out in the audience. In 1604, the Jesuits in Mainz had to use clubs to bring the chaos
under control.[490]

Sometimes plays by outside authors were performed. Besides ancient
dramas, scenes from Molière's *The Imaginary Invalid* or adaptations of
dramas by Corneille and Voltaire were put onstage.[491] In general, however, the Jesuits themselves primarily wrote the plays they performed.
Franz Lang, S.J., a dramatist from early eighteenth-century Munich, is
said to have written 120 plays. That was possible because such prolific
writers not only borrowed the subjects of their plays from other Jesuits
but the boundary between reworking older topics and outright "copying" was sometimes hard to draw.[492] Here and there, "several pens collaborated" to compose a play, especially when it had to be done quickly,
as the important dramatist Nicola Avancini, S.J., once admitted in
1650.[493] Jesuit dramaturgy was thus, to a certain extent, a collective activity that reflected a wide-ranging, institutionalized culture of writing.
With respect to artistic production, the Society furnished a network
within which ideas, drafts, literary trends, and even competent personnel could roam effortlessly across Europe.

That is also true of other areas of Jesuit literature. In addition to
countless Latin dramas, the Jesuits produced an extremely wide range
of Latin poetry and prose.[494] Some subjects of Jesuit poetry are unsurprising. The several thousand verses that Tommaso Ceva composed in
1690 for his work *Iesus Puer* (Jesus as a boy) are no more unexpected of
a Catholic clergyman than the epic that Jakob Bidermann wrote about
the Massacre of the Innocents, Herod's execution of the male children
of Bethlehem. The three books of his *Herodiad* (1622) are full of gruesome depictions of the children's mutilated bodies and scenes of grief

and lamentation. In the end, it shows heaven and the murdered children, on one side, and hell with Herod and his helpers, on the other. Bidermann's biblical epic was divided into numbered sections, which may indicate that the individual passages were intended as textual reference points for meditation.[495] René Rapin's heroic epic *Christus Patiens* (The sufferings of Christ) from 1674 was similarly based on meditations during Holy Week.[496]

The Jesuits also liked to put outstanding events of their own history in verse. The life story of Ignatius was embellished by Jesuit epicists in such works as Laurent Le Brun's *Ignatiad* of 1661.[497] Loyola's life is presented as a paradigmatic conversion story, guided by Providence, written with an obvious pro-French bias.[498] And in 1640, the year of the Society's first centennial, the Portuguese Jesuit Bartolomeu Pereira published an epic composed of some six thousand verses, the *Paciecid*, which told the tale of the martyrdom of Francisco Pacheco, S.J., in Japan, in 1626.[499] The poet framed the historical action with numerous edifying and allegorical passages—angels speak with God, pagan and ancient Greek gods intermingle, pagan rulers travel to hell, personified virtues (and vices) speak, a council of pagan gods meets. Pereira even invented an angel named Japoniel responsible for Japan. The epic jumps forward and backward in time, reports about missions in other lands, and juxtaposes scenes set in China and Japan with depictions of the Roman Curia of the Society. In this way, the action is embedded in a complex interplay of wide-ranging references to ancient, Portuguese, and other European literature.

Such epic poetry, which was regarded as especially sublime, played to the triumphant piety of the decades around 1600, with its hero cult of the martyrs and saints. In the process, the ancient genre was recast with Christian values. Whereas in ancient epics, military excellence (the original sense of *virtus*) is regarded as the key quality of a hero, this is no longer unambiguously true in a Christian context. The very first line of Le Brun's poem highlights this shift of emphasis in light of Ignatius's life: "Let others sing of wars; we call him who has abandoned war a renowned hero." With these words, the Jesuit poet is obviously alluding to the beginning of Vergil's *Aeneid*: "I sing of arms and the man . . ."[500]

Le Brun, in contrast, casts his hero Ignatius linguistically and formally as an improved reshaping of ancient ideals, indeed virtually as the antithesis of the ancient hero—and he does so by simultaneously referring to another ancient verse, namely, by Ovid: "Let others sing of Caesar's arms; we sing of Caesar's altars."[501] The Jesuits regularly inverted the essence of heroism in this way. Bidermann made helpless, murdered children into heroes in his *Herodiad*; Pereira, the defenseless martyr Pacheco.

But classical, martial heroes might also still be useful and attractive, especially when they served to manifest and propagate the faith. In that case, the Jesuits could also sing of feats of war, as Jean de Bussières did in the roughly six thousand verses of his *Scanderbergus* (Skanderbeg, 1656), wherein the deeds of the eponymous hero, an Albanian who battled the Turks in the fifteenth century, are praised.[502] In Tommaso Ceva's *Iesus Puer* of 1690, the Christians' victory over the Turks at Vienna from just a few years earlier appears in the form of a dream. The *Rhea liberata* (The liberation of Ré), also by Bussières, was no less framed in terms of *militia Christiana*—or *Catholica*: this work was dedicated to the war between the heretical English and the good Catholic King Louis XIII on the Île de Ré.[503] The poet's Catholic position is unmistakable in these works: in *Rhea liberata*, a demon named Haeresis (Heresy) fights alongside the Protestant English army. The archangel Michael thereupon takes up the fight for the French, giving counsel to Cardinal Richelieu.

Another specialty of large-scale Jesuit Latin poetry was almost as extensive as Christian epic: didactic poetry. In this case, the Jesuits reworked the ancient model of Vergil's *Georgics*. The key work in this very popular genre was the poem *Horti* (Gardens) by René Rapin, published in 1665. He was followed in the seventeenth and eighteenth centuries by more than 250 verse treatises on all kinds of things—the Jesuits wrote didactic poems on musical instruments, gunpowder, chocolate, coffee beans, fisheries, navigation, and much, much more.[504] Scientific subjects were also presented in this manner. Carlo Noceti's (1694–1741) *De iride et aurora boreali carmina* is dedicated to rainbows and the northern lights. In 1768, Bernardo Zamagna produced a poetic interpretation of

Lana Terzi's airship idea that discussed not only the physical principles behind it but also the construction and navigation of the airship, including what to do when becalmed and when landing.[505] A year later, his confrere Giuseppe Maria Mazzolari composed the *Electrica*, on electricity, in six books of hexameters. Even the great scholar Boscovich began composing didactic verses on solar and lunar eclipses in 1735.[506]

The minor poetic genres were far more pointed than the thousands of hexameters of epic and didactic verse. The Jesuits composed countless odes, elegies, and epigrams. It was obvious to Jesuit poets that these brief, concise genres could serve as vehicles for Christian subjects in verse. Whole cycles of poems were dedicated to Mary Magdalene, for example.[507] Other poems imitated biblical scenes or paraphrased the Psalms. Some of the Society's poets proved to be genuine virtuosos. Bernard Bauhuis wrote the famous hexameter "Tot tibi sunt dotes, Virgo, quot sidera caelo" (You have as many gifts, virgin, as there are stars in the sky) about the Virgin Mary. The words of this verse produce a perfect hexameter in almost any combination. Another Jesuit wrote out no fewer than 1,022 permutations of it, all of which make sense.[508] Such anagrammatic games were very popular in the early modern period. They highlighted both the virtuosity of the poet and the perfection of the language and the subject celebrated in it. Bauhuis flaunted his eloquence in yet another poem. The last verse of the poem "What Is a Friend?" ends in ingenious, and inimitable, Latin wordplay: "Cernitur amicus amore, more, et ore, et re" (A true friend is recognized by his love, by his manners, and by his speech, and by the fact, i.e., by the fact of his friendship, his actions), whereby the word *amore* (by his love) is broken down one letter at a time into the other three tokens of friendship.[509] That was formally perfect and linguistically clever, and for that reason memorable despite the fact that the subject of the verse was a rather unspectacular moral platitude.

The Jesuit poets of the baroque—like preachers—also drew on playful, surprising, and even counterintuitive subjects to convey Christian insights. The "Polish Horace" Maciej Sarbiewski, S.J. (1595–1640), for example, once took advantage of a tragic event to articulate a Christian perspective on life in an apt and profound way: while the poet was living in Rome, one of his confreres by the name of Cesare fell off a stage set to his death at the theater. The event inspired Sarbiewski to compose three epigrams. In the second of these texts, the deceased addresses the reader directly:

> While I was marveling at the false stars from the theater's
>   Olympus,
> I said, "Reveal to me, God, the real stars."
> . . .
> While I was still speaking, God unveiled the real stars to me.
> But because death, which I sought, was not to be found
>   in heaven,
> I therefore had to fall to the earth to die.[510]

False stars lead to the real ones, falling to earth brings about ascent to heaven, death gives life. At the end of this poetic game of paradoxes, the poet delivers a clear, if playfully worded, theological message: "Do not weep, pious companions, Cesare did not fall from the stars, he fell up to them." Thus ends Sarbiewski's last poem on the subject.[511]

As we can see, the poets of the Society of Jesus were open to inspiration on almost any topic of everyday life. The ostensible subject did not even always have to be religious. Sarbiewski also celebrated the Polish general Jan Karol Chodkiewicz (1560–1621), his family, and his coat of arms in epigrams. Patriotic poetry and poems on political occasions were also not unknown to him.[512] The Jesuits did not shy away from harnessing their poetic skills for propagandistic purposes, cultivating their social contacts in the process—as was de rigueur for the late humanists. Beneath the superficial worldliness of these works, however, there often lurked much more than appeared at first glance. The Swabian Jesuit poet Johann Bissel, for example, composed two extensive cycles titled *Delights of Spring* and *Delights of Summer*. Each season— understood literally here, used metaphorically there—served as a common denominator linking the most diverse subjects: Bissel, for instance, wrote about the river Günz and local fishing holes, about his personal experiences in storms, and about raising a maypole. The poet could use the theme of the seasons to highlight a wide range of individual and local topics. But the way that Bissel and his colleagues observed man and nature was always oriented toward God, and that was also true of their poetry. As Jakob Balde wrote in Latin, "Whence this certain alternation of day and night? Who directs the hazy clouds, the sun, and the wandering stars? . . . Everything obeys a law. GOD, GOD presides over the world as supreme arbiter."[513]

Like so many other late humanist Latin poets, Sarbiewski, Bidermann, Bissel, and Balde saw themselves as *poetae docti* (learned poets). For writers like them, this meant that they deliberately composed in ongoing discussion with the entire literary tradition. Hence, first and foremost, the ancient poets and their works were critical reference points, as was all poetry of the Middle Ages and Renaissance. Artistic success meant making one's own mark, presenting one's own experiences, and addressing the present day, all in constant and deliberate engagement with these models and within a more or less obvious Christian framework. In the process, whole literary traditions might be artfully reworked. In love poetry, for instance, pagan carnal love was transformed into spiritual Christian love. The genre of *heroides*, that is, "letters from heroines," is a good example in the context of Jesuit poetry.[514] This genre went back to the Roman poet Ovid. Twenty-one verse letters are transmitted under his name in which the wives or lovers of famous mythological figures like Jason, Theseus, and Aeneas lament the heroes' absence and/or infidelity. Building on a long late antique and medieval tradition, the Jesuits Christianized the genre. In the Jesuits' letters, now Christian wives spoke to "their" husbands.

Influential educational theorists in the Society like Antonio Possevino regarded elegiac poetry, which aimed to "stir minds" (and included letters like the *Heroides*), as "a great opportunity for those who love God." Such emotionally charged poetry could give one a "passionate instruction in ethics." Thus, in the hands of the Jesuits, the pagan heroines of Ovid became biblical figures, women of the Christian church, or allegorical personifications. Hence, there were not only numerous letters from women of the Old Testament to various recipients or fictional verse epistles from Emperor Charles V to Francisco de Borja, but also letters from the Society of Jesus to "her" members, from the church to "her" faithful, or from the soul to the body.

On closer inspection, it is not at all surprising that members of religious orders like the Jesuits labored over such learned, playful, and exquisite Latin poems.[515] For as long as Europe was influenced by the late humanist fascination with Latin antiquity, Jesuit poetry and its ongoing engagement with ancient models continued to contribute to the dominant culture. And the Jesuits were happy to keep things that way. When fierce controversy broke out in Italy and elsewhere in 1700 over the relationship between vernacular and Latin poetry, the Jesuits were important advocates of Latin Catholic culture. Tommaso Ceva, for example, was willing to undertake a cautious modernization and updating of the ancient language in light of contemporary vernaculars, but he stayed resolutely true to Latin as a cultural medium.[516]

This Latin culture, moreover, showed that the Jesuit colleges were doing outstanding work. It was, after all, professors at the order's schools for the most part who published as poets. Their poems showed that the combination of devotion and humanistic versatility in the ancient languages, the harmonious fusion of *pietas* and *litterae*, was as successful as ever. In the context of late humanistic European culture, Latin poetry brought not only individual Jesuits but also the Society of Jesus as a whole to the fore as an intellectual heavyweight—even if we realistically must presume that even in the best of times nowhere near all graduates of the Jesuits' schools could have completely understood, let alone effortlessly read, their instructors' often intricate and difficult Latin verse.

Poetry was moreover both the means and the product of a cultural battle raging in the Society itself and beyond. In a posthumous biography of the Neapolitan poet Giannettasio, Tommaso Ceva is recorded as saying he "gave thanks to the gods for deferring so much to the Italians that they now surpassed the Gauls even in fine literature [*vel humanioribus literis*]."[517] Fierce battles for cultural supremacy were also waged among the early modern Jesuits. Since the dawn of age of humanism, verbal skirmishes across Europe pitted, measured, and judged the culture, literature, and art of the "Italians," "Germans," and "French" against one another. In 1687, for example, the French Jesuit Dominique Bouhours enthusiastically celebrated the French language, literature, and culture as the most important in Europe. The Italians retaliated with numerous pamphlets of their own. An outright controversy over the superiority of Italian or French broke out. The unmatched refinement of Giannetta-sio's didactic poems—"nothing like them had been published this century"—helped repudiate French claims.

It would be completely mistaken to view the literary production of the Jesuits as static and uniform over the decades. Various stylistic and formal standards came and went or competed with one another. Jesuit authors could also come in for criticism by their fellows. In both ser-mons and poetry, debate revolved around the question of how "ba-roque" one's rhetorical style should be. Many Jesuits advocated a mod-erate baroque, that is, they wanted to restrain the brilliant rhetorical virtuosity, the vibrant ingenuity, and the expressive richness of the ba-roque style with a harness of Christian rules.[518] In terms of rhetoric, this position coalesced into the typically Jesuit stylistic movement that epitomized its ideal with the term *argutia* (wit, incisiveness). Complex thoughts could and had to be formulated in brief figures of thought that "are acute and penetrating" (*acuta ma penetrante*).[519] An image, a brief apothegm, or a pun could accomplish that—what mattered was that the idea in question was ingenious and pointed, surprising yet apposite. That would help sear the message into a reader's or listener's memory.

In southern and Western Europe, the ex-Jesuit Emanuele Tesauro in Italy and the controversial member Baltasar Gracián in Spain were prominent spokesmen for this way of thinking. North of the Alps, Jakob Masen and the aforementioned Sarbiewski were the leading theorists of the movement. Language should aspire to subtle and pregnant so-phistication, they argued. Masen inveighed, in contrast, against wildly exuberant speech on the stage or from the pulpit. He criticized the style of his confrere Bidermann as an "all too dainty poetic stew."[520] The aforementioned "moderate" stylist Pallavicino sharply criticized his contemporary Giambattista Marino, one of the most important "opu-lent" poets of the baroque.[521] And the Jesuit cardinal advised his con-frere Paolo Segneri, who also loved rhetorical pomp, "to remove some vivid but trite and therefore [excessively] popular metaphors" from his sermons; they "might lend the speech some vigor, but that of a peasant rather than of a nobleman."[522]

With his skepticism of the lavish forms of baroque style, Pallavicino anticipated many points of a literary shift that was launched in 1690 by the poets and scholars of the Accademia dell'Arcadia in Rome. Tommaso Ceva, mentioned earlier, was one of the Jesuits who belonged to the Arcadia movement. At the transition from the baroque to the Enlightenment, he opted for a stylistic "middle way." He had no patience left for unbridled rhetorical ingenuity:

> In composing, the poet is forced, so to speak, to split himself in two, into a fool and wise man, who at the same time, in a strange alliance, both contrast and agree with one another. The one runs straight toward fantasms in search of exotic images and ideas, pushing on to track them down ultimately in the realm of the impossible, extracting from it nymphs transformed into laurels, women changed into stones, fauns, harpies, and singing sirens. The other selects, polishes [these ideas], strips off their rough skin, and clothes them in the semblance of truth. The one [i.e., the fool] is totally intent on novelty, marvels, delight; the other [i.e., the wise man] totally dedicated to utility, verisimilitude, and decorum.

Poetry, Ceva railed, now more than ever, was a "madness of phantasms, bound like madmen in the bonds of verse and kept, so to speak, at the school of morality under the rod of stern judgment and beneath the eyes of discerning intelligence."[523]

New antibaroque stylistic ideals also made their presence felt in the theater by the last quarter of the seventeenth century. In France, Jesuit poets like Charles de la Rue and Charles Porée conceived their texts according to the principles of the great and austere classicist Pierre Corneille.[524] In Germany, Franz Neumayr, S.J., in Munich spoke very highly of his style, "which the French call by the very apt designation of *belles lettres*."[525] Neumayr was also familiar with contemporary German (Protestant) dramatic theory, which he esteemed, such as the work of Johann Christoph Gottsched (1700–1766). The reception of French classicism, however, often proceeded haltingly at best. Even

Neumayr was unwilling to part ways with opulent stage productions, for example.

The literary production of Jesuit poets thus remained capable of new developments even shortly before the abolition of the Society. Despite the vivacity of Latin within the order, however, Latin poetry was on its way out in the eighteenth century, in both drama and all its other forms. After the shift in style and taste, Latin poetry at best became an esoteric hobby; at worst—in the eyes of the eighteenth-century Enlightenment—a useless dead end.

Song and Music

The Jesuits found it easier to keep up with modern tastes in a different area of culture intimately connected to poetry and drama: music. Song and music were almost ubiquitous in the Society of Jesus as means of transmitting and representing the Jesuits' particular message.[526] For one, music was part of the liturgical day for the Society of Jesus in the broadest sense of the word. Church music included songs at mass, litanies, vespers, spiritual motets, and much more. Music also played an increasingly prominent part in Jesuit drama. At first appearing only in interludes or as accompaniment, music soon became an independent element of the spectacle onstage.

The status of music in the Jesuit order was initially precarious.[527] Ignatius deliberately dispensed with singing the Liturgy of the Hours—the traditional gateway to musical activity among the regular clergy. There also was to be no singing at mass, and the possession of musical instruments "at home" was prohibited.[528] Both Ignatius and his immediate successors in the sixteenth century exhibited a clear skepticism of musical activity. Some Jesuits, such as Paul Hoffaeus, were even openly opposed to music.[529] But Ignatius was not fundamentally hostile to singing and musical instruments per se—on the contrary, he enjoyed music and occasionally even had musicians perform for his own recreation. His reservations toward ecclesiastical music within his order were primarily a cautionary measure: Ignatius wanted to prevent the reintroduction of choral singing, which the Jesuits had explicitly forbidden, by way of other singing and music.

This reservation at the heart of the Society in Rome, however, often stood at odds—sometimes right from the start—with the perspectives of local Jesuits across the world. The laity were used to music in the liturgy and requested it. The success of many Jesuit houses seemed to be due at least in part to the musical offerings of their religious services. Especially where Protestant music was well known, a similarly attractive Catholic countermodel in the liturgy was needed—whether purely choral singing or instrumental music. Hence singing was soon used both in mass and in teaching the catechism on the streets. Wherever possible, ecclesiastical music was accompanied by an organ. In 1566, Jerónimo Nadal permitted various forms of song at mass and for paraliturgical occasions in Vienna.[530] In Rome, the Collegium Germanicum became an artistic hot spot in 1573.[531] In 1575, General Mercurian then permitted the singing of "motets, masses, hymns, and other such pious pieces," if they were already available in print, had been sanctioned by the authorities, and were not the work of Protestants.[532]

Soon collections of so-called spiritual songs were being published by Jesuits everywhere. In 1580, for example, the composer Philippe de Monte, the director of the chapel at the imperial court of Prague, collaborated very closely with several Jesuits.[533] From Italy, they sent him religious texts that he then set to music as spiritual madrigals. De Monte duly dedicated his important first collection of such pieces in 1581 to the newly elected superior general Claudio Acquaviva, stressing the especially close relationship between his spiritual music and the religious projects of the Society of Jesus: "If our music could do what is said of the ancient, [these madrigals] would be useful for the purpose pursued by your order for the benefit of the whole world and the glory of God." De Monte even singled out texts by Jesuits, not least by Peter Canisius. In Munich, at the court of the Duke of Bavaria and patron of the Jesuits William V, the great Orlando di Lasso was likewise encouraged to collaborate with the Jesuits. Thus, spiritual music not only had a fixed place within the Society of Jesus by the end of the sixteenth century but also was enthusiastically cultivated. Many Jesuit schools reserved places for boarders—often needy youngsters—who were specifically connected to musical activities. The students of these "music seminaries" (*domus musicorum*) were trained to sing and play instruments; they not only performed for the Society but also were dispatched to other churches for individual engagements.[534]

Broadly speaking, music in the context of the everyday life of the Society of Jesus had to follow the order's overarching religious and pedagogical principles. Lorenzo Maggio in Paris decreed in 1587, "Nothing [should] be sung based on enticing songs of a trivial and secular nature, much less lascivious songs, or songs of war, as they are called, for it is not at all fitting to mix such profane things into divine worship. But let all the music be serious, suited to the occasion, not long-winded; and let it exude piety and inspire devotion."[535] For a long time, Jesuits were preoccupied with the fear that music might overwhelm the listener and make it more difficult to understand the lyrics. Music "should be composed in such a way that it does not bury the words but rather somehow bring them to life," it was said in accordance with the musical ideal of the Society in the seventeenth century.[536] In Rome, therefore, traditional Gregorian choir was highly recommended.[537] For the same reason, some Jesuits in Paris around 1580 were skeptical of the more modern polyphony, criticizing the fact that the wildly popular polyphonous works of Orlando di Lasso were being performed in their college. Even in Munich, the Jesuits' relationship with Lasso was not free of skepticism.[538] But despite this mistrust, they continued to use Lasso's music. One of his pieces was sung in Rome itself in 1583 at liturgical devotions at the Germanicum.[539]

Soon Lasso's compositions and music in general invaded Jesuit plays. In 1584 and 1587, Jakob Gretser explicitly requested that Lasso's motets be sung in several of his plays. And in Graz in 1589, at least six motets composed by Lasso were featured in the play *Christus judex* (Christ as judge) by the Jesuit Stefano Tucci.[540] In Jesuit dramas, his compositions took over the part of the choruses, collectively spoken or indeed sung passages that commented on the action. Around 1600, even dialogues and monologues by the protagonists began to be reinforced with music in some plays. Solos in the form of recitatives were incorporated in plays, clearly in response to the new musical genre of opera that began to emerge around the year 1600. Drama and music were fused into a new art form among the Jesuits, as well. There may have been members who vehemently opposed opera and its dramatic singing, such as Jeremias Drexel or François Antoine Le Febvre,[541] but it was not so much that they objected to the new form per se as that they wanted to keep genuinely liturgical music—that is, songs during mass—free from the new theatrical effects. The Jesuits thus made significant contributions to the history of opera on their stages in the seventeenth and eighteenth centuries.

The Society of Jesus not only promoted the fusion of song and theater but also supported the growing enthusiasm for ballet.[542] In France, for example, the Jesuits thus took up an art form that was extremely popular at the court of the young Louis XIV until approximately 1670. In terms of quality and popularity, the Jesuits' own productions were often not far behind the royal performances that they obviously knew.[543] Jesuits like Claude Ménestrier and Gabriel François Le Jay were among the most important contemporary theorists of dance.[544] Their effort to describe and establish ballet undoubtedly helped the art gain credibility and grow in popularity in the latter half of the seventeenth century. What made ballet attractive to the Jesuits was the widespread belief that one could translate things and values, moods and moral messages directly into physical movements. Dance "imitated" things, Le Jay averred. In so doing, dance even surpassed painting because, in contrast to the latter, it could also express the invisible inner state of people.

Originally conceived as interludes during spoken drama, the episodes of dancing, singing, and music on Jesuit stages soon evolved into independent pieces. In terms of content, these productions had, at best, only a tenuous connection to the actual subject of the drama, if they had not outgrown the context of school theater altogether. As had long been conventional in ballet, the action and characters were often allegorical. In 1715, for example, *L'empire de la sagesse sur les passions* (The reign of wisdom over the passions) was danced in Paris. In Blois on the Loire, *Les délices de Blois* (The graces of Blois) was performed in 1729: the dancers represented the "Courtesy," "Hilarity," and "Eloquence" of the townsfolk, among other characters. Topical subjects and developments were also taken up: in 1703, the Jesuits produced a ballet titled *Les nouvelles* (News) in which they reflected on the contemporary reality of an ever-denser network of information in Europe by means of figures and examples from antiquity.[545] Other subjects were more concrete, as for instance when the *Birth of the Heir to the Throne* or *Hope* was performed with dance and music during wartime in 1709.

The music for such spectacles was occasionally written by the Jesuits themselves. Among the few Jesuit composers were men like Jakob Gippenbusch (1612–64), in Cologne, and Tommaso Ceva, who has been mentioned several times previously.[546] Antoine Parran published an important treatise on music and composition theory in 1639.[547] But the Society of Jesus produced only a few really outstanding artists in the field of music, in contrast to poetry or architecture. One of the exceptions was Domenico Zipoli, S.J. (1688–1726), a student of Alessandro Scarlatti in Naples who was the organist at Il Gesù and achieved great contemporary fame as a composer—but Zipoli joined the Society relatively late at the age of twenty-eight and long after he had embarked on his musical career.[548] The Jesuits in Europe generally preferred to employ outside composers. The bigger schools often collaborated with the most important composers of the day. The famed Johann Hieronymus Kapsberger wrote the music to the opera *Apotheosis sive consecratio SS. Ignatii et Francisci Xaverii* (The apotheosis of Saints Ignatius and Francis Xavier) for the Collegio Romano, which produced it on the occasion of the canonization of the two great Jesuits. Marc-Antoine Charpentier, who was employed by the Jesuits in Paris from 1687 to 1698, wrote the famous music to *David et Jonathas* for them in 1688.[549]

Charpentier's liturgical music for the Jesuits was, like all music at the time, highly "rhetorical." By means of stylistic effects, it attempted to emphasize the message of the lyrics or script. To highlight the passage "the earth shook" from the story of the Passion, for example, Charpentier composed a rumbling and grumbling in the low registers of the orchestra that were underscored by an organ. The music was supposed to heighten the audience's interest in the script and reinforce and make audible its message. By adhering to such principles, Charpentier followed the Jesuits' interests in a typically contemporary way. The Jesuits strove to utilize every media—image, word, music—to illustrate their message.[550]

The Jesuits still maintained close contacts with leading composers in the eighteenth century. Jean-Philippe Rameau (1683–1764), the great French composer of the first half of the century, not only had been educated by the Jesuits but also maintained several contacts with them later in life and served as the Society's organist in Paris. Jean Castel, S.J., was an especially important contact and sounding board of his, until their relationship ended in conflict.[551] Castel himself was famous for his synesthetic theory that combined sounds and colors in the form of an "ocular harpsichord" (*clavecin oculaire*). He also took sides in the "Querelle des Bouffons," a dispute over the superiority of French or Italian opera that raged from 1752 to 1754. Jean-Jacques Rousseau and other French philosophes declared in favor of the livelier, less strict, and definitely more modern Italian music. The Jesuits were divided. Castel remained loyal to the established "geometric" French music in the spirit of Rameau, while Guillaume-François Berthier, the editor of the *Journal de Trévoux*, broadly supported Rousseau's position.[552] The Jesuits' positions show that the order had an easier time keeping up with current developments in music than in many other cultural areas.

The Jesuits collaborated with professional artists for music and dance performances, hiring, for example, ensemble members of the Parisian opera house. Primarily, however, they relied on students from the colleges. Hence, many schools soon employed dance and ballet masters who were responsible for the design and choreography of shows and often also served as composers. The first ballet master, active at Louis-le-Grand on a permanent basis since the 1660s, was Pierre Beauchamp, one of the greatest dance authorities of his time. He was the dance instructor of the Sun King himself, Louis XIV, and also the second director of the royal Académie de la danse. This cooperation with dancers and ballet masters of the opera continued for a long time, as for instance with Beauchamp's nephew Michel Blondy after 1713.[553]

Jesuit schools were also often important centers of music overseas. The Jesuits even cultivated a vigorous musical life in Quebec on the St. Lawrence Seaway, a humble outpost of Europe in North America.[554] Their missions were among the few places where European music was played at all. The Jesuits organized the importation of musical instruments and trained musicians, and thus Quebec was soon able to take part in current trends. They even once managed to get Marc-Antoine Charpentier to send an autographed copy of one of his pieces to Canada.[555]

Despite the Jesuits' tireless musical dedication, however, much was left to improvisation and chance in the colonies, as they learned again and again in Quebec. When the Jesuits there wanted to perform a four-part piece in the church for Christmas 1646, they were missing a singer who could take the soprano part. Only after a Huguenot soldier who happened to command the high registers coincidentally converted to Catholicism could the show go on.[556] Other problems could not be solved.[557] The Jesuits therefore relied regularly on indigenous musicians, and so Native Americans, Japanese, and Filipinos regularly played together with the European students. Sometimes, though, the quality of colonial music was simply bad: the Jesuits in Quebec themselves noted at Christmas in 1657 that the music for the midnight mass had been "worth nothing" and thought the performance was almost embarrassing because "they forgot to sing the *Te Deum* at the beginning."[558]

Outside colonial cities, there were virtually no European musicians (or those of European ancestry) at all, with the exception of the Jesuits themselves. And still the members of the Society of Jesus frequently cultivated an intense musical life in their lonely mission stations. Out in the field, everything depended on the enthusiasm of the indigenous population for music. The extraordinary musicality of the native peoples of North and South America and the Philippines often astonished the Jesuit missionaries. They lacked formal training, no one in the mission stations could read music, and nobody understood the principles by which European music was composed, yet the Native Americans compensated for this ignorance with a good ear and intuitive skill, as the German missionary Ignaz Pfefferkorn reported from the Mexican Sonora.[559]

The Jesuits used their regional and international networks to provide these music-loving peoples with European instruments and sheet music. Even mobile organs made it in this way to the unexplored regions of the modern borderland between Mexico and the United States, far from major colonial cities.[560] The missionary and musician Martin

Schmid reported with obvious pride from the reductions of South America in 1744: "Today, all our towns have an organ and sets of violins, cellos, and basses, all made of cedarwood; they have harpsichords, spinets, harps, trumpets, and shawms etc., all of my making, and I have taught the Indians how to play them . . . if they were to perform in any European city, they would astound the community of the faithful gathered in the church."[561] Everywhere we have reports of missionary efforts in remote and lonely regions in the early modern period, we find references to a flourishing and well-working Catholic musical life—the Jesuits played a major part in that.

Music gave the Jesuits a precious entry point into these foreign cultures that could then serve as a basis for imparting Christian values and messages. It had a decidedly catechetical function in the missions, serving as a vehicle for transmitting religious content. In Europe, there was a long tradition of harnessing musical resources to transmit catechisms. Simple vernacular religious songs, so-called *laude* or *villancicos*, were composed all over Europe for this purpose, and the Jesuits' very first written catechism—Diego de Ledesma's *Modo per insegnar* of 1574— eagerly took up this tradition.[562] Music, Ledesma wrote, was a "fisher of souls" (*piscatore di anime*), citing an idea of Filipe Neri's and his Oratorians, who were pioneers in this area. The Jesuits' propagation of the faith through music in the New World applied this principle under new conditions. Success seemed to justify the method. "Since we have set their prayers to music they take a remarkable pleasure in attending them," reported French Jesuits from North America in 1644.[563]

It would be an oversimplification to claim either that European music was adopted wholesale or that it supplanted pre-European music making. Instead, a fusion of Jesuit and local practices took place. At the mission station of Carigara on the island of Leyte in the Philippines, the local population was taught how to intone polyphonous music, but old songs (*canto antiguo*) were also provided with Christian lyrics—a musical hybrid of Christian and indigenous elements thus came into being.[564] Among the Mapouche people of Chile, Jesuit missionaries relied on Christian messages in the local language, sung to simple European melodies.[565] The Jesuits did not hesitate to fuse even exquisite

European music with this indigenous enthusiasm. In the Abenaki mission in Canada, under the Jesuits' direction, the natives sang catechetical texts in their own language to melodies taken from the oratories of Marc-Antoine Charpentier.[566] In the mission to the Moxos in the primeval forest of South America, pieces by the major European composers Arcangelo Corelli and Antonio Vivaldi were reworked for these novel environs and regularly performed.[567] In Paraguay, the mutual influence was so great that the mission opera *St. Francis Xavier* was produced around 1740 in the indigenous language—presumably by a native composer.[568]

Sometimes, though, European and indigenous musical practices were not such a perfect fit. In 1657, for example, the missionaries to Canada stressed the great differences between them:

> Concerning the sense of hearing, although the Savages take much pleasure in singing, a concert of music sounds to them like a confusion of voices, and a roulade like a bird's twittering. I admit that the warbling of birds is not disagreeable to them; but their own songs, which are so heavy and dismal as to give us ideas of night, seem to them as beautiful as the blush of dawn. They sing amid dangers; in torments, and at the approach of death; while the French usually preserve a deep silence on all such occasions.[569]

European music was also sometimes panned and rejected at the Chinese imperial court in Beijing, where the Jesuits introduced keyboard instruments in the early seventeenth century. The Kangxi Emperor is said to have once cut short a performance because it offended his ears. At the same time, of course, in spite of everything, he also had Chinese music written down in Western notation and cultivated contacts with Jesuit musicians.[570] On the whole, music was one of the Jesuits' most effective strategies for transmitting their wishes and messages.

Building and Painting

The Jesuits needed space and place: to sleep, to gather and work, for theaters and offices, for kitchens, for chapels, and above all else for churches. Wherever they first settled, members of the Society of Jesus

turned to existing facilities and made do with whatever rooms or buildings were available. The longer the Jesuits stayed at a place and the more
extensive their engagement there became, the more probable it was that
they would become active as builders. In the 1570s, they began to construct a rapidly growing number of churches and other buildings for
their establishments.[571]

As with so many of their projects, the Jesuits approached the herculean task of designing and executing their building plans with a typical
mixture of local autonomy and central coordination with the Society's
Roman Curia.[572] At no point in time did the Society ever seek to impose
a standard design and decorating style. The final form of Jesuit buildings
accordingly was manifold, diverse, and flexible. But the Jesuits on the
ground were not supposed to go about building in just any way. The
order's leadership took great care to ensure that Jesuit structures shared
certain features and projected a consistent image.[573] The Jesuits' buildings were visual representations of the Society; they gave the order a
face, highlighted its presence, and were thought to reflect its self-
conception. They made its existence impossible to miss. As the Society
built, so did it work. Therefore, the superiors general reserved for themselves some influence over this powerful medium for broadcasting their
public image. Rome also wanted to ensure that Jesuit schools and
churches were as functional as possible. Last but not least, it was also
important to guarantee the *decorum* of all new buildings. The Jesuits
thus sometimes devised "master plans" when they settled somewhere,
as in the case of the Roman novitiate on the Quirinal and the professed
house of Valencia.[574]

Concerns about functionality, craftsmanship, and aesthetic quality
induced the Roman Curia to monitor all Jesuit architectural plans
worldwide on a constant basis. As was typical of the administrative culture of the Society of Jesus, a review procedure was introduced for all
building plans. In 1565, at the Second General Congregation, it was decreed that all blueprints had to be sent to Rome for approval before
buildings could be constructed. When it subsequently was determined
in 1613 that all such plans had to be sent to the Curia in duplicate, the
cornerstone of a Roman archive of blueprints was laid.[575] To judge the

projects submitted to them, the superiors general turned to practicing architects from their own ranks for advice. In this way, down to the year 1610, Giovanni Tristano, Giuseppe Valeriano, and Giovanni de Rosis, the Italian master builders of the Society, shaped Jesuit architecture. After de Rosis's death, the professors of mathematics at the Collegio Romano, such as Christoph Grienberger or Orazio Grassi, became the generals' most important advisers in architectural matters—yet again we see the prominence of "applied mathematics" (*mathematica mixta*) in the Society of Jesus.[576] Even in this artistic area, the final decision on individual projects within the Society of Jesus was a product of this interaction of individual ability and engagement, on the one hand, and mechanisms of collective control and authorization, on the other. The planning of many Jesuit building projects was a communal enterprise.[577]

The Society's Roman leadership knew precisely what was *not* appropriate for Jesuits. Designs submitted from the provinces were regularly critiqued and corrected. Some buildings thus had to be redesigned several times. The new church in Antwerp is a good example: rejected designs from 1613 envisioned a rotunda as a central structure with a cupola, an extraordinary plan that was rejected in Rome precisely for that reason, with reference to the more conventional "solid and simple architecture" of the order.[578] Elsewhere, of course, the Jesuits constructed churches as central structures, such as the church at the symbolic site of Loyola, where an extraordinary round church designed by Carlo Fontana, a student of Gian Lorenzo Bernini, was built around the former family manor of the founder of the Society in 1682.[579] The Roman censors thus did not mandate a universal stylistic ideal, but rather judged each project on its own merits in the context of the conventions of the Society. The Jesuits' approach to architecture revolved around regulating building plans broadly, not dictating the stylistic design of individual buildings or churches in exhaustive detail.

There were primarily two different building tasks. On the one hand, the Society of Jesus needed relatively austere, purpose-built structures for its colleges; on the other, it hoped to boast magnificent and lavishly designed churches with high theatrical potential and complex theological symbolism.[580] Insofar as the colleges of the Society of Jesus, with their diverse functions, were an innovative, typically Jesuit institution, they also were a novel job for architects.[581] The First General Congregation had decreed in 1558 that the new structures had to be "sound buildings, sturdy and well built, suited to be our residences," and should not be "too fancy" or "luxurious" like "palaces befitting the nobility." "Our poverty" militated against that.[582] Just how opulent or "poor" new buildings actually were supposed to be was the subject of recurrent discussion.[583] Colleges and novitiates readily dispensed with excessive outward ornamentation. The instructions of the General Congregation of 1558 were respected at least to the extent that these buildings did not normally feature columns of precious stone or elaborate window frames— proposed details for which the original plans for the college in Florence were criticized. The first design, for all its simplicity, still included a roof terrace and a massive IHS monogram, but both of these features were dropped in the interest of "simplicity." In 1662, conflict broke out during the renovation of the college in Milan when Vicar-General Gianpaolo Oliva from Rome complained bitterly about its "opulent design" and "superfluous ornamentation." Oliva generally urged restraint and moderation in building colleges—they ultimately were only buildings "intended for us, not for Christ," he wrote.

This adherence to a "poor" style did not mean that the Jesuits built shabbily and badly. They used high-quality materials, but not necessarily for ostentation. The point of the relatively minimalistic architecture of the Jesuit colleges was rather to cultivate a certain image of humility rather than impoverishment. And yet the Society still was either unwilling or unable to realize this aspiration everywhere. The central court in Milan remained clad in marble despite Oliva's protests, and at the Collegio Romano, where Pope Gregory XIII financed a massive renovation beginning in 1582, he had a wall torn down because it had been constructed "in a rather simple style." Patrons who invested large amounts of money in Jesuit buildings wanted to ensure that their munificence was obvious at first sight. Jesuit architecture shaped not only the public image of the Society itself but also that of its supporters, and at least in the case of popes and other powerful personages, their wishes had to be respected.[584] The Collegio Romano thus received more expensive and elaborate brickwork.

The architectural challenge of Jesuit colleges lay in the fact that they housed many distinct parts with very different purposes that had to be integrated into a harmonious whole. Living quarters for the many students and numerous Jesuits, meeting rooms and dining rooms, libraries and classrooms, theaters, gardens, and sick wards—all had to be accommodated in often limited and contorted properties in the heart of cities. Last but not least, a major church had to be fitted into the assemblage. The products were usually symmetrical, quadrangular, "block-like" facilities with several interior courtyards, in which the church was preferably located on one of the outer corners—quite in contrast to the influential alternative model of the Spanish monastery of El Escorial, which was contemporary to the development of Jesuit architecture. Massive monumental building complexes arose, demolishing conventions of scale in the sixteenth and early seventeenth centuries. Jesuit complexes were among the largest buildings in many cities (fig. 20).

Far more spectacular than the purpose-built colleges were the many churches that the Jesuits erected for a vast range of establishments. Although the churches of the Society of Jesus may have been conceived first for the needs of the Jesuits themselves, every one of them—no matter whether in a college, professed house, residence, or novitiate—was also explicitly dedicated to pastoral ministry at large. Jesuit churches had to appeal to the laity, visitors, members of the congregation, and the general public.[585] They were the showplaces and media of religious communication with a large audience. The Jesuits impressively illustrated how these needs could be met with one of their very first new churches: their mother church in Rome, Il Gesù, on which construction began in 1558.[586] Sant'Ignazio, the church of the Collegio Romano from the following century, was also extremely influential.[587] Other benchmark Jesuit churches include San Fedele in Milan and Valeriano's Gesù churches in Naples and Genoa. While Milan was conceived along similar lines as Il Gesù, Valeriano followed an alternative, triple-nave model that ultimately enjoyed a subordinate status in the Society.[588] Sant'Andrea, the famous church of the novitiate on the Quirinal Hill

FIGURE 20. The model of the city of Munich by Jakob Sandtner (1570) illustrates the vast scale of major Jesuit colleges in the urban landscape. The Jesuit college of Munich dominates the city in the foreground (right). © Bayerisches Nationalmuseum München.

built by Bernini beginning in 1658, remained a singular creation that was neither typical of the Jesuit order nor broadly received elsewhere.[589]

Jesuit churches north of the Alps were modeled on their Italian forerunners, but by no means exclusively. In the kingdom of Poland, the Italian Jesuit architects Giuseppe Brizio and Giovanni Maria Bernardoni, who had been stationed there, began to build churches in the southern style in 1575. The new churches in Nieśwież (begun in 1586) and Kraków (begun in 1597) were heavily influenced by Il Gesù.[590] St. Michael's in Munich, the largest and most important Jesuit church immediately north of the Alps, likewise incorporated the new Italian ideas when construction began in 1583, as did the church of the professed house of Antwerp begun in 1615, for which Peter Paul Rubens collaborated on the decoration. Brussels, Bruges, and Namur likewise followed the new stylistic ideas. But Il Gesù, Sant'Ignazio, and even St. Michael's, with their rich decoration and generous patrons, were not only models but also exceptions. Many of the Jesuits' small and midsize churches neither could nor would imitate this opulence.[591] The great churches of the Society thus served as inspiration rather than as prototypes that one might really imitate. And it might also happen that the Roman style did not initially dominate. At the same time as the Jesuit church of Antwerp was being built, other Belgian members of the order still built predominantly in the northern European Gothic style. A majority of Jesuit churches in the early decades of the seventeenth century adhered to older, local models, which the Jesuit architects Hendrik Hoeymaker (1559–1626) and Jean du Blocq (1583–1656) particularly favored.[592]

The interior of Jesuit churches catered to the most important aspects of pastoral care in the eyes of the order.[593] The area reserved for the choir was often relatively small, because in contrast to other religious orders the members of Society of Jesus did not need a place for regular choral prayer. Choir and rood screens were also superfluous because the Society did not seek to separate laity and monks. In accord with the special emphasis they placed on communion, however, in place of the usual choir screens the Jesuits built a low barrier in many of their churches where the faithful could kneel to receive the sacrament: the communion rail.[594] In this way, the parishioners still had an unobstructed view of the high altar where the most important part of the liturgy, the celebration of the Eucharist, took place. The altar itself was visually highlighted and in many cases framed by lavish decoration. The pulpits were also prominently placed, often in the middle of the nave to improve the audibility of sermons.[595] Confessionals, which had recently been invented, also had to be sensibly integrated into the church interior so that they did not block processions. If we set aside the exceptions discussed here, it was for these reasons that the Jesuits usually preferred churches that had a single open space for pastoral ministry—an important difference from Gothic churches with multiple naves divided by columns or pillars.[596] The Jesuits liked to cover the interior with a barrel vault. Cardinal Alessandro Farnese, who financed Il Gesù, had insisted on this kind of roof, which he believed conveyed special majesty in accordance with humanist ideals.[597] A dome, which the cardinal had also demanded, could not always be built everywhere.

Churches were explicitly excepted from the prohibition on opulence and ornamentation issued in 1558.[598] This greatly benefited their interior furnishings. As with Counter-Reformation architecture generally, the Society of Jesus did not view richly decorated churches as a contradiction of the church's message, but rather as one of its most important means of expression. Jean Crasset, a French member of the Society of Jesus, wrote to this effect in 1679: "Nothing gives our religion more luster and brilliance than the magnificence of our churches, the beauty of their adornments, and the majesty of their ceremonies. . . . It is a very good and very holy thing to spend lavishly to build temples, adorn their images, and dress the altars." "No one can deny," Crasset added, that the people are "incited to praise and honor God by the rich ornaments of our churches."[599]

The Jesuits therefore subsequently conceived of a sacred aesthetic that would make a direct impact on the congregation and observers, stirring them in their heart of hearts and inciting them to change.[600] To achieve that end, departing from the decorations of many earlier churches, the Jesuits worked with coherent pictorial programs and subordinated interior rooms to overarching plans.[601] The subjects of frescoes and altarpieces, statues, the positioning of the confessionals— everything served to remind the congregation of the most important elements of Jesuit personal development. Even though there certainly were favorite themes, it usually was not the subjects of the images that were particularly typical of the Jesuits. Rather than the choice of certain motifs per se, the Jesuit utilization of images was characterized first and foremost by the ensemble of different paintings and the overall composition of religious space. The chapel of the meditation house of Vannes, for example, featured images that were intended to illustrate "the state of sin, the state of grace, and the transition from the one to the other." It was concluded that this strategy was "like an epitome of all Christian ethics. Experience has shown that nothing is better suited to teaching people than these images."[602]

In a much more extensive but functionally comparable way, the pictorial program of St. Michael's Church in Munich also served to guide the faithful.[603] The three pairs of chapels in the nave are furnished with corresponding altarpieces: the first pair, Mary Magdalene as penitent on the left and St. Ursula on the right, symbolizes conversion and steadfastness—subjects that should motivate the observer to examine his conscience. The second pair depicts the martyrdoms of St. Andrew and St. Sebastian, each of them in a cross-like pose or nailed to a cross. Without directly invoking the death of Christ on the side altars, the altarpiece nonetheless asks the observer to follow Christ even to one's death. This interpretation is reinforced by the larger-than-life-size statues of angels with the implements of martyrdom placed along the nave. The third pair of chapels finally presents the Annunciation, referring to the coming of Christ's redemption of man, and opposite it *Christ Giving the Keys of the Church to Peter and Paul*—a visual representation of the New Testament origin of the church as the most important authority for winning salvation. The side altars at the crossing show, on the left, a vague foreshadowing of divine salvation in the Old Testament story of Israel (a Trinity altarpiece populated with Old Testament figures) and, on the right, the New Testament's clear anticipation of salvation through the *Altar of the Name of Christ*. Finally, the high altar features a large image of St. Michael triumphing over the dragon Lucifer—an image that evoked the cosmic conflict of good and evil and dramatized Catholic confidence of victory in the fight against heresy.

The architecture, interior decoration, and art that the Jesuits desired were sometimes executed by some of the most famous artists of the day from outside the Society. Peter Paul Rubens and Gian Lorenzo Bernini, a friend of Superior General Oliva, worked for the Jesuits, as did Anthony van Dyck in Antwerp.[604] This cooperation with influential contemporary artists continued until shortly before the dissolution of the Society. As late as 1767, Pompeo Batoni painted one of the most important religious artworks of the day in his *Sacred Heart of Jesus* for Il Gesù.[605]

But alongside major secular architects and painters, the best artists from the Society itself had no reason to hide. The most important Jesuit architects of the sixteenth century, Valeriano, Tristano, and de Rosis, have already been mentioned. Étienne Martellange, S.J. (1569–1641), in France, may serve as an example for the first half of the following

2 Veüe du Bâtiment de l'Eglise du Collège de Roanne.

FIGURE 21. The Jesuit college of Roanne under construction. Sketch by Étienne
Martellange, *Veüe du Bâtiment de l'Eglise du Collège de Roanne. Second année de la Batisse*, 1618.
© Bibliothèque Nationale de France, départment Estampes et photographie,
RESERVE UB-9-BOITE FT 4.

century.[606] Martellange traveled constantly as an architect for the order
and oversaw the construction or renovation of many of its buildings
after the Society was restored in France in 1603. In fact, he only sporadically supervised construction in person because he usually was not on
site for very long. He was in such high demand as a building specialist
that he had to rush from one work site to the next (fig. 21).

The international influence of Andrea Pozzo (1642–1709), painter,
plasterer, and architect of the Society of Jesus in the final decades of the
seventeenth century, surpassed even that of Martellange.[607] This Jesuit
lay brother had begun his career in Milan, where he initially had designed
and executed stages and settings for solemn occasions and decorations
for the Quarant'ore.[608] Pozzo's church decorations were influenced by

visual stage effects and backdrops. He staggered the architecture of church interiors so that their decoration resembled a series of backdrops. The interior of the church itself became artfully framed and designed scenery. Pozzo specialized in creating optical illusions with perspective painting; his trademark was painted pseudo-architecture (fig. 22). The illusion of his frescoes, however, emerges only from a single, "ideal" viewing point; the illusion is immediately broken for anyone not standing on that point. There was a message behind this fact: one should not blindly trust what reason and the senses present to one. And yet, if one viewed these semblances of reality correctly from the ideal viewing point, one could blur the boundary between this world and the next, between mortal church and the divine. The senses and sensuality had to be channeled, not condemned.

Pozzo transmitted his experience and techniques to a large group of engaged students from inside and outside the Jesuit order in well-attended classes at the Collegio Romano. He also published on the basics of his technique and their underlying ideas in 1693 and 1700, in a much-read Latin treatise that was subsequently translated into many languages, *Perspectiva pictorum et architectorum* (Perspective in painting and architecture). A school came into being and, in the decades around and after 1700, Pozzo's influence reached places where the master had never worked—even China in the Far East, where Pozzo's famous treatise was translated, printed, and read. Giuseppe Castiglione (1688–1766), a Jesuit brother and painter in Beijing, edited the book and published a Chinese abridgement titled *Shixue jingyun* (視學精蘊; The essence of Perspective) in 1729 together with his friend and collaborator Nian Xiyao (年希堯).

Castiglione was one of many Jesuits artists at the imperial court.[609] Before him, other members of the Society, such as Giovanni Gherardini (1655–1729), had familiarized Chinese artists with the principles of European perspective painting. Illusionist pseudo-architecture fascinated the emperors in Beijing, and so Castiglione and his workshop produced several frescoes that—like Pozzo's ceiling paintings—seemed to enlarge and extend rooms. Of course, the Jesuits quickly realized that their European pictures, art, and architectural conventions could not simply be used unaltered in China. Conventions of viewing and design are

FIGURE 22. Andrea Pozzo's masterpiece: the ceiling of Sant'Ignazio in Rome.
Courtesy akg-images/Andrea Jemolo.

influenced by culture—Asian and European opinions about what a
"correct" and "beautiful" depiction of objects or people was could be
miles apart. Because some Chinese courtiers harshly criticized central
perspective, Jesuit artists like Castiglione in Beijing created a hybrid
variety. Three-dimensionality, shadowing, realistic depictions of horses,

and oil painting in general had to be reconciled with traditional Chinese conventions.[610]

Whereas Chinese Jesuit painting generally subsumed European techniques in a predominantly "Chinese" final product, it was usually the opposite in Paraguay and all of South and Central America.[611] Here, churches were built and artworks fashioned that seemed predominantly European at first glance, but elements of indigenous pictorial conventions and craftsmanship can be detected on closer inspection.[612] In the early days among the Guaraní, for example, an autonomous art form emerged: highly symmetrical and rather abstract-looking statutes were created with a cylindrical shape, depicting individuals primarily in a strict frontal view. The artists had no interest in achieving absolute realism.

Around 1700, a new wave of Italian and Central European Jesuit artists brought baroque art to Paraguay. Giuseppe Brasanelli (1659–1728) and Angelo Camillo Petragrassa (1656–1729) were especially influential.[613] Despite initial difficulties, an enduring aesthetic compromise was reached. After long hesitation, Brasanelli integrated some aspects of Guaraní visual culture in his baroque installations. Numerous churches, statues, and paintings were created in this spirit in the eighteenth century and are today known as examples of Jesuit-Guaraní art. The style of Brasanelli's mission church in the reduction of San Borja was highly influential: a triple-nave church with a cross-shaped plan and dome. Contemporaries enthusiastically described the church as fitted with columns and flooded with light. The altar was especially striking; it was clearly inspired by European predecessors created by Gian Lorenzo Bernini.

As in the case of music, Jesuits at the missions frequently trained indigenous artisans. At Nagasaki in Japan, a groundbreaking academy directed by the Italian Jesuit Giovanni Niccolò (1560–?) produced several Japanese Christian painters. A school for painting, carpentry, and sculpture was also established in the mission village of San Luis in Paraguay in 1650. It was run by the Spanish Jesuits Antonio de la Cuesta and one Brother Carnigal. Elsewhere, goldsmithing, weaving, and embroidery were taught.[614] Most of the sculptures that adorned the mission churches or were otherwise intended for devotions came from indigenous workshops. The sculptors often used copperplate engravings, usually from Belgium, as models, adapting them to South American stylistic ideals (figs. 23 and 24; similarly, see also figs. 27 and 28 in chapter 4).[615]

Small-scale illustrations, like those used as models for large statues or paintings in Paraguay, were very important in the early modern period and especially in the Society of Jesus. The power of images in the Society of Jesus was by no means limited to large panel paintings or frescoes. On the contrary, the Jesuits also systematically produced and encouraged the production of small etchings and woodcuts and disseminated them as devotional objects.[616]

Images had already been integrated in meditative practices in the Middle Ages, for example, in the form of illustrated books of hours. Ignatius followed this tradition and is said to have regularly viewed pictures prior to meditating.[617] Hence it was only logical that, at the end of his life, he told Jerónimo Nadal to produce an illustrated version of biblical texts for meditation. Nadal took up the project, but it would be a long time before the final product appeared. Nadal's *Adnotationes et meditationes in Evangelia* (Notes and meditations on the Gospels) was published in Antwerp in 1595, fifteen years after his death and a long and complicated origin story. The work was a commentary on the New Testament with 153 copperplates by the Wierix brothers, which had appeared separately two years earlier. Nadal's idea to provide the images with a legend of sorts was innovative.[618] Important elements of the illustration were marked with small letters that were then explained in brief notes. In this way, Nadal could ensure that his readers did not miss anything and at the same time could highlight particularly inspirational elements.

The fusion of text and image that Nadal introduced in his devotional book soon became a popular model. Many further texts were made along the same lines. The Spanish Netherlands led the way with their rich publishing culture and outstanding engravers. The books may have differed in aesthetic, quality, theme, and spiritual objectives, but this literature always returned to the functional principle of internalizing the underlying text in the imagination with the help of images. Antoine Sucquet's *Via vitae aeternae* (Way of Eternal Life) of 1622 or Étienne

FIGURE 23. Model and adaptation of art at the mission: *Auferstandener Christus*. Copperplate engraving by Hieronymus Wierix and Johann Baptist Vrints after a painting by Martin de Vos. © SLUB Dresden/ Deutsche Fotothek.

Binet's book of meditations on Mary of 1632 (*Méditations affectueuses sur la vie de la Vierge* [Loving meditations on the life of the Virgin]) may be cited as examples. Since the turn of the century, a growing number of illustrated editions of the life of Ignatius were also published—these works by Jesuits for Jesuits likewise presented scenes suitable for meditation. Peter Paul Rubens himself had played an important part in designing the first illustrated biography of Ignatius.[619] A handful of illustrated editions of the *Exercises* also appeared in 1609. Illustrations of

FIGURE 24. Sculptural adaptation by South American
craftsmen from the Guaraní mission. Photograph from
Gauvin Bailey, *Art on the Jesuit Missions in Asia and Latin
America, 1542–1773* (Toronto 1999).

individual parts of the *Exercises* were also available as separate sheets
that could be hung up.[620]

Finally, the *Pia desideria* by the Flemish Jesuit Hermann Hugo (1588–
1629), which appeared in Antwerp in 1624, was an extremely important
work. Hugo's book was no longer (only) about the illustration of biblical episodes. Instead, it covered general aspects of Christian life and
devotion in forty-five sections of poems and prose. An emblem appeared at the top of each section epitomizing the subject of meditation.
Hugo's images were linked by the figure of a small boy, who symbolized

the human soul. Another boy, Jesus, was his counterpart. These figures then were worked into images that helped the reader meditate on central tenets of Catholic doctrine: the one boy leads the other with a rope (Jesus as guide for the human soul); the soul as a boy in a cart used by toddlers to learn how to walk (Jesus calls the human soul to step closer to him). Even relatively abstract concepts could be visualized with the help of such allusive depictions. In Hugo's version of devotional exercises with the support of images, the incredibly popular contemporary symbolic medium of the emblem reached its religious peak. The *Pia desideria* was widely read and translated and was even influential in Protestant Germany. It was illustrations like these that ultimately became models for the works of the Guaraní artists of South America. We see precisely in the use of art and media that, in just a few decades, the Society of Jesus had truly become a global order.

4

The Global Society

IN THE *Imago primi saeculi* of 1640, the opulent commemorative book produced for the centennial jubilee of the Society of Jesus, two emblems proudly illustrate the Jesuits' global reach (fig. 25). Both emblems show maps of the two hemispheres.[1] The maps are littered with crosses surmounting the Society's anagram IHS, signifying Jesuit establishments worldwide. A prophecy of the Old Testament prophet Malachi (1:11) appears below by way of explanation: "For from the rising of the sun to its setting my name is great among the nations." The Jesuits believed they themselves would fulfill this biblical prediction, placing themselves directly in the tradition of the prophets. In the second emblem, the propagandists from Antwerp combined a very similar image with the aphorism "One world is not enough." Those words, adapted from Juvenal's Tenth Satire, alluded to the ancient conqueror Alexander the Great. In this context, the phrase likewise evoked the Jesuits' global ambitions, but in a totally different spirit, namely, the spirit of curiosity, conquest, and heroism. Biblical prophecy and pagan curiosity thus came together. The Jesuits enthusiastically set out to conquer the world for the faith and strove to rival even Alexander's boldness and courage. The first part of this chapter surveys how the Jesuits' worldwide expansion unfolded. It presents the places on which the Society's overseas ministry concentrated and where the successors of Ignatius maintained only a rather superficial presence. The global network of the Society of Jesus was impressive, but it was spun with varying density.

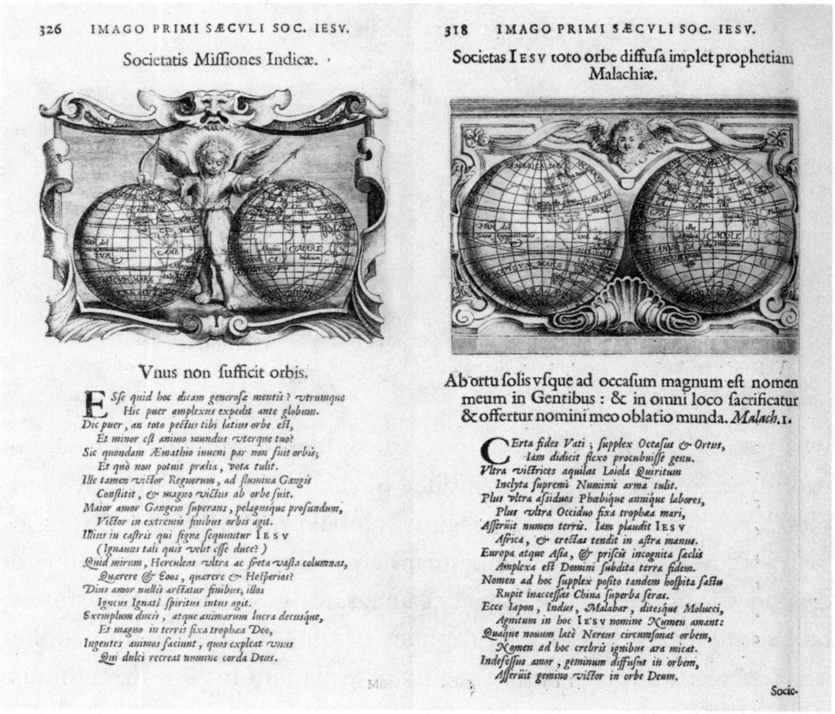

326   IMAGO PRIMI SÆCVLI SOC. IESV.

Societatis Missiones Indicæ. ·

Vnus non sufficit orbis.

ESse quid hoc dicam generosæ mentis? vtrumque
  Hic puer amplexus expedit ante globum.
Dic puer, an toto pectus tibi latius orbe est,
  Et minor est animo mundus vterque tuo?
Sic quondam Æmathio iuueni par non fuit orbis,
  Et quò non potuit prælia, vota tulit.
Ille tamen victor Regnorum, ad flumina Gangis
  Constitit, & magno victus ab orbe fuit.
Maior amor Gangem superans, pelagúmque profundum,
  Victor in extremis finibus orbis agit.
Illius in castris qui signa sequuntur IESV
  (Ignauus tali quis velit esse duce?)
Quid mirum, Herculeas vltra ac freta vasta columnas,
  Quærere & Eoos, quærere & Hesperios?
Dius amor nullis arctatur finibus, illos
  Igneus Ignati spiritus intus agit.
Exemplum ducis, atque animarum lucra decusque,
  Et magno in terris fixa trophæa Deo,
Ingentes animos faciunt, quos explicat vnus
  Qui dulci recreat nomine corda Deus.

M.

318   IMAGO PRIMI SÆCVLI SOC. IESV.

Societas IESV toto orbe diffusa implet prophetiam
Malachiæ.

Ab ortu solis vsque ad occasum magnum est nomen
meum in Gentibus : & in omni loco sacrificatur
& offertur nomini meo oblatio munda. Malach.1.

CErta fides Vati ; supplex Occasus & Ortus,
  Iam didicit flexo procubuisse genu.
Vltra victrices aquilas Loiola Quiritum
  Inclyta supremi Numinis arma tulit.
Plus vltra assiduos Phœbíque anníque labores,
  Plus vltra Occiduo fixa trophæa mari,
Asseruit numen terris. Iam plaudit IESV
  Africa, & erectas tendit in astra manus.
Europa atque Asia, & priscis incognita sæclis
  Amplexa est Domini subdita terra fidem.
Nomen ad hoc supplex posito tandem hospita fastu
  Rupit inaccessas China superba feras.
Ecce Iapon, Indus, Malabar, ditésque Molucci,
  Agnitum in hoc IESV nomine Numen amant:
Quáque nouum latè Nereus circumsonat orbem,
  Nomen ad hoc crebris ignibus ara micat.
Indefessus amor, geminum diffusus in orbem,
  Asseruit gemino victor in orbe Deum.

Socie-

FIGURE 25. Two emblems from the *Imago Primi Saeculi* document the Society's claim to global influence by means of biblical and ancient pagan motifs. Antwerp 1640, 318 and 326.

In the second part, I ask what the Jesuits actually did overseas and what motives drove members of the order to undertake the often long, hard, and dangerous journey. Europeans in the early modern period left the Continent behind and traveled to the New World for many reasons. Sometimes their decision was motivated by political problems, sometimes by economic distress. Some left their homes willingly, others under duress. Some were driven out; others looked at the New World full of hope. The Jesuits, like many other clergymen, went primarily for religious reasons. To put it somewhat schematically, we can distinguish two focuses of their ministry: on the one hand, the Jesuits ministered to the colonists; on the other, they worked to Christianize the indigenous population. These were very different remits: the one revolved around working in, with, and for the incipient colonial societies and was concentrated mainly in the major cities overseas—Mexico City, Lima, Goa, Manila.

The Jesuits there soon lived in conditions modeled on those in Europe. The other was the mission, which often took them far from the European colonial centers. The mission captured the imagination of contemporaries, as the goal of "converting the heathen" constantly drove the Jesuits (and their colleagues) to undertake new adventures and experiments. The fact that the Jesuits managed to approach Native American, Indian, Japanese, and Chinese people at all and engage them on a religious level is one of their most remarkable accomplishments.

The relationship between these two fields—working with the colonists, working with the natives—was by no means tension-free. The superiors sometimes found it difficult to strike a balance between the two objectives. Nicolás Durán Mastrilli, the provincial of Paraguay, critically surmised in 1628, "It is very edifying that the padres think so highly of the ministry to the Indios that they prefer it to that to the Spanish. But experience has taught us that an exclusive apostolate leads us 'bit by bit' to neglect the Spanish."[2] Other members of the Society agreed. In fact, it can hardly be claimed that the mission dominated. Even if it remained incredibly important for both the Jesuits' self-conception and their perception by others, the mission soon occupied only a minority of them.[3] Both these areas of Jesuit ministry will be surveyed here. The chapter concludes with a glance at the Society as an agent of incipient globalization. Even if the success of the worldwide network of the Society of Jesus should by no means be exaggerated, by the standards of the time it is still very impressive how often the Society successfully moved information, objects, and people on something at least approaching a global scale. No treatment of the order's ministry would be complete without taking this point into consideration.

The Jesuits' Global Reach

The Portuguese World

The actual beginning of Jesuit ministry outside of Europe can be dated to April 7, 1541. On this day, Francis Xavier, one of Ignatius's first companions, set sail for India with two other Jesuits on a Portuguese ship from Lisbon. They arrived a year later. Francis Xavier became the prototypical Catholic missionary par excellence and an icon in his order; his influence was overshadowed only by Ignatius himself.[4] Strict with himself but selfless toward others, fearless, tough, ever the optimist, unshakably devout, and utterly convinced of the righteousness of his own actions, Francis Xavier traveled tirelessly across Asia. For the next ten years, he explored what would become, in the medium and long term, the Society's most important missionary territories in the Far East. He first spent several years in India before setting out for the Maluku Islands—the Spice Islands of legend—in 1544. By 1548, he was back in Goa, but he had gotten new ideas during his travels. He had heard of Japan and China and dedicated his final years before his premature death in 1552 to these two countries.

GOA

Before Francis Xavier set out on his final journey from India to the Far East, however, he remained for about a year in Goa to perform his administrative duties as the superior of all Jesuits in Asia. Goa was not only the center of Portugal's Asian colonial empire but also the headquarters of the Society of Jesus there. Arising from various predecessors, the Jesuit college of São Paolo, which included a school for Indians, was officially established in 1544. By 1556, it had a printing press. At that point, there were already 450 boys in the college's classes. Roughly 180 Jesuits lived in Goa in the seventeenth century. From here, they could maintain official correspondence especially well, and that was important to Francis Xavier. This pioneer of the Jesuit mission constantly wrote letters, which were eagerly read in Europe. Francis Xavier's letters and example inspired many future Jesuit missionaries to go to the colonies and become missionaries themselves. Goa was the first port of call for newcomers in Asia. There, the Jesuits received supplies, an introduction to local conditions, and often additional training. When Francis Xavier returned to Goa from the Maluku Islands in 1548, he found twenty Jesuits who had arrived from Europe in the meantime already there. Twenty-five more Jesuits were active in other parts of Asia: in Hormuz, in Malacca, and on the Spice Islands. A network of Jesuit mission stations—initially thin but already quite far-flung—began to span the vast territory between East Africa and East Asia.[5]

On Palm Sunday 1549, after he had taken care of many details concerning these missions, Francis Xavier and two other Jesuits set out from Goa. Months later, on August 15, he landed in southern Japan. The people there captivated the Jesuit. Francis Xavier initially lived with a Japanese man whom he had met and baptized in India. An attempt to meet the emperor of Japan in Kyoto failed, but his introduction to the daimyo of Yamaguchi proved much more successful. Francis Xavier had learned from his misadventure in Kyoto that certain polite formalities and an official appearance were necessary before one could meet the Japanese rulers. Gifts in particular were indispensable. Hence the missionary now appeared before the daimyo well-dressed and equipped with clocks, music boxes, and other European products. The latter was impressed and bid welcome to the missionaries and their strange message.

Francis Xavier's time in Japan, however, soon came to an end. In fall 1551, he received news from India that the local Jesuit mission was in a sorry state. The brothers were divided by internal conflict, and so Francis Xavier set out on the long journey back to set things aright. His two Jesuit companions stayed behind in Japan. Business in Goa occupied Francis Xavier for only two months. Then he boarded another ship, this time bound for China. He had long heard of the Middle Kingdom, and his stay in Japan had only reinforced his conviction that the actual center of Asian high culture could be found there. But this goal ultimately remained out of his reach: Francis Xavier died on December 3, 1552, on a small island off the coast of Guangzhou, in sight of the Chinese mainland. His early death was a bitter blow, but a growing number of newcomers from Europe constantly reinforced the Jesuit presence in Asia over the succeeding decades. By 1607, there were already 559 members of the order active between East Africa and China. Often following in the footsteps of their great model Francis Xavier, they constantly expanded the Society's missions in Asia. The Jesuits could tout a number of successes down to the early seventeenth century, before a phase of setbacks and stagnation commenced around 1610.

North of Goa, the missionaries of the Society of Jesus on the Indian subcontinent rapidly founded a relatively dense string of missions.[6] In 1548, the Jesuits began to work in Baçaim (Vasai), north of Mumbai, where they maintained a college since 1559. Damão farther to the north followed suit in 1581, and by 1600 some Jesuits were permanently active in Diu far up India's northwestern coast. Since about 1598, at least some isolated Jesuits had also worked in Bengal, although political and military conflicts largely obstructed the mission throughout the following century.[7]

THE MUGHAL EMPIRE

Bengal and the entire northern part of the subcontinent, as well as parts of the modern states of Pakistan and Afghanistan in the early modern period, belonged to the powerful Islamic Mughal Empire. Its capital was the city of Agra, some two hundred kilometers south of New Delhi. The Jesuits first met the Mughal in his capital in 1573, in the context of a politically motivated missionary journey on behalf of the Portuguese.[8] This first visit made an impression, and six years later the Mughal Muhammad Akbar the Great (r. 1556–1605) officially invited the Jesuits to his court so that they could explain Christian doctrine to him. Rudolfo Acquaviva, a nephew of Claudio Acquaviva, who was elected superior general shortly thereafter, and two other Jesuits set out for the north. The court of the great Mughal in the late sixteenth century was a unique place of cultural and religious openness. Akbar himself was eclectic in choosing his own religion, and so the most diverse belief systems could coexist here. Remarkable religious colloquiums took place before the Mughal in which Muslims, Jains, followers of Zoroastrianism, Hindus, and Christian Jesuits debated the respective advantages of their systems of belief.

At least initially, the Jesuits hoped they might win over the entire empire to Christianity by converting Akbar. They thus concentrated on the court and its members. But they also did not forget to secure a broader social base.[9] Despite intense cultural and religious experiences, however, the mission failed to produce any notable results: neither Akbar himself nor his son Jahangir (1605–27) wanted to subscribe to a specific religion, including Christianity. At least a handful of Jesuits nonetheless lingered in the Mughal Empire until the suppression of the Society in 1773. They could often be found in close proximity to the Mughal and discussed religious, scientific, and philosophical questions with him. But there also were constant difficulties with officials and segments of the population that were skeptical of such religious openness. In 1627, serious interest in foreign religious experts gradually began to wane. Now there were periods of hostility and open persecution. In the eighteenth century, only some soldiers remained loyal to the Christian faith.

The Mughal mission was the point of departure for some of the Jesuits' remotest expeditions: to Kashmir, Kafiristan (Afghanistan), and Jaipur and deeper into Central Asia. A trip undertaken by the lay brother Bento de Góis (1561/2–1607), who set out from Agra in 1603, was especially spectacular, albeit also especially mysterious and buried in secrecy at the time. The head of the Mughal mission at the time, Jerónimo Xavier, a grandnephew of Francis Xavier, dispatched Góis in search of a land route to China from northern India via Muslim Central Asia. Góis traveled to Afghanistan, brushed along the Pamir Mountains and the Taklamakan Desert, crossed the Gobi Desert, and after four years died in Suzhou in northern China, near the modern boundary with Mongolia. Traveling for years totally alone, the Jesuit pretended to be a Muslim, wore a turban, rode camels, and hid under the assumed name of Abdallah Isâwî. "As I walk, some take me for a *sayyid*, that is, 'kin of Mohammed'; others take me for a great lord of the Kingdom of Mecca," as he described his disguise.[10] He managed to survive in foreign lands undoubtedly because of the religious ambiguity he skillfully showed, such as observing Ramadan and refusing to eat pork. Even if we can detect a certain fusion of Christianity and Islam in this traveling Jesuit, Góis felt tied to his original religious community to the very end. In order to celebrate Christian holidays, he had a kind of pocket calendar that gave the exact dates of Easter, Pentecost, and other high feasts. He also kept a crucifix and the Gospel with him.[11] Obviously, preaching Christianity was out of the question. His bold expedition was rather a journey of exploration.

TIBET

No less bold was the small Jesuit mission to Tibet, which commenced in 1624.[12] It began with sporadic forays by the Jesuit missionaries António de Andrade, Estêvão Cacella, João Cabral, and Francisco de Azevedo. They reached the region bordering Ladakh near Tsaparang in western Tibet and then crossed Bhutan en route to southeastern Tibet. The Jesuits met with constant adversity in both the east and west of the country, from political threats to bandit attacks and incarceration, to say nothing of the climate. As Andrade reported in his account of his journey: "We had no feeling in our feet, in our hands, in our faces, since on account of the extreme cold we were left deprived of all sensation. It happened that when I bumped into something, a good piece of a finger fell off; I would not have become aware of it and noticed the injury had it not bled copiously."[13] But despite the impressive perseverance that the Jesuits displayed, their ministry largely ceased in the 1630s after the king of Ladakh overthrew the dynasty that had been more open them. The Society of Jesus would not take up the project of Christianizing the Himalayas again until after 1700.

An Italian Jesuit was instrumental in this new beginning: Ippolito Desideri (1684–1733), who set out for the mountains via Kashmir in 1715, reached Lhasa and lived in Tibet for six years as a solitary Jesuit.[14] He learned Tibetan and even wrote about Christianity in it. Desideri appears to have established good relations with the local ruler in Lhasa, but this mission also came to a fruitless end in the medium term. This time, the reason for retreat was of the Jesuits' own making: the Society became involved in a jurisdictional dispute with the Capuchins, who claimed Lhasa as their missionary territory since 1703, citing a ruling of the Propaganda Fide. In the end, Desideri was recalled and traveled back south.

THE SOUTHERN INDIAN SUBCONTINENT

In terms of numbers, the Jesuits' efforts south of Goa were initially more successful than these initiatives north of the Indian subcontinent. The Jesuit college in Kochi on the southwestern coast of the subcontinent stood at the center of this development. Kochi eventually became the headquarters of the Jesuit province of Malabar—officially founded in 1605—which comprised southern India and the islands as far as the Malukus. Step by step, Jesuits from Kochi scouted the deep south of India around Cape Comorin for missionary work, and soon a loose string of Jesuit footholds dotted the landscape. The first stretch of southeastern India's coastline, the Coromandel Coast with its center at Tuticorin (Thoothukudi), was especially important to the Jesuits. Here lived the Paravars, who were fishermen and famous pearl divers. Both local Hindu rulers and their Muslim neighbors took interest in this region and its inhabitants, in addition to the Christian Portuguese, so that the Paravars lived in the crossfire of international conflict. Their decision in favor of Christianity should therefore be interpreted as an attempt to win themselves an at least semireliable ally in this complicated power struggle—political motives always played a major part in the behavior of indigenous peoples toward the mission.

Portuguese Franciscans had already conducted mass baptisms among the Paravers for some time, and Francis Xavier himself had briefly visited the region. Other Jesuits soon followed in his footsteps. Anrique Anriquez, S.J. (1520–1600), not only established a confraternity for the Christian Paravars to intensify their religious life but also may have been the first European to learn to speak Tamil. By 1601, there were about twenty Jesuits present there, in charge of an equal number of churches.[15] Despite various disputes in the following decades, some of which could be traced back to conflicts among the Europeans, a Jesuit could proudly report about the region in 1644 that he "had come to a Christian land." Even deep into the hinterland, there now were many Christians, who had often wandered away from the coast and dwelled scattered in villages and hamlets.[16]

About two hundred kilometers inland from the Coromandel Coast lies the city of Madurai, which was closely connected to the coastal mission. It was from this base that the Jesuits explored the region, roughly equivalent to the modern state of Tamil Nadu, in the first half of the seventeenth century. This was accomplished not least through the efforts of a famous member of the order who would have a profound influence on Jesuit modus operandi: Roberto de Nobili (1577–1657). He was one of those Jesuit missionaries who firmly believed that one could propagate the faith most efficiently by adapting to the local culture as far as possible and adopting the customs, conventions, and values of the country. For de Nobili, that meant that presenting himself as a member of the powerful Brahmin caste in appearance, manner, and attitude. He accordingly soon dressed in yellow as is typical of this Indian religious elite, became a vegetarian, and decorated his face with sandalwood paste. He enjoyed significant success with this strategy. By the end of the seventeenth century, there were well over a hundred thousand Christians in the area. De Nobili's methods were adopted in other missionary territories of southern India, such as Mysuru. He remained a controversial but enormously influential model until well into the eighteenth century.

In 1632, the provincial of Malabar in Kochi—who oversaw the southern Indian missionaries—had more than 180 Jesuits at his disposal. Just half a century later, in 1697, only 42 were left. After the sometimes explosive, euphoric expansion of the Society in the first decades after Francis Xavier's arrival, setbacks, stagnation, and even contraction set in in many of Portugal's Asian territories in the seventeenth century. In northern India, the missions to the Mughal Empire, Tibet, and Bengal ultimately proved to be failures, even if a few Jesuits were still stationed there. In the south, the Jesuits' undeniable successes were initially threatened and subsequently destroyed by the rise of the Netherlands to a leading colonial power. Only a handful of conversion efforts, such as de Nobili's mission in Madurai, survived. The Dutch were Calvinists, and so European confessional rivalries were injected into the colonial power struggle. Wherever the Dutch drove out the Portuguese, the Jesuits also had to go. The Dutch conquest of Malacca, that important crossroads south of modern Kuala Lumpur in Malaysia, was a painful loss in 1641. The small Jesuit college there had to be closed, and so the Society lost an important transit point on the route from Goa to the east and southeast. But worse lay in store. When Kochi in southwestern India was conquered on January 7, 1663, only scraps remained of the

Jesuit province of Malabar. At many places in southern India, the Jesuits were driven underground. They occasionally disguised themselves as Franciscans so as not to be identified as members of the Society so intensely hated by the Dutch.[17] Without the protection of Portuguese colonial power, the Jesuits were also drawn into local power struggles between Indian rulers. The mission on the Coromandel Coast suffered in particular. The Jesuits there risked their lives, and in 1700 several of them were tortured and executed.

The conflict with the Netherlands also decided the fate of the episodic Jesuit mission on Sri Lanka. Individual Jesuits had visited the island several times since Francis Xavier's brief stay in 1545, but the Society was not really established there until 1602.[18] By then, the Franciscans had been active locally for a good half century. They were not happy about the new competition, and even fighting and attacks broke out between the two orders in the capital Colombo. When the Dominicans and Augustinians then also showed up in 1606, the four orders divided the country into separate spheres of influence. The Jesuits expanded their presence in the following years and dedicated themselves to converting the natives in the areas reserved for them. But Ceylon remained hotly contested. In 1630, the Portuguese suffered a dramatic defeat at the hands of the Singhalese from the Kingdom of Kandy in the interior of the island, where several Jesuits had already been killed. Kandy allied itself with the Dutch in 1638, which quickly brought about the end of Portuguese rule and with it the Jesuit mission. From 1641 on, Ignatius's followers were restricted de facto to Colombo. In 1656, Ceylon was lost permanently to the Dutch.

MELANESIA

History played out similarly on the islands of Southeast Asia, which correspond roughly to the territory of Indonesia. Although this region was one of the most remote in the world from an early modern perspective, the Portuguese had established a presence there early and the Jesuits could point to some conversions to Christianity as early as the

1530s. The Portuguese had come on account of the spices produced on the Maluku Islands at the extreme eastern end of this island world. With the exception of various failed projects, the Jesuit presence on the islands of Southeast Asia was limited primarily to the Malukus.[19] Francis Xavier himself was the first Jesuit active on the Spice Islands in 1546 and 1547 and had Christianized Ambon, Ternate, and Halmahera. The first contingent of missionaries arrived in 1547, making Ternate their base under the protection of the local Portuguese fort and also settling on the neighboring island of Tidore. A handful or two of Jesuits were constantly present thereafter. Setting out from Ternate, Tidore, and Ambon, they established a series of mission stations on the neighboring islands. There supposedly were as many as seventy thousand Christians on Ambon by the 1570s as a result of these efforts.

But here too the Jesuits' labors were ultimately only an episode. Life was hard and full of deprivation in the small European settlements— the clergymen often suffered hunger, just as royal officials and merchants did, and were exposed to the whims of the indigenous population. The spiritual condition of the mission also usually gave cause for concern.[20] The attitude of the local Muslim rulers toward the missionaries was volatile, and even the support of the Portuguese regularly left much to be desired. The vast distance between these Jesuits and their nearest confreres and superiors in Malacca, Goa, let alone Rome, meant that they worked in relative isolation from the rest of the Society. When by 1600 the influence of Spain emanating from the nearby Philippines began to make itself felt on the Maluku Islands, the region's political allegiance gradually shifted from the one Iberian power to the other. The Jesuits, however, who now found themselves living in the Spanish sphere of influence, belonged to India and hence to Portugal in the eyes of the church and the Society until 1642. Only then were the Maluku Islands attached to the Society's much closer Spanish province in the Philippines. This long balancing act between political and ecclesiastical poles seriously complicated the missionaries' situation on the ground.[21] As Dutch aggression mounted after 1600, ever more Jesuits were driven out. The mission of the Society of Jesus to the Maluku Islands ended in 1677.

JAPAN

The Jesuits' famous and important mission to Japan came to an end even more quickly—notwithstanding the fact that it initially achieved resounding successes.[22] Francis Xavier himself had sent home glowing letters about Japan, and the Jesuits viewed the mission there almost as a kind of crown jewel. At its peak, in 1626, more than eight hundred thousand Japanese had reportedly become Christians. The Jesuits were initially active primarily on Kyushu, the southernmost major island of Japan. In 1559, they reached central Japan. After Francis Xavier's departure, it fell to Cosme de Torres (1510–70) to direct the Society's ministry; he was able to expand the Jesuits' presence significantly. In 1560, the Jesuits were permitted to settle in Kyoto. Then, in 1563, the regional ruler Ōmura Sumitada (1533–87) converted, taking the name Dom Bartolomeu, and inspired thousands of his subjects to do the same. This conversion had major consequences for the subsequent history of the mission because the port city of Nagasaki lay in Sumitada's territory. In 1571, it became the most important trading post for Europeans and Japanese. The fate of the Jesuits in Japan was intimately bound up in the daily economic, political, and military desires of local potentates. The protection of rulers like Dom Bartolomeu or Oda Nobunaga (1534–82) in the 1570s ensured that a dozen Jesuits could minister to the new Christians in Japan. Nine years later, there were fifty-five Jesuits present, including seven Japanese natives, a rapid development that was unparalleled elsewhere.

In 1579, Alessandro Valignano (1539–1606) set out on the first of his three visits to Japan.[23] Valignano was the son of an Italian nobleman and a friend of the future general Acquaviva. General Mercurian dispatched him to Asia as visitor in 1573. In this capacity, he proceeded to evaluate and organize the affairs of the Jesuit missions between Africa, the Maluku Islands, India, and Japan. The most important legacy of his visitation, however, was the Jesuits' broad commitment to an approach that was not based on outright confrontation with indigenous cultures, but rather advocated adaptation in all possible areas. Valignano's experience in Japan was instrumental in this decision: "In no way can [this new Japanese church] be governed by our European legislation, because customs here are completely different and this church is young and evolving every day." This feeling for the peculiarities of non-European conditions and willingness to permit adaptation characterized the visitor's message.[24] It was in this spirit that Valignano ordered two training institutions be founded in Usuki and Funai, where Japanese and Europeans would each receive an introduction to the other's culture. Both these institutions were founded in the territory of Dom Bartolomeu, who yet again proved to be an important patron of the Society.

But the first threats shook the mission at almost the same time. Toyotomi Hideyoshi emerged from fierce infighting among various Japanese warrior-princes as a strongman. He viewed his European competitors and the missionaries as the harbingers of European aggression. In 1587, he banished the missionaries. He may have retracted the decree shortly thereafter, but he still forbade the Jesuits to preach the Christian faith publicly. The Jesuits continued to work intensively in Japan—there were still 142 Jesuits in Japan in 1591—but they were already confined to a semilegal demimonde. In 1597, the first 26 Christians, including three Japanese Jesuits, were executed. They attained global fame in no time as the "martyrs of Nagasaki." Although Hideyoshi died the following year, ushering in a phase of peace, Christianity remained in jeopardy, as did the Jesuit mission. New anti-Christian laws were issued in 1612 and 1614. Eighty-eight Jesuits left the country in response, leaving just 27 behind. Further persecution and the execution of Christians of European and especially Japanese backgrounds took place. The most important decree that closed Japan off to outside influence was issued in 1639. Although two small contingents of Jesuits traveled again to Japan in 1642 and 1643, vainly attempting to support the native Christian population, the end of the mission had come. Later attempts to revive it evaporated.[25] Instead, the Jesuit personnel that had thus become available were deployed elsewhere, especially in Thailand, Vietnam, and Cambodia. For the first time, this region now came under the Jesuits' focus.[26]

SOUTHEAST ASIA

A small Jesuit mission existed thereafter in Cambodia until the early eighteenth century, although it could serve only a small number of indigenous Christians. In Thailand (Siam), the Jesuits first attempted to establish a mission between 1625 and 1632, but success eluded them until 1655.[27] The Jesuits enjoyed even greater success in southern Vietnam (Cochinchina), where they had been present since 1615, after their expulsion from Japan. Several years later, Alexandre de Rhodes (1591 or 1593–1660) was able to build on this foundation. Although he was a Frenchman, de Rhodes formally answered to the pope and the province of Rome.[28] He was an unusual figure who visited Cochinchina twice between 1624 and 1630 and four times between 1640 and 1645. He was also one of the first missionaries to visit northern Vietnam (Tonkin). He learned the local language (for which he also drafted the first Latin transliteration) and shrewdly utilized philosophy, science, and European craftsmanship to draw attention to his real message.[29] But de Rhodes was also brash and confrontational, which not only created problems with other Jesuits but also led to repeated banishment from the kingdoms of Vietnam. He was permanently expelled from Vietnam and forced to return to Europe in 1645.

Back in France, de Rhodes became one of the founders of the Missions Étrangères de Paris (MEP), a worldwide Catholic missionary organization. The mission, which collaborated closely with the Propaganda Fide in Rome and its apostolic vicars, usually had a tense relationship with the Society of Jesus in Europe and on the ground in the missions, which sometimes seriously weakened the MEP. The conflict can be traced in part back to theological differences, but it also was a result of the fact that the MEP and the Propaganda Fide prioritized recruiting indigenous clergy more than the Jesuits did. From 1682 to 1692, the Propaganda Fide even forbade the Jesuits to work in Vietnam at the request of the MEP.

The Jesuits' Christianization effort in northern Vietnam was more successful. The small kingdom of Tonkin may have had more Christians in 1650 than the massive Chinese empire did a full generation later. But in both kingdoms of Vietnam, the mission remained plagued by an unpredictable succession of phases of toleration and persecution. Sometimes the Jesuits openly proselytized; sometimes the Christians were persecuted and the ministry could take place only underground. During the persecutions, Jesuits who were good scientists often still enjoyed the best status. Johannes Koffler, for example, a Bohemian, was allowed to stay in Cochinchina as a court physician for five years after the final expulsion of the missionaries in 1750.[30]

CHINA

The presence of Jesuit scholars at court reminded some observers of conditions in China at the same time.[31] The mission to China had been Francis Xavier's last great project, which he himself had proved unable to realize. After his death, thirty-one years would pass before Michele Ruggieri (1543–1607) and Matteo Ricci (1552–1610), the actual founder of the mission to China, at last established the first permanent mission on the Chinese mainland opposite Macao in 1583. Ricci not only established the Society in China but also, by skillfully and doggedly pursuing his goals all his life, managed to penetrate from provincial southern China to the capital of Beijing. He also laid the foundation for the missionaries' subsequent approach, construing a social role for himself and his confreres that copied the type of the Confucian intellectual. Ricci thus was undoubtedly one of the Jesuits who conformed especially closely to the spirit and views of Valignano and developed them independently.

The mission to China initially stood very much in the shadow of Japan. Despite some successes, the early years were a phase of small steps forward amid countless imponderables. Beginning circa 1620, after the end of this pioneering phase, the Jesuits gained an ever more secure foothold at the imperial court, particularly by virtue of their scholarly activity as mathematicians and astronomers. Until the end of the mission after 1773, Jesuit scientists were engaged in the imperial department of astronomy. In 1644, the reigning Ming dynasty was overthrown by the Qing. This was a dramatic caesura in Chinese history, but for the history of the Jesuit mission, with the exception of some short-lived problems, the violent accession of the new dynasty did not bring about significant change. Most Jesuits were temporarily banished to Guangzhou from 1664 to 1671, with only four permitted to stay in Beijing as astronomers. But after their rehabilitation, they were able to pick up more or less seamlessly where they had left off in their previous areas of operations. The long reign of the Kangxi Emperor (r. 1662–1722) was simultaneously a climax and a phase of transition. The Jesuits initially enjoyed good relations with the emperor, culminating in the so-called Edict of Toleration of 1692. But internal conflict between French Jesuits and all other members of the order dramatically weakened the mission by 1700. Missionaries from other orders also took an ever more hostile view of the Jesuits and their evangelizing tactics. In the late seventeenth century, in China and Rome and all across Europe, a major debate broke out over the so-called Chinese rites, a form of Sinicized Christianity that the Jesuits tolerated, but their adversaries abhorred. Around 1705, not least on account of these internal European conflicts, the emperor's trust in missionaries generally, including the Jesuits, gradually began to crumble.[32] After his death, the decline was swift. Christianity was outlawed in 1724, and the missionaries—with the exception of a handful of mathematicians in Beijing—were expelled.

The mission to China attracted the utmost attention in Europe, but in point of fact the Society of Jesus never maintained an especially strong presence in the Middle Kingdom. At no point were there more than a few dozen Jesuits active there at the same time, and often there were far fewer. The four "colleges," in Beijing, Nanjing, Hangzhou, and Ganzhou, did not offer academic instruction. Most of the time, the Jesuits were pushed to the limit, and many of their projects could not be carried out even halfway without the greatest exertion. Until about 1700, however, the Society was nonetheless able to build a far-flung network of several dozen rural and provincial communities in which probably about two hundred thousand Christians lived. The special fascination of the China mission derived, rather, from its cultural significance. Ever since Ricci, the Jesuits strove to understand the complex high culture of the Far East. They learned the language and read the literature; they translated in both directions and published a large number of works about China in Europe and about Europe in Chinese. The Jesuits' encounter with China was also a European encounter with a culture of equal standing. The exceptional status of China was undeniable, even if the Europeans never voiced any doubt at least about the superiority of the Christianity.

BRAZIL

At roughly the same time that Francis Xavier launched his missionary undertakings in Asia, the Jesuits also established themselves in Portuguese America—and their successes here were more enduring than those in most regions of the Far East. Portuguese holdings in the New World consisted primarily of Brazil, for which the first contingent of Jesuits set sail in 1549 under the leadership of Manuel da Nóbrega (1517–70).[33] One thousand soldiers sailed with the same fleet to Brazil, including Tomé de Sousa, the first royal governor-general. The force was intended to tie the colony more closely to the motherland and integrate it within the administrative structures of the Portuguese empire. The year 1549 is therefore also regarded as the beginning of Portugal's colonial policy for Brazil, and it was no coincidence that the Jesuits were part of the process from the start. The focused proselytization of the indigenous population was conceived as a means of bolstering the king's plans to extend his power beyond the few coastal strongholds established thitherto. The Jesuits soon erected the first colleges: Salvador de Bahía (1549), Rio de Janeiro (1567), and Olinda in Pernambuco (1568). In 1553, the province of Brazil was established as the first in the Americas, for which the aforementioned colleges and cities long served as hubs. By 1568, some 61 names were listed on the provincial staff; by 1600, the number had grown to 169. Significant growth beyond these numbers did not take place until the very end of the seventeenth century, when a new boom in personnel brought the total to well over 400. The delay after 1600 was caused above all by the two major Dutch invasions in 1624/5 and 1630–54. The Dutch occupied large stretches of Brazil (e.g., Bahía and Pernambuco), albeit not all, during this period. The Jesuits lost some of their footholds, and new ones were not established until after midcentury, when five new colleges were founded in relatively quick succession. On the whole, Brazil developed into one of the most successful, indeed perhaps *the* most successful, part of the Jesuit mission in the Portuguese world.[34]

The Jesuits had high hopes of converting the heathen, and their missionary experiences in Brazil, together with the early impressions of Francis Xavier, had a profound influence on the subsequent ministry of the Society in this area. In the early years, da Nóbrega was still starry-eyed and saw his work as child's play. He thought he could impart Christian and European values on the dominant Tupí people of Brazil, "as if on an unwritten page." But it quickly emerged that the various Tupí tribes either had no interest in such values or even openly resisted. Even in the best circumstances, da Nóbrega's missionary efforts were crowned with only very superficial success. In order to monitor the natives better and to pace their efforts more precisely, the Jesuits set up mission villages for the natives in Brazil (*aldeias*). There were supposedly already 150 of them along the coast and in the immediate hinterland as early as the year 1601. Here, as everywhere else in the Americas, these mission villages were an attempt to compensate, at least somewhat, for the numerical imbalance between the handful of Jesuit missionaries and the thousands of natives. By settling segments of the indigenous population permanently at a single place, the Jesuits hoped they could magnify their own influence on the people. The *aldeias* also served to protect the natives from the unsupervised actions of Portuguese colonists, who viewed the indigenous population primarily as a source of labor and had long brutally and unscrupulously captured and exploited them as slaves. The Jesuits intervened in this long-term conflict between the Portuguese and the natives, taking the side of the latter, and their skill and political influence in Lisbon helped curtail at least the most repellent excesses on the part of the former—but that earned them the enmity of the settlers in Brazil already in the sixteenth century.[35] The first attacks by colonists on the Jesuits broke out in 1609. Many more physical disputes ensued over the following decades. The Jesuits were repeatedly driven out and threatened. The college in São Paulo, for example, was more or less closed from 1640 to 1653. The Society's reputation was permanently damaged, and the Jesuits' status remained controversial.

MARANHÃO

These problems with the settlers plagued not only the province of Brazil but also—and especially—the Maranhão region, that is, the Caribbean coast and the Amazon basin. The Jesuits, as well as Portuguese settlers, did not reach this region until the seventeenth century, since the colonial bases had been concentrated on the southeastern and eastern coasts. Individual Jesuits had made excursions to the north here and there since at least 1607, but it was Luís Figueira who first seriously set out to familiarize himself with the pathless region in 1636. A year later, he was in Lisbon to negotiate with the crown to open a mission. The outcome was better than expected: the monarch not only supported the Society's plans but also granted the Society of Jesus supreme ecclesiastical authority over Maranhão—in other words, he transferred authority over the mission territory from the jurisdiction of the bishop of Bahía, who had hitherto been nominally responsible for it, to the Jesuits.

Figueira and seventeen more Jesuits were at last able to return to the Amazon in 1643. Only three of them, however, survived a shipwreck off the coast, and these survivors were murdered in a native revolt in 1649. A new group of missionaries came in 1652 under the leadership of António Vieira (1608–97), one of the most remarkable Jesuits of his day. Vieira had been an adviser to the king of Portugal and a celebrated preacher before he turned to South America. In about ten years, he built a network of fifty-four missions along the Amazon and its most important tributaries. Again, he was able to rely on extensive ecclesiastical privileges that invested the Society of Jesus with general ecclesiastical authority in the area. Over the course of his career, Vieira tried ever more forcefully to prevent the enslavement of the natives. Massive anti-Jesuit riots therefore broke out in 1662, leading to the expulsion of some of the padres.

The Jesuits remained active in Maranhão after this setback, but their rights were significantly curtailed. Whereas they previously had authority to supervise all dealings between the settlers and the natives, they now were forced to stand by more or less helplessly when Portuguese settlers compelled the native people to labor for them. The Jesuits repeatedly made enemies of the settlers in subsequent decades, too, and sometimes found support at court. But their position in this constantly tense situation was precarious. The Brazilian Jesuits lost many of their Christianized natives when they fled to their Jesuit confreres across the border in French Guyana on account of "the good treatment they received."[36] It was not until 1686, not least on account of the influence of the expelled missionary Johann Philipp Bettendorff (1625–98) at the court in Lisbon, that the Jesuits' old rights were restored. They thereafter acted as the appointed protectors of the native people. Now, only the Jesuits were supposed to govern native settlements, and only for real pay were the Tupí supposed to work for the settlers. The Jesuits were involved in every matter touching the indigenous population, at least officially.

The mission in Maranhão now expanded on a vast scale. In the following decades, more new Jesuits came there than to Brazil itself. It was made a vice-province in 1727. And still conflicts over the Jesuits' protective measures for the natives raged on. The Jesuits' persistent defense of the natives roused anti-Jesuit sentiment that the enemies of the Society of Jesus propagated loudly in Brazil and Europe. The Jesuits' response was equally loud, and so a fierce debate broke out in the royal administration. Disputes over the status of the natives and arguments for or against the Society converged. Decades later, this debate would significantly bear fruit in the campaign to suppress the order.

AFRICA

There were still other missions closely associated with Brazil in the Portuguese sphere of influence in which the Jesuits placed high hopes—in Africa. There were three regions in which they succeeded in establishing at least a semipermanent presence: Kongo and Angola in the southwest, Mozambique and the Zambezi region in the southeast, and Ethiopia in East Africa. Europeans of the sixteenth century often regarded Ethiopia, with its Coptic Christians, as the kingdom of Prester John, a mythical figure who was feverishly sought for in the real world. In 1554, some dozen Jesuits were dispatched to the reigning king Galawdewos (his Christian name was Claudius) to persuade him to acknowledge the supremacy of Rome. Led by João Nunes Barreto (1517–62), who was, exceptionally, the first Jesuit to be consecrated bishop for this purpose, the group set out. It soon became apparent, however, that their hopes would be dashed because Claudius was far too insecure domestically. Hence the entire mission failed, even though a handful of Jesuits stayed behind in the country for several decades. One of them, Manuel Fernandes, spent thirteen years of his life, from 1583 to 1596, totally alone in this alien society. In the seventeenth century, the Jesuits in Goa revived their ministry to Ethiopia, and a small group of Jesuits actually resided intermittently at the court of the Ethiopian emperors at the time. The mission seemed to be rapidly evolving into an even bigger enterprise in the 1620s, but for all their extraordinary efforts, the Society of Jesus could never secure stable backing. The Jesuits were expelled from the country in 1634; the last Jesuits in Ethiopia were hung in 1641.

Southeast Africa, first and foremost, was an important stopover for the Portuguese on their way around the Cape of Good Hope to India. The Jesuit mission launched in Mozambique in 1560 never amounted de facto to more than a supply station. Despite several attempts, the Society failed to establish itself in the sixteenth century. A new push was made in 1607, though, and this time the Society of Jesus succeeded in putting down roots. A series of small missions was built along the Zambezi River heading inland. Even though the Jesuits were able to situate themselves in this region over the long term and their houses became economically self-sufficient, the Mozambique mission remained a peripheral endeavor.

The projects in southwestern Africa, in the Kongo and neighboring Angola, initially seemed more promising. The Kingdom of Kongo at the time was a relatively rigidly organized, centralized state. The king of Kongo had converted to Christianity, albeit in a highly syncretized form, in 1491, long before the founding of the Society of Jesus. Since the kingdom had voluntarily embraced the new religion, the cultural and religious balance of power here differed from that in most other colonies. The Christian church of Kongo was much more autonomous and confident.[37] Despite this spectacular start, however, success in winning converts outside the royal house was rather meager, even though several Catholic orders tried to do so. The Jesuits joined the Kongo mission in 1547. In light of the confidence of the local church, the Jesuits were confronted with very precise ideas. That swiftly led to conflict, and the Jesuits repeatedly had to retreat. Hence, around 1560, the Society of Jesus set its sights farther south, on Angola. But here too the missionaries were initially unsuccessful. The situation remained the same until 1575, when a major Portuguese military expedition violently interceded. A year later, the Jesuits were able to establish their headquarters in Luanda. But their ministry continued to rely on provisions from the Portuguese occupiers. Converting the indigenous population proved to be extremely difficult and progressed hardly beyond scant initial successes. Angola was furthermore severely harmed by the rivalry between Portugal and Holland. Luanda was occupied by the Dutch for years.

These conflicts were fought primarily for control of the transatlantic slave trade, for which the Kongo and Angola were the most important supply centers. From the mid-seventeenth century on, the Jesuits faced growing competition from the Capuchins in the Kongo, who proved to be far more engaged and effective than the Jesuits. When the central government of the Kongo collapsed and the kingdom splintered in the mid-1660s after protracted civil war, the Jesuits withdrew forever in 1666. The mission in southwest Africa never amounted to more than a sideshow. On the whole, that is true for Africa generally.

The Spanish World

FLORIDA AND NORTHERN SOUTH AMERICA

The Jesuits were not initially present in Spain's overseas territory, in contrast to Portugal's colonial empire. Several decades passed before King Philip II invited the Society to enter the possessions of the Spanish crown.[38] It all began in 1565, when some Jesuit missionaries were summoned for a Spanish expedition to Florida.[39] The Spanish had no luck there, however, and so the Jesuits were unable to leave any lasting impression. Few Spanish Jesuits were lured to the Caribbean, where some missionaries resided (especially in Havana) after their failure in Florida, or to southern Central America, although they maintained a certain presence in modern Venezuela. The Society's presence in the central port city of Cartagena de las Indias in modern Colombia was more important. The Society of Jesus gained a foothold there in several steps around 1600. From there, the Jesuits penetrated to the interior, where they founded important colleges at Santa Fe de Bogotá and Popayán (1640), among others, far to the southwest. The Jesuits repeatedly made great effort, but enjoyed very little success, to establish a permanent mission to the natives east of Bogotá in the Casanare region on the edge of the Amazon basin.

PERU

The heart of the Jesuits' South American ministry initially lay farther to the south in the Viceroyalty of Peru, which could be reached from the Pacific Ocean via Panama. Peru at the time covered far more than the territory of the modern state. The name referred to the entire western half of central South America. The Jesuits looked to this territory with high hopes, and it was here where the Society of Jesus enjoyed its first lasting success in Spanish America. Under the leadership of the Jesuit Jerónimo Ruiz de Portillo (1532–89), the first group of missionaries arrived in Lima after leaving some brothers behind in Panama along the way. The phase of military conquest was already over when Ruiz de Portillo brought his contingent of eight Jesuits to the capital of Peru. These men thus arrived in a zone that was already visibly permeated to some extent by European rule, organization, and society. The colonial cities were therefore the natural starting point for the Jesuits, and at first they tried to establish their ministry there just as they had done in the cities of Europe. They entrenched themselves in the more important colonial cities and soon also in the smaller ones at an astonishing pace. Lima and Cuzco (1571) in modern Peru, and La Paz (1582), the mining city of Potosí, and La Plata (today

Sucre; 1593) in modern Bolivia became important bases. Farther north, in modern Ecuador, one of the leading Jesuit settlements, with several institutions, was founded in Quito in 1586. Bit by bit, the massive province of Peru was cut up into smaller administrative parts: Quito, Nuevo Reyno de Granada (Bogotá), and Paraguay.

The Jesuits also ministered to indigenous peoples, slaves, and mestizos in the cities. For the sons of indigenous "chiefs," a number of schools were opened, such as the Colegio del Príncipe in Lima and the Colegio de San Francisco Borja in Cuzco. In the early years, the Jesuits attempted to reach the natives in the countryside with short excursions in the manner of temporary "flying missions." This proved unsuccessful, though, and so the Jesuits scrapped the practice more or less entirely.[40] In its place, they turned to establishing stable mission villages. The Jesuits of Peru first took over a mission village, namely, the *doctrina* of Julí on the western shore of Lake Titicaca, by order of the viceroy Francisco de Toledo in 1576. They were initially highly critical of the *doctrinas* but soon recognized their advantages. A *doctrina* was a kind of indigenous village that fell exclusively under the jurisdiction of one order and represented a kind of outpost of Christianity in heathen surroundings. Schools and a hospital were built in Julí. Step by step, the Jesuits then built their own establishments, such as the tertiate of the province of Peru. They soon called Julí the "holy village" and the "Rome of Peru."[41] The experiment was enormously influential over the long term.[42]

One of the most important and influential Jesuits who ever worked in the Americas was closely associated with the Julí project: José de Acosta (1539–1600). He was transferred to the Andes in 1571, served as the provincial of Peru from 1576 to 1583, spent time thereafter in Mexico, and returned to Spain in 1587. Acosta's outstanding importance is based above all on two books he wrote. His *Natural and Moral History of the Indies* (*Historia natural y moral de las Indias*) became the standard account of the land and peoples of Spanish America for future generations even outside the Catholic world; his theoretical treatise on missions, *On Securing Salvation for the Indians* (*De procuranda Indorum salute*), summarized the fundamental knowledge of the early missionaries and became a kind of textbook for missionaries both inside and outside the order.

AMAZONIA

Spreading outward from Peru, with the model of Julí lurking in the background, a series of relatively large mission districts emerged beyond the Andes, stretching in a large semicircle around the area where the headwaters of the Amazon rose. This mission started in the Mainas region to the north, in the modern borderland between Ecuador and Colombia. In 1601, Rafael Ferrer, S.J. (1570–1611), set out from Quito on a decade-long journey to various tribes on the tributaries of the great rivers of the Amazon. He mapped parts of the region, described important plants and languages, and introduced at least a vague form of Christianity. The Jesuits' Mainas mission, however, was not officially established until 1638. A Spanish expedition in which the Jesuits participated explored the upper reaches of the Amazon in the northeast of modern Peru in 1639, and over the ensuing decades the Jesuits established about a dozen mission villages along the riverbanks of this inaccessible region.

A generation later, the Bohemian missionary Samuel Fritz was active along the upper Amazon, likewise founding several dozen mission villages, which are collectively known as the Omaguas Missions. In 1689, he traveled down the Amazon almost to its mouth, where he was apprehended by the Portuguese and detained for several months. By the beginning of the eighteenth century, the mission's problems were impossible to ignore: it spanned a massive, impassable territory that was inhabited by numerous indigenous tribes hostile to the Jesuits. These tribes had successfully resisted military subjugation, while the native people whom the Jesuits had successfully befriended in their villages faced rising pressure from Portuguese adventurers and slavers. By the end of the early modern period, in 1760, the mission of Mainas ministered to some twelve thousand Christians in approximately thirty settlements.

CENTRAL SOUTH AMERICA

The second major missionary expansion spearheaded by the Jesuits beyond the Andes played out farther to the south. Immediately east of Lake Titicaca, in the modern border region between Bolivia and Brazil, the flourishing Moxos mission was founded in the late seventeenth century.[43] The Society of Jesus had already been present on the southern edge of the territory since 1587, with a base at Santa Cruz de la Sierra.[44] Spanish soldiers of fortune regularly set out for the region from this border city, often in search of native slaves. This created an ambivalent situation for the Jesuits: on the one hand, the Spaniards' behavior was the biggest obstacle to close cooperation with the natives; on the other, the Jesuits constantly accompanied the Spanish on their raids to familiarize themselves with the area. Hence a mission was long out of the question, even though the Jesuits had dreamed of one since about 1600. Only after the Spanish raids subsided did the situation slowly change. The Jesuits redoubled their efforts in the 1670s, and in 1682, without the direct support of the Spanish settlers, Pedro Marbán, Cipriano Barace, and José del Castillo founded the mission to Moxos. The missionaries established their typical mission villages, often bolstered by the natives' fear of further Spanish slave raids from Santa Cruz. The following decades witnessed gradual expansion. By 1688, already twelve Jesuits were working in the new mission. One to two dozen villages— often only short-lived—were founded. There were setbacks, too. Barace, one of the founding fathers of the mission, became its first martyr in 1703. The Jesuits petitioned the governor of Santa Cruz for a punitive expedition to avenge his death. The missionaries repeatedly had to call on the secular authorities for assistance, although they normally tried to win the natives peoples' sympathy by other, more peaceful means. The mission reached its zenith for about two or three decades after 1720. Thirty-five thousand natives lived under the influence of up to fifty-three Jesuits, who had covered the region more or less systematically with their settlements. Most of the people were now Christians, albeit many elements of pre-Christian culture had been integrated in their faith. The lives of the Jesuits and their protégés became settled. Churches were built, and communities organized. Agriculture, fields, and herds along with regularly planned adobe villages were the hallmarks of the mission. At the end of its existence, the Moxos mission collectively owned no fewer than 5,398 books—an astonishing number at the time. Even if life in the missions was neither free of tension nor completely in keeping with the Jesuits' ideal, these mission settlements in the wilderness, hundreds of kilometers away from the nearest Spanish towns, were a veritable marvel for visitors. A "new world in the midst of the New World," one of them remarked.[45]

Things began to change for the worse, however, around 1750. A catastrophic flood led to a crop failure, forcing many natives and Jesuits to resettle. There also was political conflict originating in Europe. The Spanish and Portuguese clashed everywhere in South America. The latter fanned out from Brazil ever farther to the west, southwest, and south, colliding with the Spanish sphere of influence. This created insecurity, border disputes, and finally conflict over the political, religious, and social order itself. The Moxos mission was also affected, as Portuguese traders and soldiers began to crop up there. The Jesuits, who sought to shield their villages and their natives from European influence, carefully but unambiguously opposed the Portuguese newcomers. The letters of the Moxos missionaries are full of revulsion for the infiltrators.[46] Around 1750, this European rivalry escalated to open warfare, and the missions and their inhabitants fell victim. As we shall see, the Society of Jesus would be one of the most prominent casualties of the new balance of power struck by the colonial powers of Europe in South America.

Relatively close by the Jesuit villages in Moxos lay the mission regions of Chiquitos and Gran Chaco. The name Chiquitos designated the native peoples of a relatively compact area in eastern Bolivia on the border with Paraguay and Brazil. The Jesuit José de Arce established the first of a total of seven mission villages here in 1691, which developed into prosperous settlements over the following decades. One of the most renowned missionaries of this area was the dynamic and artistically versatile Martin Schmid, whom we have already come to know as a musician and composer. It was in these villages and their great baroque churches that the Jesuits gave the musical performances with indigenous musicians described earlier. In terms of organization, the Chiquitos missions did not belong to the province of Peru on the western side of the continent, but rather were oriented toward Paraguay in the east. That was also the case for the missions of Gran Chaco, a massive territory that today comprises the part of Argentina north of

Buenos Aires and west of Asunción in Paraguay.[47] For early modern
Europeans, Gran Chaco was an inhospitable, forbidding region—damp
and often swampy with insufficient clean drinking water and arable
land. The landscape was dotted with almost impassable thorny forests
and scrubland. The climate was more tolerable only along the river
courses. Here and there the land was suitable to pasturing cattle, and the
natives there had indeed adapted to horses at an early date. They knew
how to handle their steeds and were formidable mounted warriors. The
Jesuits tried again and again over the entire seventeenth century to establish contact with the indigenous population from their base in
Paraguay—normally with no success, or at least no resounding success.
One factor behind the effort to open up the area was the founding of a
Jesuit college in Tarija in 1690, in the far northwest of the region (today
in southern Bolivia). The mission in Chaco only seriously began afterward. These missions saw their heyday in the late phase of the Society's
early modern history, beginning around 1750.[48] The Jesuits gained a
foothold farther south in the Pampas of northern Patagonia at a similarly late date. The indigenous people there had successfully warded off
colonial expansion until well into the eighteenth century. In 1739/40,
however, a treaty struck after military conflict granted the Jesuit missionaries access to the region. Their ministry here focused on the coastal
region around modern Mar del Plata and Tandil some three to four
hundred kilometers south of Buenos Aires.

PARAGUAY

The Jesuit presence north of Buenos Aires was more effective and more
prominent. The early modern Jesuits called the area Paraquaria, a name
that was applied to a much wider territory than the eponymous modern
nation-state of Paraguay. The Jesuit province created in 1607 encompassed Paraguay, modern Uruguay, northern and central Argentina,
small parts of southern Brazil, and border regions of modern Bolivia—
it was the Jesuits from Paraguay who founded the aforementioned college in Tarija. The Jesuits had first come to this expansive region in the
final years of the sixteenth century, arriving simultaneously from Brazil

and Peru.[49] A house was opened in Asunción in 1588, followed in 1599 by another in the regional Spanish capital of Córdoba (today in northern Argentina). Shortly thereafter, yet another house was founded farther north in Santiago del Estero. The status of Paraguay was initially uncertain, wavering between Peru and Brazil, but it was elevated to a province and received its first provincial in 1607. The number of Jesuit houses and members there grew dramatically in the following years. The Society of Jesus soon found support from a variety of sources in the cities of Paraguay where it established itself. The bishop of Santiago del Estero, for example, financed a new novitiate in Córdoba in 1613 and donated his property to the Society to found a central college there as well. Two years later, the province had 122 Jesuits and eighteen houses, although they were usually rather humble affairs.

Only the central college of Córdoba provided the entire education that one needed for an ecclesiastical career. The Jesuits in Chile—the Society was active over the long term not only in Santiago but also on the remote Chiloé islands—initially fell under Paraguay's jurisdiction, but General Vitelleschi attached them to the province of Peru in 1624. That caused Paraguay to lose a significant number of members, but by the eighteenth century up to four hundred Jesuits lived in the province.

Paraguay was and still is synonymous with the famous mission villages of the Guaraní, the "reductions." The first reduction, San Ignacio Guazú, was founded south of Asunción in 1610. Although the most important pioneer of this early phase, Roque González de Santa Cruz (1576–1628), was murdered by natives, the Jesuits were still able to establish several dozen remote mission settlements in the region that existed as small autonomous communities. The need to protect the natives from raids emanating from Brazil to the north was an important motive behind the creation of these settlements. Large expeditions of adventurers set out annually from São Paulo to enslave natives to work the incipient Brazilian sugar plantations. At first, the raiders did not even spare the reductions. Only after the natives were supplied with European weapons at the Jesuits' discretion and successfully defended themselves did the raids subside, although they never stopped completely.[50] The exact number and location of the villages changed constantly for that very reason, but the reductions stabilized as institutions by the mid-eighteenth century. There now were thirty villages that were regarded as a network of interconnected settlements. There, the Jesuits built the magnificent churches mentioned previously, Guaraní art was produced, and musical life flourished—just as in the Chiquitos and Moxos missions. Under Jesuit leadership, prosperous settlements arose in the tropical wilderness, to the astonishment of European observers.

In the eighteenth century, the reductions of Paraguay were increasingly swept into the vortex of the border conflicts between Spain and Portugal mentioned earlier. A treaty struck in early 1750 was intended to clarify the border between the two colonial empires. In it, the Spanish conceded parts of Paraguay to Portugal. The areas in question contained seven Jesuit reductions, and the Portuguese ordered the Society of Jesus to withdraw from the region. The natives were told to stay or leave (along with their Jesuit leaders). Almost thirty thousand Guaraní were reportedly affected by the measure.

The Jesuits turned to diplomatic resistance. That in turn angered the Portuguese. Soon it was assumed that the Jesuits were playing for time so they could mobilize the military resources of the reductions—a claim that dramatically kindled anti-Jesuit sentiment prior to the suppression of the Society. The Jesuits had no interest in military opposition, but the Guaraní steeled themselves for a fight. Relations between the Jesuits and the natives became increasingly fraught. A violent rebellion of the indigenous population against the Spanish and Portuguese broke out in 1754 and raged for two years, going down in history as the War of the Seven Reductions. Some thirteen hundred natives lost the decisive battle against twice as many opponents at Caíbaté in February 1756. Soon thereafter the Jesuits evacuated thousands of indigenous inhabitants from the newly Portuguese reductions. The Jesuits remained active in Spanish territory until they were driven out there, too, in the wake of the suppression of the Society. But even then the reductions of Paraguay never completely disappeared. Under the direction of a secular Spanish colonial official, the reductions carried on for decades, albeit in a far less prosperous state.

NORTHWESTERN MEXICO

From Paraguay to Peru, from La Plata to La Paz, Lima, and still farther northward to Santa Fé de Bogotá and Cartagena on the Caribbean coast, South America was profoundly influenced by the Society of Jesus and its missionaries after the failure of the Florida mission in 1568. In only one other territory of the Spanish Americas did the Society play a similar part: Mexico. Some of the Jesuits who survived the unlucky Florida mission arrived there in 1572. They quickly established themselves in the capital, where they found support almost immediately. The Colegio Máximo de San Pedro y San Pablo was founded in the same year. Further colleges and houses followed in other colonial cities. The Jesuits soon expanded their ministry beyond the urban centers and, in 1591, turned to missions. The northwest of the modern state of Mexico and the southwestern border region of the United States became dense mission districts. Some Franciscans and infrequent Spanish military expeditions had previously visited the region, but the Spanish had never devised a successful strategy for controlling the area.[51] The Jesuits initiated and were part of a new approach that chased success with a subtle mixture of violence and a willingness to make cultural compromises.

The Jesuit missionaries focused their efforts on two regions of northwestern Mexico that were close enough to each other to exert a mutual influence. First, the Jesuits opened up the coast along the Pacific to the north—the regions of Sinaloa and Sonora. Their starting point was the border town of Culiacán. From there, the first Jesuit missionaries of Mexico, Martín Pérez and Gonzalo de Tapia, headed north and settled with other Spaniards at Villa de Sinaloa. Tapia became the first Jesuit martyr of this mission in 1594. The region by the sea is characterized by a series of river valleys running east to west and emptying into the Sea of Cortés. The Jesuit missionaries became acquainted with valley after valley—and so also tribe after tribe—on their way north. They founded the northernmost and most important of these missions in 1617 among a population of perhaps thirty thousand Yaqui on the eponymous river.[52]

The other major missionary territory comprised the adjacent territory of the interior. This was often rugged, mountainous terrain. The point of departure for these missions was the colonial border town of Durango in 1600. Hernando de Santarén and Gerónimo Ramírez were among the most influential figures of the Society in this area, which was predominantly inhabited by tribes of Acaxee, Xixime, and Tepehuán. Devastating revolts repeatedly erupted here over the following years and decades, first in 1601 and again from 1616 to 1619. Eight Jesuits were beaten to death at the time. But step by step, the missions here also pushed north. At least from the Jesuits' perspective, the missions created a kind of domino effect among the natives. "The good impression [literally, "good smell"] and enthusiasm of this Acaxee people have inspired the neighboring heathens for our holy faith, and they have come to us many times for instruction," wrote one of the missionaries in 1604.[53] The Jesuits' expansion was intimately linked to Spanish military advances. Economic or military contact usually preceded religious encounters. The Jesuits were rarely the first Europeans whom the natives had met.[54] The mountain regions known as Pimera Baja and Tarahumara were opened up in the 1620s and 1630s in the course of this two-pronged religious-military initiative.

Despite numerous conflicts in the Tarahumara region and elsewhere, the decades around 1650 in northwestern New Spain were a time of tense but at least partly viable peace.[55] The Spanish repeatedly said that many natives were at least "semi-pacified" ("indios de media paz"). Relationships with such groups required what modern scholars call a "colonial pact," implying that the Spanish and the native tribes were equally matched. The Yaqui tribe is perhaps the best example: although they had initially offered the Spanish violent resistance and long posed a military threat that could strike at any time, this well-organized people soon cultivated a close alliance with the colonial power.[56] On both sides, the "semi-peace" between the Europeans and the indigenous population of Mexico was based on a mixture of threats and calculated, occasional violence, on the one hand, and cooperative diplomacy, shrewd negotiations, and strategic aid, on the other. Despite various setbacks, the Jesuits and their new religion exerted a certain influence on the Yaqui and many other tribes—but we should not exaggerate it. Even after their encounter with the missionaries, these tribes never entirely lost their autonomy.

A new age dawned at the end of the seventeenth century after this phase of pacification. It witnessed many new and far-reaching Jesuit initiatives but was also marked by crisis and incipient decline. Spectacular successes immediately catch the eye: Eusebio Kino (1645–1711), one of the most important and famous Jesuits of Mexico, acquainted his order with the northernmost part of New Spain in 1700. He crisscrossed the vast territory on either side of the modern border of Mexico and the United States "for 15 years on over 40 exploration expeditions totally alone with my servants and 50, 60, and 100 horses and mules," pushing as far as the area of modern Tucson, Arizona.[57] The Jesuits had not come so far prior to his arrival, although there had long been a trickle of Spanish settlers, adventurers, and soldiers. Numerous Jesuits followed in Kino's footsteps in the mid-eighteenth century, including such influential missionaries as the Swiss Philipp Segesser (1689–1762).

Kino himself selected the second new major missionary territory in which the Jesuits then set foot, although it was another member of the order, his good friend Juan María de Salvatierra (1648–1717), who carried out the pioneering work. Under Salvatierra's leadership, the Jesuits succeeded in establishing a permanent foothold in Baja California opposite the mainland of northwestern Mexico.[58] The Jesuits went on to found over a dozen mission villages there in the following decades, dotting the lower two-thirds of the peninsula.

But despite these new initiatives, a long phase of crisis and decline set in in northwestern Mexico around 1700. As more and more colonists with economic interests flowed into the erstwhile border regions, administrative, social, and economic pressure on the missions rose. By around 1725, the number of nonnative inhabitants in the region may have surpassed that of the remaining indigenous population for the first time. Indigenous languages faded away in various places, to be replaced by Spanish or a local form of Nahuatl. Individual native leaders dressed like the Spanish and wore silk stockings with heeled shoes.[59] The settlements under Jesuit supervision were no longer outposts of the empire but rather were now viewed as obstacles or as relics of a pioneer phase that belonged to the past.[60] Numerous uprisings created additional unrest. In 1697, the relatively autonomous Tarahumara attempted to revolt.

Another major revolt broke out in the region in 1740, this time lasting four years. The reign of the French Bourbons in Spain, established in 1701, also eroded the traditionally prominent role of the clergy.[61]

The ministry in northwestern Mexico also slowly exceeded the capacities of the Society of Jesus. In 1740, there were 112 missionaries for some three hundred mission villages, to which even more numerous, smaller stations were attached.[62] Even the Jesuits were forced to admit that many of their mission stations were in poor condition. And so, by order of Superior General Franz Retz, the Jesuits of Mexico decided to transfer part of their missions to the secular clergy to maintain. This was an unusual step because the Society of Jesus usually insisted on keeping its ministry to convert the heathen and guide new Christians in its own hands. But in light of the increasingly alienated and even hostile attitude of Spanish colonial society toward the missionaries, joining forces with the secular clergy seemed to be the only solution. Thus, twenty-two mission stations were finally transferred to the king for secularization in 1745. The dissolution of Jesuit institutions was underway. The process would continue over the following decades, culminating in the expulsion of the Jesuits in 1767.

THE PHILIPPINES

The Society of Jesus made yet another major leap from Mexico: in 1571, Spanish soldiers seized the fort of Manila from the Muslim ruler of the Philippines. Ten years later, at the request of King Philip II, the first four Jesuits set out for the Philippines from Mexico.[63] The leader of the first Jesuit expedition across the Pacific was Antonio Sedeño. He was a remarkable man: a member of the unsuccessful Florida mission, in 1572 he became one of the first Jesuits in Mexico. Now he became a pioneer for the third time in his life. Like Mexico, the Philippines became a highly successful field of operations. At first, the Jesuits often had the impression that their presence was superfluous: the Augustinians and Franciscans were already doing very good work, the conversion of the natives was in full swing, and the few Spanish colonists present were already being tended to. But, once on the ground, they soon found enough to do, and so they finally persuaded General Acquaviva to allow the mission to continue. The Jesuits of Manila got their wish: in 1595, a college was opened in the city to provide educational opportunities to the Spanish colonists and aspiring clergymen. The Philippines was elevated to a vice-province in the same year.

By then, the first attempts to convert the indigenous population had already been made, starting in 1590. These efforts would be redoubled in the following years, despite a shortage of personnel. As everywhere else, the balance between flying missions and permanent stations had to be negotiated, particularly since constantly wandering the countryside was not a real option in light of often difficult conditions on the ground. The Jesuits subsequently proselytized from semipermanent bases where they often set up schools for indigenous children. Some of these sites became real draws. The indigenous people of the Philippines often took great interest in Christianity, and the mission made rapid advances. In 1605, General Acquaviva elevated the vice-province to a full province. The Jesuits traveled ever more frequently to the Philippines, often accompanying Spanish expeditions. There were 43 Jesuits in the Philippines in 1597; by 1621, there were exactly 100 men. The personnel strength of the mission over the following decades usually hovered between 100 and 150 Jesuits. It was their job in 1755 to tend to 130 communities with 212,153 Christians. From the Philippines, the Jesuits launched a mission to the Mariana Islands in 1668, roughly fifteen hundred kilometers to the east in the middle of the Pacific. Although the history of this mission was mixed, it greatly impressed contemporaries in the eighteenth century and enjoyed a high profile in early modern media. Not least on account of massive resettlement measures, the islands were almost completely Christianized by about 1740, despite serious conflicts.

The Philippines lay at the intersection of various spheres of influence—in addition to Spain and Portugal, the Dutch also became a constant presence in the region in the seventeenth century. That put the Spanish colony and the Jesuit mission under pressure and sometimes in mortal danger. Chinese, Japanese, and Muslims were also part of the political and cultural mix. The Jesuits were profoundly affected by these conflicts and clashes. Philippine Jesuits were also constantly dispatched to China, India, and the Maluku Islands. Their aptitude for cross-cultural exchange often helped them immensely: Josef Wilhelm, for example, who was stationed at Zamboanga in the far south of the Philippines in the 1740s, became a close confidant of the neighboring sultan, Muhammad Alimuddin, although the latter was initially hostile. In order to discuss religious matters with him, this Jesuit from Lower Germany learned Arabic. A lively, friendly, and engaged exchange developed between Wilhelm and the Jesuits and the sultan and his retinue in this border region between Muslim and Christian spheres of influence.[64] It was hoped that the sultan might convert to Christianity. Wilhelm's engagement may not have helped in the short term—revolts broke out against the sultan and hopes of a rapid expansion of the Christian-Spanish sphere of influence were dashed—but the Philippines remained profoundly influenced by the Catholic faith that the Jesuits and other missionaries had introduced.

The French World

The European expansion spearheaded by Spain and Portugal inspired other Christian rulers to imitate it toward the end of the sixteenth century. The colonies of the Protestant Netherlands and England, with the exception of a small Catholic mission in the tolerant American colony of Maryland, represented obstacles and challenges to the Jesuits rather than opportunities.[65] But many new doors for the Jesuits opened when Catholic France joined the mission around 1600.

CANADA

The kings of France had long cast a greedy eye at the American continent north of Spain's possessions. The first successful French colonies were founded near the modern border of Canada and the United States in 1600, after the end of the religious wars in France.[66] The peninsula of Nova Scotia and the facing stretches of the mainland were the first to be colonized—the region became famous as Acadia. The development of the small, independent settlements on Nova Scotia was a constant up and down. Initial missionary efforts there were thus likewise inconsistent and sometimes erratic. Although the first two Jesuits—Énemond Massé and Pierre Biard—visited Acadia in 1611, the Society of Jesus did not establish a permanent presence there until 1632. The mission to the Abenaki people in modern New Brunswick and the American state of Maine was especially important in this relatively remote region.[67] This massive territory remained a kind of no-man's-land between the colonial powers of England and France in the seventeenth and early eighteenth centuries, although it came under rising pressure from English settlements to the south. In 1646, the Jesuits founded a mission at Norridgewock on the Kennebec River, some three hundred kilometers north of Boston. In total, only a handful of Jesuits were active there, but they served an important function, extending even to the realm of politics. Sébastien Rale (1657–1724) is the most prominent example.[68] Rale came to Canada in 1689 and learned the Abenaki language in the backwoods of Quebec. He later was active in Norridgewock. Missionaries like Rale were often the only informants governing officials had in this sensitive yet so remote region of Quebec.[69] Jesuits like Rale also ensured that the connection between the Abenaki and the French remained intact, despite the fact that the English were much closer. Their shared Catholic faith was an important bond that kept the natives in the French sphere of influence. When all else failed, Rale ensured that the Abenaki took up arms and fought for the French against the English, even after 1713, when the entire region had officially fallen to England. In Paris, the king was very pleased, because "Father Rale continue[d] to incite the savages [i.e., the Abenaki] not to permit the English to encroach on their lands."[70] From the English point of view, however, Rale was a troublemaker and agitator, and they pursued him as such. He was killed in his mission during an English attack in 1724.

Beginning in 1608, the colony on the St. Lawrence River began to develop into a permanent center of French and Jesuit influence in New France: it was then that Quebec was founded. The Jesuits became active in Quebec in 1625, when the Recollects, who had been there for some time, asked for their help. After a brief intermission from 1629 to 1632 when the English conquered the colony, the Jesuits founded the first college in New France in 1635. For the following three decades, the Society of Jesus enjoyed a monopoly on spiritual matters. That changed, however, in 1663, when Louis XIV made the transatlantic colonies directly subject to the crown. In the course of this change, a bishop also was installed, and the secular clergy began to be built up. Now other orders and religious societies like the Sulpicians and the missionaries of the Propaganda Fide were invited to Canada. This development was connected to a decline in the Jesuits' influence in the colony's core territories, although they at least remained the dominant force in the mission to the indigenous population.

The French Jesuits had daily contact with natives almost everywhere in Canada, but some regional hubs clearly emerged. At Tadoussac, an eastern French outpost where the Saguenay empties into the St. Lawrence, the Jesuits established an annual wandering mission to the Montagnais in 1641. Adapting to the Montagnais' nomadic lifestyle, they concentrated predominantly on the summer months, when the natives could normally be found in the area to trade furs and were easier to reach. Jean de Quen (ca. 1603–59) was the most important founder of this mission. On his missionary trips in 1647, he also became the first European to learn of Lac St. Jean, two hundred kilometers northwest of Tadoussac. In the following years, he and his confreres expanded their summer missionary work to the vicinity of the lake, establishing direct contact between the Europeans and indigenous tribes living farther to the north.[71] Some very special Jesuits were stationed at Tadoussac: Gabriel Druillettes (1610–81) and Charles Albanel (1616?–96), for example, spent many winters among the natives. It was Albanel, too, who first traveled by land from Tadoussac to Hudson Bay in 1671/2.[72]

As impressive as the Jesuits' accomplishments in eastern New France and along the St. Lawrence were, the primary orientation of the Society and the entire colony lay westward. The highest hopes after the return of the French in 1632 were placed in the mission to the Huron on the southern end of the Great Lake that bears their name. Building on earlier contacts from the 1620s, the Jesuits under the leadership of Jean de Brébeuf (1593–1649) began to construct a permanent mission in

1634. Brébeuf and his companions fired up the expectations of the pious French with many impressive reports from this region. They remained there for fifteen years before the mission was wiped out in multiple attacks by the hostile Iroquois in 1649/50. Four Jesuits were tortured to death, and the conquerors displaced, killed, or absorbed the Huron.

The fall of Huronia was a heavy blow, but it was by no means the end of the Jesuits' conversion efforts, even if they never again succeeded in constructing such a compact, geographically self-contained, and intensive mission in New France. In the immediate aftermath of the bloody events, the Jesuits turned in a stunning direction at first glance: as relations began to improve after 1653, and especially after 1667, the Jesuits sent missionaries to each of the five Iroquois tribes.[73] They even acquired a certain influence over the Iroquois in the latter half of the 1670s.[74] Around 1665, however, the colony in general and the Jesuits in particular turned their attention even farther west.[75] At first, the Great Lakes became the center of their interest. The Jesuits' most important footholds there were Michillimackinac (1671) and Sault Sainte Marie (1668) at the convergence of Lake Superior, Lake Michigan, and Lake Huron, and Baie Verte on the western bank of Lake Michigan. In 1701, when Detroit was founded and the colonization of Louisiana intensified, the focus of their ministry shifted south to the Ohio and later to the Mississippi River valley. Now the territory of the Illinois around southern Lake Michigan and, somewhat later, a series of small villages along the great river became their chief field of operations. Kaskaskia, just over 120 kilometers south of St. Louis, became a hub, since it was located near the most important fortified French stronghold, Fort de Chartres. The area around Kaskaskia became the most important supply base for Louisiana, and the Jesuits were among its greatest agricultural entrepreneurs. Dozens of slaves worked their fields. In 1718, there were supposedly three mills to grind winter wheat under Jesuit supervision.[76]

Despite the emergence of such centers, the French and Jesuit presence in this vast territory was very thin. In demographic terms, Canada was a weak colony. Even as late as 1760, there were only approximately sixty-seven thousand inhabitants in the population centers along the St. Lawrence.[77] Farther west, in the so-called Pays d'en Haut (Up-Country) on the Great Lakes and in the Ohio and Mississippi valleys, the European presence consisted merely of a network of tiny outposts in the vastness of the prairie. This network was stable, however, and enabled the French to exert a significant influence. They cleverly constructed a complex web of alliances with native peoples around these outposts, where military, political, economic, and missionary interests converged. The alliance system was based precisely on this combination. Viewed as a whole, the Catholic faith usually played a subordinate role, which emerges very clearly in contrast to the heavily Christianized territories along the St. Lawrence. Missionary fervor had generally flagged in France under Louis XIV. Nonetheless, despite the Jesuits' relatively precarious position, the natives perceived them as a relatively reliable arm of the French colonial empire, and they enjoyed great influence on account of their marked willingness to adapt to native culture.

On account of its demographic weakness and geographic overextension, North America's place in the French colonial empire was ambivalent. The benefit of the colony was primarily of a strategic nature. It was a counterweight to the much more successful English settlements. New France, however, remained unproductive. Even the Jesuits' mission successes were modest in quantitative terms. In Huronia, there may have been between one and two thousand baptized Christians, and the numbers were fairly small elsewhere.[78] In the decade after 1668, there were perhaps eighteen hundred serious neophytes among the Iroquois—a fifth of the tribes.[79] Père Marquette allegedly claimed five hundred chiefs and fifteen hundred young men on the southern shore of Lake Michigan in 1675.[80] There were only a few hundred Christians, men and women, in the Christian villages along the St. Lawrence. Nowhere did whole tribes convert. Regardless of the bare numbers, however, French North America was a space of missionary visions for the Society of Jesus. High-flying plans and fervent dreams came alive in the wilderness of this unexplored continent. At least as a canvas for grandiose ideas, then, Canada was extremely important to the Jesuits. That was also partly why the ministry in Canada was publicized so loudly.

THE FRENCH CARIBBEAN

Farther south, in the French Caribbean, the situation was, in a sense, the exact opposite. The Caribbean had been the economic center of the French colonial empire since the late seventeenth century, but for the Jesuits it remained difficult terrain with limited appeal.[81] The first members of the Society of Jesus arrived in 1640. The island of Martinique had originally been intended for them, while the other French islands were ministered by other orders. But their presence was soon also requested on Guadeloupe and St. Christopher (St. Kitts). In the 1650s, the Society then began to expand in grand style. It established itself on most of the French islands, which the Jesuit Jean de la Mousse described as very beautiful and picturesque on his journey through them in 1688.[82] The heart of their pastoral ministry consisted of tending to the European settlers and the rapidly growing population of African slaves on the sugarcane plantations. In isolated cases, French members of the Society of Jesus also guided English and Dutch Catholics on neighboring islands.[83] On an international scale, the number of Jesuits in the islands remained small, and so they constantly struggled to provide sufficient spiritual services.

The mission to the indigenous population of the French Caribbean played a secondary role. The Jesuits attempted to convert the Caribs on St. Vincent from 1653 to 1701, as long as the island remained a French possession.[84] The first two missionaries were killed by the Caribs in 1654, when they went to war with the colonists. Although two Jesuits returned as the only Europeans in 1660, success remained elusive, and the Jesuits lost their enthusiasm. The mainland territory of Guayana, on the edge of the Caribbean to the south, soon appeared more attractive. The Society had stationed individual missionaries there since the 1650s but did not establish a permanent mission in Cayenne until 1667—initially housing no more than two to four Jesuits.[85] The Society subsequently was called on repeatedly to expand its religious ministry to the French and "heathen" in these remote tropical places.[86] In 1709, the fathers finally built some mission stations in the hinterland of Cayenne. Despite this modest progress, however, observers on the ground stressed that "the success in no way corresponds to the effort."[87] Even in the early eighteenth century, the mission superiors in the French Caribbean still were talking mostly about projects inspired by Paraguay and Brazil that they wanted to start at some indefinite point in the future.[88] In sum, the mission of the French Jesuits in Guayana—like the colony as a whole—amounted to no more than a relatively humble success.

ASIA

The situation of the French Jesuits in Asia was more complicated than that in the Americas. Iberian supremacy initially made it seem impossible to establish a mission of their own. In the late seventeenth century, however, Jesuits from France managed to contribute to the spread of Christianity in Southeast Asia, India, and China after all. Between 1685 and 1700, Louis XIV sent several delegations to the Kingdom of Siam (roughly equivalent to modern Thailand) to establish new trading contacts in support of incipient French expansion. On board for all of them was the adventure-loving Jesuit Guy Tachard (1648–1712).[89] Over time, Tachard became a driving force behind French policy in Siam. In 1689, he received permission from the pope to found a Jesuit mission. Individual Portuguese Jesuits had already been present from 1625 to 1632, but without success.[90] Tachard hoped for more. Since conditions in Siam, however, soon turned against the Europeans, his efforts ultimately came to naught. To some extent as an emergency measure, Tachard repeatedly withdrew to Pondicherry on the east coast of India for short spells in the 1690s and then permanently in 1701. France had maintained an important trading station there since 1673. Making the most of their predicament, Tachard and some of his compatriots launched the French mission to India from there. In the eighteenth century, this mission stretched from Pondicherry into the interior to the northwest (Karnataka).[91] A total of forty French fathers were active there over the century, albeit rarely more than six at a time. The French normally drew inspiration from the method pioneered by Roberto de Nobili somewhat farther south in Madurai, if often in a pared-down form.[92]

Five other Jesuits had accompanied Tachard on his first expedition to Siam in 1685. These included Joachim Bouvet (1656–1730), Jean-François Gerbillon (1654–1707), and Claude de Visdelou (1656–1737). As instructed, they traveled on to China and founded a French mission in Beijing in 1688.[93] On the one hand, the mission was intended as an explicit political statement by Louis XIV to the Iberian powers and the pope, whose exclusive power over the mission the king wanted to break. On the other hand, however, these men were expected in China first and foremost as scientists. They had been made corresponding members of the Académie des sciences prior to their departure. They traveled directly to the imperial court without making the usual detour via Macao and dispensed with the other conventional Portuguese channels of communication. Shortly thereafter, the Kangxi Emperor requested further contingents of French Jesuits. This growing number of Frenchmen at court soon clashed with their confreres under Portuguese command in Beijing, and a bitter feud broke out. The dispute was superficially pacified in 1705 when General Tirso González formally split off the French from the rest of the Jesuit mission. The French Jesuits now went so far as to build their own church. But these squabbles permanently damaged the missionaries' status in Beijing, as we have seen.

THE NEAR EAST

Finally, we can identify one last mission focus of the French Jesuits: the Near East and the Levant.[94] The Eastern Mediterranean and its hinterland had special significance to Christians generally, since they were home to many sites that were connected more or less directly with scripture and the early history of their religion. The region also had a continuous Christian tradition, as Eastern Christian groups of all kinds had lived there for centuries. Another special feature was the fact that Muslim rulers controlled these places so deeply rooted in Christian history.[95] The sixteenth and seventeenth centuries witnessed many political changes in the Levant: Venetian hegemony crumbled; the Ottoman Empire expanded.[96] The papacy also attempted to extend its influence in this melting pot of religions, for example, by establishing a tribunal of the Inquisition on Malta. The Jesuits' initial projects to establish themselves on Cyprus, in Constantinople (modern Istanbul), and Jerusalem in 1553 may have failed, but teaching and printing in Arabic played a part in the Society of Jesus from the start.[97] Ignatius's men regularly served the popes as ecclesiastical legates to the region: in 1561, Pius IV sent the Jesuit Giambattista Eliano to the Coptic patriarch in Cairo; in 1578 and 1580, Gregory XIII sent Eliano to the Christian Maronites in Lebanon, who were still nominally under the pope's authority. The Jesuit's trip was intended to rebuild these ties: the dream of annexing the Orthodox Church to Rome lived on. Further Jesuit delegations to Damascus, Cairo, and Jerusalem followed for that reason. Usually they discussed the relationship of Eastern Christians to the Roman church. In 1583, Giulio Mancinelli, S.J. (1537–1618), also went to Constantinople for two years at the pope's behest to establish a mission that the Christians of Galata had petitioned for.[98]

French Jesuits were increasingly active in this region, as the Eastern Mediterranean came to the center of attention in Paris in the 1620s and 1630s.[99] The first French Jesuits took up residence in Constantinople in 1609.[100] François de Canillac, the superior at this mission, viewed the entire Levant, from Constantinople to Syria and the Holy Land all the way to Egypt, as a single missionary territory. De Canillac was one of those Jesuits who shaped the Society's missions with grand visions rather than indefatigable work on the ground. De Canillac constantly devised new plans for journeys and new missions. More than one of his collaborators complained about this visionary inconsistency. But de Canillac's transregional perspective nonetheless soon became reality. The Jesuits established numerous missions in the area until well into the eighteenth century: at Izmir in 1623, Aleppo in 1625, on several Greek islands beginning in 1627, and in Damascus and three other sites in Lebanon in 1644. They repeatedly tried, albeit never successfully, to found a mission on Mount Athos in Greece. A mission to Egypt, however, was successfully opened in 1696. Of course, only a handful of Jesuits lived at most of these missions. There were forty-nine members of the order active in the region in 1717.[101]

The complex religious situation of this corner of the world forced the Society to proceed with discretion. As Nicolas de Poiresson wrote from Syria in 1659, "Since they perform their functions among the Turks, Jews, heretics, and schismatics, Christian prudence obliges them to speak little and write less so as to protect themselves from surprises and violence."[102] Often only those who ministered to European merchants and diplomats were initially permitted to settle. The Jesuits and other missionaries then gradually expanded their ministry to indigenous Christians. For example, in the early eighteenth century, the Jesuits regularly traveled across Galilee to visit and instruct the Eastern Christians living there.[103] It was obvious that these missions were intended exclusively for non–Roman Catholic Christians, not Muslims.[104] Isolated calls to convert the Muslims went considerably wide of reality.[105] The Muslim rulers seemed indifferent to this inter-Christian ministry, as long as their own interests remained untouched. There thus was also no lack of contact between the missionaries and Muslims and even Islamic scholars.

Historical geography and the religious history of the Near East were especially interesting to the Jesuits—these were the lands of the Bible, as well as of classical antiquity. Jesuits like the great Orientalist Claude Sicard (1677–1726) traveled through the region in search of ruins, manuscripts, and other monuments with which they could reconstruct the development of Judaism and Christianity, and it goes without saying that biblical sites had major spiritual significance to them. Hence the missionaries to the Holy Land, Syria, and Egypt were inspired by a combination of spiritual seeking, religious antiquarianism, and genuine interest in the Christian churches of the East.[106] Then there were the political interests of the king of France, which the Jesuits were supposed to serve: Sicard was in Egypt on a royal expedition. This alliance between king and missionary remained intact until well into the eighteenth century.

On the periphery of French missionary efforts in the Levant lay Persia. No fewer than five different religious orders were attempting to Christianize it in the seventeenth century. Both European and Persian hopes of closer cooperation against the Ottoman Empire constituted the political background to this relationship.[107] By the sixteenth century, Portuguese Jesuits had lived for years in Hurmuz on the Persian Gulf. But the Society of Jesus did not gain a foothold in the shah's kingdom until 1646, when French Jesuits in Syria launched a new push. François Rigordi (1609–79), coming from Tripoli/Lebanon, was the first Jesuit to reach Isfahan, where the Augustinians and Carmelites had been active for some time. He was succeeded by the aforementioned Alexandre de Rhodes, who died in Persia in 1660. The Jesuits soon established themselves in several other cities, including Shiraz and Trabis. Despite various conflicts, they successfully founded missions in Yerevan and other parts of Armenia around 1700. The majority of Jesuits involved were French, but they were energetically supported in Armenia by Polish Jesuits and protected by the Polish king.

The Jesuits in Colonial Society

Cooperation and Conflict with the Colonists

At least in the Iberian context, European expansion and Christianization had been intimately connected since 1493. In a variety of documents, the popes granted the kings of Spain and Portugal extensive privileges to claim foreign regions provided that they endeavored to support the Christianization of the "heathen" population in terms of logistics and supplies. This "patronage" (*patronado/patroado*) shaped the reality of Jesuit ministry overseas and had a series of profound consequences. For one, the kings put their transportation infrastructure at the church's disposal. This was a major relief because no arm of the Catholic Church—let alone its religious orders—normally had its own ships to make the long journey.[108] Under the mantle of its patronage, the crown also was responsible for supporting the missionaries economically and obligated to protect them. For all these reasons, close coordination between the Jesuits' missionary activity and royal projects was necessary. The Jesuits soon founded an institution in Seville dedicated specifically to coordinating cooperation between missionaries and the royal colonial bureaucracy, the Oficio de Indias. It was here that

passports were obtained, travel documents requested, waiting missionaries housed, and much more.[109]

This dependence on the machinery of the secular colonial administration also had many disadvantages. The Jesuits had to come to grips
with bureaucratic and political requirements and, often enough, had no
choice but to bow to them. At first, the Jesuits were flatly denied the
right to work in some areas. The Society of Jesus was excluded from the
Spanish colonial empire, for instance, until 1565. The Spanish crown
furthermore insisted, despite a serious personnel shortage, that almost
exclusively Spanish Jesuits go to the colonies, although the Society repeatedly pleaded to be allowed to employ the many German, Swiss, and
Bohemian members it had available.[110] Christianization also was by no
means always the kings' highest priority. The Iberian states definitely
helped finance the missions, but their contributions often fell far short
of their promises. The Jesuits also constantly complained about the
practical realities of transport. The fleets seldom accommodated the
Jesuits' needs; it was usually the latter who had to adjust as was expedi-
ent to the royal shipmasters. Many a Jesuit waited a long time in Seville
or Lisbon for an opportunity to set sail, while others had to set out at
breakneck speed to reach their ships before they left. The alternatives
were limited and usually unattractive—and therefore seldom used.
General Goswin Nickel, for example, sent the missionaries Johann
Grueber and Albert d'Orville to Tibet by land to avoid Portuguese
ships—a spectacular but, over the long term, impractical solution.[111]
When Portugal's logistical capacity declined in the latter half of the seventeenth century, and shipping connections to East Asia became too
infrequent, some Jesuits found themselves forced to resort to Protestant
ships from England or the Netherlands—an infrastructural advantage
purchased at the price of silence about religion on board.[112]

In the New World, relations between Jesuit missionaries and colonists ranged from genuine collaboration to pragmatic complicity, to
suspicious mistrust and open conflict. The Jesuits knew and boldly declared that they were often the first to advance the interests of European
monarchs. Juan María de Salvatierra, for example, boasted in 1701 that the
Jesuits could have integrated Baja California into the Spanish Empire

by themselves—and at a price that could only have delighted the king.[113] And not only the Jesuits but also military leaders and officials knew very well that the network of mission stations was of the utmost importance for colonizing the territory and that the missionaries were indispensable for dealing with the native population. Far from the cities and settlement centers, Jesuit missionaries were, often enough, if not the only representatives of colonial power, then by far the most reliable. The missionaries were undoubtedly the vanguard and protagonists of Catholic colonial expansion. Keeping public order depended critically on the Jesuits' presence in the early years of many colonies.

Members of the Society of Jesus were often the only or at least the best educated clergymen available at the beginning of many colonial enterprises. Canada may serve as a good example. Until 1663, the Jesuits were the only representatives of the Catholic Church there, and even after the arrival of the first bishop, there often were no other clergymen in the remote territories. Similarly, in 1732, the Jesuits pledged to take over the parishes for the settlers of Cayenne/Guyana.[114] Even in Paraguay, which had a bishop and parish clergy before the Jesuits' arrival, there were more members of religious orders living there in 1610 (thirteen Jesuits, four Franciscans, and two Mercedarians) than secular clergy (eleven), and the latter were uneducated.[115] In Brazil, the institutions of the secular clergy were likewise too weak to cover the massive territory. Here, too, the Jesuits and other orders served as long-term surrogates.[116] In the Canadian wilderness, just as on the remote islands of the Indian Ocean, in the cities of China, and in the outlying settlements of South America, any European (or converted non-European) who wanted to make confession, celebrate a Catholic marriage, or receive any other sacrament probably had to rely on the services of a missionary.[117] In some places, such as the French Caribbean, this situation was permanent because a diocesan and parish structure with secular clergy was never installed here—Jesuit missionaries simply assumed the duties of ordinary priests.

In the long run, working with the European settlers and Creole colonists consumed ever more of the Jesuits' energy. Serving as a missionary in remote regions and on semi-isolated reductions, in contrast, gradually became a specialized job within the order. In Paraguay circa 1650, three-quarters of all Jesuits were working in the (small) colonial cities. Only one-quarter was still occupied on the missions. Things were similar in the Brazilian territory of Bahía around 1600: four-fifths of all Jesuits worked predominantly with the settlers.[118] The more the colonists tried to adapt life in the new cities to European standards, the more the Jesuits did likewise. The preference of the Society of Jesus for cities and city life also prevailed overseas. Soon there were universities and schools in the colonial cities to direct and supply, just as there were in Europe: even overseas the Society of Jesus worked primarily as an educational institution. Scientific research was conducted, books were written and printed, and theological questions were discussed.[119] There were false doctrines to combat not only in Europe but also in the overseas colonies. And there were public feasts to celebrate with due solemnity. In Manila in the Philippines, the students of the Jesuit College of San Ignacio played "a thousand instruments" in 1619 at the feast of the Immaculate Conception and performed a Mexican dance to mark the occasion.[120] And of course Jesuits like Paul Klein, who arrived in Mexico City in 1682, also performed the "usual services"—preaching, hearing confession, visiting the sick, ministering to prisoners.[121] Jesuits like him also naturally met non-Europeans and indigenous non-Christians in the colonial cities. Sometimes the Jesuits stationed in the cities made flying missions to the outlying native villages. Urban Jesuits in the colonies were therefore definitely also "missionaries," but usually only on a part-time basis, and they often regarded missionary work more as a burdensome task than as a fulfilling activity.[122] The more European the cities became, the more the Society poured its energies into ministering to the urban colonists.

And yet, as much as the colonists strove to emulate European conditions, the Jesuits had to live with the fact that conditions in the new colonial societies were often far more unstable and open in comparison. José de Acosta, one of the sharpest and most perceptive observers of South America, described this situation vividly:

In the government of the Indies, particularly because our people are entering and living in new kingdoms, everything is different.

Everything is new; there are no fixed conventions, no established laws and statutes, excepting natural law. Authority and the examples of the earlier times are either nonexistent or unworthy of imitation. The outcome of every day is unpredictable; sudden and generally dangerous change, common. Municipal law sometimes unknown, sometimes not definite enough to judge. Spanish and Roman laws largely conflict with the long-standing customs of the barbarians. The state of the Republic itself is highly volatile, changing, and unlike itself, so that what is regarded most convenient and just today is in changed circumstances most unjust and pernicious.[123]

In this passage, Acosta describes the loss of control that inevitably accompanied the transplantation of Europe overseas. The unease that the Jesuits felt in such circumstances is impossible to miss.

Within a certain framework, the Jesuits' reaction to these structural difficulties and challenges was highly flexible. They recognized that some rules had to be interpreted liberally for the good of the colony and the colonists. European regulations on marital and sexual life, for example, had to be adapted in light of the initially very low number of European women. In Paraguay, socially discriminating Europeans contracted many endogamous marriages in the early decades of the colony. Such marriages between comparatively close relatives regularly required papal dispensation.[124] In the Caribbean, widows also usually observed only a very brief period of mourning after their husbands' death before remarrying; this was likewise an adaptation of European practices to colonial realities that the Jesuits tolerated.[125] Another solution for the unusual situation of a gender gap was to permit Europeans to marry unbaptized native women. It was unusual per se, but the Jesuits explicitly supported such alternatives in Canada and the Caribbean.[126] Within certain limitations, the Jesuits could and would bend the rules to put as few obstacles as possible in the colonists' way.

The interests of the Jesuits and the colonists thus overlapped considerably, albeit not completely. The mission and expansion were tightly intertwined, both in a secular and in a spiritual respect, but they were by no means identical. Cracks in this collaborative relationship could quickly appear when differences of goals and ideals came to light. Conflict might erupt at any moment over any detail of daily life. How should members of the order proceed then? This was a common question that the Jesuit superiors constantly had to decide. Sometimes they grudgingly observed restraint for tactical reasons, hiding the conflict between the goals of the mission and the colony. In 1633, the Society in Paraguay resolved "always to keep the peace with the bishop, even if it is necessary to overlook what we deem to be unreasonable . . . and so much patience and humility are necessary, and to put up with things there and not pick a fight over each one."[127] Episodes like this show how deep discontent often simmered beneath the surface. The tense and even extreme conditions in the colonies, where, for better or worse, each side depended on the other, made often difficult compromises necessary.

Sometimes, however, one of the sides let rip: the bishop of Asunción in Paraguay burned down the Jesuit college in 1649. The Jesuits' restraint evidently came to naught.[128] In the Northern Hemisphere, in Quebec, royal officials were unhappy with the Society of Jesus. Governor Augustin de Saffray de Mézy, who fought many battles with the clergymen, railed against them in 1664: "The religion of the savages is imaginary; they are Christians only for political reasons and the favors done them, and otherwise they all remain in their error [i.e., non-Christian beliefs] as before." In other words, the Jesuits' ministry had accomplished nothing, and the colony should emancipate itself from their dominance.[129]

While the gravity of the conflict with the powerful bishop in South America was unique and can be traced not least back to his personal distaste for the Jesuits, structural reasons were behind the problems on the St. Lawrence. Louis XIV and his leading minister, Jean-Baptiste Colbert, were trying to tighten the reins of the royal government. They wanted to bring the chaotic, freewheeling pioneer phase to an end and to integrate the colony more firmly in the French administration. Ever more royal officials and, for the first time, regular soldiers were dispatched there in the years after 1663. The Jesuits, who had represented not only their religion but also France itself in the early years by virtue of their fairly effective presence on the ground would now have to prove they could be part of a team and "reform their behavior," as one of these new royal delegates put it.[130] The state-driven consolidation of the colonies and the conversion of the heathen were potentially countervailing goals; if pressed, the Jesuits and royal officials made no effort to conceal that fact.

The Jesuits continued to invoke the traditional alliance between the crown and the missionaries even in changing times. Guy Tachard explained in 1688:

> I will count myself all too happy if with even greater labors and pains I can help put the French on a firm foundation in the Indies and contribute to the commercial advantages of the [French] East India Company, on which the establishment of the Christian religion absolutely depends. I am so convinced of this that I take great credit for working toward these two goals in some way, having no doubt that the Indies will soon be able to become entirely Christian when they become French.[131]

But Tachard's lifetime was a time of change. Twenty years later, in Pondicherry, he himself was harshly attacked by the local governor Guillaume André Hébert on the grounds that the broad independence of the mission Tachard oversaw would impede the exercise of royal authority.[132] By the eighteenth century, such small cracks in this once solid alliance became undeniable breaks with accelerating regularity. As the number of colonists rose in many places, their interests inevitably were represented more vocally. The Jesuits and colonists soon found themselves embroiled in the "gravest strife" with one another. The settlers' opposition to the Jesuits grew; they were increasingly viewed as holding the colony back.[133] In some regions, such as the missions to Mexico in the 1740s, the Jesuits themselves reported open mistrust and a complete breakdown of relations:

> It is a pack of passionate, biased, deceitful swindlers, whose only aim is to disgrace the religion, to turn one another against the mission and to discredit them, even publicly. And everyone has assured me that legal papers were found in the archive of the Sonora mayor's office that documented major errors by our men; which, if Don Gabriel

Pudrom had not delivered them when he was mayor, they would have waged a great war without granting any escape or pardon. But, if what they say is not true, then there is a lot of quickness to judge, to assume second intentions. There is little love, much murmuring, readiness to believe, and their assumptions out of envy.[134]

Don Manuel Bernal de Huidobro was the royal governor of northwestern Mexico. On behalf of the Spanish crown, he attempted to do what Louis XIV had tried decades earlier on the St. Lawrence: to integrate the colony more firmly in the royal administration and to exploit it more efficiently for the benefit of the state. In contrast to the days of Louis XIV, now, two generations later, people also felt much greater and much more fundamental reservations about the Jesuits. The missions and missionaries were already generally viewed with greater skepticism. Huidobro frequently allowed conflicts to escalate that revolved, in one way or another, around the question of how much importance should (still) be attached to the Jesuit missionaries and the Christianization of the heathen in the broad profile of European colonial interests. He is one example of how the alliance between the Society and royal officials could and did change into open opposition. The loss of significance and prestige that the Jesuits had suffered in Europe and overseas was impossible to ignore.

The Jesuits and Slavery

One of the most striking features of the nascent colonial societies that no one had foreseen, especially in the Americas, was the plantation economy and, intimately connected to it, African slavery. Of course, there had been fairly large numbers of slaves from foreign lands in southern Europe and the Mediterranean before 1492. Their existence was by no means unknown to the Jesuits when they were confronted with the practice again in the New World, but the vast scale of slavery in the colonies and the systematic nature of the slave trade were unique. Ever since cultivating sugarcane had proved to be a highly profitable industry, the Jesuits were confronted with the subject of slavery more and more. In light of the close ties the Jesuits maintained with European settlers overseas, whether born in Europe or abroad, it was inevitable that they themselves became thoroughly entangled in questions of slavery.[135]

Many Jesuits had strong misgivings about African slavery. Alonso de Sandoval (1576–1652), who spent his entire life with slaves in Cartagena, once wrote, "For a long time I was at a loss as to whether I should pass over slavery in silence."[136] It is typical, though, that he ultimately declared in favor of slavery, albeit without much enthusiasm. In doing so, he epitomized the attitude of the Society as a whole: Jesuit criticism of slavery is occasionally heard, but it is usually directed toward its practical consequences.[137] Instead of rejecting slavery outright, the Jesuits resorted to making the prevailing conditions tolerable in religious terms. In light of the traditional conviction "that we must take care of the well-being of their [i.e., slaves'] souls more than that of their bodies," ultimately derived from the apostle Paul, the Jesuits were not blind to the misery of the slaves, but they considered it nonetheless to be of secondary importance.[138] From Paul, a positive religious concept of the believer as the "slave of God" had been construed; the social reality of slaves here on earth tended to disappear behind this spiritual emphasis.[139] Even slaves were "half-free," António Vieira once wrote, because their captivity pertained only to the body, never to the soul. Elsewhere, the same Jesuit even described life in slavery as the most sublime imitation of Christ.[140] This legitimating and, at any rate, tolerant attitude has very aptly been called the "theology of resignation."[141]

In acting on the Pauline belief that one could reach the free soul—the only important freedom—even of persons in physical bondage, the followers of Ignatius launched a broad campaign to minister to the African slaves. Their effort went far beyond comparable initiatives of other clergymen, at least in the Spanish and French territories in the Americas.[142] It ultimately amounted to "helping souls," as one contemporary in the early seventeenth century argued: "The Society of Jesus, then, seeing the thousands of blacks that disembarked every year in Cartagena and the spiritual duress in which they came, took it upon itself to minister to them by all means at its disposal, looking after their salvation with as much care as possible, and for that reason dispatched some clerics [*Religiosos*] who would go to teach, convert, and baptize them."[143] Alonso de Sandoval, whose family emigrated to South America from Seville in his childhood, was one of these Jesuits. In Cartagena de las Indias, he ministered to the slaves who made landfall there after crossing the Atlantic. He reportedly baptized more than three thousand of them in seven years.[144] Sandoval soon received support from another Spanish Jesuit, Pedro Claver (1580–1654). Claver's influence would far surpass Sandoval's own, and he was elevated to sainthood in 1888.[145] Many other personalities from the order who dedicated themselves to this task could be mentioned, such as Diego de Torres Bollo, Gabriel Perlín, Francisco de Castillo, Alonso Messía, and Jean de la Mousse from Peru and the French Caribbean.[146] Again, we see at work the Jesuit practice of specialized ministry, whereby particular members preoccupied themselves primarily with specific tasks and groups.

For missionaries to the slaves like Claver, the arrival of new ships was no reason to grumble about one's own culture, but rather an opportunity to practice Christian charity:

> There was no news that delighted the good Father more than when he received word that a ship of negros had arrived or was near the port. Because on receiving the news, he set out with an assistant bearing gifts [*regalos*] and some interpreters—since he did not know the language—boarded the ship, and bade welcome to the miserable slaves [*esclavos miserables*]. He presented himself to them in a very friendly manner, with all possible affability, distributed the gifts he brought, embraced them one by one as if they were his brothers, freeing them of the fear with which they had come.

This description gives a realistic assessment of the situation: Claver obviously registered the newcomers' fear. This was an important point of departure for his method: in the brutal everyday world of the slaves, he attempted to present himself and his companions as their "friend" or "brother." He signed his profession with the telling formula "Petrus Claver, ever a friend of the Africans."[147] His conduct was keyed to distinguish himself conspicuously from the slave traders. The slaves were given to understand that the goodwill and devotion of the Jesuits were lasting and reliable.[148] To that end, Sandoval and Claver in particular alleviated the slaves' physical suffering. Contemporary hagiographic sources report many small good deeds that Claver did for them.[149] The Jesuit regularly brought medicine to the sick or summoned doctors when the state of the newcomers' health necessitated it.[150] Sandoval and his helpers also provided the slaves with food and water.[151] In this way, they could impart simple Christian teachings. As proof of his success, Claver led several public processions and held religious gatherings with Christianized slaves in the central square of Cartagena.[152] Soon the Roman Curia of the Society issued its own instructions for this "ministerio de los negros," initiated by Vitelleschi in 1621.[153]

As with all their other ministries, the Jesuits aspired both to impart fundamental Christian teachings and to Christianize the slaves' everyday way of life. The ministry to the slaves, however, faced several specific problems in addition to the slaves' material destitution and mental anguish. Slave traders were often uncooperative. The Jesuits repeatedly complained that the colonists showed no or too little interest in the salvation of the slaves. In the ports, where the slaves arrived only to be quickly sold on, the Jesuits' proselytizing was a constant race against time anyway.[154] The slaves' final destinations were often remote haciendas or plantations, where the Jesuits often could minister to them only sporadically; thus, they made visits of several days, following a packed Christianizing educational agenda.[155] Jean de la Mousse, for example, repeatedly wrote in his diary how he ministered to "both the healthy and the sick, both Frenchmen and Black and Indian slaves" without distinction on every occasion, eagerly seeking them out even in the most remote settlements.[156]

In some places, more permanent structures to minister to the slaves were built. At many sites in Colombia, Mexico, and Peru, as well as on the islands of the French Caribbean, special communities for African slaves were established.[157] Father Louis Charpentier was presumably the first French Jesuit since 1699 to oversee such a black community as curé des nègres on the little island of St. Christopher (St. Kitts). In many cases, the missionaries intervened on behalf of not only the slaves' salvation but also their everyday situation. Franz-Xaver Eder, for example, wanted to improve the captives' living conditions: "In my sermons, I have personally reproached many of them [sc. the Portuguese], with due severity, for these excesses of tyrannical power, in the hope of showing them that it is inhuman and unworthy of a Christian to use such unprecedented violence against another Christian."[158]

The ambiguity of the Jesuits' position on slavery was exacerbated by the fact that the Society itself owned numerous slaves. Some Jesuits in the New World struggled with the idea of a slave-owning Society of Jesus. One Jesuit from Mexico wrote in 1582, "I don't know how appropriate it is to the piety of the Society of Jesus to bring slaves loaded in irons like the laity."[159] Miguel García from Brazil agreed the following year: "The multitude of slaves that the Society of Jesus possesses in this province and particularly in this college [Bahía] is something that I cannot condone in any way, because I do not know whether their possession is lawful." García even wanted to deny his confreres absolution because they kept slaves.[160] The Society's leadership in Rome was likewise skeptical in the sixteenth century. Francisco de Borja, general from 1565 to 1572, even wrote once, "I decided a few days ago that it is not appropriate for the Society to exploit the work of slaves."[161] But in the end all this resistance came to naught. By 1600, the argument of economic exigency had triumphed over the Jesuits' scruples: "Because there are no Spaniards [in Peru] who work on them [sc. Jesuit haciendas] as in Spain, and no Indians or only very few, we are forced to buy blacks."[162] By the late seventeenth century, under General Tirso González, the Jesuit leadership was convinced of the pragmatic reasons: "The survival of the Hacienda depends on them [sc. the slaves]."[163] And so, despite all its doubts, discussions, and pangs of conscience, the Society became a major slave owner in the Americas. In 1767, the Society of Jesus reputedly owned a total of 5,095 slaves in the Viceroyalty of Peru; groups of 200 to 400 slaves per hacienda were not a rarity.[164] The Jesuits received 300 slaves a year in Angola as tribute according to local custom. At the same time, hundreds of slaves also worked for the Society in Guayana. There were at least 1,400 slaves in the five missions on the Zambezi in Africa, and regularly 1,000 to 2,000 in eighteenth-century Brazil. The Colegio Máximo in Mexico City bought and sold about 500 people in the seventeenth century. The Society also owned African and occasionally Malay or Indian slaves in Japan, India, and China and even in the motherland Portugal—often hundreds or thousands of them.[165]

Some slaves came into the Jesuits' hands as gifts, for example, when pious colonists donated their estates to the Society, complete with all their furnishings (human included).[166] Other slaves, in contrast, were systematically bought on a grand scale where they were cheap and then transported to their final destination—for example, from Panama to Peru. Some Jesuits in Central America even hit upon the idea of outfitting their own expeditions to Africa to buy slaves. The superiors rejected the plan, but on the grounds of the economic risk and the spiritual threat of reaping profits rather than any ethical reservations about involvement in the slave trade.[167] The Jesuit province of Brazil met its need for slave labor with an almost exclusive trade with nearby Angola. It was so effective that contemporaries soon thought the Society would "engage in slave-trading under the pretext of conversion."[168] Later, slaves were obtained in the Americas primarily through breeding and less from new imports.

How the Jesuits in Mexico and Guayana and along the Zambezi treated their slaves remains an important question, not least for reasons of self-representation. It has repeatedly been claimed that the Jesuits were kinder to their slaves than secular owners. But slavery was brutal even in the Society of Jesus. Among some Jesuit slave owners, the "rigor with which they punish the slaves" sometimes seemed "to run roughshod over charity and justice."[169] In the Caribbean, Jesuits recommended cutting off slaves' ears as punishment.[170] In Huaura, Peru, the Jesuits' slaves had just three or four hours a night to sleep.[171] It thus was not without reason that the local provincial congregation of 1686 identified a litany of cruelty and brutality in the treatment of its own slaves.[172] And the treatment of slaves in Maryland was notoriously bad—even pregnant women were reportedly still whipped in the nineteenth century.[173]

Of course, repeated attempts were also made to improve the living conditions of the Society's slaves.[174] The fact that the Jesuits always made time for Christian catechesis and instruction may have been some relief from work, likewise the strict observance of Sundays and holidays as days of rest. The Jesuits also regularly purchased indulgences for all their slaves at their own expense. In the coastal regions of Peru, moreover, we know that slaves on the Jesuit haciendas often could live as families that were respected. At many of the Society's establishments, old slaves or those who could no longer work for other reasons continued to be cared for and were not weeded out. These hardworking people are even supposed to have been relatively well fed. Daily rations of meat were provided in many places. Advanced forms of health care were established, and recreation for the workers was an important subject for the Jesuit stewards on the ground. Relatively large numbers of slaves on the Society's Peruvian haciendas lived to over sixty years old, and virtually no unfree people owned by the Jesuits sought their freedom in flight. Sexual exploitation might also have been far less common than it was elsewhere. Punishments were pronounced and carried out, but at the same time Jesuit slave owners constantly looked for alternatives to corporal punishment. Last but not least, the Jesuits also wanted to show themselves to be exemplary Christians in the treatment of their slaves because slaves too were the children of God and hence every Christian's neighbor. Manuel da Nóbrega, the founder of the Jesuit mission to Brazil, wrote in a letter to King João III of Portugal in 1553 that the Jesuits would distinguish themselves by the "moderate subjection" of their slaves.[175] General Vincenzo Carafa explicitly forbade Jesuit slave owners to impose excessive and brutal punishments in 1648.

Despite all this, however, we should not overlook the fact that these measures were not motivated purely by feelings of humanity and religious solicitude. There were concrete benefits to be had from treating slaves decently. Multiplying the number of slaves naturally by encouraging reproduction through well-functioning families was cost-effective and easy, and in some cases that was what the Jesuits very clearly and strategically intended; how effective the plan was, of course, is debated.[176]

More than one Jesuit discerningly noted that the relatively good treatment of slaves reduced their inclination to flee and thus prevented economic losses.[177] Thus both religious and pragmatic considerations legitimated this campaign for the humane treatment of slaves. Treatises by two Jesuit missionaries in Brazil, Jorge Benci (ca. 1650–1708) and João Antônio Andreoni (1649–1716), provided it with an elaborate Christian theoretical basis in the late seventeenth century. Andreoni regarded it as a plantation owner's most important responsibility to hire a competent clergyman to ensure that his agricultural enterprise was Christian through and through. That included, first and foremost, the slaves, whom the planter had to treat fairly.[178] Benci likewise took the fusion of economy, Christianity, and slavery for granted, as indicated by the title of his book *Economia Christiaã dos senhores no governo dos escravos* (Christian economy of masters in the management of their slaves). Both authors clearly evoked a vision of a Christian patriarchy in which the slave and his owner were bound to each other by mutual obligations. The slave owner should prove that he was not only a "master" but also a "father."

Although we can see in these texts an effort to make life easier for slaves—albeit also for reasons of economic opportunism—they also reflect the fact that the Society had at last come to accept the reality of slavery at least in a "Christianized" form. Andreoni could gauge the respective physical and mental qualities of slaves from different regions of African as coolly and objectively as a secular slave trader would have done. While giving the institution a specific Christian coloring, the Society of Jesus ultimately decided to tolerate, participate in, and support colonial society's reliance on slavery. The Society ultimately benefited from it. And this largely positive relationship with slavery was astonishingly long-lived among the Jesuits. In Maryland, where the Society managed to keep its properties even during the suppression from 1773 to 1814, the Jesuits kept slaves until well into the nineteenth century. The Jesuits did not sell their last 272 slaves until 1838—*sold*, not manumitted, because the Jesuits viewed abolitionism as a Protestant way of thinking.[179]

Converting the "Heathen": The Jesuits as Missionaries

Motives: The Mission as Spiritual Duty and Personal Desire

When the Jesuits joined the ongoing campaign to Christianize the Americas in the 1540s, the mission was already at the center of a thicket of ideological debates. Some early missionaries had interpreted the discovery and conversion of the heathen in the New World as the beginning of the end of the world. The Franciscans, who began converting the natives of central Mexico in 1523, repeatedly voiced such convictions.[180] The Jesuits viewed things differently. With a handful of exceptions, their missionary fervor was not fueled by the belief that conversion would trigger the Last Judgment.[181] That had important consequences: the Jesuits were free of the enormous urgency that eschatological expectations added. Emancipation from apocalyptic scenarios gave one flexibility. The Jesuits could afford to study the object of their mission, the indigenous population, carefully before setting out to change their lives and beliefs. This different view of the mission also gave them the time to watch for substantial catechetical success among the heathen. In this regard the Jesuits were often very strict: without compelling evidence of a serious conversion, they did not normally give baptism. For the Jesuits, the mission was systematic, long-term cultural work in the name of Christianization. That was one reason the success of the Jesuit mission was not normally the result of the heroic deeds of lone charismatic missionaries, as much as these individuals were perhaps indispensable for spectacular initial breakthroughs. A patient approach, in which the collective, not an extraordinary individual, took the lead, was much more typical and prevalent.[182]

Yet even if the conversion of the heathen did not play out in the context of the imminent end of the world and the last kingdom of God on Earth, the mission was intimately connected to biblical motifs.[183] In the view of Catholic theologians, the basis of the mission to non-Christians was the Great Commission of Jesus Christ, expressed in several passages of the New Testament, such as the Gospel of Matthew (28:19f.): "Go therefore and make disciples of all nations." Whereas the followers of

Martin Luther believed that these words had lost their meaning after the death of the apostles, the Jesuits and the entire Catholic world presumed that they were as valid as ever.[184] Hence the *Imago primi saeculi* of 1640 could present the Jesuits' missionary endeavors as the direct fulfillment of prophecy. Jesuits stationed locally counted the heathen as the "neighbors" whom the Bible commanded them to help (Mark 12:29–31).[185] In the words of Andrés Pérez de Ribas (1576–1655), a Jesuit missionary and author from Mexico: "The first truth is that Christ the Redeemer ordered His Gospel to be preached throughout the world. We will find that He entrusted every nation on this earth—large and small, lofty and humble—to His holy Apostles and those who succeeded [them]."[186] The Bible not only commanded Catholics to propagate the faith but also was urgently needed: the missionaries had something to offer—the Christian faith—for which in their view all people had an existential need, even if the "heathen" refused to see it right away. Embracing Jesus Christ was the prerequisite of salvation after death. Only those who confessed him and were received into the Christian community by baptism could escape damnation. This conviction raised another difficult question: What happened when indigenous peoples turned a deaf ear to the Good News? In response, many early modern theologians found themselves in agreement with the arguments of the medieval Pope Innocent IV (r. 1243–54), arriving at an answer that suited the European colonial powers very well: non-Christian peoples need not accept Christianity, but they had to allow missionaries to preach it. If they refused or created unfavorable conditions for the preaching of the Word, then it was the legitimate responsibility of European kings to make ready the way for the preaching of the Gospel by military means.[187] To meet his spiritual obligation to convert the heathen, kings were entitled and indeed bound to reform social structures, to compel "barbarian" cultures to assimilate European values, and to protect and promote the work of the missionaries.

But that did not mean in the eyes of the clergy that the colonists could use unlimited force. Many theologians also emphasized that the indigenous population must not be robbed of its freedom, and that Europeans were permitted to wage only "just war," if any at all, to which very specific restrictions applied. For the Jesuits, it was clear as day that indigenous peoples were human beings who enjoyed the same natural rights as Europeans. Whether that was in fact the case was hotly debated in the first half of the sixteenth century. After long and contentious discussions, however, Pope Paul III decreed in the bull *Sublimis Deus* of 1537 that non-Europeans (in point of fact, the indigenous population of the Americas) were indeed human beings. The Jesuits had shared this conviction throughout.

That put the peoples of the non-Christian corners of the world in a curiously ambivalent position. On the one hand, even the Jesuits usually considered Native Americans, Indians, and Africans to be utterly different, alien, and often tragically primitive. Some peoples and lands, from the Jesuits' perspective, had been left "by the just but obscure judgement of Our Lord in this semi-paralysis and regarded as unfertile, barren, and rejected ground."[188] The natives of North America and the lands they inhabited were regarded as the epitome of the wild—the Jesuits did not hesitate to call the indigenous people "savages" (*sauvages*).[189] On the other hand, it was clear that in principle no people could be excluded from believing in Jesus Christ. The Jesuits construed their own role in most mission territories from these two positions: the indigenous population was essentially equal, but non-Christian natives were also ultimately expected to be grateful. They were supposed to recognize their own need for instruction and therefore voluntarily submit to the Jesuits' cultural, religious, and political authority. The Jesuits, in turn, would use their superior position only in the interest of the spiritual and social welfare of the natives, who were their wards, after all. Ippolito Desideri, the missionary in Tibet, pointedly captured the essence of the Jesuits' pastoral paternalism: "They have to serve for thousands and thousands of people as a prudent father, a caring and compassionate mother, a merciful steward, a rigid censor, a teacher, a judge, or a powerful or humble intercessor; they must be cunning, naïve, severe, and pleasant."[190] Japan and China, where the Jesuits distanced themselves from this condescending, if well-intentioned, self-assuredness, were among the few exceptions where this mentality could not be applied.

The paternalism the Jesuits evinced overseas was at heart no different from the spirit in which they met the rural population of Europe. The border between the heathen in the colonies and bad Christians at home was fluid. One missionary in Canada wrote, "I naturally compare our Savages with certain villagers, because both are usually without education, though our Peasants are superior in this regard; and yet I have not seen any one thus far, of those who have come to this country, who does not confess and frankly admit that the Savages are more intelligent than our ordinary peasants." Pérez de Ribas in Mexico agreed: when he compared his natives with the rustics of Europe, the indigenous people of Mexico came out looking pretty good.[191] In essence, the "mission" in the Jesuit view was a process of teaching people the correct Christian faith, which applied equally to both European peasants and the African pagans. While all that may have served to legitimate the subjection and, in some circumstances, the violent suppression of non-Christians, it still was clear that the non-Christians of the world fundamentally should be brought into the Christian community of saints. And it was God's commission to the missionaries to bring that about. Many Jesuits accepted this divine commission with burning "desire" in their heart. For many of them, setting out overseas was a euphoric moment for which they "long harbored a very deep desire."[192] They stylized the mission virtually as a place of spiritual yearning. After a static life during their education in the colleges, they celebrated the dynamism of the mission as a spiritual new beginning, a breakthrough to the actual core of Jesuit existence. Niccolò Stagliano, for example, found the mission at the "remotest places in the world" so attractive in 1705 because "my heart distinctly told me that the Lord would be much closer to me, to attain salvation and help my neighbor, if I resolutely left my country, my friends, my family, the places I knew and definitively bade 'adieu' to this world." It was such "desire to go outside," "to leave behind everything" that was familiar (and comfortable), notions of self-sacrifice, renunciation of the world, self-abasement, and radical, self-imposed privation that lent the mission its unique spiritual appeal. By taking the men overseas, the mission enabled them "to leave the delights of the body behind," as another Jesuit believed. Hence aspiring missionaries regularly affirmed that they wanted to go on mission "to shed [their own] blood for His love." The possibility of martyrdom indeed was a major motivating factor, despite the fact that the superiors frowned upon playing such games with one's life. To demonstrate in advance their readiness for physical self-sacrifice, some mission enthusiasts went so far as to write letters to the general in their own blood. Thus, for many a Jesuit, the mission ultimately transformed from a place of yearning to a place of destiny. "I can only say that God wants me to go, and it seems to me if I don't get that, I can almost say for certain that it's a sign that I must damn myself," wrote Giulio Orsini to General Acquaviva in 1600. Even if in many cases this enthusiasm and longing may have quickly been dampened in the new work environment of the mission, and even potentially replaced by disillusionment and disappointment, this euphoric description of the mission was ubiquitous. Until the demise of the order, there were many Jesuits who kept this enthusiasm alive in word and deed.

Scenarios: The Process, Reality, and Difficulty of Christianization

Often enough, individual Jesuits' enthusiasm for the mission gave the entire movement its dynamic. Without engaged and committed missionaries, the conversion of the world would remain only a dream. Yet, on the whole, individual charisma in the Society of Jesus was subordinate to its communal, collectively structured "way of proceeding." The Society learned from painful experience in the early decades of its efforts to convert the heathen that dynamic individuals might occasionally achieve breakthroughs, but did not necessarily lay the best foundation for the systematic cultural work that they had come to understand the mission to represent. The Jesuit mission was most successful where it harnessed the individual dedication of its members within a communal culture. That was one of the most important insights that the Jesuits made over the course of their experiences in Africa, the Americas, and Asia.

During this protracted missionary learning process, the Jesuits constantly hit on new ways in which they might productively engage with the many foreign cultures, languages, and religions they encountered. The early modern mission of the Jesuits was indeed but one long experiment, a painstaking search by trial and error for strategies to communicate beliefs and culture. In the following, four mission territories are presented as illustrations of how the Jesuits proceeded to bring Christianity to people who had never heard of it and could not immediately see why they supposedly needed a new religion. Numerous compromises were inevitable, sometimes very painful ones. The Jesuits soon learned that it would take a delicately balanced approach to guarantee any chance of missionary success at all. Loyola's successors set about to rise to the occasion with resourcefulness, stubbornness, and ingenuity.

The scenarios presented here will also show, on the one hand, that a worldwide exchange of experiences and insights took place within the Society of Jesus. These resulted in something like a pool of shared experiences. Certain strategies proved viable over time and became global models. In many regards, Jesuit missions in places separated by vast distances closely resembled one another. On the other hand, the Jesuits never distilled their diverse impressions and experiences into an abstract "method," let alone a "theory." There was no explicit, official, universally binding Jesuit mission strategy; there was only a set of presumptions that all Jesuits shared as a result of their education, and a common pool of role models. But it was clear to every Jesuit involved that the mission was ultimately a local project. Models from far away and the fundamental lessons of European education had to be adapted to local conditions. Hence the Society of Jesus proceeded on its mission in an extremely wide and, in part, contradictory variety of ways.

CANADA: MISSIONARIES, SAINTS, AND APOSTATES
IN THE MIDDLE GROUND

On October 18, 1633, the Jesuit Paul Le Jeune (1591–1664) began a remarkable journey. He joined, all by himself, a group of forty-four Montagnais (Innu) natives and set out with them from Quebec. He traversed the winter wilderness of Canada with them until the next April.[193] The

Montagnais were nomads who moved camp every five or six days. While there was no snow, the missionary often slept under the stars. Later, the natives built makeshift huts in the snow at each stop. Inside, Le Jeune warmed one half of his body by the fire while the other half froze. He could not stand up because choking smoke gathered in the upper part of the hut. Dogs were everywhere. They gave warmth but also annoyed the missionary. Each shelter was intended for several people, and more than once Le Jeune was forced to overhear nocturnal activities that were forbidden to him as a Catholic priest. But the hunger was the worst. His hosts had warned him about it: "*Chibiné*, harden thy soul, resist hunger; thou wilt be sometimes two, sometimes three or four, days without food: do not let thyself be cast down, take courage; when the snow comes, we shall eat." Le Jeune described how he ate old animal hides and the ends of branches to survive. The wandering was torturous: "We did nothing but go up and go down; frequently we had to bend halfway over, to pass under partly-fallen trees, and step over others lying upon the ground whose branches sometimes knocked us over, gently enough to be sure, but always coldly, for we fell upon the snow. If it happened to thaw, Oh God, what suffering!" He remarked sarcastically in hindsight: "Now imagine a person loaded like a mule, and judge how easy is the life of the Savage."

In addition to the enormous physical toll, the adventures in ice and snow, the wild animals, and the poor food, there also were enormous social and religious challenges. Le Jeune had few friends among the natives. We should by no means exaggerate the position of the missionaries in the indigenous population, even over the long term. The Jesuits may have liked to put themselves at the center of events in their colorful accounts of their experiences, but they were often no more than marginal figures among the indigenous peoples of Canada.[194] It was not Le Jeune himself but rather his hosts who dictated what part he could play. From the natives' point of view, the Frenchman may have cut a remarkable figure, but he was still a marginal one. He was regularly in danger and had to toil to gain influence, if he succeeded in gaining any at all. The shamans were his most important adversaries. Le Jeune's account is full of anecdotes about his encounters with the natives' "sorcerer." The shaman, the key spiritual authority among the Montagnais, viewed the Catholic priest—not unreasonably—as competition. More than once the Jesuit feared for his life for that very reason. He constantly describes the "nonsense" that his adversary got up to.[195] At first, the Jesuit could not quite make out where the "sorcerer" got his ideas, not to mention his authority and eminent social position. The Jesuits often saw the devil behind the Native American shamans, whispering in their ear. But they also often viewed them as delivering a "mere" human performance. Sometimes an indigenous medicine man seemed possessed, sometimes a clever charlatan.

Over the months, the Jesuit became acquainted with the religious world of the natives from close proximity and tried hard to understand it. Through numerous conversations, Jesuit missionaries like Le Jeune developed a complex and multifaceted, if also distorted, picture of their hosts' beliefs.[196] He listened and asked questions, but he inevitably interpreted what he heard and saw through the lens of his own Christian viewpoint. He shaped the natives' ideas into a coherent, logical whole, just as he knew to do from Catholic theology. He drew inferences, analyzed, speculated, constructed.[197] Under Le Jeune's Christian gaze, a coherent "religion" emerged from individual myths, stories, and practices—although the Montagnais themselves had perhaps no need at all for a coherent system. The missionaries regarded many of the Montagnais' beliefs as false and dismissed them with negative European labels like "superstition" and "idolatry." For instance, Le Jeune wrote off the major importance of dreams for the natives as "silly ideas."[198]

In other native beliefs, however, Le Jeune and his confreres imagined they could find at least the seeds of the Christian message. The natives had a concept of the soul and considered it immortal, Le Jeune happily concluded—even if he dismissed the particulars of their doctrine as a bunch of errors. The Jesuits also identified the rudiments of biblical tales like that of the Flood in the myths of the indigenous population. They were not at all surprised: from their perspective, in light of the common ancestry of all people from the family of Adam, it was only natural that at least traces of the common tradition should survive even in heathen America. The missionaries regularly discovered vague echoes of biblical knowledge elsewhere, too. The inhabitants of the Kongo, the Jesuit missionary Mateus Cordoso concluded in 1624, had undoubtedly known of the Christian god even before the arrival of the Portuguese. The latter then merely had to acquaint them with Jesus Christ. Stone crosses were discovered in Peru—this too was considered a relic of Christian traditions. And the Guaraní told tales that suggested they had previously been visited by a Christian messenger—had not the apostle Thomas traveled the world?[199]

Such supposed traces of Christianity gave the missionaries courage. In other regards, too, Jesuits like Le Jeune, for all his criticism, found some praiseworthy things among the natives. He may have observed many vices—gluttony, filth, pride—but he also highlighted the Montagnais' good-natured ways, their physical prowess, their patience and magnanimity. Not least, the Jesuits were fascinated by some of the skills and techniques of the indigenous inhabitants. They may not have known of metal or European craftsmanship, but Le Jeune praised their deftness with a canoe, their sense of direction in the wilderness, and many of their everyday tools, such as snowshoes and certain methods of starting a fire.[200] As preposterous and baffling as the "superstition" of the natives may have been, they were ultimately God's creation and therefore capable of a Christian education.

In the dark winter months of 1633/4, both sides therefore attempted to understand and appreciate each other on the basis of their own worldviews. Both the natives and the Jesuit missionary tried to make sense of the doings of the other in light of their own convictions. Numerous misunderstandings ensued, misunderstandings that we see in retrospect were mistakes or even the results of pride. Sometimes, these misunderstandings led to conflict and even threatened life and limb. But it is also important to note that these efforts to understand one another might also be creative and productive. They created a common "middle ground" in which cultural contact could take place.[201] Each side learned to anticipate and influence the actions of the other and at least attempted to understand their motives and culture better. The natives got an idea of Christianity and the Jesuits. In doing so, they came to appreciate the newcomers from foreign lands and learned how to anticipate their attitudes and expectations better, although they by no means interpreted everything correctly. This was the way in which conversion, Christianization, and the Jesuit mission played out in Canada and everywhere else. Despite all their hardships and misunderstandings, the missionary and the natives came closer together during those long winter months of 1633/4.

Le Jeune, however, returned from his experiment not only sick and exhausted but also deflated. He knew that this could not be the right way: "I may be mistaken; but, if I can draw any conclusion from the things I see, it seems to me that not much ought to be hoped for from the Savages as long as they are wanderers."[202] Spiritual education, the Jesuit reasoned, stood a much greater chance of success with sedentary people. This conclusion, with which Le Jeune came away from his journey, essentially corresponded to the general experience and preference of the Society. The Jesuit missions indeed witnessed bold actions by individualists like Le Jeune. Francis Xavier himself, as well as Rafael Ferrer in modern Ecuador, Eusebio Kino in northwestern Mexico, Samuel Fritz in the Amazon basin bordering Colombia and Peru, and Jean de la Mousse in Guayana are all examples. Even in Canada, missions undertaken by lonely wanderers like Le Jeune did not vanish completely. But already contemporary Jesuits stressed that such heroic solo efforts usually achieved "little success." It was seldom these highly revered (even today) individualists with their erratic biographies who achieved lasting success, but rather the Society's systematic ministry efforts.[203]

It thus was not the mission to the Montagnais that became famous in Canada, but rather the mission to the Huron. This tribe, which still consisted of nearly twenty thousand people in 1635 despite dramatic loss of life, resided south of Georgian Bay on Lake Huron. Roughly a thousand kilometers west of Quebec, the most important (albeit still tiny) French settlement in New France, the Hurons' territory was remote and inaccessible. Nonetheless, or perhaps precisely for that reason, the Jesuits founded a mission there in 1634 that filled contemporaries with great hope until its tragic demise in 1649/50.[204] The French had established trading ties with the Huron shortly after settling. This trade revolved primarily around beaver pelts, which were by far the most important export commodity from New France. As early as the 1620s, several Jesuits, above all Jean de Brébeuf, spent a significant amount of time among the Huron. The Society built on those relations in 1634.

Huronia, as the region was called, was a prosperous area with extreme continental weather conditions. Summers were very hot, winters brutally cold. But the fertile soil enabled the Huron to practice agriculture. They also hunted, and fish provided an additional source of food, but they lived permanently in a handful of settlements. The Jesuits moved into these villages and established mission stations. In 1639, they established a headquarters at Sainte-Marie-des-Hurons on the shore of Lake Huron's Georgian Bay.[205] They had a church, other buildings, and, most important, storehouses for fresh supplies that were brought on a weeks-long journey by canoe from Quebec. They also practiced agriculture. Up to fifty Frenchmen lived in Sainte-Marie, including about a dozen Jesuits. Thanks to its stores, the Jesuits of Sainte-Marie became largely self-sufficient and independent of the natives. From there, they explored the region, christened the native villages with new names, and raised wayside crosses. At regular intervals, they set out from Sainte-Marie to visit the other stations, which were always only a few kilometers away. They made their home in the midst of the natives and yet, in contrast to Le Jeune in 1633/4, retained more of their own conventional way of life. A totally European lifestyle, of course, was impossible at such mission stations. In material terms, the Jesuits around Jean de Brébeuf lived—from a European perspective—an extremely humble existence. The educated Jesuits, who often came from middle- or upper-class backgrounds, found themselves reduced to satisfying basic needs. Manual labor was routine. Cleanliness, privacy, culinary variety, and culture were rare commodities. Raw materials like paper, ink, books, and even holy objects and items for celebrating mass like wine and cloth had to be procured from far away and were accordingly expensive. Even if life was not as desperately precarious as the winter Le Jeune experienced, it was still bitter cold in the Huronia in the snow. The Jesuits constantly lost their way in the wilderness, and at least one of them, Anne de Noüe (1587–1646), died in the snow when he became lost in a blizzard.

For many of the missionaries, these experiences were deeply disturbing, despite their express willingness to make sacrifices. There may have been many Jesuits who heroically defied the hard living conditions and met their new challenges with aplomb, but by no means all of them accepted these external difficulties with equanimity. Although the rhetoric of Jesuit sources again and again emphasized that the dangers and limitations of everyday life presented the men of the order a special chance at humility and should be eagerly accepted for that reason, other quieter and even desperate voices could also be heard. Uncertainty, perplexity, frustration, helplessness and purposelessness, and even outright despair were also often part of everyday life, though the Jesuits tried to hide them, especially in official communications.[206]

The Jesuits had every reason to despair in the years 1649 and 1650: the Huron tribe and, with them, the Jesuit mission were completely annihilated by multiple Iroquois attacks. Several Jesuits died as martyrs, tied to the torture pillars of the victors. Huronia ceased to exist. Yet the Jesuits remained faithful to the idea of a sedentary mission that would operate on the basis of permanent stations. As early as 1656, at the invitation of the Iroquois, they attempted to replicate the Huronia project by founding the new mission station of Sainte-Marie de Gannentaha on the shore of Lake Onondaga, but the effort was in vain.[207] The French in general and the Jesuits in particular searched for sites farther west, in the Great Lakes region and the Ohio and Mississippi River valleys, that could be inhabited by large groups of native peoples or at least visited regularly.[208]

Wherever semipermanent native settlements structures were lacking, the Jesuits themselves often did not hesitate to help them along. With a mixture of coercion and persuasion, they forced or encouraged the natives to build villages.[209] The village of Sillery, several kilometers west of the capital, Quebec, was the first. Under Le Jeune's leadership, the Jesuits tried to settle the Montagnais there in 1637, but only a handful of the Montagnais answered the call.[210] La Prairie, south of Montreal, was somewhat more successful. Several hundred Hurons and Iroquois settled there in the latter half of the century, founding the mission village of Kahnawake.[211] A church, several buildings, and fields worked by the

Jesuits complemented the fields and dwellings of the natives.[212] The goal was again to bring the new Christians together in one place where the Jesuits could supervise and give them spiritual guidance more easily. Their native catechumens would also be isolated from the profligate colonists. Indeed, the Jesuits viewed the French settlers as a threat to their new wards. Along the St. Lawrence, the missionaries sought above all to protect their new Christians from alcohol. There was a tall cross at the entrance to Kahnawake that stood for sobriety—all who entered the village had to leave their drunkenness behind. Claude Chauchetière preserved a dramatic record of this scene in a famous drawing (fig. 26).

And so it was none other than the Jesuits' Iroquois mission village near Montreal where it seemed as if the Society's religious dreams were about to come true after the fall of Huronia. Striking signs of an ecstatic religiosity appeared among the native inhabitants of Kahnawake around 1680. A group of young women in particular dedicated themselves to a radical Christian life: they swore chastity and began a series of rigorous penitential practices at Christmas 1676:

> The first who began made her first attempt about Christmas in the year 1676, when she divested herself of her clothing, and exposed herself to the air at the foot of a large Cross that stands beside our Cemetery. She did so at a time when the snow was falling, although she was pregnant; and the snow that fell upon her back caused her so much suffering that she nearly died from it—as well as her Child, whom the cold chilled in its mother's womb. It was her own idea to do this—to do penance for her sins, she said.[213]

Although the Jesuits found these practices excessive, they were delighted by the women's religious fervor. For several years, a milieu of native Christians that could serve as an example even for Europeans thrived at Kahnawake. This was particularly true of a young Iroquois woman, Kateri (Catherine) Tekakwitha, who died in April 1680 at about the age of twenty-four. In the last months of her life, she exerted a powerful fascination on the Christian natives and especially on the Jesuit priest Claude Chauchetière. She radiated an aura of holiness, he felt. Shortly after her death, visions of Tekakwitha were reported by different

FIGURE 26. Jesuit mission as isolated from European influence: at the entrance
of the mission village of Kahnawake in Canada, inhabitants had to leave
the vice of alcohol at a cross. Drawing by Fr. Claude Chauchetière from
Narration annuelle de la mission du Sault depuis sa fondation jusqu'à l'an 1686.
© Archives départmentales de la Gironde H 48.

inhabitants of the village. Chauchetière and later also his confrere Pierre
Cholenac launched a campaign to make Kateri a saint. They viewed her
as proof that God had also redeemed the (erstwhile) heathen of North
America.

Yet for as much as the Jesuits touted Tekakwitha and sundry other
Christian natives as commendable examples in their lively reports, it is

doubtful how typical these individuals were. By no means every Christianized native lived happily ever after with the faith of their choosing.
For every Kateri Tekakwitha, there was at least one Pierre-Antoine Pastedechouan, as the Jesuits themselves were forced to admit.[214] Pierre-
Antoine was one of Paul Le Jeune's companions on his winter journey
of 1633/4. The Jesuit constantly referred to him merely as "the apostate,"
because in his view Pastedechouan's dramatic and ultimately tragic life
was nothing but a great disappointment. Viewed objectively, however,
the unhappy biography of this young man shows the difficulties and
consequences that contact with the priests might have for interested
natives. Pastedechouan was born around 1608, just as the French began
to settle in Quebec. He came into contact with the first French settlers
and missionaries as a boy. At the time, the latter were Franciscan Recollects, who asked the Jesuits for support a few years later. In 1620, the boy
traveled with the Recollects from Canada to France, where he was baptized in Angers a year later in a large public ceremony. That was less
uncommon than it might seem. Catholic missionaries everywhere
began to intensively court children. They saw much more potential of
permanent conversion in them than in adults. Hence both the Recollects and the Jesuits established schools for native children along the
St. Lawrence River or brought them to Europe, like Pastedechouan. He
and numerous other boys were to be brought up like Frenchmen so they
could act as intermediaries between cultures. At the same time, these
exotic newcomers to France would serve as living illustrations of the
missionaries' tales of foreign worlds. They gave the Jesuits additional
credibility and attracted new sponsors. Catholic missionaries repeatedly
brought people from other parts of the world to Europe for this purpose. A famous Japanese "delegation" that traveled to Europe in 1582, for
example, created a sensation.[215]

Pastedechouan's European life was not as wide-ranging. During his
years-long stay, he probably remained exclusively in France. Like it or
not, he adjusted at least a little to his new social, cultural, religious, and
intellectual world. But when he was brought back to Canada in 1626,
where he was supposed to serve as a Christian model for the unconverted natives as well as a cultural and linguistic middleman, it quickly

became evident that his position was very ambivalent. His tribesmen, who had voluntarily given him to the French, were disappointed when it emerged that the young man would not simply do their bidding. While away from his tribe, he had been raised instead to reject the religious customs and rituals of his relatives and former friends as unchristian. He also never learned to survive in the American wilderness on his own. His connection to his original culture was shaken, and his embrace of Christianity led to significant tension and conflict. This was not an isolated case. Conversion to a new religion often split indigenous societies into hostile camps. Christianization broke up traditional loyalties. Sometimes the missionaries exploited preexisting quarrels. Christianity was often particularly attractive for dissidents and outsiders among the indigenous peoples.[216]

At any rate, Pastedechouan's presence led to a rift with his estranged family. He thus became even more dependent on the French. But when they were expelled by the English between 1629 and 1632, he was left without the Recollects' protection. Now he was completely at the mercy of his old tribe. When the French returned three years later, and the Recollects passed the religious baton to the Jesuits, Paul Le Jeune became Pierre-Antoine's most important Catholic contact. Pastedechouan served the Jesuit for some time as a language tutor and translator, but their relationship was increasingly undermined by mistrust and animosity. Le Jeune wanted to use Pastedechouan as a role model to compel his Christian converts to adhere to Christian rituals and ways of life, thus creating a model for future converts. Pierre-Antoine, in contrast, wanted to express an independent identity in light of his ambivalent experiences with the French. Ultimately, the multiple countervailing claims and influences to which the young man was exposed became too much for him. The "middle ground" between cultures seemed to shake under his feet, becoming a zone of uncertainty and disorientation:

> I see clearly that I am not doing right; but my misfortune is that I have not a mind strong enough to remain firm in my determination; I believe all they tell me. When I was with the English, I allowed myself to be influenced by their talk; when I am with the Savages,

I do as they do; when I am with you [sc. Le Jeune], it seems to me
your belief is the true one. Would to God I had died when I was sick
in France, and I would now be saved.[217]

The pressure Le Jeune put on Pastedechouan only made the situation
worse, and the young man took sides with the shaman, Le Jeune's greatest adversary, several times during the winter journey of 1633/4. But he
also found no way back to his tribe either—he starved to death forsaken
and alone in the forests in 1636. Pierre-Antoine's end was undoubtedly
as tragic as his life between continents, cultures, and colonizers was
complex. But the Jesuits continued to tell stories of "apostate" converts
again and again.

Pierre-Antoine ultimately had no chance of escaping Christianity.
His long years in France and his alienation from his former life gave him
no choice but to adapt to his new reality as best he could. The Montagnais, Iroquois, Huron, and Illinois, in contrast, who all more or less embraced Christianity in Canada, probably often had a real choice. If they
welcomed Jesuit missionaries and their faith with open arms, they usually did so for very specific reasons. The Jesuits ultimately saw this as
evidence of God's grace at work. But even they were forced to admit in
moments of sober reflection that there initially were far more pragmatic
reasons for the sympathetic reception of Christianity among the natives. "The spiritual interests of these Missions depend largely on temporal affairs," wrote Julien Garnier in 1672.[218] Garnier was active among
the Iroquois, who, in this case, wanted to keep the peace with the
French. Religious cooperation guaranteed military alliances and opened
privileged trading channels. For the Huron, similarly, receiving the Jesuits resulted in reinforcing their prominent position in the fur trade.
Access to European goods became easier and more stable for those
among whom the Jesuits lived. The natives may also have seen the Jesuits as ceremonial hostages, whom they exchanged in diplomatic relations to guarantee mutual goodwill.[219] The missionaries, moreover,
constantly impressed the indigenous people by shrewdly using their
scientific and technological knowledge to overpower them intellectually. "This prediction of eclipses has always been one of the things that

have most astonished our savages; and it has given them a higher opinion of their missionaries," wrote one Jesuit, for example.[220] It was the Europeans' miraculous abilities that first captivated the natives, not the content of their message. In such moments, the Jesuits radiated cultural strength and instilled new spiritual confidence. Often enough, such experiences and feelings were then transmitted within indigenous societies along ties of family and friendship.[221]

The spread of Christianity within the indigenous population of the Americas thus obeyed a social, political, and economic logic. If the natives willingly adopted the outward forms of Christianity, that by no means meant that they sympathized inwardly with the new faith. Experienced Jesuits like Julien Garnier, mentioned previously, saw through such pragmatic exploitation of particular Christian elements. When some chiefs once promised him during alliance negotiations that they wanted to pray to his god, he dryly remarked, "I could not yet see therein any great beginnings of faith."[222] He and all his fellow brothers were thus extremely careful and reserved with respect to baptism. As a rule, the Jesuits were strictly opposed to the mass baptism of (usually) anonymous native converts and hesitated long before conferring the sacrament on healthy people. From their everyday interactions with non-Christian peoples the world over, Ignatius's followers had learned that "conversion" had to be viewed as a highly multifaceted process. They were very well aware of the fact that many newly baptized Christians like Pastedechouan often remained torn and uncertain about their beliefs. "Apostasy" represented a serious danger because it was a grave sin after baptism. Converts accordingly had to be introduced to Christianity very carefully, and the Jesuits closely monitored their wards before accepting a case of genuine "conversion." They sometimes even were too careful and were angry with themselves when a native willing to convert died unbaptized, "because I was waiting until he had been educated [in the faith] a bit better."[223]

The mission territories in the Americas and the rest of the world thus had an important message to send: it was here, through their intensive everyday experience, that the Jesuits learned that cultivating a thoroughly Christian personality was a laborious process. They learned to distinguish between a religious exterior and a devout interior in people. To become truly Christian, native converts had to take more from their new faith than simply praying now and then—Garnier was absolutely right about that. This experience, which was both sobering and enriching for the missionaries, accorded very well with the ideas that Ignatius had put down in the *Exercises*: there too, he understood faith and devotion as pervading one's entire personality.

The members of the Society of Jesus spared no effort to bring about this inner acceptance of Jesus Christ in people. They lived in the simplest conditions among their protégés, in burning heat and icy cold, froze and starved with them, endured their ridicule, and, like Jean de Brébeuf and other "martyrs of Canada," even suffered torture at their hands. All this was necessary to initiate and patiently monitor the indispensable, intensive process of transformation from heathen to Christian. Conversion was a process of character development that was as difficult as it was laborious. Only if Catholic experts like the Jesuit missionaries were permanently present locally and able to guide everyday life could true, inner change definitively be established. Hence, Jesuits like Paul Le Jeune took it for granted that the mission required them to give up their life in Europe and sleep under the stars and in the snow in the Canadian wilderness, if that was what it took.

MEXICO: THE MISSIONARIES' METHODS
TO CONVERT THE INDIGENOUS PEOPLES

Sometimes, however, Jesuit missionaries felt a completely different method of proceeding was needed, as illustrated by a remarkable scene that played out in a small settlement in the territory of the Acaxee in northwestern Mexico in the summer of 1600. The village was already, at least nominally, under Christian influence. There was a church, and the natives had been assigned to a Spanish don. To prevent a potential uprising (which then happened anyway a year later), the Jesuit Hernando de Santarén (1566/7–1616), the officer Diego de Ávila, and several soldiers patrolled the area for about ten months.[224] One morning, no fewer than 239 natives gathered in the village square. Two days earlier, the two

Spaniards had instructed the natives to systematically collect and transport there all non-Christian cult objects. The natives delivered the following objects:

> twenty-nine skulls from the heads of human bodies; many shin, hand, and arm bones; more than 60 bundles of stone idols, small and large, in various shapes and styles . . . all of which the aforesaid officer ordered them to burn and throw together on a very large bonfire before the entrance of the church. And on top of that, the aforesaid [Jesuit] priest Hernando de Santarén gave many sermons and reasons to the aforesaid people as to why one should detest this idolatry and worship Our Lord, while everything burned and was reduced to ashes.

Over the following days, the group diligently set about "hauling away idols." Whoever refused to surrender his statues faced corporal punishment.

Santarén and Ávila's actions had nothing to do with blind destruction but were well planned and stood in a clearly identifiable tradition. Such acts of destruction had also occasionally been used in India, but it was the colonial rulers of Spanish America who repeatedly attempted to extinguish old religious beliefs with the selective use of force, clearing the way for Christianity. Outright campaigns against pre-Christian cult sites and "idols" were still being undertaken in the eighteenth century, with Jesuit participation.[225] This inquisitional practice took its most virulent and institutionalized form, however, farther south, in Peru. There, the viceroy decreed in 1572 that the religious experts of the indigenous population (*hechizeros*) were to be punished with death.[226] A decade later, in 1582/3, the third Council of Lima, a church council with tremendous influence, issued rules that also called for harsh measures against the indigenous religion. The screws were turned even tighter in 1609, culminating in a systematic hunt for indigenous "priests," the destruction of cult sites, corporal punishment, and even executions.[227] Well-organized campaigns to "extirpate idolatry," as the process was euphemistically called, were conducted in at least some regions. State and church institutions collaborated closely, and the Jesuits also took part more or less enthusiastically in the first half of the seventeenth century.[228] José de Arriaga, S.J. (1563–1622), a theologian in Lima, played an important part in organizing and systematizing the effort. His book *La extirpación de la idolatría en el Perú* (The extirpation of idolatry in Peru), published in 1621, was one of the most significant manifestos of this movement. Santarén may have heard of this program even in Mexico, although it was still in its infancy in 1600. The decrees of the Council of Lima were well known in the north. At any rate, beatings, burning, and destruction followed in the wake of Santarén's tour of the territory of the Acaxee.

The use of official force was a powerful means of degrading indigenous religion and its proponents. But such drastic action in the spirit of the Inquisition was feasible only where the European colonial powers had already established an adequate military presence.[229] In Mexico, soldiers usually could be found nearby where the Jesuits introduced their ministry. The Jesuits sought such military protection and felt insecure and uneasy where it was lacking. We must also emphasize, however, that the Jesuits were overall skeptical of imposing Christianity by force. "Kindness" and "amiability" were the preferred methods to which the Jesuits actually aspired.[230] The Jesuits believed that the faith could be transmitted not by the sword but rather solely by the Word. After some initial trials, the Society of Jesus broadly accepted the fact that it was impossible to turn non-Christians into Christians without convincing them and overcoming their resistance to the new religion.

To accomplish that, missionaries like Hernando de Santarén first had to find a way to communicate with the native population. In principle, there were two options: either the natives learned Spanish, or the Spaniards learned the various native languages. The Jesuits never aggressively pursued the first option, although they taught Spanish here and there, and the language developed into a lingua franca among their protégés. From the Jesuit perspective, however, it was (and continued to be) simply assumed that they would adapt to the languages spoken by native population, not vice versa. Ignatius himself had written in the *Constitutions* that the Jesuits should learn local languages.[231] In fact, in Mexico, a Jesuit was not supposed to be ordained unless he spoke at least one indigenous language. The order founded schools to teach these languages in Mexico City.[232] Although none of the Jesuits knew a single Native American language when they arrived in 1572, they had a command of a considerable number of local idioms after only a few years. By 1604, about half of all Jesuits engaged in the mission to Mexico would have had at least some proficiency in one or more indigenous languages.[233] Santarén himself was part of this group and could hear the natives' confession in their native language.[234] "All the missionaries know their respective languages," Juan Antonio Balthasar later reported from Baja California in 1743/4. "This is no little accomplishment, inasmuch as the languages are difficult and vary from region to region," he noted appreciatively in light of these enormous challenges.[235]

To familiarize themselves with these foreign languages despite such difficulties, many Jesuit missionaries became linguistic scholars. Members of the Society of Jesus were among the first Europeans to take up the systematic study of foreign languages. That is true, for instance, of Sanskrit, which Heinrich Roth, S.J., was among the first to master; it is true of Chinese, of which missionaries since Matteo Ricci acquired an impressive, even literary, command; it is true of Vietnamese, which Alexandre de Rhodes was the first to put in writing; and it is true of many indigenous languages of North, Central, and South America.[236] Santarén also studied indigenous languages closely, learning to differentiate between local dialects and thus painting a clear picture of the linguistic landscape of his mission district.[237] In northern Mexico, the Jesuits did pioneering linguistic work and published grammars for at least five local languages.[238] Such materials were often available only in manuscript form and simply circulated within the order. That sometimes worked very well. When Juan María Salvatierra, the founder of the mission to Baja California, landed there in 1697, he was carrying texts and word lists in the local language in his baggage that another Jesuit brother had compiled on an earlier, unsuccessful expedition. In this way, a kind of institutionalized linguistic knowledge developed in the Society that individual missionaries could and indeed were expected to call upon as needed.

The Jesuits' familiarity with indigenous languages, however, also had its limits.[239] Juan Antonio Balthasar, mentioned earlier, expressed not only amazement but also criticism. Apparently, the Jesuits he visited in the peninsula still had not managed to systematize the native languages. "There are no books, not even a grammar," Balthasar lamented, chastising the superiors for the deficit. And not only did the scholarly study of newly learned indigenous languages sometimes disappoint, but the actual proficiency of the missionaries often fell far short of what the superiors demanded. The missionaries' expertise tended to decline in the eighteenth century and was (still) modest in many places.[240] In 1725, the Jesuits could communicate with the indigenous inhabitants of Nayarit only in a broken mixture of Spanish, Nahuatl, and the local native language with the help of unpopular translators. Despite the Jesuits' best efforts, such attempts at broken communication were probably very often the reality. The mysteries of Christianity had to be conveyed in a kind of pidgin.

Since persuading and reasoning with language alone often failed for very practical reasons, the missionaries adopted other strategies to teach the faith. They made deliberate, skillful use of media to transmit their message. The Jesuits sometimes used technology unknown to the natives to impress them. Juan María de Salvatierra reported from Baja California in 1698:

> I wrote a note to Father Francisco María Piccolo in the Monquí language. When I had finished writing it, I called together all the Californians who had accompanied us. I read the note aloud to them; but they had no idea of its purpose. The Indian who offered to carry it was a chief. He reached Loreto at four o'clock in the afternoon, and the father and the Spanish soldiers were delighted to see letters instituted in California. The father read the letter aloud in the presence of Chief Pablo, the bearer. When he heard the padre, paper in hand, repeating what I had previously said, he was amazed. And thus all the Indians became aware of the power of letters.[241]

The ability to transmit content through writing and reading without personal contact was virtually presented as magic.

In this instance, Salvatierra does not report what this, the "first letter" sent in California, actually contained. The message was probably not the point anyway, but rather the opportunity to give an impressive demonstration of European abilities. For the many other media that the Jesuits used, however, both form *and* content mattered. The missionaries of the Society of Jesus instrumentalized images, religious objects, and especially music to convey the messages of the Christianity. That began with the churches of the many mission stations themselves: the lavishness of their decor may have varied, but all of them were furnished with paintings and statues.[242] "When the churches were completed the priests decorated them with handsome vessels, images, and silk banners," the Jesuits themselves reported, not without some pride.[243] These images and artworks were sometimes produced in the colony itself, especially in Mexico City, but some came all the way from Europe. Regardless, "these very religious ministers consider this money well spent because it greatly assists the people in understanding divine matters, much more than one might think." A painting of the Last Judgment, for example, showing the End of Days with all its details, was used to support a sermon: "When [the Yaqui] saw it painted on the retablo it made a great impression on them. As their priest wrote, the retablo struck such fear and panic in them that its memory has been powerful enough to deliver them from many temptations and close calls with sin." The Jesuits' use of such effects was deliberate and carefully calculated. A combination of media helped them transmit their messages.

At least as effective as the large, colorful paintings and statues that adorned the churches were the numerous smaller objects that the missionaries used to deliver religious messages to their newly Christianized wards. Philipp Segesser, a Swiss Jesuit active south of Tucson, Arizona, used various small devotional objects from his homeland. He found it helpful to give converted natives reproductions of the miracle-working "Salzburger Kindl" (the Christ Child of Loreto, a statue associated with miracles in Salzburg, Austria), cloths embroidered with religious motifs, indulgence medals, and small carved or wax figures as physical tokens of their new faith that they could keep.[244] Newly baptized Christians wore medals and blessed objects on necklaces.[245] The rosary also played an important part in the everyday religious life of many missions, both as an object and as a ritual. In many places in Mexico, along the

Mississippi, and farther north in Canada, it became a prominent symbol of the natives' interest in the new religion.[246] At San Ignacio in Baja California, the converts supposedly prayed the rosary daily and even, so the Jesuits claimed, without a priest present.[247] The rosary was also combined with the Christian symbol of the crucifix. Some natives were initially afraid of crucifixes on account of the gruesome suffering they depicted. But soon the new Christians not only adopted the gesture of crossing oneself but also set up crosses everywhere. They marked paths and boundaries—the landscape itself was Christianized. The natives also used crosses to accelerate the healing of the sick. Adults and little children wore crosses around their necks. They even produced these symbols themselves: "The affection they have for the holy images and the rosary is remarkable. They make these things themselves, carving them with their knives." In some places, "they try to outdo each other in fashioning artistic crosses out of special materials . . . [such as] pearl-producing blue shells, called mother-of-pearl, thinned down and polished like small mirrors." Some newly baptized Christians went even further and cut the sign of the cross into the skin of their forehead.[248]

The padres themselves undoubtedly encouraged many of these practices. Wearing crucifixes, believing in their healing power as amulets, and giving the landscape a Christian aura in the form of wayside crosses were key aspects of European folk religion, which the Jesuits simply transferred to their new protégés. The boundary between working with the rural population of Europe and the nomadic peoples of the New World was fluid. That said, it cannot be overlooked that the new converts of Mexico immediately adapted these religious symbols of their own accord. The artisanal form of the objects they produced derived at least in part from local techniques and utilized local materials, such as mother-of-pearl. Competition over the handsomest crucifix made the new cult a social affair. The self-mutilation reported by the Jesuits likewise integrated the Christian symbol in preexisting social practices. Many other Catholic rituals and conventions could likewise be superimposed on pre-Christian customs.[249]

The natives' adaptation of particular Christian elements, however, sometimes had a contrary or even subversive effect. The indigenous population also used Christian symbols to legitimate revolts.[250] In 1737, a messianic movement and rebellion swept through the Pima people in Mexico. They were led by Ariscibi, a baptized member of the Guaymas who claimed to be a prophet.[251] He prophesied an inversion of the balance of power, whereby the Spaniards would be the Pimas' servants. Ariscibi alleged a cult statue had given him his messages. But the self-proclaimed prophet combined this pre-Christian idol with rosaries and two crucifixes of lead and coral—the new Christian religion was not far off. Ariscibi dressed in black, probably imitating the Jesuits' cassock, and even adopted the gesture of making the sign of the cross, integrating it in his public appearances.[252] For a short while, the movement was able to capture the imagination of several thousand natives, not least those at the Jesuit mission stations. The Spanish felt not unreasonably threatened, sent soldiers, and finally executed Ariscibi. The middle ground of the mission in this case showed not only its extensive religious and cultural creativity but also its potential for conflict.

In the eyes of the missionaries and colonists, Ariscibi went too far with his independent Christian-indigenous hybrid religion. But as long as the indigenous version of Christianity remained peaceful and retained at least a vague orientation toward "correct" goals, the men of the Society of Jesus were often prepared to make astonishing religious compromises. They were well aware of the fact that the thorough Christianization of the new converts would be a long journey. What they forbade is often less surprising than what and how much they allowed.[253] Even Hernando de Santarén, who gladly oversaw the physical destruction of "idols" and in whose presence "apostate" indigenous Christians were beaten, could be generous. "Their way of burying the dead has been left to them," he once remarked somewhat patronizingly.[254] He evidently did not find anything immediately reprehensible about it, so he saved his strength for changing other areas of indigenous life. It was that way everywhere. In their Christianizing mission, the Jesuits took the long—often frustratingly long—approach to conversion, persevering step by step only with great patience. Every Christianizing change, however small, was a success, even if countless "heathen" customs remained. The sudden, complete transformation of the natives' way of life was all too improbable, and so the Jesuits came to terms—indeed had to come to terms—with the extensive remnants of "heathen" customs.[255]

What was taught during the missionizing process thus was not only a hybrid of Catholicism and local pre-Christian elements but also usually a minimal version of Catholicism. The Jesuits focused on the new Christians' behavior, less so on niceties of doctrine. The rudiments of Christian theology—the Trinity, sin and salvation, the Last Judgment—were mentioned and conveyed through catechisms and fundamental prayers that were learned by heart. The sacraments were important. The Jesuits also attached great importance to confession at the mission because this rite required the new converts to distance themselves explicitly from their past life and demonstrate their rejection of "diabolical superstitions."[256] Beyond this reduced theological basis, however, the missionaries did not normally measure their success by whether the natives comprehended the finer dogmatic points of Catholic theology. The padres were usually satisfied if the natives at least adapted their behavior to Christian standards. One day, for example, a Xixime was talking with the priest at the church of San André.[257] All of a sudden, he turned away and left the building without saying goodbye. When he came right back, the Jesuit was curious and asked where he had been. The man answered that he had just quickly gone outside the church to spit because he did not want to do that in the holy interior. "Such was the respect shown the church by this Indian, who just yesterday was a barbarian," the padre proudly concluded. It was commonly such simple acts with which the missionaries at first had to content themselves. And even if they sometimes vented their frustration about the often minimal progress made, the Jesuits still pointed to every tiny step forward as a token of success. They saw such changes of behavior not merely as superficial gestures but rather as signs of profound inner change on the part of the converts. The natives' outward actions reflected their inner state of mind, the Jesuits were sure, and there was an endless supply of references and examples in classical Catholic literature. And so it was in this case, too: the Xixime man's reluctance to spit in church immediately reminded the educated Jesuit of an early Christian episode reported by Gregory of Nazianzen, whose holy sister Gorgonia likewise refused to spit in church. By suggestively superimposing the mission in Mexico on early Christianity, the Native American, who presumably had adapted only superficially to the missionaries' new code of conduct, was immediately transformed into a model of Christian righteousness.

Spitting, of course, was just the beginning, as far as changing behavior was concerned. Everywhere in the missions to the Americas, from Canada to the Mississippi valley and Mexico down to the peoples of the Andes and Amazonia, the Jesuits (and all other Catholic clergymen) were confronted with a series of indigenous behaviors that were radically at odds with European, Christian standards. Sexual ethics were often a major point of contention. Christianizing them, in the Jesuits' eyes, was both an indispensable prerequisite and proof of successful conversion. While the Jesuits may have been willing to compromise in many things, with respect to sexuality and marriage compromise was utterly impossible. The Catholic clergymen were constantly beside themselves over the fact that, in many tribes, a man could have several wives. Time after time, they criticized this behavior and forced the indigenous population to give up their traditional customs. As for the fact that they were deliberately manipulating the social structures of whole societies against the will of many of those involved, thus causing enormous social problems—they either looked the other way or approvingly accepted it. Andrés Pérez de Ribas, one of the most influential missionaries of the first half of the seventeenth century, openly admitted: "On innumerable occasions I saw with my own eyes and heard [with my own ears] the angry clamor of those women who had been cast aside." It is telling that Pérez de Ribas could not completely rebut this allegation. His answer was vague and unspecific: "I could find no better answer than to tell each of them to forget about their husband's indifference. . . . I told them I would marry them in the Christian fashion to someone who would love them."[258] How persuasive the women found this answer is unknown. It is undeniable, however, that Christianization seriously warped established social structures, leading to significant tensions.

From the missionaries' perspective, however, social crises might also have their good side: moments in which established worldviews and beliefs were cast into doubt, were shaken, or proved to be ineffective were occasions on which the Europeans' new ideas and new behaviors might have greater appeal.[259] The Jesuits often registered success when they encountered people whose own convictions were already under fire. In Mexico—and in principle likewise in Canada—two types of crisis repeatedly helped the missionaries creep in: plague and famine. From north to south, the indigenous population of the Americas in the early modern period was exposed to European pathogens usually without any natural immunity. Although there were major differences in detail, the decimation of native peoples everywhere took on catastrophic dimensions. Predominantly on account of imported diseases— combined with the behavior of the colonizers themselves—up to 90 percent of the indigenous population of Mexico perished in the sixteenth century.[260] The early modern Jesuits and their contemporaries lacked a clear understanding of the causes of this mass mortality. They saw themselves all the more called on to tend to the sick and to give them the best possible care, selflessly and with unstinting personal engagement. For the Jesuits, epidemics traditionally were occasions on which to demonstrate that fundamental virtue, Christian charity. Just as they tended to plague victims in Europe, often suffering enormous loss of life in their own ranks, so too they tended to the sick in Mexico, whether baptized or not. A paradoxical logic spurred them on: "So that these precious acts of charity might be performed, we can further understand that God often chooses not to perform or make use of those sudden miracles of healing referred to by Christ our Lord in the Gospel."[261] The suffering of one was a test of piety for the other. The Jesuits also enjoyed some success. Although the medicine available and the application of relics in combination with prayers did not usually help, their intensive care for the sick was a lifesaving factor again and again. Indigenous plague victims who were cared for by the Jesuits probably had a significantly better chance of survival.[262]

Of course, from the missionaries' perspective, the bodies of the sick were a secondary concern. Concern for the salvation of the soul always lurked behind their care for the health of the body. Deathly ill natives were immediately baptized without further instruction to ensure that their souls were not shut off from eternal life. This was the only occasion when the Society of Jesus' otherwise very high standards for baptism were suspended. Mortal death and eternal life lay so close together that they were nearly two sides of the same coin. The missionaries' feelings as they attempted to process this depressing experience were accordingly ambivalent: "Although it is true that at times our priests could not help but feel natural sorrow over seeing so many children die, and also over the fact the sorcerers accused them of killing them, nevertheless they have found some consolation in the fact that these souls nevertheless have been saved."[263] The unconverted natives of Mexico, like those in Canada, often drew a different conclusion: baptism meant death. From their perspective, baptism was not a life-giving but rather a life-ending ritual because it occurred so frequently in connection with sickness and death.[264] This helpless logic in the face of mass mortality created real threats for the missionaries. They sometimes could only secretly baptize the deathly ill, often with considerable risk to their own lives.

But overall the epidemics probably enhanced rather than diminished the status of Christianity and the Jesuits among the survivors.[265] The Europeans, who were immune, seemed to be invincible beings. Their unflagging care for the sick won them sympathy. Above all, the Jesuits had something to offer that the indigenous population, which had never experienced such dramatic waves of plague, lacked: a comprehensive, spiritual explanatory model that they propounded with conviction. Like their brothers in Europe, the Jesuits in Mexico interpreted sicknesses primarily as a sign from God. The people's behavior had to change; they had to recognize and worship God more intensely. Pious, newly baptized Christians were on the right path, but they had not yet gone far enough. When the normal social life of the natives collapsed during an epidemic, the spiritual interpretations offered by the Jesuits often proved to be especially persuasive. The new religion was worth a try after all.

After plague, famine was the second major topic. Arguably no other aspect of everyday life in northwestern Mexico was more influential than the constant shortage of food. The Jesuits regularly reported that the natives lived from hand to mouth without any regular food supply. This permanent shortage was particularly serious in Baja California. Salvatierra reported that the people there could meet their needs only by traveling vast distances as nomads. The Jesuits themselves were frequently affected by this lack of resources during the founding phase of the various missions, particularly since they were at a loss for how to provide for themselves in the inhospitable conditions of Baja California. They normally relied on the generosity of the natives to obtain food. Often enough, the friendly indigenous population shared some of their meager yield from hunting and gathering and thus ensured the missionaries' survival.[266]

Over the long term, however, the balance of power shifted. In time, the Jesuits established semireliable supply lines almost everywhere: Baja California, for example, was supplied by regular shipments from the fruitful territory of Sinaloa across the Gulf of California. Jesuits like Philipp Segesser on their mainland mission stations and the many experts on Jesuit haciendas that supplied the Society elsewhere reaped good harvests.[267] When the indigenous population was hungry, however, the uneven distribution of resources often led to conflict. The very first violent confrontation in Baja California in 1697, for example, revolved around supplies the Europeans had brought with them. When a cold spring wiped out the Yaquis' crop in 1736, in their distress they stole and slaughtered half a dozen horses and a mule belonging to the missionary Philipp Segesser—to which he turned a blind eye in light of the circumstances.[268] Even in normal times, however, the natives knew that the missionaries usually had supplies. Mission stations often became trading hubs for foodstuffs and other goods. Segesser, for instance, mentions that "some [Yaquis] come daily with salt to trade for maize and wheat."[269] In some cases, the natives became largely dependent on food provided by the mission.[270]

Food and drink were not the Jesuits' only attractions. The indigenous population also found a complex material culture to marvel at, far surpassing the capabilities of the native peoples of North, Central, and South America. This gave the missionaries and their faith considerable appeal.[271] Segesser ordered objects like waffle irons, knives, spoons, and other devices and tools from Europe—they may have initially served the missionaries' own needs, but the Jesuit was also well aware of the fact that the new material culture would, step by step, enhance the position of the Europeans vis-à-vis the indigenous population. "But how will the things for which I am asking help the Indians? Answer: one thing leads to another," Segesser explained before elaborating on the indirect missionary benefit he anticipated from individual objects.[272]

European weapons had special significance. Guns and cannons by no means guaranteed military superiority: at the occupation of Loreto by Salvatierra and his little band of soldiers in 1697, some European munitions exploded and posed a greater threat to the occupiers than to their adversaries. The Spanish were nonetheless sought-after allies in native conflicts. At the very beginning of the mission to Sinaloa, several Ximes, "who waged constant war on our Christians, but not with the Spanish," approached the governor and said "they wanted to be our friends, but not those of the [baptized] Indians."[273] In this way, the European newcomers were drawn into alliances and pacts with the natives, and the Jesuits along with them.

The missionaries in Mexico, Canada, and elsewhere thus had a variety of things to offer that promised something like greater security for the indigenous population: new military alliances, a strict new mental and spiritual orientation preached with enthusiasm, supplies, and care. Intentionally or not, the colonizers and missionaries had often created the crises that produced this greater need for security. But once the natives' world had been uprooted and set in motion, European goods and alliances proved to be a great temptation. The path to them often lay through the missionaries of the Society of Jesus, especially in the early days.

In order to wield this influence as effectively as possible, the Jesuits devised a concise organizational structure for their missions.[274] The Jesuits' way of proceeding in Mexico was (just as it was in Canada and everywhere else) to dispatch missionaries to live in the midst of the people to be converted. Mere visits, for instance, by Jesuits setting out from the colonial cities, were considered inadequate. Hence, in practical terms, they drew small mission districts at the heart of which—as in Huronia—lay a permanent headquarters (cabecera). Over time, dozens of such cabeceras were founded. The main church in the region, the missionaries' supplies, and—if there were any—schools were located there. In theory, two missionaries were supposed to live there, as stipulated by the rules and precepts of the Society. De facto, however, it was usually only a single Jesuit.[275] He was responsible for ministering not just to the natives who lived in the immediate vicinity of the cabecera; these outposts were only the point of departure for Christianizing the entire region. To facilitate that goal, further smaller, temporary mission stations (*visitas*) were established in the district of each cabecera—two or three or even more such *visitas* per cabecera were common. These smaller stations were often located several hours away, so that the padres sometimes could visit them only sporadically.

In order to create an organization along the lines of European culture and religion, the Jesuits appointed a whole series of indigenous officials. Imitating European administrative structures, the Jesuits appointed *gobernadores*, *capitanes*, *alcaldes*, *fiscales*, and other "officials" to watch over everyday business. Sometimes they even trained real "catechists" who could take over at least some simple forms of ministry.[276] They liked to give such positions to natives they regarded as military or political leaders. To emphasize such natives' status as officials, the padres also conferred European insignia—such as a scepter or a ceremonial sword.[277] The offices gave their incumbents special authority and prestige and thus were undoubtedly an efficient way to secure their loyalty in the long term.[278]

Ideally, these indigenous officials always exercised their office in consultation with the missionary or only in his absence. As far as possible, the Jesuits wanted to prevent indigenous elites from building their own power bases. In light of their patriarchal sense of superiority to the natives, there was no doubt that they saw themselves as the highest authorities in the converts' villages. Obedience to the clergymen, pious belief in their authority, and respect for European social hierarchies were the values that ideally shaped life in the missions and fostered the spread of Christianity.

The system of *visitas* was a compromise, like so much else in this and in every mission. It resulted from the sobering experience that it often was impossible to compel the seminomadic indigenous population to become completely sedentary and settle in mission villages. It was not for want of trying. In 1730, for example, Father José de Echeverría proposed to force the natives in Baja California to settle near the headquarters of the missions "with gentle pressure, or, if that were insufficient, with harsh means."[279] As in Canada, the history of the Jesuit mission in Mexico also contains several episodes in which the population was compelled to move, settle, and become sedentary. By far the most famous example of the founding of real mission towns, however, involved the both heavily criticized and fascinating reductions (*reducciones*) of the province of Paraguay.

PARAGUAY: ISOLATION OR EUROPEANIZATION UNDER THE "JESUIT STATE"

After relatively brief training in Córdoba and ordination in Santiago del Estero, Father Antonio Ruiz de Montoya was sent to one of these reductions in 1612. Loreto, southeast of Asunción on the right bank of the Rio Paraná, was the first place where Ruiz de Montoya was deployed as a missionary. We thus can appreciate the state of exhilaration in which he described his first days there. Completely different experiences remained in his memory. He was glad to meet the two other Jesuits stationed there, Giuseppe Cataldini (1571–1653) and Simone Mascetta (1577–1658). Both missionaries were "impoverished, but rich in happiness." Their frocks were so threadbare that the original cloth could scarcely be seen beneath all the patches. The shoes they had brought from Asunción had been repaired with strips of material they had cut off from their cassocks. The Jesuits themselves had to grow the grain for the hosts, and they rationed the wine for celebrating mass to the last drop. Otherwise, their food consisted almost exclusively of potatoes, manioc (cassava), and bananas. These poor living conditions reminded the newcomer of the stories he had read during his education about the anchorites, early Christian monks who withdrew from the world to practice radical asceticism in wastelands, rejecting every physical comfort. Ruiz de Montoya now wanted to join the ranks of these ecclesiastical heroes. The reductions of Paraguay seemed to him to be an arena for feats of religious devotion. "I counted myself blessed to be in their company," he noted exuberantly.[280] But not only Ruiz de Montoya, but also the Guaraní people of the region seemed to appreciate the missionaries' presence. They repeatedly asked the Spanish authorities to send clergymen. The Jesuits' readiness to go and the indigenous population's willingness to cooperate resulted in one of the most successful Jesuit mission projects ever.[281] There soon was no more talk of poor conditions reminiscent of the ancient anchorites.

Prior to the Europeans' arrival, the Guaraní had lived primarily "in forests, hill country, and valleys, and along hidden streams in clumps of three, four, or six dwellings," often several kilometers apart. In 1610, the Jesuits began to bring them together "into large settlements," as Ruiz de Montoya described.[282] Compelling these small groups of different people, who were often enemies, culturally distinct, and highly mobile, to relocate and settle permanently in the same place was complicated business.[283] The process usually was peaceful, but violence was also always in play on the Jesuits' part.[284] After numerous changes, the Jesuits had established thirty such mission villages in the eighteenth century, in which up to 140,000 indigenous people lived. Compared with most Spanish settlements in the New World, and even in the motherland, they were outstandingly organized and prosperous cities of considerable size. Few colonial cities will have had more inhabitants.[285] In the context of these new artificial settlements, the Jesuits wanted to Christianize the indigenous population with catechesis, education, sermons, sacraments, pastoral care, and constant habituation.[286] Native people who did not live in these villages for whatever reason were only sporadically touched by the Jesuits' mission in Paraguay.

The Jesuits called these settlements "reductions." The etymological root of the word is derived from the Latin verb reducere. The original meaning was "to lead" or "bring back" or "restore," but in the Spanish of the day the verb reducir meant "to convert" or "to bring to an orderly way of life."[287] A reduction, from the Jesuit point of view, was accordingly not only a place but also an extensive, life-changing process.[288] Inducing the scattered native peoples to resettle and live together was only the first step in this evolution, albeit an important one. The Jesuits were not the first, however, to hit upon the idea that changing the settlement geography of a region would facilitate the mission.[289] Bishop Bartolomé de Las Casas, for example, a harsh critic of the excessive colonial exploitation of the indigenous population, had developed very specific ideas for artificial mission villages decades beforehand. In Paraguay itself, the Franciscans had instituted such settlements prior to the Jesuits' arrival.[290] In nearby Brazil, under the leadership of Manuel da Nóbrega, the Jesuits began to establish mission villages (*aldeias*) in the mid-sixteenth century. The Spanish Laws of the Indies (Leyes de Indias) explicitly prescribed the settlement of indigenous natives in permanent villages. We have already become acquainted with the influential mission village of Julí on the west bank of Lake Titicaca, which the Jesuits took over in 1576. In 1609 in Paraguay, it was explicitly said that mission villages should be founded "in the manner of those in Peru."[291] From Paraguay, this model spread across the world. Whether in North America, Baja California, or the Caribbean, Jesuits everywhere drew inspiration from the successes of the reductions.[292]

Since each reduction was built from the ground up, with careful planning it was possible to illustrate important norms and principles of Christian life. The reductions accordingly all followed more or less the same layout.[293] A large square, usually measuring more than one hundred meters long and wide, was located at the center of a reduction. Featuring a cross in the middle and a church on one side, it unmistakably illustrated the Christian character of the new settlement. On the one hand, the square was the reduction's commons, in which communal activities could take place and assemblies met. The area was in fact large enough for the Jesuits to address the entire population. Feasts and festivals were held here, and punishments were carried out, as well. On the other hand, the central square served to divide the reduction, splitting it into two areas: on one side stood the church, cemetery, and the Jesuits' houses, which usually constituted a coherent architectural complex of stone buildings. This sphere of clergymen and Europeans also included the storehouses and the many workshops that were found in every reduction. On the other side of the central square were the dwellings and living quarters of the Guaraní, which were often built of wood or adobe. Streets and alleys separated these residential blocks by rank and file. Thus, this urbanistic structure served to symbolize social hierarchies. The section around the church represented the power and prominence of the two Jesuits who normally lived in each reduction. Opposite them lay the area for thousands of native people. The latter had, in a sense, to leave their "neighborhood," cross the square by the church, and enter the Jesuits' area to go to work in their workshops.

The living quarters for the native people were conceived for small nuclear families—a vivid rejection of the communal cohabitation of large native clans. Even if this transition from clan to family living quarters actually took centuries, it was still planned from the outset to build the villages "after the fashion of Spanish cities, so that everyone lives in his own house and is kept within certain boundaries and walls, so there is no way from one house into another." That would ensure that the occupants "would not have their usual opportunity for sinning."[294] The reductions were thus physical representations of European values and social ideas and simultaneously served as architectural means of suppressing indigenous sexual relations. Women who for various reasons were permanently or temporarily alone had to move into a special, closed-off house (*coty guazú*). With this prisonlike measure, the Jesuits hoped to ensure that the indigenous people observed European sexual norms. In sum, the simple layout and rational planning of the reductions enabled the two or three priests on hand to maintain control over a large population. Every few days, the padres could and indeed were required to take a walk through the straight streets of the indigenous quarter of the mission village to find and put a stop to any potential transgressions, such as drunkenness.[295] This architectural restructuring of the natives' everyday lives shows how the Jesuits at the mission were attempting to direct cultural transformation understood in very broad terms.[296] They by no means felt as if they had to educate the indigenous population of the Americas exclusively in terms of religion, but rather also wanted to reform them on a social, political, organizational, and cultural level. Indeed, the Jesuits did not have a very high opinion of the native people: José de Acosta, for example, the most famous Jesuit mission theorist and erstwhile provincial of Peru, divided the non-Christian peoples of the world into three categories: high cultures with sophisticated writing and literature (like Japan and China), civilized cultures (he cites the Inca and Aztecs as examples), and barbarians without culture or civilization (he placed the natives of North and South America within this category).[297] The high cultures of Asia might also have been "barbaric," but they still deserved respect on account of their advanced literary culture. The way of life of the native peoples of South America, however, seemed lacking in almost every way for Acosta and his many readers: they had no writing, no philosophy, no education, and no permanent settlements. Jesuits like Acosta were regularly astonished that native peoples seemingly lacked all of the hallmarks of a formal public order. According to one very common prejudice, they lived "like animals, almost without any human sense, without law, without a king, without treaties, without a clear magistrate and state." Hence the missionaries wanted to impart far more than the Christian religion to the natives. "We must teach all these people, or rather barely people, the fundamentals of human life [*humana*] so that they might learn to be human," Acosta concluded. The reductions were an appropriate means of doing so. Their goal was to situate the indigenous people "in a polity" (*ponerles en policía*).[298]

The Jesuits therefore tried to impose European social structures on indigenous society. As in the *visitas* of Mexico, they created a series of institutions previously unknown to the natives to govern and administer the reductions. At the top of each reduction was a kind of administrative council, the cabildo. The most important member of the cabildo was the *corregidor*, who presided over it. He was assisted by a deputy and several subordinate officials (regidores and alcaldes), a secretary, a beadle, and further officials. The Jesuits had decisive influence on appointments to these positions, even if the *corregidor* had to be authorized by the Spanish colonial administration. The cabildo was responsible for maintaining and structuring the public order. It had a coordinating, mediating, and even a punishing function. From the Jesuits' perspective, the indigenous members of the cabildo served not only to monitor the natives living in the mission but also to introduce them to European Christian conventions. The Jesuits, however, wanted to keep a firm grip on authority and responsibility for the reductions. Hence, as they understood things, the cabildo could take action only after consulting and winning the approval of the padres.

How great an influence the new institutions of the reductions had on the everyday life of the people remains doubtful. Below and outside the cabildos, the traditional division of the indigenous population into *caci-cazgos* still existed. These were small units of perhaps twenty or thirty families that were led by a chief (cacique). This traditional social structure remained intact in the reductions, and it may have been a major, indeed perhaps the decisive, factor that made the settlements successful. The Jesuits might try to "Europeanize" these people and their functions, as reflected in the very way they were addressed: the cacique and his wife were styled *don* and *doña*, but otherwise the reductions remained marked by traditional social structures.[299] In this way, a hybrid of traditional and European social orders emerged at the reductions rather than a purely European society. Nowhere could it be claimed that the indigenous population had been totally Europeanized. It would have been a utopian goal for practical reasons alone, as the Jesuits themselves acknowledged. This admission, however, sometimes led to conflict with the colonial powers, which often had grander ambitions. In Canada, for example, the French minister Colbert and his most important local official, Intendant Jean Talon, were upset that the missionaries had simply abandoned their intention to Gallicize the natives. And yet the colonial officials also reluctantly had to accept the fact that it was impossible to integrate the indigenous population into European social and political structures. No one, for example, could enforce European (criminal) law to its full extent, even if the subjugated natives, as subjects of the king, were bound de jure to the laws of the motherland in the eyes of the European colonists. In reality, many actions that were crimes according to European standards were often not, or not seriously, punished when they were committed by natives.[300]

There also was the problem that the missionaries of the Society of Jesus sometimes viewed Europeanization not only as impossible and impracticable but also even as harmful. Large segments of European émigrés had a markedly bad reputation. Spanish laws regularly cited the bad example set for the natives by the colonists.[301] Many clergymen shared these reservations. "Father, take my advice and run away from those Indians [i.e., the colonists], unless you want to put your soul in danger!"—with these words, Domingo de Soto, the great Dominican scholar and professor in Salamanca, supposedly bade farewell to his student and good acquaintance, the young Jesuit Bartolomé Hernández, as the latter set out for the New World in 1568.[302] Hence, the Jesuits very clearly tried to contain the influence of the European settlers, and the reductions were extremely helpful at doing so. Provincial Torres Bollo therefore ordered in 1609 that the missionaries should "ensure with all possible fortitude, prudence, and caution that the Spanish do not set foot in the reductions."[303] In contrast to Franciscan precedent, and also in distinction to the Jesuit reductions in Brazil (*aldeias*), the missionaries established many of their reductions in Paraguay far from the central Spanish settlements and major commerce routes.[304] That better ensured their isolation.

The clearest European threat from which the native inhabitants had to be protected was slavery. On the one hand, the Spanish settlers had claims to the labor of the Guaraní in the context of the official encomienda system; on the other, Portuguese adventurers originating from nearby São Paulo regularly preyed on native people by the thousand in the first half of the seventeenth century with brutal slave raids. The Spanish authorities viewed the raids as completely illegal.

The Spanish introduced the encomienda system in all their colonial holdings in the Americas shortly after conquest. Insofar as the natives had been subjugated (by military force), they were viewed as vassals of the king who had to pay tribute to their monarch according to European convention. They would do so in the form of labor for the Spanish settlers. The settlers (encomenderos) accordingly believed they had a legal right to indigenous labor.[305] There in fact were extensive Spanish laws that regulated the nature and extent of the labor to be performed by native peoples. At least de jure the natives were not at the colonists' mercy. De facto, however, many Spanish encomenderos did their utmost to exploit indigenous labor, in some cases imposing slave-like conditions, at least temporarily. Many Europeans in the New World viewed the system as the key to the survival of the Spanish colonies: without indigenous labor, they argued, they could not produce anything from either agriculture or mining.

As early as the sixteenth century, however, heated discussions about the practice were already taking place in Spain. The encomienda was successively curtailed or at least put under stricter regulations. Some colonial officials, such as Francisco de Alfaro, who energetically supported the Jesuits in Paraguay after 1600, took action against the excesses of the system and attempted to monitor it much more rigorously. In this confused situation, the Jesuits broadly took the view that native peoples who were the targets of their mission or who had already converted should be exempt from the encomienda and any personal obligation to perform labor. The Jesuits of Paraguay therefore styled themselves as fighting for the "freedom of the Indians."[306] Nicolás Durán Mastrilli, the provincial of Paraguay, stressed that the Jesuit fathers would do their utmost to fight against the encomienda on behalf of the natives living under their protection.[307] The Jesuits actually managed to ensure that the natives who lived on most of their reductions were exempt from the encomienda—one of the major attractions of Jesuit mission villages. This was one of the key differences between them and their Franciscan counterparts in Paraguay, where the encomienda was universally in force.[308]

Even Durán Mastrilli had to concede, however, that the padres by no means successfully freed all the natives from the encomienda. At least two reductions in Paraguay—Loreto and San Ignacio Guazú—permanently remained part of the system because the natives living there had been subject to the encomienda before the reductions were founded.[309] Spanish officials therefore occasionally entered the village and prepared lists detailing which natives were obligated to perform labor for which colonists. No matter how bitterly the Jesuits complained and how scrupulously they strove to ensure that royal regulations were observed, they still could not bring about the complete abolishment of the system. The Jesuits repeatedly learned that difficult compromises with the colonists in cases of doubt were inevitable. Nowhere could they realize the ideal of complete isolation, and in borderline cases they more or less accepted the inevitable.[310] Whether in Santa Cruz de la Sierra in Bolivia, in Brazil, or in northwestern Mexico, the missionaries always had to yield to the colonists' demands and tolerate the abduction of large groups of natives to work the mines and fields. Wherever the encomienda had been introduced, the Jesuits often had to content themselves with small improvements.[311]

The survival of the reductions themselves ultimately depended on the labor of their indigenous inhabitants. Without their contribution, only a "miracle" could have kept the Jesuit project going, as it was repeatedly stated, directly echoing the position of the encomenderos.[312] The Jesuits had to provide for the sustenance of the reduction inhabitants, and that was impossible without the labor of the natives themselves.[313] They therefore tried to convince the Guaraní living in the reductions of the merits of planned agriculture. Four days a week, the natives were supposed to work their small plots of land (abambaé). They were theoretically autonomous and responsible for their own crops, but in reality the missionaries largely controlled the proceedings and the harvest. The remaining two days were spent in communal labor (tupambaé) on common land. The missionaries thus also systematically called on the natives to work, albeit under different conditions than under the encomenderos. The work was strictly organized. The Jesuits tried to teach the natives European production standards. The villagers were awoken at four or five in the morning; after morning mass, the missionaries distributed the daily agenda to the cabildos, which then passed on the tasks to be carried out to the men and women fit to work. In addition to agriculture, a variety of crafts were also practiced— indeed, they flourished in the reductions. Despite the Jesuits' efforts, however, the reductions usually were not completely self-sufficient. The missionaries complained that the natives did not work hard enough and had no interest in the European logic of property and maximizing yields—whether for these or for other reasons, at any rate, the yields usually sufficed for only part of the year. Their food was supplemented by large amounts of beef, which came initially from massive wild herds in the area, and later from the reductions' own herds on numerous ranches. Their dependence on beef was so great that the Jesuits even deliberated whether to permit them to consume it exceptionally during fasting periods.[314] Finally, yerba maté was important to the reductions. The leaves of this plant were (and are) used to make a beverage known as maté, a kind of tea. Drinking this beverage was extremely important to the Guaraní, and so every year they spent several months away from the missions harvesting and preparing the leaves. To prevent them from leaving, the Jesuits began around 1700 to establish their own yerba maté plantations in the vicinity of the reductions. Despite all these activities, however, the missions continued to rely on external contacts to obtain certain commodities and to sell their own products. European goods— knives, axes, and so on—had to make their way to the reductions, just like the personal equipment of the Jesuits themselves. They sold their own products—maté, textiles produced by the women in the reduc-tions—at a profit in relatively distant cities like Buenos Aires. Without a doubt, the reductions were deeply and profitably integrated within the regional economy—all thanks to the labor of the indigenous population.

The native inhabitants living on the reductions could never be totally isolated from colonial society—that was neither feasible nor in-tended.[315] For one, the Jesuits themselves regularly selected inhabitants of the reductions to travel to the Spanish settlements to deliver mes-sages or obtain supplies. The natives naturally also were responsible for transporting the products of the mission villages to markets. The Jesuits, however, were also neither willing nor able to prevent the Spanish from visiting the reductions entirely. The door was obviously open for royal officials. And the originally strict order that ideally no travelers should be taken in had been softened already by 1610.[316] Now they talked of receiving Spanish guests "with love" and even cautiously "inviting" se-lect people. It of course was still stipulated that such visits by colonists from outside should last only a few days. Not until the eighteenth century, when such visits became increasingly common, did the Jesuits return to stricter rules. Despite those reservations, at least six particu-larly accessible mission villages had actual guesthouses (*tambos*) where travelers and traders could be housed.

It was much less complicated for the Jesuits of Paraguay to take an uncompromising stance against the raids of Portuguese *bandeirantes* from São Paulo. The Paulistas carried off thousands of native people in large-scale campaigns with several hundred participants.[317] Whereas the Portuguese Jesuits in São Paulo themselves were sometimes suspected of opportunistically looking the other way or even profiting from this business, the Spanish Jesuits railed against the *bandeirantes* almost without exception from Moxos to Chiquitos to Paraguay. Regarding the Paulistas, Ruiz de Montoya contended, "Their way of life is the destruction of the human race."[318] The German missionary Franz Xaver Eder also complained bitterly about the scandalous practices of these "mamelukes." His all-out attack on the *bandeirantes* culminated in a dramatic juxtaposition of the converted natives and the pseudo-Christian Paulistas: "Behold the New World: the Indians, who were brutes a short while ago have become men and Christians! The whites, in contrast, often descending from European families, have transformed into savage beasts and brutes."[319]

On account of their proximity to São Paulo, the reductions of Paraguay were especially vulnerable to these raids. Some sixty thousand natives were abducted by the dreaded Paulistas in the three years from 1628 to 1631 alone to provide labor for the sugar plantations then being built in Brazil. In 1630, in a dramatic rescue operation, Ruiz de Montoya evacuated some ten thousand natives by river and through virgin forest. Well over half of them perished on the long journey. Dramatic reports penned by Jesuit hands detailed the brutality and unscrupulousness of the *bandeirantes*, who killed at will, plundered, and burned, sparing not even the churches and clergymen, but even humiliating and ridiculing the Jesuits.[320] In light of these attacks, the Jesuits saw only one way to defend the natives and the reductions from European greed: by taking up arms.[321] The Jesuits began to advocate giving firearms to the natives in the missions in 1627, and in 1637 Ruiz de Montoya successfully petitioned Madrid to arm them. The reductions indeed took up arms in the ensuing years, although the measure long remained controversial. Even small cannons were used. In 1639, the Paulistas suffered the first of a series of defeats to the increasingly well-organized militias. From the start, the Jesuits personally were near the scene of the fighting, not least to defend their churches. Father Luis Ernot reported, for instance, that he and two other members of the order "had to physically strike and knock them down in order to stop their villainy, even though they often aimed their muskets at our stomachs."[322] Another Jesuit, Diego de Alfaro, the son of the royal official friendly toward the indigenous people, was killed by the Paulistas in battle. Once founded, the Guaraní army also became interesting to the Spanish colonial power. Although it had initially been established to defend the reductions from attacks originating in Brazil, indigenous soldiers were mobilized at least sixty times at the request of the Spanish from 1644 to 1766. The reductions were by no means completely segregated and autonomous in this respect either.

The "freedom of the Indians," however, which the reductions represented in the eyes of the Jesuits, could never completely be realized—nor indeed was that intended—given the paternalism of the Jesuits themselves. They were never interested in granting the natives equal rights; at no point did they give the natives a real say in their own fate. The missionaries were also not intractable opponents of the use of indigenous people as labor for European interests. Instead, they were more like middlemen and trusted partners who wanted to ensure a fair and appropriate balance. The purpose of the reduction system was not to bring about genuine freedom for the native people but rather to mediate between different models, degrees, and types of European influence to which they were subject.[323]

The reductions were nonetheless remarkable projects. They represented an attempt to organize the indigenous population of Paraguay, living in a Stone Age seminomadic culture, in such a way that the prime objective of the mission—the propagation of Christianity, leading to conversion—could be achieved as effectively as possible (according to the Jesuits' standards at the time) in the context of colonialization. The structure, appearance, and even the remarkable resilience and prosperity of the reductions were the product of a complex variety of causes: the Jesuits implemented long-standing royal regulations that they then fused with a clear vision of what the mission should actually be. They shrewdly took advantage of the conditions of the natural environment. Not least, the Jesuit missionaries had access to global expertise, which provided them with clear guidelines—that they then always applied in the light of local idiosyncrasies and circumstances. The reductions ulti- mately were the product of a protracted historical learning process.

We therefore should not read more than is warranted into the reduc- tions of Paraguay, which in many respects ranked among the Society's most spectacular successes. That has happened many times in the past. This mission in particular has been invested with sometimes grotesquely exaggerated significance. The utopification and mystification of the re- ductions commenced in the eighteenth century and were aided and abet- ted by ex-Jesuits themselves. José Manuel Peramás (1732–93), for exam- ple, composed a treatise titled *La República de Platón y los guaraníes* (The Republic of Plato and the Guaraní) that was published immediately after his death. Other authors tried in all seriousness to discover not merely Plato's ideal state but also typical Renaissance utopias like those de- scribed in Campanella's *City of the Sun*, St. Thomas More's *Utopia*, and Sidney's *Arcadia* in the reductions.[324] Even a "Jesuit state" was posited here, essentially as a countermodel to the Spanish colonial empire. Later observers found both communistic and capitalistic principles at work in the reductions. As popular as such literary caricatures of the South American missions were (and are), they also were historically untenable. These exaggerations eclipsed the embeddedness of the mission villages in their context and traditions, idealizing them as utopias. The reduc- tions, however, were not devised by the Jesuits as abstract social experi- ments. They were pragmatic reactions to specific circumstances. The social realities created by the Jesuits were a means, not an end.

CHINA: THE MISSION AS CULTURAL EXCHANGE BETWEEN PEERS

As they did often, the educated elite of the coastal Chinese city of Fu- zhou met one day in early 1625 to discuss and socialize at the local acad- emy. These meetings began when everyone bowed before a plaque bear- ing the name of Confucius that was placed at the entrance to the assembly hall. The opening ceremony was followed by music, which was heavy and sustained so as to enable those present to focus their feelings. The hall became quiet, after which one of the men rose up and read aloud some verses from the most important Confucian classic, the *Zhongyong*, the *Doctrine of the Mean*: "Man has received his *nature* from *Heaven*. Conduct in accordance with that nature constitutes what is right and true,—is a pursuing of the proper *Path*. The cultivation or regulation of that path is what is called *Instruction*."[325] After the speaker fell silent, another participant, Ai Rulüe, was asked to interpret the passage. He began a fairly long speech: The heaven mentioned in the *Zhongyong* was not the material heaven with stars and the sun. By "Heaven," the text meant rather the "faculty of understanding" (*magistero d'intendimento*), a rational principle that pervaded nature. People learned from "Heaven" to recognize themselves and live as men. Instead of "Heaven," in fact, it would be more appropriate to say "Lord of Heaven." Confucius himself will also have intended the phrase in that sense. Now, the Lord of Heaven is none other than God, who in his infinite goodness created all things, including man. In the soul of man, in turn, the Lord of Heaven planted the divine law of nature. Ai Rulüe's audience was both captivated and surprised by this speech. Probably no one had ever interpreted Confucius in this way before. Ai Rulüe had given a new interpretation that "did not destroy, but rather built on the foundations of their most ancient wisdom."[326]

Ai Rulüe (1582–1649), who presented this sensational elaboration of Confucianism, had arrived in Fuzhou only a few weeks earlier, in the retinue of Ye Xianggao (1559–1627), a high state official who had fallen into disgrace and returned to his native city.[327] Ye and Ai had met farther to the north, in Hangzhou, where Ai had won a reputation as an outstanding scientist.[328] He had published an atlas that showed the regions beyond those that paid tribute to the emperor—in other words, the lands beyond China itself (*Zhifāng wàijì*, 職方外紀).[329] The book proved to be extremely successful and remained in use for decades. Hence the scholar Ai came to the attention of the official Ye, perhaps also because Ye himself had once composed a geographical work about the barbarians of the four directions of heaven (*Sìyí kāo*, 四夷考).[330]

When Ye was traveling home to Fuzhou after he had been deposed and passed Hangzhou, he abruptly took Ai along with him.

Ai made many friends in Fuzhou in the succeeding years. To many who spoke with him, Ai's scholarly abilities and in particular his powerful and innovative interpretation of Confucius seemed like the answer to a burning question. In the early seventeenth century, an increasingly urgent sense of crisis pervaded the Chinese literati. Everywhere, they lamented the decline of the intellectual foundation of the country. A variety of reforms were proposed. Among them was a greater scholarly interest in practical subjects like acoustics, crafts, and agriculture. People looked in many philosophical and religious directions to find new, helpful supplements to Confucian culture.[331] With his scientific expertise and his moral-philosophical reinterpretation of the Confucian "heaven," Ai Rulüe seemed like he could contribute to this political, intellectual, and social revival—and in his geographic work, had not Ai even told of a faraway continent where these ideas had already been implemented? Worshipping the "heaven" as Ai proposed led to ideal conditions there: "They see all under Heaven as one family, and all people on earth as one body. . . . This is how, in general, Europe honours Heaven and loves people."[332] This was received as good news in the atmosphere of crisis prevailing in China. People who heard Ai, like Gou Bangyong, a student at the beginning of his official career, took up his ideas and carried them far beyond the city of Fuzhou.[333] Soon Ai Rulüe's followers made up a network spanning the entire province of Fujian.

Over time, Ai expanded his teachings. He now also explained, for example, how the "Lord of Heaven," whom he had introduced in 1625 as the principle of order and righteousness, had transformed into a man. In 1637, he even published a biography of this man, for which he supplied multiple illustrations (figs. 27 and 28). The people who appeared in these pictures wore strange clothing, and the rooms in which they appeared were built in a completely different way from what was the norm in China. Now Ai also talked about a special initiation ritual, which he offered to everyone who wanted to commit wholeheartedly to his ideas. These more recent ideas of Ai Rulüe—or rather Giulio Aleni,

IN NOCTE NATALIS DOMINI.
Natiuitas Christi.
Luc. ij.   Anno 1.

A. Bethlehem ciuitas Dauid.
B. Forum vbi soluitur tributum.
C. Spelunca, vbi natus est Christus.
D. IESVS recens natus, ante Prasepe hœnu in fœno iacens; quem pannis Virgo Mater inuoluit.
E. Angeli adorant Puerum natum.
F. Ad Prasepe bos & asinus nouo lumine commoti.
G. Lux è Christo nato fugat tenebras noctis.
H. Turris Heder, idest gregis.
I. Pastores ad turrim cum gregibus.
K. Angelus apparet Pastoribus, & cum eo Militia cœlestis exercitus.
L. Angelus, qui pie creditur missus in Limbum ad Patres nuncius.
M. Stella & Angelus ad Magos missi, eos primum ad iter impellunt.

FIGURE 27. Model and adaptation at the mission: depiction of the birth of Jesus Christ in Nadal's *Adnotationes et meditationes in Evangelia quae in sacrosancto Missae sacrificio toto anno leguntur*, 1595.

the Italian birth name of this Jesuit missionary—were not received as warmly now. With few exceptions, senior officials and high-ranking scholars distanced themselves.[334] The number of converts that the Jesuit Aleni was able to baptize in Fuzhou over the decades may have slowly grown, but it remained small and largely comprised people from the middle and lower social classes. In the latter half of the seventeenth

FIGURE 28. Ai Rulüe/Giulio Aleni's Chinese adaptation of Nadal's
Adnotationes. Giulio Aleni/Ai Rulüe, Tianzhu jiangsheng yanxing
jixiang [天主降生言行紀像, *Records and Illustrations of the Works and
Deeds of the Incarnation of the Lord [Jesus]*], ca. 1640. © Houghton
Library, Harvard University, 52-1049 f. 6, p. f. 6 (seq. 13).

century, there may have been no more than four thousand Christians in
the entire province of Fujian.[335]

The transformation of the Italian priest, Jesuit, theologian, and Christian Giulio Aleni into the Chinese philosopher, technological expert,
intellectual, and moral counselor Ai Rulüe is typical of the Jesuits' way

of proceeding in China. The Jesuits may have been perceived as "strange" when they first arrived in the Middle Kingdom, but they soon came to be viewed as venerable "lone traveler(s)," having proved themselves to be outstanding men "of encyclopedic knowledge and of certain special arts."[336] This positive impression was a result of the fact that they did not simply confront the Chinese with their foreign and novel teachings but rather struck a shrewd balance between familiar and new, Chinese and foreign. Jesuits like Aleni roused the curiosity of the Chinese and offered them things they could relate to, without overwhelming them.[337] They moreover skillfully presented Christianity in their first encounters with a Chinese audience as a higher form of Confucianism. Aleni knew the *Zhongyong* and the other Confucian classics well enough to interpret these texts competently in an innovative way. He integrated Christian elements in his interpretations, while he spared his audience as far as possible the difficult aspects of Christianity and those that defied rational explanation—no mention at first of the Incarnation, the Trinity, or transubstantiation, and even original sin, which he actually mentioned, was reduced to moral and social aspects. The crucifixion and details of the death of Jesus Christ in particular were often passed over in silence since the late seventeenth century. Some Chinese adversaries of Christianity had inferred from this method of execution the polemical conclusion that Christ had been killed as a criminal and rebel. The Jesuits thereafter held back on this point.[338] When they spoke to Chinese non-Christians, they therefore did not immediately launch into the summa of all Christian dogma. Instead, the Jesuits showed good instincts for presenting their interests in a way that maintained a fluid continuum between their own ideas and concepts that were already familiar to their Chinese interlocutors.

In this way, Aleni continued down the path blazed by the first two Jesuit missionaries to China: Michele Ruggieri (1543–1607) and Matteo Ricci (1552–1610).[339] In 1583, these two pioneers had succeeded where Francis Xavier and many after him had failed: by many little steps, they patiently and skillfully established social connections to leading officials in Guangzhou and Zhaoqing and so finally were able to establish the first Jesuit mission in continental China.

There were at least two reasons for the enormous difficulty of gaining a foothold in China. First—in contrast to the Americas and India— with the exception of Macao, there were no European colonists on hand, let alone any European military power. A mission could be established exclusively according to the rules of the Chinese hosts, in contrast to the peoples of the New World who had been subjugated by force. Second, the highly educated Jesuits in Asia encountered no less nuanced, literate, and technically sophisticated cultures of writing, arguing, and philosophizing. The Jesuits constantly acknowledged and emphasized this fact—one could and indeed had no choice but to anticipate demanding, rational intellectual cultures here. The condescending, patriarchal attitude of superiority that the Jesuits showed the cultures of Africa and the Americas was seldom to be found in China.[340] Therefore, the Jesuits had to "become Chinese in order to win China for Christ."[341] They began by laboriously learning the Chinese language and broadly adopting Chinese customs and clothing. Ruggieri and Ricci also learned that European knowledge and technology aroused the curiosity of the Chinese. The fascination with exotica and novelties was great among educated Chinese at the time, and both Jesuits skillfully exploited it—for instance, by effectively presenting sophisticated European mechanical devices, such as clocks.[342] In this way, Ruggieri and Ricci attained regional notoriety. They managed to translate their cultural appeal into viable social networks. Step by step, Ricci strengthened these networks by skillfully emulating Chinese forms of cultivating relations, which he found all the easier to do insofar as there were major parallels to the social conventions of Western scholars: Chinese sympathizers wrote forewords to the Europeans' texts, just like late humanist authors in Europe; academies, salons, and club-like associations bound the people together, just like scholarly circles and religious confraternities in Europe.[343]

Ruggieri initially, however, emulated the "wrong" social role: that of a Buddhist monk. Although Buddhism was then in vogue with some officials and intellectuals, it was rejected by the overwhelming majority of educated Confucian elites. Confucianism, not Buddhism—that was the lesson learned in the early years. Hence a famous change of tack came about that can be traced back primarily to Matteo Ricci. It was complete by 1595: the Jesuits now literally stepped into the shoes of Confucian scholars.[344] Contemporary portraits of Ricci and many other Jesuits depict them with long beards and wearing the silk robes of the Confucian Chinese intelligentsia. Their foreign origins were unmistakable, but the Jesuits otherwise presented themselves now as the respectable colleagues of Chinese scholars.[345] Giulio Aleni seemed to one of his friends no less than a "Confucius from the West" (xīlaí Kongzi, 西來孔子; fig. 29). Henceforth, an anti-Buddhist attitude also became part of the Jesuits' self-presentation.

This new identity soon produced results. Ricci's goal from the start was to get a foothold at the imperial court in Beijing. He was first able to live in the capital in 1601 and then settle permanently, albeit unofficially, in 1602. The emperor tolerated his presence but did not explicitly authorize it. Ricci's determination to go to Beijing grew out of his order's fundamental conviction that close ties to the high and mighty were essential. They wanted to begin to Christianize people at the pinnacle of the social hierarchy because that promised to amplify the effects of conversion the most. Ricci quickly noticed, however, that the only road to Beijing was by way of social connections. With consummate skill, he thus deliberately won the favor of midlevel, high, and leading imperial officials.

Ricci was especially successful in the case of Xu Guangqi (1562–1633), who was baptized in 1603 under the Christian name Paul, and a few years later in the case of three other eminent officials (Li Zhizao/Leo; Yang Tingyun/Michael; Wang Zheng/Philip).[346] In many regards, Xu shared the contemporary feeling of crisis and worked feverishly to improve the intellectual, military, and economic state of China. He explicitly took the view that "[the missionaries'] teaching is suitable to supplement Confucianism and to replace Buddhism."[347] As he enjoyed a meteoric rise in the state bureaucracy, he therefore sponsored many Jesuit missionaries, including Giulio Aleni.[348] Later, when Xu was working in his highest function as the minister of rites in Beijing, he also arranged for a handful of Jesuits to be permitted to reside in Beijing, now officially. Had the Jesuits not changed models, from that of a

FIGURE 29. Jesuits as Confucian scholars: Nicolas Trigault in
Chinese dress. Peter Paul Rubens, portrait of Nicolas Trigault, S.J.,
in Chinese clothing. Private collection/photograph © Christie's
Images/Bridgeman Images.

Buddhist monk to a Confucian scholar, none of this would have been
possible.

The Jesuits understood Confucianism less as a religion than as a rational philosophy.[349] To that effect, Ricci made Confucianism suit his
needs: "It was very helpful to bring the leader of the scholars' sect,

Confucius, over to our side by interpreting some obscure passages he had left behind to our advantage. That increased our prestige in the eyes of the scholars who do not worship idols."[350] Just as he had learned during his late humanist education at home in Italy, Ricci marshaled Confucian texts in his readings by making careful selections and exhausting the interpretive possibilities of the texts. Given their "obscurity," alternative interpretations could always be found.

Ricci's Chinese friends, both those who converted and those who did not, were very much aware of his tendentious purpose. In contrast to the Jesuits, they did not want to interpret away differences of worldview. Even a man who had embraced Christianity like Yang Tingyun/Michael insisted on differences: "The theory that the Lord is without voice or smell and surpasses the human's sense of hearing, seeing, and thinking is similar, but the great Lord's coming down to redeem and save the world, [the distinct stages of] the teaching of the Word . . . are all differences from the concept that people now are not as good as those of ancient times."[351] For Chinese Christians, it was and remained essential that new foreign ideas did not irreparably damage the Confucian orthodoxy, and so converted intellectuals often rearranged the building blocks of Christian doctrine into their own religious constructs in highly creative fashion.[352]

Chinese scholars could not follow Ricci's Christianizing reinterpretation of Confucius in numerous particulars. For example, the Jesuit wanted to accept only the earliest Confucian texts as genuine and dismiss all later additions as spurious, especially the neo-Confucianism of the Song dynasty of the eleventh and twelfth centuries. This view was cemented in Europe in 1687, when a team of Jesuits in Paris published an epoch-making translation of basic Confucian texts in Latin under the title *Confucius sinarum philosophus*. Their Chinese counterparts, however, found this negative verdict unnecessary and viewed the interpretive schools of the Song in a more positive light. This difference may ultimately have deterred some of Ricci's Chinese contacts from converting, despite their great sympathy for him. Only later, around 1700, did the Jesuits learn to view the Confucianism of the Song dynasty in a more positive light.[353]

Another important difference concerned the Jesuits' view of mankind. From their perspective, original sin had profoundly corrupted the once good nature of man. In conversation with Chinese people, they therefore formulated the maxim that the goal of a good life was to "overcome [corrupt] human nature." That took direct aim at (neo-)Confucian textbooks that presumed that human nature was fundamentally good and made it their supreme rule "to follow [human] nature is the Way." This significant difference was ample grounds for discussion, and for many Chinese people it was a reason not to embrace Christianity.[354] Even converts like Yang Tingyun often simply omitted original sin from their reflections.[355] But these anthropological differences did not prevent either party from debating questions of practical ethics. Despite their difficulties with the dogma of original sin, many Chinese shared the Jesuits' view that people had to work hard on themselves to lead a moral life. Confucius himself had spoken of the necessity of "overcoming the self" (kèjǐ fùlǐ, 克己復禮); Christian missionaries saw things very similarly and liked to cite the passage in question. In both cultures there was a rich tradition of edifying literature that sought to inspire the reader to introspection and taught him to overcome vice and cultivate virtue.[356] Ricci shrewdly took up this overlapping culture of ethical instruction in the first book he published in Chinese, a treatise on friendship in 1595. From a European point of view, the work was hardly noteworthy: it was a fairly typical late humanistic collection of excerpts from ancient authors like Cicero and Seneca. From a Chinese perspective, however, it confirmed that this foreign author had something to contribute to the moral-philosophical debate in their own country.[357] In light of such overlap and parallels, Ricci soon made so bold as to report home in exaggerated euphoria that the Confucian scholars "agree almost completely with us in ethics."[358]

Drawing on these shared cross-cultural interests in ethics, the Jesuits and Chinese Christians devised specific social projects together. For example, the Jesuits widely publicized the need to care for exposed children in China. The practice of leaving unwanted newborns on the roadside was a widespread social reality in China; the Jesuits and other European missionaries viewed it as a violation of Christian norms. They began to establish care facilities and gathered exposed infants into them. Christian preoccupations soon fused with Chinese traditions of care in such projects. In eighteenth-century Beijing, the Jesuits regularly paid Chinese workers—Christian and otherwise—to gather the infants exposed outside the city gates every morning, to bury the dead, and to bring the living to hospitals. The baptism of the infants was delegated to these laymen. The Jesuits often dispensed with Christian names "because these heathens neither understand our saints' names nor can they remember them, and anyway that is not critically important for baptism."[359] The orphanage in Beijing was sponsored by the Bavarian countess Maria-Theresia von Fugger-Wellenburg, while an orphanage in Shanghai was a result of the energetic support of the Chinese Christian Candida Xu (1607–80, a granddaughter of Xu Guangqi).[360] Candida compelled her son to found this orphanage with moral arguments of Christian and Confucian provenance. In circles of Chinese society exposed to Christian influence, social pressure to engage in active social welfare could be brought to bear. In twenty-one years, some 5,480 infants were saved in the orphanage of Candida's son.

After moral philosophy, the technological and scientific study of nature was the second major tie between the Jesuits and the Chinese educated elite. The Jesuits exploited the fact that their Chinese counterparts took avid interest in the Europeans' superior scientific theories and technological abilities. The Jesuits' scientific expertise and abilities brought enormous respect and prestige. But to the Jesuits' way of thinking, nature and religion had always been intimately connected. Whoever attentively "observe[d] the earth" like the "spectators in a theater" almost inevitably arrived at questions about the origin of order and beauty, Giulio Aleni wrote in the foreword to his famous Chinese atlas. From there it was but a small step to discussing the Christian God. "For the beauty of all creatures constitutes evidence of his real existence," Aleni's confrere Adam Schall von Bell assented in one of his own Chinese-language texts.[361] The Jesuits deftly maneuvered in this gray zone between religion and natural science for the next several decades in the hope of winning over Chinese intellectuals first on scientific grounds so as to then influence them in religious terms.

Geography and cartography quickly proved to be especially fruitful subjects for discussion in the Jesuits' eyes. Ricci attained wide fame as a scientific expert above all on account of his massive Chinese world map, several versions of which he had printed over the years in various exemplars. In this case, it proved advantageous that he had studied in Rome under the groundbreaking mathematician Christoph Clavius. Ricci soon taught his Chinese acquaintances at least the basics of Western mathematics. Together with Xu Guangqi and other scholars, he began to translate and publish several classical texts of Western mathematics in 1607.[362] Once again the Jesuits and their native sympathizers made use of the art of printing in China to popularize their interests. The categories of "Western knowledge" (xīxué, 西學) and the "science of heaven" (tiānxué, 天學) were thereby created—and as specialists in this field the Jesuits became sought-after contacts.

Astronomy and calendrical calculation were another area of Jesuit applied mathematics that attracted great interest. In China, the emperor was responsible for issuing the calendar and establishing important dates; hence, the best possible calculations were not only practical but also of the utmost symbolic importance. Although the Europeans' Aristotelian cosmology clashed with Chinese ideas, their astronomical calculations and observations were far more precise thanks to the new instruments they used, such as the recently invented telescope. Xu Guangqi wanted to harness the Jesuits' technological expertise for the imperial administration and successfully petitioned the emperor in 1630 to appoint two members of the Society permanently in the office of the Ministry of Rites responsible for the calendar. Over the ensuing decades, barring short interruptions, several Jesuits were always on hand in Beijing as calendrical and technological experts, even after the prohibition of Christianity in 1724. The Society always ensured that eminent scientists held these positions. Among the extraordinary personages to do so were Johann Schreck, also known as Terrenz (1576–1630), Johann Adam Schall von Bell (1592–1666), and Ferdinand Verbiest (1623–88).[363] These Jesuits also shared their knowledge far beyond Beijing through a variety of scholarly publications in Chinese. Many of their native students, colleagues, and contacts—Christian and non-Christian alike—took up aspects of Western science and wrote a plethora of new books on the most diverse scientific subjects.

This soon applied not only to mathematics but also to a whole series of European fine arts and crafts. Full-fledged workshops under Jesuit supervision were established in Beijing. Besides casting cannons and drawing maps, clockmaking, glassmaking, music, and painting all attracted Chinese interest.[364] We have already encountered Giuseppe Castiglione, who shrewdly fused perspective painting with Chinese tradition. Individual Jesuits were even employed as imperial diplomats—in 1689, Tomás Pereira and Jean-François Gerbillon took part in negotiations with the Russian Empire in Siberian Nerchinsk in an effort to put border disputes to rest.[365]

Despite these manifold worldly preoccupations, the Jesuits never forgot why they really had come to China. Adam Schall von Bell wrote to the emperor in 1642: "I came from the West to the East to propagate the teachings [of the Lord]. Because, in my youth, I did [some] calendar studies, You mistakenly ordered me to hold office. In fact, the calendar was only my secondary study, while the propagation of the teachings was my fundamental study."[366] Even after 1724, when the mission became virtually impossible, the few Jesuits who stayed behind in Beijing explicitly saw themselves as the champions of Christianity.[367] From the Society's perspective, science served to propagate religion, but most of the order's Chinese contacts turned these hierarchies on their head and separated science from religion entirely. That was also true of the emperor himself, as an episode from May 1690 illustrates. When a religious painting of Mary and various technological devices were presented to him, he accepted the instruments with great interest but politely gave the painting back—a telling choice.[368] And Mei Wending, perhaps the greatest Chinese mathematician circa 1700, wrote in a roughly contemporary poem, "Although you never served Jesus, / Yet you were able to fathom their techniques."[369] It ultimately was not the religious content of their message that made the Jesuits sought-after among intellectuals and at court.

The Jesuits were acutely aware of this problem. Individual Jesuits openly voiced their frustration about their failure to convert the mandarins, who were simply not interested in Christianity.[370] In the 1630s, the Jesuits therefore loosened their previously close ties to high scholarly officials. The connection to the circle of Confucian intellectuals, which provided the Jesuits such indispensable aid early on, was never completely cut but became significantly more tenuous over time.[371] Many influential Jesuits saw a promising alternative in concentrating their efforts more intently on the emperor. This shift away from Confucian intellectuals and toward the imperial court culminated in the efforts of the French Jesuits, who had arrived in China in 1689 and never showed much real interest in missionary work in the provinces.

It was among the French Jesuits that the "figurism" movement was born, which was the clearest sign of this policy shift and reappraisal of the cultural basis for the mission.[372] The movement took its name from the Jesuits' belief that they could identify encoded signs (*figurae*) of the Christian revelation in Chinese texts and in Chinese culture broadly. That went far beyond the thinking of Ricci and Aleni, who had merely pointed out promising parallels between Chinese teachings and Christian dogma.[373] The figurists were convinced that ancient China was in fact a kind of encoded prototype for Christianity. As Joachim Bouvet saw things, for example, there was a direct link from the Old Testament and Greek philosophy to the earliest Chinese emperors and scholars. All these different cultures and thinkers, in his eyes, were part of a universal "original theology" (*prisca theologia*), as Bouvet liked to say, borrowing the late humanist esoteric ideas of Athanasius Kircher. No wonder, then, that they also found the ancient Jewish Kabbalah in ancient Chinese texts.[374] Louis-Daniel Le Comte thought he could prove the existence of all the Christian mysteries in ancient Chinese civilization.[375] He claimed that during the two thousand years before the Incarnation, it was not the West but rather China where the "spirit of God" was preserved in the world most purely.

These claims blew up the framework of the Jesuit worldview. Both in the Society and in Paris, these positions were prohibited and censored. Figurism and its proponents were suspected of heterodoxy.

Bouvet based his esoteric interpretation of Chinese culture primarily on the *Book of Changes* (*Yijing*), which at the time was considered the earliest Chinese classic. The Jesuits were aware of the book, but they admitted that it "has little for us."[376] Bouvet changed their preferences. He in fact had hit upon a trend, because the *Yijing* was enjoying a broad revival in popularity. The Kangxi Emperor himself was very interested in this text around the year 1700.[377] Chinese Christians had taken part in current debates about this difficult book for some time, drawing on the *Yijing* to produce novel fusions of Confucian and Catholic views that paved the way toward Bouvet's figurism.[378] Li Zubai (d. 1665) first wrote that the Chinese were direct descendants of Adam and Eve in 1664.[379] The French Jesuit then built on these trends by publishing a heavily Christianized interpretation of the *Yijing* in Chinese.[380] Figurism thus was a remarkable attempt to renew and update the Jesuit approach toward China. By 1711, Bouvet also began to express his views in personal conversations with Kangxi, who took great pleasure in such considerations until at least 1716.

The Jesuits' concentration on the emperor resulted in enormous short- and medium-term benefits. Financial support from the court was crucial and did a lot of good for the poor Jesuit mission.[381] Above all, however, the Jesuits' focus on Beijing guaranteed that they enjoyed the emperor's protection for many years. The presence of the mathematician Schall von Bell in the capital in 1644 was vitally important in ensuring that they weathered the fall of the Ming and rise of the Qing dynasty relatively unscathed. Even in the chaos and banishments of the late 1660s, it was clear to everyone involved that the prestige and indispensability of the scientists at the imperial court had guaranteed the survival of the mission.[382] And the fact that Kangxi permitted the Jesuits to instruct him in Western knowledge for decades since around 1670 reinforced the emperor's trust in the men of the order. Without their influence, Kangxi's edict of toleration of 1692 would never have been issued.[383] Only toward the end of his reign, as the emperor's favor slowly began to fade, did it emerge how vulnerable the mission had become in spite—or rather precisely because—of its proximity to the emperor. When Kangxi's successor took radical action against Christianity in 1724, there was too little support in the imperial administration to change his mind.

There was yet another consequence of the spectacular presence of Jesuits at the imperial court in Beijing: even today, their fame and many publications have largely obscured the fact that in many regards they were an atypical and, in a certain sense, marginal group whose successes are also very much open to debate. Conversions at the highest level, like that of Xu Guangqi, were very rare. Likewise, despite the Jesuits' best efforts, relatively few people in the emperor's immediate circle converted, and what few conversion successes there were did not bring major consequences.[384] If we presume that there were roughly two hundred thousand Christians living in China in 1700, then these elite conversions were a minuscule fraction. By far the largest numbers of converts came from much humbler backgrounds. It usually was local midlevel or low officials and other educated people, as well as many simple rural inhabitants, who took the step of receiving baptism.[385]

By far the vast majority of Jesuits in China were preoccupied with ministering to these people in provincial cities and in the countryside, far from the national centers of power—that is the other side to the history of the Society in China that continues to be somewhat overlooked even today.[386] Very early on, around 1600, while Ricci laboriously made his way northward to Beijing as the companion of ever more new friends from the ranks of scholars and officials, his first comrades in arms were already at work in some provincial hubs.[387] Hangzhou became an important field of operations for the mission.[388] And in Guangdong, Niccolò Langobardo wanted to "see whether we might accomplish something outside the city." He crisscrossed the countryside preaching and teaching and actually converted several hundred people this way.[389] In a high culture like China, establishing mission villages in the style of the reductions, with mechanisms of repression always lurking in the background, was out of the question without the presence of European settlers and soldiers. There was no alternative to flying, wandering missions, and so soon other Jesuits also regularly left their houses in the provincial cities on excursions into the hinterland, where they sought to win followers for Christ. These missionaries worked under completely different conditions than their brothers in Beijing.[390]

Giulio Aleni was a member of this group during his time in Fujian. Despite the fact that he also was one of the Jesuits with scientific interests and cultivated such contacts with Chinese intellectuals, he spent most of his years in the order as a missionary in the countryside. Over his twenty-five-year career, he founded approximately twenty churches across the region.[391] Aleni constantly rode from village to village, visited individual Christians, received guests in turn, and occasionally battled storms and a wide variety of complications.[392] That started with language. In theory, the Jesuits had been permitted to celebrate mass in Chinese since 1615, but it appears that the missionaries still stuck with Latin.[393] The Jesuits also usually spoke fluent Mandarin Chinese, the high language of the educated class. It was widely understood in the northern and central regions of the empire, but in the south, such as in Fujian, that was not the case. Women in particular, who were already regarded as inaccessible, usually spoke only local dialects, which the Jesuits never took great pains to master.[394] As a result, Aleni could communicate directly with educated people but presumably not with the vast majority of the population. The Jesuits could address large assemblies only with the help of translators.

In conversation, the Chinese Christians Aleni encountered struck him as highly motivated and proactive: they confidently declared their needs, concerns, and troubles. Simple people in the countryside discussed the weather or the harvest with the missionaries.[395] Others were frustrated that Christianity played only a marginal part in their city and failed to catch on like wildfire—some new Christians were perhaps having second thoughts about the path they had taken.[396] Others had discussed certain topics among themselves, and Aleni was now asked to give his authoritative opinion.[397] Of their own accord, the Chinese faithful asked about communion,[398] posed questions about natural phenomena,[399] and demonstrated a clear need for a better understanding of their new religion. They sometimes brought up difficult topics for the Jesuit, questions that had led to complex theological debates in Europe. In Haikou in 1632, for instance, Aleni had to answer the fraught question of what became of the souls of those who had lived virtuously but had died before the missionaries' arrival—the classic problem of the salvation of the heathen. Aleni calmed his audience, telling them that even in such circumstances it was possible to be redeemed.[400] He also routinely had to mediate between the teachings of Christianity and local traditions. Normally, the Jesuit took the typical approach of his order, understanding most Confucian rituals as purely secular customs and therefore permitting them.[401] When pressed (but probably only then), however, he encouraged the local Christians to take aggressive measures against Buddhist rituals.[402] It is obvious that the Jesuit was thought of as a person of authority who was an esteemed adviser, even in economic concerns and family affairs, at least among the Christians and their sympathizers.[403]

Aleni thought very carefully about how to communicate his teachings as effectively as possible. He skillfully took advantage of his provincial audience's fascination with novel Western technology, for example, by belaboring metaphors with a clavichord or telescope to explain Christian ethics.[404] He also employed pictures to illustrate his message, not to mention the whole store of biblical tales and saints' legends, which Aleni often elaborated in vivid detail. If these images seemed to stay with his listeners especially well, it was not least because an illustrative, anecdotal teaching method aligned very closely with Chinese traditions.[405] Sometimes, of course, the Jesuits had to caution against misunderstandings. Pictures of Mary, for example, occasionally led people to believe that the Christian god was female, which immediately prompted the Jesuits to replace the images with depictions of Jesus Christ.[406] This rural mission relied to a considerable extent on ritual gestures and spectacular actions that seemed almost magical—reading the mass, miraculous healings, processions. Exorcisms and the expulsion of demons in particular were religious acts that the population expected and demanded the Jesuits perform.[407] This brand of Christianity differed markedly from the rationalized and pared-down version that was offered to scholars and the upper classes. By the same token, however, it came much closer to the popular missions in Europe.

The missionaries' tours and conversations at numerous hamlets and villages laid the indispensable foundation of Christian religious life in these small communities. Yet throughout the early modern period, there were far too few Jesuits to minister to these Christians.[408] There were tens of thousands of Christians in Shanghai and its hinterland alone by 1700 but only three or four Jesuits. Various forms of lay ministry therefore became increasingly important in the early Chinese church as a way to compensate. Meetings of the faithful often took place without a priest present; lay catechists normally presided.[409] This was a peculiarity of the Jesuit mission in Asia: both in Japan and later in Vietnam and China, motivated native Christians were trained to answer religious questions and to keep their community on a Christian course in everyday life. They baptized often, sometimes by the hundreds.[410] Conditions in China inevitably blurred boundaries between priests and laity. There also were lay organizations to help maintain Christianity without the help of priests. Christian converts frequently formed groups on their own initiative, since such associations were deeply embedded in Chinese society. The Jesuit missionaries later encouraged these associations, often drawing on the confraternities of Europe for inspiration.[411] There were congregations in honor of Mary, as well as *bona mors* (good death) confraternities.[412] The Jesuits and Chinese Christians published a rich body of catechetical literature, which they purposefully disseminated.[413]

These indigenous lay structures served to embed Christianity in Chinese society and proved very efficient over the long term. Not only were there too few missionaries but the Jesuits also were intermittently banished for several years, during which they could not minister to the faithful. The survival of these Christian communities in such cases depended entirely on the native laity. The Chinese Christians had already survived the first persecutions around the year 1620 largely unscathed in this way. Lay catechists became even more important during the Jesuits' forced absence in the 1660s.[414] And even the propagation of Christianity began to be carried forward by Chinese laymen in the mid-seventeenth century.[415] Most new Christians were no longer converted by the missionaries but rather by the transmission of the Christian faith within families and social networks. This structure was of the utmost importance after 1724, when Christianity was outlawed and the missionaries were permanently driven out. Some Jesuits and several

Chinese priests may have still labored on underground, but now lay catechists became the bulwark of the new religion. They ensured that Christianity remained entrenched among the population at least in some villages.[416]

In many other areas and social milieus, however, this Western religion never secured a permanent foothold, or rather no more than a marginal one at best. The Jesuits themselves were forced to admit in 1700, at the height of the mission, "People are not yet turning out in droves to receive Holy Baptism."[417] That certainly had nothing to do with the supposed fundamental incompatibility of Christianity and the Chinese worldview, as Jacques Gernet claimed decades ago.[418] It rather was initially a pragmatic consequence of the numbers: given the massive population of China, Christianity was never more than a marginal sect in the early modern period. The Jesuits moreover not only were few in number but also had limited freedom of action in China because they were constrained by the political agenda of Portugal or France and the religious instructions of Rome. They had to satisfy both European and Chinese demands, which frequently were irreconcilable. Matters were complicated still further by the fact that the powerbrokers in Europe and China knew too little about each other or had no interest in learning more. The Jesuits neither succeeded in conveying a truly convincing picture of local realities in China to those at home in Rome, Paris, and Lisbon, nor could they or would they initiate the Chinese emperor in the power struggles and conflicts of interest between rival European powers.

The fact that the Jesuits nonetheless still managed to walk the fine line between cultures and powers was a remarkable achievement. Ultimately, however, this difficult and often virtually impossible situation proved to be the undoing of the Jesuit mission to China. The Jesuits and their allies were neither able to control the will of the emperor nor willing to disregard orders from Europe. By 1700, the Jesuits began to be criticized more vocally for their support of cultural adaptation, and the popes and the Holy Office in Rome turned against the fusion of Confucianism and Christianity that Ricci, Aleni, and others had developed. The emperor in Beijing, meanwhile, insisted on this adaptation.

Without broad integration in Chinese culture, they faced the prospect of banishment. This predicament was exacerbated by growing internal tensions in the Christian mission: national animosities and quarrels among the religious orders belied the clerics' claim that the Christian religion and society was one harmonious whole. That raised the imperial court's suspicions—and the Jesuits were more or less at its mercy since they had loosened their alliance with leading officials. The Europeans' ultimately self-inflicted loss of prestige could not be compensated with violence on the part of kings and colonists as it had been in the mission territories of the Americas, which had been subjugated by military force and colonized. The missionaries had no direct European protector in China, and so were largely helpless to protect themselves against local preferences. The Kangxi Emperor gradually withdrew from the Europeans in his final years. The conversion of native Chinese was prohibited in 1717, and Kangxi's successor, Yongzheng, finally outlawed Christianity in 1724. Christianity now was considered "heretical," and Chinese Christians were monitored by the mistrustful authorities for the rest of the century.[419] Two Jesuits on mission in Suzhou were even executed in 1748. In the following years, only an extremely limited and semilegal ministry was possible. A few missionaries, however, were permitted to remain at court as scientific experts—a tradition that did not finally lapse until 1773.

Criticism: The Debate over Jesuit "Accommodation"

The expulsion of the Jesuits from China in 1724 was also a consequence of constant disputes over the methods used by the Jesuit mission. Across the world, and almost from the start, the Jesuits were criticized for their Christianizing methods. In Brazil in 1552, just three years after the arrival of Manuel da Nóbrega, a bitter feud broke out between the Jesuits and the first bishop of Bahía, Dom Pedro Fernandes Sardinha.[420] The bishop was displeased with how accommodating the Jesuits were toward the natives. They permitted the natives to sing their "heathen" songs and keep their "heathen" hairstyles, and they relied on mestizos as translators. The Jesuits were not at all sufficiently strict and consistent in his view. "I did not come here to make gentiles out of Christians, but to train gentiles to be Christians," the bishop stated. The Jesuits would hear these accusations again and again in countless iterations over the next two centuries.[421]

Many Jesuits believed, on the contrary, that the success of their mission depended on their willingness to accommodate local preferences. They vocally defended this approach. Da Nóbrega thought it was permissible "to adopt some indigenous customs that are not contrary to our Catholic faith and are not rites dedicated to idols."[422] The first Jesuit missionary to Vietnam, Francesco Buzomi, likewise thought in 1628 that one should propagate the faith first and worry about publicizing prohibitions later.[423] A clear, practical insight lay behind this approach: it was impossible to change everything all at once, and some things perhaps need not be changed at all: "Our indulgence and goodwill toward such customs enable us to suppress other, much worse customs."[424] In everyday practice, the mission thus involved a constant cost-benefit analysis, even though that was often tangled up in intellectual quandaries. The nudity of many (South) American indigenous peoples, for example, was a difficult case. Da Nóbrega himself was initially inclined to tolerate it, despite the fact that he considered it a violation of natural law: "Because they come naked, should one deny them baptism and access to the church to hear mass and teaching, if they are otherwise prepared for it?" In contrast to the stricter bishop, da Nóbrega leaned toward compromise for pragmatic reasons.

Fifty years later, colleagues in India like the great missionary Roberto de Nobili agreed.[425] In de Nobili's young community, it was not nudity but rather a certain clothing practice that was the problem. The Brahmin in Madurai wore threads across their bodies to indicate their social status and caste. Some of the Portuguese wanted to suppress the custom, suspecting that it was based on "superstition." De Nobili retorted,

> It is undeniable that these men find themselves in a painful dilemma. If they refuse to believe, they risk falling into the greatest of spiritual evils, the loss of their souls; if they embrace the faith and do not wear the thread, they incur the greatest of temporal evils, the loss of

personal dignity, and the forfeiture of their family goods and property. What sort of philosophy is this? Is it thinkable that for the sake of a trivial and false opinion put forward by a few men, it would become necessary to ordain that these converts of ours should subject themselves inevitably to either of these evils?[426]

There was no reason, in his opinion, to put additional obstacles in the way of those willing to convert because these threads and other controversial Indian customs had merely social and cultural, not religious, significance.[427]

De Nobili not only let his Brahmin converts keep their threads but also attempted to raise his chances of successfully converting the Indian population by presenting himself like a Brahmin. One contemporary reported, "He wore velvet slippers which people would kiss, he bathed twice a day before meals as Brahmans do, but without reciting prayers. . . . This he did not do out of love of cleanliness, but to show himself as a Brahman, and when he went out, he used to go in a *palanquim* [a litter]."[428] Analogously, Matteo Ricci in China was soon also being carried in a litter like a distinguished Confucian scholar.[429] And he likewise viewed this accommodation of local customs as the most promising way to raise the level of acceptance shown the missionaries. By changing their appearance and way of life, the Jesuits fit more comfortably in the worldview of their hosts and improved their chances of being heard.

The debate over strictness versus leniency in engaging with non-Christian cultures had a long tradition in Christianity. Essentially, these two opposing attitudes had existed since the days of the apostles.[430] "Accommodation," adapting to local conditions, was also not a unique feature of the Society of Jesus in the early modern period. Many missionaries from other religious orders later saw things similarly. And even contemporaries acknowledged that, in addition to Manuel da Nóbrega, it was the triumvirate of Jesuit missionaries in Asia—Alessandro Valignano, Matteo Ricci, and Roberto de Nobili—who had pioneered this approach in an especially prominent and precedent-setting way. The question thus remains as to why missionaries from the Society of Jesus in particular were so willing to adapt to strange new environments and able to integrate into new social conditions. The widest variety of reasons have been offered as answers. The Jesuits have even been mistaken for early advocates of religious inculturation or even of "interreligious dialogue."

Such exaggerated interpretations do not bring us forward. In most cases, there is far less theory and far more pragmatism behind the Jesuit missionaries' methods. Concepts of cultural—let alone religious— relativity were as alien to de Nobili as they were to Ricci or da Nóbrega.[431] The early modern Jesuits were and remained firmly convinced that Christianity was the exclusive truth that led to salvation. In the Jesuits' view, the practices that they accommodatingly tolerated were precisely *not* the religion of the Indians, Chinese, or Tupí. Their approach was calculated much more, rather, to lead people of different faiths to accept Christianity. There was no place in their views for ideas of necessarily adapting essential Christian truths to cultural contexts.

Far from a product of overarching theories, the Jesuits' capacity for adaptation was the result of the religious and academic training they received in the Society's schools and of the social background of many members. Years of practicing the *Exercises* inculcated in Jesuit missionaries the idea of viewing everything in creation as a means to a religious end—by extension, one could also take a pragmatic view of customs and traditions. Some Jesuits inferred from this attitude permission to be somewhat flexible. There was no need to impart and enforce every aspect of Christianity all at once, Jerónimo Nadal stressed.[432] The Jesuits' pastoral ministry, with its therapeutic orientation and broad focus on edification, consolation, and positive guidance, and the Jesuits' relatively positive theological view of mankind may have bolstered their inclination to look for ways to cooperate with non-Christian cultures.

We also may point to the fact that de Nobili, da Nóbrega, and Valignano, among others, came from the nobility. The aristocratic courtly culture of the sixteenth and seventeenth centuries attached the utmost importance to courteous behavior. For nobles like them, it was second nature to play a variety of social roles without losing oneself. This skill was mandatory for life at court and also helped missionaries adapt their appearance.[433] The effortlessness with which de Nobili grasped the strict social differentiation between castes according to outward symbols may also have been connected to his roots as a nobleman in the European society of estates. At bottom, arrangements in India may not have looked so different from the social reality of Europe, where distinctions of social status could clearly be seen at many religious events.[434]

The Jesuits' outstanding education in ancient rhetoric may have encouraged and reinforced such views. It had long been a basic principle of humanist rhetoric that one should key one's speech to the circumstances and audience. From there, it was only a short step to viewing a missionary's appearance, his *actio*, as something that also needed to be calibrated. Another legacy of late humanist scholarly practice was the Jesuits' adroitness at reconciling non-Christian texts with Christianity—theoretically, what they did every day with Aristotle and Cicero could also work with Confucius and Hindu treatises.[435]

Jesuit missionaries therefore felt their overall approach was justified because they judged foreign cultures and their ways of life only on the basis of the most diligent scholarly assessment: "It is risky to pronounce on the customs of the people here, unless a person has first diligently gone through their books and familiarized himself with these same customs and usages, guided by knowledge of their origin and source."[436] In this case, spiritual reflections about missionary strategies productively collided with the Jesuits' enthusiasm for scientific observation. Their superior knowledge of indigenous cultures was one of the Jesuits' most important weapons because they used all their expertise to differentiate the many customs known to them into those that were merely "secular" and those that were truly "religious" or "heathen" or "superstitious." "Secular" or social conventions could be tolerated, whereas the Jesuits banned genuinely "heathen" practices as a matter of course. The Jesuits' ability and willingness to draw this distinction between religious and social, spiritual and cultural spheres, and to divide indigenous customs into those that were prohibited and the many others that were allowed, were among the key intellectual foundations of their way of proceeding worldwide. Whoever questioned this distinction, from the Jesuits' perspective, merely proved that he had not yet familiarized himself sufficiently with the local culture: "As soon as they see the Christians depart a little bit from the customs in Spain, they think it all is heathenism and idolatry. They don't know how to distinguish between a pagoda and heathen cult from the custom of the country or province."[437] Whoever failed to accept this distinction, failed to temper "zeal" with "knowledge." The scientific analysis of indigenous cultures facilitated and legitimated cultural adaptation, while Christian rigorism appeared to be symptomatic of ignorance.

The Jesuits' adversaries obviously rejected this position. They were more intransigent and rigorous, and they considered it indispensable for religious reasons to implement as complete a version of European Christianity as possible among the "heathen." It all depended on whether one made the distinction that Jesuits drew between religious and civil, spiritual and social conventions. And it was precisely this question in the seventeenth and eighteenth centuries that ignited a bitter international debate that far surpassed in duration, impact, and importance earlier conflicts of a similar nature. The missions in Madurai/Malabar and China stood in the eye of the storm.[438] In addition to the traditional threads of the Brahmin, the Indian Malabar rites controversy also revolved around the sandalwood paste that they wore on their foreheads. Jesuits in Malabar also omitted touching those receiving baptism with saliva, as prescribed, because the Indians took offense at that element of the ritual. There were also allegations floating around that Jesuits like de Nobili accepted the existence of "Untouchables," whom, as "Brahmin Christians," they were disinclined to serve. The missionaries in fact had become so involved in the caste system that they built churches in which members of the congregation who belonged to the untouchable castes were clearly separated from the other people celebrating mass and had no contact with the missionaries themselves.[439] This practice became one of the most controversial aspects of the mission.

The Chinese rites controversy concerned the question of whether Chinese Christians might still take part in Confucian ancestor veneration.[440] It was alleged that these rituals were not simply a memorial celebration of the deceased but rather amounted to actual ancestor worship. Leading Chinese Christians in fact often practiced a combination of Christian and Confucian funeral rituals.[441] There also were language problems in China. That pertained especially to the term used to translate the European word "God." Various words that appeared in classical Chinese literature could be considered potential counterparts to "God." The Jesuits accepted two "ancient Chinese" terms from classical Confucian literature: tiān (天, "sky," "Heaven") and shàngdì (上帝, "Highest Deity")—but they preferred the newly coined "Western" word tiānzhǔ (天主, "Lord of Heaven") as the official term.[442] The admissibility of the nuanced traditional terms became a point of contention. Similar terminological problems arose almost everywhere in the Jesuit mission because no non-European language had adequate vocabulary to express the religious content of Christianity. The Chinese case, however, was the most hotly debated.

The Jesuits themselves had quibbled over these aspects. Even for some Jesuits, this inexactitude in proselytizing was simply too great.[443] And it moreover was not at all clear at first whether the unusual methods of de Nobili, for instance, were not "most unfruitful."[444] Pope Gregory XV nonetheless permitted de Nobili's approach in 1623. Internal conflicts in China pushed their way out into the open in the church somewhat later. In 1643, the Dominican Juan Bautista de Morales (1597–1664) presented seventeen problematic aspects about the Jesuit mission in Rome and thus transformed the Society's internal discussions into an international Catholic debate over the Chinese rites. Two years later, the pope assented to the Dominican's skepticism and banned the Chinese rites. The Society of Jesus responded by sending one of their most competent missionaries from China to Rome. With a skillfully orchestrated campaign, Martino Martini (1614–61) was able to captivate Europe and obtain a decree to the contrary in 1656. For decades, the question remained undecided, left floating in limbo, especially since the Holy Office declared in 1669 that both decisions were valid. The question of the Malabar rites also was left up in the air for the time being.

After these preludes came the main act, when Charles Maigrot, a member of the Mission Étrangère de Paris and an apostolic vicar in the service of the Propaganda Fide, traveled to China. He prohibited the

Chinese rites in 1693. At the same time, the question of local Jesuit rites in southern India again came under discussion. Papal officials were already looking into the mission's practices in 1702. In 1703, the Capuchin missionary François-Marie de Tours wrote and published an indictment that he sent to the Propaganda Fide in Rome. The controversy became public.[445] All the chief protagonists of the decades-long controversy have now been named: the Jesuits on the one side, most of the other orders and the Propaganda Fide on the other. In both disputed cases, Rome authorized a long series of commissions and hearings that repeatedly investigated the question. Then, in 1704, the pope banned the Chinese rites with the decree *Cum Deus optimus*. The Jesuits sent several representatives from the Society to Europe to present their position in word and text. By the same token, Rome also dispatched several high representatives of the church to assess the situation in Asia. The most famous of these Roman emissaries was the papal legate Charles-Thomas Maillard de Tournon (1668–1710). Tournon took decisive action against the Jesuits both in India and in China. The Holy Office in Rome ratified his criticism of the Indian missionaries in 1706, and in 1709, 1712, and 1715 the papal ban on the Chinese and Indian rites was renewed. The superior general of the Society at the time, Michelangelo Tamburini, had to pledge obedience to the pope in a humiliating audience in 1711. After further back-and-forth, the papal bull *Ex quo singulari* of 1742 ended the rites controversy for the Jesuits in a definitive defeat.

These conflicts by no means remained hidden locally at the missions. Indian and Chinese observers—Christian and non-Christian—actively took sides from their own perspective, significantly influencing the events.[446] On October 7, 1702, for example, the Chinese Jesuit Blasius Liu Yunde gathered nineteen other Christians together at a meeting in Nanjing to discuss current developments among the missionaries. In no uncertain terms, they questioned the anti-Jesuit decisions taken by Maigrot in a letter sent to Rome and pleaded with the pope to permit the Chinese rites that had been introduced. When *shàngdì* now was explicitly prohibited as a designation for God, other Chinese Christians argued that the prohibition would hurt their Christian reading of Confucianism. The cultural synthesis of both intellectual edifices, after all, was based on the presumption that the earliest texts (which contain *shàngdì*) anticipated Christianity.[447] The one Chinese person who was willing and able to influence the course of events the most, however, was not a Chinese Christian but rather the emperor. He had heard the Jesuits' reactions in several audiences. In 1700, he then issued an official proclamation in which he confirmed, from the Chinese perspective, the Jesuit interpretation of Confucian ancestor veneration: these were civil, not religious, rites. At the same time, he expressed his misgivings to Tournon in 1706 about the hard line taken by Rome. That only induced the legate to come down even harder on the missionaries. Since the Christians in Zhangzhou in southern Fujian refused to abandon the Chinese rites, they were forbidden to receive the sacraments.[448]

The Jesuit missionaries deeply regretted the local consequences of these conflicts. It was the indigenous Christians, their well-being, and their perception of Christianity that were at stake. And yet the Jesuits were also under no illusion that the last resort that would decide over these matters was not in India or China but rather in Rome. Hence the Jesuits attached particularly great importance to contesting their side of the debate in Europe. The controversy over the Indian and Chinese rites, however, was soon magnified by many more religious and ecclesiastical debates that had long been simmering. Soon, conflicts not only revolved around the mission and theology but also broke out in the form of institutional rivalries (the Jesuits versus other orders; the Jesuits versus the Propaganda Fide), power struggles between different church institutions (bishops versus vicars), conflicts between European powers (the Portuguese *patroado* versus French vicars), and Jansenist opposition to the Jesuits (the Jansenists naturally opposed the Indian and Chinese rites). For all these reasons, the various parties engaged in the most complicated bureaucratic and institutional maneuvering in Rome. The whole business was spurred on by mountains of printed and especially manuscript texts, some of which were intended to influence a wide audience, others only individual decision makers.

Even in the remote villages of Europe, clergymen discussed the doings in Asia and the Eternal City and ever more frequently arrived at a damning condemnation of the Jesuits. In Chaise-Dieu, a village in central France, the Benedictine monk Jacques Boyer followed developments with interest in 1712. When news of the death of Tournon (1710) arrived in February, he praised the man in his diary as a shining example. The Jesuits, in contrast, seemed to Boyer to be "enemies of the church" who were responsible for the legate's death.[449] The Chinese and Malabar rites also regularly came in for similarly harsh condemnation. The rites controversy did much to brand the Jesuits as deviants and a threat to Christianity. There were sporadic positive statements, such as that of Gottfried Wilhelm Leibniz, who declared, "I favor the Jesuits' side in the Chinese controversy being discussed today in Rome,"[450] but barring those, the Jesuits ultimately lost the public debate over the methods of their missionaries in India and China. The negative image that became attached to the Jesuits over the course of these disputes led directly to the conflicts they faced at midcentury and ultimately culminated in the suppression of the Society.

Networking through Transfers: At the Dawn of Globalization

If you paid a visit to Father Segesser in the province of Mexico and had some luck, he invited you to have a cup of hot chocolate.[451] Segesser may have lived in a deserted location on the extreme fringe of the European sphere of influence, but he was by no means cut off from the rest of the world. He regularly received a fresh supply of an exotic luxury good, chocolate, which was not produced locally. The world of the early modern missionaries was astonishingly well-connected, and the men of the Society of Jesus worked especially hard to lay the groundwork for global communication. Segesser's steady supply of chocolate, which he even served in Chinese porcelain or European stoneware, is just one such example.

There were probably few global commodities with which the Jesuits were not involved. Goods material and immaterial, precious and commonplace, living and dead all made the rounds worldwide in the service of the Jesuits or under their supervision. The Society was thus one of the most important factors in the growing integration of different regions of the world since 1492. Both in collaboration and in competition with the great Dutch and English trading companies, the colonial administrations of France, Spain, and Portugal, papal authorities operating globally, and other religious orders, the Society of Jesus bolstered the growing intercontinental interconnectivity of the day.[452] The incipient globalization of the sixteenth, seventeenth, and eighteenth centuries had a definite ecclesiastical dimension. With its key harbors like Seville, Lisbon, Brest, and Toulon, Europe was also often the center from which the Jesuits requested and shipped goods and coordinated their distribution. But as early as the sixteenth century they also established transshipment points outside Europe that were at least as important on a regional scale. The Jesuit province of Mexico, for example, was the crucial hub of all transpacific connections. Contact between the Philippines and Europe, for instance, passed through Mexico.[453]

From the perspective of Catholic clergymen like the Jesuits, there was no doubt as to which goods should circulate worldwide above all others and bind their distant brothers together in their isolation: prayers, Christian charity, and communal devotional practices.[454] Like all Catholics, the Jesuits presumed that prayers were effective completely independent of geographical distance. Accordingly, Segesser wrote, "The affairs of [my] honorable brother I will support through prayer and the offering of the Holy mass," and "I want to repay all [my relations in Switzerland] to the utmost of my abilities through prayer and the offering of holy Masses."[455] Vice versa, people back home in Europe prayed for the success of particular missions. Adam Gilg (1653–1709), another Jesuit missionary to Mexico, even suggested to the papal Curia that special masses for the propagation of the faith should be introduced in the mission.[456] The Jesuits in Asia in turn—often together with their newly converted communities—prayed for concerns in Europe. A reciprocal give-and-take of pious thoughts, prayers, and charitable remembrance bound together and connected the Jesuits both to one another and to sympathetic laymen across vast distances.[457]

The Jesuits were also very much aware that well-wishing and prayers alone did not suffice. Material gifts were indispensable for advancing the global spread of Christianity. The geographic remoteness of the missions must not lead to disinterest, the Jesuits stressed.[458] Indeed, donations crisscrossed the globe in the early modern Catholic world: people in New Spain financed benevolent undertakings by European Jesuits in North Africa, while the dukes of Bavaria sent money and materials to Jesuit missionaries in China.[459] José de la Puente, Marqués of Villapuente de Peña (1670–1739), who himself had lived in Spain and Mexico and thus was familiar with two continents, financed projects in Spain (at Manresa and Santander), Africa (ransoming slaves), Macao (an orphanage), India (catechists in Pondicherry), and of course Mexico (significant contributions to the mission in Baja California)—a truly global portfolio of charitable acts that benefited the Jesuits to a significant extent, albeit not exclusively.[460]

The Jesuits were not too proud to help themselves by making specific requests when they needed additional resources and had their sights set on potential donors. They launched downright campaigns to acquire the necessary support. The limitless zeal of the missionaries had to be matched by the limitless generosity of wealthy French supporters. Louis Le Valois urged one well-to-do noblewoman in a long appeal from 1726: "Help them, madame, help them. Help the poor infidels, who are what they are because there are not enough missionaries to preach the true Faith to them. . . . Help to pull them from the ignorance in which they live."[461] Such rhetorically charged appeals skillfully reminded lay addressees of their Christian duty, and the fundraising campaigns of the Society of Jesus were often very successful. That may have regularly led to insinuations that the Jesuits had taken advantage of the pious naivete of wealthy men and women to enrich themselves by dubious means, but the generosity of the donors was not a product of sinister scheming. The Jesuits simply knew how to pitch appeals to Christian charity extremely effectively.

In their fundraising, the missionaries shrewdly capitalized on Europe's growing thirst for knowledge of distant lands. In a famous letter to Gaspar Barzaeus in India in 1554, Ignatius explicitly urged the missionary to send exotic details about flora and fauna because people in Rome were extremely interested in these things.[462] In a short time, such propagandistic considerations evolved into a veritable information system. The Jesuit missions combined the conversion of foreign peoples with their meticulous observation and literary description.[463] Knowledge therefore was transmitted across the entire world through the structures of the Society of Jesus, a feat that was admired by contemporaries of all stripes. This Jesuit information system could cover virtually every field of the sciences of the day. The Jesuits observed anything and everything and transmitted their knowledge to interested parties both inside and outside the order. Foreign peoples and their customs were one central subject. But also anyone who wanted to learn about Asiatic musk or the medicinal rhubarb plant that grew in China, anyone who wanted information about quipus in Peru or the canoes of the native peoples of North America, anyone who wanted to learn about Hindu gods or the landscape of the Himalayas, anyone who wanted to learn exotic languages—with great probability, they could find information in Europe that had been transmitted, directly or indirectly, through Jesuit channels.

The scientific machinery and the procurement and transport logistics of the Society of Jesus not only were available to members but also could be accessed by outsiders and even Protestants in certain circumstances. Famous scholars like the (Lutheran) philosopher Gottfried Wilhelm Leibniz or reliable donors like the (Catholic) countess Maria-Theresia von Fugger-Wellenburg could make direct contact with far-away members of the order.[464] Kings and princes could also approach Jesuits with specific requests at any time. The Jesuits regularly made skillful use of their competences in the worldwide circulation of the most various goods to secure the goodwill of the powerful and cultivate social ties.

This knowledge also reached people outside major trading hubs at second and third hand. Most of the Society's scholarly output was intended for publication from the start. Countless books by Jesuit authors told of distant lands and did so in the most diverse genres, from scholarly treatises to travelogues, magazine articles, and edifying mission reports. There was something for every reader's taste. Some regions, such as Canada, even published reports in an annual rhythm. The famous *Relations* from New France, in which the Jesuit missionaries to North America wrote about the events of the past year, were printed in Paris annually from 1632 to 1673. In addition to religious affairs, these much-read volumes routinely contained information about the country and people. In the eighteenth century, the Jesuits of Paris founded the *Lettres édifiantes*, a kind of journal that published redacted letters from missionaries across the world. It was a very popular medium for information from overseas in its day. The Jesuits' texts were then digested across Europe in a variety of ways. There were translations, collections, abridgments, and plagiarism. Even in Protestant territories, readers eagerly devoured Jesuit knowledge, which was accessible in printed form across confessional boundaries, occasionally after it had been pruned of excessively Catholic passages. Protestants had no reservations about drawing on the Jesuits' objective information, because, as the English Protestant and publisher John Lockman acknowledged in 1742,

> no Men are better qualified to describe Nations and Countries than the Jesuits. Their Education, their extensive Learning; the Pains they take to acquire the Languages of the several Regions they visit; the Opportunities they have, by their Skill in the Arts and Sciences knowledge of indigenous languages, and their engagement with foreign cultures through science and the arts . . . must necessarily give our Jesuits a much more perfect Insight into the Genius and Character of a Nation.[465]

Hence it was not surprising that when the English took control of Canada in 1763 after conquering the territory, they turned to the Jesuits' writings to acquaint themselves with local conditions.[466]

Knowledge, although an immaterial good per se, necessarily circulated in various material forms, whether in letters or books or exemplary specimens of plants and animals. The enormous importance of letters to the Jesuits has been mentioned several times already. Correspondence was firmly anchored in the cultural bedrock of the Society of Jesus, and even the missions to the most remote places on earth were correctly confident that their letters would eventually be delivered. Vast efforts were made to maintain epistolary contact. Sometimes the

missionaries wrote "hastily, now in one place, now in another; sometimes upon the water, sometimes upon the land."[467] They wrote everywhere and down to the very last moment, sometimes even beyond it.
In 1611, Pierre Biard, S.J., in Port-Royal, Acadia, was not ashamed to
paddle in a canoe after a departing French ship to send his last letters to
the superior general on their way.[468]

After letters, books were by far the most important bearers of information and knowledge in the early modern period. Literature of all
kinds was regarded as a scarce commodity overseas. Matteo Ricci had
already lamented the "terrible lack of books" at the China mission. His
successors likewise took a burning interest in new publications; as one
of them remarked, "It is incredible how much the mind yearns to know
in this exile of sorts what books have been published since our departure."[469] To satisfy their thirst for knowledge, the missionaries constantly sent wish lists of books back home. The mission procurators in
Europe then set out in search of the requested titles. Sometimes extensive gifts of books were made especially for a given mission. Paul V, for
example, bequeathed a large number of printed books to the Jesuits in
China. Large shipments of books crossed the oceans at the Society's
behest. In this way, impressive libraries were created in some of the order's overseas missions, where one could find many European works as
a matter of course.[470]

Vice versa, the missionaries were in the best position to provide Europe with foreign texts. They often shipped home printed and manuscript literature from exotic mission territories. Joachim Bouvet, for
example, brought no fewer than three hundred Chinese books with him
on his brief return to France from China (1693–97).[471] The king of
France and his ministers explicitly requested further shipments from
China, Tibet, and India to furnish the royal library with exotic titles.[472]
The Jesuits were often dispatched specifically on acquisitions tours in
the mission territories, and they did not hesitate to take the books they
sought even against their owners' will. When a search for manuscripts
was to be conducted in Syria in 1673, it was suggested that the task be
entrusted to Father Joseph Besson (1607–91) because he "once dragged
about 50 volumes from the libraries of some great men here and from

some old synagogues of the Jews in the Levant, which no one before him had ever dared to attempt."[473] In India, some books, especially the sacred scriptures of the Veda, had to be "torn away" from the Brahmin, "even for money."[474] Jesuit missionaries were deeply implicated in the theft of cultural property.

In addition to printed books and manuscripts, the Jesuits shipped curiosities and other objects from distant lands back to the home countries, such as ancient coins and artworks from the Near East.[475] Plants, animals, clothing, and foodstuffs also made their way across the sea to Europe in the Jesuits' luggage and through their organization.[476] Chocolate reached not only Philipp Segesser in northwestern Mexico through Jesuit channels but also his Spanish confreres in the European motherland. And Chinese porcelain, which was primarily imported along Portuguese trading routes, at least occasionally came directly to Europe by way of the Philippines via Mexico.[477] Medicinal supplies also flowed freely through the logistical services of the Society. Exotic medicinal plants and foreign remedies like "Jesuit powder" (quinine) were intimately associated with the Society of Jesus in the early modern period.

In the opposite direction, the missionaries also carried heavy bags on departure from Europe. A contemporary described the cargo that Trigault took with him to Asia in 1617 as follows:

> It was then that we saw the great preparations for the East Indies, where fifty Jesuit priests were preparing to go, with all sorts of mathematical instruments, like charts, globes, astrolabes, planispheres, spheres, spherical triangles, cross-staffs, geometric squares, diopters, and more, and a bunch of musical instruments, and many packs of books of all kinds. All the Christian princes sent gifts, the Duke of Bavaria sent, inter alia, a manuscript of the Bible in four languages; the queen, the mother of our King, sent two fine, rich tapestries for the King of China.[478]

Valuable scientific instruments were a typical and exclusive European export that the Jesuits took with them almost everywhere they went. But the Jesuits were also involved in the circulation of much simpler

everyday items that were indispensable but virtually unobtainable overseas. In Mexico, for example, Segesser received extensive shipments of
tools and other iron implements from his family in Switzerland through
Jesuit channels—even, illicitly, weapons.[479]

In addition to everyday items and their many books, the Jesuits also
organized the global transport of artworks. For example, European
paintings regularly reached Mexico via Spain.[480] These works of art provided important artistic inspiration in Mexico, but, in light of the long
way they had traveled, they also were especially valuable status symbols.
Vice versa, the Jesuits acquired and exported indigenous artworks,
sending them halfway around the world. The Society of Jesus shipped
Japanese enamels to Europe and Mexico via Macao and sent the famous
paintings and garments that the many indigenous tribes of the Americas
produced from feathers to Europe and even the Far East.[481] Insofar as
these feather paintings employed indigenous techniques and materials
(that was their special allure, after all), yet depicted Christian themes
like the portraits of saints, their shipment to Japan and China under the
Jesuits' watch seamlessly tied together the cultures of three
continents.

Perhaps the most important form of circulation that the Society of
Jesus organized on a global scale, however, was the incredible mobility
of its own members. The Society was an institution that regularly
brought people from different cultures and backgrounds and with the
most varied experiences and worldviews into contact with one another.
Of course, by no means all Jesuits led an international life, let alone a
global one: we have already observed a degree of regionalization several
times.[482] Yet even, and perhaps especially, for the Jesuits who stayed
home within their limited geographic horizon, the Society constantly
provided opportunities for personal encounters with confreres who had
traveled widely. The frequent journeys of the Jesuits' delegates from the
missions to Europe (the provincial procurators) are well known. These
homecomers typically had very specific legal or economic responsibilities, such as representing the provinces of China and India in the rites
controversy. But they also served as advertisements, bringing a little of
the exoticism of foreign lands back to Europe. Missionaries from China,

like the Belgian Nicolas Trigault or the Italian Martino Martini, spent months making a triumphal procession across Europe as they visited courts and princes and countless Jesuits establishments. There, with their stories and the fascinating aura of an eyewitness, they courted— often with great success—money, political support, and new volunteers before they traveled back to their missions.[483] Their efforts were successful even in Protestant northern Germany, where they used their exotic allure as a pro-Catholic advertisement and propaganda.[484]

It is at least equally noteworthy that the Society of Jesus represented an opportunity for many Creoles to "travel abroad" to Europe. Jesuits born overseas received a profoundly "European" education in the Society of Jesus. They read the authors of ancient Rome and used teaching and learning methods that had been devised in French and Italian scholarly milieus. Yet they had never seen the places mentioned in their texts. They were part of a global religious apparatus, yet its most important symbolic centers were entirely unknown to them. When the global network of the Society of Jesus gave Creole Jesuits the opportunity to visit Europe, powerful impressions were the result.

Juan Antonio de Oviedo (1670–1756) is a good example. Born in Bogotá, he became a Jesuit in Mexico—that already attests to significant geographic mobility. From Mexico, he subsequently crossed the Pacific at the Society's behest, traveling to the Philippines before returning. The worldwide correspondence that he maintained spanned these regions and stretched as far as China and all of Spanish America. In 1716, Oviedo was sent to Europe to take part in the congregation of procurators in Rome. Even if his experiences in Asia may have been perhaps a bit more exotic than his encounter with Europe, he was nonetheless astonished by Spain, France, and Italy, which were previously unknown to him. The king of Spain, who had always been so far away from Mexico, was suddenly before his very eyes, as Oviedo was permitted to kiss his hand in Madrid. His visit to Rome, with its "spectacles" and an audience with the pope, likewise must have made the global nature of the Catholic Church palpable to him in a new way. Europe was an unfamiliar but also very pleasant experience for Oviedo. He was glad he did not have to travel "extremely inconveniently" on mules as he did back home, but rather in a coach, and not through barren deserts but rather "through cities, villages, and inns." His journey across Europe was "sweet recreation." Oviedo enjoyed the trip to the utmost, "reflected on everything he saw," and let "nothing escape his attention." Naturally, he had come prepared to satisfy the European thirst for exotica: he brought herbs and medicines in his luggage, but the chief attraction was a recently baptized native, who created something of a sensation in Rome. Oviedo spoke there not without some sense of pride. He told the pope not only that Mexico City had more inhabitants than Rome but also that the unity of the Catholic Church was maintained there much more successfully than in Europe.[485]

Oviedo met many famous personages in Rome: Superior General Tamburini, the Jesuit cardinal Tolomei, Pope Clement XI. He also met colleagues from Asia and the other overseas Spanish provinces at the congregation of procurators, which was the reason he had been sent to Europe in the first place. The institutional assemblies of the Society of Jesus in Rome were truly astonishing meetings of global dimensions. A small circle of Jesuits from all corners of the world gathered at them. At these congregations, it was evident how the Society's networks of contacts crisscrossed Europe and the whole world. At the General Congregation in Rome in 1645/6, the Jesuit Nithart Biber from Mainz met the missionary to Asia António Francisco Cardim. The Portuguese missionary and others not only vividly recounted the dangers and triumphs of their proselytizing work in China and India but also pressed Nithart about the fate of his brother, who had died decades earlier in Germany.[486] Through the lives of individual men, India, Portugal, and Germany were all connected in the Jesuit order.

And at least some members of the Jesuit order led a truly global life. That means more than the fact that many missionaries left one continent and spent years or the rest of their lives working on another. Many Jesuits were genuine globetrotters who far exceeded usual mobility of missionaries. Many of the men we have met in the preceding chapters knew vast spaces from firsthand experience. Jerónimo Nadal traveled to several missions in southern, Western, and Central Europe at Ignatius's behest in 1550. In the sixteenth century, Antonio Possevino traversed central, northern, and eastern Europe by order of the pope. Sebastian Rale spent parts of his life in France, Acadia, and along the Mississippi. Alexandre de Rhodes had seen Vietnam, China, Europe, and Persia. Juan Antonio de Ovieda, in addition to South and Central America, journeyed to the Philippines, China, and all of southern Europe. Guy Tachard traveled back and forth between Southeast Asia and France several times in his life; he also crossed the Bay of Bengal fairly often. Before that, he presumably had also once visited the Caribbean. Alonso Sánchez (1547–93), from Spain, initially served as a missionary in Mexico and then in the Philippines. From there, he traveled twice to Macao in China before he then returned to Spain and died before his planned return trip. The Jesuit visitors, however, represented perhaps the pinnacle of this mobility. In their case, global mobility was built directly into the institutions of the Society itself. Men like Alessandro Valignano and André Palmeira traveled tens of thousands of kilometers in the sixteenth and seventeenth centuries.[487]

Valignano, Palmeira, Tachard, and many other Jesuits obviously ran into countless difficulties on their global travels. The distances were so vast that effective communication was severely limited and even prevented—if letters arrived at all. Ignatius was still writing to Francis Xavier from Rome because he still had not received the sad news of his death months after the fact. There also were plenty of regions of the world where the early modern Jesuits never succeeded in gaining a foothold. Moreover, despite the occasional delivery of letters and supplies, missionaries on the fringes of the Europeanized world felt loneliness and isolation rather than a connection to a functioning society. Travel was always unpleasant, frequently impossible, and often life-threatening—in some phases, only about half of all missionaries sent to China survived the voyage there.[488] Information was wrong or outdated, shipments ended up in the wrong hands all too easily. More than one Jesuit felt so cut off from the European world that he claimed, according to a popular saying, that he had forgotten his native language.[489] Just like merchants and royal governors, the Jesuits of the early modern period also experienced the brutal reality of how vast the world really was and how difficult it was, indeed sometimes even impossible, to keep the Europeans scattered at remote outposts and colonies in contact with one another.[490]

Yet even though this worldwide network of Europeans was and remained precarious, and voyages in the early modern period could not guarantee the success of the many intercontinental exchanges the Jesuits planned, many Jesuits nonetheless tied the continents together through their lives and their experiences as wanderers between worlds. All this happened first and foremost in the name of the mission. That was the decisive purpose that brought the Jesuits overseas, inspired them to undertake their sundry ministries, and warranted the global network they created. Even though they were well aware of the dangers and difficulties, the world was often smaller for the Jesuits than perhaps even they thought. And through the Society of Jesus, an organization with a global reach was pivotal in making the world even smaller for people both inside and outside the order with its manifold feats of intercontinental cultural transfer since the sixteenth century.

5

A World without the Society of Jesus

HOSTILITY, SUPPRESSION, REVIVAL

ON FEBRUARY 26, 1748, a son was born to the merchant Dionysius Fortis and his wife, Theresa Ferro of Verona. They named him Luigi. The boy soon showed an inclination toward theological matters, and so they permitted him to join the Society of Jesus at the unusually young age of fourteen. He completed his novitiate at Bologna from 1762 to 1764 and took the lower classes and philosophy there until 1770.

As was customary for the Society, he then was employed as a teacher of the humanities, namely, in Ferrara. There, on July 21, 1773, he lived through the most dramatic episode that ever befell the Jesuit order in its long history: Pope Clement XIV suppressed the Society with the brief *Dominus ac redemptor*. The order henceforth ceased to exist. Its property was gradually seized by the authorities, its members in part imprisoned and expelled, its libraries sold.[1]

The now ex-Jesuit Fortis, who was only twenty-five years old but had already lived in the order for ten years, got by like many who shared his fate: he worked as a teacher and was finally ordained in 1778. Former Jesuits often still found a place in society that suited their inclinations, abilities, and previous education in such ways. Fortis first taught languages and philosophy in Verona and Parma; after the French under Napoleon invaded in 1804, he taught in Naples, Orvieto, and Verona.

He kept in touch with old and new sympathizers of the suppressed Society as best he could at these places. Even after the suppression of the Society of Jesus, many men—some of whom had never been members—tried to carry on its culture, spirit, and organization, and even to revive it.

This revival of the Society of Jesus really happened in 1814, after new sympathy for the Society emerged more prominently in Europe and the United States of America after the conclusion of the French Revolution. Pope Pius VII was able to link the restitution of the Society to a happy coincidence: namely, the fact that the papal brief *Dominus ac redemptor* had never been enforced in the Russian Empire. A kind of skeleton order had survived there the whole time, at first with hazy authority and later, from about 1800, with increasingly official sanction. The first superior general after 1814 was the superior elected for Russia in 1805, Tadeusz Brzozowski. But by 1820, when Brzozowski died and a General Congregation met for the first time since 1758, the Society's center of gravity shifted again back to Italy. The Congregation deliberately elected as its new general a man who had been a Jesuit before 1773 and had not abandoned his Jesuit values since then: Luigi Fortis, now an old man of seventy-two. For the last nine years of his life, Fortis was the first elected head of the "new" Society of Jesus. His biography encompasses and reflects the key events that will be discussed in this chapter.

The events of 1773 that came crashing down on the Society of Jesus had a long prehistory. The global suppression ordered by Clement XIV had been coming for decades. The Society had already been banned in Portugal and Brazil in 1759. France and Spain, as well as several Italian principalities, followed suit, respectively, in 1764 and 1767. This wave of intense hostility to the Jesuits becomes intelligible only when one views it in the light of a long tradition of anti-Jesuit polemic and literature that essentially began shortly after the founding of the Society in 1540. Hence, short-, medium-, and long-term causes and occasions coincided in the suppression of the Society of Jesus, and the dramatic events that affected the lives of Luigi Fortis and so many other Jesuits ultimately proved to be the consequences of protracted developments that rapidly escalated on account of local and temporary circumstances around the year 1750. This chapter accordingly will first explore the long-term structures of anti-Jesuitism, before describing the dynamic events at midcentury that culminated in the wave of suppressions. The final section will cover the life and doings of the ex-Jesuits until 1814. The conclusion takes a glance at the restoration of the Society of Jesus after 1801.

The Many Enemies of the Society

With the exception of the Inquisition, probably no other ecclesiastical institution attracted as much aversion as the Society of Jesus. We have already heard of the countless local economic, social, and cultural conflicts with the Society's institutions in cities. That was neither surprising nor unusual—the economically powerful and socially influential colleges and their residents were almost inevitably implicated in many everyday local quarrels over students and their behavior, property claims, rights of way, or the administration of fields. That could scarcely be avoided, and that alone would not have put the order in any real danger.[2] For the Jesuits, however, this negative background music that accompanied every confident social group rapidly transformed into a much more deep-set aversion. A torrent of anti-Jesuit Catholic literature soon washed over the reading public of the early modern period, and with growing regularity it was no longer about this or that particular problem. The Society itself became a symbol and scapegoat for the most diverse evils that one identified in the church, politics, or society. Social anxieties and political fears were projected onto the Society.[3] These anti-Jesuit, critical texts therefore ultimately tell us more about their authors than they do about the Society of Jesus.

It almost goes without saying that the Protestants took a hostile view of the Jesuits. Far more significant was the fact that the Society became the target of entrenched hostility in Catholic Europe itself. To some extent, the Jesuits were victims of their own success and their typical way of proceeding. There soon was no missing them—the Jesuits' very ubiquity commanded attention. Eloquent, prolific speakers and writers, dynamic and resourceful in debate—the Jesuits were in the spotlight and did nothing to step out of it. Nearly no job was too delicate for them. They trumpeted their triumphs, and their critics attacked them publicly. The Jesuits lived confidently and deliberately cultivated their prominence in European society—that attracted ill will.

Criticism initially centered on their novel constitution and devotional practices, which were suspected of heterodoxy. Their rejection of choral prayer, their centralization, their unusually long training, their curious "simple vows," the supposedly arrogant name of the Society—opponents of the Jesuits like the Dominican Melchor Cano and many others raised all these points of criticism again and again in the sixteenth century. In late sixteenth-century France, these rather technical lines of attack became politically charged. One of the key authors there, who would have a long-lasting influence on anti-Jesuit literature, was Étienne Pasquier (1529–1615).[4] He had already taken on the Jesuits as lawyer in 1563/4, when he took over the Sorbonne's lawsuit against the founding of a Jesuit college in Paris—the venerable university was afraid of the new competition, particularly competition that would take its cues from Rome, the pope, and the Jesuit superior general.[5] Pasquier was one of the first at the time to view the institutional structure of the Society not merely as unusual but even as politically dangerous because it supposedly sought to undermine the traditional Gallicanism of France. Pasquier expressed this view yet again in his famous work Le catéchisme des Jésuites (Catechism of the Jesuits), which appeared in 1602 after several years of preparation.[6]

In the Catéchisme, Pasquier likened the Jesuits to "filth" or "scum" with a biting pun in French, replacing ordre (order) with ordure (excrement).[7] The Catéchisme also attacked the structure of the Society of Jesus: "Their sect is a new bastard religious order, a mishmash of all our orders but lacking anything pure and clean from our old church."[8] Pasquier was irritated by the variety of vows (simple, solemn, three or four) that were customary in the order. In his eyes, it was symptomatic of the wrong and completely exaggerated importance of obedience within the Society.[9] The strictly hierarchical, centralized, and—from a hostile standpoint—even tyrannical government of the Society was a recurring theme ever after. According to the Anticoton of 1610, another aggressively anti-Jesuit contemporary text, the root of all evil was "the vow that the Jesuits take whereby they promise to obey their superiors, that is, the generals of their order, who necessarily must be subjects of the Spanish crown, and their other superiors with an obedience that is simple and absolute and without any exception, even without asking why."[10]

This thought ultimately led to the grotesque caricature of the Society of Jesus as a ruthlessly efficient, perfectly streamlined organization, an institution that acted in concert with an incomparably effective world-wide information network.[11] The eighteenth century added a new layer of metaphor. "Their monarchy is a machine in which all the wheels turn smoothly as soon as the drive wheel is engaged," one German author pointedly claimed in 1761.[12] In this way, by the mid-eighteenth century, the Jesuit order had been stylized as the epitome of an unlimited and therefore despotic monarchy. Enlightenment opponents of monarchy like Louis-Adrien Le Paige saw to it that the *Constitutions* were widely discredited as a blueprint for absolute tyrannical power. Anti-Jesuit agitation was thus part of a broad political debate on the eve of the French Revolution.[13]

A second basic motif centered around the groundless exaggeration of Jesuit administrative control. The real problem with the Jesuits, in their adversaries' view, was that they used their (allegedly) efficient organization to execute orders from foreign powers. There were two basic alternatives: the Jesuits' instructions might come either from Rome, in which case they were portrayed as agents of the pope, or from Spain, in which case it was alleged that the Society of Jesus was ultimately the extended arm of the Iberian monarchy (as in the *Anticoton* quoted earlier).[14] Fear of the Jesuits as a fifth column in the service of a foreign power was already in the air in France around the year 1600, and similar allegations were also made in Poland and England. The attacks always amounted to claims that the Jesuits would advance political and religious positions ultimately detrimental to the commonwealth, that they would incite rebellion and even maintain their own fortresses.[15] A Bavarian commentator summarized the logical conclusion of these suppositions in 1770: it was clear "that the constitution of the Jesuit order and its provinces could not coexist with the welfare of individual states."[16] Abolishing the Society was in the interest of the common good, adversaries concluded.

After the failed assassination attempt on Henry IV of France in 1594, it was alleged that the Jesuits even were capable of carrying out assassinations and making attempts on the lives of European kings. The *Anticoton*, for example, produced pages of supposed proof, all of which seemed to show that, although the Jesuits may not have explicitly ordered various attacks on European princes, they certainly had advocated and watched them with pleasure.[17] The reasoning was highly tendentious and relied on weak arguments ex silentio, but the fact that the order had not distanced itself sufficiently (to the author's taste) from particular assassins was harnessed as a positive argument for its involvement in or at least condonement of such deeds.[18] Despite the weakness of the arguments, a rich tradition of portraying the Jesuits as unscrupulous conspirators took root in England and France. The fact that the Jesuits were blamed for the Gunpowder Plot in 1605 and the Popish Plot in 1678 was one of the high points of this polemic. Even though the Jesuits could not even semiplausibly be implicated in any of these cases, they were still imputed at least a hidden role as architects and instigators.[19] The Jesuits never shook this image of being subversives who would resort to sedition and violence to achieve their political goals.

Even the Jesuits' opponents knew that the Society had explicitly distanced itself from such radical actions. But they were unconvinced: the Jesuits, another typical claim alleged, knew how to hide their "real" goals and methods. According to this hostile depiction, they were not only a strictly hierarchical, politically subversive organization but also adept at hiding their true nature. The Jesuits were two-faced or, as contemporaries already often said, "wolves in sheep's clothing." That resonated with Pasquier: he wrote that the Jesuits regularly preceded secretly in political affairs, emulating the controversial Italian Niccolò Machiavelli.[20] Ambiguous, divided, and hidden loyalties were, in Pasquier's view, inherent in the Jesuits' character.[21]

Hence, the literary posture of revealing or unmasking the truth became one of the most important ingredients in anti-Jesuit literature: the enemies of the Jesuit order routinely speculated that behind the pious

Catholic facade the Jesuits presented to the outside world, a hidden, secretive inner life played out where the public could not go. Paulo Sarpi, for example, one of the harshest critics of the Jesuits of his time, remarked in 1608:

> I have always admired the Jesuits' policy and especially their sense of secrecy. It's wonderful that their constitutions have been printed, although it's still impossible to see a copy. I don't mean the rules printed in Lyon, which are puerile, but their governing laws, which are so full of secrets. . . . Nowhere in the world are there as many people to conspire together for the same end, to maneuver with such care, to bring such passion and zeal to their actions. I would willingly believe that it would be highly beneficial to penetrate the secret of their administration and to uncover their arts and political treatises so as to oppose them on occasion.[22]

Sarpi's wish for better insight into the inner life of the Society seemed to have been granted in 1614, when the *Monita secreta* (*Secret Instructions*) of the Society of Jesus became public.[23] The text seemed to confirm what everyone had long conjectured: the Jesuits' real purpose, as one could read there, was the implacable, unethical pursuit of wealth and power, to which the Society subordinated all moral and religious principles. Obviously the scandalous *Monita secreta*, which would be reprinted in several dozen editions again and again since the *editio princeps*, was a forgery. A disappointed Polish ex-Jesuit by the name of Hieronim Zahorowski had written it to take revenge on the order. At least some seventeenth-century contemporaries, however, believed the *Monita* were authentic—and despite their spurious nature they furnished an important stockpile of anti-Jesuit prejudices that would long remain in use. Subsequent editions of the *Monita* were moreover always slightly altered and expanded in response to new developments. Hence, the fake text remained "up to date" and continued to help unmask the "true" goals of the Society even in new contexts.

It was no coincidence that a (former) member of the order like Zahorowski provided anti-Jesuit authors with important arguments. Several other Jesuits also had helped lay the foundation of anti-Jesuit polemic, albeit unintentionally, in contrast to Zahorowski. Around 1600, several members of the order forcefully voiced their dissatisfaction with the status quo inside the Society and called on General Acquaviva to undertake various changes and reforms.[24] These texts have been described as "Jesuit anti-Jesuitism." Some of them were printed—sometimes against their author's will—and kindled debate over the governance and inner life of the Society of Jesus. The two most important works of harsh internal criticism that were published and dissected by the enemies of the order were Juan de Mariana's *Discurso de los grandes defectos que hay en la forma del gobierno de los Jesuitas* (Discourse on the major flaws in the form of governance of the Jesuits) and Hernando de Mendoça's *Advis de ce qu'il y a à reformer en la Compagnie des Iesuites* (Note on what needs to be reformed in the Society of Jesus), both of which were made public shortly after 1600.[25] They criticized the Society's personnel management, educational policy, and spirituality as it appeared at the time. Other authors during these years criticized the oppressive power of the superiors or lamented the Society's dependence on central decisions. The fact that these complaints were "authentic material" was of the utmost importance for the claims to plausibility of anti-Jesuit literature.[26] Even later, we regularly encounter Jesuits critical of the order or dismissed ex-Jesuits who supposedly had insider information on the real workings of the Society of Jesus. Giulio Clemente Scotti and Melchior Inchofer produced further specimens of this revelatory literature in the seventeenth century that projected an aura of authenticity.[27] The *Historia interna documentada de la Compañía de Jesús* (Documented internal history of the Society of Jesus) by the Spanish ex-Jesuit Miguel Mir (1841–1912), published posthumously in 1913, enjoyed similar significance. The fact that anti-Jesuit literature drew on such insider information long lent it much of its effectiveness—like every successful prejudice, anti-Jesuitism did not simply invent its allegations out of thin air but rather generated them with a distorting interpretation of grains of truth. The voices of disappointed, dismissed, and enraged (ex-)Jesuits, of course, were especially helpful.

These new anti-Jesuit texts put the Jesuits ever more frequently on the defensive. That was not at all because their claims had substance.

Objectively speaking, almost every accusation could more or less be refuted or at least blunted. The Society's growing difficulties had more to do with a change in style and readership.[28] The debate moved ever farther from the realm of academic, ecclesiastical, and legal debate and into the expanding arena of popular literature. Some of the countless anti-Jesuit publications capitalized very skillfully on current trends and fashions in the book market.[29]

By the mid-seventeenth century, the Jesuits' response to these nimble, subtle and ambiguous, literary and popular smear tactics was increasingly flatfooted. All too often, Jesuit authors clung to an earnest, unflashy, stubbornly earnest style of polemic that soon came to be derided as blinkered. What one of these adroit literary opponents wrote with sneering malignancy about the Jesuit François Garasse may have applied to many of the Society's authors: "When he tries to write something amusing (which he almost always tries to do), he has to pay the people to laugh."[30] The Jesuits never cultivated the field of pleasant literature—when their enemies then seized it, the Jesuits had little to offer in response.

The men of the Society of Jesus thus did not stand a chance against arguably the most brilliant anti-Jesuit satire ever, the *Lettres provinciales* of 1656/7, in which the mathematician, philosopher, and religious author Blaise Pascal caricatured the ethical teachings and religious attitude of the Jesuits, holding them up for ridicule from a Jansenist perspective. Pascal had his fictional letter writer, one Mr. Louis de Montalte, pen eighteen letters to an imaginary friend in the province. In his letters, Montalte first reports his encounters with a fictional Jesuit. The overwhelming comical and ironic effect of the letters derives from the fact that this invented Jesuit—a naive, gullible, nice contemporary with no evil intentions, but of limited intelligence—says one thing after another in his conversations with Montalte that either makes a mockery of the Society or would inevitably rouse the reader's indignation. Montalte tells of pleasant and unprepossessing conversations in which the Jesuit puts his foot in his mouth again and again. Unintentionally, and yet irresistibly for that very reason, the fictional Jesuit exposes the unscrupulousness, thoughtlessness, and moral degeneration of his order. Only toward the end of the series of letters does Pascal progressively abandon the style of biting satire in a conversational tone and adopt a register of aggressive, open attack.

In addition to the familiar accusations against the Society, the Jansenist Pascal's letters to the province also immortalized a relatively new theme: the *Lettres provinciales* stigmatized the Jesuits as the proponents of unprincipled, wildly lax morals. The theme played only a marginal part in early attacks, such as Pasquier's *Catéchisme* or the *Anticoton*. The anti-Jesuit polemic of Pascal's letters cemented the image of the Jesuit confessor for the following decades and centuries: you could do whatever you wanted under his spiritual guidance because with the skillful application of casuistry he could always produce an excuse. The Jesuits as paragons of immorality in the guise of high-sounding moral theology: Pascal left a lasting impression with this image and exerted a profound influence on subsequent anti-Jesuit literature.[31] The stereotype was reinforced in the multivolume *Morale pratique des Jésuites* (Practical ethics of the Jesuits, 1669), and soon enough the equivocation of the Society with perverted morals became an anti-Jesuit commonplace. When the Society of Jesus was suppressed in France in 1762, several official edicts justified the measure with explicit reference to the corrosive moral influence of Jesuit ethics.

The missions began to reinforce existing prejudices against the Jesuits with fresh examples and arguments in the latter half of the seventeenth century. Claims that the Society preached only a pseudo-theology gained new momentum from the controversy over the Chinese and Malabar rites. Pascal himself had blazed the way in the *Lettres provinciales*, portraying the Jesuits' methods in the mission as yet another indication of their lack of principles.[32] The later stages of the Chinese rites controversy in particular were instrumentalized against the Society in almost paradoxical fashion: since the Jesuits did their utmost to circumvent the papal bans on their rites, they now were accused of disobedience to the pope and church.[33] When the archbishop of Salamanca tried to legitimate the suppression of the Society of Jesus in 1769, he accordingly alleged that the Society had "for a century and a half, with public and manifest resistance, disobeyed the decrees of the Propaganda

Fide and the Inquisition and repeated apostolic constitutions." The Jesuits' oath of obedience to the pope now appeared to make them guilty of perjury, and they supposedly were jeopardizing the unity of the church.

The colonies and mission territories provided ample new material to recast the anti-Jesuit argument that the Jesuits were plotting to undermine the political order. There were numerous everyday examples that one could use to depict the Jesuits as standing in the way of progress in the colonies.[34] The old dispute over the enslavement of the native peoples, for example, constantly produced new arguments against the Society, all of them generally to the effect that the Jesuits were blocking the economic prosperity of the settlements out of economic and political self-interest. Spanish and Portuguese authors both at home and abroad had made such claims against the Jesuits since the sixteenth century, but it was in the eighteenth century that this strain of argumentation intensified with redoubled strength. Anti-Jesuit attention in this context focused especially on the reductions of Paraguay, which had come to the forefront of the debate since the Treaty of Madrid of 1750 and the Guaraní War. In Portugal, a veritable campaign against the Society was launched after 1750, spurred on by the leading minister of Portugal, Sebastião José de Carvalho e Melo, later known as the Marquis de Pombal.[35] He initiated and sponsored the large-scale publication of anti-Jesuit texts, in which events in the colonies featured prominently.[36]

One of the key texts of this new campaign was the anonymous *Relação abreviada da República, que os religiosos jesuitas das províncias de Portugal e Hespagna estabeleceram nos domínios ultramarinos das duas monarchias* (Brief report on the republic that the Jesuit clerics from the provinces of Portugal and Spain established in the overseas domains of the two monarchies, 1757). Initially published in Lisbon in Portuguese, the text was quickly reprinted in several other European languages.[37] It presented the reductions as the basis of the Jesuits' sinister "power" while also characterizing them as an insidious system that the Society secretly used to exploit the natives. The *Relação* claimed the Jesuits would instill their typical "blind obedience" in the natives, turning them

into willing "slaves" that the Jesuits tyrannized with "inhuman despotism." The missionaries' talk of converting the native inhabitants was
nothing but a "holy pretext" because what the Jesuits really desired was
material advantages, political power, and military autonomy. That posed
the greatest threat from the authorities' perspective: "The fathers of the
Society have conceived and clandestinely pursued a bold and terrible
project, with the usurpation of the entire state of Brazil, and with such
cunning and such violent progress that, if it is not immediately and effectively stopped, [Brazil] will become inaccessible and unconquerable
by combined might of Europe within a span of fewer than ten years."[38]
This theory could even be taken a step further: in his second important
anti-Jesuit work, the *Dedução chronologica e analytica* (Chronological
and analytical deduction), published in two copious volumes in 1767
and 1768, Pombal blamed the Jesuits broadly for the political and cultural decline of Portugal in the early modern period. He asked rhetorically "whether the Jesuits or Luther and Calvin had done Christendom
greater harm." In the mid-eighteenth century, it suddenly seemed clear
even to Catholics that the Protestants had been the lesser evil.[39]

Anti-Jesuitism had taken on such vast proportions that the very fate
of European society and civilization seemed to hang in the balance. The
thinkers of the Enlightenment grew increasingly hostile to churches and
especially to Catholicism over the eighteenth century. As an institution
tied to Rome and the pope, the Society of Jesus epitomized the "obscu-
rantism" of traditional society in their view: the Society became a symbol of unenlightened backwardness. That was true in many areas, but it
was debated especially fiercely with respect to pedagogy and education,
as we have seen. The philosophes constantly drew an antithesis between
modernity, rationality, and individualism, on the one hand, and antiquity, the church, and the Jesuits, on the other. Anti-Jesuitism thus dramatically escalated once more: the war against the Society of Jesus had
ceased to be about individual troublemakers, harmful outside influence,
or even feigned disbelief and instead now rather was being waged in the
name of the civilizing progress of an entire society, indeed ultimately of
all mankind. The Society had been blown up so far out of proportion
that fundamental questions of European history seemed to hinge on it:

progress or stagnation, modern statehood or age-old particularism, progressive education and cosmopolitanism or traditional superstition and parochialism?

To lend plausibility to this dramatic picture, critics revived the old idea of the extreme "uniformity" and "solidarity" of the Society of Jesus. Attacks on the Jesuits had long ago moved beyond individual members, events, or views. Pascal and his contemporaries wrote about the Society of Jesus in a stereotypical manner: *the* Jesuit had become a recognizable type.[40] The anti-Jesuit polemic of the eighteenth century deindividualized the members of the order until only caricatures were left: the collective, *the* Society was behind every single action by every single Jesuit, behind every single statement, every book, every text that they published anywhere in the anti-Jesuits' eyes, always pursuing the order's grand, clearly defined plan. As one German anti-Jesuit concluded in 1761, after stressing the strict obedience cultivated in the order, it was "eminently reasonable that one also call the superiors of the Society to account for the transgressions of individual members, seeing as they necessarily must have known these things in advance."[41] The Society of Jesus no longer appeared to comprise thousands of individuals but rather was a cipher for broad historical trends. "The Jesuits are the same everywhere," was one credo of anti-Jesuit literature that was cited again and again at least since the Jesuit-hater Antoine Arnauld used it in 1683.[42] Anti-Jesuitism became a conspiracy theory.

These traditions lived on during the suppression of the Society of Jesus and drew newfound strength from anti-Jesuit sentiment in the nineteenth century. Now the Society was identified with a specific ecclesiastical-political attitude and cultural model: ultramontanism.[43] The Jesuits' (allegedly) fanatical devotion to the pope, who plied his dark schemes "beyond the mountains" (Latin: *ultra montes,* i.e. the Alps), was widely reviled. Both Protestant Germans under Bismarck and liberal Catholics in France viewed ultramontanism primarily as a reactionary political movement, while even conservative Catholics in France feared its Roman centralism. At any rate, the Jesuit order served as a blank canvas onto which hostile authors could project everything they feared or abhorred for political, religious, or cultural reasons. The

Society transformed into an amorphous, opposing force that attacked one's own values and ideals. A German poem from 1845 captures the sinister and somber, anti-Enlightenment and dark, gloomy, alien, impersonal, and demonic nature of this hostile image of the Jesuits:

> A gloomy being flits about
> That calls itself a Jesuit;
> It does not speak, is quiet and mute,
> And sneaking comes its kick.
> A robe of mourning long it wears,
> Together with its close-cropped hair,
> And brings the night back to the land
> Where dawn had just appeared.[44]

This frightening image of the grim, shifty Jesuit could be combined at any time with the now prominent rhetoric of conspiracy theories. Fascination with secret societies had flourished in the heated political atmosphere of the 1780s and then the revolutionary period. Secret alliances that steered events were conjectured everywhere—part of a new, paranoid style of political agitation. The Jesuits were prominent victims of this way of thinking.[45] The schools in particular were debated like never before. The famous historian and public intellectual Jules Michelet, for example, alleged that the Jesuits would undermine paternal authority in the family with their schools and confessionals and thus, ultimately, the foundation of society itself. The questions of whether and, if so, what influence ecclesiastical and particularly Jesuit teachers should have on rearing the next generation was a major point of contention in both France and Germany. And even the papacy suddenly no longer seemed safe from the Jesuit conspiracy. From a conspiratorial angle, the Jesuits' support for the dogma of papal infallibility, which was finally proclaimed in 1869/70, looked like a plot to capture the papacy itself. It may have been at this point in time, the middle of the nineteenth century, that the description of the Jesuit superior general as a "black pope" first appeared, supposedly diverting the power of the true pope to himself.[46]

This centuries-long debate, despite or perhaps precisely because of its sometimes vast distance from reality, is an impressive example of the invention of social prejudices on a pan-European, indeed global, scale. Important texts circulated and were translated at breakneck pace. Arguments were borrowed, and Jesuit (mis)deeds from all corners of the world were fused into a single image. For all the local contextuality of its various strains, anti-Jesuit literature was an international phenomenon, just like the Society of Jesus itself. Every enemy of the Jesuits had access to a pool of models and angles of attack that most authors used very generously. The vast majority of these texts, unsurprisingly, were clichéd and predictable. Numerous contradictions also pervaded the debate. For example, proponents of enlightened absolutism like Pombal and impassioned adversaries of a strong monarchy like Le Paige could blame the Jesuits for the prevailing evils of the day at virtually the same time—the one, because the Society refused to accept its place in a strong kingdom; the other, because the Society seemed to provide an all too perfect blueprint for absolute monarchy. Remarkable anti-Jesuit alliances between incompatible schools of thought were forged again and again.

By the early 1600s, this incessant literary denigration turned the figure of *the* Jesuit into a template that could explain one event after the next. For the Jesuits themselves, this soon meant that they could and increasingly had to anticipate the anti-Jesuit perception of their actions—if only to distance themselves from it. The Jesuits themselves therefore soon came to find themselves living in the shadow of their enemies' anti-Jesuit image. They fared no better than "the Jew" or "the witch," two other negative stereotypes that were used to explain the world in the early modern period and long thereafter while stigmatizing and endangering a specific group of people.[47] The Jesuits differed from Jews and witches, however, in that they were far more actively involved in the discursive fashioning of the negative stereotype that was used against them. For all its distortion and exaggeration, anti-Jesuitism still drew on texts and reports that the Jesuits published about themselves. And in contrast to Jews and witches, the Jesuits also could defend themselves. They responded to their literary enemies in kind—every anti-Jesuit treatise elicited a rebuttal from the Society. Often enough, it was the members of the Society of Jesus themselves who prompted the hostile debate or at least poured fuel on the fire with their own writings and actions. Even in Portugal, where anti-Jesuit sentiment in the late 1750s took on unprecedented dimensions, resulting in an open anti-Jesuit policy, the Jesuits themselves were very actively entangled in such polemical debates.[48]

The Suppression of the Society of Jesus

The earth shook in Portugal in 1755. One of the severest earthquakes in European history reduced Lisbon to rubble and ashes. The aftershock was felt across Europe, and not just in a geological sense. The earthquake gave rise to extensive discussion as intellectuals—not only locally but also in Paris, London, and many other cities—tried to come to terms with the devastating catastrophe.[49] They felt an acute need to interpret and understand the disaster. Some embraced the new ideas of the age wholeheartedly. The Marquis de Pombal, for example, since 1750 the leading minister of Portugal and responsible for the immediate response to the devastation, advocated an entirely scientific explanation for the earthquake. He therefore turned his gaze to the future and he launched a dynamic and innovative rebuilding program to repair the damage as quickly as possible in grand style. In his eyes, the horrific disaster was a moment that required the state to act as decisively as possible free of constraints and to pursue its goals purely on the basis of rational criteria. With skillful measures, politicians like Pombal helped people put such setbacks as the Lisbon earthquake behind them.

The Jesuit Gabriel Malagrida (1689–1761) saw things differently. In 1756, he published a famous sermon on the earthquake.[50] In his view, God had decreed the destruction of the capital as punishment for the sinful lives of its inhabitants and especially the Portuguese court; the earthquake was "solely" the result of "our intolerable sins." Malagrida believed the disaster had long been presaged by various signs and prophetic warnings. The effort to explain the earthquake solely in physical or geological terms, in his view, was misguided and sinfully missed the heart of the matter: moral improvement, not natural science, was needed. Jesuits elsewhere agreed.[51] Hence Malagrida roundly attacked

Pombal's rebuilding campaign in the strongest language. When Pombal's rebuilding efforts subsequently met with resistance in several places for various reasons, the Jesuits were quickly suspected of inciting it. In 1757, the wine merchants of Porto revolted. The origins of the revolt can be traced back to the new economic measures introduced in 1755—but the Jesuits were blamed without hesitation.[52] In 1757, Pombal thereupon banished all the confessors from the Society of Jesus in Lisbon from court. Malagrida himself had already been expelled.

The earthquake discussion showed that the Jesuits and the willful minister held different views about how the community should be governed and who had the authority to interpret events and take decisive action. Fundamental differences in their assessment of policy and power collided. Did not the Jesuits ultimately have to submit to Pombal's authority?[53] Malagrida and Pombal had clashed over this question before, with respect to Portugal's colonial policy in South America. Malagrida had spent long years in Brazil, where he had picked a fight with Pombal's brother, the governor at the time. The latter had been entrusted with enforcing the Treaty of Madrid, which the Jesuits, as we have seen, rejected and tried to rescind on behalf of the reductions—the impression that the Society refused to obey royal commands spread rapidly in a short time.[54] There also were conflicts between Pombal and the Jesuits at court over the marriage plans for King José's firstborn daughter.[55] The earthquake was just another bone of contention. In 1758, Pombal then took action against this supposed rival to royal power. Through his proxies in Rome, he launched a papal review of the Jesuits in Portugal. Even though this visitation failed to produce any major results, it significantly raised the pressure on the Jesuits. Things escalated few months later.

A love story was the beginning of the end. José I had an affair with a young noblewoman whose mother's confessor was none other than the Jesuit Malagrida. As the king was returning from visiting his lover in the night between September 3 and 4, 1758, someone opened fire on his coach. Numerous prominent personages were soon arrested, and eventually Malagrida and other Jesuits, too. The first executions followed on January 13, 1759. More and more Jesuits found their way into the prisons, as the search for the instigators expanded. Even though there was no material evidence against them, the Jesuits rapidly became subjects of general suspicion, both in government circles and in the international press. In the person of Malagrida, the old "regicide" stereotype merged beautifully with the Society's political disrepute (fig. 30). All Jesuits who had not already been incarcerated were placed under house arrest. In January 1759, the government confiscated all the property of the Society of Jesus in the country; in June, Pombal stripped the Society of its schools and replaced their instruction with new curricula and textbooks. Finally, on the first anniversary of the attack on the king, the Jesuits were expelled from Portugal by royal decree. Some were imprisoned and forced to spend more than a decade in jail, among them the German Maurice Thoman. The majority of the Jesuits were transported by ship from the colonies and motherland to the Papal States. Malagrida was then tried before the Inquisition (and not, as Pombal had wanted, before secular courts, since the pope objected) in a sensational but one-sided trial. Now a slightly confused old man, he was publicly executed in 1761. The Society ceased to exist in Portugal, after Pombal thus skillfully exploited a series of unpredictable events to take action against it.[56]

Expulsion from Portugal was followed by suppression in France, but neither case really resembled the other: whereas the king was the source of anti-Jesuit measures in Portugal, the Jesuits in France were the victims of an age-old political conflict between the king and the highest courts of the land (the *parlements*). The dispute had deep roots, stretching back to the late Middle Ages, and no less than the balance of power in France was at stake.[57] The years around 1750 were an especially intense phase of domestic controversy, not least because they once again revolved around religious affairs. The power struggle between *parlements* and the king had become amalgamated with the old fight over Jansenism. The Parlement of Paris in particular leaned in favor of the Jansenists and stubbornly resisted a series of anti-Jansenist measures taken by Rome and Paris in 1750, which it depicted as a tyrannical abuse of power by the king, the Jesuits, and the pope.

This heated religious and political climate intensified on January 5, 1757, when Robert-François Damiens attempted to stab the king in his coach. The attack failed, but it fanned the flames of the debate over

FIGURE 30. Regicidal Jesuits as propaganda: a caricature of Gabriel Malagrida.
© Bibliothèque National de France, M97447.

fundamental political questions in the kingdom into a blaze.[58] The Parlement brought the well-known stereotype of the Jesuits as regicides
into play, although there was not a shred of evidence for it. Two years
later, though, when word of the attack on José I reached France, it
seemed to confirm the general suspicion against the Society.

In this chaotic situation of rampant rumors and fears, treachery and age-old prejudices, the Jesuits themselves provided the spark for the ensuing conflagration with an astounding spectacle of local reckless-ness. In 1755, scandal engulfed the Jesuit Antoine Lavalette in France. As procurator for the Society, Lavalette was responsible for Jesuit commercial enterprises in the Caribbean, particularly on the island of Martinique. In speculative and frivolous fashion, he invested vast amounts of money in the construction of sugar plantations. The mis-sion in Martinique was soon deep in debt. When war broke out with England in 1755 and some sugar deliveries were lost, Lavalette could no longer pay his creditors.[59] At first the Jesuits back home intervened, but eventually they ran out of money, too. Now the creditors began to collect the arrears before the courts. In 1760, they secured an impor-tant victory against the Society of Jesus, when a Parisian court ruled that the entire French Society was liable, and the creditors could have the possessions of the Society of Jesus in France confiscated. What happened next is difficult to understand: in order to appeal this dan-gerous ruling, the Jesuits turned precisely to the—generally hostile— Parlement of Paris. The court obviously upheld the ruling of the first instance. After intense scrutiny, including the perusal of anti-Jesuit literature, the court arrived at the conclusion that, in light of the strict internal obedience of the Society and the bloc-like solidarity of its members, the actions of individuals should always be imputed directly to the entire order. The Parlement therefore ruled that the superior general in Rome, as the head of the entire organization, was respon-sible for satisfying the debt.

The economic disaster of the Lavalette affair also enabled the Par-lement, over the course of the year 1761, to launch a judicial review of the constitution of the Society of Jesus. In this context it was Louis-Adrien Le Paige who impressed on the public the political threat the *Constitutions* posed—they were a blueprint for tyranny, he argued. Now the fight over this anti-Jesuit stereotype ceased to be a literary battle and became a legal one, to be decided by the Parlement. It soon became obvious where the trial and campaign were headed, and so the king at last attempted to intervene. Both to defy the Parlement with his own initiative and to save the Jesuits at least in part, he proposed a drastic reform of the French branch of the Society. On August 6, 1761, the Parlement reached a decision that de facto amounted to the suppression of the order, the nullification of its legal underpinnings, and the closing or repurposing of the colleges and other properties. The king nonetheless managed to secure a twelve-month stay for transition and review. That year was then filled with the widest variety of initiatives on all sides, leaving observers unsure of how it would all play out. As late as December 1761, some Jesuits believed "the affairs of the Society in this kingdom look good for now."[60] And still it was unsurprising when after the year had passed, in the latter half of 1762, more and more *parlements* definitively banned the Society and ordered the Jesuits to renounce their vows. In contrast to Portugal, the Jesuits were not expelled, but they were prohibited from living together: they were not to have any contact with one another. If they wished to remain active as clergymen or teachers, they had to swear an oath to the king and explicitly renounce the teachings of the Society. These measures were not ratified by the *parlements* everywhere in France, and so the order initially survived in some parts of the country. Finally, in 1764, the king took action to standardize the legal status of ex-Jesuits: they were permitted to remain in France, even if they had not sworn the unpalatable oath, but they were ineligible for public office until they did so. Several subsequent decrees modified and exacerbated the rights, duties, and burdens of former Jesuits. It was not until the 1770s that the tense situation for French ex-Jesuits began to ease.

As in Portugal, we also cannot identify any long-term political plan to annihilate the Society in France. The Society fell because a vocal and shrewd group of active opponents knew how to seize the moment, and the Society failed to marshal an effective defense. The new leading minister, Étienne-François de Choiseul, in office since 1758, was no friend of the Jesuits. He needed the sympathy of the *parlements* and regarded the order as a pawn he could sacrifice. The king, Choiseul himself noted, was undecided as to whether he should take decisive action to save the Society; he ultimately bowed to the supposed short-term advantage of its suppression.[61]

In Spain, the king (like his counterpart in Portugal) was actively hostile to the Jesuits. Charles III, who had reigned since 1759, had appointed two enemies of the Society, Bernardo Wall and Pedro Rodríguez de Campomanes, as his ministers.[62] As king of the Two Sicilies, he had previously worked with Prime Minister Bernardo Tanucci, who was likewise at the forefront of the wave of anti-Jesuitism in the style of Pombal.[63] Charles also no longer had a Jesuit confessor, although Jesuits very probably were still assigned to other members of the royal family. This new group of decision makers received the news about the reductions and finally the Guaraní War in South America with anti-Jesuit ears.[64] They were especially annoyed by the large number of "foreign," that is, non-Iberian, Jesuit missionaries. The anti-Jesuit atmosphere was only heightened by the fact that, even in the mid-eighteenth century, the Jesuits were still unwilling to pay the tithe to the bishops in the Spanish colonies.[65] Hence, it was a clear anti-Jesuit sign when Madrid explicitly supported the official canonization of the famous adversary of the Jesuits Juan de Palafox launched in 1760. The bishop of Puebla's battle with the Jesuits now looked like a blueprint for real conflict. And the death of the queen mother Isabella Farnese in 1766 weakened the Jesuits' standing at court even more.

As this sense of crisis grew, a revolt then broke out in Madrid and several provinces in late March 1766. It was primarily a spontaneous revolt over food shortages with very specific goals and no broader political ambitions, as was quite common in early modern Europe. But almost immediately many observers interpreted the events as a plot for which—initially unnamed—"priests" were to blame. Campomanes took up the tune, and a tribunal to identify the perpetrators was established under his supervision. The investigation was to be conducted in strict secrecy. As the year wore on, Campomanes ensured that the focus of the investigation came to rest ever more fixedly on the Jesuits. By the end of the year, on December 31, 1766, the Jesuits' "guilt" was officially established. The tribunal had heard most of the familiar anti-Jesuit prejudices, from lax morals to regicidal conspiracy theories. The king accepted the court's ruling in the spring of 1767, thereby ratifying it. Up until then, the entire affair had been conducted in secrecy. It thus came as a complete surprise to both the public and the Jesuits themselves when in a large-scale action on April 1 and 2, 1767, all the houses of the Society in Madrid and everywhere else on the Iberian Peninsula were closed. Given the complete secrecy of the discussion, judgment, and execution of the prohibition of the Society, virtually no resistance of any kind was offered anywhere in Spain. The Spanish Jesuits also seem to have largely isolated themselves: in contrast to France, the Spanish clergy had little sympathy left for the order. Whereas the French bishops had still reiterated the enormous usefulness of the Jesuits in 1761, the messages of their Spanish counterparts after the closing of the local Jesuit houses betrayed sympathy only for the king and his decision.[66]

Further expulsions followed: from Naples, Sicily, and Parma. Initially, all these anti-Jesuit measures were purely local events that resulted from the specific circumstances of each country in question. Contemporaries soon had the impression, however, that they were connected. The media reported the events all across Europe, leading people everywhere to talk about the fate of the Jesuit order and draw a connection between the events in Portugal, France, and Spain.[67] Bit by bit, circumstances reinforced the impression that the Jesuits' time had run out. Their growing isolation became conspicuous. Powerful patrons withdrew their support for the Jesuits because they did not want to jeopardize their monarchs' favor.[68] The unrest and foreboding were palpable in Rome.[69] Even in the village taverns of Germany, people seized on the faraway events to criticize the Jesuits at home.[70] By the late 1760s, the hypothetical connection between the events had transformed into a genuine anti-Jesuit alliance. The kings of Spain, France, and Naples and the Duke of Parma—all of them from the house of Bourbon and so bound by ties of kinship—launched a coordinated international campaign that put the Holy See under more and more pressure. The goal was the complete dissolution of the Society by the pope.[71]

The reason that induced the Bourbons to take concerted action to compel the pope to dissolve the Society was a long-standing feud between Clement XIII and Parma, which originally had nothing to do with the Jesuits. The pope had tried to intervene in the religious affairs of Parma; Parma defended itself. Things finally escalated into military confrontation. The Bourbons closed ranks, and the conflict with the pope became a matter of family honor; France then occupied some papal territories. The Bourbons sent the pope a long list of conditions that had to be met before they would restore his territories and end the conflict. In addition to many other points, they also demanded the suppression of the Society of Jesus, the banishment of Superior General Ricci, and the dismissal of Cardinal Secretary Torrigiani, who was regarded as a friend of the Jesuits. Thus, the call for the complete abolition of the Society was on the table. The decisive, final stage of the conflict commenced. The French minister Choiseul noted in 1769, "The kings of France, Spain, and Naples are making open war against the Jesuits and their followers. Will it come to abolition or not? Will the kings or the Jesuits be victorious? That is the question that every cabinet is pondering."[72] The Bourbons did not get very far with Pope Clement XIII, who was considered a friend of the Jesuits. He viewed his actions against Parma as a matter of conscience and refused to relent.[73] The Bourbons thus placed great hopes in his homonymous successor, Clement XIV, who was elected in 1769. In contrast to his predecessor, Clement XIV considered the restoration of peace with the Bourbons and Portugal a matter of the utmost urgency. The pope also distanced himself from the embattled order with a display of symbolic coolness toward the Jesuit superior general.[74] But contrary to the Bourbons' expectations, Clement XIV was also disinclined to yield with respect to the Jesuit question. Instead, he maneuvered between the fronts with ambiguous statements for years. One of the pope's most important reasons for dragging out the decision was the fact that he could not anticipate the international consequences the suppression of the Society might have in the rest of Europe outside of Bourbon control. Even the French ambassador recognized that the pope had to tread carefully here: "The pope . . . is a secular prince and so must take great care with respect to the courts of Vienna and Turin."[75]

Vienna in particular was the deciding factor for both the pope and the Bourbons. There were various openly anti-Jesuit cliques at the imperial court. Empress Maria Theresa herself wanted to rein in the Society of Jesus significantly on certain particulars, especially as she launched an education and school reform. But on the whole, she was not openly opposed to the Society; she even initially protected it, and not until the very end did she see any reason to promote its suppression. In 1770, however, after her daughter Marie Antoinette married the Dauphin, she gave in to France's agitation to the extent that she would at least not stand in the way of the suppression of the Society by the pope—a position that she reiterated crucially in 1773. Now the pope had lost his last and most important argument against suppressing the order. After years of delay, on July 21, 1773, the papal brief *Dominus ac redemptor* suppressed the Jesuit order throughout the Catholic Church. The Spanish ambassador to the Vatican, José Moñino y Redondo, had worked for months on the text of this document: in its composition and wording, the document was the product of Bourbon diplomacy.

It would be mistaken to view the events from 1759 to 1773 simplistically as implacable opposition to the church, let alone religion. The leading ministers—Tanucci, Campomanes, and Pombal—were guided foremost by a "royalist" agenda. That is, they were concerned first and foremost with strengthening royal authority vis-à-vis recalcitrant or ungovernable social groups. That included the Jesuits, but was by no means exclusive to them.[76] The ministers' fight was not against the church as such, let alone against Christianity, but merely against an ecclesiastical institution (namely, the Society of Jesus) that seemed to interfere to an intolerable extent in the shaping of state and society. The kings understood their agitation against the Society as evidence of constructive engagement on behalf of the church and the pope. *Dominus ac redemptor* made this perspective its own. The suppression of the Society, the document claimed, was a step toward liberating the church. In the early modern period, and even as late as the nineteenth century, anti-Jesuitism was by no means automatically identical with criticism of the church. On the contrary, the "bad Jesuits" often enough served as a foil for the otherwise positive image of the church.[77]

The Jesuits themselves obviously saw things completely differently, and yet they were astonishingly passive during these dramatic years. They failed to devise a smart, universal defensive strategy. Instead of acting jointly in the Lavalette affair, for example, the French provinces sued one another in court in an attempt to shift the financial damage to other parts of the Society. General Lorenzo Ricci, who had just been elected in 1758, likewise was unable or unwilling to intervene effectively. Even friends within the order itself regarded the election of the "inexperienced" Ricci as inappropriate—by his very nature, Ricci was incapable of "treating unusual ills with unusual remedies."[78] Another contemporary observed: "The general does not want to compromise at all, and that forces him to retreat."[79] Ricci indeed rejected every last resort: when Paris demanded that the French branch of the Society split from Rome, the French superiors quickly agreed, but the general vetoed the measure. And when the French clergy rallied behind the Jesuits on December 31, 1761, on the condition that they submitted to Gallicanism, Ricci forbade that, too. He strove—undoubtedly for honorable and upstanding reasons—to maintain an unbending loyalty to the traditions and identity of the order. Either he or Pope Clement XIII, after all, supposedly said of the Society of Jesus, "Let them be as they are or not at all" (Sint ut sunt aut non sint). Compromise, which inevitably would have resulted in dramatic reform, was unthinkable. With this inflexible determination, however, the Jesuits could no longer cope with the incredible force of events, which could no longer be influenced with conventional ways of thinking and acting. They may also have simply underestimated the danger when they still had options. Many Jesuits hardly perceived any existential threat prior to 1773.[80] Some Jesuits caught unawares received the actions taken by Portugal in 1759 as a "bolt from the blue."[81] Even as late as 1768, the Jesuits in Rome seemed blind to the looming threat of suppression, although the entire city was already talking about it. Only the events of the suppression itself, when it was already too late, impressed on them the gravity of the situation.[82]

Ex-Jesuits: The Years from 1759 and 1773 to 1814

Almost everywhere in the weeks and months after July 21, 1773, local bishops appeared before the various Jesuit houses and read aloud the papal brief *Dominus ac redemptor*: the house in question was thereby closed and the local history of the Society of Jesus at an end—for the time being. The brief simultaneously inaugurated a new history because in many places implementing it was a herculean task that posed enormous challenges. That started with the Jesuits' landholdings and property: something had to be done with it! The prospect of enrichment from the Jesuits' properties may not have ranked among the most important motives for the suppression, but the Society's property became an international bone of contention before the brief had even been promulgated. In the draft of the brief, Clement XIV had entrusted the administration of Jesuit property to the bishops, as usual. It thus would remain in the church's hands. But the powers of Europe had other plans: the Bourbons proposed a very vaguely worded alternative that did not mention the bishops: they had long since seized the Jesuits' landholdings in their countries as state property.[83] The empress in Vienna in particular insisted on a nonecclesiastical, state administration of the immense properties.[84] Bavaria was of the same opinion and charged ahead to be safe: "We took possession of the *temporalia* even before the promulgation of the bull[!]," the government openly admitted to underscore its claim to the Jesuits' properties.[85] The bishops of Bavaria did not offer serious resistance; they probably saw little prospect of success in doing so. Things were similar elsewhere.

In many cases, the government created special officials for dismantling the Society and administering its property. Normally, the first course of action was to conduct a detailed inventory to determine what the Society had actually possessed. The auditors naturally made use of the Jesuits' own files and records and in some cases also questioned the former procurators of the Society. It still proved to be an enormous test of endurance to delve into the complex and sometimes centuries-old ownership structures. Then the land and buildings had to be reallocated for use. Very different strategies were adopted. In Spain, for example, the state began to sell off the Jesuits' property both at home and abroad in grand style in 1767.[86] In Bavaria, in contrast, the state kept most of the Jesuits' lands and merely leased them to tenants. The real estate, especially the college buildings, preferably remained in use as schools, but they also might conceivably be repurposed as hospitals or seminaries. In both Bavaria and Spain, the large profits that were raised from Jesuit property in one form or another were supposed to be put to use for charitable purposes. In Bavaria, as in most places, the money was used to finance new schools that now were under closer state supervision. That remained the case, however, for only a few years because in 1781 the property was reallocated to a new, far less charitable project: Charles Theodore, elector of Bavaria, used the proceeds to outfit the newly founded Bavarian branch of the Order of Malta—that was how he provided for his own illegitimate children from various flings and for those of other high noblemen at court. In Spain, large amounts of the proceeds from Jesuit property were soon spent on transporting the men out of Spain. The remarkable conditions in Maryland were the only exception in this panorama: there, there was neither a bishop nor—in light of the ongoing War of Independence and the separation of church and state in the newly founded United States of America—any ecclesiastical or public officials who might have confiscated the Society's property. Thus, the Society of Jesus remained de facto in possession of its landholdings, from which it set about to secure its restoration in 1805.[87]

The property of the Society could be managed—albeit with great effort. But what was supposed to happen with the men who had made up the Society of Jesus? There may not have been any "Jesuits" anymore after the suppression, but as ex-Jesuits the men were still around. What place in society should this special social group now take? Some authorities viewed the ex-Jesuits as a valuable personnel resource; others considered the men a problem that had to be addressed as effectively as possible. The treatment that the Jesuits received varied in the extreme.

There were cases of hardship. General Ricci was thrown into the papal prison in Castel Sant'Angelo, where he died miserably two years later on account of the poor conditions there. Some two hundred Jesuits were also incarcerated in Portugal. Maurice Thoman, the German missionary mentioned previously, spent a total of sixteen years in jail, as did many other ex-Jesuits.[88] Whoever was not imprisoned was deported at state expense. The king of Spain deployed the army and navy to arrange for the transportation of the Jesuits from the motherland and colonies in a generally well-organized and remarkably efficient manner.[89] The Jesuits were initially confined to their houses before they then traveled

to the ports—on foot, on mounts, in coaches—along specifically designated routes and under strict surveillance. Since the authorities feared
(with good reason) popular protests against the expulsion in places like
Mexico, they tried to avoid letting the men come into contact with the
population as best they could. Hence, the ex-Jesuits took remote routes,
traveled swiftly, and were permitted only brief stops, ideally in places
that had no Jesuit tradition. It was not a convoy of prisoners, but the
resemblance cannot simply be dismissed.

The Papal States was the common destination of the ships bearing all
the Jesuits from Portugal, Spain, and the Iberian colonies. Beginning in
1759, in several stages, around a thousand Portuguese Jesuits arrived.
The first were still welcomed personally in Civitavecchia by the newly
elected Superior General Ricci. They remained in Rome until they
could be dispersed across the Italian peninsula.[90] The capacity of Italy,
however, seemed exhausted. When shortly thereafter the exiles from
Spain were also supposed to be shipped to Italy, Clement XIII refused
to receive them. After sundry diplomatic entanglements, the Spanish
Jesuits were sent to Corsica, which at the time still belonged to Genoa.
When the island was conquered by France in 1768, Louis XV expelled
the remaining Jesuits from there, as well. Now the Spanish refugees
reached Italy via Genoa in small groups after all, where they were placed
predominantly on papal possessions.[91] The ex-Jesuits were often unwel-
come outsiders in the cities and usually lived in impoverished conditions. "On arriving in Italy, they had to preoccupy themselves more with
working for their sustenance than with scholarly studies for their own
edification or that of others," one of them remarked.[92] They moreover
were closely watched by the Spanish authorities, who still feared the
Jesuits' political and seditious potential. Until 1773, however, the Spanish Jesuits nevertheless found ways to continue their common life together as an order, at least in rudimentary form, even in exile.[93] Provinces and colleges continued to exist, and the men who had once lived
together in Spain still viewed themselves as a group in Italy. As one
observer commented, "You would say that the Spanish Society had not
at all been destroyed, but only transferred to Italy."[94] Many non-Iberian
missionaries, however, did not make the journey to Italy and instead

returned to their respective homelands. Maurice Thoman, for example, spent the twilight of his life in Bolzano. The suppression in southwestern Europe temporarily caused a dramatic reinforcement of the Society elsewhere, such as Austria, where the Jesuits could work even more intensively by virtue of the added personnel.[95]

In contrast to the Iberian Peninsula, the expulsion of the Jesuits was not the immediate objective in France.[96] That did not mean, however, that the Jesuits were unmolested: quite the opposite. The intensity, though, with which the Jesuits were monitored and regulated in the ten years after 1762 varied dramatically. In some phases, they were required to report to authorities twice annually. Members of the Jesuit order who renounced their vows by swearing the oath and pledging obedience to the king and Gallicanism were permitted to take on public responsibilities under certain conditions. The king also promised ex-Jesuits over the age of thirty-three a public pension, for which many Jesuits successfully applied. Conditions here also varied considerably, and this material incentive was moreover used to pressure ex-Jesuits to swear loyalty to the king. Many of the pensioners returned to their families, often after long years of life in the order, or lived with a housekeeper. They now were the heads of households and responsible (at least in part) for providing sustenance for their relatives. These were new life experiences for many ex-Jesuits.[97] Other former members of the Society rejected the pension in protest or took refuge in the employ of sympathetic bishops. The situation in France did not calm down until the 1770s.

The situation for ex-Jesuits east of the Rhine stood in marked contrast to that in Western Europe.[98] In Poland, Bavaria, and Austria, official policy was to make the fate of the men as "tolerable" as possible.[99] At least until the death of Maria Theresa in 1780, the climate in Vienna remained largely sympathetic to the Jesuits.[100] Several ex-Jesuits even remained employed as confessors at the imperial court, such as in the service of the archduchess Maria Anna.[101] The empress even granted individual ex-Jesuits an audience at Schönbrunn, to the amazement of the Jesuits themselves.[102] Former members of the order also received pensions in Bavaria and Austria. In Landsberg, a kind of nursing home was founded for elderly and sick Jesuits.

Even when they obeyed official restrictions, fairly large groups of ex-Jesuits still could live together or at least develop tight networks in European cities and towns. Even in Paris and France, where it was actually prohibited or at least made very difficult, groups of ex-Jesuits lived in direct proximity to one another.[103] In Bologna, Genoa, Vienna, and Graz around 1770, large communities of Spanish, South and Central American, Italian, and Austrian ex-Jesuits could be found.[104] As late as 1798, around a hundred ex-Jesuits were still living in the former professed house in Rome.[105] The Bollandists were permitted to continue to live and work together in Antwerp.[106] Ex-Jesuits remembered one another in their wills.[107] On at least a regional level, groups of such Jesuits corresponded by letter.[108] And many ex-Jesuits were generally well-informed about one another, closely following news of any deaths in the ranks, for example.[109] Although European governments were extremely apprehensive of the community of ex-Jesuits and occasionally prohibited meetings, the ex-Jesuits were neither scattered to the four winds geographically nor necessarily driven into social isolation.[110]

It sometimes was perhaps the shared spirituality of the ex-Jesuits that allowed them to maintain their sense of solidarity for years and decades. In Bologna, refugees from Mexico gathered for years around the cult of the Virgin of Guadalupe; even as late as 1812, a small group of ex-Jesuits still held memorial masses there for their deceased confreres, as had been customary in the past.[111] There were religious songs in which together they attempted to process what had happened. Ex-Jesuits often found a defiant spiritual refuge in the intensely reviled devotion of the Sacred Heart.[112] Manuel Luengo (1735–1814) mentions in his diary from 1767 and 1768 how many of the Jesuits' customary spiritual practices were still a matter of course. Thirty years later, in the volume from 1798, however, he hardly mentions such spiritual exercises anymore.[113] Jesuit piety could now scarcely be found. Nostalgia had perhaps become more important for the men's feeling of solidarity. Ex-Jesuits clung to old customs and convictions. For Luengo, even a quarter century after the suppression, it was a "ridiculous spectacle" when other clerics heard confession in Il Gesù.[114] He evidently still identified himself and his suffering confreres with this church.

Cherished hostilities from the days before 1773 were also still cultivated. Even as late as the 1790s, Luengo continued to compose virulent
attacks on the probabiliorists and the Jansenists. He likewise still cultivated the Jesuits' aversion to various other orders.[115] Old reference
points and mindsets theoretically helped one come to terms with the
new reality.

Other ex-Jesuits kept the memory of the Society alive with historical
publications. The Society of Jesus had a long tradition of cultivating its
identity through history. This tradition lived on past 1773. Several ex-
Jesuits now published books that described their previous ministry as
missionaries. Franz Xaver Eder's book on the Moxos mission may serve
as an example; it was published posthumously in 1791. Maurice Thoman
(1722–1805), one of the last Jesuit missionaries in Mozambique, published an account of his travels and life in 1788. It contained, on the one
hand, mission reports and natural observations and, on the other, an
account of his arrest in 1759 and his sixteen-year imprisonment in Lisbon. The conversational and fairly nonpolemical text was undoubtedly
intended to depict the Jesuits as the victims of persecution.[116] Other
ex-Jesuits ensured that the great heroes of the Society of Jesus maintained a literary presence. Soon after the suppression, a group of Jesuits
in Rome set out to collect Ignatius's letters. The project lurched forward,
and it was not until 1804 that the ex-Jesuit Roque Menchaca, drawing
on earlier preliminary work, managed to publish a groundbreaking collection of the letters of Ignatius of Loyola that met modern scholarly
standards. He had published the letters of Francis Xavier shortly
beforehand.[117]

Ongoing reflection on the events from 1759 to 1773 was also part of
the ex-Jesuit culture of memory. Giulio Cesare Cordara, for example,
wrote a comprehensive history of the suppression in which he showed
an astonishing degree of sympathy for Pope Clement XIV.[118] Many
other ex-Jesuits spoke disparagingly of Clement XIV and his order (the
Franciscans) only in hindsight.[119] Carlo Borgo, an Italian ex-Jesuit, composed a harsh attack on the pope and his brief *Dominus ac redemptor* in
a widely read and widely censored pamphlet shortly after Clement's
death.[120] Borgo presented himself and his former order as the victims

of "an illegitimate act." He defended the glorified order in the name of "oppressed innocence, slandered truth, insulted religion, damaged faith, and the tyrannized universal church."

For many Jesuits, this perception of themselves as the victims of hostile religious intrigue soon became amalgamated with very specific political opposition to everything connected to the Enlightenment and enlightened politics. As we have seen, previously the Jesuits had penned texts and sermons explicitly against the Enlightenment. The suppression, however, dramatically reinforced this tendency. After the prohibition of the Society in France in 1762, numerous ex-Jesuits became involved in the agile and dynamic conservative demimonde of the Counter-Enlightenment. Julien Louis Geoffroy (1743–1814) and Louis Abel Bonafous, known as Fontenai (1736–1806), for example, operated in this milieu as authors, journalists, and journal editors.[121] German ex-Jesuits like Aloys Merz of Augsburg likewise vociferously opposed the change of course toward the Enlightenment that Joseph II set in motion in 1781 in Austria.[122]

The anti-Enlightenment sentiment of many ex-Jesuits took on yet another dimension in 1789, when the Revolution broke out in France. The ex-Jesuits fused the course of world history with their own fate. Luengo wrote, for example, that it was Pope Clement XIV who ultimately took the decisive step toward the revolutionary upheaval of the world.[123] The years 1773 and 1789 now seemed to be directly linked. Luengo's French confrere Augustin Barruel went even further. In his *Memoirs Illustrating the History of Jacobinism* (*Mémoires pour servir à l'histoire du Jacobinisme*), published in 1797–98 and translated into English in 1799, Barruel interpreted the Revolution as a conspiracy of philosophes, in allegiance with the devil, against traditional religious and monarchic values. His Spanish confrere Lorenzo Hervás y Pandura largely agreed in his own book *Causas de la revolución de Francia* (Causes of the French Revolution), published in 1807.[124] Ex-Jesuits of this political and cultural bent viewed the Revolution as the result of a coordinated project to de-Christianize Europe, of which the suppression of the Society of Jesus was merely one step—albeit an important one. In this way, for many Jesuits like Luengo, Barruel, and Hervás y Pandura, the experience of the suppression and the French Revolution culminated in an antimodern, rigidly papocentric, conservative Christian attitude.

By no means all former members of the Society of Jesus, however, landed in the reactionary camp.[125] Not a few former Jesuits in fact utterly rejected the old values and the brand of conservatism that sprang from them. For these ex-Jesuits, the years around 1770 were a moment of liberation and escape from oppressive living conditions.[126] The prominent Portuguese ex-Jesuit and mathematician José Monteiro da Rocha (1734–1819) began cooperating closely with Pombal to reform the University of Coimbra in the spirit of the Enlightenment. He even supposedly praised the minister for suppressing the Society of Jesus in a public speech, calling the suppression "an extraordinary and difficult enterprise—a superhuman undertaking, more worthy of fame than all the victories of generals and the heroic achievements of history."[127] His former confrere Pedro de Mondengón is another example of an ex-Jesuit who changed cultural and intellectual sides, as are the five ex-Jesuits in Paris who sided with the revolutionary Third Estate in the Estates General of 1789.[128]

And standing in the shadow of these small groups of ex-Jesuit political extremists were many others who used the suppression, quietly and without much fuss, to close that chapter of their life. Not a few Spanish and Portuguese Jesuits left the Society of Jesus more or less promptly without any need for coercion when the expulsion gave them the opportunity to do so. The king of Spain was delighted: he soon offered additional support to any Jesuits willing to leave the order. A Jesuit who left the Society altogether was better than one shunted off to Italy, they thought in Madrid. Many men seized the chance: some 10 percent of all Mexican Jesuits voluntarily left the order before 1773, and in the case of Peru the rate was as high as 55 percent. Even in Russia, where the Society continued to exist, a good 10 percent of the members left in 1774.[129] Especially younger Jesuits decided to take this step. Perhaps they were less tied to the Society than their older confreres; perhaps they were also more optimistic that they could strike out in a new direction. Novices and scholastics in particular, who had not yet been ordained, had endless possibilities. In France, we find ex-Jesuits as diplomats, doctors, and advocates after 1773.[130] Hundreds of men from this group of unordained Jesuits went on to found families in the ensuing years and decades.[131] Even Cordara openly acknowledged that the suppression of the Society had many "advantages" and good sides for priests, such as the possibility of reviving ties to one's families and relatives.[132] Many former members of the Society of Jesus were simply reintegrated into society at large and absorbed during the suppression without shedding tears for their former life in the order. And even for some ex-Jesuits who faithfully sought to keep the memory of the old order, its culture, and values alive, the suppression not only represented a caesura but also opened new opportunities. The disappearance of familiar structures and mechanisms of surveillance made experiments possible and unleashed new forces.

In Germany, ex-Jesuits now often made contact with the Freemasons: they could now explore social milieus that had been previously closed to them.[133] It also was certainly not a coincidence that a sudden rise in ex-Jesuit activity in journalism can be observed after the suppression of the Society. Interested former Jesuits now tested such previously inaccessible (to them) forms of publishing to propagate their goals and views.[134] They quickly discerned that they could use the new media very profitably to spread their conservative ideology in the spirit of Barruel. It was thanks to the ex-Jesuits that European conservatives learned how to erase the head start in literature and communications that the Enlightenment had taken. This development had enormous long-term consequences.

For other ex-Jesuits, expulsion and the suppression of the Society of Jesus led to fruitful new intellectual encounters. Many an older debate was reinvigorated by the controversies of 1773. The English ex-Jesuits who continued to run their schools in Liège as secular clergy until 1794 still seized on the upheaval to introduce major innovations to the curriculum, despite their institutional continuity.[135] Since 1769, the arrival of Iberian and American ex-Jesuits in Italy had greatly helped disseminate Spanish and American views and knowledge in the European debate during the Enlightenment.[136] The newcomers entered local universities, visited libraries, and wrote books, and over the years some of them became important figures of Italian cultural life, although not always without some intellectual conflict. The Spaniard Luengo complained about the Italians' sense of cultural superiority right after his arrival in 1768.[137] His diagnosis was not entirely off the mark, as for instance the thirteen-volume *Storia della letteratura italiana* (History of Italian literature, 1772–82) by Girolamo Tiraboschi demonstrated. The Italian ex-Jesuit not only romanticized his own literary tradition but also presented Spanish literature as an inferior counterexample. This topos of Spanish backwardness was widespread at the time. Now that a large number of accomplished Spanish Jesuits were on hand, however, a fierce countermovement was foreseeable. The Catalan ex-Jesuit Saverio Llampillas soon responded to Tiraboschi's insult and published—in Italian, in Italy—a defense of Spanish literature. Many of his compatriots and confreres contributed to the pro-Spanish campaign in Italy, conferring new prominence on their country. They received support from a surprising source, namely, from the authorities in Madrid. Count Floridablanca, who as Spanish ambassador had once incessantly called for the suppression of the Society (then under the name José Moñino y Redondo), now lent this pro-Spanish campaign his direct support as leading minister in Madrid in 1777. His battle against the anti-Spanish prejudice of European Enlightenment thinkers led to an unanticipated, albeit in no way complete, rapprochement between the Iberian ex-Jesuits and the Spanish government.[138] Patriotism and national pride were identity-defining categories even for the Jesuits.

It was perhaps even more significant that the ex-Jesuits' Italian exile helped integrate the Americas in the European Enlightenment. European philosophes had been writing about the Americas for a long time—Montesquieu, Voltaire, and Diderot all discussed the continents. But the subject became especially prominent in the last quarter of the eighteenth century, evolving into a downright "debate about the Americas." Now key monographs about the Americas began to appear, including famous works by Cornelius de Pauw, William Robertson, and Guillaume Thomas François Raynal. The Americas did not enjoy a good reputation: the aforementioned authors generally described the New World as inhospitable, dangerous, and culturally and morally backward.

They also ranked the European colonizers—and here the philosophes normally attacked Spain but not, for example, England—among the factors that prevented culture from blossoming and instead made a negative impact on the Americas. The Enlightenment theorists of civilization had little interest in Creole peoples and societies.[139]

American ex-Jesuits (or those with extensive experience in the Americas) joined this debate in the 1770s and 1780s in numerous publications: Filippo Salvatore Gilii with his treatise on (South) American history (*Saggio di storia americana*, 1780–84), Francisco Javier Clavijero with his history of Mexico (*Storica antica di Messico*, 1780), and Juan Ignacio Molina with his *Compendio di storia geografica, naturale e civile del Regno del Chile* (Compendium of the geographic, natural, and civil history of the Kingdom of Chile, 1776). The Jesuits expelled from the Americas presented their erstwhile home in a completely different, more positive light than de Pauw and his Enlightenment successors. The ex-Jesuits from the New World made effective use of their authentic familiarity with the nature, geography, ethnography, and culture of the Americas against the condescension of de Pauw and others. Not only were the indigenous inhabitants shown in a much better light than in the Europeans' works, but Creole peoples were also depicted in much more positive terms. In this way, having been challenged by the summary, negative verdict of the European philosophes, ex-Jesuits from overseas became the champions of an autonomous Spanish-language Creole culture that had no reason to fear comparison with Europe. They helped articulate the cultural confidence and independence of a new American elite. Authors from the New World regularly downplayed the importance of Spain and the conquistadors for the development of their civilization.[140] In these works, the rise of Creole autonomy and the growing distance between Creole-American elites and Europe are unmistakable. Even though we should not draw a direct line from American ex-Jesuits to the independence movements of the early nineteenth century in Spanish America, it is nonetheless indicative that some of them, like Juan José Godoy (1728–87) from Chile and Juan Pablo Viscardo y Guzmán (1748–98) from Peru, openly advocated the independence of their homelands from Spain.

Finally, we must address the question of what the end of the Society of Jesus meant for the Catholic Church and its culture. The popes soon noticed that the suppression of the Society had done nothing to dispel the dissatisfaction of the philosophes, Jansenists, and absolutist monarchs with the church. On the contrary, the papacy remained under pressure in the last quarter of the eighteenth century. While it is doubtful that the Jesuits would have brought any relief, the suppression had not fundamentally improved the situation for Rome. Emperor Joseph II in Austria and his brother (and later successor) Leopold in Tuscany enacted an enlightened religious policy that dramatically increased the power of the state over the church. Pope Pius VI was duly displeased. The Italian Jansenists held a synod in Pistoia in 1786, where they adopted unexpectedly belligerent antipapal positions. Clement XIV's sacrifice of the Jesuit order failed to confer any long-term benefits on the papacy.

On the contrary, Rome soon noticed that the suppression of the Jesuits had created massive gaps in the ministry and cultural work of the church. That was true, for example, with respect to the mission.[141] Wherever Jesuits still lived in the missions in 1773, the brief *Dominus ac redemptor* was more or less promptly enforced, depending on the infrastructure, but many reports reveal that local bishops and apostolic vicars simply had no replacements for the Jesuits at their disposal. Many of these local church officials emphasized that, in contrast to "Christian regions," there were no alternatives to the Jesuits in the mission territories: "The missions [in the Americas] then stay empty, because there are no other missionaries, neither from the secular nor from the regular clergy." Even in the territories controlled by Portugal, not all the Jesuits were actually expelled. In Aleppo, *Dominus ac redemptor* was not fully enforced until 1798. In many cases—for example, in Beijing—ex-Jesuits soldiered on as secular priests. In Canada, now under British rule, where the pope had virtually no influence, the suppression could be carried out only in secrecy. For years, with the exception of a handful of people in the know, no one was aware that the Society had ceased to exist. The Jesuits carried on as if nothing had happened. They were forbidden to have novices, however, and so the group of twelve men slowly died out.

The last of them, Jean Joseph Casiot, died in March 1800, at the age of seventy-two.[142]

The pope and the Propaganda Fide tried to reassign the Jesuits' former responsibilities. Employing other missionary orders was an attractive option. They turned to the Lazarists, for example, whom Vincent de Paul had founded as the Congregation of the Mission in 1625. Their members were entrusted with the mission in China and also to some extent in the Levant and Africa. Discalced Carmelites were employed in Madurai. In Mexico, the Franciscans took over, and together with the Dominicans and Mercedarians they likewise replaced the Jesuits in Paraguay, albeit with only moderate success.

In sum, the events of 1759 to 1773 did not bring the Catholic mission to an abrupt end, but the demise of the Society of Jesus, together with the upheaval and challenges brought about by the French Revolution and the Napoleonic Wars, was undeniably a major reason for the temporary decline in Catholic missionary endeavors that could be observed everywhere in the decades around 1800.[143]

Even secular authorities soon had to acknowledge that it was not easy to organize certain areas of social life sensibly without the Jesuits. This was especially obvious in the case of schools. Enlightened governments found it astonishingly hard to translate the demise of Jesuit schools into the dawn of a new pedagogical era. They therefore often went right back to the ex-Jesuits for teachers.[144] All the reservations that they had harbored against Jesuit colleges shortly beforehand now suddenly seemed to be forgotten. First and foremost, that was a consequence of practical necessity: there often were only a few weeks between the suppression of the old schools and the beginning of the new school year. The ex-Jesuits, who were in part already provided with pensions, were moreover cheap instructors. In Ellwangen, for example, the suppressed Jesuit school was simply turned into Ignatius College. The municipal government and the bishop, who were now responsible for this school, were instructed "to leave the whole thing as it was as far as possible and practical."[145] In Bavaria, where the desire to strip the Jesuits of their teaching positions had been quite fierce, this goal was achieved at best only in phases. The ex-Jesuits and other clergymen quickly regained their former influence.[146] Even in France, where ex-Jesuits had no way back into the schools, the curricula and teaching methods remained essentially the same after the state and local communities had taken over the schools.[147] What is potentially most telling, however, is the case of the Collegio Romano.[148] The seminary of Rome—itself formerly under Jesuit control—was transferred to the Collegio in 1774, now under the direction of three cardinals. But nothing much changed, whether in curricular or pedagogical terms. The Catholic world was not well prepared for the abolition of the Society of Jesus. The hopes that many groups had placed in this event could at best be realized only piecemeal. The Society was, in many ways, a key institution of the Catholic Church that had shaped it for centuries: it was impossible simply to carry on without it.

Survival in Russia and Restoration in 1814

Despite foreseeable difficulties, princes and bishops across the world put the papal brief *Dominus ac redemptor* into effect after July 21, 1773. Some of them, such as Frederick the Great, did so reluctantly and took their time—until 1776 in the case of the Prussian king.[149] But ultimately, rulers everywhere carried out what Clement XIV had ordered—or almost everywhere, it must be said. One European monarch refused to promulgate the brief: Catherine II of Russia. The czarina simply ignored the document from Rome, and so the Society of Jesus continued to exist in Russia without interruption. Catherine's territory was initially an isolated exception, but beginning around 1800 it became the center of the campaign to restore the Society.[150]

The only reason Catherine had anything to do with the Jesuits at all was because Russia had annexed a strip of Polish territory in the First Partition of Poland in 1772 that was inhabited predominantly by Catholics. The religious needs of her new subjects had to be met, and in contrast to southwestern Europe the Jesuits were well liked in Poland. Although the Society of Jesus had been present in Russia only unofficially since 1719, Catherine wasted little time before deciding in 1772 to tolerate the Polish Jesuits. She stood by that decision even after *Dominus ac redemptor*, not least because the czarina saw no alternatives to the Jesuits in the area of education and schools. She moreover viewed the Jesuit question as a good opportunity to demonstrate the newfound confidence and independence of Russia with respect to Europe. The czarina wanted to show not least that she was the absolute ruler of her country, also and especially in regard to church affairs. Paradoxically, therefore, the Society of Jesus owed its survival to the same royalist ideal that had annihilated the Society in Portugal and Spain. It was no less paradoxical that the Society continued to exist as an institutional community in a country that belonged to the (from a Catholic perspective, schismatic) Orthodox Church. The czarina was untroubled by such religious niceties; in 1780, she even permitted the Jesuits to found a new novitiate in Polotsk in the north of modern Belarus. There soon were dozens of new members there. In 1782, a general congregation met there and, nine years after the papal suppression of the Society, a new head was elected with the title of vicar-general: Stanislaus Czerniewicz. Pope Pius VI, whose initially vehement opposition to Catherine's behavior gradually gave way to disapproving tolerance, officially recognized the election, albeit only orally.[151]

The Polish Jesuits who lived in Russia on the periphery of Latin Christendom, in a region with an extremely complex religious, ethnic, and political makeup, were engaged primarily in everyday pastoral care. After 1773, they quickly took up the Jesuits' "customary ministries" again—confraternities, helping the poor, the mission to the people. With few exceptions, sophisticated intellectual debate and involvement in broad questions of religious policy were rather atypical. Whereas the ex-Jesuits of Italy or Austria were at least moderately influenced by Enlightenment discourses—though often only *ex negativo*—such points of contact were largely lacking in the introverted Jesuit community of Russia. Their educational work in Russia was praised precisely because they were not attached to the new ideas that had been broadly received everywhere else in Europe.[152] The Society survived not only geographically but also culturally "on the margins of Europe," as the poet Novalis remarked in 1799.[153] The Russian superiors made little attempt to intervene in the affairs of ex-Jesuits outside the Russian Empire by dispatching letters or delegates.[154] Instead, they concentrated on their colleges in Polotsk and St. Petersburg and on the growing number of missions among Latin Christians of German background.[155] Turning inward, not fanning outward: that was both the reality and their motto.

The relative isolation of the Russian Jesuit community remained intact when the first small wave of ex-Jesuits from Western, southern, and Central Europe began to trickle into Catherine's territory around 1780 once word had gotten around that the Society could probably continue to exist there indefinitely.[156] The future superior general Luigi Fortis also initially planned to journey to Russia, but he ultimately spared himself the long march eastward. His enthusiasm, however, is nonetheless indicative of the burgeoning hopes that many Jesuits placed in Russia. Although Pope Pius VI explicitly declared his support for his predecessor's decrees (despite his personal toleration of Polotsk), friends of the order gradually became confident that the Society of Jesus would someday be back. The Spanish diarist Luengo, like many others, was animated by anticipation of the future revival of the Society despite the present prohibition: "With respect to the Jesuits, those who duly regret what happened and who completely drop the false ideas and preoccupations against [the Jesuits] will always be few in number. But, whether they like it or not, they will see they are in no position to do anything to prevent [the Jesuits'] restoration."[157] Luengo was proved right in the end, although there was a long way to go before the complete restoration of the Society in 1814. Still, the years around 1800 were a turning point of sorts.[158] Ever more widely, initiatives and projects were launched to bring old members together and to recruit new ones. Nikolaus Joseph Albert von Diesbach (1732–98), for example, who lived in Turin and then in Vienna after 1773, founded Amicizia Cristiana (Christian Friendship). This organization consisted of small, loose-knit groups that operated in secrecy at many different places throughout Europe. These groups made systematic use of print media to influence further Catholic social circles.[159] In Vienna, Diesbach's circle included both many former members of the Society of Jesus and new sympathizers.

Diesbach's groups had ties to several roughly contemporary religious associations in France, Italy, and Austria that explicitly dedicated themselves to the cause of reviving the Society of Jesus.[160] Pierre-Joseph de

Clorivière (1735–1820), an ex-Jesuit, had founded several such groups in France in 1791.[161] In Antwerp in 1794, Léonor-François de Tournély (1767–97), who was not an ex-Jesuit, founded the Fathers of the Sacred Heart (Pères du Sacré-Cœur)—whose name alone indicated a clear ecclesiastical-political position. They soon resettled in Vienna, where they were received by the old friend of the Jesuits Cardinal Migazzi. The Pères were a community of about fifty educated men, primarily French, who had fled the Revolution. Their spiritual practices included the complete *Exercises* of Ignatius.[162] In 1800, a network of congregations influenced by the ex-Jesuit Jean-Baptiste Bordier Delpuits began to emerge in Paris and soon in many other French cities.[163] The most spectacular among these new pro-Jesuit groups was the "Fathers of Faith" (Pères de la Foi), which was founded by Niccolò Paccanari in 1797 and merged with Tournély's society in 1799. Paccanari was "a young man full of fire who felt he had been called by God to restore the old Society," in the assessment of one contemporary.[164] He was an exciting and highly complex character with idiosyncratic ideas. In 1808, those ideas brought him before the Holy Office, which condemned him to ten years in prison. His society, however, was a decisive force in favor of the restoration of the Society of Jesus in several parts of Europe.

The founders and members of the various religious societies inspired by Ignatius of Loyola were aware of each other, knew one another, and corresponded regularly. All of them embodied the intention and will to continue or reinstitute essential aspects of the Society of Jesus. Pope Pius VI conferred official recognition on all these new groups. There were significant differences, however, with respect to what exactly they hoped to accomplish. In particular, serious controversy broke out between older ex-Jesuits and the usually younger Paccanarists over how the revival of the order should proceed. Paccanari embodied an interest in the Society that focused predominantly on its opposition to the Enlightenment and the Revolution to the exclusion of other aspects. In light of the postrevolutionary atmosphere, this bias amounted to a modernizing narrowing of Jesuit identity that suppressed the diversity of the earlier tradition. Many ex-Jesuits were accordingly critical of Paccanari. "For I cannot look upon the Society of the Faith of Jesus as the same as our Society. I acknowledge they are Jesuits, but they are also something more; and that more I don't like," commented one English ex-Jesuit in 1800.[165] In Rome, several cardinals were likewise of the opinion that the Paccanarists were not the true heirs of the Society despite everything they had borrowed from it.[166] The superiors in Russia shared this assessment and were willing to admit the Paccanarists to the Society only after thorough individual screening.[167]

Although the Paccanarists thus fell short of their ambitions, their significance for the history of the Society should not be underestimated. Over time, one out of six of the Pères de la Foi still became a Jesuit despite all these reservations.[168] These roughly fifty young men gave the Society an undoubtedly necessary dose of contemporary relevance and an urgently needed feeling for the new zeitgeist, since the Jesuits who provided direct personal continuity with the past were all aging or old men. Some of the most important Jesuits of the nineteenth century found their way into the order by way of the Pères de la Foi. In many places, moreover, such as Switzerland, it was the Paccanarists who laid the cornerstone for the revival of the Society. The Pères de la Foi thus had a considerable influence on the Society of Jesus.

Officially, however, the "Russian way" prevailed. Pope Pius VII ostentatiously approved it by officially recognizing the Russian Society of Jesus in 1801 in the brief *Catholicae fidei* and by hauling Paccanari before court in 1808. It thus was clear that the revival of the Society would commence in Russia, and that meant in strictest adherence to the old model. Step by step, the influence of the generals in Russia expanded. They began to speak for the order as a whole, and donations began to flow to St. Petersburg to finance their work. Ex-Jesuits from across Europe traveled to Russia or at least stayed abreast of events there by letter.[169] Vice versa, Italian, German, and many other ex-Jesuits were officially permitted to join the Russian Society of Jesus in their homelands. One of them was Luigi Fortis, the future superior general, who joined the Russian order in 1793. Even in Beijing, at the Chinese imperial court, there was still one old ex-Jesuit, Louis Poirot (1735–1813), who now resumed his connection with the Society.[170] Vows were renewed, the *Exercises* made, and individual Jesuit careers planned.[171] In central, western, and southern Europe, Jesuit life was initially still confined to small local networks of (former) Jesuits, some Paccanarists, and interested laypersons. Connected to one another by letter, acquaintance, and visits and connected to the general in St. Petersburg by new or renewed vows and regular correspondence, these communities again gave rise to institutional structures.

At many places outside of Russia, all this amounted to the refounding of the Society. By 1794, the Society of Jesus was unofficially tolerated in Parma by the same ruler who decades earlier had agitated for its suppression with special zeal. Now, Duke Ferdinand of Parma sent a letter, written in his own hand, to the czarina to ask her personally and explicitly to send some "real" Jesuits from Russia to facilitate the revival of the Society.[172] Under the leadership of Father José María Pignatelli, who was often called the "second founder" of the Society, a lively Jesuit community flourished in the newly established Vice-Province of Parma. Luigi Fortis also found a new home there. The Society of Jesus was then officially reestablished in Holland and then in Maryland and England in 1803; in Naples with the involvement of Pignatelli in 1804; in Düsseldorf in 1805 (albeit without lasting success); and in Sion, Switzerland, in the same year by a group of Paccanarists led by Giuseppe Sineo della Torre. Mission plans were now discussed again for the first time—Greece, North America, China, and various parts of the Russia Empire crop up in the general's letters.[173]

In the chaos of Napoleon's first exile in 1814, when Pope Pius VII—like all major European political players—took stock of the situation and began devising new goals and plans for the future, he also decided to restore the Society of Jesus.[174] Since his accession in 1800, Pius had simply been waiting for an opportune moment to reinstate the Society of Jesus. The papal brief *Catholicae fide* of 1801 was the first clear signal. Now that Napoleon seemed to have been beaten, that time had come. The moment looked favorable politically, too, given that the leading politicians were preoccupied with the Congress of Vienna that had just gotten underway. Not every cardinal, however, saw things the same way. Some considered the measure premature; others pointed (not unreasonably) to the still considerable reservations harbored against the

Jesuits in Portugal, Spain, and France. But Pius VII stuck to his plan. In order to undercut foreseeable objections, he informed very few people about it at all. Ultimately, however, the measure accorded perfectly with the spirit of the times. Monarchs across Europe were interested in sacralizing their restored power after the tumultuous decades of the French Revolution and Napoleonic Wars. On August 7, 1814, the bull *Sollicitudo omnium ecclesiarum* was read in Il Gesù. The world without the Jesuits was over; the Society had been restored.[175]

The Modern Society

GIULIO CESARE CORDARA (1704–85) made his order partly to blame for its suppression in 1773.[1] In particular, Cordara faulted himself and his confreres for the great pride they had taken in their many "signal successes," writing, "There were many glorious things that easily produced and fed pride." The Jesuits, he criticized, had become "complacent" in the strength of their faith. Healthy confidence had degenerated into hubris. *Dominus ac redemptor* was God's punishment, to which Cordara was not unwilling to submit: "I do not think the Society is to be restored before that self-importance of Ours is completely deflated." In his view, the Society of Jesus needed moral and religious renewal—it needed reform.

For the Jesuits, the forty years between 1773 and 1814 were indeed a period in the Society's history in which a wide-reaching reorientation would have made sense. In contrast to many other orders, the Society of Jesus had not previously experienced an organized reform movement. But were the decades of suppression such a period of real and profound reform? Was the "new" order (re)founded in 1814 really a fundamentally changed Society of Jesus? The first section of this epilogue will show that, on the whole, that was not the case. The Jesuits may have reacted to the changed circumstances of new times, the order may have adapted to new challenges and opportunities, it may have abandoned various venerable traditions and adopted some modern innovations, but at heart a conservative insistence on continuity and tradition prevailed even after the restoration.

It was not until after the Second World War and in particular after the Second Vatican Council that the Society of Jesus underwent real, fundamental spiritual and cultural renewal. Now the Jesuits became in many regards the leading advocates of the aggiornamento, the church's rapprochement with modern culture and society. For Ignatius's order, this inaugurated a troubled period marked both by charismatic initiatives and by resistance and tests of endurance. One of the major results of the Jesuits' reorientation was that it acquired a new role and position within the church itself. The final section of this book will give an overview of some of the important changes of this "third" Society of Jesus since the 1950s.

The Early Nineteenth Century: An Old Order, a New Outlook

Tentative First Steps

Just as the suppression of the Society was in no way a single, unique act, the revival of the Society likewise did not take place overnight. It was an open question as to what direction the order would take after 1814. It was not even clear what exactly was being restored in 1814. *Sollicitudo omnium ecclesiarum* had restored the Society as it had been founded in 1540. It was not until 1826 that Pope Leo XII confirmed all the subsequent legal privileges that had been conferred on it between 1540 and 1773. Prior to that date, was the Society supposed to come back to life less in the spirit of the eighteenth century and more in that of the sixteenth? Was it perhaps necessary to go back to the sources and leave established traditions behind?[2]

There was social friction in addition to these structural uncertainties. The six hundred or so members of the Jesuit order in 1814 can be divided into three groups: a handful of old men who had been Jesuits before 1773 and had rejoined the Society as early as 1801; Jesuits who had joined in Russia but who generally had received no more than a brief and summary education; and men who had been socialized in the other religious groups mentioned earlier. Which of these groups would shape the

Society was a crucial but initially open question. At first, under the continuing generalship of Tadeusz Brzozowski until 1820, the Society maintained a Russian focus. The czar had forbidden the superior general to relocate to Rome. The leadership of the Society of Jesus therefore remained in Russia for a few years, while several vicars held office in Italy—Luigi Fortis was one of them. It was not until 1820, at the Twentieth General Congregation, that the Society moved back to its old hub in Rome. At the same time, social differences came out into the open.[3] A group of old Italian Jesuits from the days before 1773 took a highly critical view of the younger Russian Jesuits and especially the former Paccanarists. It was also debated whether the administrative structure of the order should be adapted in several ways. Personal animosity between Mariano Petrucci, one of the "old-timers," and Giuseppe Sineo, one of the ex-Paccanarists with significant influence in Switzerland and Italy, broke out along this front. Only after some disgruntled Italian Jesuits had been excluded (and Petrucci had died) was Luigi Fortis finally elected superior general. Fortis generally supported the old Italian line; one of his first official acts was to propose that the General Congregation should declare the immense body of rules and norms from the period prior to 1773 binding yet again. The *Institutum* was recommended to all members of the order in 1820. These were unmistakable signs that Fortis intended to return to the old ways, marginalizing both the Russian tradition and especially the Paccanarists.[4] The goal was to restore former conditions as far as possible.

The Russian focus vanished from the Jesuits' sight in 1820 because Czar Alexander expelled the Society immediately after Brzozowski's death. The Jesuits were prohibited in Russia until the fall of Communism. And Russia was only the opening act: the history of the Jesuits in the nineteenth and twentieth centuries is the history of constant bans, expulsion, and reinstatement. By no means did the Jesuits return permanently and en masse to their old workplaces at a stroke in 1814. In many places, very little happened in 1814—and sometimes nothing at all. In Portugal and Austria, the Jesuits were not reinstated until 1829, not until 1836 in Argentina, and the restoration of the Society of Jesus in Germany had to wait until 1849. In France, the Society was initially tolerated again, but then Jesuit schools were banned again in 1828. Until 1850, the Jesuits managed to survive by attracting as little attention as possible.[5] They were permitted to return to Spain with some reservations in 1814 and without any in 1816, but they were expelled again in 1820; they were recalled yet again in 1823, only to be driven out once more from 1834 to 1851. They often could work only underground, as they long did in Seville.[6] Wherever they had not already been banned, the wave of revolutions in 1848/9 brought about their expulsion, at least temporarily.[7] Since these revolutions generally failed, the conservative reaction in many countries played right into the Jesuits' hands. One Roman Jesuit thought, after the end of the revolutionary movement, that conditions in the Eternal City were "even better now than before."[8] In France, the Falloux Law passed in 1850 permitted clergymen to run institutions of higher education again. The Society experienced a new heyday until it faced expulsion another time in the context of a widespread Kulturkampf: from Spain in 1868 (until 1875), from Rome in 1870 (until 1872), and from Germany in accordance with the Jesuit Law of 1872 (until 1917). In the twentieth century, under fascist, communist, and other dictatorial regimes, numerous further episodes of anti-Jesuit policy ensued in Spain, Germany, and the Eastern Bloc.

Living in a New World

Luigi Fortis, newly elected general, remarked in 1825: "God has shaped the circumstances of the reborn Society greatly, indeed very differently from those in which it was born."[9] In many ways, political, cultural, religious, and social realities had profoundly changed. The French Revolution and the Napoleonic Wars had redrawn the political map of Europe. Unimaginably powerful and aggressive new political actors had arisen in the form of nation-states, which now paid less and less attention to ecclesiastical and religious affairs. The idea of democracy was ubiquitous, and even though monarchy remained the dominant form of state, there now were parliaments almost everywhere to counterbalance the power of kings. In cultural terms, idealism and historicism created new intellectual paradigms, as the bourgeoisie moved ever more to the center of public life. By the same token, it became less and less clear what place the church and the Society could and should (still) hold in public life. Whereas there had previously been isolated and even serious conflicts between state and church, politics and religion, it was not until the nineteenth century that a genuine, fundamental antithesis seemed conceivable and, often enough, became reality. The Society of Jesus and the church itself often no longer fit in modern states' visions of the future. Opposition to the Society now became a mass phenomenon.[10] Open anti-Jesuit policies were often the result. Hence, when a wave of national-liberal enthusiasm washed over the Continent during the revolutions of 1848, violent anti-Jesuit riots broke out in many places. The Society was duly banned in many locations, and more than one Jesuit viewed this new wave of suppressions as parallel to 1773.[11]

Even if signs in 1814 seemed to point toward restoration after the end of the French Revolution and Napoleon's defeat, the Jesuits by no means came back to a stable world that was well-disposed toward them. On the contrary, they had to carefully anticipate the political consequences of their actions even more than before. They could not simply pursue their own goals proactively and aggressively: under the new, headstrong nation-states, they were forced to take careful, and deliberate, defensive action. Although religion, the church, and the Society of Jesus still held a prominent position, they were much more fragmented and limited, and thus also much less secure in the nineteenth century than they had been in the eighteenth, let alone the seventeenth. They thus were often compelled to accept very difficult and painful compromises.

It would be many years before the Society regained its old sense of purpose and clout. Even if the order's traditions had not been completely severed (as we have seen), it still was not immediately obvious which of the old traditions might still matter and define the Jesuits' identity in the new world. What did it mean now to be a "Jesuit" in light of this general change? What parts of the legacy of the past should the Jesuits take up, and on what parts could they build a common future? The members of the order first had to relearn what being a Jesuit meant to themselves. Guidelines had to be devised and tested. All this happened fairly sluggishly in the immediate aftermath of 1814, then more purpose-fully after 1830.

One difficulty in updating the old legacy of the Society was a result of the fact that its geography had been dramatically altered after 1814. On account of the new political landscape, the newly restored Society lost some of its former domains and gained others in which it placed its hopes for the future. The Jesuits' old heartlands in Germany and Aus-tria, for example, were initially still off-limits after 1814, while formerly peripheral areas like Switzerland and Galicia became their first new strongholds. The geographic balance of power and influence within the order also shifted considerably after the Restoration. With the Jesuits' reorientation toward new territories, different traditions and interests became important to Jesuit identity.

The most remarkable geographic expansion and shift of focus oc-curred with the rapid rise of the English and especially the American branches of the Society. The English Jesuit community, which had pre-viously resided on the Continent in Saint-Omer (since 1593), Bruges (since 1762), and Liège (since 1773), relocated to Stonyhurst, Lan-cashire, as early as 1774, where the Jesuits managed to establish them-selves despite numerous difficulties. Catholicism was legalized in England in 1829, and the Society was unmolested, officially, ever after. Protestant England was one of few countries where the Jesuits were never banned again.

The even more remarkable rapid growth of the Society of Jesus in the United States was the result of two of the most dramatic political up-heavals of the modern era: the American Revolution and mass migra-tion to the United States from Europe after about 1800. Shortly after the suppression of the Society, the thirteen colonies fought for their inde-pendence from England from 1775 to 1783. Freedom of religion was a key principle of the American Constitution passed in 1787—that was the cue taken by the church as a whole and the Jesuits in particular. Some Jesuits were already in the country, since around two dozen members ministered to the small Catholic population of Maryland. They stayed put after the suppression of the Society.[12] One of them, John Carroll—who became the first bishop of Baltimore in 1789—ensured that the

Jesuits survived as an organized group. The ex-Jesuits even kept control of the old property of the Society during the suppression. From the start, Carroll recognized that American independence opened up new opportunities for his confession. In 1791, a group of ex-Jesuits founded the first Catholic college in Georgetown (Washington, DC). Beginning in 1805, more and more members of the order from Belgium and Russia traveled to the New World to support them. Another wave of Jesuit immigrants followed after the annexation of the Mexican Cession at the conclusion of the Mexican-American War in 1848. Since revolutions and anti-Jesuit sentiment were raging in Europe at the same time, this vast area became an opportunity for a total of about four hundred Italian Jesuits who fled their homes and settled in the American West.

The massive immigration of Jesuits from Europe was not only the result of anti-Jesuit agitation at home. Jesuit immigration was intimately linked to the mass migration of Europeans to the United States after independence. Tens of millions of people from many European countries crossed the Atlantic to escape poverty or political oppression or in search of personal advancement. Many of the new arrivals came from Catholic countries. American Catholicism, arguably, was to a significant degree "immigrant Catholicism." More than a thousand Jesuits arrived with these Catholics and worked primarily for the newly founded immigrant communities. For a long time, most of the Jesuits stood "at the helm of the ethnic subcultures."[13] It took well into the twentieth century for American Jesuits to completely shed their attachment to these immigration experiences. These enormous cultural difficulties notwithstanding, however, the United States became an important cornerstone of the new Society of Jesus. Nowhere else did more Jesuits go than to America.[14]

On the ground, the complex mixture of old traditions and new men could easily lead to conflict and uncertainty. As established conventions clashed with new contexts, the parameters that governed Jesuit life changed and became controversial. The early Jesuits of Maryland in the 1820s and 1830s may serve as an example of the mental, cultural, and religious divides that the restored Society had to bridge. The old American Jesuits soon found themselves opposite a large number of European newcomers from Russia, Italy, and Belgium. For want of new recruits, the Society in the United States relied on immigrants for a long time. Anton/Anthony Kohlmann, Adam Britt, and Giovanni Antonio Grassi—who was actually supposed to go to China—were the foremost among the early men that General Brzozowski sent. But American and European Jesuits had different values. Jesuits from different historical contexts and eras, with widely different experiences, views, and visions of the future were encountering one another in the United States. One example of this was the subject of slavery, which was taken for granted by the American Jesuits of Maryland.[15] Another was the question of where they saw the future of Catholic America headed: the old, established Jesuits insisted on maintaining their remote but traditional rural parishes, while the European newcomers viewed the rapidly growing cities as profitable targets. In the cities, the immigrants hoped, they might at last be able to revive an orderly and communal Jesuit way of life in accordance with the rules, but the Americans seemed to have no real interest in that.[16] The two groups also had different ideas about the role of Rome, the general, and the pope in defining what Jesuits in America should, and should not, be. Contrasting visions of what a proper Jesuit way of life was and what it entailed collided here obviously and openly.

That was also the case with political views: the American Jesuits viewed the Europeans as reactionary monarchists and insisted on their own hard-fought "republican simplicity." The "Polish" and "Russian" Jesuits supposedly had "strange notions about their privileges and exemptions" in the state. Vice versa, the Italian Grassi and the Pole Franz Dzierozynski—both of them superiors with significant power and influence—looked down on American republicanism and the "unlimited freedom" that prevailed in the United States. They could not comprehend the strict separation of church and state in the American Constitution.[17] The Americans "wish for revolutions [and] adopt the condemned position: *that the sovereignty [in the state] rests essentially in the people,*" another European complained.[18] In America, the Jesuits long remained divided according to their geographic origin. That ultimately raised the question of how "American" the Society in the United

States could and should be. Similar conflict between a stronger American focus and a stronger attachment to Rome broke out around the year 1900 in the so-called Americanist Controversy.

Religious and spiritual sea changes accompanied the political. With the pontificate of Pius VII (1800–1823), a new understanding of the faith and the church became entrenched that was Romano-centric and hierarchical to an unprecedented degree. After the humiliations inflicted on it by the Revolution and Napoleon, which Pius VII had successfully weathered, the papacy entered a new era after 1815 as the reliable constant of Catholic identity. It became an identification figure that roused strong feelings.[19] The adoption of the dogma of papal infallibility by the First Vatican Council in 1869/70 was the hotly contested climax of this pious enthusiasm for Rome. This papocentrism went hand in hand with a boom in religious life across Europe that persisted until at least the eve of the First World War despite sundry points of criticism. In France in the years following the Bourbon Restoration, a domestic mission campaign in the interior attracted widespread attention.[20] An intense "devotional Catholicism" was touted far and wide here and elsewhere.[21] This brand of piety included pilgrimages and public devotions, as well as a variety of now mass-produced devotional objects. Much of it had roots in the seventeenth and eighteenth centuries—such as the ever more popular devotion of the Sacred Heart or a new campaign to promote the frequent reception of communion around 1900.[22] In its breadth and degree of mobilization, however, this wave of regulated, controlled, ostentatious devotion was a clearly recognizable, innovative movement.

Over the course of the century, this Catholic revival—including that of the Jesuits—took on a hefty dose of passion and emotion, which were supposed to inspire a naive, "saccharine devotion."[23] A mixture of controlled homogenization and folksy emotionality again shaped the faith in many ways, after the strict and more austere piety of the Enlightenment and Jansenism had held sway in the years without the Jesuits. The miraculous, supernatural, and mystical often played a major part, and many members of the Society of Jesus shared this enthusiasm. The Jesuits from continental Europe who were active in Maryland around

1820 were ecstatic when a series of miraculous healings occurred in and around Baltimore in connection with the Eucharist.[24] The nineteenth century was also the great era of Marian apparitions.[25] In Lourdes, France, and somewhat later in Marpingen, Germany, witnesses to the apparition of the Virgin Mary elevated her already popular cult to even greater heights. This adoration of the Virgin Mary, which often went hand in hand with an uninhibited, emotional focus on her supernatural dimensions, reached a climax in 1854, when the Immaculate Conception was formally established as an indisputable church dogma. It was clear enough that the Jesuits had won a belated dogmatic and religious victory within Catholicism. No wonder, then, that many Jesuits shared the belief in these Marian miracles. Even eminent Jesuits like the theologian Joseph Kleutgen or Superior General Peter Jan Beckx thought it was plausible that Mary the Mother of God might communicate with individual people through celestial letters or that the devil might do his wicked work in the guise of a beautiful nun.[26]

Meanwhile, alternatives to this dominant form of Catholicism certainly persisted. In some places, the traditions of the "regulated devotion" of the Age of Enlightenment remained en vogue. Early Anglo-American Jesuits insisted on a pragmatic, pared-down devotional practice.[27] They dismissed miracles and miraculous healings out of hand and saw only "fanaticism" in the religiosity of their European confreres. But a highly emotional faith, extending to belief in the supernatural, was not everyone's cup of tea even in Europe. The Jesuit general Jan Philipp Roothaan, in office since 1829, instead advocated a more ascetic and disciplined Catholicism.[28]

General Roothaan Recenters the Society

The Dutch superior general Roothan was of towering importance for the history of the Society in the nineteenth century. He renewed the order's obligation to perform a series of core duties that he associated with the "old Society" so as to reinforce Jesuit identity. The general understood that excessively rapid, ambitious expansion threatened to undermine the "adolescent" new Society, if its "alumni" were not yet properly grounded in an articulated corporate identity.[29] Roothaan insisted on making haste slowly, ensuring that members imbibe the Jesuit spirit over the long term. "Formation first, labor second," he said and placed special emphasis on the "heritage of our fathers."[30] His regular insistence on tradition therefore was not merely backward-looking but rather, in the complex situation of an almost seventy-year loss of tradition, an innovative step forward. Roothan returned to the order its profile, its mission, and its spirituality.

Renewed emphasis on the *Exercises* in Jesuit life initially stood at the heart of this process. Roothaan was profoundly devout and a constant seeker through prayer. The *Spiritual Exercises* were of paramount importance to him.[31] A philological detail warrants our attention first: Roothaan played a key part in popularizing Ignatius's original, the Spanish *Autograph*, supplanting the Latin translation (the so-called *Vulgata*) by André des Freux in 1548 that had previously been the primary text in use. Making this original text accessible was a scholarly accomplishment that made its historical dimension much more palpable. But much more significant than this textual-critical detail work was the fact that his promotion of the *Exercises* helped ensure that the Society of Jesus (re)acquired a clearly discernible spiritual profile. Religious training, spiritual formation (again) had the highest priority—only on that basis could all the practical questions of pastoral care be addressed.[32] Returning to this foundational Ignatian text was therefore an important step in the restored Society's quest for an identity. The general aspired to no less than "to revive where necessary or to conserve, nourish, and grow . . . the spirit."[33]

We also cannot overlook the fact that Roothaan's fundamental, forward-looking return to the *Exercises* went hand in hand with a narrow reading of the text. Now more than ever, the Jesuits understood them as an ascetic exercise of self-formation that one should follow exactly. Roothaan firmly rejected romanticism and its proclivity toward the miraculous. He likewise had little time for the mystical elements of the *Exercises*. Spiritual texts of the early modern era went unread under his leadership.[34] He was generally not in favor of "especulación" and rejected it in particular with respect to the *Exercises*.[35] The outcome thus was an often arid and dry, sometimes even harsh and hard, form of religiosity with a heavily moralizing tendency. Even if this moralizing, ascetic reading cast a long, at times repressive, shadow over the history of the next generations of Jesuits, we still must concede that Roothaan's spiritual endeavors represented a turning point. He gave his community a common purpose again, a spiritual core. Although it was by no means self-evident, his renewed emphasis on the *Exercises* in their original form linked the "new" Society of Jesus of the nineteenth century deliberately and effectively with the early phase of the "old" Societas Iesu. In a similar vein, Roothaan also guided the Society back to missionary and educational activities.

MISSIONS RESTARTED

Roothaan frequently insisted that the mission ranked among the Society's most important responsibilities.[36] A circular letter to that effect went out in 1833.[37] Soon numerous *patres* caught the general's enthusiasm for the mission. Just as before 1773, they signed up in droves for deployment overseas. Numerous letters still survive today in which individual Jesuits passionately (albeit in completely stereotyped language) begged to be sent to one of the new mission territories.[38] Roothaan's reactivation of the missions obviously incited his confreres to redouble their collaboration.

In this field, too, Roothaan and his confreres sought inspiration for the tasks at hand from their order's tradition. Missionaries of the old Society like Roberto de Nobili or the reductions of Paraguay, or Paolo Segneri served as role models for nineteenth-century Jesuits. The established methods of the early modern period, though, had been systematized by the new theological discipline of missiology (i.e., mission studies).[39] In contrast to their past rivalry, the Society now maintained a broadly cooperative relationship with the Propaganda Fide.[40] The Society's renewed focus on the mission gelled with corresponding initiatives launched by Pope Gregory XVI—the former head of the Propaganda Fide—who in 1831 had likewise begun working to revive missionary activity. This improved cooperation also extended to a more positive attitude toward the question of whether there should be an indigenous clergy. In India, for example, seminaries were founded for native men. Traditional engagement with the mission was undeniably integrated in the new religious conditions of the nineteenth century.

The Jesuits departed significantly from earlier times also with respect to their geographical reach. They returned to some of their former mission territories, but many other areas of the world now came to the Jesuits' attention for the first time. In India, for example, the Society opened a mission in Bengal and Calcutta in 1834; prior to 1773, the order had maintained only a superficial presence there at best. In North America, the Society began in 1823 to expand into the vast Midwest, the Rocky Mountains (fig. 31), and finally the far Pacific coast. By 1895, no fewer than 160 Jesuits were active among the Native Americans in the northwestern United States.[41] The Jesuits also expanded to Algeria in 1830, the year in which Charles X of France conquered the territory. Almost simultaneously, new initiatives were launched on Madagascar, and in 1847 an expedition set out south from Cairo with the Polish Jesuit Maximilian Ryllo—who had already made a significant impact in the Near East—to open up Khartoum as a missionary gateway to central Africa. The expedition ultimately failed, but the order's arduous return to the Zambezi, commencing in 1879, proved to be a greater long-term success.[42] The first Jesuits to reach the Kongo arrived in 1893. The Society also expanded its previously marginal presence in the Pacific and Oceania.[43]

The revived missions of the Society of Jesus encountered a changed world. Infrastructure had changed dramatically. Life on the periphery of European civilization may still have been an adventure, but new modes of transportation like colonial railways and bicycles provided greater mobility in many places.[44] Advances in communications technology like the telegraph strengthened links between the faraway missionaries and their friends and colleagues at home.[45] The ecclesiastical structures of the mission had also dramatically changed. The old *padronado* system no longer existed; mission territories could now be distributed much more evenly among all the European Jesuit provinces. Hence, for example, Poland was responsible for Southeast Africa, and

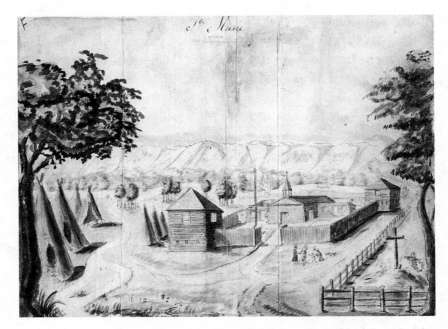

FIGURE 31. Revived and new Jesuit mission territories after 1814: the mission station of St. Mary, Maryland, 1841, by Nicholas Point. @ Jesuit Archives, Central United States.

Italy for the American West. An unprecedented internationalization of Jesuit missionary activity took place. Every province in the Society could now have "its own" mission, no longer merely those of the colonial powers. All of this gave the *patres* even greater global mobility, as they now—not least thanks to improved travel conditions—established an even denser Catholic network around the globe.[46] Above all, however, it was the cultural and political conditions of the mission that changed in the aftermath of colonialism and imperialism.

The mission in the age of colonialism was animated by new forms of sponsorship and organization. The established orders were now no longer the only—and often not even the primary—arbiters of missionary activity. Missionary societies, which first appeared in France in 1819 and soon spread to other European countries, systematically integrated the laity in missionary activities.[47] Societies like the Société pour la Propagation du Foi founded in Lyon by Pauline Jaricot or the

Franz-Xaver-Verein founded in Aachen in 1842 by Heinrich Hahn asked their members to make small, daily donations for the missionaries. Journals also reported the results, challenges, and problems of evangelizing overseas—the Jesuits alone had at least three dozen such journals worldwide.[48]

New missionary congregations were also founded, often in close association with lay societies. For example, the Society of Mary or Marianists (Societas Mariae)—founded in 1824, inspired by the Society of Jesus—was primarily active in Oceania. The Jesuits also founded their own training centers for missionaries—a half dozen of these so-called apostolic schools that sprouted up across Europe after 1865 traced their origins back to Fr. Albéric de Foresta. Not only Jesuits received instruction there but also missionaries from other orders.[49] The Jesuits now often maintained better relations with their various missionary comrades in arms than had been the case before—despite the fact that the Lazarists, for example, had moved into the Jesuits' former buildings in Syria in 1835.[50] The Society also collaborated far more closely with female missionary orders in the nineteenth century than in the early modern period, when only sporadic collaboration had been possible.

The Jesuits had a more competitive relationship with now numerous Protestant missionary organizations. If we set aside important predecessors, the Protestant mission began in earnest in the middle of the eighteenth century. By the time the Jesuits had been restored and set about proselytizing overseas again, they often found their confessional rivals already there. In some cases, the Jesuits became active in certain missionary territories just to beat their confessional competitors to the punch.[51] The Jesuit missionaries' confident self-presentation sometimes had a blatantly anti-Protestant edge. Alexandre Brou gave a vivid description of it in the year 1908, praising the beauty of the Society's African mission stations: "Taken together, all this gives Catholicism an outward profile that is by no means negligible, but which in fact proves to be indispensable when there is competition with Protestantism."[52] Even when Jesuits and Protestants encountered one another in remote corners of the world, their confessional differences tended to take center stage.[53] They not only hurled mutual recriminations at one another in matters theological but also criticized each other's methods of inter-acting with the indigenous population.[54] The Jesuits claimed the Prot-estant missionaries bought conversions with money—the Protestants answered in kind.[55] Jesuit and Protestant missionaries were in direct competition, but that did not prevent Catholics and Protestants from supporting one another if the need arose. "Well, they do good to many natives whom we could not reach; anyhow it is better to have them as friends than enemies," wrote Jules Torrend (1861–1936), a Jesuit mis-sionary on the Zambezi, summarizing his attitude toward the Protes-tants. In faraway and exotic locales, European solidarity and confes-sional quarrels did not stand in a fixed hierarchy.[56]

REFORMING THE *RATIO STUDIORUM* AND NEW EDUCATIONAL INITIATIVES

Much more controversial than the Jesuits' resumption of missionary work was their return to education. The *patres* became schoolteachers again more or less quickly in many countries. In Italy, individual colleges were transferred to them within a few years. The return of the Society of Jesus to the Collegio Romano in 1824 was undoubtedly a symbolic climax, although the Jesuits essentially had to bring the Collegio back to life. Yet it was again Roothaan who gave key impulses to the Society's renewed educational work.

One of the biggest changes the Jesuits had to come to terms with after 1814 was the growing influence of the state on education. In contrast to the period before 1773, there now were real, viable alternatives to ecclesi-astical and specifically Jesuit education. In the decades without the Jesuits, nation-states had made questions of instruction and science their own, tackling them in an innovative way. Even where ecclesiastical educational institutions were still permitted to exist, they had to submit to state super-vision. Now, even in the best circumstances, Jesuit schools also had to operate within an external framework—in the worst circumstances, eccle-siastical schools were prohibited outright. In light of that fact, the Jesuits' educational engagement not only had to be restarted but also had to be recalibrated in terms of both content and concept. It was telling that the

Jesuits compared the curricula of secular schools when they began to think about how they might reform the *Ratio studiorum*.[57]

The process of reforming the *Ratio* was launched at the Twentieth General Congregation in 1820. Intense discussions in the following years, however, only highlighted the contradictory positions held inside the order. Some Jesuits were open to adding new subjects and emphases, while others could accept, at most, only a linguistic and potentially pedagogical adjustment. Some Jesuits approached the question pragmatically and took a cue from their contemporaries' new needs, many of which they considered justified and innocuous. Others preoccupied themselves with fundamentals, focusing particularly on the *Constitutions'* demand for "uniformity" and "orthodoxy" of doctrine.[58] The reform made little headway in light of these conflicting priorities. It was not until Roothaan's urgent initiative in 1829 that a new version of the *Ratio studiorum* could be presented. Before his election, Roothaan had worked for several years as rector in Turin, and he brought this personal experience to bear in the reform process.[59] After long, intensive consultation, which strongly resembled the work carried out 230 years earlier under General Acquaviva, the new document was published in 1832.

It is undeniable that the *Ratio* of 1832 was intended to continue the earlier tradition in many respects. Roothaan insisted that even the "slightest change" was to be made only with "great care" and "prudence."[60] Hence, a humanistic education remained the basis of Jesuit pedagogy. The Society also initially still believed that it was possible to determine the content and guidelines of Jesuit pedagogy by decree from Rome as in the early modern period. The Society did not finally break with this unrealistic and obsolete requirement until 1906.[61]

Despite all the continuity, change was unmistakable. References to school theater were dropped.[62] Church history, vernacular languages, and the natural sciences were at last added to the curriculum—as had become inevitable at least since the Enlightenment.[63] And the traditional educational focuses on rhetoric and philology—which incidentally were not at all incompatible with the neo-humanistic educational movement of the nineteenth century—began to be taught with new pedagogical techniques. Even in pedagogy, the order showed that it was at least somewhat open to new developments of the preceding fifty years.[64] That extended to a new willingness to include vernacular literature in the curriculum. The *Ratio* of 1832 also reflected the fact that neither the Society nor the Catholic Church itself had a standard philosophy or theology anymore at the dawn of the new century. The old models had fallen away: there was little room for Aristotelianism left in the *Ratio*, and the teachings of St. Thomas Aquinas were praised but explicitly not prescribed. And even though the basic philosophical orientation of the Society was still strongly opposed to Enlightenment ideals, engagement with modern philosophy became a key element of the *Ratio* at least *ex negativo*. More room was also made in the regular curriculum for physics and mathematics, while philosophy was reduced from three to two years. These too were adjustments made to accommodate students' new needs.

Throughout the century, we can find Jesuit educational institutions here and there that thoroughly exhausted the possibilities opened up by the new *Ratio* for integrating modern subjects. That is true not only of Spain, where the Jesuits opened a school of engineering (Instituto Católico de Artes e Industrias) in 1908, but also of England: initially at Stonyhurst (in the innovative tradition of the schools of Liège) and since the 1870s in Liverpool, where now scientific and commercial instruction was even offered in middle school. Even the General Congregations recognized economic subjects as relevant.[65] At the Collegio Romano, where the classical subjects of the Jesuit educational canon were still the order of the day, experiments and lectures in physics and chemistry were held shortly after the restoration of the Society.[66] The Jesuit Angelo Secchi (1818–78), one of the most important astronomers and spectroscopists of the entire nineteenth century, taught there—and intermittently also at Stonyhurst and Georgetown.[67]

This groundbreaking revival resulted in a new boom in Jesuit educational institutions. In many places, the nineteenth century was a phase of expansion for Jesuit schools. The Society's first educational institution in the United States, for example, Georgetown, was founded in 1791. Many more universities and simple schools followed in the ensuing decades. Most of them, such as Boston College, were closely tied to immigrant subcultures. But since the schools became arguably the most sensitive public arena for confessional Kulturkampf, they implicated the Jesuits in countless conflicts all over the world. Liberal governments in the Netherlands, France, and elsewhere tried to place the ecclesiastical training under government supervision. Rome resisted. Pope Pius IX condemned the idea of complete state control of schools in 1864.[68] In many places, the legitimacy and supervision of Catholic and Jesuit schools were contested, and the Jesuits as teachers found themselves entangled in debates big and small. The debate took an especially drastic turn in France. Policy shifted with the prevailing political winds. Whereas ecclesiastical (and that meant especially Jesuit) institutions of higher learning were initially banned, the Falloux Laws of 1850/1 permitted them until the Ferry Laws prohibited them again in 1882. Jesuits at schools on the ground had an uncomfortably close view of these conflicts and reversals. In Ellsworth, Maine, John Bapst, a former Swiss Jesuit and refugee of the Revolution of 1848, was tarred and feathered in 1854 for trying to found a Catholic school before moving on to becoming the first president of Boston College in 1863.[69] Often enough the Jesuits found themselves in the eye of the storm raging over educational policy. It was obvious that a fundamental conflict over the basic values and outlook of modern society was playing out in the debate over Jesuit and Catholic schools.

Times of Ambivalence: Mid-nineteenth to Mid-twentieth Century

Revolutions and Kulturkampf

The debates over the role of religion, church, and religious orders in the modern world and modern nation-states escalated dramatically after 1850. The wave of revolutions in 1848/9 marked a turning point in many ways. Almost everywhere, members of religious orders experienced attempts to overthrow the government as a personal and existential threat. The brief success of the revolutionaries meant expulsion and exile for many Jesuits. To many, 1848 looked like a new 1773. Only a small fringe group of Jesuits joined the March Revolution of 1848, leaving the

Society as quickly as possible.[70] For most of the *patres*, in contrast, the events only hardened the front against the modern political ideas of democracy, liberalism, and nationalism.

But the revolutions in Europe failed, the exile was lifted, and the revolutionary years culminated generally only in exacerbated religious and political reactionism. Thus, over the medium term, the March Revolution paradoxically even played right into the hands of the Jesuits and their Catholic allies; among the Catholic victors of 1848/9, ultramontanism increasingly became the default. Even Protestant authorities took a positive view of the Jesuits' resolute antirevolutionary intervention.[71] This Catholic revival peaked in the decade after 1850. Together with many other Catholic orders and organizations, the Jesuits launched an intensive new phase of popular missions in the Catholic regions of Germany and elsewhere.[72] Perpetuating earlier traditions, the *patres* tried to fill whole villages with a new enthusiasm for the faith through intense religious guidance. A mixture of highly emotional piety and an intense moralization of private and public life set the tone. The missionaries insisted that people exhibit correct behavior, which explicitly included political positions. Wrong political views were discussed as a moral problem and sin.

By the same token, the revolutionary unrest had driven anti-Jesuit and anti-Catholic prejudices to new heights. The virulent anti-Jesuit protests of the revolutionary period not only stuck fast in the memory of the *patres* but also acquired exemplary status among opponents of the Society. Political and cultural antipathies became entrenched, conflicts grew (even) fiercer. The popes in Rome—and with them, the Society of Jesus—embraced an explicitly antimodern, reactionary attitude, culminating in the *Syllabus errorum* of 1864. While we can interpret the first decades of the nineteenth century under General Roothaan as a phase of Catholic revival marked by romanticism and restoration, the latter half of the century and the early twentieth century are often considered a period of ultramontanist dogmatic and cultural sclerosis. The Society now explicitly pitted itself against the modern zeitgeist.

All this was bound up in strong confessional antagonism. It is not for nothing that scholars have labeled the nineteenth century the

"second" or even the "real" age of confessional schism. In many contexts, it was *now* that Catholic anti-Protestantism peaked—as was
equally true of Protestant anti-Catholicism. The battle had long ceased
to be fought over dogmatic or liturgical details; now it was about a
supposed Kulturkampf.[73] Conservative Catholics battled Protestantism as epitomizing "modernity," while the Protestants battled (Jesuit)
Catholicism as epitomizing cultural backwardness. This idea of the
hated Catholic enemy helped the liberal Protestant losers of the revolutions of 1848 formulate their own identity more clearly. Anti-
Catholicism and anti-Jesuitism became part of the liberal Protestant
self-conception more than ever—first in the euphoria of revolution
and then in the disappointment of the reactionary 1850s. On the other
side, Protestantism and liberalism fused in the Catholics' imagination
into one and the same adversary. When Otto von Bismarck, chancellor
of unified Germany after 1871, launched a full-scale attack on Catholicism and the church (first and foremost, the Jesuits), this was as much
a tactical political move as it was an attack on a widely shared way of
life. An entire culture, including associated mindsets, institutions, habits, and social practices, was to be purged. For Catholics and especially
for Jesuits in the German Empire, this meant years and decades of persecution, banishment, hostility, and public marginalization. Catholicism took refuge in a subculture, and the *patres* of the Society of Jesus
were a prominent part of it.

MODERN ANTIMODERNISTS

Much of what most Jesuits in the latter half of the nineteenth century
rejected so bitterly ultimately came to be labeled "modernism." This concept designated an often somewhat diffuse collection of positions and
ideas that were supposedly at odds with the Catholic truth. The most
abominable "modern" ideas from a Roman perspective included many
scientific discoveries (like Darwin's theory of evolution) and political
and moral views like republicanism or liberalism, which threatened to
degenerate into "subjectivism" and "individualism." Fear of religious autonomy, of the emancipation of the faithful from church authority, and

of a growing self-confidence of Catholics decisively marked Roman antimodernism of the nineteenth century.[74]

Even though the idea of "modernism" was genuinely connected to real consequences of the comprehensive political, economic, and cultural modernization in the nineteenth century, "modernism" nonetheless was at first a polemical battle cry, an ideological cipher. What the popes and Jesuits were battling was at least as much a chimera, a negative stereotype, as it was a social reality. Antimodernism accordingly was not at all a consistent, homogeneous mindset. On the contrary, there were many nuances, also in the Society of Jesus. We can observe a strong strand of conservative and even reactionary philosophy among many Jesuits of the nineteenth century; these Jesuits placed their trust in the alliance between the altar and the throne, monarchy and the church.[75] This antimodernist attitude held by many Jesuits was reflected in their support of Pius IX's *Syllabus* in 1864, in their advocacy of papal infallibility at Vatican I, and in the sometimes guiding role of individual members of the Society in the composition of numerous antimodernist papal decrees.

But even conservative Jesuits had to acknowledge that they were no longer living under the ancien regime. Pope Pius VIII saw things the same way in 1830, when the July Revolution overturned the political system of France and brought a new king, Louis-Philippe, to power: after the "citizen king" declared that he was prepared to preserve the church's rights, the pope saw no reason not to recognize him. The papacy could easily adapt to the new political reality as long as the church's claims appeared secure.[76] The pope and the Jesuits also had few reasons not to recognize the independence of the new states of Latin America, despite Spanish protests—in many places that meant the Society could return to its old stomping grounds. A certain form of moderate nationalism, thus, seemed acceptable even to mainstream Jesuits.[77] Of course, even the European Jesuits who had been socialized under monarchic and authoritarian governments soon recognized at least the pragmatic advantages of the new democratic, liberal structures. In republican American, the Society of Jesus "[did] not have to combat one of the principle obstacles which block it elsewhere, which is that the civil authority in our days seems completely to favor irreligion and error," as

Grassi himself conceded. And a Belgian confrere insisted with the superior general only a few years later that "liberty as realized in America is better for the church than the protection of absolute monarchies."[78] The Jesuits never cut themselves off entirely from the modern world.

The Jesuits' partial openness to modernity and their willingness to adapt to modern structures is especially visible in the communications media that the Society used. Beginning in 1850, the Jesuits founded a plethora of journals of the most diverse kinds in quick succession, thus productively seizing on one of the most modern media of the time. In addition to publishing scholarly articles, many of these journals provided Catholic Christian commentary on current events. The first and arguably most important was Civiltà Cattolica, edited by Carlo Curci, a weekly and now bi-weekly magazine run exclusively by Jesuits (even today).[79] It was published in Italian, not Latin, and was addressed to broad segments of the population. The journal was founded in a demonstratively reactionary spirit, in close association with conservative neo-Thomism. General Roothaan in fact wanted to prevent its founding because he viewed its strict focus on contemporary politics as a politicization of the Society. But the general was overruled by his own men, as well as by the pope. With its conservative agenda, Civiltà became a powerful mouthpiece of the Vatican, an unofficial function that it still performs today. Similar journal and magazine projects soon followed. In 1856, the Études began to appear in France; in 1865, The Month in England (shuttered in 2001); and in 1871, Stimmen aus Maria Laach (since 1914: Stimmen der Zeit).

The depth and presentation of these publications varied. The border between them and scholarly journals was always fluid, and eminent academics from the Society often wrote in them. Some outlets were purely Jesuit affairs; others involved suitable laymen. Many of these journals were extremely conservative at the start. Civiltà Cattolica was regarded as the voice of antimodernism and moreover propagated a virulent, aggressive anti-Judaism in the early twentieth century. Many journals' outlooks gradually changed, however, during the interwar period and especially after the Second World War. After a highly antimodernist early phase, some outlets, like Stimmen under the Weimar Republic, advocated a willingness to engage with people of different schools of thought.[80] Many other periodicals, too, slowly transitioned to a more moderate traditional line. Pius XII congratulated *Études* in 1956 on the occasion of its centennial and thanked it in a handwritten letter for its long years of "upholding Catholic teaching against 'rationalism,'" while using "commendable moderation and firmness without weakness."[81] *Civiltà Cattolica*, on the other hand, being de facto censored and approved by the popes, usually adhered very closely to the intellectual, cultural, and political agenda of the Vatican, anchoring itself firmly in a Roman and curial perspective.

The question of the philosophical and theological outlook of Christianity was an important battleground in this confessional Kulturkampf. It was no coincidence that Curci, the founder of *Civiltà Cattolica*, had a decidedly neo-Thomist background.[82] For the Roman Catholic Church, antimodernism increasingly meant declaring for a Thomistic brand of neo-scholasticism. It also was understood as a rejection of the idealism of more recent (German) philosophy since Immanuel Kant and Georg Wilhelm Friedrich Hegel, which was perceived as Protestant. Before 1850, adherents of strict Thomism did not yet constitute a majority in the Catholic world. Even among the Jesuits, the early decades of the nineteenth century were regarded as a time of limited philosophical plurality. A "period of peace" prevailed between the Thomists and their opponents.[83] After 1850, though, the proponents of strict Thomism began to prevail.[84] For several years, conflict raged within the order over the question of whether and how exclusively the Society of Jesus should embrace Thomistic neo-scholasticism. The movement came to be viewed increasingly as a bulwark against the science and philosophy of the modern age. Hence it was no surprise when Pope Pius IX, with the key support of the German Jesuit Joseph Kleutgen (1811–83), elevated Thomism to the dogmatic norm.[85] Thomistic hard-liners, like the Jesuit Giovanni Mari Cornoldi (1822–92), now regarded modern science as atheism. The heated exchange between Cornoldi and Angelo Secchi, an internationally renowned astronomer who worked out of the Collegio Romano, is a perfect example.[86] While ostensibly harking back to tradition, ultramontane neo-scholasticism had in fact emerged as a powerful new weapon against "modernism" that had been forged in an extraordinarily creative process of cultural innovation. Pope Leo XIII brought this development to its conclusion in 1879 by declaring Thomistic neo-scholasticism the mandatory Catholic philosophy in his encyclical *Aeterni Patris*: it was to serve as a weapon against "modern philosophy," which the church now roundly rejected.

Pius X condemned modernism yet again in the syllabus *Lamentabili sane exitu* and the encyclical *Pascendi dominici gregis*. The Society of Jesus, too, now pivoted to fighting modernity and modern science.[87] Antimodernism and reactional sociopolitical views now became fused in neo-Thomism under Jesuit leadership.[88] Shortly thereafter, the idiosyncratic and atypical Irish Jesuit George Tyrrell (1861–1909) was dismissed from the Society and excommunicated because he had come uncomfortably close to embracing condemned doctrines. Yet we still cannot overlook certain nuances. Tyrrell's tragic case was by no means the only template for the Jesuits' response to modernism. For all the Jesuits' ultramontane and conservative values, which pointedly manifested themselves in their overwhelming support of Vatican I, these were also decades of contradiction, upheaval, and new approaches. Neither the history of the papacy, nor the Jesuits, nor Catholicism itself can simply be pigeonholed as antimodernist. Even in this phase of extreme ideological division, the Jesuits went with the flow, at least in part. Being an "antimodern," neo-scholastic Thomist was in and of itself a modern position: antimodernist ideology was as much a recent innovation as the ideas it opposed. The Jesuits' antimodernism was always only selective, never total.

FROM WORLD WAR I TO WORLD WAR II: GENERAL LEDÓCHOWSKI AND THE JESUITS BETWEEN FASCISM AND ANTICOMMUNISM

The First World War introduced change for Jesuits in many places. The men of the Jesuit order frequently took part in the enthusiastic mobilization of the masses at the beginning of the war. The nationalism of the times had seized them, too. Even before the Great War, the Jesuits at *Civiltà Cattolica* closely monitored the debates over a (potential) link between the army and Catholicism, after the state of Italy had radically secularized its armed forces after 1870.[89] The Jesuits overwhelmingly supported a new alliance between the church and the military. Hence several dozen Italian fathers went directly to the battlefields as chaplains in 1914 and witnessed the gruesomeness of the trenches at first hand. The Jesuits served as chaplains in the armies of other Catholic belligerents.[90] In Italy, where clergymen had been required to perform military service since 1870, Jesuits who had not yet been ordained fought on the front.

When these Jesuits came home from the war, they not only had experienced many things that called their traditional worldview into question in many respects but also returned to a society in flux. Political ideologization, in particular, entered a new phase. The gradual transition to democracy affected many European states after 1918, but it was also a highly controversial and, in many places, a violently contested change. During this phase of social and political upheaval after the end of the war, which was often accompanied by civil war–like violence and dramatic ideological divides, the Jesuits also had to position themselves anew between political camps. When communism and fascism emerged as radical alternatives to democracy, the *patres'* cultural situation became only more complicated.

The destiny of the Society of Jesus in this turbulent age was guided by Superior General Włodzimierz Ledóchowski, who served an extraordinarily long tenure (1915–42).[91] On the one hand, this Polish nobleman at the head of the Society stood out for starkly anti-Semitic views and an authoritarian disposition; on the other, his generalship was a time of important and forward-thinking adaptation for the Society. In 1931, for example, the Society took over the newly founded Vatican radio station at the pope's request—yet again, we find the Jesuits as protagonists in the progressive use of modern mass media. Under Ledóchowski's leadership, the Society also adapted to a new ecclesiastical legal basis in important ways. After Pope Benedict XV issued a new code of canon law in 1917 (*Codex iuris canonici*), a thorough revision of the statutes of the order was needed. The educational system of the Society of Jesus was also recalibrated under Ledóchowski. Already in 1915, he had turned on the radical, reactionary use of neo-scholasticism by a small group of extremely antimodernist Jesuit theologians and undercut their influence.[92] In 1938, an extraordinary General Congregation ensured that the Society revamped its educational policy. Pius XI had issued the apostolic constitution *Deus Scientiarum Dominus* in 1931, reforming theological education and ecclesiastical studies generally.[93] For the first time ever, a pope had taken legislative action to issue a universal educational program. Education in ecclesiastical subjects was not just centralized and put on a higher level. The subject of the constitution in particular was a reassessment of the Church's relationship to historical-critical ("positive") approaches to the Bible and dogma. Although no doubt was cast on the abiding primacy of dogmatic and speculative theology, the constitution recognized the basic admissibility of new disciplines and perspectives, albeit within narrow limits.[94] At the same time, it was asked how strictly and inflexibly the church should insist on the absolute authority of Thomism in its antimodernist position. A milder, moderate position was formulated under the guiding influence of the Jesuits Ledóchowski and Augustin Bea. It both retained the special precedence of Thomism and accepted the premise that the interpretation of Thomas was always subject to historical change.[95]

Like all other Catholic educators, the Jesuits also had to adapt to the new papal doctrinal policy. At the Thirty-Eighth General Congregation, a series of adjustments were made. Even though the Jesuits continued to attack Protestant historical-critical theology under Ledóchowski, the general also was somewhat sympathetic to historical approaches to Church history. Already one of Ledóchowski's predecessors, the Spaniard Luis Martín (1846–1906, general since 1892), had ordered that historical-critical editions of the sources of the Society be published—the key series *Monumenta Historica Societatis Iesu*, which remains crucial today, can be traced back to these efforts of the late nineteenth century to adopt modern forms of scholarly historiography. Under Ledóchowski, these efforts were redoubled and institutionalized. The general founded an institution at the Roman Curia dedicated to preserving the history of the Society, the still-functioning Institutum Historicum Societatis Iesu.[96]

In the field of missionary work, too, Ledóchowski's generalship was a period of remarkable acceleration and intensification. While the total number of Jesuits rose from seventeen thousand to twenty-seven thousand during his term, the number of Jesuit missionaries quadrupled. New places attracted the *patres'* attention and kindled their hopes, such as Shanghai, where the Society had operated a university with a famous observatory since 1903. Besides China, Russia also played a key part as an evocative target of mission hopes.[97]

With respect to politics, Ledóchowski's generalship was defined by the major contemporary conflict between communism and fascism.[98] Fear of communism gained the upper hand among clergymen of this period, casting the authoritarian and totalitarian tendencies of European fascism in a positive light. The general himself set the tone for the Jesuits in that regard, while Edmund A. Walsh, S.J., became the champion of "Catholic anti-communism" in America.[99] Like many other Catholics, he was gravely afraid of the materialistic implications of the new ideology. Anticlerical, materialist, collectivist socialism seemed to have nothing in common with Christianity.[100]

Again and again, this attitude drove the Jesuits into the hands of the fascists. There may have been some dedicated democrats among them, as seen, for example, in the Irish fight for independence,[101] but many others, including numerous Irish, saw better prospects for their goals with the fascists.[102] In Spain, many Jesuits embraced the nationalist-Catholic line of the fascist dictator Francisco Franco.[103] The Jesuits profited enormously in 1938 from the fascists' imminent victory in the Spanish Civil War, which had shaken the country since 1936. After they had been prohibited and in some cases persecuted under the Second Spanish Republic since 1931, the Jesuits under Franco now enjoyed great esteem as "an eminently Spanish order," which was reflected not least in their restoration immediately after the end of the war. Franco's state posed as the defender of the church and counted on its cooperation. This led to significant growth in the order, which actively joined the Catholic Church's broad initiative to "re-Christianize Spain," as the unholy alliance of church and state was propagandistically labeled. It thus was no surprise that the Society maintained a close and positive relationship with the generalissimo.

But the Jesuits' support was not simply the result of gratitude for restoration and patronage. At least some members of the Society held

views of state and society that converged closely with basic fascist assumptions. The ideas of Christian corporatism and the "Christian concept of autarky," which the Jesuit social ethicist (and engineer) José
Agustín Pérez del Pulgar (1875–1939) advocated in his homonymous
book in 1940, resembled the nationalistic ideas of the Franco regime.
He considered the economic policy of Nazi Germany to be exemplary.
The ideas of the Jesuit Joaquín Azpiazu Zulaica (1887–1953), another
prominent social theorist, also converged with those of the Franco regime on the role of a strong (authoritarian) state as a way to mitigate the
excesses of capitalism.[104] Not every Jesuit thought along these lines, of
course. There were some exceptions of republican-minded Jesuits.
Basque and Catalan Jesuits were systematically oppressed by the Franco
regime and were considered opponents rather than supporters. But on
the whole, they made up only a small, critical minority. Even after the
experiences of the Second World War, which proved a decisive turning
point elsewhere, fascism and the alliance between the Franco regime
and the church, and especially the Society of Jesus, remained intact.

Many Jesuits also identified with Italian fascism. The conquest of
Ethiopia was acclaimed with great enthusiasm.[105] *Civiltà Cattolica* in
Rome voiced considerable sympathy for Benito Mussolini's movement
since 1922, often adding vitriolic anti-Judaism to a toxic ideological mixture.[106] Fr. Pietro Tacchi Venturi (1861–1956), a prominent historian and
collaborator with *Civiltà Cattolica*, was a close associate of Mussolini's
and may even have temporarily been his confessor. He served for years
as a liaison between Il Duce and the Vatican and worked on a fusion of
fascism and Catholicism.

At the same time, however, Tacchi Venturi also was involved in saving
Jews from fascist race laws.[107] Here, he shared a broader Roman ambivalence: while many embraced right-wing totalitarianism, far fewer Jesuits
and churchmen endorsed the specifically racist version propagated by
the German National Socialists and, in later years, by Mussolini himself.[108] There can be no doubt about the centuries-long hostility of the
Society of Jesus toward the Jews, but the Society by and large rejected
the racist variety of anti-Semitism. Jakob Nötges, for example, accused
Adolf Hitler in 1931 of "deliberately putting raceology [*Rassologie*] above

religious ethics."[109] Following the same train of thought, *Civiltà Cattolica*, though calling for anti-Jewish legislation in Italy, still called Nazism the "heresy of the century."[110] *Stimmen der Zeit* expressed similar criticism in Germany, for which it was banned first in 1935/6 for a few months and, after 1941, until the fall of the Third Reich. In 1938, the Twenty-Eighth General Congregation condemned all "errors that, subverting the right order among natural and supernatural goods and between the human person and human society, extol the cult of race or nation or state to such an extent that they deny or completely weaken the most fundamental rights of the human person, the family, other nations, and the very Church of Christ"—an unmistakable rebuke of Nazism.[111] At the same time, the Jesuits Gustav Gundlach and John LaFarge were drafting an encyclical against racism for Pius XI, but it was never promulgated on account of the pope's death in February 1939.[112] The fact that General Ledóchowski probably played a major part in halting the publication of the encyclical testifies once again to the divided attitudes of the Society of Jesus in these matters. Although several hundred Jesuits served actively in the Wehrmacht and even voiced their enthusiastic support for the war from the field on several occasions, the Society's relationship with Nazism ranged predominantly from cool distance to open criticism.[113]

SIGNS OF CHANGE

As conservative as the Society remained during the interwar period, like the church as a whole, we still can identify numerous breaks from tradition and new developments, at least in hindsight. The decades between approximately 1900 and the beginning of Vatican II may therefore be seen as a long period of transition in which old customs remained officially in force but had already begun to crumble.[114] Tensions and contradictions became evident but did not break down the established framework. It became possible to make individual changes without profoundly altering the existing image of the Catholic Church or the Society of Jesus. Many early changes were of a pragmatic nature and did not attract much attention.

It was especially the Jesuits' experiences during the Second World War that sparked or at least accelerated the transformation. War, experiences on the front lines, and the persecution that many Jesuits were forced to endure—going as far as internment in concentration camps—shattered old conventions. In a notable radio address at Christmas in 1944, Pope Pius XII became the first pope to talk about democracy at length and in positive terms, declaring the "liberation" of mankind an objective—a completely new message.[115] Some Jesuits aligned themselves with such standpoints early. John Courtney Murray, S.J. (1904–67), was a pioneer of religious freedom since the 1940s. Although he sometimes found himself in serious trouble with the Vatican, he nonetheless played a key part in formulating a positive ecclesiastical vision of democracy.

A number of Jesuits were also seeking to rethink and give a new profile to the Catholic faith during the interwar period. One school, labeled "new theology" (*nouvelle théologie*) comprised a diverse group of theologians, including many Dominicans and Jesuits. Henri de Lubac was perhaps the most important Jesuit in this connection, although his confreres Jean Daniélou and Josef Andreas Jungmann also were key contributors. They all shared a desire to return to the sources of Christianity so as to break away from rigid neo-scholastic theology and to discover new ways of reflecting on and expressing the Christian faith. Patristics, the rich literature of the early Christian Church fathers, gave these theologians inspiration and ideas of how one might reinterpret the mysteries of the faith without abstract dogmatic systems.[116] Other Jesuits, primarily but not exclusively from France, embraced a new kind of religious literature, often subsumed under the rubric of *Renouveau catholique* (Catholic renewal). Novelists like Georges Bernanos, who had judged the Jesuits very harshly from an antifascist position, Paul Claudel, and Gertrud von Le Fort represented this trend and the interest in powerfully articulating personal religious experiences. Jesuits like Gaston Fessard (1897–1978), who composed an innovatively intense, dialectical interpretation of the *Spiritual Exercises* (1957), Pierre Teilhard de Chardin, and Hans Urs von Balthasar (a Jesuit until he left the order in 1950) drew inspiration from this new reading of the faith. The Jesuit François

Varillon (1905–78) published his friend Claudel's diary in two volumes in 1968/9.[117]

In the 1950s, pastoral and liturgical topics also came to the fore in the church, namely, with respect to the question of how the church could convey the relevance of the faith to the community. Jesuits of the older generation regarded this as a potentially dangerous development, arguing that this pastoral approach would emphasize only the comfortable and easily digested aspects of the faith. At the end of his life in 1961, the prominent German Jesuit Gustav Gundlach derided the "practical-pastoral acrobatics" that pushed clear dogmatic positions into the background.[118] Others, however, such as Gundlach's younger contemporary and confrere Klemens Brockmöller, were much more open to questions of propagating the faith through pastoral care. Signs of a change of religious style and mood began to appear in the Catholic Church overall and in the Society of Jesus specifically. American Jesuits described the transition in hindsight as one from "religion" to "spirituality," from "something of the intellect" to a "something of the heart," as a transition from an institutional to a personal framework for a life of faith, from God the "stern judge" to a notion of God centered around love and affection—in a word: even the Society of Jesus turned away from traditional "rosary Catholicism."[119]

This impulse resulted in particular from the rediscovery of the mystic aspects of the Society's history. The importance of this new appreciation of the Jesuits' rich spiritual tradition can hardly be overstated: for the first time in centuries, Ignatius of Loyola again figured as a mystic author in his own right, as interpreted by Jesuits like Joseph de Guibert or Hugo Rahner. From 1932 to 1995, under the direction of the Society, the groundbreaking *Dictionnaire de la spiritualité* in seventeen volumes was compiled to facilitate research on and the dissemination of this tradition.[120] In the midst of these efforts, in 1957, the Thirtieth General Congregation resolved to revisit the foundational spiritual works of the Jesuit order.[121] The Society of Jesus "rediscovered" the *Spiritual Exercises* as the spiritual origin of its existence. The *Constitutions* likewise came to be understood in new ways: less rigidly, more spiritually. Only in 1970 did the complete text finally become available in a modern English translation for easy inspection also by those Jesuits overwhelmed by the Latin or Spanish originals. Easy access was all the more important as it now was obvious that the "order's statutes [were] more a spiritual handbook than a legal codex."[122]

Ideological renewal was accompanied by a transformation of everyday life in the Society of Jesus. Life as a Jesuit gradually took on a new look. After 1945, traditional life in the colleges became increasingly unfamiliar, in particular for the many Jesuits directly affected by the war.[123] The strict, hierarchical style of the church, which had shaped life in the Jesuit houses and colleges, began to relax.[124] Seating arrangements at table became more intimate, and shared living arrangements outside the major houses became more common. The cassock ceased to be the inevitable dress and hallmark of a Jesuit. Plain clothes became accepted. The Jesuits spoke with one another more familiarly, dropping formal terms of address for the informal "you" in non-English languages (e.g., German Du instead of the formal Sie). Latin was rendered meaningless as a lingua franca. The rhythm of a Jesuit's day also adapted to more recent customs. "One may go to bed later and get up later," General Jean-Baptiste Janssens conceded in 1959. New pastimes were permitted or tolerated: the Jesuits could play soccer, even without a robe at times. After initial disapproval, televisions were permitted in German Jesuit houses from about 1962.

After 1965: Toward a "New" Society of Jesus

These slow, initially often isolated and sporadic changes coalesced into a program in the 1960s. Vatican II, the student revolts of 1968, the sexual revolution, and the attempt to revive Christianity as a lived and experienced religion changed the Catholic Church and the Society of Jesus. A "third," contemporary phase of the Society's history commenced. In hindsight, the transformation that came at an ever greater pace after about 1960 seems almost inexplicable: "How does one explain that Jesuit theologians nowadays are just as likely to be living in non-institutional settings, sometimes in working-class suburbs . . . as heretofore in great institutions like the Gregorianum in Rome?"[125]

The Rise of the "Social Apostolate"

It was of the utmost importance for the culture change within the Society of Jesus that it recognized ever more clearly since the nineteenth century, just as did the entire Catholic Church, that the Christianity of modern times existed in a fundamentally different society. Reject modernism as the Jesuits might, there still was no denying that the living conditions of most people had radically changed since 1800. Industrialization and urbanization had created undreamt-of social misery. It was up to the church, in very practical terms, to alleviate it, but beyond such specific aid efforts, the church also had to reimagine ideal Christian society in a forward-thinking way. We can identify a new focus of religious questions and topics precisely in this attention to social realities.

Since roughly the 1850s, Catholic pioneers like Adolph Kolping and Wilhelm Emmanuel von Ketteler, archbishop of Mainz, had understood the social misery of the working poor as a new and unprecedented religious problem. With various projects and writings, these two clergymen laid the foundations for a new Christian social doctrine. Catholic laymen like Count Albert de Mun of France came to similar conclusions. Drawing inspiration from various models, de Mun founded a network of Christian workers' clubs in 1871. Conservative in outlook and organized along paternalistic, ecclesiastical lines, these clubs offered a variety of programs for interested laborers with the goal of giving them a Christian education. De Mun thus understood the social question essentially as a problem of deficient or incorrect education. This new Catholic social doctrine thus came to be seen as a Christian alternative and answer to the burgeoning socialist movement. Building on this preliminary work, Pope Leo XIII formulated the first comprehensive program of modern Christian social ethics in the encyclical *Rerum novarum* of 1891: drawing on traditional Catholic values and convictions, it was intended as a response to the new social developments of the day. In contrast to the socialists, however, it did not call on the people to revolutionize existing social structures.

Even though it was a Jesuit who coined the term "social justice" (Luigi Taparelli d'Azeglio [1793–1862]), thereby exercising a profound influence on Leo XIII, for a long time the Jesuits were *not* the leaders of this movement. They only gradually embraced its goals and strategies. At first, only a few individuals took up the new ministry. Fr. Antonio Vicent (1837–1912) popularized the new ideas in Spain. His book *Socialismo y Anarquismo*, published in 1893, built on Leo XIII's ideas. After some attempts in the 1870s, Vicent adapted de Mun's model of workers' clubs in 1880 in the vicinity of Valencia. The goal here was first and foremost education and instruction. Vicent declared that his organization sought above all "to spread religious, moral, and technological knowledge, the sciences and arts, and literary and artistic knowledge among workers."[126] Sunday and night school, popular lectures, special university programs for workers, and even library and theater activities constituted the package of planned offerings. Soon this workers' ministry became even more specialized. Fr. Narciso Basté Basté (1866–1936), for example, began founding special institutions for young people in 1900.[127] This kind of social ministry might also include a lively, broadly pitched lecture program.[128]

After 1918, the Jesuits' presence in the growing Catholic social movement intensified greatly. German Jesuits like Gustav Gundlach (1891–1963) and Oswald von Nell-Breuning (1890–1991) became leading proponents of Catholic social doctrine.[129] These two men played a vital part in the formulation of the second fundamental social encyclical, *Quadragesimo anno*, which Pope Pius XI issued on the fortieth anniversary of *Rerum novarum* in 1931. The Twenty-Eighth General Congregation in 1938 explicitly recognized the "social apostolate" among workers as a field of ministry.[130]

For a long time, these intensive efforts to give the Catholic Church a social dimension remained tied to traditional ways of thinking and acting. The forms of Jesuit social work illustrated here continued earlier approaches—congregations, education, pilgrimages, the devotion of Mary and the Sacred Heart of Jesus.[131] With its paternalistic approach, Catholic social doctrine also long remained beholden to long-standing traditional social concepts. That was not least a consequence of the Church's instinctive rejection of socialism, which it viewed as antireligious and materialistic. Often enough, moderate forms of social democracy were lumped together with it. Pioneers of Catholic social thought like Gustav Gundlach in Germany, for example, remained critical even of the "democratic socialism" of the German Social Democratic Party (Sozialdemokratische Partei).[132] Gundlach, accordingly, was one of the few Jesuits who considered it necessary in 1955 to found a separate Christian trade union independent of the existing German trade union confederation (Deutscher Gewerkschaftsbund).[133] In a famous text from 1959, he argued in lonely extremism that nuclear war was justified in defense of Christian values against communism, even if the end of the world was the foreseeable consequence. Taking action for the right values became a matter of principle during the Cold War. "The state, the principle task of which is to provide for the law, cannot practice the Sermon on the Mount," claimed Gundlach.[134]

Such arguments, however, had long since lost touch with engaged Catholics' perception of the needs of the day. It became increasingly evident that traditional forms and ways of thinking no longer sufficed to check the rising tide of social alienation from Christianity. Around 1945, it was frequently claimed that the working class consisted of de facto neo-pagans (néo-païens).[135] Capitalism and industrialization created new social conditions that were difficult or impossible to reach with the traditional categories and practices of pastoral care. Rapid urbanization sapped the strength of traditional "agrarian religiosity," which had exerted a powerful influence on Catholicism until well into the twentieth century.[136] The social misery of industrialization, the material distress of the working class, and the cultural deracination of the "proletariat" that was already being diagnosed rendered established forms of piety ineffective. A younger, more radical group of Catholics turned to new, much more politicized forms of organization. Their goals now were engagement in political parties, voter turnout, and political agitation. More radical forms of social work were deemed necessary.

Some Jesuits like the Frenchman Henri Perrin therefore took part in a "worker-priest" project launched in 1944: these priests took on paid labor in factories or ports in order to be close to the socially vulnerable working class of metropoles. "Yesterday I filed [iron] for five hours," as Perrin once noted.[137] Even though "worker-priests" were initially controversial—they were banned in 1954 but permanently reinstituted in 1964—the growing urgency of a new justification for the social apostolate in the Society overall was undeniable. In 1949, Superior General Jean-Baptiste Janssens issued a groundbreaking instruction on the subject.[138] Janssens declared that he did not want to leave the question to "atheistic materialists." The Society's leadership now recognized that the material living conditions of people had an important influence on their inclination to the faith and their ability to practice it. Social "injustice" hindered the "gracious plan of Divine Providence." Important impulses for this groundbreaking text came from the Chilean Jesuit Alberto Hurtado (1901–52), who had encountered the topic in his work with homeless children before he became a driving force behind the Society's new orientation. Soon these new approaches were also elaborated in theoretical terms. After the Second World War, the Jesuits founded twenty-six sociopolitical research centers to provide their social ministry with scholarly support.[139]

This gradual transformation also led to a partial reassessment of socialism.[140] Klemens Brockmöller, a Jesuit from Germany, exemplifies the new generation's greater openness to the idea of Christian socialism. His book *Christianity at the Dawn of the Atomic Age* (*Christentum am Morgen des Atomzeitalters*), published in 1954, was a "theological bestseller."[141] Brockmöller's work, which was innovative and groundbreaking in its pastoral-theological reflections, played with the idea that positive engagement with Marxism was possible. In the new atomic age, the Western idea of pronounced individualism was no longer tenable— Marxism had also recognized this, and hence it was possible to adopt some of its thoughts. Conservative forces and the Jesuit hierarchy were dismayed and wanted to ban the book. But it enjoyed a positive reception among the young members of the Society and in the public at large or was at least regarded as an important attempt to give an appropriate diagnosis of the times. Print, radio, and television media reported it.[142]

Contemporaries already put Brockmöller's book alongside the scientific works of his Austrian confrere Gustav Wetter, who taught in

Rome. Wetter's own book *Dialectical Materialism* (*Der dialektische Materialismus*) had appeared in 1952. In it, he identified certain parallels between socialist and Christian thought. Other Jesuits in Rome were responsible for maintaining diplomatic ties to Soviet ambassadors and attachés. By the mid-1950s, at least part of the Society was regarded as the vanguard of "leftist Catholicism." Jesuits in direct contact with Pope Pius XII stressed that Brockmöller's thinking was "representative" of a strong current in the Society. Even in Spain under Franco, there now were Jesuits who belonged to the Spanish Communist Party, such as José María de Llanos (1906–92). Initially a supporter of Franco, whose exercises he directed in 1943, de Llanos, the most famous "worker-priest" in Spain, became a Communist after 1955. His was not an isolated case.[143] The Jesuits' rigid, intransigently antidemocratic, anticommunist, and anti-Marxist position began to crumble.

Vatican II, General Arrupe, and "Social Justice"

Change culminated in late 1962 in the convening of the Second Vatican Council.[144] For the next three years, the council worked to give the Catholic Church a new profile and image. The buzzword of the day was "aggiornamento," adapting the church to modern times and its problems. That definitely did not mean a merely grudging adjustment to inevitable change. The goal, rather, was to devise a new, positive vision of Catholic life. From the start, a majority viewed the council as a pastoral event, while only a minority insisted on a meeting focused strictly on dogma. In their view, the council should preoccupy itself with condemning the latest excrescences and dictating the conservative consensus. It was the gentler majority view that prevailed, however, which saw the council as a vehicle for updating the church and its public image so that it could reach people in the twentieth century.

Jesuits were engaged at the council in a variety of functions. They attended predominantly as "theologians," that is, as expert advisers to the decision-making bishops. Among these Jesuit theologians there were conservative speakers like the Dutchman Sebastiaan Tromp, but a majority supported the current reform movement: Henri de Lubac,

Karl Rahner, and Jean Daniélou, among others, were present as experts. Above all, Cardinal Augustin Bea, S.J., had an immense impact on the spirit and outcome of the council. Bea was a cautious reformer who saw the need for change and acted accordingly, but he moreover knew how to achieve his goals by the force of his personality. With all the authority of his eighty-one years when Vatican II was convened, he became one of its leading figures.

For the Society of Jesus, the question of the significance of Vatican II was raised before it had officially concluded. General Jean-Baptiste Janssens died on October 5, 1964; the now necessary Thirty-First General Congregation was convened in the summer of 1965.[145] After the Basque Pedro Arrupe had been elected as the Society's new superior general, the congregation adjourned, in an unprecedented act, for a full year until after the conclusion of the council so that it could reconvene from September to November 1966 to deliberate the consequences. The result was a comprehensive mandate for Arrupe to reform the Jesuit order in light of Vatican II.

In Arrupe, the Jesuits had elected the right man to open the Society up to new ways.[146] He considered himself and his Society as obligated first and foremost to the mission, to proclaiming the faith. To do so successfully, he viewed an aggiornamento of the Society as an absolute, even existential necessity. "I am afraid we may repeat yesterday's answer to tomorrow's problems," he warned. Arrupe was also the first superior general who took advantage of modern means of transportation, traveling tirelessly around the world. For the first time for a large number of Jesuits, direct personal contact with the general became possible. Arrupe's enthusiasm for personal encounters became his trademark. He also cultivated an open relationship with the media, which made him almost a "star."[147]

The task of modernizing the governance, spirituality, and missions of the Society preoccupied the Jesuits for the following decades.[148] They followed the council's general call to go back to the historical sources (*ressourcement*) and recommended reacquainting oneself with the "authentic" Ignatius. The Society encouraged this spiritual engagement with its venerable foundation texts so that it could rediscover its own charismatic origins and become acquainted with the roots of its identity.[149] For the first time in their history, the Jesuits now also said they were prepared, at least in theory, to take over parishes (that had previously been only the exception in the context of the missions). The pope also commissioned the Society with two new objects of pastoral care and mission: dialogue with atheism and ecumenical exchange. A certain democratization of the Society's institutions also took place. For example, provincial congregations were henceforth to be elected. In order to test further which way forward would be helpful for the Jesuits, the decrees of the General Congregation explicitly called for "experiments."

In fact, the following years were a phase of very heterogeneous, far-reaching, and even sometimes radical attempts at renewal. As the sexual revolution got underway, some especially liberal Jesuits even took up critical positions on the celibacy and chastity of priests and on the sexual ethics of the church.[150] In Amsterdam, several Jesuits associated with the famous hymnist and then student preacher Huub Oosterhuis, S.J., advocated marriage for priests among many other innovations (for which he was ultimately dismissed from the Society).[151] The college and school rectors did away with much of the traditional humanistic curriculum, now viewed as "bourgeois."

Undoubtedly the most well-known "experiment" of the period after Vatican II was liberation theology. Drawing on a Marxist critique of social conditions in Central and South America, Jesuit thinkers like Jon Sobrino, Ignacio Ellacuría, and Juan Luis Segundo, together with numerous personalities from the secular clergy, developed a theology that actively advocated social and economic change on the basis of the Christian commitment to justice, charity, and responsibility. The goal for Christians should not be the "development" of the so-called Third World, but rather the "liberation" of the people who lived there. At their conference in Medellín, Colombia, in 1968, the bishops of Central and South America championed this "preferential option for the poor" inspired by liberation theology. Liberation theologians rejected the long-standing traditional Christian social doctrine of cooperation between the bourgeoisie and the working class, pointing to the inherent paternalism of the rulers. Jesuit authors subsequently worked not only to elaborate liberation theology in terms of social ethics or pastoral theology but also to integrate it in core theological areas like Christology. This strain of theology was and still is highly controversial both inside and outside the order.

"The whirlwind of the experimental phase was occasionally very fierce," Fr. Ignacio Ellacuría from El Salvador remarked in hindsight with complete contentment.[152] In some places, these experiments, bolstered by Arrupe's enormous personal charisma, gave the order new wind and new impetus. Elsewhere, they soon resulted in a chaotic juxtaposition of contradictory initiatives. Mistakes were inevitable and accepted.[153] Arrupe painstakingly had to guide the Society forward through these dynamic times by trial and error. Not everything was stringent and coherent: on the one hand, he once had no problem drawing a direct link between Che Guevara's militant revolution and the words of Christ from the New Testament; on the other, though, he expelled Oosterhuis and several other Jesuits of Amsterdam who opposed celibacy and obedience.[154] Hence he angered both conservatives and radical progressives.[155] Generations and positions often violently collided in the Society.[156]

The 1960s and 1970s were a time of spiritual seeking and inner uncertainty. Numerous open conflicts erupted over the question of how one could reconcile the acknowledged necessity of comprehensive reform with equally indispensable faithfulness to the Ignatian tradition.[157] To what extent could and should criticizing and changing the social structures of earthly life be the responsibility of a religious order? Many of the sometimes heated controversies within the Jesuit order at this time revolved around this question of the right balance between this world and the next, between material and spiritual perspectives. Although many viewed Arrupe as a groundbreaking source of inspiration in this difficult time, doubts persisted as to whether his leadership style was the right one to guide the Society unscathed through these problems. Paul VI had initially been sympathetic to the Jesuits, but sometimes serious conflict broke out on account of the Jesuits' seemingly uncoordinated leadership of the Society. At the Vatican, there was talk of "crisis" in the Society in 1970, and around 1974 the Jesuits began to play with the idea of somehow removing Arrupe from office.[158] By no means all Jesuits were still convinced that the years since the end of the council had been used profitably.[159] Many Jesuits wondered, "Where is the Society headed?"[160] Even loyal followers of Arrupe confronted the general with impatient questions and urgently pointed to many problems.[161] In Spain, conservative dissatisfaction with the situation in the early 1970s produced an open splinter group. Traditionalists, often with close ties to the fascist Franco regime, worked to establish autonomous organizational structures. These Iberian Jesuits formed the radical group Jesuits in Fidelity (Jesuitas en fidelidad) and openly worked to have General Arrupe deposed.[162]

Another General Congregation was necessary in 1974 to set the future course of the Society of Jesus more clearly on the basis of the experiences it had gained—many of them painful and chaotic. This was the famous Thirty-Second General Congregation that provided the decisive guidelines for the modern image of the Society.[163] It now was becoming clear what aspects of the religious renewal since the council could continue permanently—and what aspects could not. Many of the now classical formulations of Jesuit activity were officially adopted at this time. It was at this moment that the Society of Jesus received the form that still dominates it today. "Justice" became the central subject of the meeting—Medellín and liberation theology had become impossible to ignore. Arrupe saw a need for action: "The Society has not, in fact, effectively been oriented toward the apostolate for social justice; it has always been more focused, in accordance with a strategy justified essentially by historical conditions, on making an impact on the ruling social classes and the formation of their leaders."[164] That now would finally and officially change.

In the famous fourth decree of the congregation, the Society committed itself to the social apostolate and explicitly acknowledged "the promotion of justice" as its duty. Justice thus was not merely one goal among many, but rather now the basis of the entire Jesuit ministry. The promotion of "justice" was understood not only as a social duty but also as a genuine religious affair. As epitomized in a key tenet, "The mission of the Society of Jesus today is the service of faith, of which the promotion of justice is an absolute requirement." Echoing contemporary leftist criticism, a call went out to undertake a rigorous, scholarly analysis of the political, economic, and social structures that promoted injustice.[165] From now on, overcoming social injustice and disadvantage stood at the top of the Society's agenda.

One of the most impressive consequences of this new attitude was the founding, in 1980, of a formally independent nongovernmental organization dedicated to providing sustenance and political support for refugees, the Jesuit Refugee Service (JRS).[166] Originally established to help the Vietnamese boat people, the JRS soon became a care and advocacy institution that has dedicated itself to the welfare and interests of refugees worldwide. The fact that the JRS—following North American organizational models—explicitly relies on a partnership with the laity reflects the greater openness of the Jesuit order to people outside the church and even outside Christianity.[167] Also, for the Society's thousands of schools and hundreds of universities all over the world, which often rely predominantly on the work of laymen, this form of partnership became the successful way forward.[168] Jesuit universities and schools now operate with greater autonomy from the Society than before. Cooperative relationships between these independent Jesuit organizations are being formed to carry out the Society's missions in a modern fashion appropriate to the globalized world of the twenty-first century. One example is the Jesuit Worldwide Learning initiative, in which Jesuit universities (together with other institutions of higher education) are offering online educational opportunities for refugees under the auspices of the JRS.[169]

Difficult Modernity: From Arrupe to Pope Francis

Arrupe's generalship ended de facto with the stroke he suffered in 1981. When Arrupe officially resigned in 1983 (he lived until 1991, debilitated and largely unable to speak), he had profoundly changed the style, orientation, and appearance of the Society. Besides all his individual measures, Arrupe epitomized and still epitomizes the effort to lead the

Society of Jesus in a new direction in the modern age. At least in retrospect, now that all the controversies have subsided and his legacy is
firmly accepted as the basis for recent Jesuit successes, Arrupe is regarded as a trailblazer and the founder of the third, contemporary Society of Jesus. That new direction entailed a conscious "break with the
general guidelines of the apostolate heretofore" and a reawakened "feeling for confrontation," as liberation theologian Ignacio Ellacuría once
approvingly put it.[170] Many, but not all, Jesuits would have agreed and
shared his enthusiasm. The outcome of the opening up of the Society
after Arrupe was mixed. Despite the power of the Society's new focus
on social justice in shaping Jesuit identity, the order has constantly
struggled since then not to lose sight of its spiritual focus.

Arrupe was well aware of the dangers and conflicts that his men
would encounter on account of their new mission of social justice. Former pillars of the traditional social order, often in a traditionalist spirit,
became advocates of change, even revolution. In many places, especially
the Third World of the 1980s and 1990s, Jesuits joined ranks with opposition movements. Ellacuría likewise anticipated "confrontation with
ruling circles" if the Jesuits continued down their new path. And he was
indeed proved right: with their increasingly critical stance on society,
some Jesuits found themselves literally in the crosshairs of the powerful.
Dozens of Jesuits have since paid for their dedication to justice with
their lives. A tragic culmination of this development was the murder of
six Jesuits and two domestic employees in San Salvador by government
thugs during the Salvadoran Civil War in 1989. Ellacuría himself was
among the dead.[171]

The Jesuits' sharply defined social policy brought them into conflict
not only with secular powers but also with ecclesiastical authorities. The
Society's new orientation under Arrupe changed its self-conception and
image and significantly raised its social relevance, but it also thrust the
Jesuits into the role of a distrusted alternative to the prevailing orthodoxy. Serious observers in the 1990s even declared that the Jesuits had
transformed from a "subculture" into a "counterculture" within the
church.[172] At the latest, this development had become impossible to
ignore by the election of John Paul II in 1978. Arrupe was under no

illusion that the election of the Polish cardinal Karol Wojtyla, whose background had instilled in him profoundly anticommunist convictions, would lead to new conflicts. In 1980, relations had deteriorated to such an extent that the Vatican actually began to deliberate compelling Arrupe to resign and placing the Society under a papal superintendent.[173] John Paul II was presumably already considering a Jesuit he could trust, the Italian Paolo Dezza, for this role. When Arrupe was surprisingly sidelined by the stroke he suffered in August 1981, this very scenario played out: for just under two years, Dezza was entrusted with leading the Society as the pope's "personal delegate" (*delegato personale*). Dezza had a reputation for his experience and moderation and was definitely not a proponent of the offensive, adventurous style of Arrupe, let alone the liberation theologians. Dezza had taught Thomist theology and metaphysics as a professor at the Gregoriana in Rome. He thus embodied a Roman perspective and focus within the order without, however, figuring as a conservative hard-liner. Dezza respected Arrupe, although he had often opposed Arrupe's preferences and his leadership. Hence, it was not so much Dezza himself as it was the pope's actions that elicited the most diverse reactions among the Jesuits. While some viewed the proceedings as a necessary change of course, most felt humiliated and misunderstood when they were placed under papal supervision.

All in all, though, Dezza succeeded in improving relations within a relatively short time. The belated convocation of a new General Congregation in 1983, which Arrupe's illness had made necessary, was a consequence of Dezza's steady hand at the helm of the Society in this difficult phase.[174] At the Thirty-Third General Congregation, the Society set out on a course that self-critically acknowledged and sought to correct the mistakes of past years while also essentially holding true to its new policy and orientation.[175] Significantly, Peter Hans Kolvenbach was elected general; a Jesuit who had lived and worked in Lebanon, he had not been a member of either party to the conflict.

Despite this return of calm, over the following years the Society continued to search for the right balance between its spiritual foundation and its sundry operations. The Society first had to "learn," the new general repeatedly emphasized, how best to approach the subject of "faith and justice" and to strike the right balance.[176] Crises continued to break out. As early as 1984, Kolvenbach had to wrestle with the conflict surrounding Fernando Cardenal, S.J. It put into particularly sharp focus the typical issues of the day: Cardenal, a member of the leftist Sandinistas in Nicaragua, rose up to become minister for education in this revolutionary movement. The Vatican demanded that he terminate this political arrangement; Cardenal objected, and after long deliberations, Kolvenbach was forced to dismiss his confrere from the order (only to welcome him back later, though, after Cardenal broke with the Sandinistas).[177] Critical questions about the spirituality and activities of the Society continued to be raised, and they came not just from the outside. There were also complaints inside the order to the effect that prayer and communal religious life were given short shrift in the everyday life of the Jesuits.[178] Education and pedagogy were also subjects in which the Society had to integrate a new perspective.[179] The supposedly impractical intellectualism of traditional pedagogical work made it an unappealing field for many *patres* in the 1980s and 1990s. Kolvenbach addressed the subject several times and tried to set necessary new priorities. A speech he delivered in Santa Clara in October 2000 set forth sweeping new ideas. Titled "The Service of Faith and the Promotion of Justice in American Jesuit Higher Education," the general's speech now applied the guiding concept of "social justice" in full to the area of education.[180]

When Kolvenbach was elected general, he extended another trend that had already been in motion for some time. The Jesuit General Assistant Jean-Yves Calvez described it in 1975 as follows: "For the first time in its 400-year history, the Society of Jesus is truly international; or more precisely, it is starting to become so."[181] The growing clout of the non-European provinces of the Society had been making itself felt for some time. A new Assistancy of Latin America, for example, had been established at the Twenty-Eighth General Congregation in 1938. At the Thirtieth General Congregation in 1957, an Assistancy of India and East Asia followed.[182] The Church as a whole had explicitly and deliberately recognized and accepted the challenges of modern globalization by Vatican II. The question of the unity of the World Church played a prominent part in some of the key documents produced by the council (*Lumen gentium, Gaudium et spes*).[183] Jesuit theologians like Karl Rahner and John Courtney Murray had no small part in their formulation. Step by step the personnel structure of the Society also became globalized in the latter half of the century. A disproportionately steep decline in members from Europe and North America was compensated at least in part by a sharp rise in new vocations from places like India and Africa. Nowhere are the growing globalization of the Society and the growing prominence of the former margins and peripheries of the Western world more palpable than in the biographies of the superior generals after 1965. All of them served outside of Europe to an unprecedented extent: Arrupe was a missionary to Japan, where he was profoundly shocked by the dropping of the atomic bombs in 1945. Kolvenbach likewise came to Rome as an "outsider"; he did not have ties to liberation theology but rather brought his years of experience in interfaith collaboration in war-torn Lebanon.[184] The next father general, Adolfo Nicolás, prior to his election in 2008, had long served in Japan. This long-term development reached its logical culmination when Arturo Sosa became the first non-European Jesuit to be elected superior general in 2016. Sosa, born in Caracas, Venezuela, in 1948, became Adolfo Nicolás's successor when the latter stepped down on account of his advanced age.

Given this shift of focus away from Europe, it is fitting that the principle of "inculturation" has become prominent in the Society. Already in 1944, the French worker-priests had talked about the "need to 'bathe' among people in order to Christianize them."[185] Ideas like this were taken up again later. Decree 5 of the Thirty-Second General Congregation had highlighted the topic in 1975. But it was really during the following years that Arrupe elaborated the concept. He proposed "total inculturation," which he understood as "total immersion" in the life of the poor and marginalized. Circumstances permitting, Jesuit missionaries were to live right in the slums as "inserted communities."[186] Arrupe started to regard inculturation as the implementation and logical consequence of the Incarnation, a thought that goes far beyond its early modern antecedents.[187] The Jesuits may like to stress that inculturation extends older traditions of the order, but "dialogue with cultures" as it is understood today is de facto something far more extensive and fundamental.[188] Today, for example, inculturation no longer pertains exclusively to missionary practice but rather, as Arrupe argued, must figure as *the* central way of life for the Christian faith: even in Europe, the constant "re-inculturation" of Christianity is necessary because also and especially in Europe there often is a wide gap between popular culture and traditional faith. The purpose of inculturation is precisely to bridge this gap. The decrees of the Thirty-Fourth General Congregation of 1995 elaborated on inculturation even more exhaustively and expanded it by defining interfaith dialogue as a key element of the Jesuit ministry. Inculturation is now also defined as a crucial aspect of justice. Decree 26 addresses the "poor" of the world in particular: "They show us the way to enculturate gospel values in situations where God is forgotten. Through such solidarity [with the poor] we become 'agents of inculturation.'"[189] The Thirty-Fourth General Congregation thus resulted in a major reinvigoration of missionary self-conception not least because, for the first time in decades, Jesuit contact with non-Christians was formulated as a religious topic in an innovative way independently of the ideological controversies of the 1970s and 1980s.

In this way, the Society of Jesus has become an important vehicle for bringing the sensibilities of Christians outside of Europe into the conversation in Rome, and doing so in a theologically well-considered, organizationally prominent, and medially effective way. This input includes harsh, even radical criticism of the Roman central administration by the Jesuit periphery: "If you will permit me to speak with complete sincerity, I do not feel 'at home' in this world of curias, diplomacy, calculations, power, etc. Being far away from 'this world,' even though I have not sought that out, does not give me any grief. To make myself clear, I even feel relieved." Thus Jon Sobrino, S.J., the oft-chastised liberation theologian from El Salvador, whom the Vatican repeatedly admonished, relayed the dissatisfaction of many Latin American Christians in 2007.[190] The Jesuits' advocacy of an alternative, critical form of Catholic religiosity won them little sympathy under John Paul II and Benedict XVI in the new millennium. Sobrino's words, quoted here, were spoken in the context of his reprimand by the Congregation for the Doctrine of the Faith, which charged him with making doctrinally "erroneous or dangerous" statements in 2007—and this was only the culmination of a long series of doctrinal reprimands given to prominent Jesuit theologians in preceding years.[191] Not a few cardinals diagnosed a "growing distance from the Hierarchy" among the Jesuits during these years.[192] The Vatican's dissatisfaction with the Society of Jesus may have become so great in 2008 that people close to Pope Benedict again deliberated installing a papal superintendent as in 1982. The Thirty-Fifth General Congregation, at which General Kolvenbach officially stepped down on account of his advanced age, had been the reason behind such thoughts. In the end, it never came to pass, not least because the person allegedly designated to serve as the special papal delegate, the Jesuit archbishop of Buenos Aires, Jorge Mario Bergoglio, vehemently opposed the idea. And still there could be no doubt about the ongoing discontent of the popes. Benedict XVI reminded the General Congregation in 2008 of the Jesuits' obligation to obey the pope and submit to papal magisterium in unusually harsh, blunt terms. In the context of the polemics surrounding Sobrino, that was an unmistakable sign of impatience and mistrust.[193]

"I don't know Rome. I know only a few things [here]," Bergoglio said only a few years later, in 2013. He likewise called for the church to change its perspective.[194] As Pope Francis, he would personally help answer that call. Bergoglio shared some experiences with the liberation theologian Sobrino—but he had taken a different approach to engaging the poor in the turbulent 1970s and 1980s.[195] Bergoglio advocated, then and now, a specific, popular theology of the poor that emphatically distanced itself from the intellectual-seeming, scholarly social analysis of other theologians: he supported a "theology of the people." Bergoglio viewed popular piety as the way of the future; his Jesuit adversaries, in contrast, viewed the popular religion from a Marxist perspective as a relic of unjust social structures that had to be swept away. Bergoglio viewed simple Catholics as *the* decisive force for the spiritual renewal of the church; the liberation theologians wanted to change society. Bergoglio avoided open conflict and confrontation, just as he does now. In the difficult political circumstances of a military dictatorship in Argentina, he kept his channels to the people in power open—something that brought him criticism from more radical resistance forces, even if it gave him room to maneuver at the time. On the whole, by proceeding in this way, he continued the old traditions of his order, which had always accepted that the courts of the powerful were important, albeit extremely dangerous, arenas. These positions eventually put Bergoglio at odds with General Arrupe and, after 1985 and particularly from 1990 to 1992, led to his own sidelining within the order and de facto house arrest.[196] But Bergoglio made an astonishing comeback, undoubtedly supported by John Paul II, who took a very critical stance toward the Society. Here was an opportunity for opponents of the mainstream—for Jesuits like Bergoglio. At the instigation of the archbishop of Buenos Aires at the time, Antonio Quarracino, the Vatican appointed the Jesuit coadjutor bishop in 1992.

Now many signs point toward a reconciliation between the Vatican and the bulk of liberation theology. The fact that a Latin American is now sitting on the throne of St. Peter undoubtedly has played an important part.[197] It was perhaps not least the traditional role of the Society of Jesus as a link between Rome and the rest of the world that made a member of the order so eminently qualified to become the first pope from overseas.[198] Francis himself wants to bring the perspective of the marginalized and forgotten peoples of the world to the fore in Rome. At the congregation of cardinals before the conclave, Bergoglio reportedly impressed his colleagues in an appeal that called on the church to "go outside itself" so as to "go to the peripheries," not only to those of a geographic nature but also to "existential peripheries," where it would find "evil, injustice, and pain."[199] Liberating the church—and the Society—from self-absorption has been the new pope's primary objective, and he regards the members of his own order as important ambassadors of the church and pioneers in facing its new, modern challenges.[200] Bergoglio views his idol from the Society, Pierre Favre, as an especially good embodiment of the simplicity and openness that the church should emulate in addressing the needs of the world.

At any rate, the rich legacy of the Jesuit tradition can clearly be recognized in the actions of the pope himself.[201] Prominent Jesuits today have often seen the legacy of their order in the pope.[202] Francis himself has highlighted his restored ties to the Society, for instance, by celebrating July 31, the memorial day of Ignatius of Loyola, in the company of his confreres almost every year since 2013.[203] Francis traces his own missionary engagement, his need to "reignite the hearts of the faithful, the closeness, the conviviality," back to his Jesuit roots.[204] Bergoglio cites none other than Pedro Arrupe for the idea that one must "insert" oneself as a missionary in contemporary border zones and frontiers—a personal adaptation of the imperative of inculturation.[205] The Jesuit pope prefers to invoke the Ignatian call for *discretio*, the ability and also the willingness to search for the right way of proceeding in complex situations instead of falling back on preexisting patterns of behavior. Francis's mistrust of fixed standpoints, ideologies, and theories is unmistakable.[206] Perhaps that is why Francis would like to change the church not so much with new dogmatic or moral-theological pronouncements as he would with a policy composed of numerous, small symbolic steps and gestures, changes of rhetoric, and unmistakable shifts of emphasis.[207] Even if the Argentinean archbishop was not explicitly elected pope because he was a Jesuit, his affiliation with the order shapes his vision in many ways. The example of Pope Francis shows that a Society of Jesus that presents itself as a modern institution in both style and religious practice, in both theology and image, can still be a major player in the twenty-first century.

ACKNOWLEDGMENTS

THIS BOOK began with an email from Kristin Rotter and Ulrich Wank from the Piper publishing house, asking whether I might be interested in writing a book about the Jesuits. Without the encouragement of Mona Garloff, I might never have taken on the project. Without the patience of the press, it would have ended prematurely long ago. But Kristin Rotter, Maren Wetcke, and Martin Janik met all the imponderables with charming obstinacy and the greatest understanding for me and my everyday difficulties. My sincere thanks for their wonderful guidance at Piper! Ulrike Strerath-Bolz put the entire manuscript into presentable form with great enthusiasm for the subject matter and equally great stylistic finesse. Wolfgang Gartmann magisterially carried out the work of proofreading the final product.

If Kim Breitmoser, Sonja Döhring, and Judith Lipperheide had not provided me with mountains of books and photocopies—which often enough entailed recalling overdue books—I would have had no chance of coming to grips with the literature. They and everyone else at the University of Hamburg—Martin Foerster, Jacob Schilling, Kai Schwahn—were instrumental in preparing this book. Andreea Badea, Jost Eickmeyer, Marc Föcking, Michael Friedrich, Margit Kern, Christian Kühner, and Ivana Rentsch read longer and shorter sections of the text—I also extend my thanks to them! Judith Lipperheide and Christoph Dartmann performed great service as test readers of the manuscript.

In the middle of the work, Frieda was born. She had to share me with "the Jesuit book" from the start, against which—thank God!—she constantly protested. It therefore is her book. I owe the fact that my bad conscience stayed within tolerable bounds while writing despite this addition to my family, first of all, to the loving devotion of Julia and, second, to the countless kind "baby services" of Moni and Dieter Isbarn. My warmest "Vergelt's Gott!" My mother passed away in the middle of the work. She would have liked to have seen this book in its finished form.

AFTERWORD TO THE ENGLISH EDITION

THIS ENGLISH translation of the book preserves the text essentially unchanged. Some small slips and errors were tacitly eliminated. Several passages of the epilogue were revised and expanded in response to the stimulating remarks of Simon Ditchfield and in light of current events. The entire text was supplemented at least sporadically with references to the most important scholarly literature since 2016. There otherwise was no real need to carry out extensive revisions.

Once more, I thank John Noël Dillon for a magisterial translation— his feeling for language astonished me again and again! He moreover very helpfully qualified or supplemented my argumentation in various passages with his own research.

Easter 2020
Markus Friedrich

TRANSLATOR'S NOTE

"PER ASPERA AD ASTRA," a Jesuit history teacher once told me in college. Undertaking a translation of this magnitude was not so much a rocky road as a long one, but finishing the journey was complicated by the outbreak of the coronavirus pandemic, which brought both Germany and the United States to a standstill in March 2020, just as I was finalizing and revising the translation. As a freelancer used to working from home, I cannot say having my two boys, John and James, at home full-time did wonders for my own or my wife Yii-Jan Lin's productivity. But I got through it in the end, and now Markus and I find ourselves celebrating finishing this manuscript a day after we celebrated Bayern Munich winning the Champions League. What a year!

With the exception of a handful of books that we simply could not obtain in current circumstances, I have gone back to the original Latin, Spanish, Italian, French, and even occasionally Portuguese texts of Markus's sundry sources to translate quotations directly rather than (re)translate them from his own German translations. In the process of tracking down and reworking all these quotations, we sometimes expanded them to give the reader more context and a better impression of the historical actors' statements. The translation also preserves a dating convention of the German original: a slash is used occasionally in dates (e.g. 1582/3) to indicate events or episodes that straddled successive years, especially in winter. Other, more distant alternative dates that were indicated by this shorthand in the original have been revised for the sake of clarity. With the exception of the epilogue, which has been extensively revised, the notes correspond to the German version; the bibliography has been standardized.

I count myself lucky to have collaborated with Markus twice now on major projects. As with *The Birth of the Archive,* I learned so much along the way.

August 2020
John Noël Dillon

NOTES

Prologue

1. FontNarr 2:450f. The latest biography: García Hernán, *Ignacio*.
2. Homza, "Religious Milieu," 14.
3. Boyle, *Loyola's Acts*.
4. Rahner, *Ignatius von Loyola*, 214 (quotation there).
5. Pavone, "Preti riformati."
6. Reminisc. § 85; Const § 258.
7. Olin, "Idea of Pilgrimage," 393f. (quotation is from Ex 146).
8. Ignatius of Loyola, *Spiritual Diary* (included in Ex, trans. Munitz and Endean).
9. García de Castro Valdés, *Polanco*.
10. Cohen, "Why the Jesuits Joined."
11. Leturia, *El gentilhombre*; Schneider, "Der weltliche Heilige"; García Mateo, "Ignatius" (1990).
12. FontNarr 2:62; see García Mateo, "Ignatius" (1990), 31f.
13. O'Malley, *Trent*.

Chapter One

1. For a self-critical account, see Cordara, *Suppression*, 178–85.
2. Imago, esp. 204–330; Salviucci Insolera, *L'Imago*; O'Malley (ed.), *Art*.
3. BN Vittorio Emmanuele mss Ges 1442, fol. 242v: "Oriuolo," Tuscan for *orologio*; see http://www.treccani.it/vocabolario/oriolo1/.
4. Original statistics taken from ARSI Hist Soc 10–19. For a summary, see Boehmer, *Die Jesuiten*, 188–91.
5. Soto Artuñedo, "La Compañía," 244; Alden, *Making*, 581.
6. For a general overview, see Bangert, *A History*.
7. Alden, *Making*, 24–229, 603–13; Assunção, *Negócios*.
8. Assunção, *Negócios*, 29.
9. Egido, *Los jesuitas*, 49–255.
10. Soto Artuñedo, "La Compañía," 241–76.
11. Imago, 211. For the early phase, see Pasquier, *Le catéchisme*, 1–121 (introduction).
12. Bergin, *Politics*, 58.
13. Martin, *Henry III*, passim.
14. Nelson, *Jesuits*; Waele, "Pour la sauvegarde"; Bergin, *Politics*.

15. Bergin, *Politics*, 75.

16. Gay, "Voués à quel royaume?"; Gay, *Jesuit Civil Wars*.

17. Imago, 212.

18. Shore, *Jesuits*.

19. Hoffmann, "Theodor Moretus."

20. Shore, *The Eagle*, 6f.

21. Scaduto, "Le missioni"; Scaduto, "La missione del nunzio"; Donnelly, "Antonio Possevino."

22. Parker, *Faith*, esp. 38f.; Vanden Bosch, "Saving Souls."

23. For Scandinavia: Garstein, *Rome*; for the British Isles: McCoog, *Society of Jesus*; McGoog (ed.), *Reckoned Expense*; McGoog, *"And Touching Our Society."*

24. Imago, 215.

25. Chadwick, *St. Omers*; Promitzer, "Die merkwürdige Flucht"; Murphy, *Ingleses de Sevilla*; Lukács, "Die nordischen Seminare."

26. Steinhuber, *Geschichte*; Schmidt, *Das Collegium Germanicum*.

27. Imago, 208.

28. In general, see Schurhammer, *Franz Xaver*; on Pamplona, see 1:51–54.

29. García de Castro Valdés, "Ignatius," 76f.

30. See Geger, "First First Companions."

31. In general, see Ruiz Jurado, *Orígenes*, 89–96.

32. Le Valois, *Œuvres*, vol. 1, p. IIj.

33. For a brief overview, see Cohen, "Racial and Ethnic Minorities."

34. Coello de la Rosa, "De mestizos," 40–51; Pacheco, *Los Jesuitas*, 49f., 168–71; Duve, "Das Konzil."

35. Acosta, *De procuranda*, 485–87.

36. Hyland, *The Jesuit*.

37. Brockey, *Journey*, 140–51; Brockey, *Visitor*, 369–73; Mungello, *Forgotten Christians*, 47f.; Chan, "Chinese Church."

38. Cohen, "Racial and Ethnic Minorities," 208.

39. Pacheco, *Los Jesuitas*, 168–71.

40. On Mercurian, see MonPeru 2:433; on Acquaviva: MonPeru 4:333.

41. Cf. Zeron, "From Farce," 411f.

42. Coello de la Rosa, "De mestizos," 55–59.

43. Astrain, *Historia*, 5:420f.

44. CG 5, d. 52 and 53, p. 204f.; see now esp. Maryks, *Jesuit Order*.

45. CG 6, d. 28, p. 231f.

46. Soto Artuñedo, "Jesuitas," 4, with examples from southern Spain in the sixteenth century.

47. Reinhard, "Kirche als Mobilitätskanal."

48. Chaumonot, "Autobiographie," 20–21.

49. Cf., e.g., Martin, "Jesuits," 6f.

50. EpIgn 4:7–9 (no. 4); MonPaed 3:350 with nos. 1–4; Prosperi, *La vocazione*, 75–126.

51. Number taken from Martin, "Jesuits," 8.

52. For examples, see Gioia, "Saggio introduttivo," 23; Coreth, "Priesterliches Wirken," 72f.; Arranz Roa, "Las Indias," 399.

53. Boschet, *Le parfait missionnaire*, 31f.

54. EpIgn 6:410f.

55. Ayrault, *Petri Aerodii*. See Prosperi, *La vocazione*, 170–87.

56. Bibliothèque Royale, Brussels, ms 4156, pp. 83–87.

57. Gisolfo, *Vita*, 9–12 (quotation on p. 10: "viva forza").

58. Sander, *Geschichte*, 503–5.

59. Deslandres, *Croire*, 101f.; Diefendorf, "Give Us Back." See further the papers collected in University of Angers (ed.), *La vocation religieuse*.

60. MonFab 253–55.

61. Bouuaert-Claeys, "Une visite," 112f.

62. Cf., e.g., Lukács, "De graduum diversitate," 240.

63. Ruiz Jurado, *Orígenes*, 93.

64. Ruiz Jurado, *Orígenes*, 95; Pillorget, "Vocation religieuse," 9f.

65. EpIgn 12:110f.; MonPaed 1:128 (§ 2), 335 (no. 15).

66. MonPaed 2:47f. (no. 9).

67. Bourdaloue, *Œuvres*, 5:1–33. The quotation appears on p. 4.

68. Lancicius, *Opera*, 199–201, 382–453.

69. GE no. 61. Cf. Const. no. 246.

70. Manaraeus, *Exhortationes*, 453–60 (*spiritualis*); Biblioteca Casanatense ms 2135, fol. 33^v (Claudio Filippo Grimaldi in a eulogy for de Noyelle, 1687); Ranum (ed.), *Beginning*, 172, 180 ("moderate"); Martin, "Jesuits," 3–5.

71. For an example, see RAA Jes 65, unfol. (October 27, 1684, after a death).

72. EpIgn 5:418–20 and 6:49–51.

73. ARSI Inst 107, fol. 6^r.

74. Quotation from Hoffmann, "Theodor Moretus," 123.

75. BayHStA Jes 665, unfol. (to Veihelin, June 24, 1663).

76. ARSI FG 700, fol. 259^r–260^v.

77. Ranum (ed.), *Beginning*, 172, 180.

78. EpIgn 6:474f. Adorno, however, cited GE 62.

79. Campeau, "Le voyage," 72.

80. "Unwillingly," according to Ricci in 1751 (ARSI Germ Sup 16, 152f.).

81. Martin, "Jesuits," 9–16.

82. Viguerie, "La vocation." See now also Prosperi, *La vocazione*.

83. Gilardi, "Autobiografie," 14f.

84. Machielsen, *Martin Delrio*, 52.

85. Gilardi, "Autobiografie," 31.

86. Quotation taken from Diefendorf, "Give Us Back," 279.

87. Gilardi, "Autobiografie," 30.

88. Boschet, *Le parfait missionnaire*, 11–16.

89. Cf. CG 1, d. 127, p. 100; Inst 3:122–24 (1580); Lancicius, *Opera*, 542–46.

90. Châtellier, *Tradition chrétienne*, 235f.

91. CG 2, d. 14, p. 115. Ruiz Jurado, "Jesuit Formation"; Ruiz Jurado, *Orígenes*, 114–16; Guibert, *The Jesuits*, 229, 233f. n. 9; Terhalle, *S. Andrea*, esp. 15–54; EpIgn 1:603–6.

92. CG 2, d. 14, p. 115; Inst 3:126.

93. For the Middle Ages, see Breitenstein, *Das Noviziat*, 67f., 137f., 249f., 400–403, 485f.; Puente, *Vida*, cap. 1.

94. Cf. the rules of 1526 in Kunkel, *Theatines*, 167.

95. See Ruiz Jurado, *Orígenes*, 16–18.

96. Boschet, *Le parfait missionnaire*, 14. Cf. Ranum (ed.), *Beginning*. The rules of Paris are essentially a local application of Inst 3:128–30.

97. Stoeckius, *Untersuchungen*, 49–59.

98. On these goals, see Ranum (ed.), *Beginning*, 59, 145, 184. Maunoir soon internalized important principles of Jesuit thought: "Just as God always thinks of me, so I will always think of him." In Paris, special importance was attached to conveying to new members the Ignatian maxim of "finding God in all things"; Boschet, *Le parfait missionnaire*, 14.

99. For the early history, see Ruiz Jurado, *Orígenes*, 73–83.

100. Chaumonot, "Autobiographie," 22. For the identification of Colanelli, I am indebted to Dr. Andreea Badea of Rome. For his biographical data, see Sommervogel 2:1278.

101. Ranum (ed.), *Beginning*, 177.

102. GE 64–70.

103. For Ignatius's reservation, see EpIgn 6:203. On maintaining them, see Inst 3:124f. For an example, see Gensac, "Antoine Le Gaudier," 339.

104. Boschet, *Le parfait missionnaire*, 17.

105. Boschet, *Le parfait missionnaire*, 36, 41, 48f.

106. Boschet, *Le parfait missionnaire*, 51.

107. Dupont-Ferrier, *Vie quotidienne*, 1:69f.

108. Ruiz Jurado, "La tercera probación," 291, 294.

109. Inst 3:262, 275; Boschet, *Le parfait missionnaire*, 52. First mentioned as "P. Maunoir" on p. 64.

110. Boschet, *Le parfait missionnaire*, 64.

111. For the following remarks, see Ruiz Jurado, "La tercera probación"; Inst 3:262.

112. Puente, *Vida*, cap. 47.

113. Le Gaudier, *Introductio*, 2–10; Inst 3:265. On missions overseas, see Molina, *To Overcome*, 100f.; Puente, *Vida*, cap. 47.

114. Boschet, *Le parfait missionnaire*, 64, 69. Cf. Le Gaudier, *Introductio*, 11, passim.

115. de la Palma, *Praxis*, 25–31: internal and external novitiate.

116. Bremond, *Histoire*, 5:4–65; Jimenez Berguecio, *Louis Lallemant*, 183–238.

117. Inst 3:118. On spatial separation, see Gensac, "Antoine Le Gaudier," 351n73; Inst 3:262; Ruiz Jurado, "La tercera probación," 315.

118. Inst 1:88.

119. Österreichische Nationalbibliothek cod 11956, fol. 13^v f.

120. Gerhartz, *"Insuper promitto,"* 25f.; Maire, "La Critique gallicane."

121. "precariato a vita": Catto, *La compagnia divisa*, 45–47; cf. pp. 134–36 for Francesco della Torre.

122. Cf., e.g., AN M 242, no. 2 (anno 1701).

123. Inst 1:89f.; 1:94.

124. In general, see Olivares, *Los votos*. For critical voices, see ACDF St. St. O 5 h. Concerning a property question, cf. Biblioteca Casanatense ms 2117, fol. 290^r–300^v.

125. Olivares, "Los coadjutores"; Lukács, "De graduum diversitate"; O'Malley, *First Jesuits*, 345–48.

126. Inst 1:92f.

127. Ganss, "Toward Understanding."

128. Quotation from Bovelette, "Die Laienbrüder," 200.

129. Schurhammer, "Die Anfänge."

130. EpMixt 1:141f.

131. Ganss, "Toward Understanding," 24, 31, 61.

132. Errichetti, "L'antico Collegio," 237n22.

133. Rehg, "Value," 7f.

134. Cf. CG 1, d. 95, p. 92. On the biretta, see the brief references and sketch in Rocca (ed.), *La sostanza*, 57.

135. Cf., e.g., Possevino's criticism of *coadiutores* in ARSI Congr 26, fol. 43^v–44^r.

136. ARSI FG 678 no. 12; CG 7, d. 24 and 27, p. 259f. Cf. CG 9, d. 24, p. 306.

137. Inst 3:10 (rule no. 14); Ganss, "Toward Understanding," 32, 35–37.

138. Archivio Segreto, Vatican City, Fondo Gesuiti 49, unfol. (August 28, 1681).

139. DHCJ, 281; Shore, *The Eagle*, 4 and passim; Steinbicker, "Westfalen," 151f.

140. Inst 1:4.

141. GE 3.

142. EpNad 4:214.

143. Paolucci, *Missioni*, 1f.

144. Van Ginhoven Rey, *Instruments*.

145. On apostolicity, see Foresta, *"Wie ein Apostel,"* 123–81. On the original church as a reference point, see Mongini, "Censura," 178f.

146. EpNad 4:651 (my emphasis).

147. Witwer, *"Contemplativus"*; Coreth, "In actione contemplativus."

148. Champion, *Vie du Père Vincent Huby*, 54.

149. Lallemant, *Doctrine spirituelle*, 194f., 236–38.

150. Const § 288.

151. EpIgn 3:510.

152. Stierli, "Das ignatianische Gebet"; Sudbrack, "Gott in allen Dingen."

153. Ex §§ 23, 166.

154. On the tradition, see Marno, "Attention," 237–47.

155. Ex § 23.

156. AN M 242, fol. 66^r (a fragment, presumably from Canada).

157. Coleman, *Virtues*, 53f. and passim.

158. Ex § 179.

159. Marno, "Attention," 235.

160. Cf. Pizzorusso, "Le choix," 889f.

161. O'Malley, *Saints or Devils*, 147–64; quotations from EpNad 5:54, 364f., 773f. (in order).

162. Reyero, *Misiones*, 13.

163. Ex §§ 152, 155, and more in García Mateo, "Origines"; Bertrand, *Un corps*, 27; Bertrand, *La Politique*, 23.

164. Friedrich, *Der lange Arm*, 372–78.

165. E.g., EpIgn 1:341.

166. For variants, see Knauer, "Unsere Weise."

167. E.g., MonBor 7:186; EpIgn 2:46.

168. EpIgn 11:277.

169. Cf., e.g., MonMex 2:581f., 5:224.

170. Expressed polemically in ARSI Hisp 143, fol. 24ᵛ ("primero modo de proceder nostro"), 275ᵛ, and very frequently passim.

171. E.g., Castelnau-L'Estoile, *Les ouvriers*, 61f.

172. Possevino's metaphor taken from Endean, "Original Line," 39 with n. 17.

173. SJ (ed.), *Epistolae* (1847), 1:440f.

174. For the history of the composition of the *Exercises*, see Leturia, "Génesis"; Arzubialde, *Ejercicios*, esp. 35–63; Prosperi, "Two Standards."

175. Albuquerque, "Historia."

176. Ex § 1.

177. E.g., Diertins, *Exercitia*, 12 f.

178. Ex § 1.

179. Demoustier, "La primera anotación."

180. O'Reilly, "Spiritual Exercises," esp. 204–10; Zarri, "Introduzione," 36; Mongini, "Devozione," 250f.

181. Ex § 25.

182. Ex §§ 90, 160, 207.

183. de' Pazzi, *L'epistolario*, 239.

184. Brunner, *Dramata Sacra*, unpag., fol. D5ᵛ ("Sechster Unterricht," par. 20); Karant-Nunn, *Reformation*, 13–62, esp. 42–47.

185. For Kisel's calculation of drops of blood, see Karant-Nunn, *Reformation*, 42–47.

186. Ex §§ 65–70.

187. For criticism and qualification, see Levy, "Early Modern Jesuit Arts."

188. Iparraguirre (ed.), *Historia*, 1:258–63.

189. Canisius, *Das Testament*, 37.

190. Boschet, *Le parfait missionnaire*, 29.

191. Segneri, *Opere*, 4:951–53.

192. Cf. Mongini, "Devozione," 264f.

193. Iparraguirre, *Historia*.

194. Inst 3:120–31.

195. Cf., e.g., Le Gaudier, *Introductio*. On the value and duration of the *Exercises*, see p. 23.

196. For a translation, see Palmer, *On Giving*, 290–346, esp. 292 (no. 10).

197. EpMixt 4:819.

198. SJ (ed.), *Epistolae* (1847), 1:281, 287. For an example, see Palomo, "Malos panes," 13.

199. From Japan 1592, quoted by Iparraguirre, *Historia*, 2:309.

200. CG 6, d. 29, p. 232; 7, d. 25, p. 260 (temporary withdrawal from *consueta ministeria*); CG 8, d. 38, p. 294 (suspension only by provincials); CG 18, d. 22, p. 400; Iparraguirre, *Historia*, 3:461–81. For an example, see Zanardi, "Il padre," 180.

201. Diertins, *Exercitia*, 11f., 311–34.

202. Iparraguirre, *Historia*, 2:281–84, 288–90.

203. Iparraguirre, *Historia*, 2:278.

204. Ceccotti, *Apparatus*, esp. 35–41.

205. See the fundamental studies collected in Plazaola (ed.), *Las fuentes*; cf. also Prosperi, "Two Standards."

206. Shore, "*Vita Christi.*"

207. Reminisc. no. 7.

208. Ex §§ 136–48. See Leturia, "La conversión," 22f.

209. Solignac, "Le 'Compendio breve.'"

210. Rho, *Achates*; Cajetanus, *De religiosa*. See Orlandi, "L. A. Muratori," 289.

211. Poggi, "Para una lectura," esp. 5.

212. Zarncke, *Die Exercitia*.

213. Habsburg, *Catholic and Protestant*, esp. 179–242.

214. Boyle, "Angels"; Weinczyk, "Zur Rezeption."

215. Dudon, *St. Ignatius*, 212, 457–62.

216. Ceccotti, *Apparatus*, 9.

217. Cf. the now lost texts in Braunsberger, "Ein Meister," 83; cf. also Begheyn, "Pierre Fabre."

218. Stroppa, *Sic arescit*, passim.

219. Márquez, "Origen."

220. For apophatic and affective mysticism, see Van Dyke, "Mysticism." On pious "self-ownership," see Coleman, *Virtues*. Coleman's entire book discusses this.

221. Rodríguez, *Practice*; Donnelly, "Alonso Rodríguez"; Hendrickson, *Jesuit Polymath*, 12–16, 131–36.

222. García Hernán, *Ignacio*, 113–38; Mongini, "Le teologie"; Mongini, "Per un profilo"; Fernández Martín, "Iñigo de Loyola."

223. Reminisc. nos. 29 and 30.

224. O'Reilly, "Spiritual Exercises."

225. EpIgn 2:233–37.

226. O'Reilly, "Spiritual Exercises."

227. Hamilton, *Heresy*; cf. also Andrés Martin, *Los recogidos*.

228. EpIgn 2:316–20; Ruiz Jurado, "San Juan."

229. Mercurian in a circular from January 1578, quoted in Pastore, "La 'svolta antimistica.'"

230. Dalmases, "Santa Teresa"; Elizalde, "Teresa de Jesús"; Iglesias, "Santa Teresa"; Mujica, "Encuentro."

231. Irving, *Colonial Counterpoint*, 51.

232. Ruiz Jurado, "Un caso de profetismo"; Milhou, "La tentación"; García Hernán (ed.), *Francisco de Borja*, esp. the chapters by Broggio (597–617), Pastore (619–31), and Navarro Sorní (669–79).

233. EpIgn 12:632–52; EpIgn 6:79f.

234. EpIgn 8:362f. Cf. Jiménez Pablo, "La lucha," 129f. and passim.

235. Palmio criticized Borja's tendencies: Navarro Sorní, "La espiritualidad," 676.

236. MonPaed 4:583f.

237. Schoeters, "Johannes Berchmans"; Cepari, *Essercitio*, "Al Lectore," unpag., and pt. 2, 221–23, 355–59.

238. de' Pazzi, *L'epistolario*, 226f.

239. Gioia, "Saggio introduttivo"; Mostaccio, "Per via."

240. Gagliardi, *Breve compendio*, 182 (*annihilatione*), 183f., 194, 335–38.

241. Pirri, "Il P. Achille Gagliardi," 17.

242. For Poiret, see Gioia, "Saggio introduttivo," 161; for de' Pazzi, see Mostaccio, "Au carrefour." For her contacts with Coton, see de' Pazzi, *L'epistolario*, 232–36.

243. Jiménez Pablo, "La lucha."

244. Krumenacker, *L'école française*, 113–18, 131–34. When the first Carmelite house was at last founded in Paris, it was placed under the direction of the Spanish Carmelite nun Ana de Jesús—whose confessor also was Balthasar Álvarez.

245. Krumenacker, *L'école française*, 141–43.

246. Certeau, *Die mystische Fabel*, 391–441; Faesen, "Great Silence"; Loupès, "Un grand centre."

247. Vidal, *Jean de Labadie*, 17, 23.

248. Faesen, "Great Silence"; Ghielmi, "Al crocevia," 194. Cf. Jimenez Berguecio, *Louis Lallemant*.

249. In general, see Goujon, *Prendre part*.

250. Surin, *Dialogues spirituels*, 1:228f.

251. Surin, *Dialogues spirituels*, 1:225–27.

252. Surin, *Dialogues spirituels*, 1:225; Surin, *Correspondance*, 1530.

253. Surin, *Dialogues spirituels*, 1:164, 2:201–6.

254. Surin, *Dialogues spirituels*, 1:167f., 2:206–13.

255. Lezcano Tosca, "Antonio Cordeses" (quotations on pp. 1299 and 1302); Endean, "Strange Style," 352–60; Jiménez Pablo, "La lucha," 195–206; Andrés Martin, *Los recogidos*, 450–514.

256. Suárez, *Tractatus IV*, 23f., 158f.

257. Godínez, *Practica*, 54–101.

258. Godínez, *Praxis*, 1:496, § 147.

259. For *mysticus*, see Jimenez Berguecio, *Louis Lallemant*, 220. Cf. Guibert, *The Jesuits*, 566–72.

260. MonPaed 4:576–78.

261. In general, see Vidal, *Jean de Labadie*; Saxby, *The Quest*.

262. Surin, *Correspondance*, 435.

263. Quoted in Molina, *To Overcome*, 29.

264. Surin, *Correspondance*, 453, 455.

265. Faesen, "Dupliciter."

266. Godínez, *Practica*, 54–101; Suárez, *Tractatus IV*.

267. Sandaeus, *Pro theologia mystica clavis*, 1–2, referring to his *Theologia mystica*. See further Spica, "La 'Pro Theologia Mystica Clavis.'" See also Cepari, *Essercitio*, 2:340, on mystic language as a "linguaggio nuovo, & incognito."

268. See Goddard, "Canada."

269. See Houdard, *Les invasions*.

270. Quotation taken from Levy, *Propaganda*, 72; cf. p. 81f.

271. EpIgn 1:687–93.

272. Const § 547. For the Franciscan connection, see Mostaccio, "Perinde ac si cadaver," 61–65.

273. For Ignatius and *vana gloria* in general, see Boyle, *Loyola's Acts*. Rule of St. Benedict: cap. 49, § 9, quoted by Bernard (*Patrologia Latina*, vol. 183, col. 866 B), quoted in EpIgn 1:691f.

274. The great letter on obedience (EpIgn 4:669–81) is included in the edition of Ex (trans. Mundiz and Endean), 251–61.

275. Ex (trans. Mundiz and Endean), 258.

276. Lallemant, *La vie*, 23f.

277. EpIgn 4:675.

278. EpIgn 4:669–81.

279. Mostaccio, "Perinde ac si cadaver," 65–71.

280. ARSI Naples 181, fol. 457^r–458^r.

281. In general, see Alfieri and Ferlan, "Storie."

282. Quoted by Majorana, "Predicare," 153.

283. RAA Jes 2844, unfol. (July 14, 1682; February 16, 1682).

284. RAA Jes 2845, unfol. (May 29, 1682). On its unusualness, see Fechner, *Entscheidungsfindung*, 257n388 (with quotation).

285. Quoted in Broggio, "Potere," 192.

286. EpNad 4:733.

287. Inst 1:3–7.

288. See, in general, Friedrich, "Archive."

289. Friedrich, *Der lange Arm*, 206–10.

290. García de Castro Valdés, *Polanco*, 109–47, 219–41.

291. In general, see Coupeau, *From Inspiration*.

292. Arranz Roa, "Las Casas Profesas"; on Ribadeneira, see p. 132f.

293. Friedrich, *Der lange Arm*, 150f.; McCoog, "English Province," 166–80.

294. MonPaed 4:479.

295. Number from Bösel, "Jesuit Architecture," 66. For a different number (twenty-six), see Arranz Roa, "Las Casas Profesas," 135.

296. Bouuaert-Claeys, "Une visite," 63; analogously, p. 74.

297. MonRib 2:495.

298. In general, see Fechner, *Entscheidungsfindung*.

299. Historical Archive of Cologne Jes. 16b.

300. CG 2, d. 19, p. 116f.

301. Inst 1:177–79, 262–69.

302. Menniti Ippolito, *Il governo*, 22; Meyer, *Frankreich*, 25–31.

303. In general, see García de Castro Valdés, *Polanco*. On Polanco, now see the major new book by Nelles, *Information Order*.

304. See now McCoog (ed.), *With Eyes and Ears Open*.

305. Friedrich, *Der lange Arm*, 87f.

306. See in general Schurhammer, "Die Anfänge."

307. EpIgn 1:236–38.

308. See Rahner, *Ignacio*.

309. Cf., e.g., Vitelleschi's extensive correspondence with Jakob Canisius in ARSI Germ 111.

310. Cf., e.g., BayHStA Jes 5#4, fol. 1ʳ–[15ʳ], an early modern manuscript German translation.

311. Pfeiffer, "Iconography," 201f. Cf. Lazar, "Belief," 14.

312. Levy, "Jesuit Identity."

313. Polanco, *Breve directorium*, fol. A2ʳ (my emphasis).

314. Files in ARSI Inst 213.

315. Friedrich, "Theologische Einheit."

316. See Schürer, *Das Exemplum*; Ertl, *Religion*.

317. Motta, "La compagine sacra"; Bilinkoff, "Many 'Lives'"; König-Nordhoff, *Ignatius*; García de Castro Valdés, "Ignatius," 76–81.

318. FontNarr 3:609.

319. Levy, "Jesuit identity," 135–37.

320. E.g., Hevenesi, *Scintillae*; Le Brun, *Virgilius*.

321. For Ignatius's rooms, see Friedrich, *Der lange Arm*, 145; on the archives, see Friedrich, "Archive"; on the process of selection, see Mongini, "Censura."

322. Orlandini, *Historia*.

323. E.g., Techo, *Historia*; Schmidl, *Historia*.

324. BN mss Ges 1328, no. V, fol. 40ʳ.

325. See, e.g., the letters edited by Aricò, "Fra teologia," 115–19.

326. BN mss Ges. 1328, no. VI, fols. 74ʳ–151ᵛ.

327. BN mss Ges. 1328, no. V, fols. 55ʳ⁻ᵛ, etc.

328. Orlandini, *Historia*, 201: *conglutinandosque in dies magis universorum animos*. Peter Canisius uses the same metaphor in a letter to Count Oswald II. See Hansen, (ed.), *Rheinische Akten*, no. 18, p. 29: *quae non praesentes modo conglutinare possit*. For details on dissemination, see Friedrich, "Circulating."

329. In general, see Friedrich, "Circulating"; Nelles, "*Cosas*."

330. MonPaed 3:258f.

331. E.g., Sander, *Geschichte*, 488–89. For a very similar case, see Opfermann (ed.), *Geschichte*, 1:113.

332. Opfermann (ed.), *Geschichte*, 1:22.

333. E.g., RAA Jes 65, unfol. (December 2, 1684).

334. RAA Jes 3159, "Informatio," 1; RAA Jes 2844, unfol. (*Historia de Domino de Vos*).

335. Files in ARSI Hist Soc 140; cf. the vague account in Cordara, *Historiae*, 140f. Cf. the more explicit, but also more apologetic, account in Lyraeus, *De imitatione*, 250.

336. See Coello de la Rosa, "Lights and Shadows."

337. See Lang, *Reverendi*.

338. Quoted by Martin, "Vocational Crises," 215.

339. Forschungsbibliothek Gotha Chart A, fol. 158ᵛ.

340. Chevallier (ed.), *Old Regime*, 59–87.

341. Carrasco, "Le crime."

342. Folsom, *The Yaquis*, 184–88.

343. Manucci, *Storia do Mogor*, 2:155.

344. Brockey, "Death."

345. Martin, "Vocational Crises," 205.

346. ARSI Germ 111, fol. 213^{r-v}.

347. ARSI Germ 111, fol. 343^{r-v}.

348. ARSI Germ Sup 8, fol. 380^r.

349. Quoted in Martin, "Vocational Crises," 211.

350. Gisolfo, *Vita*, 14–16.

351. Carrasco, "Le crime."

352. Quoted in Pavone, "I dimessi," 473, 474; cf. Prosperi, *La vocazione*, 220–35.

353. Bouuaert-Claeys, "Une visite," 51.

354. On Ribadeneira's treatise on *dimissi*, see, e.g., Moreno Martínez, "Obediencias."

355. ARSI Germ Sup 10, fol. 452^v.

356. ARSI Germ 111, fol. 339^r. What exactly happened to Marell after his sins were discovered is uncertain. Two decades later, however, he still was a respected and extremely active member of the order, although he apparently had been transferred out of Augsburg to Austria. Cf. BayHStA Jes 691, passim.

357. Catto, *La compagnia divisa*. See also Mostaccio, *Early Modern Jesuits*.

358. Friedrich, *Der lange Arm*, 124–40.

359. ARSI Congr 74, fol. 171^r (1651).

360. SJ (ed.), *Epistolae* (1711), 477f.

361. SJ, *Regulae*, 25.

362. Wielewicki (ed.), *Historicum*, 238f. (*motus in provincia, animorum motus*).

363. Nebgen, *Missionarsberufungen*.

364. Quoted in Pignatelli, "Il P. Virgilio Cepari," 11. Cf. Friedrich, *Der lange Arm*, 427.

365. Quoted in Bösel, "Jesuitenkirche," 59n8.

Chapter Two

1. Ex §§ 352–70.

2. Mostaccio, *Early Modern Jesuits*, 83–85.

3. Guida, "Antonio Possevino"; Possevino, *The Moscovia*; Donnelly, "Antonio Possevino."

4. For an exemplary account, see Shore, *Jesuits*.

5. Dalmases, *Ignatius*, 193–99; Wolff, "Boscovich"; Hamilton, *The Copts*; Heyberger, *Les chrétiens*.

6. Inst 3:46. For broader assessments of the relationship between Jesuits and the Society of Jesus, see also Catto and Ferlan (eds.), *I gesuiti*; O'Malley, *Jesuits and the Popes*.

7. Const no. 605.

8. Inst 1:4.

9. For example, it does not appear at all in the entire third volume of the Inst.

10. Giulio Cesare Cordara quoted in Cajani and Foa, "CLEMENTE XIII, papa."

11. Dandelet, *Spanish Rome*, 142–45.

12. Fois, "Il Generale."

13. Taken from Santos Hernández, *Jesuitas y obispados*, 166f. The quotation comes from the Venetian ambassador to the Curia.

14. Godman, *The Saint*, 50f.

15. Baum, "Luigi Maria Torrigiani." Garampi downplayed Ricci's influence somewhat: Vanysacker, *Cardinal Giuseppe Garampi*, 115f.

16. CG 3, d. 5 (*ante electionem*), p. 137, no. 5. On Gregory XIII, see Martínez Millán, "Transformación."

17. Paglia, *La pietà*, 81.

18. Wicki, "Die Jesuiten-Beichtväter."

19. Pagano (ed.), *Documenti*, esp. 99f. (Benedetto Giustiniani as theologian), 139–48 (Melchior Inchofer).

20. Godman, *The Saint*. For the date: ACDF SO Juramenta 1575–1655, fol. 102ʳ.

21. ARSI Hist Soc 25, fol. 24ʳ.

22. Santos Hernández, *Jesuitas y obispados*, 168. On the personnel of the Sanctum Officium in the eighteenth century, see Wolf (ed.), *Prosopographie*. I wish to thank Dr. Andreea Badea for further information.

23. Alcaraz Gómez, *Jesuitas*, 399–422.

24. Romeo, *Ricerche*, 35–62; Brambilla, *Alle origini*, 475–93; Ianuzzi, "Mentalidad"; Herzig, *Der Zwang*, 118 (the Inquisition was directed "more against the Jesuits than against the Lutherans").

25. [Faure], *Commentarium*, e.g., 31–47. See also this work's extensive table of contents. Cf. also Schwedt, "Fra giansenisti."

26. Wolf (ed.), *Prosopographie*, 1:476.

27. Borges, "Nuevos datos."

28. Pizzorusso, "Le pape rouge"; Pizzorusso, "La Congregazione"; Pizzorusso, *Roma nei Caraibi*.

29. Launay (ed.), *Documents*, 1:242; Codignola (ed.), *Calendar*, 2:26–33.

30. Condemnation of the Jesuits in China in 1645, mandatory general congregations in 1646; support for Palafox: see Alvarez de Toledo, *Politics*, 254f., 275. For ridicule of the Jesuits' Quarant'ore, see Imorde, *Präsenz*, 127f.

31. Carayon (ed.), *Première mission*, 257–59.

32. Cf., e.g., AFSJ Brotier 69, unfol. (December 12, 1722).

33. Cf. the example of the Netherlands: Spiertz, *L'église*; Van Hoeck, "Romeinische correspondentie."

34. Quotation taken from the Chinese rites controversy in 1679: Launay (ed.), *Documents*, 1:84.

35. Launay (ed.), *Documents*, 1:256 (quotation), 258, 260.

36. Pizzorusso, "Per servitio."

37. Schneider, "Die Jesuiten."

38. Jaitner (ed.), *Die Hauptinstruktionen*, 1:65, 325 (quotation); 2:485, 569 (quotation), 712, 717. Cf. Metzler, "Die Missionsinitiativen," 39.

39. Schneider, "Die Jesuiten," 296f.

40. Schneider, "Die Jesuiten," 282–84 with quotes.

41. Quotation taken from Hengerer, *Kaiser Ferdinand III*, 426n74.

42. Schüller, "Die Eifelmission," 86f. Cf. also Nanni, "Réformistes," 266f.

43. Const no. 817; EpIgn 1:451. See in general, also on the infrequent exceptions, Santos Hernández, *Jesuitas y obispados*.

44. Santos Hernández, *Jesuitas y obispados*, 96–98.

45. E.g., Lugo, *Responsa moralia*, 106–18.

46. Samerski, "Olmütz," 254; Ferlan, *Dentro e fuori*, 112f. and passim.

47. Baer, "Die Gründung."

48. Breuer, "Der Anteil."

49. AN G 8, unfol. (circular from February 21, 1668). For examples, including Caulet, see Doublet, "Caulet."

50. Catalano, *La Boemia*, esp. 83–105; Shore, *The Eagle*, 20–23; for Harrach's views, see Keller and Catalano (eds.), *Die Diarien*, passim.

51. See in general Alvarez de Toledo, *Politics*.

52. Astrain, *Historia*, 5:366.

53. Torre, "Politics Cloaked," esp. 48–50.

54. Rurale, *Monaci*, 71f. (quotation by Marino Berengo).

55. Rosa, *Clero cattolico*, 53–89, esp. 53–63.

56. Musart, *Manuale*, unfol. ("Prooemium, mens autoris" [*sic*]).

57. Sage, *Le "bon prêtre."*

58. Foresti, *La Strada*, esp. 132–44; Herzig, *Manuale parochi*.

59. Fantappiè, "Problemi"; Negruzzo, *Collegij a forma*.

60. CG 2, d. 18, p. 116.

61. Samerski, "Olmütz."

62. Groll, "Das jesuitische Studien- und Erziehungsprogramm," 271–90.

63. Negruzzo, *Collegij a forma*, 52–70.

64. CG 12, d. 25 and 26, p. 341f. See the important edition in Gay, *Morales*, 769–71.

65. Deregnaucourt, "La formation."

66. Rurale, *Monaci*, 38f.

67. Reminisc. no. 7.

68. Cf., e.g., EpIgn 1:495–510.

69. See Hsü, *Texts*; Hsü, *Dominican Presence*; García de Castro Valdés, *Polanco*, 120f.

70. Kammann, *Die Kartause*, 335–50; Greven, *Die Koelner Kartause*, 86–112.

71. Cohen, "Why the Jesuits Joined." For requests to transfer: Braunsberger 3, no. 521; ARSI Germ Sup 3, fol. 145ʳ⁻ᵛ (November 12, 1605); ARSI Germ Sup 6, 314f. (January 11, 1631), 378f. (August 30, 1631); ARSI Germ 111, 123 (September 6, 1629). Cf. also Guibert, *The Jesuits*, 222. On the difficulty of returning: CG 3, d. 45; 4, d. 66

72. CG 5, d. 26 (*societas fraternitatis*). On 1544, cf. the document in Greven, *Die Koelner Kartause*, 100f.

73. For two examples, see Stenmans, *Litterae annuae*, 93f., 106.

74. Dolinar, *Das Jesuitenkolleg*, 28–31.

75. Nickel, "Zwischen Stadt," 478–81, 535, 554f.

76. Wrba, "Ignatius." Quotations taken from EpIgn 6:132; 7:64. Cf. also Assunção, *Negócios*, 108–14.

77. See, e.g., O'Reilly, "Spiritual Exercises"; O'Malley, *First Jesuits*, 292–94; Jiménez Pablo, "The Evolution."

78. Cf. Ianuzzi, "Mentalidad."

79. [Faure], *Commentarium*, 31–47.

80. Alonso Romo, "Dominicos."

81. Negruzzo, *Collegij a forma*, 272.

82. CG 11, d. 19 (echoing CG 8, d. 12).

83. Molina, *To Overcome*, 64f.

84. Joassart, "Jean-Paul Oliva," 179.

85. Gori, *Lettere filosofiche*, 128.

86. Weber, "Los jesuitas." The quotation from Mercurian's circular letter of March 1578 appears on page 109.

87. Joassart, "Jean-Paul Oliva," 139–52.

88. Joassart, "Jean-Paul Oliva," 145, 179.

89. Joassart, "Jean-Paul Oliva," 184.

90. O'Malley, *First Jesuits*, 68f.

91. Castaldo, *De beati Caietani*; Negrone, *Historica disputatio*; Castaldo, *Pacificum certamen*.

92. Vanni, *"Fare diligente inquisitione."*

93. FontNarr 4:246.

94. EpIgn 1:114–18. On the discussion of whether this was in fact a letter sent or intended to be sent to Carafa, cf. Bottereau, "La 'lettre' d'Ignace."

95. In general, see Bonora, *I conflitti*; cf. Ellero, "Vergini cristiane," 49–51, 62–65; Rurale, "Lo spazio," 142–47.

96. Tanturri, "Ordres."

97. Tanturri, "Scolopi"; León Navarro and Hernández, "La pugna."

98. For a somewhat sensational account, see Liebreich, *Fallen Order*, esp. 185f.

99. For an overview, see Beyer, "Der Einfluß."

100. Conrad, *Zwischen Kloster*; Le Bourgeois, *Les Ursulines*; Schneider, *Kloster*.

101. Bottereau, "Jésuites et Ursulines"; Dawdy, *Building*.

102. Dirmeier (ed.), *Mary Ward*.

103. Loupès, "Un grand centre," 400.

104. Cf., e.g., Vitelleschi's letter of 1640 in Bottereau, "Jésuites et Ursulines," 354.

105. Stenmans, *Litterae annuae*, 72 (examples reversed).

106. Opfermann (ed.), *Geschichte*, 1:62–64.

107. Stenmans, *Litterae annuae*, 187f. (abridged slightly).

108. Cf., e.g., Franco, *Synopsis*, 158.

109. For examples, see Friedrich, *Der lange Arm*, 365.

110. In general, see Clark, *Thinking*, esp. 149–311. On the Jesuits, see Waddell, *Jesuit Science*, 29–53. On Delrio, see Machielsen, *Martin Delrio*.

111. Opfermann (ed.), *Geschichte*, 1:36.

112. Braunsberger 6:255f., 392f., 398f., and passim; cf. Lederer, *Madness*, esp. 206–10, 288f.

113. Duhr, *Die Stellung*, 81; Sobiech, "Friedrich Spee," 181 (quotation taken from there).

114. For examples, see Opfermann (ed.), *Geschichte*, 1:37, 39, 42, 48f., 84; Sander, *Geschichte*, 63, 65, 141, 255, 257, 961; Heiss, "Konfessionelle Propaganda"; Barth, "Die Seelsorgetätigkeit," 391–94; Sobiech, "Friedrich Spee," 180–88.

115. Cf. Certeau, *The Possession*; Sluhovsky, "The Devil."

116. The standard work is Duhr, *Die Stellung*. Important information can also be found in Behringer, *Hexenverfolgung*, 233–36, 333–40, 369; and Lederer, *Madness*, esp. 205, 231–40. On Spee, see, e.g., Dillinger, "Friedrich Spee"; and now Sobiech, *Jesuit Prison Ministry*. For Spee and Delrio, see Machielsen, *Martin Delrio*, 264, 292.

117. Cf. esp. Delumeau, *Rassurer*, 293–339; Dompnier, "Des anges"; Manevy, "Le droit chemin"; Petrocchi, *Storia*, 2:187–93.

118. Albertino, *Trattato*; Johnson, "Guardian Angels," 197–200.

119. Barry, *La devotion*, fol. A3^r, A4^v.

120. Barry, *La devotion*, 109f.

121. Coret, *L'Ange Gardien*; Coret, *La bonne morte*. On Coret, cf. Carel, "La dévotion."

122. Motta, "La politica."

123. Albertino, *Trattato*, 80–86.

124. Barry, *La devotion*, 79–114.

125. Dompnier, "La dévotion"; Delumeau, *Rassurer*, 340–52.

126. Faesen, "Great Silence." For examples, see Lallemant, *La vie*, passim; Boschet, *Le parfait missionnaire*, 13; Chaumonot, "Autobiographie," 26.

127. See the example from 1733 in Burkhardt and Habermehl (eds.), *Die Neustadter Pfarr-chronik*, 98f.

128. Rosa, *Settecento religioso*, esp. 17–45; Coreth, *Liebe ohne Maß*, 13–22; Morgan, *Sacred Heart*; Gennaro, "Mistica Gesuitica," 179–81; Ghielmi, "La vita spirituale," 19f.

129. Schwaller, *Kurtzer Begriff*; Sonnenberg, *Neüe vom Himmel*.

130. AN M 745 no. 29, unfol. (p. 7 of the "préface").

131. Jonas, *France*, 34–53.

132. AN M 745 no. 29, unfol. (p. 7 of the "préface"). Cf. De' Pazzi, *L'epistolario*, 235f.

133. Quotation taken from Coreth, *Liebe ohne Maß*, 60. On corporeality, see Jonas, *France*, 31.

134. For examples, see Molina, *To Overcome*, 184–92.

135. Froeschlé-Chopard, "La dévotion," 532 (quoting J. Le Brun).

136. Quotation from Coreth, *Liebe ohne Maß*, 41n50. See also p. 226.

137. Croiset, *La dévotion*, unpag. ("Preface"), with reference to St. Gertrude and St. Mechthilde.

138. Ghielmi, "Al crocevia," 193f.

139. Froeschlé-Chopard, "La dévotion." Cf. also Lazar, "Belief," 10–15.

140. Sander, *Geschichte*, 117.

141. Meisner, *Nachreformatorische Frömmigkeitsformen*, 123–82.

142. For an example, see Burkhardt and Habermehl (eds.), *Die Neustadter Pfarrchronik*, 35.

143. Dumoutet, *Le désir*, esp. 91–98.

144. Dompnier, "Un aspect"; Di Santi, *L'orazione*; Imorde, *Präsenz*, 127f.; Cargnoni, *Le Quarantore*.

145. For an example of posting notice of the Quarant'ore in advance, see LittQuadr 6:97.

146. LittQuadr 6:239f.

147. For an overview, see Bösel and Salviucci Insolera (eds.), *Andrea Pozzo*, 230–47; on financing the Quarant'ore, see Maher, "Financing Reform"; on stage construction, see Weil, "The Devotion."

148. Quoted in Imorde, *Präsenz*, 146.

149. For criticism of such lavishness, see ARSI Congr 72, fol. 217^r.

150. Imorde, *Präsenz*, 146.

151. Quotation from 1585: see Cargnoni, *Le Quarantore*, 31.

152. Châtellier, "À l'origine," 208.

153. Baillet, *De la dévotion*; Crasset, *Des congrégations*.

154. Reeves, *Painting*, 141–44; Broggio, "Teologia"; Broggio, "Immacolata Concezione"; Delfosse, "Autour de l'*Instructio*."

155. Stricher, *Le vœu*, esp. 1:19–21, 52–63.

156. BayHStA Jes 253, fol. 3^v (no. 34).

157. Iacovella, "'Fabbricatori.'"

158. For examples and parallels between the physical and spiritual "plague," see [Budrioli], *La madre di Dio*.

159. Iacovella, "'Fabbricatori,'" 178; Rosa, *Settecento religioso*, 46–74.

160. Coreth, *Liebe ohne Maß*, 45, 153–56.

161. In general, see Jonas, *France*, passim; Menozzi, *Sacro Cuore*.

162. Binet, *Quel est*.

163. Le Moyne, *La dévotion aisée*, 52, from the headings of chapters 1 and 2 of book 2, respectively.

164. Le Moyne, *La dévotion aisée*, fol. ēiij^v–ēiiij^v, pp. 3–4; Goujon, "Nicolas Caussin," 192; Course, "La dévotion honnête."

165. Neercassel, *L'Amour pénitent*, 1:4.

166. "A forza di braccia con atti frequentati." Cepari, *Essercitio*, pt. 2:3–5.

167. McCall Probes, "'L'Amour de Dieu'"; Stella, "Attrizione"; Jouslin, *"Rien ne nous plaît,"* 1:339–45; Myers, *"Poor, Sinning Folk,"* 15–26. For the Middle Ages, see Spykman, *Attrition*.

168. For examples of sermons, see Spykman, *Attrition*, 6–9.

169. Moriarty, *Disguised Vices*, 172–75.

170. Sánchez, *Selectae*, 56 (no. 16); Quantin, *Le rigorisme*, 67f.

171. See Toulmin and Jonsen, *Abuse*.

172. Gay, *Morales*, 520–50; Stone and van Houdt, "Probabilism," 362–66.

173. On two teachers in Oviedo, see García Sánchez (ed.), *Los jesuitas*, 411.

174. On the numbers: Hurtubise, *La casuistique*, 26, 63, 65–67.

175. Quantin, *Le rigorisme*, 54.

176. García Sánchez (ed.), *Los Jesuitas*, 411.

177. Gay, "Doctrina Societatis?"; Gay, *Morales*, 548f., however, emphasizes that often one and the same Jesuit was employed as a casuist and *praefectus spiritualis*; there thus was a certain link after all.

178. Clm 27439, no pages (no. 1: *De juramento fidelitatis Benedictinorum S. Udalirci erga Regem Sueciae Gustavum Adolphum (tempore tricennalis belli 1632)*).

179. Quotation from Orlandi, "Il Regno," 162.

180. Gay, *Jesuit Civil Wars*, 94–104, 112.

181. Quantin, "Le Saint-Office," 905–7.

182. Quotation from Quantin, "Le Saint-Office," 876.

183. Stella, *Il giansenismo*, 1:81.

184. Gay, *Jesuit Civil Wars*; Friedrich, *Der lange Arm*, 177–80.

185. Hurtubise, *La casuistique*, 165–69, on Antoine.

186. Bibliotheca Casanatense mss 2984, fol. 96^r–135^v; Gay, *Jesuit Civil Wars*, 79–85.

187. That at least is how his position was perceived; cf. the polemical assessment in the contemporary report by Carlo Antonio Casnedi in Peloso, *Antonio Vieira*, 199–201.

188. Broggio, *La teologia*, 45–170.

189. Neveu, "Juge suprême," 404f.; Quantin, *Le catholicisme*, 144, 148 ("exaltation patristique").

190. Albert, "Jansenismus."

191. On its compilation and new sources, see Burkard, "Zur Vorgeschichte."

192. Maire, *De la cause*, 22–48; Hildesheimer, *Le jansénisme*.

193. The term "Jansenist" (*Jansenistisch*) first appeared in 1641: Thanner, "Zur Entstehungsgeschichte, 283.

194. For details, see Franceschi, "La prédétermination"; Franceschi, "Le moment pascalien."

195. Neveu, "Culture Religieuse," 259–64; Stella, *Il giansenismo*, 1:73–80.

196. For the political dimension, see Maire, *De la cause*; Van Kley, *Religious Origins*.

197. Stella, *Il giansenismo*, 1:95, 103, 159.

198. Patouillet, *Dictionnaire*, vol. 1, p. x.

199. Neveu, "Culture Religieuse," 264f.

200. Stella, *Il giansenismo*, 1:153.

201. For the seventeenth century, see Stella, *Il giansenismo*, 1:263–65; for turning of the tide after 1700, see Hurtubise, *La casuistique*, 149 and passim; Gay, *Morales*, passim.

202. EpIgn 2:189f.

203. Arranz Roa, "Educar a rudos."

204. García-Garrido, "Cuando los jesuitas."

205. See Polenghi, "Militia," 48–55.

206. Cf. Parhamer, *Vollkommener Bericht*, with numerous lists and overviews.

207. FontNarr 2:346f.

208. Cavallo, *Charity*, 23–33; Pullan, "Support," esp. 181 and 193 for "redemptive, 'new philanthropy'"; Alves, "Christian Social Organism."

209. Guévarre, *La mendicità*, vi–vii.

210. For overviews, see O'Malley, *First Jesuits*, 178–85; Lazar, *Working*.

211. On these dowries, see Ciammitti, "Quanto costa."

212. Cohen, *The Evolution*, 34f., mentions examples from Florence in the 1520s.

213. Pullan, *Rich and Poor*, 384f.

214. de León, *Grandeza*, 43–45. Cf. Moreno Mengíbar and Vázquez García, "Poderes," 43f. On the New World, see Cohen, *The Evolution*, 127–29. On Naples, see Novi Chavarria, *Il governo*, 278.

215. Lunardon, "Le zitelle"; Ellero, "Vergini cristiane"; Boccazzi Mazza, "Governare."

216. Romanello, *Le spose*, 48–52, 57 f., 167–79 (statutes). On Milan, see Lunardon, "Le zitelle," 18f.

217. Hickey, *Local Hospitals*, esp. 57–60, 100–133.

218. Gutton, *Dévots*, 65–79; Paultre, *De la répression*, 207–311; McHugh, *Hospital Politics*, 43–46.

219. On continuity with earlier efforts, see Guévarre, *La mendicità*, 88–92.

220. Carayon (ed.), *Documents* 23:360–71, 386f. On Grenoble in 1712, see Norberg, *Rich and Poor*, 82.

221. Cf. Hickey, *Local Hospitals*, 110f.

222. BnF ms fr. 21.802, fol. 349^v; Hickey, *Local Hospitals*, 112.

223. Cf., e.g., the printed propaganda pamphlet in BnF ms fr. 21.802, fol. 345^r.

224. BnF ms fr. 21.802, fol. 345^v.

225. Norberg, *Rich and Poor*, 88; Carayon (ed.), *Documents*, 23:372–429. On Guévarre, cf. Zanardi, "Il padre."

226. BnF ms fr. 21.802, fol. 349$^{r–v}$: transition from a "Capuchin" to a "Benedictine" financial basis is conceivable.

227. For Caën, see Le Valois, *Œuvres* (1758), 1:x–xi.

228. BnF ms fr. 21.802, fol. 345^v.

229. Zanardi, "Il padre," 170–72.

230. Cf. Cavallo, *Charity*, 182–96.

231. Quotations taken from Paultre, *De la répression*, 227. On the role of labor, see Gutton, *Dévots*, 72; contrast Norberg, *Rich and Poor*, 89f.; on Venice, see Lunardon, "Le zitelle," 27; for criticism, Polenghi, "Militia," 54.

232. Described as a "take-over bid" by Pullan, *Rich and Poor*, 384–91 (here, p. 390).

233. Guévarre, *La mendicità*, 1.

234. Parhamer, *Vollkommener Bericht*, passim. Parhamer sets the daily agenda for holidays, work days, and feast days, all presented in the form of lists and bullet points. For the "exercising" of the boys, see pp. 62–68. In general, see Polenghi, "Militia."

235. Romanello, *Le spose*, 45 ("governo").

236. Paultre, *De la répression*, 227: "almost prisons" ("presque des prisons"). On everyday life there, p. 231f.

237. BnF ms fr. 21.802, fol. 345^r. See Guévarre, *La mendicità*, 8–9: quartering the poor brings "comodi non ordinari" and "utili spirituali." For critical voices (Jeremias Drexel), see Lazar, *Working*, 19f.

238. Paultre, *De la répression*, 225 and passim, attaches (too much) importance to Chaurand's role as royal agent.

239. Lavenia, "Non arma."

240. For developments down to 1570, see Civale, "Francesco Borgia"; Bangert, *Jerome Nadal*, 75–81 (quotation on p. 77).

241. LittQuadr 4:438f., 663f.

242. Civale, "Francesco Borgia," 212–14; Martin, *Henry III*, 34f.

243. Martin, *Henry III*, 36f.

244. Duhr 1:517f.

245. Lavenia, "Non arma," 75f.; Borja Medina, "Jesuitas en la armada," 14f. Sailly's later deployment in Spinola's army after 1620 is mentioned in ARSI Boh 94, fol. 110^r. See Brouwers, "L'Elogium."

246. Duhr 1:518f.

247. Chennevieres, *Détails*, 2:146f.

248. Possevino, *Il soldato christiano* (1583), 48–50, 55f.

249. Quotation taken from Lavenia, "Non arma," 73.

250. Sailly, *Guidon*, 62f.

251. AFSJ Brotier 37, fol. 77^v.

252. Le Valois, *Œuvres* (1726), 2:73f.

253. Quotation from Sander, *Geschichte*, 626.

254. Sailly, *Guidon*, 9. On the humanization of soldiers' conduct, see pp. 63–66.

255. Mayr, *Mariæ Stammen buech*, 179–81.

256. Sailly, *Guidon*, unpag. (foreword to Alexander Farnese).

257. Possevino, *Il soldato christiano* (1583), 137f., 139–45 (litanies), 146–50 (prayers), 151f. (examination of conscience).

258. Sailly, *Guidon*, 309–18.

259. Possevino, *Il soldato christiano* (1604), 188–200.

260. Quoted in Duhr 1:520.

261. Quotations translated from the title: Pleiner, *Der in Lebensgefahr*. Cf. Pleiner, *Glaubens- und Sitten-Lehre*.

262. Shore, *The Eagle*, 101f., on the year 1760.

263. BayHStA Jes 691/II, unfol. (August 25, 1717); ARSI Germ Sup 6, p. 408.

264. A paraphrasis of his instruction for the papal expeditionary force: Lavenia, "Non arma," 66.

265. Sailly, *Guidon*, 167–76.

266. Riezler (ed.), *Kriegstagebücher*, passim.

267. In Brest and Toulon, naval hospitals were under their supervision: cf. Boudet, *Histoire*, 330f. Cf. esp. Chennevieres, *Détails*, 2:146f. (with quotation).

268. Possevino, *Il soldato christiano* (1583), 10–13, 39–45; Sailly, *Guidon*, 20–23.

269. Sailly, *Guidon*, 3 (on war, paraphrasing Pindar, fr. 110), 6–9, 11–13, 14 ("confidence"), and more; Riezler (ed.), *Kriegstagebücher*, 144f., 149 (quotation there).

270. Lavenia, "Non arma."

271. García Hernán, "La asistencia," esp. 243–49 and passim.

272. Borja Medina, "Jesuitas en la armada."

273. Pottier, *Le père Pierre Champion*, 92–105.

274. AN Marine B8/24, unfol. B3/239, fol. 118^{r-v}, 121^r–147^v and passim; B3/247, passim; AN M 242 no. 3; AFSJ Brotier 37, fol. 76^r–77^v; Boudet, *Histoire*, 330f.

275. Shore, *The Eagle*, 101f. On negligence in Toulon, see AFSJ Brotier 33, fol. 53^r.

276. Riezler (ed.), *Kriegstagebücher*, 130, 132.

277. Mayr, *Mariæ Stammen buech*, 281.

278. Riezler (ed.), *Kriegstagebücher*, 128, 134f., 171, 178.

279. Mayr, *Mariæ Stammen buech*, 281.

280. E.g., Le Valois, *Œuvres* (1726), 2:231f.

281. LittQuadr 1:574f.; LittQuadr 2:114, 117. See these sources for further information about Vienna.

282. Copete, "L'assistance"; de León, *Grandeza*, 193–392.

283. de León, *Grandeza*, 377.

284. LittQuadr 1:20.

285. Quotation taken from Paglia, *La pietà*, 254.

286. Paglia, *La pietà*, esp. 93–149, 162–90.

287. de León, *Grandeza*, 221, 368–71.

288. de León, *Grandeza*, 393–606.

289. See, in general, Van Dülmen, *Theater*.

290. Sander, *Geschichte*, 850 (*hilarus, gaudenter*).

291. LittQuadr 2:507 (Evora, 1554).

292. de León, *Grandeza*, 393 ("bien morir").

293. Sander, *Geschichte*, 727.

294. de León, *Grandeza*, 246.

295. Le Valois, *Œuvres* (1726), 2:234.

296. de León, *Grandeza*, 245.

297. For the number, see Egido, "Los sermones," 88. For an overview, see McManners, *Church*, 2:58–77; Smith, *Preaching*; Fumaroli, *L'âge*.

298. Chinchilla, *De la* compositio, 54f.; Norman, "Social History," passim, on *movere*.

299. Caussin, *Eloquentiae sacrae*, 608.

300. SJ (ed.), *Epistolae* (1847), 1:342.

301. Quoted by Castillo Gómez, "El Taller," 17f.

302. For the early phase, see O'Malley, *First Jesuits*, 91–104.

303. Saugnieux, *Les jansénistes*, 39–77, esp. 52f.; Norman, "Social History," 151f.; Smith, *Preaching*, 91–93.

304. Quoted in Díez Coronado, "Juan Bautista Escordó," 651.

305. Rauscher, *Oel und Wein*, 3:6.

306. Rauscher, *Oel und Wein*, 3:479–86.

307. Coreth, "Priesterliches Wirken," 78–80.

308. Ledda, "Predicar"; Orozco Díaz, "Sobre la teatralización"; Egido, "Los sermones"; Herzog, *Geistliche Wohlredenheit*, 58.

309. For examples, see Caussin, *Eloquentiae sacrae*, esp. 594–606; Moss and Wallace (eds.), *Rhetoric*, 396–98 (Carbone; quotation on p. 355); Díez Coronado, "Juan Bautista Escordó." Cf. Baffetti, "Teoria e prassi."

310. Novi Chavarria, *Il governo*, 269–90.

311. Pascual, *El misionero*, 235–39.

312. Smith, *Preaching*, 78–88, 106–10; Chinchilla, *De la* compositio, e.g., 32, 198–245; Cull, "The Baroque," 241, 243; Norman, "Social History," 155; Edwards, "Varieties," 6–8; Rodríguez de Flor, "Picta Poesis."

313. Vieira, *El semejante*.

314. For an overview, see Baffetti, "Teoria e prassi."

315. SJ (ed.), *Epistolae* (1847), 1:344. On stylistic debates over theories of sermons, see Norman, "Social History," 152–55; Battistini, "Forme e tendenze."

316. Caussin, *Eloquentiae sacrae*, 618.

317. Pallavicino, *Lettere* 1:165f. (to Segneri). Cf. Hendrickson, *Jesuit Polymath*, 58f.; Rauscher, *Oel und Wein*, vol. 1 (unpaged preface to the reader); Worcester, "Classical Sermon"; Houdry, *La bibliothèque*, 1:j–ij. Further information may be found there. On the author himself, see Varachaud, *Le père Houdry.*

318. See the excerpts from "Gravissimum praedicandi ministerium" in Pastor 15:517n2; Francisco de Isla, *Crisis.*

319. Worcester, "Catholic Sermons."

320. Const no. 402f.

321. Moss and Wallace (eds.), *Rhetoric*, 405–7.

322. Herrero Salgado, *La oratoria*, 357–58 (quotation); Chinchilla, *De la* compositio, 76–78.

323. Landry, "Bourdaloue." On preaching reform, see Blanco, "Ambiguïtés"; Rico Callado, "La reforma"; Saugnieux, *Les jansénistes.*

324. Quoted in Herzog, *Geistliche Wohlredenheit*, 198.

325. Norman, "Social History," 138–42; Chinchilla, *De la* compositio, 92–125; Saugnieux, *Les jansénistes*, 79–117.

326. Mercier, *Tableau*, 7:215f.

327. On the production of sermons, see Castillo Gómez, "El Taller."

328. Herzog, *Geistliche Wohlredenheit*, 28–80.

329. Houdry, *La bibliothèque*, 1:566–89.

330. Quoted in Castillo Gómez, "El Taller," 12.

331. Herzog, *Geistliche Wohlredenheit*, 55 (quotation there).

332. On these differences, see Majorana, "Missionarius/concionator"; Battistini, "Forme e tendenze," 39f.

333. Herzog, *Geistliche Wohlredenheit*, 302–11; Fumaroli, *L'âge*, 356.

334. Castillo Gómez, "El Taller," 12–16; Herzog, *Geistliche Wohlredenheit*, 298–302.

335. Bers, "Jülich," 200. On the duration of sermons, cf. Herzog, *Geistliche Wohlredenheit*, 175f.; and Egido, "Los sermones," 98. See p. 94 on "broken" threads; McManners, *Church*, 2:64.

336. For an example, see Opfermann (ed.), *Geschichte*, 1:218.

337. Majorana, "Missionarius/concionator," 816.

338. Varachaud, *Le père Houdry*, 51.

339. Quoted in Duhr 1:440. For further similar quotations, see pp. 1:439–42.

340. E.g., Myers, *"Poor, Sinning Folk,"* 15–105, 191–93; Romeo, *Ricerche*, 35–62; Prosperi, *Tribunali*, esp. 213–549; Brambilla, *Alle origini*, esp. 469–94; O'Malley, *First Jesuits*, 136–52; Boer, *Conquest.*

341. Polanco, *Breve directorium*, fol. 21^v–22^v; Bruno, *Brevis tractatio*, 62; O'Malley, *First Jesuits*, 140f.

342. Polanco, *Breve directorium*, fol. B3^v. For context, see Lederer, *Madness*, 50–95.

343. Quotation (from 1566) in Romeo, *Ricerche*, 40.

344. Bruno, *Brevis tractatio*, 39–51, here pp. 45 and 47.

345. Coster, *Libellus*, 14.

346. Lederer, *Madness*, 94; Myers, *"Poor, Sinning Folk,"* 52, 131–42. For exceptions, cf. Veress (ed.), *Annuae litterae*, 157.

347. Orlandi, "L. A. Muratori," 217; on shame, see Veress (ed.), *Annuae litterae*, 63.

348. Müller, *KirchenGeschmuck*, 160. I thank Dr. Christian Kühner (Freiburg) for this reference.

349. Ex § 44. See O'Malley, *First Jesuits*, 137f.; Myers, *"Poor, Sinning Folk,"* 168–84; Sluhovsky, "General Confession"; Sluhovsky, *Becoming*. For criticism, see Prosperi, *Tribunali*, 494f.

350. Coster, *Libellus*, 17–52. Cf. Ex § 44.

351. Orlandi, "L. A. Muratori," 217.

352. Ex §§ 24–43.

353. Motta, "La politica," 221.

354. Bruno, *Brevis tractatio*, 50.

355. See Hosne, "Assessing," 182f.

356. Bouuaert-Claeys, "Une visite," 79, 82.

357. For examples, see Stenmans, *Litterae annuae*, 47; Sander, *Geschichte*, 295.

358. Stenmans, *Litterae annuae*, 50.

359. For examples, see Stenmans, *Litterae annuae*, 29f., 41; Veress (ed.), *Annuae litterae*, 44.

360. Thus, Stenmans, *Litterae annuae*, 53; Veress (ed.), *Annuae litterae*, 96.

361. Bouuaert-Claeys, "Une visite," 56.

362. For the example of Peru, see Broggio, "I gesuiti," 40f. (with quotation).

363. For an example, see Eichhorn, *Beichtzettel*, 21.

364. Lederer, *Madness*, 52f.; Boer, *Conquest*, 77–79, 177f.

365. Quantin, *Le rigorisme*, esp. 18f.; Spiertz, *L'église*, 90f.

366. As reproduced by the Jesuits in Van Hoeck, "Romeinische correspondentie," 120.

367. E.g., Bruno, *Brevis tractatio*, 62–67, esp. 65f. The book concludes with a mediation on the Eucharist.

368. Cf. Dougherty, *From Altar-Throne*, 1–41.

369. Andrés Martin, "La espiritualidad," 265f.

370. O'Malley, *First Jesuits*, 152

371. For examples, see Villaret, "Les premières origines," 46; for context, see Jiménez Pablo, "La lucha," 127–31; Gennaro, "Mistica Gesuitica," 187f.

372. PolChron 2:23, 589, 625 and passim.

373. Dudon, "Le 'Libellus'" (quotations on p. 270); de Madrid, *De frequenti usu*, fol. Aiij[r].

374. Cf., e.g., Hogan, "Jansenism," who also discusses their impact.

375. Arnauld, *De la fréquente communion*, fol. aiij[r]. On the origin of this work, see the helpful essay by Mochizuki, "La conversion."

376. Quotation taken from Opfermann (ed.), *Geschichte*, 2:133. Cf. Arnauld, *De la fréquente communion*, fol. eij[v]. For earlier parallels, see O'Malley, *First Jesuits*, 154.

377. MonPaed 3:286; Nadal, *Scholia*, 114; Bouuaert-Claeys, "Une visite," 64, 83; Feitler, "Le refus," 214 (with quotation).

378. Dougherty, *From Altar-Throne*, 8.

379. Toledo, *In Summam* 4:282 (with Bonaventura); Toledo, *Summa casuum*, 604–6, is briefer and less explicit.

380. Perlín, *Sacrum convivium*, 231–84, esp. 249.

381. Not only on feast days and holidays but at every mass: Opfermann (ed.), *Geschichte*, 2:17.

382. O'Malley, *First Jesuits*, 156.

383. Opfermann (ed.), *Geschichte*, 133.

384. ARSI Germ Sup 8, fol. 370^r, 375^{r-v}; BayHStA M Jes 665, unfol. (September 11, 1657).

385. For an example, see Sander, *Geschichte*, 839, 841.

386. Stenmans, *Litterae annuae*, 43.

387. Opfermann (ed.), *Geschichte*, 1:28.

388. Sander, *Geschichte*, 1041.

389. For examples, see Opfermann (ed.), *Geschichte*, 1:57, 206, 207, 303; 2:35; Sander, *Geschichte*, 927.

390. Opfermann (ed.), *Geschichte*, 1:268.

391. Suggested by Stenmans, *Litterae annuae*, 41, 70, 73.

392. Stenmans, *Litterae annuae*, 79.

393. Myers, *"Poor, Sinning Folk,"* 189f.; Boer, *Conquest*, 182f., is more critical.

394. Cf. the title of the book by Bilinkoff, *Related Lives*.

395. On this subject in general, see Zarri and Filoramo (eds.), *Storia*; Catto (ed.), *Direzione spirituale tra ortodossia*; Catto (ed.), *La direzione spirituale tra medioevo*. For an overview, see Egido, *Los jesuitas*, 124–27. For an important contextualization, see also Prosperi, *Tribunali*, 489f. See also Sluhovsky, *Becoming*.

396. Bilinkoff, *Related Lives*, 17–27; Zarri, "Introduzione."

397. Guilloré, *La Manière*, 324.

398. Guilloré, *La Manière*, 4.

399. Guilloré, *Maximes spirituelles*, 1f.

400. Ex §§ 4, 8–10, 18–20.

401. Guilloré, *La Manière*, unfol. (preface), 121.

402. Guilloré, *Maximes spirituelles*, 37–55.

403. Guilloré, *La Manière*, 355–58; Guilloré, *Maximes spirituelles*, 94–97.

404. Guilloré, *La Manière*, 339.

405. Pirri, "Il P. Achille Gagliardi," 3–7. The following quotations are taken from this source.

406. Mostaccio, "Per via."

407. Gagliardi, *Breve compendio*; on the composition of these texts, cf. also Bilinkoff, *Related Lives*, 41–44; Pirri, "Il P. Achille Gagliardi," 10f.

408. See esp. Le Valois, *Œuvres* (1726), 2:1–90 (quotation on p. 9).

409. Le Valois, *Œuvres* (1726), 2:64.

410. Quoted in Lozano Navarro, "Los jesuitas," 123.

411. Quoted in Arranz Roa, "Las Casas Profesas," 128f.

412. RAA Jes 2844, unfol. (May 30, 1682).

413. Bibliothèque de l'Arsenal ms 3384, fol. 53–60, "Extraits des livres de Père Guilloré."

414. Quoted in Stroppa, "Il direttore," 414f.

415. Orlandi, "L. A. Muratori," 198–226 (quotations on pp. 198, 227, 205, 220).

416. In general, see Châtellier, *Religion*; Novi Chavarria, *Il governo*. For biographical information, see Guidetti, *Le missioni*.

417. Fiorani, "Missioni."

418. Quoted in Fiorani, "Missioni," 220; see p. 220 further on the lack of teachers, especially for children.

419. Orlandi, "L. A. Muratori," 198 (quoting Paolo Segneri the Younger).

420. Lazar, *Working*, 25f.

421. Reminisc. no. 95.

422. Cf., e.g., Parente, "Nicolo Bobadilla e gli esordi"; Parente, "Nicolas Bobadilla (1509–1590)."

423. Luongo, *Silvestro Landini*. Cf. also Moresco, "1552."

424. Copete and Vincent, "Missions," 275f., call this "nearby missions."

425. For a chronology, see Novi Chavarria, *Il governo*, 44f.; Majorana, "Une pastorale"; Majorana, "La pauvreté"; Palomo, "Malos panes"; Johnson, "Blood," 182–202, 272–75.

426. The essential texts are collected and translated in Lécrivain, "Les missions."

427. Cf., e.g., Boschet, *Le parfait missionnaire*, 273f., 276 and passim.

428. Novi Chavarria, *Il governo*, 91, with an explicit quotation.

429. Copete and Palomo, "Des carêmes," 369; Palomo, "Limosnas impresas," 242f.

430. This is illustrated very impressively in Lebec (ed.), *Miracles*, 81f.

431. Order for whips (1715) from Bers, "Jülich," 203. On flagellation, see Majorana, "L'Arte"; Majorana, "Le missioni"; Largier, *In Praise*, 175–98; Novi Chavarria, *Il governo*, 58f. For Spain, see Broggio, "L'Acto," 237.

432. Palomo, "Malos panes," 19–23.

433. Boschet, *Le parfait missionnaire*, 296.

434. Quoted in Rico Callado, "Las misiones," 108n16.

435. Paolucci, *Missioni*, 23.

436. Segneri, *Pratica*, 150f.

437. Fiorani, "Missioni"; Rico Callado, "Las misiones," 109f. On lighting effects, see Palomo, "Limosnas impresas," 245f.

438. Palomo, "Malos panes," 7–12. On the transition to full-time employment: Broggio, "L'Acto," 233f. On the semantics, cf. the article by Majorana, "Missionarius/concionator."

439. On lumber, cf. Segneri, *Pratica*, 104; for improvised sermons, see Lebec (ed.), *Miracles*, 59; Palomo, "Malos panes," 17. On the weather, see Lebec (ed.), *Miracles*, 90.

440. Oswald (ed.), *"Auch auf Erd,"* 61.

441. Deslandres, *Croire*, 159–171. For an example, see Orlandi, "L. A. Muratori," 168.

442. Paolucci, *Missioni*, 24. On weeping, see Copete and Palomo, "Des carêmes," 368.

443. Segneri, *Pratica*, 157.

444. Majorana, "L'Arte," 213–19.

445. For a good example, see Orlandi, "L. A. Muratori," 230f.

446. Segneri, *Pratica*, 99–101.

447. See the texts collected in Lécrivain, "Les missions."

448. Châtellier, *Religion*, 188.

449. For Spain, see Broggio, "L'Acto," 237; for Germany, see Johnson, "Blood," 193. Maunoir makes no mention of flagellation: Boschet, *Le parfait missionnaire*, 270–306.

450. Palomo, "Malos panes," 8f. and passim; Egido, *Los jesuitas*, 167f.

451. For the Lower Rhine, see Bers, "Jülich"; Brzosa, *Geschichte*, 297–300; for the Upper Palatinate, see Johnson, "Blood." On the translation of Fontana's sermons, see Ettlin, *Dr. Johann Baptist Dillier*, 215.

452. Orlandi, "L. A. Muratori," 280, 281 (ball), 285 (pomp). Cf. also Fiorani, "Missioni."

453. See Nanni, "Réformistes," 265 (quotation).

454. For bans in Bavaria, see Johnson, "Blood"; for (disregarded) bans in Jülich in 1702, see Bers, "Jülich," 198; Duhr 4.2:195. For bans in Molsheim in 1717 and 1742, see Barth, "Die Seelsorgetätigkeit," 367f.

455. Lazzarelli may have drawn some inspiration from the Jansenists, given that he quoted the most important critic of flagellation against the Jesuits, namely, Boileau, *Histoire*; cf. Orlandi, "L. A. Muratori," 282f.

456. Broggio, "L'Acto," 237f.; on nighttime in Europe, see Koslofsky, *Evening's Empire*; on respect for working hours, cf. Segneri, *Pratica*, 97; Schüller, "Die Eifelmission," 91.

457. Orlandi, "L. A. Muratori," 166–69.

458. Polenghi, "Militia."

459. Schüller, "Die Eifelmission," 92.

460. Shore, *The Eagle*, 121f.

461. Vismara Chiappa, "L'abolizione."

462. Rosa, *Settecento religioso*, 251–56.

463. Boschet, *Le parfait missionnaire*, 280.

464. See Füssenich, "Die Volksmission," 128n1.

465. Segneri, *Pratica*, 107a–b.

466. Oswald (ed.), *"Auch auf Erd,"* 30 (Oswald's introduction); Deslandres, *Croire*, 166 with references. Cf. Lebec (ed.), *Miracles*, 58: "méfiance." Cf. also p. 69 and passim.

467. Quotation taken from Van der Veldt, *Franz Neumayr*, 28n68.

468. Orlandi, "L. A. Muratori," 229.

469. Lebec (ed.), *Miracles*, 59.

470. Bers, "Jülich," 188f.

471. Palomo, "Limosnas impresas"; Bers, "Jülich," 198. On parish priests and missions, see Schüller, "Die Eifelmission," 86f.

472. Johnson, "Blood," 195–202; Sieber, *Jesuitische Missionierung*, 28, 134–51.

473. Lebec (ed.), *Miracles*, 59, 65 and passim; Novi Chavarria, *Il governo*, 87f.

474. Brzosa, *Geschichte*, 298n322.

475. On the number and concentration of missions, see Copete and Vincent, "Missions," 261–71.

476. Lebec (ed.), *Miracles*, 55f.

477. Lebec (ed.), *Miracles*, 88f.

478. Novi Chavarria, *Il governo*, 96–100.

479. Selwyn, *Paradise*, 81f.

480. For examples, see Schinosi, *Istoria*, 2:93; Orlandi, "L. A. Muratori," 281f.; Deslandres, *Croire*, 162.

481. Châtellier, *Religion*, 185 and passim. Put in a broader context, the theory that Europe was not really Christianized until the late Middle Ages derives from Jean Delumeau. Cf. also Copete and Palomo, "Des carêmes," 364.

482. See O'Reilly, "Spiritual Exercises."

483. E.g., Palmer, *On Giving*, 105–9, 159, 293, 304–7.

484. SJ (ed.), *Epistolae* (1847), 1:276–79; Palmer, *On Giving*, 292–94.

485. Gisolfo, *Vita*, 55f.

486. On Borromeo, see Iparraguirre (ed.), *Historia*, 2:20; Giussano, *Life of St. Charles Borromeo*, 109f.; Hayden, *Catholicisms*, 163–66.

487. Iparraguirre (ed.), *Historia*, 3:17.

488. Inst 1:180f.; Iparraguirre (ed.), *Historia*, 3:245f.

489. Mostaccio, "Shaping"; Quéniart, "La 'retraite de Vannes'"; Iparraguirre (ed.), *Historia*, 3:20–44; Rosignoli, *Notizie*, 43–47. On the chaotic beginnings, see Chaurand, "Copie," 316.

490. Champion, *Vie du Père Vincent Huby*, 57; Rosignoli, *Notizie*, 43. Cf. Huby, *Œuvres*, 388f. A century after Huby, exercitants there are divided into three groups: clergymen, laymen, and women.

491. Guilloré, *Einsamkeit*.

492. Surin, *Correspondance*, 1529–33.

493. Croiset, *Retraite spirituelle*, 1:4f.

494. Le Valois, *Œuvres* (1726), e.g., 2:200f.

495. Huby, *Œuvres*, 362–88 (quotation on p. 380).

496. Croiset, *Retraite spirituelle*, 1–5 (quotations on p. 3f.), 28.

497. Ranum (ed.), *Beginning*, 128.

498. Croiset, *Retraite spirituelle*, 16.

499. Chaurand, "Copie," 326.

500. Champion, *Vie du Père Vincent Huby*, 65f.

501. Chaurand, "Copie," 317, 327f.; Champion, *Vie du Père Vincent Huby*, 68.

502. Across classes: Champion, *Vie du Père Vincent Huby*, 58; Quéniart, "La 'retraite de Vannes,'" 552. Watered down: Le Valois, *Œuvres* (1758), 1:xvij. On habits: Chaurand, "Copie," 318.

503. Iparraguirre (ed.), *Historia*, 3:173–77, 3:189–93. Despite his own abridgment, de la Palma still stressed the four-week duration as ideal: *Praxis*, 9.

504. Chaurand, "Copie," 343.

505. SJ (ed.), *Epistolae* (1847), 1:278.

506. For the number, see Iparraguirre (ed.), *Historia*, 3:86.

507. Chaurand, "Copie," 336, 342f.

508. Châtellier, *Religion*, 47.

509. Schüller, "Die Eifelmission," 115.

510. Orlandi, "L. A. Muratori," 288f.

511. On Spinelli, see Selwyn, *Paradise*, passim On Naples, see Iparraguirre (ed.), *Historia*, 3:173, 3:200–225, 3:233.

512. Iparraguirre (ed.), *Historia*, 3:284–86; Debiaggi, "Una testimonianza"; Novi Chavarria, *Il governo*, 50, 292 on Carafa, and passim on the training of priests in southern Italy.

513. Molina, *To Overcome*, 131–37.

514. Coreth, "Priesterliches Wirken," 82.

515. See the contributions to Dompnier and Vismara (eds.), *Confréries*, and Terpstra (ed.), *The Politics*; Terpstra, *Lay Confraternities*.

516. Mallinckrodt, *Struktur*, 97, 131.

517. EpSalm 1:107f.

518. Lewis, "Development." On Parma, see Villaret, "Les premières origines," 42–44.

519. See Lazar, "First Jesuit Confraternities"; Lazar, *Working*.

520. On the cost of sermons, see McManners, *Church*, 2:58f.

521. See Mullan, *The Sodality*; Villaret, *Les congrégations mariales*; Châtellier, *L'Europe*; Châtellier, "À l'origine"; O'Malley, *First Jesuits*, 192–199. For predecessors, see Villaret, "Les premières origines"; Crasset, *Des congrégations*, 9. On Leunis, see Wicki, *Le père Leunis*.

522. Coreth, "Die ersten Sodalitäten"; Lewis, "The Development," 221–27; Châtellier, "Les premières congrégations."

523. Crasset, *Des congrégations*, 38f. Cf. Mallinckrodt, *Struktur*, 132, 140–43, 211; Schneider, "Reform," 219, 221. On a sodality of women in Erfurt, 1622, see Meisner, *Nachreformatorische Frömmigkeitsformen*, 27, 50–58.

524. For a list, see Crasset, *Des congrégations*, 85–128.

525. Coreth, "Die ersten Sodalitäten," 42–48.

526. Meisner, *Nachreformatorische Frömmigkeitsformen*, 49.

527. For numbers, see Mullan, *The Sodality*, 30f.

528. Crasset, *Des congrégations*, 14f.

529. Lewis, "The Development," 215f.; Mallinckrodt, *Struktur*, 146f.

530. Quotation from Brzosa, *Geschichte*, 453. An analogous example may be found from 1575 in Cologne, cited in Châtellier, "À l'origine," 204f.

531. Crasset, *Des congrégations*, 70–74, 81; Coster, *Libellus*, 192–342.

532. Miller, "Die marianischen Kongregationen," 99.

533. Mallinckrodt, *Struktur*, 16–20, 47, 154 with n. 100 and passim.

534. Le Valois, *Œuvres* (1726), 2:236–46.

535. Quotation taken from Rädle, "Jesuit Theatre," 262.

536. Deslandres, *Croire*, 153; Dompnier, *Le venin*. On the early phase, see Schatz, "Deutschland"; O'Malley, *First Jesuits*, 272–83.

537. Cf. Inst 1:4 and 1:23.

538. MonPaed 3:335.

539. MonFab, 159f.

540. EpIgn 12:260.

541. MonPaed 3:335f.

542. MonPaed 3:336.

543. On the early phase, see O'Malley, *First Jesuits*, 115–26.

544. Begheyn, "The Catechism."

545. Hendrickson, *Jesuit Polymath*, 50–63. For an overview, see Carter, *Creating Catholics*, esp. 30f., 64f. See now also Flüchter and Wirbser (eds.), *Translating*.

546. EpIgn 7:399–403.

547. For an overview, see Herzig, *Der Zwang*, esp. 95–118.

548. Johnson, *Magistrates*; Châtellier, *Tradition chrétienne*, esp. 269–94.

549. Burkhardt and Habermehl (eds.), *Die Neustadter Pfarrchronik*, 67.

550. Steinwascher, "Die konfessionellen Folgen," esp. 62–65 (quotation on p. 63n56).

551. See, in general, Schatz, "Deutschland."

552. EpIgn 12:262; MonPaed 3:54, 337, 498f.; MonPaed 4:486f. Cf. Mancia, "La controversia."

553. For instance, in their teachings about original sin: see Schubert, *Das Ende*.

554. Cf., e.g., Galeota, "La teologia."

555. For a late example, see Herzig, *Manuale controversisticum*. Cf., e.g., p. 8 on how to deal with opponents who claim to possess "the truth."

556. Kaufmann, *Konfession*, 243–49.

557. Frusius [des Freux], *Epigrammata*. Cf. also the many poems in Masen, *Ars nova*.

558. Frusius, *Epigrammata*, fol. 18^r, epigram no. 83, lines 3–4: "Materia haec adeo nam foetet, ut orta cloacam | Vix tactam cogat nausea iam fugere" (This substance/subject matter is already so foul that as soon as it emerges it forces the sewer to flee from nausea having hardly touched it).

559. Examples and analyses in Bremer, *Religionsstreitigkeiten*; Niemetz, *Antijesuitische Bildpublizistik*.

560. For a nice example, see Opfermann (ed.), *Geschichte*, 1:26. Cf. also Kaufmann, *Konfession*, 249–54.

561. Questier, "'Like Locusts.'"

562. BayHStA Jes 253, fol. 5^r on the geographic works of Matthäus Merian.

563. Clm 24076, fol. 66^r.

564. BayHStA Jes 641, fol. 8^r–9^v. For a similar case, see MonPaed 7:555–61 (Poland).

565. Cf. the reference to Germany in Bellarmine's words in Tutino, *Empire*, 331n20, and in BayHStA Jes 641, fol. 26^{r-v}.

566. Quotations compiled from Neumayr, *Heilige Streitt-Reden*, vol. 1, "Vorrede an den Leser," and p. 162.

567. Neumayr, *Heilige Streitt-Reden*, 1:167.

568. Neumayr, *Heilige Streitt-Reden*, 1:154 (marginal note), 163.

569. Neumayr, *Heilige Streitt-Reden*, 1:156.

570. Neumayr, *Heilige Streitt-Reden*, vol. 1, title page. For a very similar comment, see EpIgn 7:399.

571. For case studies, see Nugent, *Ecumenism*; Bauer, "Das Regensburger Religionsgespräch."

572. Santarelli, *Tractatus*, 87–124.

573. Stillig, *Jesuiten*, 73–91.

574. McCoog, "'Playing the Champion,'" 159f.

575. Now available in Latin and English translation in Houliston et al. (eds.), *Correspondence*, 79f. and 82. Pierre Coton (quoted in Dompnier, *Le venin*, 177) was of a different opinion.

576. Opfermann (ed.), *Geschichte*, 1:47.

577. Flucke (ed.), *Die litterae annuae*, 1:187, *a.* 1655. See now also Friedrich, "Jesuiten und Lutheraner."

578. Krumenacker, *L'école française*, 308–12.

579. Parker, *Faith*, 42: in contrast to apostolic vicars, the Jesuits permitted Catholics to study in Leiden and invest in the Dutch East India Company.

580. Questier, "Like Locusts," 357 with n. 36.

581. For an example, see Stenmans, *Litterae annuae*, 117, 133f.; Gerard, *Autobiography*, 209.

582. Houliston et al. (eds.), *Correspondence*, 387 (Italian), 399 (English).

583. SJ, *Florus anglo-bavaricus*, 30.

584. Gerard, *Autobiography*, 207.

585. Both points are brought up in Forschungsbibliothek Gotha Chart A 298, fol. 153^{r-v}.

586. For examples, see Stenmans, *Litterae annuae*, 110, 116; Opfermann (ed.), *Geschichte*, 2:47f.

587. For an example, see Gerard, *Autobiography*, 207.

588. Sander, *Geschichte*, 712, 713.

589. Stenmans, *Litterae annuae*, 152.

590. For an exception, noted as such, see Stenmans, *Litterae annuae*, 141.

591. Barth, "Die Seelsorgetätigkeit," 331f.

592. For examples from Erfurt, see Meisner, *Nachreformatorische Frömmigkeitsformen*, 18.

593. In general, see Garstein, *Rome*; Parker, *Faith*. "Prudence" is therefore indispensable: Hicks (ed.), *Letters*, 316.

594. Nadasi, *Annus dierum*, 6.

595. Forbes-Leith (ed.), *Memoirs*, 1:76.

596. Begheyn, "Pastoral Journeys," 190, 191, 194, etc.

597. Quotation from Garstein, *Rome*, 2:255f.

598. ARSI Germ Sup 8, fol. 370^v.

599. BayHStA Jes 1079, p. 22 (1586, school instruction).

600. Quotations from Brennan, "John Bargrave."

601. Marti, "Gesellschaftliches Leben," 200.

602. Spener, *Insignium*, "Ad lectorem."

603. Hoffmann, "Theodor Moretus," 150–53.

604. Pohle, "Jakob Masen," 109.

605. Hengst, *Jesuiten*, 77 (Rinteln visits Osnabruck, Altdorf visits Bamberg).

606. Barth, "Die Seelsorgetätigkeit," 366; Opfermann (ed.), *Geschichte*, 2:119f.; Kast (ed.), *Die Jahresberichte*, 109, 167.

Chapter Three

1. FontNarr 2:494; FontNarr 3:611.

2. Hufton, "Altruism"; Hufton, "Faith," 592f. Quotation: Schurhammer, *Franz Xaver*, 1:461.

3. EpIgn 1:134–36.

4. Quotation from Bartoli, *Della vita*, 493: "a cui [sc. a pontifice] era carissimo." Cf. also Lucas, *Landmarking*, 92f.

5. Burrieza Sánchez, "La fundación."

6. Lozano Navarro, *La Compañía*, 173–75 (quotation on p. 175).

7. Cf. parallels from Mantua in Hufton, "Faith," 597. In general, see Hufton, "Every Tub."

8. Carrasco Martínez, "Los Mendoza"; Cavallo, *Charity*, 98–152.

9. Hufton, "Faith," 587.

10. E.g., Bibliotheque Royal Brüssel ms Jes. 4861 and 7052.

11. Scribani, *Superior religiosus*, 92–104.

12. For an example, see ARSI Rom 205, fol. 18^r. For criticism on the absence of these points, cf. BayHStA Jes 253, fol. 2^v (no. 20).

13. Errichetti, "L'antico Collegio," 220.

14. Bangert, *A History*, 105.

15. Madonia, *La Compagnia*, passim.

16. Dupont-Ferrier, *Vie quotidienne*, 3:1–11.

17. Rochemonteix, *Le Collège*, 1:35–61, esp. 52–57 on the conditions in which it was founded.

18. Rurale, *Monaci*, 49–56.

19. Const no. 624.

20. Burrieza Sánchez, "La fundación," 479–83; Giard, "Jesuit College," 1–5; Venard, "Y a-t-il une 'stratégie scolaire,'" 79f.

21. Bösel, *Jesuitenarchitektur*, 2:157.

22. Const no. 622.

23. Copete and Vincent, "Missions," 263f.

24. Rosa, "Strategia."

25. On the Capuchins, see Novi Chavarria, *Il governo*, 32; on the Recollects, see Meyer, *Pauvreté*, 51.

26. Turtas, *La nascita*, 53–57 and passim.

27. ARSI Germ Sup 6, 393–95.

28. EpIgn 4:412; Lucas, *Landmarking*, 140f.; Fonseca, "Collegio e città." On exceptions such as Padova, Straubing, and Hall in Tirol, cf. Schwab, "Das Jesuitenkollegium," 47f.

29. Lombaerde, "The Facade."

30. Cf. the example of Valladolid 1579/80 in Arranz Roa, "Las Casas Profesas," 146–48.

31. Arranz Roa, "Las Casas Profesas," 160–62.

32. Paolucci, *Missioni*, 4.

33. On Colombia: quotation taken from Pacheco, *Los Jesuitas*, 161.

34. Surin, *Correspondance*, 1418f., 1430, 1643f., 1652, 1659f.

35. Ignatius of Loyola, *Spiritual Diary* (included in Ex, trans. Munitz and Endean).

36. Arranz Roa, "Las Casas Profesas."

37. On conventional acquisition strategies, see Assunção, *Negócios*, 105, 113f.

38. AD Loir-et-Cher D 8; AD Loir-et-Cher 11 H 114, fol. 29^r.

39. Müller, "Zur Finanzierung," 158–68.

40. Const no. 561; Lugo, *Responsa moralia*, 183–89; Bouuaert-Claeys, "Une visite," 63; Borja Medina, "El esclavo," 90.

41. ARSI Germ 171, fol. 90^r–101^v, 123^r–124^v, 331^r–332^r.

42. See in general Paringer, *Die bayerische Landschaft*. I wish to thank Dr. Paringer for his additional information in an email from December 12, 2014.

43. Duhr, "Die deutschen Jesuiten"; Duhr 1:713–30; Braunsberger 6:287, 390f., 403, 410, 416f., 7:10f., 16, 129, 156f., etc.; Flynn, "Jasper Heywood."

44. Vismara, "Les jésuites."

45. EpIgn 6:483f., 630f.

46. Van Houdt, "'Lack of Money.'"

47. This chronology follows Vismara, "Les jésuites." See also Guitton, "En marge de l'histoire," 64–69.

48. Schlachta, "Stiftungen," 272.

49. Maher, "Financing Reform," 135.

50. Thompson, "The Lavalette Affair," 211.

51. Konrad, *Jesuit Hacienda*, 77.

52. Müller, "Zur Finanzierung," 156.

53. Arranz Roa, "Las Casas Profesas," 137, 140.

54. Astrain, *Historia*, 5:40–44.

55. Kast (ed.), *Die Jahresberichte*, 28. This was reported because they were finally (in 1673) able to move the activities into a dedicated house, thus restoring the peace they had missed.

56. Kast (ed.), *Die Jahresberichte*, 42.

57. Cf. Herzig, "Die Jesuiten."

58. For a survey, see Thummerer, "Besitzgeschichte." For further details, see Graf, *Geschichte*.

59. The college in Koblenz in 1600, for example, became involved in a long dispute with the peasants in the village of Güls. The dispute was about the extent to which the peasants could be compelled to perform labor for the Jesuits during the vintage: Landeshauptarchiv Koblenz 117/440, fasc. I. See Friedrich, *Der lange Arm*, 431–33; in general, Herzig, "Die Jesuiten."

60. Dolinar, *Das Jesuitenkolleg*, 106–23.

61. Didier, "Entre l'Europe." On the Carmelites, see Windler, "Regelobservanz," 56–58.

62. See Clossey, *Salvation*.

63. Assunção, *Negócios*, 151.

64. Hausberger, *Für Gott*, 452–57.

65. Rea, *Economics*, 48, on this and on the distinction to the Dominicans.

66. Alden, *Making*, 380.

67. Negro, "Arquitectura," 451f., on Peru.

68. Alden, *Making*, 407.

69. Cushner, *Jesuit Ranches*, 49–65.

70. In general, see Thompson, "The Lavalette Affair."

71. Alden, *Making*, 412f., makes this very clear.

72. Alden, *Making*, 529–51; Borges, *Economics*, passim.

73. Assunção, *Negócios*, 115f.

74. Schlachta, "Stiftungen."

75. Assunção, *Negócios*, 127–30.

76. Konrad, *Jesuit Hacienda*, 70f., with an explicit quotation.

77. E.g., Cushner, *Jesuit Ranches*, 40f.; Konrad, *Jesuit Hacienda*, 126–51.

78. Friedrich, *Der lange Arm*, 214–16.

79. ARSI Fondo Gesuitico 678, unfol. (no. 14).

80. See Centorrino, *Il trattato*; Quattrone, "Accounting."

81. Orlandi, "L. A. Muratori," 221–24.

82. Alden, *Making*, 405f., 427–29; Hausberger, *Für Gott*, 440.

83. BayHStA Jes 14.

84. For an example, see Stenmans, *Litterae annuae*, 50.

85. Pierre, *La monarchie ecclésiale*.

86. On Vienna, see Bireley, *Jesuits*.

87. Reinhardt, "Spin Doctor." Now see also the author's major monograph: Reinhardt, *Voices*.

88. Dudik, "Korrespondenz," 268, 278.

89. Pierre, *La monarchie ecclésiale*, 84, on Louis XII.

90. Richelieu, *Lettres*, 2:155–58. See also Pierre, *La monarchie ecclésiale*, 361f.; Bergin, "The Royal Confessor," 189f.

91. Schröer (ed.), *Die Korrespondenz*, 453–55 (*bona conscientia*).

92. Leibniz I/20, p. 148f., etc. Quotation taken from Leibniz I/21, p. 477.

93. Fouqueray, *Histoire*, 3:468–74.

94. Cf. Bireley, *Maximilian*; Bireley, *Religion*.

95. On Lamormaini's everyday work, see Dudik, "Korrespondenz," 260, 268, 272.

96. Dudik, "Korrespondenz," 270, 277.

97. Bireley, *Jesuits*, 225.

98. Hansen, "Briefe."

99. Rurale, "Confessori," 304f.

100. Fleischer, "Father Wolff."

101. Pierre, *La monarchie ecclésiale*; Bergin, "The Royal Confessor." See now also Reinhardt, *Voices*.

102. Negredo del Cerro, "La hacienda."

103. Rurale, "Confessori," 296f.

104. Guillaume-Alonso, "Les jésuites d'Olivares." Quotation taken from López Arandia, "Velando," 264 with n. 39, 268. On Bermúdez and Philip V, see Tessé, *Mémoires*, 2:351f.

105. Alcaraz Gómez, *Jesuitas*, 442 (with quotation).

106. Langewiesche and Westphal (eds.), *Die Briefe*, 243f.

107. Quotation taken from Alcaraz Gómez, *Jesuitas*, 399.

108. Bergin, "The Royal Confessor."

109. Quotations taken from Hengerer, *Kaiser Ferdinand III*, 426f., n. 72); cf. Bireley, "Acquaviva's 'Instruction,'" 64.

110. Lozano Navarro, "Los jesuitas," 115–17.

111. Gay, "Voués à quel royaume?"

112. See Fernández Terricabras, "Surviving."

113. Lucca, *Jesuits and Fortifications*, 123, 142.

114. Fouqueray, *Histoire*, 3:470f.

115. Tessé, *Mémoires et lettres*, 2:365.

116. Ex § 40.

117. Bireley, "Acquaviva's 'Instruction'"; Inst 3:281–84.

118. Batllori, "Los Jesuitas."

119. ARSI Germ 111, fol. 339ᵛ.

120. Rurale, "Confessori"; Rurale, "Il confessore."

121. Quoted in Forer, *Anatomia*, 34; Argenti, *Apologeticus*, 41; cf. Noringus, *Dissertatio*, 164–66. On the following, see Höpfl, *Jesuit Political Thought*.

122. Nieremberg, *Theopoliticus*, 340–45, 347f. On the author, see Chaparro Martínez, "Juan Eusebio de Nieremberg."

123. On Jesuit anti-Machiavellianism, see Chaparro Martínez, "Maquiavelo"; Barbuto, *Il principe*, 249–76; SJ, *Leontius*.

124. Nieremberg, *Corona virtuosa.*

125. Tutino, *Empire;* Frajese, "Regno ecclesiastico."

126. For exceptions, see Barbuto, *Il principe,* 153 with n. 11.

127. On Bellarmin generally, see Motta, *Bellarmino.*

128. Höpfl, *Jesuit Political Thought,* 345 with quotation in n. 23.

129. In general, see Tutino, *Empire.*

130. Friedrich, *Der lange Arm,* 125–29; Broggio, *La teologia,* 88f.

131. Broggio, *La teologia;* Jiménez Pablo, "The Evolution."

132. Höpfl, *Jesuit Political Thought,* 224–62.

133. Höpfl, *Jesuit Political Thought,* 235 (quotation on p. 236).

134. In general, see Braun, *Juan de Mariana.*

135. Lezza, "I Decreti."

136. Fritsch, "Naturrecht."

137. Schwarz, *Institutiones,* 5–8, 55–57, 60–68, 228–30, 243–48.

138. Schwarz, *Institutiones,* 245.

139. Schwarz, *Institutiones,* 245 (*corruptela de potestate sacrorum, quam profanant protestantici Moralistae*); 427 (*infelix Protestantismus . . . male suffultus;* summary of positions, no. XXVIII).

140. Leturia, "Perché la Compagnia"; O'Malley, *First Jesuits,* 200–242.

141. Julia, "Entre universel," 17f.

142. Zanardi, "La 'Ratio.'"

143. O'Malley, *The Jesuits,* 115f.; Giard, "Jesuit College," 1f.

144. Aricò and Basile, "L'insediamento," 39.

145. Grendler, *Schooling,* 368.

146. Kraus, *Das Gymnasium,* 21 and passim.

147. For examples, see Carlsmith, "Struggling."

148. Fois, "Il Collegio Romano," 576; Villoslada, *Storia,* 23f.

149. Huppert, *Public Schools,* 104–29.

150. On German universities, see Hengst, *Jesuiten.*

151. Grendler, *University of Mantua,* 17–23. For cases in Italy, see now the monumental survey by Grendler, *Jesuits and Italian Universities.*

152. For an assessment, see Grendler, *University of Mantua,* 22. Cf. Sangalli, *Cultura,* 31–54, 317–22.

153. Turtas, *La nascita,* esp. 73f. on its elevation to a university.

154. Cf. O'Keefe, "Pedagogy."

155. Henryot and Henryot, "Savoirs," 70; Anagnostou, *Missionspharmazie.*

156. E.g., MonPaed 3:362–64, 377–82.

157. MonPaed 3:304–6.

158. MonPaed 7:590 (no. 10).

159. For Naples, see Errichetti, "L'antico Collegio," 232; for Germany, see Kraus, *Das Gymnasium,* 11.

160. Ratio, p. 424.

161. Ratio, p. 401.

162. Romano, *La Contre-Réforme.*

163. Ratio, pp. 383–84.

164. Ratio, pp. 420, 427, 424f.; Const no. 356. See Brader, "Die Entwicklung"; Dainville, *L'éducation*, 427–54; Puchowski, "Between *Orator Christianus*," 234.

165. Benci, *Orationes*, fol. 72ʳ–79ʳ.

166. MonPaed 7:639.

167. Neddermeyer, "Das katholische Geschichtslehrbuch."

168. Puchowski, "Between *Orator Christianus*," 235f.

169. Jouvency, *De ratione docendi*, 87–91. On the author, cf. Dainville, *L'éducation*, 209–66.

170. Pachtler (ed.), *Ratio Studiorum*, 4:107f.

171. Dainville, *L'éducation*, 437–44; Palasi, *Jeux de cartes*.

172. Grendler, *Schooling*, 372–76. On the social history of the students, see Kraus, *Das Gymnasium*, 31.

173. Dainville, *L'éducation*, 159, 291. For Munich, see Kraus, *Das Gymnasium*; Van der Veldt, *Franz Neumayr*, 30. Quotation taken from Dupont-Ferrier, *Vie quotidienne*, 1:64n2.

174. I wish to thank Dr. Martin Holý (Prague) for this information, sent by email December 10, 2014.

175. Mariani, "Le strategie educative," 304.

176. Mariani, "Le strategie educative," 308–12.

177. Brizzi, *La formazione*, list of schools on p. 25f.; Ferrante and Mattone, "Il Collegio"; Turrini, *Il "giovin signore."*

178. Turrini, *Il "giovin signore,"* 85–98, 165–81.

179. Conrads, *Ritterakademien*.

180. Bonifacio, *Institutio*, unpag. (*Dedicatio*).

181. Bonifacio, *Institutio*, fol. § 3ʳ, pp. 147–219 (*laus pueritiae*) (quotation on p. 211).

182. Sacchini, *Protrepticon*, 48–52.

183. Sacchini, *Paraenesis*, 38f.

184. Porteman, *Emblematic Exhibitions*, 26 (figure).

185. Ratio, p. 403.

186. MonPaed 3:397f.

187. Ratio, pp. 421, 425, 429, etc.

188. Ratio, pp. 428, 433.

189. Leinsle, "Dichtungen," 270–81, with the example of Dillingen.

190. Steiner, *Die Ordnung*; for an example from 1762, see Puchowski, "Between *Orator Christianus*," 244.

191. Porteman, "Use of the Visual"; Porteman, *Emblematic Exhibitions*, passim.

192. Lacotte, "La notion de jeu."

193. Palasi, *Jeux de cartes*, 79–102; Barthet, *Science*, 95f.

194. Lacotte, "La notion de jeu," 262.

195. O'Keefe, "Pedagogy."

196. Sacchini, *Paraenesis*, 39.

197. Sacchini, *Paraenesis*, 39–46.

198. Carlsmith, "Struggling," 236–38.

199. Cited in Turrini, *Il "giovin signore,"* 276.

200. Langewiesche and Westphal (eds.), *Die Briefe*, 48.

201. Cf., e.g., Grafton and Jardine, *From Humanism*.

202. For fundamental treatments, see Codina Mir, *Aux sources*; Scaglione, *The Liberal Arts*.

203. Huppert, *Style of Paris*.

204. Huppert, *Public Schools*, 47–60.

205. Codina Mir, *Aux sources*, 258–68 (quotation on p. 260).

206. Huppert, *Style of Paris*, 92–97.

207. Sacchini, *Protrepticon*, 2.

208. Anselmi, "Per un'archeologia"; Turrini, *Il "giovin signore,"* 214–16.

209. Périn, *Communis vitae*, unpag. (publisher's *dedicatio*).

210. Périn, *Communis vitae*, unpag. (publisher's *dedicatio*).

211. Masen, *Ars nova*, 123.

212. On cleanliness, see Turrini, *Il "giovin signore,"* 56–67. On "self-ownership," see Coleman, *Virtues*.

213. Anselmi, "Per un'archeologia."

214. Errichetti, "L'antico Collegio," 234.

215. Quoted in Capoccia and Lojacono, "Giulio Gori," 329.

216. Eickmeyer, "Kadavergehorsam?"

217. On "civilité" as the goal of education, see Croiset, *Règlements*.

218. In general, see Gill, *Educational Philosophy*; Snyders, *La pédagogie*, 345–55.

219. On common features, see Snyders, *La pédagogie*, 417, etc.

220. Quoted in Crosby, *Antigua California*, 431n68.

221. Blanchard, *Préceptes*. See the commendatory remarks in vol. 1, viii–xv.

222. Const no. 307f.

223. Ratio, p. 363.

224. SJ, *Florus anglo-bavaricus*, 31. See also Opsomer, "La science," 215; and, in general, Feingold, "Fama," 765f.

225. Van Damme, "Ecriture."

226. Begheyn, *Jesuit Books*, 19f., based on Sommervogel.

227. ARSI Rom 78c; MonPaed 4:486f.

228. Tüskés, *Johannes Nádasi*; Friedrich, "Circulating."

229. Baldini, *Legem impone*, 75–123. Cf. also Hellyer, "'Because the Authority'"; Biasiori, "Il controllo interno."

230. The office of *revisores* was eventually codified in the mid-seventeenth century; see Inst 3:65–68.

231. ARSI Germ Sup 8, fol. 377^{r-v}.

232. ARSI Germ Sup 12/II, fol. 159^r, 172^v–173^r.

233. See Aricò, "Fra teologia."

234. Heigel, "Geschichte des Censurwesens"; BayHStA Jes 84, unfol. (Landsberg, 1625).

235. BayHStA Jes 256, fol. 31^{r-v}; Inst 3:66 (no. 4). For dedications, see Van Damme, *Le temple*, 57, 91–113.

236. Siebert, "Kircher"; Stolzenberg, "Utility"; Stolzenberg, *Egyptian Oedipus*, 180–91.

237. BayHStA Jes 256, fol. 31^{r-v}.

238. ARSI Germ Sup 15/I, p. 176: a Jesuit author was permitted to decide where his book would go through the censorship process (1735).

239. Feingold, "Fama," 763, 772.

240. Stolzenberg, "Utility," 343f.

241. MonPaed 3:320f.

242. Boschet, *Le parfait missionnaire*, 17.

243. Le Valois, *Œuvres* (1758), 1:vj.

244. Feingold, "Fama," passim; Van Damme, *Le temple*, 54–60.

245. SJ, *Florus anglo-bavaricus*, 48: *Cum vitae nostrae ratio, & pia Fundatoris intentio in solem et pulveremque nos potius educat, quam in umbram litterariam scribendis libris vacare permittat: Mirum non esset, si pauca tantum litterarum monumenta nostrorum industria in lucem prodiissent.*

246. On Lyon, see Van Damme, *Le temple*, 207–474.

247. Dainville, "Projet d'un corps."

248. Const no. 372.

249. Inst 3:146.

250. Mech, "Les bibliothèques," 60.

251. MonPaed 4:420.

252. Ratio, p. 364; Dainville, "Livres de comptes."

253. See, in general, Martínez, "Las librerías."

254. Martínez, "Las librerías," 319.

255. Hansen (ed.), *Rheinische Akten*, 239.

256. Wallnig and Stockinger (eds.), *Die gelehrte Korrespondenz*, 1:90.

257. Quoted in Trombetta, "Libri e biblioteche," 130.

258. Trombetta, "Libri e biblioteche," 129.

259. Quoted in Errichetti, "L'antico Collegio," 237. For skepticism of such decoration, cf. Martínez, "Las librerías," 358.

260. Châtellier, "Genèse"; Guibovich Pérez, "Libros antiguos."

261. Trombetta, "Libri e biblioteche," 131f.

262. Mech, "Les bibliothèques," 61.

263. Krempel, "Die Orbansche Sammlung."

264. See Leibniz I/24, p. 120 (Leibniz to LeLong, November 11, 1704). During the following years, Orban exchanged many letters with Leibniz, though mostly on matters of religious policy.

265. Findlen, "Science."

266. Udías, *Searching*, 21–35.

267. Kircher, *Primitiae*, unpag. (dedicatory preface): *Nam immensa caelorum volumina in epitomen veluti quandam redacta, eo mox descripsit artificio et industria, ut illa caelorum miracula, ad quae penetranda nullum hactenus sufficiens erat oculorum acumen, clare et absque difficultate conspicienda ac pervolvenda coram mox exhibuerit.*

268. Van Damme, "Sociabilité," 80f.

269. Romani, "Note"; Hein and Mader, "La Stamperia."

270. Martínez, "Las librerías," 330f. See p. 341f. on Villagarcía.

271. Braunsberger 2:528f. (*nota*).

272. CG 7, d. 84, p. 276. It was discussed but not banned in 1558 at CG 1, d. 105, p. 9.

273. McShea, "Cultivating Empire," 48–60; O'Keefe, "Pedagogy," 433f.; Ronsin, "L'éditeur," esp. 352–57.

274. Van Damme, "Les livres," 15–18.

275. Golvers, "XVIIth-Century Jesuit Mission."

276. Hoffmann, "Theodor Moretus."

277. Begheyn, *Jesuit Books*, 33, 40.

278. Bosmans, "Théodore Moretus."

279. Begheyn, *Jesuit Books*, 8–13, 44f.

280. MonPaed 3:347.

281. Romano, "Les collèges jésuites," 10.

282. Quoted in Van Damme, "Sociabilité," 85.

283. Harris, "Confession-Building"; Harris, "Mapping"; Harris, "Long-Distance Corporations."

284. Ferlan, *Dentro e fuori*, 213–15; Shore, *The Eagle*, 173.

285. See Hoffmann, "Theodor Moretus."

286. Faux, "La fondation"; ARSI Epp NN 9, pp. 71–73.

287. Faux, "La fondation"; Sgard and Weil, "Les anecdotes"; Pappas, *Berthier's* Journal, 14.

288. For the estimate, see Harris, "Mapping," 223f.

289. Stepling, *Commercium*, 329–34.

290. Gaubil, *Correspondance*, 792f.

291. García Mateo, "San Ignacio."

292. Cf., e.g., O'Malley, *Saints or Devils*, 181–98.

293. O'Malley, *Saints or Devils*, 190–94; Maryks, *Saint Cicero*.

294. O'Malley, "Concluding Remarks," 517–19 (Const no. 728 = Cicero, *De officiis*, 1.20.66); Coupeau, *From Inspiration*.

295. EpIgn 1:519–26.

296. EpIgn 2:445f., 5:421f.

297. FontNarr 2:498.

298. Clm 9201, fol. 7^{r-v}.

299. EpIgn 4:99–106, 484; 5:94f.; Elizalde Armendáriz, "Luis Vives"; García Hernán, *Ignacio*, 190–92.

300. MonPaed 3:258f.

301. Bezzel, "Erasmusdrucke."

302. EpIgn 5:421f.

303. Clm 9201, fol. 7^{r-v}; EpIgn 7:612.

304. Albuquerque, "Historia," 17–19.

305. Frusius, *De utraque copia*.

306. Soarez, *De arte rhetorica*.

307. Grafton and Jardine, *From Humanism*.

308. Nelles, "*Libros de papel*." Now see also Nelles, *Information Order*, passim.

309. Clement, *Musei*, 479–518; Drexel, *Aurifodina*.

310. Pontanus, *Philokalia*.

311. Turner, *Philology*.

312. Sawilla, *Antiquarianismus*.

313. Rosweyde, *Fasti*. See p. 11f. on his working principles. See also Godding, "L'œuvre."

314. For the sixteenth century, see Boesch Gajano, "Delle raccolte."

315. Rosweyde, *Vitae patrum*.

316. Daub (ed.), *Auf heiliger Jagd*.

317. See Joassart (ed.), *Pierre-François Chifflet*; Babin, "Leibniz' Verbindungen"; UB Frankfurt Ms Ludolf (Briefe), s.v. "Papebroch."

318. Grafton, "Jean Hardouin" (the first of the following quotes is from p. 248).

319. BnF ms lat 3422, fol. 1^r.

320. In general, see Stolzenberg, *Egyptian Oedipus*; Findlen (ed.), *Athanasius Kircher*.

321. Kircher, *Arca Noë*, 16–30.

322. Breidbach and Ghiselin, "Athanasius Kircher."

323. Pena González, *La Escuela*; Belda Plans, *La Escuela*; Belda Plans, "Hacia una noción."

324. Belda Plans, *La Escuela*, 853–72; Baldini, *Legem impone*, 37f.

325. Bayón, "La escuela jesuitica"; Jansen, *Pflege der Philosophie*.

326. Belda Plans, "Hacia una noción," 380f.; Pozo, "La facoltà."

327. Belda Plans, *La Escuela*, 856f.

328. Biffi, "La figura."

329. Galdos (ed.), *Miscellanea*, 64.

330. Galdos (ed.), *Miscellanea*, 134. Cf. p. 138.

331. Galdos (ed.), *Miscellanea*, 127.

332. Cf. Stone, "Scholastic Schools"; Jansen, "Die scholastische Philosophie."

333. Schmutz, "Bellum scholasticum."

334. For examples, see Brockliss, *French Higher Education*, 338.

335. Pererius [Benito Pereira], *De communibus*, fol. ++^{r}.

336. Gioia, "Saggio introduttivo," 109; Leinsle, "Antike Lebenskonzepte," 815f.; MonPaed 3:414–16n4.

337. Belda Plans, *La Escuela*, 866–68; Motta, "Analisi."

338. Bremer, "Das Gutachten"; Bauer, "Jacob Pontanus," 85–87; Leinsle, "Werke," 114.

339. Bayón, "La escuela jesuitica"; Jansen, "Deutsche Jesuiten-Philosophen."

340. Rapin, *Réflexions*, 235. On Rapin, see Popkin, *Traditionalism*.

341. Ariew, *Descartes*, 140–54.

342. Errichetti, "L'antico Collegio," 244; De Ferrari, "DE BENEDICTIS"; Stella, *Il giansenismo*, 1:168–75.

343. Le Valois, *Sentimens*.

344. Bouillier, *Histoire*, 1:430f., 571–603.

345. Jansen, "Deutsche Jesuiten-Philosophen"; Jansen, "Philosophen katholischen Bekenntnisses," 35–45.

346. Ariew, *Descartes*, 140f., 152–54.

347. Alcaraz Gómez, *Jesuitas*, 555, 559–69.

348. Capoccia, "Modernità"; Jansen, "Die scholastische Philosophie," 437f.; Bayón, "La escuela jesuitica," 57–65. Tommaso Ceva was a parallel case; cf. Colombo, "Milano bilingue."

349. Gori, *Lettere filosofiche*, 3.

350. For Spain, see Guasti, "I gesuiti spagnoli" (2009), 57–60. For France, see Northeast, *Parisian Jesuits*.

351. Garagnon, "Les Mémoires."

352. Burson, "Claude G. Buffier"; Burson, "Crystallization"; Burson, "Abdication"; Burson, *Rise and Fall*.

353. Stone, "Scholastic Schools"; Bayón, "La escuela jesuitica," 65–71.

354. Lehner, "Benedict Stattler."

355. Fritsch, *Vernunft*; Jansen, *Pflege der Philosophie*, 78–81.

356. Northeast, *Parisian Jesuits*, 16–23.

357. Outram, *Enlightenment*.

358. See Friedrich, "Gottfried Wilhelm Leibniz."

359. Charma and Mancel (eds.), *Le Père André*, 99f.

360. Pappas, *Berthier's Journal*, 138–62.

361. Alcaraz Gómez, *Jesuitas*, 559f.

362. Pappas, "L'influence"; Pappas, *Berthier's Journal*, 85–137.

363. Ehrard, "Une 'amitié'"; Flamarion, "Castel, Father (S.J.)"; Pappas, *Berthier's Journal*, 65–84.

364. Bastid, "Montesquieu"; Flamarion, "Jesuites"; Pappas, *Berthier's Journal*, 67f.

365. Laboulaye (ed.), *Œuvres*, 361; Northeast, *Parisian Jesuits*, 6 with n. 19.

366. Marchal, *Madame de Lambert*, 244f., 366f.

367. Masson, *Madame de Tencin*, 60, 216.

368. Reilly, "A Catalogue."

369. Masseau, *Les ennemis*, 81.

370. Paschoud, *Le monde amérindien*, 1–6; Rétat, "Mémoires"; Pappas, *Berthier's Journal*.

371. For much smaller examples from the Benedictines, see Lehner, *Enlightened Monks*, 80–103.

372. In general, see Sgard and Weil, "Les anecdotes."

373. Pappas, *Berthier's Journal*; Masseau, *Les ennemis*, 120f.

374. For Spain, see Alcaraz Gómez, *Jesuitas*, 569; for China, see Golvers, *Libraries*, 78f., 106f.

375. González, *Die jesuitische Berichterstattung*.

376. Mariani, *I gesuiti*, 267–80.

377. *Journal de Trévoux* 47 (January 1747): 185. The concept of a moderate Catholic Enlightenment has received additional attention lately; see, e.g., Lehner, *Catholic Enlightenment*; Overhoff and Oberndorf (eds.), *Katholische Aufklärung*.

378. Quoted in Colombo, "Milano bilingue," 80.

379. In general, see Masseau, *Les ennemis*.

380. Israel, *Enlightenment Contested*, 840–62; Burson, *Rise and Fall*, 153–61; Pappas, *Berthier's Journal*, 163–96; Daoust, "Les Jésuites."

381. Masseau, *Les ennemis*, 120–23.

382. McMahon, *Enemies*.

383. Kelter, "Refusal."

384. Dollo, "Le ragioni."

385. Wallace, "Jesuit Influences"; Dear, "Jesuit Mathematical Science."

386. Romano, *La Contre-Réforme*.

387. E.g., Feldhay, "Knowledge," 198.

388. Steinmetz, *Die Gregorianische Kalenderreform*.

389. Dollo, "Le ragioni," 138–43.

390. For Grienberger and Grassi, see Feingold, "Grounds for Conflict"; Gorman, "Mathematics." For Biancani, see Reeves, *Painting*, 221–25.

391. Cf. Ceglia, "*Additio*," 159.

392. Dollo, "Le ragioni," 119 with n. 57.

393. In general, see Godman, *The Saint*; see specifically Pagano (ed.), *Documenti*, esp. 100–102, 125–28. Further on Bellarmine, see Baldini, *Legem impone*, 285–344.

394. Cf. Feingold, "Grounds for Conflict," 131f.

395. In general, see Kelter, "Refusal"; Remmert, "Picturing." Cf. Hellyer, *Catholic Physics*, 132. As early as 1604 in Jean Lorin: cf. Dollo, "Le ragioni," 113.

396. On the famous case of the temporary censorship of Biancani, cf., e.g., Ceglia, "*Additio*."

397. Reeves, *Painting*, 138–225.

398. On Riccioli, see Borgato (ed.), *Giambattista Riccioli*. On Bologna, see Cavazza, "La scienza"; Battistini, "La cultura scientifica."

399. Aricò, "'Yeux d'Argos.'"

400. Heilbron, *The Sun*, 188–97; Elazar, *Honoré Fabri*.

401. Pallavicino, *Lettere*, 1:141.

402. Quotation from Bosmans, "Théodore Moretus," 64. See further Bruycker, "'To the Adornment'"; Van der Vyver, "L'école"; Vanpaemel, "Jesuit Science."

403. Mercer, *Leibniz's Metaphysics*, 143, 157.

404. Van der Vyver, "Lettres."

405. On Belgium, see Vanpaemel, "Jesuit Mathematicians." For a survey, see Lucca, *Jesuits and Fortifications*. Poza's quotation taken from the epigram to Lucca's book.

406. Leitao, "Jesuit Mathematical Practice."

407. AFSJ Collection Brotier 37, fol. 76^{r-v}, 76^v–77^v.

408. Hoste, *Art des Armées navales*; Hoste, *Théorie*; Hoste, *Recueil*. See Ferreiro, *Ships and Science*, 259–62.

409. Lana Terzi, *Prodromo*, 52–74.

410. Fiocca, "Ferrara."

411. Konrad, *Jesuit Hacienda*, 64.

412. Gagliano and Ronan (eds.), *Jesuit Encounters*. For South America, see Asúa, *Science*, 164–210.

413. On d'Anville, see Ribeiro and O'Malley (eds.), *Jesuit Mapmaking*.

414. Cams, "Early Qing."

415. Bardell, "Hodierna's 'The Eye of the Fly'"; Armogathe, "L'œil vivant."

416. Asúa, *Science*, 113–47.

417. Reyes, "Botany"; see p. 263 for *botanicus*.

418. In general, see Anagnostou, *Missionspharmazie*, including Knuist in Münster and the pharmacy of the Collegio Romano.

419. Bisschop, *Pharmacia*.

420. Cf. Amidei, "Le decorazioni," 240–51.

421. For Pont-à-Mousson, I rely on Henryot and Henryot, "Savoirs."

422. Asúa, *Science*, 99–113.

423. Barthet, *Science*, 221–333; Baldwin, "Alchemy"; Matton, "Les théologiens"; Hellyer, *Catholic Physics*, 82.

424. Gábor, "'Difficiles nugae,'" 464f. On Kircher and alchemy, see Asmussen, "'Ein grausamer Alchemysten Feind,'" 226–32.

425. Lana Terzi, *Prodromo*, 109–21, esp. p. 112 ("quale io hò veduto").

426. Martin, "With Aristotelians," 146–48.

427. Vanpaemel, "Jesuit Science," 404f.

428. Gábor, "Johann Misch" (with English summary and edition of the most important pieces, as well as notes 38 and 43).

429. Anagnostou, *Missionspharmazie*, 313, for Trier.

430. Bisschop, *Pharmacia*, 319–26, here esp. 321f.

431. Menochius, *Hieropoliticon*, 369–71.

432. Pallavicino, *Opere*, 294 ("Al padre Michele d'Elizalda").

433. Leibniz II/1, p. 79f. (to Leibniz, June 7, 1670).

434. See, in general, Heilbron, *Electricity*.

435. Ugaglia, "Science of Magnetism."

436. Martin, "With Aristotelians."

437. Faure, *Congetture*, 6–12, 66–124 (quotation on p. 72). Cf. Heilbron, *Electricity*, 46–58, 239–41.

438. Dainville, *L'éducation*, 373; Moss, "Newton"; Hellyer, *Catholic Physics*, 227–33.

439. Gorman, "Jesuit Explorations," 23; Gavagna, "I gesuiti"; Hellyer, *Catholic Physics*, 103f., 131–68.

440. Hellyer, *Catholic Physics*, 219–22.

441. Udías, *Jesuit Contribution*, 27.

442. Dainville, *L'éducation*, 362–78; Hellyer, *Catholic Physics*, 82f., 125f., 130f., 159, 181–201.

443. Croiset, *Règlements*, 1:84f.

444. Hellyer, *Catholic Physics*, 186–88.

445. Battistini, "La cultura scientifica," 167f.

446. Stepling, *Commercium*, 257–61.

447. Hellyer, *Catholic Physics*, 232–36.

448. In general, see Boer and Göttler (eds.), *Religion*; Hall and Cooper (eds.), *The Sensuous*; O'Malley, *Trent*, 244, 273.

449. Levy, *Propaganda*, 49 (quotation).

450. Gaston, "How Words Control Images."

451. MonPaed 3:267.

452. Rädle, "Jesuit Theatre"; Valentin, *Les jésuites*.

453. In Domingo Malvadi, *La producción*, 271.

454. Flamarion, "Une 'peinture animée'" (quotation on p. 166).

455. Zampelli, "'Lascivi Spettacoli'"; Pohle, *Glaube*, 245–47; Flamarion, *Théâtre Jésuite*, 157–91.

456. EpIgn 6:286; Villoslada, *Storia*, 32, 41.

457. EpIgn 10:185.

458. Actresses were inconceivable; even female parts (which were played by men) were avoided. There were, however, exceptions: ARSI Germ Sup 12 II, fol. 165^r–167^r. See Drozd, *Schul- und Ordenstheater*, 106–10.

459. Van Damme, *Le temple*, 217–21.

460. Flamarion, *Théâtre Jésuite*, 126.

461. On Spain, see Fernández Guerrero (ed.), "La *Iudithis Tragoedia Tertia*," 8f.; Domingo Malvadi, *La producción*, 149–52. For Germany, see Pohle, *Glaube*, 462f. For examples, see Stenmans, *Litterae annuae*, 90; Bauer-Mahlmann, "Deutsch"; Pérez González, *Bilingualität*.

462. Szarota, *Jesuitendrama*.

463. Quoted in Rädle, "Jesuit Theatre," 219.

464. Flamarion, "Une 'peinture animée,'" 173.

465. Cf., e.g., Petrus Telonarius from Münster, 1604, in Stork, *Das Theater*, 283–89.

466. See Stork, *Das Theater*. This *Coena Magna* from Münster, 1632, combined Luke 14 and Matthew 22 with further, fairytale-like elements.

467. Dürrwächter, *Jakob Gretser*, 35f. and generally.

468. Filippi, "Le corps suspendu."

469. Villoslada, *Storia*, 162–66.

470. Stork, *Das Theater*, 182f. The Latin title is *Fortuna Westphaliae sive Westphalia a paganismo ad fidem christianam traducta*.

471. Friedrich, "Politikberatung," 190–93.

472. Friedrich, *Der lange Arm*, 348, 350f.

473. See Hsia (ed.), *Mission*.

474. Proot and Verberckmoes, "Japonica," 33 (with following quote).

475. Pallavicino, *Ermenegildo*, 141–45. Cf. also Chevalier, "Jesuit Neo-Latin Tragedy," 427f.

476. Burschel, *Sterben*, 197–285.

477. Pohle, "Jakob Masen," 105f.; Filippi, "Le corps suspendu," 231. See Burschel, *Sterben*, 274, for a similar chronology.

478. Chevalier, "Jesuit Neo-Latin Tragedy," 450–54.

479. Flamarion, *Théâtre Jésuite*.

480. MonPaed 3:390.

481. Turrini, *Il "giovin signore*," 315–25.

482. E.g., MonPaed 3:267; ARSI Germ 162, fol. 112^r; Griffin, "Lewin Brecht," 22–27; Domingo Malvadi, *La producción*, 153f.; Chevalier, "Jesuit Neo-Latin Tragedy," 423f.

483. Pohle, "Jakob Masen," 103.

484. Pohle, *Glaube*, 399–427.

485. Dubreuil, *La Perspective*, "Traité IV," 2:92–107.

486. Flamarion, *Théâtre Jésuite*, 126–31; Pohle, *Glaube*, 378–87. A play was performed in a field in Ettlingen, 1664: see Kast (ed.), *Die Jahresberichte*, 9; for rain, see Stenmans, *Litterae annuae*, 90.

487. Flamarion, *Théâtre Jésuite*, 128–29.

488. Van der Veldt, *Franz Neumayr*, 98f. Further examples are mentioned there.

489. Rädle, "Jesuit Theatre," 238.

490. MonPaed 7:545.

491. AD Loir-et-Cher F 647, p. 10 (Blois); Pohle, *Glaube*, 302f., and Wirthensohn, *Anton Claus*, 249–82 on Corneille and Voltaire.

492. Pohle, *Glaube*, 262–310, 434–72.

493. Drozd, *Schul- und Ordenstheater*, 91. See p. 89 for critiques.

494. Haskell, *Loyola's Bees*; Haskell, "The Passion(s)"; Haskell, "Vineyard of Verse."

495. Haskell, "Child Murder," 93.

496. Braun, *Ancilla Calliopeae*, 587–93.

497. Cf. Braun, *Ancilla Calliopeae*, 551–73.

498. Le Brun, *Virgilius*, 256f.; Klecker, "'Imperium Minervae,'" 202–4.

499. Urbano, "The *Paciecidos*."

500. Le Brun, *Virgilius*, 5 (1.1): *Bella canant alij; nos clarum Marte relicto | Dicimus Heroëm.* Cf. Vergil Aen. 1.1: *Arma virumque cano.*

501. Ovid, *Fasti* 1.13; Le Brun, *Virgilius*, 212–23 ("Prolusio").

502. Braun, *Ancilla Calliopeae*, 482–505.

503. Braun, *Ancilla Calliopeae*, 469–82.

504. Haskell, *Loyola's Bees*, 4 (for the number of didactic poems). On Giannettasio, see Schindler, "Nicolò Partenio Giannettasio"; on Le Febvre, see Winnacker, "Populärmusik."

505. Bitzel, *Bernardo Zamagna*.

506. Boscovich, *De solis*.

507. Cabilliau, *Magdalena*; Sautel, *Divae Magdalenae*.

508. Hallyn, "Puteanus."

509. Mertz and Murphy (eds.), *Jesuit Latin Poets*, 66.

510. Sarbiewski, *Poemata omnia*, 303 (epigrams 114–16).

511. Rieder, "Sternenhimmelbetrachtung." As was not unusual in epigrams, the poet also incorporates a witty pagan and political allusion in his pious message. The victim's name also evoked the emperors of ancient Rome, who all bore the name "Caesar" and (at least sometimes) were "elevated to the stars" as gods (*divi*)—but apotheosis is ultimately denied them. In connection with the tragic story of Cesare's accident, the epigram thus also has a powerful moral message, whether on the transience of power or the invalidity of paganism. As the punch line of the first epigram puts it, "Heights are always bad for Caesars: whatever Caesar comes up to the heavens above [literally, to the gods—*superos*] will fall from there" (*Noxia Caesaribus semper sublimia: quisquam | Ad superos veniat Caesar, et inde ruet*). I thank John N. Dillon for helping further clarify this passage.

512. Schäfer, "Sarbiewskis patriotische Lyrik."

513. Quoted in Claren, Eickmeyer, and Kühlmann (eds.), *Johannes Bisselius*, 19–20.

514. Eickmeyer, *Der jesuitische Heroidenbrief*, 241–44 (Possevino); Wiegand, "*Supplicium Cupidinis*."

515. Guzzardi, "Introduzione," 12–14; Haskell, *Loyola's Bees*; Schindler, "Nicolò Partenio Giannettasio," 42–44, 49–51.

516. Leone, *Geminae voces*, 71–94; Milani, "Introduzione," xviii–xxiv, xxix; Colombo, "Milano bilingue," 89–91.

517. Milani, "Introduzione," xxvn20.

518. Croce, "I critici"; Bellini and Scarpati, *Il vero*, 73–190; Delbeke, *Art of Religion*, 80–86.

519. Pallavicino, *Lettere*, 1:164.

520. Eickmeyer, *Der jesuitische Heroidenbrief*, 283.

521. Pallavicino, *Vindicationes*, 123.

522. Pallavicino, *Lettere*, 1:163.

523. Ceva, *Memorie*, 132–33, 134. On Ceva, see Leone, *Geminae voces*, 74f.

524. Valentin, "La diffusion"; Pohle, *Glaube*, 299–302, 461. On Corneille and the Jesuits, see now also Wirthensohn, *Anton Claus*, 249–56.

525. Van der Veldt, *Franz Neumayr*, 84, 86–97, 103.

526. This probably even includes Spain, which is sometimes viewed as an exception to the rule: see Jorquera, "Nuevas fuentes."

527. Culley and McNaspy, "Music"; Guillot, *Les jésuites*, esp. 65–145; Kennedy, "Jesuits and Music" (1982) and (2005).

528. Const nos. 266, 268.

529. Culley, *Jesuits and Music*, 32f.; Kennedy, "Jesuits and Music" (1982), 19f., 27–31.

530. Kennedy, "Jesuits and Music" (2005), 418.

531. Culley, *Jesuits and Music*.

532. Clm 9201, fol. 8^r (August 20, 1575).

533. On this (and for the following quotes), see Filippi, "Earthly Music."

534. Kochanowicz, "Jesuit Music Seminaries"; Bobková, "Studienstiftungen."

535. Crook, "'A Certain Indulgence,'" 472.

536. Quoted in Drozd, *Schul- und Ordenstheater*, 127.

537. Culley, *Jesuits and Music*, 77, with quotation.

538. Fisher, "'Per mia particolare devotione,'" 183f.

539. Culley, *Jesuits and Music*, 84, with quotation.

540. Körndle, "'Ad te perenne gaudium'"; Körndle, "Between Stage."

541. Winnacker, "Populärmusik."

542. Rock, *Terpsichore*; Walsdorf, *Die politische Bühne*.

543. Walsdorf, *Die politische Bühne*, 67.

544. Le Jay, *Bibliotheca rhetorum*, 477–91; Ménestrier, *Des ballets*.

545. SJ, *L'empire de la sagesse*; SJ, *Les delices de Blois*, in AD Loir-et-Cher F 647 (the *periocha* is fragmentary); SJ, *Les nouvelles*.

546. Guillot, *Les jésuites*, 70, 95.

547. Parran, *Traité*. For a list of treatises on music by Jesuits, see Guillot, *Les jésuites*, 245–50.

548. Gasta, *Transatlantic Arias*, 151–220.

549. Ranum, "Charting"; Culley, *Jesuits and Music*, 266–70.

550. Gosine and Oland, "*Docere.*"

551. Jam, "Castel et Rameau"; Gepner, *Le père Castel*, 52–58. Cf. also Grove Music, s.v. "Rameau, Jean-Philipp."

552. Pappas, *Berthier's* Journal, 142–49, 155–57; Vendrix, "Castel," 132–34.

553. Astier, "Pierre Beauchamps"; Lecomte, "Un danseur."

554. Koegel, "Spanish and French Mission Music," 42–46.

555. Cessac, "Le Regina caeli."

556. JR 27:247.

557. JR 32:87, 97.

558. JR 43:75.

559. Koegel, "Spanish and French Mission Music," 24.

560. Koegel, "Spanish and French Mission Music."

561. Quoted in Kennedy, "Colonial Music," 3.

562. Kennedy, "Music and the Jesuit Mission," 17–20 (quotation on p. 19); Rostirolla, "La musica."

563. JR 28:31.

564. Irving, *Colonial Counterpoint*, 118–27.

565. Aracena, "Viewing."

566. Dubois, "Marc-Antoine Charpentier."

567. Waisman, "Arcadia."

568. Gasta, *Transatlantic Arias*, 151–220.

569. JR 44:277.

570. Lindorff, "Missionaries."

571. For a chronology, see Smith, *Sensuous Worship*, 55.

572. Bösel, "La *ratio*," 39–41.

573. Levy, *Propaganda*.

574. On Rome, see Terhalle, *S. Andrea*, 46–49; on Valencia, see Gómez-Ferrer, "La arquitectura."

575. Vallery-Radot, *Le recueil*.

576. Bösel, "La *ratio*," 44f.

577. Bösel, "Meglio soli," 159.

578. Quotation from Snaet and de Jonge, "Architecture," 266f.; Oevermanns, "Die Pläne."

579. Rodríguez G. de Ceballos, "Loyola"; Rodríguez G. de Ceballos, "La arquitectura"; Bösel, "Jesuit Architecture," 91.

580. In general, see Bösel, "Jesuit Architecture."

581. Nising, *". . . in keiner Weise prächtig"*; Terhalle, ". . . ha della Grandezza."

582. CG 1, d. 113.

583. Terhalle, ". . . ha della Grandezza," 87–90 (Florence), 98–100 (building materials); Bösel, *Jesuitenarchitektur*, 2:232, 239 (Milan); Sale, *Pauperismo*, 50f. (Oliva). On Rome, see Bösel, "Meglio soli," 152 (with quotation).

584. Levy, *Propaganda*, 84f.

585. Terhalle, *S. Andrea*, 56f.

586. Schwager, "La chiesa"; Bösel, *Jesuitenarchitektur*, 1:160–79.

587. Strinati, "La Chiesa"; Bösel, *Jesuitenarchitektur*, 1:191–200.

588. Bösel, *Jesuitenarchitektur*, 1:84–86.

589. Terhalle, *S. Andrea*, esp. 267–87; Bösel, *Jesuitenarchitektur*, 1:86.

590. Betlej, "Jesuit Architecture," 282; Bösel, "Jesuit Architecture," 71.

591. Smith, *Sensuous Worship*, 108; Bösel, "Jesuit Architecture," 77–79.

592. Snaet and de Jonge, "Architecture," 242–46.

593. Smith, *Sensuous Worship*, 66, 122.

594. Muller, "Jesuit Uses," 139.

595. Muller, "Jesuit Uses," 135.

596. Rosario Nobile, "La provincia," 98; Knaap, "Meditation," 156–81.

597. Terhalle, ". . . ha della Grandezza," 84.

598. Bailey, "Italian Renaissance Painting"; Tapié (ed.), *Baroque vision*.

599. Crasset, *La véritable dévotion*, pt. 2, 106–31 (quotations on pp. 106, 107, 110).

600. Terhalle, ". . . ha della Grandezza," 100.

601. Smith, *Sensuous Worship*, 78f.; Torre, "Politics Cloaked," 48.

602. Champion, *Vie du Père Vincent Huby*, 68.

603. Smith, *Sensuous Worship*, 81–90.

604. Filipczak, "Van Dyck's 'Life of St. Rosalie.'"

605. Edmunds, "French Sources"; Seydl, "Il pittore."

606. Sénard, "Étienne Martellange."

607. See Bösel and Salviucci Insolera (eds.), *Andrea Pozzo*.

608. Bösel, "Jesuit Architecture," 69f.

609. Corsi, *La fábrica*; Picard, *Les peintres*.

610. Musillo, "Reconciling"; Boda, "Castiglione."

611. Bailey, *Art on the Jesuit Missions*; O'Malley, Bailey, and Sale (eds.), *The Jesuits and the Arts*; Plá, *El barroco*.

612. Bailey, *Art on the Jesuit Missions*, 144–81. On the quincha construction technique, whereby walls and vaults in the Andes were constructed not of brick but rather of straw, wattle and daub, and leather, cf. Rodríguez-Camilloni, "Constantino de Vasconcelos"; Rodríguez-Camilloni, "Quincha Architecture."

613. Sustersic, "El 'insigne artífice.'"

614. Plá, *El barroco*, 57–92.

615. Bailey, *Art on the Jesuit Missions*, 173f.; Plá, *El barroco*, 79f.

616. Salviucci Insolera, "Livres d'emblèmes," 61–65.

617. Rodríguez G. de Ceballos, "Las *Imágenes*."

618. Bailey, "Italian Renaissance Painting," 127.

619. König-Nordhoff, *Ignatius*.

620. Salviucci Insolera, "Le illustrazioni."

Chapter Four

1. Imago, 318, 326. See the articles collected in O'Malley (ed.), *Art*.

2. Quotation taken from Carbonell de Masy, "Las ordenaciones," 41. Cf. García Recio, "Los jesuitas en Santa Cruz," 78f.

3. ARSI Gal 110, fol. 370^v–371^r; Burrus and Zubillaga (eds.), *Misiones mexicanas*, 125, 128. Cf. Brockey, *Visitor*, 84.

4. On Francis Xavier the man and the mission to Asia generally, see the fundamental work by Schurhammer, *Franz Xaver*.

5. Alden, *Making*, 41–71; Brockey, *Visitor*.

6. See Neill, *History of Christianity*.

7. Alden, *Making*, 150f.; Maclagan, *Jesuits*, 127–29; Brockey, *Visitor*, 139f.

8. See generally Maclagan, *Jesuits*.

9. Didier, "Entre l'Europe," 361–63.

10. Didier (ed.), *Fantômes d'Islam*, 57.

11. Didier (ed.), *Fantômes d'Islam*, 60, 63.

12. Caraman, *Tibet*; Pomplun, *Jesuit on the Roof*.

13. Didier (ed.), *Les Portugais*, 44f.

14. Desideri, *Mission to Tibet*.

15. For the number, see Neill, *History of Christianity*, 1:353, 355 (with quotation).

16. Brockey, *Visitor*, 133f. (with quotation).

17. Alden, *Making*, 187–205.

18. Alden, *Making*, 153f., 168f., 177f., 188; Perera, *Jesuits in Ceylon*; on printing see p. 18.

19. Jacobs, "An Abortive Mission."

20. Brockey, *Visitor*, 136–40.

21. On regional power relations, see Villiers, "Manila and Maluku."

22. Schwade, "Frühgeschichte"; Üçerler, "Jesuit Enterprise."

23. On Alessandro Valignano, see Üçerler, "Alessandro Valignano"; and further Üçerler, *Alessandro Valignano*; and the classic study by Schütte, *Valignano's Mission Principles*.

24. Valignano, *Les jésuites*, 116.

25. Burrus (ed.), *Kino Writes*, 29–32, 118.

26. Brockey, *Visitor*, 333–41. On Cambodia, see Loureiro, "Jesuits in Cambodia."

27. Smithies and Bressan, *Siam*, 24–27.

28. Schatz, ". . . Dass diese Mission."

29. Maggs, "Science."

30. Hsia (ed.), *Noble Patronage*, 74–77.

31. For an overview, see Standaert (ed.), *Handbook*; Brockey, *Journey*; Standaert, "Jesuits in China"; Peterson, "Learning."

32. Jami (ed.), *Statecraft*, 253–55. On the several rites controversies, see now Županov and Fabre (eds.), *Rites Controversies*.

33. Amado Aymoré, *Die Jesuiten*; Alden, *Making*, 71–75, 206–27; Castelnau-L'Estoile, *Les ouvriers*.

34. Alden, *Making*, 474.

35. Zeron, *Ligne de foi*.

36. Cf. de la Mousse, *Les indiens*, 152f.

37. Thornton, "Development."

38. For a survey, see Egido, *Los jesuitas*, 186–224; Santos Hernández, *Los jesuitas en América*.

39. Cushner, *Why Have You Come Here?*, 31–48.

40. Cushner, *Why Have You Come Here?*, 80f.; Meiklejohn, *La iglesia*, 202–4.

41. Meiklejohn, *La iglesia*, 227n25.

42. Cushner, *Why Have You Come Here?*, 79–99; Echánove, "Origen y evolución"; Morales, "Los comienzos," 5–32.

43. Block, *Mission Culture.*

44. García Recio, "Los jesuitas en Santa Cruz."

45. Eder, *Missionnaire,* 59.

46. Eder, *Missionnaire,* 62, 165–71, etc.

47. Saeger, *Chaco Mission.*

48. Kitzmantel, "Die Jesuitenmissionare."

49. Morales, "Los comienzos," 57–63.

50. Ganson, *Guaraní,* 45–47.

51. Folsom, *The Yaquis,* 13–43. On the "new strategy" since the 1590s, see p. 64; Burrus (ed.), *Kino Writes,* 17.

52. Folsom, *The Yaquis.*

53. González, "La etnografía acaxee," 391.

54. Haubert, *La vie quotidienne,* 46f. For background, see Provost-Smith, "New Constantinianism."

55. Deeds, *Defiance,* 56–85 ("counterfeit peace"; "indios de media paz"), 86–103 ("crises of the 1690s").

56. Folsom, *The Yaquis,* e.g., 6, 72–74.

57. Burrus (ed.), *Kino Reports,* 111.

58. Crosby, *Antigua California.*

59. Folsom, *The Yaquis,* 133.

60. Deeds, *Defiance,* 115f., 121f., 127.

61. Folsom, *The Yaquis,* 120–26.

62. Deeds, *Defiance,* 131–52, 156.

63. See Costa, *Jesuits.*

64. Costa, "Muhammad Alimuddin," 203.

65. See Curran (ed.), *American Jesuit.*

66. Deslandres, *Croire,* 201–445.

67. Morrison, *Embattled Northeast.*

68. Charland, "RALE, SÉBASTIEN."

69. AN Marine B1, 8, fol. 238^r–240^v.

70. Archives nationales d'outre-mer COL E 345bis, dossier "Rasle," fol. 2^r.

71. Tremblay, "QUEN, JEAN DE."

72. Campeau, "DRUILLETTES, GABRIEL"; Giguere, "ALBANEL, CHARLES."

73. Richter, "Iroquois vs. Iroquois."

74. Greer, *Mohawk Saint,* 50.

75. Palm, *Jesuit Missions*; Havard, *Empire et métissages,* esp. 294–98, 681–737.

76. Ekberg, *French Roots,* 146, 153, 265f.

77. Moogk, *La Nouvelle France,* 10.

78. At most 170 baptisms per year until 1646, and 500 thereafter: Campeau, *La mission,* 252, 261.

79. Richter, "Iroquois vs. Iroquois," 8.

80. Palm, *Jesuit Missions,* 17.

81. Boucher, *France.*

82. de la Mousse, *Les indiens,* 154–69.

83. de la Mousse, *Les indiens*, 159.

84. Boucher, *Cannibal Encounters*; de la Mousse, *Les indiens*, 160f.

85. Le Roux, Auger, and Cazelles, *Les jésuites et l'esclavage*; Verwimp, *Les jésuites*.

86. AN M 242, no. 1, unfol. (August 4, 1674, general assembly of the Compagnie de Cayenne).

87. Montezon (ed.), *Mission*, 528 (1711).

88. Montezon (ed.), *Mission*, 525f.

89. Vongsuravatana, *Un jésuite*; Hsia, *Sojourners*, 51–92; Smithies and Bressan, *Siam*.

90. Brockey, *Visitor*, 337f.

91. Neill, *History of Christianity*, 1:358, 2:90–93; Hambye, *History of Christianity*, 170–85.

92. On a lack of linguistic competence: Colas, "Vie légumineuse"; p. 204 for the quotation from 1732.

93. Jami, *Emperor's New Mathematics*; Hsia, *Sojourners*; Witek, "Understanding."

94. Heyberger, *Les chrétiens*; Levenq, *La première mission*.

95. Heyberger and Verdeil, "Spirituality."

96. Greene, *Catholic Pirates*.

97. Poggi, "Arabismo," 343. The following remarks are based on this work. On Eliano, now see Clines, *Jewish Jesuit*.

98. Capoccia, "MANCINELLI, Giulio."

99. On the "patronage" of France, see Heyberger, *Les chrétiens*, 260–71.

100. Ruiu, "Conflicting Visions."

101. On missions in Greece, see Hofmann, "Apostolato"; Heyberger, *Les chrétiens*, 284, 292, 299. On Mount Athos, see Hofmann, "Die Jesuiten."

102. Besson, *La Syrie*, xi; Ruiu, "Conflicting Visions," 271.

103. Heyberger, *Les chrétiens*, 275, 278, 349f., 370–77.

104. Heyberger, "Le catholicisme."

105. Aggressive passages: Besson, *La Syrie*, 199f.

106. Heyberger and Verdeil, "Spirituality."

107. Matthee, "Jesuits"; Matthee, "Die Beziehung"; Windler, "Regelobservanz." On Persia, now see the monumental study Windler, *Missionare*.

108. For exceptions, see Crosby, *Antigua California*, 20, 40; Alden, *Making*, 531.

109. Galán García, El *"Oficio de Indias."*

110. Nebgen, *Missionarsberufungen*.

111. Caraman, *Tibet*, 84.

112. Golvers, "XVIIth-Century Jesuit Mission," 158; Campeau, *La mission*, 66.

113. Salvatierra, *Selected Letters*, 203–6.

114. Montezon (ed.), *Mission*, 486f.

115. Morales, "Los comienzos," 32f. On Santa Cruz de la Sierra, see García Recio, "Los jesuitas en Santa Cruz."

116. Amado Aymoré, *Die Jesuiten*, 71f.

117. Burrus (ed.), *Kino Writes*, 131; Hausberger, *Für Gott*, 506; Polzer (ed.), *Rules*, 62.

118. For the numbers, see Santos Hernández, *Los jesuitas en América*, 188; Amado Aymoré, *Die Jesuiten*, 96.

119. ARSI Franc 49, fol. 118^r.

120. Irving, *Colonial Counterpoint*, 178–82, 223, 224–26.

121. Burrus (ed.), *Kino Writes*, 115–17. On Paraguay, see Nieva Ocampo, "Cimentar las identidades locales," 1409–18. On Pedro Claver in Cartagena, see Suarez de Somoza, *Vida*, fol. 76^r–81^v.

122. Morales (ed.), *A mis manos*, 385 (1628), 418 (1630), 453 (1633); Leonhardt (ed.), *Cartas anuas*, 2:390–93, and many more.

123. Acosta, *De procuranda* (1670), 163f.

124. Nieva Ocampo, "Cimentar las identidades locales," 1414.

125. Verwimp, *Les jésuites*, 90f.

126. ARSI Gal 110, fol. 356^r–357^v; BN mss Ges. 1328, fol. 112^{r-v}.

127. Morales (ed.), *A mis manos*, 500f.

128. Abou, *Jesuit "Republic,"* 57f.

129. AN M 242 no. 1, unfol.

130. Talon, "Correspondance," 32 (quotation), 79, 110; AN M 242 no. 1, here fol. 44^r.

131. Quoted in Vongsuravatana, *Un jésuite*, 209f.

132. Archives Nationales d'Outre-mer COL E 219, dossier Hébert, fol. 2^v–4^v, in Olagnier, "Les Jésuites," 398f.

133. Maeder, "Las encomiendas," 126 (with quotation); Carbonell de Masy, *Estrategias*, 79f.; Lacombe, *Guaranis et jésuites*.

134. Burrus and Zubillaga (eds.), *El noroeste*, 166f.

135. Tardieu, *L'église*.

136. Sandoval, *Naturaleza, policia*, fol. 65^r; Sweet, "Black Robes," 94–101. On Jesuit attitudes toward slavery, now also see Priesching, *Sklaverei*.

137. Examples: de la Mousse, *Les indiens*, 160f.; Eder, *Missionnaire*, 45f.

138. Borja Medina, "El esclavo," 97.

139. Murphy, *Jesuit Slaveholding*, 92–129.

140. Sweet, "Black Robes," 107, 112; cf. Murphy, *Jesuit Slaveholding*, 92–129.

141. Tardieu, "La esclavitud," 71; Borja Medina, "El esclavo," 88f.; Zeron, *Ligne de foi*, 64, 483f.

142. Tardieu, "Les jésuites," 532; Amado Aymoré, *Die Jesuiten*, 29.

143. Suarez de Somoza, *Vida*, fol. 41^{r-v}.

144. Franklin, "Alonso De Sandoval," 351; Sandoval, *Naturaleza, policia*; cf. Sandoval, *Treatise on Slavery*.

145. See Suarez de Somoza, *Vida*, fol. 41^r–46^r; the following long quotation comes from fol. 42^{r-v}.

146. Tardieu, *L'église*, 454–522; de la Mousse, *Les indiens*, passim.

147. Aristizábal, "Las cinco vocaciones," 889.

148. Sandoval, *Naturaleza, policia*, fol. 231^v.

149. Splendiani, "La Cartegena," 402; Pacheco, *Los Jesuitas*, 250.

150. Sandoval, *Naturaleza, policia*, fol. 231^v, 233^{r-v}.

151. Morgan, "Jesuit Confessors," 231.

152. Splendiani, "La Cartegena," 384.

153. Borja Medina, "El esclavo," 95.

154. Morgan, "Jesuit Confessors." For an example, see de la Mousse, *Les indiens*, 145f.

155. Tardieu, "Les jésuites," 538–44; de la Mousse, *Les indiens*, passim.

156. E.g., de la Mousse, *Les indiens*, 127.

157. Peabody, "'A Dangerous Zeal'"; Pacheco, *Los Jesuitas*, 246; Borja Medina, "El esclavo," 85 (Peru); Tardieu, "Les jésuites," 535f.

158. Eder, *Missionnaire*, 46.

159. MonMex 3:701.

160. Zeron, *Ligne de foi*, 156f.

161. Quoted in Zeron, *Ligne de foi*, 101.

162. Quoted in Tardieu, "La esclavitud," 68. For Brazil, see Zeron, *Ligne de foi*, 92.

163. Quoted in Borja Medina, "El esclavo," 91.

164. Tardieu, "La esclavitud," 76; Cushner, *Lords*, 89f.

165. Alden, *Making*, 513–25; Borges, *Economics*, 47–49; Rea, *Economics*, 117–29; Konrad, *Jesuit Hacienda*, 247; Zeron, *Ligne de foi*, 42f.; Le Roux, Auger, and Cazelles, *Les jésuites et l'esclavage*, 111–33.

166. Tardieu, "L'église," 145–48.

167. Borja Medina, "El esclavo," 89.

168. Quoted in Zeron, "Les jésuites," 43f.

169. Quoted in Borja Medina, "El esclavo," 106.

170. Le Roux, Auger, and Cazelles, *Les jésuites et l'esclavage*, 112 (with quotation).

171. Tardieu, *L'église*, 159.

172. Borja Medina, "El esclavo," 108–10.

173. Curran, *Shaping*, 35, 96–98; Murphy, *Jesuit Slaveholding*, 91–128.

174. Negro, "Arquitectura"; Tardieu, "La esclavitud," 72–78; Tardieu, *L'église*, 191, 223–82; Borja Medina, "El esclavo," 101–18; Konrad, *Jesuit Hacienda*, 253f., 258–66.

175. da Nóbrega, *Cartas*, 191.

176. For different findings, see Konrad, *Jesuit Hacienda*, 248f.; Tardieu, *L'église*, 166.

177. See Polderman, *La Guyane*, 260; de la Mousse, *Les indiens*, 128; Borja Medina, "El esclavo," 92.

178. Antonil, *Brazil*, 25–28, 39–44; Zeron, "From Farce"; Marquese and Duarte Joly, "Panis"; Sweet, "Black Robes," 123–28.

179. Murphy, *Jesuit Slaveholding*.

180. Prosperi, "L'Europa cristiana," 198–203.

181. Exceptions: Milhou, "La tentación," 231–35; Pastore, "La otra cara," 620–22.

182. Prosperi, "L'Europa cristiana," 210, Brockey, *Visitor*, 353f.

183. Prosperi, "L'Europa cristiana"; Prosperi, *Tribunali*, 551–86; Vantard, "Les vocations," 238–70. Cf. Deslandres, *Croire*, 19–107.

184. Friedrich, "Gottfried Wilhelm Leibniz." For a good overview, see Sievernich, *Die christliche Mission*, 106–39.

185. Laborie and Lima (eds.), *La mission*, 201.

186. Pérez de Ribas, *History*, 436.

187. Costa, *Jesuits*, 26f. On Innocent IV, see Sievernich, *Die christliche Mission*, 116f.

188. In the words of Alessandro Valignano, quoted in Üçerler, "Alessandro Valignano," 353f.

189. Blackburn, *Harvest*, 42–69.

190. Desideri, *Mission to Tibet*, 521.

191. JR 6:227–29; Pérez de Ribas, *History*, 436.

192. Capoccia, "Le destin," 91 (quoting Stagliano); Capoccia, "Per una lettura"; Guerra, "Per un'archeologia," 133, 143f. (with quotations); Nebgen, "'dahin zillet'"; Pizzorusso, "Le choix"; Roscioni, *Il desiderio*, 7–26 (Orsini); Vantard, "Les vocations."

193. JR 6:143–55; JR 7:41–55, 109f.

194. Folsom, *The Yaquis*, 100f. and passim.

195. JR 6:169 may serve as an example.

196. See esp. JR 6:155–225.

197. E.g., JR 6:187: "I am inclined to think . . ." Cf. pp. 175–79, his discussion of the natives' "doctrine of salvation."

198. JR 6:181.

199. Thornton, "Development," 152. On Peru: Brosseder, *Power*, passim. On Thomas in South America: Techo, *History*, 724f.; Wilde, *Religión*, 116–22. In general on Thomas, see Sievernich, *Die christliche Mission*, 106–9.

200. JR 6:215 (fire).

201. See White, *Middle Ground*.

202. JR 6:145.

203. Block, *Mission Culture*, 35f.; Montezon (ed.), *Mission*, 491 ("peu de succès"); de la Mousse, *Les indiens*, esp. 7f. (introduction); JR 56:67–89.

204. Campeau, *La mission*.

205. Moogk, *La Nouvelle France*, 30. The site has been reconstructed as a living museum: http://www.saintemarieamongthehurons.on.ca/sm/en/Home/index.htm.

206. Greer, *Mohawk Saint*, 5; Laborie and Lima (eds.), *La mission*, 195–216; Valle, *Escribiendo*.

207. Greer, *Mohawk Saint*, 50.

208. White, *Middle Ground*, 23f.

209. Moogk, *La Nouvelle France*, 36–41; Jetten, *Enclaves amérindiennes*; Ronda, "The Sillery Experiment"; Ronda, "The European Indian"; Délage, "Les iroquois chrétiens."

210. JR 66:42–50.

211. Greer, *Mohawk Saint*. Cf. also Blanchard, "To the Other Side."

212. Description in JR 62:173; see, more broadly, JR 62:166–89. The following quotations are taken from here.

213. JR 62:173.

214. Anderson, *Betrayal*.

215. Donattini, "Ambasciatori giapponesi."

216. Richter, "Iroquois vs. Iroquois"; Ronda, "The Sillery Experiment"; Délage, "Les iroquois chrétiens."

217. JR 7:89–91.

218. JR 56:59.

219. Richter, "Iroquois vs. Iroquois," 4.

220. JR 62:199f. Cf. JR 12:139f.; JR 15:137.

221. Richter, "Iroquois vs. Iroquois," 9; Greer, *Mohawk Saint*, 57f.

222. JR 56:59.

223. de la Mousse, *Les indiens*, 60. On the opposite "grand embarras" (when natives baptized in sickness surprisingly recover), see p. 147.

224. SJ, *Colección*, 4:209–17 (quotation on p. 215); Cushner, *Why Have You Come Here?*, 72–78; González, "La etnografía acaxee"; Hausberger, *Für Gott*, 248–58.

225. On Nayarit, see Moreno de los Arcos, "Autos seguidos"; Moreno Martínez, "Jesuitas y franciscanos." Moreno Martínez also discusses Tomás de Solchaga, S.J., who declared in favor of the use of force.

226. In general, see Brosseder, *Power*, esp. 104–35. Cf. Broggio, "I gesuiti."

227. Cordero Fernández, "Las penas."

228. For the chronology, see Cordero Fernández, "Rol de la Compañía," 369.

229. Poole, "Some Observations," 338f.

230. Burrus (ed.), *Kino Writes*, 135.

231. Const no. 402.

232. Burrus, "Language Problem," 170.

233. Burrus, "Pioneer." For a different assessment of the same figures, see Cushner, *Why Have You Come Here?*, 61.

234. González, "La etnografía acaxee," 390.

235. Burrus (ed.), *Jesuit Relations*, 224f.

236. For an exemplary account, see Brockey, *Journey*, 243–55. On Canada, see True, *Masters*, esp. 27–82; Hernández de León-Portilla, "Paradigmas gramaticales," 82, 91–96.

237. González, "La etnografía acaxee," 380n40.

238. Guadalajara, *Gramática tarahumara*. On Guadalajara's biography, see González Rodríguez, "Thomás de Guadalaxara."

239. For a helpful, if exaggerated, account, see Hausberger, *Für Gott*, 230–48 (quotation on 234n170).

240. Reff, *Plagues*, 240f.

241. Crosby, *Antigua California*, 41, 43. In general, see Wogan, "Perceptions."

242. Bargellini and Komanecky, *El arte*.

243. This and the following quotations are from Pérez de Ribas, *History*, 371.

244. Thompson (ed.), *Jesuit Missionary*, 133.

245. Pérez de Ribas, *History*, 189 (a medal of Ignatius).

246. Pérez de Ribas, *History*, 258, 322, 417, etc.; Leavelle, "Catholic Rosary."

247. Burrus (ed.), *Jesuit Relations*, 117 (anno 1744). Cf. p. 152 (anno 1730).

248. Examples: Burrus (ed.), *Jesuit Relations*, 122 (anno 1744); Pérez de Ribas, *History*, 447, 553; Burrus (ed.), *Kino Reports*, 53 (fear of a crucifix).

249. González, "La etnografía acaxee," 377; Folsom, *The Yaquis*, 56–59.

250. E.g., in the rebellion of the Tepehuanes under Quautlatas in 1616–19. See Deeds, *Defiance*, 29–35.

251. Mirafuentes Galván, "Agustín Ascuhul."

252. Thompson (ed.), *Jesuit Missionary*, 246–54.

253. Greer, *Mohawk Saint*, 54f.

254. González, "La etnografía acaxee," 391.

255. Folsom, *The Yaquis*, 48f., 104–6. On patience, see Eder, *Missionnaire*, 60.

256. Pérez de Ribas, *History*, 448f. On confession, see Brosseder, *Power*, 41–46.

257. Pérez de Ribas, *History*, 553.

258. Pérez de Ribas, *History*, 451.

259. JR 56:27; Greer, *Mohawk Saint*, 50; Richter, "Iroquois vs. Iroquois," 6.

260. On the number, see Reff, *Plagues*, 127.

261. Pérez de Ribas, *History*, 456.

262. Reff, *Disease*, 262.

263. Pérez de Ribas, *History*, 450.

264. Cushner, *Why Have You Come Here?*, 57–59.

265. Reff, *Disease*, 243–274; Reff, *Plagues*.

266. Crosby, *Antigua California*, 212f.

267. Thompson (ed.), *Jesuit Missionary*, 138. Cf. also p. 170f.

268. Thompson (ed.), *Jesuit Missionary*, 175.

269. Thompson (ed.), *Jesuit Missionary*, 175, 196f.

270. Deeds, *Defiance*, 105.

271. JR 64:231; Block, "Links," 166f.; Meiklejohn, *La iglesia*, 204f. Reff, *Disease*, 254–59, is more critical.

272. Thompson (ed.), *Jesuit Missionary*, 137–44 (quotation on p. 138).

273. González, "La etnografía acaxee," 380f.

274. Deeds, *Defiance*, 18; Crosby, *Antigua California*, 197–200.

275. Polzer (ed.), *Rules*, 61f.

276. Burrus (ed.), *Jesuit Relations*, 143.

277. Hausberger, *Für Gott*, 219f., 299–317.

278. Burrus (ed.), *Jesuit Relations*, 143.

279. Quoted in Crosby, *Antigua California*, 199.

280. Ruiz de Montoya, *Spiritual Conquest*, 46.

281. Sarreal, *Guaraní*, 1–5.

282. Ruiz de Montoya, *Spiritual Conquest*, 37f.

283. Carbonell de Masy, *Estrategias*, 52–55.

284. Wilde, *Religión*, 96f.

285. Numbers taken from Carbonell de Masy, *Estrategias*, 41, 95.

286. Furlong, *Misiones*, 272–86.

287. Morales, "Introducción," 30*.

288. Pérez de Ribas, *History*, 289: ". . . when we reached the Mayo and began their reduction."

289. Morales, "Introducción," 36*–39*; Morales, "Los comienzos," 5f.

290. Salinas, "Jesuitas."

291. Hernández, *Organización*, 1:582; Carbonell de Masy, *Estrategias*, 43f.

292. JR 3:141–45; JR 12:217–19; Crosby, *Antigua California*, 430n38 (with quote); Montezon (ed.), *Mission*, 489–92.

293. Hernández, *Organización*, 1:582 (§8); Sarreal, *Guaraní*, 39–64; Ganson, *Guaraní*, 69–74.

294. Leonhardt (ed.), *Cartas anuas*, 1:344.

295. Hernández, *Organización*, 1:587 (§12).

296. Reinhard, "Gelenkter Kulturwandel." Cf. Folsom, *The Yaquis*, 72; Ruiz de Montoya, *Spiritual Conquest*, 37f.

297. Acosta, *De procuranda* (1670), unpag. ("Prooemium"); Blackburn, *Harvest*, 70–104.

298. Hernández, *Organización*, 1:582 (§9).

299. Wilde, *Religión*, 23, 73–79, 82–86, 107f., and passim.

300. Using Canada as an example: Moogk, *La Nouvelle France*, 41–45; Dêlage, "Les iroquois chrétiens," 65f.

301. Mörner, "Guaraní Missions."

302. MonPeru 1:228.

303. Hernández, *Organización*, 1:584 (§15).

304. Furlong, *Misiones*, 293. On Brazil, see Zeron, *Ligne de foi*, 80f. On the Franciscans, see Salinas, "Jesuitas," 228.

305. Matienzo Castillo, "La encomienda."

306. Quotation from Matienzo Castillo, "La encomienda," 75f.; MonPeru 8:458–82; Morales, "Los comienzos," 68–125.

307. Maeder, "Las encomiendas," 126.

308. Salinas, "Jesuitas."

309. Maeder, "Las encomiendas."

310. Zeron, *Ligne de foi*, passim, e.g., 485–88; Sweet, "Black Robes," 94.

311. García Recio, "Los jesuitas en Santa Cruz," 81f.; Deeds, *Defiance*, 75, 110, etc.; Alden, *Making*, 474–501; Costa, *Jesuits*, 126 and passim.

312. MonBras 2:409.

313. Carbonell de Masy, *Estrategias*; Sarreal, *Guaraní*, esp. 65–92.

314. Morales (ed.), *A mis manos*, 228.

315. Mörner, "Guaraní Missions"; on "relative isolation," see Furlong, *Misiones*, 292–96. On contact with indigenous peoples outside the system, see Wilde, *Religión*, 124f., 144–52.

316. Hernández, *Organización*, 1.588 (§15).

317. Cf., e.g., Furlong, *Misiones*, 117–27.

318. Ruiz de Montoya, *Spiritual Conquest*, 101. On the laxity of the Jesuits in São Paulo, see Morales (ed.), *A mis manos*, 498f. with note; Fechner, *Entscheidungsfindung*, 245n332.

319. Eder, *Missionnaire*, 165–71 (quotation on p. 167).

320. Ruiz de Montoya, *Spiritual Conquest*, 100–105, 177–86.

321. Ganson, *Guaraní*, 45–47.

322. Abou, *Jesuit "Republic,"* 53f. (with quotation), 81–83.

323. Alden, *Making*, 478, 499f.; Zeron, *Ligne de foi*, 147.

324. Abou, *Jesuit "Republic,"* 23.

325. Legge, *Confucian Analects*.

326. Bartoli, *Dell'historia*, 811–13; Zürcher, "Jesuit Mission." Cf. the interpretation of the *Zhongyong* by Schall von Bell in his treatise *Zhujiao yuanqi zonglun*, in Dudink, "Religious Works," 857.

327. On Ai Rulüe, see Lippiello and Malek (eds.), *"Scholar"*; Song, "Learning."

328. Menegon, *Ancestors*, 28f.

329. Luk, "A Study."

330. Luk, "A Serious Matter."

331. Übelhör, *Hsü Kuang-ch'i*; Übelhör, "Geistesströmungen"; Peterson, "Why Did They Become Christians?," 134f., 147f.; Standaert, *Yang Tingyun*, 217f.

332. Luk, "A Study," 73. For parallels, see Dudink, "Religious Works," 842f. with n91.

333. Menegon, *Ancestors*, 24–27.

334. Liu, "Spiritual Journey."

335. Standaert (ed.), *Handbook*, 387.

336. Quotations from Liu, "Spiritual Journey," 441f.

337. Peterson, "Learning," 789, 802; Song, "Learning," 156f.

338. Mungello, *Forgotten Christians*, 85f.

339. Hsia, *Jesuit*; Laven, *Mission*.

340. There were, however, also negative opinions. Cf. Voiret (ed.), *Gespräch*, passim.

341. Quoted in Peterson, "Learning," 794.

342. Zhang, *Making*, 38–47.

343. Standaert (ed.), *Handbook*, 540–42; Standaert, *Yang Tingyun*, 58f.

344. FontRicc 1:335–38; Hsia, *Jesuit*, 89–92, 188–98; Standaert, *Yang Tingyun*, 52–60.

345. Mungello, *Forgotten Christians*, 77f. Quotation from Song, "Learning," 133.

346. Peterson, "Why Did They Become Christians"; Standaert (ed.), *Handbook*, 404–9; Übelhör, *Hsü Kuang-ch'i*; Jami (ed.), *Statecraft*; Standaert, *Yang Tingyun*.

347. Quoted in Übelhör, *Hsü Kuang-ch'i*, 91.

348. Luk, "A Study," 62.

349. Ricci, *True Meaning*, 59. On their image of Confucius, see Rule, *K'ung-tzu or Confucius?*

350. FontRicc 2:296; Ricci, *Lettere*, 518; Goodman and Grafton, "Ricci."

351. Peterson, "Learning," 827; Zürcher, "Jesuit Accommodation," 43–47.

352. Mungello, *Forgotten Christians*; Liu, "Spiritual Journey"; Zürcher, "Jesuit Accommodation"; Standaert, *Yang Tingyun*.

353. Mungello, *Forgotten Christians*, 79–81; Mungello, "Reconciliation."

354. Song, "Learning," 354–59; Standaert (ed.), *Handbook*, 653–59. For texts, see Ricci, *True Meaning*, 347–407. For Aleni, see Zürcher (ed.), *Kouduo richao*, 273f.; for Schall von Bell, see Dudink, "Religious Works," 857–60.

355. Standaert, *Yang Tingyun*, 141–43.

356. Gernet, *China*, 161f.; Standaert, *Yang Tingyun*, 61f.

357. Hsia, *Jesuit*, 155–57.

358. Ricci, *Lettere*, 520.

359. Hsia (ed.), *Noble Patronage*, 119 (Florian Bahr from Beijing in 1743).

360. Hsia (ed.), *Noble Patronage*, passim. For a parallel case, see Voiret (ed.), *Gespräch*, 339–42; King, "Christian Charity," 24 for the quotation. For the important role of Chinese women in the Jesuit mission, see now Amsler, *Jesuits and Matriarchs*.

361. On Aleni, see Luk, "A Study," 64. For Schall von Bell, see Dudink, "Religious Works," 834–36, here 834; Ricci, *True Meaning*, 63.

362. Jami, *Emperor's New Mathematics*; Zhang, *Making*.

363. Cf. Malek (ed.), *Western Learning*; Golvers, *Ferdinand Verbiest*.

364. On music theory, see Gild, "Introduction."

365. Sebes (ed.), *Jesuits*.

366. Quoted in Dudink, "Religious Works," 866.

367. Voiret (ed.), *Gespräch*, 362–66.

368. Jami, *Emperor's New Mathematics*, 153.

369. Quoted in Jami, *Emperor's New Mathematics*, 85f. Cf. Zhang, *Making*, 360–62.

370. Voiret (ed.), *Gespräch*, 69.

371. Brockey, *Journey*, 91; Mungello, *Forgotten Christians*, 17; Jami, *Emperor's New Mathematics*, 54.

372. Standaert (ed.), *Handbook*, 668–79; Mungello, *Curious Land*, 300–307.

373. SJ, *Confucius*, "Prooemium."

374. Collani, "Cabbala."

375. Mungello, *Curious Land*, 310f., 334f.

376. Mungello, *Curious Land*, 342 (on Le Comte); Brockey, *Journey*, 264 (with quotation); Mungello, *Forgotten Christians*, 98f.

377. Mungello, *Curious Land*, 306f., 313f.; Smith, "Jesuit Interpretations." On the *Yijing* in a Jesuit context, see Goodman and Grafton, "Ricci," 122–48.

378. Mungello, *Forgotten Christians*, 96f., 100f., and passim.

379. Jami, *Emperor's New Mathematics*, 51.

380. Smith, "Jesuit Interpretations," 34f.

381. Musillo, "Reconciling," 57.

382. Brockey, *Journey*, 136f.

383. Jami, *Emperor's New Mathematics*, 239.

384. Standaert (ed.), *Handbook*, 384f. (number), 438–41 (names); Dudink, "Religious Works," 837–54.

385. Standaert (ed.), *Handbook*, 380–404; see in general Brockey, *Journey*; Mungello, *Forgotten Christians*, 72.

386. Standaert (ed.), *Handbook*, 143; Peterson, "Western Natural Philosophy."

387. Cf. Brockey, *Journey*, 47f., 77f., esp. 92–98, 290–95.

388. Mungello, *Forgotten Christians*.

389. FontRicc 2:192–215 (quotation on p. 193); Hsia, *Jesuit*, 247f.

390. That did not prevent, for example, Schall von Bell from experiencing both types of apostolate as two successive phases of his life. All of his religious works were composed, significantly, prior to his arrival in Beijing. Cf. Dudink, "Religious Works."

391. Cf. his obituary in Zürcher (ed.), *Kouduo richao*, 21f., 176–78. On the order's regional strategies overall, including China, see also Standaert (ed.), *Handbook*, 538–43.

392. Zürcher (ed.), *Kouduo richao*, 355 (riding).

393. Entenmann, "Chinese Catholic Clergy," 399.

394. On working with women and linguistic problems, see Voiret (ed.), *Gespräch*, 71f. On ignorance of dialects, see Zürcher (ed.), *Kouduo richao*, 13; Brockey, *Journey*, 258f. See now also Amsler, *Jesuits and Matriarchs*.

395. Lin, *Wu Li*, 132–40.

396. Zürcher (ed.), *Kouduo richao*, 351, 354f., 567f.

397. Zürcher (ed.), *Kouduo richao*, 510.

398. Zürcher (ed.), *Kouduo richao*, 466.

399. Zürcher (ed.), *Kouduo richao*, 257, about calendrical issues; 469, about the theory of the elements; 471, about the moon.

400. Zürcher (ed.), *Kouduo richao*, 376f. Cf. pp. 229–31. On the theological debate in Europe, see Schatz, "... *Dass diese Mission*," 127–32.

401. Cf. esp. Zürcher (ed.), *Kouduo richao*, 479, about the portraits of ancestors in private houses.

402. Zürcher (ed.), *Kouduo richao*, 481. Cf. p. 228.

403. Zürcher (ed.), *Kouduo richao*, 223f.

404. Zürcher (ed.), *Kouduo richao*, 207–12, 263, 264f., 354f.

405. On pictures, see FontRicc 2:193f.; Zürcher (ed.), *Kouduo richao*, 225, 266; Zürcher, "Lord of Heaven"; Dudink, "Religious Works," 805–9.

406. FontRicc 1:193f.; Hsia, *Jesuit*, 88f.

407. Zürcher, "Lord of Heaven," 362f.; FontRicc 2:191–95; Voiret (ed.), *Gespräch*, 72f.

408. Brockey, *Journey*; on Shanghai, see p. 171.

409. Standaert (ed.), *Handbook*, 470–73; Brockey, *Journey*, 172f., 357–60.

410. Schatz, "... *Dass diese Mission*," 82–85, 153–56; Brockey, *Visitor*, 365–69.

411. Zürcher (ed.), *Kouduo richao*, 43f.; Brockey, *Journey*, 133f., 331–401.

412. Zürcher (ed.), *Kouduo richao*, 219, 501, 520.

413. Dehergne, "Catéchismes."

414. Brockey, *Journey*, 70f. (1620s), 135f. (1660s).

415. Menegon, *Ancestors*, 17–27; Brockey, *Journey*, 138f.

416. On the eighteenth century, see Entenmann, "Chinese Catholic Clergy"; Laamann, *Christian Heretics*; Lin, *Wu Li*.

417. Voiret (ed.), *Gespräch*, 333.

418. Gernet, *China*.

419. Laamann, *Christian Heretics*.

420. MonBras 1:358–66.

421. At best, the heathen would become "semi-Christians" in this way, in the opinion of the French *gouverneur* d'Hébert in Pondicherry (1708), quoted in Olagnier, "Les Jésuites," 351.

422. Quotations from Laborie and Lima (eds.), *La mission*, 133f.

423. Brockey, *Visitor*, 346f.

424. Laborie and Lima (eds.), *La mission*, 133 (following quotation on p. 134).

425. Sanfilippo and Prezzolini (eds.), *Roberto De Nobili*; Županov, *Disputed Mission*; Brockey, *Visitor*, 88–97, 109–15.

426. De Nobili, *Preaching Wisdom*, 168.

427. De Nobili, *Preaching Wisdom*, 161. De Nobili argues here that even if the practice was pagan in nature, that did not necessarily mean it had to be suppressed.

428. Quoted in Županov, *Disputed Mission*, 58.

429. Ricci, *Lettere*, 172.

430. For a brief overview, see Sievernich, *Die christliche Mission*, 110–22.

431. Aranha, "Sacramenti"; Colas, "Vie légumineuse," 210–13.

432. Ex § 23. See Mongini, "Le teologie," 40–45; EpNad 4:849; Brockey, *Journey*, 44.

433. Laven, *Mission*, 21f.

434. Županov, *Disputed Mission*, passim; Pavone, "Tra Roma," 664.

435. Goodman and Grafton, "Ricci," esp. 106f.

436. de Nobili, *Preaching Wisdom*, 139.

437. MonInd 6:682.

438. Hambye, *History of Christianity*, 211–37; Mungello (ed.), *Chinese Rites*; Minamiki, *Chinese Rites Controversy*. On the rites controversies, see now Županov and Fabre (eds.), *Rites Controversies*.

439. Aranha, "Social and Physical Spaces"; Pavone, "Tra Roma," 665f.

440. Standaert (ed.), *Handbook*, 680–88.

441. Standaert, *Yang Tingyun*, 55.

442. Standaert, *Fascinating God*, 61f.

443. Pomplun, *Jesuit on the Roof*, 152; Brockey, *Journey*, 85–89; Brockey, *Visitor*, 348.

444. Brockey, *Visitor*, 111 (*infructuosissima*, from 1619). On ineffectiveness, see p. 114; Olagnier, "Les Jésuites," 352.

445. For the chronology, see Aranha, "'Glocal' Conflicts," 93f.

446. Standaert, *Chinese Voices*. The following episode can be found there on p. 7f.; Standaert, *Fascinating God*.

447. Standaert, *Fascinating God*, 58; Zürcher, "Jesuit Accommodation," 50–52.

448. Standaert, *Fascinating God*, 12f.

449. Vernière (ed.), *Journal*, 172–74.

450. Friedrich, "Gottfried Wilhelm Leibniz."

451. Thompson (ed.), *Jesuit Missionary*, 234f., etc.

452. Cook, *Matters*, is exemplary.

453. Clossey, "Merchants."

454. Clossey, *Salvation*, 216–37.

455. Thompson (ed.), *Jesuit Missionary*, 14, 46, etc.

456. Brüning, "Zur Vorgeschichte."

457. Hsia (ed.), *Noble Patronage*, 108, 221.

458. SJ, *Nouveaux mémoires des missions*, 8:iij–vj; Voiret (ed.), *Gespräch*, 331–38.

459. Melvin, "Charity"; Münsterberg, "Die Beziehungen"; Wilczek, "Ingolstadt."

460. Lazcano, *Vida exemplar*, 184–86.

461. Le Valois, *Œuvres* (1726), 2:291–322 (quotation on p. 297).

462. EpIgn 6:357–59.

463. True, *Masters*.

464. Hsia (ed.), *Noble Patronage*.

465. Lockman, *Travels*, viii–ix; Widmaier (ed.), *Gottfried Wilhelm Leibniz*; Friedrich, *Der lange Arm*, 382–84.

466. Lawson, *Imperial Challenge*, 29f., 117f.

467. JR 9:303.

468. JR 1:189.

469. Golvers, *Libraries*, 13, 109.

470. Del Rey Fajardo, *Las bibliotecas Jesuíticas.*

471. Widmaier (ed.), *Gottfried Wilhelm Leibniz*, 109.

472. Omont (ed.), *Missions archéologiques*, 806–50.

473. Omont (ed.), *Missions archéologiques*, 223, 224–27.

474. Omont (ed.), *Missions archéologiques*, 843 (from 1730).

475. Omont (ed.), *Missions archéologiques*, 274f., 278.

476. Martínez-Serna, "Procurators," 194–208.

477. Alcalá, "The Jesuits," 135.

478. Golvers, *Libraries*, 211f.

479. Thompson (ed.), *Jesuit Missionary*, passim.

480. Alcalá, "The Jesuits," esp. 126–71 and 303–99.

481. Curvelo, "Artistic Circulation," 64f.

482. Steinbicker, "Westfalen."

483. Golvers, "Viaggio"; Lamalle, "La propagande."

484. Flucke (ed.), *Die litterae annuae*, 206f.

485. Lazcano, *Vida exemplar*, 104 (quotations), 108.

486. Hansen, "Briefe," 141f., 155.

487. Brockey, *Visitor.*

488. Numbers vary: Brockey, "Largos Caminhos," 45; Golvers, "Distance," 107 (6.8 percent).

489. Valle, *Escribiendo*, 31f. and passim.

490. See the critical remarks by Brockey, *Visitor*, 428–31. For one such case, now see Zampol D'Ortia, "Cape of the Devil."

Chapter Five

1. DHCJ col. 1662–70.

2. McManners, *Church*, 2:530–35.

3. Cubitt, *Jesuit Myth.*

4. For a brief introduction, see Bergin, *Politics*, 58–61. For detail, see the editor's introduction in Pasquier, *Le catéchisme*, 1–121.

5. Pasquier, *Le catéchisme*, 254–60.

6. Giard, "Le Catéchisme."

7. Pasquier, *Le catéchisme*, 230.

8. Pasquier, *Le catéchisme*, 205.

9. Maire, "La Critique gallicane."

10. Anonymous, *L'Anticoton*, 30.

11. Nelson, "Jesuit Legend," 101f.

12. McKenzie-McHarg, "History as Subversion," 318n152.

13. Maire, *De la cause*; Maire, "Des comptes-rendus." For background, see Baker, *Inventing.*

14. Anonymous, *L'Anticoton*, 38 and passim.

15. Lichy, "Das Böse," 65f.

16. Anonymous, *Vorstellung*, 4.

17. Anonymous, *L'Anticoton*, 7–28, 38.

18. Anonymous, *L'Anticoton*, 18.

19. McKenzie-McHarg, "History as Subversion," 323–30.

20. Pasquier, *Le catéchisme*, 319.

21. Pasquier, *Le catéchisme*, 413.

22. Quoted in Pavone, "Antijésuitisme politique," 143f.

23. Pavone, *Le astuzie*.

24. Catto, *La compagnia divisa*; Carrasco, "Le crime."

25. Mariana, *Discurso*; Mendoça, *Advis*.

26. Anonymous, *Le Mercure iesuite*, vol. 2, "Ami Lecteur," unpag.

27. Dümmerth, "Les combats"; Stefanovska, "La monarchie."

28. Gay, *Jesuit Civil Wars*, 285f., 295. Cf. Bombart, "Un antijésuitisme 'littéraire'?"; Vogel, *Der Untergang*, 32; Bianchini, "Un mondo," 57–60.

29. Cf. *Le Mercure Iesuite*, which appeared in two volumes in the 1620s. The title alluded to the new trend of journals just coming into vogue. The foreword to the first volume explicitly mentions the *Mercure françois* and the *Mercure gallobelgique* as reference publications.

30. Quoted in Bombart, "Un antijésuitisme 'littéraire'?," 184.

31. Gay, "Le Jésuite improbable."

32. Duteil, "La 'Querelle des rites'"; Hsia, *Sojourners*, 40f.

33. St. Clair Segurado, "La cuestión," esp. 110–21 (quotation on p. 110).

34. St. Clair Segurado, *Flagellum iesuitarum*; Zeron and Dias, "L'antijésuitisme."

35. Franco, "L'antijésuitisme."

36. St. Clair Segurado, *Flagellum iesuitarum*.

37. E.g., in German: Carvalho e Melo, *Kurtze Nachricht*.

38. Quoted in Franco, "L'antijésuitisme," 370.

39. Carvalho e Melo, *Relation abrégée*, iv.

40. Gabriel, *"An tyrannum opprimere fas sit?,"* 263.

41. Quoted in McKenzie-McHarg, "History as Subversion," 311n135.

42. Vogel, *Der Untergang*, 187; Ferrer Benimeli, *Expulsión*, 220 (Tanucci).

43. Cubitt, *Jesuit Myth*; Leroy, *Le mythe jésuite*, esp. 145–50 ("complot permanent").

44. "Es geht ein finstres Wesen um | Das nennt sich Jesuit | Es redet nicht, ist still und stumm | Und schleichend ist sein Tritt. | Es trägt ein langes Trau'rgewand | Und kurzgeschornes Haar | Und bringt die Nacht zurück ins Land | Wo schon die Dämm'rung war." Quoted in German in Healy, *Jesuit Specter*, 38n72.

45. Healy, *Jesuit Specter*, 33.

46. For one of the first contrasts between the "white" (i.e., good) and "black" (bad) popes, see Guettée, *Histoire*, 1:154.

47. Nelson, "Jesuit Legend."

48. On the suppression, see esp. Burson and Wright (eds.), *Jesuit Suppression*.

49. Löffler, *Lissabons Fall*, 167–77; Marques, "A acção da igreja," 273–81.

50. Malagrida, *Juizo* (following quote on p. 4).

51. Flucke (ed.), *Die litterae annuae*, 1079.

52. Gatzhammer, "Politisch-diplomatische Beziehungen," 365–70 (quotation on p. 369).

53. Gatzhammer, "Politisch-diplomatische Beziehungen," 385 and passim, very clearly.

54. Assunção, *Negócios*, 29–41.

55. Cordara, *De suis ac suorum rebus*, 222.

56. Gatzhammer, "Politisch-diplomatische Beziehungen," 374.

57. For a summary, see Vogel, *Der Untergang*, 199–238. The fundamental work is Van Kley, *Jansenists*.

58. McManners, *Church*, 2:542–46.

59. Thompson, "French Jesuit Leaders"; Thompson, "The Lavalette Affair."

60. Quoted in Mestre Sanchis, "Reacciones," 109.

61. Beaurepaire, *La France*, 445–60.

62. Guasti, *Lotta politica*; Egido, *Los jesuitas*, 250–76; Ferrer Benimeli, "De la expulsión."

63. Renda, *Bernardo Tanucci*.

64. Andrés-Gallego, "1767."

65. Mörner, "Expulsion."

66. Ferrer Benimeli, *Expulsión*, 275–79.

67. Vogel, *Der Untergang*, 49, 122–43; Gatzhammer, "Antijésuitismo europeu," 201n231.

68. Cordara, *Suppression*, 103f., 111.

69. McCoog, "'Lost in the Title,'" 162–66.

70. Schüller, "Die Eifelmission," 111.

71. Pastor, vol. 16. See Ferrer Benimeli, *Expulsión*, 219–355; Chadwick, *Popes*, 345–90.

72. Quoted in Pastor, vol. 16, pt. 2, 117.

73. On this characterization, cf. the outstanding article by Cajani and Foa, "CLEMENTE XIII, papa."

74. Cordara, *Suppression*, 125f. and passim.

75. Quoted in Pastor, vol. 16, pt. 2, 118.

76. Mörner, "Expulsion"; Egido, *Los jesuitas*, 259; Andrés-Gallego, "1767," 87–91 (on Tanucci); Ferrer Benimeli, *Expulsión*, 219.

77. Cubitt, *Jesuit Myth*, 22 and passim.

78. Cordara, *De suis ac suorum rebus*, 228; Thompson, "General Ricci."

79. Quoted in Mestre Sanchis, "Reacciones," 109.

80. Shore, *The Eagle*, 166.

81. Thoman, *Reise*, 96 ("Donnerschlag," a "thunderclap").

82. Cordara, *Suppression*, 7; McCoog, "Lost in the Title," esp. 167.

83. Ferrer Benimeli, *Expulsión*, 331–38.

84. Trampus, *I gesuiti*, 25.

85. On Bavaria, see Müller, "Aufhebung," 325 (quotation). On Austria, see Trampus, *I gesuiti*, 29.

86. Martínez Tornero, "La administración," 172–91.

87. Curran, *Shaping*; Buckley, *Stephen Larigaudelle Dubuisson*, 72–76.

88. Russo, "L'espulsione," 92f.; see further Thoman, *Reise*.

89. Giménez López, "El ejército"; St. Clair Segurado, *Expulsión*; St. Clair Segurado, "La expulsión"; St. Clair Segurado, "Arresto"; Russo, "L'espulsione."

90. Russo, "La grande dispersione."

91. Baldini and Brizzi (eds.), *La presenza.*

92. Russo, "La grande dispersione," 32.

93. Guasti, "I gesuiti spagnoli" (2006).

94. Cordara, *Suppression,* 106.

95. Trampus, *I gesuiti,* 19.

96. Thompson, *Modern Persecution;* Thompson, "Persecution of French Jesuits"; Lécrivain, "Une prosopographie."

97. Scherer, "Aus Petersburger Briefen," 176f.

98. Schatz 1:8–32.

99. Quoted in Müller, "Aufhebung," 340. On Poland, see Pavone, *Una strana alleanza,* 34f.

100. On the date, see Trampus, *I gesuiti,* 105f.

101. Thoman, *Reise,* 238f., 241f.

102. Lécrivain, "Une prosopographie," nos. 23–28.

103. Thoman, *Reise,* 238–40.

104. Giménez López and Martínez Gomis, "La secularización," 302; Trampus, *I gesuiti,* 41–45.

105. Luengo, *Memorias,* 57.

106. Vanysacker, *Cardinal Giuseppe Garampi,* 193–96; Whitehead, "Jesuit Secondary Education."

107. Guerrini, "Il lungo esilio," 175f.

108. Trampus, *I gesuiti,* 87f.

109. Luengo, *Memorias,* 59f., 75f., etc.; Trampus, *I gesuiti,* 97.

110. On the prohibition of meetings of ex-Jesuits, see Guasti, "I gesuiti spagnoli" (2006), 30; Thoman, *Reise,* 234.

111. Marchetti, "Bartolomeo Dal Monte," 220–24; Guerrini, "Il lungo esilio," 173f.

112. Fernández Arrillaga, "Profecías."

113. For samples, see Luengo, *El retorno;* Luengo, *Memorias.*

114. Luengo, *El retorno,* 80.

115. Luengo, *El retorno,* 77f.

116. Thoman, *Reise.*

117. Ignatius of Loyola, *Epistolae,* 1, pp. iii–iv; Verd Conradi, "El P. Roque Menchaca."

118. Cordara, *Suppression,* 125–27, 157–59.

119. Luengo, *El retorno,* 69.

120. Borgo, *Memoria cattolica,* 11 (with following quotations).

121. McMahon, "Counter-Enlightenment," esp. 100–105.

122. Trampus, *I gesuiti,* 146–57; Horstmann, *Aloys Merz.*

123. Luengo, *El retorno,* 69, 82, 87.

124. Mücke, *Gegen Aufklärung,* 168–87.

125. Luengo, *El retorno,* 63, 79, 99.

126. Guasti, "I gesuiti spagnoli" (2009), 54.

127. SJ, "Voyage," 128; Figueiredo, "José Monteiro."

128. Lécrivain, "Une prosopographie," nos. 38–43.

129. Pavone, *Una strana alleanza,* 93n157.

130. Lécrivain, "Une prosopographie," no. 32.

131. Giménez López and Martínez Gomis, "La secularización" (numbers on p. 291); St. Clair Segurado, *Expulsión*, 331–44.

132. Cordara, *Suppression*, 150f., 160.

133. Trampus, *I gesuiti*, 167–215.

134. Bianchini, "Un mondo."

135. Whitehead, "Jesuit Secondary Education," 37–40.

136. Baldini and Brizzi (eds.), *La presenza*; Guasti, *L'esilio italiano.*

137. Luengo, *Memorias*, 802–5, 807f.

138. Guasti, "I gesuiti spagnoli" (2006), 44–52; Guasti, "I gesuiti spagnoli" (2009), 66f.; Domergue, "Les jésuites espagnols"; Mücke, *Gegen Aufklärung*, 185–87.

139. Browning, "Cornelius de Pauw"; Cañizares-Esguerra, *How to Write the History.*

140. Guasti, "I gesuiti spagnoli" (2009), 73f.

141. Pastor vol. 16, pt. 2, 342–67; quoted in Nanni, "Le missioni," 81; Otto, *Gründung*, 53–64. See now Correa Etchegaray, Colombo, and Wilde (eds.), *Las misiones.*

142. Lavoie, *C'est ma seigneurie*, 71–193.

143. For a critical assessment and overview, see Sievernich, *Die christliche Mission*, 91–97. For a specific example, see Ganson, *Guaraní*, 117–63.

144. Müller, "Aufhebung"; Trampus, *I gesuiti*, 49f.

145. Quoted in Eberl, "Die Umwandlung," 71.

146. Müller, "Aufhebung."

147. Bailey, "French Secondary Education."

148. Quesada, "Il Collegio Romano"; Martina, *Storia*, 47–71; Altamore and Maffeo (eds.), *Angelo Secchi.*

149. Hoffmann, *Friedrich II.*

150. On Russia, see Pavone, *Una strana alleanza*; Inglot, *La Compagnia di Gesù.*

151. On Pius VI's change of heart, see Guasti, *L'esilio italiano*, 356–59.

152. Pavone, *Una strana alleanza*, 191.

153. Quoted in Schatz 1:18: "an den Grenzen von Europa."

154. See Van Hoeck, "Lettres."

155. Van Hoeck, "Lettres," 287f. (December 13, 1803).

156. Trampus, *I gesuiti*, 164f.; Pavone, *Una strana alleanza*, 80f.

157. Luengo, *El retorno*, 70.

158. Schatz 1:18–32.

159. Decot, "Klemens Maria Hofbauer."

160. Fontana Castelli, "The Society of Jesus"; Fontana Castelli, *La Compagnia di Gesù.*

161. Rayez, "Clorivière."

162. Rayez, "Clorivière," 307.

163. Buckley, *Stephen Larigaudelle Dubuisson*, 23–27.

164. Quoted in Rayez, "Clorivière," 321.

165. Chadwick, "Paccanarists," 148f. (quotation on p. 149); Pavone, *Una strana alleanza*, 149f. For an exception (Fr. Adam Britt), cf., e.g., Van Miert, "Some Historical Documents," 343f.

166. Rayez, "Clorivière," 318 (with quotations).

167. Van Hoeck, "Lettres," 289f.

168. Fontana Castelli, "The Society of Jesus," 198f. Cf. by way of example the letter from Fr. Anton Kohlmann (1804) in Van Miert, "Some Historical Documents," 339f.

169. Scherer, "Aus Petersburger Briefen."

170. SJ, "Voyage," 115f.

171. For examples, see Van Hoeck, "Lettres"; Scherer, "Aus Petersburger Briefen."

172. Pavone, *Una strana alleanza*, 197f.

173. Van Hoeck, "Lettres," passim; Van Miert, "Some Historical Documents"; see also SJ, "Voyage"; Inglot, "Le missioni."

174. Inglot, *La Compagnia di Gesù*, 153–55, 249–51.

175. Bangert, *A History*, 426–29.

Epilogue

1. Cordara, *Suppression*, 178–87 (quotations on pp. 178, 182, 187).

2. Worcester, "Restored Society," 23f.

3. Alfieri, "'Unearthing Chaos'"; DHCJ, vol. 4, s.v. "Petrucci, Mariano Luigi."

4. CG 20, d. 6, 9, and 15, pp. 428f., 432f.; d. 8, p. 430, on the insinuation that Russian Jesuits had not completed a sufficient novitiate.

5. Cubitt, *Jesuit Myth*, 20f.

6. Soto Artuñedo, "La Compañía."

7. Schatz 1:108–14.

8. Quoted in McKevitt, *Brokers*, 29.

9. Quoted in Colombo and Massimi, *In viaggio*, 43.

10. See, e.g., Healy, *Jesuit Specter*.

11. On parallels with 1773, see McGreevy, *American Jesuits*, 13.

12. Curran, *Shaping*.

13. Quotation from McDonough, *Men*, xi. See also McKevitt, *Brokers*.

14. McGreevy, *American Jesuits*, 4.

15. Curran, *Shaping*, 4, 100; Farrelly, "Catholicism."

16. McKevitt, *Brokers*, 70–74.

17. Curran, *Shaping*, 33f. The first and second quotations are taken from Kuzniewski, "Francis Dzierozynski," 56n20, 63f. The second and immediately following quotation by Grassi are taken from Schlafly, "'Russian' Society," 363.

18. Kuzniewski, "Francis Dzierozynski," 55.

19. Duffy, *Saints*, 266f., 275f.

20. Sevrin, *Les missions religieuses*.

21. Also called "Catholic devotionalism." See Light, "Reformation"; Duffy, *Saints*, 291–94; Aston, *Christianity*; Atkin and Tallett, *Priests*.

22. Dougherty, *From Altar-Throne*, passim.

23. Atkin and Tallett, *Priests*, 132. "Conformist homogeneity and popular emotionality" in the words of Mario Rosa, describing devotional trends after 1773; cf. his article "Clemente XIV, papa."

24. Schultz, *Mrs. Mattingly's Miracle*, esp. 124–32, 142–52.

25. Blackbourn, *Marpingen*.

26. For illuminating case studies of how these people and cultural trends were connected, see Wolf (ed.), *The Nuns*.

27. Curran, *Shaping*, 78–81 (quotation on p. 80); Buckley, *Stephen Larigaudelle Dubuisson*, 72f., 91f., 96, 107–18; McKevitt, *Brokers*, 7, 65–75, 265–95; Schultz, *Mrs. Mattingly's Miracle*, esp. 124–32, 142–52.

28. Martina, *Storia*, 27–34; Schatz 1:37; Sudbrack, "Gott in allen Dingen," 172f.

29. See SJ (ed.), *Epistolae* (1847), 2:311 (written 1830).

30. SJ (ed.), *Epistolae* (1847), 2:312, 322 (written 1830).

31. Guibert, *The Jesuits*, 465f., 468.

32. Cebollada Silvestre, "La significación," 395f.

33. Quoted from Cebollada Silvestre, "La significación," 403.

34. Martina, *Storia*, 155, 158.

35. See the quotation from 1844 (concerning Germany) in Cebollada Silvestre, "La significación," 404.

36. Otto, *Gründung*; Brou, *Les Jésuites*.

37. SJ (ed.), *Epistolae* (1847), 2:347–65.

38. On *indipetae* after 1814, see Colombo and Massimi, *In viaggio*; Colombo and Rochini, "Four Hundred Years."

39. Otto, *Gründung*, 93n216, 205–9; Brou, *Les Jésuites*, 66 ("petit Paraguay"); McKevitt, *Brokers*, 93, 120–49.

40. Schatz 1:39; Curran, *Shaping*, 25.

41. McKevitt, *Brokers*, 120.

42. Murphy (ed.), *History*.

43. Coello de la Rosa, "Gathering Souls."

44. On bicycles in Africa, see Murphy (ed.), *History*, 198.

45. For an example, see McGreevy, *American Jesuits*, 5f.

46. McGreevy, *American Jesuits*, 4f. and passim, emphasizes the new intensity of global Jesuit connectedness.

47. Arens, *Die katholischen Missionsvereine*; Arens, *Jesuitenorden*. On France, see Essertel, *L'aventure*.

48. For a list, see Arens, *Jesuitenorden*, 49–54.

49. Arens, *Jesuitenorden*, 57–63.

50. Rabbath (ed.), *Documents inédits*, 2:136f.

51. Otto, *Gründung*, 90.

52. Brou, *Les Jésuites*, 73.

53. Rabbath (ed.), *Documents inédits*, 2:137f.

54. Brou, *Les Jésuites*, 81–84.

55. Jean, *Le Maduré*, 2:30, 32f.

56. Otto, *Gründung*, 95; Murphy (ed.), *History*, 146, 216; 189 (quoting Torrend).

57. Cf. Bianchini, "*Ratio studiorum*," 331n9: the provincials should assess what is taught in secular institutions and how.

58. Bianchini, "*Ratio studiorum*," 332f. Cf. Sulas, "La riforma"; Abbate, "Luigi Taparelli."

59. On Roothaan's time in Turin, cf. now Lindeijer, "Aptus."

60. Roothaan quoted in Casalini, "Włodzimierz Ledóchowski's Call," 125n3.

61. CG 25, d. 12, p. 496f.

62. Pachtler (ed.), *Ratio Studorium*, 2:273.

63. Pachtler (ed.), *Ratio Studorium*, 2:320–23, 346–49, 358f., 382f., 390f.

64. Bianchini, "*Ratio studiorum*," 337.

65. Egido, *Los jesuitas*, 330f.; Whitehead, "Jesuit Contribution"; CG 22, d. 39, p. 456.

66. Quesada, "Il Collegio Romano," 138.

67. Altamore and Maffeo (eds.), *Angelo Secchi*.

68. In paragraph 47 of the *Syllabus errorum*. Cf. Unterburger, *Vom Lehramt*, 133 and passim, for a broad panorama of the conflicts and developments with respect to academic instruction.

69. For Ellsworth, see McGreevy, *American Jesuits*, 37–41. On France, see Gontard, "Les Jésuites," 109–27.

70. McKevitt, *Brokers*, 38.

71. Sperber, *Popular Catholicism*, 61.

72. Sperber, *Popular Catholicism*, 56–63.

73. I rely in particular on Gross, *War*; Bennette, *Fighting*.

74. For a wide-ranging survey, see Neuner, *Der Streit*. Neuner also highlights the many nuances and ambivalence that made Catholic antimodernism much less uniform than may appear at first sight. On Jesuit opposition to "religious individualism," see also McGreevy, *American Jesuits*, 52–54.

75. Codignola, "Roman Catholic Conservatism."

76. Aston, *Christianity*, 307f.

77. McGreevy, *American Jesuits*, 75f.

78. Quoted in McKevitt, *Brokers*, 237f. Schatz 1:128.

79. Dante, *Storia*.

80. Schatz 2:120–26, 143–46; 3:87–96, 347–52, 357–60; 4:119–24.

81. Reproduced in *Études* 291 (December 1956): 321f.

82. Abbate, "Luigi Taparelli," 500.

83. See Malusa, *Neotomismo* (quotation on 2:155). See also Peitz, *Anfänge*; Unterburger, *Vom Lehramt*, 200–222.

84. Cf. Unterburger, *Vom Lehramt*, 200–222.

85. Wolf (ed.), *The Nuns*, 376–83; CG 21, d. 13, p. 440; 22, d. 31, p. 454. Not yet visible in CG 22, d. 37, p. 455.

86. Altamore and Maffeo (eds.), *Angelo Secchi*, 58; Malusa, *Neotomismo*, 1:54–58, 81–87; 2:235–92, 383–425.

87. CG 23 (1883), d. 12, p. 465f.; d. 15, p. 466f.; 26, d. 18, p. 510.

88. Unterburger, *Vom Lehramt*, 215f., 219.

89. For Italy, see Paiano, "Italian Jesuits."

90. For Ireland, see Burke (ed.), *Irish Jesuit*.

91. See the brief but pointed passage on Ledóchowski, in Colombo and Massimi, *In viaggio*, 52–66.

92. Unterburger, *Vom Lehramt*, 219f.

93. See the comprehensive study by Unterburger, *Vom Lehramt*.

94. On this, see the retrospective interpretation by Bea, "Apostolic Constitution," esp. 37, 46.

95. Unterburger, *Vom Lehramt*, 432–45. Cf. already Ledóchowski, "Epistola" (from 1918).

96. CG 28, d. 35, p. 609.

97. On China and Russia, cf. the remarks in Colombo and Massimi, *In viaggio*, 57–61.

98. Kertzer, *Pope and Mussolini*.

99. See Kertzer, *Pope and Mussolini*; MacNamara, *Catholic Cold War*.

100. CG 28, d. 29, p. 607.

101. Frehill, "Republican Dissent."

102. Cronin, "Catholicising Fascism"; Heffernan, "Discerning."

103. Egido, *Los jesuitas*, 365–57; Álvarez Bolado, "La Compañía," following quotation taken from p. 148.

104. Camprubí, *Engineers*, 57–61.

105. D'Agostino, *Rome*, 172f., 220f., 236, 244f.

106. Nelis, "Clerical Response."

107. Maryks, *"Pouring Jewish Water."*

108. Schatz 3:321–451; Lapomarda, *Jesuits*.

109. Plöckinger, *Geschichte*, 286f. (with quotation).

110. Quoted in Nelis, "Clerical Response," 268; Malusa, *Neotomismo*, 1:437–40.

111. CG 28, d. 29, p. 607.

112. Schwarte, *Gustav Gundlach*, 72–105. On Ledóchowski, see Kertzer, *Pope and Mussolini*, 364f.

113. On Jesuits in the Wehrmacht, see Leugers, *Jesuiten*.

114. For the United States, see McGreevy, *American Jesuits*, 23f. For a general assessment, see McDonough, *Men*, xii and 1. See also, more generally, O'Malley, *What Happened*.

115. O'Malley, *What Happened*, 83.

116. Mettepenningen, *Nouvelle théologie*, esp. 83–114; O'Malley, *What Happened*, 65–80.

117. Balthasar, *Gelebte Kirche*; Kapp, "Die katholischen Dichter"; Tilliette, *Le jésuite*, esp. 171–85; Claudel, *Journal*.

118. Schwarte, *Gustav Gundlach*, 187–89 (quotation on p. 187), 587 (on Brockmöller).

119. McDonough and Bianchi, *Passionate Uncertainty*, 112f.

120. O'Malley, *The Jesuits: A History*, 98.

121. CG 30, d. 9, p. 651f.

122. Stierli, "Das ignatianische Gebet," 161.

123. Murphy (ed.), *History*, 287–97, esp. 296f.

124. Schatz 4:411f., 450f., 75–98 (Janssens quoted on p. 92), 161–64; La Bella and Maier (eds.), *Pedro Arrupe*, 90–97; Whitfield, *Paying*, 22f., 28f. (on soccer).

125. O'Hanlon, "Jesuits," 25f.

126. Quoted in Ruiz Rodrigo, "La educación," 131.

127. Martínez Herrer, "Una experiencia."

128. Höltershinken, *Jesuiten*.

129. Schatz 4:116–19.

130. CG 28, d. 29, p. 606f.

131. Sperber, *Popular Catholicism*, 180–84.

132. Rauscher (ed.), *Gustav Gundlach*, 80f., 84–88.

133. Schatz 4:170–77.

134. Gundlach, "Die Lehre," 131, 124; Schwarte, *Gustav Gundlach*, 171–74.

135. "Neo-pagans": General Janssens in 1947, quoted in Barré, *Jésuites et ouvriers*, 40.

136. On this concept, cf. the groundbreaking work by Hersche, *Agrarische Religiosität*.

137. Perrin, *Tagebuch*, 13, 249; Straßner, "Die Arbeiterpriester." Cf. Barré, *Jésuites et ouvriers*.

138. Janssens's "Instruction on the Social Apostolate" is available at http://www.sjweb.info/sjs/documents/Janssens_eng.pdf.

139. Based on CG 29, d. 29, p. 639; Martina, *Storia*, 329f.

140. "Töten oder Taufen?," *Der Spiegel*, December 21, 1955, 25–28 (p. 27: "Linkskatholizismus"); cf. https://www.spiegel.de/spiegel/print/d-31971836.html (accessed March 6, 2020).

141. Schatz 4:165–70 (p. 166: "sozialistisch"); Höltershinken, *Jesuiten*, S. 71, 86–98 (p. 87: "einem theologischen Bestseller").

142. Schildt, *Zwischen Abendland*, 105 (NDR feature, October 8, 1954), 253 (conservative criticism from outside the order). Northwest German Broadcasting (NWDR) aired a thirty-minute "discussion" at 8:15 p.m. on December 8, 1954; cf. the television listings recorded at http://www.tvprogramme.net/50/1954/19541208.htm (accessed March 6, 2020).

143. On the worker-priests and communism, see Barré, *Jésuites et ouvriers*, 44 and passim.

144. See generally O'Malley, *What Happened*.

145. Schatz 4:335–53.

146. La Bella and Maier (eds.), *Pedro Arrupe*; Lamet, *Arrupe*, 287 (with quotation). See now also La Bella, *I gesuiti*, for the entire period.

147. La Bella and Maier (eds.), *Pedro Arrupe*, 31f., 90, etc.

148. CG 31, d. 2 no. 3, p. 74

149. La Bella and Maier (eds.), *Pedro Arrupe*, 27 and passim.

150. Lamet, *Arrupe*, 306f.; La Bella and Maier (eds.), *Pedro Arrupe*, 98f.

151. Schatz 4:368. Cf. the interview with Mario Schoenenberger in *Der Spiegel* 15 (1969): 89–97.

152. Ellacuría, "Pedro Arrupe," 125.

153. La Bella and Maier (eds.), *Pedro Arrupe*, 27.

154. Lamet, *Arrupe*, 320.

155. Padberg, "Society True to Itself," 38f.; Lamet, *Arrupe*, 294f., 332, 344, and passim. The editors of *Spiegel* repeatedly attempted to depict Arrupe as a reactionary. Cf. *Der Spiegel* 15 (1969): 89–97. In a similar vein, H. J. Herbort, "Ein Kampf gegen Rom. Der Aufstand der Jesuiten—'Fall Schoenenberger'—nur ein Glied in einer langen Kette," *Die Zeit*, May 2, 1969.

156. On Central America, see Whitfield, *Paying*, 37–47, 52–55, 58f.

157. The profound uncertainty of the Society of Jesus is illustrated by La Bella, *I gesuiti*, 1–130.

158. Martina, *Storia*, 377f. On conflicts with Paul VI, see La Bella, *I gesuiti*, 115 and passim.

159. Ivereigh, *Great Reformer*, 83–165 passim.

160. Autorenkollektiv (eds.), *Jesuiten.*

161. Cf. Giuseppe de Rosa's letter to Arrupe dated September 8, 1970, in La Bella, *I gesuiti,* 87–89.

162. La Bella, *I gesuiti,* 90–98; Álvarez Bolado, "La Compañía," 407–9.

163. Padberg, "Society True to Itself."

164. Quoted in Lamet, *Arrupe,* 293.

165. For the relevant material, see Padberg (ed.), *Documents.*

166. La Bella and Maier (eds.), *Pedro Arrupe,* 268–75. See also Balleis, "Global Human Mobility."

167. Cf. the remark by Peter Hans Kolvenbach in McDermott, "Let Us Look Together."

168. Martina, *Storia,* 383f.; Banchoff, "Jesuit Higher Education."

169. Home page: https://www.jwl.org/en/home. Cf. Balleis, "Global Human Mobility."

170. Ellacuría, "Pedro Arrupe," 114, 124.

171. Whitfield, *Paying.*

172. McDonough and Bianchi, *Passionate Uncertainty,* 2, 290.

173. La Bella, *I gesuiti,* 160–65.

174. La Bella, *I gesuiti,* 166–74.

175. See the long first decree of CG 33 at https://jesuitportal.bc.edu/research/documents /1983_decree1gc33/.

176. Thus wrote Kolvenbach in 1990; cf. the text in La Bella, *I gesuiti,* 247n124.

177. See Cardenal, *Faith.*

178. La Bella, *I gesuiti,* 234.

179. La Bella, *I gesuiti,* 235f.

180. The text can be found in Kolvenbach, "Service of Faith," 13–29. The impact of this speech is illustrated by Combs, *Transforming.*

181. Quoted in Autorenkollektiv (eds.), *Jesuiten,* 113.

182. CG 28, d. 19, p. 601; 30, d. 55, p. 675.

183. On this, and the following, see Hollenbach, "Jesuits."

184. Cf. Kolvenbach's self-assessment in McDermott, "Let Us Look Together."

185. From Barré, *Jésuites et ouvriers,* 35.

186. Lucchetti Bingemer, "Jesuits and Social Justice," 195.

187. See Arrupe's letter to the entire Society of Jesus, May 14, 1978: Arrupe, "On Inculturation," available at https://jesuitportal.bc.edu/research/documents/1978_arrupeinculturationsociety/. The worker-priests of France also saw their descent into the working class as a process of "incarnation"; see Barré, *Jésuites et ouvriers,* 46 (with quotation).

188. Sievernich, "Von der Akkommodation."

189. CG 34, d. 26, no. 14. A phrase of Arrupe's is cited at the end. Cf. also CG 34, d. 4. The decrees of this General Congregation are available at https://jesuitportal.bc.edu/research /general-congregations/general-congregation-34/ (accessed March 10, 2020). General Congregations 31 through 35 are available at the same site under the heading "General Congregations."

190. For the Spanish original, see http://2006.atrio.org/?p=565 (accessed March 10, 2020). Cf. similar positions in a subjective and biased selection in Kaiser, *Inside.*

191. On this and the following remarks, see La Bella, *I gesuiti*, 295–303.

192. Thus Cardinal Franc Rodé, in the context of a homily to the Jesuits, at https://www
.saintpeters.edu/wp-content/uploads/blogs.dir/135/files/2012/08/GC35_Decrees.pdf.

193. See the letter by Benedict XVI from January 10, 2008: Benedict XVI, "To Kolvenbach," at
https://www.saintpeters.edu/wp-content/uploads/blogs.dir/135/files/2012/08/GC35_Decrees
.pdf

194. See Spadaro, "Interview," 4.

195. The best biography is Ivereigh, *Great Reformer*; updated now in Ivereigh, *Wounded Shepherd*. Cf. also Deckers, *Papst Franziskus*.

196. Ivereigh, *Great Reformer*, 190–97; Erbacher, *Ein radikaler Papst*, 125–37.

197. Erbacher, *Ein radikaler Papst*, 120–25.

198. Gregory III (731–41) from Syria is generally regarded as the last non-European pope
before Francis.

199. Cf. the quotations in "Un cardinal cubain révèle l'intervention du futur Pape," *Le Point*,
March 27, 2013, https://www.lepoint.fr/monde/un-cardinal-cubain-revele-l-intervention-du
-futur-pape-avant-le-conclave-27-03-2013-1646616_24.php (accessed March 10, 2020).

200. Ivereigh, *Wounded Shepherd*; La Bella, *I gesuiti*, 335f. In depth on Bergoglio's intellectual
background and his grounding in twentieth-century Jesuit theology, see now Borghesi, *Mind of
Pope Francis*.

201. Kevin C. Shelly, "Francis Sounds Like a Jesuit, Not a Pope," *PhillyVoice*, September 21,
2015, http://www.phillyvoice.com/francis-sounds-jesuit-not-pope (accessed March 10, 2020).
Cf. also Kaiser, *Inside*.

202. For a typical example, see Kiechle, *Grenzen Überschreiten*.

203. Francis rested in 2015; cf. "Festtag für Franziskus: Papst feiert Ignatius-Tag 'in Ruhe,'"
Radio Vatikan, July 31, 2015, http://www.archivioradiovaticana.va/storico/2015/07/31/festtag
_f%C3%BCr_franziskus_papst_feiert_ignatius-tag_%E2%80%9Ein_ruhe%E2%80%9C/de
-1162118 (accessed March 10, 2020). As of this writing, in 2019, Francis paid a private visit to the
Jesuit headquarters for a private dinner with General Sosa. See "Pope Visits Jesuit Headquarters," *Vatican News*, July 8, 2019, https://www.vaticannews.va/en/pope/news/2019-07/pope
-francis-jesuit-curia-private-visit.html (accessed March 10, 2020).

204. See Spadaro, "Interview," 14: "I see clearly that the thing that the Church needs most
today is the ability to heal the wounds and reignite the hearts of the faithful, closeness,
conviviality."

205. Spadaro, "Interview," 27.

206. Spadaro, "Interview," 6–7 (concerning "discernement").

207. Eamon Duffy, "Who Is the Pope?," *New York Review of Books*, February 19, 2015, 11–14;
Erbacher, *Ein radikaler Papst*, 145f., 188–96.

WORKS CITED

Abbate, Emma. "Luigi Taparelli D'Azeglio e l'istruzione nei collegi gesuitici del XIX° secolo." *Archivio storico per le province napoletane* 115 (1997): 467–516.

Abou, Sélim. *The Jesuit "Republic" of the Guaranís (1609–1768) and Its Heritage.* New York 1997.

Acosta, José de. *De procuranda Indorum salute.* Lyon 1670. First published Salamanca 1588.

Albert, Marcel. "Jansenismus als diplomatisches Problem. Fabio Chigi und die Bekämpfung des Jansenismus in der Kölner Nuntiatur 1640–1651." In *Der Jansenismus–eine "katholische Häresie"? Das Ringen um Gnade, Rechtfertigung und die Autorität Augustins in der frühen Neuzeit*, edited by Dominik Burkard and Tanja Thanner, 193–239. Münster 2014.

Albertino, Francesco. *Trattato dell'angelo custode.* Rome 1612.

Albuquerque, Antonio. "Historia de la Vulgata." In *Las fuentes de los Ejercicios espirituales de san Ignacio. Actas del simposio internacional, Loyola, 15–19 septiembre*, edited by Juan Plazaola, 13–63. Bilbao 1998.

Alcalá, Luisa Elena. "The Jesuits and the Visual Arts in New Spain, 1670–1767." PhD diss., New York University, 1998.

Alcaraz Gómez, José F. *Jesuitas y reformismo. El Padre Francisco de Rávago (1747–1755).* Valencia 1995.

Alden, Dauril. *The Making of an Enterprise: The Society of Jesus in Portugal, Its Empire, and Beyond, 1540–1750.* Stanford, CA, 1996.

Alfieri, Fernanda. "'Unearthing Chaos and Giving Shape to It': The Society of Jesus after Suppression: Hiatus and Continuity." In *The Historiography of Transition: Critical Phases in the Development of Modernity (1494–1973)*, edited by Paolo Pombeni and Ralph Nisbet, 105–21. London 2015.

Alfieri, Fernanda, and Claudio Ferlan. "Storie die obbedienza negoziata." In *Avventure dell'obbedienza nella Compagnia di Gesù. Teorie e prassi fra XVI e XIX secolo*, edited by Fernanda Alfieri and Claudio Ferlan, 7–17. Bologna 2012.

Alonso Romo, Eduardo Javier. "Dominicos peninsulares amigos de los jesuitas." *Archivo Dominicano* 26 (2005): 75–101; 27 (2006): 117–42.

Altamore, Aldo, and Sabino Maffeo, eds. *Angelo Secchi. L'avventura scientifica del Collegio romano.* Foligno 2012.

Álvarez Bolado, Alfonso. "La Compañía de Jesús en España, entre 1936 y 1989." *Estudios eclesiásticos* 76 (2001): 145–91, 383–436.

Alvarez de Toledo, Cayetana. *Politics and Reform in Spain and Viceregal Mexico: The Life and Thought of Juan de Palafox, 1600–1659.* Oxford 2004.

Alves, Abel Athouguia. "The Christian Social Organism and Social Welfare: The Case of Vives, Calvin and Loyola." *Sixteenth Century Journal* 20 (1989): 3–22.

Amado Aymoré, Fernando. *Die Jesuiten im kolonialen Brasilien. Katechese als Kulturpolitik und Gesellschaftsphänomen (1549–1760)*. Frankfurt 2009.

Amidei, Rosanna Barbiellini. "Le decorazioni del Collegio Romano. 'Lo sforzo Gregoriano 1581–1585.'" In *Il Collegio Romano dalle origini al Ministero per i beni culturali e ambientali*, edited by Claudia Cerchiai, 201–64. Rome 2003.

Amsler, Nadine. *Jesuits and Matriarchs: Domestic Worship in Early Modern China*. Seattle 2018.

Anagnostou, Sabine. *Missionspharmazie. Konzepte, Praxis, Organisation und wissenschaftliche Ausstrahlung*. Stuttgart 2011.

Anderson, Emma. *The Betrayal of Faith: The Tragic Journey of a Colonial Native Convert*. Cambridge, MA, 2007.

Andrés-Gallego, José. "1767: Por qué los jesuitas." In *Los Jesuitas españoles expulsos. Su imagen y su contribución al saber sobre el mundo hispánico en la Europa del siglo XVIII*, edited by Manfred Tietz and Dietrich Briesemeister, 77–102. Madrid 2001.

Andrés Martin, Melquiades. "La espiritualidad española en el siglo XVII." In *Historia de la Teología española. II. Desde fines del siglo XVI hasta la actualidad*, edited by Melquiades Andrés Martin, 209–310. Madrid 1987.

———. *Los recogidos. Nueva visión de la mística española (1500–1700)*. Madrid 1975.

Anonymous. *L'Anticoton ou refutation de la lettre declaratoire du père Cotton*. [Paris] 1610.

———. *Le Mercure iesuite: ou, recueil des pieces, concernants le Progrés de Iesuites, leurs Escrits, et Differents*. 2 vols. Geneva 1631.

———. *Relação abreviada da República, que os religiosos jesuitas das províncias de Portugal e Hespagna estabeleceram nos domínios ultramarinos das duas monarchias*. N.p. 1757.

———. *Vorstellung des P. Provinzialen der oberdeutschen Provinz S.J. wider die Aufhebung des Nexus mit Ausländern und Gegen-Antwort*. N.p. 1770.

Anselmi, Gian-Mario. "Per un'archeologia della Ratio: dalla 'pedagogia' al 'governo.'" In *La "Ratio studiorum": Modelli culturali e pratiche educative dei Gesuiti in Italia tra Cinque e Seicento*, edited by Gian Paolo Brizzi, 11–42. Rome 1981.

Antonil, André João. *Brazil at the Dawn of the Eighteenth Century*. Dartmouth, MA, 2012.

Aracena, Beth K. "Viewing the Ethnomusicological Past: Jesuit Influences on Araucanian Music in Colonial Chile." *Latin American Music Review* 18 (1997): 1–29.

Aranha, Paolo. "'Glocal' Conflicts: Missionary Controversies on the Coromandel Coast between the XVII and the XVIII Centuries." In *Evangelizzazione e globalizzazione*, edited by Guido Mongini and Silvia Mostaccio, 79–104. Castello 2010.

———. "Sacramenti o *saṃskārāḥ*? L'illusione dell'*accommodatio* nella controversia dei riti malabarici." *Cristianesimo nella storia* 31 (2010): 621–46.

———. "The Social and Physical Spaces of the Malabar Rites Controversy." In *Space and Conversion in Global Perspective, Fifteenth–Nineteenth Centuries*, edited by Giuseppe Marcocci, 214–31. Leiden 2014.

Arens, Bernard. *Die katholischen Missionsvereine: Darstellung ihres Werdens und Wirkens*, Freiburg 1922.

———. *Jesuitenorden und Weltmission. Darstellung der heimatlichen Missionshilfe der Gesellschaft Jesu*. Regensburg 1937.

Argenti, Johannes. *Apologeticus pro Societate IESU*. Cologne 1616.

Aricò, Denise. "Fra teologia e censura. Lettere inedite di Daniello Bartoli a Giovanni Battista Riccioli." *Filologia e critica* 19 (1994): 91–131.

———. "Les 'yeux d'Argos' et les 'étoiles d'astrée' pour mesurer l'univers. Les Jésuites italiens et la science nouvelle." *Revue de synthèse* 120 (1999): 285–303.

Aricò, Nicola, and Fabio Basile. "L'insediamento della Compagnia di Gesù a Messina dal 1547 all'espulsione tanucciana." *Annali di storia delle università italiane* 2 (1998): 39–72.

Ariew, Roger. *Descartes and the Last Scholastics*. Ithaca, NY, 1999.

Aristizábal, Tulio. "Las cinco vocaciones de San Pedro Claver en defensa de la vida y de la dignidad humanas." *Boletín de historia y antigüedades* 827 (2004): 881–91.

Armogathe, Jean Robert. "L'œil vivant. Optique et représentation en Sicile au XVIIe siècle." In *Baroque vision jésuite. Du Tintoret à Rubens*, edited by Alain Tapié, 93–97. Paris 2003.

Arnauld, Antoine. *De la fréquente communion*. Paris 1643.

Arranz Roa, Íñigo. "Educar a rudos y pobres. La Casa de los Niños del Amor de Dios (Valladolid, 1595–1860)." In *Los jesuitas. Religión, política y educación, siglos XVI–XVIII*, edited by José Martínez Millán, Henar Pizarro Llorente, and Esther Jiménez Pablo, 491–526. Madrid 2012.

———. "Las Casas Profesas de la Compañía de Jesús: Centros de actividad apostólica y social. La Casa Profesa de Valladolid y Colegio de San Ignacio (1545–1767)." *Cuadernos de historia moderna* 28 (2003): 125–63.

———. "Las Indias de aquí. Misiones interiores en Castilla, siglos XVI–XVII." *Estudios eclesiásticos* 82, no. 321 (2007): 389–409.

Arrupe, Pedro, S.J. "On Inculturation, to the Whole Society." In *Other Apostolates Today: Selected Letters and Addresses*, ed. Jerome Aixala, vol. 3. (St. Louis 1981), 171–81.

Arzubialde, Santiago. *Ejercicios espirituales de S. Ignacio. Historia y análisis*. 2nd ed. Bilbao 2009.

Asmussen, Tina. "'Ein grausamer Alchemysten Feind.' Athanasius Kircher als Akteur und Figur gelehrter Polemik im 17. Jahrhundert." In *Scharlatan! Eine Figur der Relegation in der frühneuzeitlichen Gelehrtenkultur*, edited by Tina Asmussen and Hole Rössler, 215–44. Frankfurt 2013.

Assunção, Paolo de. *Negócios jesuíticos: O cotidiano da administração dos bens divinos*. Sao Paulo 2004.

Astier, Régine. "Pierre Beauchamps and the Ballet du Collège." *Dance Chronicle* 6 (1983): 138–63.

Aston, Nigel. *Christianity and Revolutionary Europe, 1750–1830*. Cambridge, UK, 2002.

Astrain, Antonio, S.J. *Historia de la Compañía de Jesús en la asistencia de España*. Vol. 5, *Vitelleschi, Carafa, Piccolomini, 1615–1652*. Madrid 1916.

Asúa, Miguel de. *Science in the Vanished Arcadia: Knowledge of Nature in the Jesuit Missions of Paraguay and Río de la Plata*. Leiden 2014.

Atkin, Nicholas, and Frank Tallett. *Priests, Prelates, and People: A History of European Catholicism since 1750*. Oxford 2003.

Autorenkollektiv, S.J., eds. *Jesuiten. Wohin steuert der Orden? Eine kritische Selbstdarstellung von einem Autorenteam S.J.* Freiburg 1975.

Ayrault, Pierre. *Petri Aerodii hochberühmten JCti Send-Schreiben und Unterricht von Vaterrechte* [. . .]. N.p. 1683.

Babin, Malte-Ludolf. "Leibniz' Verbindungen in die Niederlande." In *Leibniz als Sammler und Herausgeber historischer Quellen*, edited by Nora Gädeke, 139–54. Wiesbaden 2012.

Baer, Wolfram. "Die Gründung des Jesuitenkollegs St. Salvator." In *Die Jesuiten und ihre Schule St. Salvator in Augsburg 1582*, edited by Wolfram Baer, 17–22. Munich 1982.

Baffetti, Giovanni. "Teoria e prassi dell'oratoria sacra nella Compagnia di Gesù." In *La predicazione nel Seicento*, edited by Maria Luisa Doglio and Carlo Delcorno, 149–68. Bologna 2009.

Bailey, Charles R. "French Secondary Education, 1763–1790: The Secularization of Ex-Jesuit Collèges." *Transactions of the American Philosophical Society* 68, no. 6 (1978): 1–124.

Bailey, Gauvin Alexander. *Art on the Jesuit Missions in Asia and Latin America, 1542–1773*. Toronto 1999.

———. "Italian Renaissance Painting and Baroque Painting under the Jesuits and Its Legacy throughout Catholic Europe, 1565–1773." In *The Jesuits and the Arts, 1540–1773*, edited by John W. O'Malley, Gauvin A. Bailey, and Giovanni Sale, 125–98. Philadelphia 2005.

Baillet, Adrien. *De la dévotion à la Sainte Vierge et du culte qui est luis du*. 2nd ed. Tournai 1712.

Baker, Keith Michael. *Inventing the French Revolution: Essays on French Political Culture in the Eighteenth Century*. Cambridge, UK, 1990.

Baldini, Ugo. *Legem impone subactis. Studi su filosofia e scienza dei gesuiti in Italia 1540–1632*. Rome 1992.

Baldini, Ugo, and Gianpaolo Brizzi, eds. *La presenza in Italia dei gesuiti iberici espulsi. Aspetti religiosi, politici, culturali*. Bologna 2010.

Baldwin, Martha. "Alchemy and the Society of Jesus in the Seventeenth Century: Strange Bedfellows?" *Ambix* 40 (1993): 41–64.

Balleis, Peter. "Global Human Mobility, Refugees, and Jesuit Education at the Margins." In *The Jesuits and Globalization: Historical Legacies and Contemporary Challenges*, edited by José Casanova and Thomas F. Banchoff, 224–38. Washington, DC, 2016.

Balthasar, Hans Urs von. *Gelebte Kirche: Bernanos*. 2nd ed. Einsiedeln 1954.

Banchoff, Thomas F. "Jesuit Higher Education and the Global Common Good." In *Historical Legacies and Contemporary Challenges*, edited by José Casanova and Thomas F. Banchoff, 239–60. Washington, DC, 2016.

Bangert, William V. *A History of the Society of Jesus*. 2nd ed. St. Louis, MO, 1986.

———. *Jerome Nadal, S.J., 1507–1580: Tracking the First Generation of Jesuits*. Edited by Thomas M. McCoog, S.J. Chicago 1992.

Barbuto, Gennaro Maria. *Il principe e l'Anticristo: Gesuiti e ideologiche politiche*. Naples 1994.

Bardell, David. "Hodierna's 'The Eye of the Fly': The First Book of Microscopic Observations." *Bio Science* 43 (1993): 570–73.

Bargellini, Clara, and Michael Komanecky. *El arte de las misiones del norte de la Nueva España, 1600–1821*. Mexico City 2009.

Barré, Noël. *Jésuites et ouvriers. La mission ouvrière jésuite de 1944 à la fin des années 1990*. Paris 2014.

Barruel, Augustin. *Mémoires pour servir à l'histoire du Jacobinisme*. 4 vols. Hamburg 1797–98.

———. *Memoirs Illustrating the History of Jacobinism*. Translated by Robert Clifford. New York 1799.

Barry, Paul de. *La devotion aux anges*. Lyon 1644.

Barth, Medard. "Die Seelsorgetätigkeit der Molsheimer Jesuiten von 1580 bis 1765." *Archiv für elsässische Kirchengeschichte* 6 (1931): 325–400.

Barthet, Bernard. *Science, histoire et thématiques ésotériques chez les jésuites en France (1680–1764)*. Pessac 2012.

Bartoli, Daniele. *Della vita e dell'istituto di S. Ignatio: Fondatore della compagnia di Giesù, libri cinque*. Rome 1650.

———. *Dell'historia della Compagnia de Giesù. La Cina. Terza parte dell'Asia*. Rome 1663.

Bastid, Paul. "Montesquieu et les Jésuites." In *Actes du Congrès Montesquieu. Réuni à Bordeaux du 23 au 26 mai 1955 pour commémorer le deuxième centenaire de la mort de Montesquieu*, edited by Louis Desgraves, 305–26. Bordeaux 1956.

Batllori, Miguel. "Los Jesuitas y la guerra de Cataluña: 1640–1659." *Boletín de la academia de la historia* 146 (1960): 141–198.

Battistini, Andrea. "Forme e tendenze della predicazione barocca." In *La predicazione nel Seicento*, edited by Maria Luisa Doglio and Carlo Delcorno, 23–48. Bologna 2009.

———. "La cultura scientifica nel collegio bolognese." In *Dall'isola alla città. I gesuiti a Bologna*, edited by Gian Paolo Brizzi, 157–69. Bologna 1988.

Bauer, Barbara. "Das Regensburger Religionsgespräch." In *Wittelsbach und Bayern*. Pt. 2, *Um Glauben und Reich*, edited by Hubert Glaser, 90–101. Munich 1980.

———. "Jacob Pontanus SJ, ein oberdeutscher Lipsius. Ein Augsburger Schulmann zwischen italienischer Renaissancegelehrsamkeit und jesuitischer Dichtungstradition." *Zeitschrift für Bayerische Landesgeschichte* 47 (1984): 77–120.

Bauer-Mahlmann, Barbara. "Deutsch und Latein in den Schulen der Jesuiten." In *Latein und Nationalsprachen in der Renaissance*, edited by Bodo Guthmöller, 227–57. Wiesbaden 1998.

Baum, W. "Luigi Maria Torrigiani (1697–1777). Kardinalstaatssekretär Papst Klemens XIII." *Zeitschrift für katholische Theologie* 94 (1972): 46–78.

Bayón, Amalio. "La escuela jesuitica desde Suarez y Molina hasta la guerra de sucesión." In *Historia de la teología española. II. Desde fines del siglo XVI hasta la actualidad*, edited by Melquiades Andrés Martin, 39–74. Madrid 1987.

Bea, A., S.J. "The Apostolic Constitution *Deus Scientiarum Dominus*: Its Origin and Spirit." *Theological Studies* 4 (1943): 34–52.

Beaurepaire, Pierre-Yves. *La France des Lumières (1715–1789)*. Paris 2011.

Begheyn, Paul. "The Catechism (1555) of Peter Canisius, the Most Published Book by a Dutch Author in History." *Quaerendo* 36 (2006): 51–84.

———. *Jesuit Books in the Dutch Republic and Its Generality Lands 1567–1773: A Bibliography*. Leiden 2014.

———. "The Pastoral Journeys of the Dutch Jesuit Roeland de Pottere (1584–1675) in Delft and Environs: An Eyewitness about the Years 1621–1622." *Lias* 35 (2008): 187–208.

———. "Pierre Fabre as Director of the Spiritual Exercises: The Case of Peter Canisius." In *Ite, inflammate omnia: Selected Historical Papers from Conferences Held at Loyola and Rome in 2006*, edited by Thomas M. McCoog, 71–84. Rome 2010.

Behringer, Wolfgang. *Hexenverfolgung in Bayern. Volksmagie, Glaubenseifer und Staatsräson in der Frühen Neuzeit*. 3rd ed. Munich 1997.

Belda Plans, Juan. "Hacia una noción crítica de la 'Escuela de Salamanca.'" *Scripta heologica* 31 (1999): 376–411.

———. *La Escuela de Salamanca y la renovación de la teología en el siglo XVI*. Madrid 2000.

Bellini, Eraldo, and Claudio Scarpati. *Il vero e il falso dei poeti: Tasso, Tesauro, Pallavicino, Muratori*. Milan 1990.

Benci, Francesco. *Orationes et carmina, cum disputatione de stylo et scriptione*. 2nd ed. Cologne 1617.

Benci, Jorge. *Economia Christiaã dos senhores no governo dos escravos*. Rome 1705.

Benedict XVI. "To the Reverend Father Peter-Hans Kolvebach, S.J., Superior General of the Society of Jesus." In *Decrees of General Congregation 35*, ed. SJ (Washington, D.C.), 69–71.

Bennette, Rebecca Ayako. *Fighting for the Soul of Germany: The Catholic Struggle for Inclusion after Unification*. Berlin 2012.

Bergin, Joseph. *The Politics of Religion in Early Modern France*. New Haven, CT, 2014.

———. "The Royal Confessor and His Rivals in Seventeenth-Century France." *French History* 21 (2007): 187–204.

Bers, Günter. "Jülich in Sack und Asche. Religiöse Massenphänomene in einer rheinischen Stadt im Jahre 1714." *Zeitschrift des Aachener Geschichtsvereins* 102 (1999/2000): 185–217.

Bertrand, Dominique. *La Politique de Saint Ignace de Loyola. L'analyse social*. Paris 1985.

———. *Un corps pour l'esprit. Essai sur l'expérience communautaire d'après les Constitutions de la Compagnie de Jésus*. Paris 1974.

Besson, Joseph. *La Syrie et la Terre sainte au XVIIe siècle (Nouvelle édition)*. Edited by Augustin de Carayon. Paris 1862.

Betlej, Andrzej. "Jesuit Architecture in the Polish-Lithuanian Commonwealth in 1564–1772." In *La arquitectura jesuítica*, edited by María Isabel Alvaro Zamora, Javier Ibáñez Fernández, and Jesús Criado Mainar, 277–304. Zaragoza 2012.

Beyer, Jean. "Der Einfluß der Konstitutionen der Gesellschaft Jesu auf das moderne Ordensleben." *Geist und Leben* 29 (1956): 440–54; 30 (1957): 47–59.

Bezzel, Irmgard. "Erasmusdrucke in bayerischen Jesuitenbibliotheken." In *Das Verhältnis der Humanisten zum Buch*, edited by Fritz Krafft and Dieter Wuttke, 145–62. Boppard 1977.

Bianchini, Paolo. "La *Ratio studiorum* alla prova della modernità. Le revisioni del piano di studi e della pedagogia della Compagnia di Gesù tra XVIII e XIX secolo." *Rivista di storia del cristianesimo* 11 (2014): 325–40.

———. "Un mondo al plurale: I gesuiti e la società francese tra la fine del Settecento e i primi decenni dell'Ottocento." In *Morte e resurrezione di un Ordine religioso. Le strategie culturali ed educative della Conpagnia di Gesù durante la soppressione (1759–1814)*, edited by Paolo Bianchini, 53–88. Milan 2006.

Biasiori, Lucio. "Il controllo interno della produzione libraria nella Compagnia di Gesù e la formazione del Collegio dei Revisori generali (1550–1650)." *Annali della Scuola normale superiore di Pisa. Classe di lettere e filosofia* 5 (2010): 221–50.

Biffi, Inos. "La figura della teologia in Juan de Maldonado: Tra rinnovamento e fedeltà." In *Figure moderne della teologia nei secoli XV–XVII*, edited by Inos Biffi and Constante Marabelli, 137–56. Lugano 2007.

Bilinkoff, Jodi. "The Many 'Lives' of Pedro de Ribadeneira." *Renaissance Quarterly* 52 (1999): 180–96.

———. *Related Lives: Confessors and Their Female Penitents, 1450–1750*. Ithaca, NY, 2005.

Binet, Étienne. *Quel est le meilleur gouvernement, le rigoureux ou le doux?* Paris 1884.

Bireley, Robert. "Acquaviva's 'Instruction for Confessors of Princes' (1602/1608): A Document and Its Interpretation." In *Los jesuitas. Religión, política y educación, siglos XVI–XVIII*, edited by José Martínez Millán, Henar Pizarro Llorente, and Esther Jiménez Pablo, 45–68. Madrid 2012.

———. *The Jesuits and the Thirty Years War: Kings, Courts, and Confessors.* Cambridge, UK, 2003.

———. *Maximilian von Bayern, Adam Contzen S.J. und die Gegenreformation in Deutschland 1624–1635.* Göttingen 1975.

———. *Religion and Politics in the Age of the Counterreformation: Emperor Ferdinand II, William Lamormaini, S.J. and the Formation of Imperial Policy.* Chapel Hill, NC, 1981.

Bisschop, Jan. *Pharmacia Galenica & Chymica, Dat is de Apotheker ende Alchymiste ofte Distillerkonste.* 2nd ed. Amsterdam 1657.

Bitzel, Diane. *Bernardo Zamagna, Navis aëria. Eine Metamorphose des Lehrgedichts im Zeichen des technischen Fortschritts.* Frankfurt 1997.

Blackbourn, David. *Marpingen: Apparitions of the Virgin Mary in Bismarckian Germany.* New York 1994.

Blackburn, Carole. *Harvest of Souls: The Jesuit Missions and Colonialism in North America, 1632–1650.* Montreal 2000.

Blanchard, David. "To the Other Side of the Sky: Catholicism at Kahnawake." *Anthropologica* 25 (1982): 77–102.

Blanchard, Jean-Baptiste. *Préceptes pour l'éducation des deux sexes à l'usage des familles chrétiennes.* 2 vols. Lyon 1803.

Blanco, Mercedes. "Ambiguïtés d'une réforme: La critique de la prédiction conceptiste au XVIIIe siècle." *Mélanges de la Casa de Velazquez* 24 (1988): 153–75.

Block, David. "Links to the Frontier: Jesuit Supply of Its Moxos Missions, 1683–1767." *The Americas* 37 (1980): 161–78.

———. *Mission Culture on the Upper Amazon: Native tradition, Jesuit Enterprise and Secular Policy in Moxos, 1660–1880.* Lincoln, NE, 1994.

Bobková, Katerina. "Studienstiftungen für Schüler der Jesuitenschulen der Böhmischen Ordensprovinz." In *Schulstiftungen und Studienfinanzierung. Bildungsmäzenatentum in den böhmischen, österreichischen und ungarischen Ländern, 1500–1800,* edited by Joachim Bahlcke and Thomas Winkelbauer, 231–51. Vienna 2011.

Boccazzi Mazza, Barbara. "Governare i 'luoghi pii': La casa delle zitelle." *Studi veneziani* 50 (2005): 293–99.

Boda, Yang. "Castiglione at the Qing Court: An Important Artistic Contribution." *Orientations* 19 (1988): 44–50.

Boehmer, Heinrich. *Die Jesuiten. Auf Grund der Vorarbeiten von Hans Leube.* Edited by Kurt Dietrich Schmidt. Stuttgart 1957.

Boer, Wietse de. *The Conquest of the Soul: Confession, Discipline, and Public Order in Counter-Reformation Milan.* Leiden 2001.

Boer, Witse de, and Christine Göttler, eds. *Religion and the Senses in Early Modern Europe.* Leiden 2013.

Boesch Gajano, Sofia. "Delle raccolte di vite di Santi agli Acta Sanctorum. Persistenze e trasformazioni fra umanesimo e controriforma." In *De Rosweyde aux Acta Sanctorum. La recherche hagiographique des Bollandistes à travers quatre siècles,* edited by Robert Godding, 5–35. Brussels 2009.

Boileau, Jacques. *Histoire des flagellants.* Amsterdam 1701.

Bombart, Mathilde. "Un antijésuitisme 'littéraire'? La polémique contre François Garasse." In *Les antijésuites. Discours, figures et lieux de l'antijésuitisme à l'époque moderne,* edited by Pierre-Antoine Fabre and Catherine Maire, 179–96. Rennes 2010.

Bonifacio, Juan. *Institutio pueri christiani.* Ingolstadt 1607.

Bonora, Elena. *I conflitti della Controriforma. Sanità e obbedienza nell'esperienza religiosa dei primi barnabiti.* Florence 1998.

Borgato, Maria Teresa, ed. *Giambattista Riccioli e il merito scientifico dei gesuiti nell'Età barocca.* Florence 2002.

Borges, Charles J. *The Economics of the Goa Jesuits, 1542–1759: An Explanation of Their Rise and Fall.* New Delhi 1994.

Borges, Pedro. "Nuevos datos sobre la Comisión Pontifica para Indias de 1568." *Missionalia Hispanica* 46 (1959): 213–41.

Borghesi, Mossimo. *The Mind of Pope Francis: Jorge Mario Bergoglio's Intellectual Journey.* Collegeville, MN, 2017.

Borgo, Carlo. *Memoria cattolica da presentarsi a Sua Santità.* Cosmopolis [Rome] 1780.

Borja Medina, Francisco de. "El esclavo: Bien mueble o persona? Algunas observaciones sobre la evangelización del negro en las haciendas jesuíticas." In *Esclavitud, economía y evangelización. Las haciendas jesuitas en la América virreinal,* edited by Sandra Negro and Manuel M. Marzal, 83–122. Lima 2005.

———. "Jesuitas en la armada contra Inglaterra (1588). Notas para un centenario." *Archivum historicum Societatis Iesu* 58 (1989): 3–42.

Boschet, Antoine, S.J. *Le parfait missionnaire ou la vie du R. P. Julien Maunoir de la Compagnie de Jésus, missionnaire en Bretagne.* Paris 1697.

Boscovich, Roger J. *De solis ac lunae defectibus libri V.* London 1760.

———. *Edizione nazionale delle opere e della corrispondenza di Ruggiero Giuseppe Boscovich.* Vol. 13, pt. 2, *Opere scientifiche in versi. Les eclipses. Poème en six chants.* Edited by Luca Guzzardi. Rome 2012.

Bösel, Richard. "Die Jesuitenkirche in Mondoví. Zur Raumarchitektur eines Perspektivmalers." In *Andrea Pozzo (1642–1709). Der Maler-Architekt und die Räume der Jesuiten,* edited by Herbert Karner and Stefanie Linsboth, 57–68. Vienna 2012.

———. "Jesuit Architecture in Europe." In *The Jesuits and the Arts, 1540–1773,* edited by John W. O'Malley, Gauvin A. Bailey, and Giovanni Sale, 65–122. Philadelphia 2005.

———. *Jesuitenarchitektur in Italien (1540–1773).* 2 vols. Vienna 1985–2007.

———. "La *ratio aedificorum* di un'istituzione globale tra autorità centrale e infinità del territorio." In *La arquitectura jesuítica,* edited by María Isabel Alvaro Zamora, Javier Ibáñez Fernández, and Jesús Criado Mainar, 39–70. Zaragoza 2012.

———. "Meglio soli che 'boncompagnati'? La facciata del Collegio Romano tra magnificenza papale e pauperismo religioso." *Römische historische Mitteilungen* 52 (2011): 147–98.

Bösel, Richard, and Lydia Salviucci Insolera, eds. *Andrea Pozzo.* Rome 2011.

Bosmans, Henri. "Théodore Moretus de la Compagnie de Jésus, mathématicien. D'après sa correspondance et ses manuscrits." *De Gulden Passer* 6 (1928): 57–163.

Bottereau, Georges. "Jésuites et Ursulines au Canada de 1639–1645." *Archivum historicum Societatis Iesu* 47 (1978): 350–60.

———. "La 'lettre' d'Ignace de Loyola à Gian Pietro Carafa." *Archivum historicum Societatis Iesu* 44 (1975): 139–52.

Boucher, Philip P. *Cannibal Encounters: Europeans and Island Caribs, 1492–1763*. Baltimore 1992.

———. *France and the American Tropics to 1700: Tropics of Discontent?* Baltimore 2008.

Boudet, Antoine. *Histoire générale de la Marine: Contenant son origine chez tous les peuples du monde, ses progrès, son état actuel, & les expéditions maritimes, anciennes & modernes*. Vol. 3. Amsterdam 1758.

Bouillier, Francisque. *Histoire de la philosophie cartésienne*. 2 vols. Paris 1868.

Bourdaloue, Louis. *Œuvres complètes de Bourdaloue, de la Compagnie de Jésus*. 16 vols. Versailles 1812.

Bouuaert-Claeys, F. "Une visite canonique des Maisons de la Compagnie de Jésus en Belgique (1603–1604)." *Bulletin de l'Institut Historique Belge de Rome* 7 (1927): 5–116.

Bovelette, Heinrich. "Die Laienbrüder der Dürener Jesuiten." *Dürener Geschichts-Blätter* (1955): 199–202.

Boyle, Marjorie O'Rourke. "Angels Black and White: Loyola's Spiritual Discernment in Historical Perspective." *Theological Studies* 44 (1983): 241–57.

———. *Loyola's Acts: The Rhetoric of the Self*. Berkeley 1997.

Brader, David. "Die Entwicklung des Geschichtsunterrichts an den Jesuitenschulen Deutschlands und Oesterreichs (1540–1774)." *Historisches Jahrbuch* 31 (1910): 728–59.

Brambilla, Elena. *Alle origini del Sant'Uffizio. Penitenza confessione e giustizia spirituale dal medioevo al XVI secolo*. Bologna 2000.

Braun, Harald E. *Juan de Mariana and Early Modern Spanish Political Thought*. Aldershot 2007.

Braun, Ludwig. *Ancilla Calliopeae. Ein Repertorium der neulateinischen Epik Frankreichs (1500–1700)*. Leiden 2007.

Braunsberger, Otto. "Ein Meister des inneren Gebets." *Stimmen der Zeit* 105 (1923): 81–91.

Breidbach, Olaf, and Michael T. Ghiselin. "Athanasius Kircher (1602–1680) on Noah's Ark: Baroque 'Intelligent Design' Theory." *Proceedings of the California Academy of Sciences* 57, no. 36 (2006): 991–1002.

Breitenstein, Mirko. *Das Noviziat im hohen Mittelalter. Zur Organisation des Eintrittes bei den Cluniazensern, Cisterziensern und Franziskanern*. Berlin 2008.

Bremer, H. "Das Gutachten des Jakob Pontanus über die humanistischen Studien in den deutschen Jesuitenschulen." *Zeitschrift für katholische Theologie* 28 (1904): 621–31.

Bremer, Kai. *Religionsstreitigkeiten. Volkssprachliche Kontroversen zwischen altgläubigen und evangelischen Theologen im 16. Jahrhundert*. Tübingen 2005.

Bremond, Henri. *Histoire Littéraire du sentiment religieux en France depuis la fin des Guerres de Religion jusqu'à nos jours*. 8 vols. Paris 1923.

Brendle, Franz, and Anton Schindling, eds. *Geistliche im Krieg*. Münster 2009.

Brennan, Michael G. "John Bargrave and the Jesuits." *Catholic Historical Review* 88 (2002): 655–76.

Breuer, Dieter. "Der Anteil der Jesuiten an der Kulturentwicklung im Hochstift Ermland und im Herzogtum Preußen (Braunsberg, Rössel, Königsberg)." In *Kulturgeschichte Ostpreussens in der Frühen Neuzeit*, edited by Klaus Garber, Manfred Komorowski, and Axel E. Walter, 319–33. Tübingen 2001.

Brizzi, Gian Paolo. *La formazione della classe dirigente nel Sei-Settecento*. Bologna 1976.

Brockey, Liam Matthew. "The Death and 'Disappearance' of Nicolas Trigault S. J." *Journal of the Metropolitan Museum of Art* 38 (2003): 161–67.

———. *Journey to the East: The Jesuit Mission to China 1579–1724*. Cambridge, MA, 2007.

———. "Largos Caminhos e Vastos Mares. Jesuit Missionaries and the Journey to China in the Sixteenth and Seventeenth Centuries." *Bulletin of Portuguese Japanese Studies* 1 (2001): 45–72.

———. *The Visitor: André Palmeiro and the Jesuits in Asia*. Cambridge, MA, 2014.

Brockliss, Laurence W. B. *French Higher Education in the Seventeenth and Eighteenth Centuries: A Cultural History*. Oxford 1987.

Broggio, Paolo. "I gesuiti e la confessione sacramentale nel Perù coloniale. ipotesi di ricerca." *Archivio per l'antropologia e la etnologia* 135 (2005): 39–56.

———. "Immacolata Concezione." *Bruniana & Campanelliana* 17 (2011): 233–42.

———. "L'Acto de contrición entre Europe et nouveaux mondes. Diego Luis de Sanvítores et la circulation des stratégies d'évangélisation de la compagnie de Jésus en XVIIe siècle." In *Missions religieuses modernes. "Notre lieu est le monde,"* edited by Pierre-Antoine Fabre and Bernard Vincent, 229–59. Rome 2007.

———. *La teologia e la politica. Controversie dottrinali, curia romana e monarchia spagnola tra Cinque e Seicento*. Florence 2009.

———. "Potere, fedeltà e obbedienza. Johann Eberhard Nithard e la coscienza della regina nella Spagna del Seicento." In *Avventure dell'obbedienza nella Compagnia di Gesù. Teorie e prassi fra XVI e XIX secolo*, edited by Fernanda Alfieri and Claudio Ferlan, 165–94. Bologna 2012.

———. "Teologia, ordini religiosi e rapporti politici. La questione dell'Immaculata concezione di Maria tra Roma e Madrid (1614–1663)." *Hispania sacra* 65 (2013): 255–81.

Brosseder, Claudia. *The Power of Huacas: Change and Resistance in the Andean World of Colonial Peru*. Austin, TX, 2014.

Brou, Alexandre. *Les Jésuites missionnaires au XIX siècle*. Brussels 1908.

Brouwers, Louis. "L'*Elogium* du père Thomas Sailly S.I. (1553–1623) composé par le père Carolus Scribani S.I." *Archivum historicum Societatis Iesu* 48 (1979): 87–124.

Browning, John D. "Cornelius de Pauw and Exiled Jesuits: The Development of Nationalism in Spanish America." *Eighteenth-Century Studies* 11 (1978): 289–307.

Brüning, Walter M. "Zur Vorgeschichte der Messe 'Pro Propagatione Fidei.' Eine Bittschrift aus der Sonoramission im Jahre 1707." *Archivum historicum Societatis Iesu* 8 (1939): 319–27.

Brunner, Andreas. *Dramata Sacra oder Hertzrührende Schaubühne auff welcher [...] das H. Leiden Christi [...] vorgestellet*. Salzburg 1684.

Bruno, Vincenzo. *Brevis tractatio de sacramento poenitentiae, cum examine generale ad confessionem de tota vita*. Cologne 1599.

Bruycker, Angelo de. "'To the Adornment and Honour of the City': The Mathematics Course of the Flemish Jesuits in the Seventeenth Century." *Journal of the British Society for the History of Mathematics* 24 (2009): 135–46.

Brzosa, Ulrich. *Die Geschichte der katholischen Kirche in Düsseldorf*. Cologne 2001.

Buckley, Cornelius Michael. *Stephen Larigaudelle Dubuisson, S.J. (1786–1864) and the Reform of the American Jesuits*. Lanham, MD, 2013.

[Budrioli, Andrea.] *La madre di Dio preservata dalla peste del peccato originale ec. convenientissima preservatrice, o liberatrice dalla peste si' dell'anima, che del corpo.* Padova 1752.

Burkard, Dominik. "Zur Vorgeschichte der 'fünf Propositionen' aus dem Augustinus von Cornelius Jansen (1649–1652). Das unbekannte Memorandum der Pariser Augustinisten für Innozenz X." In *Der Jansenismus–eine "katholische Häresie"? Das Ringen um Gnade, Rechtfertigung und die Autorität Augustins in der frühen Neuzeit*, edited by Dominik Burkard and Tanja Thanner, 241–79. Münster 2014.

Burke, Damien, ed. *Irish Jesuit Chaplains in the First World War.* Dublin 2014.

Burkhardt, Friedrich, and Paul Habermehl, eds. *Die Neustadter Pfarrchronik der Jesuiten 1686–1755. Ein Dokument der Gegenreformation.* Neustadt an der Weinstraße 2008.

Burrieza Sánchez, Javier. "La fundación de colegios y el mundo femenino." In *Los jesuitas. Religión, política y educación, siglos XVI–XVIII*, edited by José Martínez Millán, Henar Pizarro Llorente, and Esther Jiménez Pablo, 443–89. Madrid 2012.

Burrus, Ernest, ed. *Jesuit Relations: Baja California, 1716–1762.* Los Angeles 1984.

———, ed. *Kino Reports to Headquarters: Correspondence of Eusebio F. Kino, S.J., from New Spain with Rome.* Rome 1954.

———, ed. *Kino Writes to the Duchess: Letters of Eusebio Francisco Kino to the Duchess of Aveiro.* St. Louis. MO, 1965.

———. "The Language Problem in Spain's Overseas Dominions." *Neue Zeitschrift für Missionswissenschaft* 35 (1979): 161–70.

———. "Pioneer Jesuit Apostles among the Indians of New Spain (1572–1604): Ignatian Principles Put into Practice." *Archivum historicum Societatis Iesu* 25 (1956): 574–95.

Burrus, Ernest, and Felix Zubillaga, eds. *El noroeste de México. Documentos sobre las misiones jesuíticas 1600–1769.* Mexico City 1986.

———, eds. *Misiones mexicanas de la Compañía de Jesús, 1618–1745: Cartas e informes conservados en la "Colección Mateu."* Madrid 1982.

Burschel, Peter. *Sterben und Unsterblichkeit. Zur Kultur des Martyriums in der frühen Neuzeit.* Munich 2004.

Burson, Jeffrey D. "Abdication of Legitimate Heirs: The Use and Abuse of Locke in the Jesuit Journal de Trévoux and the Origins of Counter-Enlightenment, 1737–1767." *Studies on Voltaire and the Eighteenth Century* 2005, no. 7 (2005): 297–325.

———. "Claude G. Buffier and the Maturation of the Jesuit Synthesis in the Age of Enlightenment." *Intellectual History Review* 21 (2011): 449–72.

———. "The Crystallization of Counter-Enlightenment and Philosophe Identities: Theological Controversy and Catholic Enlightenment in Pre-Revolutionary France." *Church History* 77 (2008): 955–1002.

———. *The Rise and Fall of Theological Enlightenment: Jean-Martin de Prades and Ideological Polarization in Eighteenth-Century France.* Notre Dame, IN, 2010.

Burson, Jeffrey D., and Jonathan Wright, eds. *The Jesuit Suppression in Global Context: Causes, Events, and Consequences.* Cambridge 2015.

Cabilliau, Baudouin [Balduinus Cabilliavus]. *Magdalena.* Antwerp 1625.

Cajani, Luigi, and Anna Foa. "CLEMENTE XIII, papa." DBI 26 (1982). http://www.treccani.it /enciclopedia/papa-clemente-xiii_%28Dizionario-Biografico%29/. Accessed February 24, 2020.

Cajetanus, Constantinus [Costantino Caetano]. *De religiosa S. Ignatii, sive S. Enneconis fundatoris societatis Jesu, per patres Benedictinos institutione, deque libello exercitiorum eiusdem, ab exercitatorio venerabilis servi dei, Garciae Cisnerii, abbatis Benedictini, magna ex parte desumpto.* Venice 1641.

Campeau, Lucien. "DRUILLETTES (Dreuillettes, Drouillettes, Drouillet, Droulletes, Drueillettes Druilletes), GABRIEL." In *Dictionary of Canadian Biography*. Vol. 1. University of Toronto/Université Laval, 2003–present. http://www.biographi.ca/en/bio/druillettes _gabriel_1E.html. Accessed January 13, 2020.

———. *La mission dés jésuites chez les Hurons, 1634–1650.* Montreal 1987.

———. "Le voyage du Père Alexandre de Rhodes en France, 1653–1654." *Archivum historicum Societatis Iesu* 48 (1979): 65–86.

Camprubí, Lino. *Engineers and the Making of the Francoist Regime.* London 2014.

Cams, Mario. "The Early Qing Geographical Surveys (1708–1716) as a Case of Collaboration between the Jesuits and the Kangxi Court." *Sino-Western Cultural Relations Journal* 34 (2012): 1–20.

Canisius, Peter. *Das Testament des Petrus Canisius. Vermächtnis und Auftrag.* Edited by Rita Haub and Julius Oswald. Frankfurt 1997.

Cañizares-Esguerra, Jorge. *How to Write the History of the New World: Histories, Epistemologies, and Identities in the Eighteenth-Century Atlantic World.* Stanford CA, 2001.

Capoccia, Anna Rita. "Le destin des *indipetae* au-delà du XVIe siècle." In *Missions religieuses modernes. "Notre lieu est le monde,"* edited by Pierre-Antoine Fabre and Bernard Vincent, 88–103. Rome 2007.

———. "MANCINELLI, Giulio." DBI 68 (2007). http://www.treccani.it/enciclopedia/giulio -mancinelli_(Dizionario-Biografico)/. Accessed January 17, 2020.

———. "Modernità e ortodossia: Strategie di conciliazione e dissidenza nell'insegnamento della filosofia nei collegi gesuitici del primo Settecento." *Le Dossiers du Grihl* 2009-2 (2009). https://journals.openedition.org/dossiersgrihl/3678.

———. "Per una lettura delle *indipetae* italiane del Settecento: 'Indifferenza' e desiderio di martirio." *Nouvelles de la république des lettres* 1 (2000): 7–43.

Capoccia, Anna Rita, and Ettore Lojacono. "Giulio Gori, un gesuita singolare, teorico della dissimulazione. Il problema del suo insegnamento della filosofia cartesiana al Collegio Romano nei primi decenni del XVIII secolo." In *Descartes e l'eredità cartesiana nell'Europa seisettecentesca,* edited by Maria Teresa Marcialis and Francesca Maria Crasta, 327–55. Lecce 2002.

Caraman, Philip. *Tibet: The Jesuit Century.* Tiverton 1998.

Carayon, Auguste, ed. *Documents inédits concernant la Compagnie de Jesus.* 23 vols. Poitiers 1863–86.

———, ed. *Première mission des Jésuites au Canada.* Paris 1864.

Carbonell de Masy, Rafael. *Estrategias de desarrollo rural en los pueblos guaranies (1609–1767).* Barcelona 1992.

———. "Las ordenaciones del P. Nicolas Duran Mastrilli para la Provincia jesuítica del Paraguay. Libertad evangélica y opción preferencial por los indios." *Folia historica del nordeste* 8 (1989): 5–43.

Cardenal, Fernando. *Faith and Joy: Memoirs of a Revolutionary Priest*. Maryknoll, NY, 2015.

Carel, Jacques. "La dévotion à l'ange gardien dans le nord de la Lorraine." *Cahiers lorrains* 1 (1995): 23–34.

Cargnoni, Costanzo. *Le quarantore ieri e oggi: Viaggio nella storia della predicazione cattolica, della devozione popolare e della spiritualità cappuccina*. Rome 1986.

Carlsmith, Christopher. "Struggling toward Success: Jesuit Education in Italy, 1540–1600." *History of Education Quarterly* 42 (2002): 217–46.

Carrasco, Raphael. "Le crime de frère Hernando. Un drame au collège de Grenade en 1616." In *Les Jésuites en Espagne et en Amérique. Jeux et enjeux du pouvoir (XVIe–XVIIIe siècles)*, edited by Annie Molinié, 433–48. Paris 2007.

Carrasco Martínez, Adolfo. "Los Mendoza y lo sagrado. Piedad y símbolo religioso en la cultura nobiliaria." *Cuadernos de historia moderna* 25 (2000): 233–69.

Carter, Karen E. *Creating Catholics: Catechism and Primary Education in Early Modern France*. Notre Dame, IN, 2010.

Carvalho e Melo, Sebastião José de. *Kurtze Nachricht von der Republique, so von denen R. R. P. P. der Gesellschafft Jesu der portugiessisch- und spanischen Provinzen in den über Meer gelegenen diesen zweyen Mächten gehörigen Königreichen aufgerichtet worden*. Lisbon 1760.

———. *Relation abrégée, concernant la république que les religieux, nommes Jésuites, des provinces de Portugal & d'Espagne, ont établie dans les pays & domaines d'outremer de ces deux monarchies*. Paris 1758.

Casalini, Cristiano. "Włodzimierz Ledóchowski's Call for Cura Personalis: Humanist Roots and Jesuit Distinctiveness in Education." *Studia paedagogica ignatiana* 22 (2020): 123–34.

Castaldo, Giovanni Battista. *De beati Caietani Thienaei cum B. Ignatio Loiolo consuetudine deque huius in clericorum regularium ordinem propensione*. Vicenza 1618.

———. *Pacificum certamen seu in Rev. P. Iulij Negroni Genuensis Societatem presbyteri opusculum posthumum contines disputationem [. . .] animadversiones*. Sorrento 1637.

Castelnau-L'Estoile, Charlotte de. *Les ouvriers d'une vigne stérile. Les jésuites et la conversion des indiens au Brésil*. Lisbon 2000.

Castillo Gómez, Antonio. "El Taller del Predicador. Lectura y escritura en el sermón barroco." *Via spiritus* 11 (2004): 7–26.

Catalano, Alessandro. *La Boemia e la riconquista delle coscienze. Ernst Adalbert von Harrach e la Controriforma in Europa centrale (1620–1667)*. Rome 2005.

Catto, Michela, ed. *Direzione spirituale tra ortodossia ed eresia. Dalle scuole filosofiche antiche al Novecento*. Brescia 2002.

———. *La compagnia divisa. Il dissenso nell'ordine gesuitico tra '500 e '600*. Brescia 2009.

———, ed. *La direzione spirituale tra medioevo ed età moderna. Percorsi di ricerca e contesti specifici*. Bologna 2004.

Catto, Michela, and Claudio Ferlan, eds. *I gesuiti e i papi*. Annali dell'Istituto storico italo-germanico in Trento, Quaderni, 97. Bologna 2016.

Caussin, Nicolas. *Eloquentiae sacrae et humanae parallela, libri XVI*. Paris 1619.

Cavallo, Sandra. *Charity and Power in Early Modern Italy: Benefactors and Their Motives in Turin, 1541–1789*. Cambridge 1995.

Cavazza, Marta. "La scienza, lo studio, i gesuiti a Bologna nella metà del Seicento." *Giornale di astronomia* 32 (2006): 11–19.

Cebollada Silvestre, Pascual. "La significación de Jan Philip Roothaan, S.J. en la historia de los Ejercicios espirituales ignacianos." *Estudios eclesiásticos* 91 (2016): 391–410.

Ceccotti, Giovanni B. *Apparatus ad meditationes vitae domini nostri Iesu Christi*. Rome 1631.

Ceglia, Francesco Paolo de. "*Additio ILLA Non Videtur Edenda*: Giuseppe Biancani, Reader of Galileo in an Unedited Censored Text." In *The New Science and Jesuit Science: Seventeenth Century Perspectives*, edited by Mordechai Feingold, 159–86. Dordrecht 2003.

Centorrino, Giovanna. *Il trattato di padre Ludovico Flori. Analisi del contenuto e trasposizione in linguaggio contemporaneo*. Rome 2008.

Cepari, Virgilio. *Essercitio della presenza di Dio*. 2 parts in 1 vol. Rome 1621.

Certeau, Michel de. *Die mystische Fabel*. Frankfurt 2010.

———. *The Possession at Loudun*. Chicago 2000.

Cessac, Catherine. "Le Regina caeli (H 32) conservé à Québec: Un nouveau regard." *Bulletin Charpentier* 1 (2008): 1–14.

Ceva, Tommaso. *Memorie d'alcune virtù del signor conte Francesco De Lemene con alcune riflessioni su le sue poesie*. Milan 1706.

Chadwick, Hubert. "Paccanarists in England." *Archivum historicum Societatis Iesu* 20 (1961): 143–66.

———. *St. Omers to Stonyhurst: A History of Two Centuries: St. Omers, 1593; Bruges, 1762; Liege, 1773; Stonyhurst, 1794*. London 1962.

Chadwick, Owen. *The Popes and European Revolution*. Oxford 1981.

Champion, Pierre. *Vie du Père Vincent Huby, de Mademoiselle de Francheville, et de Monsieur de Kerlivio*. Edited by P. Watringant. Lille 1886.

Chan, Albert. "Towards a Chinese Church: The Contribution of Philippe Couplet (1622–1693)." In *Philippe Couplet, S.J. (1623–1693): The Man Who Brought China to Europe*, edited by Jerome Heyndrickx, 55–86. Nettetal 1990.

Chaparro Martínez, Sandra. "Juan Eusebio de Nieremberg (1595–1658). Un intelectual de la monarquía católica hispana." *Razón y fe* 264, no. 1358 (2011): 427–36.

———. "Maquiavelo y la política de Dios. Los teóricos políticos de la compañía de Jesús ante el reto del realismo maquiaveliano." In *Los jesuitas. Religión, política y educación, siglos XVI–XVIII*, edited by José Martínez Millán, Henar Pizarro Llorente, and Esther Jiménez Pablo, 1197–219. Madrid 2012.

Charland, Thomas. "RALE (Râle, Rasle, Rasles), SÉBASTIEN." In *Dictionary of Canadian Biography*. Vol. 2. University of Toronto and Université Laval, 2003–present. http://www.biographi.ca/en/bio/rale_sebastien_2E.html. Last accessed January 10, 2020.

Charma, Antoine, and Georges Mancel, eds. *Le Père André, jésuite, documents inédits pour servir à l'histoire philosophique, religieuse et littéraire du XVIIIe siècle*. Caen 1844.

Châtellier, Louis. "À l'origine d'une société catholique. Le rôle des congrégations mariales au XVIème–XVIIIème siècles." *Histoire, économie et société* 3 (1984): 203–20.

———. "Genèse de bibliothèques. Les jésuites et les oratoriens en Alsace et en Lorraine vers 1630." In *Les religieux et leurs livres à l'époque moderne*, edited by Bernard Dompnier and Marie-Hélène Froeschlé-Chopard, 39–49. Clerment-Ferrand 2000.

———. "Les premières congrégations mariales dans les pays de langue français." *Revue de l'histoire de l'église de France* 75 (1989): 167–76.

———. *L'Europe des dévots*. Paris 1987.

———. *The Religion of the Poor: Rural Missions in Europe and the Formation of Modern Catholicism, c. 1500–1800*. Cambridge 1997.

———. *Tradition chrétienne et renouveau catholique. Dans le cadre de l'ancien diocèse de Strasbourg (1650–1770)*. Paris 1981.

Chaumonot, Pierre. "Autobiographie du P. Pierre Chaumonot de la Compagnie de Jésus." In *Documents inédits concernant la Compagnie de Jésus*, vol. 13, edited by Auguste Carayon, 1–82. Poitiers 1869.

Chaurand, Honoré. "Copie d'une lettre au R. P. Galien, de la même Compagnie, provincial en la province de Lyon, touchant la maison des retraites establies à Vannes." In *Documents inédits concernant la Compagnie de Jésus*, vol. 23, edited by Auguste Carayon, 315–48. Poitiers 1874–86.

Chennevieres, François de. *Détails militaires: Dont la connaissance est nécessaire à tous les officiers, et principalement aux commissaires des guerres*. 2 vols. Paris 1750.

Chevalier, Jean-Frédéric. "Jesuit Neo-Latin Tragedy in France." In *Neo-Latin Drama in Early Modern Europe*, edited by Jan Bloemendal and Howard Norland, 415–69. Leiden 2013.

Chevallier, Jim, ed. *The Old Regime Police Blotter II: Sodomites, Tribads and "Crimes against Nature."* North Hollywood, CA, 2010.

Chinchilla, Perla. *De la* compositio loci *a la república de las letras. Predicación jesuita en el siglo XVII novohispano*. Mexico City 2004.

Ciammitti, Luisa. "Quanto costa essere normali. La dote nel Conservatorio femminile di Santa Maria del Baraccano (1630–1680)." *Quaderni storici* 53 (1983): 469–97.

Civale, Gianclaudio. "Francesco Borgia e gli esordi della pastorale gesuitica nei confronti dei soldati." In *Francisco de Borja y su tiempo. Política, religión y cultura en la edad moderna*, edited by Enrique García Hernán, 207–21. Valencia 2012.

Claren, Lutz, Jost Eickmeyer, and Wilhelm Kühlmann, eds. *Johannes Bisselius. Deliciae Veris—Frühlingsfreuden. Lateinischer Text, Übersetzung, Einführungen und Kommentar*. Berlin 2013.

Clark, Stuart. *Thinking with Demons: The Idea of Witchcraft in Early Modern Europe*. Oxford 1997.

Claudel, Paul. *Journal*. Edited by François Varillon. 2 vols. Paris 1968–69.

Clavijero, Francisco Javier [Francesco Saverio Clavigero]. *Storia antica del Messico*. 4 vols. Cesena 1780.

Clement, Claude. *Musei sive bibliothecae tam privatae quam publicae extructio, instructio*. Lyon 1635.

Clines, Robert. *A Jewish Jesuit in the Eastern Mediterranean: Early Modern Conversion, Mission, and the Construction of Identity*. New York 2020.

Clossey, Luke. "Merchants, Migrants, Missionaries, and Globalization in the Early-Modern Pacific." *Journal of Global History* 1 (2006): 41–58.

———. *Salvation and Globalization in the Early Jesuit Missions*. Cambridge 2008.

Codignola, Luca, ed. *Calendar of Documents Relating to French and British North America in the Archives of the Sacred Congregation "De Propaganda Fide."* 6 vols. Ottawa 1983.

———. "Roman Catholic Conservatism in a New Atlantic World, 1760–1829." *William and Mary Quarterly* 64 (2007): 717–56.

Codina Mir, Gabriel. *Aux sources de la pédagogie des Jésuites. Le "modus parisiensis."* Rome 1968.

Coello de la Rosa, Alexandre. "De mestizos y criollos en la Compañía de Jesús (Perú, siglos XVI–XVII)." *Revista de Indias* 243 (2008): 37–66.

———. "Gathering Souls: Jesuit Missions and Missionaries in Oceania (1668–1945)." *Brill Research Perspectives in Jesuit Studies* 1, no. 2 (2019): 1–115.

———. "Lights and Shadows: The Inquisitorial Process against the Jesuit Congregation of Nuestra Señora de la Luz on the Mariana Islands (1758–1776)." *Journal of Religious History* 37 (2013): 206–27.

Cohen, Sherrill. *The Evolution of Women's Asylums since 1500: From Refuges for Ex-prostitutes to Shelters for Battered Women.* New York 1992.

Cohen, Thomas V. "Racial and Ethnic Minorities in the Society of Jesus." In *The Cambridge Companion to the Jesuits*, edited by Thomas Worcester, 199–215. Cambridge 2008.

———. "Why the Jesuits Joined, 1540–1600." In *Historical Papers / Communications historiques*, edited by Peter Gillis, 237–58. Ottawa 1974.

Colas, Gerard. "Vie légumineuse et pensée travestie. À propos de l'adaptation des Jésuites en Inde aux XVIIe et XVIIIe siècles." *Purusartha* 19 (1996): 199–220.

Coleman, Charly. *The Virtues of Abandon: An Anti-individualist History of the French Enlightenment.* Stanford, CA, 2014.

Collani, Claudia von. "Cabbala in China." In *From Kaifeng . . . to Shanghai: Jews in China*, edited by Roman Malek, 527–58. Nettetal 2000.

Colombo, Emanuele. "Milano bilingue. Il Gesuita Tommaso Ceva (1648–1737)." In *La cultura della rappresentazione nella Milano del settecento. Discontinuità e permanenze*, edited by Roberta Carpani, 77–97. Milan 2010.

Colombo, Emanuele, and Marina Massimi. *In viaggio. Gesuiti italiani candidati alle missioni tra antica e nuova Compagnia.* La Compagnia di Gesù, 10. Milan 2014.

Colombo, Emanuele, and Marco Rochini. "Four Hundred Years of Desire: Ongoing Research into the Nineteenth-Century Italian *indipetae* (1829–1856)." In *Representations of the Other and Intercultural Experiences in a Global Perspective (16th–20th Centuries)*, edited by Niccolò Guasti, 83–108. Sesto San Giovanni 2017.

Combs, Mary Beth, ed. *Transforming Ourselves, Transforming the World: Justice in Jesuit Higher Education.* New York 2013.

Conrad, Anne. *Zwischen Kloster und Welt. Ursulinen und Jesuitinnen in der katholischen Reformbewegung des 16./17. Jahrhunderts.* Mainz 1991.

Conrads, Norbert. *Ritterakademien der frühen Neuzeit. Bildung als Standesprivileg im 16. und 17. Jahrhundert.* Göttingen 1982.

Cook, Harold John. *Matters of Exchange: Commerce, Medicine, and Science in the Dutch Golden Age.* New Haven, CT, 2007.

Copete, Marie-Lucie. "L'assistance aux prisonniers pauvres en Espagne (XVIe–XVIIe siècles)." *Archives de sciences sociales des religions* 153 (2011): 23–42.

Copete, Marie-Lucie, and Federico Palomo. "Des carêmes après le carême. Stratégies de conversion et fonctions politiques des missions intérieures en Espagne et Portugal." *Revue de synthèse* 120 (1999): 359–80.

Copete, Marie-Lucie, and Bernard Vincent. "Missions en Bétique. Pour une typologie des missions intérieures." In *Missions religieuses modernes. "Notre lieu est le monde,"* edited by Pierre-Antoine Fabre and Bernard Vincent, 261–85. Rome 2007.

Cordara, Giulio Cesare. *De suis ac suorum rebus alijsque suorum temporum usque ad occasum Societatis Jesu commentarij ad Franciscum fratrem comitem calamandranae.* Edited by Agostino Faggiotto. Turin 1932.

———. *Historiae Societatis Jesu pars sexta complectens res gestas sub Mutio Vitelleschio. Tomus Prior.* Rome 1750.

———. *The Suppression of the Society of Jesus: A Contemporary Account.* Translated by John P. Murphy. Chicago 1999.

Cordero Fernández, Macarena. "Las penas y los castigos para la idolatría aplicados en las visitas de idolatría en Lima durante el siglo XVII." *Revista de estudios histórico-jurídicos* 32 (2010): 351–79.

———. "Rol de la Compañía de Jesús en las visitas de idolatrías. Siglo XVII." *Anuario de historia de la Iglesia* 21 (2012): 361–86.

Coret, Jacques. *La bonne morte sous la protection des SS. Anges Gardiens.* Paris 1663.

———. *L'Ange Gardien protecteur des mourans.* Paris 1662.

Coreth, Anna. "Die ersten Sodalitäten der Jesuiten in Österreich. Geistigkeit und Entwicklung." *Jahrbuch für mystische Theologie* 11 (1965): 7–50.

———. *Liebe ohne Maß. Geschichte der Herz-Jesu-Verehrung in Österreich.* Vienna 1994.

———. "Priesterliches Wirken im barocken Wien. P. Antonius Khabes 1687–1771." *Archivum historicum Societatis Iesu* 61 (1992): 71–89.

Coreth, Emerich. "In actione contemplativus." *Zeitschrift für katholische Theologie* 76 (1954): 55–82.

Correa Etchegaray, Leonor, Emanuele Colombo, and Guillermo Wilde, eds. *Las misiones antes y después de la restauración de la Compañía de Jesús. Continuidades y cambios.* Puebla 2014.

Corsi, Elisabetta. *La fábrica de las ilusiones. Los jesuitas y la difusión de la perspectiva lineal en China, 1698–1766.* Mexico City 2004.

Costa, Horacio de la. *The Jesuits in the Philippines 1581–1768.* Cambridge, MA, 1961.

———. "Muhammad Alimuddin I of Sulu: The Early Years." *Asian Studies* 2 (1964): 199–212.

Coster, Francis. *Libellus Sodalitatis.* Cologne 1610.

Coupeau, Carlos. *From Inspiration to Invention: Rhetoric in the Constitutions of the Society of Jesus.* St. Louis, MO, 2010.

Course, Didier. "La dévotion honnête du Père Le Moyne." *Œuvres & Critiques* 35 (2010): 33–42.

Crasset, Jean. *Des congrégations de Notre-Dame érigées dans les maisons des Pères de la Compagnie de Jésus.* Paris 1694.

———. *La véritable dévotion envers la Ste Vierge.* 2 parts in 1 vol. Paris 1679.

Croce, Franco. "I critici moderato-barocchi III. Sforza Pallavicino." *Rassegna della letteratura italiana* 60 (1956): 438–70.

Croiset, Jean. *La dévotion au Sacré Cœur de N. S. Jesus-Christ par un P. de la Compagnie de Jésus. Nouvelle edition augmentée.* Lyon 1691.

———. *Règlements pour Messieurs les pensionnaires des pères jésuites du Collège de Lyon*. 2 vols. Lyon 1733.

———. *Retraite spirituelle pour un jour du chaque moins*. 2 vols. Paris 1713.

Cronin, Mike. "Catholicising Fascism, Fascistising Catholicism? The Blueshirts and the Jesuits in 1930s Ireland." *Totalitarian Movements and Political Religions* 8 (2007): 401–11.

Crook, David. "'A Certain Indulgence': Music at the Jesuit College in Paris, 1575–1590." In *The Jesuits II: Cultures, Sciences, and the Arts 1540–1773*, edited by John W. O'Malley, 454–78. Toronto 2006.

Crosby, Harry W. *Antigua California: Mission and Colony on the Peninsular Frontier, 1697–1768*. Albuquerque, NM, 1994.

Cubitt, Geoffrey. *The Jesuit Myth: Conspiracy Theory and Politics in Nineteenth-Century France*. Oxford 1993.

Cull, John T. "The Baroque at Play: Homiletic and Pedagogical Emblems in Francisco Garau and Other Spanish Golden Age Preachers." In *Writing for the Eyes in the Spanish Golden Age*, edited by Frederick A. de Armas, 235–56. Lewisburg, PA, 2004.

Culley, Thomas D. *Jesuits and Music: A Study of the Musicians Connected with the German College in Rome during the 17th Century and of Their Activities in Northern Europe*. Rome 1970.

Culley, Thomas D., and Clement J. McNaspy. "Music and the Early Jesuits (1540–1565)." *Archivum historicum Societatis Iesu* 40 (1971): 213–45.

Curran, Robert Emmett, ed. *American Jesuit Spirituality: The Maryland Tradition, 1634–1900*. New York 1988.

———. *Shaping American Catholicism: Maryland and New York, 1805–1915*. Washington, DC, 2012.

Curvelo, Alexandra. "The Artistic Circulation between Japan, China and the New Spain in the 16th–17th Centuries." *Bulletin of Portuguese Japanese Studies* 16 (2008): 59–69.

Cushner, Nicholas P. *Jesuit Ranches and the Agrarian Development of Colonial Argentina, 1650–1767*. New York 1983.

———. *Lords of the Land: Sugar, Wine, and Jesuit Estates of Coastal Peru, 1600–1767*. Albany, NY, 1980.

———. *Why Have You Come Here? The Jesuits and the First Evangelization of Native America*. Oxford 2006.

D'Agostino, Peter R. *Rome in America: Transnational Catholic Ideology from the Risorgimento to Fascism*. Chapel Hill, NC, 2004.

Dainville, François de. *L'éducation des Jésuites (XVIe–XVIIe siècles)*. Paris 1978.

———. "Livres de comptes et histoire de la culture." *Archivum historicum Societatis Iesu* 18 (1949): 226–52.

———. "Projet d'un corps d'écrivains à Toulouse en 1712." *Archivum historicum Societatis Iesu* 7 (1938): 285–91.

Dalmases, Candido de. *Ignatius von Loyola. Versuch einer Gesamtbiographie*. Munich 2006.

———. "Santa Teresa de Jesús y los jesuitas." *Archivum historicum Societatis Iesu* 53 (1966): 343–78.

Dandelet, Thomas James. *Spanish Rome: 1500–1700*. New Haven, CT, 2001.

Da Nóbrega, Manuel. *Cartas do Brasil e mais escritos (opera omnia)*. Edited by Serafim Leite. Coimbra 1955.

Dante, Francesco. *Storia della "Civiltà Cattolica" (1850–1891). Il laboratorio del papa*. Rome 1990.

Daoust, Joseph. "Les Jésuites contre l'Encyclopédie (1751–1752)." *Bulletin de la Société historique et archéologique de Langres* 12 (1952–54): 29–44.

Daub, Susanne, ed. *Auf heiliger Jagd in Florenz. Aus dem Tagebuch des Jesuiten Daniel Papebroch*. Erlangen 2010.

Dawdy, Shannon Lee. *Building the Devil's Empire: French Colonial New Orleans*. Chicago 2008.

Dear, Peter. "Jesuit Mathematical Science and the Reconstruction of Experience in the Early Seventeenth Century." *Studies in History and Philosophy of Science* 18 (1987): 133–75.

Debiaggi, Casimiro. "Una testimonianza pittorica sul conte Olivero e la Casa degli Esercizi fuori Porta Susina." In *La Compagnia di Gesù nella provincia di Torino. Dagli anni di Emanuele Filiberto a quelli di Carlo Alberto*, edited by Bruno Signorelli and Pietro Uscello, 247–58. Turin 1998.

Deckers, Daniel. *Papst Franziskus. Wider die Trägheit des Herzens*. Munich 2014.

Decot, Rolf. "Klemens Maria Hofbauer im politisch-geistlichen Umfeld seiner Wiener Zeit." *Spicilegium historicum Congregationis Ssmi Redemptoris* 49 (2001): 3–28.

Deeds, Susan M. *Defiance and Deference in Mexico's Colonial North: Indians under Spanish Rule in Nueva Vizcaya*. Austin, TX, 2003.

De Ferrari, Augusto. "DE BENEDICTIS, Giovanni Battista." DBI 33 (1987). http://www.treccani.it/enciclopedia/de-benedictis-giovanni-battista_%28Dizionario-Biografico%29/. Accessed July 20, 2020.

Dehergne, Joseph. "Catéchismes et cetéchèse des Jésuites en Chine de 1584–1800." *Monumenta Serica* 47 (1999): 397–478.

Dêlage, Denys. "Les iroquois chrétiens des réductions." *Recherches amerindiennes au Quebec* 21, 1/2 and 3 (1991): 59–70, 39–50.

de la Mousse, Jean. *Les indiens de la Sinnamary. Journal du père Jean de la Mousse en Guyane, 1684–1691*. Paris 2006.

de la Palma, Luis. *Praxis et brevis declaratio viae spiritualis*. Antwerp 1637.

Delbeke, Maarten. *The Art of Religion: Sforza Pallavicino and Art Theory in Bernini's Rome*. Farnham 2012.

de León, Pedro. *Grandeza y miseria en Andalucía. Testimonio de una encrucijada histórica*. Edited by P. Herrera Puga, S.J. Granada 1981.

Delfosse, Annick. "Autour de l'*Instructio ad tyronem* (1672). Les enjeux d'une définition dogmatique de l'Immaculée Conception." In *Le jansénisme et l'Europe*, edited by Raymond Baustert, 201–21. Tübingen 2010.

D'Elia, Pasquale, ed. *Fonti Ricciane*. 3 vols. Rome 1942–49.

Del Rey Fajardo, José. *Las bibliotecas jesuíticas en la Venezuela colonial*. 2 vols. Caracas 1999.

Delumeau, Jean. *Rassurer et protéger. Le sentiment de sécurité dans l'Occident d'autrefois*. Paris 1989.

de Madrid, Cristóbal. *De frequenti usu sanctissimi Eucharistiae sacramenti libellus*. Rome 1557.

Demoustier, Adrien. "La primera anotación de los Ejercicios espirituales y su contexto histórico." In *Las fuentes de los Ejercicios espirituales de san Ignacio. Actas del symposio internacional*, edited by J. Plazaola, 281–97. Bilbao 1998.

De Nobili, Roberto. *Preaching Wisdom to the Wise: Three Treatises by Roberto de Nobili, S.J., Missionary and Scholar in 17th Century India*. Translated by Anand Amaladass and Francis X. Clooney. St. Louis, MO, 2001.

de' Pazzi, Maria Maddalena. *L'epistolario completo*. Edited by Chiara Vasciaveo. Florence 2009.

Deregnaucourt, Gilles. "La formation des prêtres et les séminaires dans les Pays-Bas catholiques du XVIe au XVIIIe siècle." In *Eglise, éducation, Lumières [. . .] Histoires culturelles de la France, 1500–1830: En l'honneur de Jean Quéniart*, edited by Alain Croix, André Lespagnol, and Georges Provost, 17–24. Rennes 1999.

Desideri, Ippolito. *Mission to Tibet: The Extraordinary Eighteenth-Century Account of Father Ippolito Desideri, S.J.* Translated by Michael J. Sweet. Edited by Leonard Zwillig. Boston 2010.

Deslandres, Dominique. *Croire et faire croire. Les missions françaises au XVIIe siècle, 1600–1650*. Paris 2003.

Didier, Hugues. "Entre l'Europe et les missions lointaines, les Jésuites premiers mondialisateurs." In *Les Jésuites en Espagne et en Amérique. Jeux et enjeux du pouvoir (XVIe–XVIIIe siècles)*, edited by Annie Molinié, 355–67. Paris 2007.

———, ed. *Fantômes d'Islam et de Chine. Le voyage de Bento de Góis (1603–1607)*. Paris 2003.

———, ed. *Les portugais au Tibet*. Paris 2000.

Diefendorf, Barbara. "Give Us Back Our Children: Patriarchal Authority and Parental Consent to Religious Vocations in Early Counter-Reformation France." *Journal of Modern History* 68 (1996): 265–307.

Diertins, Ignatius. *Exercitia spiritualia S. P. Ignatii Loyolae [. . .]*. 4th ed. Antwerp 1693.

Díez Coronado, A. "Juan Bautista Escordó y la oratoria sagrada barroca." In *Memoria de la palabra*, edited by María Luisa Lobato, 647–55. Madrid 2004.

Dillinger, Johannes. "Friedrich Spee und Adam Tanner. Zwei Gegner der Hexenverfolgung aus dem Jesuitenorden." *Spee-Jahrbuch* 7 (2000): 31–58.

Dirmeier, Ursula, ed. *Mary Ward und ihre Gründung. Die Quellentexte bis 1645*. 4 vols. Münster 2007.

Di Santi, Angelo. *L'orazione delle Quarant'ore e i tempi di calamità e di guerra*. Rome 1919.

Dolinar, France Martin. *Das Jesuitenkolleg in Laibach und die Residenz Pleterje. 1597–1704*. Laibach 1977.

Dollo, Corrado. "Le ragioni del geocentrismo nel Collegio Romano (1562–1612)." In *La diffusione del copernicanesimo in Italia 1543–1610*, edited by Massimo Bucciantini, 99–167. Florence 1997.

Domergue, Lucienne. "Les jésuites espagnols écrivains et l'appareil d'État (1767–1808)." In *Los jesuitas españoles expulsos. Su imagen y su contribución al saber sobre el mundo hispánico en la Europa del siglo XVIII*, edited by Manfred Tietz and Dietrich Briesemeister, 265–94. Madrid 2001.

Domingo Malvadi, Arantxa. *La producción escénica del Padre Pedro Pablo Acevedo. Un capítulo en la pedagogía del latín de la Compañía de Jesús en el siglo XVI*. Salamanca 2001.

Dompnier, Bernard. "Des anges et des signes. Littérature de dévotion à l'ange gardien et image des anges au XVIIe siècle." In *Les signes de Dieu aux XVIe et XVIIe siècles*, edited by Geneviève Demerson, 213–23. Clermont-Ferrand 1993.

———. "La dévotion à Saint Joseph au miroir des confréries (XVIIe–XVIIIe siècles)." In *Confréries et dévotions dans la catholicité moderne (mi-XVe–début XIXe siècle)*, edited by Bernard Dompnier and Paola Vismara, 285–309. Rome 2008.

———. *Le venin de l'hérésie. Image du protestantisme et combat catholique au XVIIe siècle*. Paris 1985.

———. "Un aspect de la dévotion eucharistique dans la France du XVIIe siècle. Les prières des Quarante-Heures." *Revue d'histoire de l'église de France* 67 (1981): 5–31.

Dompnier, Bernard, and Paola Vismara, eds. *Confréries et dévotions dans la catholicité moderne (mi-XVe–début XIXe siècle)*. Rome 2008.

Donattini, Massimo. "Ambasciatori giapponesi ed esiliati americani. Vicende della presenza gesuitica a Bologna." In *Dall'isola alla città. I gesuiti a Bologna*, edited by Gian Paolo Brizzi, 193–201. Bologna 1988.

Donnelly, John Patrick. "Alonso Rodriguez' *Ejercicio*: A Neglected Classic." *Sixteenth Century Journal* 11 (1980): 16–24.

———. "Antonio Possevino: From Secretary to Papal Legate in Sweden." In *The Mercurian Project: Forming Jesuit Culture, 1573–1580*, edited by Thomas McCoog, 323–50. St. Louis, MO, 2004.

Doublet, Georges. "Caulet, évêque de Pamiers et les jésuites." *Annales du Midi* 9 (1897): 201–26, 323–33.

Dougherty, Joseph. *From Altar-Throne to Table: The Campaign for Frequent Holy Communion in the Catholic Church*. Lanham, MD, 2010.

Drexel, Jeremias. *Aurifodina artium et scientiarum omnium excerpendi solertia*. Munich 1636.

Drozd, Kurt Wolfgang. *Schul- und Ordenstheater am Collegium S. J. Klagenfurt, 1604–1773*. Klagenfurt 1965.

Dubois, Paul-André. "Marc-Antoine Charpentier chez les Abénaquis ou la petite histoire d'une 'Chanson des Bergers' au Nouveau-Monde." *Études d'histoire religieuse* 72 (2006): 55–73.

Dubreuil, Pierre. *La perspective pratique*. 2nd ed. 3 vols. Paris 1679.

Dudik, Beda. "Korrespondenz Kaiser Ferdinands und seiner erlauchten Familie mit P. Martinus Becanus und Pater Wilhelm Lamormaini, Kaiserlichen Beichtvätern S.J." *Archiv für österreichische Geschichte* 54 (1876): 219–350.

Dudink, Adrian. "The Religious Works Composed by Johann Adam Schall von Bell, Especially His *Zhuzhi Qunzheng* and His Efforts to Convert the Last Ming Emperor." In *Western Learning and Christianity in China: The Contribution and Impact of Johann Adam Schall von Bell, S.J. (1592–1666)*, edited by Roman Malek, 805–99. Nettetal 1998.

Dudon, Paul. "Le 'Libellus' du P. Bobadilla sur la communion fréquente et quotidienne." *Archivum historicum Societatis Iesu* 2 (1933): 258–79.

———. *St. Ignatius of Loyola*. Translated by William J. Young. Milwaukee, WI, 1949.

Duffy, Eamon. *Saints and Sinners: A History of the Popes*. New Haven, CT, 2002.

Duhr, Bernhard. "Die deutschen Jesuiten im 5%-Streit des 16. Jahrhunderts." *Zeitschrift für katholische Theologie* 24 (1900): 209–48.

———. *Die Stellung der Jesuiten in den deutschen Hexenprozessen*. Cologne 1900.

Dümmerth, Desco. "Les combats et la tragédie du Père Melchior Inchofer S. J. à Rome (1641–1648)." *Annales Universitatis Scientiarum Budapestiensis de Rolando Eötvös nominatae, Sectio historica* 17 (1976): 81–112.

Dumoutet, Édouard. *Le désir de voir l'hostie et les origines de la dévotion au Saint-Sacrement*. Paris 1926.

Dupont-Ferrier, Gustave. *La vie quotidienne d'un collège parisien pendant plus de 350 ans. Du collège de Clermont au lycée Louis-le-Grand.* 3 vols. Paris 1921.

Dürrwächter, Anton. *Jakob Gretser und seine Dramen. Ein Beitrag zur Geschichte des Jesuitendramas in Deutschland.* Freiburg 1912.

Duteil, Jean-Pierre. "La 'Querelle des rites' au coeur des disputes religieuses des XVIIe et XVIIIe siècles." *Mélanges de science religieuse* 61, no. 2 (2004): 59–74.

Duve, Thomas. "Das Konzil als Autorisierungsinstanz. Die Priesterweihe von Mestizos vor dem Dritten Limaneser Konzil (1582/83) und die Kommunikation über Rechte in der spanischen Monarchie." *Rechtsgeschichte* 16 (2010): 132–53.

Eberl, Immo. "Die Umwandlung des Jesuitengymnasiums in Ellwangen in das Collegium Ignatianum und dessen Tätigkeit bis zur Säkularisation." In *Jesuiten in Ellwangen. Oberdeutsche Provinz, Wallfahrt, Weltmission,* edited by Franz Brendle, Fabian Fechner, and Anselm Grupp, 61–109. Stuttgart 2012.

Echánove, Alfonso. "Origen y evolución del a idea jesuítica de 'reducciones' en las misiones del Virreinato del Perú." *Missionalia hispanica* 12 (1955): 95–144.

Eder, Franz-Xaver. *Missionnaire en Amazonie. Récit du dix-huitième siècle d'un jésuite au Pérou, en Bolivie et dans les réductions indiennes, traduit du latin par Joseph Laure.* Paris 2009.

Edmunds, Martha Mel. "French Sources for Pompeo Batoni's 'Sacred Heart of Jesus' in the Jesuit Church in Rome." *Burlington Magazine* 149 (2007): 785–89.

Edwards, Otis Carl. "Varieties of Sermon: A Survey of Preaching in the Long Eighteenth Century." In *Preaching, Sermon and Cultural Change in the Long Eighteenth Century,* edited by Joris van Eijnatten, 3–53. Leiden 2009.

Egido, Teófanes. *Los jesuitas en España y en el mundo hispánico.* Madrid 2004.

———. "Los sermones. Retórica e espectáculo." In *Trabajo y ocio en la época moderna,* edited by Luis Antonio Ribot García and Luigi de Rosa, 87–110. Madrid 2001.

Ehrard, Jean. "Une 'amitié de trente ans.' Castel et Montesquieu." In *Autour du Père Castel et du clavecin oculaire,* edited by Roland Mortier and Hervé Hasquin, 69–81. Brussels 1996.

Eichhorn, Gertraud K. *Beichtzettel und Bürgerrecht in Passau, 1570–1630. Die administrativen Praktiken der Passauer Gegenreformation unter den Fürstbischöfen Urban von Trenbach und Leopold I., Erzherzog von Österreich.* Passau 1997.

Eickmeyer, Jost. *Der jesuitische Heroidenbrief. Zur Christianisierung und Kontextualisierung einer antiken Gattung in der Frühen Neuzeit.* Berlin 2012.

———. "Kadavergehorsam? Zur 'Totalität' jesuitischer Pädagogik in der Frühen Neuzeit. Ein institutions- und literaturgeschichtlicher Durchgang." In *Totale Erziehung in europäischer und amerikanischer Literatur,* edited by Richard Faber, 51–75. Frankfurt 2013.

Ekberg, Carl J. *French Roots in the Illinois Country: The Mississippi Frontier in Colonial Times.* Urbana, IL, 2000.

Elazar, Michael. *Honoré Fabri and the Concept of Impetus: A Bridge between Conceptual Frameworks.* Dordrecht 2011.

Elizalde, Ignacio. "Teresa de Jesús y los jesuitas." In *Teresa de Jesús. Estudios histórico-literarios. Studi storico-letterati,* edited by the Pontifical Theological Faculty Teresianum, 151–75. Rome 1982.

Elizalde Armendáriz, Ignacio. "Luis Vives y Ignacio de Loyola." *Hispania sacra* 33 (1981): 541–47.

Ellacuría, Ignacio. "Pedro Arrupe, Erneuerer des Ordenslebens." In *Offen für die Zeichen der Zeit. Pedro Arrupe im Zeugnis seiner Mitarbeiter*, edited by Stefan Bamberger, 109–35. Kevelaer 1986.

Ellero, Giuseppe. "Vergini cristiane e donne di valore." In *Le Zitelle. Architettura, arte e storia di un'istituzione veneziana*, edited by Lionello Puppi and Giuseppe Ellero, 49–95. Venice 1992.

Endean, Philip. "'The Original Line of Our Father Ignatius': Mercurian and the Spirituality of the Exercises." In *The Mercurian Project: Forming Jesuit Culture, 1573–1580*, edited by Thomas McCoog, 35–48. Rome 2004.

———. "'The Strange Style of Prayer': Mercurian, Cordeses and Álvarez." In *The Mercurian Project: Forming Jesuit Culture, 1573–1580*, edited by Thomas McCoog, 351–97. St. Louis, MO, 2004.

Entenmann, Robert. "Chinese Catholic Clergy and Catechists in Eighteenth-Century Szechwan." In *Images de la Chine: Le contexte occidental de la sinologie naissante*, edited by Edward J. Malatesta, 389–410. Paris 1995.

Erbacher, Jürgen. *Ein radikaler Papst. Die franziskanische Wende*. Munich 2014.

Errichetti, Michele. "L'antico Collegio Massimo dei gesuiti a Napoli (1552–1806)." *Campania sacra* 7 (1976): 170–264.

Ertl, Thomas. *Religion und Disziplin. Selbstdeutung und Weltordnung im frühen deutschen Franziskanertum*. Berlin 2006.

Essertel, Yannick. *L'aventure missionnaire lyonnaise. 1815–1962: De Pauline Jaricot à Jules Monchan*. Paris 2001.

Ettlin, Leo. *Dr. Johann Baptist Dillier 1668–1745*. Sarnen 1969.

Faesen, Rob. "'Dupliciter intelligi potest': Jan van Ruusbroec in the First Century of the Society of Jesus (1540–1640)." In *De letter levend maken. Opstellen aangeboden aan Guido de Baere bij zijn zeventigste verjaardag*, edited by Kees Schepers and Frans Hendrickx, 285–307. Leuven 2010.

———. "The Great Silence of Saint Joseph: Devotion to Saint Joseph and the 17th Century Crisis of Mysticism in the Jesuit Order." In *Instruments of Devotion: The Practices and Objects of Religious Piety from the Late Middle Ages to the 20th Century*, edited by Henning Lagerud and Laura Katrine Skinnebach, 73–92. Aarhus 2007.

Fantappiè, Carlo. "Problemi della formazione del clero nell'età moderna." In *Istituzioni e società in Toscana nell'età moderna*, edited by Claudio Lamioni, 730–50. Rome 1994.

Farrelly, Maura Jane. "Catholicism in the Early South." *Journal of Southern Religion* 14 (2012). http://jsr.fsu.edu/issues/vol14/farrelly.html.

[Faure, Giambattista.] *Commentarium in bullam Pauli III Licet ab initio, datam anno 1542, qua Romanam Inquisitionem constituit, et eius regimen non regularibus, sed clero seculari commisit*. N.p. 1750.

Faure, Giambattista [Giovanni Battista]. *Congetture fisiche intorno alle cagioni de' fenomeni osservati in Roma nella macchina elettrica*. Rome 1747.

Faux, Jean M. "La fondation et les premiers rédacteurs des *Mémoires de Trévoux* d'après quelques documents inédits." *Archivum historicum Societatis Iesu* 23 (1954): 131–51.

Fechner, Fabian. *Entscheidungsfindung in der Gesellschaft Jesu. Die Provinzkongregationen der Jesuiten in Paraguay (1608–1762)*. Regensburg 2015.

Feingold, Mordechai. "Fama. Les savants jésuites et la quête de la renommée." *Dix-septième siècle* 237 (2007): 755–74.

———. "The Grounds for Conflict: Grienberger, Grassi, Galileo, and Posterity." In *The New Science and Jesuit Science: Seventeenth Century Perspectives*, edited by Mordechai Feingold, 121–57. Dordrecht 2003.

Feitler, Bruno. "Le refus de la communion aux nouveaux-chrétiens. La tendance rigoriste de l'Inquisition portugaise sous la présidence du dominicain João Vasconcelos (1640)." *Revue d'histoire ecclésiastique* 108 (2013): 199–227.

Feldhay, Rivka. "Knowledge and Salvation in Jesuit Culture." *Science in Context* 1 (1987): 195–213.

Ferlan, Claudio. *Dentro e fuori le aule. La Compagnia di Gesù a Gorizia e nell'Austria interna (secoli XVI–XVII)*. Bologna 2012.

Fernández Arrillaga, Inmaculada. "Profecías, coplas, creencias y devociones de los Jesuitas expulsos durante su exilio en Italia." In *Y en el tercero perecerán. Gloria, caída y exilio de los jesuitas españoles en el s. XVIII*, edited by Enrique Giménez López, 513–30. Alicante 2002.

Fernández Guerrero, Eduardo, ed. "La *Iudithis Tragoedia Tertia* de Jusé Guimerá. Estudio y edición de una tragedia jesuítica en el ms. 383 de la Real Academia de la Historia." https://www.academia.edu/4903538/La_Iudithis_Tragoedia_Tertia_estudio_y_edici%C3%B3n_de_una_tragedia_jesu%C3%ADtica_en_el_ms._383_de_la_Real_Academia_de_la_Historia.

Fernández Martín, Luis. "Iñigo de Loyola y los alumbrados." *Hispania sacra* 35 (1983): 585–680.

Fernández Terricabras, Ignasi. "Surviving between Spain and France: Religious Orders and the Papacy in Catalonia (1640–1659)." In *Papacy, Religious Orders, and International Politics in the Sixteenth and Seventeenth Centuries*, edited by Massimo Carlo Giannini, 145–64. Rome 2013.

Ferrante, Carla, and Antonello Mattone. "Il Collegio dei Nobili di Cagliari e la formazione della classe dirigente del Regno di Sardegna (XVIII–XIX secolo)." In *Dai collegi medievali alle residenze universitarie*, edited by Gian Paolo Brizzi and Antonello Mattone, 69–97. Bologna 2010.

Ferreiro, Larrie D. *Ships and Science: The Birth of Naval Architecture in the Scientific Revolution*. Cambridge, MA, 2007.

Ferrer Benimeli, José Antonio. "De la expulsión de los jesuitas a la extinción de la Compañía de Jesús. Parte I: 1766–1770." 2000. http://www.larramendi.es/i18n/consulta/registro.cmd?id=1207.

———. *Expulsión y extinción de los jesuitas, 1759–1773*. Bilbao 2013.

Figueiredo, Fernando B. "José Monteiro da Rocha (1734–1819)." In *Dicionário biográfico de cientistas, engenheiros e médicos portugueses ou trabalhando em Portugal*. Forthcoming. https://www.academia.edu/2505723/Jos%C3%A9_Monteiro_da_Rocha_1734_1819_. Accessed February 10, 2021.

Filipczak, Zirka Zaremba. "Van Dyck's 'Life of St. Rosalie.'" *Burlington Magazine* 131 (1989): 693–98.

Filippi, Bruna. "Le corps suspendu. Le martyr dans le théâtre jésuite." *Littératures classiques* 73 (2010): 229–39.

Filippi, Daniele V. "Earthly Music, Interior Hearing, and Celestial Harmonies: Philippe de Monte's First Book of Spiritual Madrigals (1581)." *Journal of the Alamire Foundation* 3 (2011): 208–34.

Findlen, Paula, ed. *Athanasius Kircher: The Last Man Who Knew Everything.* London 2003.

———. "Science, History, and Erudition: Athanasius Kircher's Museum at the Collegio Romano." In *The Great Art of Knowing: The Baroque Encyclopedia of Athanasius Kircher*, edited by Daniel Stolzenberg, 17–26. Stanford, CA, 2001.

Fiocca, Alessandra. "Ferrara e i gesuiti periti in materia d'acque." In *Gesuiti e università in Europa (sec. XVI–XVIII)*, edited by Gian Paolo Brizzi and Roberto Greci, 339–60. Bologna 2002.

Fiorani, Luigi. "Missioni della Compagnia di Gesù nell'agro romano nel XVII secolo." *Dimensioni e problemi della ricerca storica* 2 (1994): 216–34.

Fisher, Alexander J. "'Per mia particolare devotione': Orlando di Lasso's *Lagrime di San Pietro* and Catholic Spirituality in Counter-Reformation Munich." *Journal of the Royal Musical Association* 132 (2007): 167–220.

Flamarion, Edith. "Castel, Father (S.J.)." Translated by Philip Stewart. In *Dictionnaire Montesquieu*, edited by Catherine Volpilhac-Auger. September 2013. http://dictionnaire -montesquieu.ens-lyon.fr/fr/article/1377616334/en.

———. "Jesuites." In *Dictionnaire Montesquieu*, edited by Catherine Volpilhac-Auger. September 2013. http://dictionnaire-montesquieu.ens-lyon.fr/fr/article/1377616473/en/.

———. *Théâtre Jésuite néo-latin et antiquité. Sur le "Brutus" de Charles Porée (1708).* Rome 2002.

———. "Une 'peinture animée.' Le théâtre selon Charles Porée (1676–1741)." In *La chair et le verbe. Les jésuites de France au XVIIIe siècle et l'image*, edited by Edith Flamarion, 159–78. Paris 2008.

Fleischer, Manfred P. "Father Wolff: The Epitome of a Jesuit Courtier." *Catholic Historical Review* 64 (1978): 581–613.

Flüchter, Antje, and Rouven Wirbser, eds. *Translating Catechisms, Translating Cultures: The Expansion of Catholicism in the Early Modern World.* Studies in Christian Mission 52. Leiden 2017.

Flucke, Christoph, ed. *Die litterae annuae. Die Jahresberichte der Gesellschaft Jesu aus Altona und Hamburg (1598–1781).* 2 vols. Münster 2015.

Flynn, Dennis Owen. "Jasper Heywood and the German Usury Controversy." In *The Mercurian Project: Forming Jesuit Culture, 1573–1580*, edited by Thomas McCoog, 183–211. St. Louis, MO, 2004.

Fois, Mario. "Il Collegio Romano. L'istituzione, la struttura, il primo secolo di vita." *Roma moderna e contemporanea* 3 (1995): 571–99.

———. "Il generale dei gesuiti Claudio Acquaviva (1581–1615), i sommi pontefici e la difesa dell'*Istituto* ignatiano." *Archivum historiae pontificiae* 40 (2002): 199–233.

Folsom, Raphael B. *The Yaquis and the Empire: Violence, Spanish Imperial Power, and Native Resilience in Colonial Mexico.* New Haven, CT, 2014.

Fonseca, Cosimo Damiano. "Collegio e città: Progetto culturale e scelte strategiche." In *Alle origini dell'Università dell'Aquila. Cultura, università, collegi gesuitici all'inizio dell'età moderna in Italia meridionale*, edited by Filippo Iapelli and Ulderico Parente, 91–106. Rome 2000.

Fontana Castelli, Eva. *La Compagnia di Gesù sotto altro nome. Niccolò Paccanari e la Compagnia della fede di Gesù.* Rome 2007.

———. "The Society of Jesus under Another Name. The Paccanarists in the Restored Society of Jesus." In *Jesuit Survival and Restoration: A Global History, 1773–1900,* edited by Robert A. Maryks, 197–211. Leiden 2015.

Forbes-Leith, William, ed. *Memoirs of Scottish Catholics during the XVIIth and XVIIIth Centuries, Selected from Hitherto Inedited Mss.* 2 vols. London 1909.

Forer, Laurenz. *Anatomia anatomiae Societatis Jesu.* Innsbruck 1634.

Foresta, Patrizio. *"Wie ein Apostel Deutschlands." Apostolat, Obrigkeit und jesuitisches Selbstverständnis am Beispiel des Petrus Canisius.* Göttingen 2015.

Foresti, Antonio. *La strada al santuario mostrata a'cherici, i quali aspirano al sacerdozio.* 3rd ed. Rome 1709.

Fouqueray, Henri. *Histoire de la Compagnie de Jésus en France des origines à la suppression (1528–1762).* 5 vols. Paris 1910–25.

Frajese, Vittorio. "Regno ecclesiastico e Stato moderno. La polemica fra Francisco Pena e Roberto Bellarmino sull'esenzione dei chierici." *Annali dell'Istituto storico italo-germanico in Trento* 14 (1988): 273–339.

Franceschi, Sylvio Hermann de. "La prédétermination physique au tribunal du magistère romain. Tomás de Lemos et la défense augustinienne du Thomisme au temps des congrégations de auxiliis." *Roma moderna e contemporanea* 18 (2010): 125–50.

———. "Le moment pascalien dans la querelle de la grâce. Pascal à la croisée des chemins (1656–1657)." *Revue de synthèse* 130 (2009): 595–635.

Francisco de Isla, José, S.J. *Crisis de los predicadores y de los sermones y otros escritos (1725–29).* Edited by José Martínez de la Escalera, S.J. Madrid 1994.

Franco, Antonio. *Synopsis annalium Societatis Jesu in Lusitania ab annis 1540 usque ad annum 1725.* Augsburg 1726.

Franco, José Eduardo. "L'antijésuitisme au Portugal. Composition, fonctionnalités et signification du mythe des Jésuites (De Pombal à la 1er République)." In *Les antijésuites. Discours, figures et lieux de l'antijésuitisme à l'époque moderne,* edited by Pierre-Antoine Fabre and Catherine Maire, 353–81. Rennes 2010.

Franklin, Vincent P. "Alonso De Sandoval and the Jesuit Conception of the Negro." *Journal of Negro History* 58 (1973): 349–60.

Frehill, Olivia. "Republican Dissent among Irish Jesuits during the Civil War, 1922–23." *Studies: An Irish Quarterly Review* 107 (2018): 57–75.

Friedrich, Markus. "Archive und Verwaltung im frühneuzeitlichen Europa. Das Beispiel der Gesellschaft Jesu." *Zeitschrift für Historische Forschung* 35 (2008): 369–403.

———. "Circulating and Compiling the Litterae Annuae: Towards a History of the Jesuit System of Communication." *Archivum historicum Societatis Iesu* (2008): 1–39.

———. *Der lange Arm Roms? Globale Verwaltung und Kommunikation im Jesuitenorden 1540–1773.* Frankfurt 2011.

———. "Gottfried Wilhelm Leibniz und die protestantische Diskussion über Heidenmission. Zur Eigenart und historischen Stellung seines Chinainteresses im Vergleich zu Conrad Mel und der lutherischen Theologie um 1700." In *Umwelt und Weltgestaltung. Leibniz' politisches*

Denken in seiner Zeit, edited by Friedrich Beiderbeck, Irene Dingel, and Wenchao Li, 641–77. Göttingen 2014.

———. "Jesuiten und Lutheraner im frühneuzeitlichen Hamburg. Katholische Seelsorge im Norden des Reichs zwischen Konversionen, Konfessionskonflikten und interkonfessionellen Kontakten." *Zeitschrift für Hamburgische Geschichte* 104 (2018): 1–78.

———. "Politikberatung durch 'Intellektuelle'? Das Verhältnis des Jesuitenordens zu den frühneuzeitlichen Fürstenhöfen im Spiegel von Giulio Negronis Traktat *Aulicismus, sive de fuga aulae dissertatio.*" In *Gab es Intellektuelle in der Frühen Neuzeit?*, edited by Luise Schorn-Schütte, 175–209. Berlin 2008.

———. "Theologische Einheit und soziale Kohärenz. Debatten um die Homogenität von doctrina im Jesuitenorden um 1600." In *Vera Doctrina. Zur Begriffsgeschichte der Lehre von Augustinus bis Descartes*, edited by Philippe Büttgen, 297–324. Wiesbaden 2009.

Fritsch, Matthias J. "Naturrecht und katholische Aufklärung im 18. Jahrhundert." In *Macht und Moral. Politisches Denken im 17. und 18. Jahrhundert*, edited by Markus Kremer and Hans-Richard Reuter, 92–103. Stuttgart 2007.

———. *Vernunft—Offenbarung—Religion. Eine historisch-systematische Untersuchung zu Sigismund von Storchenau*. Frankfurt 1997.

Froeschlé-Chopard, Marie-Hélène. "La dévotion au Sacré-Cœur. Confréries et livres de piété." *Revue de l'histoire des religions* 217 (2000): 531–46.

———. "La dévotion du saint-sacrement. Livres et confréries." In *Confréries et dévotions dans la catholicité moderne (mi-XVe–début XIXe siècle)*, edited by Bernard Dompnier and Paola Vismara, 77–102. Rome 2008.

Frusius, Andreas [André des Freux]. *De utraque copia, verborum et rerum, praecepta.* [Antwerp] 1568.

———. *Epigrammata in Haereticos*. Douai 1596.

Fumaroli, Marc. *L'âge de l'éloquence. Rhétorique et "res literaria" de la Renaissance au seuil de l'époque classique*. Geneva 2003.

Furlong, Guillermo. *Misiones y sus pueblos de guaranies*. Buenos Aires 1962.

Füssenich, Karl. "Die Volksmission in den Herzogtümern Jülich und Berg während des 18. Jahrhunderts." *Annalen des Historischen Vereins für den Niederrhein* 78 (1904): 117–41.

Gábor, Kiss Farkas. "'Difficiles nugae.' Athanasius Kircher magyaroszági kapcsolatai." *Irodalomtörténeti Közlemények* 109 (2005): 436–68.

———. "Johann Misch Astrophilos Nagyszombatban." *Magyar Könyvszemle* 121 (2005): 140–66.

Gabriel, Frédéric. "*An tyrannum opprimere fas sit?* Construction d'un lieu commun: La réception française du *De rege et regis institutione* de Juan de Mariana (Tolède, 1599)." In *Les antijésuites. Discours, figures et lieux de l'antijésuitisme à l'époque moderne*, edited by Pierre-Antoine Fabre and Catherine Maire, 241–63. Rennes 2010.

Gagliano, Joseph A., and Charles E. Ronan, eds. *Jesuit Encounters in the New World: Jesuit Chroniclers, Geographers, Educators and Missionaries in the Americas, 1549–1767*. Rome 1997.

Gagliardi, Achille, S.J. *Breve compendio di perfezione cristiana*. Edited and with an introduction by Mario Gioia. Rome 1996.

Galán García, Agustín. *El "Oficio de Indias" de Sevilla y la organización económica y misional de la Companía de Jesús (1566–1767)*. Seville 1995.

Galdos, Romualdus, ed. *Miscellanea de Maldonato. Anno ab eius nativitate quater centenario (1534?–1934)*. Madrid 1947.

Galeota, Gustavo. "La teologia controversista." In *Storia della teologia II. Da Pietro Abelardo a Roberto Bellarmino*, edited by Giuseppe Occhipinti, 523–65. Rome 1996.

Ganson, Barbara. *The Guaraní under the Spanish Rule in the Rio de la Plata*. Stanford, CA, 2003.

Ganss, George E. "Toward Understanding the Jesuits Brothers' Vocation, Especially as Described in the Papal and Jesuit Documents." *Studies in the Spirituality of Jesuits* 13 (1981): 1–63.

Garagnon, Jean. "*Les Mémoires de Trévoux* et l'événement, ou Jean-Jacques Rousseau vu par les Jésuites." *Dix-huitième siècle* 8 (1976): 215–36.

García de Castro Valdés, José. "Ignatius of Loyola and His First Companions." In *A Companion to Ignatius of Loyola: Life, Writings, Spirituality, Influence*, edited by Robert A. Maryks, 66–83. Leiden 2014.

——. *Polanco. El humanismo de los jesuitas. (Burgos 1517–Roma 1576)*. Bilbao 2012.

García-Garrido, Manuela-Águeda. "Cuando los jesuitas toman la palabra. Poder y predicación en la Sevilla del Siglo XVII." In *Les jésuites en Espagne et en Amérique. Jeux et enjeux du pouvoir (XVIe–XVIIIe siècles)*, edited by Annie Molinié, 265–83. Paris 2007.

García Hernán, Enrique, ed. *Francisco de Borja y su tiempo. Política, religión y cultura en la edad moderna*. Valencia 2012.

——. *Ignacio de Loyola*. Madrid 2014.

——. "La asistencia religiosa en la Armada de Lepanto." *Anthologica annua* 43 (1996): 213–63.

García Mateo, Rogelio. "Ignatius von Loyola in seiner sozio-kulturellen Umwelt. Spanien 1491–1527." In *Ignatianisch. Eigenart und Methode der Gesellschaft Jesu*, edited by Michael Sievernich and Günter Switek, 19–41. Freiburg 1990.

——. "Ignatius von Loyola vor seiner Bekehrung." *Geist und Leben* 61 (1988): 42–257.

——. "Origines del 'más' ignaciano." In *Ignacio de Loyola en Castilla. Juventud, formación, espiritualidad*, edited by Pedro de Leturia, 115–29. Valladolid 1989.

——. "San Ignacio de Loyola y el humanismo." *Gregorianum* 72 (1991): 261–88.

García Recio, José María. "Los jesuitas en Santa Cruz de la Sierra hasta los inicios de las reducciones de Moxos y Chiquitos. Posibilidades y limitaciones de la tarea misional." *Quinto Centenario* 14 (1988): 73–92.

García Sánchez, Justo, ed. *Los jesuitas en Asturias. Documentos*. [Oviedo] 1992.

Garstein, Oskar. *Rome and the Counter-Reformation in Scandinavia*. 4 vols. Leiden 1992.

Gasta, Chad M. *Transatlantic Arias: Early Opera in Spain and the New World*. Frankfurt 2013.

Gaston, Robert W. "How Words Control Images: The Rhetoric of Decorum in Counter-Reformation Italy." In *The Sensuous in the Counter-Reformation Church*, edited by Marcia B. Hall and Tracy Elizabeth Cooper, 74–90. New York 2013.

Gatzhammer, Stefan. "Antijésuitismo europeu. Relações político-diplomáticas e culturais entre a Bavaria e Portugal (1750–1780)." *Lusitania sacra*, 2nd ser., 5 (1993): 159–250.

——. "Politisch-diplomatische Beziehungen zwischen Portugal und Österreich im 18. Jahrhundert vor dem Hintergrund der Jesuitenfrage." *Mitteilungen des Instituts für Österreichische Geschichtsforschung* 102 (1994): 359–408.

Gaubil, Antoine. *Correspondance de Pékin 1722–1759*. Edited by Renée Simon. Geneva 1970.

Gavagna, Veronica. "I gesuiti e la polemica sul vuoto. Il contributo di Paolo Casati." In *Gesuiti e università in Europa (sec. XVI–XVIII)*, edited by Gian Paolo Brizzi and Roberto Greci, 325–38. Bologna 2002.

Gay, Jean-Pascal. "Doctrina Societatis? Le rapport entre probabilisme et discernement des esprits dans la culture jésuite (XVIe–XVIIe siècles)." In *Le discernement spirituel au dix-septième siècle*, edited by Simon Icard, 23–43. Paris 2011.

———. *Jesuit Civil Wars: Theology, Politics and Government under Tirso González (1687–1705)*. Farnham 2012.

———. "Le Jésuite improbable. Remarques sur la mise en place du mythe du Jésuite corrupteur de la morale en France à l'époque moderne." In *Les antijésuites. Discours, figures et lieux de l'antijésuitisme à l'époque moderne*, edited by Pierre-Antoine Fabre and Catherine Maire, 305–27. Rennes 2010.

———. *Morales en conflit. Théologie et polémique au Grand Siècle, 1640–1700*. Paris 2011.

———. "Voués à quel royaume? Les Jésuites entre vœux de religion et fidélité monarchique. À propos d'un mémoire inédit du P. de La Chaize." *XVIIe siècle* 57 (2005): 285–314.

Geger, Barton T. "The First First Companions: The Continuing Impact of the Men Who Left Ignatius." *Studies in the Spirituality of Jesuits* 44, no. 2 (2012): 1–38.

Gennaro, Giuseppe de. "Mistica Gesuitica nell '600." In *Alle origini dell'Università dell'Aquila. Cultura, università, collegi gesuitici all'inizio dell'età moderna in Italia meridionale*, edited by Filippo Iapelli and Ulderico Parente, 167–99. Rome 2000.

Gensac, Henri de. "Le P. Antoine Le Gaudier S. I. 1572–1622. Étude bio-bibliographique." *Archivum historicum Societatis Iesu* 37 (1968): 335–69.

Gepner, Corinna. *Le père Castel et le clavecin oculaire. Carrefour de l'esthétique et des savoirs dans la première moitié du 18e siècle*. Paris 2014.

Gerard, John. *The Autobiography of a Hunted Priest*. Translated from the Latin by Philipp Camaran. San Francisco 2012.

Gerhartz, Johannes Günter. *"Insuper promitto [. . .]." Die feierlichen Sondergelübde katholischer Orden*. Rome 1966.

Gernet, Jacques. *China and the Christian Impact: A Conflict of Cultures*. Cambridge 1987.

Ghielmi, Maria Pia. "Al crocevia tra antica e nuovo. L'insegnamento di Jean-Baptiste Saint-Jure (1588–1657) e la 'questione mistica' nella Compagnia di Gesù." *Ignaziana* 16 (2013): 178–200.

———. "La vita spirituale cristiana nell'insegnamento di Jean-Baptise Saint-Jure." *Ignaziana* 11 (2011): 3–39.

Giard, Luce. "The Jesuit College: A Center for Knowledge, Art, and Faith, 1548–1773." *Studies in the Spirituality of Jesuits* 40 (2008): 1–31.

———. "Le Catéchisme des Jésuites d'Étienne Pasquier, une attaque en règle." In *Les antijésuites. Discours, figures et lieux de l'antijésuitisme à l'époque moderne*, edited by Pierre-Antoine Fabre and Catherine Maire, 73–90. Rennes 2010.

Giguere, Georges-Émile. "ALBANEL, CHARLES." In *Dictionary of Canadian Biography*. Vol. 1. University of Toronto and Université Laval, 2003–present. http://www.biographi.ca/en/bio/albanel_charles_1E.html. Accessed January 13, 2020.

Gilardi, Lorenzo M. S.J. "Autobiografie di gesuiti in Italia (1540–1640). Storia e interpretazione." *Archivum historicum Societatis Iesu* 64 (1995): 3–39.

Gild, Gerlinde. "The Introduction of European Musical Theory during the Early Qing Dynasty: The Achievements of Thomas Pereira and Theodorico Pedrini." In *Western Learning and Christianity in China: The Contribution and Impact of Johann Adam Schall von Bell, S.J. (1592–1666)*, edited by Roman Malek, 1189–201. Nettetal 1998.

Gilii, Filippo Salvatore. *Saggio di storia americana o sia storia naturale, civile, e sacra de regni, e delle provincie Spagnuole di Terra-firma nell'America meridionale.* 4 vols. Rome 1780–84.

Gill, Natasha. *Educational Philosophy in the French Enlightenment: From Nature to Second Nature.* Farnham 2010.

Giménez López, Enrique. "El ejército y la marina en la expulsión de los jesuitas de Espana." In *Expulsión y exilio de los jesuitas españoles,* edited by Enrique Giménez López, 67–113. Alicante 1997.

Giménez López, Enrique, and Mario Martínez Gomis. "La secularización de los jesuitas expulsos (1767–1773)." In *Expulsión y exilio de los jesuitas españoles,* edited by Enrique Giménez López, 259–304. Alicante 1997.

Gioia, Mario. "Saggio introduttivo." In *Breve compendio di perfezione cristiana,* by Achille Gagliardi, edited by M. Gioia, 15–176. Rome 1996.

Gisolfo, Pietro. *Vita del P. D. Carlo Carafa fondatore della Congregatione de' P. P. Pij Operarij di Napoli.* Naples 1667.

Giussano, Giovanni Pietro. *The Life of St. Charles Borromeo.* London 1884. First published in 1610.

Goddard, Peter A. "Canada in Seventeenth-Century Jesuit Thought: Backwater or Opportunity?" In *Decentring the Renaissance: Canada and Europe in Multidisciplinary Perspective, 1500–1700,* edited by Germaine Warkentin and Carolyn Podruchny, 186–199. Toronto 2001.

Godding, Robert. "L'œuvre hagiographique d'Héribert Rosweyde." In *De Rosweyde aux* Acta sanctorum. *La recherche hagiographique des Bollandistes à travers quatre siècles,* edited by Robert Godding, 35–62. Brussels 2009.

Godínez, Miguel. *Practica de la theologia mystica.* Seville 1682.

———. *Praxis theologiae mysticae opusculum selectum.* 2 vols. Rome 1740.

Godman, Peter. *The Saint as Censor: Robert Bellarmine between Inquisition and Index.* Leiden 2000.

Golvers, Noël. "Distance as an Inconvenient Factor in the Scientific Communication between Europe and the Jesuits in China." *Bulletin of Portuguese Japanese Studies* 18/19 (2009): 105–4.

———. *Ferdinand Verbiest, S.J. (1623–1688) and the Chinese Heaven: The Composition of the Astronomical Corpus, Its Diffusion and Reception in the European Republic of Letters.* Leuven 2003.

———. *Libraries of Western Learning for China: Circulation of Western Books between Europe and China in the Jesuit Mission (ca. 1650–ca. 1750). I. Logistics of Book Acquisition and Circulation.* Leuven 2012.

———. "Viaggio di reclutamento di M. Martini S. J. attraverso i paesi bassi nel 1654. A proposito di bussole geomantiche, collezioni di oggetti cinesi, proiezioni di lanterna magica, e del R. P. Wilhelm von Aelst S. J." *Studi Trentini di Scienze Storiche* 74 (1995): 447–74.

———. "The XVIIth-Century Jesuit Mission in China and Its 'Antwerp Connections' (1): The Moretus Family (1660–1700)." In *Ex officina Plantiniana Moretorum. Studies over het drukkersgeslacht Moretus*, edited by Marcus de Schepper and Francine de Nave, 157–88. Antwerp 1996.

Gómez-Ferrer, Mercedes. "La arquitectura jesuítica en Valencia. Estado de la cuestión." In *La arquitectura jesuítica*, edited by María Isabel Alvaro Zamora, Javier Ibáñez Fernández, and Jesús Criado Mainar, 355–92. Zaragoza 2012.

Gontard, Maurice. "Les Jésuites et l'enseignement secondaire en France de la Restauration à la loi Falloux." *Paedagogica historica* 25 (1984): 109–27.

González, Galaxis Borja. *Die jesuitische Berichterstattung über die Neue Welt, Zur Veröffentlichungs, Verbreitungs- und Rezeptionsgeschichte jesuitischer Americana auf dem deutschen Buchmarkt im Zeitalter der Aufklärung.* Göttingen 2011.

González, Luis. "La etnografía acaxee de Hernando de Santarén." *Tlalocan* 8 (1980): 355–94.

González Rodríguez, Luis. "Thomás de Guadalaxara (1648–1720), misionero de la Trahumara, historiador, lingüista, y pacificador." *Estudios de historia novohispana* 15 (1995): 9–34.

Goodman, Howard, and Anthony Grafton. "Ricci, the Chinese, and the Toolkits of Textualists." *Asia Major*, 3rd ser., 2, no. 2 (1990): 95–148.

Gori, Giulio. *Lettere filosofiche. In appendice: "Dissertazioni epistolari sopra le bugie e circa l'anima delle bestie."* Edited by Anna Rita Capoccio. Florence 2011.

Gorman, Michael John. "Jesuit Explorations of the Torricellian Space: Carp-Bladders and Sulphurous Fumes." *Mélanges de l'Ecole française à Rome* 106 (1994): 7–32.

———. "Mathematics and Modesty in the Society of Jesus: The Problems of Christoph Grienberger." In *The New Science and Jesuit Science: Seventeenth Century Perspectives*, edited by Mordechai Feingold, 1–119. Dordrecht 2003.

Gosine, C. Jane, and Erik Oland. "*Docere, delectare, movere*: Marc-Antoine Charpentier and Jesuit Spirituality." *Early Music* 32 (2004): 511–38.

Goujon, Patrick. "Nicolas Caussin et le *Traité de la conduite spirituelle selon l'esprit du B. Francois de Sales.*" In *Nicolas Caussin: Rhétorique et spiritualité à l'époque de Louis XIII*, edited by Sylvie Conte, 191–205. Münster 2007.

———. *Prendre part à l'intransmissible. La communication spirituelle à travers la correspondance de Jean-Joseph Surin.* Grenoble 2008.

Graf, Matthias. *Geschichte der Hofmark Kissing an der Paar. Eine lokalhistorische Studie.* Edited by Adelheid Hoechstetter-Müller. Augsburg 2008. First published in 1894.

Grafton, Anthony. "Jean Hardouin: The Antiquary as Pariah." *Journal of the Warburg and Courtauld Institutes* 62 (1999): 241–67.

Grafton, Anthony, and Lisa Jardine. *From Humanism to the Humanities: Education and the Liberal Arts in Fifteenth and Sixteenth Century Europe.* London 1986.

Greene, Molly. *Catholic Pirates and Greek Merchants: A Maritime History of the Mediterranean.* Princeton, NJ, 2010.

Greer, Allan. *Mohawk Saint: Catherine Tekakwitha and the Jesuits.* New York 2005.

Grendler, Paul F. *The Jesuits and Italian Universities, 1548–1773.* Washington, DC, 2017.

———. *Schooling in Renaissance Italy: Literacy and Learning, 1300–1600.* Princeton, NJ, 1989.

———. *The University of Mantua, the Gonzaga and the Jesuits, 1584–1630.* Baltimore 2009.

Greven, Joseph. *Die Koelner Kartause und die Anfänge der katholischen Reform in Deutschland.* Münster 1935.

Griffin, Nigel. "Lewin Brecht, Miguel Venegas, and the School Drama: Some Further Observations." *Humanitas* 35–36 (1983–84): 19–86.

Groll, Thomas. "Das jesuitische Studien- und Erziehungsprogramm und seine Umsetzung in der Priesterausbildung." In *Die Univerisität Dillingen und ihre Nachfolger. Stationen und Aspekte einer Hochschule in Schwaben. Festschrift zum 450jährigen Gründungsjubiläums*, edited by Rolf Kiessling, 271–90. Dillingen 1999.

Gross, Michael B. *The War against Catholicism: Liberalism and the Anti-Catholic Imagination in Nineteenth-Century Germany.* Ann Arbor, MI, 2004.

Grove Music. S.v. "Rameau, Jean-Philipp." *The New Grove II.* http://www.musictheory21.com/documents/rameau-studies/rameau-grove-ii.pdf. Accessed January 15, 2020.

Guadalajara, Tomás de. *Gramática tarahumara.* Edited by Abel Rodríguez López. Ciudad Juárez 2010. First published in 1683.

Guasti, Niccoló. "I gesuiti spagnoli espulsi (1767–1815). Politica, economia, cultura." In *Morte e resurrezione di un ordine religioso. Le strategie culturali ed educative della Conpagnia di Gesù durante la soppressione (1759–1814)*, edited by Paolo Bianchini, 15–52. Milan 2006.

———. "I gesuiti spagnoli espulsi e la culture del settecento." *Ricerche di storia sociale e religiose* 38 (2009): 45–77.

———. *L'esilio italiano dei gesuiti spagnoli. Identità, controllo sociale e pratiche culturali, 1767–1798.* Rome 2006.

———. *Lotta politica e riforme all'inizio del regno di Carlo III. Campomanes e l'espulsione dei gesuiti dalla monarchia spagnola (1759–1768).* Florence 2006.

Guerra, Alessandro. "Per un'archeologia della strategia missionaria dei gesuiti. Le Indipetae e il sacrificio nella 'vigna del Signore.'" *Archivio italiano per la storia della pietà* 13 (2000): 109–92.

Guerrini, Maria Teresa. "Il lungo esilio. Forme di convivenza e integrazione nella società bolognese dei gesuiti espulsi." In *La presenza in Italia dei gesuiti iberici espulsi. Aspetti religiosi, politici, culturali*, edited by Ugo Baldini and Gian Paolo Brizzi, 157–86. Bologna 2010.

Guettée, Wladimir. *Histoire des jésuites.* 3 vols. Paris 1858–59.

Guévarre, André. *La mendicità sbandita col sovvenimento de' poveri.* Turin 1717.

Guibert, Joseph de. *The Jesuits: Their Spiritual Doctrine and Practice: A Historical Study.* St. Louis, MO, 1986.

Guibovich Pérez, Pedro. "Libros antiguos en la Universidad del Cuzco. La 'Biblioteca de los Jesuitas.'" *Histórica* 24, no. 1 (2000): 171–81.

Guida, Francesco. "Antonio Possevino e la Livonia. Un episodio della Controriforma (1582–1585)." *Europa orientalis* 2 (1983): 73–105.

Guidetti, Armando. *Le missioni popolari. I grandi gesuiti italiani.* Milan 1988.

Guillaume-Alonso, Araceli. "Les jésuites d'Olivares. Confession, absolution et exercice du pouvoir." In *Les jésuites en Espagne et en Amérique. Jeux et enjeux du pouvoir (XVIe–XVIIIe siècles)*, edited by Annie Molinié, 35–61. Paris 2007.

Guilloré, François. *Einsamkeit Für das Frauenzimmer.* Dillingen 1719.

———. *La Manière de conduire les âmes.* Paris 1676.

———. *Maximes spirituelles pour la conduite des âmes.* 2nd ed. Paris 1675.

Guillot, Pierre. *Les jésuites et la musique. Le Collège de la Trinité à Lyon, 1565–1762.* Liège 1991.

Guitton, Georges. "En marge de l'histoire du prêt à l'intérêt. Lyon jaloux d'Anvers et d'Amsterdam (1654–1678)." *Nouvelle Revue théologique* 75 (1953): 59–69.

Gundlach, Gustav. "Die Lehre Pius XII. vom modernen Krieg." In *Kann der atomare Verteidigungskrieg ein gerechter Krieg sein?*, edited by Karl Forster, 105–34. Munich 1960.

Gutton, Jean-Pierre. *Dévots et société au XVIIe siècle. Construire le ciel sur la terre.* Paris 2004.

Guzzardi, Luca. "Introduzione." In *Edizione nazionale delle opere e della corrispondenza di Ruggiero Giuseppe Boscovich*, vol. 13, pt. 2, *Opere scientifiche in versi. Les eclipses. Poeme en six chants*, edited by Luca Guzzardi, 11–34. Rome 2012.

Habsburg, Maximilian von. *Catholic and Protestant Translations of the* Imitatio Christi, *1425–1650: From Late Medieval Classic to Early Modern Bestseller.* Farnham 2011.

Hall, Marcia B., and Tracy Elisabeth Cooper, eds. *The Sensuous in the Counter-Reformation Church.* New York 2013.

Hallyn, Fernand. "Puteanus sur l'anagramme." *Humanistica lovaniensia* 49 (2000): 255–67.

Hambye, Edward René. *History of Christianity in India.* Vol. 3, *Eighteenth Century.* Bangalore 1997.

Hamilton, Alastair. *The Copts and the West, 1439–1822: The European Discovery of the Egyptian Church.* Oxford 2006.

———. *Heresy and Mysticism in Sixteenth Century Spain: The Alumbrados.* Toronto 1992.

Hansen, Georg. "Briefe des Jesuitenpaters Nithard Biber an den Churfürsten Anselm Casimir von Mainz, geschrieben auf seiner Romreise 1645/6." *Archivalische Zeitschrift* 9 (1900): 132–75.

Hansen, Joseph, ed. *Rheinische Akten zur Geschichte des Jesuitenordens 1541–1582.* Bonn 1896.

Harris, Steven. "Confession-Building, Long-Distance Networks, and the Organization of Jesuit Science." *Early Science and Medicine* 1 (1996): 287–318.

———. "Long-Distance Corporations, Big Science, and the Geography of Knowledge." *Configurations* 6 (1998): 269–304.

———. "Mapping Jesuit Science: The Role of Travel in the Geography of Knowledge." In *The Jesuits: Cultures, Sciences, and the Arts 1540–1773*, edited by John W. O'Malley, 212–39. Toronto 2000.

Haskell, Yasmin. "Child Murder and Child's Play: The Emotions of Children in Jakob Bidermann's Epic on the Massacre of the Innocents (*Herodiados libri iii*, 1622)." *International Journal of the Classical Tradition* 20 (2013): 83–100.

———. *Loyola's Bees: Ideology and Industry in Jesuit Latin Didactic Poetry.* Oxford 2003.

———. "The Passion(s) of Jesuit Latin." In *Brill's Encyclopaedia of the Neo-Latin World*, edited by Philip Ford, Jan Bloemendal, and Charles Fantazzi, 775–88. Leiden 2014.

———. "The Vineyard of Verse: The State of Scholarship on Latin Poetry of the Old Society of Jesus." *Journal of Jesuit Studies* 1 (2014): 26–46.

Haubert, Maxime. *La vie quotidienne au Paraguay sous les Jésuites.* Paris 1967.

Hausberger, Bernd. *Für Gott und König. Die Mission der Jesuiten im kolonialen Mexiko.* Munich 2000.

Havard, Gilles. *Empire et métissages. Indiens et français dans le Pays d'en Haut, 1660–1715.* Paris 2003.

Hayden, J. Michael. *The Catholicisms of Coutances: Varieties of Religion in Early Modern France, 1350–1789.* Montreal 2013.

Healy, Róisín. *The Jesuit Specter in Imperial Germany*. Boston 2003.

Heffernan, Brian. "Discerning the Spirits: The Irish Jesuits and Political Violence, 1919–1921." *Studies: An Irish Quarterly Review* 103 (2014): 552–61.

Heigel, Karl Theodor von. "Zur Geschichte des Censurwesens in der Gesellschaft Jesu." *Archiv für Geschichte des deutschen Buchhandels* 6 (1881): 162–67.

Heilbron, Jon L. *Electricity in the 17th and 18th Centuries: A Study of Early Modern Physics*. Berkeley 1979.

———. *The Sun in the Church: Cathedrals as Solar Observatories*. Cambridge, MA, 1999.

Hein, Olaf, and Rolf Mader. "La Stamperia del Collegio Romano." *Archivio della Società romana di storia patria* 115 (1992): 133–46.

Heiss, Gernot. "Konfessionelle Propaganda und kirchliche Magie. Berichte der Jesuiten über den Teufel aus der Zeit der Gegenreformation in den mitteleuropäischen Ländern der Habsburger." *Römische historische Mitteilungen* 32/33 (1990): 103–52.

Hellyer, Marcus. "'Because the Authority of My Superiors Commands': Censorship, Physics and the German Jesuits." *Early Science and Medicine* 1 (1996): 319–54.

———. *Catholic Physics: Jesuit Natural Philosophy in Early Modern Germany*. Notre Dame, IN, 2005.

Hendrickson, D. Scott. *Jesuit Polymath of Madrid: The Literary Enterprise of Juan Eusebio Nieremberg (1595–1658)*. Leiden 2015.

Hengerer, Mark. *Kaiser Ferdinand III. (1608–1657). Eine Biographie*. Vienna 2012.

Hengst, Karl. *Jesuiten an Universitäten und Jesuiten-Universitäten. Zur Geschichte der Universitäten in der Oberdeutschen und Rheinischen Provinz der Gesellschaft Jesu im konfessionellen Zeitalter*. Paderborn 1981.

Henryot, Anne-Hélène, and Fabienne Henryot. "Savoirs et savoir-faire pharmaceutiques au collège des jésuites de Pont-à-Mousson au XVIIIe siècle." *Annales de l'Est* 61 (2011): 69–93.

Hermann, Hugo, S.J. *Pia desideria emblematis*. Antwerp 1624.

Hernández, Pablo. *Organización social de las doctrinas guaraníes de la Compañía de Jesús*. 2 vols. Barcelona 1913.

Hernández de León-Portilla, Ascención. "Paradigmas gramaticales del nuevo mundo: Un acercamiento." *Boletín de la Sociedad española de historiografía lingüística* 7 (2010): 73–108.

Herrero Salgado, Félix. *La oratoria sagrada española de los siglos XVI y XVII*. Madrid 1996.

Hersche, Peter. *Agrarische Religiosität. Landbevölkerung und traditionaler Katholizismus in der voralpinen Schweiz 1945–1960*. Baden 2013.

Hervás y Pandura, Lorenzo. *Causas de la revolución de Francia en el ano de 1789, y medios de que se han valido para efectuarla los enemigos de la religion y del estado*. Madrid 1807.

Herzig, Arno. *Der Zwang zum wahren Glauben. Rekatholisierung vom 16. bis zum 18. Jahrhundert*. Göttingen 2000.

———. "Die Jesuiten im feudalen Nexus. Der Aufstand der Ordensuntertanen in der Grafschaft Glaz im ausgehenden 17. Jahrhundert." *Prague Papers on History of International Relations* (1999): 41–62.

Herzig, Franciscus. *Manuale controversisticum*. Tyrnau 1745.

———. *Manuale parochi, seu methodus compendiosa munus parochi apostolicum ritè obeundi*. Augsburg 1716.

Herzog, Urs. *Geistliche Wohlredenheit. Die katholische Barockpredigt*. Munich 1991.

Hevenesi, Gabriel. *Scintillae ignatianae, sive Sancti Ignatii de Loyola Societatis Iesu fundatoris apophthegmata sacra. Per singulos dies anni distributa.* Cologne 1705.

Heyberger, Bernard. "Le catholicisme tridentin au Levant (XVIIe–XVIIIe siècles)." *Mélanges de l'Ecole française à Rome* 101 (1989): 897–909.

———. *Les chrétiens du Proche-Orient au temps de la réforme catholique. Syrie, Liban, Palestine, XVIIe–XVIIIe siècles.* Rome 1994.

Heyberger, Bernard, and Chantal Verdeil. "Spirituality and Scholarship: The Holy Land in Jesuit Eyes (Seventeenth to Nineteenth Centuries). In *New Faith in Ancient Lands: Western Missions in the Middle East in the Nineteenth and Early Twentieth Centuries,* edited by Hendrika L Murre-van den Berg, 19–41. Leiden 2006.

Hickey, Daniel. *Local Hospitals in Ancien Régime France: Rationalization, Resistance, Renewal, 1530–1789.* Montreal 1997.

Hicks, Leo, ed. *Letters and Memorials of Father Robert Persons S.J.* London 1942.

Hildesheimer, Françoise. *Le jansénisme. L'histoire et l'héritage.* Paris 1992.

Hoffmann, Hermann. *Friedrich II. von Preussen und die Aufhebung der Gesellschaft Jesu.* Rome 1969.

———. "Theodor Moretus S.J. Professor der Theologie und Mathematik in Breslau." *Jahresbericht der Schlesischen Gesellschaft für Vaterländische Cultur* 107 (1934): 118–55.

Hofmann, Georg. "Apostolato dei gesuiti nell'Oriente greco, 1583–1773." *Orientalia Christiana Periodica* 1 (1935): 139–63.

———. "Die Jesuiten und der Athos." *Archivum historicum Societatis Iesu* 8 (1939): 3–33.

Hogan, Edmund H. "Jansenism and Frequent Communion: A Consideration of the Bremond Thesis." *Irish Theological Quarterly* 53 (1987): 144–50.

Hollenbach, David. "The Jesuits and the 'More Universal Good' at Vatican II and Today." In *The Jesuits and Globalization: Historical Legacies and Contemporary Challenges,* edited by José Casanova and Thomas F. Banchoff, 169–87. Washington, DC, 2016.

Höltershinken, Dieter. *Jesuiten in Dortmund. In der geistigen Auseinandersetzung mit den Themen der Moderne.* Bochum 2015.

Homza, Lu Ann. "The Religious Milieu of the Young Ignatius." In *The Cambridge Companion to the Jesuits,* edited by Thomas Worcester, 13–31. Cambridge 2008.

Höpfl, Harro. *Jesuit Political Thought: The Society of Jesus and the State, c. 1540–1630.* Cambridge 2004.

Horstmann, Fred. *Aloys Merz, Dom- und Kontroversprediger von Augsburg, als Opponent der Aufklärung.* Frankfurt 1997.

Hosne, Ana Carolina. "Assessing Indigenous Forms of Writing: José de Acosta's View of Andean Quipus in Contrast with Chinese 'Letters.'" *Journal of Jesuit Studies* 1 (2014): 177–91.

Hoste, Paul. *Art des armées navales ou traité des évolutions, qui contient des règles utiles aux officiers généraux, et particulières d'une armée navale.* Lyon 1697.

———. *Recueil des traités mathématiques.* Lyon 1692.

———. *Théorie de la construction des vaisseaux.* Paris 1697.

Houdard, Sophie. *Les invasions mystiques. Spiritualités, hétérodoxies et censures au début de l'époque moderne.* Paris 2008.

Houdry, Vincent. *La bibliothèque des prédicateurs.* 8 vols. Lyon 1716.

Houliston, Victor, Ginevra Crosignani, Thomas M. McCoog, and Robert Parsons, eds. *The Correspondence and Unpublished Papers of Robert Persons, SJ.* Vol. 1. Catholic and Recusant Texts of the Late Medieval and Early Modern Periods, 4. Toronto 2017.

Hsia, Adrian, ed. *Mission und Theater: Japan und China auf den Bühnen der Gesellschaft Jesu.* Regensburg 2005.

Hsia, Florence C. *Sojourners in a Strange Land: Jesuits and Their Scientific Missions in Late Imperial China.* Chicago 2009.

Hsia, Ronnie Po-chia. *Jesuit in the Forbidden City: Matteo Ricci 1552–1610.* New York 2010.

———, ed. *Noble Patronage and Jesuit Missions: Maria Theresia von Fugger-Wellenburg (1690–1762) and Jesuit Missionaries in China and Vietnam.* Rome 2006.

Hsü, Alois. *Dominican Presence in the Constitutions of the Society of Jesus: A Study of Dominican Influence on the Textual Make-up of the Jesuit Constitutions in Regard to the Formation of Novices and the Rules for the Novice Master Based on an Unpublished Manuscript of Juan A. Polanco (1517–1576).* Rome 1971.

———. *Texts of Collectanea Polanci: Regulae aliarum Religionum.* Rome 1971.

Huby, Vincent. *Œuvres spirituelles.* Paris 1772.

Hufton, Olwen. "Altruism and Reciprocity: The Early Jesuits and Their Female Patrons." *Renaissance Studies* 15 (2001): 328–53.

———. "Every Tub on Its Own Bottom: Funding a Jesuit College in Early Modern Europe." In *The Jesuits II: Cultures, Sciences, and the Arts 1540–1773,* edited by John W. O'Malley, 5–23. Toronto 2006.

———. "Faith, Hope and Money: The Jesuits and the Genesis of Fundraising for Education, 1550–1650." *Historical Research* 81 (2008): 585–609.

Huppert, George. *Public Schools in Renaissance France.* Urbana, IL, 1984.

———. *The Style of Paris: Renaissance Origins of the French Enlightenment.* Indianapolis, IN, 1999.

Hurtubise, Pierre. *La casuistique dans tous ses états. De Martin Azpilcueta à Alphonse de Ligouri.* Ottawa 2005.

Hyland, Sabine. *The Jesuit and the Incas: The Extraordinary Life of Padre Blas Valera S.J.* Ann Arbor, MI, 2003.

Iacovella, Marco. "'Fabbricatori di ciarle.' La disputa sul 'voto sanguinario' attraverso il carteggio muratoriano (1740–1743)." *Rivista di storia e letteratura religiosa* 49 (2013): 175–200.

Ianuzzi, Isabella. "Mentalidad inquisitorial y jesuitas. El enfrentamiento entre el Cardenal Silíceo y la Compañía de Jesús." *Cuadernos de historia moderna* 24 (2000): 11–31.

Iglesias, Ignacio. "Santa Teresa de Jesús y la espiritualidad ignaciana." *Manresa* 54 (1982): 291–311.

Ignatius of Loyola. *Epistolae Sancti Ignatii Loyolae Societatis Jesu fundatoris.* Edited by Roque Menchaca. 4 vols. Bologna 1804.

Imorde, Joseph. *Präsenz und Repräsentanz, oder, Die Kunst, den Leib Christi auszustellen (das vierzigstündige Gebet von den Anfängen bis in das Pontifikat Innocenz X.).* Emsdetten 1997.

Inglot, Marek. *La Compagnia di Gesù nell'Impero Russo (1772–1820) e la sua parte nella restaurazione generale della Compagnia.* Rome 1997.

———. "Le missioni della Compagnia di Gesù di Russia Bianca." *Studia missionalia* 60 (2011): 319–54.

Iparraguirre, Ignacio, ed. *Historia de los Ejercicios de San Ignacio.* Vol. 1, *Prática de los ejercicios de San Ignacio de Loyola en vida de su autor (1522–1556).* Rome 1946.

———. *Historia de los Ejercicios de San Ignacio.* Vol. 2, *Desde la muerte de San Ignacio hasta la promulgación del directorio oficial (1556–1599).* Rome 1955.

———. *Historia de los Ejercicios de San Ignacio.* Vol. 3, *Evolucion en Europa durante el siglo XVII.* Rome 1973.

Irving, David R. M. *Colonial Counterpoint: Music in Early Modern Manila.* Oxford 2010.

Israel, Jonathan I. *Enlightenment Contested: Philosophy, Modernity, and the Emancipation of Man, 1670–1752.* Oxford 2006.

Ivereigh, Austen. *The Great Reformer: Francis and the Making of a Radical Pope.* New York 2014.

———. *Wounded Shepherd: Pope Francis and the Struggle to Convert the Catholic Church.* New York 2019.

Jacobs, Hubert. "An Abortive Mission Effort: The Island of Bali in 1635." *Archivum historicum Societatis Iesu* 53 (1984): 313–30.

Jaitner, Klaus, ed. *Die Hauptinstruktionen Clemens' VIII. für die Nuntien und Legaten an den Europäischen Fürstenhöfen.* 2 vols. Tübingen 1984.

Jam, Jean-Louis. "Castel et Rameau." In *Autour du Père Castel et du clavecin oculaire,* edited by Roland Mortier and Hervé Hasquin, 59–67. Brussels 1996.

Jami, Catherine. *The Emperor's New Mathematics: Western Learning and Imperial Authority during the Kangxi Reign (1662–1722).* Oxford 2012.

———, ed. *Statecraft and Intellectual Renewal in Late Ming China: The Cross-Cultural Synthesis of Xu Guangxi (1562–1633).* Leiden 2001.

Jansen, Bernhard. "Deutsche Jesuiten-Philosophen des 18. Jahrhunderts in ihrer Stellung zur neuzeitlichen Naturauffassung." *Zeitschrift für katholische Theologie* 57 (1933): 384–410.

———. *Die Pflege der Philosophie im Jesuitenorden während des 17./18. Jahrhunderts.* Fulda 1938.

———. "Die scholastische Philosophie des 17. Jahrhunderts." *Philosophisches Jahrbuch der Görres Gesellschaft* 50 (1937): 401–44.

———. "Philosophen katholischen Bekenntnisses in ihrer Stellung zur Aufklärung." *Scholastik* 11 (1936): 1–51.

Jean, Auguste. *Le Maduré. L'ancienne et la nouvelle mission.* 2 vols. Paris 1894.

Jetten, Marc. *Enclaves amérindiennes. Les "réductions" du Canada, 1637–1701.* Sillery 1994.

Jimenez Berguecio, Julio. *Louis Lallemant S.J., 1588–1635. Estudios sobre su vida y su "Doctrine spirituelle."* Santiago de Chile 1988.

Jiménez Pablo, Esther. "The Evolution of the Society of Jesus during the Sixteenth and Seventeenth Centuries: An Order That Favoured the Papacy or the Hispanic Monarchy?" In *Papacy, Religious Orders, and International Politics in the Sixteenth and Seventeenth Centuries,* edited by Massimo Carlo Giannini, 47–66. Rome 2013.

———. "La lucha por la identidad en la Compañía de Jesús. Entre el servicio a Roma y el influjo de la monarquía hispana (1573–1648)." PhD diss., Autonomous University of Madrid, 2011.

Joassart, Bernard. "Jean-Paul Oliva, Charles de Noyelle et les Bollandistes d'après les archive bollandiennes." *Analecta Bollandiana* 125 (2007): 139–97.

———, ed. *Pierre-François Chifflet, Charles Du Cange et les Bollandistes. Correspondance.* Brussels 2005.

Johnson, Trevor. "Blood, Tears, and Xavier-Waters: Jesuit Missionaries and Popular Religion in the Eighteenth-Century Upper Palatinate." In *Popular Religion in Germany and Central Europe*, edited by Robert W. Scribner, 182–202, 272–75. Basingstoke 1996.

———. "Guardian Angels and the Society of Jesus." In *Angels in the Early Modern World*, edited by Alexandra Walsham and Peter Marshall, 194–213. Cambridge 2006.

———. *Magistrates, Madonnas, and Miracles: The Counter Reformation in the Upper Palatinate.* Farnham 2009.

Jonas, Raymond Anthony. *France and the Cult of the Sacred Heart: An Epic Tale for Modern Times.* Berkeley 2000.

Jorquera, Juan Lorenzo. "Nuevas fuentes musicales para el estudio de la actividad musical en la Compañía de Jesús de Madrid durante el siglo XVII." In *Los jesuitas. Religión, política y educación, siglos XVI–XVIII*, edited by José Martínez Millán, Henar Pizarro Llorente, and Esther Jiménez Pablo, 751–62. Madrid 2012.

Jouslin, Olivier. *"Rien ne nous plaît que le combat." La campagne des* Provinciales *de Pascal. Étude d'un dialogue polémique.* 2 vols. Clermont-Ferrand 2007.

Jouvency, Joseph de. *De ratione docendi et discendi.* Paris 1725. First published 1691.

Julia, Dominique. "Entre universel et local. Le collège jésuite à l'époque moderne." *Paedagogica historica* 40 (2004): 15–31.

Kaiser, Robert Blair. *Inside the Jesuits: How Pope Francis Is Changing the Church and the World.* London 2014.

Kammann, Bruno. *Die Kartause St. Barbara in Köln (1334 bis 1953). Kontinuität und Wandel; ein Beitrag zur Kirchen- und Stadtgeschichte Kölns.* Cologne 2010.

Kapp, Volker. "Die katholischen Dichter in Frankreich und das deutsche Geistesleben. Hans Urs von Balthasar als Deuter und Mittler des Renouveau Catholique." *Moderne und Antimoderne. Der "Renouveau catholique" und die deutsche Literatur*, edited by Wilhelm Kühlmann, 397–412. Freiburg 2008.

Karant-Nunn, Susan C. *The Reformation of Feeling: Shaping the Religious Emotions in Early Modern Germany.* Oxford 2010.

Kast, Augustin, ed. *Die Jahresberichte des Ettlinger Jesuitenkollegs 1661–1769.* Karlsruhe 1934.

Kaufmann, Thomas. *Konfession und Kultur. Lutherischer Protestantismus in der zweiten Hälfte des Reformationsjahrhunderts.* Tübingen 2006.

Keller, Katrin, and Alessandro Catalano, eds. *Die Diarien und Tagzettel des Kardinals Ernst Adalbert von Harrach (1598–1667).* Vienna 2010.

Kelter, Irving A. "The Refusal to Accommodate: Jesuit Exegetes and the Copernican System." *Sixteenth Century Journal* 26 (1995): 273–83.

Kennedy, T. Frank. "Colonial Music from the Episcopal Archive of Concepción, Bolivia." *Latin American Music Review* 9 (1988): 1–17.

———. "Jesuits and Music." In *The Jesuits and the Arts, 1540–1773*, edited by John W. O'Malley, Gauvin A. Bailey, and Giovanni Sale, 415–26. Philadelphia 2005.

———. "Jesuits and Music: The European Tradition, 1547–1622." PhD diss., University of California, Santa Barbara, 1982.

———. "Music and the Jesuit Mission in the New World." *Studies in the Spirituality of Jesuits* 29 (2007): 1–24.

Kertzer, David I. *The Pope and Mussolini: The Secret History of Pius XI and the Rise of Fascism in Europe*. New York 2014.

Kiechle, Stefan. *Grenzen Überschreiten. Papst Franziskus und seine jesuitischen Wurzeln*. Würzburg 2015.

King, Gail. "Christian Charity in Seventeenth-Century China." *Sino-Western Cultural Relations Journal* 22 (2000): 13–30.

Kircher, Athanasius. *Arca Noë*. Amsterdam 1675.

———. *Primitiae gnomonicae catoptricae, hoc est, Horologiographiae novae specularis*. Avignon 1635.

Kisel, Philipp. *Duodecim scintillae ex ardenti pectore et corde Jesu crucifixi*. Bamberg 1674.

———. *Iesv Siebenfältig-Blutiges Schau-Spiel Deß Siebenströmigen Geistlichen Nili-Flusses*. Bamberg 1679.

Kitzmantel, Angelika. "Die Jesuitenmissionare Martin Dobritzhoffer und Florian Paucke und ihre Beiträge zur Ethnographie des Gran Chaco im 18. Jahrhundert." PhD diss., Ludwig Maximilian University of Munich, 2004.

Klecker, Ellisabeth. "'Imperium Minervae.' Jesuitische Bildungspropaganda in der Ignatias des António Figueria Durao." In *Imperium minervae. Studien zur brasilianischen, iberischen und mosambikanischen Literatur*, edited by Dietrich Briesemeister, 179–209. Frankfurt 2003.

Knaap, Anna C. "Meditation, Ministry, and Visual Rhetoric in Peter Paul Rubens's Program for the Jesuit Church in Antwerp." In *The Jesuits II. Cultures, Sciences, and the Arts 1540–1773*, edited by John W. O'Malley, 156–81. Toronto 2006.

Knauer, Peter. "'Unsere Weise voranzugehen' nach den Satzungen der Gesellschaft Jesu." In *Ignatianisch. Eigenart und Methode der Gesellschaft Jesu*, edited by Michael Sievernich and Günter Switek, 131–48. Freiburg 1990.

Kochanowicz, Jerzy. "Jesuit Music Seminaries in Poland and Lithuania during the 17th and 18th Centuries." *Studia Comeniana et Historica* 36 (2006): 172–79.

Koegel, John. "Spanish and French Mission Music in Colonial North America." *Journal of the Royal Musical Association* 126 (2001): 1–53.

Kolvenbach, Peter-Hans, S.J. "The Service of Faith and the Promotion of Justice in American Jesuit Higher Education." *Studies in the Spirituality of the Jesuits* 33 (2001): 13–29.

König-Nordhoff, Ursula. *Ignatius von Loyola. Studien zur Entwicklung einer neuen Heiligen-Ikonographie im Rahmen einer Kanonisationskampagne um 1600*. Berlin 1982.

Konrad, Herman W. *A Jesuit Hacienda in Colonial Mexico: Santa Lucía, 1576–1767*. Stanford, CA, 1980.

Körndle, Franz. "'Ad te perenne gaudium.' Lassos Musik zum 'Ultimum Judicium.'" *Die Musikforschung* 53 (2000): 68–70.

———. "Between Stage and Divine Service: Jesuits and Theatrical Music." In *The Jesuits II. Cultures, Sciences, and the Arts 1540–1773*, edited by John W. O'Malley, 479–97. Toronto 2006.

Koslofsky, Craig. *Evening's Empire: A History of the Night in Early Modern Europe*. Cambridge 2011.

Kraus, Andreas. *Das Gymnasium der Jesuiten zu München (1559–1773). Staatspolitische, sozialgeschichtliche, behördengeschichtliche und kulturgeschichtliche Bedeutung*. Munich 2001.

Krempel, Ulla. "Die Orbansche Sammlung, eine Raritätenkammer des 18. Jahrhunderts." *Münchner Jahrbuch der bildenden Kunst* 19 (1968): 169–84.

Krumenacker, Yves. *L'école française de spiritualité. Des mystiques, des fondateurs, des courants et leurs interprètes*. Paris 1998.

Kunkel, Paul A. *The Theatines in the History of Catholic Reform before the Establishment of Lutheranism.* Washington, DC, 1941.

Kuzniewski, Anthony J. "Francis Dzierozynski and the Jesuit Restoration in the United States." *Catholic Historical Review* 78 (1992): 51–73.

Laamann, Lars Peter. *Christian Heretics in Late Imperial China: Chinese Inculturation and State Control, 1720–1850.* New York 2006.

La Bella, Gianni. *I gesuiti: dal Vaticano II a Papa Francisco.* Milan 2019.

La Bella, Gianni, and Martin Maier, eds. *Pedro Arrupe, Generaloberer der Jesuiten. Neue biographische Perspektiven.* Freiburg 2008.

Laborie, Jean-Claude, and Anne Lima, eds. *La mission jésuite du Brésil. Lettres et autres documents, 1549–1570.* Paris 1998.

Laboulaye, Édouard, ed. *Œuvres complètes de Montesquieu.* Vol. 7, *Discours, Lettres, Voyage à Paphos.* Paris 1879.

Lacombe, Robert. *Guaranis et jésuites. Un combat pour la liberté.* Paris 1993.

Lacotte, Jacqueline. "La notion de jeu dans la pédagogie des Jésuites au XVII' siècle." *Revue des sciences humaines* 158 (1975): 251–68.

Lallemant, Louis. *Doctrine spirituelle.* Edited by Dominique Salin, S.J. Paris 2011.

———. *La vie et la doctrine spirituelle.* Edited by Paul Champion. Lyon 1735. First published in 1694.

Lamalle, Edmond. "La propagande du P. Nicolas Trigault en faveur des missions de Chine (1616)." *Archivum historicum Societatis Iesu* 9 (1940): 49–120.

Lamet, Pedro Miguel. *Arrupe. Una explosión en la iglesia.* Madrid 1989.

Lana Terzi, Francesco. *Prodromo overo Saggio di alcune inventioni nuove premesso all'arte maestra [. . .] per mostrare li più reconditi principi della naturale filosofia.* Brescia 1670.

Lancicius, Nicolaus. *Opera omnia spiritualia XXI opusculis comprehensa.* Ingolstadt 1724.

Landry, Jean-Pierre. "Bourdaloue face à la querelle de l'éloquence sacrée." *XVIIe siècle* 143 (1984): 133–39.

Lang, Karl Heinrich von, ed. *Reverendi in Christo patris Jacobi Marelli S.J. amores e scriniis provinciae Superioris Germaniae Monachii nuper apertis brevi libello expositi.* Munich 1815.

Langewiesche, Wilhelm, and Margarethe Westphal, eds. *Die Briefe der Liselotte von der Pfalz.* Ebenhausen 1958.

Lapomarda, Vincent A. *The Jesuits and the Third Reich.* Lewiston, NY, 1989.

Largier, Niklaus. *In Praise of the Whip.* Translated by Graham Harman. New York 2006.

Launay, Adrien, ed. *Documents historiques relatifs à la Société des Missions étrangères.* 2 vols. Paris 1905.

Laven, Mary. *Mission to China: Matteo Ricci and the Jesuit Encounter with the East.* London 2011.

Lavenia, Vincenzo. "'Non arma tractare sed animas.' Cappellani cattolici, soldati e catechesi di guerra in età moderna." *Annali di storia dell'esegesi* 26 (2009): 47–100.

Lavoie, Michel. *C'est ma seigneurie que je réclame. La lutte des Hurons de Lorette pour la seigneurie de Sillery, 1650–1900.* Montreal 2010.

Lawson, Philip. *The Imperial Challenge: Quebec and Britain in the Age of the American Revolution.* Montreal 1989.

Lazar, Lance. "Belief, Devotion, and Memory in Early Modern Italian Confraternities." *Confraternitas* 15 (2004): 3–33.

———. "The First Jesuit Confraternities and Marginalized Groups in Sixteenth-Century Rome." In *The Politics of Ritual Kinship: Confraternities and Social Order in Early Modern Italy*, edited by Nicholas Terpstra, 132–49. Cambridge 2000.

———. *Working in the Vineyard of the Lord: Jesuit Confraternities in Early Modern Italy*. Toronto 2005.

Lazcano, Francisco Xavier. *Vida exemplar y virtudes heroicas del venerable padre Juan Antonio de Oviedo*. Mexico City, 1760.

Leavelle, Tracy Neal. "The Catholic Rosary, Gendered Practice, and Female Power in French-Indian Spiritual Encounters." In *Native Americans, Christianity, and the Reshaping of the American Religious Landscape*, edited by Joel W. Martin and Mark A. Nicholas, 159–77. Chapel Hill, NC, 2010.

Lebec, Monique, ed. *Miracles et sabbats. Journal du Père Julien Maunoir. Missions en Bretagne*. Paris 1997.

Le Bourgeois, Marie-Amélie. *Les Ursulines d'Anne de Xainctonge (1606). Contribution à l'histoire des communautés religieuses féminines sans clôture*. Saint-Étienne 2003.

Le Brun, Laurent. *Virgilius christianus*. Paris 1661.

Lecomte, Nathalie. "Un danseur d'exception sur les tréteaux de Louis-le-Grand. Michel Blondy (1676?–1739)." In *La chair et le verbe. Les jésuites de France au XVIIIe siècle et l'image*, edited by Edith Flamarion, 135–57. Paris 2008.

Lécrivain, Philippe. "Les missions de l'intérieur. Un Ministère privilégié de la Compagnie de Jésus sous Ignace de Loyola et Claudio Acquaviva." *Studia Missionalia* 60 (2011): 195–214.

———. "Une prosopographie des ex-jésuites 'parisiens' (1762–1848)." *Mélanges de l'Ecole française à Rome* 126 (2014). https://journals.openedition.org/mefrim/1670. Accessed September 25, 2019.

Ledda, Giuseppina. "Predicar a los ojos." *Edad de Oro* 8 (1989): 129–42.

Lederer, David. *Madness, Religion and the State in Early Modern Europe: A Bavarian Beacon*. Cambridge 2006.

Ledóchowski, Włodzimierz. "Epistola A. R. P. Wlodimiri Ledóchowski Praepositi Generalis Societatis Jesu de Doctrina S. Thomae magis magisque in Societate fovenda." *Zeitschrift für katholische Theologie* 42 (1918): 205–53.

Le Gaudier, Antoine. *Introductio ad solidam perfectionem per manducationem ad Sancti P. N. Ignatii Exercitia spiritualia integro mense obeunda*. Munich 1656.

Legge, James. *Confucian Analects, the Great Learning, and the Doctrine of the Mean*. 2nd ed. 1893. Repr., Oxford 2006.

Lehner, Ulrich L. "Benedict Stattler (1728–1797): The Reinvention of Catholic Theology with the Help of Wolffian Metaphysics." In *Enlightenment and Catholicism in Europe: A Transnational History*, edited by Jeffrey D. Burson and Ulrich L. Lehner, 167–89. Notre Dame, IN, 2014.

———. *The Catholic Enlightenment: The Forgotten History of a Global Movement*. New York 2016.

———. *Enlightened Monks: The German Benedictines, 1740–1803*. Oxford 2011.

Leinsle, Ulrich G. "Antike Lebenskonzepte in jesuitischer Wirklichkeit. Die akademischen Reden und *Progymnasmata Latinitatis* des Jakob Pontanus." In *Welche Antike?*

Konkurrierende Rezeptionen des Altertums im Barock, edited by Ulrich Heinen, 809–33. Wiesbaden 2011.

———. "Dichtungen Jakob Pontanus' in der Handschrift Studienbibliothek Dillingen XV 399." *Jahrbuch des Historischen Vereins Dillingen an der Donau* 107 (2006): 258–321.

———. "Werke Jakob Pontanus' in der Handschrift Studienbibliothek Dillingen XV 399." *Jahrbuch des Historischen Vereins Dillingen an der Donau* 106 (2005): 87–146.

Leitao, Henrique. "Jesuit Mathematical Practice in Portugal, 1540–1759." In *The New Science and Jesuit Science: Seventeenth Century Perspectives*, edited by Mordechai Feingold, 229–47. Dordrecht 2003.

Le Jay, Gabriel. *Bibliotheca rhetorum, praecepta et exempla complectens*. Vol. 2, *In quo orationes sacrae et panegyricae*. Venice 1747.

Le Moyne, Pierre. *La dévotion aisée*. 2nd ed. Paris 1658.

León Navarro, Vicente, and Telesforo M. Hernández. "La pugna entre jesuitas y escolapios en Valencia por el control de la enseñanza secundaria (1737–1760)." *Estudis. Revista de historia moderna de la Universidad de Valencia* 24 (1998): 307–37.

Leone, Marco. *Geminae voces. Poesia in latino tra barocco e Arcadia*. Lecce 2007.

Leonhardt, Carlos, ed. *Cartas anuas de la provincia de Paraguay, Chile y Tucumán, de la Compañía de Jesús*. 2 vols. Buenos Aires 1927–29.

Le Roux, Yannick, Réginald Auger, and Nathalie Cazelles. *Les jésuites et l'esclavage. Loyola. L'habitation des jésuites de Rémire en Guyane française*. Sainte-Foy 2010.

Leroy, Michel. *Le mythe jésuite: De Béranger à Michelet*. Paris 1992.

Leturia, Pedro de. *El gentilhombre Iñigo López de Loyola en su patria y su siglo*. 2nd ed. Barcelona 1949.

———. "Génesis de los Ejercicios de S. Ignacio y su influjo en la fundación de la Compañía de Jesús (1521–1540)." *Archivum historicum Societatis Iesu* 10 (1941): 17–59.

———. "La conversión de S. Ignacio. Nuevos datos y ensayo de síntesis." *Archivum historicum Societatis Iesu* 5 (1936): 1–35.

———. "Perché la Compagnia di Gesù divenne un ordine insegnante." *Gregorianum* 21 (1940): 350–82.

Leugers, Antonia. *Jesuiten in Hitlers Wehrmacht. Kriegslegitimation und Kriegserfahrung*. Paderborn 2009.

Le Valois, Louis. *Œuvres spirituelles*. Vol. 1, *Contenant les lettres sur la nécessité de la retraite, & sur divers sujets de piété*. Paris 1758.

———. *Œuvres spirituelles*. Vol. 2. Paris 1726.

———. *Sentimens de M. Descartes touchant l'essence et les propriétés du corps, opposés à la doctrine de l'église, et conformes aux erreurs de Calvin sur le sujet de l'Eucharistie*. Paris 1680.

Levenq, Gabriel. *La première mission de la Compagnie de Jésus en Syrie 1625–1775*. Beirut 1925.

Levy, Evonne. "Early Modern Jesuit Arts and Jesuit Visual Culture: A View from the Twenty-First Century." *Journal of Jesuit Studies* 1 (2014): 66–87.

———. "Jesuit Identity, Identifiable Jesuits? Jesuit Dress in Theory and in Image." In *Le monde est une peinture. Jesuitische Identität und die Rolle der Bilder*, edited by Elisabeth Oy-Marra and Volker R. Remmert, 127–52. Berlin 2011.

———. *Propaganda and the Jesuit Baroque*. Berkeley 2004.

Lewis, Mark A. "The Development of Jesuit Confraternity Activity in the Kingdom of Naples in the Sixteenth and Seventeenth Century." In *The Politics of Ritual Kinship: Confraternities and Social Order in Early Modern Italy*, edited by Nicholas Terpstra, 210–27. Cambridge 2000.

Lezcano Tosca, Hugo. "Antonio Cordeses. Lectura y mística en la espiritualidad de la Primera Compañía." In *Los jesuitas. Religión, política y educación, siglos XVI–XVIII*, edited by José Martínez Millán, Henar Pizarro Llorente, and Esther Jiménez Pablo, 1281–307. Madrid 2012.

Lezza, Antonia. "I Decreti sul tirannocido di Claudio Acquaviva." In *Letteratura fra centro e periferia. Studi in memoria di Pasquale Alberto De Lisio*, edited by Gioacchino Paparelli, 399–417. Naples 1987.

Lichy, Kolja. "Das Böse ist immer und überall. Antijesuitismus in Polen-Litauen um 1600." In *Streitkultur und Öffentlichkeit im konfessionellen Zeitalter*, edited by Henning P. Jürgens and Thomas Weller, 57–83. Göttingen 2013.

Liebreich, Karen. *Fallen Order: Intrigue, Heresy, and Scandal in the Rome of Galileo and Caravaggio*. New York 2004.

Light, Dale. "The Reformation of Philadelphia Catholicism, 1830–1860." *Pennsylvania Magazine of History and Biography* 112 (1988): 375–404.

Lin, Xiaoping. *Wu Li (1632–1718): His Life, His Paintings*. Lanham, MD, 2000.

Lindeijer, Marc. "'Aptus ad gubernandum': The Formation of Fr. Jan Roothaan in the Principles and Practices of Good Governance of the Restored Society of Jesus (1823–1829)." In *The Survival of the Jesuits in the Low Countries, 1773–1850*, edited by Leo Kenis and Marc Lindeijer, 233–53. Leuven 2019.

Lindorff, Joyce. "Missionaries, Keyboards and Musical Exchange in the Ming and Qing Courts." *Early Music* 32 (2004): 403–14.

Lippiello, Tiziana, and Roman Malek, eds. *"Scholar from the West": Giulio Aleni S.J. (1582–1649) and the Dialogue between Christianity and China*. Sankt Augustin 1997.

Liu, Yu. "The Spiritual Journey of an Independent Thinker: The Conversion of Li Zhizao to Catholicism." *Journal of World History* 22 (2011): 433–53.

Lockman, John. *Travels of the Jesuits, into Various Parts of the World: Particularly China and the East-Indies*. London 1742.

Löffler, Ulrich. *Lissabons Fall—Europas Schrecken. Die Deutung des Erdbebens von Lissabon im deutschsprachigen Protestantismus des 18. Jahrhunderts*. Berlin 1999.

Lombaerde, Piet. "The Facade and the Towers of the Jesuit Church in the Urban Landscape of Antwerp during the Seventeenth Century." In *Innovation and Experience in the Early Baroque in the Southern Netherlands: The Case of the Jesuit Church in Antwerp*, edited by Piet Lombaerde, 77–96. Turnhout 2008.

López Arandia, María Amparo. "Velando por el ánima del rey católico. Gabriel Bermúdez, confesor de Felipe V (1723–1726)." In *Los jesuitas. Religión, política y educación, siglos XVI–XVIII*, edited by José Martínez Millán, Henar Pizarro Llorente, and Esther Jiménez Pablo, 255–77. Madrid 2012.

Loupès, Philippe. "Un grand centre de formation des Jésuites. Bordeaux à l'époque du père Surin (1600–1665)." In *Los jesuitas. Religión, política y educación, siglos XVI–XVIII*, edited by José Martínez Millán, Henar Pizarro Llorente, and Esther Jiménez Pablo, 393–406. Madrid 2012.

Loureiro, Vanessa. "The Jesuits in Cambodia: A Look upon Cambodian Religiousness." *Bulletin of Portuguese Japanese Studies* 10/11 (2005): 193–222.

Lozano Navarro, Julián José. *La Compañía de Jesús en el Estado de los duques de Arcos. El colegio de Marchena (siglos XVI–XVIII)*. Granada 2002.

———. "Los jesuitas, paradigmas del orden, la obediencia y la dependencia." *Historia Social* 65 (2009): 113–24.

Lucas, Thomas M. *Landmarking: City, Church and Jesuit Urban Strategy*. Chicago 1997.

Lucca, Denis de. *Jesuits and Fortifications: The Contribution of the Jesuits to Military Architecture in the Baroque Age*. Boston 2012.

Lucchetti Bingemer, Maria Clara. "The Jesuits and Social Justice in Latin America." In *The Jesuits and Globalization: Historical Legacies and Contemporary Challenges*, edited by José Casanova and Thomas F. Banchoff, 188–205. Washington, DC, 2016.

Luengo, Manuel. *El retorno de un jesuita desterrado: Viaje del Padre Luengo desde Bolonia a Nava del Rey (1798)*. Edited by Inmaculada Fernández Arrillaga. Alicante 2010.

———. *Memorias de un exilio. Diario de la expulsión de los jesuitas de los dominios del Rey de España (1767–1768)*. Edited by Inmaculada Fernández Arrillaga. Alicante 2010.

Lugo, Juan de. *Responsa moralia*. Lyon 1651.

Luk, Bernard Hung-kay. "A Serious Matter of Life and Death: Learned Conversations at Foochow in 1627." In *East Meets West: The Jesuits in China, 1582–1773*, edited by Charles E. Ronan, 173–206. Chicago 1988.

———. "A Study of Giulio Aleni's *Chih-fang wai chi*." *Bulletin of the School for Oriental and African Studies* 40 (1977): 58–84.

Lukács, Ladislaus. "De graduum diversitate in Societate Iesu." *Archivum historicum Societatis Iesu* 37 (1968): 237–316.

———. "Die nordischen päpstlichen Seminare und P. Possevino (1577–1587)." *Archivum historicum Societatis Iesu* 24 (1955): 33–95.

Lunardon, Silvia. "Le zitelle alla Giudecca. Una storia lunga quattrocento anni." In *Le Zitelle. Architettura, arte e storia di un'istituzione veneziana*, edited by Lionello Puppi and Giuseppe Ellero, 9–49. Venice 1992.

Luongo, Carlo. *Silvestro Landini e le "nostre Indie." Un pioniere delle missioni popolari gesuitiche nell'Italia del Cinquecento*. Scandicci 2008.

Lyraeus, Hadrian. *De imitatione Iesu patientis sive de morte et vita in Christo Iesu patiente abscondita in carne vero nostra mortali ad similitudinem eius exprimenda libri VII*. Antwerp 1655.

Machielsen, Johannes M. *Martin Delrio: Demonology and Scholarship in the Counter-Reformation*. Oxford 2015.

Maclagan, Edward. *The Jesuits and the Great Mogul*. London 1932.

MacNamara, Patrick H. *A Catholic Cold War: Edmund A. Walsh, S.J., and the Politics of American Anticommunism*. New York 2005.

Madonia, Claudio. *La Compagnia di Gesù e la riconquista cattolica dell'Europa orientale nella seconda metà del XVI secolo*. Genoa 2002.

Maeder, Ernesto J. A. "Las encomiendas en las misiones jesuíticas." *Folia histórica del Nordeste* 6 (1984): 119–37.

Maggs, Barbara Widenor. "Science, Mathematics, and Reason: The Missionary Methods of the Jesuit Alexandre de Rhodes in Seventeenth-Century Vietnam." *Catholic Historical Review* 86 (2000): 439–58.

Maher, Michael W. "Financing Reform: The Society of Jesus, the Congregation of the Assumption and the Funding of the Exposition of the Sacrament in Early Modern Rome." *Archiv für Reformationsgeschichte* 93 (2002): 126–44.

Maire, Catherine. *De la cause de Dieu à la cause de la nation. Le jansénisme au XVIIIe siècle.* Paris 1998.

———. "Des comptes-rendus des constitutions jésuites à la Constitution civile du clergé." In *Les antijésuites. Discours, figures et lieux de l'antijésuitisme à l'époque moderne*, edited by Pierre-Antoine Fabre and Catherine Maire, 401–27. Rennes 2010.

———. "La Critique gallicane et politique des Voeux de religion." *Cahiers du Centre de recherches historiques* 24 (2000): 121–40.

Majorana, Bernadette. "La pauvreté visible. Réflexions sur le style missionnaire jésuite dans les *Avvertimenti* de Antonio Baldinucci (environ 1705)." *Memorandum* 4 (2003): 86–103.

———. "L'Arte della disciplina corporale nella predicazione popolare dei Gesuiti." *Teatro e storia* 13/14 (1998–99): 209–30.

———. "Le missioni popolari dei gesuiti Italiani nel XVII secolo. Il teatro della compassione." In *Les missions intérieures en France et en Italie du XVIe siècle au XXe siècle*, edited by Christian Sorrel and Frédéric Meyer, 87–102. Chambery 2001.

———. "Missionarius/concionator. Note sulla predicazione dei gesuiti nelle campagne (XVII–XVIII secolo)." *Aevum* 73 (1999): 807–29.

———. "Predicare per obbedienza. Note sull'ultima attività di Paolo Segneri (1692–1694)." In *Avventure dell'obbedienza nella Compagnia di Gesù. Teorie e prassi fra XVI e XIX secolo*, edited by Fernanda Alfieri and Claudio Ferlan, 139–64. Bologna 2012.

———. "Une pastorale spectaculaire. Missions et missionnaires jésuites en Italie (XVIe–XVIIIe siècles)." *Annales. Histoire, Sciences Sociales* 2 (2002): 297–320.

Malagrida, Gabriel. *Juizo da verdadeira causa do terremoto.* Lissabon 1756.

Malek, Roman, ed. *Western Learning and Christianity in China: The Contribution and Impact of Johann Adam Schall von Bell, S.J. (1592–1666).* Nettetal 1998.

Mallinckrodt, Rebekka von. *Struktur und kollektiver Eigensinn. Kölner Laienbruderschaften im Zeitalter der Konfessionalisierung.* Göttingen 2005.

Malusa, Luciano. *Neotomismo e intransigentismo cattolico. Il contributo di Giovanni Maria Cornoldi per la rinascita del tomismo.* 2 vols. Milan 1986.

Manaraeus, Oliver, S.J. *Exhortationes super Instituto et Regulis Societatis Jesu quas ante trecentos amplius annos provinciis Germaniae et Belgii tradidit.* Edited by B. Losschaert. Brussels 1912.

Mancia, Anita. "La controversia con i protestanti e i programmi degli studi teologici nella Compagnia di Gesù 1547–1599." *Archivum historicum Societatis Iesu* 54 (1985): 3–43, 209–66.

Manevy, Anne. "Le droit chemin. L'ange gardien, instrument de la disciplinarisation après la Contre-Réforme." *Revue de l'histoire des religions* 2 (2006): 195–227.

Manucci, Niccoló. *Storia do Mogor; or, Mogul India 1653–1708.* Translated by William Irvine. 2 vols. London 1907.

Marchal, Roger. *Madame de Lambert et son milieu.* Oxford 1991.

Marchetti, Elisabetta. "Bartolomeo Dal Monte e i gesuiti espulsi a Bologna." In *La presenza in Italia dei gesuiti iberici espulsi. Aspetti religiosi, politici, culturali*, edited by Ugo Baldini and Gian Paolo Brizzi, 211–27. Bologna 2010.

Mariana, Juan de. *Discurso de los grandes defectos que hay en la forma del gobierno de los Jesuitas*. Burdeos 1625.

Mariani, Andrea. *I gesuiti e la nobiltà polacco-lituana nel tardo periodo sassone (1724–1763). Cultura e istruzione fra tradizione e innovazione*. Poznan 2014.

———. "Le strategie educative dell'aristocrazia polacco-lituana. Il ruolo dei Gesuiti fra ideale retorico-umanistico e pratica pedagogica." *History of Education and Children's Literature* 8 (2013): 295–318.

Marno, David. "Attention and Indifference in Ignatius's *Spiritual Exercises*." In *A Companion to Ignatius of Loyola: Life, Writings, Spirituality, Influence*, edited by Robert A. Maryks, 232–47. Leiden 2014.

Marques, João Francisco. "A acção da igreja no terramoto de Lisboa de 1755. Ministério espiritual epregação." *Lusitania sacra*, 2nd ser., 18 (2006): 219–329.

Marquese, Rafael de Bivar, and Fábio Duarte Joly. "Panis, disciplina, et opus servo. The Jesuit Ideology in Portuguese America and Greco-Roman Ideas of Slavery." In *Slave Systems: Ancient and Modern*, edited by Enrico Dal Lago and Constantina Katsari, 214–29. Cambridge 2008.

Márquez, Antonio. "Origen y caracterización del iluminismo (según un parecer de Melchor Cano)." *Revista de Occidente* 21 (1968): 320–33.

Marti, Hanspeter. "Gesellschaftliches Leben und *unio mystica* am Beispiel der Mystiktheorie des Jesuiten Maximilian Sandäus (1578–1656)." In *Geselligkeit und Gesellschaft im Barockzeitalter*, edited by Wolfgang Adam, 199–209. Wiesbaden 1997.

Martin, Austin Lynn. *Henry III and the Jesuit Politicians*. Geneva 1973.

———. "Jesuits and Their Families: The Experience in Sixteenth Century France." *Sixteenth Century Journal* 13 (1982): 3–24.

———. "Vocational Crises and the Crisis in Vocations among Jesuits in France during the Sixteenth Century." *Catholic Historical Review* 72 (1986): 201–21.

Martin, Craig. "With Aristotelians Like These, Who Needs Anti-Aristotelians? Chymical Corpuscular Matter Theory in Niccolò Cabeo's *Meteorology*." *Early Science and Medicine* 11 (2006): 135–61.

Martina, Giacomo. *Storia della Compagnia di Gesù in Italia (1814–1983)*. Brescia 2003.

Martínez, Barnabé Bartolomé. "Las librerías e imprentas de los jesuitas (1540–1767). Una aportación notable a la cultura española." *Hispania sacra* 40 (1988): 315–88.

Martínez Herrer, Carlos. "Una experiencia de acceso a la cultura en la clase obrera. La Congregación Mariana del Patronato de la Juventud Obrera de Valencia a principios del siglo XX." In *El largo camino hacia una educación inclusiva. La educación especial y social del siglo XIX a nuestros días*, edited by Reyes Berruezo Albéniz, 507–14. Pamplona 2009.

Martínez Millán, José. "Transformación y crisis de la Compañía de Jesús (1578–1594)." In *I religiosi a corte. Teologia, politica e diplomazia in antico regime*, edited by Flavio Rurale, 101–30. Rome 1998.

Martínez-Serna, J. Gabriel. "Procurators and the Making of the Jesuits' Atlantic Network." In *Soundings in the Atlantic: Latent Structures and Intellectual Currents, 1500–1830*, edited by Bernard Bailyn and Patricia L. Denault, 181–209. Cambridge, MA, 2009.

Martínez Tornero, Carlos Alberto. "La administración de las temporalidades de la Compañía de Jesús: El destino de los colegios valencianos." PhD diss., University of Alicante, 2009.

Maryks, Robert A. *The Jesuit Order as a Synagogue of Jews: Jesuits of Jewish Ancestry and Purity-of-Blood Laws in the Early Society of Jesus.* Leiden 2010.

———. *"Pouring Jewish Water into Fascist Wine": Untold Stories of (Catholic) Jews from the Archive of Mussolini's Jesuit Pietro Tacchi Venturi.* Leiden 2012.

———. *Saint Cicero and the Jesuits: The Influence of the Liberal Arts on the Adoption of Moral Probabilism.* Aldershot 2008.

Masen, Jakob. *Ars nova argutiarum.* Cologne 1660.

Masseau, Didier. *Les ennemis des philosophes. L'antiphilosophie au temps des Lumières.* Paris 2000.

Masson, Pierre-Maurice. *Madame de Tencin (1682–1749).* Paris 1909.

Matienzo Castillo, W. Javier. "La encomienda y las reducciones jesuíticas de América meridional." *Temas americanistas* 21 (2008): 66–88.

Matthee, Rudi. "Die Beziehung des Iran zu Europa in der Safawidenzeit. Diplomaten, Missionare, Kaufleute und Reisen." In *Sehnsucht Persien. Austausch und Rezeption in der Kunst Persiens und Europas im 17. Jahrhundert & Gegenwartskunst aus Teheran*, edited by Axel Langer, 6–39. Zurich 2013.

———. "Jesuits in Safavid Persia." In *Encyclopaedia Iranica*, edited by Ehsan Yarshater, vol. 14, 634–38. London 2008. https://iranicaonline.org/articles/jesuits-in-safavid-persia. Accessed February 18, 2021.

Matton, Sylva. "Les théologiens de la Compagnie de Jésus et l'alchimie." In *Aspects de la tradition alchimique au XVIIe siècle*, edited by Frank Greiner, 383–428. Milan 1998.

Mayr, Leonhard. *Mariæ Stammen buech. Denkhwirdige Historien auff alle tag des Jars.* Dillingen 1632.

McCall Probes, Christine. "'L'Amour de Dieu': Rhetorical Strategies of the Controversy." *Papers on French Seventeenth Century Literature* 71 (2009): 529–40.

McCoog, Thomas M. *"And Touching Our Society": Fashioning Jesuit Identity in Elizabethan England.* Toronto 2013.

———. "The English Province of the Society of Jesus 1623–1699: An Institutional History." PhD diss., University of Warwick, 1983.

———. "'Lost in the Title': John Thorpe's Eyewitness Account of the Suppression." In *The Jesuit Suppression in Global Context: Causes, Events, and Consequences*, edited by Jeffrey D. Burson and Jonathan Wright, 161–81. Cambridge 2015.

———. "'Playing the Champion': The Role of Disputation in the Jesuit Mission." In *The Reckoned Expense: Edmund Campion and the Early English Jesuits*, edited by Thomas M. McCoog, 139–63. Rome 2007.

———, ed. *The Reckoned Expense: Edmund Campion and the Early English Jesuits.* Rome 2007.

———. *The Society of Jesus in Ireland, Scotland, and England 1541–1588: "Our Way of Proceeding?"* Leiden 1996.

———, ed. *With Eyes and Ears Open: The Role of Visitators in the Society of Jesus.* Leiden 2019.

McDermott, Jim. "Let Us Look Together to Christ: An Interview with Jesuit General Peter-Hans Kolvenbach." *America: The National Catholic Review*, November 26, 2007. https://www.americamagazine.org/sites/default/files/issues/cf/pdfs/635_1.pdf.

McDonough, Peter. *Men Astutely Trained: A History of the Jesuits in the American Century*. New York 1992.

McDonough, Peter, and Eugene C. Bianchi. *Passionate Uncertainty: Inside the American Jesuits*. Berkeley 2002.

McGreevy, John T. *American Jesuits and the World: How an Embattled Religious Order Made Modern Catholicism Global*. Princeton, NJ, 2016.

McHugh, Tim. *Hospital Politics in Seventeenth-Century France: The Crown, Urban Elites, and the Poor*. Aldershot 2007.

McKenzie-McHarg, Andrew. "History as Subversion: Conspiracy Theory as a Modern Concept and as an Early Modern Facet of Anti-Jesuit Polemic." PhD diss., University of Erfurt, 2013.

McKevitt, Gerald. *Brokers of Culture: Italian Jesuits in the American West, 1848–1919*. Stanford, CA, 2007.

McMahon, Darrin M. "The Counter-Enlightenment and the Low-Life of Literature in Pre-revolutionary France." *Past and Present* 159 (1998): 77–112.

———. *Enemies of the Enlightenment: The French Counter-Enlightenment and the Making of Modernity*. New York 2002.

McManners, John. *Church and Society in Eighteenth-Century France*. 2 vols. Oxford 1998.

McShea, Bronwen Catherine. "Cultivating Empire through Print: The Jesuit Strategy for New France and the Parisian Relations of 1632 to 1673." PhD diss., Yale University, 2010.

Mech, Paul. "Les bibliothèques de la Compagnie de Jésus." In *Les bibliothèques sous l'ancien régime, 1530–1789*, edited by Claude Jolly, 57–63. Paris 1988.

Meiklejohn, Norman. *La iglesia y los Lupaqas de Chucuito durante la colonia*. Cusco 1988.

Meisner, Joachim. *Nachreformatorische katholische Frömmigkeitsformen in Erfurt*. Leipzig 1971.

Melvin, Karen. "Charity without Borders: Alms-Giving in New Spain for Captives in North Africa." *Colonial Latin American Review* 18 (2009): 75–97.

Mendoça, Hernando de. *Advis de ce qu'il y a à reformer en la Compagnie des Iesuites, presenté au Pape & à la congregation generale*. [Paris] 1605.

Menegon, Eugenio. *Ancestors, Virgins, and Friars: Christianity as a Local Religion in Late Imperial China*. Cambridge, MA, 2009.

Ménestrier, Claude-François. *Des ballets anciens et modernes selon les regles du theatre*. Paris 1682.

Menniti Ippolito, Antonio. *Il governo dei papi nell'età moderna. Carriere, gerarchie, organizzazione curiale*. Rome 2007.

Menochius [Menochio], Stephan. *Hieropoliticon, sive Institutionis politicae e S. scripturis depromptae, libri tres*. Cologne 1626.

Menozzi, Daniele. *Sacro Cuore. Un culto tra devozione interiore e restaurazione cristiana della società*. Rome 2001.

Mercer, Christia. *Leibniz's Metaphysics: Its Origins and Development*. Cambridge, MA, 2001.

Mercier, Louis-Sébastien. *Tableau de Paris*. 12 vols. Paris 1782–88.

Mertz, James J., and John P. Murphy, eds. *Jesuit Latin Poets of the 17th and 18th Centuries: An Anthology of Neo-Latin Poets*. Wauconda, IL, 1989.

Mestre Sanchis, Antonio. "Reacciones en España ante la expulsión de los Jesuitas de Francia." *Revista de historia moderna* 15 (1996): 101–28.

Mettepenningen, Jürgen. *Nouvelle théologie—New Theology: Inheritor of Modernism, Precursor of Vatican II.* London 2010.

Metzler, Josef. "Die Missionsinitiativen und Unionsbemühungen in den Hauptinstruktionen Clemens' VIII." In *Das Papsttum, die Christenheit und die Staaten Europas 1592–1605. Forschungen zu den Hauptinstruktionen Clemens VIII,* edited by Stefano Andretta and Georg Lutz, 35–52. Tübingen 1994.

Meyer, Frédéric. *Pauvreté et assistance spirituelle. Les franciscains récollets de la province de Lyon aux XVIIe et XVIIIe siècles.* St. Étienne 1997.

Meyer, Jean. *Frankreich im Zeitalter des Absolutismus 1515–1789.* Stuttgart 1990.

Milani, Felice. "Introduzione." In *Iesus puer* by Tommaso Ceva, translated by Felice Milani, ix–lxv. Milan 2009.

Milhou, Alain. "La tentación joaquinita en los principios de la Compañía de Jesús. El caso de Francisco de Borja y Andrés de Oviedo." *Florensia* 8/9 (1994): 193–239.

Miller, Josef. "Die marianischen Kongregationen im 16. und 17. Jahrhundert." *Zeitschrift für katholische Theologie* 58 (1934): 83–109.

Minamiki, George. *The Chinese Rites Controversy: From Its Beginning to Modern Times.* Chicago 1985.

Mirafuentes Galván, José Luis. "Agustín Ascuhul, el profeta de Moctezuma. Milenarismo y aculturación en Sonora (Guaymas, 1737)." *Estudios de historia novohispana* 12 (1992): 123–41.

Mochizuki, Yuka. "La conversion de la princesse de Guéméné et la genèse de *La Fréquente Communion*: Spiritualité et polémique." 武蔵大学人文学会雑誌 [*Musashi University Journal of Humanities*] 42 (2010): 234–180 (1–54). https://repository.musashi.ac.jp/dspace/handle /11149/896.

Molina, J. Michelle. *To Overcome Oneself: The Jesuit Ethic and Spirit of Global Expansion, 1540–1767.* Berkeley 2013.

Molina, Juan Ignacio. *Compendio di storia geografica, naturale e civile del Regno del Chile.* Bologna 1776.

Molina, Luis de. *Concordia liberi arbitrii cum gratiae donis, divina praescientia, providentia, praedestinatione, et reprobatione.* Lisbon 1588.

Mongini, Guido. "Censura e identità nella prima storiografia gesuitica (1547–1572)." In *Nunc alia tempora, alii mores. Storici e storia in età posttridentina,* edited by Luigi Firpo, 169–88. Florence 2005.

———. "Devozione e illuminazione. Direzione spirituale e esperienza religiosa negli Esercizi spirituali di Ignazio di Loyola." In *Storia della direzione spiritual,* vol. 3, *L' età moderna,* edited by Gabriella Zarri and Giovanni Filoramo, 241–88. Brescia 2008.

———. "Le teologie gesuitiche delle origini. Lo spiritualismo radicale come matrice comune del dissenso e della fedeltà all'ortodossia." In *Avventure dell'obbedienza nella Compagnia di Gesù. Teorie e prassi fra XVI e XIX secolo,* edited by Fernanda Alfieri and Claudio Ferlan, 19–48. Bologna 2012.

———. "Per un profilo dell'eresia gesuitica. La Compagnia di Gesù sotto processo." *Rivista storica italiana* 117 (2005): 26–63.

Montezon, Fortuné de, ed. *Mission de Cayenne et de la Guyane française.* Paris 1857.

Moogk, Peter N. *La Nouvelle France: The Making of a French Canada; a Cultural History*. East Lansing, MI, 2000.

Morales, Martín María, ed. *A mis manos han llegado. Cartas de los PP. Generales a la antigua Provincia del Paraguay (1608–1639)*. Madrid 2005.

———. "Introducción." In *A mis manos han llegado. Cartas de los PP. Generales a la antigua Provincia del Paraguay (1608–1639)*, ed. Martín María Morales, 7*–77*. Madrid 2005.

———. "Los comienzos de las reducciones de la provincia del Paraguay en relación con el derecho indiano y el instituto de la Compañía de Jesús. Evolución y conflictos." *Archivum historicum Societatis Iesu* 67 (1998): 3–129.

Moreno de los Arcos, Roberto. "Autos seguidos por el provisor de naturales del arzobispado de México contra el ídolo del Gran Nayar, 1722–1723." *Tlalocan* 10 (1985): 377–447.

Moreno Martínez, Alida Genoveva. "Jesuitas y franciscanos en la sierra de Nayarit durante el siglo XVIII." In *Angeli novi. Prácticas evangelizadoras, representaciones artísticas y construcciones del catolicismo en América (siglos XVII–XX)*, edited by Fernando Armas Asin, 19–32. Lima 2004.

Moreno Martínez, Doris. "Obediencias negociadas y desobediencias silenciadas en la Compañía de Jesús en Espana, ss. XVI–XVII." *Hispania* 74 (2014): 661–86.

Moreno Mengíbar, Andrés, and Francisco Vázquez García. "Poderes y prostitución en España (siglos XIV–XVII). El caso de Sevilla." *Criticón* 69 (1997): 33–49.

Moresco, Roberto. "1552—Silvestro Landini e Emanuele Gomez de Montemayor: Due gesuiti a Capraia nel Cinquecento." https://storiaisoladicapraia.com/2013/06/27/1552-silvestro-landini-e-emanuele-gomez-de-montemayor-due-gesuiti-a-capraia-nel-cinquecento/. Accessed September 23, 2019.

Morgan, David. *The Sacred Heart of Jesus: The Visual Evolution of a Devotion*. Amsterdam 2008.

Morgan, Ronald J. "Jesuit Confessors, African Slaves and the Practice of Confession in Seventeenth-Century Cartagena." In *Penitence in the Age of Reformations*, edited by Katharine Jackson Lualdi and Anne T. Thayer, 222–39. Aldershot 2000.

Moriarty, Michael. *Disguised Vices: Theories of Virtue in Early Modern French Thought*. Oxford 2011.

Mörner, Magnus. "The Expulsion of the Jesuits from Spain and Spanish America in 1767 in Light of Eighteenth-Century Regalism." *The Americas* 23 (1966): 156–64.

———. "The Guaraní Missions and the Segregation Policy of the Spanish Crown." *Archivum historicum Societatis Iesu* 30 (1961): 367–88.

Morrison, Kenneth M. *The Embattled Northeast: The Elusive Ideal of Alliance in Abenaki-Euramerican Relations*. Berkeley 1984.

Moss, Jean Dietz. "Newton and the Jesuits in the Philosophical Transactions." In *Newton and the New Direction in Science: Proceedings of the Cracow Conference, 25 to 28 May 1987*, edited by George V. Coyne, Michał Heller, and Józef Życiński, 117–34. Vatican City 1988.

Moss, Jean Dietz, and William Wallace, eds. *Rhetoric and Dialectic in the Time of Galileo*. Washington, DC, 2003.

Mostaccio, Silvia. "Au carrefour des regards. Le théologien et la mystique. Virgilio Cepari et Maria Maddalena de' Pazzi." In *Fiction sacrée. Spiritualité et esthétique durant le premier âge moderne*, edited by Ralph Dekoninck, Agnès Guiderdoni, and Émilie Granjon, 319–36. Leuven 2013.

————. *Early Modern Jesuits between Obedience and Conscience during the Generalate of Claudio Acquaviva.* Aldershot 2014.

————. "'Perinde ac si cadaver essent.' Les jésuites dans une perspective comparative: La tension constitutive entre l'obéissance et le 'representar' dans les sources normatives des réguliers." *Revue d'histoire ecclésiastique* 105 (2010): 44–73.

————. "Per via di donna. Il laboratorio della mistica al servizio degli Esercizi spirituali: Il caso Gagliardi/Berinzaga. In *Storia della direzione spiritual,* vol. 3, *L' età moderna,* edited by Gabriella Zarri and Giovanni Filoramo, 311–29. Brescia 2008.

————. "Shaping the *Spiritual Exercises*: The Maisons de Retraites in Brittany as a Gendered Pastoral Tool." *Journal of Jesuit Studies* 2 (2015): 659–84.

Motta, Franco. "Analisi della fede e sintesi dell'autorità. La verità secolarizzata di Gregorio di Valencia." In *Avventure dell'obbedienza nella Compagnia di Gesù. Teorie e prassi fra XVI e XIX secolo,* edited by Fernanda Alfieri and Claudio Ferlan, 49–67. Bologna 2012.

————. *Bellarmino. Una teologia politica della Controriforma.* Brescia 2005.

————. "La compagine sacra. Elementi di un mito delle origini nella storiografia sulla Compagnia di Gesù." *Rivista storica italiana* 117 (2005): 5–25.

————. "La politica degli istanti ultimi. Morte, santità, autorità nella devozione gesuitica del secolo XVII." *Archivio italiano per la storia della pietà* 300 (2000): 217–73.

Mücke, Ulrich. *Gegen Aufklärung und Revolution. Die Entstehung konservativen Denkens in der iberischen Welt (1770–1840).* Cologne 2008.

Mujica, Bárbara. "Encuentro de santos. Francisco de Borja y Teresa de Jesús." In *Francisco de Borja y su tiempo. Política, religión y cultura en la edad moderna,* edited by Enrique García Hernán, 745–53. Valencia 2012.

Mullan, Elder. *The Sodality of Our Lady.* New York 1916.

Müller, Jacob. *KirchenGeschmuck. Das ist: Kurtzer Begriff der fürnembsten Dingen, damit ein jede recht und wol zugerichte Kirchen geziert und auffgebußt seyn solle.* Munich 1591.

Muller, Jeffrey. "Jesuit Uses of Art in the Province of Flanders." In *The Jesuits II. Cultures, Sciences, and the Arts 1540–1773,* edited by John W. O'Malley, 113–55. Toronto 2006.

Müller, Rainer A. "Zur Finanzierung der Kollegien und Hochschulen der oberdeutschen Ordensprovinz der Societas Jesu in der Frühen Neuzeit." In *Finanzierung von Universität und Wissenschaft in Vergangenheit und Gegenwart,* edited by Rainer Christoph Schwinges, 143–73. Basel 2005.

Müller, Winfried. "Die Aufhebung des Jesuitenordens in Bayern. Vorgeschichte, Durchführung, Administrative Bewältigung." *Zeitschrift für Bayerische Landesgeschichte* 48 (1985): 285–352.

Mungello, David E., ed. *The Chinese Rites Controversy: Its History and Meaning.* Nettetal 1994.

————. *Curious Land: Jesuit Accommodation and the Origins of Sinology.* Stuttgart 1985.

————. *The Forgotten Christians of Hangzhou.* Honolulu 1994.

————. "The Reconciliation of Neo-Confucianism with Christianity in the Writings of Joseph de Prémare S.J." *Philosophy East and West* 26 (1976): 389–410.

Münsterberg, Oskar. "Die Beziehungen Bayerns mit Ostasien durch die Jesuiten über Spanien und Portugal." *Zeitschrift des Münchener Altertumsvereins* 6 (1894): 12–37.

Murphy, Joseph, ed. *A History of the Jesuits in Zambia: A Mission Becomes a Province.* Nairobi 2003.

Murphy, Martin. *Ingleses de Sevilla. El Colegio de San Gregorio, 1592–1767.* Seville 2012.

Murphy, Thomas. *Jesuit Slaveholding in Maryland, 1717–1838.* London 2001.

Musart, Charles. *Manuale parochorum sive institutiones et praxes tum vitae tum officij pastoralis.* Augsburg 1713. First published in 1652.

Musillo, Marco. "Reconciling Two Careers: The Jesuit Memoire of Giuseppe Castiglione, Lay Brother and Qing Imperial Painter." *Eighteenth Century Studies* 42 (2008): 45–59.

Myers, W. David. *"Poor, Sinning Folk": Confession and Conscience in Counter-Reformation Germany.* Ithaca, NY, 1996.

Nadal, Jerónimo. *Scholia in Constitutiones S.I.* Edited by Manuel Ruiz Jurado. Granada 1976.

Nadasi, Johannes. *Annus dierum memorabilium Societatis Jesu.* Antwerp 1665.

Nanni, Stefania. "Le missioni nell'età della crisi." In *L'età di papa Clemente XIV. Religione, politica cultura,* edited by Mario Rosa, 79–102. Rome 2010.

———. "Réformistes et rigoristes. Les missions italiennes et la crise religieuse du XVIIIe siècle." In *Les missions intérieures en France et en Italie du XVIe siècle au XXe siècle,* edited by Christian Sorrel and Frédéric Meyer, 263–70. Chambery 2001.

Navarro Sorní, Miguel. "La espiritualidad valenciana del siglo XVI y san Francisco de Borja." In *Francisco de Borja y su tiempo. Política, religión y cultura en la edad moderna,* edited by Enrique García Hernán, 669–80. Valencia 2012.

Nebgen, Christoph. "'dahin zillet mein verlangen und begierd.' Epistolae Indipetarum der Deutschen Assistenz der Gesellschaft Jesu als Quellengattung." In *Sendung–Eroberung–Begegnung. Franz Xaver, die Gesellschaft Jesu und die katholische Weltkirche im Zeitalter des Barock,* edited by Johannes Meier, 67–98. Wiesbaden 2005.

———. *Missionarsberufungen nach Übersee in drei Provinzen der Gesellschaft Jesu im 17. und 18. Jahrhundert.* Regensburg 2007.

Neddermeyer, Uwe. "Das katholische Geschichtslehrbuch des 17. Jahrhunderts. Orazio Torsellinis *Epitome Historiarum.*" *Historisches Jahrbuch* 108 (1988): 469–83.

Neercassel, Jean de. *L'Amour pénitent.* 3 vols. Utrecht 1741.

Negredo del Cerro, Fernando. "La hacienda y la conciencia. Las propuestas del confesor del Conde Duque para el saneamiento de las finanzas reales (1625)." *Cuadernos de historia moderna* 27 (2002): 171–96.

Negro, Sandra. "Arquitectura, poder y esclavitud en las haciendas jesuitas de la Nasca en el Perú." In *Esclavitud, economía y evangelización. Las haciendas jesuitas en la América virreinal,* edited by Sandra Negro and Manuel M. Marzal, 449–92. Lima 2005.

Negrone, Giulio. *Historica disputatio de S. Ignatio Loiola, eiusdem Societatis Iesu fundatore, & de B. Caietano Thienaeo, institutore Ordinis clericorum regularium.* Cologne 1630.

Negruzzo, Simona. *Collegij a forma di seminario. Il sistema di formazione teologica nello stato di Milano in età spagnola.* Brescia 2001.

Neill, Stephen. *A History of Christianity in India.* 2 vols. Cambridge 1984.

Nelis, Jan. "The Clerical Response to a Totalitarian Political Religion. La Civiltà Cattolica and Italian Fascism." *Journal of Contemporary History* 46 (2011): 245–70.

Nelles, Paul. "*Cosas y cartas*: Scribal Production and Material Pathways in Jesuit Global Communication (1547–1573)." *Journal of Jesuit Studies* 2 (2015): 421–50.

———. *The Information Order: Writing, Mobility and Distance in the Making of the Society of Jesus (1540–1573).* Cambridge, MA, 2021.

———. "*Libros de papel, libri bianchi, libri papyracei*. Note-Taking Techniques and the Role of Student Notebooks in the Early Jesuit Colleges." *Archivum historicum Societatis Iesu* (2007): 75–112.

Nelson, Eric. "The Jesuit Legend: Superstition and Myth-Making." In *Religion and Superstition in Reformation Europe*, edited by Helen L. Parish and William G. Naphy, 94–117. Manchester 2002.

———. *The Jesuits and the Monarchy: Catholic Reform and Political Authority in France (1590–1615)*. Williston 2005.

Neumayr, Franz. *Heilige Streitt-Reden uber wichtige Glaubens-Fragen*. 2 vols. Augsburg 1757.

Neuner, Peter. *Der Streit um den katholischen Modernismus*. Frankfurt 2009.

Neveu, Bruno. "Culture Religieuse et Aspirations réformistes à la Cour d'Innocent XI." In *Érudition et religion aux XVIIe et XVIIIe siècles*, 235–76. Paris 1991.

———. "Juge suprême et docteur infaillible. Le pontificat romain de la bulle *In eminenti* (1643) à la bulle *Auctorem fidei* (1794)." In *Érudition et religion aux XVIIe et XVIIIe siècles*, 385–450. Paris 1991.

Nickel, Ralf Michael. "Zwischen Stadt, Territorium und Kirche. Franziskus' Söhne in Westfalen bis zum Dreißigjährigen Krieg." PhD diss., Ruhr University Bochum, 2007.

Niemetz, Michael. *Antijesuitische Bildpublizistik in der Frühen Neuzeit. Geschichte, Ikonographie und Ikonologie*. Regensburg 2008.

Nieremberg, Eusebius. *Corona virtuosa, y virtud coronada*. Madrid 1643.

———. *Theopoliticus*. Antwerp 1641.

Nieva Ocampo, Guillermo. "Cimentar las identidades locales. Los Jesuitas y las élites sociales del Tucumán (1600–1650)." In *Los jesuitas. Religión, política y educación, siglos XVI–XVIII*, edited by José Martínez Millán, Henar Pizarro Llorente, and Esther Jiménez Pablo, 1399–418. Madrid 2012.

Nising, Horst. "*. . . in keiner Weise prächtig." Die Jesuitenkollegien der süddeutschen Provinz des Ordens und ihre städtebauliche Lage im 16.–18. Jahrhundert*. Petersburg 2004.

Norberg, Kathryn. *Rich and Poor in Grenoble, 1600–1814*. Berkeley 1985.

Noringus, Livius [Negrone, Giulio]. *Dissertatio de aulae et aulicismi Fuga*. Milan 1626.

Norman, Corrie. "The Social History of Preaching: Italy." In *Preachers and People in the Reformations and Early Modern Period*, edited by Larissa Taylor, 125–91. Leiden 2001.

Northeast, Catherine M. *The Parisian Jesuits and the Enlightenment 1700–1762*. Oxford 1991.

Novi Chavarria, Elisa. *Il governo delle Anime. Azione pastorale, predicazione e missioni nel Mezzogiorno d'Italia. Secoli XVI–XVIII*. Naples 2001.

Nugent, Donald. *Ecumenism in the Age of the Reformation: The Colloquy of Poissy*. Cambridge, MA, 1974.

Oevermanns, Michael. "Die Pläne François Aguilons für den Bau der Antwerpener Jesuitenkirche." In *Intellektuelle in der Frühen Neuzeit*, edited by Jutta Held, 119–45. Munich 2002.

O'Hanlon, Gerard. "The Jesuits and Modern Theology—Rahner, von Balthasar and Liberation Theology." *Irish Theological Quarterly* 58 (1992): 25–45.

O'Keefe, Joseph M. "The Pedagogy of Persuasion: The Culture of the University of Pont-Mousson." *Paedagogica historica* 34 (1998): 421–42.

Olagnier, Paul. "Les Jésuites à Pondichéry de 1703 à 1721, et l'affaire Naniappa." *Revue d'histoire des colonies françaises* 19 (1931): 345–407, 517–50.

Olin, John C. "The Idea of Pilgrimage in the Experience of Ignatius Loyola." *Church History* 48 (1979): 387–97.

Olivares, Stanislaus. "Los coadjutores, espirituales y temporales, de la Compania de Jesús. Su origen y sus votos." *Archivum historicum Societatis Iesu* 33 (1964): 102–21.

———. *Los votos de los escolares de la Compagnia de Jesús. Su evolución jurídica.* Rome 1961.

Oliverius, Horatius [Orazio Olivieri, S.J.], ed. *Epistolae praepositorum generalium ad patres et fratres Societatis Jesu.* Prague 1711.

O'Malley, John W., ed. *Art, Controversy, and the Jesuits: The* Imago Primi Saeculi *(1640)*. Philadelphia 2015.

———. "Concluding Remarks." In *I gesuiti e la Ratio studiorum*, edited by Manfred Hinz, Roberto Righi, and Danilo Zardin, 509–21. Rome 2004.

———. *The First Jesuits.* Cambridge, MA, 1993.

———. *The Jesuits: A History from Ignatius to the Present.* London 2014.

———. *The Jesuits and the Popes: A Historical Sketch of Their Relationship.* Philadelphia 2016.

———. *Saints or Devils Incarnate? Studies in Jesuit History.* Leiden 2012.

———. *Trent: What Happened at the Council.* Cambridge, MA, 2013.

———. *What Happened at Vatican II.* Cambridge, MA, 2008.

O'Malley, John W., Gauvin A. Bailey, and Giovanni Sale, eds. *The Jesuits and the Arts, 1540–1773.* Philadelphia 2005.

Omont, Henri, ed. *Missions archéologiques françaises en Orient aux XVIIe et XVIIIe siècles.* 2 vols. Paris 1902.

Opfermann, Bernhard, ed. *Die Geschichte des Heiligenstädter Jesuitenkollegs.* 2 vols. Duderstadt 1989.

Opsomer, Carmélia. "La science au service de l'apostolat. L'enseignement des jésuites anglais à Liège aux XVIIe et XVIIIe siècles." *Archives internationales d'histoire des sciences* 148 (2002): 212–26.

O'Reilly, Terence. "The Spiritual Exercises and Illuminism in Spain: Dominican Critics of the Early Society of Jesus." In *Ite, inflammate omnia: Selected Historical Papers from Conferences Held at Loyola and Rome in 2006*, edited by Thomas M. McCoog, 199–228. Rome 2010.

Orlandi, Giuseppe. "Il Regno di Napoli nel Settecento. Il mondo di S. Alfonso de Liguori." *Spicilegium historicum Congregationis SSmi Redemptoris* 44 (1996): 5–389.

———. "L. A. Muratori e le Missioni de P. Segneri." *Spicilegium historicum Congregationis SSmi Redemptoris* 20 (1971): 158–294.

Orlandini, Nicola. *Historia Societatis Iesu, prima pars.* Cologne 1615.

Orozco Díaz, Emilio. "Sobre la teatralización del templo y la función religiosa en el Barroco. El predicador y el comediante." *Cuadernos de investigación para la literatura hispánica* 2–3 (1980): 171–88.

Oswald, Julius, ed. *"Auch auf Erd ist Gott mein Himmel." Pater Philipp Jeningen SJ, Missionar und Mystiker. Leben und Briefe.* Ostfildern 2004.

Otto, Josef Albert. *Gründung der neuen Jesuitenmission durch General Pater Johann Philipp Roothaan.* Freiburg 1939.

Outram, Dorinda. *The Enlightenment.* Cambridge 1995.

Overhoff, Jürgen, and Andreas Oberdorf, eds. *Katholische Aufklärung in Europa und Nordamerika*. Göttingen 2019.

Pacheco, Juan Manuel. *Los jesuitas en Colombia. Tomo I (1567–1654)*. Bogotá 1959.

Pachtler, Georg M., ed. *Ratio studiorum et Institutiones scholasticae Societatis Jesu per Germaniam olim vigentes*. 4 vols. Berlin 1887.

Padberg, John W., ed. *Documents of the 31st and 32nd General Congregations of the Society of Jesus: An English Translation of the Official Latin Texts of the General Congregations and of the Accompanying Papal Documents*. Saint Louis, MO, 1977.

———. "The Society True to Itself: A Brief History of the 32st General Congregation of the Society of Jesus." *Studies in the Spirituality of Jesuits* 15 (1983): 1–101.

Pagano, Sergio, ed. *Documenti del processo di Galileo Galilei*. Vatican City 1984.

Paglia, Vincenzo. *La pietà dei carcerati. Confraternite e società a Roma nei secoli XVI–XVIII*. Rome 1980.

Paiano, Maria. "Italian Jesuits and the Great War: Chaplains and Priest-Soldiers of the Province of Rome." *Journal of Jesuit Studies* 4 (2017): 637–57.

Palasi, Philippe. *Jeux de cartes et jeux de l'oie héraldiques aux XVIIe et XVIIIe siècles. Une pédagogie ludique en France sous l'Ancien Régime*. Paris 2000.

Pallavicino, [Pietro] Sforza. *Ermenegildo martire*. Rome 1644.

———. *Lettere*. 2 vols. Biblioteca Classica Sacra, 20. Rome 1848.

———. *Opere edite ed inedite*. Vol. 5, *Lettere*. Rome 1848.

———. *Vindicationes Societatis Iesu, quibus multorum accusationes in eius Institutum, leges, gymnasia, mores refelluntur*. Rome 1649.

Palm, Mary Borgias. *The Jesuit Missions of the Illinois Country, 1673–1763*. St. Louis, MO, 1931.

Palmer, Martin E. *On Giving the Spiritual Exercises: The Early Jesuit Manuscript Directories and the Official Directory of 1599*. St. Louis, MO, 1996.

Palomo, Federico. "Limosnas impresas. Escritos e imágenes en las prácticas misioneras de interior en la península Ibérica (siglos XVI–XVIII)." *Manuscrits* 25 (2007): 239–65.

———. "Malos panes para buenos hambres. Comunicación e identidad religiosa de los misioneros de interior en la península Iberíca." *Penélope* 28 (2003): 7–30.

Paolucci, Scipione. *Missioni de padri della Compagnia di Giesù nel Regno di Napoli*. Naples 1651.

Pappas, John N. *Berthier's* Journal de Trévoux *and the Philosophes*. Geneva 1957.

———. "L'influence de René-Joseph Tournemine sur Voltaire." *Annales de Bretagne et des pays de l'Ouest* 83 (1976): 727–35.

Parente, Ulderico. "Nicolas Bobadilla (1509–1590)." *Archivum historicum Societatis Iesu* 59 (1990): 323–44.

———. "Nicolo Bobadilla e gli esordi della Compagnia di Gesù in Calabria." In *I gesuiti e la Calabria*, edited by Vincenzo Sibilio, 19–56. Reggio Calabria 1992.

Parhamer, Ignaz. *Vollkommener Bericht von der Beschaffenheit des Waisenhauses Unserer lieben Frau auf dem Rennwege in Wien zu Oesterreich*. 3rd ed. Vienna 1774.

Paringer, Thomas. *Die bayerische Landschaft. Zusammensetzung, Aufgaben und Wirkungskreis der landständischen Vertretung im Kurfürstentum Bayern (1715–1740)*. Munich 2007.

Parker, Charles H. *Faith on the Margins: Catholics and Catholicism in the Dutch Golden Age*. Cambridge, MA, 2008.

Parran, Antoine. *Traité de la musique théorique et pratique contenant les précepts de la composition.* Paris 1639.

Paschoud, Adrien. *Le monde amérindien au miroir des Lettres édifiantes et curieuses.* Oxford 2008.

Pascual, Miguel Angel. *El misionero instruido, y en él los demás operarios de la Iglesia.* Madrid 1698.

Pasquier, Étienne. *Le catéchisme des Jésuites.* Edited by Claude Sutto. Sherbrooke 1982.

Pastore, Stefania. "La otra cara de la Compañía. Francisco de Borja tra profetismo e Inquisizione." In *Francisco de Borja y su tiempo. Política, religión y cultura en la edad moderna,* edited by Enrique García Hernán, 619–31. Valencia 2012.

———. "La 'svolta antimistica' di Mercuriano. I retroscena spagnoli." *Dimensioni e problemi della ricerca storica* 1 (2005): 81–93.

Patouillet, Louis. *Dictionnaire des livres jansénistes ou qui favorisent le Jansénisme.* 4 vols. Antwerp 1752.

Paultre, Christian. *De la répression de la mendicité et du vagabondage en France sous l'ancien régime.* Paris 1906.

Pavone, Sabina. "Antijésuitisme politique et antijésuitisme jésuite. Une comparaison de quelques textes." In *Les antijésuites. Discours, figures et lieux de l'antijésuitisme à l'époque moderne,* edited by Pierre-Antoine Fabre and Catherine Maire, 139–64. Rennes 2010.

———. "I dimessi della Compagnia negli anni del generalato di Francesco Borgia. Una nuova questione storiografica." In *Francisco de Borja y su tiempo. Política, religión y cultura en la edad moderna,* edited by Enrique García Hernán, 465–80. Valencia 2012.

———. *Le astuzie dei Gesuiti. Le false istruzioni segrete della Compagnia di Gesù e la polemica antigesuita nei secoli XVII e XVIII.* Rome 2000.

———. "'Preti riformati' e riforma della chiesa. I gesuiti al concilio di trento." *Rivista storica italiana* 117 (2005): 110–35.

———. "Tra Roma e il Malabar. Il dibattito intorno ai sacramenti ai paria nelle carte dell'Inquisizione romana (secc. XVII–XVIII)." *Cristianesimo nella storia* 31 (2010): 647–80.

———. *Una strana alleanza. La Compagnia di Gesù in Russia dal 1772 al 1820.* Naples 2008.

Peabody, Sue. "'A Dangerous Zeal': Catholic Missions to Slaves in the French Antilles, 1635–1800." *French Historical Studies* 25 (2002): 53–90.

Peitz, Detlef. *Die Anfänge der Neuscholastik in Deutschland und Italien (1818–1870).* Bonn 2006.

Peloso, Silvano. *Antonio Vieira e l'impero universale. La Clavis prophetarum e i documenti inquisitoriali.* Viterbo 2005.

Pena González, Miguel Anxo. *La Escuela de Salamanca. De la monarquía hispánica al orbe católico.* Madrid 2009.

Perera, Simon Gregory. *The Jesuits in Ceylon in the 16th and 17th Centuries.* Madura 1941.

Pererius, Benedictus [Benito Pereira]. *De communibus omnium rerum naturalium principiis et affectionibus libri XV.* Rome 1576.

Pérez de Ribas, Andrés. *History of the Triumphs of Our Holy Faith amongst the Most Barbarous and Fierce Peoples of the New World.* Translated by Daniel T. Reff, Maureen Ahem, and Richard K. Danford. Tucson, AZ, 1999.

Pérez González, Christiane. *Bilingualität auf der Jesuitenbühne. Latein und Volkssprache im spanischen Schultheater des 16. und 17. Jahrhunderts.* Münster 2014.

Périn, Léonard. *Communis vitae inter homines scita urbanitas.* Augsburg 1618.

Perlín, Juan. *Sacrum convivium, Hoc est: De frequentia et usu S. Eucharistiae.* Cologne 1632.

Perrin, Henri. *Tagebuch eines Arbeiterpriesters. Aufzeichnungen 1943/44.* Munich 1964.

Peterson, Williard J. "Learning from Heaven: The Introduction of Christianity and Other Western Ideas into Late Ming China." In *The Cambridge History of China*, vol. 8, pt. 2, *The Ming Dynasty, 1368–1644*, edited by Denis Twitchett and Frederick W. Mote, 789–839. Cambridge 1998.

———. "Western Natural Philosophy in Late Ming China." *Proceedings of the American Philosophical Society* 117 (1973): 295–322.

———. "Why Did They Become Christians? Yang T'ing-yün, Li Chih-tsao, and Hsü Kuangch'i." In *East Meets West: The Jesuits in China, 1582–1773*, edited by Charles E. Ronan, 129–52. Chicago 1988.

Petrocchi, Massimo. *Storia della spiritualità italiana.* Vol. 2, *Il Cinquecento e il Seicento.* Rome 1978.

Pfeiffer, Heinrich. "The Iconography of the Society of Jesus." In *The Jesuits and the Arts, 1540–1773*, edited by J. W. O'Malley, Gauvin A. Bailey, and Giovanni Sale, 201–28. Philadelphia 2005.

Picard, René. *Les peintres jésuites à la cour de Chine.* Grenoble 1973.

Pierre, Benoist. *La monarchie ecclésiale. Le clergé de cour en France à l'époque moderne.* Seyssel 2013.

Pignatelli, Antonio. "Il P. Virgilio Cepari S.J. La formazione e la prima attività, 1582–1601." *Archivum historicum Societatis Iesu* 51 (1982): 3–44.

Pillorget, René. "Vocation religieuse et état en France aux XVIe et XVIIe siècles." In *La vocation religieuse et sacerdotale en France. XVII–XIX siècles*, edited by the University of Angers, Centre de recherches d'Histoire religieuse, 9–18. Angers 1979.

Pirri, Pietro. "Il P. Achille Gagliardi, la Dama milanese, la riforma dello spirito e il movimento degli zelatori." *Archivum historicum Societatis Iesu* 14 (1945): 1–72.

Pizzorusso, Giovanni. "La Congregazione de Propaganda Fide e gli ordini religiosi. Conflittualità nel mondo delle missioni del XVII secolo." *Cheiron* 43/44 (2005): 197–240.

———. "Le choix indifférent. Mentalités et attentes des jésuites aspirants missionnaires dans l'Amérique française au XVIIe siècle." *Mélanges de l'Ecole française à Rome* 109 (1997): 881–94.

———. "Le pape rouge et le pape noir. Aux origines des conflits entre la Congrégation 'de Propaganda Fide' et la Compagnie de Jésus au XVIIe siècle." In *Les antijésuites. Discours, figures et lieux de l'antijésuitisme à l'époque moderne*, edited by Pierre-Antoine Fabre and Catherine Maire, 539–62. Rennes 2010.

———. "'Per servitio della Sacra Congregatione de Propaganda Fide': I nunzi apostolici e le missioni tra centralità romana e Chiesa universale (1622–1660)." *Cheiron* 30 (1998): 201–27.

———. *Roma nei Caraibi. L'organizzazione delle missioni cattoliche nelle Antille e in Guyana (1635–1675).* Rome 1995.

Plá, Josefina. *El barroco hispano-guaraní.* Asunción 2006.

Plazaola, Juan, ed. *Las fuentes de los Ejercicios espirituales de san Ignacio. Actas del symposio internacional.* Bilbao 1998.

Pleiner, Joachim. *Der in Lebensgefahr begriffene Soldat, durch trostreiche Ermahnungen und anmutige Gebeter zu einem christlichen Tode, auch in Ermanglung eines priesterlichen Beystandes, zum Trost dem in sächsischen Diensten befindlichen Soldaten vorbereitet.* Dresden 1748.

———. *Glaubens- und Sitten-Lehre auff die heiligen Evangelia des Jahres gerichtet, und zum Trost deren in Königl. Pohl. und Churfl. Sächss Diensten stehenden Catholischen Soldaten.* Dresden 1746.

Plöckinger, Othmar. *Geschichte eines Buches: Adolf Hitlers "Mein Kampf," 1922–1945.* Munich 2011.

Poggi, Vincenzo. "Arabismo gesuita nei secoli XVI–XVIII." In *Eulogema: Studies in Honor of Robert Taft,* edited by Ephrem Carr, 337–72. Rome 1993.

———. "Para una lectura oriental de los Ejercicios." *Manresa* 69 (1997): 5–18.

Pohle, Frank. *Glaube und Beredsamkeit. Katholisches Schultheater in Jülich-Berg: Ravenstein und Aachen (1601–1817).* Münster 2010.

———. "Jakob Masen als Dramatiker." *Spee-Jahrbuch* 14 (2007): 97–117.

Polanco, Johannes. *Breve directorium ad confessarii ac confitentis munus rite obeundum.* Louvain 1554.

Polderman, Marie. *La Guyane française 1676–1763. Mise en place et évolution de la société coloniale, tensions et métissages.* Matoury 2004.

Polenghi, Simonetta. "'Militia est vita hominis.' Die 'militärische' Erziehung des Jesuitenpaters Ignaz Parhamer im Zeitalter Maria Theresias." *History of Education and Children's Literature* 4 (2009): 41–68.

Polzer, Charles W., ed. *Rules and Precepts of the Jesuit Missions of Northwestern New Spain.* Tucson 1979.

Pomplun, Trent. *Jesuit on the Roof of the World: Ippolito Desideri's Mission to Eighteenth-Century Tibet.* New York 2010.

Pontanus, Jakob. *Philokalia sive excerptorum e sacris et externis auctoribus [. . .] opus.* Augsburg 1626.

Poole, Stafford. "Some Observations on Mission Methods and Native Reactions in Sixteenth-Century New Spain." *The Americas* 50 (1994): 337–49.

Popkin, Richard A. *The Traditionalism, Modernism and Scepticism of René Rapin.* Turin 1964.

Porteman, Karel. *Emblematic Exhibitions (Affixiones) at the Brussels Jesuit College (1630–1685): A Study of the Commemorative Manuscripts (Royal Library, Brussels).* Turnhout 1996.

———. "The Use of the Visual in Classical Jesuit Teaching and Education." *Paedagogica historica* 36 (2000): 178–96.

Possevino, Antonio. *Il soldato christiano, con l'instruttione de' capi dell'essercito catolico.* Macerata 1583.

———. *Il soldato christiano, con nuove aggiunte, et la forma di un vero principe et principessa espressi nelle vite di Stepano Batori Rè di Polonia, di Lodovico Gonzaga Duca di Nivers; di Eleonora Arciduchessa di Austria, Duchessa di Mantova.* Venice 1604.

———. *The Moscovia of Antonio Possevino, S.J.* Translated by Hugh F. Graham. UCIS Series in Russian and East European Studies 1. Pittsburgh 1977.

Pottier, Aloys. *Le père Pierre Champion. L'évangélisation du père Louis Lallemant et de son école au XVIIe siècle. 1631–1701.* Paris 1938.

Pozo, Candido. "La facoltà di teologia del Collegio Romano nel XVI secolo." *Archivum historiae pontificiae* 29 (1991): 17–32.

Pozzo, Andrea. *Shixue jingyun* [視學精蘊]. Edited and translated by Giuseppe Castiglione and Nian Xiyao. Beijing 1729.

Priesching, Nicole. *Sklaverei im Urteil der Jesuiten. Eine theologiegeschichtliche Spurensuche im Collegio Romano.* Hildesheim 2017.

Promitzer, Christian. "Die merkwürdige Flucht eines Jesuitenzöglings im Jahre 1735." In *Aspekte der Bildungs- und Universitätsgeschichte. 16. bis 19. Jahrhundert,* edited by Kurt Mühlberger, 271–303. Vienna 1993.

Proot, Goran, and Johan Verberckmoes. "Japonica in the Jesuit Drama of the Southern Netherlands." *Bulletin of Portuguese Japanese Studies* 5 (2003): 27–47.

Prosperi, Adriano. *La vocazione. Storie di gesuiti tra Cinquecento e Seicento.* Turin 2016.

———. "L'Europa cristiana e il mondo. Alle origini dell'idea di missione." *Dimensioni e problemi della ricerca storica* 2 (1992): 189–220.

———. *Tribunali della coscienza. Inquisitori, confessori, missionari.* Turin 1996.

———. "The Two Standards: The Origin and Development of a Celebrated Ignatian Meditation." *Journal of Jesuit Studies* 2 (2015): 361–86.

Provost-Smith, Patrick. "The New Constantinianism. Late Antique Paradigms and Sixteenth-Century Strategies for the Conversion of China." In *Conversion to Christianity: From Late Antiquity to the Modern Age; Considering the Process in Europe, Asia, and the Americas,* edited by Calvin B. Kendall, 223–58. Minneapolis, MN, 2009.

Puchowski, Kazimierz. "Between *Orator Christianus* and *Orator Politicus*: History Teaching and Books in Jesuit Colleges in Poland and Lithuania (1565–1773)." *Paedagogica historica* 38 (2002): 228–49.

Puente, Luis de la. *Vida del P. Baltasar Álvarez.* Edited by Camilo María Abad. Online edition at Biblioteca Virtual Miguel de Cervantes. Based on *Obras escogidas del V.P. Luis de la Puente,* edited by Camilo María Abad, 19–292, 429–39. Madrid 1958. http://www.cervantesvirtual .com/obra-visor/vida-del-p-baltasar-alvarez—o/html/. Accessed January 15, 2020.

Pullan, Brian. *Rich and Poor in Renaissance Venice: The Social Institutions of a Catholic State, to 1620.* Oxford 1971.

———. "Support and Redeem: Charity and Poor Relief in Italian Cities from the Fourteenth to the Seventeenth Century." *Continuity and Change* 3 (1988): 177–208.

Quantin, Jean-Louis. *Le catholicisme classique et les pères de l'église. Un retour aux sources (1669–1713).* Paris 1999.

———. *Le rigorisme chrétien.* Paris 2001.

———. "Le Saint-Office et le Probabilisme (1677–1679). Contribution à l'histoire de la théologie morale à l'époque moderne." *Mélanges de l'Ecole française à Rome* 114 (2002): 875–960.

Quattrone, Paolo. "Accounting for God: Accounting and Accountability Practices in the Society of Jesus (Italy, XVI–XVII Centuries)." *Accounting, Organizations and Society* 29 (2004): 647–83.

Quéniart, Jean. "La 'retraite de Vannes' à la fin du XVIIe siècle." *Revue de l'histoire des religions* 217 (2000): 547–61.

Quesada, Maria Antonietta. "Il Collegio Romano negli anni della soppressione della Compagnia di Gesù (1773–1824)." In *Il Collegio Romano dalle origini al Ministero per i beni culturali e ambientali*, edited by Claudia Cerchiai, 125–48. Rome 2003.

Questier, Michael C. "'Like Locusts over All the World': Conversion, Indoctrination and the Society of Jesus in Late Elizabethan and Jacobean England." In *The Reckoned Expense: Edmund Campion and the Early English Jesuits*, edited by Thomas M. McCoog, 347–69. Rome 2007.

Rabbath, Antoine, ed. *Documents inédits pour servir à l'histoire du christianisme en orient*. 2 vols. Paris 1910.

Rädle, Fidel. "Jesuit Theatre in Germany, Austria and Switzerland." In *Neo-Latin Drama in Early Modern Europe*, edited by Jan Bloemendal and Howard Norland, 185–293. Leiden 2013.

Rahner, Hugo. *Ignacio. Briefwechsel mit Frauen*. Freiburg 1956.

———. *Ignatius von Loyola als Mensch und Theologe*. Freiburg 1964.

Ranum, Patricia M, ed. *Beginning to Be a Jesuit: Instructions for the Paris Novitiate circa 1685*. St. Louis, MO, 2011.

———. "Charting Charpentier's 'Worlds' through His Mélanges." In *New Perspectives on Marc-Antoine Charpentier*, edited by Shirley Thompson, 1–29. Farnham 2010.

Rapin, René. *Réflexions sur la philosophie ancienne et moderne, et sur l'usage qu'on en doit faire pour la religion*. Paris 1676.

Rauscher, Anton, ed. *Gustav Gundlach 1892–1963*. Paderborn 1988.

Rauscher, Wolfgang. *Oel und Wein Deß Mitleidigen Samaritans Für die Wunden der Sünder*. 3 vols. Dillingen 1689.

Rayez, André. "Clorivière et les Pères de la Foi." *Archivum historicum Societatis Iesu* 21 (1952): 300–328.

Rea, William F. *The Economics of the Zambezi Missions, 1580–1759*. Rome 1976.

Reeves, Eileen. *Painting the Heavens: Art and Science in the Age of Galileo*. Princeton, NJ, 1999.

Reff, Daniel T. *Disease, Depopulation, and Culture Change in Northwestern New Spain*. Salt Lake City, UT, 1991.

———. *Plagues, Priests, and Demons: Sacred Narratives and the Rise of Christianity in the Old World and the New*. Cambridge 2005.

Rehg, William. "The Value and Viability of the Jesuit Brother's Vocation: An American Perspective." *Studies in the Spirituality of Jesuits* 40 (2008): 2–39.

Reilly, Conor. "A Catalogue of Jesuitica in the *Philosophical Transactions of the Royal Society of London* (1665–1715)." *Archivum historicum Societatis Iesu* 27 (1958): 339–62.

Reinhard, Wolfgang. "Gelenkter Kulturwandel im 17. Jahrhundert. Akkulturation in den Jesuitenmissionen als universalhistorisches Problem." *Historische Zeitschrift* 223 (1976): 529–90.

———. "Kirche als Mobilitätskanal der frühneuzeitlichen Gesellschaft." In *Ständische Gesellschaft und soziale Mobilität*, edited by Winfried Schulze, 333–52. Munich 1988.

Reinhardt, Nicole. "Spin Doctor of Conscience? The Royal Confessor and the Christian Prince." *Renaissance Studies* 23 (2009): 568–90.

———. *Voices of Conscience: Royal Confessors and Political Counsel in Seventeenth-Century Spain and France*. Oxford 2016.

Remmert, Volker R. "Picturing Jesuit Anti-Copernican Consensus: Astronomy and Biblical Exegesis in the Engraved Title-Page of Clavius' *Opera mathematica* (1612)." In *The Jesuits II. Cultures, Sciences, and the Arts 1540–1773*, edited by John W. O'Malley, 291–312. Toronto 2006.

Renda, Francesco. *Bernardo Tanucci e i beni dei gesuiti in Sicilia*. Rome 1974.

Rétat, Pierre. "*Mémoires pour l'histoire des sciences et des beaux-arts*. Signification d'un titre et d'une entreprise journalistique." *Dix-huitième siècle* 8 (1976): 167–88.

Reyero, Elias. *Misiones del M. R. P. Tirso González de Santalla*. Santiago 1913.

Reyes, Raquel A. G. "Botany and Zoology in the Late Seventeenth-Century Philippines: The Work of Georg Josef Camel SJ (1661–1706)." *Archives of Natural History* 36 (2009): 262–76.

Rho, Giovanni. *Achates ad D. Constantinum Caietanum*. Lyon 1644.

Ribeiro, Roberto M., and John W. O'Malley, eds. *Jesuit Mapmaking in China: D'Anville's Nouvelle atlas de la Chine (1737)*. Philadelphia 2014.

Ricci, Matteo. *Lettere: 1580–1609*. Edited by Francesco D'Arelli. Macerata 2001.

———. *The True Meaning of the Lord of Heaven*. Translated by Douglas Lancashire and Peter Hu Kuo-chen. Taipei 1985.

Richelieu, Armand Jean du Plessis cardinal duc de. *Lettres, instructions diplomatiques et papiers d'état du cardinal de Richelieu*. 8 vols. Paris 1856.

Richter, Daniel K. "Iroquois vs. Iroquois: Jesuit Mission and Christianity in Village Politics." *Ethnohistory* 32 (1985): 1–16.

Rico Callado, Francisco Luis. "La reforma de la predicación en la orden ignaciana. 'El nuevo predicador instruido' (1740) de Antonio Codorniu." *Revista de historia moderna* 18 (2000): 311–40.

———. "Las misiones populares y la difusión de las prácticas religiosas posttridentinas en la España moderna." *Obradoiro de historia moderna* 13 (2004): 101–25.

Rieder, Bruno. "Sternenhimmelbetrachtung als geistliche Übung. Zu einem Motiv aus der Biographie des heiligen Ignatius von Loyola in der neulateinischen Jesuitenlyrik des 17. Jahrhunderts." *Geist und Leben* 65 (1992): 450–65.

Riezler, Sigismund, ed. *Kriegstagebücher aus dem ligistischen Hauptquartier 1620*. Munich 1903.

Rocca, Giancarlo, ed. *La sostanza dell'effimero. Gli abiti degli ordini religiosi in Occidente*. Rome 2000.

Rochemonteix, Camille de. *Le Collège Henri IV de La Flèche*. 4 vols. Le Mans 1889.

Rock, Judith. *Terpsichore at Louis-le-Grand: Baroque Dance on the Jesuit Stage in Paris*. St. Louis, MO, 1996.

Rodé, Franc, S.J. "Homily of His Eminence, the Most Reverend Franc Card. Rodé, C.M." In *Decrees of General Congregation 35*, ed. SJ (Washington, D.C.), 89–92.

Rodríguez, Alonso [Alphonsus]. *Practice of Perfection and Christian Virtues*. Translated by Joseph Rickaby. 2 vols. London 1929.

Rodríguez-Camilloni, Humberto. "Constantino de Vasconcelos and quincha architecture in Spanish Colonial Peru." In *Structures and Architecture*, edited by Paolo J. da Sousa Cruz, 311–13. London 2010.

———. "Quincha Architecture: The Development of an Antiseismic Structural System in Seventeenth Century Lima." In *Construction History*, ed. Santiago Huerta Fernández, 1741–52. Madrid 2003.

Rodríguez de Flor, Fernando. "Picta Poesis. Un sermón en jeroglíficos, dedicado por Alonso de Ledesma a la fiesta de beatificación de San Ignacio, en 1610." *Anales de literatura española* 1 (1982): 119–33.

Rodríguez G. de Ceballos, Alfonso. "La arquitectura jesuítica en Castilla. Estado de la cuestión." In *La arquitectura jesuítica*, edited by María Isabel Alvaro Zamora, Javier Ibáñez Fernández, and Jesús Criado Mainar, 305–26. Zaragoza 2012.

———. "Las *Imágenes de la historia evangélica* del P. Jerónimo Nadal en el marco del Jesuitismo y la Contrarreforma." *Traza y baza* 5 (1974): 77–95.

———. "Loyola e il suo santuario." *FMR. Rivista bimestrale d'arte e cultura visiva* 16 (2006): 92–116.

Romanello, Marina. *Le spose del principe: Una storia di donne. La casa secolare delle zitelle in Udine. 1595–1995.* Milan 1997.

Romani, Valentino. "Note e documenti sulla prima editoria gesuitica." *Archivio della Società romana di storia patria* 117 (1994): 187–214.

Romano, Antonella. *La Contre-Réforme mathématique. Constitution et diffusion d'une culture mathématique jésuite à la Renaissance (1540–1640).* Rome 1999.

———. "Les collèges jésuites, lieux de la sociabilité scientifique 1540–1640." *Bulletin de la Société d'histoire moderne et contemporaine* 3–4 (1997): 6–21.

Romeo, Giovanni. *Ricerche sulla confessione dei peccati e Inquisizione nell'Italia del Cinquecento.* Naples 1997.

Ronda, James P. "The European Indian: Jesuit Civilisation Planning in New France." *Church History* 41 (1972): 385–95.

———. "The Sillery Experiment: A Jesuit-Indian Village in New France, 1637–1663." *American Indian Culture and Research Journal* 3 (1979): 1–18.

Ronsin, Albert. "L'éditeur Sébastian Cramoisy et l'université de Pont-à-Mousson." In *L'université de Pont-à-Mousson et les problèmes de son temps. Actes du colloque organisé par l'Institut de recherche régionale en sciences sociales, humaines et économiques de Nancy*, 345–63. Nancy 1974.

Rosa, Mario. "Clemente XIV, papa." DBI 26 (1982). http://www.treccani.it/enciclopedia/papa-clemente-xiv_%28Dizionario-Biografico%29/. Accessed July 20, 2020.

———. *Clero cattolico e società europea nell'età moderna.* Rome 2006.

———. *Settecento religioso. Politica della ragione e religione del cuore.* Venice 1999.

———. "Strategia missionaria gesuitica in Puglia agli inizi del Seicento." In *Religione e società nel Mezzogiorno tra Cinque e Seicento*, 245–72. Bari 1976.

Rosario Nobile, Marco. "La provincia di Sicilia." In *La arquitectura jesuítica*, edited by María Isabel Alvaro Zamora, Javier Ibáñez Fernández, and Jesús Criado Mainar, 91–140. Zaragoza 2012.

Roscioni, Gian Carlo. *Il desiderio delle Indie. Storie, sogni e fughe di giovani gesuiti italiani.* Turin 2001.

Rosignoli, Carlo Giuseppe. *Notizie memorabili degli Esercizj spirituali di Sant' Ignazio, fondatore della Compagnia di Gesù.* Venice 1713.

Rostirolla, Giancarlo. "La musica negli istituti religiosi della Compagnia di Gesù nel XVI e XVII secolo. Le tradizioni laudistiche fiorentina e romana." In *Alle origini dell'Università dell'Aquila. Cultura, università, collegi gesuitici all'inizio dell'età moderna in Italia meridionale*, edited by Filippo Iapelli and Ulderico Parente, 261–358. Rome 2000.

Rosweyde, Heribert. *Fasti sanctorum quorum vitae in belgicis bibliothecis manuscriptae.* Antwerp 1607.

———. *Vitae patrum.* Antwerp 1615.

Ruiu, Adina. "Conflicting Visions of the Jesuit Mission to the Ottoman Empire, 1609–1628." *Journal of Jesuit Studies* 1 (2014): 260–80.

Ruiz de Montoya, Antonio. *The Spiritual Conquest Accomplished by the Religious of the Society of Jesus in the Provinces of Paraguay, Paraná, Uruguay, and Tape.* St. Louis, MO, 1993.

Ruiz Jurado, Manuel. "Jesuit Formation during Mercurian's Generalate." In *The Mercurian Project: Forming Jesuit Culture, 1573–1580,* edited by Thomas McCoog, 399–419. St. Louis, MO, 2004.

———. "La tercera probación en la Compañía de Jesús." *Archivum historicum Societatis Iesu* 60 (1990): 265–351.

———. *Orígenes del noviciado en la Compañía de Jesús.* Rome 1980.

———. "San Juan de Ávila y la Compañía de Jesús." *Archivum historicum Societatis Iesu* 40 (1971): 153–72.

———. "Un caso de profetismo reformista en la Compañía de Jesús. Gandía 1547–1549." *Archivum historicum Societatis Iesu* 43 (1974): 217–66.

Ruiz Rodrigo, Candido. "La educación del obrero. Los inicios del catolicismo social en Valencia." *Historia de la educación* 1 (1982): 123–44.

Rule, Paul A. *K'ung-tzu or Confucius? The Jesuit Interpretation of Confucianism.* Sydney 1986.

Rurale, Flavio. "Confessori consiglieri di principi. Alcuni casi seicenteschi dell'area estense." In *Archivi, territori, poteri in area estense (secc. XVI–XVIII),* edited by Euride Fregni, 289–316. Rome 1999.

———. "Il confessore e il governatore. Teologi e moralisti tra casi di coscienza e questioni politiche nella Milano del primo Seicento." In *La Lombardia spagnola. Nuovi indirizzi di ricerca,* edited by Elena Brambilla and Giovanni Muto, 343–70. Milan 1997.

———. "Lo spazio religioso milanese tra Sei e Settecento. Gesuiti e barnabiti." In *Clelia Grillo Borromeo Arese. Un salotto letterario tra arte, scienza e politica,* edited by Andrea Spiriti, 127–49. Florence 2011.

———. *Monaci, frati, chierici. Gli ordini religiosi in età moderna.* Rome 2008.

Russo, Mariagrazia. "La grande dispersione in Italie dei gesuiti portoghesi espulsi. processi di catalogazione e documentazione inedita." In *La presenza in Italia dei gesuiti iberici espulsi. Aspetti religiosi, politici, culturali,* edited by Ugo Baldini and Gian Paolo Brizzi, 27–55. Bologna 2010.

———. "L'espulsione dei gesuiti di Portogallo e il loro arrivo in Italia." *Ricerche di storia sociale e religiose* 38 (2009): 87–100.

Sacchini, Francesco. *Paraenesis ad magistros scholarum inferiorum.* Dillingen 1626.

———. *Protrepticon ad magistros scholarum inferiorum.* Dillingen 1626.

Saeger, James Schofield. *The Chaco Mission Frontier: The Guaycuruan Experience.* Tucson 2000.

Sage, Pierre. *Le "bon prêtre" dans la littérature française d'Amadis de Gaule au Génie du christianisme.* Geneva/Lille 1951.

Sailly [Saillius], Thomas. *Guidon et practicque spirituelle du soldat chrestien, reveu et augmenté pour l'armee de sa Majesté catholicque au Pays-Bas.* Paris 1590.

Sale, Giovanni. *Pauperismo architettonico e architettura gesuitica. Dalla chiesa ad aula al Gesù di Roma*. Milan 2001.

Salinas, María Laura. "Jesuitas y franciscanas en las misiones del Paraguay en perspectiva comparada, siglo XVII." In *Fronteiras e identidades. Encontros e desencontros entre povos indígenas e missões religiosas*, edited by Graciela Chamorro, Thiago Leandro Vieira Calvacante, and Carlos Barros Gonçalves, 223–46. São Bernardo do Campo 2011.

Salvatierra, Juan María de. *Selected Letters about Lower California*. Translated by Ernest J. Burrus, S.J. Los Angeles 1971.

Salviucci Insolera, Lydia. "Le illustrazioni per gli Esercizi spirituali intorno al 1600." *Archivum historicum Societatis Iesu* 60 (1991): 161–229.

———. *L'Imago primi saeculi (1640) e il significato dell'immagine allegorica nella Compagnia di Gesù. Genesi e fortuna del libro*. Rome 2004.

———. "Livres d'emblèmes, livres d'oraisons." In *Baroque vision jésuite. Du Tintoret à Rubens*, edited by Alain Tapié, 61–65. Paris 2003.

Samerski, Stefan. "Olmütz als Drehkreuz des ostmitteleuropäischen Priesternachwuchses? Das Bildungsmäzenatentum der Olmützer Jesuiten im 16. bis 18. Jahrhundert." *Schulstiftungen und Studienfinanzierung. Bildungsmäzenatentum in den böhmischen, österreichischen und ungarischen Ländern, 1500–1800*, edited by Joachim Bahlcke and Thomas Winkelbauer, 253–62. Vienna 2011.

Sánchez, Juan. *Selectae et practicae disputationes de rebus in administratione Sacramentorum, praesertim Eucharistiae & Poenitentiae*. Lyon 1643.

Sandaeus [van der Sandt], Maximilian. *Pro theologia mystica clavis*. Cologne 1640.

———. *Theologia mystica sive Contemplatio divina religiosorum a calumniis vindicata*. Mainz 1627.

Sander, Johannes, S.J. *Geschichte des Jesuitenkollegs in Paderborn 1580–1659*. Edited and translated by Gerhard Ludwig Kneißler. Notes by Friedrich Gerhard Hohmann. Paderborn 2011.

Sandoval, Alonso de. *Naturaleza, policia sagrada i profana, costumbres i ritos, disciplina i catechismo evangelico de todos Etiopes*. Seville 1627.

———. *Treatise on Slavery: Selections from* De Instauranda Aethiopum Salute. Edited by Nicole von Germeten. Indianapolis, IN, 2008.

Sanfilippo, Matteo, and Carlo Prezzolini, eds. *Roberto De Nobili (1577–1656). Missionario gesuita poliziano*. Perugia 2008.

Sangalli, Maurizio. *Cultura, politica e religione nella repubblica di Venezia tra Cinque e Seicento. Gesuiti e somaschi a Venezia*. Venice 1999.

Santarelli, Antonio. *Tractatus de haeresi, schismate, apostasia, sollicitatione in sacramento Poenitentiae*. Rome 1625.

Santos Hernández, Ángel. *Jesuitas y obispados. La Compañía de Jesús y las dignidades eclesiásticas*. Madrid 1999.

———. *Los jesuitas en América*. Madrid 1992.

Sarbiewski, Maciej. *Poemata omnia*. Leipzig 1840.

Sarreal, Julia. *The Guaraní and Their Missions: A Socioeconomic History*. Stanford, CA, 2014.

Saugnieux, Joël. *Les jansénistes et le renouveau de la prédication dans l'Espagne de la seconde moitié du XVIIIe siècle*. Lyon 1976.

Sautel, Pierre-Juste, S.J. *Divae Magdalenae ignes sacri et piae lachrimae sive Selecta de diva Magdalena*. Lyon 1656.

Sawilla, Jan Marco. *Antiquarianismus, Hagiographie und Historie im 17. Jahrhundert. Zum Werk der Bollandisten. Ein wissenschaftshistorischer Versuch*. Tübingen 2009.

Saxby, Trevor J. *The Quest for the New Jerusalem: Jean de Labadie and the Labadists, 1610–1744*. Dordrecht 1987.

Scaduto, Mario. "La missione del nunzio. Due memoriali di Possevino ambasciatore, 1581, 1582." *Archivum historicum Societatis Iesu* 49 (1980): 135–60.

———. "Le missioni di A. Possevino in Piemonte. Propaganda calvinista e restaurazione cattolica, 1560–1563." *Archivum historicum Societatis Iesu* 28 (1959): 51–191.

Scaglione, Aldo. *The Liberal Arts and the Jesuit College System*. Amsterdam 1986.

Schäfer, Eckart. "Sarbiewskis patriotische Lyrik und sein 'polnischer Horaz' Jan Kochanowski." In *Sarbiewski. Der polnische Horaz*, edited by Eckart Schäfer, 145–76. Tübingen 2006.

Schatz, Klaus. "... *Dass diese Mission eine der blühendsten des Ostens werde*..." *P. Alexander de Rhodes (1539–1660) und die frühe Jesuitenmission in Vietnam*. Münster 2015.

———. "Deutschland und die Reformation in der Sicht Peter Fabers." *Geist und Leben* 4 (1996): 259–72.

———. *Geschichte der deutschen Jesuiten (1814–1983)*. 5 vols. Münster 2013.

Scherer, Emil Clemens. "Aus Petersburger Briefen an einen Strassburger Exjesuiten." *Archivum historicum Societatis Iesu* 20 (1951): 167–80.

Schildt, Axel. *Zwischen Abendland und Amerika. Studien zur westdeutschen Ideenlandschaft der 50er Jahre*. Munich 1999.

Schindler, Claudia. "Nicolò Partenio Giannettasio (1648–1715) und die neulateinische Gelehrtenkultur der Jesuiten in Neapel." *Scientia poetica* 18 (2014): 28–59.

Schinosi, Francesco. *Istoria della compagnia di Giesu, appartenente al regno di Napoli*. 4 vols. Naples 1706–57.

Schlachta, Astrid von. "Stiftungen, Stipendien und Kredite. Die Bildungsstätten der Jesuiten in Tirol." In *Schulstiftungen und Studienfinanzierung. Bildungsmäzenatentum in den böhmischen, österreichischen und ungarischen Ländern, 1500–1800*, edited by Joachim Bahlcke and Thomas Winkelbauer, 263–78. Vienna 2011.

Schlafly, Daniel. "The 'Russian' Society and the American Jesuits: Giovanni Grassi's Crucial Role." In *Jesuit Survival and Restoration: A Global History, 1773–1900*, edited by Robert A. Maryks, 353–67. Leiden 2015.

Schmidl, Johann. *Historia provinciae Bohemiae Societatis Iesu*. 4 vols. Prague 1747–59.

Schmidt, Peter. *Das Collegium Germanicum in Rom und die Germaniker. Zur Funktion eines römischen Ausländerseminars (1552–1914)*. Tübingen 1984.

Schmutz, Jacob. "Bellum scholasticum. Thomisme et antithomisme dans les débats doctrinaux modernes." *Revue thomiste* 109 (2008): 131–82.

Schneider, Bernhard. "Reform durch Elitenbildung. Die Bürgersodalität Trier im Kontext der jesuitischen Reforminitiative. Ein Beitrag zur 400-Feier." *Kurtrierisches Jahrbuch* 50 (2010): 215–25.

Schneider, Burkhart. "Der weltliche Heilige. Ignatius von Loyola und die Fürsten seiner Zeit." *Geist und Leben* 27 (1954): 35–58.

———. "Die Jesuiten als Gehilfen der päpstlichen Nuntien und Legaten in Deutschland zur Zeit der Gegenreformation." *Miscellanea Historiae Pontificiae* 21 (1959): 269–303.

Schneider, Christine. *Kloster als Lebensform. Der Wiener Ursulinenkonvent in der zweiten Hälfte des 18. Jahrhunderts (1740–1790)*. Cologne 2005.

Schoeters, Karl. "War Johannes Berchmans Mystiker?" *Zeitschrift für Aszese und Mystik* 13 (1938): 239–65.

Schröer, Alois, ed. *Die Korrespondenz des Münsterer Fürstbischofs Christoph Bernhard von Galen mit dem Heiligen Stuhl (1650–1678)*. Münster 1972.

Schubert, Anselm. *Das Ende der Sünde. Anthropologie und Erbsünde zwischen Reformation und Aufklärung*. Göttingen 2002.

Schüller, Andreas. "Die Eifelmission der Jesuiten 1704–1773." *Annalen des Historischen Vereins für den Niederrhein* 121 (1932): 79–130.

Schultz, Nancy Lusignan. *Mrs. Mattingly's Miracle: The Prince, the Widow, and the Cure That Shocked Washington City*. New Haven, CT, 2011.

Schürer, Markus. *Das Exemplum oder die erzählte Institution. Studien zum Beispielgebrauch bei den Dominikanern und Franziskanern des 13. Jahrhunderts*. Hamburg 2005.

Schurhammer, Georg. "Die Anfänge des römischen Archivs der Gesellschaft Jesu." *Archivum historicum Societatis Iesu* 12 (1943): 89–118.

———. *Franz Xaver. Sein Leben und Seine Zeit*. 4 vols. Freiburg 1955.

Schütte, Josef Franz. *Valignano's Mission Principles for Japan*. St. Louis, MO, 1980.

Schwab, Ludwig. "Das Jesuitenkollegium des 16. und 17. Jahrhunderts in der Oberdeutschen Ordensprovinz." PhD diss., Technical University of Darmstadt, 2001.

Schwade, Arcadio. "Die Frühgeschichte des Christentums in Japan im Überblick." In *Mission und Theater. Japan und China auf den Bühnen der Gesellschaft Jesu*, edited by Adrian Hsia, 289–353. Regensburg 2005.

Schwager, Klaus. "La chiesa del Gesù del Vignola." *Bollettino del Centro internazionale di studi di architettura Andrea Palladio* 19 (1977): 251–71.

Schwaller, Thaddäus. *Kurtzer Begriff von der wahren Andacht zu dem Hochwürdigen Hertzen Jesu Unsers Welt Heylands*. Einsiedeln 1695.

Schwarte, Johannes. *Gustav Gundlach S.J. (1892–1963). Repräsentant der katholischen Soziallehre während der Pontifikate Pius' XI. und Pius' XII*. Paderborn 1975.

Schwarz, Ignaz. *Institutiones in iuris publici universalis naturae et gentium*. Venice 1760.

Schwedt, Hermann H. "Fra giansenisti e filonapoleonici. I domenicani al S. Offizio romano e alla Congregazione dell'Indice nel Settecento." In *Praedicatores, inquisitores III. I Domenicani e l'Inquisizione romana*, edited by Carlo Longo, 591–613. Rome 2008.

Scribani, Carolus. *Superior religiosus. De prudenti ac religiosa gubernatione*. Lyon 1620.

Sebes, Josef, ed. *The Jesuits and the Sino-Russian Treaty of Nerchinsk (1689): The Diary of Thomas Pereira, S.I.* Rome 1961.

Segneri, Paolo. *Opere del padre Paolo Segneri*. Vol. 4, *Opere ascetiche*. Milan 1847.

———. *Pratica delle missioni del Padre Segneri della Compagnia di Gesù, predicatore pontifico, continuata dal P. Fluvio Fontana della medesima Religione*. Venice 1739.

Selwyn, Jennifer D. *A Paradise Inhabited by Devils: The Jesuits' Civilizing Mission in Early Modern Naples*. Aldershot 2004.

Sénard, Adriana. "Étienne Martellange. Un architecte de la Compagnie de Jésus en France au XVIIe siècle." In *La arquitectura jesuítica*, edited by María Isabel Alvaro Zamora, Javier Ibáñez Fernández, and Jesús Criado Mainar, 213–38. Zaragoza 2012.

Sevrin, Ernest. *Les missions religieuses en France sous la Restauration, 1815–1830.* 2 vols. Paris 1948–59.

Seydl, Jon L. "Il pittore del Sacro Cuore." In *Pompeo Batoni, 1708–1787. L'Europa delle corti e il grand tour,* edited by Liliana Barroero, 120–25. Cinisello Balsamo 2008.

Sgard, Jean, and Françoise Weil. "Les anecdotes inédites des *Mémoires de Trévoux.*" *Dix-huitième siècle* 8 (1976): 193–204.

Shore, Paul. *The Eagle and the Cross: Jesuits in Late Baroque Prague.* St. Louis, MO, 2002.

———. *Jesuits and the Politics of Religious Pluralism in Eighteenth-Century Transylvania: Culture, Politics and Religion, 1693–1773.* Aldershot 2007.

———. "The *Vita Christi* of Ludolf of Saxony and Its Influence on the Spiritual Exercises of Ignatius of Loyola." *Studies in the Spirituality of Jesuits* 30 (1998): 1–34.

Sieber, Dominik. *Jesuitische Missionierung, priesterliche Liebe und sakramentale Magie. Volkskulturen in Luzern 1563–1614.* Basel 2005.

Siebert, Harald. "Kircher and His Critics: Censorial Practice and Pragmatic Disregard in the Society of Jesus." In *Athanasius Kircher: The Last Man Who Knew Everything,* edited by Paula Findlen, 79–104. London 2003.

Sievernich, Michael. *Die christliche Mission. Geschichte und Gegenwart.* Darmstadt 2009.

———. "Von der Akkommodation zur Inkulturation. Missionarische Leitideen der Gesellschaft Jesu." *Zeitschrift für Missionswissenschaft und Religionswissenschaft* 86 (2002): 260–76.

Sievernich, Michael, and Günter Switek, eds. *Ignatianisch. Eigenart und Methode der Gesellschaft Jesu.* Freiburg 1990.

Sluhovsky, Moshe. *Becoming a New Self: Practices of Belief in Early Modern Catholicism.* Chicago 2017.

———. "The Devil in the Convent." *American Historical Review* 107 (2002): 1379–411.

———. "General Confession and Self-Knowledge in Early Modern Catholicism." In *Knowledge and Religion in Early Modern Europe: Studies in Honor of Michael Heyd,* edited by Asaph Ben-Tov, Yaacov Deutsch, and Tamar Herzig, 25–46. Leiden 2013.

Smith, Hilary Dansey. *Preaching in the Spanish Golden Age: A Study of Some Preachers of the Reign of Philip III.* Oxford 1978.

Smith, Jeffrey Chipps. *Sensuous Worship: Jesuits and the Art of Early Catholic Reformation in Germany.* Princeton, NJ, 2002.

Smith, Richard J. "Jesuit Interpretations of the *Yijing* (Classic of Changes) in Historical and Comparative Perspective." http://ikgf.fau.de/content/articles/Richard_J_Smith_-_Jesuits_and_Yijing.pdf. Accessed January 15, 2020.

Smithies, Michael, and Luigi Bressan. *Siam and the Vatican in the Seventeenth Century.* Bangkok 2001.

Snaet, Joris, and Krista de Jonge. "The Architecture of the Jesuits in the Southern Low Countries: A State of the Art." In *La arquitectura jesuítica,* edited by María Isabel Alvaro Zamora, Javier Ibáñez Fernández, and Jesús Criado Mainar, 239–76. Zaragoza 2012.

Snyders, Georges. *La pédagogie en France aux XVII et XVIII siècles.* Paris 1964.

Soarez, Cyprian. *De arte rhetorica.* Seville 1569.

Sobiech, Frank. "Friedrich Spee S.J. (1591–1635) und Bernhard Löper S.J. (1609–1670). Der Verfasser der *Cautio Criminalis* und ein Exorzist in Zeiten der Hexenverfolgung." In *Die Academia Theodoriana. Von der Jesuitenuniversität zur Theologischen Fakultät Paderborn, 1614–2014,* edited by Josef Meyer zu Schlochtern, 175–90. Paderborn 2014.

———. *Jesuit Prison Ministry in the Witch Trials of the Holy Roman Empire: Friedrich Spee SJ and His* Cautio Criminalis *(1631).* Bibliotheca Instituti Historici Societatis Iesu 80. Rome 2019.

Society of Jesus [SJ]. *Colección de documentos para la historia de México, Cuarta serie.* 7 vols. Mexico City, 1856–57.

——— [Collegium Anglorum Leodii]. *Florus anglo-bavaricus serenissimo principi Maximiliano Emmanueli Duci Bavariae etc. et Mariae Antoniae Leopoldi Caesaris filiae.* Liège 1685.

———. *Confucius sinarum philosophus sive scientia sinensis latine exposita.* Translated and edited by Philippe Couplet, Christian Herdtrich, Prospero Intorcetta, and Francis Rougemont. Paris 1687.

———, ed. *Epistolae praepositorum generalium.* 3 vols. Ghent 1847.

———, ed. *Epistolae praepositorum generalium ad patres et fratres SJ.* Prague 1711.

———. *L'empire de la sagesse sur les passions, ballet, qui sera dansé au collège de Louis le Grand, mercredi 7 d'août 1715 à midi précis pour servir d'intermèdes à la tragédie latine.* Paris 1715.

———. *Les delices de Blois, ballet, qui sera dansé au college Royal de Blois de la Compagnie de Jesus. Pour servir d'Intermede a la Tragedie d'Isac.* AD Loir-et-Cher F 647. Blois 1729.

———. *Les nouvelles. Ballet qui sera dansé au College de Louis le Grand, a la tragedie de Posthumius.* Paris 1703.

——— [Lycaeum Catholicum]. *Leontius sive Pseudo-politicus punitus. Dramation.* Lucerne 1670.

———. *Nouveaux mémoires des missions de la Compagnie de Jésus dans le Levant.* 9 vols. Paris 1715–55.

———. *Regulae Societatis Iesu.* Dillingen 1609.

———. "Voyage of Very Reverend Fr. John Anthony Grassi, S.J. from Russia to America. Jan. 1805–Oct. 1810." *Woodstock Letters* 4, no. 2 (1875): 115–36.

Solignac, Aimé. "Le 'Compendio breve' de l' 'Exercitatorio' de Cisneros et les 'Exercices spirituels.'" *Archivum historicum Societatis Iesu* 63 (1994): 141–60.

Song, Gang. "Learning from the Other: Giulio Aleni, the Koudou Richao, and Late Ming Dialogic Hybridization." PhD diss., University of Southern California, 2006.

Sonnenberg, Bernhard. *Neüe vom Himmel gesandte Andacht Gegen dem Göttlichen Hertz Jesu Christi* [. . .] Munich 1695.

Soto Artuñedo, Wenceslao. "Jesuitas, Moriscos y Musulmanes. Algunos datos de Granada y Malaga." *Encuentro islamo-cristiano* 422 (2007): 2–15.

———. "La Compañía de Jesús en Andalucía y Canarias. La Provincia Bética." *Proyección* 61 (2014): 241–76.

Spadaro, Fr. Antonio, S.J. "Interview du pape François aux revues culturelles jésuites." *Études* 419, no. 10 (2013): 1–30. http://www.jesuites.com/v3/wp-content/uploads/2013/09/Interview-Pape-Fran%C3%A7ois_long.pdf?967019.

Spener, Philipp Jakob. *Insignium theorie seu Operis heraldici pars generalis.* Frankfurt 1690.

Sperber, Jonathan. *Popular Catholicism in Nineteenth-Century Germany*. Princeton, NJ, 1984.

Spica, Anne-Élisabeth. "La 'Pro Theologia Mystica Clavis' de Maximilian van der Sandt. Un inventaire lexical à valeur encyclopédique?" In *Pour un vocabulaire mystique au XVIIe siècle*, edited by François Trémolières, 23–41. Turin 2004.

Spiertz, Mathieu G. *L'église catholique des Provinces-Unies et le Saint-Siège pendant la deuxième moitié du XVIIe siècle*. Leuven 1975.

Splendiani, Ana María. "La Cartegena de Pedro Claver." *Boletín de historia y antigüedades* 821 (2003): 371–418.

Spykman, Gordon J. *Attrition and Contrition at the Council of Trent*. Kampen 1955.

Standaert, Nicolas. *Chinese Voices in the Rites Controversy: Travelling Books, Community Networks, Intercultural Arguments*. Rome 2012.

———. *The Fascinating God: A Challenge to Modern Chinese Theology Presented by a Text on the Name of God Written by a 17th-Century Chinese Student of Theology*. Rome 1995.

———, ed. *Handbook of Christianity in China*. Vol. 1, *635–1800*. Leiden 2001.

———. "Jesuits in China." In *The Cambridge Companion to the Jesuits*, edited by Thomas Worcester, 169–85. Cambridge 2008.

———. *Yang Tingyun, Confucian and Christian in Late Ming China: His Life and Thought*. Leiden 1988.

St. Clair Segurado, Eva María. "Arresto y conducción a Veracruz de los jesuitas mexicanos." In *Y en el tercero perecerán. Gloria, caída y exilio de los jesuitas españoles en el s. XVIII*, edited by Enrique Giménez López, 221–50. Alicante 2002.

———. *Expulsión y exilio de la provincia jesuita mexicana, 1767–1820*. Alicante 2005.

———. *Flagellum iesuitarum. La polémica sobre los jesuitas en México (1754–1767)*. Alicante 2004.

———. "La cuestión de los ritos chinos y malabres. Desobediencia e idolatría en la Compañía de Jesús." *Hispania sacra* 54 (2002): 109–39.

———. "La expulsión de los jesuitas de América. Reflexiones sobre el caso de Nueva España." In *La Compañía de Jesús en la América española (siglos XVI–XVIII)*, edited by Francisco Javier Gómez Díez, 165–204. Vitoria 2005.

Stefanovska, Malina. "La monarchie des jésuites. Solipsisme et politique." *Dix-huitième siècle* 37 (2005): 359–81.

Steinbicker, Clemens. "Westfalen in der niederrheinischen Provinz der Gesellschaft Jesu 1626–1773." *Beiträge zur westfälischen Familienforschung* 51 (1993): 149–223.

Steiner, Benjam *Die Ordnung der Geschichte. Historische Tabellenwerke in der Frühen Neuzeit*. Cologne 2008.

Steinhuber, Andreas. *Geschichte des Collegium Germanicum Hungaricum in Rom*. 2 vols. 2nd ed. Freiburg 1906.

Steinmetz, Dirk. *Die Gregorianische Kalenderreform von 1582. Korrektur der christlichen Zeitrechnung in der Frühen Neuzeit*. Oftersheim 2011.

Steinwascher, Gerd. "Die konfessionellen Folgen des Westfälischen Friedens für das Fürstbistum Osnabrück." *Niedersächsisches Jahrbuch für Landesgeschichte* 71 (1999): 51–80.

Stella, Pietro. "Attrizione e contrizione in età moderna. L'importanza storica di una disputa irrisolta." *Annali di scienze religiose* 3 (1998): 151–72.

———. *Il giansenismo in Italia*. 3 vols. Rome 2006.

Stenmans, Peter. *Litterae annuae. Die Jahresberichte des Neusser Jesuitenkollegs 1616–1773*. Neuss 1966.

Stepling, Josef. *Commercium litterarum*. Bratislava 1782.

Stierli, Josef. "Das ignatianische Gebet. 'Gott suchen in allen Dingen.'" In *Ignatius von Loyola. Seine geistliche Gestalt und sein Vermächtnis*, edited by Friedrich Wulf, 153–82. Würzburg 1956.

Stillig, Jürgen. *Jesuiten, Ketzer und Konvertiten in Niedersachsen. Untersuchungen zum Religions- und Bildungswesen im Hochstift Hildesheim in der Frühen Neuzeit*. Hildesheim 1993.

Stoeckius, Hermann. *Untersuchungen zur Geschichte des Noviziates in der Gesellschaft Jesu*. Bonn 1918.

Stolzenberg, Daniel. *Egyptian Oedipus: Athanasius Kircher and the Secrets of Antiquity*. Chicago 2013.

———. "Utility, Edification, and Superstition: Jesuit Censorship and Athanasius Kircher's *Oedipus Aegyptiacus*." In *The Jesuits II. Cultures, Sciences, and the Arts 1540–1773*, edited by John W. O'Malley, 336–53. Toronto 2006.

Stone, Martin. "Scholastic Schools and Early Modern Philosophy." In *The Cambridge Companion to Early Modern Philosophy*, edited by Donald Rutherford, 299–327. Cambridge 2006.

Stone, Martin, and Toon van Houdt. "Probabilism and Its Methods: Leonardus Lessius and His Contribution to the Development of Jesuit Casuistry." *Ephemerides Theologicae Lovanienses* 75 (1999): 359–94.

Stork, Sieglind. *Das Theater der Jesuiten in Münster (1588–1773). Mit Editionen des* Petrus Telonarius *von 1604 und der* Coena magna *von 1632*. Münster 2013.

Straßner, Veit. "Die Arbeiterpriester. Geschichte und Entwicklungstendenzen einer in Vergessenheit geratenen Bewegung." https://arbeitergeschwister.wordpress.com/intern/intern-werkstatt/veit-strassner-arbeiterpriester-gesichte/. Accessed March 9, 2020.

Stricher, Julien. *Le vœu du sang en faveur de l'Immaculée Conception. Histoire et bilan théologique d'une controverse*. 2 vols. Rome 1959.

Strinati, Claudio. "La Chiesa di Sant'Ignazio di Loyola." In *Il Collegio Romano dalle origini al Ministero per i beni culturali e ambientali*, edited by Claudia Cerchiai, 165–97. Rome 2003.

Stroppa, Sabrina. "Il direttore spirituale nel Seicento francese e italiano. Teoria e pratica." In *Storia della direzione spirituale*. Vol. 3, *L' età moderna*, edited by Gabriella Zarri and Giovanni Filoramo, 411–36. Brescia 2008.

———. *Sic arescit. Letteratura mistica del Seicento italiano*. Florence 1998.

Suárez, Francesco. *Tractatus IV de religione*. In *Opera omnia*, edited by Charles Berton, vol. 14, 4–440. Paris 1859.

Suarez de Somoza, Geronimo. *Vida del padre Pedro Claver de la Compañía de Iesus*. Madrid 1657.

Sudbrack, Josef. "'Gott in allen Dingen finden.' Eine ignatianische Maxime und ihr metahistorischer Hintergrund." *Geist und Leben* 65 (1992): 165–86.

Sulas, Cinzia. "La riforma della *Ratio studiorum* di fronte al paradigma scientifico moderno. La prospettiva di Luigi Taparelli SJ, rettore al Collegio Romano (1824–1829)." *Archivum historicum Societatis Iesu* 86 (2018): 301–36.

Surin, Jean-Joseph. *Correspondance*. Edited by Michel de Certeau. Bruges 1966.

———. *Dialogues spirituels, où La perfection chrétienne est expliquée*. 2 vols. Lyon 1831.

Sustersic, Bozidar. "El 'insigne artífice' José Brasanelli. Su participación en la conformación de un nuevo lenguaje figurativo en las misiones jesuíticas-guaraníes." In *Actas III Congreso internacional del barroco americano. Territorio, arte, espacio y sociedad*, edited by Universidad Pablo de Olavide, Sevilla, 533–49. Seville 2001.

Sweet, David G. "Black Robes and 'Black Destiny': Jesuit Views of African Slavery in 17th-Century Latin America." *Revista de historia de América* 86 (1978): 87–133.

Szarota, Elida Maria. *Das Jesuitendrama im deutschen Sprachgebiet. Eine Periochen-Edition. Texte und Kommentare.* 4 vols. Munich 1979–87.

Talon, Jean. "Correspondance échangée entre la cour de France et l'intendant Talon pendant ses deux administrations dans la Nouvelle France." In *Rapport de l'archiviste de la province de Québec 1930–1931*, 1–182. Québec 1931.

Tanturri, Alberto. "Ordres et congrégations enseignants à l'époque de la Contre-Réforme. Barnabites, somasques, scolopes." *Revue historique* 660 (2011): 811–52.

———. "Scolopi e Gesuiti all'epoca di S. Giuseppe Calasanzio." *Archivio italiano per la storia della pietà* 13 (2009): 193–216.

Tapié, Alain, ed. *Baroque vision jésuite. Du Tintoret à Rubens.* Paris 2003.

Tardieu, Jean-Pierre. "La esclavitud de los negros y el plan de Dios. La dialéctica de los jesuitas del virreinato del Perú." In *Esclavitud, economía y evangelización. Las haciendas jesuitas en la América virreinal*, edited by Sandra Negro and Manuel M. Marzal, 67–81. Lima 2005.

———. *L'église et les noirs au Pérou, XVIe et XVIIe siècles.* 2 vols. Paris 1993.

———. "Les jésuites et la pastoral des Noirs en Nouvelle-Espagne (XVIe siècle)." *Iberoamerikanisches Archiv*, n.s., 16 (1990): 529–44.

Techo, Nicolás del. *Historia provinciae Paraquariae Societatis Iesu.* Liege 1673

———. *The History of the Provinces of Paraguay, Tucuman, Rio de la Plata, Parana, Guaira and Urvaica. And Something of the Kingdom of Chili, in South America.* Abridged translation. London 1703.

Terhalle, Johannes. ". . . ha della Grandezza de padri Gesuiti. Die Architektur der Jesuiten um 1600 und St. Michael in München." In *Rom in Bayern. Kunst und Spiritualität der ersten Jesuiten*, edited by Reinhold Baumstark, 83–145. Munich 1997.

———. *S. Andrea al Quirinale von Gian Lorenzo Bernini in Rom. Von den Anfängen bis zur Grundsteinlegung.* Weimar 2011.

Terpstra, Nicholas. *Lay Confraternities and Civic Religion in Renaissance Bologna.* Cambridge 1995.

———, ed. *The Politics of Ritual Kinship: Confraternities and Social Order in Early Modern Italy.* Cambridge 2000.

Tessé, René de Froulay de. *Mémoires et lettres.* 2 vols. Paris 1806.

Thanner, Tanja. "Zur Entstehungsgeschichte der Bulle *Cum occasione*. Die Zensurierung der fünf Lehrsätze durch Mitglieder des Augustinerordens." In *Der Jansenismus–eine "katholische Häresie"? Das Ringen um Gnade, Rechtfertigung und die Autorität Augustins in der frühen Neuzeit*, edited by Dominik Burkard and Tanja Thanner, 281–309. Münster 2014.

Thoman, Maurice. *Reise und Lebensbeschreibung.* Augsburg 1788.

Thompson, D. Gillian. "The French Jesuit Leaders and the Destruction of the Jesuit Order in France, 1756–1762." *French History* 2 (1988): 237–63.

———. "General Ricci and the Suppression of the Jesuit Order in France 1760–4." *Journal of Ecclesiastical History* 37 (1986): 426–41.

———. "The Lavalette Affair and the Jesuit Superiors." *French History* 10 (1996): 206–39.

———. *A Modern Persecution: Breton Jesuits under the Suppression of 1762–1814.* Oxford 1999.

———. "The Persecution of French Jesuits by the Parlement of Paris 1761–71." *Studies in Church History* 21 (1984): 289–301.

Thompson, Raymond H., ed. *A Jesuit Missionary in Eighteenth-Century Sonora: The Family Correspondence of Philipp Segesser.* Albuquerque, NM, 2014.

Thornton, John K. "The Development of an African Catholic Church in the Kingdom of Kongo, 1491–1750." *Journal of African History* 25 (1984): 147–67.

Thummerer, Hilda. "Besitzgeschichte des Kollegs St. Salvator." In *Die Jesuiten und ihre Schule St. Salvator in Augsburg 1582*, edited by Wolfram Baer, 54–59. Munich 1982.

Tilliette, Xavier. *Le jésuite et le poète. Éloge jubilaire à Paul Claudel.* Versailles 2005.

Tiraboschi, Girolamo. *Storia della letteratura italiana.* 13 vols. Modena 1772–82.

Toledo, Francisco de [Franciscus Toletus]. *In Summam theologiae S. Thomae Aquinatis enarratio.* 4 vols. Rome 1869–70.

———. *Summa casuum conscientiae, sive de instructione sacerdotum.* Cologne 1601.

Torre, Angelo. "Politics Cloaked in Worship: State, Church, and Local Power in Piedmont 1570–1770." *Past and Present* 134 (1992): 42–92.

Toulmin, Stephen, and Albert R. Jonsen. *The Abuse of Casuistry: A History of Moral Reasoning.* Berkeley 1988.

Trampus, Antonio. *I gesuiti e l'illuminismo. Politica e religione in Austria e nell'Europa centrale (1773–1798).* Florence 2000.

Tremblay, Victor. "QUEN, JEAN DE." In *Dictionary of Canadian Biography.* Vol. 1. University of Toronto/Université Laval 2003–present. http://www.biographi.ca/en/bio/quen_jean _de_1E.html. Accessed January 13, 2020.

Trombetta, Vincenzo. "Libri e biblioteche della Compagnia di Gesù a Napoli dalle origini all'Unità d'Italia." *Hereditas monasteriorum* 4 (2014): 127–60.

True, Micah. *Masters and Students: Jesuit Mission Ethnography in Seventeenth-Century New France.* Montreal 2015.

Turner, James. *Philology: The Forgotten Origins of the Modern Humanities.* Princeton, NJ, 2014.

Turrini, Miriam. *Il "giovin signore" in collegio. I gesuiti e l'educazione della nobiltà nelle consuetudini del Collegio ducale di Parma.* Bologna 2006.

Turtas, Raimondo. *La nascita dell'università in Sardegna. La politica culturale dei sovrani spagnoli nella formazione degli Atenei di Sassari e di Cagliari (1543–1632).* Sassari 1988.

Tüskés, Gábor. *Johannes Nádasi. Europäische Verbindungen der geistlichen Erzählliteratur Ungarns im 17. Jahrhundert.* Tübingen 2001.

Tutino, Stefania. *Empire of Souls: Robert Bellarmine and the Christian Commonwealth.* Oxford 2010.

Übelhör, Monika. "Geistesströmungen der späten Ming-Zeit, die das Wirken der Jesuiten in China begünstigten." *Saeculum* 23 (1972): 172–85.

———. *Hsü Kuang-ch'i (1562–1633) und seine Einstellung zum Christentum. Ein Beitrag zur Geistesgeschichte der Späten Ming-Zeit.* Hamburg 1969.

Üçerler, M. Antoni. "Alessandro Valignano: Man, Missionary, and Writer." *Renaissance Studies* 17 (2003): 337–66.

———, ed. *Alessandro Valignano S.I. Uomo del Rinascimento. Ponte tra Oriente e Occidente.* Rome 2008.

———. "The Jesuit Enterprise in Sixteenth- and Seventeenth-Century Japan." In *The Cambridge Companion to the Jesuits,* edited by Thomas Worcester, 153–68. Cambridge 2008.

Udías, Augustín. *Jesuit Contribution to Science: A History.* New York 2014.

———. *Searching the Heavens and the Earth: The History of Jesuit Observatories.* Dordrecht 2003.

Ugaglia, Monica. "The Science of Magnetism before Gilbert Leonardo Garzoni's Treatise on the Loadstone." *Annals of Science* 63 (2006): 59–84.

University of Angers, Centre de recherches d'Histoire religieuse, ed. *La vocation religieuse et sacerdotale en France. XVII–XIX siècles.* Angers 1979.

Unterburger, Klaus. *Vom Lehramt der Theologen zum Lehramt der Päpste? Pius XI., die Apostolische Konstitution "Deus scientiarum Dominus" und die Reform der Universitätstheologie.* Freiburg 2010.

Urbano, Carlota. "The *Paciecidos* by Bartolomeu Pereira S.J.: An Epic Interpretation of Evangelisation and Martyrdom in 17th-Century Japan." *Bulletin of Portuguese-Japanese Studies* 10/11 (2005): 61–95.

Valentin, Jean-Marie. "La diffusion de Corneille en Allemagne au XVIIIe siècle à travers les poétiques jésuites." *Arcadia* 7 (1972): 171–99.

———. *Les jésuites et le théâtre (1554–1680). Contribution à l'histoire culturelle du monde catholique dans le Saint-Empire romain germanique.* Paris 2001.

Valignano, Alessandro. *Les jésuites au Japon. Relation missionnaire (1583).* Translated and commented by Jacques Bésineau, S.J. Paris 1990.

Valle, Ivonne del. *Escribiendo desde los márgenes. Colonialismo y jesuitas en el siglo XVIII.* México 2009.

Vallery-Radot, Jean. *Le recueil de plans d'édifices de la Compagnie de Jésus conservé a la Bibliothèque nationale de Paris.* Rome 1960.

Van Damme, Stéphan. "Ecriture, institution et société. Le travail littéraire dans la Compagnie de Jésus en France (1620–1720)." *Revue de synthèse* 120 (1999): 261–83.

———. "Les livres du P. Claude-François Ménestrier (1631–1705) et leur cheminement." *Revue d'histoire moderne et contemporaine* 42 (1995): 5–45.

———. *Le temple de la sagesse. Savoirs, écriture et sociabilité urbaine (Lyon, 17–18e siècles).* Paris 2004.

———. "Sociabilité et culture urbaines. Le rôle du collège de la Trinité à Lyon (1640–1730)." *Histoire de l'Education* 90 (2001): 79–100.

Vanden Bosch, Gerrit. "Saving Souls in the Dutch Vineyard. The *Missio Hollandica* of the Jesuits (1592–1708)." In *The Jesuits of the Low Countries: Identity and Impact (1540–1773),* edited by Rob Faesen, 139–51. Leuven 2012.

Van der Veldt, Petrus Thomas. *Franz Neumayr SJ (1697–1765). Leben und Werk eines spätbarocken geistlichen Autors.* Amsterdam 1992.

Van der Vyver, Omer. "L'école de mathématique des jésuites de la province flandro-belgique au XVIIe siècle." *Archivum historicum Societatis Iesu* 49 (1980): 265–78.

———. "Lettres de J-CH. Della Faille S. J., cosmographe du roi à Madrid, à M.-F. Van Langren, cosmographe du roi à Bruxelles, 1634–1645." *Archivum historicum Societatis Iesu* 46 (1977): 73–183.

Van Dülmen, Richard. *Theater des Schreckens. Gerichtspraxis und Strafrituale in der frühen Neuzeit.* Munich 1988.

Van Dyke, Christina. "Mysticism." In *The Cambridge History of Medieval Philosophy*, edited by Robert Pasnau, 720–34. Cambridge 2010.

Van Ginhoven Rey, Christopher. *Instruments of the Divinity: Providence and Praxis in the Foundation of the Society of Jesus.* Leiden 2014.

Van Hoeck, François. "Lettres des supérieurs de la Compagnie de Jésus en Russie-Blanche aux Jésuites de Hollande (1797–1806)." *Archivum historicum Societatis Iesu* 3 (1934): 279–99.

———. "Romeinische correspondentie over het conflict tusschen den Apostolischen Vicaris en de Jezuiten in de Hollandsche missie 1669–1671." *Archief voor de geschiedenis van het aartsbisdom Utrecht* 65 (1945): 113–77.

Van Houdt, Toon. "'Lack of Money': A Reappraisal of Lessius' Contribution to the Scholastic Analysis of Money-Lending and Interest-Taking." *European Journal of the History of Economic Thought* 5 (1998): 1–35.

Van Kley, Dale K. *The Jansenists and the Expulsion of the Jesuits from France, 1757–1765.* New Haven, CT, 1975.

———. *The Religious Origins of the French Revolution: From Calvin to the Civil Constitution, 1560–1791.* New Haven, CT, 1996.

Van Miert, Louis. "Some Historical Documents Concerning the Mission of Maryland." *Woodstock Letters* 30, no. 3 (1901): 333–52.

Vanni, Andrea. *"Fare diligente inquisitione." Gian Piero Carafa e le origini dei chierici regolari teatini.* Rome 2010.

Vanpaemel, Gert. "Jesuit Mathematicians, Military Architecture and the Transmission of Technical Knowledge." In *The Jesuits of the Low Countries: Identity and Impact (1540–1773)*, edited by Rob Faesen, 109–28. Leuven 2012.

———. "Jesuit Science in the Spanish Netherlands." In *Jesuit Science and the Republic of Letters*, edited by Mordechai Feingold, 389–432. Cambridge, MA, 2003.

Vantard, Amélie. "Les vocations pour les missions ad gentes (France, 1650–1750)." PhD diss., Le Mans University, 2010. http://cyberdoc.univ-lemans.fr/theses/2010/2010LEMA3007 .pdf. Accessed January 22, 2020.

Vanysacker, Dries. *Cardinal Giuseppe Garampi (1725–1792): An Enlightened Ultramontane.* Turnhout 1995.

Varachaud, Marie-Christine. *Le père Houdry S.J. (1631–1729). Prédication et pénitence.* Paris 1993.

Venard, Marc. "Y a-t-il une 'stratégie scolaire' des jésuites en France au XVI e siècle?" In *L'Université de Pont-à-Mousson et les problèmes de son temps. Actes du colloque organisé par l'Institut de recherche régionale en sciences sociales, humaines et économiques de l'Université de Nancy II*, 67–85. Nancy 1974.

Vendrix, Philippe. "Castel et la musique. Quelques aspects inédits." In *Autour du Père Castel et du clavecin oculaire*, edited by Roland Mortier and Hervé Hasquin, 129–37. Brussels 1996.

Verd Conradi, Gabriel María. "El P. Roque Menchaca, San Ignacio y el Soneto 'No me mueve, mi Dios, para quererte.'" *Archivo teologico grandadino* 67 (2004): 109–45.

Veress, Endre, ed. *Annuae litterae societatis Jesu de rebus transylvanicis.* Budapest 1921.

Vernière, Antoine, ed. *Journal de voyage de Dom Jacques Boyer, Religieux Bénédictin de la Congrégation de Saint-Maur (1710–1714).* Clermont-Ferrand 1886.

Verwimp, Régis. *Les jésuites en Guyane française sous l'Ancien Régime, 1498–1768.* Matoury 2011.

Vidal, Daniel. *Jean de Labadie, 1610–1674. Passion mystique et esprit de Réforme.* Grenoble 2009.

Vieira, Antonio. *El semejante sin semejante San Ignacio de Loyola.* Valencia 1680.

Viguerie, Jean de. "La vocation sacerdotale et religieuse aux XVIIe et XVIIIe siècles. La théorie et la réalité." In *La vocation religieuse et sacerdotale en France. XVII–XIX siècles,* edited by the University of Angers, Centre de recherches d'Histoire religieuse, 27–39. Angers 1979.

Villaret, Émile, S.J. *Les congrégations mariales. Des origines à la suppression de la Compagnie de Jésus (1540–1773).* Paris 1947.

———. "Les premières origines des Congrégations mariales dans la Compagnie de Jésus." *Archivum historicum Societatis Iesu* 6 (1937): 25–57.

Villiers, John. "Manila and Maluku: Trade and Warfare in the Eastern Archipelago, 1580–1640." *Philippine Studies* 34 (1986): 146–61.

Villoslada, Riccardo. *Storia del Collegio Romano dal suo inizio (1551) alla soppressione della Compagnia di Gesù (1773).* Rome 1954.

Vismara, Paola. "Les jésuites et la morale économique." *XVIIe siècle* 59 (2007): 739–54.

Vismara Chiappa, Paola. "L'abolizione delle missioni urbane dei gesuiti a Milano (1767)." *Nuova rivista storica* 62 (1978): 549–71.

Vogel, Christine. *Der Untergang der Gesellschaft Jesu als europäisches Medienereignis (1758–1773). Publizistische Debatten im Spannungsfeld von Aufklärung und Gegenaufklärung.* Mainz 2006.

Voiret, Jean-Pierre, ed. *Gespräch mit dem Kaiser und andere Geschichten. Auserlesene Stücke aus den "erbaulichen und seltsamen Briefen" aus dem Reich der Mitte.* Bern 1996.

Vongsuravatana, Raphaël. *Un jésuite à la cour de Siam.* Paris 1992.

Waddell, Mark A. *Jesuit Science and the End of Nature's Secrets.* Aldershot 2015.

Waele, Michel de. "Pour la sauvegarde du roi et du royaume. L'expulsion des Jésuites de France à la Fin des guerres de religion." *Canadian Journal of History* 39 (1994): 267–80.

Waisman, Leonardo. "Arcadia Meets Utopia: Corelli in the South-American Wilderness." In *Arcangelo Corelli fra mito e realtà storica. Nuove prospettive d'indagine musicologica e interdisciplinare nel 350. anniversario della nascita,* edited by Gregory Barnett, 633–65. Florence 2007.

Wallace, William A. "Jesuit Influences on Galileo's Science." In *The Jesuits II. Cultures, Sciences, and the Arts 1540–1773,* edited by John W. O'Malley, 314–34. Toronto 2006.

Wallnig, Thomas, and Thomas Stockinger, eds. *Die gelehrte Korrespondenz der Brüder Pez. Text, Regesten, Kommentare.* 2 vols. Vienna 2010–15.

Walsdorf, Hanna. *Die politische Bühne. Ballett und Ritual im Jesuitenkolleg Louis-le-Grand 1701–1762.* Würzburg 2012.

Weber, Alison. "Los jesuitas y las carmelitas descalzas en tiempos de san Francisco de Borja. Amistad, rivalidad y recelos." In *Francisco de Borja y su tiempo. Política, religión y cultura en la edad moderna,* edited by Enrique García Hernán, 103–14. Valencia 2012.

Weil, Mark S. "The Devotion of the Forty Hours and Roman Baroque Illusions." *Journal of the Warburg and Courtauld Institutes* 37 (1974): 218–48.

Weinczyk, Raimund. "Zur Rezeption des Erasmus von Rotterdam bei den Jesuiten des 16. Jahrhunderts." In *Erasmus-Rezeption im 16. Jahrhundert*, edited by Christoph Galle and Tobias Sarx, 153–76. Frankfurt 2012.

White, Richard. *The Middle Ground: Indians, Empires, and Republics in the Great Lakes Region, 1650–1815.* Cambridge 1991.

Whitehead, Maurice. "The Jesuit Contribution to Science and Technical Education in Late-Nineteenth-Century Liverpool." *Annals of Science* 43 (1986): 353–68.

———. "Jesuit Secondary Education Revolutionized: The Académie anglaise, Liège, 1773–1794." *Paedagogica historica* 40 (2004): 33–44.

Whitfield, Teresa. *Paying the Price: Ignacio Ellacuría and the Murdered Jesuits of El Salvador.* Philadelphia 1994.

Wicki, Josef. "Die Jesuiten-Beichtväter in St. Peter, Rom, 1569–1773. Ein geschichtlicher Überblick." *Archivum historicum Societatis Iesu* 56 (1987): 83–115.

———. *Le père Leunis.* Rome 1951.

Widmaier, Rita, ed. *Gottfried Wilhelm Leibniz. Der Briefwechsel mit den Jesuiten in China (1689–1714). Französisch/lateinisch–deutsch.* Translated by Malte Rudolf Babin. Hamburg 2006.

Wiegand, Hermann. "*Supplicium Cupidinis.* Zur Rezeption der römischen Liebesdichtung in der lateinischen Jesuitendichtung." In *Studia humanitatis ac litterarum Trifolio Heidelbergensi dedicata*, edited by Angela Hornung, Christian Jäkel, and Werner Schubert, 377–92. Frankfurt 2004.

Wielewicki, Johannes, ed. *Historicum diarium domus professae S.J. ad S. Barbaram, Cracoviae (1609–1619).* Kraków 1889.

Wilczek, Gerhard. "Ingolstadt, Macao, Peking. Die Jesuiten und die Chinamission." *Sammelblatt des historischen Vereins Ingolstadt* 102–3 (1993–94): 405–38.

Wilde, Guillermo. *Religión y poder en las misiones de guaraníes.* Buenos Aires 2009.

Windler, Christian. *Missionare in Persien. Kulturelle Diversität und Normenkonkurrenz im globalen Katholizismus (17.–18. Jahrhundert).* Cologne 2018.

———. "Regelobservanz und Mission. Katholische Ordensgeistliche im Safavidenreich (17. und frühes 18. Jahrhundert)." In *Normenkonkurrenz in historischer Perspektive*, edited by Hillard von Thiessen and Arne Karsten, 39–63. Berlin 2015.

Winnacker, Julia. "Populärmusik oder Kunstmusik? Franciscus Antonius Le Febvres Lehrgedicht *Musica* (1704)." *Neulateinisches Jahrbuch* 16 (2014): 291–308.

Wirthensohn, Simon. *Anton Claus, Leben und Werk. Studie zum späten Jesuitentheater.* Berlin 2019.

Witek, John W. "Understanding the Chinese: A Comparison of Matteo Ricci and the French Jesuit Mathematicians Sent by Louis XIV." In *East Meets West: The Jesuits in China, 1582–1773*, edited by Charles E. Ronan, 60–102. Chicago 1988.

Witwer, Toni. "*Contemplativus in actione.* Beschaulich im Handeln." *Geist und Leben* 83 (2010): 241–52.

Wogan, Peter. "Perceptions of European Literacy in Early Contact Situations." *Ethnohistory* 41 (1994): 407–29.

Wolf, Hubert, ed. *The Nuns of Sant'Ambrogio. The True Story of a Convent in Scandal.* New York 2015.

———, ed. *Prosopographie von römischer Inquisition und Indexkongregation 1701–1813.* 2 vols. Paderborn 2010.

Wolff, Larry. "Boscovich in the Balkans: A Jesuit Perspective on Orthodox Christianity in the Age of Enlightenment." In *The Jesuits II. Cultures, Sciences, and the Arts 1540–1773,* edited by John W. O'Malley, 738–57. Toronto 2006.

Worcester, Thomas. "Catholic Sermons." In *Preachers and People in the Reformations and Early Modern Period,* edited by Larissa Taylor, 3–33. Leiden 2001.

———. "The Classical Sermon." In *Preaching, Sermon and Cultural Change in the Long Eighteenth Century,* edited by Joris van Eijnatten, 133–72. Leiden 2009.

———. "A Restored Society or a New Society of Jesus?" In *Jesuit Survival and Restoration: A Global History, 1773–1900,* edited by Robert A. Maryks, 13–33. Leiden 2015.

Wrba, Johannes. "Ignatius, die Jesuiten und Wien." In *Aspekte der Bildungs- und Universitätsgeschichte. 16. bis 19. Jahrhundert,* edited by Kurt Mühlberger, 61–90. Vienna 1993.

Zampelli, Michael. "'Lascivi Spettacoli': Jesuits and Theatre (from the Underside)." In *The Jesuits II. Cultures, Sciences, and the Arts 1540–1773,* edited by John W. O'Malley, 550–71. Toronto 2006.

Zampol D'Ortia, Linda "The Cape of the Devil: Salvation in the Japanese Jesuit Mission under Francisco Cabral (1570–1579)." PhD diss., University of Otago, 2016.

Zanardi, Mario. "Il padre Andrea Guevarre della Compagnia di Gesù. Linee biografiche di un protagonista della 'Mendacità sbandita.'" In *La Compagnia di Gesù nella provincia di Torino. Dagli anni di Emanuele Filiberto a quelli di Carlo Alberto,* edited by Bruno Signorelli and Petro Bruno, 161–220. Turin 1998.

———. "La 'Ratio atque institutio studiorum Societatis Iesu.' Tappe e vicende della sua progressiva formazione (1541–1616)." *Annali di storia dell'educazione* 5 (1998): 135–64.

Zarncke, Lilly. *Die Exercitia Spiritualia des Ignatius von Loyola in ihren geistesgeschichtlichen Zusammenhängen.* Leipzig 1931.

Zarri, Gabriella. "Introduzione." In *Storia della direzione spirituale.* Vol. 3, *L'età moderna,* edited by Gabriella Zarri and Giovanni Filoramo, 5–53. Brescia 2008.

Zarri, Gabriella, and Giovanni Filoramo, eds. *Storia della direzione spirituale.* Vol. 3, *L'età moderna.* Brescia 2008.

Zeron, Carlos. "From Farce to Hybris: António Vieira's Hubris in a War of Factions." *Journal of Jesuit Studies* 2 (2015): 387–420.

———. "Les jésuites et le commerce d'esclaves entre le Brésil et l'Angola à la fin du XVIe siècle: contribution à un débat." *Traverse* 3 (1996): 34–50.

———. *Ligne de foi. La Compagnie de Jésus et l'esclavage dans le processus de formation de la société coloniale en Amérique portugais (XVIe–XVIIe siècles).* Paris 2009.

Zeron, Carlos, and Camila Loureiro Dias. "L'antijésuitisme dans l'Amérique portugaise (XVIe–XVIIIe siècle)." In *Les antijésuites. Discours, figures et lieux de l'antijésuitisme à l'époque moderne,* edited by Pierre-Antoine Fabre and Catherine Maire, 563–83. Rennes 2010.

Zhang, Qiong. *Making the New World Their Own: Chinese Encounters with Jesuit Science in the Age of Discovery.* Leiden 2015.

Županov, Ines G. *Disputed Mission: Jesuit Experiments and Brahmanical Knowledge in Seventeenth-Century India*. Oxford 1999. http://www.ineszupanov.com/publications/DisputedMission .pdf. Accessed February 10, 2020.

Županov, Ines G., and Pierre Antoine Fabre, eds. *The Rites Controversies in the Early Modern World*. Leiden 2018.

Zürcher, Erik. "Jesuit Accommodation and the Chinese Cultural Imperative." In *The Chinese Rites Controversy: Its History and Meaning*, edited by David E. Mungello, 31–64. Nettetal 1994.

———. "The Jesuit Mission in Fujian in Late Ming Times: Levels of Response." In *Development and Decline of Fukien Province in the 17th and 18th Centuries*, edited by Eduard B. Vermeer, 417–57. Leiden 1990.

———, ed. *Kouduo richao. Li Jiubiao's Diary of Oral Admonitions: A Late Ming Christian Journal*. St. Augustine 2007.

———. "The Lord of Heaven and the Demons: Strange Stories from a Late Ming Christian Manuscript." In *Religion und Philosophie in Ostasien. Festschrift für Hans Steininger zum 65. Geburtstag*, edited by Gert Naudorf, 359–76. Würzburg 1985.

NAMES INDEX

Acarie, Madame (Marie of the Incarnation), 90
Acevedo, Pedro Pablo de, 385
Acosta, José de, 43–44, 47–48, 451, 476–477, 524–525
Acquaviva, Claudio, 23, 27, 62, 109, 111, 307–308, 582–583; on bureaucratic control, 21–22, 55, 116, 119, 283; on censorship, 327; Clement VIII and, 135; on conversos, 45, 46; on Creoles, 33; critics of, 128, 251; *Instruction for the Confessors of Princes*, 295; on libraries, 332; on Marian congregations, 243; on military chaplains, 193–194, 196; on Philippine mission, 462; political theories of, 298–299; *Ratio studiorum* of, 119, 173, 304–305, 310–314, 317–318, 637; on rural missions, 227; on sermons, 202, 205; on *Spiritual Exercises*, 22, 79–80, 119, 236; on spiritual renewal, 114; on tertianships, 58; on Thomism, 367; on witchcraft, 161
Acquaviva, Rudolfo, 432
Adorno, Francesco, 53, 88
Afonso VI of Portugal, 26
Aguilon, François, 370, 379
Ai Rulüe. *See* Aleni, Giulio
Akbar I, Mughal Emperor, 432
Alacoque, Marguerite-Marie, 164–165, 222
Alba, Duke of, 36
Albanel, Charles, 465
Alberoni, Giulio, 287
Albertino, Francesco, 162
Aleni, Giulio (Ai Rulüe), 534–538, 540, 544, 547, 550–551, 553

Alexander I of Russia, 623
Alexander VII (pope), 135–136, 181, 237, 379
Alexander VIII (pope), 178
Alexander the Great of Macedonia, 427
Alfaro, Diego de, 532
Alfaro, Francisco de, 528
Álvarez, Balthasar, 87, 92
Álvarez de Paz, Diego, 92, 164
Ana de Jesús, 686n244
Andrade, António de, 434
André, Yves-Marie, 358
Andreoni, João Antônio, 487
Andrew, St., 417
Annat, François, 181
Anne de Xainctonge, 154
Anriquez, Anrique, 435
Antoine, Paul-Gabriel, 177
Aperger, Sigismund, 376
Aquinas. *See* Thomas Aquinas
Araoz, Antonio de, 28–29, 45
Arce, José de, 454
Ariscibi (Pima prophet), 513
Aristotle, 119, 312, 351, 353, 364, 380, 389, 558
Arnauld, Angélique, 182
Arnauld, Antoine, 177, 182–183, 216–217, 587
Arndt, Johann, 220
Arnold, Gottfried, 258
Arnoux, Jean, 290, 294
Arriaga, José de, 508
Arrupe, Pedro, 659, 661–665, 667–668, 670–671
Auger, Edmond, 30–31, 193–194, 227
Augustine of Hippo, Saint, 179, 181, 347
Avancini, Nicola, 393

Averroës (Ibn Rushd), 353
Ávila, Diego de, 506–507
Ávila, Juan de, 87, 88, 202, 215
Ayrault, Pierre, 48–49, 54
Azevedo, Francisco de, 434
Azim ud-Din I of Sulu (Muhammad
    Alimuddin), 463
Azpiazu Zulaica, Joaquín, 649

Bacon, Francis, 257
Baegert, Jacob, 325
Baiole, Jean-Jerôme, 90
Baius, Michel, 179
Balde, Jakob, 397–398
Balthasar, Hans Urs von, 651
Balthasar, Juan Antonio, 509–510
Bapst, John, 639
Barace, Cipriano, 453
Barberini, Lucrezia, 223
Barbier, Guillaume, 337
Barclay, William, 297
Bargrave, John, 258
Barras de la Penne, Jean-Antoine de, 373
Barreto, João Nunes, 448
Barruel, Augustin, 607, 609
Barry, Paul de, 162–163
Barzaeus, Gaspar, 565
Basté Basté, Narciso, 655
Batoni, Pompeo, 418
Bauhuis, Bernard, 396
Bayle, Pierre, 360
Bea, Augustin, 647, 659
Beauchamp, Pierre, 407
Beckx, Peter Jan, 109, 630
Bellarmine, Robert, 54, 89, 136–137, 179, 250,
    297–298, 337, 366–367
Bellefonds, Bernardin Gigault de, 222–223
Benci, Francesco, 313
Benci, Jorge, 487
Benedict, Saint, 95, 687n273
Benedict XIII (pope), 206
Benedict XIV (pope), 382
Benedict XV (pope), 646
Benedict XVI (pope), 668–669

Benedictis, Giambattista de, 356
Benoît de Canfeld, 90
Berchmans, John, 88
Bergoglio, Jorge Mario, 669–671
Berinzaga, Isabel, 89, 221–222
Berkeley, George, 356
Bermúdez, Gabriel, 30, 292, 294
Bernanos, Georges, 651
Bernard, Pierre, 48
Bernardino of Siena, 225
Bernard of Clairvaux, 83, 95, 148
Bernardoni, Giovanni Maria, 415
Bernini, Gian Lorenzo, 27, 168, 412, 415,
    418, 422
Berthier, Guillaume-François, 358, 361–363,
    407
Bérulle, Pierre de, 90, 164, 237
Besson, Joseph, 568
Bettendorff, Johann Philipp, 447
Bettini, Mario, 366, 368
Beza, Theodore, 30, 253
Biancani, Giuseppe, 366, 368
Biard, Pierre, 464, 568
Biber, Nithart, 291, 572
Bidermann, Jakob, 393–395, 398, 400
Binet, Étienne, 90, 203, 423–424
Bismarck, Otto von, 587, 641
Bisschop, Jan, 378–379
Bissel, Johann, 397–398
Blaeu, Willem, 337
Blanchard, Jean-Baptiste, 325
Blondy, Michel, 407
Bobadilla, Nicolás, 6–7, 12–13, 32, 41, 100,
    104, 113, 116, 140, 215, 217, 226
Bochet, Jean, 41
Bolland, Jean, 345
Bondinarus, Hieronymus, 124
Bonifacio, Juan, 304, 316
Bordier Delpuits, Jean-Baptiste, 617
Borgo, Carlo, 606–607
Borja, Francisco de, 22, 43, 120, 127, 202–203,
    264, 290, 391, 398, 484; Araoz and, 28–29;
    Dominicans and, 151; Gandía college of,
    303, 304; on missionary work, 138;

mysticism of, 87–88; on tertianships, 58;
  Valdés and, 46
Borromeo, Carlo, 27, 146, 212
Boscovich, Roger, 360, 382, 396
Bouhours, Dominique, 399
Bourdaloue, Louis, 50, 205
Bouvet, Joachim, 470, 547–548, 568
Boyer, Jacques, 563
Brahe, Tycho, 367–368
Brasanelli, Giuseppe, 422
Brébeuf, Jean de, 93, 465–466, 498
Brecht, Lewin, 387
Britt, Adam, 628
Brizio, Giuseppe, 415
Brockmöller, Klemens, 652, 657
Broët, Paschase, 6–7, 37, 41, 54
Brou, Alexandre, 635
Brunner, Andreas, 77
Bruno, Vincenzo, 213
Brzozowski, Tadeusz, 576, 623, 628
Budé, Guillaume, 332
Buffier, Claude, 359
Burriel, Andrés Marcos, 357–358
Busembaum, Heinrich, 176
Buslidius, Johann, 197
Bussières, Jean de, 395
Buzomi, Francesco, 555

Cabeo, Niccolò, 368, 379–380
Cabral, João, 434
Cacella, Estêvão, 434
Cáceres, Diego de, 41
Caesar, Julius, 312, 341
Caille, Robert J. B. de la, 337
Calasanz, José, 153
Calatayud, Pedro de, 232
Calixt, Georg, 253
Calloët-Querbrat, Gabriel, 190, 192
Calvez, Jean-Yves, 666
Calvin, John, 245–246, 586
Campanella, Tommaso, 533
Campion, Edmund, 38, 253
Campomanes, Pedro Rodríguez de, 596, 599
Camus, Jean-Baptiste, 172

Canillac, François de, 471
Canisius, Peter, 198–199, 303, 307, 403;
  Carthusians and, 149, 164; catechisms
  of, 247–248; family of, 49, 50; Favre and,
  33, 78; mysticism of, 84, 87; on papal
  diplomacy, 140; on witchcraft, 159–161
Cano, Melchor, 150–151, 235, 350, 578
Caputo, Sertorio, 227
Carafa, Carlo, 48, 51, 126, 236, 240
Carafa, Gian Pietro, 152–153, 235. See also
  Paul IV
Carafa, Roberto, 264
Carafa, Vincenzo, 45, 73, 114, 139, 374, 486
Carbone, Giovanni Battista, 26
Carbone, Ludovico, 206
Cardell, Franciscus, 340
Cardenal, Fernando, 666
Cardim, António Francisco, 572
Carillo, Alfonso, 33
Carranza, Bartholomé de, 13, 28
Carroll, John, 626–627
Carvalho, Andrés, 79
Carvalho e Melo, Sebastião José. See
  Pombal, Marquis de
Casiot, Jean-Joseph, 613
Casnedi, Carlo Antonio, 695n187
Castel, Jean, 407
Castel, Louis-Bertrand, 359–360
Castiglione, Baldassare, 322
Castiglione, Giuseppe, 420–421, 546
Castillo, Francisco de, 482
Castillo, José de, 453
Cataldini, Giuseppe, 521
Catherine II of Russia, 614–616, 619
Catullus, 311, 342
Caulet, François de, 143
Caussin, Nicolas, 170, 177, 203, 205, 294
Ceccotti, Giovanni, 81, 84
Centurione, Luigi, 114
Cepari, Virgilio, 77, 88–89
Cerutti, Joseph-Antoine, 360
Cesari, Nicholas Peter, 52
Ceva, Tommaso, 362, 393, 395, 399, 401, 406
Champion, Pierre, 67–68, 197

Charles I of England, 39

Charles II of England, 39

Charles III of Spain, 596–597

Charles V, Holy Roman Emperor, 10, 28–29, 263, 398

Charles X of France, 633

Charles of Lorraine, 334

Charles Theodore of Bavaria, 602

Charlet, Étienne, 356

Charpentier, Louis, 483

Charpentier, Marc-Antoine, 406, 408, 410

Chauchetière, Claude, 500–501

Chaumonot, Pierre, 46–47, 57

Chaurand, Honoré, 189–192

Chigi, Fabio, 135–136, 181, 237, 379

Chodkiewicz, Jan Karol, 397

Choiseul, Étienne-François de, 595, 598

Cholenac, Pierre, 501

Cicero, Marcus Tullius, 203, 205, 311–312, 319, 341, 347, 543, 558

Ciermans, Jan, 294, 370

Cisneros, García de, 82–83

Clarke, William, 292

Claudel, Paul, 651–652

Claver, Pedro, Saint, 482–483

Clavijero, Francisco Javier, 611

Clavius, Christoph, 364–366, 545

Clemens, Josef, 141

Clement, Claude, 344

Clement VIII (pope), 135, 140, 180, 226, 351

Clement XI (pope), 572

Clement XIII (pope), 135–136, 596, 598, 600, 603

Clement XIV (pope), 16, 575–576, 598, 601, 606–607, 612, 614

Clorivière, Pierre-Joseph de, 616–617

Codacio, Pietro, 262

Codorniu, Antonio, 206

Codure, Jean, 6–7, 41, 73

Colanelli, Lidanus, 57

Colbert, Jean-Baptiste, 190–191, 478, 526

Commolet, Jacques, 31

Concho, Arnoldo, 123

Confucius, 533–535, 542, 558

Contarini, Gasparo, 262

Contzen, Adam, 161, 251, 290

Copernicus, Nicolaus, 364, 367–369

Coral, Benoît, 337

Cordara, Giulio Cesare, 606, 609, 621

Cordeses, Antonio, 92

Cordoso, Mateus, 496

Corelli, Arcangelo, 410

Coret, Jacques, 162

Corneille, Pierre, 393, 401

Cornoldi, Giovanni Maria, 644

Coster, Francis, 211

Coton, Pierre, 49, 54–55, 89–90, 294

Cramoisy, Sébastian, 337

Crasset, Jean, 417

Crema, Battista de, 153

Croiset, Jean, 164

Croll, Oswald, 379

Cromwell, Oliver, 39

Cuéllar, Juan Velázquez de, 2–3, 11, 113

Cuesta, Antonio de la, 422

Curci, Carlos Maria, 643–644

Curtius Rufus, 312

Czerniewicz, Stanislaus, 615

Damiens, Robert-François, 592

Daniel, Antoine, 93

Daniel, Edmund, 38

Daniélou, Jean, 651, 659

d'Anville, Jean-Baptiste Bourguignon, 374

Darwin, Charles, 641

Daubenton, Guillaume, 30, 183

Delrio, Martin, 54, 159–161, 378

Delumeau, Jean, 703n481

de Mun, Albert, 654–655

Derkennis, Ignatius, 379

Descartes, René, 330, 355–356, 381

Desfontaines, Pierre François Guyot, 125

Desideri, Ippolito, 434, 490

d'Estrées, Comte, 197

Dezza, Paolo, 665

d'Hébert, Guillaume André, 736n421

Diderot, Denis, 362–363, 610

Diego de Zúñiga, 364

Diesbach, Nikolaus Joseph Albert von, 616

Digby, Everard, 255

Dinet, Jacques, 356

Doménech, Jerónimo, 303

Dominic, Saint, 5, 82, 148, 151

Donati, Alessandro, 314

d'Orville, Albert, 474

Drexel, Jeremias, 195, 337, 344, 405

Druillettes, Grabriel, 465

du Blocq, Jean, 416

Dubreuil, Jean, 391–393, 392

Dufrène, Maximilian, 314

du Fresne du Cange, Charles, 346

Dunod, Pierre-Joseph, 189

du Noyer, Catherine Olympe, 359

Duns Scotus, John, 352

Duprat, Guillaume, 265

Du Val, André, 237

Du Vergier de Haranne, Jean (Abbé de Saint-Cyran), 172, 182, 216–217

Dzierozynski, Franz, 628

Echeverría, José de, 521

Eder, Franz Xaver, 484, 531, 606

Egen, Johannes, 275

Eguía, Miguel de, 83

Eliano, Giambattista, 471

Elijah, 152

Elizabeth I of England, 38

Elizalde, Miguel de, 177

Ellacuría, Ignacio, 660–661, 664

Emerson, Ralph, 38

Enrique, León, 80

Erasmus, Desiderius, 83, 123, 321, 341–343

Ernest of Bavaria, 35

Ernfelder, Jakob, 209–210

Ernot, Luis, 531

Errada, José de, 208

Erwitte, Othmar von, 194

Estrada, Francisco de, 35, 198

Eudes, Jean, 164

Eudocia, 389

Euler, Leonhard, 382

Fabi, Fabio, 267

Fabri, Honoré, 176, 369

Fabrini, Nicolò, 195, 197

Faille, Jean-Charles della, 294, 339, 370

Farnese, Alessandro, 36, 193, 195, 416

Farnese, Elisabeth, 294

Farnese, Isabella, 596

Farnese, Ottavio, 263

Faure, Giovanni Battista, 137–138, 380

Favre, Pierre, 6, 73, 113, 140, 149, 161, 263, 303; Araoz and, 28; Bergoglio on, 670; Canisius and, 33, 78; Lutheranism and, 32–33, 246–247, 249,306–307; on parental consent, 50; in Paris, 41; in Parma, 242; portrait of, 7

Ferdinand I, Holy Roman Emperor, 32, 150, 333

Ferdinand II, Holy Roman Emperor, 144, 288, 290, 292

Ferdinand II of Aragon, 81

Ferdinand III, Holy Roman Emperor, 288, 292

Ferdinand VI of Spain, 292, 357

Fernandes, Manuel, 448

Ferrer, Rafael, 452, 497

Ferrer, Vincent, 215, 225

Fessard, Gaston, 651

Figueira, Luís, 446

Firmian, Karl Joseph von, 28, 233

Fleury, André-Hercule de, 287

Flori, Lodovico, 284

Floridablanca, Count (José Moñino y Redondo), 599, 610

Fontana, Carlo, 412

Fontana, Flavio, 232

Fontenai, Louis Abel Bonafous de, 607

Foresta, Albéric de, 635

Foresti, Antonio, 145

Fortis, Luigi, 575–576, 616, 618–619, 623–624

Foscarini, Paolo, 364

Fournier, Georges, 294, 371

Francis I of France, 1

Francis I (pope), 16–17, 142, 669–671

Francis of Assisi, Saint, 4, 82, 148, 271

Francis Xavier, Saint, 6, 19, 144, 320, 444–445, 573; dramas about, 121, 406, 410; correspondence of, 113, 430, 439, 606; missions of, 429–431, 435–439, 442, 497, 538; Nadal and, 54; on *padronado*, 279; in Paris, 41; pedagogical guides of, 304–305; portrait of, 7; prayers to, 157–158; Rodrigues and, 25

Franco, Francisco, 648–649, 658

François, Guillaume, 361

François de Sales, Saint, 164, 220

Frederick I of Prussia, 291

Frederick II of Prussia, 614

Freux, André des, 73, 250, 303, 343, 386, 631

Frey, Bernhard, 160

Fritz, Samuel, 452, 497

Fugger family, 274, 277, 279

Fugger-Wellenburg, Maria-Theresia von, 544, 566

Gaar, Georg, 161

Gaetano da Thiene, 152–153

Gagliardi, Achille, 47, 81, 89–90, 221–222, 353

Galawdewos of Ethiopia, 448

Galen, Bernhard von, 289–290

Gandía, Duke of. *See* Borja, Francisco de

Galilei, Galileo, 338, 364–369, 382

Gans, Johannes, 140, 288, 292

Garasse, François, 583

García, Miguel, 484

Garnier, Julien, 504–506

Garzoni, Lorenzo, 380

Gassendi, Pierre, 355

Gaubil, Antoine, 340

Geoffroy, Julien Louis, 607

Gerard, John, 255

Gerard of Zutphen, 83

Gerbillon, Jean-François, 470, 546

Gerhard, Johann, 220

Gernet, Jacques, 553

Geronimo, Francesco de, 203

Gherardini, Giovanni, 420

Giannettasio, Niccolò Partenio, 399–400

Gilbert, William, 380

Gilg, Adam, 564

Gilii, Filippo Salvatore, 611

Gippenbusch, Jakob, 406

Godínez, Miguel (Michael Wadding), 48, 92–93

Godoy, Juan José, 611

Goethe, Johann Caspar, 333

Góis, Bento de, 433

Gómez Dávila, Hernando, 125

Gonzaga, Aloysius (Luigi), 59, 88, 121, 161

Gonzaga, Ferdinando, 308

Gonzaga, Silvio Valenti, 382

González, Tirso, 24, 27, 47, 71, 111, 128, 177, 191, 232, 293, 470, 484

González de Santa Cruz, Roque, 456

Good, William, 38

Gori, Giulio, 323, 357

Gottifredi, Luigi, 109

Gottsched, Johann Christoph, 401

Gou Bangyong, 535

Gouda, Nikolaas Floris de, 38

Gracián, Baltasar, 400

Granada, Luis de, 151, 202, 215

Grandier, Urbain, 160

Grassi, Giovanni Antonio, 628, 643

Grassi, Orazio, 366, 412

Gregory III (pope), 749n198

Gregory XIII (pope), 43, 61, 120, 135–136, 141, 242, 281, 365, 413, 471

Gregory XV (pope), 138, 560

Gregory XVI (pope), 632

Gregory of Nazianzen, 514–515

Gretser, Jakob, 161, 227, 388, 404

Grienberger, Christoph, 366, 368, 412

Grimaldi, Filippo, 681n70

Grimaldi, Francesco Maria, 368

Grotius, Hugo, 300

Grueber, Johann, 474

Guarini, Guarino, 321

Guden, Corrado, 63

Guericke, Otto von, 258

Guevara, Ernesto "Che," 661
Guévarre, André, 189–191
Guibert, Joseph de, 652
Guilloré, François, 220–221, 224
Gundlach, Gustav, 650, 652, 655–656
Gustavus Adolfus, 174

Hahn, Heinrich, 635
Hannover, Maximilian Wilhelm von, 290
Hardouin, Jean, 347
Harley, Achille IV de, 333
Harrach, Ernst Adalbert von, 143–144
Hauser, Berthold, 355, 357
Hay, Edmund, 38
Hébert, Guillaume-André, 479
Hegel, Georg Wilhelm Friedrich, 644
Hell, Maximilian, 335, 382
Henriquéz, Enrique, 298
Henry II of France, 30
Henry III of France, 31
Henry IV of France, 31, 48, 265, 296, 580
Henschen, Gottfried, 345–346
Herdegen, Konrad, 232
Hernández, Bartolomé, 527
Hernández, Pablo, 330
Herod, 393–394
Herp, Hendrik, 92
Hervás y Pandura, Lorenzo, 607
Herzig, Franciscus, 145
Hitler, Adolf, 649
Hobbes, Thomas, 300
Hoces, Diego, 41
Hodierna, Giovanni Battista, 376
Hoeymaker, Hendrik, 415
Hoffaeus, Paul, 402
Horace, 312, 342, 347, 396
Hosius, Stanislaus, 142, 265
Hoste, Paul, 371–373
Houdry, Vincent, 205, 207–209
Huby, Vincent, 60, 237–239
Huet, Pierre-Daniel, 333
Hugo, Hermann, 424–425
Huidobro, Manuel Bernal de, 480
Hurtado, Alberto, 657

Ibn Rushd (Averroës), 353
Ignatius of Loyola, Saint, 1–14, 19–25, 147–158, 239, 262–263, 295, 316, 423; on banned books, 342–343; biographies of, 424; on bishops' authority, 141–142; childbirth prayers to, 156–158; on confession, 212–215; on congregations of procurators, 108; on conversos, 46; on corporal punishment, 320; correspondence of, 113–114, 606; dramas about 389, 394–395, 406; early life of, 2–3, 341; on family attachments, 48, 52–53; on "finding God in all things," 682n98; "first companions" of, 6, 7, 9, 41–42, 325–326; on Jesuit identity, 117–118; on language learning, 508–509; on "living in the world," 260; on marginalized groups, 186–188, 198, 266; memorial day of, 671; on missionaries, 226; on music, 402; on mysticism, 88, 652; Nadal and, 54, 66, 67, 70; on noble patronage, 266; on novitiates, 57; on obedience, 70, 94–97, 111, 134–135; on pedagogy, 301–304; portraits of, 4, 7; on printing presses, 336; on Protestantism, 246–250; on spiritual coadjutors, 62–63; on tertianship, 58, 60; Thomas à Kempis and, 83, 215; Vieira's sermon on, 204
Ignatius of Loyola, works of: Autobiography, 3–8, 13, 82, 120–121, 220; Formula Instituti, 101; "Meditation on the Two Standards," 75–79; Spiritual Diary, 271. See also Constitutions and Spiritual Exercises in the subject index
Inchofer, Melchior, 582
Innocent IV (pope), 489
Innocent X (pope), 108, 139, 154
Innocent XI (pope), 32
Innocent XII (pope), 98, 136, 191
Isabella of Castile, 81
Isasi, Francesco, 294
Isla, José Francisco de, 206

Jacobus da Varagine, 4, 81
Jacquinot, Barthélémy, 90

Jahangir, Mughal Emperor, 433
James I of England, 297
Jansen, Cornelius, 181–182
Janssens, Jean-Baptiste, 653, 657, 659
Jaricot, Pauline, 634
Jason, 398
Jay, Claude, 6–7, 32–33, 41, 140, 150,
    303, 307
Jégou, Jean, 239
Jeningen, Philipp, 228, 233
Jiménez de Cisneros, Francisco, 287
Joachim of Fiore, 88
Joanna of Austria, 29, 263
João III of Portugal, 25, 28, 263, 279, 486
João IV of Portugal, 26
João V of Portugal, 26
Jogues, Isaac, 93
Johann Wilhelm, Elector Palatine, 334
John Climacus, 83
John Paul II (pope), 664–665, 668, 670
José I of Portugal, 591, 593
Joseph (father of Jesus), 50, 163, 168
Joseph II of Austria, 28, 607, 612
Jouvency, Joseph de, 304, 314
Joyeuse, Cardinal de, 332–333
Juan de Ávila, 87, 88, 202, 215
Julius III (pope), 246
Jungmann, Josef Andreas, 651
Juvenal, 427

Kalckbrenner, Gerhard, 149
Kamel, Georg Josef, 376–377
Kangxi Emperor, 376, 410, 443, 470, 548,
    554, 562
Kant, Immanuel, 644
Kapsberger, Johann Hieronymus, 406
Kaunitz, Wenzel Anton von, 233
Kempis, Thomas à, 83, 215
Kepler, Johannes, 368
Kerlivio, Louis Eudo de, 237
Kessel, Leonhard, 79
Ketteler, Wilhelm Emmanuel von, 654
Keudel, Katharina von, 157
Khabes, Anton, 203

Khlesl, Melchior, 287
Kino, Eusebio, 460, 497
Kircher, Athanasius, 329, 335, 348–349,
    378–380, 547
Kisel, Philipp, 78, 164, 684n185
Klein, Paul, 476
Kleutgen, Joseph, 630, 644
Knuist, Joseph, 718n418
Kochański, Adam, 369
Koffler, Johannes, 442
Kohlmann, Anton (Anthony), 628
Kolping, Adolph, 654
Kolvenbach, Peter Hans, 665–667, 669,
    748n167
Körler, Theodor, 289–290
Kostka, Stanislaus, 121, 157
Kropf, Francis Xavier, 304

Labadie, Jean de, 92
La Chaise, Pierre de, 293
La Colombière, Claude, 164–165
LaFarge, John, 650
Laínez, Diego, 6–7, 22, 30, 41, 46, 50, 193,
    252, 303, 309, 342
Lallemant, Jacques-Philippe, 183
Lallemant, Louis, 60, 68, 90, 92–93
Lambert, Marquise de (Anne-Thérèse de
    Marguenat de Courcelles), 359
Lamormaini, Wilhelm, 290, 292
La Mousse, Jean de, 468, 482–483, 497
Lana Terzi, Francesco, 373–374, 379, 396
Lancicius, Nicolaus, 50–51
Landini, Silvestro, 226
Lang, Franz, 393
Langobardo, Niccolò, 549
La Quintinye, Pierre, 177–178
Las Casas, Bartolomé de, 523
Lasso, Orlando di, 403–404
Laval, François, 139
Lavalette, Antoine, 280, 594, 599
Laymann, Paul, 160
Lazzarelli, Alessandro, 232
Le Brun, Laurent, 394–395
Le Comte, Louis-Daniel, 547

Ledesma, Diego de, 409
Ledóchowski, Włodzimierz, 646–648, 650
Le Febvre, François Antoine, 405
Leibniz, Gottfried Wilhelm, 258, 334, 346, 358, 370, 373, 381, 563, 565
Le Jay, Gabriel François, 405
Le Jeune, Paul, 60, 93, 493–499, 502–504, 506
Lemius, Gottfried, 245–246, 255
Le Moyne, Pierre, 170
Léon, Pedro de, 198–201
Leopold I, Holy Roman Emperor, 291
Leopold II, Holy Roman Emperor, 612
Leo XII (pope), 622
Leo XIII (pope), 645, 654–655
Le Paige, Louis-Adrien, 579, 589, 594
Lessius, Leonard, 181, 274
Lestonnac, Jeanne de, 154
Le Tellier, Michel, 360
Leubenstain, Martin, 140
Leunis, Jean, 242
Le Valois, Louis, 42, 222–223, 245, 330–331, 356, 565
Ligouri, Alphonsus, 232
Linnaeus, Karl, 376
Lippomano, Andrea, 188
Liselotte von der Pfalz (Madame Palatine), 292
Liu Yunde, Blasius, 561
Livy, 312
Li Zhizao, 540
Li Zubai, 548
Llampillas, Saverio, 610
Llanos, José María de, 658
Loarte, Gaspar de, 88
Locke, John, 300, 324–325, 357
Lockman, John, 567
Loferer, Georg, 232
Lombard, Peter, 215
Löpen, Bernard, 249
López, Jerónimo, 70–71, 232
Lorin, Jean, 366
Lossada, Luis de, 355
Louis XII of France, 288

Louis XIII of France, 90, 177, 289–290, 294, 356, 395
Louis XIV of France, 32–33, 36, 192, 265, 360, 405, 407; absolutism of, 287; colonial policies of, 465, 467, 469, 470, 472, 478, 480; confessors of, 289, 291, 293; Strasbourg and, 248
Louis XV of France, 32, 603
Louis-Auguste de Bourbon, 360
Louis-Philippe of France, 642
Loyola, Ignatius of. See Ignatius of Loyola
Lubac, Henri de, 651, 658
Ludger, Saint, 389
Ludolf, Hiob, 346
Ludolph of Saxony, 4, 81–82
Luengo, Manuel, 605–607, 609, 616
Lugo, Juan de, 137, 273
Luther, Martin, 51, 68, 137, 172, 179, 245, 247, 249, 251, 489, 586
Luynes, Charles d'Albert de, 294

Machiavelli, Niccolò, 297, 580
Madrid, Cristóbal de, 215–217
Magdeburg, Mechthild of, 92
Maggio, Lorenzo, 52, 90, 404
Maigrot, Charles, 560–561
Malachi, 427
Malagrida, Gabriel, 590–593
Maldonado, Juan de, 350–352
Malebranche, Nicolas, 356, 358
Mambrianus, Philippus, 124
Manaraeus, Oliver, 127
Mancinelli, Giulio, 471
Manutius, Aldus Jr., 338
Manutius, Paulus, 338
Marbán, Pedro, 453
Marcellus II (pope), 136
Marell, Jakob, 124, 127
Margaret of Parma, 263
Maria Anna of Austria, 604
Maria Anna von Jülich, 232
Maria Manuela of Portugal, 28
Mariana, Juan de, 108, 299, 582
Mariana of Austria, 29, 99, 291

Maria of Austria, 263

Maria Theresa of Austria, 28, 34–35, 170, 185, 598–599, 601, 604

Marie Antoinette of France, 599

Marie of the Incarnation (Madame Acarie), 90

Marino, Giambattista, 400

Marquette, Jacques, 467

Martellange, Étienne, 418–419

Martial, 342

Martínez Silíceo, Juan, 28, 46

Martín, Luis, 647

Martini, Martino, 560, 571

Mary, Queen of Scots, 38

Mascareñas, Leonor de, 29, 263

Mascareñas, Pedro, 263

Mascetta, Simone, 521

Masen, Jakob, 323, 390–391, 400

Massé, Énemond, 464

Mastrilli, Nicolás Durán, 429

Mattei, Gaspare, 140

Matthieu, Claude, 31

Maugeraye, François de la, 373, 381

Maunoir, Julien, 54–58, 61, 64–65, 78–79, 229, 233–234, 239, 330, 682n98

Maximilian I, Duke of Bavaria, 161, 197, 277, 290–291, 569

Maximilian II, Holy Roman Emperor 263

Mayans, Gregorio, 358

Mayr, Anton, 355

Mazarin, Jules, 287

Mazzolari, Giuseppe Maria, 396

Medici, Anna Maria Luisa de', 232

Medina, Bartolomé de, 176

Mei Wending, 546

Menchaca, Roque, 606

Mendoça, Hernando de, 582

Ménestrier, Claude, 337, 405

Ménestrier, François de, 258

Menochio, Giovanni Stefano, 379–380

Mercurian, Everard, 25, 38, 44, 55, 58, 79, 141; on banned books, 342, 343; on Carmelites, 151; on English mission, 253; mysticism and, 92, 93; on religious music, 403

Merici, Angela, 154

Merz, Aloys

Mesland, Denis, 356

Messía, Alonso, 482

Michael (archangel), 387, 395, 418

Michallat, Étienne, 337

Michelet, Jules, 588

Migazzi, Christoph, 185, 617

Mir, Miguel, 582

Mirabeau, Honoré Gabriel Riqueti de, 360

Miró, Diego, 25, 63

Misch, Johannes, 379

Moëlo, Olive, 235

Molière (Jean-Baptiste Poquelin), 393

Molina, Juan Ignacio, 611

Molina, Luis de, 179–181, 274, 297–298

Mondengón, Pedro de, 608

Moñino y Redondo, José (Count Floridablanca), 599, 610

Monte, Philippe de, 402

Monteiro de Rocha, José, 608

Montenegro, Pedro, 376

Montesino, Ambrosio, 81

Montesquieu, Charles-Louis de Secondat, Baron de La Brède et de, 359, 362, 610

Montoya, Juan de, 127

Morales, Juan Bautista de, 560

More, Thomas, Saint, 533

Moretus, Theodore, 52, 258, 337, 339

Morone, Giovanni, 12–13

Mousse, Jean de la, 468, 482–483, 497

Mousson, Pierre, 390

Muhammad Alimuddin (Azim ud-Din I of Sulu), 463

Müller, Jacob, 212

Mun, Adrien Albert Marie de, 654–655

Muratori, Ludovico Antonio, 169, 183, 233

Murray, John Courtney, 651, 667

Musart, Charles, 145

Musch, Adam, 123

Mussolini, Benito, 649

Nadal, Jerónimo, 249, 303–304, 403, 536–537, 557, 572; *Adnotations et meditations in*

Evangelia, 423; on communion, 217; *Constitutions* and, 12; on conversos, 46; as military chaplain, 193; Polanco and, 20; on spirituality, 66–68; on traveling, 70; on vocational choice, 53–54

Nádasi, Johannes, 327

Napoleon Bonaparte, 575, 619, 625, 629

Neercassel, Jean, 170, 214

Nell-Breuning, Oswald von, 655

Neri, Filipe, 409

Neumayr, Franz, 252, 401–402

Newton, Isaac, 370, 380–382

Nian Xiyao, 420

Niccolò, Giovanni, 422

Nicephorus I of Constantinople, Saint, 333

Nickel, Goswin, 24, 27, 97–98, 257, 328, 474

Nicolás, Adolfo, 667

Nicole, Pierre, 182

Nieremberg, Eusebius, 85, 296

Nithard, Eberhard, 29, 99–100

Nobili, Roberto de, 436, 469, 555–560, 632, 736n427

Nóbrega, Manuel da, 25, 444–445, 486, 523, 554–557

Noceti, Carlo, 395

Nötges, Jakob, 649

Nouë, Anne de, 498

Novalis (Georg Philipp Friedrich von Hardenberg), 615

Noyelle, Charles de, 24, 27

Nzinga-a-Nkuwu (João I of Kongo), 448

Ockham, William of, 352

Oda Nobunaga, 439

Olier, Jean-Jacques, 147

Oliva, Gianpaolo, 24, 27, 99, 130, 151–152, 177, 291, 413, 418

Oliva, Jean, 359

Olivares, Count-Duke of (Gaspar de Guzmán), 291

Ōmura Sumitada, 439–440

Oosterhuis, Huub, 660–661

Orban, Ferdinand, 334–335, 340, 714n264

Orsini, Giulio, 492

Ortíz, Francesco, 125

Osorio, Leonora, 263

Osuna, Francisco de, 215

Ovid, 311, 342, 395, 398

Oviedo, Andrea, 304

Oviedo, Juan Antonio de, 571–573

Paccanari, Niccolò, 617–618

Pacheco, Francisco, 394–395

Palafox y Mendoza, Juan de, 143–144, 282, 596

Palatine, Madame (Liselotte von der Pfalz), 292

Paleotti, Gabriele, 383

Pallavicino, Sforza, 27, 135–137, 177, 205, 369, 380, 400–401

Palma, Luis de la, 239, 704n503

Palmeira, André, 573

Palmio, Benedetto, 45, 188–189

Pamphili, Giofanni Battista. *See* Innocent X

Paolucci, Scipione, 66–67, 270

Papebroch, Daniel, 152, 345–346

Paracelsus, 379

Parhamer, Ignaz, 185, 191, 233, 696n234

Parma, Duke of, 619

Parran, Antoine, 406

Pascal, Blaise, 182, 583–584, 587

Pascual, Miguel Angel, 203

Pasquier, Étienne, 578, 580, 548

Pastedechouan, Pierre-Antoine, 502–505

Patino, Gabriel, 374

Patouillet, Louis, 183

Paul (apostle), 67, 418, 481

Paul III (pope), 10–11, 66, 73, 100–101, 134, 185, 490

Paul IV (pope), 12–13, 135, 235

Paul V (pope), 27, 180–181, 568

Paul VI (pope), 661

Pauw, Cornelius de, 610–611

Pazzi, Maria Maddalena de', Saint, 89, 221

Pedro II of Portugal, 26

Peña, Francisco, 297

Peña, Juan de la, 151

Peñafiel, Leonardo de, 45

Peramás, José Manuel, 533

Pereira, Bartolomeu, 394–395
Pereira, Benito, 353, 365, 378
Pereira, Tomás, 546
Pérez, Martín, 458
Pérez del Pulgar, José Agustín, 649
Pérez de Ribas, Andrés, 489, 491, 515
Périn, Léonard, 322–323
Perlín, Gabriel, 482
Perlín, Juan, 217
Perrin, Henri, 656–657
Persons, Robert, 38–39, 297, 299
Pétau, Denis, 203, 314, 390
Peter, Saint, 418
Petragrassa, Angelo Camillo, 422
Petrarca, Francesco, 341
Petrucci, Mariano, 623
Pfefferkorn, Ignaz, 408
Philip II of Spain, 28–29, 39, 43, 169, 449, 461
Philip III of Spain, 29
Philip IV of Spain, 29, 99, 282, 291
Philip V of Spain, 183, 292, 294
Piccolo, Francisco María, 510
Piccolomini, Francesco, 295–296
Pietrasanta, Silvestro da, 154
Pignatelli, José María, 619
Pineda, Juan de, 379
Pius IV (pope), 471
Pius V (pope), 58, 193
Pius VI (pope), 612, 615–617
Pius VII (pope), 576, 618–620, 629
Pius VIII (pope), 642
Pius IX (pope), 168, 639, 642, 644
Pius X (pope), 645
Pius XI (pope), 647, 650, 655
Pius XII (pope), 644, 651, 658
Plato, 351, 533
Plautus, 342
Pleiner, Joachim, 195
Pliny the Elder, 347
Poiresson, Nicolas de, 472
Poiret, Pierre, 89
Poirot, Louis, 618
Polanco, Juan Alfonso de, 46–47, 73, 111–116, 274, 317; on communion, 217;

congregation of procurators and, 108; *Constitutions* and, 11–12, 71, 100–101; on Counter-Reformation, 246; Dominicans and, 148–149; on Jesuit identity, 119; on Jesuit publications, 336; Laínez and, 342; Nadal and, 20; on spirituality, 68; on tertianship, 58, 60
Pombal, Marquis de, 585–586, 589–592, 596, 599, 608
Pontanus, Jakob, 311, 319, 321, 343–344, 354
Porée, Charles, 385–386, 390, 401
Possevino, Antonio, 46, 193–196, 572–573; on heretics, 196; as papal diplomat, 37, 133, 290; on poetry, 398; on *Spiritual Exercises*, 72–73
Possevino, Giovanni Battista, 124
Postel, Guillaume, 56
Poza, Juan Baptista, 370, 718n405
Pozzo, Andrea, 63, 120, 130, 168, 419–421
Prádanos, Juan de, 223–224
Prat, Raymundo, 87
Précipiano, Humbert-Guillaume de, 183
Propertius, Sextus, 342
Prusinovský z Víckova, Vilém, 142
Ptolemy, 364
Pudrom, Gabriel, 479–480
Puente, José de la, 565
Pufendorf, Samuel, 300

Quarracino, Antonio, 670
Quen, Jean de, 465
Quesnel, Pasquier, 183
Quintilian, 203
Quiroga, José, 374

Rahner, Hugo, 652
Rahner, Karl, 659, 667
Rale, Sébastien, 464, 573
Rameau, Jean-Philippe, 407
Ramírez, Gerónimo, 459
Ramírez, Juan, 391
Rapin, René, 355–356, 394–395
Rauscher, Wolfgang, 203, 205
Rávago, Francisco de, 292, 357

Ray, John, 376
Raynal, Guillaume Thomas François, 610
Reccati, Vincenzo, 382
Reggio, Carlo, 205
Reittemberger, Franz, 124
Retz, Franz, 24, 27, 461
Rhey, Kaspar, 389
Rhodes, Alexandre de, 441, 473, 509, 573
Ribadeneira, Pedro de, 103, 105, 113, 120, 127,
    268–269
Ricci, Lorenzo, 109, 136, 598, 600, 602–603
Ricci, Matteo, 442–443, 509, 538–543, 545,
    547, 549, 553, 556–557, 568
Riccioli, Giovanni Battista, 328, 368–369
Richelieu, Cardinal (Armand Jean du
    Plessis), 32, 177, 193, 287, 289, 395
Rigoleuc, Jean, 60, 237, 239
Rigordi, François, 473
Robertson, William, 610
Rocco, Gregorio, 203
Rodrigues, Simão, 6–7, 12, 41
Rodríguez, Alonso, Saint, 43, 63, 85–85
Roothaan, Johan Philipp, 86, 630–632,
    636–637, 640, 643
Rosis, Giovanni de, 412, 418
Rossi, Andrea, 221
Rosweyde, Heribert, 345–346
Roth, Heinrich, 509
Rousseau, Jean-Jacques, 324–325, 358, 407
Rubens, Peter Paul, 76, 415, 418, 424, 541
Rue, Charles de la, 401
Ruggieri, Michele, 442, 538–539
Ruiz de Montoya, Antonio, 521–522, 531
Ruiz de Portillo, Jerónimo, 450
Ryllo, Maximilian, 633

Sacchini, Francesco, 304, 316, 319–320, 344
Saffray de Mézy, Augustin de, 478
Sailly, Thomas, 193–197, 696n245
Saint-Cyran, Abbé de (Jean Du Vergier de
    Hauranne), 172, 182, 216–217
Saint-Jure, Jean-Baptiste, 164
Saint-Vincent, Grégoire de, 339, 370
Salazar, Hernando de, 125

Sales, François de, Saint, 164, 220
Sallust, 312
Salmerón, Alfonso, 6–7, 37, 41, 73, 113, 241,
    249, 307
Salutati, Coluccio, 341
Salvatierra, Juan María de, 144, 460, 474,
    509–510, 518–519
Samier, Henri, 31
Sánchez, Alonso, 573
Sánchez, Juan, 172–173
Sandaeus (van der Sandt), Maximilian, 93,
    258
Sandoval, Alonso de, 481–483
Sandoval, Francisco Gómez de, 29
Santarén, Hernando de, 459, 506–509
Sarbiewski, Maciej, 396–398, 400
Sardinha, Pedro Fernandes, 554
Sarpi, Paolo, 581
Satan, 74–75, 77, 159, 162, 179, 387, 418, 495,
    607, 630
Savonarola, Girolamo, 88, 215
Scarlatti, Alessandro, 406
Schacht, Heinrich, 256
Schall von Bell, Adam, 544–546, 548, 733n326
Scheiner, Christoph, 366
Schmid, Martin, 408–409, 454
Schott, Andreas, 203
Schreck, Johann (Terrenz Constantiensis),
    545
Schurhammer, Georg, 262
Schwaller, Thaddäus, 164
Schwarz, Ignaz, 300
Scotti, Giulio Clemente, 582
Scribani, Carlo, 264
Sebastião I of Portugal, 25
Secchi, Angelo, 638, 644
Sedeño, Antonio, 461
Segesser, Philipp, 460, 511, 518–519, 563–564,
    569–570
Segneri, Paolo, Jr., 212, 225
Segneri, Paolo, Sr., 79, 98–99, 136, 229,
    231–232, 285, 400–401, 632
Segundo, Juan Luis, 660
Seneca, 543

Sicard, Claude, 472
Sidney, Philip, 533
Sigismund III of Poland, 33
Sineo della Torre, Giuseppe, 619, 623
Sirmond, Antoine, 172
Sixtus V (pope), 132, 135, 195, 242
Skanderbeg, Gjergi Kastrioti, 395
Skarga, Piotr, 33
Soarez, Cyprian, 312, 343
Sobrino, Jon, 660, 668–669
Solchaga, Tomás de, 731n225
Sonnenberg, Bernhard von, 164
Sosa, Arturo, 667
Soto, Domingo de, 350, 527
Soto, Francisco de, 185
Sousa, Tomé de, 444
Spaur, Christoph Andreas von, 142
Spee, Friedrich, 160
Spener, Jakob Philipp, 220, 258
Spinelli, Pierantonio, 240
Spinoza, Baruch, 356
Staglianon, Niccolò, 491
Stattler, Benedict, 358
Stefonio, Bernardino, 389
Stepling, Josef, 382
Storchenau, Sigismund von, 358
Sturm, Johannes, 257
Suárez, Francisco, 92, 297, 299–300
Sucquet, Antoine, 423
Suffren, Jean, 289
Surin, Jean-Joseph, 60, 91, 93, 160, 270

Tacchi Venturi, Pietro, 649
Tachard, Guy, 469, 479, 573
Tacquet, André, 370
Takayama Ukon (Justo), 389
Talon, Jean, 526
Tamburini, Michelangelo, 24, 109, 561, 572
Tamburini, Tommaso, 176
Tanner, Adam, 160–161
Tanucci, Bernardo, 596, 599
Taparelli d'Azeglio, Luigi, 655
Tapia, Gonzalo de, 458
Tauler, Johannes, 87, 92

Tavono, Giovanni Battista, 274
Teilhard de Chardin, Pierre, 651
Tejeda, Juan de, 87–88
Tekakwitha, Kateri, 500–502
Tellier, Jean, 199
Tellino, Ignatio, 137
Telonarius, Petrus, 720n465
Tencin, Madame de, 359–360
Terence, 342
Teresa de Ávila, Saint, 87, 90, 151, 163, 220
Tertullian, 383
Tesauro, Emanuele, 400
Theodosius II, Roman Emperor, 389
Theseus, 398
Thoman, Maurice, 582, 602, 606
Thomas (apostle), 496
Thomas à Kempis, 83, 215
Thomas Aquinas, Saint, 68, 119, 215, 313, 347, 352–354, 638
Thomasius, Christian, 300
Tibullus, 342
Tiraboschi, Girolamo, 610
Toledo, Fernando Álvarez de, 36
Toledo, Francisco de, 135, 180, 215, 217, 350–351, 451
Tolomei, Giovanni Battista, 137, 151
Torrend, Jules, 636
Torres, Cosme de, 439
Torres Bollo, Diego de, 482, 527
Torricelli, Evangelista, 381
Torrigiani, Luigi Maria, 136, 598
Torsellini, Orazio, 313
Toulouse, Pierre Gregoire de, 308
Tournély, Léonor-François de, 617
Tournemine, René-Joseph, 358–359, 361
Tournon, Charles-Thomas Maillard de, 561–563
Tours, François-Marie de, 561
Tourville, Anne-Hilarion de, 371
Toyotomi Hideyoshi, 389, 440
Travaglia, Camilla, 221
Trigault, Nicolas, 126, 541, 569, 571
Tristano, Giovanni, 412, 418
Tristano, Lorenzo, 94–95, 98

Tromp, Sebastiaan, 658
Truchsess, Eusebius, 52
Truchsess von Waldburg, Otto, 142
Tucci, Stefano, 404
Turriani, Augustin, 253
Tyrrell, George, 645

Ulloa, Magdalena de, 223–224
Urban VIII (pope), 181

Valdés, Juan de, 46
Valencia, Gregory of, 354
Valens, Robert, 256
Valera, Blas, 44
Valeriano, Giuseppe, 412, 414, 418
Valignano, Alessandro, 439–440, 442,
    556–557, 573
Valla, Lorenzo, 341
van der Sandt (Sandaeus), Maximilian, 93,
    258
Van Dyck, Anthony, 418
Van Helmont, Jan Baptist, 379
Varillon, François, 651–652
Vasconcelos, João de, 26
Verbiest, Ferdinand, 545
Vergerio, Pier Paolo, 321
Vergil, 312, 347, 394–395
Verveaux, Johannes, 291, 295–296
Vetter, Konrad, 227
Vicent, Antonio, 655
Victor Amadeus II, Duke of Savoy, 191
Vieira, António, 44, 178, 204, 206–207,
    446, 481
Villanueva, Francisco de, 29
Villar Goitia, Andrés de, 276
Vincent de Paul, 147, 189, 220, 237, 613
Vinck, Anton, 193
Viscardo y Guzmán, Juan Pablo, 611
Visdelou, Claude de, 470
Vitelleschi, Muzio, 23, 109, 456, 483; English
    mission of, 39; mysticism and, 92–93,
    163; on politics, 129–130, 266–267, 295;
    Propaganda Fide and, 139
Vitoria, Francisco de, 350

Vitoria, Juan Alfonso de, 78
Vivaldi, Antonio, 410
Vives, Juan Luis, 341–342
Voltaire (François-Marie Arouet), 125,
    324–325, 358–359, 362, 393, 610
Von Guericke, Otto, 381
Von Le Fort, Gertrud, 651
Vos, Jakob de, 98–99, 123, 224
Vos, Martin de, 424
Vrints, Johann Baptist, 424

Wadding, Lucas, 48
Wadding, Michael (Miguel Godínez), 48,
    92–93
Wall, Bernardo, 596
Walsh, Edmund A., 648
Wang Zheng, 540
Ward, Mary, 154
Wetter, Gustav, 657–658
Wilhelm, Josef, 463
William V, Duke of Bavaria, 274, 403
Wischaven, Cornelis, 35
Wojtyla, Karol. See John Paul II
Wolf, Johannes, 290
Wolfe, David, 38–39
Wolff, Christian, 358, 382
Wolff, Friedrich von Lüdinghausen zu, 291
Wurz, Ignaz, 207

Xavier, Francis. See Francis Xavier
Xavier, Jerónimo, 433
Ximenes, Diego, 226
Xu, Candida, 544
Xu Guangqi, 540, 544–545, 549

Yang Tingyun, 540, 542–543
Ye Xianggao, 534–535
Yongzheng Emperor, 554

Zaccari, Antonio Maria, 153
Zahorowski, Hieronim, 581–582
Zamagna, Bernardo, 395
Zipoli, Domenico, 406
Zucchi, Niccolò, 368

SUBJECT INDEX

Note: Page numbers in italics indicate illustrations

Abenaki people, 464

accommodationalism, 554–563

Aeterni Patris (encyclical), 645

Afghanistan, 433

Africa, 104, 447–449, 565, 633–634, 667

aggiornamento, 658–659

airship design, 371–372, *373*, 379

alchemy, 378–380

alcohol abuse, 500, *501*

Algeria, 633

allegorical dramas, 390–391, 394. *See also* theater

alumbrados, 8, 86–87. *See also* Enlightenment

American Revolution, 602, 626–627

amulets, 158, 512. *See also* superstitions

ancestor veneration, 551, 559–560

angels, guardian, 161–163, 387

Angola, 447, 449, 485

anti-communism, 646, 648, 656–658

Anticoton, 578–580, 584

"anti-modernists," 641–645

anti-Semitism, 589, 643, 646, 649–650

Apostolic Penitentiary, 136

apostolic vicars, 139

Apostolic Visitator, 154

Arabic language, 471

architecture, 410–422, *415*, *419*

Argentina, 240, 455; Jesuit land in, 280; Jesuit reinstatement in, 623

asceticism, 84–94, 170

astrology, 380

astronomy, 364–370, *369*, 545, 638; observatories for, 335–336, 340, 648

attritio/contritio dispute, 171–174, 177

Augustinians, 118, 148; in Ceylon, 437; in Philippines, 461

Austria, 28, 32–35, 65, 106, 129, 263; Enlightenment in, 28, 35, 607; Jesuit reinstatement in, 623; Jesuit suppression in, 598–599, 601, 604, 605; Nordic Seminary in, 40; orphanages in, 185; prison ministry in, 199. *See also* Holy Roman Empire

Austrian Succession, War of the (1740–48), 34, 376

bandeirantes (slave hunters), 531–532

baptism, 535–537, 540, 544, 549; of indigenous people, 516–517; by lay ministers, 551

Barnabites, 148, 153, 167

Bavaria, 34, 196, 197, 248, 273; court confessors in, 295–296; Jesuit properties in, *415*, 601–602

Belgium, 35–36, 378, 379; Carmelites of, 152; church architecture in, 416; Louis XIV's wars in, 36; printing in, 345, 423–426

Benedictines, 82–83, 95, 105; casuistry of, 174–175; habits of, 118; on Jesuit conversion campaigns, 232; monasticism of, 147–148; poorhouses of, 190

benefactors of religious institutions, 264–265. *See also* patronage

biblical dramas, 387–388. *See also* theater

biretta, 63–64

Bolivia, 450–455, 529

Bollandists, 345–346, 605

bookkeeping methods, 283–286, 284–285

Book of Changes (*Yijing*), 547–548

Boston College, 638, 639

botanical studies, 376–378, 377

Brazil, 130, 178, 444–447; accommodationalism in, 554–555; *encomienda* system in,
529; Jesuit ban in, 576; Jesuit land in, 280,
281; slavery in, 485–487, 531–532

Brethren of the Common Life, 321

Buddhism, 539, 540–541

bureaucratic control, 100–117; Acquaviva
on, 21–22, 55, 116, 119, 283; bookkeeping
for, 283–286, 284–285; of novices, 55;
"our way of proceeding" and, 72

calculus, 370, 381

calendars, 365, 545–546

Calvinism, 179, 200, 248–249, 255. *See also*
Protestant Reformation

Cambodia, 441

Canada, 46, 139, 463–467, 475, 478, 491;
annual reports from, 566; conversion
campaigns in, 493–506, 501; European
law in, 526; indigenous music of, 410;
Jesuit music in, 407–408; Jesuit suppression and, 612–613; marriage customs in,
477; Ursulines in, 154

canon law, 50, 132, 646; on profit, 281, 285

Capuchins, 48–49; missionary work of, 138,
434, 449; poorhouses of, 190; Quarant'ore
and, 167

Carmelites, 90, 148, 151–152, 613

Carnival (pre-Lenten festival), 167

Cartesianism, 355–357

Carthusians, 149, 164

cartography, 370, 374–375, 375; Chinese, 545;
lunar, 368, 369

Casa de Citelle (Venice), 189

Casa Pia (Seville), 188

Casa Santa Catarina (Rome), 188

Casa Santa Marta (Rome), 187–188

casuistry, 174–181, 175, 313. *See also* theology

catechism, 514, 520; of Canisius, 247–248; of
Ledesma, 409; of Luther, 247; of Pasquier,
578, 580, 584

Catholicae fidei (papal brief), 618, 619

Catholic League, 31

Cayenne, 197, 468–469, 475

celibacy, 43, 660–661

censorship, 342–343, 356; of Index Liborum
Prohibitorum, 328, 382

"central missions," 231–232

Ceylon, 437

chastity, 43, 61, 94, 123–125, 271, 524, 660–661

childbirth, perils of, 156–158

Chile, 456, 611

China, 44, 129, 150, 442–444, 533–563;
Christianity banned in, 552–554; European
music in, 410; European painting in,
420–422; Góis's mission to, 433; Lazarists
in, 613; Louis XIV and, 470; Macao and,
282, 442, 470, 539, 565, 570; maps of,
374, 376; Shanghai University in, 648;
Xavier's mission to, 431, 442, 538.
See also Confucianism

Chinese rites controversy, 443, 559–563, 584

Cistercians, 108, 147–148, 150

"civilizing mission," 524–526

Civiltà Cattolica (journal), 643–646, 650

"clerics regular," 148

Cluniacs, 148, 150

coadjutors (*coadjutores*), 61–64

Collège de Clermont, 265

Collège de Montaigu (Paris), 321

Collège Henri IV (La Flèche), 265

Collegio Romano, 27, 306; curriculum of,
638; after Jesuit suppression, 614, 636;
pharmacy of, 378; printing press of, 336,
338; Sant'Ignazio Church of, 414, 420,
421; theater of, 389

Colombia, 450, 452, 482–483

color theory, 370

communion. *See* Eucharist

Compagnie de Marie-Notre-Dame, 155

confession, 132, 209–218; *attritio/contritio*
dispute of, 171–174, 177; communion and,

215, 216, 218; of court nobles, 288–296;
Protestant views of, 255; spiritual directors and, 219. *See also* penance
confraternities, 166, 199, 241–245
Confucianism, 442, 533–535, 539–542, 547,
551–554; ancestor veneration of, 551,
559–560; classical rhetoric and, 558;
neo-Confucianism and, 542–543
Congregation for the Doctrine of the Faith,
669
consilium (spiritual counsel), 220
Constitutions (Loyola), 11–13, 21, 66, 71–73,
100–113; on Aquinas, 119; on bishops'
authority, 141–142; criticisms of, 581; on
educational mission, 304, 326; Enlightenment and, 362; on family attachments,
51–53; on "finding God in all things," 68;
on income from rural houses, 273; leadership structure of, 109–110, 128; on
learning local languages, 508–509; legal/
spiritual aspects of, 101–102; on member
qualifications, 42–53; on scholarship, 340;
on sermons, 206; on "testing experiences,"
57; on "union of hearts," 118, 128, 130.
See also Society of Jesus
contritio/attritio dispute, 171–174, 177
controversialist theology, 250–253,
300–301
conversion campaigns: in Canada, 493–506,
501; in Europe, 225–235, *230, 231*, 240; in
Mexico, 506–521
conversos, 26, 45–46
Coptic Church, 133, 348, 448, 471
Corpus Christi, Feast of, 166
Counter-Reformation, 145, 248; Hosius on,
142; Paleotti on, 383; spiritual goals of,
155–156, 246
Creoles, 43–45, 571–572, 611
Cuba, 450
cultural dialogue, 667–668, 671
Cum Deus optimus (papal bull), 561
curiosities, cabinets of, 334
curriculum. *See Ratio studiorum*
customary ministries, 184–185

dance, 405–407
demonology, 158–161, 378. *See also* witchcraft
Deus Scientiarum Dominus (apostolic
constitution), 647
dispassion (*apatheia*), 68–69
disputationes, 322
doctrinas (indigenous mission jurisdictions),
451
Dominicans, 67, 108, 578; casuistry of, 176,
180–181; in Ceylon, 437; on Chinese rites
controversy, 560; habits of, 118; Inquisition
and, 137, 138, 150; on Marian worship, 169;
other religious orders and, 148, 150–151;
scholasticism of, 350, 353; on usury, 274
Dominus ac redemptor (papal brief), 575,
576, 599–601, 612; Cordara on, 621;
criticisms of, 606–607
dying, "art" of, 162–163, 200, 244

Eastern Orthodox Church, 133, 470, 471,
615
economic endeavors, 271–296, 278, 284–285;
moneylending as, 274, 286; profits from,
281–282, 285
Ecuador, 451, 452
Egypt, 472
electricity, 380, 396
El Salvador, 664
emperor versus pope conflicts, 287–288,
297–298
encomienda system, 527–529
Encyclopédie, 362–363
England, 38–40, 256; anti-Jesuit bias in, 579,
580; Catholic reconversions in, 254–255
English College (Rome), 40
"English Ladies" (Mary Ward), 154, 155
Enlightenment, 24, 333; in Austria, 28, 35,
607; "Catholic," 355–363; definitions
of, 355–356; *Encyclopédie* of, 362–363;
pedagogy of, 324–325; philosophes
of, 166, 324–325, 361–362, 607–611;
"regulated devotion" of, 630
epic poetry, 394–396
Ethiopia, 133, 348, 447–448, 471

etiquette manuals, 322–323
Eucharist, 166–168, 215–218; in China, 538;
    confession and, 215, 216, 218; Jansenists on,
    216–217; miraculous healings with, 630
European diseases in New World, 516–517
European law in New World, 526–527
Everyman plays, 387
executions, public, 199–200
exorcisms, 159–161, 551. *See also* witchcraft
Exponi nobis (papal brief), 63

Falloux Law (1850), 624, 639
famine, 517–518
fascism, 646, 648–650
Fathers of Faith, 617–619, 623
Fathers of the Sacred Heart, 617
figurism, 547, 548
fine arts, 382–385, 415–418, 511, 546, 570;
    perspective tradition in, 420–422, 421
flood control projects, 374
Florida, 450, 458, 461
"flying boat," 371–372, 373, 379
"flying missions," 451, 462, 476, 549
fortifications, 370–371, 371
Forty Hours' Devotion (Quarant'ore),
    166–168, 275, 419
founders of religious institutions, 264–265.
    See also patronage
France, 30–32, 129; colonies of, 463–473;
    court confessors in, 289–294; Falloux
    Law of, 624, 639; Jesuit reinstatement
    in, 623–624; Jesuit schools in, 614, 639;
    Jesuit suppression in, 31, 576, 592–595,
    597–600, 604, 605; Wars of Religion in,
    30, 193–194, 306. *See also* Gallicanism
Franciscans, 67, 95, 137, 606; in Ceylon, 437;
    in India, 435; on Marian worship, 169; as
    mendicant friars, 148; in Mexico, 488; in
    Paraguay, 523; in Philippines, 461
Freemasons, 609
French Guayana, 197, 468–469, 475
French Revolution, 607, 624, 625
funeral rites, 513, 560

Gallicanism, 31, 32, 48, 360, 604; Colbert on,
    526; Pasquier on, 578; Lorenzo Ricci on,
    600
Gandía college (Spain), 303, 304
Georgetown University, 638
Germany, 623; Kulturkampf in, 624, 639–641,
    644; Nazi, 649–650; Social Democratic
    Party of, 656; Weimar, 643–644. *See also*
    Holy Roman Empire
global networks, 40, 304, 429, 563–574, 579,
    663–667
Goa, 430–432, 436, 448
Great Commission of Jesus Christ, 488–489
Gregorian calendar, 365
Guadeloupe, 468
Guaraní people, 496, 521–533; art of, 422,
    425, 426, 457; reductions of, 456–457,
    521–533, 585–586
Guaraní War (1754–56), 457, 585, 596
guardian angels, 161–163, 387
Guayana, 468, 475
Gunpowder Plot (1605), 39, 580

"helping souls," 9, 66–67, 184–201, 303–304;
    of paupers, 186–187, 189–192; of prisoners,
    198–201; of prostitutes, 186–189, 191; of
    slaves, 481–482; of soldiers, 192–198
heretics, 33, 119, 137–138, 161, 211, 245–246;
    Bussières on, 395; in China, 5541;
    Copernicus and, 367; Diderot and, 362;
    Freux on, 250; La Qintinye on, 178; in
    Ottoman Empire, 472; Possevino on,
    196; probabilists as, 176
Hindu converts, 432, 555–559
Holy Roman Empire, 32–35, 65, 142; court
    confessors in, 288–291, 295–296; Jesuit
    schools in, 306–308; Lutherans of,
    246–247; Marian worship in, 169; retreat
    houses in, 240. *See also* Austria; Germany
homilies, 206–208. *See also* sermons
homosexuality, 124–125, 194
humanism, 326, 340–349, 558; educational
    programs of, 311–312, 321, 575, 637; of

Erasmus, 83, 321, 341–343; of Hardouin, 347; Jesuit dramas and, 390; of Kircher, 348–349, 547; scholasticism and, 6, 350, 352–354

Hungary, 33, 34, 40, 129

Huron people, 465–466, 497–500, 504

Imago primi saeculi (1640), 20, 21, 36–37, 427, 428

Immaculate Conception, 168–169, 184, 328, 367, 630

Index Liborum Prohibitorum, 328, 382

India, 44, 129, 565, 666–667; Hindu converts in, 432, 555–559; Jesuit missions in, 430–437, 469; Jesuit seminaries in, 633; Malabar rites controversy in, 559, 560, 563, 584; Portuguese presence in, 430–432, 436, 448; Vedas of, 569

indigenous peoples, 178, 489–490; accommodationalism with, 554–563; Acosta's writings on, 451; alcohol abuse among, 500, *501*; baptism of, 516–517; "colonial pacts" with, 456, 473–480, 527–529; confession rituals of, 213–214, 500; European diseases among, 516–517; European peasants versus, 491; famine among, 517–518; funeral rites of, 513; Jesuit-appointed officials among, 520, 525–526; Jesuit art for, 422; Jesuit exclusion of, 43–44; marriage customs among, 515; music of, 410; suppression of religious beliefs of, 507–508, 513. *See also particular tribes*

Indonesia, 437–438

infallibility of pope, 588, 629, 642

infectious diseases, 52, 164–165, 169, 218; Kircher on, 329; mass mortality from, 516–517

inheritance rights, 61, 112

Innu (Montagnais) people, 465, 493–497, 499, 502

Inquisition, 26, 577; confession sacrament and, 210, 211; Dominicans and, 137–138,

150; Roman, 12–13, 136–137, 366–367; Spanish, 8, 28, 46, 152

Institutum Societatis Iesu, 101

Ireland, 37–39, 40

Iroquois people, 466, 467, 499, 500, 504

Italy, 26–28, 267–270, *269*; aristocratic support in, 262–263; fascism in, 649; Jesuit schools in, 303–304, 308; Jesuit suppression in, 27, 597–600, 603–605, 609–610

Jains, 432

Jansenists, 36, 143, 181–184, 606, 612; on communion, 216–217; on confession, 214–215; as Jesuit critics, 584, 592

Japan, 44, 439–440, 502, 667; Christian artists of, 422; Jesuit land in, 280; silk trade of, 282; Xavier's mission to, 431

Jesuit Refugee Service (JRS), 663

Jesuits: career paths of, 57–58, 64–65, 309, 575–576, 608–609; categories of, 61; disputes among, 12, 61, 123; diversity of, 17; families of, 42–53; first generation of, 6–9, *7*, 41–42, 65, 302; Freemasons and, 609; fundraising by, 565–567; indigenous officials appointed by, 520, 525–526; "living in the world," 260–262; nicknames of, 385; Protestants and, 245–259; radical, 592–593, *593*, 662; scholarship by, 325–331, 340, 363–382; spiritual callings of, 53–55; during suppression, 32, 575–576, 600–614. *See also* Society of Jesus; *Spiritual Exercises*

Jesuit schools, 301–302, 309–310, 451; critics of, 586, 588, 592; discipline at, 320, 323–324; Enlightenment philosophy and, 324–325; financing of, 272; networks of, 304; note-taking methods at, 344; online education and, 663; patronage of, 266; physics courses at, 381–382; Protestants and, 257–258; rationale for, 302–310; social training at, 322–323; student competition in, 317, *318*; during suppression, 613; theater at, 321, 386, 637. *See also* pedagogy

Jews, 26, 45–46, 547; animus toward, 589, 643, 646, 649–650
Julian calendar, 365
justice, social, 655, 657, 660–666

Kabbalah, 547
Kongo, Kingdom of, 447–449, 496, 633
Kulturkampf, 624, 639–641, 644

Lateran Council, Fourth, 210, 215
latifundia, 280
lay brothers, 62–63
lay ministry, 44, 551–553
Lazarists, 613, 635
Lettres édifiantes et curieuses (journal), 360, 361, 567
liberation theology, 660–662, 664, 669–670
linguistic studies, 508–510, 631
Lisbon earthquake (1755), 590
Lithuanian Orthodox Church, 133
"living in the world," 260–262, 322
Louisiana, 154, 466. See also Mississippi River valley
Lutherans, 68, 157; catechisms of, 247; on contrition, 172; on grace, 179; Jesuits and, 32, 245–246, 249–255; missionary efforts of, 489. See also Protestants

Macao, 282, 442, 470, 539, 565, 570
Madagascar, 633
Madrid, Treaty of (1750), 585, 591
magnetism, 380
Malabar rites controversy, 559, 560, 563, 584
malaria, 377
Malaysia, 436
Malta, Order of, 602
Maluku Islands, 430, 435, 438
Mantua, University of, 308
Manuale parochorum, 145
Marian apparitions, 630
Marian congregations, 242–245, 309
Marian worship, 168–169, 546, 655

marriage, 475; celibacy and, 43, 660–661; endogamous, 477; interfaith, 255; of nobility, 295–296, 591; polygamous, 515
Martinique, 468, 594
Maryland, 463, 602, 626–627; miraculous healings in, 629–630; slavery in, 485, 487, 628
mathematics, 364–365, 382, 545; architecture and, 412; astronomy and, 365–369; calculus and, 370, 381; teaching of, 312–313, 339
Melanesia, 437–438
Mémoires de Trévoux (journal), 360–362
mendicant friars, 148, 225, 235
"mental prayer," 91–92
Mercedarians, 613
Messina college, 303–304
mestizos, 43–44, 554
Mexico, 143–144, 458–461, 476, 479–480; Colegio Máximo of, 275; conversion campaigns in, 506–521; donations to, 565; encomienda system in, 529; Franciscans in, 613; global networks and, 564; history of, 611; indigenous people of, 491; Jesuit expulsion from, 603; Jesuit lands in, 280–281; music of, 408–409; slaves in, 482–483; Virgin of Guadalupe and, 605
military chaplains, 192–198, 290
military science, 370–372, 371, 372. See also warfare
Missions Étrangères de Paris (MEP), 441, 560–561
mission villages, 497; in Brazil, 445, 452, 527; China and, 549; in Mexico, 461, 519–521, 523; in Paraguay, 429, 454–457, 475–476, 521–533, 585–586; in Peru, 445, 523; in Philippines, 462; utopianism of, 533
Mississippi River valley, 154, 466–467, 499, 511–512, 515
modernism, 663–671; Jesuit reforms and, 653–654, 658–659; reactions against, 641–645, 653–654; social justice and, 655, 657, 660–666
Molinism, 182

Montagnais (Innu) people, 465, 493–497, 499, 502
Monumenta Historica Societatis Iesu, 647
moon, 367, 368, 369
Morale pratique des Jésuits (1669), 584
morality versus mercy dispute, 171–184
"Mother of the church" (patronage title), 264
Mozambique, 447, 448, 606
Mughal Empire, 432–433
museums, 334–335, 340
music, 402–410, 511, 534
Muslims, 432, 435; China and, 433; conversion of, 45–46, 472
mysticism, 75, 652; asceticism and, 84–94; Guilloré on, 221; Loyola on, 88, 652; Protestant, 258; Sandaeus on, 258

Napoleonic Wars, 620, 624–626
natural law, 300–301, 477
natural philosophy, 365, 381, 544
naval tactics, 371–372, 372
navy chaplains, 197. *See also* military chaplains
Nazism, 649–650
neo-Confucianism, 542–543
neo-pagans, 656
Netherlands, 214, 257, 639; as colonial power, 436–437, 463; independence from Spain, 35–37, 257; Louis XIV's war with, 289–290
networks. *See* global networks
Newton, Isaac, 370, 380, 381, 382
Nicaragua, 666
note-taking methods, 344
noviciates, 47, 53–58, 59, 65, 270; "little rules" of, 56–57; probationary period for, 55; property rights of, 61, 112; simple vows of, 57, 60–61, 126, 578; *Spiritual Exercises* for, 79
nuncios, 140–141

obedience vow, 61, 123, 271, 578–579; perjury and, 585; self-initiative versus, 94–100; social justice and, 661

Omagua people, 452
optics, 370
Oratorians, 167, 215, 409
ordination, 58, 61
orphans, 185, 191–192, 543–544, 565
Orthodox Christianity. *See* Eastern Orthodox Church
Ottoman Empire, 10, 470–473

Paccanarists, 617–619, 623
painting. *See* fine arts
Pamplona, siege of (1421), 1–2, 13, 73
papal infallibility, 588, 629, 642
Paraguay, 374, 375, 521–533, 613; Creole marriages in, 477; European law in, 526–527; Jesuit art of, 422–423, 425, 426; mission villages in, 429, 454–457, 475–476, 521–533, 585–586
Parma, University of, 308
Pascendi dominici gregis (encyclical), 645
patronage, 262–270, 279–280, 473, 633
pedagogy, 310–325, 586; Enlightenment, 324–325; humanistic, 321, 340–349, 637–638, 660; modern reforms of, 647; "Parisian style" of, 322; of persuasion, 319–320; playfulness of, 319; standardization of, 316–317; textbooks for, 343; visual aids of, 317–318, 417, 423, 511. *See also* Jesuit schools; *Ratio studiorum*
penance, 171–173, 500; self-flagellation as, 227, 229, 230, 232. *See also* confession
periochae, 386, 389
Persia, 472–473
Peru, 213, 217, 450–451, 486; Jesuit land in, 280; schools of, 524–525; slaves in, 482–483; suppression of indigenous religions in, 507–508
pharmaceuticals, 376–379
Philippines, 408, 438, 461–463, 476, 564
philology, 346, 351–352
philosophes, 166, 324–325, 361–362, 607–611. *See also* Enlightenment
"philosophical sin," 178. *See also* heretics
Piarists, 148, 153–154, 310

Pietà dei Carcerati (confraternity), 199
Pietism, 92, 258
Pima people, 513
plagues. *See* Infectious diseases
poetry, 394–402
Poland, 129, 361, 369; anti-Jesuit bias in, 579,
    581–582; First Partition of, 614–615;
    missionaries from, 633–634; Orthodox
    Church of, 133
pope versus emperor conflicts, 287–288,
    297–298
Popish Plot (1678), 39, 580
Port-Royal, 182, 183, 216–217
Portugal, 24–26, 293; colonies of, 429–449;
    Goa and, 430–432, 436, 448; Jesuit prop-
    erties in, 280; Jesuit reinstatement in,
    623; Jesuit suppression in, 576, 592, 600,
    603; Lisbon earthquake in, 590; Macao
    and, 282, 442, 470, 539, 565, 570; silk trade
    of, 282; Spanish rule of, 282–283
poverty, 413; educational mission and, 305;
    Francis of Assisi on, 271; poorhouses
    and, 189–192, 242; vow of, 61, 94, 103,
    271–273
Prester John legend, 448
prison ministries, 198–201
probabilism/probabiliorism, 175–177, 606
procurators, 107–112, 283
"professed fathers," 61
profit, 274, 281–282, 285, 286. *See also*
    economic pursuits
Propaganda Fide congregation, 44, 138–139,
    434, 632–635; Canadian missions of, 465;
    on Chinese rites, 560–561; Missions
    étrangères de Paris and, 441
property rights, 61, 112
Prospero felicique (papal bull), 108–109
prostitution, 186–189, 191
Protestant Reformation, 11, 15, 132–133; of
    Calvin, 179, 200, 245–249, 266; casuistry
    of, 175, 179; Enlightenment and, 358; in
    France, 30–31; Loyola on, 246–250. *See also*
    Lutheranism

Protestants, 587, 641; colloquies with,
    252–253; historical-critical theology
    of, 647; Jesuit disputes with, 245–259;
    missionaries of, 636; music of, 403;
    schools of, 315, 321. *See also* Lutherans

Quarant'ore (Forty Hours' Devotion),
    166–168, 275, 419
Quietists, 69
quinine, 377, 569

Ratio studiorum, 119, 173, 304–305, 310–314;
    Enlightenment and, 362; reform of,
    636–639; on scholarship, 326, 340; on
    theology, 354–355; on visual teaching
    aids, 317–318. *See also* pedagogy
Recollects (religious order), 464, 502, 503
Redemptorists (religious order), 232
reductions, 456–457, 521–533; critics of,
    585–586. *See also* mission villages
refugees, 663
regicide, 298–299, 592–593, 593
Regimini militantis ecclesiae (papal bull), 11,
    100, 101
Rerum novarum (encyclical), 654, 655
retreat movement, 237–240, 245
revolutions of 1848, 624, 625, 639–641
"rigorism" doctrine, 177–178, 184, 214–216;
    accommodationalism versus, 556–559;
    "easiness" principle versus, 170–173;
    money-lending and, 274–275
rosary, 511–513, 652
Russia, 546, 648; Jesuits in, 576, 614–619,
    622–623; Orthodox Church of, 133

sacramentals (*sacramentalia*), 158, 163, 166,
    234
Sacred Heart of Jesus, 617; veneration of,
    163–166, 170, 184, 363, 655
saints' legends, 345–346, 388–390
salons (*sociétés littéraires*), 359–360
Sant'Ignazio Church (Rome), 414, 420, 421
Scandinavia, 37, 40, 256

scholasticism, 313, 349–355; definition of, 349; humanism and, 6, 350, 352–354. *See also* Thomism

scholastics (*scholastici*), 58, 61, 126

scientific knowledge, 325–331, 363–382, 546; atheism and, 644; of missionaries, 301–302, 505; of physics, 381–382, 638; theology versus, 354–355, 365–369

Scolopi. *See* Piarists

Scotland, 38

self-flagellation, 227, 229, 230, 232. *See also* penance

self-initiative, 94–100

sermons, 201–210, 656; classical sources for, 203–205, 204, 342; of conversion campaigns, 225–227; homiletics and, 206–208; on Lisbon earthquake, 590–591; of missionaries, 208–209; props for, 202–203, 227–228, 231; rhetorical effects of, 202–204, 558; Vieira on, 204, 206–207

Seven Reductions, War of (1754–56), 457, 585, 596

shamanism, 494–495. *See also* witchcraft

Shanghai University, 648

shipbuilding, 373

siege warfare, 370–371, 371

slaves, 449, 480–487, 628; of *encomienda* system, 527–529; ransoming of, 565

social apostolate, 654–658

social justice, 655, 657, 660–666

social welfare programs, 185

Société pour la Propagation du Foi, 634–635

Society of Jesus, 10–11, 22–41; centennial of, 20; economic pursuits of, 271–296, 278, 284–285; enemies of, 577–590; Inquisition trials of, 12–13; legal foundations of, 101; monogram of, 117, 118; noble patronage of, 262–270; other religious orders and, 147–155; restoration of, 16; restoration of, 576; suppression of, 16, 575–576, 592–614. *See also Constitutions*; Jesuits

sodalities. *See* confraternities

solidarity (*unio*), 97, 117

Sollicitudo omnium ecclesiarum (papal bull), 620, 622

Spain, 28–30, 129, 263, 267; colonies of, 449–463, 473–480, 528–529; court confessors in, 291–294, 596; Dutch independence from, 35, 36; Jesuit properties in, 601–602; Jesuit reinstatement in, 624; Jesuit suppression in, 576, 596–597, 603; Reconquista of, 81

Spanish Armada (1588), 39, 197

Spanish Civil War (1936–39), 648–649

Spanish Succession, War of (1701–14), 30, 278

"spiritual directors," 219–225

Spiritual Exercises (Loyola), 8, 17, 21, 65, 72–84, 506; accommodationalism and, 557; Acquaviva on, 22, 80, 119, 236; Canisius on, 84; Cano on, 150; Ceccotti on, 84; on confession, 212; dramatic elements of, 385; Fessard on, 651; illustrations for, 424–425; on individual's needs, 221; Latin translation of, 73, 631; Marian congregations and, 244; "Meditation on the Two Standards" in, 75–79; on moral self-assessment, 75–77, 76; on obedience, 97; on political involvement, 295; Possevino on, 73; for retreats, 235–240; Roothaan on, 630–631; on "true attitude of mind," 131; Spanish version of, 631; on "true impulses," 97; Ursulines and, 154. *See also* Jesuits

spirituality, 66–72, 155–156; Acquaviva on, 114; of Baroque period, 156–171, 204; of Counter-Reformation, 155–156; Nadal on, 66; Polanco on, 68; religious practice and, 65–66

Sri Lanka, 437

Sublimis Deus (papal bull), 490

Sudan, 633

suicide, 125–126

Sulpicians (religious order), 465

sumptuary laws, 117–118, 653

superstitions, 184, 495–497, 514; of childbirth, 156–158; of guardian angels, 161–163; Muratori on, 169–170. *See also* witchcraft

Syllabus errorum, 640, 642

syncretic religion, 513–514, 553–563

Syrian Christians, 133

tertiates, 58–61, 59, 65, 79, 270. *See also* noviciates

Tertullian, 383

textual criticism, 346–347

Thailand, 441, 469–470

theater, 258, 385–393, 392, 404–405; allegorical, 387, 390–391, 394; biblical, 387–388; at Jesuit schools, 321, 386, 637; Terence and, 342, 383; Tertullian on, 383

Theatines (religious order), 56; as clerics regular, 148; Jesuits and, 152–153

theology, 313, 351–352; casuistry and, 174–181, 175, 313; controversialist, 250–253, 300–301; historical-critical, 647; liberation, 660–662, 664, 669–670; morality versus mercy dispute in, 171–184; "new," 651; scientific knowledge versus, 354–355, 364–370; teaching of, 313, 354–355; uniformity of doctrine and, 119

Thirty Years' War (1618–48), 23, 33–34, 278, 288

Thomism, 68, 119, 215, 313, 347, 367; criticisms of, 352–354; neo-Thomism and, 643–647 (*See also* scholasticism); teaching of, 638

Tibet, 434, 474, 490

Toleration, Chinese Edict of (1692), 443

Trent, Council of (1545–63), 6, 15, 33; on confession, 172, 210; on grace, 179; on pastoral care, 265; on sacred images, 383; on sermons, 201–210, 202

Tupí people, 445, 447, 557

tutiorism, 175–176

tyrannicide. *See* regicide

ultramontanism, 587, 640, 644–645

Unigenitus (apostolic constitution), 183

"union of hearts," 118, 128, 130

United States, 602, 626–628, 633, 634, 638–639

Ursulines, 154, 155, 160

Uruguay, 455

usury, 274, 286. *See also* profit

utopianism, 533

Vatican Council: First, 629, 642, 645; Second, 650, 653, 658–660, 666–667

Venezuela, 450

vernacular instruction, 311

Vienna, Battle of (1683), 334

Vietnam, 441–442, 555

Vietnamese boat people, 665

visitas (temporary mission stations), 520–521

visitations, 112–113, 439

visual teaching aids, 78, 239, 317–318, 417, 423, 511

vocational callings, 53–55

vows: of chastity, 43, 61, 94, 123–125, 271, 524, 660–661; of obedience, 61, 94–100, 123, 271, 578–579, 585, 661; of poverty, 61, 94, 103, 123, 271–273; simple, 57, 60–61, 126, 578; solemn, 61, 65

Vulgate Bible, 351

warfare, 370–372, 489–490; chaplains during, 192–198, 290

witchcraft, 158–161, 589; alchemy and, 378; exorcisms and, 159–161, 551; indigenous religions as, 507–508, 513; shamanism and, 494–495. *See also* superstitions

worker-priests, 656–657

"worldly helpers," 61–64

World War I, 645–647

World War II, 649–651, 667

Yaqui people, 458–459, 511, 518

zoology, 376

Zoroastrianism, 432

A NOTE ON THE TYPE

This book has been composed in Arno, an Old-style serif typeface in the classic Venetian tradition, designed by Robert Slimbach at Adobe.